Siberia
ASIA
Lake Baikal
Ulaanbaatar
MONGOLIA
Mountains
Gobi Desert
Shenyang
Beijing
NORTH KOREA
P'yongyang
Seoul
SOUTH KOREA
Pusan
Sea of Japan
Sapporo
JAPAN
Tokyo
Kobe
Osaka
Fukuoka
Kyushu
Yellow Sea
CHINA
Huang River
Chengdu
Chang River
Shanghai
30°N
East China Sea
Okinawa
Naha
Taipei
TAIWAN
PACIFIC OCEAN
BHUTAN
Brahmaputra R.
Irrawaddy R.
Dhaka
MYANMAR (BURMA)
Red River
Guangzhou
Hong Kong
Macao
Hanoi
LAOS
Chiang Mai
Vientiane
Mekong River
Udon Thani
Yangon
THAILAND
South China Sea
Luzon
Philippine Sea
Manila
PHILIPPINES
VIETNAM
Bangkok
Tonle Sap
CAMBODIA
Andaman Islands
Phnom Penh
Ho Chi Minh City
Gulf of Thailand
Spratly Islands
Cebu
Mindanao
PALAU
Koror
Nicobar Islands
Songkhla
Strait of Malacca
Bandar Seri Begawan
BRUNEI
MALAYSIA
Medan
Kuala Lumpur
Sarawak
Singapore
SINGAPORE
Sumatra
Kalimantan
Borneo
0°
Irian Jaya
INDONESIA
PAPUA NEW GUINEA
Jakarta
Surabaya
Java
Bali
Dili
EAST TIMOR
Port Moresby
OCEAN
120°E
150°E
90°E
AUSTRALIA

# Encyclopedia of Modern Asia

# Editorial Board

# Encyclopedia of Modern Asia

Volume 3

Iaido to Malay-Indonesian Language

A Berkshire Reference Work

David Levinson · Karen Christensen, Editors

CHARLES SCRIBNER'S SONS®

New York • Detroit • San Diego • San Francisco • Cleveland • New Haven, Conn. • Waterville, Maine • London • Munich

**Encyclopedia of Modern Asia**

David Levinson and Karen Christensen, Editors



Charles Scribner's Sons
An imprint of The Gale Group
300 Park Avenue South
New York, NY 10010



*For more information, contact*
The Gale Group, Inc.
27500 Drake Rd.
Farmington Hills, MI 48331–3535
Or you can visit our Internet site at
http://www.gale.com



The paper used in this publication meets the requirements of ANSI/NISO Z39.48-1992 (Permanence of Paper).



**LIBRARY OF CONGRESS CATALOGING-IN-PUBLICATION DATA**

Levinson, David, 1947-
Encyclopedia of modern Asia : / David Levinson, Karen Christensen,
p. cm.
Includes bibliographical references and index.
ISBN 0-684-80617-7 (set hardcover : alk. paper)
1. Asia—Encyclopedias. I. Christensen, Karen, 1957- II. Title.
DS4 .L48 2002
950'.03—dc21

2002008712

Printed in United States of America
1 3 5 7 9 11 13 15 17 19 20 18 16 14 12 10 8 6 4 2

# Contents

# List of Maps

**Front Matter of All Volumes**



**Volume 1**



**Volume 2**



**Volume 3**



**Volume 4**

**Volume 5**



**Volume 6**

# Survey of Asia's Regions and Nations

The *Encyclopedia of Modern Asia* covers thirty-three nations in depth and also the Caucasus and Siberia. We have divided Asia into five major subregions and assigned the thirty-three nations to each.

**West and Southwest Asia**

The West Asian nations covered in detail here are Turkey, Iran, and Iraq. Afghanistan and Pakistan form Southwest Asia, although in some classifications they are placed in Central and South Asia, respectively. Afghanistan, on the crossroads of civilizations for thousands of years, is especially difficult to classify and displays features typical of Central, West, and South Asia.

Despite diversity in language (Persian in Iran, Arabic in Iraq, Turkish in Turkey) form of government (theocracy in Iran, dictatorship in Iraq, and unstable democracy in Turkey) and international ties (Iran to the Islamic world, Iraq to the Arab Middle East, Turkey to the West), there are several sources of unity across West Asia. Perhaps the oldest is geographical location as the site of transportation routes between Europe and Central, East, and South Asia. Since ancient times, people, goods, wealth, and ideas have flowed across the region. In 2002 the flow of oil was most important, from the wells of Iran and Iraq through the pipelines of Turkey. Another source of unity is Sunni Islam, a major feature of life since the seventh century, although Iran is mainly the minority Shi'a tradition and there have long been Zoroastrian, Jewish, Christian, and Baha'i minorities in the region. Diversity is also evident in the fact that Turkey is a "secular" state while Iran is a theocracy, and in the conflict between fundamentalist and mainstream Islam in all the nations.

Another important common thread is the shared historical experience of being part of the Ottoman Empire and having to cope with British and Russian designs on their territory and, more recently, American influence. And, in the twentieth century, all three nations have sought to deal with the Kurdish minority and its demands for a Kurdish state to be established on land taken from all three nations.

Unity across Afghanistan and Pakistan is created by adherence to Sunni Islam (although there is a Shi'ite minority in Afghanistan) and the prominence of the Pashtun ethnic group in each nation. Both nations also experienced British colonialism, although the long-term British influence is more notable in Pakistan, which had been tied to India under British rule. West Asia is the only region in the world never colonized by Britain, although some experts argue that it did experience significant British cultural influence. In all nations resistance to external control—British, Russian, or United States—is another common historical experience.

Across the region (although less so in Afghanistan) is the stark contrast between the traditional culture and the modernity of liberation from imperial rule, still not complete across the region. This contrast is apparent in clothing styles, manners, architecture, recreation, marriage practices, and many elements of daily life.

In 2002 all the nations faced a water crisis of both too little water and water pollution. They all also faced issues of economic and social development, including reducing external debt, controlling inflation, reducing unemployment, improving education and health care, and continually reacting to the ongoing Arab-Israeli conflict, which exacerbates many of these problems. The governments also faced the difficult task of solving these problems while resisting Americanization and also while controlling internal political unrest. Political unrest is often tied to efforts at creating democratic governments and the persistence of elite collaboration with tyrannical governments.

**Central Asia**

Central Asia is known by many names, including Eurasia, Middle Asia, and Inner Asia. At its core, the region is composed of five states that became independent nations following the collapse of the Soviet Union in 1991: Kazakhstan, Kyrgyzstan, Tajikistan, Turkmenistan, and Uzbekistan. Scholars sometimes include Afghanistan, Mongolia and the Xinjiang province of China within the label Central Asia. For this project, Central Asia is restricted to the five former Soviet countries, while Afghanistan is classified in Southwest Asia, and Mongolia and Xinjiang as part of East Asia. These states have a shared landmass of 1.5 million square miles, about one-half the size of the United States.

The region's unity comes from a shared history and religion. Central Asia saw two cultural and economic traditions blossom and intermix along the famed Silk Road: nomadic and sedentary. Nomadic herdsmen, organized into kinship groupings of clans, lived beside sedentary farmers and oasis city dwellers. Four of the countries share Turkic roots, while the Tajiks are of Indo-European descent, linguistically related to the Iranians. While still recognizable today, this shared heritage has developed into distinct ethnic communities.

The peoples of Central Asia have seen centuries of invasion, notably the legendary Mongol leader Genghis Khan in the thirteenth century, the Russians in the nineteenth and the Soviets in the twentieth century. For better or worse, each invader left behind markers of their presence: the Arabs introduced Islam in the seventh century. Today Islam is the predominant religion in the region, and most Central Asians are Sunni Muslims. The Russians brought the mixed legacy of modernism, including an educated populace, alarming infant mortality rates, strong economic and political participation by women, high agricultural development, and environmental disasters such as the shrinking of the Aral Sea. It was under Russian colonialism that distinct ethno-national boundaries were created to divide the people of the region. These divisions largely shape the contemporary Central Asian landscape.

Today the five Central Asian nations face similar challenges: building robust economies, developing stable, democratic governments, and integrating themselves into the regional and international communities as independent states. They come to these challenges with varied resources: Kazakhstan and Turkmenistan have rich oil reserves; several countries have extensive mineral deposits; and the Fergana Valley is but one example of the region's rich agricultural regions.

Finally, the tragic events of September 11, 2001, cast world attention on Afghanistan's neighbors in Central Asia. The "war on terrorism" forged new alliances and offered a mix of political pressure and economic support for the nations' leaders to suppress their countries' internal fundamentalist Muslim movements.

**Southeast Asia**

Southeast Asia is conventionally defined as that subregion of Asia consisting of the eleven nation-states of Brunei, Cambodia, East Timor, Indonesia, Laos, Malaysia, Myanmar, Philippines, Singapore, Thailand, and Vietnam. Myanmar is sometimes alternatively classified as part of South Asia and Vietnam as in East Asia. The region may be subdivided into Mainland Southeast Asia (Cambodia, Laos, Myanmar, Thailand, and Vietnam) and Insular Southeast Asia (Brunei, East Timor, Indonesia, Philippines, and Singapore). Malaysia is the one nation in the region that is located both on the mainland and islands, though ethnically it is more linked to the island nations of Indonesia, Brunei, and the Philippines.

Perhaps the key defining features for the region and those that are most widespread are the tropical monsoon climate, rich natural resources, and a way of life in rural areas based on cooperative wet-rice agriculture that goes back several thousand years. In the past unity was also created in various places by major civilizations, including those of Funan, Angkor, Pagan, Sukhothai, Majapahit, Srivijaya, Champa, Ayutthaya, and Melaka. Monarchies continue to be significant in several nation—Brunei, Cambodia, Malaysia, and Thailand—today. Subregional unity has also been created since ancient times by the continued use of written languages, including Vietnamese, Thai, Lao, Khmer and the rich literary traditions associated with those languages.

The region can also be defined as being located between China and India and has been influenced by both, with Indian influence generally broader, deeper, and longer lasting, especially on the mainland, except for Vietnam and Singapore, where influences from China have been more important. Islamic influence is also present in all eleven of the Southeast Asian nations. Culturally, Southeast Asia is notable for the central importance of the family, religion (mainly Buddhism and Islam), and aesthetics in daily life and national consciousness.

In the post–World War II Cold War era, there was a lack of regional unity. Some nations, such as Indonesia under Sukarno, were leaders of the nonaligned nations. Countries such as Thailand and the Philippines joined the U.S. side in the Cold War by being part of the Southeast Asia Treaty Organization (SEATO). A move toward greater unity was achieved with the establishment of the Association of Southeast Asian Nations (ASEAN) in 1967, with the founding members being Indonesia, Malaysia, the Philippines, Singapore, and Thailand. Subsequently other Southeast Asian nations joined ASEAN (Brunei, 1984; Laos, Myanmar, and Vietnam 1997; Cambodia 1999). As of 2002, communism was still the system in Laos and Vietnam and capitalism in Brunei, Cambodia, East Timor, the Philippines Thailand, Indonesia, Malaysia and Singapore. Political, economic, and cultural cooperation is fostered by the Association of Southeast Asian Nations (ASEAN), with headquarters in Jakarta, Indonesia. Economically, all the nations have attempted to move, although at different speeds and with different results, from a reliance on agriculture to an industrial or service-based economy. All nations also suffered in the Asian economic crisis beginning in July 1997.

Alongside these sources of similarity or unity that allow us to speak of Southeast Asia as a region is also considerable diversity. In the past religion, ethnicity, and diverse colonial experience (British, Dutch, French, American) were major sources of diversity. Today, the three major sources of diversity are religion, form of government, and level of economic development. Three nations (Indonesia, Malaysia,

Brunei) are predominately Islamic, five are mainly Buddhist (Vietnam, Laos, Cambodia, Thailand, Myanmar), two are mainly Christian (Philippines and East Timor), and Singapore is religiously heterogeneous. In addition, there is religious diversity within nations, as all these nations have sizeable and visible religious minorities and indigenous religions, in both traditional and syncretic forms, also remain important.

In terms of government, there is considerable variation: communism in Vietnam and Laos; state socialism in Myanmar; absolute monarchy in Brunei; evolving democracy in the Philippines, Thailand, Cambodia, and Indonesia; and authoritarian democracy in Malaysia and Singapore. The economic variation that exists among the nations and also across regions within nations is reflected in different levels of urbanization and economic development, with Singapore and Malaysia at one end of the spectrum and Laos and Cambodia at the other. Myanmar is economically underdeveloped, although it is urbanized, while Brunei is one of the wealthiest nations in the world but not very urbanized.

In 2002, Southeast Asia faced major environmental, political, economic, and health issues. All Southeast Asian nations suffer from serious environmental degradation, including water pollution, soil erosion, air pollution in and around cities, traffic congestion, and species extinctions. To a significant extent all these problems are the result of rapid industrial expansion and overexploitation of natural resources for international trade. The economic crisis has hampered efforts to address these issues and has threatened the economies of some nations, making them more dependent on international loans and assistance from nations such as Japan, Australia, and China. The persisting economic disparities between the rich and the poor are actually exacerbated by rapid economic growth. Related to poverty is the AIDS epidemic, which is especially serious in Cambodia, Myanmar, and Thailand and becoming more serious in Vietnam; in all these nations it associated with the commercial sex industry.

Politically, many Southeast Asian nations faced one or more threats to their stability. Political corruption, lack of transparency, and weak civic institutions are a problem to varying degrees in all the nations but are most severe in Indonesia, which faces threats to its sovereignty. Cambodia and Thailand face problems involving monarch succession, and several nations have had difficulty finding effective leaders. Myanmar's authoritarian rulers face a continual threat from the political opposition and from ethnic and religious separatists.

In addition, several nations faced continuing religious or ethnic-based conflicts that disrupt political stability and economic growth in some provinces. The major conflicts involve Muslim separatists in the southern Philippines, Muslims and Christians in some Indonesian islands and Aceh separatists in northern Sumatra, and Muslims and the Karen and other ethnic groups against the Burman government in Myanmar. Since the economic crisis of 1997, ethnic and religion-based conflict has intensified, as wealthier ethnic or religious minorities have increasingly been attacked by members of the dominant ethnic group. A related issue is the cultural and political future of indigenous peoples, including the so-called hill tribes of the mainland and horticulturalists and former hunter-gatherers of the islands.

In looking to the future, among the region's positive features are the following. First, there is Southeast Asia's strategic location between India and China, between Japan and Europe, and between Europe and Oceania. It stands in close proximity to the world's two most populous countries, China and India. Singapore, the centrally located port in Southeast Asia, is one of two major gateways to the dynamic Pacific Basin (the other is the Panama Canal). Second, there is the region's huge population and related economic market, with a total population approaching that of one half of China's. Indonesia is the world's fourth most populous nation. Third, there is enormous tourist potential in sites and recreational locales such as Angkor Wat, Bali, Borobudur, Phuket, and Ha Long Bay. Fourth, there is the region's notable eclecticism in borrowing from the outside and resiliency in transcending tragedies such as experienced by Cambodia and Vietnam. Fifth, there is the region's significant economic potential: Southeast Asia may well have the world's highest-quality labor force relative to cost. And, sixth, there is the region's openness to new technologies and ideas, an important feature in the modern global community.

### South Asia

South Asia is the easiest region to demarcate, as it is bounded by the Hindu Kush and Himalayan ranges to the north and the Bay of Bengal and Arabian Sea to the south. It contains the nation-states of Bangladesh, Bhutan, India, Nepal, and Sri Lanka and the more distant island nations of the Maldives and Mauritius. Myanmar and Pakistan, which are considered part of South Asia in some schemes, are here classified in Southeast Asia and Southwest Asia, respectively.

While the region is diverse economically, culturally, linguistically, and religiously, there is unity that, in some form, has existed for several thousand years. One source of unity is the historical influence of two major civilizations (Indus and Dravidian) and three major religions (Hinduism, Buddhism, and Islam). Regionally, Sikhism and Jainism have been of great importance. There is also considerable economic unity, as the majority of people continue to live by farming, with rice and especially wet-rice the primary crop. In addition, three-quarters of the people continue to live in rural, agricultural villages, although this has now become an important source of diversity, with clear distinctions between urban and rural life. A third source of unity is the caste system, which continues to define life for most people in the three mainland nations. Another source of unity is the nature and structure of society, which was heavily influenced by the several centuries of British rule. A final source of political unity in the twentieth century—although sometimes weakened by ethnic and religious differences—has been nationalism in each nation.

South Asia is diverse linguistically, ethnically, religiously, and economically. This diversity is most obvious in India, but exists in various forms in other nations, except for the isolated Maldives, which is the home of one ethnic group, the Divehi, who are Muslims and who have an economy based largely on tourism and fishing.

The dozens of languages of South Asia fall into four major families: Indo-European, Austroasiatic, Dravidian, and Tibeto-Burman and several cannot be classified at all. Because of its linguistic diversity, India is divided into "linguistic" states with Hindi and English serving as the national languages.

Hinduism is the dominant religion in South Asia, but India is the home also to Buddhism, Jainism, and Sikhism. India also has over 120 million Muslims and the world's largest Zoroastrian population (known in India as Parsis) and Bangladesh is a predominately Muslim nation. India also has about twenty-five million Christians and until recently India had several small but thriving Jewish communities. Nepal is mainly Hindu with a Buddhist minority, and Bhutan the reverse. Sri Lanka is mainly Theravada Buddhist with Hindu, Muslim, and Christian minorities. Mauritius, which has no indigenous population, is about 50 percent Hindu, with a large Christian and smaller Muslim and Buddhist minorities.

Linguistic and religious diversity is more than matched by social diversity. One classification suggests that the sociocultural groups of South Asia can be divided into four general and several subcategories: (1) castes (Hindu and Muslim); (2) modern urban classes (including laborers, non-Hindus, and the Westernized elite); (3) hill tribes of at least six types; and (4) peripatetics.

Economically, there are major distinctions between the rural poor and the urban middle class and elite, and also between the urban poor and urban middle class and elite. There are also significant wealth distinctions based on caste and gender, and a sizeable and wealthy Indian diaspora. There is political diversity as well, with India and Sri Lanka being democracies, Bangladesh shifting back and forth between Islamic democracy and military rule, the Maldives being an Islamic state, and Nepal and Bhutan being constitutional monarchies.

In 2002, South Asia faced several categories of issues. Among the most serious are the ongoing ethnic and religious conflicts between Muslims and Hindus in India, the conflict between the nations of Pakistan and India; the ethnic conflict between the Sinhalese and Sri Lankan Tamils in Sri Lanka; and the conflict between the Nepalese and Bhutanese in both nations. There are also various ethnic separatists movements in the region, as involving some Sikhs in India. The most threatening to order in the region and beyond is the conflict between India and Pakistan over the Kashmir region, as both have nuclear weapons and armies gathered at their respective borders.

A second serious issue is the host of related environmental problems, including pollution; limited water resources; overexploitation of natural resources; destruction and death caused by typhoons, flooding, and earthquakes; famine (less of a problem today), and epidemics of tropical and other diseases. The Maldives faces the unique problem of disappearing into the sea as global warming melts glaciers and raises the sea level. Coastal regions of Bangladesh could also suffer from this.

There are pressing social, economic, and political issues as well. Socially, there are wide and growing gaps between the rich and middle classes and the poor, who are disproportionately women and children and rural. Tribal peoples and untouchables still do not enjoy full civil rights, and women are often discriminated against, although India, Sri Lanka, and Bangladesh have all had women prime ministers. Economically, all the nations continue to wrestle with the issues involved in transforming themselves from mainly rural, agricultural nations to ones with strong industrial and service sectors. Politically, all still also struggle with the task of establishing strong, central governments that can control ethnic, religious, and region variation and provide services to the entire population. Despite these difficulties, there are also positive developments. India continues to benefit from the inflow of wealth earned by Indians outside India and is emerging as a major technological center. And, in Sri Lanka, an early 2002 cease-fire has led to the prospect of a series of peace negotiations in the near future..

### East Asia

East Asia is defined here as the nations of Japan, South Korea, North Korea, China, Taiwan, and Mongolia. It should be noted that Taiwan is part of China although the People's Republic of China and the Republic of China (Taiwan) differ over whether it is a province or not. The inclusion of China in East Asia is not entirely geographically and culturally valid, as parts of southern China could be classified as Southeast Asian from a geographical and cultural standpoint, while western China could be classified as Central Asian. However, there is a long tradition of classifying China as part of East Asia, and that is the approach taken here. Likewise, Mongolia is sometimes classified in Central Asia. As noted above, Siberia can be considered as forming North and Northeast Asia.

Economic, political, ideological, and social similarity across China, Korea (North and South), and Japan is the result of several thousand years of Chinese influence (at times strong, at other times weak), which has created considerable similarity on a base of pre-existing Japanese and Korean cultures and civilizations. China's influence was greatest before the modern period and Chinese culture thus in some ways forms the core of East Asian culture and society. At the same time, it must be stressed that Chinese cultural elements merged with existing and new Korean and Japanese ones in ways that produced the unique Japanese and Korean cultures and civilizations, which deserve consideration in their own right.

Among the major cultural elements brought from China were Buddhism and Confucianism, the written language, government bureaucracy, various techniques of rice agriculture, and a patrilineal kinship system based on male dominance and male control of family resources. All of these were shaped over the centuries to fit with existing or developing forms in Korea and Japan. For example, Buddhism coexists with Shinto in Japan. In Korea, it coexists with the indigenous shamanistic religion. In China and Korea traditional folk religion remains strong, while Japan has been the home to dozens of new indigenous religions over the past 150 years.

Diversity in the region has been largely a product of continuing efforts by the Japanese and Koreans to resist Chinese influence and develop and stress Japanese and Korean culture and civilization. In the twentieth century diversity was mainly political and economic. Japanese invasions and conquests of parts of China and all of Korea beginning in the late nineteenth century led to hostile relations that had not been completely overcome in 2002.

In the post–World War II era and after, Taiwan, Japan, and South Korea have been closely allied with the United States and the West; they have all developed powerful industrial and postindustrial economies. During the same period, China became a Communist state; significant ties to the West and economic development did not begin until the late 1980s. North Korea is also a Communist state; it lags behind the other nations in economic development and in recent years has not been able to produce enough food to feed its population. In 2002 China was the emerging economic power in the region, while Taiwan and South Korea hold on and Japan shows signs of serious and long-term economic decline, although it remains the second-largest (after the United States) economy in the world. Mongolia, freed from Soviet rule, is attempting to build its economy following a capitalist model.

Politically, China remains a Communist state despite significant moves toward market capitalism, North Korea is a Communist dictatorship, Japan a democracy, and South Korea and Taiwan in 1990s seem to have become relatively stable democracies following periods of authoritarian rule. Significant contact among the nations is mainly economic, as efforts at forging closer political ties remain stalled over past grievances. For example, in 2001, people in China and South Korea protested publicly about a new Japanese high school history textbook that they believed did not fully describe Japanese atrocities committed toward Chinese and Koreans before and during World War II. Japan has refused to revise the textbook. Similarly, tension remains between Mongolia and China over Mongolian fears about Chinese designs on Mongolian territory. Inner Mongolia is a province of China.

Major issues with regional and broader implications are the reunification of Taiwan and China and North and South Korea, and threat of war should reunification efforts go awry. Other major regional issues include environmental pollution, including air pollution from China that spreads east, and pollution of the Yellow Sea, Taiwan Strait, and South China Sea. A third issue is economic development and stability, and the role of each nation, and the region as a unit, in the growing global economy. A final major issue is the emergence of China as a major world political, economic, and military power at the expense of Taiwan, South Korea, and Japan, and the consequences for regional political relations and stability.

### Overview

As the above survey indicates, Asia is a varied and dynamic construct. To some extent the notion of Asia, as well as regions within Asia, are artificial constructs imposed by outside observers to provide some structure to a place and subject matter that might otherwise be incomprehensible. The nations of Asia have rich and deep pasts that continue to inform and shape the present—and that play a significant role in relations with other nations and regions. The nations of Asia also face considerable issues—some unique to the region, others shared by nations around the world—as well as enormous potential for future growth and development. We expect that the next edition of this encyclopedia will portray a very different Asia than does this one, but still an Asia that is in many ways in harmony with its pasts.

*David Levinson (with contributions from Virginia Aksan, Edward Beauchamp, Anthony and Rebecca Bichel, Linsun Cheng, Gerald Fry, Bruce Fulton, and Paul Hockings)*

# Regional Maps

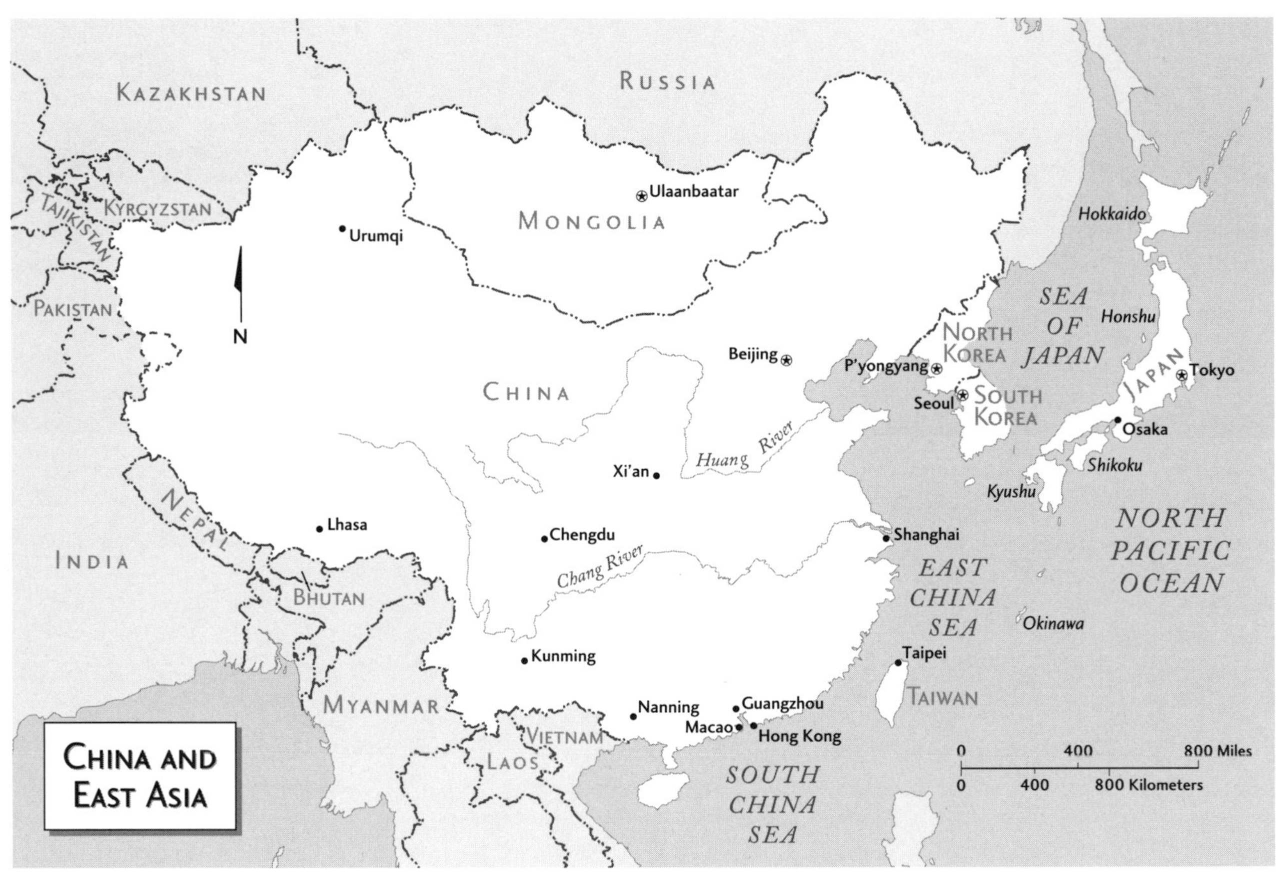
CHINA AND EAST ASIA
KAZAKHSTAN
RUSSIA
KYRGYZSTAN
TAJIKISTAN
PAKISTAN
MONGOLIA
Ulaanbaatar
Urumqi
N
CHINA
Beijing
P'yongyang
NORTH KOREA
SOUTH KOREA
Seoul
SEA OF JAPAN
JAPAN
Hokkaido
Honshu
Tokyo
Osaka
Shikoku
Kyushu
Huang River
Xi'an
Lhasa
NEPAL
Chengdu
Chang River
INDIA
BHUTAN
Shanghai
EAST CHINA SEA
NORTH PACIFIC OCEAN
Okinawa
Taipei
TAIWAN
Kunming
MYANMAR
Nanning
Guangzhou
Macao
Hong Kong
VIETNAM
LAOS
SOUTH CHINA SEA
0 400 800 Miles
0 400 800 Kilometers

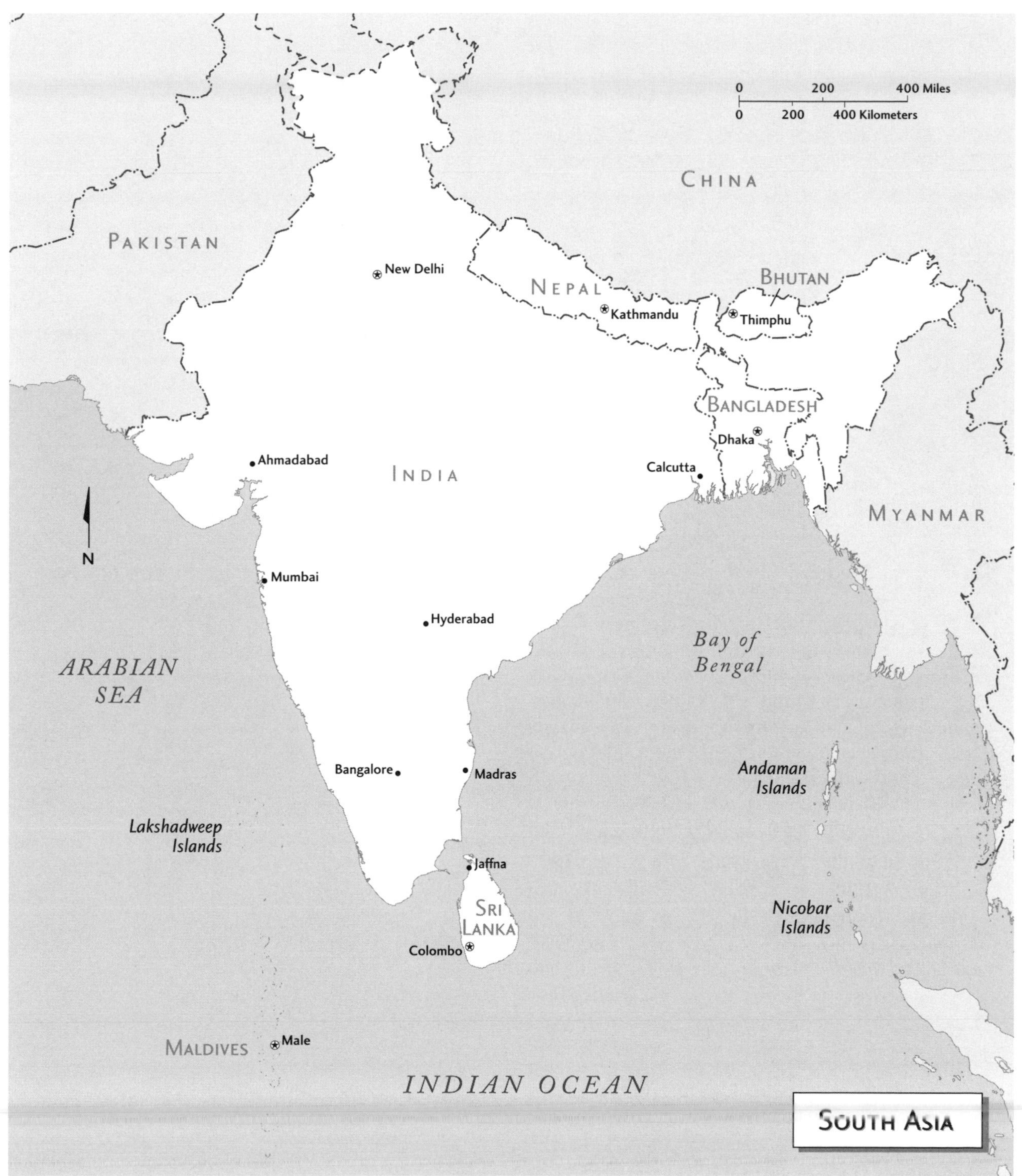
0 200 400 Miles
0 200 400 Kilometers
CHINA
PAKISTAN
New Delhi
NEPAL
Kathmandu
BHUTAN
Thimphu
BANGLADESH
Dhaka
Calcutta
Ahmadabad
INDIA
MYANMAR
N
Mumbai
Hyderabad
Bay of Bengal
ARABIAN SEA
Bangalore
Madras
Andaman Islands
Lakshadweep Islands
Jaffna
SRI LANKA
Nicobar Islands
Colombo
MALDIVES
Male
INDIAN OCEAN
SOUTH ASIA

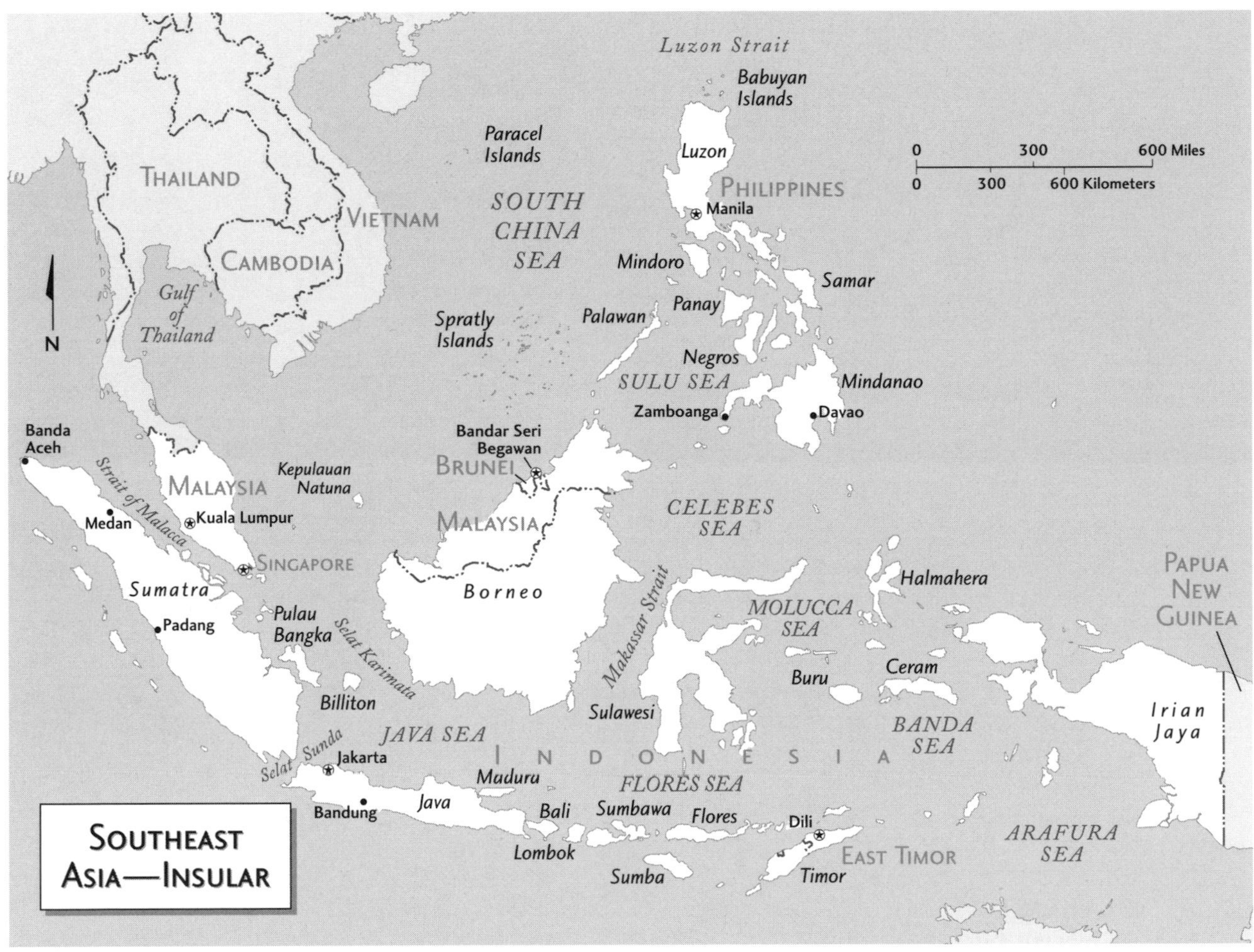
Luzon Strait
Babuyan Islands
Paracel Islands
Luzon
0 300 600 Miles
0 300 600 Kilometers
THAILAND
PHILIPPINES
Manila
VIETNAM
SOUTH CHINA SEA
CAMBODIA
Mindoro
Samar
Gulf of Thailand
Panay
Spratly Islands
Palawan
N
Negros
SULU SEA
Mindanao
Zamboanga
Davao
Banda Aceh
Bandar Seri Begawan
BRUNEI
Kepulauan Natuna
Strait of Malacca
MALAYSIA
CELEBES SEA
Medan
Kuala Lumpur
MALAYSIA
SINGAPORE
Halmahera
PAPUA NEW GUINEA
Sumatra
Borneo
MOLUCCA SEA
Makassar Strait
Padang
Pulau Bangka
Selat Karimata
Buru
Ceram
Billiton
Sulawesi
Irian Jaya
BANDA SEA
JAVA SEA
INDONESIA
Selat Sunda
Jakarta
Madura
FLORES SEA
Bandung
Java
Bali
Sumbawa
Flores
Dili
ARAFURA SEA
SOUTHEAST ASIA—INSULAR
Lombok
EAST TIMOR
Sumba
Timor

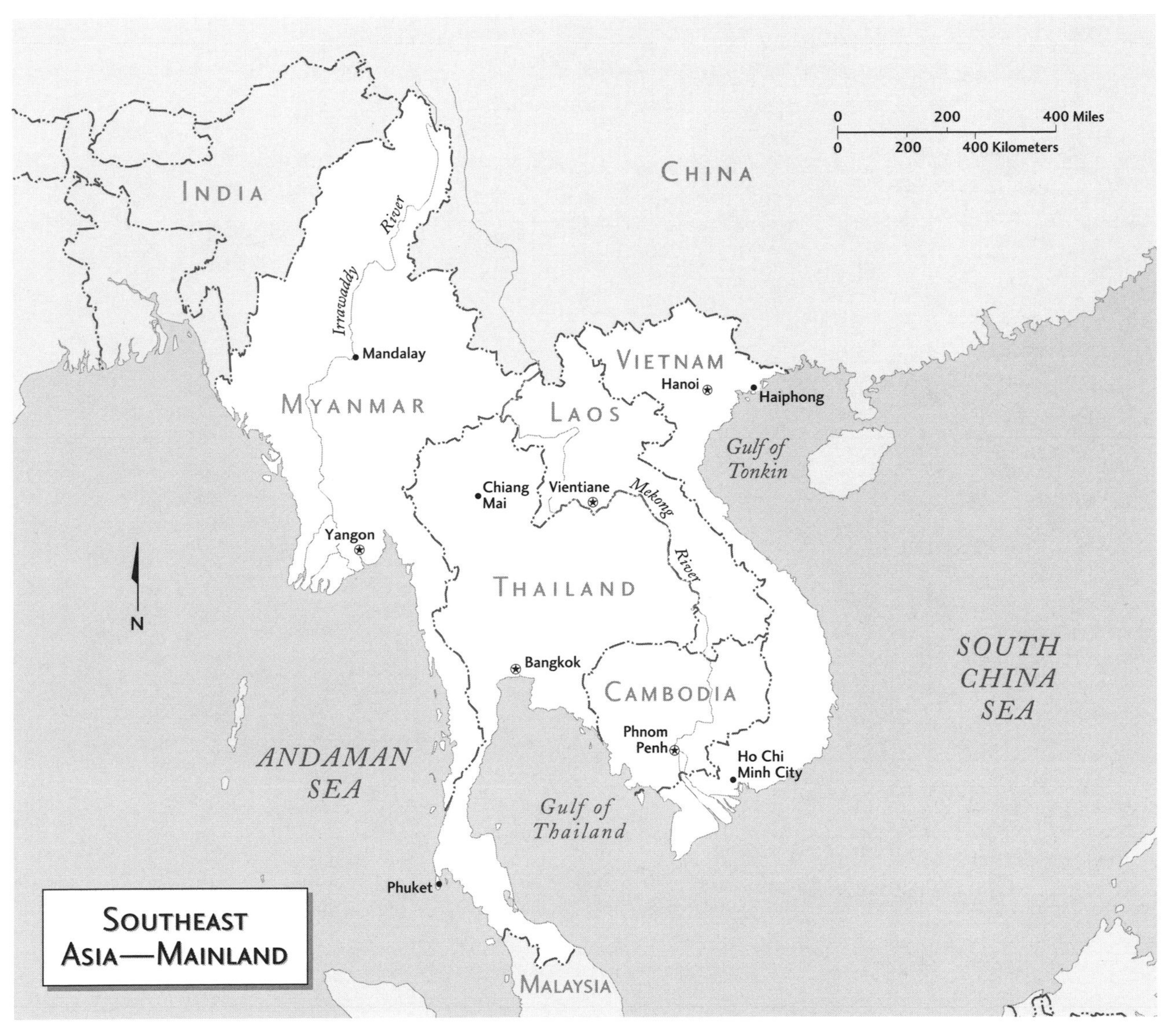
SOUTHEAST ASIA—MAINLAND
0
200
400 Miles
0
200
400 Kilometers
CHINA
INDIA
Irrawaddy River
Mandalay
MYANMAR
VIETNAM
Hanoi
Haiphong
LAOS
Gulf of Tonkin
Chiang Mai
Vientiane
Mekong River
Yangon
N
THAILAND
Bangkok
CAMBODIA
SOUTH CHINA SEA
Phnom Penh
Ho Chi Minh City
ANDAMAN SEA
Gulf of Thailand
Phuket
MALAYSIA

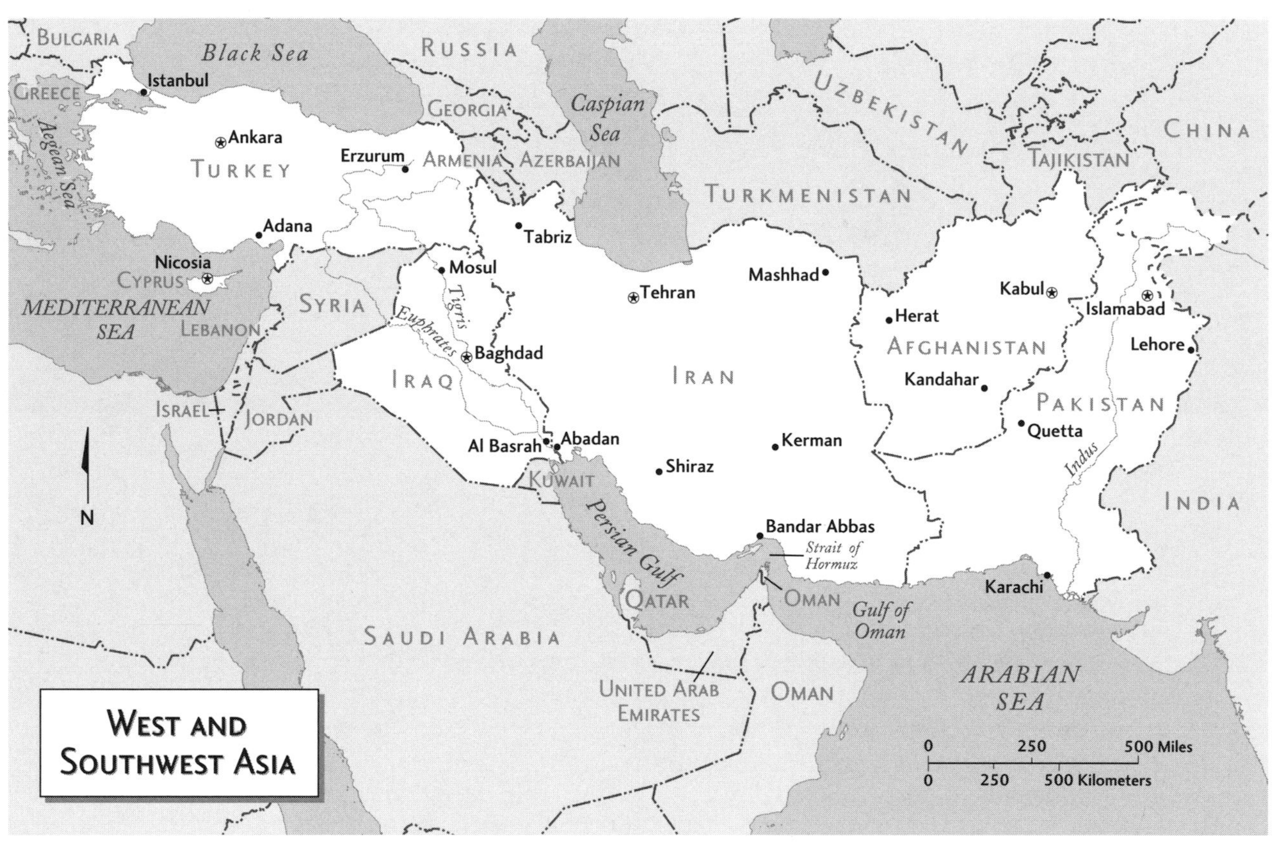
Bulgaria
Black Sea
Russia
Istanbul
Greece
Aegean Sea
Georgia
Caspian Sea
Uzbekistan
China
Ankara
Turkey
Erzurum
Armenia
Azerbaijan
Tajikistan
Turkmenistan
Adana
Tabriz
Nicosia
Cyprus
Mosul
Tigris
Mashhad
Tehran
Kabul
Mediterranean Sea
Syria
Euphrates
Herat
Islamabad
Lebanon
Baghdad
Afghanistan
Lehore
Iraq
Iran
Kandahar
Pakistan
Israel
Jordan
Quetta
Al Basrah
Abadan
Kerman
Indus
Kuwait
Shiraz
N
India
Persian Gulf
Bandar Abbas
Strait of Hormuz
Karachi
Qatar
Oman
Gulf of Oman
Saudi Arabia
Arabian Sea
United Arab Emirates
Oman
West and Southwest Asia
0 250 500 Miles
0 250 500 Kilometers

# Reader's Guide

**ASIA** *(continued)*

**International Relations** *(continued)*

Europe-Asia Relations
International Monetary Fund
Land Mines
New Zealand-Asia Relations
Nuclear Arms
United Nations
World War I
World War II

**Language and Communication**

Altaic Languages
Austroasiatic Languages
English in Asia
Hmong-Mien Languages
Indo-European Languages
Language Purification
Media
Self-Censorship
Sinitic Languages
Tibeto-Burman Languages
Turkic Languages
Uralic Languages

**Peoples, Cultures, and Society**

Fertility
Homosexuality
New Rich
Orientalism

**Religion and Philosophy**

Asian-Christian Religious Dialogue
Baraka
Muslim Saints
Religious Self-Mortification
Shamanism
Shariʿa
Zoroastrianism

**Science,Technology, and Health**

AIDS
Disease, Tropical
Terrace Irrigation

**CENTRAL ASIA**

**Arts, Literature, and Recreation**

Alpamish
Architectural Decoration—Central Asia
Architecture—Central Asia
Buzkashi
Carpets—Central Asia
Chagatay
Cuisine—Central Asia
Dance—Central Asia
Dastan, Turkic
Dombra
Edige
Felting—Central Asia
Fine Arts—Central Asia
Folklore—Central Asia
Gorkut Ata
Koroghli
Literature—Central Asia
Minaret
Music—Central Asia
Nava'i, Mir' Ali Shir
Tile Work—Central Asia
Woodworking—Central Asia

*Kazakhstan*

Auezov, Mukhtar
Dauylpaz
Dulatov, Mirzhaqyp
Kalmakanov, Bukharzhrau
Kobyz
Kunanbaev, Abai
Mailin, Beiimbet
Makhambet Utemisov
Seifullin, Saduakas
Taimanov, Isatai
Valikhanov, Chokan
Aitmatov, Chingis
Manas Epic

*Tajikistan*

Bun Bang Fai

*Turkmenistan*

Kuli, Maktum

*Uzbekistan*

Abdalrauf Fitrat
Abdullah Quaisi
Mamadali Mahmudov

**Economics, Commerce, and Transportation**

Agriculture—Central Asia
Caravans
Energy—Central Asia
Oil and Mineral Industries—Central Asia

*Kazakhstan*

Kazakhstan—Economic System

*Kyrgyzstan*

Kyrgyzstan—Economic System

*Tajikistan*

Tajikistan—Economic System

*Turkmenistan*

Turkmenistan—Economic System

*Uzbekistan*

Uzbekistan—Economic System

**Education**

Madrasahs

*Kazakhstan*

Altynsarin, Ibrahim
Kazakhstan—Education System

*Kyrgyzstan*
Kyrgyzstan—Education System
*Tajikistan*
Tajikistan—Education System
*Turkmenistan*
Turkmenistan—Education System
*Uzbekistan*
Alisher Navoiy Samarkand State University
Uzbekistan—Education System

**Geography and the Natural World**

Altay Mountains
Aral Sea
Bactria
Balkhash, Lake
Camel, Arvana Dromedary
Fergana Valley
Horse, Akhal-teke
Horse, Karabair
Horse, Lokai
Kara-Kum Desert
Khwarizm
Leopard, Snow
Murgab River
Pamir Range
Paracel Islands
Radioactive Waste and Contamination—Central Asia
Sheep, Karakul
Sheep, Marco Polo
Syr Dar'ya
Tedzhen River
Tobol River
Trans Alai
Tura Lowland
Turugart Pass
Ustyurt Plateau
Zerafshan River
*Kazakhstan*
Irtysh River
Ishim River
Kazakh Uplands
Mangyshlak Peninsula
Turgay Plateau
*Tajikistan*
Kafirnigan River
Sarez Lake
*Turkmenistan*
Garabil Plateau

**Government, Politics, and Law**

Basmachi Movement
Communism—Central Asia
Great Game
Russification and Sovietization—Central Asia
Timur
Tribes and Tribal Federations—Central Asia
Urgench
*Kazakhstan*
Almaty
Astana
Bokeikhanov, Alikhan
Kazakhstan—Political System
Kunaev, Dinmukhamed
Nazarbaev, Nursultan
Oral
Petropavlovsk
Saryshaghan
Semipalatinsk Movement
Seralin, Mukhammedzhan
Suleimenov, Olzhas
*Kyrgyzstan*
Akaev, Askar
Aksakal
Bishkek
Kurmanjan Datka
Kyrgyzstan—Political System
Osh
Usubaliev, Turdakun Usubalievich
*Tajikistan*
Dushanbe
Gafurov, Bobojan Gafurovich
Islamic Renaissance Party—Tajikistan
Khorog
Khujand
Kulob
Nabiev, Rakhmon
Qurghonteppa
Rakhmonov, Imomali
Tajikistan—Political System
Tajikistan Civil War
*Turkmenistan*
Ashgabat
Mary
Niyazov, Saparmurat
Turkmenabat
Turkmenistan—Political System
*Uzbekistan*
Bukhara
Guliston
Karakalpakstan
Karimov, Islam
Karshi
Mahalla
Nukus
Rashidov, Sharof Rashidovich
Samarqand
Tashkent
Termez
Uzbekistan—Political System

**CENTRAL ASIA** *(continued)*

**History and Profile**

Bukhara, Khanate of
Central Asia—Early Medieval Period
Central Asia—Late Medieval and Early Modern
Central Asia—Modern
Khiva, Khanate of
Paleoanthropology—Central Asia
Quqon, Khanate of

*Kazakhstan*

Kazakhstan—History
Kazakhstan—Profile

*Kyrgyzstan*

Kyrgyzstan—History
Kyrgyzstan—Profile

*Tajikistan*

Tajikistan—History
Tajikistan—Profile

*Turkmenistan*

Turkmenistan—History
Turkmenistan—Profile

*Uzbekistan*

Uzbekistan—History
Uzbekistan—Profile

**International Relations**

Central Asia—Human Rights
Central Asia-China Relations
Central Asian Regionalism
Central Asia-Russia Relations

**Language and Communication**

Central Asian Languages
Farsi-Tajiki
Media—Central Asia

*Kazakhstan*

Ai Qap
Baitursynov, Akhmet
Kazak
Leninshil Zhas

**Peoples, Cultures, and Society**

Dungans
Germans in Central Asia
Kalym
Kishlak
Koreans in Central Asia
Marriage and Family—Central Asia
Nomadic Pastoralism—Central Asia
Pamir Peoples
Russians in Central Asia
Westernization—Central Asia
Women in Central Asia
Yurt

*Kazakhstan*

Kazakhs

*Kyrgyzstan*

Clothing, Traditional—Kyrgyzstan
Kyrgyz

*Tajikistan*

Clothing, Traditional—Tajikistan
Tajiks

*Turkmenistan*

Clothing, Traditional—Turkmenistan
Turkmen

*Uzbekistan*

Clothing, Traditional—Uzbekistan
Karakalpaks
Uzbeks

**Religion and Philosophy**

Buddhism—Central Asia
Bukharian Jews
Christianity—Central Asia
Islam—Central Asia
Ismaili Sects—Central Asia
Jadidism
Minaret
Muslim Religious Board of Central Asia
Naqshbandiya

**Science,Technology, and Health**

Ariq Water System
Ibn Sina
Kara-Kum Canal
Kariz Irrigation System
Medicine, Traditional—Central Asia

**EAST ASIA**

**Arts, Literature, and Recreation**

*China*

Ang Lee
Architecture—China
Architecture, Vernacular—China
Ba Jin
Beijing Opera
Birds and Bird Cages
Calligraphy—China
Cao Xueqin
Chen Kaige
Chuci
Ci
Cinema—China
Cloisonne
Cui Jian
Cuisine—China
Dazu Rock Carvings
Ding Ling
Dragon Boat Festival
Drama—China
Du Fu
Five Classics

Fu Baoshi
Gao Xingjian
Gardening—China
Ginseng
Gong Li
Guo Moruo
Hong lou meng
Hong Shen
Humor in Chinese History
Hungry Ghost Festival
Imperial Palace
International Labor Day—China
Jin ping mei
Lao She
Li Bai
Literature—China
Longmen Grottoes
Lu Xun
Mei Lanfang
Mid-Autumn Festival
Mogao Caves
Music—China
National Day—China
Nu Shooting
Painting—China
Poetry—China
Qi Baishi
Qigong
Qin Tomb
Qingming
Qiu Jin
Quan Tangshi
Shadow Plays and Puppetry
Shen Congwen
Shi
Shijing
Social Realism—China
Sports—China
Spring Festival—China
Summer Palace
Tai Chi
Tea—China
Temple of Heaven
Thirteen Ming Tombs
Tian Han
Tofu
Twelve Muqam
Wang Yiting
Wu Changshi
Wushu
Xiqu
Xu Beihong
Xu Zhimo
Zhang Yimou
Dance, Modern— East Asia
Lacquerware
Masks—East Asia
Porcelain—East Asia

*Japan*

Aikido
Ando Tadao
Anime
Aoi Matsuri
Arata Isozaki
Architecture—Japan
Architecture—Modern Japan
Baseball—Japan
Basho
Bento
Biwa
Bon Matsuri
Bonsai
Bunjinga
Bunraku
Calligraphy—Japan
Ceramics—Japan
Children's Day—Japan
Chugen
Cinema—Japan
Cinema, Contemporary—Japan
Cuisine—Japan
Dazai Osamu
Drama—Japan
Edogawa Rampo
Emakimono
Enchi Fumiko
Endo Shusaku
Eto Jun
Fugu
Fujieda Shizuo
Fujisawa Takeo
Fujita Tsuguhara
Fukuchi Gen'ichiro
Fukuzawa Yukichi
Funakoshi Gichin
Futabatei, Shimei
Geisha
Gion Matsuri
Haiku
Hakata Matsuri
Hayashi
Hina Matsuri
Hiratsuka Raicho
Iaido
Ito Noe
Judo
Jujutsu
Kabuki

Economic Planning Agency
Economic Stabilization Program
Electronics Industry—Japan
Farmer's Movement
Financial Crisis of 1927
Fishing Industry—Japan
Furukawa Ichibei
Japan—Economic System
Japan—Money
Japanese Firms Abroad
Japanese Foreign Investments
Japanese International Cooperation Agency
Kawasaki
Nikkyoso
Overseas Economic Cooperation Fund
Quality Circles
Ringi System
Settai
Shibusawa Eiichi
Shunto
Whaling—Japan

*Koreas*

Chaebol
Fishing Industry—Korea
Food Crisis—North Korea
North and South Korean Economic Ventures
North Korea—Economic System
South Korea—Economic System
Steel Industry—Korea

*Mongolia*

Cashmere Industry
Forest Industry—Mongolia
Mongolia—Economic System
Trans-Mongolian Railway

**Education**

*China*

Academia Sinica
China—Education System
Hu Shi
National Taiwan University
Peking University
Taiwan—Education System

*Japan*

Asiatic Society of Japan
Cram Schools
Daigaku
Ebina Danjo
Gakureki Shakai
Ienaga Saburo
Imperial Rescript on Education
Japan—Education System
Kyoiku Mama
Nitobe Inazo
Shiga Shigetaka

*Koreas*

Korea Institute of Science and Technology
North Korea—Education System
Seoul National University
South Korea—Education System

*Mongolia*

Mongolia—Education System

**Geography and the Natural World**

Siberia
Yellow Sea

*China*

Bramaputra River
Cathaya Tree
Chang River
East China Sea
Emei, Mount
Famine—China
Greater Xing'an Range
Hengduan Ranges
Huang River
Huang Shan
Huanglongsi
Jiuzhaigou
Kunlun Mountains
Lu, Mount
Panda
Qinling Range
Tai Shan
Taiwan Strait
Taklimakan Desert
Tarim Basin
Tian Shan
Wudang Shan
Wulingyuan
Wuyi, Mount
Yak

*Japan*

Amami Islands
Chrysanthemum
Chubu
Chugoku
Etorofu Island
Fuji, Mount
Hokkaido
Honshu
Iriomotejima Island
Kansai Region
Kanto Region
Kinki Region
Kunashiro Island
Kyushu
Sado Island
Setouchi Region
Shikoku

**EAST ASIA** *(continued)*

**Geography and the Natural World** *(continued)*

*Japan (continued)*

Tohoku Region
Tokaimura Nuclear Disaster
Tsushima Island
Yakushima Island

*Koreas*

Amnok River
Han River
Kaema Plateau
Keumkang, Mount
Korea Bay
Korea Strait
Kum River
Naktong River and Delta
Nangnim Range
T'aebaek Mountains
Taedong River
Tumen River

*Mongolia*

Gobi Desert
Hangai Mountains
Hentii Mountains
Horse, Przewalski's

**Government, Politics, and Law**

*China*

Anhui
Beijing
Cadre System—China
Chen Duxiu
Chen Shui-bian
Chen Yun
Chengde
Chengdu
Chiang Kai-shek
Chilung
China—Political System
Chinese Civil War of 1945–1949
Chinese Communist Party
Chongqing
Ci Xi, Empress Dowager
Civil-Service Examination System—China
Communism—China
Corruption—China
Cultural Revolution—China
Deng Xiaoping
Fujian
Gang of Four
Gansu
Great Leap Forward
Guangdong
Guangxi
Guangzhou
Guizhou
Guomindang
Hainan
Hangzhou
Harbin
Hebei
Heilongjiang
Henan
Hong Kong
Hu Jintao
Hu Yaobang
Hubei
Hunan
Hundred Days Reform
Hundred Flowers Campaign
Jiang Zemin
Jiangsu
Jiangxi
Jilin
Kang Youwei
Kao-hsiung
Kong Xiangxi
Lee Teng-hui
Lhasa
Li Hongzhang
Li Peng
Liang Qichao
Liaoning
Lin Biao
Liu Shaoqi
Long March
Macao
Manchuria
Manchurian Incident
Mao Zedong
May Fourth Movement
Nanjing
Nei Monggol
Ningxia
Northern Expedition
People's Liberation Army
Political Participation, Unofficial—China
Qinghai
Quemoy and Matsu
Red Guard Organizations
Republican Revolution of 1911
Self-Strengthening Movement
Shaanxi
Shandong
Shanghai
Shanxi
Sichuan
Socialist Spiritual Civilization—China
Song Ziwen

Sun Yat-sen
Suzhou
Tainan
Taipei
Taiping Rebellion
Taiwan—Political System
Thought Work—China
Three and Five Antis Campaigns
Tiananmen Square
Tianjin
Tibet
Tibetan Uprising
Wang Jingwei
White Terror
Wu Zetian
Xi'an
Xi'an Incident
Xinjiang
Yen, Y.C. James
Yuan Shikai
Yunnan
Zeng Guofan
Zhang Zhidong
Zhao Ziyang
Zhejiang
Zhou Enlai
Zhu De
Zhu Rongji
Zuo Zongtang

**Government, Politics, and Law**

*Japan*

Abe Iso
Aichi
Akita
Aomori
Araki Sadao
Aum Shinrikyo Scandal
Baba Tatsui
Buraku Liberation League
Chiba
Citizen's Movement
Constitution, Postwar—Japan
Constitutional Crisis of 1881
Democratic Socialist Party—Japan
Eda Saburo
Ehime
Enomoto Takeaki
Fukuda Hideko
Fukuda Takeo
Fukui
Fukumoto Kazuo
Fukuoka
Fukushima
Gifu
Goto Shinpei
Gumma
Hara Takashi
Hatoyama Ichiro
Higashikuni Naruhiko
Hirohito
Hiroshima
Hyogo
Ibaraki
Ichikawa Fusae
Ikeda Hayato
Ishihara Shintaro
Ishikawa
Iwate
Japan—Political System
Japan Communist Party
Japan Socialist Party
Kagawa
Kagoshima
Kanagawa
Kanno Suga
Kato Takaaki
Kishi Nobusuke
Kochi
Kodama Yoshio
Komeito
Konoe Fumimaro
Kumamoto
Kyoto
Liberal Democratic Party—Japan
Lockheed Scandal
Maruyama Masao
Mie
Minobe Tatsukichi
Miyagi
Miyazaki
Mori Arinori
Nagano
Nagasaki
Nakasone Yasuhiro
Nara
Niigata
Ogasawara
Oita
Okayama
Okinawa
Osaka
Recruit Scandal
Saga
Saionji Kinmochi
Saitama
Sapporo
Sasagawa Ryoichi
Sato Eisaku

**EAST ASIA** *(continued)*
**Government, Politics, and Law** *(continued)*
*Japan (continued)*
Sendai
Shiga
Shimane
Shipbuilding Scandal
Shizuoka
Showa Denko Scandal
Siemens Incident
Tanaka Giichi
Textbook Scandal
Tochigi
Tojo Hideki
Tokushima
Tokyo
Tottori
Toyama
Wakayama
Yamagata
Yamagata Aritomo
Yamaguchi
Yamamoto Isoroku
Yamanashi
Yoshida Shigeru
Yoshida Shoin
*Koreas*
April 19 Revolution—Korea
Chagang Province
Cheju Province
Ch'ongjin
Chun Doo Hwan
Communism—North Korea
Corruption—Korea
Democratization—South Korea
Haeju
Hamhung
Han Yong-un
Inchon
Juche
Kaesong
Kangwon Province
Kim Dae Jung
Kim Il Sung
Kim Jong Il
Kim Pu-shik
Kim Young-sam
Kim Yu-sin
Kwangju
Kwangju Uprising
Kyonggi Province
March First Independence Movement
Namp'o
North Cholla Province
North Ch'ungch'ong Province
North Hamgyong Province
North Hwanghae Province
North Korea—Political System
North Kyongsang Province
North P'yongan Province
Park Chung Hee
Pusan
Pyongyang
Rhee, Syngman
Roh Tae Woo
Sadaejuui
Sejong, King
Seoul
Sinuiju
South Cholla Province
South Ch'ungch'ong Province
South Hamgyong Province
South Hwanghae Province
South Korea—Political System
South Kyongsang Province
South P'yongan Province
Taegu
Taejon
Three Revolutions Movement
Ulchi Mundok
Wang Kon
Yanggang Province
Yi Ha-ung
Yi Song-gye
Yi T'ae-yong
Yu Kwan Sun
Yushin
*Mongolia*
Aimag
Batmonkh, Jambyn
Choybalsan, Horloogiyn
Chormaqan, Noyan
Darhan
Erdenet
Genghis Khan
Golden Horde
Gurragchaa, Jugderdemidiyn
Karakorum
Khubilai Khan
Mongolia—Political System
Mongolian Social Democratic Party
Narantsatsralt, Janlavyn
Ochirbat, Punsalmaagiyn
Sukhbaatar, Damdiny
Tsedenbel, Yumjaagiyn
Ulaanbaatar
United Party of Mongolia

**History and Profile**

*East Asia*

Paleoanthropology—East Asia

*China*

China—Profile
Han Dynasty
Hongcun and Xidi
Jurchen Jin Dynasty
Lijiang, Old Town of
Ming Dynasty
Pingyao, Ancient City of
Qin Dynasty
Qing Dynasty
Republican China
Shang Dynasty
Sixteen Kingdoms
Song Dynasty
Sui Dynasty
Taiwan—Profile
Taiwan, Modern
Tang Dynasty
Warring States Period—China
Yuan Dynasty
Zhou Dynasty

*Japan*

Choshu Expeditions
Heian Period
Heisei Period
Japan—Profile
Jomon Period
Kamakura Period
Meiji Period
Muromachi Period
Nara Period
Showa Period
Taisho Period
Tokugawa Period
Yayoi Period

*Koreas*

Choson Kingdom
Korea—History
Koryo Kingdom
North Korea—Profile
Parhae Kingdom
South Korea—Profile
Three Kingdoms Period
Unified Shilla Kingdom

*Mongolia*

Mongol Empire
Mongolia—History
Mongolia—Profile

**International Relations**

Chinese Influence in East Asia
United Front Strategy

*China*

Boxer Rebellion
Central Asia-China Relations
China—Human Rights
China-India Relations
China-Japan Peace and Friendship Treaty
China-Japan Relations
China-Korea Relations
China-Russia Relations
China-Taiwan Relations
China-United States Relations
China-Vietnam Relations
Chinese Influence in East Asia
Chinese Influence in Southeast Asia
Hart, Robert
Japan-Taiwan Relations
Mongolia-China-Russia Relations
Nanjing Massacre
Open Door Policy
Opium War
Sino-French War
Spratly Islands Dispute
Taiwan—Human Rights
Taiwan-United States Relations
Tibet—Image in the Modern West

*Japan*

China-Japan Peace and Friendship Treaty
China-Japan Relations
Comfort Women
Japan—Human Rights
Japan-Africa Relations
Japan-France Relations
Japan-Germany Relations
Japan-Korea Relations
Japan-Latin America Relations
Japan-Pacific Islands Relations
Japan-Philippines Relations
Japan-Russia Relations
Japan-Taiwan Relations
Japan–United Kingdom Relations
Japan–United States Relations
Japanese Expansion
Nixon Shock
Northern Territories
Nuclear Allergy
Plaza Accord
Russo-Japanese War
San Francisco Peace Treaty
Sino-Japanese Conflict, Second
Sino-Japanese War
Status of Forces Agreement
United States Military Bases—Japan
United States-Japan Security Treaty
Yasukuni Shrine Controversy

**EAST ASIA** *(continued)*

**History and Profile** *(continued)*

*Koreas*

China-Korea Relations
Japan-Korea Relations
Korea-Japan Treaty of 1965
Korean War
North Korea—Human Rights
North Korea-South Korea Relations
North Korea-United States Relations
South Korea—Human Rights
South Korea-European Union Relations
South Korea-United States Relations

*Mongolia*

Mongolia—Human Rights
Mongolia-China-Russia Relations
Mongolia-Soviet Union Relations
Polo, Marco

**Language and Communication**

*China*

Chinese, Classical
Dai Qing
Hakka Languages
Mandarin
Media—China
Min
Romanization Systems, Chinese
Sino-Tibetan Languages
Wu
Xiang
Yue

*Japan*

Feminine Language
Japanese Language
Matsumoto Shigeharu
Media—Japan

*Koreas*

Hangul Script
Korean Language
Media—South Korea
Romanization Systems, Korean

*Mongolia*

Khalkha
Mongolian Languages
Tungus Languages

**Peoples, Cultures, and Society**

Marriage and Family—East Asia
Westernization—East Asia

*China*

Aboriginal Peoples—Taiwan
China—Internal Migration
China—Population Resettlement
Chinese, Overseas
Clothing, Traditional—China
Clothing, Traditional—Hong Kong
Clothing, Traditional—Taiwan
Clothing, Traditional—Tibet
Courtyards
Foot Binding
Guanxi
Hakka
Han
Hmong
Hui
Manchu
Marriage and Family—China
Miao—China
Moso
Muslim Peoples in China
National Minorities—China
Qingke
Single-Child Phenomenon—China
Social Associations—China
Social Stratification—China
Tibetans
Tujia
Uighurs
Women in China
Yao
Yi
Zhuang

*Japan*

Aging Population—Japan
Ainu
Burakumin
Chinese in Japan
Clothing, Traditional—Japan
Ijime
Koreans in Japan
Social Relations—Japan
Women in Japan

*Koreas*

Ch'onmin
Clothing, Traditional—Korea
Koreans
Koreans, Overseas
Kye
Nobi
Women in Korea
Yangban

*Mongolia*

Clothing, Traditional—Mongolia
Mongols
Russians in Mongolia

**Religion and Philosophy**

Ancestor Worship—East Asia
Zodiac System—East Asia

**SOUTH ASIA** *(continued)*

**Arts, Literature, and Recreation** *(continued)*

Jatra
Kama Sutra
Kipling, Joseph Rudyard
Literature, Bengali
Literature, Sanskrit
Literature, Tamil
Mahabharata
Manto, Sadaat Hasan
Nur Jehan
Painting—South Asia
Persian Miniature Painting
Raga
Ramayana
Rubab
Sarangi
Sarod
Sculpture—South Asia
Shah, Lalon
Shehnai
Veena

*Bangladesh*

Dance—Bangladesh
Music—Bangladesh

*Bhutan*

Textiles—Bhutan

*India*

Anand, Mulk Raj
Architecture—India
Bachchan, Amitabh
Chatterjee, Bankim Chandra
Chaudhuri, Nirad Chandra
Chughtai, Ismat
Cinema—India
Dance—India
Diwali
Drama—India
Forster, E. M.
Ghalib, Mirza Asadullah Khan
Holi
Kalidasa
Khan, Vilayat
Khusrau, Amir
Kumar, Dilip
Literature—India
Mangeshkar, Lata
Music—India
Music, Devotional—India
Narayan, R.K.
Nataka
Poetry—India
Prakarana
Premchand
Rahman, A.R.
Rao, Raja
Rasa
Ray, Satyajit
Sports—India
Taj Mahal

*Sri Lanka*

Coomaraswamy, Ananda Kentish
Dance, Kandyan
Literature, Sinhalese

**Economics, Commerce, and Transportation**

Agriculture—South Asia
British East India Company
French East India Company
Hawkins, William
Nomadic Pastoralism—South Asia
Tea—South Asia

*Bangladesh*

Bangladesh—Economic System
Grameen Bank

*India*

Agriculture—South Asia
British East India Company
French East India Company
Hawkins, William
India—Economic System
Nomadic Pastoralism—South Asia
Remittances
Salt Tax
Tea—South Asia

*Nepal*

Nepal—Economic System

*Sri Lanka*

Sri Lanka—Economic System

**Education**

Panini
Sayyid, Ahmad Khan

*Bangladesh*

Bangladesh—Education System

*India*

India—Education System

*Nepal*

Nepal—Education System

*Sri Lanka*

Sri Lanka—Education System

**Geography and the Natural World**

Andaman Sea
Bay of Bengal
Bramaputra River
Bustard, Hubara
Chagos Archipelago
Elephant, Asian
Green Revolution—South Asia
Himalaya Range

**SOUTH ASIA** *(continued)*

**Religion and Philosophy** *(continued)*

Islam—South Asia
Jones, William
Judaism—South Asia
Khwaja Mu'in al-Din Chishti
Nurbakhshiya
Pilgrimage—South Asia
Sankara
Siddhartha Gautama
Sufism—South Asia
Vivekananda, Swami
Wali Allah, Shah

*Bhutan*

Bhutan—Religion

*India*

Blavatsky, Helena Petrovna
Bhakti
Dev, Nanak Guru
Hindu Philosophy
Hindu Values
Hinduism—India
Jainism
Jesuits— India
Lingayat
Nagarjuna
Nizam ad-din Awliya
Possession
Ramakrishna
Ramanuja
Sai Baba, Satya
Sikhism
Tagore, Rabindranath
Teresa, Mother
Upanishads

**Science,Technology, and Health**

Calendars—South Asia
Climatology—South Asia

*India*

Medicine, Ayurvedic
Medicine, Unani

**SOUTHEAST ASIA**

**Arts, Literature, and Recreation**

Architecture—Southeast Asia
Batik
Cockfighting
Drama—Southeast Asia
Hari Raya Puasa
Kain Batik
Kain Songket
Mendu
Sepak Takraw
Thaipusam

*Cambodia*

Angkor Wat
Literature, Khmer

*Indonesia*

Arja
Bali Barong-Rangda
Balinese Sanghyang
Bedaya
Borobudur
Cuisine—Indonesia
Dance—Bali
Gambang Kromong
Gambuh
Gamelan
Hikayat Amir Hamza
Ludruk
Masks, Javanese
Music—Indonesia
Noer, Arifin C.
Pramoedya Ananta Toer
Puisi
Randai
Rendra, W.S.
Riantiarno, Nano
Sandiwara
Wayang Beber
Wayang Golek
Wayang Kulit
Wayang Topeng
Wayang Wong
Wijaya, Putu

*Laos*

Ikat Dyeing
Luang Prabang
Music, Folk—Laos
Palm-Leaf Manuscripts
Textiles—Laos
That Luang Festival
Wat Xieng Khouan

*Malaysia*

Bangsawan
Chang Fee Ming
Chuah Thean Teng
Cuisine—Malaysia
Dance—Malaysia
Dikir Barat
Gawai Dayak
Jikey
Jit, Krishen
Labu Sayong
Lim, Shirley
Mak Yong
Maniam, K.S.
Manora

**SOUTHEAST ASIA** *(continued)*

**Education**

*Brunei*

Universiti Brunei Darussalam

*Cambodia*

Cambodia—Education System
Royal University of Phnom Penh

*Indonesia*

Bandung Institute of Technology
Gadjah Mada University
Indonesia—Education System
University of Indonesia

*Laos*

Laos—Education System
Sisavangvong University

*Malaysia*

Malaysia—Education System
Universiti Sains Malaysia
University of Malaya

*Myanmar*

Myanmar—Education System

*Philippines*

Philippines—Education System

*Singapore*

Nanyang Technological University
National University of Singapore
Singapore—Education System

*Thailand*

Chulalongkorn University
Thailand—Education System

*Vietnam*

Vietnam—Education System

**Geography and the Natural World**

Andaman Sea
Banteng
Borneo
Dangrek Range
Green Revolution—Southeast Asia
Leopard, Clouded
Mongoose
Orangutan
Sun Bear

*Cambodia*

Cardamon Mountains
Elephant Range
Kompong Som Bay
Tonle Sap

*Indonesia*

Babirusa
Bali
Banda Sea
Flores Sea
Java Sea
Komodo Dragon
Maluku
Nusa Tenggara
Timor Sea

*Laos*

Bolovens Plateau
Plain of Jars

*Malaysia*

Cameron Highlands
Kinabalu, Mount
Strait of Malacca

*Myanmar*

Arakan Yoma Mountains
Inle Lake Region
Irrawaddy River and Delta
Salween River
Sittang River

*Philippines*

Agno River
Cagayan River
Caraballo Mountains
Celebes Sea
Cordillera Central
Luzon Group
Maguey
Mindanao
Philippine Sea
Sierra Madre
Sulu Archipelago
Visayan Islands
Zambales Mountains

*Thailand*

Chao Phraya River and Delta
Doi Inthanon
Gulf of Thailand
Khon Kaen
Nakhon Ratchasima
Peninsular Thailand
Three Pagodas Pass

*Vietnam*

Cam Ranh Bay
Central Highlands of Vietnam
Con Dao Islands
Ha Long Bay
Ho Dynasty Citadel
Hoan Kiem Lake
Karun River and Shatt al Arab River
Mekong River and Delta
Red River and Delta
Tonkin Gulf

**Government, Politics, and Law**

Albuquerque, Afonso de
British Military Administration
Doumer, Paul
Dutch East India Company

Romusha
Weld, Frederick
*Brunei*
Azahari, A.M.
Bandar Seri Begawan
Brooke, James
Hassanal Bolkaih
Parti Rakyat Brunei
*Cambodia*
Buddhist Liberal Democratic Party—Cambodia
Cambodia—Civil War of 1970-1975
Cambodia—Political System
Cambodian People's Party
Fa Ngoum
FUNCINPEC
Heng Samrin
Hun Sen
Jayavarman II
Jayavarman VII
Khieu Samphan
Khmer Rouge
Killing Fields
Lon Nol
Phnom Penh
Phnom Penh Evacuation
Pol Pot
Ranariddh, Norodom
Sam Rainsy
Sihanouk, Norodom
*East Timor*
Belo, Bishop Carlos
Dili
Dili Massacre
Fretilin
Gusmao, Xanana
Ramos-Horta, José
*Indonesia*
Airlangga
Amboina Massacre
Bandung
Batavia
Bosch, Johannes van den
Budi Utomo
Coen, Jan Pieterszoon
Cukong
Daendels, Herman
Darul Islam
Ethnic Colonial Policy—Indonesia
Gajah Mada
Gerindo
Gestapu Affair
Golkar
Habibie, B.J.
Hamengku Buwono IX, Sri Sultan
Hatta, Mohammad
Hizbullah
Indonesia—Political Parties
Indonesia—Political System
Indonesian Democratic Party
Indonesian Revolution
Irian Jaya
Jakarta
Jakarta Riots of May 1998
Java
Kalimantan
Malik, Adam
Medan
Megawati Sukarnoputri
Military, Indonesia
Moerdani, Leonardus Benjamin
New Order
Old Order
Pancasila
Partai Kebangkitan Bangsa
Partai Persatuan Pembangunan
Rais, Muhammad Amien
Sarekat Islam
Solo
Speelman, Cornelius
Suharto
Sukarno
Sulawesi
Sumatra
Surabaya
Taman Siswa
Treaty of Giyanti
Umar, Teuku
Wahid, Abdurrahman
Yogyakarta
*Laos*
Bokeo
Chao Anou
Civil War of 1956–1975—Laos
Kaysone Phomvihan
Lao People's Revolutionary Party
Laos—Political System
Louangnamtha
Pathet Lao
Setthathirat
Souphanuvong, Prince
Souvanna Phouma, Prince
Vientiane
Xayabury
*Malaysia*
Abdul Razak
Abu Bakar
Anwar, Ibrahim
Badawi, Abdullah Ahmed

**SOUTHEAST ASIA** *(continued)*

**Government, Politics, and Law** *(continued)*

*Malaysia (continued)*

Bendahara
Birch, James W. W.
Bumiputra
Clifford, Hugh
Federal Territories—Malaysia
Federation of Malaysia
Haji, Raja
Hussein Onn
Iskandar Muda
Johor
Kapitan Cina
Kedah
Kelantan
Kota Kinabalu
Kuala Lumpur
Kuching
Laksamana
Light, Francis
Lim Chong Eu
Mahathir Mohamad
Mahmud Shah
Malay States, Unfederated
Malayan People's Anti-Japanese Army
Malayan Union
Malaysia—Political System
Malaysian Chinese Association
Mansur Shah
Mat Salleh Rebellion
May 13 Ethnic Riots— Malaysia
Melaka
Negeri Sembilan
Ningkan, Stephen Kalong
Onn Bin Jaafar
Pahang
Pangkor Treaty
Penang
Perak
Perlis
Raffles, Thomas Stamford
Resident System
Rukunegara
Sabah
Sarawak
Straits Settlements
Swettenham, Frank
Tan Siew Sin
Temenggong
Templer, Gerald
Trengganu
Wan Ahmad
Yap Ah Loy

*Myanmar*

All Burma Students Democratic Front
Anawratha
Anti-Fascist People's Freedom League—Myanmar
Aung San
Aung San Suu Kyi
Bassein
Burma Independence Army
Chin State
Communist Party of Burma
Irrawaddy Division
Kachin Independence Organization
Kachin State
Karen National Union
Karen State
Kayah State
Magwe Division
Mandalay
Mandalay Division
Mon State
Mong Tai Army
Moulmein
Myanmar—Political System
National League for Democracy—Myanmar
National Unity Party—Myanmar
Ne Win, U
Nu, U
Palaung State Liberation Party
Pao National Organization
Pegu
Rakhine State
Sagaing Division
Shan State
Shan State Army
State Law and Order Restoration Council—Myanmar
Tenasserim Division
Thakins
Than Shwe
Thant, U
Union Solidarity and Development Association—Mya
United Wa State Party
Yangon
Yangon Division

*Philippines*

Aquino, Benigno
Aquino, Corazon
Autonomous Region of Muslim Mindanao
Baguio
Cebu
Davao
Estrada, Joseph
Garcia, Carlos P.

**SOUTHEAST ASIA** *(continued)*

**History and Profile** *(continued)*

Paleoanthropology—Southeast Asia
Portuguese in Southeast Asia
Srivijaya

*Brunei*

Brunei—Political System
Brunei—Profile

*Cambodia*

Cambodia—History
Cambodia—Profile
Khmer Empire

*East Timor*

East Timor—Profile

*Indonesia*

Aceh Rebellion
Amangkurat
British-Dutch Wars
Candi of Java
Indonesia—History
Indonesia—Profile
Java War
Konfrontasi
Majapahit
Mataram
Netherlands East Indies
Padri War
Pakualaman
Sailendra

*Laos*

Laos—History
Laos—Profile

*Malaysia*

Anglo-Dutch Treaty
Federated Malay States
Malaysia—History
Malaysia—Profile
Melaka Sultanate
White Rajas

*Myanmar*

Myanmar—History
Myanmar—Profile
Pagan

*Philippines*

Philippines—History
Philippines—Profile

*Singapore*

Singapore—History
Singapore—Profile

*Thailand*

Ayutthaya, Kingdom of
Ban Chiang
Sukhothai
Thailand—History
Thailand—Profile

*Vietnam*

Vietnam—History
Vietnam—Profile

**International Relations**

Association of South-East Asian Nations
Bali Summit
Bandung Conference
Bangkok Declaration
Chinese Influence in Southeast Asia
Five Power Defence Arrangements
India-Southeast Asia Relations
Indochina War of 1940–1941
Piracy—Southeast Asia
Southeast Asia—Human Rights
Southeast Asia Treaty Organization
Treaty of Amity and Co-operation of 1976
ZOPFAN

*Cambodia*

Cambodia-Laos Relations
Cambodia-Vietnam Relations
United Nations Transitional Authority in Cambodia

*East Timor*

United Nations in East Timor

*Indonesia*

Indonesia-Malaysia Relations
Indonesia–United States Relations
Irian Jaya Conquest
Volksraad

*Laos*

Cambodia-Laos Relations
Laos-Thailand Relations
Laos-Vietnam Relations

*Malaysia*

Indonesia-Malaysia Relations
Malayan Emergency
Malaysia-Europe Relations
Sabah Dispute

*Myanmar*

India-Myanmar Relations
Myanmar—Foreign Relations
Myanmar—Human Rights

*Philippines*

Japan-Philippines Relations
Philippines—Human Rights
Philippines–United States Relations

*Thailand*

Laos-Thailand Relations

*Vietnam*

Cambodia-Vietnam Relations
China-Vietnam Relations
Franco-Viet Minh War
Laos-Vietnam Relations
Soviet-Vietnamese TFOC

**SOUTHEAST ASIA** *(continued)*

**Religion and Philosophy** *(continued)*

*Malaysia*

Angkatan Belia Islam Malaysia
Islam—Malaysia

*Myanmar*

Christianity—Myanmar
Islam—Myanmar
Spirit Cults

*Philippines*

Catholicism, Roman—Philippines
Iglesia ni Christo
Islam—Philippines
Philippine Independent Church
Ruiz, Saint Lorenzo
Sin, Jaime

*Thailand*

Buddhadasa, Bhikku
Dhammayut Sect
Hinduism—Thailand
Phra Pathom Chedi

*Vietnam*

Buddhism—Vietnam
Cao Dai
Catholicism, Roman—Vietnam
Hoa Hao
Thich Nhat Hanh

**Science,Technology, and Health**

Bedil
Calendars—Southeast Asia
Gunpowder and Rocketry

**SOUTHWEST ASIA**

**Arts, Literature, and Recreation**

Alghoza
Bhitai, Shah Abdul Latif
Jami, 'Abdurrahman
Khushal Khan Khatak
Shah, Waris

*Afghanistan*

Cuisine—Afghanistan

*Pakistan*

Ali Khan, Bade Ghulam
Bhit Shah
Faiz Ahmed Faiz
Gulgee
Hir Ranjha Story
Iqbal, Muhammad
Makli Hill
Naqsh, Jamil
Nusrat Fateh Ali Khan
Sabri Brothers
Sadequain

**Economics, Commerce, and Transportation**

*Afghanistan*

Afghanistan—Economic System

*Pakistan*

Karakoram Highway
Pakistan—Economic System

**Education**

*Pakistan*

Pakistan—Education System

**Geography and the Natural World**

Badakhshan
Kabul River
Karakoram Mountains
Khyber Pass
Ravi River

*Afghanistan*

Afghan Hound
Dasht-e Margo
Hunza
Wakhan

*Pakistan*

Azad Kashmir
Baltistan
Bolan Pass
Indus River
Indus River Dolphin
Khunjerab Pass
Sutlej River

**Government, Politics, and Law**

Afghani, Jamal ad-din
Baluchistan
Dost Muhammad
Taxila

*Afghanistan*

Afghanistan—Political System
Amanollah
Bagram
Bamian
Bin Laden, Osama
Daud, Muhammad
Dawai, Abdul Hadi
Din Mohammad, Mushk-e Alam
Ghazna
Herat
Kabul
Mahmud of Ghazna
Mazar-e Sharif
Mujahideen
Omar, Mullah Muhammad
Taliban
Zahir Shah

*Pakistan*

Abdullah, Muhammad
Anarkali

Ayub Khan
Bhutto, Benazir
Bhutto, Zulfiqar Ali
David, Collin
Hadood
Islamabad
Jamaʿat-e-Islami
Jinnah, Mohammed Ali
Karachi
Khan, Abdul Ghaffar
Lahore
Mohenjo Daro
Muhajir Qawmi Movement
Multan
Musharraf, Pervez
North-West Frontier Province Sarhad
Pakistan—Political System
Pakistan People's Party
Peshawar
Rahmat Ali, Chauduri
Rohtas Fort
Sehwan
Sind
Zia-ul-Haq, Mohammad

**History and Profile**

*Afghanistan*

Afghanistan—History
Afghanistan—Profile
Durrani

*Pakistan*

Federally Administered Tribal Areas—Pakistan
Pakistan—History
Pakistan—Profile

**International Relations**

*Afghanistan*

Afghanistan—Human Rights
Treaty of Gandomak

*Pakistan*

Bangladesh-Pakistan Relations
India-Pakistan Relations
Pakistan—Human Rights

**Language and Communication**

Pashto

*Afghanistan*

Dari

**Peoples, Cultures, and Society**

Afridi
Baluchi
Brahui
Pashtun
Pashtunwali
Waziri
Clothing, Traditional—Afghanistan
Ethnic Conflict—Afghanistan
Hazara

*Pakistan*

Sindhi
Siraiki
Women in Pakistan

**Religion and Philosophy**

Bakhsh, Data Ganj
Islam—Southwest Asia
Shah, Mihr Ali
Shahbaz Qalandar Lal
Sufism—Southwest Asia

*Afghanistan*

Ansari, Abdullah
Bitab, Sufi

*Pakistan*

Mawdudi, Abu'l-A'la
Muhajir

**WEST ASIA**

**Arts, Literature, and Recreation**

Architecture—West Asia
Architecture, Islamic—West Asia
Cinema—West Asia
Music—West Asia
Rudaki
Shahnameh Epic
Sports—Islamic Asia
Twelver Shiʿism

*Iran*

Cuisine—Iran
No-ruz
Literature, Persian

*Iraq*

Cuisine—Iraq
Poetry—Iraq

*Turkey*

Children's Day—Turkey
Cuisine—Turkey
Guney, Yilmaz
Literature—Turkey
Music—Turkey
Nesin, Aziz
Pamuk, Orhan

**Economics, Commerce, and Transportation**

Agriculture—West Asia
Industry—West Asia
Oil Industry—West Asia
Organization of Petroleum Exporting Countries

*Iran*

Iran—Economic System

*Iraq*

Iraq—Economic System

*Turkey*

Etatism—Turkey

**WEST ASIA** *(continued)*

**Economics, Commerce, and Transportation** *(continued)*

Turkey—Economic System

**Education**

*Iran*

Iran—Education System

*Iraq*

Iraq—Education System

*Turkey*

Turkey—Education System

**Geography and the Natural World**

Caucasia
Euphrates River
Sistan
Tigris River

*Iran*

Abkhazia
Amu Dar'ya
Dagestan
Elburz
Gulf of Oman
Persian Gulf
Zagros Mountains

*Turkey*

Aegean Sea
Anti-Taurus
Ararat, Mount
Black Sea
Bosporus
Cappadocia
Cilician Gates
Dardanelles
Gaziantep
Izmir
Kizel Irmak River
Marmara, Sca of
Tarsus
Taurus Mountains
Yesilirmak River

**Government, Politics, and Law**

Aleppo
Karabag
Yerevan

*Iran*

Abadan
Ardabil
Azerbaijan
Bakhtaran
Bandar Abbas
Bazargan, Mehdi
Constitution, Islamic—Iran
Esfahan
Fars
Hamadan
Iran—Political System
Islamic Revolution—Iran
Kandahar
Kerman
Khomeini, Ayatollah
Khurasan
Khuzestan
Mashhad
Qom
Sana'i
Shariati, Ali
Shiraz
Tabriz
Tehran
Veleyet-e Faqih

*Iraq*

Al-Najaf
Baghdad
Basra
Hussein, Saddam
Iraq—Political System
Karbala
Kirkuk
Mosul
Sulaymaniya

*Turkey*

Adalet Partisi
Adana
Afyon
Amasya
Anatolia
Ankara
Antakya
Antalya
Ataturk
Bayar, Mahmut Celal
Bodrum
Bursa
Constitution—Turkey
Demirel, Suleyman
Democrat Party—Turkey
Diyarbakir
Edirne
Erzurum
Halide Edib Adivar
Hikmet, Nazim
Inonu, Mustafa Ismet
Istanbul
Iznik
Kars
Kas
Kemal, Yasar
Konya

Kutahya
Menderes, Adnan
Mersin
North Cyprus, Turkish Republic of
Ozal, Turgut
Pergamon
Refah and Fazilet Parties
Republican People's Party—Turkey
Rize
Samsun
Sardis
Sinop
Sivas
Tanzimat
Trabzon
Turkey—Political System
Urfa
Van
Zonguldak

**History and Profile**

*Iran*

Iran—History
Iran—Profile
Pahlavi Dynasty
Qajar Dynasty

*Iraq*

Iraq—History
Iraq—Profile

*Turkey*

Archaeology—Turkey
Byzantines
Hittites
Ottoman Empire
Turkey—Profile
Turkey, Republic of

**International Relations**

Ibn Battutah

*Iran*

Iran—Human Rights
Iran-Iraq Relations
Iran-Russia Relations
Iran–United States Hostage Crisis
Iran–United States Relations

*Iraq*

Iran-Iraq Relations
Iraq—Human Rights
Iraq-Turkey Relations
Persian Gulf War

*Turkey*

European Union and Turkey
Iraq-Turkey Relations
North Atlantic Treaty Organization and Turkey
Turkey—Human Rights
Turkey-Russia Relations
Turkey–United States Relations

**Language and Communication**

Arabic
Media—West Asia
Persian

**Peoples, Cultures, and Society**

Arabs
Armenians
Kurds
Marriage and Family—West Asia
Turks—West Asia
Westernization—West Asia
Women in West Asia

*Iran*

Azerbaijanis
Bakhtiari
Persepolis
Persians

*Iraq*

Clothing, Traditional—Iraq
Marsh Arabs

*Turkey*

Albanians
Bulgarians
Circassians
Clothing, Traditional—Turkey
Greeks in Turkey
Miletus
Tatars

**Religion and Philosophy**

Alevi Muslims
Baha'i
Islam—West Asia
Judaism—West Asia
Muslims, Shi'ite
Muslims, Sunni
Oriental Orthodox Church
Qadiriya
Saint Paul

*Iran*

Babism

*Turkey*

Eastern Orthodox Church

**Science, Technology, and Health**

Calendars—West Asia
Kariz Irrigation System
Medicine, Traditional—West Asia

# Encyclopedia of Modern Asia

**IAIDO** *Iaido* is a Japanese martial art that is practiced primarily for personal physical and spiritual development, but also for competition. *Iaido* is characterized by drawing a sword from the scabbard and cutting in one motion; the name means "having the presence of mind to be flexible in response to an emergency." Developed during the Tokugawa period (1600/1603–1868), when a symbol of samurai authority was the long, curved, single-edged sword, the art was perfected by Jinsuke Shinenobu (c. 1546–1621) and his students. *Iaido* practice involves drawing the sword, making the initial cut, making the finishing cuts, cleaning the blade, and sheathing the sword. Different techniques are used depending on the position of the opponent and the number of opponents. *Iaido* is generally performed alone, with the performer facing an imaginary opponent. In competitions, the performers stand side by side and their technique is rated by judges. *Iaido* is less popular than other Japanese martial arts and has been less influenced by efforts to make it an international competitive sport.

*Kim Taylor*

**Further Reading**

Craig, Darrell. (1988) *Iai: The Art of Drawing the Sword.* Tokyo: Charles E. Tuttle.

Obata Toshishiro. (1987) *Crimson Steel: The Sword Technique of the Samurai.* Westlake Village, CA: Dragon Enterprises.

Taylor, Kim. (1994) *Kim's Big Book of Iaido.* 5 vols. Guelph, Canada: Sei DoKai.

**IBARAKI** (2002 est. pop. 3.1 million). Ibaraki Prefecture is situated in the central region of Japan's island of Honshu, where it occupies an area of 6,095 square kilometers. Ibaraki's main geographical features are the Abukuma and Yamizo mountains in the north and the broad plains of the Kanto in the south. The prefecture is bordered by the Pacific Ocean and by Chiba, Tochigi, Saitama, and Fukushima prefectures. Once known as Hitachi Province, Ibaraki assumed its present name and borders in 1875.

The prefecture's capital is Mito, which grew around a castle erected during the Kamakura period (1185–1333) by the Daijo family. After the Battle of Sekigahara (1600), it was taken over as castle town by a son of the first Tokugawa shogun. The Tokugawa, or Edo, period (1600/1603–1868) was an era of political and cultural predominance for the Mito domain, comprised of parts of Hitachi and Shimotsuke Provinces. Its rulers founded two schools of imperial learning, the Shokokan and later the Kodokan, together known as the Mito school. In 1864, at the outset of the Mito Civil War, pro-imperial rebels led a major uprising against the Tokugawa shogunate; they were crushed, but the shogunate itself soon crumbled. The focus of present-day Mito is commercial activity, including the production of *natto* (fermented soybeans). The prefecture's other important cities are Hitachi, Tsuchiura, and Koga.

Ibaraki Prefecture has large areas of arable land, producing great quantities of vegetables, fruit, rice, and other grain primarily for the Tokyo market. Fishing remains a leading activity as well. In recent decades heavy industries from the Keihin Industrial Zone have spread into the prefecture. Among them are facilities for the manufacture and processing of electrical equipment, steel, petrochemicals, and foodstuffs.

This transformation has been accompanied by such mammoth projects as Tsukuba Academic New Town and the Kashima Coastal Industrial Region. There is also a city named Ibaraki in northern Osaka Prefecture.

*E. L. S. Weber*

**Further Reading**

"Ibaraki Prefecture." (1993) *Japan: An Illustrated Encyclopedia*. Tokyo: Kodansha.

**IBN AL-QASIM, MUHAMMAD** (d. 715), Arab conqueror of Sind in India. An Arab military commander from the tribe of Thaqif, Muhammad ibn al-Qasim is famous in Islamic history as the conqueror of the western Indian province of Sind under the Umayyad dynasty (661–750). He won favor with the Umayyad governor of Iraq, al-Hajjaj, who dispatched him to Sind at the head of a military expedition between 708 and 711; Ibn al-Qasim was probably about fifteen or seventeen years old at this time.

He arrived by land in India to punish Dahir, the ruler of Sind, who had failed to curb pirates operating off the coast of his province and who were disrupting Muslim shipping. His forces conquered several Indian cities, among them the Hindu pilgrim city of Multan, and killed Dahir.

In some Arabic sources, Ibn al-Qasim is said to have accorded the Hindus the status of "protected people" (*ahl al-dhimma*). This status is traditionally reserved under Islamic law for Jews and Christians, who as kindred followers of a revealed scripture, are granted protection by the Islamic state upon payment of a poll tax. On account of this concession to the Hindus, Ibn al-Qasim is regarded by modern Muslims in particular as a paragon of religious tolerance. He is also greatly admired for his youthful military prowess. Ibn al-Qasim's career came to an abrupt end, however, with the death of al-Hajjaj in 715. Under the new administration, he was dismissed from his post and brutally put to death.

*Asma Afsaruddin*

**Further Reading**

Friedmann, Y. (1960) "Muhammad b. al-Kasim." In *The Encyclopaedia of Islam*, edited by H. A. R. Gibb et al. Leiden, Netherlands: Brill, 7:405–406.

**IBN BATTUTAH** (1304–1368/69), Arab traveler and writer. Abu'Abd Allah Muhammad ibn'Abd Allah al-Lawati at-Tanji ibn Battutah, one of the greatest travelers of the Middle Ages, spent thirty years visiting every Muslim country of his day and recorded in accurate detail the social and political life he observed on his journeys. Born in Tangier, a seaport in present-day Morocco in North Africa, he began to travel at the age of twenty-one years, when he made the hajj (pilgrimage to Mecca). On his way he passed through today's Egypt and Syria and returned through Iran and Iraq. On a second journey, he explored southern Arabia, East Africa, and the Persian Gulf.

Ibn Battutah next traveled north to Constantinople and crossed southern Russia, Samarqand (now in Uzbekistan), and Afghanistan to arrive in Delhi, India, around 1333. In 1342, Muhammad ibn Tughluq (c. 1290–1351), the son of the sultan of Delhi, sent him as an envoy to the Chinese emperor. Ibn Battutah reached present-day Beijing via the Maldive Islands in the Indian Ocean, Ceylon (today's Sri Lanka), and Assam (a state in India) and from the East returned to Fes (Fez) in northern Morocco, thereby crossing half of the Earth. From Fes he went north to al-Andalus (Muslim Spain) in Europe and later traveled south across the Sahara Desert to the Sudan in north central Africa.

Although historians and geographers largely ignored his journals until the late twentieth century, Ibn Battutah is estimated to have traveled about 125,000 kilometers, much farther than Marco Polo (1254–1324) and other medieval travelers, and his observations of the countries he visited are far more detailed and accurate than those of Polo.

*David Levinson*

**Further Reading**

Ibn Battuta. (1958–2000) *The Travels of Ibn Battuta, A.D. 1325–1354*. Trans. with revisions and notes from Arabic text ed. by C. Defrémery and B. R. Sanguinetti, by H. A. R. Gibb. 5 vols. London and Cambridge, U.K.: Published for the Hakluyt Society by Cambridge University Press.

**IBN SINA** (980–1037), philosopher, scientist, physician. Ibn Sina was a philosopher, scientist, and physician better known in the West as Avicenna. His full name was Abu 'Ali al-Husain ibn Sina. Ibn Sina was born in Bukhara, Uzbekistan, in 980 CE and died in Hamadan, Persia, in 1037. By age sixteen, Ibn Sina had learned all he could from his teachers and went on to complete his education at the library of the Samanid dynasty (864–999 CE) of Bukhara, to which he was granted access after curing a member of the dynasty.

## IBN BATTUTAH

The markets around the Umayyad mosque in Damascus as described by Ibn Battutah:

> An eastern door, the largest of the doors of the mosque, called the Jairun Door. It has a large vestibule, leading out to a vast and broad arcade, entered through a quintuple gateway [of arches] formed by six tall columns. . . . Along both sides of this arcade there are pillars upon which are supported circular passages, where the cloth-merchants amongst others have their shops; above these again are long passages in which are the shops of jewellers and booksellers and makers of admirable glassware. In the square adjoining the first door are stalls belonging to the principal legal witness, two stalls among them belonging to the Shafi-ites [a legal school] and the rest to those of various schools. In each stall there may be five or six notaries [that is, a legal witness known for honesty whose testimony would be readily accepted by an Islamic judge and employed for witnessing contracts] and the person authorized to draw up contracts of marriage on behalf of the qadi [Islamic judge]. The other notaries are scattered throughout the city. In the vicinity of these stalls is the bazaar of the stationers, who sell paper, pens and ink. In the centre of the vestibule which we have been describing there is a large circular basing, made of marble, surmounted by an unroofed cupola, which is supported by marble columns, and in the centre of the basin is a copper pipe which violently forces out water so that it rises into the air more than a man's height. They call it the Waterspout, and its aspect is striking.

*Source:* Ibn Battuta. (1958) *The Travels of Ibn Battuta, A.D. 1325–1354.* Translated by H.A.R. Gibb. London: Hakluyt Society, 131.

Unfortunately, he lived in very unsettled times and was never able to stay for very long in one place. Ibn Sina was actually imprisoned and forced into hiding more than once. He did enjoy two reasonably stable times at the courts of princes in Hamadan and later in Isfahan, Persia. He died accompanying the latter prince on a campaign against Hamadan.

Ibn Sina is best remembered for his two books, *Shifa* (Book of Healing) and *Qanun*. *Shifa* is a book on philosophy drawn largely from the works of Aristotle. *Qanun* is a medical text drawn mostly from the works of the ancient Greek physicians Hippocrates (c. 460–c. 377 BCE) and Galen (129–c. 199 CE). *Qanun*, however, recast their ideas along with his own observations into a highly accessible form and became the most widely used medical text in Europe and the Middle East for nearly seven hundred years.

*Andrew Sharp*

### Further Reading

Browne, Edward G. (1921) *Arabian Medicine*. London: Cambridge University Press.

**ICHIKAWA FUSAE** (1893–1981), leading Japanese politician, activist in Japan's women's liberation movement. Ichikawa Fusae was born in Aichi Prefecture and graduated from Aichi Women's Normal

School, after which she first pursued a career in elementary school teaching and journalism. In 1919, she entered the Yuaikai, a leading labor union, and took an active part in promoting the status of women workers. In the following year, she established the New Woman's Association with the feminist Hiratsuka Raicho (1886–1971). Resigning from the Association in 1921, Ichikawa went to the United States for two and a half years to study women's issues.

While working for the Tokyo branch of the International Labor Organization, Ichikawa formed the League for Women's Suffrage in 1924 and worked in the popular rights movement until the dissolution of the League in 1940. During World War II, Ichikawa played a significant role in numerous activities of the suffrage movement, which faced difficult compromises with the government over wartime collaboration. After the war, she established the New Japan Women's League (changing the name to The Japanese League of Women Voters in 1950), and she devoted herself to enlightening the public about women's issues and to promoting electoral ideals and political reform. From 1953, Ichikawa was elected five times to the House of Councilors, the last time being in 1980, the year before she died.

*Kyoko Murakami*

**IENAGA SABURO** (b. 1913), Japanese historian. Born in Aichi Prefecture in 1913, Ienaga Saburo graduated from Tokyo Imperial University (now the University of Tokyo) in 1937. He began his career as a high school teacher, later moving to Tokyo University of Education and, subsequently, to Chuo University. In 1948, he was awarded the Japan Academy Prize and became professor emeritus at Tokyo University of Education.

Ienaga brought three lawsuits (1965, 1967, and 1984) against the Ministry of Education, challenging the constitutional legitimacy of the textbook-screening system to which his high school Japanese history textbooks had been subjected. These suits raised a number of fundamental issues about the powers and qualifications of government officials to make decisions on curriculum content and the extent to which those powers could be reviewed in the courts. Although Ienaga lost the first two cases in the Supreme Court, he achieved a partial victory in his third court battle in the 1997 Supreme Court decision, which ruled that government may not tamper with historical truth in textbooks. Ienaga's lawsuits have had a significant influence, not only on the administrative procedure of the textbook-screening system, but also on diplomatic relations between Japan and its neighbors as well as on human rights issues worldwide.

*Kyoko Murakami*

**Further Reading**

Horio Teruhisa. (1988) *Textbook Control on Trial: The Sugimoto Decision and Textbook Authors on Trial: The Takatsu Decision in Educational Thought and Ideology in Modern Japan.* Tokyo: University of Tokyo Press.

Ienaga Saburo. (1997) *Ienaga Saburo: Ichirekishi Gakusha no Ayumi* (Ienaga Saburo: Autobiography of a Historian). Tokyo: Nippon Tosho Senta.

———. (2001) *Japan's Past, Japan's Future: One Historian's Odyssey*. Trans. by Richard H. Minear. New York: Rowman & Littlefield.

**IGLESIA NI CHRISTO** The Iglesia ni Christo ("Church of Christ") was founded in the Philippines in 1913 by Felix Manalo (1886–1963). Manalo was raised a Roman Catholic but as a teenager was influenced by a secretive local spiritual sect, as well as by Methodist and Presbyterian churches, the Church of Christ, and Seventh-Day Adventism. Following a religious experience, he founded the Iglesia ni Christo, which he incorporated with twelve followers in 1914. In 1922 he proclaimed that he was God's final messenger, and around 1930 he began to preach the church's most controversial claim, that Christ was not divine.

The church aggressively sought new members and after World War II expanded rapidly: it claimed 60,000 adherents in 1948 and 200,000 in 1960. The church also expanded outside the Philippines, particularly in Philippine diaspora communities in Hawaii and California. In 2002 it is second only to the Roman Catholic Church in the Philippines, with 2,500 congregations in the Philippines and several hundred more overseas. Its worldwide membership is estimated at between three and six million.

In part because of its perceived anti-Christ and anti-Trinitarian doctrines, its secrecy, and its aggressive proselytizing, the church has received much attention from organizations that oppose cults. Much of what is known of the church is from what it publishes in its magazine, *Pasugo*, which began publication in 1939 and is now available in Pilipino and English.

*David Levinson*

**Further Reading**

Let Us Reason. (2002) *Iglesia ni Christo.* Retrieved 15 April 2002, from: http://www.letusreason.org/Igleidir.htm.

**IJIME** *Ijime* is a considered a major social problem in Japan. Although translated as "bullying," *ijime* is really collective bullying and may include everything from name-calling to extortion or physical violence. The collective nature of *ijime* makes it difficult for adults to observe, and peer pressure silences students; most *ijime* occurs among peers. Audiences often play a significant role in promoting *ijime*.

Within Japan, popular opinion has linked *ijime* with excess academic competition and the growth of *juku* (cram schools). Academic research suggests that the contemporary characteristics of *ijime* have appeared largely since the end of the 1970s. Characteristics such as the collective nature of *ijime* and its "invisibility" to adults have been linked to school features such as high levels of social homogeneity, limited physical space, and uniformity-oriented curricular goals. Scholars have also linked some types of *ijime* to the influence of mass media and a cultural cynicism. Economic changes in society also may have weakened traditional social controls that restricted adolescent behavior in the past.

*Motoko Akiba*

*See also:* **Cram Schools**

**Further Reading**

Inamura Hiroshi, and Yukio Saito. (1995) *Ijime Jisatsu* (Suicide Related to Bullying). Tokyo: Shibundo.

Morita Youji, and Kenji Kiyonaga. (1996) *Ijime—Kyoshitu-no Yamai* (Bullying—Pathology in Classroom). Tokyo: Kaneko Shobo.

Sugano Tateki. (1995) *Ijime—Gakkyu no Ningengaku* (Bullying—Human Science in Classroom). Tokyo: Shinyosya.

Takekawa Ikuo. (1995) *Ijime to Futoko-no Syakaigaku* (Sociology of Bullying and Absenteeism). Kyoto, Japan: Houritu Bunkasya.

Zeng, Kangmin, and Gerald LeTendre. (1999) "The Dark Side of . . .: Suicide, Violence, and Drug Use in Japanese Schools." In *Competitor or Ally? Japan's Role in American Educational Debates*, edited by Gerald LeTendre. New York: Falmer Press.

**IKAT DYEING** Lowland Lao women primarily use *ikat* dyeing to decorate their lower garment, the tube skirt (*sin*). *Ikat* patterns are created before the textile is actually woven. Either the vertical threads, the warp, or the horizontal threads, the weft, are bound by strips of plant or plastic fiber to form the patterns for a textile, and then the tied threads are dyed. The plant fiber ties are removed in stages so the threads can be dipped in subsequent dye baths until the dyeing process is complete. After the dyed threads are dry, they are carefully woven to line up the patterns of the thread to form the cloth.

Only a few groups, such as the Tai Daeng, continue to utilize a simple warp *ikat*. Weft *ikat* is more common and is used to decorate the body of the tube skirt. The weft *ikat* patterns are dyed in rows separated by plain stripes *(sin mii khan)* or bands of supplementary patterns, or the patterns cover the entire body of the tube skirt with repetitive patterns. The origin of the patterns comes from the weaver's surrounding environment. Plant and animal motifs such as scorpions, spiders, birds, elephants, jasmine flowers, and trees or religious iconography such as mythical animals are abundant. The *naga* (or *naak*) is one mythical creature important to both Buddhist and animist beliefs and is a common image. An exception to the confinement of *ikat* to women's clothing is its use to decorate large, rectangular coffin covers. The design of the cloth is inspired by Khmer silk *ikats* and ultimately Indian *ikats (patolas)*. The use of *ikat* dyeing by Lao women is a distinguishing characteristic of their dress and identity.

*Linda McIntosh*

*See also:* **Textiles—Laos; Women in Southeast Asia**

**Further Reading**

*Beyond Tradition: Lao Textiles Revisited: The Handwoven Textiles of Carol Cassidy.* (1995) New York: Museum at the Fashion Institute of Technology.

Connors, Mary. (1996) *Lao Textiles and Traditions.* Singapore: Oxford University Press.

Gittinger, Mattiebelle, and H. L. Lefferts. (1992) *Textiles and the Tai Experience in Southeast Asia.* Washington, DC: Textile Museum of America.

**IKEDA HAYATO** (1899–1965), prime minister of Japan. A finance ministry bureaucrat who served as Japan's prime minister from 1960 to 1964, Ikeda is associated with the high economic growth in Japan of the 1960s, which he helped promote with his celebrated campaign for a doubling of national income in ten years.

A native of Hiroshima Prefecture, Ikeda graduated from Kyoto University in 1925, after which he worked in several prefectural tax offices. He was elected to the Lower House of the Japanese Diet (parliament) in January 1949 as a member of the Democratic Liberal Party *(Minshu Jiyuto)*. Ikeda served as vice minister of finance (1947–1948), minister of finance (1949–1952), and minister of international trade and industry (1950) under Japan's most powerful early postwar politician, Prime Minister Yoshida Shigeru (1878–1967). He and

Sato Eisaku constituted the core of what was known as the Yoshida school.

Ikeda served in Japan's delegation to the San Francisco Peace Conference in 1951. And he played a critical role in normalizing U.S.-Japanese security relations as Yoshida's special emissary in Washington for talks with Assistant Secretary of State Walter S. Robertson over Japanese rearmament in October 1953.

*Frederick R. Dickinson*

**Further Reading**

Ito, Masaya. (1985) *Ikeda Hayato.* Tokyo: Jiji Tsushinsha.

Waldner, G. W. (1975) "Japanese Foreign Policy and Economic Growth: Ikeda Hayato's Approach to the Liberalization Issue." Ph.D. diss. Princeton University.

**IKKYU** (1394–1481), Japanese Zen monk. Born in Kyoto and reputedly the son of the emperor Go-Komatsu (1377–1433) and a noblewoman who was expelled from court by a jealous imperial consort, by the age of five, Ikkyu (also called Ikkyu Sojun) was sent to a Zen temple to be raised. Early on, he was recognized as a brilliant student, quick-witted and mischievous. Appalled at the corrupt behavior of the senior monks, he fled the temple at the age of sixteen to commence instruction under the eccentric Rinzai Zen priest Kenno Soi (d. 1415), who gave him the name Sojun. Kenno had earlier caused consternation by refusing a certificate of enlightenment, necessary for obtaining a position at a major temple. Such uncompromising behavior matched Ikku's temperament closely.

Upon the death of this master, Ikkyu continued training under Kaso Sodon (1352–1428) at a small retreat on the shores of Lake Biwa, east of the ancient capital of Kyoto. Under Kaso, Ikkyu's firmness of purpose in achieving enlightenment turned to uncompromising, righteous indignation, perhaps partly motivated by his resentment at the manner in which his mother had been banished from the court. He condemned the trivialization of Zen teaching and the indolence of pleasure-seeking priests and the general populace. Ikkyu became known for his unconventional behavior and humane character. His best-known work is *Kyounshu* (The Crazy Cloud Collection), a compilation of more than one thousand Chinese poems.

*James M. Vardaman, Jr.*

**Further Reading**

Kashiwahara Yusen, and Koyu Sonoda, eds. (1994) *Shapers of Japanese Buddhism.* Trans. by Gaynor Sekimori. Tokyo: Kosei Publishing Co.

Stevens, John. (1993) *Three Zen Masters: Ikkyu, Hakuin, and Ryokan.* Tokyo: Kodansha International.

**IMPERIAL PALACE** Located in the heart of Beijing, the Imperial Palace is the largest and best-preserved palace complex in China and the city's most famous tourist attraction. Formerly known as the Forbidden City, the palace took fifteen years to build and was home to twenty-four emperors from Yongle (1360–1424), at the start of the fifteenth century, to Pu Yi (1905–1967), the last Chinese emperor, who finally left in 1924. The complex also housed Communist leaders in Zhongnanhai, which lies a short distance to the west of Imperial Palace, and Mao Zedong proclaimed the birth of the People's Republic of China on 1 October 1949 from the Gate of Heavenly Peace, at the southernmost point of the complex.

A portion of the interior of the Imperial Palace or Forbidden City in Beijing. In 2001 restoration continued on the site, which became a major tourist attraction. (CHARLES & JOSETTE LENARS/CORBIS)

## IMPERIAL PALACE— WORLD HERITAGE SITE

The Ming and Qing dynasties' Imperial Palace (the Forbidden City) was designated a UNESCO World Heritage Site in 1987. The nine thousand furnished rooms in the palace are an invaluable testament to the culture and civilization of imperial China.

The Imperial Palace, once banned to all commoners, covers an area of 250 acres and contains 800 buildings, all made of wood and brick, with more than nine thousand rooms. The Forbidden City was located at the center of the imperial capital and is still considered to be the heart of the modern city. Within the Imperial Palace, there is a clear progression of important buildings along its north-south axis. Beyond the Gate of Heavenly Peace lie the three grand halls of the Outer Court, in which the emperor and his officials carried out administrative and ceremonial duties, and the sumptuous Inner Court, formerly the living quarters of the emperors and their families. The Imperial Palace today houses a museum that contains a vast array of precious artifacts, including paintings, bronze artifacts, and calligraphy as well as a collection of several million official documents.

*Julian Ward*

**Further Reading**

MacFarquhar, Roderick. (1972) *The Forbidden City*. London: Reader's Digest Association.

Meyer, Jeffrey F. (1991) *Dragons of Tiananmen: Beijing as a Sacred City*. Columbia, SC: University of South Carolina Press.

## IMPERIAL RESCRIPT ON EDUCATION

The Imperial Rescript on Education *(Kyooiku Chokugo)* of 1890 is one of the most controversial documents in prewar modern Japan. It governed the basic purpose of education from its promulgation in 1890 to the end of World War II.

The modern era of Japanese education is commonly dated from 1872 with the *Gakusei* (First National Plan for Education) issued just four years after the Meiji Restoration (1868–1912) brought to a close 350 years of the feudal Tokugawa military regime (1600/1603–1868). The *Gakusei* set up a national school system patterned after educational practices in the West. Of all the modern reforms of feudal educational patterns carried out in the 1870s and 1880s by the Japanese oligarchy, however, the most prominent was the replacement of traditional morals education based on Confucian classics from China. As the core of the curricula, Confucian teaching was overshadowed by science, mathematics, and technology imported from the West.

A controversy emerged when figures within the Imperial Household such as the Confucian scholar Motoda Nagazane (1818–1891), acting on behalf of Emperor Meiji, protested these trends. The Imperial Will on Education *(Kyoogaku Taishi)* of 1879, written by Motoda, called for education in the modern world based on the teachings from the ancient world, particularly those of the Confucian classics. *Kyoogaku Taishi* led to a confrontation between the modernizers, such as the great statesman Ito Hirobumi (1841–1909) and his political confident Inoue Kowashi (1843–1895), along with Mori Arinori (1847–1899), first Minister of Education, pitted against conservatives like Motoda and other like-minded officials within the Imperial Household and the government, including Prime Minister Yamagata Aritomo (1838–1922).

The struggles ended with a unique compromise. Inoue Kowashi, author of the first Japanese Constitution of 1889, which was patterned after the German Constitution, wrote the initial draft of the Imperial Rescript during the summer of 1890. He referred to the modern constitutional state and the necessity of abiding by the laws. Motoda, representing the Emperor, submitted revisions based on cherished Confucian concepts previously included in the 1879 Imperial Will on Education. When Inoue, the German-oriented modernist, incorporated Motoda's recommendations, an East-West compromise was achieved. The Imperial Rescript on Education combined traditional Confucian moral principles governing the relationship between the Emperor and his people with a modern sovereign state based on constitutional laws. Its purpose was to develop a spirit of nationhood and love and respect for the Imperial tradition.

With the rise of Japanese militarism in the first half of the 1900s, however, nationalists turned to the Rescript as a means to foster extreme nationalism and ultramilitarism in the name of the emperor. The Rescript became a sacred document read with great reverence at special school meetings. The original intent of 1890 was subverted, rendering the Rescript a repressive instrument of social and political control. It was controlled by militarists and used to repress any opposition to government policy leading to World War II and the ensuing defeat of Japan. During the Occupation of Japan, American authorities abolished the Rescript as an antidemocratic document of state repression. It was replaced in 1947 by the Fundamental Law of Education, which gave the purpose of education in a democratic society as the development of the individual.

*Benjamin Duke*

**Further Reading**

Kaigo Tokiomi. (1981) *Chosaku Shu: Kyoiku Chokugo Seiritsu Shi no Kenkyu* (The Collected Works of Kaigo Tokiomi: The Formation of the Imperial Rescript on Education). Tokyo: Shoseki.

Morikawa Terumichi. (1994) *Kyoiku Chokugo e no Michi* (The Road to the Imperial Rescript on Education). Tokyo: Sangensha.

Noguchi Isaaki. (1994) *Inoue Kowashi no Kyoiku Shiso* (The Educational Thought of Inoue Kowashi). Tokyo: Kazama Shobo.

Yamazumi Masami. (1980) *Kyoiku Chokugo* (The Imperial Rescript on Education). Tokyo: Asahi Shimbunsha.

**IMPHAL** (2001 pop. 217,000). The capital of Manipur State in northeastern India, Imphal lies in a Manipur River valley at an altitude of around 792 meters. It is believed to have existed as early as the third century BCE. Imphal was the seat of the kings of Manipur before the British took control of the region in 1926. In 1944 it was the site of a decisive battle in which a British garrison held off advancing Japanese troops, thereby halting the Japanese march through Myanmar (Burma) and ending Japan's attempt to invade India.

Women in the market with their piles of textiles for sale. (LINDSAY HEBBERD/CORBIS)

A polo field dominates the city center; the Manipuri game of *Sagol Kangjei* (*Kangjei* means a stick made of cane) is considered the original form of polo. The city is a major trade center, noted for its weaving, brassware, and bronze ware. The market of Khwairamband is run by 3,000 women. Half is devoted to textiles, including the *moirangphee*, the traditional Methei dress. (The Methei are Hindus of Mongoloid stock.) The other half of the market sells fish, vegetables, and basic provisions. The Shri Govindjee temple is an important center for Vaishnavite Hindus. Two cemeteries commemorate heroes of World War II. The Khonghampat Orchidariums feature 110 species of orchids. Nearby are zoological gardens, famous for rare indigenous brow-antlered deer.

*C. Roger Davis*

**Further Reading**

Rooney, David. (1992) *Burma Victory: Imphal, Kohima and the Chindit Issue, March 1944 to May 1945*. London: Arms & Armour.

**INCHON** (2002 est. pop. 2.4 million). Located on the northwestern coast of South Korea at the mouth of the Han River and bordering the Yellow Sea, Inchon (Inch'on) is perhaps best known as the site of General Douglas MacArthur's Inchon Landing on 15 September 1950, when U.N. troops landed behind North Korean forces, effectively cutting the North Korean army in two and reversing the tide of the Korean War.

Formerly known as Chemulpo (Chemulp'o), Inchon was founded during the Unified Shilla dynasty (668–935 CE). Throughout much of its history Inchon has played second fiddle to Seoul, its larger eastern neighbor, serving as Seoul's chief port and manufacturing base. Inchon International Airport is the Koreas' largest.

*Keith Leitich*

**Further Reading**

Eckert, Carter J., Ki-baik Lee, Young Ick Lew, Michael Robinson, and Edward W. Wagner. (1990) *Korea Old and New: A History*. Seoul: Ilchokak.

Edwards, Paul. (1994) *The Inchon Landing, Korea, 1950: An Annotated Bibliography*. London: Greenwood Press.

**INDIA—PROFILE** (2001 pop. 1 billion). The spatial dimension of what came to be known as the Republic of India (in Sanskrit, Bharata), kept changing until it became independent on 15 August 1947. Although the concept of India as a nation-state emerged after British colonial rule, the idea of Bharata had been there from time immemorial. Deriving from geography, history, and culture, a sense of unity has been present throughout its history. Despite the presence of diverse elements, a unifying force is present in India's literature, music, dance, art, behavioral patterns, and societal norms. The concept of *Bharatavarsa* (the idea of Bharata as a territorial entity) is a part of Indians' common psyche.

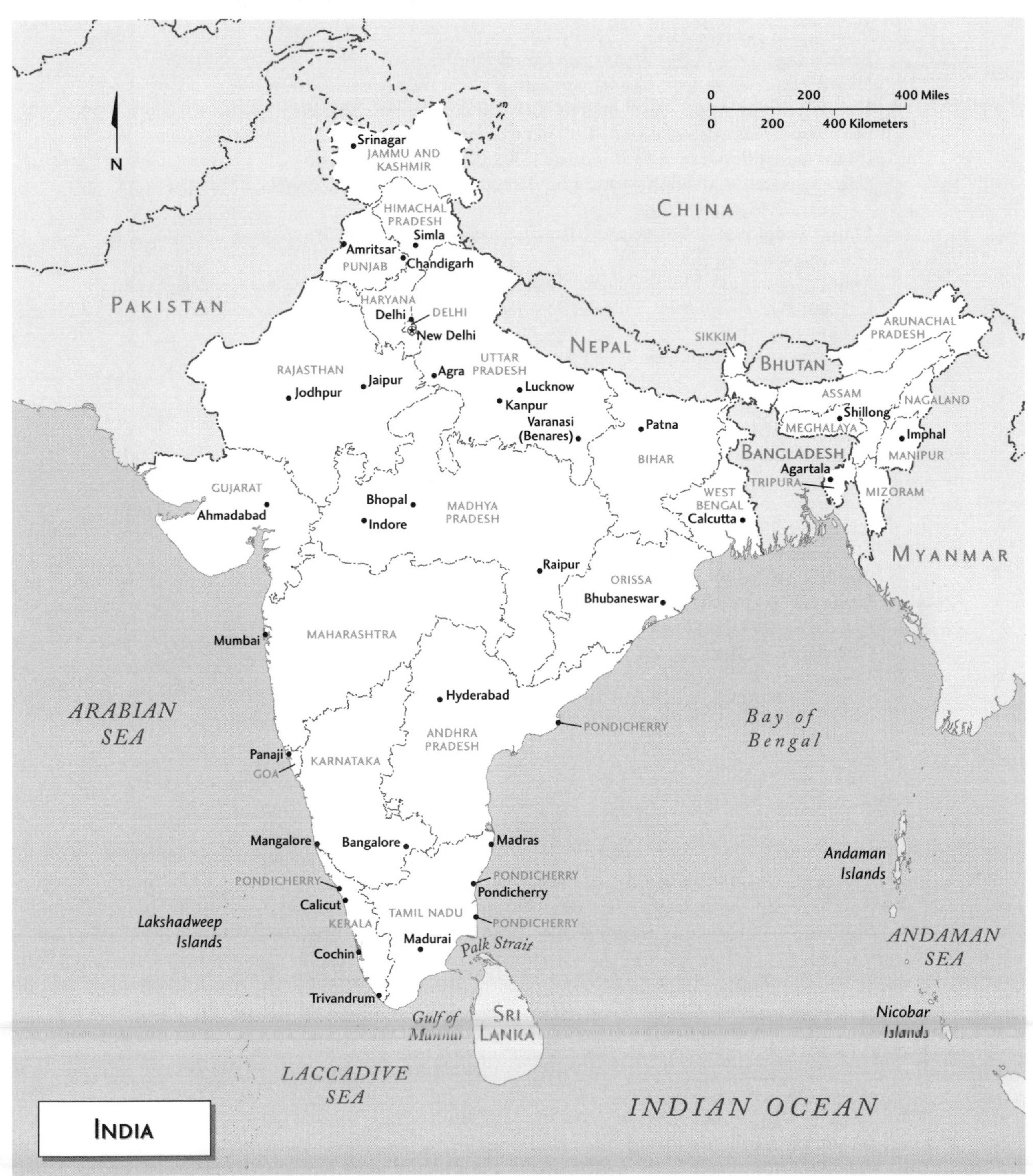

## INDIA

**Country name:** Republic of India
**Area:** 3,287,590 sq km
**Population:** 1,029,991,145 (July 2001 est.)
**Population growth rate:** 1.55% (2001 est.)
**Birth rate:** 24.28 births/1,000 population (2001 est.)
**Death rate:** 8.74 deaths/1,000 population (2001 est.)
**Net migration rate:** -0.08 migrant(s)/1,000 population (2001 est.)
**Sex ratio—total population:** 1.07 male(s)/female (2001 est.)
**Infant mortality rate:** 63.19 deaths/1,000 live births (2001 est.)
**Life expectancy at birth—total population:** 62.86 years; male: 62.22 years, female: 63.53 years (2001 est.)
**Major religions:** Hinduism, Islam, Christianity, Sikhism, Buddhism, Jainism, Zoroastrianism (Parsi)
**Major languages:** Hindi, Bengali, Telugu, Marathi, Tamil, Urdu, Gujarati, Malayalam, Kannada, Oriya, Punjabi, Assamese, Kashmiri, Sindhi, Sanskrit, Hindustani, English
**Literacy—total population:** 52%; male: 65.5%, female: 37.7% (1995 est.)
**Government type:** federal republic
**Capital:** New Delhi
**Administrative divisions:** 28 states and 7 union territories
**Independence:** 15 August 1947 (from UK)
**National holiday:** Republic Day, 26 January (1950)
**Suffrage:** 18 years of age; universal
**GDP—real growth rate:** 6% (2000 est.)
**GDP—per capita (purchasing power parity):** $2,200 (2000 est.)
**Population below poverty line:** 35% (1994 est.)
**Exports:** $43.1 billion (f.o.b., 2000 est.)
**Imports:** $60.8 billion (f.o.b., 2000 est.)
**Currency:** Indian rupee (INR)

*Source:* Central Intelligence Agency. (2001) *The World Factbook* 2001. Retrieved 18 October 2001, from: http://www.cia.gov/cia/publications/factbook.

### Geography

The second most populous nation and the seventh largest nation in land area in the world, India covers 3,287,590 square kilometers, stretching from the Bay of Bengal in the east to the Arabian Sea in the west. It shares borders with Bangladesh, Bhutan, Myanmar (Burma), the People's Republic of China, Nepal, and Pakistan. The Himalayas rise above peninsular India in the north, and here the three great rivers of the subcontinent—the Indus, the Ganges, and the Brahmaputra originate. The southern tip of India ends in Kanya Kumari, where the peninsula merges into the Indian Ocean. The Palk Strait and Gulf of Mannar divide India from Sri Lanka. The terrain varies from mountains to flat river valleys. The Vindhya range of mountains divides north from south India. The alluvial plain of the Ganges in the north contains much of the country's arable land. Between Gujarat in the southwest and Delhi in the northeast lies the Aravalli range. Two mountain ranges, the Eastern and Western Ghats, border the rocky and triangular Deccan plateau in the south. The Godavari, Krishna, and Kaveri rivers flow eastward in this region. The climate of India varies according to area and elevation, but is generally tropical. Dependent on two monsoons, India's rainfall also varies from region to region.

### People

India occupies about 2.4 percent of the world's land area, but 17 percent of the world's population is found here. The population has crossed the 1 billion mark. The influx of alien peoples down the centuries has resulted in a remarkable racial and cultural synthesis as well as considerable ethnic and linguistic diversity. The age-old caste system is present, although caste distinctions are gradually disappearing due to social mobility, modern perceptions, and the policy of reservation (seats reserved for admission to colleges, jobs, political offices, and so on). The scheduled castes and tribes (that is, the lower castes), which make up 16.5 percent of the total population, are coming into the mainstream.

With eighteen officially recognized languages (Assamese, Bengali, Gujarati, Hindi, Kannada, Kashmiri, Konkani, Malalayam, Manipuri, Marathi, Nepali, Oriya, Punjabi, Sanskrit, Sindhi, Tamil, Telugu, and Urdu) and sixteen hundred dialects, India is truly a Tower of Babel. Hindi is the official language and is the mother tongue of about 18 percent of the population. English enjoys an important status as an official language and the language of urban India and is used extensively in such fields as education, international business, science, medicine, information technology, and communication.

India is a nation of religious diversity. Hindus constitute 83.5 percent of the total population. India also has the second largest number of Muslims, after Indonesia. They form about 13 percent of the population. India, which does not have a state religion and professes secularism, also is home to Christians, Sikhs, Buddhists, Jains, and Parsis (Zoroastrians).

### Historical Overview

Human activity began in India about a half million years ago. Archaeological excavations have brought to light the urban civilization commonly referred to as the Indus Valley civilization, concentrated in India and modern-day Pakistan, during the period between 2700 and 1500 BCE. The Vedic civilization preceded the rise of cities in India. The invasion of Alexander of Macedon (356–323 BCE) in 326 BCE was followed by the Maurya empire (c. 324–c. 200 BCE), the first unified empire to cover most of present-day India and Pakistan. Asoka (d. 238 or 232 BCE) was the greatest of the Mauryan emperors. A period of chaos and foreign invasions by the Scythians, Parthians, Huns, and others followed until political stability was achieved under the Gupta dynasty (c. 320–c. 500 CE). In south India, the Pallavas and Chalukyas emerged as powerful kingdoms during the seventh century. Harsha (606–647), Sasanka (606–637), and Pulakeshin II (609–642) carved out kingdoms in north India, Bengal, and south India, respectively, in the seventh century. In the early medieval period, spanning the eighth to fourteenth centuries, north India witnessed the coming of Islam from the northwest.

Muhammad bin Qasim (invaded Sind in 712), Mahmud of Ghanza (raided India 1000–1025), and Muhammad of Ghur (reigned 1192–1206) brought the north Indian subcontinent under their domain, and it was the establishment of the Delhi sultanate (1192–1526) that resulted in the consolidation of Muslim power. India's Muslim conquerors had been drawn to the subcontinent by the desire for territorial conquest, the lure of wealth, and religious zeal. Powerful regional kingdoms such as the Palas, Senas, Ahoms, Gangas, and Cholas rose and fell in different parts of India. The Gajapati empire of Orissa and the Vijayanagar empire of the south were able to survive until the 1560s. The Mughals (1526–1857) brought almost all of north India under their control, and Akbar (1542–1605) was one of India's greatest monarchs.

From the eighteenth century onward, the Mughal empire began to crumble. The Marathas under the intrepid leader Sivaji (1627 or 1630–1680) had already encroached on Mughal power. The coming of the Europeans as traders and later as seekers of political power sounded the final death knell. The British East India Company became the master of the subcontinent. By adroit diplomacy, warfare, and political conspiracy, the British subjugated the subcontinent. The Indian Mutiny, or the First War of Independence (1857), gave a serious jolt to the colonial power, and the administration was transferred from the East India Company to the British throne. Mohandas (Mahatma) Gandhi (1869–1948) used nonviolence and mass movements to shatter the foundation of Britain's Indian empire. A tenacious struggle for freedom by people of all classes, led by nationalists such as Jawaharlal Nehru (1889–1964), Subhas Chandra Bose (1897–1945), and Sardar Vallabhbhai Patel (1875–1950), resulted in India's independence on 15 August 1947. However, the subcontinent was partitioned at that time between India and Pakistan.

### Economy

The Indian economy, which encompasses traditional village agriculture, the use of modern technology in farming, heavy industries, and a multitude of support industries, is often seen as two entities: one rural and one urban. About 30 percent of the people live below the poverty line, and India's gross national product is $450 billion. In terms of purchasing parity, India is the

## CREATING A UNIFIED, CIVIL INDIA

One of the major problems facing India as a new nation was the tremendous ethnic, religious, and linguistic diversity of its people. One attempt to create national unity amidst this diversity was a pledge to affirm India as a civilized and peaceful society. The pledge was signed by national leaders and the people of India at public meetings on 2 October 1962.

> The National Integration Conference held in 1961 decided that a pledge should be taken by every adult Indian to affirm his faith in the universal principle of civilised society to resolve civil disputes by peaceful means and to abstain from resort to violence.
>
> A campaign for such a pledge to be taken by all the people of our country will be inaugurated on the birthday of Mahatma Gandhi on October 2, 1962. The campaign will be continuous and will be carried on during all the months of the year, but the week from October 2 to 9 will be particularly devoted to it.
>
> No person should be asked to sign the pledge unless its meaning and significance have been fully explained to and understood by him.
>
> Emotional integration is the essence of national integration. Even with all the outward attributes of nationhood, a people would still be lacking in real national cohesion in the absence of complete emotional integration. India has always had a basic unity and a peculiar and distinctive identity and this should provide a basis for the task of national integration.
>
> A serious obstacle to the emotional integration of our people is the resort to violence in the course of disputes arising out of regional, linguistic, religious and other similar matters. In a large country like India with its many diversities, it is but natural that differences between sections or groups of people should arise from time to time. But it is not so much the existence of such differences and disputes which endangers the integrity of the nation as the manner in which we conduct them. When brothers quarrel and settle their differences peacefully, the spirit of fraternal accord remains unbroken. Should they, however, in their quarrel become violent and strike each other, the feeling of brotherhood may come to an end. Similarly, when Indians assault or kill Indians and burn and loot in the name of caste, sect, religion, language or religion, the resulting hatred, bitterness and spirit of vengeance create a psychological estrangement which makes it difficult for people to feel that they all belong to one another as citizens of the same nation.
>
> It was in pursuance of this line of thought that the National Integration Conference decided to launch this campaign. It is to be hoped that a countrywide campaign of this nature will create a powerful psychological climate which will help in every way in promoting national integration.
>
> *Source:* Jagdish Saran Sharma. (1965) *India's Struggle for Freedom: Select Documents and Sources*. Vol. 2. Delhi: S. Chand & Co., 481–482.

world's fifth-largest economy. Agriculture employs about 70 percent of the people and contributes about 25 percent of the gross domestic product (GDP). The industry and service sectors account for 30 and 45 percent of GDP, respectively.

India has seen broad-based industrial development for the last five decades. The most important crops are rice, wheat, millet, oilseeds, jute, and tea. Rubber, coffee, pepper, and sugarcane are other profitable cash crops. Foreign trade is important to India's economic development. Exports cover such items as agriculture and allied products, coffee, tea, spices, iron ore, textiles, leather, and computer software. Export earnings for 2000 were $43.1 billion. Petroleum and its products, fertilizers, cereals, edible oils, drugs and pharmaceuticals, and precious and semiprecious stones are major items of import, with imports amounting to $60.8 billion in 2000. The United States is India's largest trading and investment partner.

Planning is a major instrument of India's economic development. Planned economic development began in 1951 with the first five-year plan; the period 1997–2002 was covered by the ninth plan. The objectives were rapid economic growth, modernization, self-reliance, and social justice. During the 1990s, India shifted to a market-driven economy from its decades-old centralized planning model.

## Culture

India's cultural richness may be seen in religion, philosophy, literature, science, music, dance, painting, and architecture. The Vedas, the Upanishads, and the *Bhagavad Gita*, ancient Hindu texts, deal with such metaphysical concepts as the doctrine of Brahma (universal self), atman (individual self), and *moksa* (liberation). India is also the birthplace of Buddhism and Jainism. With the coming of Islam, Indian culture was confronted with a new religion. However, gradually there was an attempt at rapprochement. In art and architecture, literature, and social norms, a common culture began to evolve, which contained elements of both Islam and Hinduism. The Sufi and Bhakti saints, with their simple message of egalitarianism, brought about a reconciliation of the two communities. Monuments like the Taj Mahal and the Red Fort are great contributions to Indian culture, as are the Buddhist remains at Sarnath, the sun temple of Konarak, or the Sri Minakshi temple complex at Madurai.

## Contemporary Government and Politics

After independence, India continued as a dominion within the British Commonwealth until 26 January 1950, when it became a sovereign, democratic republic with a parliamentary form of government upon the promulgation of a new constitution. The president of India, elected for a five-year term, possesses full executive power, but the prime minister, who normally belongs to the majority party in the parliament and the cabinet, exercises real power.

Jawaharlal Nehru was premier from independence until his death in 1964. He espoused socialism, nonalignment, a planned economy, and industrialization. The 362 princely states, such as Hyderabad and Junagarh, merged with the Indian Union; a war occurred with Pakistan in 1948 over Kashmir; and Mahatma Gandhi was assassinated in 1948. A Chinese attack on India in 1962 resulted in a humiliating defeat for India. Another war with Pakistan occurred in 1965; in 1974 India successfully tested nuclear weapons at Pokhran. Sikh militants became active in the 1980s, and in 1984 Indira Gandhi (1917–1984), then prime minister, was assassinated by a Sikh bodyguard following her order of an attack on the Golden Temple, a sacred site for Sikhs. In the last decade of the twentieth century, the Congress Party lost its monopoly on power, and a trend to the right was visible with the emergence of the BJP (Bharatiya Janata Party) and the proliferation of regional parties. Relations with Pakistan took a nose-dive, and again a limited war, known as the Kargil conflict, occurred in Kashmir. Militancy in Kashmir has become one of India's main problems. Eradicating poverty, maintaining steady economic growth, and fighting overpopulation remain India's other major problems.

*Patit Paban Mishra*

## Further Reading

Basham, A. L. (1992) *The Wonder That Was India.* Reprint ed. Calcutta, India: Rupa.

Hasan, Zoya. (2000) *Politics and State in India.* New Delhi: Sage.

Kulke, Hermann, and Dietmar Rothermund. (1994) *History of India.* Calcutta, India: Rupa.

Malik, Yogendra, and Ashok Kapur. (2000) *India: Fifty Years of Democracy and Development.* New Delhi: DK.

Mathew, K. M., ed. (2001) *Manorama Yearbook 2001.* Kottayam, India: Malayala Manorama.

Nehru, Jawaharlal. (1991) *The Discovery of India.* 3d ed. New Delhi: ICCR.

Radhakrishnan, S. (1998), *Indian Philosophy.* 4th ed. Delhi: Oxford University Press.

Spear, P. (1977) *A History of India 2.* Reprint ed. Aylesbury, U.K.: Penguin.

Thapar, Romila. (1977) *A History of India.* Reprint ed. Aylesbury, U.K.: Penguin.

**INDIA—ECONOMIC SYSTEM** India's economy is one of the largest in the world. Converting Indian rupees to U.S. dollars at the rate of exchange in 1995, that year India ranked fifteenth in the world in total gross domestic product. When measured in purchasing power parity terms (that is, the number of rupees required to buy the same amount of goods and services in India as one dollar would buy in the United States), India's gross domestic product was the fifth highest in the world in 1995, exceeded only by the United States, China, Japan, and Germany.

However, using the conventional 1995 rate of exchange measure, India ranked 107th in the world in per capita income, with an average of $340 per annum. That figure was a result of an average annual growth rate in the gross national product of 5.5 percent and a growth rate in per capita income of 2.2 percent from 1950 to 1995. The half-century before 1950 was a period of economic stagnation during which growth in economic output barely kept up with India's population increase. During the second half of the twentieth century India achieved significant growth and improved well-being compared with the first half. In 1995 approximately 2.5 times as many Indians produced 5 times the output of 1950, so each Indian had on average twice as many goods and services in 1995 as in 1950.

## FIVE LARGEST COMPANIES IN INDIA

According to *Asia Week* the five largest companies in India are as follows:

| Company | Sector | Sales ($ millions) | Rank in Asia |
|---|---|---|---|
| Indian Oil | Oil Refining | 28,504.6 | 34 |
| Hindustan Petroleum | Oil Refining | 10,806.6 | 121 |
| Bharat Petroleum | Oil Refining | 10,322.8 | 130 |
| Reliance Petroleum | Oil Refining | 6,889.5 | 192 |
| Reliance Industries | Textiles, Chemicals | 6,232.0 | 209 |

*Source:* "The Asia Week 1000." (2001) *Asia Week* (9 November): 112.

Despite this massive increase in overall output, in 1993 and 1994 approximately 320 million Indians, or over one-third of all the Indian people lived below a very low level of poverty, measured by their spending less than $10 per month (at the 1995 exchange rate) for food. Also almost one-half of the entire population—male and female—are illiterate, but two-thirds of all females are, reflecting both the low levels of education throughout society and the low level of educational opportunity for women in particular. In addition many villages and urban slums lack clean water, decent sanitation, and basic health care.

India's rural population has benefited less than its urban population from the economic growth after 1950. Consequently rates of poverty, illiteracy, and poor health are higher in rural areas than in the cities. India has achieved major industrial advances since 1950. Industrial output has increased by over twenty times, and employment in the organized sector (largely industrial and government) has tripled. The share of industrial and services output in the total national income increased from about 40 percent in 1950 to over 70 percent in 1997. Yet of the more than 300 million workers in 1991, over 240 million—two-thirds of the workforce—were rural workers. India remains a mainly agricultural economy as far as its population is concerned. While farm output has exceeded population growth and the country has experienced no famines since independence, the overall well-being of its population is largely determined by the experiences of the agricultural sector.

### Goals, Policies, and Problems after Independence

India's economic achievements and history have not matched the hopes of the country's political, business, and intellectual leaders at independence in 1947. Prior to independence, India's political and business leaders put forth plans that sought, as a medium-term goal of about fifteen years, to end poverty in the country. They planned to reach this goal by increasing the growth of the economy as a whole and by shifting from a predominantly agricultural economy to an industrialized one. Their anticipated result was higher incomes, which would end extreme poverty. The experiences of the 1930s depression, the wartime economic controls in the country, the apparent Soviet achievements of industrialization and military power, and the decline of world trade during the depression provided rationales for a socialist, planned economy that emphasized an industrialization policy based on import-substitution and heavy capital goods. Mohandas (Mahatma) Gandhi (1869–1948) urged policies to strengthen agriculture, improve rural life, and encourage small-scale rural industrialization. Those policy directions were largely downplayed after his assassination in 1948.

The Indian constitution, written in 1950, included in its directive principles various economic and social goals. It aimed toward an equal economic and social order in which all people have a right to be educated, to work, and to receive unemployment benefits, health assistance, and disability benefits. These were not legal rights but goals. Prime Minister Jawaharlal Nehru (1889–1964) headed a planning commission, set up in 1950, to prepare outlines and policies for legislation to achieve those goals within the framework of a socialistic pattern of society. Indian socialism was a mixture of private property and ownership in the agricultural sector. Existing private industrial and commercial firms in large part remained private, but the government controlled the private sector and also engaged extensively in economic activities, including manufacturing, banking, and infrastructure construction. It was a mixed economy within a democratic political framework.

Under Nehru and a Congress Party government, a series of five-year plans was prepared, and policies were adopted to promote the growth of heavy industry under government ownership. The government ensured protection against imports and prohibited or tightly controlled foreign investment or ownership of industries. The aims of this industrial policy included self-sufficiency and little foreign control based on the substitution of domestic production for imports. The agricultural sector was seen essentially as a source of capital, labor, and raw materials for industrial growth. The Green Revolution of the mid-1960s introduced new, high-yield varieties of grains into India, and government policies encouraged their adoption. The results were positive for the first twenty years. Industrial and national growth did accelerate, and stimulated by the Green Revolution, agricultural output also grew substantially. Despite these positive results, poverty and inequality continued on a large scale, and by the late 1960s economic growth had slowed significantly.

The public-sector industrial firms were relatively inefficient and unprofitable. Constrained by a network of controls, they needed permission for expansion or output changes. Banks had been nationalized, and financial markets were tightly restricted. Foreign trade and investment were discouraged by high tariffs, overvalued exchange rates, and direct governmental controls. The so-called license-permit raj these controls created resulted in stagnation in terms of the quality of goods and services produced and the introduction of new technology. Corruption increased at all levels as businesses and individuals sought the permits required for production and trading rights and access to scarce domestic goods, services, imports, foreign exchange, or credits. The bureaucracy administering the controls became a powerful political and economic force at both the national and the local levels, and various social inequalities strengthened rather than declined. While agricultural output rose, the rural sector subsidized the urban and industrial sectors. The controlled prices of farm products were substantially below world prices and the potential internal free-market prices that would have resulted if exports had been permitted freely. To balance these losses of income within the farm sector, the government subsidized below-cost prices for government-supplied electric power, for water supplies for irrigation, for fertilizer from public-sector plants, and for transportation facilities. Functioning at a loss, the public agencies supplying those infrastructure inputs could not expand to meet the growing demands of industry and urbanization. This placed a heavy burden on public utility users, which raised the costs of industrial production. It also burdened the fiscal resources of the central and state governments, which had to support the loss-incurring infrastructure enterprises with budget subsidies. It was estimated in 1997 that subsidies totaled over 15 percent of India's gross domestic product, almost equaling the tax revenues. This had been the case for many years.

These systemic problems were apparent even to the supporters of socialism and the government officials administering the economic programs. In the early 1980s the administration of Indira Gandhi (1917–1984), considering possibilities for reducing controls, set up various committees to explore particular problem areas and to recommend policies to deal with them. After Indira Gandhi was assassinated in 1984, Rajiv Gandhi (1944–1991) introduced a number of reforms to reduce governmental control of industry.

### The Economic Reforms of the 1980s and 1990s

The economic reforms of the 1980s reduced the controls on industry with respect to licensing, prohibitions against firms producing related products in addition to their major products, and the monopoly restrictions on large Indian firms. These first steps did not receive wide popular or political support. Nevertheless, together with good harvests and an expansionary fiscal policy, they contributed to the acceleration of industrial growth and national output in the second half of the 1980s. From 1985 to 1990, real national income rose at its highest annual rate since independence, and industrial production rose at its highest rate since the early 1960s.

Despite this acceleration in economic growth, Rajiv Gandhi's government was defeated in the 1989 elections. The expansionary fiscal policies of Rajiv Gandhi's government also produced an inflationary price rise. India's foreign-trade position then worsened and its foreign-exchange holdings fell. These low standings forced the government to ask the World Bank for emergency aid in 1991. The government collapsed, and the elections in 1991 reinstated the Congress Party, though in a minority position. The new government—headed by Prime Minister R. V. N. Rao and Finance Minister Manmohan Singh—quickly introduced further reforms in the financial, foreign trade and investment, and industrial sectors. The economic crisis broadened popular support for reform in general, and public and political attitudes toward the economic goals and the reform process changed strikingly. The extensive corruption of the "license-permit raj" forced public recognition of the desirability of reducing those controls not only among businesspeople but also within the Communist Party governments in West Bengal and Kerala. However, various economic groups and political parties in the governing coalition disagreed over the specific actions required, reflecting their anticipated effects on each group.

In the end the government ceased licensing for all but eight industries; granted foreign investors automatic approval for equity holdings of 51 percent in most Indian industries; lifted entirely restrictions on imports of technology; removed the priority for public-sector investment except in petroleum, infrastructure, and defense-related industries; abolished the restrictions on growth or expansion by purchase of "monopoly firms"; and ended limitations on credit to larger firms and subsidies for credit to small and medium-size firms, so credit rating and safety became the determining elements in credit availability. The government continued its review of the policy of reserving production of 851 products for small-scale firms only. These new policies were intended to encourage competition within India's industries, to provide India's firms with access to new and better technology, and to give Indian consumers access to higher-quality products than had been available in the past. The rupee was devalued to reflect internal price increases and to encourage exports. Free convertibility of foreign currency was introduced, and exporters were allowed to retain overseas earnings for six months. The new system allowed a certain amount of foreign portfolio investment in India's security markets and in the securities of Indian firms, and permitted Indian firms to enter foreign bond markets and to borrow funds overseas. Of major importance, tariff rates were reduced from an average rate of 87 percent in 1991 to 27 percent in 1995, and the maximum rate fell from 150 percent to 50 percent. As a result India's foreign trade, particularly exports, rose significantly, as did foreign investment in India. The foreign-exchange problem that had led to the 1991 crisis ended and with it the need for assistance.

The government also reformed the financial system. Its goals were to increase the lending flexibility of banks, thereby encouraging the growth of financial markets, and to increase the transparency of the financial sector as a whole. At the same time the Reserve Bank of India established broad supervisory agencies to monitor the financial markets, in part in response to a major financial scandal in those markets. The new oversight agencies proved effective. Interestingly, India avoided the financial collapse that affected the Southeast Asian countries and Korea in the late 1990s. India's limitations on foreign exchange flows may have contributed to its immunity.

While reforms in the industrial, trade, and financial sectors have stimulated the Indian economy, further reforms in other major areas would spur further economic growth and improve the overall quality of life. One such possibility is raising the performance of the government-owned industrial enterprises. Except for the petroleum industry, most of the other public-sector firms are of low profitability and are a drain on the economy and the budget. Reform of these enterprises is difficult because of their bureaucratic management and their political connections. Also, if they are shut down in the absence of unemployment support and a retraining program for workers, unemployment is an understandable fear. Beneficial programs to assist the unemployed and to retrain workers unemployed by closures have not been developed, in part owing to fiscal problems.

In many fields India lags in technological advances. Expenditures on research and development in Indian manufacturing firms are still comparatively low overall, although in the information-technology and pharmaceutical industries such expenditures are higher. Policies to encourage relevant programs are important if Indian industry is to be competitive in the global economy.

India's inadequate and poorly performing infrastructure sectors—power, communication, transportation, and shipping—seriously hamper the economy and raise production costs. Many of these sectors are the responsibilities of the state governments, which continue to face fiscal shortages from past inefficiencies and cost overruns. While the central government permits foreign investment in those areas, bureaucratic and political barriers in the decision-making processes discourage investment.

In agriculture, past policies and the resulting subsidization have made financial changes politically difficult and costly. Improvements in rural infrastructure, reductions of subsidies, and limiting public distribution of low-priced grains to the genuinely poor portion of the population would stimulate output growth and spread the benefits of that growth to a larger portion of the population. Improving education and making health services more accessible in rural areas, along with encouraging industries to move to rural and semirural locations, would improve the lives of the rural poor.

### The Future of India's Economy

India has achieved major successes in economic policy reform, but further advances are necessary if the country is to accomplish its long-standing goals of ending poverty and ensuring social equality. With widespread agreement on the general desirability of economic reform, India's political parties have the opportunity to develop an effective program and convince the voting public of the possibilities of a better quality of life. Indian political democracy might then accomplish its long-term goals of ending poverty and significantly reducing social inequality.

*George Rosen*

### Further Reading


Adams, John. (1996) "Reforming India's Economy in an Era of Global Change." *Current History* 95, 600: 151–157.

Ahluwalia, Isher. (1991) *Productivity and Growth in Indian Manufacturing*. New York: Oxford University Press.

———, and I. M. D. Little, eds. (1998) *India's Economic Reforms and Development*. New York: Oxford University Press.

Bardhan, Pranab. (1984) *The Political Economy of Development in India*. New York: B. Blackwell.

Bhagwati, Jagdish. (1993) *India in Transition*. Oxford, U.K.: Clarendon Press; New York: Oxford University Press.

Dhar, P. N. (2000) *Indira Gandhi, the "Emergency," and Indian Democracy*. New York: Oxford University Press.

Government of India, Ministry of Finance. (1998) *Economic Survey, 1997–1998*. New Delhi: Ministry of Finance.

Joshi, Vijay, and I. M. D. Little. (1994) *India: Macroeconomics and Political Economy, 1964–1991*. Washington, DC: World Bank.

———. (1996) *India's Economic Reforms, 1991–2001*. Oxford: Clarendon Press.

Lal, Deepak. (1999) *Unfinished Business: India in the World Economy*. New York: Oxford University Press.

Parikh, Kirit S. (1999) "Economy." In *India Briefing*, edited by Marshall Bouton and Philip Oldenburg. Armonk, NY: M. E. Sharpe, 39–89.

Sen, Amartya. (1999) *Development as Freedom*. New York: Alfred A. Knopf.

Srinivasan, T. N. (1994) *Agriculture and Trade in China and India*. San Francisco: ICS Press.

Vaidyanathan, A. (1995) *The Indian Economy*. New Delhi: Orient Longman.

Weiner, Myron. (1991) *The Child and the State in India*. Princeton, NJ: Princeton University Press.

World Bank. (1997) *India: Achievements and Challenges in Reducing Poverty*. Washington, DC: World Bank.


## INDIA—EDUCATION SYSTEM

Indian education in the modern era shows the influence of two traditions, British and native Indian. Remnants of the British education system in the modern Indian system show the durability of British influence, but while independent India has preserved much of the British educational system, "national education," initiated by Indian nationalists and reformers in the latter half of the twentieth century, has left its own legacy. It seeks to revive the glorious heritage of knowledge and culture originating in India itself.

### Indian Education before British Colonization

Ancient Indian civilization required an elaborate system of education for the transmission of its cultural heritage. Scriptures of great length were not written down; instead, the text was learned by heart. Each generation of Brahmans was thoroughly trained in this way. Sanskrit words had to be pronounced faultlessly, as mistakes were believed to cause spiritual harm. The main educational institution was the *gurukul* ("family of the teacher"), a term used in ancient and medieval times, but revived by Hindu reformers in the twentieth century. Students lived with the teacher for twelve to sixteen years, joining him as young boys and leaving him as young men ready to establish a household of their own. While the boys stayed in the *gurukul*, they had to observe chastity and lead a disciplined life.

This education was available only to the higher castes, and women and the lower classes were excluded. The teachers were mostly Brahmans. In addition to religious lore, the Brahmans transmitted worldly knowledge of law, political science, mathematics, astronomy, and medicine. Brahmans also invented the zero and introduced algebra, designed calendars, and even taught martial arts. Students specialized in such subjects and continued the tradition of their teacher. With the advent of Muslim invasions of India (beginning c. 1000 CE), schools devoted to the

Indian schoolchildren and their parents in Mumbai in July 2001 protest a government decision to cut tuition grants for students attending English-language schools. (AFP/CORBIS)

Muslim tradition sprang up, and the Hindu and Muslim systems of education coexisted side by side for centuries. Interaction between the two systems of education was limited. Muslim schools taught the Qur'an and texts on science and mathematics of Arab and Persian origin. Hindu schools reflected a variety of different traditions with their specific sacred texts and specializations in astrology, astronomy, mathematics, etc.

### Indian Education under the British

Under British rule (from 1858) a new system of education was introduced in India; it too was not aimed at mass education. The highest educational institution became the college. Entrance qualifications often were obtained by means of private tuition. Wealth replaced caste distinction as the key to educational success, although Brahman families with little wealth still secured education for their sons, so as to get them positions in government service. The Hindus showed greater interest in British education than did the Muslims, who feared that it would affect their religion. Thomas Babington Macaulay, who served on the Supreme Council in India, wrote in his "Minute on Education" (1835) that the British should aim to educate gentlemen—Indian in blood only, British in every other respect. He also deprecated all Asian learning, although he knew little about it. At the time there was a debate in British circles in India on how to spend the limited funds available for Indian education. Those who wished to spend it on teaching of Arabic, Persian, and Sanskrit, etc. were called Orientalists; their adversaries, who favored English education, were termed Anglicists. Macaulay settled the debate in favor of the latter. Later generations of Indians, who knew more about English literature and philosophy than did the British, actually made Maucaulay's words come true to such an extent that the British felt threatened. Although British civil servants in India were selected after completing their studies at Oxford or Cambridge, they often could not match the English literary erudition of the most brilliant Indians.

In 1858 three universities were established in Mumbai (Bombay), Calcutta, and Madras as examining institutions. These universities were initially not teaching institutions; rather they determined the syllabi and curricula and controlled the examinations of affiliated colleges throughout India. This standardization produced large numbers of educated Indians imbued with the same ideas and values, and able to contribute to a common discourse.

Under the British administration in the nineteenth and early twentieth centuries, hundreds of primary, middle, and secondary schools were established. These schools were most commonly run by Christian missionaries, who received some financial support from the provincial government. The schools were important in teaching basic literacy and numeracy.

British higher institutions focused primarily on the liberal arts, law, and medicine, with little emphasis on engineering and technology. The Victoria Jubilee Institute in Mumbai, which trained Indian spinning and weaving masters for the cotton textile industry, and a school of civil engineering at Roorkee in northern India were the only exceptions. When the great industrialist Jamsetji Nasarwanji Tata (1839–1904) donated a large sum of money for the establishment in 1907 of the Indian Institute of Science in Bangalore, the British did not take kindly to the idea, believing that no one would want to employ Indian scientists. Because of the obstacles to its founding, the institute came into being only after Tata's death. It was a testament to Tata's vision, but India had very few wealthy visionaries of this kind.

## FROM ENGLISH TO INDIAN LANGUAGES

Advocates of Indian independence proposed broad changes in the education system to make it relevant to life in India. One call for reform was instruction in the indigenous languages of India, the benefits of which are listed in the following extract from the *Report of the Zakir Hussian Committee* published in 1939.

> The proper teaching of the mother-tongue is the foundation of all education. Without the capacity to speak effectively and to read and write correctly and lucidly, no one can develop precision of thought or clarity of ideas. Moreover, it is a means of introducing the child to the rich heritage of his people's ideas, emotions and aspirations, and can therefore be made a valuable means of social education, whilst also instilling right ethical and moral values. Also, it is a natural outlet for the expression of the child's aesthetic sense and appreciation, and if the proper approach is adopted, the study of literature becomes a source of joy and creative appreciation. More specifically, by the end of the seven years' course, the following objectives should be achieved:
>
> 1. The capacity to converse freely, naturally and confidently about the objects, people and happenings within the child's environment. This capacity should gradually develop into:
>
> 2. The capacity to speak lucidly, coherently and relevantly on any given topic of every-day interest.
>
> 3. The capacity to read silently, intelligently and with speed written passages of average difficulty. (This capacity should be developed at least to such an extent that the student may read newspapers and magazines of every-day interest.)
>
> 4. The capacity to read aloud—clearly, expressively and with enjoyment—both prose and poetry. (The student should be able to discard the usual lifeless, monotonous and bored style of reading.)
>
> 5. The capacity to use the list of contents and the index and to consult dictionaries and reference books, and generally to utilize the library as a source of information and enjoyment.
>
> 6. The capacity to write legible, correctly, and with reasonable speed.
>
> 7. The capacity to describe in writing, in a simple and clear style, every-day happenings and occurrences, *e.g.*, to make reports of meetings held in the village for some co-operative purpose.
>
> 8. The capacity to write personal letters and business communications of a simple kind.
>
> 9. An acquaintance with, and interest in, the writings of standard authors, through a study of their writings or extracts from them.

*Source:* Jagdish S. Sharma, ed. (1965) *India's Struggle for Freedom: Select Documents and Sources*. Delhi: S. Chand & Co., 107–108.

In the early twentieth century, two denominational universities were founded: Aligarh Muslim University in Aligarh and Banaras Hindu University in Varanasi. The secular principles of post-1947 independent India would not have permitted the establishment of such universities but, because they were founded earlier, they survived as "central universities." Their curriculums closely follow those of hundreds of other universities in India.

There were several attempts to set up national institutions of education in the twentieth century, for example, Gurukul Kangri at Haridwar and the university set up at Shantiniketan by poet and Nobel laureate Rabindranath Tagore (1861–1941). There were many varieties of "national education" that focused on indigenous rather than English traditions. For example, Gurukul Kangri intended to revive ancient Indian education by teaching Sanskrit texts whereas at Shantiniketan the emphasis was on contemporary Indian literature and art. Mohandas Gandhi sponsored a scheme of basic education closely linked to his idea of constructive work in villages. But such institutions had a basic flaw—they did not confer degrees recognized by the government and, thus, could not help people to find employment.

### Education in Independent India

Independent India preserved the British educational heritage. No attempts were made to revive the initiatives of "national education." Shantiniketan survived as a central university, with government funding. The only new departure was a proliferation of engineering colleges, including the five Indian Institutes of Technology (IIT), one each in Chennai (Madras), Kanpur, Kharagpur, Mumbai (Bombay), and New Delhi. These elite institutions select their students from hundreds of thousands of applicants. Their graduates are highly qualified—about 50 percent of each class secures a job in the United States. Many of those who remain in India acquire an additional Master of Business Administration degree (MBA) so as to qualify for administrative posts in the private corporate sector, which are better paid than those in production or research and development. Management positions were more attractive because until the end of the twentieth century, Indian industry mostly worked with imported technology and therefore invested very little in research and development.

The most neglected sector of education is still primary schooling. Official statistics show about one hundred million pupils in primary schools, but there are high dropout rates. Approximately half of the population of India is illiterate. There are frequent complaints that village schoolmasters take their jobs as sinecures and therefore do not teach regularly. This deficiency at the primary level has had serious consequences. At the end of the twentieth century, suicides occurred among peasants grieving crop losses in southern India. Not knowing to get the soil examined, they had shifted to cotton cultivation, although the soil was unsuitable. The fruition of Mohandas Gandhi's quest for combined primary and practical education at the village level is still unrealized.

*Dietmar Rothermund*

### Further Reading

Altekar, A. S. (1975) *Education in Ancient India, Varanasi*. 7th ed. Varanasi, India: Nand.

Kishore Mukerji, S. N. (1974) *History of Education in India, Baroda*. 6th ed. Baroda, India: Acharya Book Depot.

**INDIA—HISTORY.** See **British Indian Empire; Gupta Empire; Harappa; India—Medieval Period; Mauryan Empire; Mughal Empire; Mohenjo Daro; Paleoanthropology—South Asia; Quit India Movement; South Asia—History.**

**INDIA—HUMAN RIGHTS** The architects of the Indian constitution envisioned a democratic, secular polity to guarantee people's fundamental rights without distinction of caste, color, creed, religion, or sex. Fundamental rights and freedom, as incorporated in India's constitution, reflect the ethos and spirit of the charter of the United Nations, reaffirming faith in "the dignity and worth of the human person, in the equal rights of men and women" (Levin 1996: 5). The judiciary acts as custodian to uphold these rights.

Despite built-in safeguards, violation of human rights has become common in India, often at the hands of lawmakers and law enforcers. In a tightly knit hierarchical social order reinforced by abject poverty, illiteracy, and lack of social awareness about constitutional rights, the rule of law is not strictly adhered to by law-enforcement agencies. Incorrigible corruption and criminalization of politics offer a fertile ground for human rights abuses by these agencies, which make an overt distinction between privileged and nonprivileged, majority and minority groups, elite and nonelite classes. A result is profound social unrest among marginalized and minority sections of society, with some even taking up arms against the state.

To deal with the increase in militancy, insurgencies, and ethnopolitical and community violence in India, state agencies often misuse laws such as the Armed Forces (Special Powers) Act of 1958, the Terrorist and Disruptive Activities (Prevention) (TADA) Act of 1985 (now in disuse), and the Jammu and Kashmir Disturbed Areas Act. These laws empower executive authorities to resort to warrantless searches, illegal detention, physical torture, harassment, and summary execution. In most cases, however, abuses happen in the name of the law without being officially sanctioned.

Most reported cases of human rights violations are custodial rapes and deaths at the hands of police. This fact has been acknowledged by India's National Human Rights Commission, established in 1993 to investigate such cases. The state authorities justify these violations on the ground that militants and insurgents indulging in indiscriminate killings of innocent people are even worse violators of human rights.

### Community Violence

Community violence between Hindus and Muslims and between Hindus and Christians took an ugly turn in the Hindu-belt Indian states of Gujarat, Madhya Pradesh, Maharashtra, and Orissa. Extremist Hindu fundamentalist groups such as Vishva Hindu Parishad, Rashtriya Sevak Sangh, and Bajrang Dal have actively fomented violence. In violent acts against Christians, churches were damaged and burned, and Christians were physically assaulted and robbed in 1999 and 2000.

Opposition parties in parliament protested these acts, especially when the media reported in January 2000 that the Bajrang Dal was responsible for burning to death an Australian missionary, Graham Stewart Staines, and his two sons, in Orissa, where Staines had spent more than two decades serving lepers. Hindu extremist groups charged him with mass conversion of Hindus to Christianity. A judicial commission appointed by the central government to probe into the incident exonerated the Bajrang Dal, and opposition parties termed this a whitewash. Amnesty International reported that the social violence against Christians, Muslims, and *Dalits* (untouchables) was the outcome of the extreme Hindu nationalist policies espoused by the Bharatiya Janata Party–led government under A. B. Vajpayee. Caste and community violence increased, especially in the eastern Indian state of Bihar. Clashes between the Ranvir Sena (government-banned private militia of upper-caste land lords) and lower-caste minorities claimed many lives. As reported by Amnesty International on 25 January 2000, "at least twenty-two Dalit ('untouchable') men, women, and children in Bihar's Jehanabad district" were killed by the Ranvir Sena (Human Rights Watch World Report 2000). In retaliation, the People's War Group, Maoist guerrillas, killed about three dozen upper-class people in the Jehanabad district in March 2000.

### Corrective Measures

To protect human rights, the government created the National Human Rights Commission under the Protection of Human Rights Act of 1993. The commission is a statutory recommendatory and advisory body, with the powers of a civil court to summon and examine witnesses under oath. It recommends a code of conduct for state and nonstate agencies, including employers in the private sector, to prevent human rights abuses by state agencies.

Because of the commission's effective intervention, the controversial TADA Act was allowed to lapse in May 1995. The commission has also conducted numerous probes into human rights violations and compelled authorities to recognize crimes in light of its recommendations.

As an autonomous body, the commission has acquired a reputation as fair and impartial in safeguarding civil liberties. It is headed by a judicial functionary with the status of a retired Supreme Court chief justice or justices. While commenting on the state of human rights in India, the commission's chairman, Justice J. S. Verma, a retired chief justice of India, observed that although India's record of human rights is comparatively good, it is important to protect and guarantee the social and economic rights of the poor and downtrodden sections of society. In its 1998–1999 report, tabled in the Indian parliament in the winter session of December 2000, the commission expressed concern about the protection of rights of the displaced population, the Dalits, and ethnic minorities. It observed that child labor, child prostitution, and sexual harassment and violence against minorities are on the rise. The commission considered 53,711 cases and disposed of 47,061 cases in the 1999–2000 year. While looking into the plight of thousands awaiting trials in jails, the commission recommended a speedy disposal of criminal cases pending in courts.

In March 2001, the Indian government decided to set up fast-track courts in each district of the country to dispose of long-standing cases awaiting trial. According to the sixty-first report of the Parliamentary Standing Committee on Home Affairs, 25 million cases are still pending in various courts of India. In March 2001, the Supreme Court ruled that if cases are not disposed of in five years, the accused should be freed from jail.

To improve the human rights record in India, it is essential to reform the police and armed and paramilitary forces, to improve the criminal judicial system, and to educate law enforcers about preventive measures to help reduce the recurrence of custodial rapes, torture, deaths, gender violence, and atrocities against poor and minority people. Good governance is essential to achieve these goals.

*B. M. Jain*

### Further Reading


Amnesty International. (2000) *Amnesty International Annual Report.* London: Amnesty International Publications.

———. (2001) *Amnesty International Watch World Report.* London: Amnesty International Publications.

Baxi, P. M. (1999) *The Constitution of India.* New Delhi: Universal Law Publishing Co.

Human Rights Watch World Report. (2000) New York: Human Rights Watch.

Jayal, Niraja Gopal. (1999) *Democracy and the State: Welfare, Secularism, and Development in Contemporary India.* Delhi: Oxford University Press.

Levin, Leah. (1996) *Human Rights: Questions and Answers.* Paris: UNESCO.

Marwah, Ved. (1995) *Uncivil Wars: Pathology of Terrorism in India.* New Delhi: Indus.

National Human Rights Commission. (1999–2000) *National Human Rights Commission Annual Report, 1999–2000.* New Delhi: National Human Rights Commission.

Widmalm, Sten. (1997) *Democracy and Violent Separatism in India.* Uppsala, Sweden: Uppsala University Press.


## INDIA—MEDIEVAL PERIOD

The medieval period (eighth–eighteenth centuries) in India is an important phase in the history of the South Asian subcontinent. Not only is it notable for cultural and political developments, but it also marked the coming of Islam and all its consequences.

### Parameters of Period

In the twentieth century, the history of medieval India became the rallying point for the two-nation theory that culminated in the partition of the Indian subcontinent. The vastly differing natures of the religions, cultures, and histories of the Hindu and Muslim communities were stressed. Ancient India was identified with Hindu rule, and the medieval period was identified with Muslim rule. That characterization is simplistic, however: although the rulers of a portion of India may have been Muslim during the medieval period, at any given time many parts of India were not under Muslim rule, so that periodization according to the ruler's religion is incorrect.

The beginning date of medieval India is controversial. Historians have taken different demarcation lines—the death of Harsa in 647 CE, the invasion of Mahmud of Ghanza, the establishment of the Delhi sultanate in 1192, and so forth—as the beginning of the period. Likewise, the end of medieval times is variously given as 1707, 1739, and 1757. Here, the medieval period is considered to cover the eighth to eighteenth centuries and the area encompassed by present-day India, Pakistan, and Bangladesh.

### Early Medieval India

In the early medieval period, roughly the eighth to thirteenth centuries, the Indian subcontinent experienced significant change. Islam came to India through territorial conquest, the lure of wealth, and religious zeal. Muhammad bin Qasim (691–716) fulfilled the Arab dream of seizing the fabulous wealth of India when he defeated King Dahir (reigned 690–712) of Sind (Sanskrit Sindhu) in 712 CE. Qasim's conquest made possible further cultural rapprochement between the Indian subcontinent and the Arab world. Mahmud of Ghazna (971–1030) attacked North India seventeen times between 997 and 1027. His aim was not political; he was interested in amassing vast wealth from the temples of India. Muhammad of Ghuri (first invaded in 1175, d. 1206) established political control after his victory over Prithviraj Chauhan (reigned 1178–1192) in the second battle of Tarai in 1192. Muhammad controlled much of northern India and parts of Gujarat and Gwalior. The Turkish conquest from Central Asia was possible because of the internecine struggles between regional powers, the prevailing feudal system, the superior military technology of the Turks, the general detachment of the masses from the defense of the king, and the Turks' religious zeal that led to jihad.

The regional kingdoms of the Rashtrakutas (in northern Deccan, eighth–tenth centuries), Pratiharas (in eastern and central India, eighth–eleventh centuries), and Palas (in Bengal, mid-eighth–mid-twelfth centuries) also rose and fell in early medieval India. These kingdoms fought one another over the capital city of Kanauj, and their internecine struggle made them weak. The Pratihara kingdom broke into small principalities. In the eleventh century, the later Chalukyas and Senas replaced the Rashtrakutas and Palas, respectively. Meanwhile, the Rajputs (c. seventh–twelfth centuries) ruled most of the kingdoms in northern India, but their disunity prevented them from resisting aggression from the northwest. The Chola kings of south India, made wealthy through trade and commerce, were the most powerful figures on the Indian peninsula during the ninth through twelfth centuries.

The early medieval period was also a time of agrarian expansion, with land grants to Brahmans, temples, and officials. Officials were granted revenue from land, and their salaries were generally equal to the amount of revenue collected. Their obligation was to send troops to the king. Feudalism and the emergence of hierarchical landed intermediaries made the position of the king weak. The peasants suffered from heavy taxation, the obligation to provide free labor, and indebtedness.

Urban centers began to grow during the ninth century as a result of trade and the rise of new markets. The mercantile community accumulated wealth and prospered. The Arabs, Chinese, Indians, and Southeast Asians were active in sea commerce. The eastern coast of India had a major share in trade with Southeast Asia, and Indian culture began to spread in that region.

A new social ethos was also developing in this period. Castes were changing position, and mixed castes were emerging; Indian social hierarchy was not static, as is evident from the social changes experienced in the period. Saints of south India were popularizing the Bhakti movement, with its message of personal devotion to God, among the masses. The intellectual movement of the eighth-century philosopher Sankara (c. 700–c. 750) emphasized the *advaitavada* (the doctrine of nondualism). Ramanujacharya (c. 1017–1137) called for spiritually experiencing God through intuition. Sanskrit was continuing to develop as the language of learning. The *Katha-sarita-sagara* (a collection of stories) and the *Gita Govinda* of the twelfth-century poet Jayadeva were two important Sanskrit works.

Linguistically, regional languages were beginning to develop, and Lahore was becoming an important center for Persian. The early medieval period also witnessed the development of unique regional temple architecture, such as the Brihadesvara temple at Tanjore and the gigantic Siva temple at Gangaikondacholapuram, both of which were famous Chola temples. The Sun temple of Konarka in Orissa and the Chandella temple at Khajuraho demonstrate exquisite craftsmanship.

### The Delhi Sultanate of 1192–1526

The Delhi sultanate took form under Muhammad of Ghuri and Qutubuddin Aibak (reigned 1206–1210). The period between 1206 and 1290 is popularly known as the slave dynasty, although no sultan was a slave when he became ruler, and there were actually three dynasties during the period. Shamsuddin Iltutmish (reigned 1210–1236) consolidated the sultanate in northern India. He bequeathed to his capable daughter Raziya (reigned 1236–1239) a large empire extending in the west to the Indus River. The struggle between the Delhi rulers and the Turkish nobility (the Forty, or *chahalgani)* had already started; the latter plotted against Raziya. It was Ghiyasuddin Balban (reigned 1265–1286) who destroyed the Forty; he also strengthened the army, ran an efficient spy system, suppressed revolts, and repulsed the ever-menacing Mongols.

The reign of the Khalji sultans (1290–1320) was marked by territorial expansion of the Delhi sultanate as well as the end of the Turkish monopoly of the ruling class. Jalauddin Khalji (reigned 1290–1296), the founder of the Khalji dynasty, was assassinated by his nephew and son-in-law Alauddin Khalji (reigned 1296–1316). Alauddin carved out a kingdom extending to south India and carried out market reforms by fixing the price of essential goods. Ghiyasuddin Tughluq (reigned 1320–1325), the founder of the Tughluq dynasty, was a capable ruler. His son Muhammed bin Tughluq (reigned 1325–1351) ruled over extensive territory. However, his ill-fated experiments, including moving the capital city and creation of token currency, created havoc. The process of disintegration had begun, and the reign of his successor, Firuz Tughluq (reigned 1351–1388), was followed by civil war. The sack of Delhi by the Mongol chief Timur (1336–1405) in 1398 further weakened the sultanate.

The Sayyid dynasty (1414–1451) was a mere shadow of a sultanate, and its control was confined to the Delhi region. The Lodi dynasty (1451–1526) witnessed the end of the sultanate, when Babur (1483– 1530) defeated Ibrahim Lodi (reigned 1517–1526) at the first battle of Panipat in 1526. While the sultanate declined, a number of kingdoms came into existence. In eastern India, the Ilyas Sahi dynasty of Bengal arose in 1350. The powerful Gajapatis of Orissa had resisted the onslaught of the sultans. In the west, the kingdoms of Malwa and Gujarat came into existence in the fifteenth century, and in north, Kashmir in the fourteenth century. In the south, the Bhamani sultanate (1347–1527) and the Vijayanagar empire (1336–1565) emerged.

The period of the Delhi sultanate marked a new era in cultural, social, and economic history of the subcontinent. The teachings of the Sufi saints appealed to the common people, and saints' *dargah* (tombs) remain places of pilgrimage for both Muslims and Hindus in the present day. The Bhakti movement saw the emergence of Kabir (1440–1518), Nanak (1469–1539), and Caitanya (1485–1533). They preached cooperation between Hindus and Muslims, egalitarianism, and the rejection of a social system based on caste. Nanak was the founder of Sikhism, which became an important religion after his death.

Indo-Islamic architecture, a fusion of the Hindu and Islamic styles, developed in this period. Arches, domes, and ornamentation of different kinds were main features of the style. Among the important structures built by the Delhi sultans are Qutab Minar, Siri fort, the city of Tughluqabad, Firozabad, and the tomb of Firuz. Murals, painted cloth, and Qur'anic calligraphy were landmarks in painting. Amir Khusrau (1253–1325), composer of Hindi and Persian verses, is credited with having introduced *qawwali*, different ragas, and the *khayal* form of singing. Such regional languages as Bengali, Assamese, Oriya, Punjabi, and Marathi developed. Interchange between the dialects of Hindi and the court language, Persian, resulted in the growth of Urdu.

The ruling class and nobility led a life of luxury. The ulamas (theologians) were an influential section of the population. (Indian Muslims [converted Hindus and their descendants] were disliked by the foreign Muslims, who thought themselves more pure and more strict in their adherence to the tenets of Islam.) The covering of a woman's face by a veil, or the *purdah* system, became more rigid. As non-Muslims, or *zimmi*s, Hindus had to pay a discriminatory tax known as *zeziyah*. However, the Hindu autonomous rajas lived well. The Hindus were in a dominant position regarding revenue, money lending, and agriculture.

In the early period of the sultanate, the territory was divided into units, or *iqta*s. The owners collected the revenue and defrayed the costs of their salaries. With urban expansion came the growth of a money economy and trade with West Asia, Southeast Asia, and China. Ports like Melaka and Aceh in Southeast Asia had large settlements of Indian traders. It was mainly Indian Muslim traders from Gujarat, Malabar, Tamil Nadu, and Bengal who brought a liberal brand of Islam to Southeast Asia.

### The Mughal Empire of 1526–1857

In the sixteenth century, Babur laid the foundation of Mughal rule in India after defeating Ibrahim Lodi. Rana Sanga and the Afghans also lost to him in the battles of Khanwa (1527) and Ghahra (1529), respectively. His son Humayun (1508–1556) inherited the difficult task of preserving the kingdom. Sher Shah Suri (c. 1486– 1545), the ambitious Afghan ruler of Bihar, defeated him at the battle of Chausa in 1539. Sher Shah's reign (1540–1545) witnessed a brilliant overhauling of the administration. Coming back from Persia, Humayun recaptured the throne of Delhi in 1555.

Akbar (1542–1605) carved out an empire bounded by Kabul in the northwest, Kashmir in the north, Bengal in the east, and beyond the Narmada River in the south. He consolidated the empire by annexation, matrimonial alliance with the Rajputs, religious tolerance, and sound administration. His broad vision, the policy of *sulh-i-kul* (universal tolerance), and his humanitarian outlook befitted his name, Akbar, which means "the Great." His son Jahangir (1569–1627) was a great dispenser of justice. Queen Nur Jahan (d. 1645), his wife, took an active interest in politics.

Shah Jahan (1592–1666), who ruled from 1628 to 1658, oversaw the Mughal empire's golden age. The last of the great Mughals, Aurangzeb (1618–1707), captured the throne by killing all his brothers and imprisoning Shah Jahan. His religious orthodoxy, wars in Deccan, and the alienation of such groups as the Sikhs, Rajputs, Marathas, and Jats marked the beginning of the end of the empire. Aurangzeb's destruction of temples might have been the result of political considerations, but it was a deviation from the policy of tolerance of his predecessors. Other factors that led to the decline of the empire after Aurangzeb included the draining of the treasury by protracted wars, crises in the bureaucracy, the decline of the army's efficiency, weak successors to Aurangzeb, and the independence of provincial governors.

After the invasion of Nadir Shah (1688–1747) in 1739, the Mughal empire remained in name only. Powerful regional kingdoms arose in this period. Sivaji (1627–1680) carved out a strong kingdom and fought relentlessly with the Mughals. Bengal, Awadh, and Hyderabad became independent. The Europeans, who had come as traders, began to interfere in states that had become independent from the Mughals. The absence of a central authority and naval technology made their task easier.

During the Mughal period, mosques, palaces, forts, and tombs expressed the rulers' relatively settled condition and the refinement of the period. The buildings of Akbar are beautiful structures, with carved and painted designs, many-sided pillars, the use of red sandstone, and so forth. The Taj Mahal, poetry in marble, stands apart for its beauty. Lavish ornamentation, use of marble, inlaid mosaic work of costly stones, engraved arches, and foliated pillar bases mark the architectural splendor of Shah Jahan's monuments. Landscape architecture as exemplified by ornamented gardens was another contribution of the Mughals. Painting reached its high-water mark under Jahangir, and Hindustani music developed.

Persian remained the court language, but Urdu was becoming popular. Regional languages were mature with lyrical poetry. Tulsidas (1543–1623) and Surdas (1483–1563) were famous Hindi poets of the times. Saints of the Bhakti movement from this period include Dadu Dayal (1544–1603) of Gujarat and Tukaram (1607–1649) of Maharashtra. The notable Sufi saints included Sheikh Salim Chisti (sixteenth century), Sheikh Abdul Kadir (1459–1533), and Sheikh Miyan Mir (1564–1624). However, certain trends developing in Sufism led to orthodoxy. Sheikh Ahmed Sarhindi (1564–1624) called for strict adherence to the Shariʿa. The missionary activity of some Sufi saints, particularly those belonging to the Qadriya order, resulted in large-scale conversion of Hindus.

The Mughal monarchs believed they had a divine right to the throne. The administration provided stability and peace in the empire. The *mansabs* (ranks) were assigned to both civil and military officers. The holders of the ranks, or *mansabdars*, were paid either in cash or in land assigned to them (*jagirs*). Abuses crept into the system of assigning ranks during the eighteenth century.

India's trade relationships with the outside world expanded, and Indian textiles were in great demand. Delhi, Agra, Lahore, Dhaka, Surat, and Masulipatnam flourished with the growth of urbanization. Asian merchants initially controlled a major share of trade, but from the eighteenth century onward, European shipping was in ascendance.

During the medieval period, Hindus and Muslims developed many common traits. There was fusion of the old with the new in the arts, literature, society, and religion. The composite culture that emerged, an amalgamation of different traditions, was the beginning of a national culture for India as a whole.

*Patit Paban Mishra*

### Further Reading


Chattopadhyaya, Brajadulal. (1998) *The Making of Early Medieval India.* Delhi: Oxford University Press.

Islam, Riazul. (1999) *Sufism and Its Impact on Muslim Society in South Asia.* Karachi, Pakistan: Oxford University Press.

Kulke, Hermann, and Dietmar Rothermund. (1994) *History of India.* Calcutta, India: Rupa.

Majumdar, R. C., ed. (1984) *The Mughal Empire, 1526–1707,* Vol. 8. 2d ed. Mumbai (Bombay), India: Bharatiya Vidya Bhavan.

Mujeeb, M. (1967) *The Indian Muslims.* London: George Allen and Unwin.

Nehru, Jawaharlal. (1991) *The Discovery of India.* 3d ed. New Delhi: ICCR.

Qamaruddin, Muhammad. (1985) *Society and Culture in Early Medieval India (712–1526).* New Delhi: Adam Publishers.

Sharma, R. S. (1965) *Indian Feudalism, c. 300–1200.* Calcutta, India: University of Calcutta.


## INDIA—POLITICAL SYSTEM

**INDIA—POLITICAL SYSTEM** With a civilization of nearly five thousand years' antiquity, India is continental in scale and displays a wide range of social, religious, racial, ethnic, caste, cultural, and linguistic diversity. Given this heterogeneity, the modern Indian political system has had to be a unique synthesis of diverse castes, cultures, and religions. India is by far the largest functioning democracy in the world and as such merits careful study. Of its more than 1 billion people—next in size to China—624 million are over eighteen years of age and have the right to vote. The vast majority of voters, mostly in rural areas, are illiterate or semiliterate, and women constitute half of the total electorate.

### Evolutionary Process

India's political system has evolved over the past fifty years against the background of the country's cultural values, its long struggle for freedom from British imperialism, and the Gandhian political and economic philosophy of nonviolence, decentralization, and democratic socialism. After becoming independent on 15 August 1947, India instituted a parliamentary democracy under which the president is the constitutional head of state, while real power is vested in a prime minister and cabinet, collectively accountable to parliament. There are three main principles of the Indian political system: democracy, secularism, and federalism.

***The Party System*** India's multiparty political system has witnessed a proliferation of political parties. Fifty-six parties participated in the first Lok Sabha (lower house) election of 1952; now there are 200, growth partly attributable to splits within parties, and partly to narrow, personal political considerations. (Political considerations are determined mainly by immediate political gains, such as offering more seats to party candidates in local and national elections to legislative bodies at the time of seat adjustments with various political parties; and offering ministerial berths in the government or lucrative positions in government-run organizations and enterprises.) In hindsight, Indian politics has been characterized by the one-party rule of the dominant Indian National Congress under the Nehru dynasty: Jawaharlal Nehru (1889–1964), Indira Gandhi (Nehru's only daughter; 1917–1984), and Indira Gandhi's son Rajiv Gandhi (1944–1991). India entered the era of coalition politics following the Congress Party's debacle in the November 1989 parliamentary elections. The Janata Party was the first non-Congress party to form the central government, in March 1977 under the leadership of Morarji Desai (1896–1995), a Gandhian and strict disciplinarian. The Desai government tried to give new direction to

Indian politics by basing it on moral values. That did not work: bickering among its coalition partners ultimately caused the fall of the Desai government in July 1979.

In the January 1980 elections, Indira Gandhi returned to power. The black days of her state of emergency rule (1975–1977) were fresh in the minds of Indians who had suffered the excesses of that time. She had failed to benefit the people and manage incremental intrastate conflicts. Her populist slogan of *garibi hatao* (eliminate poverty) rang hollow and failed to enthuse the masses.

After her assassination on 31 October 1984, her eldest son Rajiv Gandhi was sworn in as prime minister. In the 1984 elections the Congress Party again won an overwhelming majority, attributed chiefly to sympathy following Gandhi's assassination. Rajiv Gandhi, India's youngest prime minister at just over forty, had a vision of taking India into the twentieth century, making it progressive, prosperous, and powerful in the comity of nations. He advocated economic reforms to attract foreign investment and boost exports. In foreign policy, he served the country's best interests by maintaining balanced relations with both the United States and the USSR. But his image was sullied when he was charged with involvement in kickbacks in the purchase of guns from the Swedish company Bofors. This became a major issue in the parliamentary elections of November 1989, which his party lost.

Since then, Indian politics have been generally characterized by instability. The Janata government, formed under the leadership of V. P. Singh (b. 1931) in December 1989, collapsed after a year when it lost outside support. In the May 1991 elections, the Congress Party fared better and managed to form a government under P. V. Narsimha Rao (born 1921), who completed his five-year term as prime minister. The main achievement of the Rao government was the June 1991 introduction of economic reforms intended to loosen stifling export and import restrictions, promote public-sector privatization, and encourage foreign investment. This policy of liberalization was a major departure from the "Nehruvian" model of socialist economic development. But Rao compromised his and his party's image by bribing some members of parliament to stay in power. Then in the June 1996 elections, no single political party won an absolute majority, and three central governments were formed in 1996 and 1997.

In the March 1998 elections, a coalition of about two dozen parties led by the Bharatiya Janata Party (BJP) formed the government under Atal Behari Vajpayee (b. 1924). But his government was toppled after thirteen months by a single vote during a vote of confidence in the lower house of parliament. New elections were held in September–October 1999. Again the BJP-led National Democratic Alliance (NDA), an alliance of eighteen national and regional parties, formed under the leadership of Vajpayee. The NDA government, in principle based on consensus politics, has developed a common minimum program to run the government smoothly. Its ruling partners have agreed not to abrogate Article 370 of the Indian constitution guaranteeing special status to the state of Jammu and Kashmir. Nor will they advocate a common civil code also applying to Indian Muslims or raise the controversial temple issue that rocked the country following the destruction of the Babri Masjid (mosque) by Hindu fundamentalists in December 1991.

The NDA government has not, however, met the expectations of the people. Law-enforcement agencies avoid acting against powerful, influential individuals, including smugglers, drug mobsters, and economic offenders, who have direct links with ruling political leaders. Bandits such as Veerappan (charged with nu-

## PREAMBLE TO THE CONSTITUTION OF INDIA

Adopted on 26 Jan 1950

We, the people of India, having solemnly resolved to constitute India into a sovereign socialist secular democratic republic and to secure to all its citizens: justice, social, economic and political; liberty of thought, expression, belief, faith and worship; equality of status and of opportunity; and to promote among them all fraternity assuring the dignity of the individual and the unity and integrity of the nation; in our constituent assembly this twenty-sixth day of November, 1949, do hereby adopt, enact and give to ourselves this constitution.

*Source:* International Court Network. Retrieved 8 March 2002, from: http://www.uni-wuerzburg.de/law/in00000_.html.

merous murders, violent gang robberies, and kidnappings) or the hard-core Hindu fundamentalist Bal Thakeray (charged with inflammatory writings against a minority religious community, leading to a massacre in Mumbai) have a free run. Poverty is still rampant, youth unrest is on the rise due to increasing unemployment, scams and scandals in public office are commonplace, and minorities suffer physical assaults by thugs from the majority community.

India has shifted from the value-based politics of 1950s and mid-1960s to the politics of sheer opportunism, characterized by a cancerous growth of communal hatred and violence, vote buying, divisions along caste and communal lines, and power-brokering, all of which contribute to moral degeneration in both the public and private lives of politicians, legislators, and party functionaries from top to bottom. Caught in decay and degeneration, the state has miserably failed to provide social security and ensure social harmony.

### Democratic Decentralization of Power

Indian democracy is unique in its devolution of power to the grass roots, initiated with the introduction of the Panchayati Raj system in October 1959. Under this system, village councils (*panchayats*) comprise the smallest units of local self-government. Panchayati Raj is specifically designed to empower rural people to facilitate rapid socioeconomic development. The seventy-third amendment to India's constitution (adopted on 22 December 1992 and implemented on 24 April 1993) provides for a three-tier structure of local self-government, starting with the village at the bottom, ascending through the subdivision, to the district at the top. There is a 33 percent quota for representation of women in Panchayati Raj institutions. (Another radical initiative would establish a 33 percent quota for women members in the national and state legislatures.)

### Federalism

India is a federal polity with a clear-cut division of powers between the Union and states. Despite that, center-state relations have been far from satisfactory, mainly due to the centralization of power by the Union government and to its discriminatory policies in allocating funds to states for development programs. India's northeastern states, Jammu and Kashmir in particular, have often complained that the Union government fails to address their various development and socioeconomic problems, problems resulting in large-scale violence and frustration among youths. This is a main reason why people are demanding separate statehood: they are agitating for the devolution of more authority and administrative and financial powers from the Union government. The states themselves are also demanding more autonomy. On 25 June 2000, the Legislative Assembly of Jammu and Kashmir passed an autonomy resolution for the restoration of its pre-1953 status. The central government staunchly opposes this, fearing that it would threaten national unity; it has, however, agreed to consider a state's demand for autonomy within the framework of the constitution.

Indian prime minister Atal Behari Vajpayee is congratulated by dignitaries including opposition leader Sonia Gandhi on 13 October 1999 before being sworn into office in New Delhi. (AFP/CORBIS)

### Judiciary

The judiciary is an important part of the Indian political system. It is a custodian of the constitution and has the right to review legislative enactments and executive acts. Though the Indian judiciary is independent, political considerations do influence judicial appointments, promotions, and transfers. Nonetheless, it was due to independent judicial activism that the Indian Supreme Court took action against top public functionaries—including the prime minister and top bureaucrats—who either had indulged in corrupt practices or were apathetic in the discharge of their public duties.

The major challenge before the Indian judiciary is to ensure prompt resolution of the cases piling up in the courts, sometimes for decades, to restore confidence in the efficacy of the judiciary. "Justice delayed is justice denied" aptly describes the Indian judicial system. Since the judicial process is so expensive and cumbersome, people prefer to suffer injustice rather than go to court.

### Secularism

The principle of secularism in the Indian constitution requires that the state not discriminate against anyone on grounds of religion. The secular character of the Indian polity cannot be altered even through constitutional amendment. The term "secularism" was first incorporated into the preamble to the constitution through the forty-second amendment. The constitution guarantees religious minorities the right to establish and administer educational institutions in accordance with their language, culture, and script.

The credibility of Indian secularism has been eroding, however, with the emergence of *Hindutva*, a narrow Hindu cultural nationalism. This has recently been promoted as the "essence" of the Indian state by a handful of self-styled representatives of Hinduism, including Bajrang Dal and Rastriya Sevak Sangh. Consequently, religious conflict between Hindus and Muslims and between Hindus and Christians is on the rise. The destruction of the Babri Masjid (a mosque said to have been constructed by the Muslim ruler Babar) in December 1991 shook the foundation of Indian secularism. Purportedly secular political parties are now exploiting the religious card as a vote-getter.

### Freedom of the Media

The Indian media enjoy complete freedom in expressing their views without government interference, perhaps to the envy of some of their Western counterparts. Control exercised by media magnates does, however, largely nullify this freedom. Transparency is further eroded by the media's declining commitment to professional values: in a case recently disclosed by the Indian journalist Virendra Kapoor, some forty-odd Indian journalists "on a no-expense-spared conducted tour of Pakistan" accepted "expensive carpets and other gift items" from their Pakistani host (*Economic and Political Weekly* 5–11 August 2000: 2810). The media largely serve the interests of parties in power, who in return provide them with political patronage. As well, a coterie of pro-establishment intellectuals and top bureaucrats—some retired—who air their views in the media has gained tremendous influence, to the detriment of independent and incisive analysis of national, regional, and international issues.

### India's Foreign Policy

The main plank of India's foreign policy is nonalignment. Its chief architect, Prime Minster Jawaharlal Nehru, defined this as an "independent policy," taking decisions on international and regional issues on the basis of the merits or demerits of each case. This policy was motivated by several factors, including a desire to avoid Cold War superpower politics and alliances, and India's ambitions to play a significant independent role in world affairs. Nonalignment was pursued continuously and consistently during the Cold War era, except during the Morarji Desai government (1977–1979), which favored what it termed a "genuine nonaligned policy," implying a balanced policy not tilting in favor of either superpower. By prefixing "nonaligned policy" with the word "genuine," the Desai government claimed a major shift in India's policy of nonalignment: unlike Mrs. Gandhi's tilt toward the Soviet Union, the Desai government tilted neither in favor of Russia or the United States. Critics branded India's positive tilt toward the USSR during the regime of Mrs. Gandhi a clear departure from nonalignment. India's nonaligned ideology in general, and its tilt toward the USSR in particular, was the main source of irritation between India and the West, especially the United States.

After the end of the Cold War and the collapse of the USSR, India's nonalignment underwent radical transformation. Putting aside ideology, India has gone ahead and forged a defense and strategic relationship with the United States. India not only established full diplomatic relations with Israel in 1992, but has also forged close strategic and defense ties with it—unthinkable during the Cold War period. At the same time, India introduced economic reforms in 1991, giving greater weight to the economic content of its diplomacy by encouraging foreign investment, disinvestment in the public sector (privatization), and loosening of export and import restrictions to integrate its economy into the global market. India is still attempting to justify the relevance in the post–Cold War world of being a leading member of the Non-Aligned Movement (NAM). India feels NAM can contribute to restructuring the United Nations and can help establish a nondiscriminatory trade regime while safeguarding human rights. In practice, India's nonaligned policy has lost both its ideological appeal and moral moorings.

India has been dubbed a "soft state," one vulnerable to internal and external pressures, bending its laws, rules, and regulations to political exigencies: its political system is under profound strain, as it has failed to tackle underlying caste, class, cultural, and ethnoreligious tensions. That failure is likely to undermine the country's unity and integrity as well as its secular character. On the economic and foreign policy fronts, India needs to adopt a more distinct, long-term policy, as opposed to the "adhocism" practiced today, if it wants to carve out a meaningful place in the world community.

*B. M. Jain*

**Further Reading**

Bhagwati, Jagdish. (1993) *India in Transition: Freeing the Economy*. Oxford, U.K.: Clarendon Press.

Brass, Paul R. (1992) *The Politics of India since Independence*. Cambridge, U.K.: Cambridge University Press.

Gupta, Bhabani. (1993) *India in the 1990s: Politics, Economy, and Society*. Tokyo: Japan Institute of International Affairs.

Joshi, Vijay, and I. M. J. Little. (1996) *India's Economic Reforms: 1991–2001*. New Delhi: Oxford University Press.

Kapur, Harish. (1994) *India's Foreign Policy, 1947–92: Shadows and Substance*. New Delhi: Sage Publications.

Kashyap, Subhas C. (1997) *Coalition Government and Politics in India*. New Delhi: Uppal.

Kothari, Rajni. (1988) *State against Democracy: In Search of Humane Governance*. New Delhi: Ajanta Publications.

Mehta, V. R. (1988) *Ideology, Modernisation, and Politics in India*. Delhi: Manohar.

Pannikar, K. M., ed. (1992) *Communalism in Indian History, Politics, and Culture*. Delhi: Manohar.

Thakur, Ramesh. (1995) *The Government and Politics in India*. New York: St. Martin's Press.

Thomas, Raju G. C. (1996) *Democracy, Security, and Development in India*. New York: St. Martin's Press.


**INDIA-MYANMAR RELATIONS** Myanmar (Burma until 1989) became the second-largest member of the Association of Southeast Asian Nations (ASEAN) on admission in 1997. Rich in natural resources, especially oil and gas, Myanmar could emerge as an economic leader in Asia. Moreover, its strategic importance has made India, China, and Southeast Asian nations take note of Myanmar's critical role when shaping their relations as well as Indian Ocean policies.

### Historical Background

During Britain's colonial rule of India, the British considered Burma (as Myanmar was then known) an important post for monitoring activities of hostile powers such as Japan, Russia, and China. The first Anglo-Burmese War (1824–1826) was the culmination of Burma's early-nineteenth-century intrusion into India. Thereafter, Britain extended colonial rule to Burma, which remained in the Empire (though administratively separate from India) from 1886 until independence in 1948. During World War II, Burma was important for both the Axis and Allied powers for purposes of defending security and strategic interests in South and Southeast Asia. The seizure of Burma by Japanese forces during World War II made it difficult for Britain to maintain administrative control over India.

Given this background, India-Myanmar relations are of special importance. The countries have close historical and cultural ties, sharing 1,643 kilometers of common border along the Potkai Hills. They enjoyed friendly relations from 1948 to 1962, and early on India provided Rangoon (now Yangon) with military and economic assistance to fight insurgents along their common border. Prime Ministers Jawaharlal Nehru (1889–1964) of India and U Nu of Burma (1907–unknown) were instrumental in cementing initial political and diplomatic ties between two countries.

The military regime of General Ne Win (1962–1988) and India's support for Burma's pro-democracy movement were largely responsible for the two countries' estrangement. After the September 1988 coup that brought the military junta, the State Law and Order Restoration Council (SLORC), to power in Myanmar, the government of Rajiv Gandhi in India not only gave moral support to the restoration of democracy but also provided sanctuary to refugees. However, India gradually realized that its tough policy toward the new regime might complicate the problems of cross-border insurgency, drug trafficking, and smuggling in northeastern India. The Indian government also feared that rigid opposition to SLORC might drive Myanmar closer to China. This led New Delhi to adopt a policy of realism and pragmatism.

### Policy of Engagement

In March 1993 India's foreign secretary, J. N. Dixit, visited Myanmar to hold talks with Myanmar's officials on wide-ranging issues. Talks were again held in Yangon at Myanmar's initiative in 1994. A Memorandum of Understanding on cooperation between the border authorities of both countries for maintaining border tranquillity was signed in 1994. Although India assured Yangon it would not interfere in Myanmar's domestic affairs, New Delhi openly extended moral support to Myanmar's pro-democracy activist Aung San Suu Kyi. Bilateral relations deteriorated further when the Jawaharlal Nehru Award for promoting international understanding was given to Suu Kyi.

Despite such irritants, India has kept political and diplomatic channels open with Myanmar. India's foreign secretary, K. Ragunath, visited Myanmar in February 1998 to forge wider strategic cooperation on internal security and border management. He discussed several issues of mutual concern with U Khin Maung, Myanmar's deputy foreign minister, to enhance border trade between two countries. To boost momentum, a high-level India-Myanmar meeting took place in Yangon in August 2000. Under discussion was "effective border management," including steps to curb drug trafficking and smuggling. Both countries underlined the need to strengthen infrastructure and security to promote border trade.

### The China Factor

China has always been key in India-Myanmar relations, due mainly to Myanmar's strategic location and to India's and China's clashing security and strategic interests. With implementation of the 1914 McMahon Line Agreement in 1918, the India-Burma northern boundary was set near the Talu Pass. China contested this when it signed the Boundary Treaty with Myanmar in October 1960, but despite Chinese opposition, India still considers the Talu Pass demarcation valid. Furthermore, India and Myanmar agreed on their land border in December 1967, with the exception of the three-way border between China, India, and Myanmar. In March 1984 both New Delhi and Rangoon successfully concluded a maritime boundary agreement.

China has begun building a naval base on Coco Island, much to India's distress. Also, China and Myanmar have agreed to establish a 30,000-square-mile offshore economic zone to facilitate exploitation of natural resources to their mutual benefit. This will, however, affect India's maritime and economic interests.

Growing Pakistan-Myanmar ties are also of concern to India. Increasing links between Pakistan's Inter-Services Intelligence and Myanmar's intelligence agency serve Pakistani interests, as Pakistan considers Myanmar to be a safer base from which to launch militant activities in northeastern India. This rapprochement acquires added significance, since the military regimes of both Pakistan and Myanmar share common strategic perceptions and political interests. The India-Myanmar relationship presents a complex scenario, given the Sino-Myanmar, Sino-Pakistan, and Pakistan-Myanmar triangle of relations. To counter this, India is keeping tabs on developments and has launched a multipronged diplomatic effort both to engage and contain Myanmar.

### India's Connection with Myanmar through ASEAN

Myanmar became a full member of ASEAN in 1997 despite American opposition; the same year, India was admitted as a full dialogue partner. ASEAN has allowed both New Delhi and Yangon to increase and expand economic, commercial, and trade ties. India will also gain greater access to ASEAN markets: India's trade volume with ASEAN member countries has increased since India joined, first as an observer in 1993 and then as a full dialogue partner. Undoubtedly, Myanmar understands that given India's industrial, technological, military, and nuclear capabilities, it is capable of influencing the politics, economy, and security of Southeast Asia. India and Myanmar now have better opportunities collectively to address the security, defense, and strategic issues confronting Southeast Asia, since India is also a member of ASEAN's Regional Forum (ARF, established 1994).

Good India-Myanmar relations might gradually help reduce Chinese influence on Myanmar. Although China and Myanmar have drawn closer in their common goal of launching an antidemocratic movement, Myanmar does not want to remain isolated from the world and seems eager to cast off its pariah image. In pursuit of greater international ties, Myanmar's military regime has become more pragmatic. This is likely to prompt New Delhi and Yangon to cooperate in areas of mutual concern and interest, especially in the areas of cross-border insurgency, drug trafficking, and arms smuggling, threats to the security and economic interests of both countries.

*B. M. Jain*

### Further Reading

Ahmed, Abu Taher Salahuddin. (1997) "Myanmar: Politics, Economy and Foreign Relations." *BIISS Journal* 18, 2 (April): 124–159.

Aung San Suu Kyi. (1991) *Freedom from Fear and Other Writings.* Delhi, India: Penguin Books.

Linter, Bertl. (1994) "The Indo-Burmese Frontier—A Legacy of Violence." *Jane's Intelligence Review* 6, 1 (January): 38–40.

Mung, Shwe Lu. (1989) *Burma Nationalism and Ideology: An Analysis on Society, Culture and Politics.* Dhaka, Bangladesh: University Press Limited.

Silverstein, Josef. (1977) *Burma: Military Rule and the Politics of Stagnation.* Ithaca, NY: Cornell University Press.

Singh, L. P. (1992) "India–Burma Relations." *World Focus* (January): 7–10.

## INDIA-PAKISTAN RELATIONS

With India's and Pakistan's May 1998 nuclear tests, world attention focused on South Asia. The fear was not only a regional nuclear arms race, but the effect on volatile areas such as the Middle East. The fear was well-founded, because the two nations have been at odds over Kashmir since the partitioning of the Indian subcontinent in August 1947. India and Pakistan have a history of armed conflict, having fought four major wars (1947–1948, September 1965, December 1971, and May 1999). The hostilities have cost both countries economically, physically, and psychologically without producing tangible gain. Besides Kashmir, other unresolved, long-standing bilateral problems include sovereignty over the Siachen Glacier, the Sir Creek maritime boundary, and the Tulbul Project/Wuller barrage. Many factors have contributed to this

## INDIA'S EARLY VIEW ON INDIA-PAKISTAN RELATIONS

The following resolution passed by the Indian National Congress party in September 1950 sets forth several key elements in India's policy toward Pakistan, including a desire for peace and the contradictory desire to prevent peoples in India from affiliating with Pakistan.

> The Jaipur Congress drew the particular attention of the country to the menace of communalism and called upon the people to put an end to all communal and separatist tendencies which had already caused grievous injury and which imperiled the hard-won freedom of the country. Anti-national and socially reactionary forces have continued to function and come in the way of India's progress.
>
> The partition of India caused deep wounds in the political, economic and emotional life of the country. Passions were roused and many difficult problems arose, leading to continuing tension, and ill-will between India and Pakistan. These problems can only be solved satisfactorily with patience and goodwill, tolerance and firmness, keeping always in view the honour and interests of India. These interests of India, as of Pakistan, require peaceful and cooperative relations between the two countries. This Congress, therefore, commends and approves of the proposal made by the Government of Pakistan for an agreement between the two countries that all disputes should be solved by peaceful methods and without resort to armed conflict.
>
> For this reason, among others, the Congress records approval of the Indo—Pakistan Agreement of 8th April, 1950, which represents a peaceful and effective approach to the solution of a very difficult problem and which is in keeping with the traditions and policy of the Congress. It is with this approach and in this spirit that such problems can be most effectively dealt with and can yield enduring results.
>
> Whatever disputes and conflicts may exist now or may arise in future between India and Pakistan, they should be considered as political problems between the two countries and should be treated as such. In no event should the spirit of communalism or the misuse of religion be allowed to mar and distort the consideration of our internal problems. We cannot forsake our own policy in a spirit of retaliation. We have not only to treat our minorities with full justice and fairness, but should make them feel that they are so treated.
>
> This Congress, therefore, declares that it is the basic policy of the nation, as reaffirmed in the Constitution, that India is a democratic State which, while honouring every faith, neither favours nor discriminates against any particular religion or its adherents, and which gives equal rights and freedom of opportunity to all communities and individuals who form the nation. It is the primary duty of every Congressman to carry this great message and to live up to it and to combat every form of communalism or separatism in India.

*Source:* Jagdish Saran Sharma. (1965) *India's Struggle for Freedom: Select Documents and Sources*. Vol. 2. Delhi: S. Chand & Co., 242–243.

antagonism, including Cold War politics, competitive geostrategic perceptions, ideological and cultural differences, and the dynamics of extraregional politics.

### Kashmir

Hostility began with the breakaway of primarily Muslim Pakistan from predominantly Hindu India in 1947. It continued with Pakistani advances in the Kashmir Valley in October 1947, and its forceful occupation of Azad Kashmir—the one-third of the valley thenceforth known in India as "Pakistan-occupied Kashmir." Immediately thereafter, Hari Singh, ruler of Jammu and Kashmir States, signed an instrument of accession with India on 26 October 1947, making Kashmir into Indian territory. Pakistan has contested this on the grounds that Kashmir is a Muslim-dominated area. It has consistently demanded that the problem be resolved in accordance with the U.N. resolution of August 1948, which called for a plebiscite to determine the wishes of Kashmiri Muslims. The Indian government opposes this on the grounds that it would undermine India's basic secularism. Pakistan maintains that the Kashmir issue needs to be resolved before bilateral relations can be improved and sees resolution of the Kashmir problem as essential to ensure regional peace and stability. India insists that the Kashmir issue cannot be resolved unless Pakistan stops cross-border terrorism. These rigid postures have further deepened the estrangement.

### The Cold War

Geopolitics remains key in India-Pakistan relations. Pakistan's fear of India induced it to join two U.S.-sponsored military alliances, the Southeast Asia Treaty Organization and the Central Treaty Organization, in 1954 and 1955, respectively, to bolster national security and identity vis-à-vis India. In contrast, India adopted a policy of nonalignment to avoid the superpower rivalry and concentrate scarce resources on modernization and development for the well-being of its people. New Delhi and Islamabad focused on achieving their own security and development rather than addressing common geopolitical and geostrategic issues or trying to implement a subregional security system.

During the Cold War, the United States provided massive military assistance to Islamabad to help maintain the balance of power between India and Pakistan (India being by far the larger), triggering a regional arms race in the process. India gradually came to favor the USSR, becoming its chief arms buyer. India also signed the Treaty of Peace, Friendship and Cooperation with the USSR in August 1971, to ward off Chinese or U.S. adventurism during its 1971 war with Pakistan. The war proved costliest to Pakistan, which lost East Pakistan, the latter becoming Bangladesh. India's overt hand in the emergence of Bangladesh as a separate nation hardened Pakistani enmity.

### Simla Agreement

After Pakistan's defeat in the 1971 war and the surrender of its armed forces before the Indian army in Dhaka, the new capital of Bangladesh, Pakistani president Zulfikar Ali Bhutto (1928–1979) and Indian prime minister Indira Gandhi (1917–1984) met at Simla in northern India to discuss postwar relations. On 2 July 1972 they signed the historic Simla Accord, under which both countries committed themselves to resolve disputes, including Kashmir, through peaceful bilateral negotiation without third-party intervention. They also agreed to respect the line of control (LoC) resulting from the cease-fire of 17 December 1971 and not to attempt to alter it unilaterally.

### Post-Simla Developments

The Simla Accord helped prevent the outbreak of major conflict between two countries till 1999. Despite fluctuation in their bilateral relations, New Delhi and Islamabad agreed to begin composite and integrated dialogue on eight issues during talks held by their foreign secretaries in Islamabad in June 1997. Further talks in New Delhi in November 1998 dealt with contentious bilateral issues, including Kashmir. The improvement in relations picked up momentum when the new Indian prime minister, Atal Behari Vajpayee (b. 1926), undertook a bus journey to Lahore in February 1999. He signed the Lahore Declaration

In February 2000, Indians protest what they claim is Pakistan's support for terrorism against India. (AFP/Corbis)

## UPDATE: INDIA–PAKISTAN RELATIONS WORSEN AT END OF 2001

At the close of 2001 India–Pakistan relations worsened considerably following a suicide attack on the Indian Parliament that left five terrorists and nine Indians dead. India blamed the bombing on the Lashkar-e-Taiba and Jaish-e-Muhammad, two Muslim fundamentalist groups in Pakistan that support Pakistan's claims to Kashmir. Senior Indian officials also claimed that the Pakistan government supported the attack and has long supported terrorism aimed at India. India also rejected Pakistan's offers to jointly investigate the attack and denied government involvement.

*Source:* Celia A. Dugger. (2001) "India Raises the Pitch in Criticism of Pakistan." *The New York Times* (18 December): A14.

with his Pakistani counterpart, Nawaz Sharif (b. 1949), and they resolved to settle bilateral disputes in a friendly and peaceful manner. But the Lahore spirit quickly dissipated following the May 1999 Kargil conflict in Indian territory in the Kashmir Valley. In October 1999, General Pervez Musharraf (b. 1943) took power in Pakistan in a bloodless coup. In 2002, the United States acted as a third party to encourage dialogue between the two countries. The Vajpayee government has made it clear that it will not legitimize Pakistan's military regime.

### The Nuclear Dimension

Ever since India detonated its first nuclear device in May 1974, the nuclear issue has increased the tension between New Delhi and Islamabad. In reaction to the Indian nuclear test, President Bhutto called for Pakistan to make nuclear weapons even if it had to "eat grass" to make it possible. His determination was pursued by his successors, enabling Pakistan to attain nuclear parity with India in May 1998. The United States and Japan imposed economic sanctions on India and Pakistan, refusing to lift them unless India and Pakistan sign the Comprehensive Test Ban Treaty (CTBT), but India and Pakistan are proceeding with missile upgrading programs. The Indian government has emphasized that unless China stops transferring sophisticated weapons, nuclear technology, and missiles to Pakistan, nuclear restraint in the region will remain impossible. From an Indian perspective, China remains a critical factor in the India-Pakistan relationship, a view not shared by Pakistan.

Given the nuclear threat, especially in view of the unresolved Kashmir problem, India and Pakistan need to undertake a series of confidence-building measures, such as entering into arms control and no-first-use agreements, improving nuclear command-and-control systems, and undertaking risk-reduction measures. In the interest of long-term regional peace and stability, Pakistan should stop cross-border terrorism. It is equally important to encourage friendly relations by enhancing contact between the citizens of the two nations, contact that will, one hopes, reduce mutual mistrust and build friendly and harmonious relations between the former enemies.

*B. M. Jain*

### Further Reading

Ahmed, Samina, and David Cortright, eds. (1998) *Pakistan and the Bomb: Public Opinion and Nuclear Options*. Notre Dame, IN: University of Notre Dame Press.

Chopra, Pran. (1994) *India, Pakistan and the Kashmir Tangle*. New Delhi: HarperCollins.

Cohen, Stephen, ed. (1991) *Nuclear Proliferation in South Asia: The Prospects for Arms Control*. Boulder, CO: Westview Press.

Ganguly, Sumit. (1994) *The Origins of War in South Asia*. 2d ed. Boulder, CO: Westview Press.

Gupta, Sisir. (1966) *Kashmir, A Study in India-Pakistan Relations*. Delhi: Asia Publishing.

Jain, B. M. (1994) *Nuclear Politics in South Asia*. Jaipur and New Delhi, India: Rawat.

Malik, Hafeez. (1993) *Dilemmas of National Security and Cooperation in India and Pakistan*. New York: St. Martin's Press.

Thomas, Raju G. C., ed. (1992) *Perspective on Kashmir: The Roots of Conflict in South Asia*. Boulder, CO: Westview Press.

## INDIA–SOUTHEAST ASIA RELATIONS

India had close cultural interaction with Southeast Asia from prehistoric times. In modern times there were vicissitudes in the relations, but India is striving to become a major player in the regional economy and politics.

### Ancient and Medieval Periods

In the gamut of Indo-Southeast Asian relations, both Indians and Southeast Asians played an active role. In prehistoric times a land route crossed northeastern India to Burma, China, and Thailand. Apart from movements of people and racial and linguistic affinity, trading relations also united India and

**MY SON SANCTUARY**

The My Son Sanctuary, a UNESCO World Heritage Site since 1999, was the capital of the Champa Kingdom, a Hindu kingdom located on what is now the coast of Vietnam. It elegantly demonstrates a common phenomenon in Asia—the blending of seemingly divergent cultures.

Southeast Asia. Archaeological excavations produced evidence of trade between the two regions in the form of shared objects of material culture.

In the Common Era trade increased with intensified sea-borne commerce. Along with traders, Brahmans or priests from India traveled to Southeast Asia and acquainted the local elite with Indian rituals, scriptures, and literature. The Brahmans became counselors in court affairs and legitimized the position of rulers by giving them an investiture ceremony and a genealogical list. Indian elements like Sanskrit language, Hindu-Buddhist cults, *Dharmasastra*s (treatises dealing with statecraft and administration), and the concept of royalty became essential features of the early states of Southeast Asia.

The common people in Southeast Asia were influenced by stories from the *Mahabharata* and *Ramayana*. Indian religion and deities became popular, and Indian culture diffused throughout the indigenous societies of Southeast Asia, whose cultures were open foreign elements.

The "Indianized" states of Southeast Asia persisted until medieval times, when the arrival of Islam in the latter part of the thirteenth century changed the situation. From Gujarat and the Coromandel coast (whose contact with Southeast Asia preceded the coming of Islam), traders responsible for the spice and pepper trade in the Mediterranean visited the region and helped to spread Islam by establishing Muslim settlements. Islam as brought to Southeast Asia by Indian Muslims differed from the orthodox Islam of Arabia. The Southeast Asians preserved some Hindu-Buddhist characteristics acquired by their contact with India, and there was no break with the pre-Islamic past.

### Modern Period

In the nineteenth century Indian immigrants moved to the British colonies of Malaya, Singapore, and Burma (present-day Myanmar) to work on rubber, coffee, and tea plantations as indentured laborers. Indian textile merchants and moneylenders also appeared in the French colony of Indochina. These immigrants were seen as advancing the interests of colonial masters, and a feeling of antipathy developed toward them. The Indian independence movement stimulated anticolonial struggles in Southeast Asia. Indian personalities like Mohandas K. Gandhi (called Mahatma; 1869–1948) and Rabindranath Tagore (1861–1941) were much admired by Southeast Asian leaders like Sukarno of Indonesia (1901–1970), Norodom Sihanouk of Cambodia (b. 1932), Aung San of Burma (1914?–1947), and Ho Chi Minh of Vietnam (1890–1969). In the framework of the freedom struggle, Indian leaders mooted the concept of "Asianism" and called on formation of a common Asian identity to oppose the West.

After independence India pursued a dynamic policy toward Southeast Asia. Acting as intermediary, India contributed to lessening tensions by hosting conferences like the Asian Relations Conference in 1947 and the Conference on Indonesia in 1949. The Bandung Conference (1955) was the high-water mark in Indian diplomacy. The prime minister of India, Jawaharlal Nehru (1889–1964), architect of basic principles of Indian foreign policy like anticolonialism and nonalignment, believed that India could play a meaningful role in the Cold War period.

However Indian relations with Southeast Asian countries lost momentum after India's humiliating defeat in the Sino-Indian border war of 1962. Closeness with the then Soviet Union resulted in the Friendship Treaty of 1971, and an inward-looking economy and deep commitment to the cause of Arabs resulted in neglect of Southeast Asia. India was viewed with suspicion after its 1974 nuclear tests. Its wholehearted support of the Indochinese Communists in the Vietnamese conflict caused other Southeast Asian countries to stand aloof. The end of the Cold War, the onset of a liberalization process, and economic imperatives improved India–Southeast Asia relations during the 1990s.

### Contemporary Indian–Southeast Asian Relations

Free from ideological rhetoric and the Cold War phantom, India moved closer to Southeast Asia. The Indian prime minister visited Indonesia, Thailand, Vietnam, Singapore, and Malaysia in the first half of the 1990s, and Southeast Asian leaders paid reciprocal visits. India became a full dialogue partner of the Association of Southeast Asian Nations (ASEAN) in December 1995 at the fifth ASEAN summit in Bangkok. India's eastward-looking policy as well as security considerations made India a member of the ASEAN organization of security concerns, the Asian

Regional Forum. There were joint naval exercises and defense cooperation.

India also tried to improve bilateral ties and increase trade with Southeast Asia. Indian companies invested in Southeast Asia, and India invited capital from the region. Whereas India's exports and imports with ASEAN in 1993–1994 were $1.676 billion and $1.102 billion, respectively, these increased to $2.201 billion and $4.949 billion, respectively, in 1999–2000. Although the trade balance is presently tilted in favor of ASEAN, military cooperation and the January 2001 agreement for cooperation in education and information technology will redress the balance to an extent.

India also took the initiative in multilateral cooperation apart from ASEAN. The Bangladesh, India, Myanmar, Sri Lanka, and Thailand Economic Cooperation, or BIMSTEC, aims at close cooperation among member countries. The Mekong-Ganga Cooperation, an Indian initiative, was floated in November 2000 in Vientiane for better understanding among member countries (Cambodia, India, Laos, Myanmar, Thailand, and Vietnam). Promotion of tourism, development of transport networks, and educational and cultural cooperation are items on the agenda.

India's size, population, ancient cultural relations, and its emigrant population in Southeast Asia, as well as its industrial base, military strength, and scientific and technical capacity make it a major force in Southeast Asia. It is likely to continue to play a dominant role in the region as the twenty-first century unfolds.

*Patit Paban Mishra*

### Further Reading

Ghoshal, Baladas. (1996) *India and Southeast Asia: Challenges and Opportunities*. New Delhi: Konark Publishers.

Hall, D. G. E. (1981) *A History of South-East Asia*. 4th ed. New York: St. Martin's Press.

Rao, Manjushree, Sushmita Pandey, and Bhaskarnath Mishra, eds. (1996) *India's Cultural Relations with South-East Asia*. Delhi: Sharada Publishing House.

Singh, L. J. Bahadur. (1982) *Indians in Southeast Asia*. New Delhi: Sterling.

## INDIA–SRI LANKA RELATIONS

**INDIA–SRI LANKA RELATIONS** Sri Lanka (Ceylon until 1972), with its mixture of Buddhist and Hindu institutions, has always been Indian in culture, though its identity is distinct from its northern neighbor's. The Sinhalese language occurs only in Sri Lanka and has a distinguished literary tradition. Likewise, Theravada Buddhism remained the religion of the island, while Hinduism displaced it on the subcontinent.

From the third century BCE, Ceylon was involved in the politics of southern India for more than a millennium. Beginning in 177 BCE, it faced a succession of invaders from southern India and itself invaded mainland kingdoms as political alliances shifted, until they finally broke down in the twelfth century. In the fourteenth century, the Sinhalese kingdom moved near the coast, where the rulers, originally southern Indian traders, founded the Kotte Kingdom (1415–1580). Merchant communities moved back and forth between Ceylon and the mainland. These included Chettiar traders and bankers who traveled throughout South and Southeast Asia. Muslims came for trade and on pilgrimage to what they believe is the footprint of Adam on a mountain still called Adam's Peak.

European colonial rule (1517–1948) restrained relations between Ceylon and India. The British East India Company briefly united Ceylon with India, but in 1802 the British removed it from company control and ruled it directly as a Crown Colony. The governments of the two colonies were separate at the level of the British Parliament, sometimes leading to disagreements on trade, labor migration, navigation, and transport.

### People of Indian Origin

During British colonial rule, Indians and Ceylonese were British subjects, and many Indians migrated to the island to work on plantations. Administrative separation and the British compulsion to classify their subjects, however, discouraged assimilation. Earlier migrants, such as the *karava* and *salagama* castes, who arrived before the colonial era, became fully Sinhalese; but during British rule communities of Indian origin were considered "Indian" even after generations on the island.

With British support, Chettiars eventually dominated domestic finance in Ceylon. They traded between India and Ceylon and were intermediaries between British bankers and Ceylonese clients, both as guarantors for borrowers, and as moneylenders who borrowed money from banks for relending at high interest. Since many Chettiars retained their Indian identity, their role occasioned anti-Indian animosity on the part of Ceylonese traders and planters.

Plantation workers were and are primarily of southern Indian origin. The resident labor population grew as coffee, tea, and then rubber plantations advanced across central and southwestern Ceylon. The Indian government could not insist on the protection that indentured migrants had elsewhere because they could not control emigration, due to the proximity of the island. The Indian Emigration Act No. 7 of 1922 demanded reformed treatment of Indian immigrants on threat of prohibiting emigration altogether, a threat finally enforced in August 1939. Indian intervention resulted in improved wages, educational opportunities, housing, and health services for plantation laborers.

Tamil immigrants sought employment in other occupations in Ceylon, often in menial, low-wage occupations. Recent Indian immigrants made up about one-sixth of the population in the 1920s and 1930s—a serious concern for the indigenous population, and a matter of legitimate national interest for India. When the Great Depression struck, Sinhalese politicians condemned merchants, moneylenders, and laborers of Indian origin.

Under the Sinhalese-dominated State Council (1931–1946), voting rights of people of Indian origin were restricted. Jawaharlal Nehru (India's first prime minister) and D. S. Senanayake (prime minister of Ceylon, 1947–1952) met fruitlessly several times in the 1940s to settle the question of their citizenship. Ceylon finally passed three citizenship and franchise acts that effectively made people of Indian origin stateless. As recently as November 1964, only 140,185 people who had applied for citizenship by registration were granted it, while 975,000 remained stateless. That year India and Ceylon negotiated the Sirima-Shastri Pact, under which Ceylon agreed to grant citizenship to 300,000 people (later raised to 375,000) and their progeny. More than 630,000 applied, but when the pact expired in October 1981, only 162,000 people of Indian origin had been registered as Sri Lankan citizens. In the same period, 373,900 received Indian citizenship and 284,300 were repatriated to India. Legislation in the 1980s finally granted citizenship to the remainder.

India has served as a temporary home for Tamil refugees fleeing the ethnic fighting in Sri Lanka. Here, a Sri Lankan Tamil family stands with their belongings on Manar Island, Sri Lanka, after their return from India. (HOWARD DAVIES/CORBIS)

## Civil War

India has been active in several ways in the ethnic conflict ravaging Sri Lanka. India's responses were influenced by its own Tamil separatist movement, which waned in the 1960s, and its position after the 1971 Indo-Pakistan war as the most powerful South Asian state. After 1977, Sri Lanka abandoned neutralist foreign policy, becoming openly pro-Western when India was forging closer Soviet ties.

As violence against Tamils increased in Sri Lanka, militant separatists organized and trained in Tamil Nadu in southern India, possibly with Indian support. When civil war erupted in July 1983, more than 100,000 refugees from northern Sri Lanka fled to India. These events, and increased violence by security forces against Sri Lankan Tamils, made the crisis the major political issue in the Indian state of Tamil Nadu.

Mediation by India's central government began after July 1983, and Indian-facilitated proposals to resolve the conflict were presented to an All Party Conference that met fruitlessly throughout 1984. President Jayawardene of Sri Lanka and India's prime minister Rajiv Gandhi met in early June 1985, and the Sri Lankan government and Tamil organizations held peace talks in August at Thimpu in Bhutan, but these efforts failed too. In late 1986 talks were held in Delhi, which arrived at a proposal for devolution of power that would allow considerable autonomy at the provincial level.

After severe fighting in Jaffna in April and May 1987, India intervened directly. India wanted neither Sinhalese hegemony over the Tamil minority (unacceptable to Indian Tamils) nor the establishment of a separate state (which would encourage secessionist movements among India's Tamil population). An agreement between the governments of Sri Lanka and India "to establish peace and normalcy in Sri Lanka" was signed on 29 July 1987. To ensure implementation, India stationed more than 60,000 troops in the northern and eastern provinces of Sri Lanka as the Indian Peace Keeping Force (IPKF).

By October 1987, the IPKF was waging all-out war against the Liberation Tigers of Tamil Eelam (LTTE). IPKF maintained order in parts of northern Sri Lanka and helped conduct elections in 1988 and 1989, but withdrew in March 1990 after more than 1,200 soldiers had died. On 21 May 1991, an LTTE suicide bomber assassinated Rajiv Gandhi, who as prime minister had negotiated the peace agreement. India banned the LTTE and has not intervened since, although it opposes creation of a separate Tamil state and has been asked by some Tamils to facilitate peace talks.

India and Sri Lanka signed a Free Trade Agreement in 1998 and were working to eliminate trade restrictions in early 2000. Both nations are active in the South Asian Association for Regional Cooperation (SAARC), which was established in 1985 and also includes Bangladesh, Bhutan, the Maldives, Nepal, and Pakistan. Tensions between India and Pakistan have impeded progress toward multinational cooperation, however, and the November 1999 summit was postponed indefinitely because of India's protest of the military coup in Pakistan.

*Patrick Peebles*

**Further Reading**

Bullion, Alan J. (1995) *India, Sri Lanka and the Tamil Crisis, 1976–94*. New York: Pinter.

Dubey, Ravi Kant. (1993) *Indo-Sri Lankan Relations with Special Reference to the Tamil Problem*. 2d ed. New Delhi: Deep & Deep Publications.

Gunaratna, Rohan. (1993) *Indian Intervention in Sri Lanka: The Role of India's Intelligence Agencies*. Colombo, Sri Lanka: South Asian Network on Conflict Research.

Muni, S. D. (1993) *Pangs of Proximity: India and Sri Lanka's Ethnic Crisis*. Newbury Park, CA: Sage/PRIO.

Sahadevan, P. (1995) *India and Overseas Indians: The Case of Sri Lanka*. Delhi: Kalinga Publications.

## INDIA–UNITED KINGDOM RELATIONS

Relations between India and Britain (the United Kingdom was not formed until 1801) date from the founding of the East India Company in 1600, but relations between the two as sovereign nations did not begin until India became independent in 1947. Indian independence marked the beginning of a new relationship based on trade and cultural exchange. Today, the Indian diaspora and private business form strong links between India and the United Kingdom.

### Economic Relations

The United Kingdom emerged from the World War II pessimistic as to the political and economic worth of her South Asian colonies. Disengagement of private British capital from India began in the 1930s, and India's importance as a buyer of British goods or as a destination for British investment was generally in decline in the interwar period—an effect of the worldwide Great Depression. When independence came in 1947, these processes of decolonization had already made India of little value as a business partner and too costly to maintain. Trade and investment ties between India and the United Kingdom grew still weaker in the decades that followed independence. India's external transactions shifted from the United Kingdom to the United States, Germany, the USSR, and Japan. In 1947 the United Kingdom was by far the most important supplier of machinery and intermediate goods to India; after independence, other industrial countries gradually displaced it. For its part, the British external sector was integrating more closely with Europe, and tended to disengage itself from the former colonies. The early 1990s saw some slight reintegration, however, as India's trade with the former Soviet Union and Eastern Europe collapsed. The United Kingdom was among the four largest markets for India in the 1990s, and if oil imports are excluded, among its four largest sources of imports.

Economic ties have strengthened in other ways as well. The 1960s saw large-scale migration of labor to the United Kingdom from its colonies and former colonies, chiefly the West Indies and South Asia. Acute industrial labor shortages created the demand; colonial roots shaped the sources of supply. The United Kingdom was quickly becoming truly multiracial.

### Political Relations

Immigration controls were halfhearted and partially effective, though they became increasingly stringent from 1973. Twenty years later, when migration from Europe had been made considerably easier than migration from the former colonies, the United Kingdom's economic realignment away from its former colonies was complete.

The United Kingdom's influence on India's international relations has declined since India's independence. Formally, this influence can be exercised through the Commonwealth of Nations, an association

## HOLDING ON TO INDIA

The following statement by British Lord Linlithgow on the future of Indo-British relations was made on 18 June 1934 and published in the Report of the Joint Committee on Indian Constitutional Reform (Session 1933–34). It reflects the British position of retaining control of India while affording Indians more political power.

> There are moments in the affairs of nations when a way is opened for the removal of long-standing differences and misunderstandings and for the establishment between people and people of new relations more in harmony with the circumstances of the time than those which they replace. Adjustments of this order, when they involve a transference of political power, must inevitably provide a sharp test of national character; and the instinct for the time and manner of the change is the sure mark of political sagacity and experience. If there are those to whom the majestic spectacle of an Indian Empire makes so powerful an appeal that every concession appears almost as a betrayal of a trust, we would ask them to look at the other side of the picture, different indeed in content, but not less charged with realities. India also has a right to be heard before judgment is pronounced; and her plea to be allowed the opportunity of applying principles and doctrines which we ourselves have taught cannot be met by a simple traverse or by a denial of her interest in the cause.
>
> It has seemed to some that to permit India to control her own destiny is to sever the tie which unites her to the Crown and to the United Kingdom. Never could we contemplate the rupture of that beneficent and honourable association; but we believe that a union of partners may prove an even more enduring bond. We do not deny that the creation of an Indian Empire has profoundly affected the position of the United Kingdom and has magnified its influence in the affairs of the world; but we do not think that the selfish or vainglorious element predominates in the pride which this country takes in the work accomplished. The best of those who were and are responsible for it have ever regarded themselves as the servants of India and not merely as the agents of a foreign power; nor do we forget that it could not have been carried through without the cooperation of Indian hands. It has not needed our inquiry to remind us how great a place India fills in our own history. There is no part of His Majesty's Dominions with the same power to recall memories or to stir emotions, and none with so great a succession of warriors and administrators, by the story of whose achievements our hearts are still moved, as Sir Philip Sidney by the song of Percy and Douglas, more than with a trumpet. But the whole earth is the sepulchre of famous men, and those of whom we speak are now become a part no less of India than of English history. Their arduous and patient labours founded a new and mighty State; and it is upon the foundations which they have laid that, as we hope, people of India will find political contentment as well as scope for the free and orderly growth of national life.

*Source:* Jagdish Saran Sharma. (1965) *India's Struggle for Freedom: Select Documents and Sources*. Vol. II. Delhi: S. Chand & Co., 219–220.

of the United Kingdom and her former colonies. London had initially hoped that creating this association would mitigate the effects of the partition of India in 1947, and keep South Asia from veering towards Communism. However, the Commonwealth has never succeeded as an effective agent of political mediation within South Asia, though it has periodically played an important role in matters of South Asian collaboration. Its potential role as an agent of dispute settlement within South Asia has been eroded by several circumstances.

First, external mediation was resisted or failed in the two most critical disputes that beleaguer South Asia, namely, Kashmir and the citizenship of Sri Lankan Tamils. Second, the influence of the Soviet Union, the United States, and China on South Asian affairs steadily increased in the course of the Cold War. After 1970,

India's defense policy shifted toward the Soviet Union, partly in response to Pakistan's relations with the United States and China, and partly as an extension of stronger socialist leanings in economic ideology. The United Kingdom's membership in NATO also distanced her from India in its Cold War alignments.

The Commonwealth itself was weakened by several developments. As more Commonwealth members gained independence, the United Kingdom's informal leadership of the body, and consequently British foreign policy interests in Commonwealth affairs, tended to weaken. The United Nations and the Nonaligned Movement (NAM) became more effective, or at any rate competing, bodies for negotiation and dispute resolution. Finally, European integration and immigration controls weakened the relative importance for the United Kingdom of the poorer nations in the Commonwealth as partners in trade, investment, and labor exchange.

Despite these developments and a few points of difference in political interests and perspectives, Indo-U.K. relations have generally been cordial. The end of the Cold War and the retreat from socialist sentiments in India in the 1990s removed some of the old irritants. Though these developments also mildly revived trade and investment between the two countries, a clear realignment has yet to emerge. The United Kingdom and the Commonwealth continue to be of marginal importance in internal South Asian affairs.

Cultural ties between India and the United Kingdom, however, continue to grow. The presence in the United Kingdom of well over a million people of South Asian origin is the most important factor sustaining such exchanges. This population is now highly differentiated, though its constituent segments or communities display common patterns in how they have adapted their Indian heritage to their new home. This process of transplantation and transformation is now the subject of a large and growing body of scholarly and creative literature, of which travel, mixed identities, displacement, and nostalgia are major themes.

*Tirthankar Roy*

*See also:* **Anglo-Indians; British East India Company; British Indian Empire; Immigration from South Asia; Westernization in South Asia**

### Further Reading

Lipton, M., and J. Firn. (1975) *The Erosion of a Relationship: India and Britain since 1960*. London: Royal Institute of Affairs and Oxford University Press.

Vertovec, Steven, ed. (1991) *Aspects of South Asian Diaspora*. Delhi: Oxford University Press.

## INDIA–UNITED STATES RELATIONS

Relations between the United States and India since India's independence have been decidedly mixed: a former American diplomat called the countries "estranged democracies"; an Indian scholar described them as "unfriendly friends"; and one book on the relationship is subtitled *The Cold Peace*. Why have ties between the two been so fraught with tensions? Different national, regional, and global priorities, reflecting the countries' different histories, geographies, resources, societies, and cultures, explain their problematic relations.

Such differences are not unusual, and India and the United States have good relations with other countries despite such differences. They are problematic for United States–India relations because, ironically, of similarities between the two countries, such as democratic political systems, a free press, a shared language (English), and self-perception of unique importance in the world. Because India and the United States share attributes, there are expectations that they will get along; when they do not, there is puzzlement. Also, the fact that the two countries can express, and understand, their differences through public dialogue means that disputes are aired openly and passionately, with negative consequences for the relationship. Balancing unrealistic expectations against what is possible given differing priorities is a fundamental challenge for United States–India relations.

### Importance of India–United States Relations

India–United States relations are important for many reasons. First, because these countries are the two largest democracies in the world, there is the expectation they share values and interests. Some argue that democracies make better and more peaceful partners in trade and diplomacy; the example of India–United States relations may be used to confirm or refute this, and the record so far is problematic. Second, since the United States is the world's strongest power, while India, though the largest democracy, is largely poor and weak, their relations highlight the challenges facing relations between developing and industrialized countries. Third, many critical issues confronting the world—including the United States—in the twenty-first century involve India. Nearly one-sixth of humanity lives in India. So whether in fighting poverty, preventing nuclear conflict, managing population growth, limiting environmental damage, or stopping drug trafficking or AIDS, relations with India figure prominently. Finally, there are immediate, concrete reasons why Indian–United States relations matter, including the presence in the United States of many

## CONSTITUTIONAL COMMITMENTS

A shared commitment to democracy is reflected in the preambles to the United States and Indian constitutions:

From the Constitution of the United States:

> We the People of the United States, in Order to form a more perfect Union, establish Justice, insure domestic Tranquility, provide for the common defense, promote the general Welfare and secure the Blessings of Liberty to ourselves and our Posterity, do ordain and establish this Constitution for the United States of America.

From the Constitution of India:

> We, the People of India, having solemnly resolved to constitute India into a Sovereign Socialist Secular Democratic Republic and to secure to all its citizens:
>
> JUSTICE, social, economic and political;
>
> LIBERTY of thought, expression, belief, faith and worship;
>
> EQUALITY of status and of opportunity;
>
> And to promote among them all
>
> FRATERNITY assuring the dignity of the individual and the unity and integrity of the Nation
>
> In Our Constituent Assembly this twenty-sixth day of November, 1949, do Hereby Adopt, Enact and Give to Ourselves this Constitution.

*Source:* "International Constitutional Law." Retrieved 24 April 2002, from: http://www.uni-wuerzburg.de/law.

politically active Americans of Indian origin, increasing business opportunities in India, and India's growing role in Asia—a role made more critical by India's increased emphasis on political and military engagement and nuclear-weapons capability.

### Recurring Issues in India–United States Relations

Four general issues that dominated relations between the two nations from India's independence to the end of the twentieth century are likely to continue to be important. First and foremost is India's neighbor Pakistan. The end of British rule led to the creation of two hostile states, India and Pakistan, which immediately fought over an area they both claimed, Kashmir. Indians believe the United States initially sided with Pakistan in the Kashmir dispute. Much worse in Indian eyes, in 1954 the United States signed a security agreement with Pakistan to involve it in U.S. Cold War efforts to "contain" Communism. India, concerned about Pakistan, perceived the rapprochement as a direct threat and an effort to counterbalance India's superior power and resources. The first Indian prime minister, Jawaharlal Nehru (1889–1964), argued that United States–Pakistan relations would spur an arms race in the subcontinent. The next four decades saw other periods of close United States–Pakistan military and political cooperation, but in recent years India and the United States have striven to cooperate despite differences regarding Pakistan.

A second major issue involves nuclear weapons. In 1968, the United States was instrumental in negotiating the Nuclear Non-Proliferation Treaty (NPT). India refused to sign, complaining that it allowed five states (the United States, China, France, the United Kingdom, and the USSR) to possess nuclear weapons legally, while other countries were barred from possessing them. India claimed this was discriminatory, calling instead for global abolition of nuclear weapons. In 1974, however, India tested a nuclear device; again in 1998 India conducted five nuclear explosions and declared itself a nuclear-weapons state. The India–United States dispute over nuclear weapons now focuses less on the NPT and more on recent U.S. requests that India sign a treaty banning further tests, negotiate to ban production of materials for nuclear weapons, ensure that India's nuclear technology is not exported, and restrict development of ballistic missiles. The United States and India have yet to bridge their differences regarding India's nuclear and missile programs.

A third important issue concerns aid, trade, and investment. The United States was a major bilateral and multilateral donor to India for the first three decades of their relations, and this sometimes produced friction. India often perceived political strings to be attached to the aid, while the United States complained of a lack of gratitude for and poor utilization of the aid. More seriously, until the early 1990s India had a highly regulated, inward-looking economy, and U.S. businesses had few opportunities for trade with or investment in India. Since India launched economic reforms in 1991, the situation has changed somewhat. The United States and India have expanded trade and investment, though economic interchange falls short of its potential and is considerably less than U.S. trade with and investment in China or some Southeast Asian nations. The opening of India's economy and the development of its information-technology sector may provide the basis for a significant expansion of economic and technological cooperation. However, given the differing economic needs and power of the countries, there are still important disagreements regarding global trade rules and other issues bearing on economic relations.

A final contentious area is security and defense cooperation, which has been extremely limited. United States–Pakistan military relations meant India was not keen on dealing with the United States, and that the United States did not want to upset Pakistan by transferring certain military items to India. Until the early 1970s, India's nonalignment policy also made it unwilling to enter into military relations with other countries. Following the establishment of close Indo-Soviet relations in 1971, the USSR became India's principal military supplier, angering the United States, which was still involved in the Cold War. India and the United States also share few common security and strategic outlooks that could form the basis for cooperation. India showed itself a poor counterbalance to China when it was involved in the 1962 Sino-Indian border war. India has also seen the costs and conditions attached to the U.S. transfer of weapons systems as excessive. But the end of the Cold War, changing United States–Pakistan relations, the collapse of the Soviet Union, growing Chinese power, and general improvement in India–United States relations may bring better, if still limited, prospects for defense cooperation.

United States–India relations were clearly mixed over the first five decades of Indian independence. But international changes in the 1990s, particularly in Asia, and shifts in India's economic and foreign policies may yet provide the basis for warmer, more substantial relations. In 2001, the United States took on a peacekeeper role vis-à-vis India and Pakistan as both nations amassed forces on the border in response to Muslim terrorist attack on the Indian Parliament and Indian charges that Pakistan supported the terrorist activities.

*Satu P. Limaye*

**Further Reading**


Brands, H. W. (1990) *India and the United States: The Cold Peace*. Boston: G. K. Hall.

Gould, Harold A., and Sumit Ganguly. (1992) *The Hope and the Reality: U.S.-Indian Relations from Roosevelt to Reagan*. Boulder, CO: Westview Press.

Kunhi Krishnan, T. V. (1974) *The Unfriendly Friends: India and America*. New Delhi: India Book Company.

Kux, Dennis. (1993) *Estranged Democracies: India and the United States, 1941–1991*. New Delhi: Sage Publications.

Limaye, Satu. (1993) *U.S.-Indian Relations: The Pursuit of Accommodation*. Boulder, CO: Westview Press.


**INDIAN OCEAN** The Indian Ocean, with an area of 75 million square kilometers, is the smallest of the three oceans bounded by Africa, Asia, Australia, and the Antarctic. Nevertheless occupying a huge area, the Indian Ocean extends over some 10,000 kilometers from South Asia to the Antarctic on the one side, and from South Africa to Tasmania on the other. The Indian Ocean accommodates 15 percent of the earth's total surface and occupies 21 percent of all ocean surfaces. While the mean depth is around 3,900 meters, its maximum depth is 7,125 meters (Java Trench). The seabed of the Indian Ocean is rather complex, with a multifold topography that includes huge basins as well as large ridges.

The vast area of the Indian Ocean is commonly divided into various sectors. The Arabian Sea and the Bay of Bengal are the major seas that bound the Indian peninsula, while the Lakshadweep and Andaman

Sri Lankan fishermen fishing from stilts in the Indian Ocean in 2000. (KEREN SU/CORBIS)

Seas are the minor seas around the homonymous Lakshadweep and Andaman Islands; the latter are further extended by the Nicobar Islands. The Arabian Sea is straddled by two important branches, the Gulf of Oman (elongated by the Persian Gulf) and the Gulf of Aden, which extends into the Red Sea. In 1869 the Red Sea was connected with the Mediterranean Sea by the gigantic Suez Canal, opening a new era of sea trade between Europe and Asia. The Suez Canal is still the leading shipping route between the two continents. Along its southern region the Indian Ocean is commonly called the Indian South Polar Sea, except for the Great Australian Bight that bounds South Australia. For the big islands lying opposite continental land masses, such as Madagascar, Sri Lanka, and Sumatra, the Mozambique Channel, Palk Strait, and Strait of Malacca, respectively, serve as connecting seas.

The Indian Ocean accommodates many isolated islands and island groups without hosting large island archipelagos. Apart from Madagascar and Sri Lanka, large island nations, a few small island groups are of importance, some of which have nowadays become tourist destinations. Comparably big island groups include the Comoros, Amirante, Seychelles, and Mascarene Islands (including Mauritius and Réunion), the Lakshadweep, Andaman, and Nicobar Islands as well as the Maldives, Chagos Archipelago, New Amsterdam, Saint Paul, the Kergueles, Heard, Marion, Prince Edward, Crozet, Christmas, and Cocos Islands, all dispersed across the vast Indian Ocean.

Politically the various islands and island groups are independent small island nations or still belong to other countries. In the past all the islands were colonial outposts of various European powers, as their old colonial names still underline; they gained independence only after the Second World War (and sometimes decades later).

The Indian Ocean is divided by the equator in its northern part, and most of it is located south of the equator. As a result the climate incorporates (from north to south) the monsoon, the passates or the major air current also known as the tropical easterlies (south of the equator), and the temperate climates under the westerlies (farther south). Characteristic of all climate zones is the oceanic impact that weakens the temperature contrasts between the seasons. By nature the Indian Ocean and bounding coastal land surfaces rarely have tropical cyclones or storms, except for the Bay of Bengal and Mascarene Islands, which are irregularly visited by cyclones.

Since early times the northern Indian Ocean was heavily traveled between Arabia and India by Arabian seafarers who sailed with the seasonal monsoon winds. While in ancient times Egyptians, Arabs, and Chinese traveled the Indian Ocean, the European colonial discovery of the Indian Ocean occurred only in 1497, with the legendary expedition by Vasco da Gama, who first rounded the Cape of Good Hope to cross the Indian Ocean toward India. Traditionally the countries bordering the northern Indian Ocean, such as Arabia, India, and the countries of Southeast Asia, were best known to the foreign sailors and merchants because of their spices, gems, gold, ivory, and other rare goods. Only since the colonial age commencing with the sixteenth century did a regular trade develop across the Indian Ocean between Europe and Asia. In modern times air travel has absorbed much of the commerce between Europe and the countries around the Indian Ocean.

Fishing is a traditional practice on the lands bordering the Indian Ocean. Nowadays, however, oil and gas are heavily exploited, and offshore wells represent valuable resources, mostly in the Persian Gulf nations of the United Arab Emirates, Saudi Arabia, Iran, and the emirates of Kuwait, Qatar, and Bahrain.

Though most islands in the Indian Ocean are uninhabited, some are heavily populated, even seriously overpopulated, by native peoples. The mostly poor living conditions are based on marginal subsistence agriculture. Having limited resources for development, some islands and island groups benefit from tourism as a profitable industry; these include Mauritius and Réunion, Comoros and Seychelles, and the Maldives. All such islands are favored destinations, mostly for European tourists, who are attracted by the "exoticness," the tropical climate and sandy beaches, and superb diving conditions (in case of the Maldives, due to their nature as coral islands).

Life on all the small islands in the Indian Ocean may have a hazardous future, due to the impact of global warming, which will lead to rapidly shrinking island surfaces and result in coasts flooded and life conditions worsened by the impact of increasing hurricanes and typhoons in the region. Many instances of serious coastal erosion processes have already occurred on the islands in recent times. The Maldives are worst afflicted because most of the land surfaces of all 1,200 small islands are not higher than half a meter above sea level. If critical predictions of a sea level rise of 50 to 100 centimeters are borne out during this century, disastrous results must be expected for many millions of coastal inhabitants in South Asia, mostly in India and Bangladesh.

*Manfred Domroes*

### Further Reading

Arnberger, Hertha, and Erik Arnberger. (2001) *The Tropical Islands of the Indian and Pacific Oceans.* Vienna: Austrian Academy of Sciences Press.

Toussinet, Auguste. (1966) *History of the Indian Ocean.* Chicago: University of Chicago Press.

## INDIAN SUBCONTINENT

**INDIAN SUBCONTINENT** (2001 pop. 1.4 billion). "Indian subcontinent" geographically refers to the area covering the southern section of Asia (often called South Asia), but not the Southeast Asian mainland. It comprises the vast peninsula bounded on the north by the Himalayan Ranges and projecting as a triangle in the south far into the Indian Ocean, with the Bay of Bengal lying to the east and the Arabian Sea to the west. The area is divided between five major nation-states, Bangladesh, India, Nepal, Pakistan, and Sri Lanka, and includes as well the two small nations of Bhutan and the Maldives Republic. The total area can be estimated at 4.4 million square kilometers, or exactly 10 percent of the land surface of Asia. The latitudinal range is between the equator and 37°N, thus embracing various environments from desert to mountain, from dry plateau to humid rain forest. In 2000, the total population was about 22 percent of the world's population and 34 percent of the population of Asia. Life expectancy was then in the range of 55 to 64 years throughout most of the subcontinent.

*Paul Hockings*

### Further Reading

Robinson, Francis. (1989) *Cambridge Encyclopedia of India, Pakistan, Bangladesh, Sri Lanka, Nepal, Bhutan and the Maldives.* New York: Cambridge University Press.

## INDIGO

**INDIGO** An important blue dyestuff, until about 1900 indigo was obtained entirely from the plants of the genera *Indigofera* and *Isatis* but is now manufactured synthetically. Indigo plants are stiff-stemmed shrubs with pinnately compound leaves and small, reddish or reddish-yellow flowers.

The growing of indigo plants for dye was widespread, from the East Indies to the New World, although the plant originally came from India. In the sixteenth century, indigo was brought to Europe from India by Dutch, Portuguese, and English traders. During the early years of British occupation of India, natural indigo was a major export. In 1883, a German scientist, Adolf von Baeyer, elucidated its chemical structure, and indigo then was synthesized commercially.

In addition to being used as a dye, the plant has several medicinal uses. It is a stimulant, alterative (a medicine that, taken over a course of time, gradually restores health), and purgative, and also is an antiseptic and astringent. It is used particularly in the treatment of the enlargement of the liver and spleen, epilepsy, and nervous afflictions. Leaves of indigo are used in treating whooping cough, lung diseases, and kidney complaints such as dropsy. The synthetic indigo dye is used for dyeing and printing cotton and rayon and as a pigment in paints, lacquers, and printing inks.

*Sanjukta Das Gupta*

### Further Reading

Watt, George. (1996) "Indigofera (Indigo), The Dye-Yielding Species." In *The Commercial Products of India, Being an Abridgement of the Dictionary of the Economic Products of India*. New Delhi: Today and Tomorrow's Printers and Publishers, 660–685.

## INDO-ARYAN LANGUAGES

Indo-Aryan (IA) languages constitute one of the largest groups of related languages in the world, spoken by close to a billion speakers in India, Pakistan, Nepal, Bangladesh, Sri Lanka, and the Maldives. Due to migration, Indo-Aryan languages are also spoken in Fiji, Mauritius, Guyana, Trinidad, and South Africa, as well as in Britain, Canada, and the United States. Moreover there are inscriptions in Indo-Aryan languages (Sanskrit and Pali) not only on the Indian subcontinent proper and in Sri Lanka but in other areas, such as Uzbekistan and the nearby central Asian republics, Myanmar (Burma), Thailand, Vietnam, Malaysia, Indonesia, and China; some records from around the first or second century CE have been found in Egypt.

The 1991 census of India registers native speakers of the IA languages included in the eighth schedule of the Indian constitution as follows: Asamiya (Assamese): 12,962,721; Bangla (Bengali): 69,595,738; Gujarati: 40,335,889; Hindi: 337, 272,114; Konkani: 1,760,607; Marathi: 62,481,681; Nepali: 2,076,645; Oriya: 28,061,313; Panjabi: 23,085,063; Sanskrit: 49,773; Sindhi: 1,551,384; Urdu: 43,358,978.

Census data for Kashmiri are not available for 1991; the most recent earlier count (1981) showed 33,845 speakers. (Four million is a reasonable estimate of the number of speakers, as of the early twenty-first century.) Bangla and Urdu are also the national languages of Bangladesh and Pakistan; according to the most recent estimates of speakers, there are respectively 107 million and 6,403,228. There is no accurate full count for Nepali, which is the national language of Nepal (an estimated 6 million). In addition Sinhala (Sinhalese) is an official language of Sri Lanka, with the most recent estimate being 18.5 million speakers.

Hindi is not only a co-official language of the republic of India but also a lingua franca in much of the subcontinent and a language of instruction throughout a large part of northern India, from the borders of West Bengal to the Gujarat border. Moreover, the total count for Hindi includes speakers of languages with substantial numbers, such as Bhojpuri (23,102,050), Magahi (10,566,842), Maithili (7,766,597; concentrated in the state of Bihar), Chattisgarhi (10,595,199; in Madhya Pradesh), and various languages of Rajasthan. In all there are approximately 877 million speakers of IA languages on the subcontinent, accounting for 78.7 percent of the population. The Dravidian, Munda, and Tibeto-Burman families account for the rest.

The precise subgrouping of modern IA languages on the subcontinent has not been settled, although there are certain fairly well-defined groups. For example languages of the east, in particular Asamiya, Bangla, and Oriya, form a group characterized by features that set it apart from Hindi and other languages of the midlands; these eastern languages lack a construction called "ergative" and do not have lexical gender distinctions for nouns.

### Historical Background

The history of Indo-Aryan falls into three major stages: Old, Middle, and New (or modern) Indo-Aryan. These are divisions according to linguistic characteristics only; there is evidence that languages with characteristics of one stage of development coexisted with those of earlier stages. In earliest Old Indo-Aryan (OIA) some forms have Middle Indic characteristics.

Old Indo-Aryan is represented principally by literary documents in Sanskrit (*saṃskr̥ta*—refined, adorned, purified), which is also used in inscriptions, the earliest from the first century CE. The oldest stage is attested in texts of the four Vedas. The oldest of these is the Rgveda (possibly third millennium BCE); the other Vedas are the Samaveda, Yajurveda, and Atharvaveda. There is a large body of literature, including dramas and poetry such as those composed by the poet and dramatist Kalidasa and the epics *Ramayana* and *Mahabharata*, didactic works such as the *Pancatantra* and *Hitopadesa*, and treatises on logic, medicine, and mathematics. One of the most sophisticated grammars ever produced is the *Aṣṭādhyāyiī of Pāṇini* (sixth–fifth centuries BCE), describing the OIA speech of his native area (the northwest subcontinent) as well as characteristics of earlier Vedic usage. Sanskrit is not restricted to Hindu works; Buddhist and Jain scholars used Sanskrit in original texts and commentaries. Even today Sanskrit remains a vehicle for original literature as well as technical works such as modern commentaries, and periodicals are published in Sanskrit. The language is officially recognized in the eighth schedule of the Indian constitution and is used in daily newscasts on All India Radio. Moreover speakers report Sanskrit as their mother tongue in the census of India, and due to factors that are not yet clear, the number of speakers has increased in recent years: 2,212 and 6,106 for 1971 and 1981, respectively, and 49,736 for 1991.

Middle Indo-Aryan (MIA) languages are known from inscriptions, literary sources, and grammarians' descriptions. The earliest extant MIA documents are the inscriptions of Asoka (third century BCE), in various dialects according to areas of his empire, stretching from the extreme northwest (Shāhbazgaṛhī) to the south (modern Karnataka) and from the farthest reaches in the east (Kaliṅga, modern Orissa) to the west (Girnar, in modern Gujarat). Pali, the language of Theravada Buddhist works, also reflects an early MIA stage. Ardhamāgadhī is the language of the Jaina canon, and two other MIA varieties (Māhārāṣṭrī and Śaurasenī) also are used in Jaina works.

MIA languages and dialects other than Pali are known as *prākr̥ta* (a term opposed to *saṃskr̥ta*), which refers to a form of speech viewed as derived from an original source (*prakr̥ti*). Literary theoreticians of poetics and grammarians of Prakrits (generally composing in Sanskrit) usually consider the original in question to be Sanskrit. Another view, which is historically more justified, was also entertained—that the source of Prakrits was the unadorned speech of the people. These vernaculars varied according to region and were named accordingly. They were also associated with different groups in literary compositions. According to one division of literary usage, there are four major groups: Sanskrit, Prākrit, Apabhraṃśa, and mixed.

New Indo-Aryan (NIA) languages, whose earliest documents date from approximately the twelfth century, include national languages, state languages in the republic of India, and languages spoken in restricted areas. The early stages of NIA were already vehicles for literary productions such as the Ramacaritamanasa of Tulsidas (1532–1623), in Avadhi, and modern languages have been the vehicles for literary works, including those of the great Bengali author and musician Rabindranath Tagore (1861–1941).

Indo-Aryan is most closely affiliated with the Iranian language, with which it constitutes the Indo-Iranian subgroup of Indo-European languages. OIA and Old Iranian, represented by the Zoroastrian texts of the Avesta and the Achaemenid inscriptions in Old Persian, show phonological, grammatical, and lexical affinities that demonstrate their close affiliation. There is, in addition, a small group of languages, spoken in the Hindu Kush and subsumed under the name Nuristani, whose affiliation has been the object of dispute. Most informed scholars hold that these languages represent either a distinct subgroup separate from IA and Iranian or a special area in IA that remained isolated after the main group of Indo-Aryan speakers moved south into the Punjab. The majority of informed scholars also accept that the Indo-Aryans migrated into the subcontinent. There are ongoing debates, however, concerning an alternative position: that the Indo-Aryans—and indeed the Indo-Europeans—originated on the subcontinent, from where they migrated to the Iranian territory and beyond. This controversy is connected with the interpretation of the documents of the Indus Valley civilization: Those who maintain that Indo-Aryans originated on the subcontinent view this culture, which they call the Indus-Sarasvati civilization, as Indo-Aryan. Literary and archaeological evidence is not decisive, but the linguistic evidence most plausibly supports the view that Indo-Aryans migrated into the subcontinent.

## Characteristics of Indo-Aryan Languages

More than for any other group of Indo-European languages, IA inscriptional and literary evidence and descriptions by grammarians offer an extraordinarily rich picture of the earliest stages of the languages and their developments down to the present.

***Phonology*** Two characteristic features set most IA languages apart from other Indo-European languages from very earliest times. IA languages have a contrast between unaspirated and aspirated plosives, not only in the voiceless sets (*k c ṭ t p* versus *kh ch ṭh th ph*, the latter with a strong puff of air), but also in the voiced sets (*g j ḍ d b* versus *gh jh ḍh dh bh*).

In addition they have a contrast between dental and retroflex consonants: dental *t th d dh n s* versus retroflex *ṭ ṭh ḍ ḍh ṇ ṣ*. Dental consonants are produced with the tip of the tongue pressed against the roots of the upper teeth. A retroflex stop is produced by curling the tongue back and letting the top of the tongue make contact at the area just back of the ridge behind the upper teeth (the alveolar ridge); the retroflex *ṣ* has a similar position, but the air is allowed to escape in a continuous stream. The retroflex stops originally arose through particular developments involving inherited Indo-European terms, but their frequency and distribution doubtless increased under the influence of borrowing from other languages on the subcontinent.

MIA differs from OIA in several important respects. Two of the major differences are: 1) that in the course of historical development final consonants other than *-m* were lost; and 2) that MIA ceased to allow syllables in which a long vowel was followed by more than one consonant. Due to subsequent developments, including the borrowing of Sanskrit words, modern Indo-Aryan has reintroduced word-final consonants and syllables of the type noted.

***Grammar*** Old Indo-Aryan morphology and syntax were of the general type seen in other early Indo-European languages such as Greek or Latin. The nominal system (i.e., pertaining to nouns, pronouns, and adjectives) was of the inflectional type represented in these languages (e.g., Skt. *vāc-am, vāc-ā; vāc-au, vāg-bhyām; vāc-as, vāg-bhis,* in which a stem *vāc-/vāg-* "speech, voice" is followed by different accusative and instrumental singular, dual, and plural endings), with three numbers (singular, dual, plural) and seven syntactic cases in addition to a vocative. Nouns can have any of three genders (masculine, feminine, neuter). The pronominal system, including personal pronouns and demonstrative pronouns with three degrees of reference involving distance (e.g., nominative [nom.] singular [sg.] neuter [nt.] pronoun *idam* "this," *tad* "that," *adas* "that one yonder"), also has distinctive forms. The verb system is similar to but considerably richer than that of other ancient Indo-European languages. There is a contrast among six tense forms (present, aorist, imperfect, perfect, future, distant future), with several stem types for each, and five moods (indicative, imperative, subjunctive, optative, precative), with different singular, dual, and plural forms. In addition a contrast between active and mediopassive forms applies throughout.

This system was considerably simplified in MIA, where case forms and stem types were reduced and the dual was eliminated. The nominal inflectional system was gradually replaced by a system involving nominals with postpositions (parallel to English prepositions). Modern languages too are predominantly of this kind, though they all show remnants of true case forms, especially in pronouns. The verbal system also gradually changed. Here again, the dual was given up. Moreover, mediopassive endings were eliminated, with the result that the contrast involving these came to depend on different stems. For example in Pali *chijja-ti* ("is cut"), the stem *chijja-* is followed by the ending *ti,* but in the Sanskrit passive *chid-ya-te,* the root *chid* is followed by the suffix *-ya-* and the mediopassive ending *te.* In addition, the various past tense forms were gradually reduced to the point that a single type, the aorist, according to Western terminology, came to predominate in early MIA. Moreover the aorist could now be formed from a present stem instead of a root, as in Old Indo-Aryan (e.g., the Pali passive aorist *chijj-iṃsu* "were cut down" represents a type that was not permissible earlier: *chijj-* of the present stem is followed by the third plural aorist ending). In the equivalent permissible OIA form *achit-s-ata,* the root *chid* (with augment *a*) is followed by the sigmatic aorist affix and the mediopassive ending *ata.* Later the single predominant finite past form also was eliminated, and past participles served as verb forms. For example where OIA could have either *agamat* (3d sg. aorist) "went, has gone," or its participial equivalent *gataḥ* (nom. sg. masc.), *gatā* (nom. sg. fem.), *gatam* (nom. sg. nt.), the participial type Pali *gato* (nom. sg. masc.), Pkt. *gao* came to be the norm.

In modern Indo-Aryan this continues to be the norm. In addition, the majority of modern languages have what is called a semiergative verb system, such that past forms of transitive verbs agree in number and gender with an object, as opposed to the agreement of such forms with subjects for intransitive verbs. The examples from Gujarati given below serve to illustrate. Numbers 1 and 2 have the third-person future form *āvśe* construed with the phrases *tamāro bhāī* and *tamārī bahen,* in which the masculine and feminine possessive pronoun forms *tamāro* and *tamāri* are used with *bhāī* and *bahen.* In numbers 3 and 4 the perfective verb forms *āvyo* (masc. sg.) and *avī* agree in number and gender with the phrases *tamāro bhāī* and *tamārī bahen.* Numbers 5 and 6 are like 1 and 2 except for the verb *kar-* "do" instead of *āv* "come." Numbers 7 and 8, on the other hand, differ from 3 and 4: the verb *karyuṃ* (nt. sg.) agrees here with the object *śuṃ* "what" instead of with the subject, and the phrases *tamārā bhāīe* and *tamārī bahene* contain agentive forms with the postposition *-e.*

1. *tamāro* *bhāī* *kyāre* *āvśe*
   your brother when will come
   "When will your brother arrive?"

2. *tamārī* *bahen* *kyāre* *āvśe*
   your sister when will come
   "When will your sister arrive?"

3. *tamāro* *bhāī* *kyāre* *āvyo*
   your brother when came
   "When did your brother arrive?"

4. *tamārī* *bahen* *kyāre* *āvī*
   your sister when came
   "When did your sister arrive?"

5. *tamāro* *bhāī* *śuṃ* *karśe*
   your brother what will do
   "What will your brother do?"

6. *tamārī* *bahen* *śuṃ* *karśe*
   your sister what will do
   "What will your sister do?"

7. *tamārā* *bhāīe* *śuṃ* *karyuṃ*
your brother what did
"What did your brother do?"

8. *tamārī* *bahene* *śuṃ* *karyuṃ*
your sister what did
"What did your sister do?"

These examples also illustrate the neutral word order Subject-Object-Verb, which is prevalent in modern languages and was the norm for Indo-Aryan languages from earliest times.

### Scripts

The earliest scripts used for Indo-Aryan languages are Brāhmī and Kharoṣṭhī, both used in inscriptions of Asoka, whose northwestern inscriptions are in Kharoṣṭhī. Though Kharoṣṭhī continued in use for some time, the dominant script on the subcontinent was Brāhmī, and modern Indo-Aryan scripts reflect historical developments of this script in different areas. One such script that has attained a major status is known as Devanagarī. This is the officially recognized script for Hindi and is used for other Indo-Aryan languages such as Marathi and Nepali. Sanskrit texts are increasingly also written in Devanagarī, although the earlier tradition of regional scripts for Sanskrit texts continues. In addition the Perso-Arabic script is used for some Indo-Aryan languages, such as Urdu, Kashmiri, and Sindhi, with diacritic modifications for representing sounds like retroflex stops, aspirates, and implosives.

*George Cardona*

### Further Reading

Cardona, George, and Dhanesh K. Jain, eds. (2002) *The Indo-Aryan Languages*. London: Curzon.

Cardona, George. (in press) "From Vedic to Modern Indic Languages." In *Handbooks of Linguistics and Communication Science* 17.2: *Morphology*. Berlin and New York: de Gruyter, article 158.

———. (1990) *The Major Languages of South Asia, the Middle East, and Africa*, edited by Bernard Comrie. London: Routledge, 21–30.

Masica, Colin C. (1991) *The Indo-Aryan Languages*. Cambridge, U.K.: Cambridge University Press.

Salomon, Richard. (1998) *Indian Epigraphy*. Oxford: Oxford University Press.

## INDOCHINA WAR OF 1940–1941

The Japanese threat to French Indochina (Vietnam, Laos, and Cambodia) became clear in the late 1930s, when it began its war of aggression against China in 1937 and occupied the island of Hainan in February 1939, all the more so because to the west the Japanese could count on the support of the government of Siam. In fact, since the coup of Pibul Songgram (1897–1964), Siam had begun drawing nearer to Japan. It changed its name to Thailand, a clue to its expansionist position because "Thailand" seemed to correspond to pan-Thai ideology. Facing this double threat, the French colony organized its defense. When Europe entered into a state of war in 1939, the army in Indochina boasted ninety thousand men (fewer than fifteen thousand of them Europeans) but only mediocre equipment. It was a force to maintain colonial order, not an army formed to confront the troops of a great power such as Japan.

### Japan's Demands

Since 1937 Tokyo had been criticizing Paris for permitting the resupplying of Nationalist China by the Yunnan railroad. In June 1940 Japan took advantage of France's defeat by Germany. On 19 June an ultimatum was sent to Indochina's Governor-General Georges Catroux that all transport of goods toward China must be stopped and that the Japanese must be able to verify this stoppage. Catroux yielded, in the belief that the balance of power left him no other option. The Vichy government of Philippe Pétain replaced him as leader of Indochina with Admiral Jean Decoux. The latter had to face new Japanese demands and a military convention was negotiated. Since Decoux delayed signing, the Japanese sent a new ultimatum that if the matter were not settled within three days, the Japanese would force the issue. The convention was signed on the afternoon of 22 September, just before the ultimatum. It organized and limited the stationing and passage of Japanese troops to the north of Indochina. This agreement did not prevent the Japanese Army of Canton from opening hostilities that same evening. For four days, a battle raged around the city of Lang Son. The French troops were overcome and Lang Son was taken. A landing in the region of Haiphong constituted another blow to colonial France. This time Decoux did not resist. This double humiliation did not call into question the agreement of 22 September; in theory French sovereignty over Indochina remained complete. But this Japanese eruption had struck a blow at the prestige of the colonial power.

### Further Erosion of French Power

In the autumn of 1940, the French colonial government had to confront two revolts. In the north, at the Chinese border, various gangs, notably Vietnamese partisans of Prince Cuong De (1882–1951), attacked French outposts, killing isolated soldiers and local notables. Order was swiftly reestablished by the colonial army. In the south, in Cochin China, a Communist insurrection broke out on 22 November. In Saigon the Sûreté (investigation police), forewarned, nipped the movement in the bud. But in rural areas in the west (especially in the province of My Tho), the uprising lasted several weeks. The insurgents, numbering more than ten thousand, killed about thirty Vietnamese notables. Here and there a people's regime was installed, very briefly, and land was confiscated and redistributed. The foreign legion and air corps participated in a brutal repression of the insurgents. The number of insurgents killed is not known with any certainty, but courts martial pronounced one hundred death sentences. Admiral Decoux refused to show clemency in those cases, despite a recommendation to that effect from the minister of colonies in Vichy. Added to arrests made in 1939, this repression struck a harsh blow to the PCI (Indochinese Communist Party). It was from China that its leaders, still free, continued to fight. In 1941 the border region would see the creation, around the future Ho Chi Minh (born Nguyen That Thanh, 1890–1969), of the Viet Minh, a National Front with Communist tendencies.

### The End of the Conflict

The government of Thailand learned a lesson from the French difficulties. It made territorial demands, then entered into hostilities. The "war," which lasted from September 1940 to January 1941 and consisted only of skirmishes, reached its culmination in the middle of January 1941. On 16 January the French troops had to fall back when they experienced the same weaknesses they had exhibited at Lang Son, in particular the desertion of Indochinese soldiers. But on 17 January 1941, the best ships in the Thai fleet were sunk at Ko Chang, in the Gulf of Siam. Japan then imposed an armistice and its mediation. Negotiations ended in a compromise that accorded Thailand the two Lao provinces to the west of the Mekong and a third of Cambodia's territory (in short, what Siam had had to cede to Indochina at the beginning of the century). Peace was signed in Tokyo on 9 May 1941. It satisfied Thai public opinion, which had fully supported Pibul Songgram during his war against France.

The entente with Thailand was all the more useful to Japan because the latter had decided to expand toward the south rather than the north, at the expense of the colonial empires of the European powers that had been defeated or were in difficulty. The new concessions demanded by Japan in Indochina revealed this orientation. Vichy yielded. The Darlan-Kato agreements (29 July 1941) allowed Japanese troops to be stationed throughout Indochina; moreover, they instituted the principle of a common defense of the colony. At the same time, Japan imposed its economic stranglehold on Indochina. Given the state of France and the situation of its forces in the Far East, this chain of concessions could have been avoided only with the intervention of some outside support, which at the time was not forthcoming.

*Jacques Dalloz*

### Further Reading


Charivat Santaputra. (1985) *Thai Foreign Policy, 1932–1946.* Bangkok, Thailand: Thammasat University.

Dalloz, Jacques. (1998) *La Guerre d'Indochine, 1945–1954.* 3d ed. Paris: Le Seuil.

Direk, Jayanama. (1970) *Thailand im Zweiten Weltkrieg.* Tübingen, Germany: Erdmann.

Kobuka Suwannathat-Pian. (1995) *Thailand's Durable Premier, Phibun through Three Decades, 1932–1957.* Kuala Lumpur, Malaysia: Oxford University Press.

Reynolds, E. Bruce. (1994) *Thailand and Japan's Southern Advance, 1940–1945.* London: Macmillan.


## INDO-EUROPEAN LANGUAGES

The Indo-European languages form the best-known, most widely spoken, and best-explored family of undoubtedly genetically related languages. Genetically related languages are demonstrably derived from a common ancestor, a "Proto-Language," which, in the case of Indo-European, is thought to have flourished during the fourth–third millennia BCE, before it split up into the daughter languages from which scholars are able to infer its existence. No theory about the area where this language may have been spoken has become generally accepted among scholars so far, but the south Russian steppes, Anatolia, or south-central Asia are most often mentioned as likely locations.

Attempts to reconstruct key aspects of the material and spiritual culture of the people who spoke Proto-Indo-European are likewise highly controversial, but the available lexical data (reconstructed words) point to a culture that already knew the most important cultural innovations (agriculture, animal husbandry) developed during the Neolithic Period.

The discovery by the Orientalists Sir William Jones and Franz Bopp around the turn of the eighteenth and nineteenth centuries that most languages of Europe (the only exceptions being, among living languages, Finnish, Estonian, Hungarian, some other languages of Finno-Ugric stock, and isolated Basque) and some important languages of South and Southwest Asia are demonstrably related laid the foundation for the scholarly discipline of historical-comparative linguistics.

## THE BEGINNING OF COMPARATIVE LINGUISTICS

In 1786 Sir William Jones delivered his third discourse, in which he laid the foundation for modern comparative linguistics by suggesting a close relationship between Sanskrit and the classical languages of Europe.

> The *Sanskcrit* language, whatever be its antiquity, is of wonderful structure; more perfect than the Greek, more copious than the Latin, and more exquisitely refined than either, yet bearing to both of them a stronger affinity, both in the roots of verbs and in the forms of grammar, than could possibly have been produced by accident; so strong indeed, that no philologer could examine them all three, without believing them to have sprung from some common source which, perhaps, no longer exists; there is a similar reason, though not quite so forcible, for supposing that both the Gothick and the Celtick, though blended with a very different idiom, had the same origin with the Sanskcrit; and the old Persian might be added to the same family.
>
> *Source:* Lord Teignmouth, ed. (1807) *The Collected Works of Sir William Jones*. Volumes I to XIII. London: John Stockdale and John Walker, vol. III: 34–35.

On the European continent, the members of the family are Greek, Latin, and the Romance languages (languages derived from Latin), which together with some extinct languages of ancient Italy (like Oscan and Umbrian) form the Italic branch of Indo-European; the Slavic (Russian, Polish, Czech, Serbo-Croat, Bulgarian, etc.) and Baltic languages (Lithuanian, Latvian, extinct Old Prussian), the combination of which into a Balto-Slavic branch has won some support; Armenian; Albanian; Germanic (Gothic, German, Dutch, English, the Scandinavian languages); Celtic (Irish, Welsh, Breton); and some extinct and mostly only fragmentarily attested languages like Thracian and Illyrian, both once spoken on the Balkan peninsula. In Asia, Indo-Iranian and the extinct Tocharian and Anatolian language families are members of Indo-European stock.

### Anatolian Languages

After Hattushash, the capital of the Hittite (or *Nesan*, according to the self-designation of its people) empire (c. sixteenth–twelfth centuries BCE), was discovered in 1906 and excavated near the modern Boghazköy in central Anatolia, a hitherto unknown group of languages, clearly Indo-European, but not belonging to a well-known group, entered the roster of Indo-European languages. These languages came to be known as the Anatolian branch of Indo-European, its members including the Hittite language itself, which together with Palaic was written in a variant of the cuneiform script; Luwian, which was partly written in this script as well and partly in a peculiar script, which is generally known as "Luwian Hieroglyphs" (but which is not to be confused with Egyptian Hieroglyphic writing); and Lydian and Lycian. (The latter two are fragmentarily attested languages of southwest Anatolia.)

Though Anatolian languages differ greatly, both in terms of structural makeup and material commonalities, from other Indo-European languages, their membership in the family has never been seriously in doubt. The theory that Proto-Anatolian was a sister to Proto-Indo-European rather than a daughter like all other branches has sometimes been popular (the "Indo-Hittite" theory). Whether the poorer morphological system of Anatolian or the more elaborate ones of Indo-Aryan and Greek, for example, more closely reflect the situation of the parent language continues to be debated.

### Tocharian Languages

Like the Anatolian languages, Tocharian was unknown until the early twentieth century, when between

1908 and 1914 members of European and Japanese expeditions to Chinese Turkestan (modern Xinjiang Uygur) found documents written in a variety of the Indic Brāhmi script and in a hitherto unknown but clearly Indo-European language. The documents contain texts written in two dialects (or rather, separate languages), usually referred to as Tocharian A (or East Tocharian, Agnian) and B (West Tocharian, Kuchean), respectively. West Tocharian is generally viewed as more archaic.

Like Anatolian, Tocharian differs considerably from the better-known Indo-European languages, though less dramatically, and its status as one of the daughter languages of Proto-Indo-European has never been doubted. Some (especially morphological) phenomena of Tocharian, the easternmost Indo-European language, find their best parallels in the far West, in Celtic and Italic, but attempts to unite these languages into a single subgroup have been unsuccessful.

**Indo-Iranian Languages**

By far the largest and most important Indo-European branch on the Asian continent is the Indo-Iranian or Aryan group. The latter name is derived from the attested self-designation of the earliest-known speakers of these languages.

Indo-Iranian languages form an uncontroversial primary branch of Indo-European, which is further subdivided into the Indo-Aryan (or Indic) and the Iranian groups. A third group, consisting only of unwritten languages spoken in eastern Afghanistan, is the Nuristani group (formerly also known as the Kafiri languages), with languages such as Kati, Waigali, Ashkun, and Prasun.

Both Indo-Aryan and Iranian languages have been attested since at least the first millennium BCE. Old Indian is represented by Vedic, the language of the sacred literature of Brahmanic religion, and Sanskrit, the highly normed and thus to a degree artificial language of classical Indian literature.

The various Prakrit variants, which began to be attested with the inscriptions of the Mauryan emperor Asoka (273–232 BCE), and Pali, the language of the classical Buddhist canon, form the corpus of Middle Indian. From the beginning of the second millennium CE, New Indian languages are attested. Not unlike the Romance languages, which are derived from what is commonly called Vulgar Latin, New Indian languages can be seen as continuations of a protolanguage that was close to, without being identical with, an attested language, Sanskrit, which continues to be used as a language of religion and learning.

The better-known New Indian languages include: the Hindi-Urdu dialect-cluster, Panjabi, and Gujarati as the central group; Nepali and other languages of the Pahari branch, Oriya, Bengali, and Assamese (eastern group); Marathi and Konkani (southern group); Sindhi and the Lahnda dialect-cluster (northwest group); and Sinhalese on Sri Lanka, which occupies a special position in the family. In the northwest of the Indian subcontinent, the Dardic languages were often grouped with the Nuristani languages, but nowadays they are classified as a special Indo-Aryan group, the most important member of which is Kashmiri.

Old Iranian is represented by Old Persian, the language of the Achaemenid royal inscriptions, and Avestan, in which the sacred writings of the Zoroastrian religion were composed. From the Middle Iranian period onward, the Iranian family is clearly subdivided into western and eastern branches. Western Middle Iranian languages are Middle Persian and Parthian; eastern Middle Iranian languages are Bactrian, Khotanese, Sogdian, and Chorasmian. The most important modern languages of the Iranian family are (West Iranian) Persian (Farsi, Dari, and Tajiki), Tati, Baluchi, Zaza, and numerous unwritten languages spoken in Iran, which are often erroneously classified as Persian dialects, such as Mazanderani, Gilaki, Sangesari, and many others. Modern East Iranian languages are Pashto, Ossetic, and numerous unwritten languages of the Pamir region (Tajikistan), such as Wakhi, Bartangi, Sarykoli, and many others.

*Stefan Georg*

**Further Reading**

Beekes, Robert S. P. (1995) *Comparative Indo-European Linguistics: An Introduction*. Amsterdam and Philadelphia: Benjamins.

**XANTHOS-LETOON—WORLD HERITAGE SITE**

Designated a World Heritage Site in 1988 by UNESCO, Xanthos-Letoon was the capital of Lycia. The funeral art and inscriptions found on this site are an invaluable tool for studying early Indo-European languages.

Gamkrelidze, Thomas V., and Vyacheslav V. Ivanov. (1995) *Indo-European and the Indo-Europeans*. Berlin and New York: Mouton de Gruyter.

Lehmann, Winfred P. (1993) *Theoretical Bases of Indo-European Linguistics*. London and New York: Routledge.

Mallory, James P., and Douglas Q. Adams. (1997) *Encyclopedia of Indo-European Culture*. London and Chicago: Fitzroy Dearborn.

Masica, Colin P. (1991) *The Indo-Aryan Languages*. Cambridge, U.K.: Cambridge University Press.

**INDO-GANGETIC PLAIN** The Indo-Gangetic Plain stretches from the Arabian Sea in the west in a broad crescent to Bangladesh, a distance of nearly 3000 kilometers, with a huge river delta at each end. The drainage basin of the Indus River covers 960,000 square kilometers, while that of the Ganges and the Brahmaputra Rivers together embraces another 1,730,000 square kilometers. Excluding the hilly borders of these catchments, one is still left with an immense alluvial plain in excess of two million sq. km., watered by numerous large rivers, and consequently of the greatest agricultural and historical importance to India, Pakistan, and Bangladesh. This crescent-shaped plain was created geologically by the in-filling of a trough that lay between the ancient, northward-drifting Gondwana block and the recent uplifting Himalayan Ranges. This alluvial fill may be several thousands of meters deep. Today the Ganges carries some 900,000 tons and the Indus some 1 million tons of suspended matter daily, and the Brahmaputra yet more. As a consequence, each river terminates in a broad delta.

Historically, the plain has been the regular entry corridor for invaders and migrants pushing through the passes from Afghanistan to the northwest. Nearly all of the most defining and dramatic events in South Asian history have transpired primarily on this plain, from the growth and decline of the Indus Civilization, to the supposed "Aryan invasion," to the birth and development of early Buddhism, to the battle on the Plain of Kurukshetra that is commemorated in the *Mahabharata*, to the brilliant Mughal empire, to the Indian revolt of 1857, to the bloody splitting of Pakistan from India, and of Bangladesh from Pakistan.

*Paul Hockings*

## Further Reading

Spate, O. H. K. (1972). *India and Pakistan, a General and Regional Geography*. 3d ed. London: Methuen & Co. Ltd.; New York: E.P. Dutton & Co. Inc.

**INDONESIA—PROFILE** (2001 est. pop. 228.4 million). The Republic of Indonesia, with an area of 1,919,440 square kilometers, is the fourth most populous country of the world. The former Dutch colony had an advanced civilization and connections with the outside world more than two thousand years ago. The idea of the Indonesian archipelago as an entity became pronounced after the area came under the control of the Dutch East Indies in the late seventeenth century. In the twenty-first century, a common culture unifies the far-flung Indonesian archipelago.

### Geography

Situated strategically between the continents of Asia and Australia, the archipelago of Indonesia is composed of approximately 17,500 islands, of which about 13,000 are inhabited, and is bounded by the South China Sea, the Celebes Sea, and the Pacific Ocean to the north and the Indian Ocean in the south. About 85 percent of the world's east-west commercial shipping passes through Indonesian waters. The country's principal islands are Java, Sumatra, Kalimantan (South Borneo), Bali, Sulawesi (Celebes), Maluku (Moluccas), and West Papua (Irian Jaya). The archipelago experiences frequent earthquakes, and it has about one hundred volcanoes. The country has the world's longest coastline (80,000 kilometers). Indonesia has a tropical climate, with temperatures hovering between 19° and 32°C, depending on the area. Some 70 percent of the country is covered by tropical rain forest, and the landscape is covered with mountain peaks, valleys, and a network of rivers. Zoologically, the country forms a connecting link between Asian and Australian faunal species. Jakarta is the capital; the other notable cities are Surabaya, Medan, and Bandung.

### People

Indonesia is a country having diverse ethnic groups and languages. Migrations in different periods of history have resulted in a complex ethnic structure. The primary ethnic group is Javanese (45 percent); the others are Sundanese, 14 percent; Madurese, 7.5 percent; coastal Malays, 7.5 percent; and others, 26 percent. The Chinese constitute the majority of the non-indigenous population. The predominant religion is Islam (90 percent), and Christians, Hindus, and Buddhists constitute about 10, 2, and 1 percent of the population respectively. The island of Bali has the largest concentration of Hindus. Centuries-old indigenous religious beliefs still are prevalent.

Bahasa Indonesia, a form of Malay, is the official language. English replaced Dutch as the main Western language in the 1950s. Local languages, such as

## INDONESIA

**Country name:** Republic of Indonesia
**Area:** 1,919,440 sq km
**Population:** 228,437,870 (July 2001 est.)
**Population growth rate:** 1.6% (2001 est.)
**Birth rate:** 22.26 births/1,000 population (2001 est.)
**Death rate:** 6.3 deaths/1,000 population (2001 est.)
**Net migration rate:** 0 migrant(s)/1,000 population (2001 est.)
**Sex ratio:** 1 male(s)/female (2001 est.)
**Infant mortality rate:** 40.91 deaths/1,000 live births (2001 est.)
**Life expectancy at birth—total population:** 68.27 years, male: 65.9 years, female: 70.75 years (2001 est.)
**Major religion:** Muslim
**Major languages:** Bahasa Indonesia (official, modified form of Malay), English, Dutch, local dialects, the most widely spoken of which is Javanese
**Literacy—total population:** 83.8%; male: 89.6%, female: 78% (1995 est.)
**Government type:** republic
**Capital:** Jakarta
**Administrative divisions:** 27 provinces, 2 special regions, and 1 special capital city district
**Independence:** 17 August 1945 (proclaimed independence; on 27 December 1949, Indonesia became legally independent from the Netherlands)
**National holiday:** Independence Day, 17 August (1945)
**Suffrage:** 17 years of age; universal; and married persons regardless of age
**GDP—real growth rate:** 4.8% (2000 est.)
**GDP—per capita: (purchasing power parity):** $2,900 (2000 est.)
**Population below poverty line:** 20% (1998)
**Exports:** $64.7 billion (f.o.b., 2000 est.)
**Imports:** $40.4 billion (c.i.f., 2000 est.)
**Currency:** Indonesian rupiah (IDR)

*Source:* Central Intelligence Agency. (2001) *The World Book Factbook 2001.* Retrieved 5 March 2002, from: http://www.cia.gov/cia/publications/factbook.

Javanese, are also spoken. The literacy rate, currently 83.8 percent, is high. The population growth rate is 1.63 percent. Java and Madura, which have 7 percent of country's area, contain 65 percent of the population.

### History

The remains of ten-thousand-year-old *Homo sapiens* have been discovered at Wajak in East Java. Powerful kingdoms in Java, Sumatra, and Kalimantan arose from the first century CE. The greatest of the ancient Indonesian empires was the fourteenth-century Majapahit, which was based on eastern Java. Islam, which was brought by Indian traders in the late thirteenth century, became firmly entrenched in northeast Java and north Sumatra. Indonesia fell under Dutch control in the late seventeenth century. Indonesian nationalism grew through various organizations like the Budi Utomo, Sarekat Islam, the Communist Party of Indonesia, and the Indonesian Nationalist Party. The country's notable twentieth-century leaders have included Sukarno (1901–1970), Mohammad Hatta (1902–1980), and Sutan Sjahrir (1909–1966). On 17 August 1945 the Indonesian Republic was proclaimed. It achieved independence on 27 December 1949, after winning its struggle against the Dutch. Sukarno was elected president, and Hatta became the premier. Dislocation of the economy; the revolt for autonomy by Aceh, Maluku, and North Sulawesi; and the setting

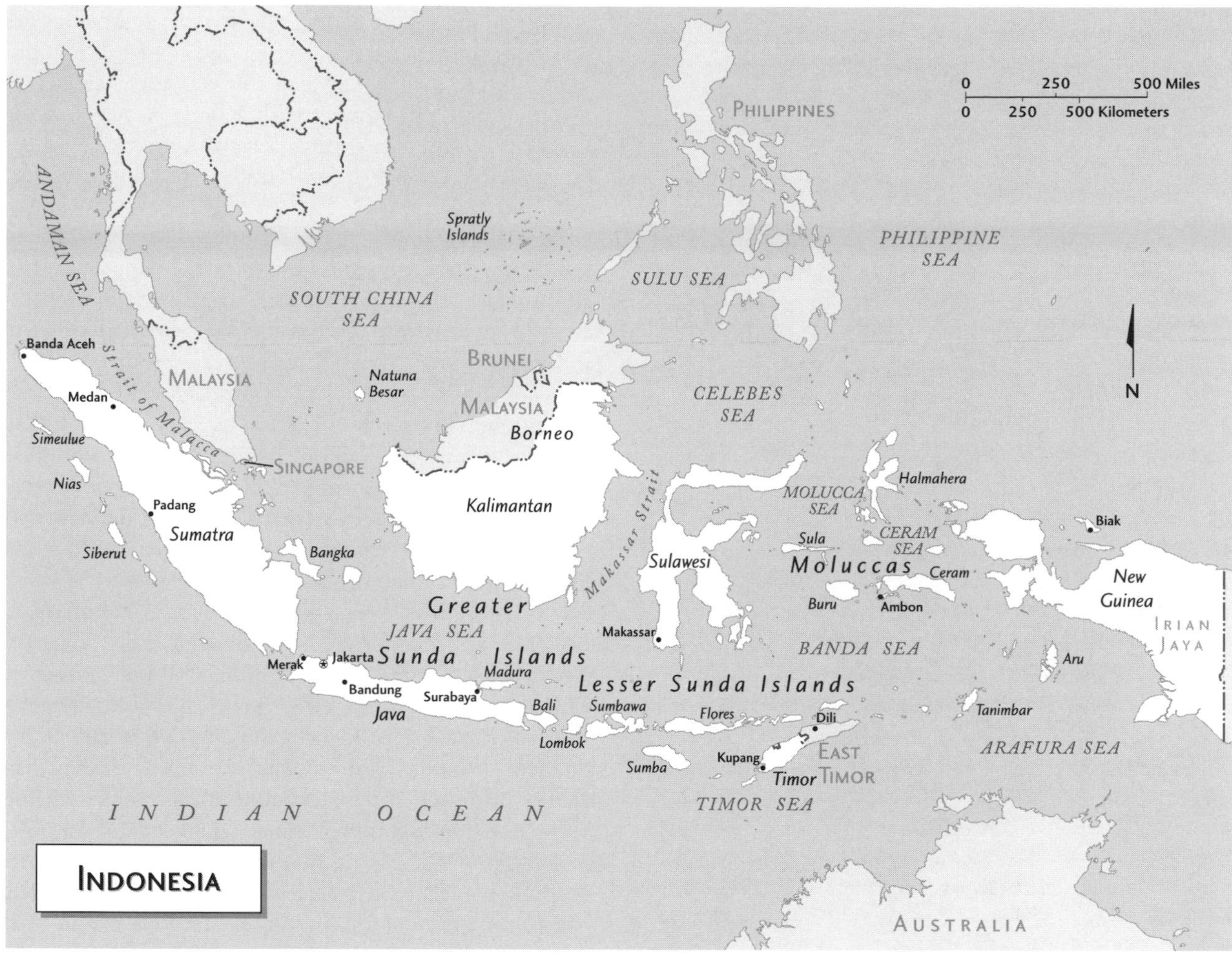


up of a rival rebel government, the Pemerintah Revolusioner Republik Indonesia (PRRI), led to the period of Guided Democracy after 1959. Suharto (b. 1921), who succeeded Sukarno as president, instituted his New Order after an abortive Communist coup in 1965. Indonesia became a member of the Association of Southeast Asian Nations (ASEAN), which was formed in 1967. Papua was recognized as Indonesian territory in 1963, and East Timor, a former Portuguese colony, was integrated into Indonesia in May 1976. In October 1997 an economic crisis paralyzed the country. Riots became widespread. Amid charges of corruption, Suharto stepped down in May 1998, and his vice president, Bacharuddin Jusuf Habibie (b. 1936), assumed the presidency. Discontent in East Timor, which had never reconciled to its incorporation into Indonesia, erupted into bitter fighting. After much bloodshed, it finally gained independence following a referendum on 30 August 1999. Calls for independence also rose in other provinces, particularly Aceh, Riau, Maluku, East Kalimantan, and Papua. Abdurrahman Wahid, better known as Gus Dur, became Indonesia's president in October 1999.

**Economy**

Indonesia is rich in natural resources, including vast supplies of rubber, timber, oil, and tin. Agriculture accounts for almost 21 percent of the gross domestic product (GDP) and more than 45 percent of the labor force. Crops include rice, coffee, maize, palm oil, and pepper. Industry and services make up 35 and 44 percent of GDP respectively. Liquefied natural gas, petroleum, rubber, tin, timber, and textiles are major foreign-exchange earners. Natural gas and oil are a major source of export revenue. The deposits are mainly located in Sumatra, and U.S. companies have heavily invested in these. The major imports are foodstuffs, chemicals, and machinery and equipment. Japan is Indonesia's largest trading partner.

Indonesia had one of world's fastest growing economies, with an average growth rate of 6 to 8 percent

The Welcome Statue at one of Jakarta's main roundabouts is used to display a political flag during the June 1999 election campaign. (AFP/CORBIS)

annually, until the Asian financial crisis hit the country in 1997, and its currency, the rupiah, lost 80 percent of its value. Inflation reached 77 percent in 1998. Locally produced products were hard hit. Unemployment rose to 20 million people, GDP contracted by an estimated 13.7 percent, and external debt was $140 billion. However, the Indonesian economy improved in 1999. A tight monetary policy reduced inflation to 2 percent in 1999. The government abolished major import monopolies, expanded the privatization program, and liberalized market access. Modest economic recovery began with stabilization of exchange and interest rates. The decision of some ASEAN members in February 2001 to set up a free-trade zone in the coming year will help Indonesia's economy.

**Culture**

Indonesia's culture is an expression of the creative genius of a people nurtured by indigenous traditions enhanced by Hindu, Buddhist, and Islamic influences. Knowledge of navigation, wet-rice cultivation, puppet shadow theater *(wayang)*, the gamelan (an orchestra composed mainly of gongs, xylophones, and percussive metal bars), batik textile dyeing, and megalithic building traditions give evidence of a developed material culture that predates contact with Indian elements in the first century CE. The greatest representative of Javanese art and architecture is the famous Buddhist stupa of Borobudur, built c. 778–850 CE. The *Ramayana*, the great Indian epic poem, has influenced the social life of the people. Islam in Indonesia was of liberal hue, with an emphasis on pantheism and a sense of divine presence in all creation. The wood and stone carvings of Indonesia, which take their themes from Indian mythology and indigenous traditions, are highly regarded, as are Indonesian metalwork, basketry, pottery, and bead making. *Pantun*, the famous poem form of interlinking four-line stanzas, are popular in some villages. Gamelan music performs an all-pervasive role in Balinese traditions: it is played at temple offerings, when immersing the ash of a cremated body in river or seawater, when driving evil spirits away, and for street dances, bull races, and so forth. The *suling*, a bamboo flute, is very common. Such nontraditional music styles as *kroncong*, which originated in the eastern part of the country and shows Portuguese influence, and *dangdut*, of Indian influence, possess Indonesian elements. Indonesian dances take their themes from Hindu mythologies and indigenous Pandji plays. The Djanger and Legong dances from Bali, Serimpi and Bedojo from Java, the candle-and-umbrella dance of West Sumatra, and the handkerchief dance of Ambon are famous throughout the archipelago.

**Looking Ahead**

The horrific violence in Maluku between Christians and Muslims, the clamor for secession by Papua and Aceh, the exodus of Muslim refugees from East Timor, and widespread riots throughout the archipelago combine to continue to threaten the stability of Indonesia. The increasing role of the military is another matter of concern, and there is a growing need for separation of the political and military agendas. For political stability, it is advisable that the ruling class look to the needs of the people and adopt some measures of decentralization for the provinces. The inherent wealth of the nation and its huge market potential should take Indonesia toward a better future.

*Patit Paban Mishra*

**Further Reading**

Legge, John D. (1980) *Indonesia*. 3d ed. Sydney: Prentice-Hall.

Leur, J. C. van. (1955) *Indonesian Trade and Society: Essays in Asian Social and Economic History*. The Hague, Netherlands: W. van Hoeve.

Mintz, Jeanne S. (1961) *Indonesia: A Profile.* New York: D. Van Nostrand Company.
Ricklefs, M. C. (1993) *A History of Modern Indonesia: c. 1300 to the Present.* Stanford, CA: Stanford University Press.

**INDONESIA—ECONOMIC SYSTEM** The Indonesian economy is based on agricultural production and extraction of natural resources, especially oil, natural gas, timber, and fish. State-sponsored attempts to promote industrialization had meager results until the 1980s and received a major setback with the Asian economic crisis of 1997. Although tourism has developed as an important service industry, Indonesia remains otherwise insignificant as an exporter of services.

### From Early Times to Independence

In precolonial times, the economy of the Indonesian archipelago was characterized by subsistence agriculture in most regions; the production of rice for export in areas with fertile volcanic soil and high rainfall (notably on Java, Bali, and parts of Sumatra); the cultivation of high-value spices (especially pepper, cloves, nutmeg, and cinnamon) for export to China, India, the Middle East, and Europe; and the collection of forest products (camphor, benzoin, gums, bird feathers, and fragrant woods), also for export. Especially on the coasts of the Strait of Melaka (Malacca) and on the northern coast of Java (known as the Pasisir), many cities developed as trading entrepôts, providing sophisticated services to merchants. Initially, trade within the archipelago and between the archipelago and China and India seems to have been mainly in the hands of indigenous merchants, but from about the thirteenth century, foreign traders, including Indians, Arabs, and Chinese, played an increasingly prominent role.

The European presence in the archipelago, beginning with the Portuguese capture of Melaka in 1511, appears to have inhibited indigenous trade. The Portuguese were effective tax gatherers, while the Dutch East Indies Company (VOC) imposed a monopoly on trade in a wide range of lucrative commodities. These restrictions increasingly choked the economic base of the entrepôt cities, shifting the balance of power within indigenous societies away from merchants and toward those controlling agriculture.

During the seventeenth century, the VOC generally left production in the hands of indigenous growers. During the eighteenth century, however, Dutch interests shifted from high-value, low-volume spices to higher-volume, lower-priced commodities such as sugar, coffee, and indigo. The Dutch also took an increasingly interventionist role in production and began to bind indigenous labor to the land, sometimes in explicitly feudal arrangements, but more often by using the traditional authority of indigenous elites to mobilize peasant farmers for work on behalf of colonial interests. Indonesians had traditionally supplied

Terraced fields like these rice fields in Bali are common in Indonesia as they make better use of the land and conserve irrigation water. (WOLFGANG KAEHLER/CORBIS)

labor services to their rulers, and this tradition was extended to serve Dutch interests. Although there was much discussion of the possible advantage of using economic incentives rather than coercion and traditional authority to mobilize labor for plantation work, duress remained a key feature of labor control throughout the colonial period. Fees collected for licenses (generally granted to Chinese entrepreneurs) to manage toll roads, gambling establishments, and the sale of opium were major sources of state income.

From the late nineteenth century, many observers identified a sharp threefold division in the colonial economy. Large European firms, which developed rapidly after the colonial government introduced a policy of economic liberalization in 1870, dominated much of the modern, capital-intensive, export-oriented sectors of the economy. Chinese firms dominated retail trade and medium-level commerce. The indigenous peoples of the archipelago occupied only the margins of the commercial economy, being engaged mainly in agriculture and state employment. Colonial economists, notably J. H. Boeke (1884–1944), attributed this stratification primarily to cultural factors, arguing that the traditional culture of village life emphasized community obligations and discouraged capital accumulation and individual advancement.

From the late nineteenth century, population growth in Java seems to have led to a declining standard of living for most Javanese, because limited resources on the island were spread ever more thinly among its people. The colonial Ethical Policy, announced in 1901, involved an attempt to overcome this problem by agricultural intensification, emigration from the island (later called transmigration), and limited industrialization. These efforts, however, had only meager results and were largely ended by the Great Depression. The decline of infrastructure during the 1930s was exacerbated during the 1940s by the Japanese occupation (1942–1945) and the war of independence (1945–1949).

### Independence

The terms of Indonesia's eventual settlement with the Dutch in 1949 left the position of Western firms intact (insofar as they had physically survived the years of warfare). Indonesia's economy in the 1950s, therefore, resembled that of the colonial era in its pronounced racial stratification and its emphasis on the export of plantation products. Except during the brief Korean War boom, however, the economy faced sluggish international commodity prices and a much-reduced political capacity to obtain cheap, partly coerced labor. Strong arguments were heard within Indonesia that political independence had failed to end the economic dimension of colonialism and that action should be taken to restrict or dispossess Western firms. Those firms responded by steadily decapitalizing their investments in Indonesia.

Successive governments attempted to strengthen the indigenous presence in the commercial economy by awarding licenses and permits to promising indigenous entrepreneurs and by restricting the access of Chinese business owners to certain sectors of the economy. These measures largely failed to stimulate an indigenous entrepreneurial class; rather, they encouraged rent seeking on the basis of political connections. From 1950, governments also sought to establish a significant state sector in the economy, nationalizing the railways and the Java Bank, the semi-private bank of circulation in the colonial era. State enterprises were also established in shipping, air transport, and industry (textiles, cement, hardboard, automobiles, and glass). A large number of government bodies, including military units and civilian departments, maintained semiformal "economic organizations" to supplement the dwindling allocations they received from the state budget. In December 1957, all Dutch enterprises in Indonesia were nationalized, most of them being placed under military management. Many of these enterprises languished because of corruption and inexperienced management; those that succeeded did so mostly because their political or military connections enabled them to function as rent collectors rather than because they showed true entrepreneurial skill.

The failure of independence to stimulate extensive industrialization in Java exacerbated tension between Java and the so-called Outer Islands, especially after the 1955 elections gave political power in Jakarta to Java-based parties. The 1953–1955 and 1956–1957 governments of Ali Sastroamidjojo (1903–1975) imposed exchange rates that favored importers (mainly in Java) and penalized exporters (many of them in Sumatra, Sulawesi, and Kalimantan). These economic tensions contributed to regional rebellions in 1956–1959.

The 1957–1965 Guided Democracy of President Sukarno (1901–1970) included a plan for rapid industrialization based on state planning and investment, but most of the planning had no grounding in economic reality, while the economy, impoverished and plagued by corruption, could not deliver the necessary tax revenues. By 1965, the central government was unable to produce a state budget, and, with recurrent expenditure being funded by printing money, serious inflation began. The infrastructure was in exceptionally poor condition, and both imports and exports stagnated, leading to hardship, including occasional starvation in some regions.

## The New Order and After

The 1967–1998 New Order government of President Suharto (b. 1921) achieved a remarkable rehabilitation of the economy. Per capita income, which had been less than $50 in 1966, reached $1,155 in 1996, and Indonesia was increasingly identified as an imminent recruit to the ranks of the Asian newly industrializing countries.

The funding for this rehabilitation came from a massive exploitation of the country's (largely nonrenewable) natural resources, chiefly oil, natural gas, and timber, as well as fish, coal, bauxite, gold, copper, and other minerals. This funding through resource exploitation was augmented by extensive marshaling of foreign aid, coordinated by the Intergovernmental Group on Indonesia until 1992 and thereafter by the Consultative Group for Indonesia. These sources of income enabled the government to invest heavily in infrastructure and to provide capital for state-owned industrial enterprises.

Although New Order Indonesia abandoned the officially tight economic planning of Guided Democracy, government intervention in the economy remained extensive. Management of the economy was principally in the hands of the National Development Planning Agency, whose leading figures were sometimes referred to as the "Berkeley mafia," because many of them had been trained at the University of California at Berkeley. State-owned banks dominated the financial sector.

Under Indonesia's constitution, all mineral resources belong to the state. In 1960, all concessions to foreign firms were abolished, and the exploitation of minerals was placed in the hands of state enterprises. A new foreign investment law in 1967 reopened the sector to foreign firms, and the Freeport corporation (now Freeport McMoRan) obtained especially favorable conditions for its massive gold and copper mine in western New Guinea (then called West Irian). Foreign investment in oil was permitted only on a joint-venture basis with the state oil corporation, Pertamina, though Pertamina's contribution was often no more than arranging official permits and taking a share of the production or the profits. During the 1970s, exports of liquefied natural gas took on major importance alongside oil exports. Indonesia's main reserves of oil and gas are located offshore in the South China Sea and near the Bird's Head peninsula of New Guinea, but important reserves also exist in Sumatra, Kalimantan, and the Java Sea.

Extensive exploitation of Indonesia's tropical forests began in 1968, and timber soon ranked as Indonesia's third-largest export after oil and gas. Whereas oil and gas exploitation remained under relatively close state supervision, timber licenses were widely allocated as patronage among individuals and groups close to the government. Sound regulations to ensure that the forests would be cut in keeping with a plan of sustainability were put in place, but until the 1990s, these regulations were virtually never enforced and were commonly ignored. During the 1980s, domestic and international environmentalists increasingly expressed concern over the irresponsible logging practices, and some attempts were made to punish firms that violated the regulations, but the firms targeted in this way were generally those with weak political connections. Fishing in Indonesia is also conducted largely as a mining operation with no attention to sustainability or maintenance of stocks. The large-scale granting of concessions to foreign tuna and shrimp fishing fleets began in 1987.

Active promotion of industry began in 1979 with the third five-year plan. The government played a major role in this process, both through state-owned enterprises and through joint ventures with private investors. Initially, such enterprises were commonly protected by tariffs and exclusive license systems, which tended to promote inefficiency and increase costs for other domestic producers. During the 1980s, increasing emphasis was placed on adding value to Indonesia's traditional exports. In 1985, the government banned the export of raw logs to promote local processing, especially the production of plywood. Processing plans for crumb rubber, rattan, palm oil, and petrochemicals were also established, as was a large aluminum smelter on the Asahan River in North Sumatra.

Workers at the Jakarta port of Sundakelpa unload lumber from Kalimantan, Borneo, Indonesia, in 1995. (SERGIO DORANTES/CORBIS)

## FIVE LARGEST COMPANIES IN INDONESIA

According to *Asia Week* the five largest companies in Indonesia are as follows:

| Company | Sector | Sales ($ millions) | Rank in Asia |
|---|---|---|---|
| Pertamina | Oil Exploration, Refining | 19,488.5 | 50 |
| Astra International | Car Assembly, Trading | 3,372.6 | 399 |
| Per. Listrik Negara | Power Generation | 2,678.4 | 498 |
| Gudang Garam | Clove Cigarettes | 1,776.9 | 743 |
| Indah Kiat Pulp & Paper | Paper, Pulp | 1,545.5 | 846 |

*Source:* "The Asia Week 1000." (2001) *Asia Week* (9 November): 113.

Coal production in Indonesia dramatically expanded in the 1980s, with Indonesia becoming the world's third-largest exporter. Gold production also expanded in this period, but reliable statistics on production levels are unavailable because of extensive illegal mining. Substantial volumes of tin and bauxite are also exported.

The importance of agriculture in the Indonesian economy declined steadily under the New Order. Whereas agricultural products accounted for 70 percent of total export value in 1969, that percentage had declined to 9 percent by 1983. Before the 1997 Asian crisis, agriculture as a whole employed around 40 percent of the Indonesian workforce in 1996, whereas in 1976 it had employed 61 percent.

Government intervention played a major role in transforming rice production. Rice is the major food crop and the preferred staple food of most Indonesians. It is cultivated mostly on small farms, but complex social arrangements that used to give most members of each community at least some share in the annual production have often given way to simple commercial arrangements for planting, weeding, harvesting, threshing, and milling. In the early 1960s, much of Indonesia's scarce foreign exchange went to pay for imported rice, but from the 1970s, a massive investment in irrigation, fertilizers, high-yielding rice varieties, pesticides, and agricultural advice (the so-called Green Revolution) led to increased production, so that Indonesia achieved self-sufficiency in rice in 1984. From the late 1980s, a sophisticated Integrated Pest Management Program dramatically reduced some of the adverse ecological consequences of the early Green Revolution.

Other food crops are generally known by the name *palawija* and include maize, cassava, soybeans, and sweet potatoes. Indonesia's main cash crops are rubber, palm oil, copra, tea, coffee, sugar, cocoa, and tobacco, all of which are produced both on large-scale plantations and by smallholders, as well as teak, which is produced in long-established government-owned plantations in Java. During and after colonial times, smallholders often competed unequally with the better-connected plantations for access to processing and export facilities. In the 1980s, however, the government delivered increased assistance to smallholders, comparable to the Green Revolution facilities given to rice producers, and established a "nucleus estate and smallholder" program to give the smallholders access to plantation facilities.

From the early 1980s, tourism developed as a major industry. International tourist arrivals rose from 366,000 in 1975 to 5 million in 1996.

Controversy has repeatedly emerged over the state sponsorship of strategic industries, including nuclear power and the aerospace industry, both backed by Suharto's technology minister and eventual successor B. J. Habibie (b. 1936). These initiatives were widely criticized as wasteful prestige projects rather than as genuine contributions to industrial development. Also criticized was President Suharto's decision to grant one of his sons a license to produce a national car, which was eventually to have a local content of more than 60 percent. Although the project was seen as useful in principle, there was widespread indignation over the fact that the project received tax and tariff concessions while importing the cars fully assembled from South Korea. Suharto's children and many other relatives were involved in commercial ventures in which their connections with the government, rather than any entrepreneurial flair, appeared to be the main factor in their success.

Successive governments in Indonesia have stressed the importance of cooperatives as a just and effective form of commercial activity for local communities, but the economic performance of cooperatives has generally been disappointing.

Throughout the New Order period, licenses, patronage, and outright corruption were extensively used to channel profits into the hands of figures in and close to the government. The fact that many of these figures were Chinese Indonesian business owners was a constant source of domestic criticism of the economic system. Much of the capital accumulated in this way, however, was productively invested in new industrial enterprises, creating a business sector that increasingly had the capacity to prosper without close government support or regulation. Nevertheless, domestic pressure and pressure from international donor countries and agencies led Indonesia to embark on a sustained deregulation of the economy from the mid-1980s. Deregulation led to strong growth in the manufacturing sector, but it contributed to the emergence of an overheated bubble economy that collapsed spectacularly in the Asian financial crisis of 1997.

The financial crisis caused serious damage to Indonesia's industrial sector, which was starved of credit and equity funds for several months, leading thousands of businesses to shut their doors and leaving hundreds of thousands of workers unemployed. Under International Monetary Fund instruction, the Habibie government established the Indonesian Bank Restructuring Agency in January 1998 to reorganize the banking sector and close down banks that were not viable. Lack of political will, however, meant that relatively little was achieved in restructuring. For the most part, economists have argued that the economic strategies of the Suharto era were sound and that the economic crisis was an acute response to investor disquiet over corruption and nepotism in ruling circles.

*Robert Cribb*

## Further Reading


Booth, Anne. (1998) *The Indonesian Economy in the Nineteenth and Twentieth Centuries: A History of Missed Opportunities.* Houndmills, U.K.: Macmillan.

Booth, Anne, ed. (1992) *The Oil Boom and After: Indonesian Economic Policy and Performance in the Suharto Era.* Singapore: Oxford University Press.

Dirkse, Jan-Paul, Frans Hüsken, and Mario Rutten, eds. (1993) *Development and Social Welfare: Indonesia's Experiences under the New Order.* Leiden, Netherlands: KITLV Press.

Hardjono, Joan, ed. (1991) *Indonesia: Resources, Ecology, and Environment.* Singapore: Oxford University Press.

Hill, Hal. (1999) *The Indonesian Economy in Crisis: Causes, Consequences and the Lessons.* St. Leonards, Australia: Allen & Unwin.

———. (1996) *The Indonesian Economy since 1966: Southeast Asia's Emerging Giant.* Cambridge, U.K.: Cambridge University Press.

Hill, Hal, ed. (1994) *Indonesia's New Order: The Dynamics of Socio-Economic Transformation.* Honolulu, HI: University of Hawaii Press.

Manning, Chris. (1998) *Indonesian Labour in Transition: An East Asian Success Story?* Cambridge, U.K.: Cambridge University Press.


# INDONESIA—EDUCATION SYSTEM

The Indonesian educational system reflects influences from Hindu, Buddhist, Islamic, and Western educational systems introduced by foreign rulers and settlers. Hindu and Buddhist educators taught royal family members in their palaces and temples, particularly between 100 and 1500 CE. The Islamic system of education was first introduced in courts, mosques, and bazaars between the seventh and the thirteenth centuries. In the sixteenth century, European traders and colonialists—particularly the Portuguese, Spanish, and Dutch—established themselves in the Indonesian archipelago and introduced their secular Western educational systems. While some signs of all these influences exist today, the Islamic and Western systems are most strongly evident.

## School Systems

Traditional Islamic schools are referred to as *pesantren* in Java, *pondok* in Sumatra, *pondok-pesantren* in Sulawesi, and *dayah* in Aceh. These are managed predominantly by Muslim philanthropists or organizations. Religious students *(santri)* study classical religious books *(kitab kuning)*, written mainly in Arabic by Muslim scholars. A guru *(kyai)* heads the institution and guides the teachers in these boarding schools. *Pesantren* recruit graduates from primary schools (both public and private schools run under Islamic or secular systems). Over a million students are enrolled in approximately six thousand *pesantren* operating across the country. While most *pesantren* provide secondary education only, some also offer a B.A. program as well as continuing education for adults. The teaching of Islamic sciences, Arabic, and theology in *pesantren* is done in the vernacular. Other subjects taught include English, the Indonesian language, and the Pancasila ("five principles"), a concept developed by Sukarno and others in 1945, which was adopted as the basis of the national ideology. (The five principles are belief in one God, humanitarianism, Indonesian nationalism, democracy based on deliberation, and social justice.) Most *pesantren* are affiliated with the Nahdlatul Ulama, a traditionalist socioreligious organization. The Muhammadiyah, another socioreligious organization, also has set up *pesantren*, which use more modern teaching methods than the Nahdlatul Ulama.

The modern system of education essentially is drawn from the Dutch educational system. While in power from the seventeenth to the mid twentieth century, the Dutch set up three types of schools patterned after those in the Netherlands. The Hollandsche Europesche School (HES) trained primarily European and Eurasian students, while the Hollandsche Chinese

School (HCS) system taught ethnic Chinese and other Far East Asian pupils. The third system, the Hollandsche Indische School (HIS), set up in the mid-nineteenth century, enrolled students from indigenous communities.

Although this system formed the basis of modern education in Indonesia, it fostered discrimination and racism in the student population, and created a breeding ground for the forces of nationalism. After Indonesia gained sovereignty in 1949, the number of educational institutions from elementary to postgraduate level increased considerably.

Most schools offer secular studies, a step encouraged by the government as a means of providing a balanced education, raising the literacy level and, hence, promoting economic development in general.

## Education Units

Education is divided into two units—learning and teaching activities—and two paths—within school and out of school. In-school education is conducted in a traditional school environment through teaching and learning activities that are gradual, hierarchical, and continuous. Out-of-school education is provided outside of the formal schooling system through teaching and learning activities that are not necessarily hierarchical and continuous. Family education is regarded as an important part of the out-of-school system. Its most crucial role is generally recognized as instilling socioreligious, moral, and cultural values. The two paths both offer general, vocational, and service-related education.

Preschooling is aimed at stimulating the mental, intellectual, spiritual, and physical development of children outside the home environment. It encourages early behavioral development and discipline, through creative, innovative, and stimulating games and playtime. Play groups are available for toddlers three years old and younger. Four- to six-year-olds attend kindergarten, where the stress is on intellectual and creative stimulation as well as on the teaching of language, religion, and social skills.

Primary and junior secondary schools are grouped by the Ministry of National Education (formerly the Minister of Education and Culture) under its compulsory basic education policy. Under this policy, general education is provided for nine years (through the third year of junior high school), divided into six years for primary school and three years for lower secondary school. The curriculum covers at least thirteen subjects: Pancasila education, religious education, citizenship education, Indonesian language, reading and writing, mathematics, introduction to science and technology, geography, national and general history, handicrafts and arts, physical education and health, drawing, and English language.

Primary school is aimed at teaching reading, writing, and arithmetic, and prepares students for lower secondary school. The latter aims at character development, building up social consciousness, civic responsibilities, and national awareness, as well as preparation for senior high school. Special schools also have been established at both levels for handicapped students. An Islamic basic education system, run parallel to this secular system, is managed by the Ministry of Religious Affairs.

Both systems (Islamic and secular) provide general secondary training (senior secondary levels) in two programs: academic and professional (vocational). The academic program includes the following subjects: Pancasila and education citizenship, religious education, Indonesian language and literature, national and general history, English language, physical and health education, mathematics, natural sciences, social sciences, and arts education.

Vocational secondary schools implement three-year programs according to the perceived present and future demands of the employment market. Programs include agriculture and forestry, industrial technology, business and management, community welfare, tourism, and arts and handicrafts.

Higher education is provided by public universities run by the government and by private colleges and institutes. Academies and polytechnic schools specialize in applied sciences, while colleges provide academic and professional training in one particular discipline. The Department of Religious Affairs also operates colleges in Islamic Studies. Institutes provide similar academic and professional programs as well but in a variety of related disciplines. The network of fourteen Institutes of Islamic Studies, for example, is managed by the Minister of Religious Affairs. Universities provide academic and/or professional education in diverse disciplines, including natural and social sciences and the arts. In 1994, the minister of national education established five consortia representing major universities to streamline the teaching of science and technology, social sciences, agriculture, medicine, and education.

## Late-Twentieth-Century Changes in Education

The educational system in Indonesia is centralized and, while this facilitates unity and uniformity under the center (Java), it also has raised fears of contributing to the demise of local languages, customs, and values.

The renaming of the Ministry of Education and Culture to Ministry of National Education in 1999 represented a move to give greater autonomy to the regions in choice of educational systems. Local communities received a say in the running of the educational system. It was hoped this would revitalize locally managed institutions and, ultimately, contribute to overall development. How successful the country will be in implementing this ideal is, however, dependent on the participation of the local population and the successful application of the autonomy policy initiated by the government in January 2001.

*Andi Faisal Bakti*

### Further Reading


Lee Kam Hing. (1995) *Education and Politics in Indonesia 1945–1965.* Kuala Lumpur, Malaysia: University of Malaya Press.

Yunus, Mahmus. (1992) *Serjarah pendidikan Islam di Indonesia* (History of Islamic Education in Indonesia). Jakarta, Indonesia: Mutiara Sumber Widya.


## INDONESIA—HISTORY

**INDONESIA—HISTORY** Once the seat of several Indianized Hindu and Buddhist empires, Indonesia, at the beginning of the twenty-first century, is the largest Muslim country in the world. Between the sixteenth and the first half of the twentieth centuries, Indonesia was under Dutch colonial control. Independence from the Netherlands in 1949 brought about a fragile democratic system under President Sukarno (1901–1970). His government having failed to meet the challenges of governance, the country faced a long period of authoritarian rule until succeeded by a democratic government in 1998. This democratic system is still fragile, and the military continue to exercise significant influence in the political affairs of the country. Nevertheless, as a founding member of the Association of Southeast Asia Nations (ASEAN), Indonesia plays an important role in the region. The country's situation on the trade route between Australia and Europe makes Indonesia a strategically important country.

Indonesia, the largest archipelago in the world, is a collection of more than 13,500 islands. The most populous of these are Java, Sumatra, Kalimantan (on the island of Borneo), Irian Jaya (western New Guinea), and Sulawesi. According to anthropologists, Java was home to one of the earliest hominids, *Pithecanthropus erectus* or Java man. Two major population groups in Indonesia are the Proto or Older Malays and the Younger or Deutero Malays.

### Foreign Influences

For centuries, wet-rice cultivation provided the subsistence basis for the people of the islands. Then, after the second century CE, trade became an equally important factor in socioeconomic, political, religious, and cultural development. The Indonesians traded with East, South, and West Asia. From early times, India, not China, had the most cultural impact on the Indonesians. As a result, Indian Hinduism and later Buddhism found a fertile soil in Indonesia. During the fifteenth and sixteenth centuries, most Indonesians embraced Islam, despite the arrival of the Portuguese, who attempted to convert the islanders to Christianity in the sixteenth century. The Dutch, who followed the Portuguese in the seventeenth century, were probably responsible for the small but significant minority of Christians.

### Early History

In the fifth century, the disintegration of the Fulan, the first historic empire in Southeast Asia, led to the establishment of many smaller successor states in the region, such as Srivijaya on the Palembang River on Sumatra. Contact with India, which was lost when Fulan disintegrated, was renewed. The increased volume of Indian trade was one reason for Srivijaya's growth into a thriving empire during the seventh century.

The empire grew to include almost all of the Malay Peninsula and dominated both the Malacca and Sunda Straits. Srivijaya remained a major force in the region for the next six centuries. An Indianized Buddhist state, Srivijaya lavishly patronized Buddhism.

In central Java, another Buddhist state, Mataram, arose in the late seventh century. Devoted to Mahayana Buddhism, Mataram was ruled by the already established Sailendra dynasty (flourished eighth–ninth centuries). Sanjaya (flourished c. 730), the first Sailendra ruler, had been a Saivite, a devotee of the Hindu god Siva. By the middle of the eighth century, the Sailendras had become Buddhists. They built the world-famous Borobudur Buddhist monuments in central Java. In 832, when the last adult member of the Sailendra dynasty, a woman, married the ruler of a rival state, the Sailendra line ended. The queen's younger brother fled to Srivijaya, where he became the ruler.

During the eleventh century, Srivijayan commercial rivalry with the eastern Java state of Mataram and the Chola rulers of southern India became intense. After establishing good relations with the Cholas, Srivijaya turned against Mataram. Between 1006 and 1007, Srivijaya attacked and burned the Mataram capital and destroyed its fleet. Meanwhile, Srivijaya's relations

## KEY EVENTS IN INDONESIA'S HISTORY

**5th century CE** With the destruction of the Fulan empire in Southeast Asia, the Srivijaya state on Sumatra emerges as a regional power.
**7th century** The Mataram state emerges as a regional power in central Java.
**13th century** The Majapahit rulers in eastern Java create a vast empire in the western islands which lasts until the arrival of the Portuguese in the sixteenth century.
**1511** The Portuguese capture Melaka.
**1641** The Dutch take Melaka from the Portuguese and begin to extend their rule.
**1795** The British become the dominant European power in the region and take some Dutch territory.
**1799** The Dutch East India Company is disbanded and the Netherlands assume direct responsibility for the Dutch East Indies.
**1830** The Dutch are reinstalled in Java.
**1920s–1930s** Indonesian nationalist organizations are repressed by the Dutch.
**1942–1945** period of Japanese occupation.
**1945** Indonesia declares independence with Sukarno its first leader.
**1949** The Dutch grant Indonesia independence.
**1955** The Bandung conference is held on Java.
**1964** Indonesia invades Malaysia but is repulsed.
**1967** Parliament removes Sukarno and he is replaced by Suharto.
**1969** Tribal elders in Irian Jaya vote to become part of Indonesia.
**1975** Indonesia annexes East Timor.
**1984** Indonesia is a founding member of ASEAN.
**1993** Suharto's rule becomes more repressive.
**1997–1998** The economy declines during the Asian economic crisis.
**1998** Suharto resigns and is replaced by B. J. Habibie.
**1999** The East Timorese vote to become an independent nation.
**1999** Abdurrahman Wahid is elected president and Megawati Sukarnoputri vice president.
**2001** Wahid is removed from office and replaced with Megawati.

with the Cholas deteriorated, leading to a Chola attack in 1025. Chola forces raided the entire Sumatran coast and captured Srivijayan territories on the Malay coast, seizing the Srivijayan king. The Cholas, however, did not follow up on their victories. In 1028, Srivijaya made peace with the Mataram ruler Airlangga (991–1049?). A Chola attack nevertheless rendered a devastating blow to Srivijayan fortunes and led to civil war in Java.

Toward the end of the thirteenth century, with the help of the Mongols (who at that time ruled China), the Javanese prince Vijaya established a new capital at Majapahit in eastern Java. The Majapahit rulers claimed control over a vast area, including Bali, Macassar (modern Ujung Pandan), Singapore, Sumatra, and western Java, until after the arrival of the Portuguese in the sixteenth century.

### The Portuguese in Southeast Asia

Portuguese entry into Southeast Asia followed the successful voyage of Vasco da Gama (c. 1460–1524) from Portugal to India in 1498. Hoping to monopolize the European spice trade, the Portuguese captured Melaka (or Malacca, as it has traditionally been spelled in English) in 1511 and slaughtered its Muslim inhabitants. The Portuguese attempt to dominate the spice trade led to open rivalry with the Javanese, who attacked Melaka in 1513 but suffered a defeat.

Since the Javanese were then unable to send spices to Melaka, coastal states like Madura, Tuban, Surabaya, and Demak all lost their independence to the new state of Mataram by the 1620s. Demak, a state on the east coast of Java, encouraged the people in the area to become Muslims in an attempt to deny the Portuguese access to the region. Such was the intensity of the Javanese opposition that the Portuguese were left with no choice but to use the north Borneo straits to reach the Spice Islands (the Moluccas).

The Chinese were also unhappy with Portuguese control of Melaka because they no longer received unconditional access to the commodities they had once enjoyed. Soon the state of Aceh, on Sumatra, at the western end of the Indonesian archipelago, became the chief Muslim rival of the Portuguese. Aceh not only defeated the Portuguese efforts to capture the Sumatran ports of Pasai and Pedir but also staged several attacks on Melaka between 1537 and 1575. Nevertheless, Aceh was forced to make peace with the Portuguese in 1587.

### The Dutch in Indonesia

Until the end of the sixteenth century, Spain and Portugal monopolized the Oriental spice trade. The Dutch, denied access to Oriental spices in Europe, were forced to seek supplies in the East itself. The English and Dutch worked together to drive the Portuguese out. Since the Dutch were not involved in the Thirty Years' War (1618–1648) in Europe, they were free to develop their trade in the East Indies. Finally, after several attempts, the Dutch dislodged the Portuguese from Melaka, captured it in 1641, and established themselves in Java, the Moluccas, and other islands.

The Dutch and English, who traded with Bantam, a well-known pepper port in western Java, were often subjected to blackmail by both the sultans and the local Chinese. Therefore, the new Dutch governor-general, Jan Pieterszoon Coen (1587–1629), decided to build a fortified place for trade in western Java. The Dutch picked Jakarta, which they renamed Batavia.

In 1588, Mataram had annexed the port city of Demak, and the sultan converted to Islam. Sultan Agung (d. 1645) of Mataram embarked on an aggressive course of conquest and expansion. Having conquered Madura (1624) and Surabaya (1625), he turned against Batavia, but the Dutch easily defeated his forces. Mataram continued as a significant power for another half-century but never completed its expansionist program.

The Dutch did not allow Indonesian ships to use the Java straits unless they carried a Dutch company passport. Indonesian crews that refused to carry the passport were subject to execution or enslavement. Macassar, which refused to accept this Dutch demand, fell in 1667. The Buginese (of Sulawesi, Indonesia) under Aru Palakka of Bone (near the Gulf of Bone) and the forces of Ternate (an island in the Moluccas) conquered most of the commercially valuable islands such as Mataram (1678–1680), Bantam, and most of the eastern islands.

After 1587, Aceh had become a powerful state, whose control extended all the way from Johor in the south to Kedah and Patani in the north of Indonesia, although Melaka remained outside its control. The sultan of Aceh tried to monopolize the cloth trade and required European traders to acquire permits to trade in pepper in the Sumatran ports. Having taken Melaka with the help of Johor and Minangkabu, the Dutch turned against Aceh and stopped its attempts to monopolize trade. Nevertheless, the interior of Kalimantan (Borneo) and Sumatra remained unaffected by the Dutch. Melaka under Dutch control never regained its importance as a shipping center.

In addition to being a trading monopoly, the Dutch East India Company also exercised sweeping authority in political, military, and diplomatic matters affecting the East Indies. Its agents exercised great freedom of action in making decisions affecting the company. Jan Pieterszoon Coen is generally regarded as the "architect" of Dutch empire in the East. His ruthlessness drove out competitors, both foreign and domestic. He defeated the Portuguese and the Spanish and made it difficult for the British to operate in the region. By 1660, the Dutch could resist any aggressor.

Dutch participation in settling local disputes enabled them to bring Sumatra under control. By extending protection to several native peoples, the Dutch also gained a trade monopoly over several groups of people, although the Dutch domination of the pepper trade was neither complete nor effective. The Dutch intervened in Java when the Madurese, with the help of pirate refugees from Macassar, attacked Mataram. The Dutch sided with Mataram, and the Madurese were defeated. As a result, the Dutch received valuable territorial and commercial privileges in western Java and Mataram.

Bantam had continued to resist the Dutch, and a domestic rivalry there helped the Dutch to bring that state under control. The eldest son of the sultan, angry that he was passed over for succession, led a successful revolt with Dutch help. As a result, the Dutch received Cheribon and other territories extending to the southern parts of Java. In 1682, they received the right to trade at Bantam. The Dutch consolidated their position in Java after the death of Amang Kurat II, son of Amang Kurat I of Mataram and puppet ruler of Mataram, in 1705.

The Dutch introduced slavery as well as forced cultivation of coffee and sugar into Java. Corrupt company officials and native middlemen worked together to exploit the peasants. Stingy with payments, the company forced its unscrupulous officials to resort to private trade. During the eighteenth century, the company no longer paid salaries after employees had established a sizable outside income. Shady business practices by employees finally forced the company to pay annual dividends to company shareholders from its capital reserves. By 1780, the situation grew so bad that the company began to force donations from its employees.

The Dutch had other problems as well. An epidemic of malaria in 1732 and the massacre of several thousand Chinese residents by the Dutch in 1740 were reasons for the decline of Bantam. Moreover, the Dutch were unable to suppress Buginese piracy in the Straits of Malacca and could not exercise effective control on the west coast of Sumatra or in pirate-infested Kalimantan. British ascendancy in India cost the Dutch their trade with the Coromandel coast of southeast India. The British defeat of the Netherlands in 1781 shattered the Dutch monopoly in Southeast Asia. Finally, the French conquest of the Netherlands in 1795 completed the dissolution of the Dutch East India Company in 1799. Between 1795 and 1825, Britain enjoyed a predominant commercial position in the region. In 1799, the Dutch East India Company was disbanded, and the Netherlands assumed direct responsibility for the Dutch East Indies.

England's territorial acquisitions in the region included Penang (1786), Melaka (1795), Province Wellesley (1800), and Java (1811). England also acquired Singapore (1819–1824) and territories in Burma (Myanmar). The Dutch ruler, living in exile in England (because of French occupation of his nation) authorized England to take control of overseas Dutch possessions. England agreed to restore the possession after the war. Local Dutch officials in Indonesia disliked this arrangement and continued to exercise their control in Ternate, Macassar, Palembang, and parts of Borneo. There was a temporary restoration of peace in 1802, and the English theoretically returned the territories to the Dutch. The creation of the kingdom of Holland (1806) under Louis Napoleon led to the reestablishment of English control over Dutch colonial possessions.

Thomas Stamford Raffles (1781–1826) was appointed English governor of Java. He reformed the administrative and judicial systems in Java. In Europe, the Napoleonic wars had come to a close with Napoleon's defeat and exile. Although Raffles was expected to leave Java in 1814, he remained there until 1816 hoping to convince his superiors to keep Java but was recalled. He was then placed in temporary charge of Melaka until it was returned to the Dutch in 1818. Raffles went on to establish an entrepôt in Singapore. In 1824, the Dutch exchanged Melaka with England for Bengkulu, a pepper port.

After the Napoleonic wars, the Dutch were fully restored in Java by 1830. They introduced the culture system to maximize production and profits. The culture system, also known as the cultivation system, was introduced by Governor Vanden Bosch. Under it, Javanese cultivators were compelled to set apart one-fifth of their land for the cultivation of commercial cash crops for export. The local chiefs were used to see that the laborers met their quota. Other aspects of the system, like assignment of land, transportation, and export, were handled by the Dutch. Native middlemen cooperated with the Dutch in exploiting the people and resources. Criticism of this government-sponsored system led to its abandonment in 1848 and the reintroduction of private enterprise in agriculture. Production increased phenomenally, but the natives did not benefit from this boom. Dutch domination of the Indonesian economy was total and complete.

The Russo-Japanese war of 1904–1905 and Russia's defeat at the hands of the Japanese encouraged the rise of nationalism throughout Asia, including Indonesia. Therefore, after the First World War, there were limited efforts to introduce local self-rule, such as the people's councils or Volksraad (1918). However, during the 1920s and 1930s, the growth of domestic radicalism met with resistance from Dutch authorities in the Netherlands as well as in Indonesia, rather than hastening the progress toward local autonomy.

A major nationalist movement of the 1920s had been Sarekat Islam ("Islamic Association"), which the Communists infiltrated. During the 1930s, the Dutch authorities turned down proposals for reform even as war broke out in Europe, and the Dutch government was forced into exile in Britain. Although the Netherlands hoped to keep Indonesia under its control indefinitely, the Japanese army was in Indonesia by 11 January 1942.

### The Japanese Occupation

The Japanese occupation of Southeast Asia (1942–1945) significantly changed the region in many ways. The Dutch East Indies surrendered to the Japanese in March 1942. The Japanese released imprisoned nationalist leaders like Sukarno and Muhammad Hatta (1902–1980, leader of the Indonesian independence movement, vice president of independent Indonesia). The Japanese attempted to win over the conquered people, and some nationalist leaders, hoping to advance the cause of Indonesian freedom, collaborated until they realized that the Japanese wanted to supplant Dutch colonialism with Japanese imperialism. The Japanese defeat of Dutch colonial rule, however, helped the growth of Indonesian nationalism.

**Independence and After (1949–1965)**

A few days after the Japanese surrendered on 17 August 1945, the Indonesians under Sukarno declared independence. Sukarno became the first president of the country. The Dutch were unwilling to grant independence, and, following on the heels of the British who had landed to disarm the Japanese, the Dutch returned to Indonesia. They took back much of Indonesia but could not completely crush the nationalists. With United Nations intervention, the Netherlands agreed to grant Indonesia independence on 27 December 1949.

The government under Sukarno could not handle the serious economic problems facing the country. Ethnic, religious, linguistic, and ideological divisions once kept in check by the desire to expel the Dutch reappeared shortly after independence. Revolts broke out in different parts of the country such as West Java, Kalimantan, south Sulawesi, and Sumatra. When people became disillusioned with Sukarno's leadership, he turned to a centralized system of government called guided democracy. Having dismissed the elected parliament (1960), he appointed a new one, which elected him president for life in 1963. His attempts to use the Communist partisans to shore up his support did not endear him to the army, which was anti-Communist.

Despite his poor record at home, Sukarno was influential in international relations. In 1955, he convened the first conference of twenty-four heads of state of the Afro-Asian countries at Bandung in West Java. The conference sought closer cooperation in economic, cultural, and political fields.

When the Dutch granted Indonesia its independence, their refusal to allow West New Guinea to become part of the new country was a source of conflict between Indonesia and the Netherlands. Indonesia threatened to use force to annex the contested territory. Finally The Netherlands agreed to hand over the territory to the UN for the Indonesians to administer. In a 1969 plebiscite in which around one thousand tribal elders voted, west Irians (Irian Jaya) agreed to become part of Indonesia, and the UN accepted that decision.

Irian Jaya was not the last of Indonesia's territorial problems. The creation of the new state of Malaysia, consisting of North Kalimantan (on Borneo), Sarawak, Malaya, and Singapore, earned Indonesia's ire. It vehemently opposed the new country as a British colonialist plot against Indonesia. In 1964, Sukarno sent his forces into the new country, but the British, with the help of the Malaysians, defeated them. In 1965, protesting the election of Malaysia as a permanent member of the U.N., Indonesia resigned from the world body. In 1975, Indonesia invaded and annexed East Timor. (In 1999, under a U.N.-sponsored referendum, East Timor voted to become independent. Unwillingly, Indonesia granted independence to the Timorese, which exacerbated secessionist tendencies in places like Aceh.)

**Suharto and the New Order**

In October 1965, thousands of people, perhaps as many as 500,000, perished in the reprisals of a leftist coup attempt by sections of the military. The Communists were blamed, but many innocent people were caught up in the violence. People of Chinese origin suffered most. Later, in March 1967, the parliament removed Sukarno from the presidency. Suharto became the acting president and in 1968 was appointed president. He remained in that capacity until political demonstrations, combined with economic problems, riots over food, international pressure, and the insistence of the Indonesian political and military elite, forced him out of office in May 1998.

During his presidency, Suharto (b. 1921) banned the Communist Party and embarked on a program to achieve economic recovery and political stability. Under Sukarno, the country had remained poor and backward, troubled by poverty, unemployment, and spiraling inflation. Suharto led the country back to the U.N., normalized relations with Malaysia, moved

Boys in Jakarta play next to a large painting of Sukarno, the first president of Indonesia, who ruled from 1945 to 1970. (SERGIO DORANTES/CORBIS)

Indonesia closer to the West, and joined with other Southeast Asian countries to form ASEAN in 1984. The government was able to reschedule its debt payment and to secure foreign loans through a consortium of Western countries, including the United States and the Netherlands. Foreign loans and investments and improvements in agriculture helped increase rice production. However, people in the outlying islands remained impoverished, and civil and political liberties and democratic institutions became casualties of the new order.

The fall of the Soviet Union in 1991 and the emergence of democratic governments in eastern Europe and in most Southeast Asian nations led Suharto to call for openness in his own country. Intellectuals, religious leaders, and even legislators began to air grievances long held back. The press began to report on a vast array of once forbidden subjects. The ruling dynasty and their business practices also were scrutinized. In 1993, when Suharto was reelected president for another five-year term, openness abruptly ended.

Repression, although neither massive nor widespread, continued. Reaction to it was expressed in many forms in different parts of the nation. In some places it led to Muslim-Christian clashes and to Muslim rioters burning churches in Java. Also during this period there was intense fighting between native Dayak people and the Javanese immigrants on the island of West Kalimantan. As a result, hundreds of people lost their lives. The protesters who turned against ethnic Chinese were angry about close cooperation between the military and the Chinese elite. Corruption, police brutality, and increased inequality in the distribution of wealth also caused resentment and protest.

On the political front, the rising popularity of the leader of the opposition Indonesian Democratic Party, Sukarno's daughter Megawati Sukarnoputri (b. 1947), invited the ire of Suharto. The government incited a faction of the party to conduct party elections without Megawati and expelled her from the party leadership. Megawati's supporters occupied the party office and refused to leave until she was reinstated. The military forcibly entered the party offices and evicted the occupiers, leading to the worst rioting in Jakarta's recent history.

In 1997 and 1998, Indonesia was caught up in the Asian economic crisis and faced severe economic troubles. Indonesian currency lost its value, the stock market fell, banks failed, and millions of people lost their jobs. Popular clamor for Suharto to step down reached feverish heights and led to violent protests in several major cities. In May 1998, Suharto resigned, and his vice president, B. J. Habibie (b. 1936), became president. In the elections held in June 1999, Megawati's party received the most votes in the house of representatives.

The following October, the people's consultative assembly elected Abdurrahman Wahid (b. 1940), the leader of the National Awakening Party, president and Megawati vice president. Wahid's tenure as president was short and tumultuous, marked by religious violence, secessionist revolts, and corruption charges. In July 2001, the People's Consultative Assembly removed Wahid from power and replaced him with Megawati, signaling a return to democratic government.

The return of democracy has not solved all of Indonesia's problems. Ethnic rivalries, religious animosities, and political squabbles continue to exist. Religious intolerance in some areas caused the torching of more than three hundred churches and the death of scores of people in the 1990s alone. Separatist tendencies exist in Aceh and Irian Jaya. Globalization continues to have its impact on the Indonesian economy. The military remains an important factor in domestic politics, and democracy is still fragile.

Nevertheless, Indonesia has come a long way; its infrastructure has improved; there are now many foreign businesses and investments; and many people's lives have improved. Indonesia has managed its oil revenues sensibly and has diversified the economy, so that it is not unduly dependent on oil revenue alone. As an active member of ASEAN, the country plays a key role in maintaining regional peace and stability. Despite its emphasis on developing closer ties to China and India, Indonesia continues to maintain good relations with Europe and North America.

*George Thadathil*

## Further Reading

Benda, Harry Jindrich. (1958) *The Crescent and the Rising Sun: Indonesian Islam under the Japanese Occupation, 1942–45.* The Hague, Netherlands: W. Van Howe.

Brown, Colin, and Robert Cribb. (1996) *Modern Indonesia: A History since 1945.* New York: Addison Wesley.

Cady, John F. (1964) *Southeast Asia: Its Historical Development.* New York: McGraw-Hill.

Dahm, Bernhard. (1971) *History of Indonesia in the Twentieth Century.* Trans. by P. S. Falla. New York: Praeger.

Friend, Theodore. (1988) *The Blue-Eyed Enemy: Japan against the West in Java and Luzon.* Princeton, NJ: Princeton University Press.

May, Brian. (1978) *The Indonesian Tragedy.* Boston: R&K Paul.

Ricklifs, M. C. (1981) *A History of Modern Indonesia: c. 1300 to the Present.* Bloomington, IN: Indiana University Press.

Schwartz, Adam. (1997) "Indonesia after Suharto." *Foreign Affairs* 76, 4: 119.

**INDONESIA—POLITICAL PARTIES** The origin of political parties in Indonesia dates back to the preindependence days of nationalist struggle against the Netherlands, which ruled Indonesia as the Dutch East Indies from the late seventeenth century until 1942, when the Japanese invaded during World War II. The PKI (Partai Komunis Indonesia, or Communist Party of Indonesia) of 1920 and PNI (Partai Nasional Indonesia, or Indonesian Nationalist Party, 1927) were major colonial-period parties. When Indonesia became independent in 1945, its constitution and the pluralist ideology of *Pancasila* (Five Principles, that is, nationalism, internationalism, consent, social justice, and belief in God) were accepted in principle by political parties. Personalities rather than ideology generally determine party affiliation.

### Political Parties under Sukarno

Sukarno (1901–1970), Indonesia's first president, held office from 1946 to 1967. In the early years of his presidency, liberal democracy and a multiparty environment were in the ascendancy. However, political instability caused the collapse of successive cabinets during this period, although the power of the president and the military was kept in check. The PNI, the Masjumi (Council of Indonesian Muslim Associations), the Indonesian Socialist Party (PSI), the PKI, and the Nahdatul Ulema (a party of Muslim scholars) were the major parties of the period. Their mutual wrangling made it difficult for party coalitions to function. Bitterness and ideological appeals marked the campaigns for the first general elections of 1955. The elections witnessed a broad party alignment: PNI and PKI on one side and the Masjumi and the Socialists on the other. The PNI fought for a state based on the ideal of *Pancasila*, whereas Masjumi's call was for an Islamic state. The PNI and the Masjumi shared fifty-seven seats in the newly elected parliament; the Nahdatul held forty-five, and the PKI held thirty-nine. With strong party discipline and maneuvering, PKI was thriving. When Sukarno later announced a change to "guided democracy," political parties were suppressed, and parliamentary democracy was nearly destroyed. In 1959 the presidential form of government was adopted, and the PSI and the Masjumi were banned the following year. A presidential decree on "party simplification" allowed just ten out of twenty-five parties to continue to function. The PNI, the PKI, and the Nahdatul Ulema were among those permitted to continue. Parliament members were nominated by Sukarno, so the parties did not have much power.

### Political Parties under Suharto

Suharto (b. 1921) acted as president from 1967 until 1998, when he was forced to resign. His New Order policy increased the membership of the House of Representatives from 347 to 460, with the president having the right to nominate 100 (later reduced to 75) members from the armed forces (ABRI). The members of three-fifths of the People's Consultative Assembly (Majelis Permusyawaratan, or MPR) were also to be selected by the president. The Golkar Party, which was composed of different groups, became the ruling party and Suharto's vehicle for holding power. Apart from Golkar, nine parties were allowed to participate in elections. In 1970 the two broad divisions of parties that were merged were the Group for Democracy and Development and the Group for Unity and Development. The 1971 elections were stage managed. The New Order was able to assure its position because opposition parties had so little power as to be almost defunct. In 1973 the opposition forces were merged into two parties: The four Islamic parties joined the Unity Development Party (PPP), and the remaining five parties joined the Indonesian Democratic Party (PDI). By the thwarting of the democratic process, Suharto was reelected in 1978, 1983, 1988, 1993, and 1998.

### Political Parties after Suharto

Since Suharto's resignation in May 1998, the office of president has been divested of much power, with a concomitant increase in the power of parliament and political parties. The earlier authoritarian regime, which ruled with government-dominated parties, has given way to a multiparty system. President Bacharuddin Jusuf Habibie (b. 1936), who served as president until 1999, lifted controls on political parties, and a special session of the MPR in November 1998 advanced the dates for elections to June 1999. The new laws allowed 48 out of the 150 parties that were formed since May 1998 to participate in the elections. The parties generally adhered to the principles of *Pancasila* and shared such common programs as provincial autonomy, clean administration, and elimination of corruption. The major difference between them seemed to be their attitude toward Islam. The nationalist parties clamored for a pluralist society and the Islamic parties advocated a religious framework. The PDI-P (Partai Demokrasi Indonesia-Perjuangan, or Indonesian Democracy Party-Struggle) of Sukarno's daughter, Megawati Sukarnoputri (b. 1947), drew support from nationalists, liberal Muslims, and minority groups. The PDI-P promoted a pluralist Indonesia, free market, and civil-military cooperation. The PKB (Partai Kebangkitan Bagsa, or National Awakening Party) epitomizing the views of Nahdatul Ulema chief Abdurrahman Wahid and its chairman, Matori Abdul Djalil, supported tolerance and accommodation befitting a diverse country. The PKB's main support was from eastern and central Java, with a sizable rural base and close rapport with PDI-P. The Golkar, led by Akbar Tanjung, faced an uphill task of winning the elections by legitimate means, but its secular credentials and money power were plus points in its favor. The former Muhammadiyah chairman, Amien Rais, led the major Muslim party PAN (Partai Amanat Nasional, or National Mandate Party). Amien, with a strong base in social and educational institutions of Muslims, advocated federalism, strong leadership, democracy, moderation, and reforms. The PPP (Partai Persatuan Pembangunan, or United Development Party) is an Islamic party chaired by Hamzah Haz. Another Islamic party, PBB (Partai Bulan Bintang, or Crescent Star Party), was established in July 1998. Its chairman, Yusril Ihza Mahendra, followed a pro-Muslim agenda. In the elections held in June 1999 for 462 seats of the House of Representatives, the PDI-P came out on top, winning 154 seats and securing 37.4 percent of the vote. Golkar came in second, with 20.9 percent of the vote and 120 seats. The breakdown for the others was PKB, 51 seats (17.4 percent); PPP, 58 seats (10.7 percent); PAN, 35 seats (7.3 percent); and, PBB 14 seats (1.8 percent). Megawati could not muster enough strength in the presidential elections of October 1999, and Wahid of the PKB became the president. Megawati was chosen as vice president.

The free and fair elections established parliamentary democracy. However, secessionist tendencies, ethnic violence, and economic problems plagued the new administration, and a day after the MPR voted to impeach Wahid in July 2001, Megawati was proclaimed president. Indonesia has democratized to a large extent and the role of political parties in the coming years will be crucial for the smooth functioning of democracy. Megawati showed political acumen after the 11 September terrorist crisis; the fundamentalists did not destabilize the nation, and nationalist parties rallied behind her. In the post-Taliban world, Indonesia can look ahead with renewed hope for a viable political process.

*Patit Paban Mishra*

*See also:* **Budi Utomo; Golkar; Indonesian Democratic Party; Indonesia—Political System; New Order; Old Order; Pancasila; Partai Persatuan Pembangunan; Sarekat Islam.**

### Further Reading

Alagappa, Muthiah, ed. (1995) *Political Legitimacy in Southeast Asia.* Stanford, CA: Stanford University Press.

Emmerson, Donald K., ed. (1999) *Indonesia beyond Suharto: Polity, Economy, Society, Transition.* New York: M. E. Sharpe.

Feith, Herbert. (1962) *The Decline of Constitutional Democracy in Indonesia.* Ithaca, NY: Cornell University Press.

## INDONESIA—POLITICAL SYSTEM

Although there have been dramatic changes to the Indonesian political system since the fall of President Suharto (b. 1921) in May 1998, Indonesia continues to operate under the constitution first promulgated by Indonesia's founding president, Sukarno (1901–1970), in 1945. The 1945 constitution, briefly surpassed by the 1950 constitution, which established a parliamentary system, was readopted in 1959, and a presidential system was returned to Indonesia. The presidential system remains to this day. While both the constitution and the Pancasila (the state philosophy) state that Indonesia must be a democratically governed country, the interpretation of what that means has changed over time. Elections held under Suharto (who ruled from 1966 to 1998) were not open to contest in Indonesia's "guided democracy," and the incumbent always won. Now the political system is marked by open political competition between parties and a greater separation of the three main branches of government—executive, legislature, and judiciary.

The constitution defines six organs of state: the Presidency, the People's Consultative Assembly (Majelis Permusyawaratan Rakyat, or MPR), the House of Representatives (Dewan Perwakilan Rakyat, or DPR), the Supreme Advisory Council (Dewan Pertimbangan Agung), the State Audit Board (Badan Pemeriksa Keuangan), and the Supreme Court (Mahkamah Agung).

### Executive Branch

Under the presidential system, the head of state has the power to initiate and give final approval to legislation and to appoint the cabinet. In a time of crisis, the president also can assume control over all of the functions of state. The president is appointed for a five-year term, but is now restricted to serving no more than two terms. If the president is incapacitated or removed, he or she is automatically succeeded by the vice president. The MPR is the highest constitutional body in Indonesia and has the power to appoint and dismiss the executive (the latter with a two-thirds majority), as well as to decide amendments to the constitution (also with a two-thirds majority). Sometimes described as an "upper house," the MPR consists of 700 representatives, who are drawn from the "lower house," or DPR (500); regional representatives (135); and "functional representatives" (65) appointed by the electoral commission. The MPR must meet at least once every five

## THE PANCASILA

On 1 June 1945 President Sukarno of Indonesia set forth the Pancasila (Pantja Sila), the five principles that form the ideological basis of the Indonesian state.

> Now that I have dealt with the question of Freedom, and Independence, I will proceed to deal with the question of principles . . .
>
> The First Principle, which is to be the foundation of Our State of Indonesia, is the *principle of Nationalism*. . . .
>
> Briefly speaking, the people of Indonesia, the Indonesian nation are not the group of individuals who, having *"le désir d'être ensemble,"* live in a small area like Minangkabau or Madura or Djokja or Pasundan or Makassar; no, the Indonesian people are those human beings who, according to God-ordained geo-politics, live throughout the entity of the entire archipelago of Indonesia from the northern tip of Sumatra to Papua! All, throughout the islands! Because amongst these seventy million human beings there exists already *"le désir d'être ensemble,"* the *"Charactergemeinschaft."* The Indonesian nation, the people of Indonesia, the Indonesian human beings which number seventy millions who have united to become one, and form one single entity . . .
>
> We must not only establish the State of Free Indonesia, but we should also aim at making one family out of all nations of the world. This is the Second Principle of my philosophy of State, the *Principle of Internationalism*. But when I say "internationalism," I do not mean cosmopolitanism, for this negates nationalism, denies the existence of such nations as Indonesia, Japan, Burma, England, America, and so on. Internationalism cannot flower if it is not rooted in the soil of nationalism. Nationalism cannot flower if it does not grow within the garden of internationalism. . . .
>
> What is the Third Principle? This is the *Principle of Consent*, the *Principle of Representative Government*. We are to establish a State "all for all," "one for all, all for one," not a State for the wealthy. . . . Allah, God of the Universe, gave us the capacity to think, so that in our daily intercourse we might constantly burnish our thoughts. Just as the pounding and husking of paddy results in our getting rice, our best food, argument and discussion in our daily intercourse results in the clarification of our thoughts.
>
> The Fourth Principle I am proposing is the *Principle of Prosperity*, the principle: that there be no poverty in free Indonesia. . . . The democracy we are seeking is not the democracy of the west, but a politico—economic democracy, which will result in the good life and social prosperity. . . . The people know what it is not to have enough to eat nor enough to wear, and now wish to create a new world of justice in accordance with the precepts of Ratu Adil. . . .
>
> Thus, the people's assembly to be established must not be a body for the discussion of political democracy only, but a body which is to translate into reality the two principles: *Political Justice* and *Social Justice*. . . .
>
> The Fifth Principle should be the recognition of the *Divine Omnipotence*, the organization of Free Indonesia on the basis of *Belief in God*. . . . The Christian should worship God according to the teachings of Jesus Christ. Moslems according to the teaching of the Prophet Mohammed, Buddhists should discharge their religious rites according to their own books. . . .
>
> Hence, if the people of Indonesia desire that the Pantja Sila I propose become a reality . . . we must not forget the condition for its realization, viz. struggle, struggle, and once again, struggle! . . . If the people of Indonesia are not united, not determined to live or die for freedom, this freedom will never come to the Indonesian people, never, until the end of time. Freedom and independence can only be won and enjoyed by a people when the soul is aflame with the determination of "MERDEKA- FREEDOM or DEATH!"

*Source: Indonesian Review*. (n.d.) Vol. 1, no. 1. Jakarta.

## THE PREAMBLE TO THE CONSTITUTION OF INDONESIA

Whereas freedom is the inalienable right of all nations, colonialism must be abolished in this world as it is not in conformity with humanity and justice;

And the moment of rejoicing has arrived in the struggle of the Indonesian freedom movement to guide the people safely and well to the threshold of the independence of the state of Indonesia which shall be free, united, sovereign, just and prosperous;

By the grace of God Almighty and impelled by the noble desire to live a free national life, the people of Indonesia hereby declare their independence.

Subsequent thereto, to form a government of the state of Indonesia which shall protect all the people of Indonesia and their entire native land, and in order to improve the public welfare, to advance the intellectual life of the people and to contribute to the establishment of a world order based on freedom, abiding peace and social justice, the national independence of Indonesia shall be formulated into a constitution of the sovereign Republic of Indonesia which is based on the belief in the One and Only God, just and humanity, the unity of Indonesia, democracy guided by the inner wisdom of deliberations amongst representatives and the realization of social justice for all of the people of Indonesia.

*Source:* Department of Information, Indonesia. Retrieved 8 March 2002, from: http://asnic.utexas.edu/asnic/countries/indonesia/ConstIndonesia.html.

years to appoint the president, although special sessions can be called by the DPR. Since the fall of Suharto, a precedent or convention has developed of holding an MPR session annually (known as *Sidang Tahunan*). So far those sessions have been landmark events and have typically called for the president to account for the government's actions over the past year. In the 2000 session, President Abdurrahman Wahid (b.1940) felt compelled to offer an apology to this body for the shortcomings of his administration. A "special session" of the MPR can also be called by the DPR. On 23 July 2001, a special session ended the presidency of Wahid and overwhelmingly selected his vice president, Megawati Sukarnoputri (b. 1946) to assume the role of executive. This represents a much-changed body politic from the more authoritarian days of President Suharto.

### Legislative Branch

The 500-member DPR is elected by popular vote, with the exception of the sixty-eight seats reserved for army and police appointees. The DPR, largely a powerless rubber-stamping institution until 1998, has now taken a crucial role in the creation and approval of legislation. Legislation must gain DPR assent (in tandem with presidential approval), and the DPR can also initiate bills.

Indonesia's freest elections since 1955 were held in June 1999. Elections for the 462 elected seats in the DPR are regarded by observers as the most complex in the world. Indonesia operates a system of proportional representation, uniquely combining it with elements of a district system. Seats gained in the DPR are determined at the provincial, not the national, level. Thus, for electoral purposes, Indonesia is split into component provinces. While the allocation of seats is broadly based on population numbers, the electoral law also stipulates that there must be a minimum of one seat at the rural *(kabupaten)* and city *(kotamadya)* district level. At the time of the 1999 election, Indonesia's then 27 provinces had 327 *kabupaten* and *kotamadya*. The rest of the 135 elected seats were allocated on the basis of population, to give provinces of higher population density a fairer representation—although this did not completely solve the problem. The number of seats a party receives is determined by the number of votes it obtains in each province. Once the number of DPR members for a given party is determined, based on its proportion of the vote for a given province, the central committee of that party then has the sole decision over who should be chosen to sit in the DPR.

The 1999 election was a strong endorsement for the Indonesia Democratic Party-Struggle (*Partai* Demokrasi Indonesia-Perjuangan, or PDI-P) of Megawati Sukarnoputri, the daughter of Sukarno and the current president, which gained nearly 34 percent of the vote. The Golkar Party, Suharto's party while he was president, was its nearest rival, with almost 22.5 percent of the vote. Most of the remaining seats were won by Islamic parties. Support for Megawati did not translate into gaining the presidency in 1999, as Wahid, from the small National Awakening Party, was able to coalesce with all the other parties during the 1999 MPR session to obtain the presidency. This was very controversial in Indonesia and has led to discussion on switching to a system whereby the president is directly elected by the voters.

## The Judicial Branch

The judiciary, established constitutionally as a separate arm of government, was in practice unable to challenge the wishes of the Suharto regime. However, even under a democratizing Indonesia, the courts struggle to revive their reputation and free themselves from past government and corporate collusion. The final court of appeal is the Supreme Court, with High Courts in provincial capitals, and District Courts beneath that. The Indonesian legal system, largely based on an antiquated code inherited from the Dutch, is placed into four distinct juridical spheres: the general court deals with criminal and civil issues; the religious court *(pangadilan agama)* applies to all Muslims (and only Muslims) in the family matters of marriage, divorce, and inheritance; the court martial for military discipline; and the administrative court for bureaucratic issues. This formal structure exists alongside more traditional notions of legality, known as *hukum adat* (traditional law), which varies markedly throughout Indonesia. There is no constitutional court in Indonesia, the MPR being the sole decision maker on constitutional issues.

## Provincial Level

Indonesia is now formally divided into thirty-two provinces, after the creation of new provinces since the 1999 election, although a division of the old Irian Jaya Province into three provinces is not operational, so the effective number is actually thirty. Three of these provinces are given a different status under Indonesia law: the two special provinces *(daerah istemewa)* of Yogyakarta and Aceh and the capital city of Jakarta *(daerah khusus ibukota)*. Below the provincial level there are now some four hundred districts. Recent plans to devolve governmental authority in such matters as schooling, health, transport, and roads, as well as in some aspects of economic planning, are centered on these districts. Indonesia has deliberately avoided any devolution of power to the thirty-two provinces on the

Students demonstrate near parliament in Jakarta in October 1999. They are calling for the military to end its involvement in Indonesian politics. (AFP/CORBIS)

grounds that this may lead to federalism—and the current government wishes to retain the unitary state structure.

**Movement toward Democracy**

Despite remaining based on a constitution it inherited from more authoritarian times, Indonesia has had since 1998 a genuine separation of powers, notably between the president and parliament. While Indonesia is not yet a consolidated democracy, it has democratized to a large degree. Parliament regularly critiques the president, while a newly freed media and an emerging civil society expose government to rigorous scrutiny.

*Anthony L. Smith*

**Further Reading**

Eklof, Stefan. (1999) *Indonesian Politics in Crisis: The Long Fall of Suharto, 1996–98*. Copenhagen, Denmark: NIAS.

Emmerson, Donald K., ed. (1999) *Indonesia beyond Suharto: Polity, Economy, Society, Transition.* New York: M. E. Sharpe.

Grayson, Lloyd, and Shannon Smith. (2001) *Indonesia Today: Challenges of History*. Singapore: Institute of Southeast Asian Studies.

Manning, Chris, and Peter van Dierman, eds. (2000) *Indonesia in Transition: Social Aspects of Reformasi and Crisis.* Singapore: Institute of Southeast Asian Studies.

Schwarz, Adam. (1999) *A Nation in Waiting: Indonesia's Search for Stability*. 2d ed. St. Leonards, Australia: Allen & Unwin.

Smith, Anthony L. (2001) "Indonesia: Transforming the Leviathan." In *Government and Politics in Southeast Asia,* edited by John Funston. Singapore: Institute of Southeast Asian Studies.

Van Dijk, Kees. (2001) *A Country in Despair: Indonesia between 1997 and 2000.* Leiden, Netherlands: KITLV (Royal Institute of Linguistics and Anthropology) Press.

Vatikiotis, Michael. (1998) *Indonesian Politics under Suharto: The Rise and Fall of the New Order*. 3d ed. New York: Routledge.

## INDONESIA-MALAYSIA RELATIONS

Indonesia-Malaysia relations are marked by normalized ties and general cordiality, albeit with a troubled past and some contemporary bilateral difficulties.

**Natural Affinities**

The majority of people in both countries are the descendants of early Austronesian peoples who have interacted with each other over maritime Southeast Asia's various trade routes since ancient times. The Malay peoples of Malaysia have close kinship, cultural, and linguistic ties with, predominantly, the Indonesian peoples of Sumatra, Java, Kalimantan, Sulawesi, and other islands. The Sumatran-based Srivijaya empire (c. eighth to c. fourteenth century) held sway over both sides of the Malacca Strait. The national languages of Malaysia and Indonesia, respectively, Malay *(Bahasa Melayu)* and Indonesian *(Bahasa Indonesia)*, share a common root in the Malay tongue, and despite some divergence are still largely mutually intelligible. Indonesia by far the largest country in Southeast Asia, has a population of 220 million, while the more developed, middle-income Malaysia has a population of just over 22 million.

**Postindependence Relations**

Postindependence relations between Indonesia and Malaysia were immediately marked by conflict. Indonesia under founding president Sukarno (1901–1970) viewed the establishment of the Federation of Malaysia, which included Malaya, Singapore, and former British Borneo (Sarawak and Sabah) on 16 September 1963 as an extension of colonial rule. Sukarno announced that he would "crush Malaysia" and launched a military campaign in Borneo known as Konfrontasi (the Confrontation). The conflict lasted until 1965 (although formally wound down in 1966) and in the latter stages included attacks on peninsular Malaysia and Singapore. When General Suharto (b. 1921) seized effective power in Jakarta in 1965, one of his first initiatives was to bring the conflict to an end in the interests of pursuing normalized relations with Malaysia, and he generally took a less radical foreign policy path than Sukarno.

The end of Konfrontasi paved the way for the establishment of the Association of Southeast Asian Nations (ASEAN), in which Indonesia and Malaysia were founding members alongside the Philippines, Singapore, and Thailand. Although Sukarno had pursued anticolonial policies, the Suharto regime saw Communism as the paramount threat to Indonesia, and relations with its non-Communist neighbors were seen as crucial to regional confidence and stability. The countries within ASEAN agreed to the principle of noninterference in each other's affairs and to renounce any claims to territory legally held by another member state (this was later formally adopted in ASEAN's Treaty of Amity and Cooperation—TAC). Subordination to this framework effectively pacified relations between Indonesia and Malaysia, and this remains the case to this day. Indonesia, for its part, discouraged supernationalists, who had, since Indonesia's declaration of independence in 1945, promoted Indonesia Raya (Greater Indonesia) that would include all Malay and related peoples. Malaysia has refused to become embroiled in

Indonesia's domestic and regional difficulties, most notably in Aceh (situated in northern Sumatra and quite close to the Malaysian peninsula), where Malaysia has continued to recognize Indonesia's state boundaries. However, given the proximity and the ties of ethnicity and sympathy of some within the Malaysian community to Aceh, stopping all lines of supply from private Malaysian channels to the Acehnese independence movement has proved difficult.

## Current Tensions

The relationship since the end of Konfrontasi has been marked by a degree of rivalry and elements of bilateral tension. There is contention over the ownership of two islands near the Sabah-Kalimantan coast—Ligitan and Sipadan. Much of the border between Kalimantan and East Malaysia is also poorly demarcated, although some progress has been made to establish part of the boundary. On two occasions (1997 and 2001) in recent years, the Malaysian authorities have had to close the border with Kalimantan because of uncontrolled ethnic violence on the Indonesian side in which elements of the Dayak community (which straddles both sides of the Borneo island) have committed acts of violence against transmigrants from other parts of Indonesia.

Although many Indonesians have entered Malaysia legally, looking to undertake employment in the domestic help and service industries, the porous land and sea boundaries have seen even larger numbers of Indonesians traveling to Malaysia through unofficial channels. It is thought that around 1 million Indonesian currently reside illegally in Malaysia. Although large numbers of these people, given the racial, cultural, religious, and linguistic similarities, have integrated themselves, often through intermarriage, into almost every Malay village and community in Malaysia, there has also been some tension with the Indonesian migrants. The presence of so many Indonesians in Malaysian society in relatively peaceful times is a sobering lesson for the Malaysian authorities about the vast numbers of Indonesians that could potentially flood Malaysia if Indonesia becomes a lot more turbulent.

In recent years Malaysia's proximity to Indonesia has made it the victim of a new hazard. In 1997, out-of-control forest fires in Sumatra and Kalimantan (later proven to be the work of large Indonesian conglomerates clearing land for plantations) saw air pollution levels rise to extremely unsafe levels in Malaysia and Singapore, and to a lesser extent Thailand. President Suharto felt compelled to apologize for the fires of 1997, and yet the same problem returned in 1998, and to a lesser extent every subsequent year during the dry season. The response of Malaysia and other affected countries has been twofold. First, with other ASEAN member nations, it subjected Indonesia to heavy criticism and joined in pressuring Indonesia to implement a "zero burning policy" in the affected regions. Second, with Singapore it gave technical assistance to help monitor "hot spots" and effectively combat them.

In the past, both countries have sought regional and Third World leadership, but in quite different ways. Indonesia has been very active in Third World forums, such as the Nonaligned Movement (NAM) and G-77. While Malaysia is an aligned state (through the Five-Power Defence Arrangements, or FPDA), the current prime minister, Mahathir Mohamad (b. 1925), has been harshly critical of the West. Elements of the Indonesian government have questioned the need for Malaysia's membership in FPDA, which links Malaysia to Australia, Britain, New Zealand, and Singapore. Indonesia's long-term goal is to remove extraregional powers from the Southeast Asian region, which it considers its own backyard. Indonesia has also been far less critical than the Malaysian leadership of internationalism and of such bodies as APEC (Asia Pacific Economic Cooperation). Differences in domestic politics have also been minor irritants. While Malaysia's prime minister has been critical of Indonesia's attempt at democracy, Indonesian officials, including the president, have openly met with Malaysian opposition figures visiting Indonesia (most notably Wan Izizah, who visited Indonesia in 2000 after the imprisonment of her husband, Anwar Ibrahim). Malaysia has asked Indonesia not to become involved in its domestic politics, deeming such involvement to be undue "interference"; however, Indonesian officials do not view such involvement as undue interference given the active multiparty environment they now must negotiate in their own country. These differences, while at times presenting bilateral difficulties, have not undermined the relationship to any significant extent.

*Anthony L. Smith*

## Further Reading

Acharya, Amitav. (2000) *The Quest for Identity: International Relations of Southeast Asia*. Singapore: Oxford University Press.

———. (2001) *Constructing a Security Community in Southeast Asia: ASEAN and the Problem of Regional Order*. New York: Routledge.

Smith, Anthony L. (2000) *Strategic Centrality: Indonesia's Changing Role in ASEAN*. Singapore: Institute of Southeast Asian Studies.

**INDONESIA–UNITED STATES RELATIONS** Indonesian leadership has long held a consensus about foreign policy, conditioned by needs of the country dating from the beginning of the struggle for independence in 1945. Indonesia has sought to be active in regional affairs without getting involved in conflict among major powers. Relations between Indonesia and the United States have fluctuated with the times and have generally, though not always, been cordial.

As conflict with the Dutch continued during the revolutionary period, Indonesia developed an anti-Western attitude, seeing Asian events as a struggle against Western imperialism. The United States was generally sympathetic to the Indonesian cause, giving it de facto recognition on 23 April 1947. Indonesia's first president, Sukarno (1901–1970), followed a policy of nonalignment while aspiring for a larger role in international affairs; he also became aggressively opposed to the West. The United States was neutral in the Dutch-Indonesian conflict concerning the status of Irian Jaya, and late in his incumbency Sukarno became markedly anti-American.

### Relations during the Suharto Era

The ascension of Suharto (b. 1921) in 1967 changed all this, and relations with the United States became warm. Indonesia was vital to U.S.-Asian security interests because of its importance as a regional power and oil-producing nation and its strategic location at the entrance of the Indian Ocean.

Though Indonesia has entered into no military alliances, it has received military assistance from the United States since 1950, with breaks in the 1965–1966 period. The military equipment grant, used for communication systems, internal security, and so forth, averaged $13 million per year up to 1978. The International Military Education and Training (IMET) program trained four thousand Indonesian military personnel between 1950 and 1992. Since 1974, Indonesia has received Foreign Military Sales (FMS) credits for purchasing military equipment. In the U.S. House International Relations Committee meeting of 7 May 1998, it was revealed that U.S. Special Operations Forces had trained elite Indonesian Kopassus special forces at a cost of $3.5 million. These forces were active against the political opponents of the government.

Presidents Sukarno and Kennedy at Andrews Air Force base in Maryland on 24 April 1961. (BETTMANN/CORBIS)

Indonesia and the United States have been involved in various multilateral organizations promoting international peace, nuclear disarmament, and economic development. Both are members of the ASEAN Regional Forum (ARF) and Asia Pacific Economic Cooperation (APEC), and Indonesia's effort to restore democracy in Cambodia and mediate in disputes concerning the South China Sea have been appreciated by the United States.

Some discord did, however, arise in bilateral relations between Jakarta and Washington in the 1990s. The United States did not support Indonesia's claim over the straits linking the Indian and Pacific Oceans and opposed Jakarta's promotion of an ASEAN nuclear-free zone. There were differences too over the issue of intellectual property rights, and under the Generalized System of Preferences (GSP) legislation, Indonesia was criticized for not meeting recognized labor standards. The U.S. Congress suspended IMET grants after Indonesian security forces killed East Timorese demonstrators in November 1991; these grants were partially restored in 1995. The United States also favored the peaceful resolution of the East Timor problem, and many Americans saw to it that U.S. policy toward Indonesia depended on the latter's actions in East Timor. The United States and nongovernmental organizations vehemently criticized human-rights violations, and U.S. president Bill Clinton announced suspension of U.S.-Indonesian military relations on 9 September 1999. Many perceived the United States as supporting secessionist forces, and anti-American demonstrations were held.

### Relations in the Post-Suharto Era

Relations improved after Abdurrahman Wahid became president and visited the United States (10–12 November 1999). President Clinton welcomed him, stressing the territorial integrity of Indonesia and the importance of building an ongoing partnership with a democratic country. The new Indonesian president, Megawati Sukarnoputri, supported the United States after the brutal events of 11 September 2001, becoming the first Islamic leader to visit the United States and meet U.S. president George W. Bush (19 September 2001) in the wake of the attack. She was receptive to U.S. appeals for assistance in antiterrorist measures but cautioned the U.S. president against any action that could be construed as revenge against Muslims.

### U.S.-Indonesian Economic Relations

The United States has long had commercial and economic interests in Indonesia, and Indonesia received $146.3 million in economic assistance and $377.2 million in credit from the United States between 1950 and 1961. The U.S. Agency for International Development (USAID) has given assistance in health care, family planning, rice production, and overseas training programs. It also provided financial and technical aid during the mid-1980s oil crisis. U.S. investors dominate mining and oil sector projects, and U.S. banks, service providers, and manufacturers began expanding in Indonesia after the reforms of the 1980s.

During the Asian economic crisis that began in 1997, Indonesia received aid from the United States, among other bilateral donors. The U.S. president urged Suharto in January 1998 to follow the International Monetary Fund (IMF) plan to mitigate the crisis. New schemes were launched to help Indonesia. A USAID program totaling $520 million was directed toward economic reform and public welfare, and Indonesia received another $450 million through other programs. USAID also made $70 million in the form of medical supplies and small construction projects available for rural people in eastern Indonesia. U.S. technical personnel came to implement economic reforms, and USAID supported democratization and civil society development activities through nongovernmental organizations. Temporary work permits were issued to Indonesian students of U.S. universities, and the U.S.-ASEAN Business Council provided financial assistance to Indonesian students so they could finish their courses. However, pouring billions of dollars of U.S. aid into Indonesia under the Suharto regime was criticized; it was felt that the beneficiaries were large corporations and members of the armed forces and Suharto's family.

Since the establishment of diplomatic relations in December 1949, Indonesia and the United States have passed through phases of understanding as well as discord. Indonesia remains vitally important to U.S. interests, both as a key to Southeast Asian security and as a moderate nation with the world's largest Muslim population. U.S. economic assistance and support of Indonesia's territorial integrity will continue to mark the relations between the two nations as primarily cordial.

*Patit Paban Mishra*

### Further Reading

Emmerson, Donald K., ed. (1999) *Indonesia beyond Suharto: Polity, Economy, Society, Transition.* New York: M. E. Sharpe.

Gardner, Paul. (1996) *Shared Hopes, Separate Fears: Fifty Years of US-Indonesian Relations.* Boulder, CO: Westview Press.

Kees, Van Dijk. (2001) *A Country in Despair: Indonesia between 1997 and 2000.* Leiden, Netherlands: KITLV Press.

Leifer, Michael. (1983) *Indonesia's Foreign Policy.* Boston and London: Allen & Unwin.

McMahon, Robert J. (1981) *Colonialism and Cold War: The United States and the Struggle for Indonesian Independence, 1945–49.* Ithaca, NY: Cornell University Press.

Suryadinata, Leo. (1996) *Indonesia's Foreign Policy under Suharto: Aspiring to International Leadership.* Singapore: Times Academic Press.

## INDONESIAN DEMOCRATIC PARTY

In 1973, the Indonesian new Order government merged all existing political parties into two: the United Development Party (PPP) and the Indonesian Democratic Party (PDI), which were allowed to form a kind of alibi "opposition" to Golkar (acronym for Golongan Karya, "functional groups"), the electoral vehicle of the government. Whereas the PPP contained four Muslim parties, the PDI incorporated the Indonesian National Party, two Christian parties, the leftist Murba, and the army-backed Association Supporting the Independence of Indonesia. The growing alienation between the then president Suharto (1921–1998) and the military over Suharto's benign attitude toward moderate strands within resurgent Islam led to Suharto's tacit support for the Christian-backed PDI, nationalist and secular in outlook, in the 1987 general elections.

In 1993, the daughter of the former president Sukarno, Megawati Sukarnoputri (b. 1947), was elected to the PDI Party chair. Her popularity led the regime to have her ousted from party leadership in 1996. This resulted in the schism between the legal PDI and the illegal Party Fighting for Indonesian Democracy (PDI-P), the latter being led by Megawati. A few months after Suharto's demise in May 1998, Megawati and her PDI-P were massively supported in a congress in Bali. Her party emerged as the winner of the general elections in June 1999. Four months later, in October, Megawati was elected as vice president of Indonesia.

*Martin Ramstedt*

### Further Reading

Cribb, Robert, and Colin Brown. (1995) *Modern Indonesia: A History since 1945*. New York: Longman.

Emmerson, Donald K. (1999) *Indonesia beyond Suharto: Polity, Economy, Society, Transition*. London: East Gate Book, with the Asia Society.

Forrester, Geoff. (1999) *Post-Soeharto Indonesia: Renewal or Chaos?* Singapore: Institute of Southeast Asian Studies.

Pompe, Sebastiaan. (1999) *De Indonesische Algemene Verkiezingen* (Indonesian General Elections). Leiden, Netherlands: KITLV Uitgeverij.

Vatikiotis, Michael R. J. (1993) *Indonesian Politics under Suharto*. New York: Routledge.

**INDONESIAN REVOLUTION** On 17 August 1945, three days after the Japanese forces occupying Indonesia had surrendered to the Allies, Sukarno and Muhammad Hatta proclaimed independence and established the Republic of Indonesia. However, it took five years of guerrilla warfare and diplomatic efforts to establish unchallenged independence.

British troops arrived in Java in September 1945, followed by the Dutch governor-general Van Mook. Dutch efforts to regain control resulted in bitter fighting and the archipelago was divided between Republican-held territory and land reoccupied by the Dutch with British help. The Republican government made diplomatic efforts, entering into the Linggarjati Agreement in November 1946. According to this agreement, ratified on 25 March 1947, the Dutch recognized Republic of Indonesia sovereignty over Java, Sumatra, and Madura, while the Republic agreed to join with the Dutch-created regional states to form the United States of Indonesia.

In July 1947, the Dutch, claiming Republican interference with rice shipments, launched a full-scale attack, the so-called first "police action." Australia and India proposed a cease-fire and the U.N. became involved. In January 1948, the Renville Agreement was signed, instituting a truce and proposing a plebiscite. The Dutch, however, blockaded Republican territory, and in December again attacked the Republic in the second "police action." The Republic's capital, Yogyakarta, was captured and Sukarno and Muhammad Hatta allowed themselves to be arrested to help galvanize world opinion. Indonesian guerrilla forces armed with primitive weapons fought bravely, and the resistance became a people's war. Even in Dutch-held territory, the colonial army was forced to retreat to urban areas. World reaction was sharp, and Indian premier Jawaharlal Nehru convened the Asian Conference on Indonesia in January 1949, urging the U.N. to intervene. The Security Council ordered an immediate cease-fire, and the Dutch government, bowing to international pressure and popular resistance, entered into negotiations. The Hague Agreement of 27 December 1949 transferred sovereignty to the Indonesian Federal Government consisting of the Republic and fifteen Dutch-created states. By 17 August 1950 the, the Dutch-created states of the Federation had joined the Republic, and the unitary state of the Republic of Indonesia was restored as originally proclaimed five years previously.

Adroit Republican diplomacy, internationalization of the issue, guerrilla warfare, and popular desire for independence foiled Dutch attempts to restore colonial rule. The revolution has become integral to Indonesian consciousness, and *Merdeka* (freedom) has acquired a special meaning.

*Patit Paban Mishra*

### Further Reading

Neill, Wilfred T. (1973) *Twentieth-Century Indonesia*. New York: Columbia University Press.

Ricklefs, M. C. (1993) *A History of Modern Indonesia: c.1300 to the Present*. 2d ed. Stanford, CA: Stanford University Press.

**INDORE** (2001 pop. 1.8 million). Indore is the largest city of Madhya Pradesh state in central India. It is situated on the banks of the Saraswati and the Khan rivers and derives its name from the eighteenth-century temple of Sangamnath, or Indreshwar, located at the confluence of the two rivers.

Indore's importance developed from its location on the route the Maratha guerrilla warriors of the Deccan took to North India. The Marathas were constantly battling against the Mughal empire (1526–1857). Their army transit camps drew the local zamindars (landlords) who, attracted by trade possibilities, settled in the villages at the confluence of the Khan and Saraswati rivers. The city grew rapidly under the Holkar dynasty (1733–1818). It became the capital of the Indore state in 1818, after the British forces defeated the Holkars. Between 1948 and 1956, Indore served as the summer capital of the former Madhya Bharat state.

Indore today is the commercial capital of Madhya Pradesh. It has the fourth largest cotton textile industry in the nation. Besides iron and steel, chemicals and machinery are also manufactured here. It is also famous for its oilseed extraction industry and manufacture of confectionery, paper, machine tools and accessories, and electronic goods. It also has one of the largest transshipment centers for truck transport.

*Sanjukta Das Gupta*

### Further Reading

Dhar, Shailendra Nath. (1936). *The Indore State and its Vicinity*. Indore, India: Indian Science Congress.

Research, Reference, and Training Division, Government of India. (2001) *India 2001: A Reference Annual*. New Delhi, India: Publications Division, Ministry of Information and Broadcasting.

## INDUS RIVER

The 3,180 kilometer–long Indus River, anciently called the Sindhu (whence our word Hindu) and mentioned as such by Greek writers, is the major river of Pakistan, running throughout the length of the country. It begins in Tibet in the glaciers of the Kailas Range (where it is known as the Xiquan He), passing through Ladakh, Kashmir, Punjab, and Sind before emptying into the Arabian Sea in a level, muddy delta near Karachi. Although this delta is little cultivated, the broad river plain was the locus of the Indus Valley civilization (also called the Harappan or Mohenjo Daro civilization). Geological research has shown that the lower course of the river has changed often; such a change is one possible explanation for the end of that civilization.

The Himalayan sections of the river's course present some of the most impressive scenery in the world, particularly where it cuts through the Ladakh Range about 160 kilometers above Leh. In this region the Indus derives from three tributaries coming out of the Kailas glaciers. The northernmost of these tributaries forms the road from Leh to the Jhalung goldfields, and the southern one forms the ancient trade route from Ladakh to Lhasa and on to China.

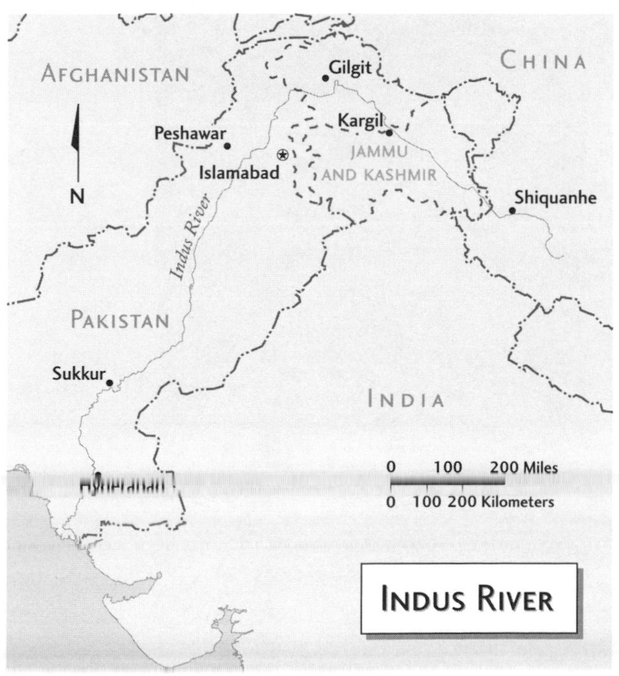


The river is navigable by small craft as far as Hyderabad in Pakistan. A modern dam at Sukkur supplies irrigation and electric power. Another vast dam is under construction at Tarbela, near Gilgit in the disputed area of Azad Kashmir. The drainage basin of the Indus has been computed at 963,400 square kilometers.

*Paul Hockings*

### Further Reading

Meadows, Azra, and Peter Meadows, eds. (1999) *The Indus River: Biodiversity, Resources, Humankind*. Oxford and New York: Oxford University Press.

Moorhouse, Geoffrey. (1984) *To the Frontier*. New York: Holt, Rinehart & Winston.

Murphy, Dervla. (1977) *Where the Indus Is Young: A Winter in Baltistan*. London: Century Hutchinson Ltd.

## INDUS RIVER DOLPHIN

The Indus River dolphin *(Platanista minor)*, known in Pakistan as the *susu*, is sometimes called the "blind dolphin" because its eyes lack lenses. This virtual blindness, scientists speculate, is due to the high silt content of its river habitat. The dolphin relies on a highly developed system of echolocation (using sound waves to locate prey) to navigate and hunt for fish.

The Indus River dolphin is a separate species from the Ganges River dolphin *(Platanista gangetica)*. It is 2 to 2.5 meters long and weighs 80 to 90 kilograms. A freshwater cetacean (aquatic mammal), the dolphin is an endangered species, having a population of about 675 in the mid-1990s. The dolphin is fully protected in Pakistan; in 1974 the Indus River Dolphin Reserve was established on the Indus River from the Sukkur Barrage to the Guddu Barrage in Sind Province in Pakistan. About 500 dolphins live in Sind Province, and about 175 live in Punjab Province. Despite legal protection, since the 1930s the dolphins have been threatened by the construction of dams throughout the Indus River system, which have degraded their habitat and impeded migration. The dams have also separated the dolphins into several small groups, which threatens the genetic diversity of the population. Occasionally, the dolphins are accidentally caught in fishing nets.

*Eric A. Strahorn*

### Further Reading

Carpino, Elizabeth. (1994) *River Dolphins—Can They Be Saved?* IRN Working Paper no. 4. Berkeley, CA: International Rivers Network.

"Dolphin." (1986) *Encyclopedia of Indian Natural History*. New Delhi: Oxford University Press.

Meadows, Azra, and Peter S. Meadows, eds. (1999) *The Indus River: Biodiversity, Resources, Humankind.* Karachi, Pakistan: Oxford University Press.

## INDUSTRY—WEST ASIA

Industry is a fundamental economic sector for West Asian nations (Iran, Iraq, and Turkey) nowadays. Since the end of the 1980s, the main sources of industrial growth in the region are local and foreign investments and the dynamism of the private sector. In the 1990s, industry contributed between 25 and 35 percent to the gross national product (GNP) of the West Asian nations and employed approximately 25 percent of their labor forces.

### Industrial Resources

West Asia has a wide range of mineral resources. Petroleum is the most important subterranean asset, found in large amounts in Iran and Iraq. These two nations are among the main producers and exporters of oil in the world. The remaining oil reserves of Iraq and Iran are estimated at 126 and 108 billion barrels, respectively. With Russia, Iran has the world's largest reserves of natural gas. Turkey has no known extensive petroleum resources, but it has large deposits of high-grade bituminous coal, which lies along the Black Sea coast, with Zonguldak as the chief mining center. Poor-quality coal is found in various locations in West Asia.

West Asia's ores are associated predominantly with the geologic fold of the Taurus and Elburz Mountains. Turkey and Iran have commercial quantities of chromites, West Asia's second most important mineral in world terms after petroleum. Turkish and Iranian deposits of iron, lead, zinc, and copper ores are found in various locations and have significance chiefly for their internal markets. Turkey also has rich deposits of boron salts, meerschaum, and perlite. Iran is rich in gypsum, manganese, lead, tin, and gold. Iraq's main raw materials excluding oil are phosphates and sulfur, though there are also deposits of glass sand, iron, copper, and salt. Iraqi natural sulfur reserves, at an estimated 515 million metric tons, are among the largest in the world. Clay, building stones, and limestone, suitable for cement production, are widespread in West Asia.

The agrarian sector also produces many raw materials needed in West Asia's manufacturing industry. Among the most important materials available for processing are cereals, cotton, sugar beets, olive oil, wool, skins, and hides. Generally, Turkey and Iran have more diverse agricultural bases for industrial development than does Iraq.

A marble quarry near the ancient city of Aphrodisias, Turkey, in 1984. (JONATHAN BLAIR/CORBIS)

### Industrial Policies

Early efforts toward industrial development in West Asia focused on the processing of local products. Factories were initially built to produce food, beverages, textiles, and leather goods. After World War II, the emphasis switched from light to heavy industry. The main goals of the governments of Turkey, Iraq, and Iran have been to build up basic industries as a means of import substitution, and in the cases of Iran and Iraq, to develop a broader industrial base to reduce reliance on oil. In Iran, state companies dominate industry, but many new private-sector companies have been formed since the 1979 Islamic Revolution. Moreover, the share of the private sector grew in the mid-1990s after approximately four hundred state-owned companies, mostly in light manufacturing, were privatized. Due to the war with Iraq (1980–1990), several major industrial schemes had to be postponed. After the end of the war, a government reconstruction program revived these projects and restored war-damaged industries. In the 1990s, the Iranian government gave priority to the development of the mining and metals processing, automotive, pharmaceuticals, and petrochemicals sectors.

During the first decades after World War II, Iraq established its basic steel and chemical industries. In the 1970s, automobile industries, as well as production of construction materials and household consumer goods, were established and expanded. Most funding, however, was directed toward petrochemicals. In the 1980s, the development of a local arms industry was the government's top priority because of the war with Iran and the arms embargo by foreign countries on both Iraq and Iran. In the 1990s, the Iraqi government gave priority to establishing downstream oil and natural gas industries (that is, industries that further process oil and natural gas). Import substitution of basic heavy goods is still an important aspect of Iraqi industrial policy.

In the early 1960s, the Turkish government introduced five-year development plans and a related annual economic program within each five-year period, which aimed to encourage industrial growth and a shift away from agriculture. In 1980, an economic stability program was adopted, followed by radical changes in the monetary, fiscal, foreign-trade, and foreign-currency exchange-rate policies. A transformation was initiated in the direction of industrialization based on exports directed to foreign markets, instead of industrialization based on substitution of imports directed to domestic markets. Free-trade zones and international fairs in the 1980s were influential in the development of Turkish industry and its integration with world markets. As a result of these efforts aimed at the development of the industrial sector, the share of industrial products in the total exports of Turkey increased from 36 percent to 77.4 percent between 1980 and 1998. Certain problems in the performance of Turkish industry arise from the State Economic Enterprises, which are a system of public-sector companies. They are generally inefficient and add a heavy burden to the government budget deficit.

### Mining Industry

Expansion of minerals production in West Asia has traditionally suffered from shortages of foreign currency for machinery and from limited technical skills. Technical cooperation and joint-venture negotiations with foreign governments and companies to develop the mining sector are important for all West Asian countries. The main minerals companies in West Asia are state owned, but governments are trying to encourage private investment in mineral exploration and production.

The main products of Turkish mining are iron ore, coal, lignite, bauxite, and copper. Turkey is also among the world's largest producers of boron and a leading exporter of chrome, meerschaum, and perlite. Other important minerals mined in Turkey are barite, mercury, and wolfram. Iraq's mining industry produces phosphates, sulfur, and building materials. Uranium is also available as a by-product of phosphates. The phosphates industry was established late, in 1982, and two towns were built, together with water-, oil- and gas-supply facilities in the sparsely populated western desert region. The Mishraq natural sulfur project near Mosul began production in 1971.

The Iranian mining industry produces iron, coal, and copper. Iran is also among the largest producers of gypsum and chrome in the world. Iran and Turkey together produce around 15 percent of the world's output of chromites each year.

### Energy

In 1998, West Asia's oil-refinery capacity was above 125,000 metric tons of oil per year. Iran is the leading nation, ensuring more than half of the whole production. (See Table 1.)

The beginnings of the oil industry in West Asia date back to 1908, when petroleum was discovered on the western side of the Zagros Mountains in southwest Iran. Iranian oil facilities were quickly expanded during World War I. As important oil discoveries were made and new oil fields were brought into production during the following decades, the geographical pattern was changed, and oil was found in other areas. However, due to geological conditions, the western slopes

**TABLE 1**

**Selected energy resource production in 1999**

(in millions of metric tons of oil equivalent)

| | | | | Production of electrical energy 1997 | | |
|---|---|---|---|---|---|---|
| Country | Coal | Crude oil | Natural gas | Net total production (million kWh) | Conventional thermal, % | Hydroelectric, % |
| Iran | .. | 175.2 | 47.3 | 95,794 | 92.0 | 8.0 |
| Iraq | .. | 125.5 | .. | 29,561 | 98.0 | 2.0 |
| Turkey | 24.4 | .. | .. | 103, 296 | 61.0 | 39.0 |

SOURCE: Euromonitor (2001).

of the Zagros Mountains near the Persian Gulf are still the site of the largest Iranian oil fields. Immediately before World War II, Iranian oil production exceeded 10 million metric tons. Starting in 1943, the development of the Iranian oil industry was accelerated when more petroleum fields were connected to the Abadan refinery on the Shatt al Arab by pipelines. In the beginning of the 1950s, the oil industry experienced troubles due to political disagreements between the Anglo-Iranian Oil Company and the Iranian government. A compromise was reached in 1954, when an agreement was signed between the Iranian government and a group of oil companies generally known as the Consortium. In the Consortium were seventeen U.S., British, Dutch, and French companies.

Iran and Iraq were among the nations that established the Organization of Petroleum Exporting Countries (OPEC) in 1960. Production of oil, gas, and electricity was seriously affected by the Iran-Iraq war. In the early 1990s, Iran rebuilt its devastated oil and gas facilities, including the 628,000-barrels-per-day Abadan oil refinery and the oil installations at the Persian Gulf port of Lavan. Several petrochemical projects realized in the 1990s have transformed Iran from a major importer of petrochemicals to a net exporter. Three state companies are now responsible for the oil, gas, and petrochemicals sectors in Iran. Oil exports are crucial to the Iranian economy, providing over 90 percent of foreign-exchange earnings.

Creation of the oil industry in Iraq began later and was carried out at a slower speed than in Iran. Petroleum was first discovered in commercial quantities along the Iranian border, in 1923. An important oil discovery took place in 1927, when oil was found at Kirkuk. Subsequently, new fields have been brought into production at Mosul, Basra, Rumaila, and other places, but Kirkuk has remained the main source of Iraqi crude oil. The monopoly position of the Iraqi Petroleum Company caused some difficulties after 1952, which strongly affected the development of the oil industry. The situation was changed in the 1970s through nationalization of the northern oil fields and most of the oil facilities. The Iraqi oil sector was seriously damaged by Iranian air raids in the early 1980s. After the war, Iraq rehabilitated its oil-refining and gas industries. However, during the Persian Gulf War (1990–1991), some oil refineries, petrochemicals plants, and about 90 percent of Iraq's electricity-generating and -distribution capacity were damaged by Allied air raids. During the 1990s, Iraqi oil and energy facilities were gradually repaired.

Although a leader in the total production of electricity in West Asia, Turkey usually experiences energy shortages. Additionally, Turkey is only 15 percent self-sufficient in its oil needs. Consequently, large quantities of crude oil have to be imported, mainly from OPEC countries, as well as some electricity. Contemporary Turkish energy policy is focused on ensuring reliable and sufficient supplies, broadening energy imports, and achieving greater energy efficiency. Investment in the energy sector has remained a priority. In comparison with the other two countries, Turkey has much better developed hydroelectric power. (See Table 1.) In 1998, West Asia's oil-refinery capacity was above 125,000 metric tons of oil per year. Iran leads in West Asia, accounting for more than half of West Asia's total refinery production.

## Manufacturing

The beginning of West Asia's manufacturing took place in Turkey and Iran, countries with a relatively diversified resource base and large populations. Coppersmithing, carpet making, and other craft industries had developed for many centuries, until textile manufacture and food production were established during the nineteenth century, using mechanical power and machines in factories. Sustained industrial development continued in the twentieth century and acceler-

**TABLE 2**

**Production of selected manufacturing products**

(in thousands of metric tons)

| Country | Crude steel (1997) | Sulphuric acid (1997) | Cement (1997) | Paper and paperboard (1998) | Cigarettes (in millions; 1999) | Meat (1999) |
|---|---|---|---|---|---|---|
| Iran | 6,322 | 200 | 17,426 | 205 | 11,860 | 1,463 |
| Iraq | 300 | .. | 18,000 | 18 | 5,794 | 106 |
| Turkey | 17,795 | 947 | 36,054 | 951 | 74,984 | 1,244 |

SOURCE: Euromonitor (2001).

ated after World War II, when a start was made on building up heavy industry. Turkey has the highest level of manufacturing development in West Asia nowadays. At the end of the 1990s, Turkish manufacturing accounted for about 80 percent of the country's total industrial production. Fourteen percent of Turkey's GDP comes from textile and apparel production, and this sector accounts for over 20 percent of manufacturing employment.

In Iran, the largest industrial conglomerate is the National Iranian Industries Organization, a state-owned group, whose companies are in nine industrial sectors: textiles, chemicals, pharmaceuticals, food, footwear and leather, electrical goods, construction, cement, and celluloid. These companies account for about 25 percent of Iran's total industrial output. In the 1980s and 1990s, West Asia's consumption of manufacturing goods fluctuated because of the war between Iraq and Iran and the lack of foreign exchange, especially for the products of heavy industry. The major metallurgy factories are in Turkey and Iran. These countries are also the main producers of chemical products, woodworking, and food and leather products. (See Table 2.)

The reconstruction programs in Iran and Iraq have greatly increased cement requirements, but Turkey is still the main producer of cement. Contemporary West Asia's machine-building industry imports machines and spare parts, and most of its branches are heavily dependent on Western technology. Moreover, the normal running of existing machinery is often interrupted by poor servicing caused by a shortage of technicians and skilled workers. The leading producer of machinery is Turkey, whose internal market shows increasing interest in a variety of items.

The increasing local demand for cars, for example, has encouraged more foreign companies to consider

The "X7"—the first entirely Iranian-conceived automobile—on display at the Tehran International Automobile Fair in June 2001. (AFP/CORBIS)

establishing a local operation in Turkey. The number of cars assembled in Turkey increased from 31,529 in 1980 to 250,000 in 1998. The biggest car maker is TOFAS (Turk Otomobil Fabrikasi A.S). In late 1988, the largest Iranian automobile manufacturer, Iran Khodro, reverted to the private sector after having been taken over for the war effort. Both Turkey and Iran manufacture trucks, cars, vans, buses and minibuses, and appliances for household use.

### Regional Disparities

West Asia is a region of grave regional disparities, to a large extent due to the pattern of industrial development. The main industrial centers are the capitals of Ankara, Tehran, and Baghdad, with their large and wealthy markets, and the major provincial towns, like Istanbul, Esfahan, and Mosul. They concentrate much of the industrial establishments and workforce, and the gap between them and the other regions is considerable. This generates the inevitable uneven development.

The future of industry in West Asia depends on several factors, mainly the economic policies of the three nations, the presence of adequate investments, both foreign and domestic, and political stability in the Middle East.

*Dimitar L. Dimitrov*

### Further Reading

Ayalon, Ami, ed. (1996) *Middle East Contemporary Survey, 1993.* Vol. 17. Boulder, CO: Westview Press.

Bates, D., and A. Rassam. (1983) *Peoples and Cultures of the Middle East.* Englewood Cliffs, NJ: Prentice Hall.

Beaumont, Peter, Gerald H. Blake, and J. Malcolm Wagstaff. (1976) *The Middle East: A Geographical Study.* London: John Wiley & Sons.

Cleveland, William L. (1994) *A History of the Modern Middle East.* Boulder, CO: Westview Press.

Cottrell, Alvin, ed. (1980) *The Persian Gulf States: A General Survey.* Baltimore: Johns Hopkins University Press.

Euromonitor. (2001) *European Marketing Data and Statistics, 2001.* London: Euromonitor.

———. (2001) *International Marketing Data and Statistics, 2001.* London: Euromonitor.

Issawi, Charles. (1995) *The Middle East Economy: Decline and Recovery: Selected Essays.* Princeton, NJ: Markus Wiener.

Peretz, Don. (1994) *The Middle East Today.* 6th ed. Westport, CT: Greenwood Press.

## INFORMATION TECHNOLOGY INDUSTRY

**INFORMATION TECHNOLOGY INDUSTRY** Emerging economies in Asia are experiencing dramatic changes in patterns of ownership and investments in their information technology (IT) sectors. Such investments continue to revolutionize societies across political frontiers, leading to a race for a larger share of global markets.

Information technology is the various ways by which communication takes place electronically, whether for personal, corporate, or intergovernmental services. It represents convergence, which is the merging of content and carriage via multimedia channels. The Asian nations that are leading in this area are Japan, South Korea, Singapore, and Taiwan. China has a vast market potential and profits from the advances made by Hong Kong. Japan took the lead when the government in the 1970s declared its pursuit of a *johoka shakai* (information society) and directly encouraged the growth of its semiconductor industry competing in global markets. South Korea led with *chaebols* (large family-owned corporations) that imported IT and adjusted technology to suit its domestic market. In Singapore and Taiwan, government-led advances in IT were directed toward export-led growth. Malaysia, Indonesia, and India lagged behind because their governments lacked political vision, leadership, and funding resources at a time when the IT sector was taking off.

Information technology is important because it contributes to the growth of all other sectors in an economy. Information technology development has made the region concentrate on its competitive strengths in global markets through continued priority in investments in the IT sectors. This has resulted in the emergence of more democratic government and greater scope for entrepreneurship.

### The Internet Economy and the Information Technology Sector in Asia

Asia has made strong inroads into the world Internet economy, which will top $1 trillion by the end of 2002, as estimated by Accenture, a U.S.-based consulting firm. Hong Kong, Singapore, Malaysia, and Taiwan have invested vast sums of money in teleports, cyberports, and technology parks to advance the use of the Internet and electronic commerce. South Korea takes the lead in using broadband (wider electromagnetic spectrum) technologies for faster access to the Internet and higher volumes of data exchange and storage. Japan takes the lead in the Third Generation (3G) wireless technology, which enables Internet access on cellular telephones. Internet users in Asia totaled 37 million in 2001, compared with 30 million in Europe. In Asia, digital networks redefine what kinds of infrastructure are possible under the sweeping trend of converging technologies. Both the Asian Tigers (Singapore, South Korea, and Taiwan) and developing nations such as Malaysia, Indonesia, and Thailand have moved to liberalize their state-owned telephone companies and introduce competition. Investments in improving access to telephones depend on the degree of liberalization as well as the willingness of the telecommunications companies to provide citizens with affordable telephone services.

E-commerce is soaring in Asia; B2B (business-to-business) transactions are expected to soar to 7.3 trillion in 2004, according to Accenture. The feverish activities of the "dot com" firms in Asia are not the full extent of the changes that the Internet is bringing to Asia. Some nations, such as Singapore, Malaysia, and Hong Kong, have invested in cybercities to house IT companies.

## China

China has the second-largest market in the world for telecommunications equipment. It invested $100 billion in its ninth Five-Year Plan between 1995 and 2000 to upgrade and extend its fiber-optic land lines, with contracts awarded to Alcatel (a French firm) and to Lucent of the United States for digitized telephone exchanges. China's gross domestic product (GDP) in 2000 was $1.08 trillion, compared with $9.87 trillion in the United States and $4.75 trillion in Japan. But what is more amazing is that China's IT sector was growing at 25 percent per annum, overtaking the growth of GDP of 12 percent per annum. Internet connections have been installed under the directive of the Ministry of Information Industries (MII) to cover forty-three cities that constitute the Chinapac network for data transmission. The MII is also connecting one thousand universities under CERN (China Educational Research Network) to use the Internet. Cisco Systems has the contract for the routers and Sprint for the telephone backbone. According to Minister Wu Jichuan, one more telephone company is to be developed to compete with China Telecom, which will provide services to the neglected provinces in the north. With so much liberalization and with China's entry into the World Trade Organization (WTO) in November 2001, China still has to make some drastic changes to its market economy. It must make it possible for other member nations of the WTO to reach its 1.3 billion consumers and lift some restrictions on foreign participation in its joint ventures, increasing to 33 percent and to 49 percent after three years. Even within its own domestic sector, it will have to give a larger role to its private enterprise. China's foreign trade now totals $475 billion per year, making it the world's seventh-largest trading nation.

China manufactures and launches its own satellites. Its satellite-launch equipment, called the Long March II and III rockets, is used for international spacecraft. China has permitted contracts with Hughes, Lockheed Martin, and Space Systems Loral for satellite equipment in the past. But when the U.S. Congress approved the Cox Commission's report (1999), all new contracts were stopped, dealing a severe blow to the U.S. satellite industry. Chinasat is a flourishing company within China. In November 2001, the MII authorized a new telecom giant called China Telecommunications Satellite Group Corporation, involving Chinasat and AP Star in Hong Kong, to serve as a telecom operator.

The wireless revolution is also overtaking China as 2 million cell phone users are being added every month, and 14 million pagers are imported each year in addition to those produced domestically. In 1994, a cell phone in China cost $2,000, but today it costs $200 because of economies of scale.

## Malaysia, Indonesia, and Thailand

Malaysia's Vision 2020 program has become the linchpin for its IT sector and has helped the nation out of its financial crisis despite the capital controls instituted by Malaysia's prime minister, Mahathir Mohamad. Vision 2020 involves a $20 billion investment in the Multimedia Super Corridor (MMSC). The corridor will include two cities based on electronic networks: Putrajaya, to house a paperless bureaucracy, and Cyberjaya, to develop convergent IT. Malaysia was the first nation to privatize its telephone authority, in 1976, and promulgated the Multimedia Communication Reform Act in 1998. The Japanese company Nippon Telephone and Telecommunications Company (NTT) invested $2.5 billion to install ATM (asynchronous transfer mode) switches and a fiber backbone for Cyberjaya. A new broadband infrastructure has been put in place to propel Malaysia to the forefront of the region's industry and to compete with neighboring Singapore. Since privatization of its telephone company, Malaysia has spent $4.5 billion to upgrade its fixed-line services and to install ISDN (integrated services digital network, a high-speed Internet infrastructure) to the interior of the peninsula. The teledensity rose to 19 percent, and the market for telecommunication services has been growing at 12 percent, overtaking GDP growth. Private-sector investment has been 15 percent of the total. A private company, Benariang, was given the contract to launch MEASAT (Malaysian East Asian Satellites), with the two first satellites' beam extending over Singapore and the Philippines. The third-generation satellite has a more extensive footprint, covering India and South Africa. It uses DTH (Direct to Home) technology for its broadcasts and attracted an investment of $1.8 billion from U.S. West in a joint venture. American computer and technology firms such as Microsoft, Sun Microsystems, and Oracle have located their subsidiaries in the Cyberjaya experiment. Japan announced an aid package of $2.1 billion in 1999 to help Malaysia expand its semiconductor export industry.

Indonesia, despite its troubled economy, was the first Asian nation to own its own domestic satellite, called Palapa. It leased the transponders (channels) of that satellite to Malaysia, Singapore, Thailand, and Papua New Guinea as far back as 1976 to earn revenues for several years. Even so, Indonesia has only two telephones per one hundred people despite having the fourth-largest population in the world. Indonesia's state monopoly, PT Telekom, sought a loan of $40 million to pay for its new satellite, Telekom I, which was launched in February 1999. The total cost of the satellite was $191 million; it was built by Lockheed Martin of the United States. It will serve Indonesia's voice and data needs for fifteen years. The best technology to link an archipelago of thirteen thousand islands has been satellite. Despite the economic malaise that hit the nation in 1997, Lockheed Martin joined a three-nation venture for a roaming access cellular system called AceS with Indonesia's Nusantara system and Jasmine International of Thailand. It will provide telephone, television, and multimedia services to all the islands. The satellite is called Garuda, and it also provides radio communication.

Thailand is also developing its telecommunications infrastructure rapidly with foreign direct investment, which increased after the partial privatization in 1995 of its telephone networks, both domestic and international. Contracts were awarded to private firms to build a 1.9-million-telephone land line throughout the nation. Telecom Asia is the biggest private company in the IT field. The goal is to build as many telephone lines in Bangkok as there are in Manhattan. The World Bank has given loans to Thailand to build public telephone booths in the rural areas of the nation. Thailand's satellite industry is entirely in the private sector, which consists of the Shinawatra Company, owned by the prime minister. Thaisat satellites supply communications throughout Thailand. The Samarat Company supplies Internet services in a joint venture with Sun Microsystems. The same company provides the Thai Tradenet, which allows foreign companies to access their subsidiaries for intranet services. As predicted by the World Bank's *Annual Development Report 1999*, IT is the driving force behind the recovery of Bangkok's economy.

**Singapore and Taiwan**

The economies of Singapore and Taiwan have been in the vanguard of the technology revolution, which enabled them to withstand the financial crisis in 1997–1998. Singapore prides itself in being the "Intelligent Island" of Asia. It retained the confidence of its foreign investors because of the integrity of its government system. Sing Tel is Asia's most efficient telecommunications company, with a market capitalization of $40 billion in joint ventures in twenty-one nations. From 2000, Sing Tel opened its local and international call services to competition and provides broadband open network services to all homes and businesses. Singapore was the first nation in Asia to set up a teleport, which it set up on Batam Island in collaboration with Indonesia and Malaysia. The teleport operates like an airport with communications traffic instead of passengers. Singapore has a Tradenet system, which documents on computers all trade that passes through its busy harbor, making it the transshipment center of the Pacific. Singapore's computerized stock exchange, Simex, is linked to the Chicago Mercantile Exchange twenty-four hours a day. A national computer board has been responsible for the development of the nation's Science Park and the computer education of all its citizens, young and old.

Despite Internet content being restricted in Singapore, the government encourages the growth of "netpreneurs" and venture capitalists and discourages resellers of telecom services. DSL (digital subscriber lines, a broadband Internet infrastructure) is proliferating on the island to provide video on demand on the same platform as other telecom services. Additionally, there is Group W network services, which houses the Asia Broadcast Center with 11-meter satellite receiving dishes for incoming signals from Panamsat 2 and 4, Apstar I, and Palapa C1, which are satellites whose footprints cover the entire Pacific Rim. Its Media One service links all homes to cable television services.

Taiwan has been one of the prosperous Asian Tigers. It planned its economic growth around its export sector to build large foreign currency reserves as high as $100 billion when the financial crisis arose in Southeast Asia in 1997. Taiwan has permitted private competition in its telephone service supplies and built a strong semiconductor industry, moving on to sophisticated computers. The nation's private sector has played a leading role in its high-tech development. Hsinchu Park is the world's third-largest technology center, making Taiwan a global leader in producing notebook computers, ahead of the United States, Japan, and South Korea. Taiwan also manufactures the lowest-priced circuit boards that go into 65 percent of the world's computers. Acer is the largest computer manufacturer in Taiwan, selling its products in China and the rest of Asia. Asustech is another Taiwanese company. It supplies 8 percent of the world's market for motherboards for computers. On the whole, Taiwan has large investments overseas, with $25 billion in China and $30 billion in Vietnam, Indonesia, and the Philippines combined.

### South Korea and Japan

In contrast to Singapore, South Korea was battered by the financial crisis. Korea Telecom had already been privatized as far back as 1989 under the Telecommunications Business Law. Dacom, which was set up for data communications, is still in the private sector and competes with Korea Telecom, in which the government still has a major stake. Dacom has set up the online infrastructure for the entire nation, which stimulates the Internet economy domestically. South Korea has attained convergence in telecommunications better than any other Asian Tiger. It distinguishes between different suppliers, which converge in their operations such as networking, programming, and broadcasting. It is the Asian leader of the broadband spectrum to provide speed and volume on the Internet. The global market for Internet-ready cell phones is likely to rise to $1 trillion in the next five years, placing South Korea in competition with Japan for the Asian market.

In Japan, the longtime monopoly of Nippon Telephone and Telecommunications (NTT) was ended by decree in December 1996, and later NTT was divided into three companies, consisting of two local exchange carriers and one long-distance carrier. Despite this decree, NTT continues to dominate the domestic market and competes with Kokusai Denshin Denwa (KDD). KDD has merged with Tokyo Telecommunications Network, which is a subsidiary of the Electric Company of Tokyo. Japan has taken the lead in wireless communications with the rollout of the new global standard called 3G (Third Generation) for its DoCoMo service, now used by 25 million Japanese. The new I-mode standard in Japan equips cell phones with cameras so that pictures taken are immediately transported on the Internet. This broadband access is thought to give the best benchmark for a nation's progress toward widespread access. South Korea still leads with 38 percent broadband access, compared with Japan's 3.4 percent.

So far, Japan has kept its telecommunications market restricted to domestic suppliers; thus in February 2001, the European Union and the United States increased their pressure on Japan to enhance competition and threatened to file a complaint to the WTO if this was not done with speed. There are an estimated 50 million Internet users in Asia, of whom 22 million are in Japan, thereby giving the advantage of a critical mass to Japanese suppliers. Fujitsu of Japan and Nokia of Finland are competing to build transmission stations around the globe for wireless telephony because it is a trillion-dollar industry. Sony of Japan is experimenting with building cell phones that will double as multimedia players.

The *Wall Street Journal* ("A Tidal Wave Sweeps Asia,"12 March 2001: 5–8) reported that "a tidal wave sweeps Asia because of the deregulation of undersea cable construction and continued leaps in fiber optic technology." Today's equipment can transmit three times more data over a given pair of fibers than could the same-priced equipment in 1999. Singapore's SEA ME WE (Southeast Asia, Middle East, Western Europe) cables, along with the PacRim cables, have linked Asia with the United States and Europe. The FLAG (Fiber Link Around the Globe) undersea cable has linked the Atlantic with the Pacific landing in Shanghai. Global Crossing Asia has completed its system linking Asia with the United States. It is equipped with an automatic backup system called a self-healing capability that reroutes data transmission if there is a break in the cable. Lack of demand perhaps led to the bankruptcy of Global Crossing, and Sing Tel and Hutchison Wahampoa considered purchasing it. In this competitive environment, Fujitsu of Japan and Alcatel of France built the Southern Cross undersea cable, which passed through Hawaii and landed in San Luis Obispo in the United States. Tyco is also a player in the Pacific, with a system called Pacific Crossing–1, connecting the United States with Japan. The principal

## INFORMATION TECHNOLOGY GIANTS

Of the ten largest information equipment firms in Asia, eight are in Japan. They are Hitachi, Toshiba, Fujitsu, NEC, Mitsubishi, Canon, IBM Japan, and Ricoh. The two non-Japanese firms are Samsung Electronics in South Korea and Flextronics in Singapore.

*Source: AsiaWeek* (9 November 2001), 121.

owners are KDD, Marubeni of Japan, and Global Crossing. The first link came into service in 2000. It is estimated that $36 billion will be spent on submarine cables worldwide, of which $15 billion will be invested in trans-Pacific routes, eclipsing the investment across the Atlantic.

**India**

In India, the Internet is cable based and is growing rapidly. The International Data Corporation predicts that India will have 5 million Internet users by 2003, making it the fourth-largest market in Asia. Currently, 200 of the Fortune 1,000 companies outsource their requirements to India. India earns considerable foreign exchange in IT-based exports, which are expected to rise to $50 billion by 2008. Even traditional corporations are investing in supply chain management, e-commerce, and e-business solutions. The nation's expertise in software production enables it to lead other Asian low-income nations in IT. India's National Association of Software and Service Companies estimates that India will earn $1 billion in 2002 from its software industry.

Minister for Information Technology and Parliamentary Affairs Pramod Mahajan of India at a press conference on 8 June 2000, where he discusses plans to expand the Indian IT sector. (AFP/CORBIS)

From 1999 onward, regulations have permitted 100 percent foreign direct investment in India's IT industry but not in retail trading. India reformed its telecommunications sector in 1999 by setting up its Telecom Regulatory Authority and a new telecommunications policy to liberalize this fastest-growing sector of the economy. The monopoly carrier has been VSNL (Videsh Sanchar Nigam Ltd.), but the government had planned to end its monopoly in April 2002. The government has licensed nine private operators of VSAT (very small aperture terminals) to supply phone services to remote and rural areas via satellite. Even for corporate communications VSATs are used for data transmission using wideband channels. In 1999, the government appointed the Commission on Convergence of Broadcasting, Telecommunications, and Information Technologies, which recommended a regulatory body to take care of spectrum allocation disputes as well as licensing of service providers. Also, the Information Technology Act of 2000 is an important milestone in India's development because it deals with electronic transactions and protects digital signatures. It also recognizes the digital filing of government documents. In India, the slow speed of web connections hinders obtaining information on the Internet.

**Bridging the Asian Digital Divide**

Asia is leading the web phone race because Asian nations have the world's newest digital networks. According to author Jeremy Rifkin, only one-fifth of the world's population has access to information technology. Half the world's population has never used a telephone. Villages in India, Indonesia, and China are isolated by their lack of communications. Farmers do not know the market prices for their crops and are swindled by businesspeople who profit from their ignorance. In emergencies farmers have to walk to get help because there is no access. The Independent Commission of the International Telecommunications Union, based in Geneva, issued its *Missing Link Report* to emphasize this disparity of access to telephones in the Third World and recommended that there be a public phone booth within twenty minutes of walking in every village around the globe. However, even in the twenty-first century the link is still missing despite the advances made in information technology and growing investments by national governments to place their nations on the global information superhighway. Although the metropolitan centers in China, India, Indonesia, and the Philippines have all the sophisticated technologies, including wireless services, the remote areas of those nations are starved for access. Such disparities have led to social

## OUTSOURCING INFORMATION TECHNOLOGY TO ASIA

A combination of high overhead in the United States and strong cultural ties between the domestic and Asian information technology industries have led many companies to outsource labor-intensive software programming to Asia and Eastern Europe.

India has always been a major player in information technology (IT); they even make their own supercomputers for predicting monsoons. It wasn't until the Y2K bug emerged that the need for legions of cheap programmers really arose, however, and American companies began to see the potential for outsourcing overseas. After Y2K the IT service industry exploded, with American companies outsourcing everything from data entry to customer service to India and other Asian countries.

India was a natural choice for outsourcing. Many American technology companies were either created by or employ nonresident Indians (NRIs) or Indian-Americans who still have strong ties to family and friends in India. This cultural bridge combined with the vast pool of cheap, technically skilled, English-speaking engineering talent produced by India's engineering colleges creates the perfect environment for information technology.

Despite its distinct advantages for companies looking to outsource their IT services, India's volatile political climate and rampant corruption present problems. Some of the 185 Fortune 500 companies that outsource software to Asia are choosing places like Vietnam or China with more predictable politics and less corruption. Other companies that outsource their customer service are finding that their customers prefer the Americanized English of the Philippines to the British English that predominates in India, though all of these countries have their drawbacks, from censored Internet lines in China and Vietnam to Muslim militancy in the Philippines.

Despite the hiccups the IT service industry continues to grow as the software industry becomes more competitive and U.S. companies try to reduce overhead. The Asian IT service market is still in its infancy, but by 2008 industry think tank Nasscom-McKinsey predicts a $17 billion IT service industry in India alone.

*James B. McGirk*

*Sources:* Manu Joseph. (2001) "Great Indian IT Jobs: $20 a Month." *Wired Magazine* (24 November). Retrieved 8 April 2002, from http://www.wired.com/news/culture/0,1284,40018,00.html.

Tim Reason. (2001) "Small World." *CFO Magazine* (1 April) Retrieved 8 April 2002, from: http://www.cfo.com.

unrest and to large migrations of people from rural regions to the cities, causing congestion and ghettos even in the United States. In 1998 and 1999, the U.S. National Telecommunications and Information Administration published two reports dealing with this problem and describing the problems of drugs and crime as a consequence of the lack of access, which also hinders education and employment.

The Group of Eight (G8) ministers of affluent economies met in Okinawa, Japan, in July 2000 to deal with the differences of affordability. The G8 recognized that IT empowers, benefits, and encourages respect among global citizens. The ministers issued the Okinawa Charter on the Global Information Society and set up the Digital Opportunities Task Force. One of the major recommendations of the charter was the principle of inclusion to provide universal, affordable access to all persons everywhere at all times, to foster the free flow of information and knowledge, and to promote human development. G8 ministers vowed to exercise their leadership to optimize global networks to bridge the digital divide, to invest in people, and to promote global participation. G8's meeting in Qatar in 2002 continued its appeals to global public and private sectors to continue efforts to bridge the digital divide.

Despite the enormous growth of investments in China's IT sector, there is great disparity in wage incomes in China. Wages in Shanghai are eight times higher than the per capita GDP. Workers in the remote areas of central and western China bordering on Mongolia are deprived of links to markets in their own nation. Unequal access in China is caused by a substantial wealth gap, leading to a poverty belt stretching from Yunnan in the south to Xinjiang in the north. Wireless communications hold the potential for closing this divide, provided that the cost is subsidized. The promise of mobile communications lies in reducing the cost of laying land lines to remote and mountainous regions by national telephone companies. In nations like India and China and Indonesia, mobile networks, including satellite-based services, are being introduced. For example, people who fish in Cochin in the state of Kerala in southern India use mobile phones for access to markets. Similarly, in Bangladesh, where the per capita income is less than $200 a year, an organization called Grameen Telecom was set up in 1997 to provide low-cost phone services to sixty-eight thousand villages. This organization is headed by women who collect the charges from users and generate revenues of $12,000 per year per village from one of the world's poorest nations. Such services are being provided through kiosks in Africa by the International Development Research Corporation of Canada and by World Space, based in the United States. Two private companies in India have provided village phones at low cost. Escotel provides mobile phones to villages in Uttar Pradesh, and BPL provides fifteen hundred mobile phones in rural areas of Kerala to boost the fishing industry there. Likewise in Mongolia, low-cost mobile phones are provided by the government to the nomads (*ghirs*) for use in selling the cashmere wool from their herds. In China, pagers are found to be more practical in providing access to rural residents.

Many conclusions can be drawn from the growth of IT investments in Asia. On the one hand, such investments are resulting in economic growth and greater human resources; on the other hand, they are deepening the digital divide. *The Asia Recovery Report 2001*, issued by the Asian Development Bank (ADB), indicates that poverty is declining, which may be a sign that the digital divide is being bridged. However, after the 11 September 2001 terrorist attacks in the United States, with the slowdown in the American economy and the global recession, with the electronics sector losing profits, Asian nations are finding it difficult to compete with exports in IT-related products. The entry of China into the WTO makes the export sectors of other Asian nations more challenging. With political unrest and the war on terrorism, investor confidence in Asia will have to be restored. The ADB forecasts that income growth in Asia may rise to 5 percent in 2002. Surviving the value chain is becoming difficult for private companies in India, and even companies like Leading Edge and China dot Com in China are not reporting high profits. Depending on the political and currency stabilities in various nations, bridging the digital divide will not be the same in China as in Thailand or Indonesia. The rising tide of IT may not lift all boats at the same time, but the IT transformation holds out hope of converting the divide into a dividend for Asia.

*Meheroo Jussawalla*

## Further Reading

Accenture. (2001) "Business Week Supplement on E.Biz Cites the Accenture Data." (May 14).

Ang Peng Hwa. (2000) "Asia's Piece of the Pie: A Region's Entry into the Dot-Com Universe." *Harvard Asia Pacific Review* 4, 2: 6–9.

Asian Development Bank. (2001) *The Asia Recovery Report, March*. Manila, Philippines: Oxford University Press.

"Connectivity for the Common Man." (2001) *The Economist* (3 March): 20–21.

Jussawalla, Meheroo. (1999) "The Impact of ICT Convergence on Development in the Asian Region." *Telecommunications Policy* 23: 217–234.

———. (2001) "The Digital Age and the Digital Divide." *Intermedia* 29 (July): 26–39.

National Telecommunications and Information Administration. (1999) *Falling through the Net*. Washington, DC: Government Printing Office.

Rifkin, Jeremy. (2000) *The Age of Access: The New Culture of Hyper-Capitalism*. New York: Tarcher/Putnam.

Semmoto, Sachio. (2001) "The Broad Band Revolution in East Asia." Paper presented to the Second Conference on E-Commerce, Honolulu, HI.

"A Tidal Wave Sweeps Asia." (2001) *Wall Street Journal* (12 March): 5–8.

Xin Hua Chinese News Agency. (2001) "Report on New Telecom Giant." *China Daily* (6 November): 1.

**INLE LAKE REGION** Inle Lake is the second-largest lake of Myanmar (Burma). Twenty-two kilometers (14 miles) long and up to four kilometers (2.5 miles) wide, it forms an integral part of a major water system that extends from the southern Shan Plateau to Kayah State, 110 kilometers (69 miles) to the south. It is also famous as the home of the Intha people, who practice a unique style of "leg rowing" and speak a distinctive dialect of Burmese that is similar to that of the Tavoyan people of the Tenasserim (Tanintharyi) Division in Myanmar's far south.

Other ethnic nationality peoples inhabit the lake and surrounding highland regions, including the Shan, Pao, Taungyo, Danu, and Palaung. The population around the lake is estimated at eighty thousand people dwelling in sixty-four villages. The largest of these villages is Haiya Ywa-ma, which is located halfway down the lake. Many of the lakeside houses are accessible only by boat and are built over the water on wooden stilts.

Fishing and farming have traditionally been the main occupations of local inhabitants. An unusual feature is the floating gardens, where crops such as tomatoes, potatoes, eggplants, cucumbers, and flowers are cultivated on artificial islands. Tourism has also become an important part of the local economy in recent years, encouraged by the proximity of the Shan State capital, Taunggyi, and the Heho airfield nearby. The main entry point to the lake is at Nyaung Shwe, which lies by the northern shores. In addition to weaving and silverware, a main attraction is the Phaung-Daw-Oo pagoda. The present buildings are of modern construction, but the temple houses five renowned Buddha images that, according to legend, date from the twelfth century CE. A major event is the boat festival each October.

The increasing number of visitors, however, has placed the fragile ecosystem of the lake under severe pressure. This has been exacerbated by declining water levels, caused by decades of oversilting from deforestation in the surrounding hills. As a result, more and more earth washes into the lake each rainy season. During the 1990s, various schemes were contemplated to increase environmental protection, including the banning of logging, reforestation, and the designation of nature sanctuaries to preserve the lake's endangered flora and fauna.

*Martin Smith*

**Further Reading**

Nath, Mohinder. (1961) *Botanical Survey of the Southern Shan States: With a Note on the Vegetation of the Inle Lake*. Yangon, Myanmar: Burma Research Society Fiftieth Anniversary Publications.

Thaw Kaung. (1998) "The Industrious Inthas of Inle Lake." *Myanmar Perspectives* 3, 2: 28–39.

**INNER MONGOLIA AUTONOMOUS REGION.** See **Nei Monggol**

**INONU, MUSTAFA ISMET** (1884–1973), Turkish president. Ismet Inonu, the second president of Turkey, oversaw the creation of a multiparty political system. Inonu, originally known as Ismet Pasha, received a military education and served as a colonel in the Ottoman army during World War I. He became a commander on the western front during the Turkish War of Independence (1919–1923), and led Turkish forces to two major victories against the Greek army near the Anatolian town of Inonu (the origin of the name he took after the victories). Subsequently, he led the Turkish delegation in peace talks with the Allies at Lausanne in 1922–1923.

Ismet Inonu served as the Turkish Republic's first prime minister and became president following the death of Mustafa Kemal Ataturk (1881–1938). As Turkey's national chief and permanent leader of Turkey's only party, the Republican People's Party (RPP), throughout World War II, Ismet Inonu worked to maintain Turkish nonbelligerency. In 1945 Ismet Inonu called for the creation of a multiparty system and worked to ensure its success. After the RPP lost to the Democrat Party, led by Celal Bayar (1884–1987), in the 1950 elections, Ismet Inonu remained active in politics, serving as chair of the RPP until 1972 and as prime minister from 1961 to 1965. In his memoirs Ismet Inonu wrote that his greatest achievement was the creation of the multiparty system.

*John M. Vanderlippe*

**Further Reading**

Heper, Metin. (1999) *Ismet Inonu: The Making of a Turkish Statesman*. Leiden, Netherlands: Brill.

Zürcher, Erik Jan. (1994) *Turkey: A Modern History*. London: I. B. Tauris.

**INTELLECTUAL PROPERTY** Intellectual property, by which is meant proprietary interest in such intangible yet commercially valuable things as trademarks, technology, and entertainment content, has proven a knotty problem in the adjustment of trade differences between East and West. Several Asian nations, most especially China, have permitted business practices that developed nations, the United States in particular, consider little better than theft. Such "piracy," as it is often called, involves using patented technology or media content without paying royalties to the patent or copyright holders. Some progress in resolving differences was made as the twenty-first century began, but substantial disagreement remains.

### Development of Issue

From the nineteenth century, it has been common practice for nearly all Western nations to regard certain processes, trade symbols, and items of manufacture as a species of property, rights to which may be vested in the inventors or those to whom they assign them. The United States came somewhat late to these agreements, being notorious during the nineteenth century for allowing its citizens to freely appropriate the work of others and sell it for profit. In the twentieth century, the Soviet Union was, likewise, notorious for its refusal to honor international copyright conventions, asserting that all humankind alike was freely entitled to the full fruits of knowledge.

The question of what constitutes legally protected intellectual property became increasingly complex during the second half of the last century as human knowledge increased. In the West, the law expanded to include such innovations as genetically engineered organisms and computer software. Some of these technologies were so vital to a modern postindustrial economy that any nation-state that lacked access to them must inevitably remain relatively backward. At the same time, however, these technologies were often so extraordinarily expensive to nurture that without commercial protection for the developers, some feared that useful innovation might disappear. There is, thus, a natural conflict of interest between wealthy nations that originate new technology and possess its property rights and less-wealthy ones that feel shut out. In practice, much of this conflict occurs between the newly industrializing countries (NICs) of East Asia and the Western industrial giants—especially the United States.

This conflict of wealth is further exacerbated by Asia's colonial legacy. It is often the case that precisely those nations that hold essential intellectual property rights are the ones that formerly colonized Asian NICs. A certain postcolonial resentment only adds bitterness to these disagreements between the haves and have-nots.

India is a prime example of an Asian country with a postcolonial entitlement. With masses of impoverished people and relatively scant financial resources, modern India cheerfully allows its domestic pharmaceutical companies to manufacture and distribute medication developed in the West at a fraction of its usual commercial price and without a penny paid to Western patent holders. Indians cite the rampaging AIDS epidemic as sufficient justification for this practice. Why, they ask, should impoverished Indian citizens die for lack of needed drugs because of the exorbitant prices charged by Western patent holders, when a cheap, Indian-made copy can save them? Western nations, which watched India spend billions of dollars to develop nuclear arms, may retort that the problem in India is priorities, not funding.

### U.S. Leadership in Protecting Rights

Regardless, the Western nations, led by the United States, have rallied to extend their concept of intellectual property throughout the world. Their overwhelming economic and technological superiority has enabled them to prevail in most, although not all, instances.

The U.S. insistence on protecting intellectual property is understandable, because it towers above all others in innovation. In 1992, for instance, an estimated 45 percent of all research and development in the world's industrialized countries occurred in the United States. By the mid-1990s, technology products constituted nearly a fifth of all U.S. exports, and the overall technological balance of trade was lopsidedly in the favor of the United States.

The United States was also peculiarly sensitive to intellectual property rights because of its vast dominance over the world entertainment market. By the 1990s, it was common for these American properties to be duplicated in Asian countries without payment of licensing fees and distributed widely via bootleg videotapes and CDs. China was a particular offender in this regard, although it was far from alone.

### Ratification of TRIPS

Thus, the United States was uniquely instrumental in drawing up the Trade Related Aspects of Intellectual Property Rights (TRIPS) agreement that was ratified by most of the international community in 1994. This convention, which codifies intellectual property rights and provides enforcement mechanisms, was in large part the work of the United States Trade Representative (USTR), an office reporting directly to the president and charged with promoting U.S. commerce. The main offenders during the 1990s, in the view of the USTR, were Thailand, South Korea, Taiwan, India, Brazil, and the Philippines, while the People's Republic of China was in a class by itself.

Tools for enforcement of TRIPS were not lacking among the Western states, especially the United States. Access to the huge U.S. market is so vital to the NICs that U.S. threats of retaliatory tariffs were taken seriously. In addition, the United States made clear that it would block application for membership in the General Agreement on Tariffs and Trade for nonmember nations, China especially, if compliance were not forthcoming. During the 1990s, pirated American CDs, movies, software, and the like, while still not difficult to obtain, became somewhat less common on the streets of such cities as Taipei and Manila.

China, however, constituted the largest obstacle to full Asian compliance with property rights as understood by the industrial West. In April 1991 the USTR targeted that country for special attention, and China quickly made certain concessions to conform its laws to international trade conventions. It did so largely because the United States threatened trade sanctions. Shortly thereafter, the Sino-U.S. dispute on intellectual property rights turned especially nasty.

By the mid-1990s, the United States was running a wide trade deficit with China in that country's favor, and loss of intellectual property rights was cited as one cause. At the same time, China was in increasingly poor odor in congressional circles because of its repressive political stance at home. In May 1996 the United States threatened especially severe trade sanctions against China but was met by retaliatory moves. While U.S. trade diplomacy had prevailed against lesser Asian nations such as South Korea, Taiwan, and even Japan, China was so large and nationalistic that it felt free to defy U.S. pressure. The United States responded more subtly by targeting especially vulnerable exporters in China's Guangdong Province, and this produced results.

### Simmering Sino-U.S. Relations

The twentieth century closed with Sino-U.S. tension over intellectual property rights being just one element of an increasingly combative trade relationship between the two powers. Nevertheless, both nations were loath to escalate the dispute to an all out trade war, and China seemed inclined to make grudgingly small, but steady, accommodation to international trade conventions in property rights. Smaller Asian nations had, likewise, begun to fall in line.

*Robert K. Whalen*

### Further Reading

Arup, Christopher. (2000) *The New World Trade Organization Agreements: Globalizing Law through Services and Intellectual Property.* New York: Cambridge University Press.

Buranen, Lise, and Alice M. Roy, eds. (1999) *Perspectives on Plagiarism and Intellectual Property in a Postmodern World.* Albany, NY: State University of New York Press.

Chao, Julie. (1993) "Intellectual Property: A Tenuous Concept." *Science* (October 15): 366.

Ryan, Michael P. (1998) *Knowledge Diplomacy: Global Competition and the Politics of Intellectual Property.* Washington, DC: Brookings Institution Press.

## INTERNATIONAL LABOR DAY—CHINA

The celebration of International Labor Day, 1 May, as an annual public holiday originated in North America in the 1880s. It was adopted by the ruling Nationalist Party (Kuomintang, or KMT) in China as early as the 1920s as a symbol of its willingness to bring all political groups into the fold. Following the founding of the People's Republic of China (PRC) in 1949, 1 May assumed much greater importance and was designated by the Chinese Communist Party as a key public holiday. In the early years of the PRC, workers enjoyed a paid day off from work and, along with party leaders, attended large-scale government-sponsored parades and other festivities in urban parks and squares throughout the country.

The celebrations included cultural activities, displays of military prowess, the carrying of banners and flags extolling the value of labor, and even mass wedding ceremonies, before climaxing with raucous fireworks displays. Recently, in a society that is more pluralistic and increasingly less dominated by the Communist Party, the focus has moved away from public ceremonies and military parades. Workers have been granted a week off from work and encouraged to travel, with the dual aims of stimulating consumer spending and developing China's tourism industry.

*Julian Ward*

### Further Reading

Hutchings, Graham. (2000) *Modern China: A Companion to a Rising Power.* London: Penguin.

## INTERNATIONAL MONETARY FUND

The International Monetary Fund (IMF, or Fund) came into official existence on 27 December 1945, when twenty-nine countries signed its Articles of Agreement (its charter), which had been agreed upon at a conference held in Bretton Woods, (in New

Hampshire, United States), 1–22 July 1944. The IMF commenced financial operations 1 March 1947. Today the IMF has near global membership of 182 countries. The Fund employs approximately 2,700 staff members from 122 countries. The Fund is headed by a managing director, who is also chairman of an executive board of twenty-four executive directors. The five largest members—the members that make the largest contributions to the fund, namely the United States, Japan, Germany, France, and Britain—are each entitled to appoint an executive director. By tradition, the managing director is a European. Most staff members work at the Fund headquarters in Washington, D.C., though a few are assigned to small offices in Paris, Geneva, Tokyo, and at the United Nations in New York. Some represent the IMF on temporary assignment in member countries. At present about seventy of these resident representatives are assigned to sixty-four member countries.

## Purpose

The purpose of the IMF as established by its charter can be summarized as follows: (1) to provide the means for consultation and collaboration between members on international monetary issues, (2) to promote exchange stability and to maintain orderly exchange arrangements among members so as to facilitate international trade, (3) to assist in the creation and expansion of markets in which members can exchange currencies without restriction, and (4) to support members that are faced with a shortage of foreign currency by making the financial resources of the IMF temporarily available to them under adequate safeguards. Under the institution's Articles of Agreement, the member countries have committed themselves to promoting global trade and deepening economic integration by maintaining a stable international monetary system. This goal is to be achieved by maintaining orderly exchange arrangements among members (in order to avoid competitive exchange depreciation) and allowing individual national currencies to be exchanged without restriction (currently only 117 members have agreed to the full convertibility of their currencies). Member countries are obligated to keep the IMF informed of any changes in their financial and monetary policies that may adversely affect fellow members' economies, and to expeditiously modify or reform national policies on the advice of the IMF in order to facilitate international trade.

In addition to supervising the international monetary system and providing financial support to member countries, the Fund also makes technical assistance available to member countries in certain specialized areas of its competence. It runs an educational institute in Washington to train personnel, and it issues a wide range of publications relating to all aspects of international monetary matters and IMF operations.

## Operations

The Fund operates much like a credit union, serving as a manager of a common pool of financial resources estimated to be over $300 billion in 1999. This resource base allows the Fund to establish a stable value for each currency and to demonstrate confidence in members by making the general resources temporarily available to them, thus providing them with the opportunity to correct maladjustments in their balance of payments without resorting to measures destructive to national or international growth. The Fund's capital comes almost entirely from quota subscriptions (membership fees), assessed on the basis of each member country's economic size and the extent of current account transactions. The size of a member's official foreign currency reserves is also taken into account. As a general rule, 25 percent of quota is required to be subscribed in an international reserve currency (international reserve currencies are the euro, the U.S. dollar, the British pound sterling, and the Japanese yen). The balance can be paid in the member's own currency. The combined contributions of the members form a pool of currencies that is known as the General Resources Account. This pool of currencies comprises the core resources from which the IMF funds lending to members. As each member has a right to borrow several times the amount it has paid in as a quota subscription, quotas may not provide enough cash to meet the borrowing needs of members in a period of great economic stress. To deal with this eventuality, the IMF has had since 1962 a line of credit for its members.

Those who contribute the most to the IMF have the strongest voice in determining its policies. The United States, with the world's largest economy, contributes about 18 percent (approximately $38 billion in 1997) of the total quota, followed by Japan and Germany, which contribute 5.67 percent each. This means that the U.S. has 18 percent of the total votes. Quotas are reviewed every five years, allowing member countries to either increase or lower their contributions. The size of quotas not only determines the voting power of the member country but also what a country can borrow in time of need. While most of the matters that go to the executive board are decided by consensus, the voting power of the individual members often provides an important backdrop to how the consensus is shaped. A simple majority of the votes is required for most matters, but the more important policy matters must receive 85 percent of the votes which means that the United States has a veto power by virtue of its 18 percent share of the total quota.

The two principal functions carried out by the IMF today are surveillance of the members' economic policies and provision of short-term conditional financing to members facing balance-of-payment difficulties. The scope of the surveillance is quite wide, and covers, for example, trade and investment policies, the financial sector (including the functioning of capital markets), and exchange-rate policy. The scope of surveillance has been bolstered in the wake of the Mexican peso crisis of 1995 and the Asian financial crisis of 1997–1998.

Conditionality is attached to all IMF loans. This generally means that IMF financing requires the recipient country to adopt economic adjustment programs. Interest is also charged on the loans made under the IMF's standard lending facilities at a rate set to cover its costs, plus a margin to cover operating expenses. For certain other IMF loan facilities, interest surcharges or concessions apply. For example, the Enhanced Structural Adjustment Facility (ESAF), established in 1987, is designed to support macroeconomic adjustment and structural reforms in low-income countries. This is a concessional facility in that the interest rate is only 0.5 percent per annum. In November 1999, the ESAF was renamed the Poverty Reduction and Growth Facility (PRGF), and its objectives were changed to support programs to strengthen economic growth in poor countries. The PRGF loans carry an interest rate of 0.5 percent and are repayable over 10 years with a 6-year grace period on principal payments.

Besides supervising the international monetary system and providing financial support to member countries, the Fund also assists its members by making technical assistance available to member countries in certain specialized areas of its competence; by running an educational institute in Washington to train personnel; and by issuing a wide range of publications relating to all aspects of international monetary matters and IMF operations.

## The IMF and the Asian Financial Crisis of 1997

The principal responsibility for dealing with the recent Asian crisis at the international level was assumed by the IMF, and the hitherto relatively unknown institution was put into the global spotlight as never before. Its every official utterance and policy move became the subject of intense public scrutiny and scathing criticism—from both the right and the left. With the benefit of hindsight, it is clear that the IMF's record in dealing with the Asian financial crisis has been mixed.

The conditions that the IMF imposed on Thailand, Indonesia, and Korea in exchange for IMF-led rescue packages consisted of three basic components. The first concentrated on macroeconomic policy reform, in particular, the introduction of tight fiscal and monetary policy (that is, an increase in interest rates and the adoption of strict limits on the growth of the money supply), in order to produce current account surpluses and to stabilize the value of the currency by slowing currency depreciation. Policy reform also included the maintenance of high interest rates to stem (or reverse) capital outflows. It was believed that such a strategy would improve the current account and the balance of payments, halt the depreciating exchange rate, reduce money growth and inflation, and reduce the government budget deficit. The second component focused on structural reforms of the financial sector. The third consisted of nonfinancial microeconomic policies, such as the removal of trade barriers, the elimination of monopolies, enterprise reform and restructuring, creating competitive factor markets, and curtailment of government budgets—in particular, the elimination of subsidies. It was presumed that all these measures could be implemented without significantly harming the real economy.

However, the initial results of the Fund-supported programs in Indonesia, Korea, and Thailand were not what had been hoped. Specifically, the programs were not successful in quickly restoring confidence. On the contrary, capital continued to exit and the currencies continued to depreciate after the IMF-supported programs had been adopted. Moreover, the economies sank deeper into recession, contrary to initial projections of only a mild slowdown. Why was this the case? Critics have asserted that the IMF's unimaginative one-model-fits-all prescriptions actually made Asia's financial turmoil worse. Suffice it to note that these issues will remain the subject for much debate for some time.

*Shalendra D. Sharma*

### Further Reading

Eichengreen, Barry. (1999) *Toward a New International Financial Architecture: A Practical Post-Asia Agenda.* Washington, DC: Institute for International Economics.

Folkerts-Landau, David, and Carl-Johan Lindgren. (1998) *Toward a Framework for Financial Stability*. Washington, DC: International Monetary Fund.

Williamson, John. (2000) "The Role of the IMF: A Guide to the Reports." International Economics Policy Brief no. 00-5. Washington, DC: Institute for International Economics.

**IQBAL, MUHAMMAD** (1877–1938), Poet-philosopher of Islam and Pakistan. Muhammad Iqbal, known as the poet-philosopher of Islam and Pakistan, was born on 9 November 1877, at Sialkot, India, and died at the peak of his fame on 21 April 1938, at Lahore. In Sialkot, Iqbal finished high school and then joined the Scotch Mission College, subsequently named Murray College. At this college, Iqbal completed two years of his education and then joined the Government College in Lahore, fifty miles from Sialkot. By this time, Iqbal had acquired a good education in Urdu, Arabic, and Farsi under the guidance of Sayyid Mir Hassan (1844–1929), who had been profoundly influenced by the Aligarh movement of Sir Sayyid Ahmed Khan (1817–1898). Under Sayyid Mir Hassan's care, Iqbal's poetic genius blossomed early.

In May 1899, a few months after Iqbal's graduation with a master's degree in philosophy, he was appointed the Macleod-Punjab reader of Arabic at the University Oriental College of Lahore. From January 1901 to March 1904, when he resigned from the position, Iqbal taught intermittently as assistant professor of English at Islamia College and at the Government College of Lahore. In 1905, Iqbal went to Europe, where he studied in England and Germany. In London, he studied at Lincoln's Inn to qualify at the bar, and, at Trinity College of Cambridge University, he enrolled as a student of philosophy while he prepared to submit a dissertation in philosophy to Munich University. Munich University exempted him from a mandatory stay of two terms on the campus before submitting his dissertation, "The Development of Metaphysics in Persia." After his successful defense of his dissertation, Iqbal was awarded a Ph.D. degree on 4 November 1907.

Iqbal was never at home in politics, but he was invariably drawn into it. In May 1908, he joined the British Committee of the All-India Muslim League. With the exception of one brief interruption, Iqbal maintained his relationships with the All-India Muslim League all his life.

When Iqbal came back from Europe in 1908 after earning three degrees in England and Germany, he started his professional career as an attorney, professor, poet, and philosopher all at once. At length, however, the poet and philosopher won out at the expense of the attorney and professor while he continued to be partially active as a political leader. Iqbal was elected a member of the Punjab Legislative Assembly from 1926 to 1930 and soon emerged as a political thinker. In 1930, the All-India Muslim League invited him to deliver a presidential address, which became a landmark in the Muslim national movement for the creation of Pakistan.

Iqbal's philosophical and political prose works are actually few in number, most notably *The Development of Metaphysics in Iran* (1908) and *The Reconstruction of Religious Thought in Islam* (1930). The latter work was actually a collection of his seven lectures that he had delivered in December 1928 in Madras. The lectures are reflective of his mature philosophical and rational approach to Islam, emphasizing a responsible *ijtihad*, the right of interpreting the Qur'an and the Sunna. A third work is *Iqbal's Presidential Address to the Annual Meeting of the All-India Muslim League* (1930). This address is an extensive review of the interaction among the British, the All-India National Congress, and the All-India Muslim League from the perspective of a Muslim thinker. In it, Iqbal expounded the concept of two nations in India. This address came to be known as the origin of the idea for an independent state of Pakistan.

Iqbal composed his poetry in Persian and Urdu. His six Persian works are *Asrar-I Khudi wa Ramuz-I Bekhudi* (1915), *Payam Mashriq* (1923), *Zabur-I Ajam* (1927), *Javid-Namah* (1932), *Pas Chas Bayad Kard Ay Aqwam-I Sharq* (1926), and *Armaghan-I Hijiz* (1938). His Urdu works, which are primarily responsible for his popularity in Pakistan as well as in India, are *Bang-I Dara* (1924), *Bal-I Jibril* (1935), and *Darb-I-Kalim* (1936). Poetry, like visual art, is susceptible to varied interpretations; consequently, his admirers, relying primarily upon his poetry, have attempted to prove him a nationalist, a Muslim nationalist, a Muslim socialist, and even a secularist.

Iqbal remained a steady supporter of the founder of Pakistan, Mohammad Ali Jinnah (1876–1948). During 1936–1937, Iqbal wrote eight letters to Jinnah, advocating the partition of India into two nations. His presidential address of 1930 formulated the two-nation theory, which Jinnah finally accepted when he presided over the All-India Muslim League's annual meeting in Lahore in 1940 and demanded that Pakistan be created by partitioning India.

*Hafeez Malik*

**Further Reading**

"Iqbal, Sir Muhammad (1876–1938)." (1949) *Dictionary of National Biography 1931–1940*. London: Oxford University Press.

Malik, Hafeez. (1970) "Iqbal's Conception of Ego." *The Muslim World* 60 (April): 2.

———, ed. (1971) *Iqbal: Poet-Philosopher of Pakistan*. New York: Columbia University Press.

Sadiq, Muhammad. (1964) *A History of Urdu Literature*. London: Oxford University Press.

Schimmel, Annemarie. (1963) *Gabriel's Wing*. Leiden, Netherlands: E. J. Brill.

**IRAN—PROFILE** (2001 pop. 66.1 million). The Islamic Republic of Iran (Iran's official name since 1979) is a nation whose social, cultural, political, and economic affairs are conducted based on the tenets of Islam. Although this theocratic republic is still in its infancy, it has faced many challenges both internal and external. Externally, its main challenges have come from the United States and Iraq. Internally, beyond staggering inflation and high unemployment rates, it currently faces demands from a youthful population for more moderate policies.

Iran covers 1.648 million square kilometers and borders Afghanistan and Pakistan in the east, Turkey and Iraq in the west, Armenia, Azerbaijan, Turkmenistan, and the Caspian Sea in the north, and the Persian Gulf and the Gulf of Oman in the south. Its main geographic features are an interior central plateau, which is arid or semiarid in nature, and mountainous regions that include the Zagros mountain range in the west, the Elburz and Talish mountains in the north, and the mountains to the east along the border with Pakistan and Afghanistan. Its climate is as varied as its topography, with temperatures ranging from minus 26°C to 55.6°C.

Iran is one of the most populous countries in the Middle East. Most Iranians live in the northwest and by the Caspian Sea. More than 50 percent of the population lives in urban areas. Besides its capital, Tehran,

## IRAN

**Country name:** Islamic Republic of Iran
**Area:** 1.648 million sq km
**Population:** 66,128,969 (July 2001 est.)
**Population growth rate:** 0.72% (2001 est.)
**Birth rate:** 17.1 births/1,000 population (2001 est.)
**Death rate:** 5.41 deaths/1,000 population (2001 est.)
**Net migration rate:** –4.51 migrant(s)/1,000 population (2001 est.)
**Sex ratio—total population:** 1.03 male(s)/female (2001 est.)
**Infant mortality rate:** 29.04 deaths/1,000 live births (2001 est.)
**Life expectancy at birth—total population:** 69.95 years, male: 68.61 years, female: 71.37 years (2001 est.)
**Major religions:** Shi'a Islam, Sunni Islam, Zoroastrianism, Judaism, Christianity, Baha'i
**Major languages:** Persian, Turkic languages, Kurdish, Luri, Balochi, Arabic, Turkish
**Literacy—total population:** 72.1%; male: 78.4%, female: 65.8% (1994 est.)
**Government type:** theocratic republic
**Capital:** Tehran
**Administrative divisions:** 28 provinces
**Independence:** 1 April 1979 (Islamic Republic of Iran proclaimed)
**National holiday:** Republic Day, 1 April (1979)
**Suffrage:** 15 years of age; universal
**GDP—real growth rate:** 3% (2000 est.)
**GDP—per capita (purchasing power parity):** $6,300 (2000 est.)
**Population below poverty line:** 53% (1996 est.)
**Exports:** $25 billion (f.o.b., 2000 est.)
**Imports:** $15 billion (f.o.b., 2000 est.)
**Currency:** Iranian rial (IRR)

*Source:* Central Intelligence Agency. (2001) *The World Factbook* 2001. Retrieved 18 October 2001 from: http://www.cia.gov/cia/publications/factbook.

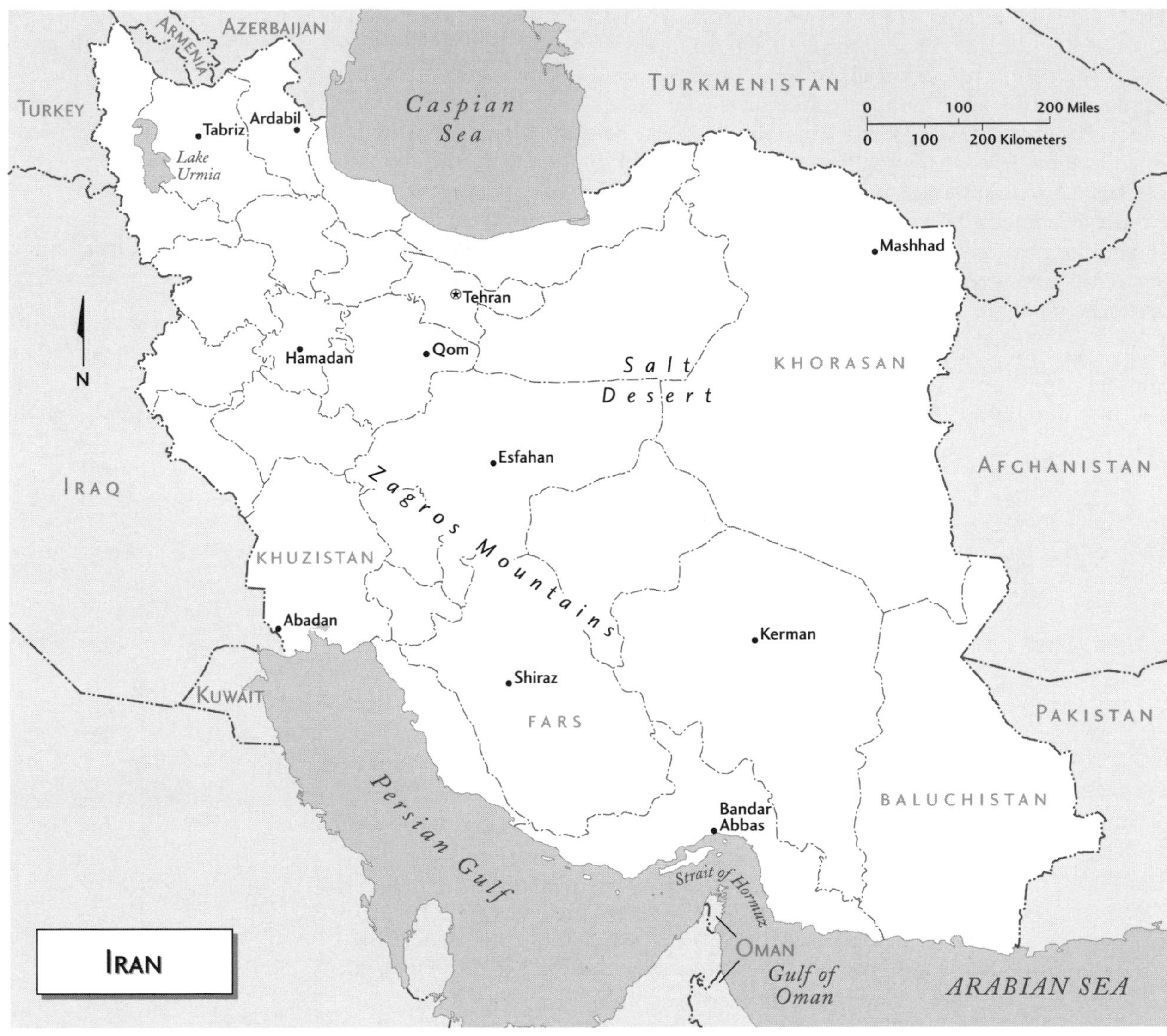


Iran's other cities and towns are Esfahan, Mashhad, Tabriz, Shiraz, Ahvaz, Bakhtaran, Orumiyeh, Qazvin, Kerman, Ardabil, Yazd, Karaj, Qom, Rasht, and Hamadan. Persians account for two-thirds of the population, with the remainder coming from a variety of ethnic groups (Azeri, Kurd, Lur, Baluch, Arab, Turkmen, Armenian, and Jewish). It is a young population, with 36 percent of the population below fourteen years of age and 60 percent of the population between the ages of fifteen and sixty-four. This youthful population has brought about the recent mass political shift and demand for reforms in the government from its conservative base to a more open forum.

### The Birth of the Islamic Republic of Iran

When Ayatollah Khomeini (1900–1989) came to power in January 1979, he gave the job of drafting a constitution to the provisional government and named Mehdi Bazargan (1907–1994) as the prime minister of the provisional government. In March 1979, a national referendum was conducted to determine what political system should be instituted. On the referendum day, however, the Islamic Republic was the only choice on the ballot. Reportedly, over 98 percent of the voters supported an Islamic republic, and the Islamic Republic of Iran was established on 1 April 1979.

By the end of the year, the constitution of the Islamic Republic had come into force. This document was originally drafted by the provisional government, then modified by the Assembly of Experts, and finally approved by a national referendum. This constitution made the concept of *veleyet-e-Faqih* (rule of religious jurisprudence) a political reality.

**Language and Culture**

Iran's official language is Persian, also known as Farsi, which is spoken by a majority of the people. Persian dialects such as Gilani and Mazandarani are also spoken throughout the country. Other regional languages found in Iran include Kurdish, Azeri, Armenian, Baloch, Luri, Arabic, and Hebrew.

Iran is a very ancient country whose history dates back to the eve of the Persian civilization and empire. Due to its colorful and rich background, it has much to offer in terms of the arts, as is evident from its architecture, paintings, and a variety of handicrafts. Moreover, Persian literature is famous for its beautiful poetry, thought-provoking stories, and epic writings.

**Government**

Similar to Western states, the political power of the Iranian government is horizontally divided into three branches: executive, legislative, and judiciary. Unlike the Western powers, however, the *faqih* (spiritual leader of the nation) oversees all three branches. The constitution clearly outlines the requirements for the *faqih*, including Islamic training and age. Ayatollah Khomeini was named the first *faqih* for life.

Several institutions were formed to monitor the government's conduct to make sure that it conformed to Islamic principles and laws. The three branches of government—executive, legislative, and judiciary—are monitored by religious leaders and institutions to make sure they operate according to the precepts of Islamic rule. Moreover, several of the government officials within all branches of government are clerics. One such institution is the Council of Guardians, half of whose members are appointed by the *faqih* (spiritual leader).

Ayatollah Sayed Ali Khamenei (b. 1939) is the current *faqih*. He succeeded Ayatollah Khomeini (1900–1989) in 1989. The constitution gives considerable powers to the *faqih* to ensure the government functions within Islamic law. The constitution also clarifies *faqih* selection criteria, which entails training in and experience with Islamic history, laws, and philosophy.

The current president is Muhammad Khatami (b. 1943) who was elected in 1997. He had been the minister of culture in the cabinet of the former president, Hashemi Rafsanjani (b. 1934). Khatami's election signaled the shifting of the political climate. The 2000 *majlis* (parliament) elections echoed that change: moderates and reformers overwhelmingly defeated more conservative candidates. The presidents and the *majlis* representatives are elected for four-year terms.

**Religion**

The constitution names the official religion in Iran as Shi'a, the branch of Islam that believes the lineage of 'Ali ibn Abi Talib, the son-in-law of the Prophet Muhammad, is the true succession. Approximately 93 percent of the population are Shi'ite Muslims. About 5 percent are Sunni Muslims; Sunni Muslims believe that Muhammad's disciples were his true successors. While there has been rivalry between the two sects, the government has worked to keep it to a minimum. Christians, Jews, and Zoroastrians are recognized as lawful religious minorities and have their own representatives in the *majlis*. The Baha'i faith, however, is not a recognized religion, and its followers face religious restrictions and even discrimination at the hands of individuals as well as the state.

This marriage of government and religion reaches out into the society, where Islamic ways have become law. Women are required by law to completely cover their body and hair, showing only their hands and face. Men are also restricted in what parts of their body they

Iranian president Muhammad Khatami at a meeting with college students in December 1999 where he agreed that students have the right to protest government policies, but urged stability. (AFP/CORBIS)

can show in public. For example, they must wear long-sleeved shirts, buttoned up to hide any chest hair. Men and women who do not comply with this dress code may be harassed by their more religious fellow citizens and can actually be arrested and charged by officials. Also, the interaction between men and women is carefully monitored. For instance, public displays of affection are not condoned.

### Education

Education is compulsory for all children from seven to thirteen years old, but it has been difficult to enforce this law in the rural areas. After the Islamic Revolution, a panel, the Cultural Revolution Headquarters, was formed to reform the educational system in accordance with Islamic values. Higher education in Iran consists of government-sponsored colleges as well as technical, vocational, and teacher-training schools.

### Human Rights

By Western standards, the human rights record of Iran has been poor both before and after the revolution. After the revolution, opponents of the new regime were severely dealt with. Illegal searches and arrests as well as quick trials and executions were the norm. Nevertheless, there have been significant improvements, especially during the Khatami era. Emphasis on human rights is one of the factors leading toward change.

Freedom of expression has been a controversial issue from time to time. The media, particularly the periodicals, are given free rein except when it is believed Islamic principles are being threatened or criticized. In one international incident, Ayatollah Khomeini publicly formally condemned British writer Salman Rushdie (b. 1947) to death for his criticisms of Islam in his book *The Satanic Verses*. The freedom of the press was seriously threatened in early 2000 when several liberal newspapers were shut down by the conservative forces before the upcoming election. This was met with outcries from the people and further represents the clash that is currently taking place between the conservative and moderate elements.

### Economy

The currency in Iran is the Iranian rial. Iran's gross domestic product (GDP) in 1998 was estimated at $100.3 billion. Its main source of income is from the sales of its natural resources, particularly fossil fuels. Iran is one of the founding members of the Organization of Petroleum Exporting Countries (OPEC). It has worked hard to diversify its economy and has faced several challenges, including the trade embargo imposed by the United States in 1995 and the high cost of the reconstruction program after the war with Iraq (1980–1990). Currently, pressure is mounting in the United States to lift the embargo, particularly from U.S. oil companies. For instance, it would be much cheaper to run an oil pipeline through Iran (rather than Turkey) in order to transport the oil of landlocked Central Asian states to the international market. One step has already been taken in the direction of relaxing U.S. pressure on Iran. Madeleine Albright, the U.S. secretary of state from 1993 to 2000, lifted the embargo on certain products (for example, carpets) in March 2000.

### Iran and the United States

The relationship between the United States and Iran since the establishment of the Islamic Republic of Iran has been strained at best. Soon after the success of the Islamic Revolution, both the Iranian and U.S. leaders demonized each other. Revolutionary Iranians claimed that the United States was pursuing a hegemonic role in the Persian Gulf region; the Americans accused Iran of sponsoring terrorism. The United States in the 1990s has been concerned about Iran achieving nuclear capability. However, toward the end of the decade there were a few signs of a thaw in relations with overtures being made by both sides, slowly and carefully. However, in 2002, U.S. President George W. Bush declared Iran, along with Iraq and North Korea, to be one of the "Axis of Evil," leading to increased hostility toward the United States.

*Houman A. Sadri*

### Further Reading

Adelkhah, Fariba. (2000) *Being Modern in Iran.* New York: Columbia University Press.

Amirahmadi, Hooshang (1990). *Revolution and Economic Transition: The Iranian Expansion.* New York: SUNY Press.

Bina, Cyrus, and Hamid Zangeneh, eds. (1992) *Modern Capitalism and Islamic Ideology in Iran.* New York: St. Martin's Press.

Katouzian, Homa. (1999) *Musaddiq and the Struggle for Power in Iran.* 2d ed. New York: St. Martin's Press.

Ramazani, R. K. (1986) *Revolutionary Iran: Challenge and Response in the Middle East.* Baltimore and London: Johns Hopkins University Press.

Sadri, Houman A. (1997) *Revolutionary States, Leaders, and Foreign Relations: A Comparative Study of China, Cuba, and Iran.* Westport, CT: Praeger.

**IRAN—ECONOMIC SYSTEM** The Iranian economic system is a combination of a centrally planned economy, public ownership of fossil-fuel and

The interior courtyard of an upper-class family's home in Na'in, Iran, in 1997. (BRIAN A. VIKANDER/CORBIS)

other large industries, village agriculture, and small market-based ventures. The economy relies on the nation's abundant natural resources but has been negatively affected by political events such as the U.S. trade embargo of the 1990s and the Iran-Iraq War (1980–1990). The current president, Mohammed Khatami (b. 1943), is working to follow in his predecessor's footsteps with regard to economic reforms and diversification. These include decreasing the military budget and improving foreign relations. However, he has found these tasks difficult to implement because of the deeply different opinions among the political elite. Ever since the establishment of the Islamic Republic, there have been heated debates in the *majlis* (parliament) and in the Council of Guardians (an organization charged with ensuring that legislation adheres to the constitution and to Islamic law) about what direction the economy should take and which policies should be enforced.

## Historical Perspective

Before World War II, agriculture was the foundation of Iranian society and economy, and the oil industry was largely in the hands of foreign interests. Not much had been developed in the manufacturing sector, with some exceptions in food processing and textiles.

After World War II some capitalistic ventures became more commonplace and the government began implementing long-term economic plans, which were instrumental in the development of the economy. The government invested large amounts of capital in infrastructure and education, plans that were financed by the export of Iranian oil. In the early 1960s, the Western powers encouraged the shah to initiate a major reform. In response, he instituted the White Revolution program, an economic plan based on land reform and industrialization. This economic reform, however, met with widespread criticism led by Ayatollah Khomeini, who began the undercurrent that eventually led to the overthrow of the shah and the establishment of the Islamic Republic.

Nevertheless, the White Revolution did succeed in raising Iran's gross national product (GNP) as well as increasing its investments in fixed capital. Metallurgical, petrochemical, and appliance businesses were developed and ultimately led to a reduction in the importance of agriculture. This industrial development led to the rapid growth of old commercial centers such as Tehran, Tabriz, Esfahan, and Abadan as well as new industrial centers like Arak, Ahvaz, Bandar-e Shah, Shiraz, and Bakhtaran.

The rapid economic achievements were halted with the advent of the 1979 Revolution. The Islamic Republic nationalized several private industries, banks, and insurance companies; skilled labor and capital fled the country. The 1979–1981 hostage crisis, in which Iranian revolutionaries seized Americans at the U.S. embassy in Tehran, seriously damaged Iranian economic relations with the United States, and the Iran-Iraq war (1980–1990) further debilitated the national economy. Several major ports were bombed, which decreased oil revenues. Since the end of the war, Iran has diligently worked to reconstruct its devastated economy. This has been a difficult task due to declining oil revenues and growing reliance on imports. In 1993, the Iranian economy experienced a crisis over exchange rates. In 1995, President Clinton instituted a trade embargo against Iran, which caused a massive devaluation of the Iranian currency. This resulted in the Iranian government linking the value of its currency to the dollar as well as to personal attacks on private foreign-currency dealers who were thought to be cheating their fellow citizens and corrupting the economy.

Currently Iran aims to diversify its economy to make it less vulnerable to the rise and fall of the price of fossil fuels in the international markets. Since the 1991 demise of the Soviet Union, the Iranian government has hoped to capitalize on its location and emerge as the main gateway to the landlocked Caspian Sea republics. It would like to take advantage of profitable transit fees exacted on imports to and exports from these states. In this regard, the Islamic Republic has succeeded in establishing cooperative working ties with these states. At the same time, the Iranian people would like the government to do more to control the rampant inflation and unemployment rates plaguing the country.

### Industries

Most of Iran's national income derives from the vast oil resources that were discovered in the southwestern part of the country in the early 1900s. They contain an estimated 48 billion barrels of petroleum, and oil comprises over 90 percent of the country's exports. A founding member of the Organization of Petroleum Exporting Countries (OPEC), Iran is one of the largest oil producers in the world. The oil industry is run by the government-owned National Iranian Oil Company. The major refineries are located at Abadan, Tehran, Bakhtaran, and Shiraz. Abadan was the largest export-producing refinery in the world until it was damaged during the war with Iraq.

### Service Industries

About half the country's GDP comes from service industries such as banks, insurance companies, restaurants, and retail shops, and from institutions such as hospitals, educational facilities, and government agencies. Almost half of all workers are employed in the service industries.

Besides oil, Iran exports carpets, hides, caviar, cotton, nuts, spices, dried fruits, and mineral ores. The nation exports a great deal of raw and semiprocessed materials and imports manufactured goods such as electrical appliances, industrial machinery, and military equipment, as well as food and medicine. Most of the trade goes through the Persian Gulf ports, with Kharg Island being the principal terminal for exporting oil. Iran's major export trading partners are Italy, Japan, Greece, France, Spain, and South Korea. Its exports were estimated at $12.2 billion in 1998, while its imports were assessed at $13.8 billion. Iran's major import trading partners are Germany, Italy, Japan, Belgium, the United Arab Emirates, and the United Kingdom. Although the United States has extensive interests in Iranian natural resources, it is operating under the restrictions of the trade embargo imposed in 1995. In March 2000, however, certain luxury products such as caviar and carpets were removed from the embargo list to reward Iran for its changing political climate.

***Transportation*** Buses are the main means of transportation throughout Iran, but more primitive means are still used in rural areas, such as horses, donkeys, mules, and bicycles. Rough terrain makes building modern transportation infrastructure difficult. There are 162,000 kilometers of highways in Iran, but only half of them are paved. The railway system extends over 7,286 kilometers. The Iranian railway system and airline are both owned by the government. There are approximately 288 airports in Iran, but only 110 of them have paved runways. The main international airport is located in Tehran, the nation's capital.

The merchant marine has 132 ships in its inventory in several classifications: bulk cargo, chemical tanker, combination bulk-container–liquefied gas tanker, multifunction large-load carrier, oil tanker, refrigerated cargo, roll-on/roll-off cargo, and short-sea passenger. Several ports and harbors exist on the Caspian Sea and Persian Gulf areas. Abadan, damaged in the Iran-Iraq war, is being rebuilt.

***Media and Communications*** Regarding communications, information is disseminated through twenty-five newspapers, over three hundred magazines, two television stations, and many radio stations. In 1999, it was estimated the Iranian population owned 13 million radios and 7 million televisions. The information distributed is monitored by the government for its content in order to make sure it is not contrary to the teachings and tenets of Islam. At various times, the government has cracked down and closed the newspapers. This happened in March 2000 when conservative elements in the government felt threatened by the upcoming *majlis* elections.

There are over 9 million telephones in Iran. In 1996, twenty-five regional telecommunications authorities were set up to oversee the development of paging and cellular services and systems. There were believed to be 230,000 cell phone subscribers in 1996.

***Agriculture and Fishing*** Iran's mountains and deserts make it hard for the country to cultivate enough land to feed its population. Only 10 percent of its land is arable. Irrigated land was estimated in 1993 at 94,000 square kilometers. Farming employs approximately 28 percent of the workforce. Most of the land is set aside to grow wheat and barley. Other crops grown are rice, cotton, corn, dates, tea, tobacco, lentils, nuts, and sugar beets. Livestock raised include cows, goats, and sheep, which provide meat and dairy products. Agriculture makes up roughly 23 percent of Iran's GDP.

Iran borders both the Caspian Sea and Persian Gulf, and has a profitable fishing industry. Sturgeon, whose eggs are processed into caviar, are the main catch for Caspian Sea fishermen. Other fish to be found in the Caspian Sea are carp, catfish, whitefish, and white salmon. Sardines, shrimp, sole, and tuna are found in the Persian Gulf.

***Manufacturing, Construction, and Mining*** Manufacturing and the construction industry employ about one-fourth of the Iranian work force and are estimated to account for 18 percent of the GDP. The principal manufactured goods are cement, fossil-fuel products, armaments, textiles, bricks, and food items. However, Iran also manufactures tools, chemicals, leather products, copper, steel, and tobacco products. Tehran is the home of over 50 percent of the factories in Iran, followed by Esfahan and Tabriz.

Although it is an important industry, mining only employs 1 percent of Iran's workers and makes up only 9 percent of the GDP. Among minerals that Iran exploits are coal, manganese, sulfur, copper, lead, zinc, chromium, iron ore, and gemstones such as turquoise. Iranian natural gas reserves are considered the second largest in the world, approximately 15 percent of the world's reserves.

***Tourism*** Tourism fell with the advent of the Islamic Revolution. However, it is on the rise due to the nation's changing image and political environment. Iran's ancient history and favorable exchange rate make it one of the most interesting and inexpensive places to visit. In this regard, the number of visitors to the historical cities of Esfahan, Tabriz, and Shiraz as well as the charming coastal cities of the Caspian Sea and Persian Gulf is gradually on the rise.

### Economic Indicators

Iran's GDP was estimated at $100.3 billion in 1998. This shows a slight decrease from the year before and represents a downtrend over the previous ten years. In 1977, the GDP was $76 billion, and in 1987 it had risen to $137.7 billion. However, this upward swing was not to continue. The average annual growth of GDP is down from 3 percent in 1997 to 1.7 percent in 1998. The gross national product per capita in 1998 was $1,770, with the GNP at $109.6 billion. The GNP per capita has likewise seen a decrease in its average annual growth, actually seeing a negative growth in 1998, standing at –0.3 percent. The early 1990s witnessed a financial crisis in Iran, which led the country to reschedule $15 billion in debt. Fluctuating oil prices dramatically affect the Iranian economy. When oil prices are high, as they were in 1996, Iran is able to make its debt service payments. But when oil prices are low, the country finds it hard to keep up with its debt service payments and is forced to decrease its imports.

The currency in Iran is the Iranian rial (IR), divided into one hundred dinars. Internationally, the IR is used for calculating figures; domestically, however, the toman (ten rials) is used. In January 1999, one U.S. dollar was worth 1,754.63 IR. However, the black market exchange rate in December 1998 was 7,000 IRs to the dollar. In 1996, it was estimated that over 53 percent of the population was below the poverty line. Despite a workforce of 15.4 million people, the country lacks highly skilled labor in terms of technology, largely because of emigration following the revolution. The unemployment rate is more than 30 percent and the inflation rate about 24 percent.

The fiscal year in Iran goes from 21 March (which is the first day of spring and the Iranian New Year) to 20 March. The budget is divided into two sections: the general budget and the development budget. For the fiscal year 1996–1997, Iran was unable to balance the budget. Revenues were $34.6 billion, but expenditures were $34.9 billion. Most of the revenues came from taxes and oil sales, while the expenditures were allotted mainly to education, housing, welfare, and defense. The government's main social expenditures for its growing population are medical coverage, unemployment, retirement, and veterans' benefits.

### The Future

The Islamic Republic has continued the practice of the previous regime in devising five-year economic plans. Its first plan was created with the vision of ultimately quadrupling GDP by 2003. Subsequent plans were designed to revitalize the economy by putting more emphasis on the private sector. Iran had an estimated external debt of $21.9 billion in 1996. In 1995, it received $116.5 million dollars in economic aid.

*Houman A. Sadri*

### Further Reading

Amirahmadi, Hooshang. (1990) *Revolution and Economic Transition: The Iranian Expansion.* New York: State University of New York Press.

Bina, Cyrus, and Hamid Zangeneh, eds. (1992) *Modern Capitalism and Islamic Ideology in Iran.* New York: St. Martin's Press.

Moghadam, Fatemeh E. (1996) *From Land Reform to Revolution: The Political Economy of Agricultural Development in Iran, 1962–1992.* New York: St. Martin's Press.

Sick, Gary G., and Lawrence G. Potter, eds. (1997) *The Persian Gulf at the Millennium: Essays in Politics, Economy, Security, and Religion.* New York: St. Martin's Press.

**IRAN—EDUCATION SYSTEM** The education system of Iran was patterned on the French system and evolved during the twentieth century to its present configuration. Although some preprimary schooling is available, the first educational cycle for most students is primary school *(debestan)* beginning at age five. This is followed by a three-year middle school *(doreh-e rahanamaii)* in which students are tested and evaluated for future educational tracking and at the end of which they receive a certificate of general education. Depending on their middle school experience, they may continue to a four-year intermediate school *(dabirestan)* whose diploma entitles them to proceed to college, to a two-year vocational school, to an agricultural secondary school that awards a trade certificate, or to a four-year technical secondary school that awards a terminal second-class technician's certificate. Women who have earned a diploma may enter a two-year normal school preparing primary teachers for rural areas. Higher education is furnished by universities offering bachelor's, master's, and doctor's degrees, institutes of technology, and one-year teacher training colleges.

Traditional education in Iran was for centuries conducted in *maktab*s, private schools conducted by Muslim clergy for boys aged seven to twelve. Located in every city and virtually every village, these free schools inculcated basic literacy in Persian and Qur'anic Arabic, as well as the fundamentals of arithmetic.

Almost as numerous were the *madrasah*s (religious schools) attached to the mosques. In these, older boys studied Arabic and Persian literature, the Qur'an, theology, philosophy, law, and other subjects suited to pursuing a religious vocation. The students who took advantage of these schools were almost always the children of the well-to-do. If their families wanted them to pursue an education broader or deeper than this curriculum provided, they were given tutors or sent abroad to study, many of them to Britain or France. In 1851, the first state-sponsored school appeared: the College of Science in Tehran, founded to provide higher studies in business, technology, and military science. Apart from some Western-style secondary schools under German, French, or English auspices, this was the only alternative to Islamic religious education until the end of the nineteenth century.

### Twentieth-Century Education before the Islamic Revolution

In 1899, publicly supported elementary and secondary schools, most of them modeled after French institutions, were established in the major cities, and in 1911, the Ministry of Education was created to develop a national system of primary schools. By 1925, there were approximately 3,300 public schools enrolling over 100,000 students.

The modernization of Iran under the Pahlavi dynasty (1925–1979) demanded the creation of an educated secularized middle class with technological and commercial expertise. Although the education system was crucial to the effort, its expansion was relatively

Older men attending a literacy class in Iran. (PAUL ALMASY/CORBIS)

slow. By the 1960s, Iranian schools offered five years of primary instruction and seven years of secondary, including both terminal and college preparatory curricula. Six universities, located in Tehran, Tabriz, Esfahan, Mashhad, Shiraz, and Ahvaz, enrolled about seventeen thousand students. To accelerate the pace of education reform, Iran created in 1963 a "knowledge corps" utilizing military inductees with secondary diplomas to teach villagers to read. When the dynasty fell in 1979, enrollment in elementary schools had reached three-quarters of the elementary-age group, but high school enrollment lagged behind at less than half of the secondary-age group.

### Education after the Revolution

The 1979 revolution brought to power a government of ayatollahs (religious leaders) to whom educational secularization was anathema. They purged teachers and texts that were perceived to be antireligious and introduced religious coursework into the curriculum. The university students resisted, often violently, and so universities were closed for four years while their curricula and personnel were reorganized. They reopened with much smaller student bodies. Although the postrevolutionary government has acted to counter this impact, the situation remains difficult, the problems many. At the end of the twentieth century, education spending had reached nearly 6 trillion rials, which was about 6 percent of the gross national product (GNP) and 18 percent of government expenditure (as compared with about 500 million rials or 7.5 percent of the GNP and 16 percent of government expenditure in 1980). More than 3,300 preprimary schools enrolled nearly 200,000 children. About 92 percent of the boys of elementary school age and 87 percent of the girls—nearly 10 million students—attended school; 79 percent of the boys of secondary school age and 69 percent of the girls—over 7.5 million students—attended school. Teacher-student ratios were 1 to 32 at the elementary level and 1 to 30 at the secondary level. Yet adult literacy was a disappointing 72 percent, unevenly distributed among males (78 percent) and females (66 percent). In 1997, a cross-national program testing mathematics and science ranked Iranian students thirty-eighth of forty-one nations studied in eighth-grade math performance and thirty-seventh in eighth-grade science. It ranked Iranian students twenty-fifth of twenty-six nations studied in both fourth-grade math and science. At all education levels, fewer women than men are enrolled, a disparity that is fairly constant over time. Higher education has not bounced back from its purging and reorganization under the revolution. The nation's thirty general universities, thirty medical universities, twelve specialized universities, and two distance-learning universities enrolled only half a million students. This enrollment drop was caused largely because the secularized economic and political elites were sending their children to university abroad in increasing numbers in the 1980s, to the detriment of Iranian universities. As if this were not bad enough, the fraction of those studying abroad who elect not to return to Iran after their studies has constituted a serious brain drain that renders national development more difficult.

*Joseph M. McCarthy*

### Further Reading


Menashri, David. (1992) *Education and the Making of Modern Iran.* Ithaca, NY: Cornell University Press.

Ringer, Monica M. (2001) *Education, Religion and the Discourse of Cultural Reform in Qajar Iran.* Costa Mesa, CA: Mazda Publishers.

Shahnazari, Fariba. (1992) *Modernization of Education: A Comparison of Japan and Iran.* Yamato-machi, Niigata-ken, Japan: Institute of Middle Eastern Studies, International University of Japan.


## IRAN—HISTORY

**IRAN—HISTORY** Iranian history is inevitably linked with that of Persia. The state was not officially named Iran until the Pahlavi dynasty, which made the name change in March 1935. But Persian history goes back to ancient times and is laced with stories of foreign invasions, battles, conflict, and glory.

### Ancient Times

In the 1500s BCE, nomads of Aryan descent began to move to southwest Asia, between the Caspian Sea and the Persian Gulf. This area is now known as Iran, which literally means "land of the Aryans." Two groups, Medes and Persians, settled in the northern and southern parts of the Iranian plateau, respectively. The Medes grew in power, ruling the Persians and other Indo-European peoples in the region. Cyrus the Great (c. 585–c. 529 BCE), a member of the Achaemenid Persian dynasty, ousted the Medes and founded the Achaemenid empire, which would bring glory to the Persian people. Cyrus went on to conquer Asia Minor, Palestine, Syria, and Babylonia. His son, Cambyses II (d. 522 BCE), added Egypt to their list of conquests. Darius I (550–486 BCE), also known as Darius the Great, came to power in 522 BCE. Although his attempt to conquer Greece failed, Darius earned his title for sound military and administrative practices, which allowed the Achaemenids to remain in power despite the less adept leaders who followed. Darius's son, Xerxes I (c. 519–465 BCE) also

## KEY EVENTS IN IRANIAN (PERSIAN) HISTORY

**7th–6th centuries BCE** The Medes rule the region.
**c.550 BCE–330/320 BCE** The period of the Ashaemenid Persians.
**312–64 BCE** Period of the Seleucid dynasty.
**224/228–651 CE** Period of the Sasanid dynasty.
**7th–10th centuries** The region is conquered and ruled by Muslim Arabs.
**1038–1157** Period of the Seljuk dynasty.
**13th–16th centuries** The region is ruled by the Mongols.
**1501–1722/1736** Period of the Safavid dynasty.
**1736** Nades Shah comes to power and extends the territory of Persia.
**1794–1925** Period of the Qajar dynasty.
**19th century** Persia is contested by Russia and Great Britain.
**1906** A constitutional monarchy is created but fails to function.
**1919** Persia becomes a British protectorate.
**1925–1979** Period of the Pahlavi dynasty.
**1941** Iran is invaded by British, Russian, and German forces.
**1951** The oil industry is nationalized.
**1979** Following the Iranian Revolution, the Islamic Republic of Iran is established.
**1980–1990** Period of Iran-Iraq War.
**1997** Mohammed Khatami, a moderate, is elected president.
**1998** A majority of moderates is elected to parliament.

tried and failed to conquer Greece, leaving his successors, Artaxerxes I and II, to make peace. Eventually, after uprisings and unrest had gradually undermined Achaemenid rule, the empire was conquered by Alexander of Macedon (356–323 BCE).

***The Seleucids and the Sasanids*** Alexander hoped to fuse the Greek and Persian cultures, even ordering his soldiers to marry Iranian women. His hopes were not realized, however, as he succumbed to fever and died without naming an heir. After his death four of his generals struggled for control of his empire; one of them, Seleucus, eventually established the Seleucid dynasty (312–64 BCE). The Seleucid dynasty was ultimately brought down by the Parthians, whose control eventually extended from India to Armenia. During this time, Ardashir (reigned 224–241 CE), who claimed to be a descendant of the legendary hero Sasan, became a Parthian governor. He used this position to consolidate his power, overthrew the Parthians, and established the Sasanid dynasty (224/228–651).

The Sasanids ruled for four hundred years within the approximate boundaries of the Achaemenid empire. It was a time of renewal of Iranian traditions, as well as of large-scale improvements in agricultural and urban development. The Sasanids proclaimed themselves *shahanshah* (king of kings) and oversaw minor rulers dispersed throughout the region. Zoroastrianism became the state religion, and priests played a major role in the government. Sasanid strength was eventually eroded by constant fighting with the Romans, who had replaced the Greeks as their main enemy. Initially, the Sasanids fought victoriously against Rome, with Shapur I (reigned 241–272), Ardashir's son and successor, at the helm. Continued fighting, however, diminished Iranian resources, and, coupled with domestic unrest, allowed the Sasanids to be conquered by the Arabs.

***Arab and Mongol Conquests*** The Arabs invaded Persia soon after they were united under the banner of Islam, a religion to which, eventually, a majority of Iranians were converted. Even though the Arabs were clearly the ruling party, Iranians were permitted to participate in and contribute to the new government; several Iranian practices were adopted by the Arabs, and Persian continued to be spoken even though Arabic became the official language. During the 900s, the Arabs began to lose control and the region broke into factions. Eventually the Seljuks, a Turkish group led by Toghril Beg (c. 990–1063), conquered the territory. Toghril Beg was given the title King of the East by the religious leadership. Malik Shah (1055–1092) succeeded him, bringing an era of cultural and scientific achievement to Iran. When he died the region once again split into warring dynasties.

At around this time the Mongol Genghis Khan (c. 1162–1227) began a conquering spree, starting in China and heading west, destroying everything in his path. Iran suffered tremendously: cities were decimated and populations massacred. Genghis Khan's death did little to ameliorate Iran's situation, however, as the Mongol rulers who followed were just as ruthless. One exception, Ghazan Khan (1271–1304), did allow improvements in agricultural techniques and road conditions, which favorably affected the Iranians. Eventually, fighting among Mongol tribes loosened their control over Iran and allowed the emergence of the Safavid dynasty (1501–1722/1736).

***The Safavid Dynasty*** The Safavids rose to power in 1501 under the leadership of Ismail, who was ultimately crowned shah of Iran. Shi'a Islam, instituted as the state religion, played a central role in the governance of the state, and resources were employed to convert the Muslim population to the Shi'a sect. Striking a balance between religion and the state, as well as between the Turkic and the Iranian populations, were among the most important challenges faced by the empire. In addition, the Safavids faced enemies in the northeast and west: the Uzbeks and Ottomans, respectively. One particular confrontation had serious repercussions: In 1524, the Ottomans occupied the Safavid capital of Tabriz; although brief, the occupation called into question the divine leadership of the Safavids.

Confrontations with the Ottomans continued until the Safavids, led by Shah Abbas I (1571–1629), counteracted Ottoman encroachment. After entering into a treaty with the Ottomans, Abbas first defeated the Uzbeks, then turned on the Ottomans, achieving control over Iraq, Georgia, and parts of the Caucasus. With his external enemies in check, Abbas worked internally to centralize his power. His reign saw a gradual distance arise between state and religion, even though the shah built mosques and donated large sums to religious institutions. The shah also actively advanced trade, architecture, and the arts. He moved the capital from Tabriz to Esfahan, the latter becoming a city of beauty, equipped with mosques, palaces, schools, and a marketplace. When Abbas died, the empire spiraled downhill, and the way was opened for Afghan tribes to take control; in 1722 they brought an end to the Safavid dynasty.

The Afghans did not rule for long. They were overthrown by a chief of the Afshar tribe, Tahmasp Qoli (1688–1747), who asserted the right to do so in the name of a member of the Safavid family. Nevertheless, soon after, he claimed the power in his own right as Nader Shah (1736). He went on to conquer Afghanistan and lead successful campaigns into India. These military incursions proved taxing on the population financially and physically, however, and resulted in the death of Nader Shah at the hands of one of his own chiefs.

***The Qajar Dynasty*** Once again, Iran erupted as petty dynasties and tribes vied for power. One tribal leader, Karim Khan Zand (c. 1705–1779), was briefly able to gain control, but when he died, chaos reigned again. Finally, Agha Muhammad Khan Qajar (1742–1797) emerged as the leader. The Qajar dynasty began in 1794, when Muhammad Qajar named himself master of the country, and ended in 1925. Qajar's successors, Fath 'Ali (reigned 1797–1834), Muhammad Shah (reigned 1834–1848), and Naser od-Din Shah (reigned 1848–1896), were able to bring some measure of stability to the country, restoring the concept of shah, which had been called into question during the Safavid era. Religion and state once again became closely associated.

## Modern Period

The history of Iran in the modern era is characterized by heavy foreign involvement—first Russia and Britain, later the United States—in the economic and political affairs of the nation, which eventually led to revolution in 1979.

In the beginning of the nineteenth century, Russia and Britain began to make their presences felt. Russia wanted Iranian territory, and in two wars that ended with two treaties—the Treaty of Gulistan (1812) and the Treaty of Turkmanchai (1828)—gained land in the Caucasus region. Later in the century Russia annexed territories in Central Asia. Britain's involvement stemmed from a desire to safeguard trade routes to India. The Treaty of Paris (1857) resulted in Britain's controlling Afghanistan.

Russia and Britain were able to exert considerable control over Iranian affairs due to their superior military and technological capabilities, and Iran's lack of centralized control. During Naser od-Din Shah's reign, attempts were made to tighten administrative processes, but these failed due to jealousy and corruption. An idea began to circulate that the way to stop foreign interference was to adopt European practices, which led to the creation of a cabinet based on the European model. Foreign involvement, however, did not

The Crown Prince of Iran and Egyptian Minister of National Defense Hussein Sabry Pacha watch a military demonstration in Egypt in March, 1939. (HULTON-DEUTSCH COLLECTION/CORBIS)

diminish, especially in commerce, where trade concessions were constantly given to Russia and Britain. The people protested these concessions; in one instance, under the leadership of the religious community, they forced the government to cancel a tobacco monopoly that had been awarded to Britain. The people became increasingly unhappy with the oppression, corruption, and foreign concessions, and Naser od-Din Shah was assassinated in 1896.

***The Constitutional Revolution*** His son and successor, Mozaffar od-Din (reigned 1896–1907) ruled in the same vein that had characterized his father's later years. He relied on Russia to provide loans—money he used extravagantly and ostentatiously, which angered the populace and ultimately led to what became known as the Constitutional Revolution. Religious leaders and merchants pressured the shah to agree to a constitutional monarchy, which would operate within the framework of law, and a constitution that limited the role of the royal family and provided for an elected parliament *(majlis)* was signed on 30 December 1906. Mozaffar, however, died just five days later, and his successor, Muhammad Ali Shah, had no intention of adhering to the constitution. He started an all-out campaign to crush it, but was defeated and forced into Russian exile. Constitutional rule did not take place, however, as once again outside influences intervened.

In 1907, Russia and Britain decided to divide Iran into spheres of influence: Russia would control the north, while Britain retained control of the south and east. A neutral area was established in the center, open to both. In a confrontation that ensued due to the hiring of a U.S. administrator, Russian troops advanced on Tehran, and the *majlis* was forced to close down and concede to Russian demands.

***The Pahlavi Dynasty*** Iran tried to maintain its neutrality during World War I, but became the battlefield for Russian, British, and Turkish forces. The end of the war brought an increased British presence, as the Russians were otherwise preoccupied with the Bolshevik revolution. The Anglo-Persian Agreement of 1919 amounted to Iran becoming a British protectorate, which enraged the population. In February 1921, a military officer, Reza Khan (1878–1944), aided by the journalist Sayyid Zia od-Din Tabatabai, seized power, first becoming war minister, then prime minister, and finally, in 1925, shah. Reza Khan changed his name to Pahlavi and thus began the Pahlavi dynasty.

The shah exerted considerable military control over the country and worked at modernization: He minimized religious influences, welcomed Westernization, and instituted economic and educational reform. The shah also worked to minimize British and Russian influence by increasing trade relations with Germany—which worked against him with the outbreak of World War II. Again, Iran tried to maintain its neutrality, but to no avail. Angered at its relationship with Germany, British and Russian troops invaded Iran in 1941, and the shah relinquished the throne to his son, Mohammad Reza Shah Pahlavi (1919–1980). Although Iran played a critical role in the war, providing passageway for military equipment and eventually declaring war on Germany, the presence of foreign troops did not create a feeling of camaraderie; in fact just the opposite occurred, and ultimately a nationalist movement took hold.

Several oil agreements had been signed with Britain and Russia. When it became apparent that Britain was benefiting more financially from the Anglo-Iranian Oil Company (AIOC) than was Iran, nationalists within the *majlis*, led by Muhammad Mosaddeq (1880–1967), began pushing for the AIOC agreement to be renegotiated, and on 15 March 1951 the *majlis* passed a bill nationalizing the oil industry. When the prime minister spoke against the law, he was assassinated and replaced by Mosaddeq. Nationalization resulted in Britain taking the case to the International Court of Justice at The Hague. Economic and political turmoil ensued, and the shah forced Mosaddeq from office. His popularity, however, proved to be such that the shah was forced into exile, and Mosaddeq assumed the reigns of government. His power was short-lived, however: the United States, finding Mosaddeq too inflexible, supported the return of the shah through a Central Intelligence Agency operation.

With the shah's return, Iran began to experience more U.S. involvement in its economic and political affairs. The shah launched several ambitious economic plans, but it was difficult for the Iranian economy to recover from the effects of the nationalist movement. Discontent with the shah's repressive practices and reliance on the United States increased. In an effort to quell these voices the shah devised the White Revolution, an ambitious plan of economic and land reform. The land reform was not met with enthusiasm by religious leaders; neither was his decision to extend the right to vote to women. In June of 1963, Ayatollah Khomeini (c.1900–1989) began speaking out against the shah and his White Revolution. Khomeini was ultimately sent into exile, but continued to speak against the shah and question his legitimacy. The shah responded by cracking down on all opposition.

***Establishment of an Islamic Republic*** In the late 1970s, Ayatollah Khomeini encouraged massive strikes throughout the country. In January of 1979, the shah left Iran under pretense of taking a vacation, allowing Khomeini to seize power. He immediately declared the shah's government illegitimate and instituted a provisional government, giving it the task of drafting a constitution establishing an Islamic republic in which the functions of government would be guided by the teachings of Islam. Several institutions, such as the Revolutionary Council, were created with the same thought in mind. Finally, Ayatollah Khomeini was named *faqih* (spiritual leader) for life.

Because of U.S. involvement in the area and its support for the shah, Khomeini regarded the United States as an enemy. These anti-American feelings were fueled in October 1978, when Washington allowed the shah to enter the United States for medical treatment—perceived as an attempt by the shah to gain support for his return to power. This resulted in Iranian students taking U.S. hostages at the embassy in Tehran. Eventually, the hostage crisis was peacefully resolved, but only after Iranian assets were frozen and a disastrous hostage rescue attempt by the United States. Negotiations began in earnest in September 1980, most likely because the Iranians were facing a new enemy: Iraq. Iraq invaded Iran in part because Iraq's president, Saddam Hussein (b. 1937), had territorial ambitions and in part because it feared the Iranian message of revolutionary Islam. The Iran-Iraq war was a brutal conflict that lasted eight years. Although it helped rally the Iranian people to a common cause, it had devastating effects on the economy, which ultimately led Khomeini to agree to a cease-fire in August 1988. The ayatollah died one year later. Ali Khamenei was named his successor as *faqih* and Hashemi Rafsanjani was elected president in 1989.

The revolutionary regime is characterized by restrictive practices and strict religious requirements. The late 1990s saw a movement calling for political reform, most likely due to the largely youthful population; as a result, a moderate, Muhammed Khatami, was elected president in 1997, and *majlis* elections in 2000 resulted in the election of a majority of moderates to the parliament.

These developments have had a positive effect on the Iranian relationship with other countries, including the United States, whose ties with Tehran have remained strained since the hostage crisis. The United States, however, is still concerned with the nature of the Iranian Islamic Republic, and with the possibility that nuclear capability might fall into the hands of revolutionary Iranian leaders as a result of the 1991 demise of the Soviet Union. Despite such considerations the United States has lifted its trade embargo on certain Iranian products, and there has been considerable pressure on the U.S. government, most notably from the oil industry, to end the trade embargo altogether. The future of Washington-Tehran ties remains unclear. From a domestic perspective, however, Iran has economic and political challenges to face in the years to come as it aims to stabilize its economy and enact the political reforms for which the people are clamoring.

*Houman A. Sadri*

**Further Reading**

Ahteshami, Anoushiravan. (1995) *After Khomeini: The Iranian Second Republic.* London, New York: Routledge.

Arjomand, Said A. (1988) *The Turban for the Crown: The Islamic Revolution in Iran.* New York: Oxford University Press.

Frye, R. N., ed. (1986) *The Cambridge History of Iran.* Cambridge, U.K.: Cambridge University Press.

Kazemi, Farhad. (1980) *Poverty and Revolution in Iran.* New York: New York University Press.

Sadri, Houman A. (1998) "Trends in the Foreign Policy of Revolutionary Iran." *Journal of Third World Studies* 1, 15.

**IRAN—HUMAN RIGHTS** The Islamic Republic of Iran was established in 1979 after a populist revolution toppled the Pahlavi monarchy. The monarchy, last headed by Mohammad Reza Shah Pahlavi (1919–1980), repressed political expression and frequently violated human rights. Unfortunately, subsequent governments of the Islamic Republic have continued this tradition.

The Islamic Republic is dominated by Muslim clergy of the Shiʿa denomination. The head of state, an ayatollah (high ranking Shiʿite cleric), holds the title of Supreme Leader of the Islamic Revolution and has direct control of the armed forces, internal security forces, and judiciary. A popularly elected unicameral Islamic Consultative Assembly, or *majlis*, legislates, but all legislation is reviewed for adherence to Islamic and constitutional principles by an appointed Council of Guardians, which has also the power to screen and disqualify candidates for elective office.

Among the agencies responsible for internal security are the Ministry of Intelligence and Security, the Ministry of Interior, and the Revolutionary Guards. Paramilitary volunteer forces known as Basijis, and gangs, known as the Ansar-e Hezbollah (Helpers of the Party of God), have acted as vigilantes who intimidate citizens suspected of counterrevolutionary activities.

Despite citizen protests, the government's human-rights record has remained poor. According to Amnesty International and Human Rights Watch, systematic abuses have included extrajudicial killings and summary executions, disappearances, widespread use of torture and other degrading treatment, arbitrary arrest and detention, and prolonged and incommunicado detention. The judiciary lacks independence and does not ensure citizens the right of due process. The government has used the courts to stifle dissent and obstruct progress on human rights.

Recent years have witnessed an intense political struggle between Iranians favoring greater liberalization in government policies, particularly in the area of human rights, and hard-liners in the government and society, who view such reforms as threats to the survival of the Islamic republic.

### Torture and Other Cruel Punishment

There have been numerous, credible reports that security forces and prison personnel torture detainees and prisoners. Some prison facilities, including Tehran's Evin prison, are notorious for the cruel and prolonged acts of torture inflicted upon the government's political opponents. Common torture methods include suspension for long periods in contorted positions, burning with cigarettes, sleep deprivation, and severe and repeated beatings with cables or other instruments on the back and on the soles of the feet. Prisoners also have reported beatings about the ears, inducing partial or complete deafness, and punching in the eyes, leading to partial or complete blindness. Prison conditions are harsh. Some prisoners are held in solitary confinement or denied adequate food or medical care in order to force confessions. Female prisoners reportedly have been raped or otherwise tortured while in detention. Prison guards reportedly intimidate family members of detainees and torture detainees in the presence of family members. The U.N. Commission on Human Rights Special Representative for Human Rights in Iran reported receiving numerous reports of overcrowding and unrest in Iranian prisons. The authorities do not allow human-rights monitors to visit imprisoned dissidents. In August 1999, however, Iranian President Mohammad Khatami (b. 1943) publicly criticized the use of torture and defended the rights of prisoners as a legitimate concern based on "Islam and human conscience."

Harsh punishments are carried out, including stoning and flogging, which are expressly mandated by the Islamic Penal Code as appropriate punishments for adultery. According to Article 102 of the code, "the stoning of an adulterer or adulteress shall be carried out while each is placed in a hole and covered with soil, he up to his waist and she up to a line above her breasts" (Bureau of Democracy, Human Rights, and Labor 1999).

### Political Executions and Arbitrary Arrest and Detention

In November 1995 the *majlis* passed a law that criminalizes dissent and applies the death penalty to offenses such as "attempts against the security of the State, outrage against high-ranking Iranian officials, and insults against the memory of Imam Khomeini and against the Supreme Leader of the Islamic Republic" (Bureau of Democracy, Human Rights, and Labor 1999). This law has been used to eliminate political dissidents.

Though the constitution prohibits arbitrary arrest and detention, these practices remain common. There is reportedly no legal time limit on incommunicado detention in jails or in local Revolutionary Guard offices. International observers believe hundreds of citizens have been imprisoned for their political beliefs.

### Denial of Fair Public Trial

Trials in the Islamic Revolutionary Courts are notorious for their disregard of international standards of fairness. Pretrial detention often is prolonged, and defendants lack access to attorneys. Indictments often lack clarity and include undefined offenses such as "antirevolutionary behavior," "moral corruption," and "siding with global arrogance." Defendants do not have the right to confront their accusers. Secret or summary trials occur. In 1992 the Lawyers Committee for Human Rights concluded that "the chronic abuses associated with the Islamic Revolutionary Courts are so numerous and so entrenched as to be beyond reform" (Bureau of Democracy, Human Rights, and Labor 1999). As of 2000 there has been no major reform of the Revolutionary Court system.

### Freedom of Speech and Press

Since the election of President Khatami in 1997 the independent press has played an increasingly important role in providing a forum for an intense debate regarding reform in the society. However, basic legal safeguards for freedom of expression are lacking, and the independent press has been subjected to arbitrary enforcement measures by elements of the government, notably the judiciary.

The 1995 Press Law prohibits the publication of material "insulting Islam and its sanctities" or "promoting subjects that might damage the foundation of the Islamic Republic." Generally prohibited topics include criticisms of the late Ayatollah Khomeini (1900–1989), direct criticism of the current Supreme Leader, questioning the tenets of certain Islamic legal principles, promotion of the views of certain dissident clerics, and promotion of rights or autonomy of ethnic minorities.

Police raid newspaper offices, and the Ansar-e Hezbollah attack the offices of liberal publications and bookstores without interference from the police or prosecution by the courts. The government directly controls and maintains a monopoly over all television and radio broadcasting facilities. Satellite dishes that receive foreign television broadcasts are forbidden, even though many wealthy citizens own them. The Ministry of Islamic Culture and Guidance screens books prior to publication and inspects foreign printed material prior to its distribution.

### Privacy Rights and Freedom of Assembly and Association

Security forces monitor the social activities of citizens, enter homes and offices, monitor telephone conversations, and open mail without court authorization. The government restricts freedom of assembly and closely monitors funeral processions and student, labor, and Friday prayer gatherings. In July 1999 students at Tehran University who were protesting the government's closure of a prominent reform-oriented newspaper as well as proposed legislation by the *majlis* that would limit press freedoms were attacked by security forces and Ansar-e Hezbollah. At least four

Author Salman Rushdie in London on 15 March 1995 while under a death sentence issued by Iran for writings critical of Islam. (AFP/CORBIS)

students were killed and three hundred were wounded. Four student leaders were later tried and sentenced to death by a Revolutionary Court for their role in the demonstrations.

### Freedom of Religion

Iran's population is 99 percent Muslim, of which 89 percent are Shiʿite and 10 percent are Sunni. Baha'i, Christian, Zoroastrian, and Jewish communities account for less than 1 percent of the population.

The Ministry of Intelligence and Security monitors religious activity closely. The Constitution declares that the official religion of Iran is Twelver sect Shiʿa Islam. It accords other Islamic denominations full respect and recognizes Zoroastrians, Christians, and Jews as protected religious minorities. Religions not specifically protected under the Constitution do not enjoy freedom of religion. This situation most directly affects the nearly 350,000 followers of the Baha'i faith.

which originated in Iran during the 1840s as a reformist movement within Shiʿa Islam. Political and religious authorities joined to suppress the movement and have always been hostile to it. They consider Baha'is to be apostates and claim the Baha'i faith is a counterrevolutionary sect historically linked to the shah's regime, even though the Baha'is had also faced discrimination under the shah.

The government does not ensure the right of citizens to change religions. Apostasy, specifically conversion from Islam, can be punishable by death.

### Political Rights

The government represses attempts to separate state and religion or to alter the state's existing theocratic foundation. Regularly scheduled elections are held for the president, members of the *majlis*, and the Assembly of Experts. (The 86-member Assembly of Experts consists of clerics who serve an eight-year term and are chosen by popular vote from a list approved by the government. It has the power to remove the Supreme Leader.) Over 90 percent of the eligible population voted in the 1997 national election. Khatami won nearly 70 percent of the vote, with his greatest support coming from the middle class, youth, minorities, and women. The election results were not disputed, and the government does not appear to have engaged in fraud.

Christians, Jews, and Zoroastrians elect deputies to specially reserved *majlis* seats. However, religious minorities are barred from holding senior government or military positions.

### Rights of Women

Women are underrepresented in government. In 1999 they held 13 of 270 *majlis* seats. There were no female cabinet members. After his election, President Khatami appointed the first female vice president (for environmental protection) since the Islamic Revolution. He also appointed a woman to serve as Presidential Adviser for Women's Affairs. The Minister of Islamic Culture and Guidance appointed a woman to the senior post of Deputy Minister for Legal and Parliamentary Affairs.

Women have access to primary and advanced education and work in many fields, including medicine, dentistry, journalism, and agriculture. A 1985 law instituted three months of paid maternity leave and two half-hour periods per day for nursing mothers. Pension benefits for women were established under the same law, which also decreed that companies hiring women should provide day-care facilities for their children.

The State enforces gender segregation in most public spaces, and prohibits women from mixing openly with men not related to them. Women are subject to harassment by the authorities if their dress or behavior is considered inappropriate, and may be sentenced to flogging or imprisonment for such violations.

Women have the right to divorce, alimony, and a share in the property that couples acquire during their marriage, in accordance with Islamic law. Mothers are granted custody of minor children in divorce cases in which the father is proven unfit. (Where the father is not proven unfit, custody varies case by case.) Muslim women may not marry non-Muslim men. The testimony of a woman is worth only half that of a man in court, and a married woman must obtain the written consent of her husband before traveling outside the country.

The government restricts the work of local human-rights groups. It denies the universality of human rights and does not permit international human rights NGOs such as Human Rights Watch and Amnesty International to establish offices or conduct regular investigative visits to Iran.

Despite the Islamic Republic's dismal human-rights record, there are some signs of improvement. In 1995 an Islamic Human-Rights Commission (IHRC) was established under the authority of the head of the judiciary, and in 1996 the government established a human-rights committee in the *majlis*. Thus far, however, these have had little impact on governmental practices.

*Paul J. Magnarella*

### Further Reading

Amnesty International. (2002) *Amnesty International Annual Reports* Retrieved 25 February 2002, from: http://www.amnesty.org/ailib/aireport/index.html.

Human Rights Watch. (2002) *Human Rights Watch World Report 2002*. Retrieved 25 February 2002, from: http://www.hrw.org/wr2k2/.

Bureau of Democracy, Human Rights, and Labor. (1999) *Iran Country Report on Human Rights Practices*. Washington, D.C.: U.S. Department of State. Retrieved 25 February 2002, from: http://www.state.gov/g/drl/hr/.

———. (2000) *Iran Country Report on Human Rights Practices*. Washington, D.C.: U.S. Department of State. Retrieved 25 February 2002, from: http://www.state.gov/g/drl/hr/.

**IRAN—POLITICAL SYSTEM** Constitutionally speaking, Iran is a theocratic republic in which the state and religion are closely intertwined. The Iranian system, which is based on Islamic law, was approved by a referendum in December 1979, soon after the success of the revolution that deposed Mohammad Reza Shah Phalavi (1919–1980), Iran's last shah (1941–1979). Before the constitution was publicly voted on, it was first modified by the Assembly of Experts, which worked on the draft provided by the provisional government established by Ayatollah Khomeini (1900–1989). Another referendum followed ten years later added forty-five amendments to the constitution. A significant change was the removal of the role of the prime minister within the government. Another major change modified the criteria for selecting the *faqih* (spiritual leader). The criteria were revised in order to allow the Assembly of Experts to choose Ali Hussein Khamanei (b. 1939) as *faqih* when Ayatollah Khomeini died in 1989 even though Khamanei was considered relatively junior at that time (his religious title was only Hojjat al-Islam) with respect to religious scholastic requirements for the role.

### Religious Oversight of the Government

The Iranian government has three branches: executive, legislative, and judiciary. However, there are several religious bodies that oversee these branches. The main religious authority is the *faqih*, who is a recognized religious scholar selected by the Assembly of Experts. The idea is that the *faqih* rules during the absence from earth of the Twelfth Imam, who, according to the main sect of Shi'a Islam, will return one day to bring salvation, peace, and prosperity to the community of believers. The *faqih*'s task is to ensure that the executive, legislative, and judiciary branches comply with the tenets of Islam; thus, he is given considerable powers. For instance, he can declare war or peace based on the recommendation of the Supreme Defense Council, half of whose membership he appoints. The *faqih* commands the military and security forces of Iran. He also appoints the office of the supreme judge and chief of the general staff as well as half the members of the Guardians Council, a council that determines whether laws proposed in the *majlis* respect the tenets of Islam and are in the spirit of the constitution. In addition, the *faqih* reserves the right to question any candidate's bid for the presidency. Ayatollah Khomeini always used this right and often prevented candidates from running when he felt they had positions contrary to the ideals of the Islamic Republic. The *faqih* has the authority as well to impeach an elected president if either the supreme court or the *majlis* (parliament) finds the president shirking his responsibilities or violating the principles of Islam. This actually happened to the first elected president of the Islamic Republic, Bani Sadr. He was impeached because he constantly clashed with the prime minister of the time, Rajai.

The Assembly of Experts is another religious body that oversees the functions of the government. It is composed solely of clerics elected by the people. The first Assembly was elected in 1982, and succeeded by a second in 1990.

### The Executive Branch

The president heads the executive branch of government and is elected for a four-year term. Currently, the president is Mohammed Khatami (b. 1943), whose election in 1997 marked a significant shift in the attitude of the people toward a more moderate system. He succeeded former President Ali Akbar Hashemi Rafsanjani (b. 1934). The president has the authority to select his cabinet called the Council of Ministers, but his appointments must be approved by the *majlis* before they can take effect.

An Election Supervisory Council manages all the election procedures. Anyone fifteen and over can vote. The minimum voting age used to be twenty but was no doubt modified due to the youthful orientation of the population. Women were given the right to vote in 1963.

### The Legislative Branch

Legislation is the jurisdiction of the 270 members of the *majlis*, who are elected for four-year terms. Lively debate occurs on the floor of the *majlis* as there is ample variety of opinion concerning economic, political, and social topics. Essentially there are three camps of thought nestled within the *majlis*: conservatives, radicals, and moderates.

Conservatives, mainly comprising the religious community and the bazaar merchants, closely follow the party line and tend to be xenophobic and wary of outside influences, particularly those of the West. They are also orthodox in the cultural application of Islamic principles, such as establishing a dress code for men and women and keeping a tight rein on the media and what it is allowed to depict. The conservatives were clearly setting the political agenda when the Islamic Republic was first established in 1979. The radicals (or followers of Imam Khomeini's line) make up another faction; they support programs for the disadvantaged classes of society. They favor fair methods of distribution of income as well as keeping a watchful eye on the private sector. They are more progressive in their social programs than the conservatives, but share their fear of the encroachment of Western ideals and dependency on foreign power. The radicals have long been present in the *majlis* and often debate issues of land reform and nationalization of industries.

## PREAMBLE TO THE CONSTITUTION OF THE ISLAMIC REPUBLIC OF IRAN

Adopted on: 24 Oct 1979

The Constitution of the Islamic Republic of Iran advances the cultural, social, political, and economic institutions of Iranian society based on Islamic principles and norms, which represent an honest aspiration of the Islamic Ummah. This aspiration was exemplified by the nature of the great Islamic Revolution of Iran, and by the course of the Muslim people's struggle, from its beginning until victory, as reflected in the decisive and forceful calls raised by all segments of the populations. Now, at the threshold of this great victory, our nation, with all its beings, seeks its fulfillment.

The basic characteristic of this revolution, which distinguishes it from other movements that have taken place in Iran during the past hundred years, is its ideological and Islamic nature. After experiencing the anti-despotic constitutional movement and the anti-colonialist movement centered on the nationalization of the oil industry, the Muslim people of Iran learned from this costly experience that the obvious and fundamental reason for the failure of those movements was their lack of an ideological basis. Although the Islamic line of thought and the direction provided by militant religious leaders played an essential role in the recent movements, nonetheless, the struggles waged in the course of those movements quickly fell into stagnation due to departure from genuine Islamic positions. Thus it was that the awakened conscience of the nation, under the leadership of Imam Khumayni, came to perceive the necessity of pursuing a genuinely Islamic and ideological line in its struggles. And this time, the militant 'ulama' of the country, who had always been in the forefront of popular movements, together with the committed writers and intellectuals, found new impetus by following his leadership.

*Source:* International Court Networks. Retrieved 8 March 2002, from: http://www.uni-wuerzburg.de/law/np00000_.html.

However, their influence was the strongest during the 1980s. The radicals mainly comprise students and members of such organizations as The Bureau for the Promotion of Unity and the Young Combatant Clerics. The moderates, also known as the centrists or pragmatists, form the last major faction. They are made up of the middle class—professionals and bureaucrats—and are more open to outside ideas and to liberalization policies. They believe in coexisting peacefully in the world and are not threatened by outside influences. The moderates took center stage in the last part of the twentieth century and the beginning of the twenty-first, as evidenced by Khatami's election to the presidency in 1997 and the landslide victory by the moderates in the 2000 *majlis* elections.

When the *majlis* passes a bill, it is reviewed by the Guardians Council to ensure its acceptability. The Guardians Council consists of twelve lawyers, six of whom are clerics appointed by the *faqih*, and six appointed by the High Council of the Judiciary and approved by the Assembly of Experts. The Guardians Council has often used its right to reject any bill proposed by the *majlis*, in particular bills relating to land reform and nationalization. When a bill is rejected by the Guardians Council, it is sent back to the *majlis* for revision. In February 1988 a committee called the Committee to Determine the Expediency of the Islamic Order was formed to mediate disputes that arise between the *majlis* and the Guardians Council. This committee was legitimized by the constitution in July of 1989.

Family members of dissidents on trial before Iran's Revolutionary Court in January 2002 protest political repression outside the court building. (REUTERS NEWMEDIA INC./CORBIS)

### The Judiciary

The judiciary is composed of a Supreme Court, with five justices, and lower criminal and civil courts. Clerics are tried in a special clerical court; people facing charges of treason against the Islamic Republic are tried in revolutionary tribunals. Judges are required to be members of the Islamic clergy and their judicial decisions must be rooted in Islamic law. A minister of justice operates as the liaison between the three branches of government.

### Freedom of the Press and Political Parties

The constitution provides for freedom of press except in cases where the press undermines Islamic ideals—a clause responsible for Iranian strained relations with the United Kingdom. Iran actually cut off diplomatic relations with the United Kingdom in March 1989 because a British company published Salman Rushdie's book *The Satanic Verses*, which was perceived to be against Islamic values. It took over a year for full diplomatic relations to be reinstated.

The same criteria of adhering to Islamic values is applied with respect to the creation of political parties and associations as well as religious institutions. Islam is listed as the official religion of Iran in the constitution. The sect that is followed is Twelver Shi'a, the dominant Shi'a sect. Other Muslim sects are recognized and represented in the government. Christians, Jews, and Zoroastrians have the status of lawful religious minorities. However, the Baha'is are not considered a recognized religious minority; they are not allowed representation in the *majlis* and their behavior is restricted by the government.

Iran's best-known political party was the Islamic Republican Party (IRP), which was created in 1978 and led by Ayatollah Khomeini. It was instrumental in the unfolding of the Islamic Revolution and became the ruling party after the Islamic Revolution's success. But Khomeini disbanded the IRP in June 1987 under pressure by the other political parties.

Other political parties that have played a part in Iranian history are the Liberation Movement of Iran, the Union of National Front Forces, the National Democratic Front, the Muslim People's Republican Party, the Party of the Masses, the Communist Party of Iran, the Party of the Toilers, the Kurdish Democratic Party, and the People's Mujahidin Organizaton of Iran. Parties may be subject to harassment if they criticize the government. For example, the Liberation Movement of Iran that was founded by Mehdi Bazargan, the first prime minister of the provisional government of the Islamic Republic, often found its offices ransacked due to its criticisms of the government, even though the government tolerated the party's existence and permitted it representation in the *majlis*. Other parties are not as fortunate. The Party of the Masses, a pro-Soviet Communist party, was banned in 1983. The Kurdish Democratic Party was prohibited in 1979. Some political parties are organized by Iranians who live abroad and are working to change the system of government. For instance, the Muslim People's Republican Party would like to see a secular government in Iran rather than a theocracy.

Other political groups are violent in nature and use terrorist tactics against the government, which in turn responds with force. Such radical groups include the People's Mujahidin Organization of Iran, Warriors of the People, the Forghan Group, and Black Wednesday. The first group originally supported the Islamic Republic and had been known for carrying out assassinations against the shah's regime and the U.S. government, but in the early 1980s a shift occurred within the organization and its members began attacking the current regime.

The recent liberalization of policies and the shift toward moderation have allowed the formation and activities of several new political parties, including Executives of Construction, Islamic Iran Solidarity Party, and the Islamic Partnership Front.

Regarding human rights, the Iranian constitution provides for the basic rights of individuals in Articles 19 through 42. But Iran is not considered a free nation by Western standards. At the start of the new republic, the revolutionary regime showed little regard for human rights. Quick trials and executions of opponents were frequent; newspapers could be closed or ransacked at a moment's notice. However, when conditions stabilized, Khomeini issued an eight-point statement, which prohibited such acts of censorship and illegal entries into homes. Although some abuses continue, conditions have significantly improved and there is a structure in place to correct the abuses. Currently, the Iranian electorate is pursuing more rights and reforms.

### The Military

Iran has four military and security forces: the regular armed forces, the Pasdaran (Revolutionary Guards), the Basij (militia), and the police. The army, navy, and air force are the components of the regular armed forces, which were heavily purged after the revolution. The Pasdaran were created with the formation of the Islamic Republic to protect the revolution, because the Ayatollah was suspicious of the loyalty of the regular forces, which had been trained by U.S. advisers in the shah's era. The Pasdaran were largely responsible for the purging of the shah's regime as well as opponents of the new government. Both the regular armed forces and the Revolutionary Guards are responsible for defending the country if threatened by a foreign power. The Basij is called upon when the government is threatened by violence.

### Local Government and the Civil Service

Iran is divided into twenty-five *ostans* (provinces). The *anjumans* (provincial councils) are slowly but surely expanding their power base. The provinces are further divided into 195 *shahrestans* (counties), then into 500 *bakhshes* (districts), and finally into 1,581 *deshitans* (groups of villages). Respectively, each level is commanded by *ostandars*, *farmandars*, *bakhshadars*, and *dehdars*. Individual villages are run by *kadkhodas* (headmen). Mayors and councils are either elected or appointed by the Ministry of Interior to run the towns and cities.

Iran has a civil service in place that still operates according to codes established in 1922 and 1966. It contains seven grade levels with fifteen in-grade steps between each grade level. To become a civil servant requires taking an entrance exam. There are over 700,000 civil servants in Iran.

### The Future

The trend toward moderation demonstrated by the 2000 *majlis* elections was encouraging. Despite pre-election crackdowns on the media, the will of the people was respected. Only time will tell how the volatility in the Middle East brought about by the U.S. responses to the 11 September 2001 terrorist attacks will affect Iran's political system.

*Houman A. Sadri*

### Further Reading

Baktiari, Bahman. (1996) *Parliamentary Politics in Revolutionary Iran: The Institutionalization of Factional Politics.* Gainesville, FL: University Press of Florida.

Sadri, Houman A. (1998) "Trends in the Foreign Policy of Revolutionary Iran." *Journal of Third World Studies* 1, 15.

Schirazi, Asghar. (1997) *The Constitution of Iran: Politics and the State in the Islamic Republic.* Trans. by John O'Kane. London: I. B. Tauris.

## IRAN-IRAQ RELATIONS

For thousands of years, the inhabitants of the neighboring areas of today's Iran and Iraq have known conflict alternating with periods of tranquillity. Both Muslim countries, Iran and Iraq share a common cultural orientation, but religious views and languages differ widely. Present-day Iranians are Shi'ite Muslims, whereas Iraqis are largely Sunni, although with a significant Shi'ite population; Persian is the official language of Iran, while Arabic is the language of Iraq, and Kurdish- and Turkish-speaking peoples also live in both countries.

### Relations up to the Nineteenth Century

Boasting long histories, both these countries are strategically situated on the Persian Gulf, a position that has shaped their unique national identities. Ancient Iraq (Mesopotamia) and Iran (Persia) were home to some of the world's first great urban civilizations. After the Arab invasion of the seventh century and the replacement of Zoroastrianism by Islam, a unique blend of Persian and Arab culture united Iran and Iraq during the long rule of the Abbasid dynasty (749/750–1258) over both countries, until both were devastated by successive Mongol invasions.

The paths of Iran and Iraq then diverged. The Safavid dynasty (1501–1722/1736) in Iran encouraged the transformation of Shi'ism, its school, and its religious hierarchy into the official religion of the region. Iraq fell under the hegemony of the Ottoman empire (1453–1922), for whom Sunni orthodoxy was the imperial religion. Ottoman-Safavid rivalries erupted across the Iran-Iraq border innumerable times for several centuries.

An Iraqi honor guard marches at the tomb of the unknown soldier in Baghdad on 8 August 1999, marking the eleventh anniversary of the end of the Iran-Iraq War. (AFP/CORBIS)

**Nineteenth- and Twentieth-Century Iran-Iraq Relations**

In the nineteenth century, the territories of Iran and Iraq were the site of the great power struggle (among Britain, France, and Russia), sometimes referred to as the "Great Game" (in the Caucasus and Iran) or the "Eastern Question" (in Iraq). Anglo-Russian-Ottoman rivalries were conducted on the ground in Iran, as conflict after conflict erupted over the Caucasus and Transcaucasus territories such as Georgia, annexed by Russia in 1801. Iraq remained under Ottoman control until World War I, when it was the scene of some of the worst fighting between the British and their Arab allies and the Turks. Iran's sovereignty was theoretically guaranteed by the presence of Russian and British forces stationed there supposedly to protect the Caucasus from Ottoman-German invasion, but in reality to keep control over the oil fields.

Iraq's present boundaries were constructed by the victorious World War I allies after Faisal led an Arab revolt against the Ottomans; the British supported Faisal as king (reigned 1921–1933). Iraq remained a kingdom until after World War II, when a dictatorship disguised as a republic eventually replaced the constitutional monarchy.

In Iran Reza Shah Pahlavi (1878–1944) seized power in 1925 and was succeeded by his son Mohammad Reza Shah, who ruled until 1979. During that time, oil catapulted the Middle East into world prominence, and both Iran and Iraq tried to consolidate their new nations through rapid economic development and attempts to unify their various peoples, an attempt that was resisted by the Kurds, an ethnic minority in both Iran and Iraq. The Kurds figure as a significant source of conflict in Iran-Iraq bilateral relations.

World War II saw increased German influence in Iran, and under Anglo-Soviet pressure Reza Shah abdicated in favor of his son Mohammad Reza. British oil interests were on the rise, and concessions were given to them in 1943, following which the Soviets asked for similar rights. Iraq was reoccupied by the British during World War II to protect British access to Iraqi oil fields. After World War II external economic pressures, especially in the competition for oil, and conflicts with ethnic minorities complicated any sense of historical unity and prevented regional cooperative development between the two neighboring states.

The Arab-Israeli war of 1973 temporarily restored Iran-Iraq bilateral relations when, in a show of anti-Zionist solidarity, the oil producing and exporting countries (OPEC) brokered a settlement between Iran and Iraq after Saddam Hussein (b. 1937), the ruler of Iraq, ordered his troops to occupy two offshore islands in the Shatt al-Arab.

The Iranian empire had begun to decay in the 1970s, and in 1979 a triumphant Ayatollah Khomeini (1900–1989) declared the new Islamic (Shi'ite) Republic of Iran, a direct threat to the Ba'ath (Socialist) Party of Saddam Hussein's secular Iraq. Hussein was fearful of the Shi'ites who formed 51 percent of Iraq's population and whose theological seminaries had been in close contact with Khomeini.

### Iran-Iraq War, 1980–1990

The roots of the Iran-Iraq War were partly planted in the question of the sovereignty of the islands in the Shatt al Arab, a waterway 193 kilometers long, flowing from the Tigris-Euphrates confluence in Iraq to the Persian Gulf near Kuwait and forming part of the Iran-Iraq border. Iraq's right to the waterway, established in 1937, was a bone of contention with Iran. Provocation had occurred in 1969 over the passage of a group of Iranian vessels flying the national flag. In 1975, after Iran-supplied weapons had allowed the Kurds in northern Iraq to revolt, Iraq agreed to recognize the Shatt al Arab as the border between the two countries if Iran agreed to stop sending weapons to the Kurds. In hopes of reversing this border agreement, with an eye on the Iranian oil fields in Khuzestan province, and also desiring to stop the threat to Iraq's secular government posed by the Islamic government of Iran, Saddam Hussein invaded Iran in 1980.

The Iran-Iraq War was a bloody conflict; it dragged on for eight years and cost a million lives. In 1980 Iraq expected an easy victory, but Iran fought back and even attempted to capture Al Basrah, Iraq's main Gulf port. Much of the time the war was a stalemate; Iran refused to surrender, but Iraq enjoyed superior military advantage and did not refrain from using gas warfare against Iranian troops. World opinion was nevertheless anti-Iranian because of the fear that an Islamic revolution would spread throughout the Middle East. This perception was shared not only by the United States, which already had a strained relationship with Iran, but also by the Arab regimes who were its allies, and by the Soviet Union.

Iraq failed in its attempts to capture the oil fields of southern Iran due to tough resistance from the Iranian army. While purges and internal strife took a toll on the Iranian army, Khomeini relied on a cadre of revolutionary guards (Pasadaran) and a massive volunteer force of young men, instant martyrs in the fight for the Iranian Islamic Revolution.

The fighting continued for eight years, in a series of offensives and counteroffensives that devastated the oil economies of both nations and wreaked havoc on a generation of young people. The conflict acquired ethnic overtones of Persian versus Arab, rather than a religious versus secular confrontation. Iraq's pipelines were damaged, and oil could be exported only though Turkey and Jordan.

By 1988 the ravaged economies of Iran and Iraq, a war-weary public, OPEC, the United States, and the Soviet Union finally combined to force both sides to the negotiating table. The efforts of the secretary-general of the United Nations resulted in a cease-fire on 20 August 1988, under the direct control of the U.N. Iran-Iraq Military Observers Group. In October 1988 Ayatollah Khomeini accepted negotiation, comparing it to drinking poison. Khomeini died in June 1989, and a new wave of enthusiasm to end the war came about. Before peace could be signed, Saddam Hussein attacked Kuwait, precipitating the Persian Gulf War. The Iran-Iraq War was not settled until August 1990, when Iraq abandoned its demand to control of the Shatt al Arab, which was divided between the two countries.

*K. N. Sethi*

### Further Reading

Cleveland, William. (2000) *A History of the Modern Middle East.* Boulder, CO: Westview Press.
Rajaee, Farhang, ed. (1993) *The Iran-Iraq War: The Politics of Aggression.* Gainesville, FL: University Press of Florida.
Chubin, Shahram, and Charles Tripp. (1988) *Iran and Iraq at War* Boulder, CO: Westview Press.

## IRAN-RUSSIA RELATIONS

Since the collapse of the Soviet Union in 1991, Iran has become Russia's principal ally in the Middle East. The two countries have cooperated in a number of regional conflicts, and Russia is Iran's primary supplier of military equipment and nuclear technology. Both Moscow and Tehran oppose what they claim are U.S. efforts to create a unipolar world. While there are some areas of dispute between the two countries, primarily over the Caspian Sea, the durability of the relationship was underscored in November 2000, when Russia unilaterally abrogated an agreement with the United States to stop selling arms to Iran when existing contracts expired at the end of 2000.

### Development of Iran-Russia Relations

Relations between Moscow and Tehran began to develop in the later part of the Gorbachev era (1985–1991). After alternately supporting first Iran and then Iraq during the Iran-Iraq war (1980–1990), by July 1987 Moscow had clearly tilted toward Iran. The relationship between the two countries was solidified in June 1989 with the visit to Moscow of the Iranian president Ali Akhbar Hashemi Rafsanjani (b. 1934), when a number of agreements, including one on military cooperation, were signed. The military agreement permitted Iran to purchase highly sophisticated military aircraft from Moscow, including MIG-29s and SU-24s.

### Russian Aid to Iran

The Iranian air force had been badly affected by the eight-year war with Iraq and by U.S. refusal to supply spare parts, let alone new planes, to replace losses in the F-14s and other aircraft that the United States had sold to the regime of Muhammad Reza Shah Pahlavi, the shah of Iran (1919–1980). Soviet military equipment was badly needed. Iran's military-supply dependence on Moscow grew as a result of the 1990–1991 Persian Gulf War. After that war, the United States, Iran's main enemy, became the primary military power in the Gulf. U.S. defense agreements with a number of Persian Gulf states included prepositioning arrangements for U.S. military equipment, and Saudi Arabia, Iran's most important Islamic challenger, acquired massive amounts of U.S. weaponry.

As Russia-Iran relations deepened, Moscow stepped up the quantity and quality of its arms sales, and by 1993 it had agreed to supply Iran with submarines that could be used to challenge the U.S. fleet operating in the region. Another Russian action angering the United States was the 1995 agreement to supply Iran with a nuclear reactor for the nuclear installation at Bushehr in southwest Iran. Under heavy U.S. pressure, Moscow did renege on a promise to provide a graphite reactor that could have been used to construct nuclear weapons. The Russian natural gas company, Gasprom, was also a major investor in Iran's South Pars natural-gas field, reaching an agreement to help develop the field in 1997.

### Iran's Support of Russia

In addition to supplying Tehran with military equipment and nuclear reactors and investing in one of Iran's major natural gas fields, Moscow, whose position in the world had been eroding as its economy and military power weakened, found Iran to be a helpful ally in dealing with a number of sensitive Middle Eastern, Caucasian, Transcaucasian, and Central and Southwest Asian hot spots. These included Chechnya, where Iran has kept a low profile during both Russian-Chechen wars, despite the Chechen rebels' use of Islamic themes in their conflict with Russia; Tajikistan, where Iran helped Russia achieve a political settlement of the civil war, albeit a shaky one; Afghanistan, where both Russia and Iran have stood together against the Taliban; and Azerbaijan, which neither Iran, with a sizable Azeri population of its own, nor Russia wishes to see emerge as a significant economic and military power, particularly as it develops closer relations with the United States. Furthermore, as NATO expands eastward, many Russians have called for a closer Russia-Iran relationship as a counterbalance. Turkey is seen by many in the Russian elite as closely cooperating with its NATO allies in expanding its influence in both Transcaucasia and Central Asia—areas that Moscow regards in its own sphere of influence. Finally, Moscow also considers Tehran as an ally in resisting what both the Iranian and Russian regimes see as an attempt by the United States to create a unipolar world that it would dominate.

Russian and Iranian foreign ministers Igor Ivanov and Karmal Kharazi at talks on the Middle East in Damascus, Syria, in October 2000. (AFP/CORBIS)

### Problems in Russia-Iran Relations

Despite these areas of cooperation, the Russian-Iranian relationship has not been without its problems. First, with a chronically weak economy, Iran has not always been able to pay for its military and other imports from Russia and by the year 2000 had run up a trade deficit of $2.5 billion. Second, the Bushehr nuclear-reactor project has lagged badly. The then director of Russia's Ministry of Atomic Energy, Yevgeny Adamov, to spur on the project, signed an agreement with Iran in 1998 to transform Bushehr into a turnkey installation, in which Russian, not Iranian, technicians would build the project, whose completion date was set for 2003.

A third problem lay in the supply of Russian missile technology to Iran. The United States brought heavy pressure against Russia, including sanctions against Russian companies accused of supplying the technology. Iran, in the eyes of the United States, was a rogue state, and its development of the Shihab III intermediate range (1,300-kilometer) missile threatened a number of U.S. allies in the region. First Boris

Yeltsin (b. 1931) and then Vladimir Putin (b. 1952) denied that supplying missile technology was official Russian policy. Nevertheless, the missile agreement severely damaged relations with the United States, especially with the Congress, and an economically weak Russia, particularly after the economic collapse of August 1998, was hard put to deflect the U.S. pressure. The rise in oil prices in 1999 and 2000 gave Iran some breathing room and allowed funds to pay down its debt to Moscow. Nevertheless, the missile-technology issue remains a serious problem in U.S.-Russia relations, which may well affect Russian-Iranian relations as well.

A fourth area of conflict lay in the issue of developing the oil and natural-gas resources of the Caspian Sea. Moscow initially shared Iran's opposition to the division of the Caspian into national sectors for the exploitation of oil and natural gas deposits (Iran called for joint development and joint sharing of the profits on a 20 percent basis for each of the five countries bordering the Caspian). By the mid-1990s, however, Moscow had changed its position and called for limited national sectors. By 1998, it had moved further and signed an agreement with Kazakhstan on the division of the Caspian. In January 2001, Moscow signed a similar agreement with Azerbaijan. The improvement in Russian-Azeri relations displeased Iran, which, unlike the other four Caspian riparian states (Russia, Azerbaijan, Kazakhstan, and Turkmenistan), had found little oil or natural gas in its small portion of the Caspian shoreline.

### The Future Course of Russia-Iran Relations

A final Russian-Iranian conflict is more of a future possibility than a current problem for the relationship. It involves a rapprochement between Iran and the United States. Some Russian observers had first feared such a rapprochement following the overtures of the Iranian president Mohammed Khatami (b. 1943) to the United States in late 1997, and again after the overwhelming victory of the reformers in the February 2000 Majlis (Iranian parliament) election. On both occasions, a strong counterattack by Iran's conservative forces prevented any rapprochement. Nonetheless, should a reconciliation occur, Russia and Iran would become competitors in providing export routes for Caspian oil and natural gas. The major fruits of an Iranian-American rapprochement would be the lifting of sanctions on the construction of oil and natural gas facilities in Iran, including pipelines. And Iran, as many U.S. oil executives continue to point out, is the shortest, safest, and most secure export route for Caspian oil to travel to the outside world.

In sum, Russia and Iran enjoyed a fruitful relationship in the first decade following the collapse of the Soviet Union. Whether the relationship will remain as close in the second decade remains to be seen.

*Robert O. Freedman*

### Further Reading

Avery, Peter et al., eds. (1968–1991) *The Cambridge History of Iran. Volume 7. From Nadir Shah to the Islamic Republic.* Cambridge, U.K.: Cambridge University Press.

Chaqueri, Cosroe. (1995) *The Soviet Socialist Republic of Iran, 1920–1921: Birth of the Trauma.* Pittsburgh, PA: Pittsburgh University Press.

## IRAN–UNITED STATES HOSTAGE CRISIS

**IRAN–UNITED STATES HOSTAGE CRISIS** On 4 November 1979, a group of Iranian students occupied the U.S. embassy compound in Tehran and took U.S. diplomats hostage. This event was a major turning point in American-Iranian relations in the period following the Iranian Revolution earlier that year. The causes of the hostage crisis are rooted in the late 1970s political environment.

### Relations in the 1970s

The Islamic Revolution had heralded the end of the monarchy in Iran. The shah had left the country at the urging of the prime minister, Shapour Bakhtiar (1935–1991). This paved the way for Ayatollah Khomeini (1900–1989) to return to Iran from his exile in France and establish the Islamic Republic. Anti-American sentiments were high, encouraged by Ayatollah Khomeini, who spoke of the United States as the Great Satan and fueled people's anger at foreign intervention in Iran.

Iranian history had been replete with foreign interference in national economic and political affairs, commencing with the Russians and British and then the Americans. However, the government of the prime minister Mehdi Bazargan (1907–1994) continued to maintain a working relationship with the United States, procuring military equipment and receiving U.S. intelligence reports concerning Soviet and Iraqi activities in Iran.

In a pivotal moment in October 1979, the United States allowed the shah to enter the country to receive medical treatment. This news was received skeptically and violently by the Iranian people. They believed the shah was trying to secure American support to regain power in Iran as he had done in 1953 in an American-engineered coup. Khomeini and hundreds of thousands of Iranians, who marched in Tehran on 1

November 1979, demanded the extradition of the shah. Unfortunately for Premier Bazargan, on that very day, he was meeting with the U.S. national security adviser Zbigniew Brzezinski in Algiers and was lambasted in the Iranian press for it.

### The U.S. Embassy Takeover and Its Aftermath

Three days later, the U.S. embassy was occupied by young men who called themselves Students of the Imam Line, a reference to the ayatollah's ideas and policies. The students took sixty-six American diplomats as hostages. Bazargan tried to secure the release of the hostages, even pleading with Khomeini for his support, to no avail. Two days later, disillusioned with his powerlessness, Bazargan resigned. No one replaced him at that time. Elections were held in January 1980, and Abolhasan Bani-Sadr (b. 1931) was elected president.

Bani-Sadr also tried to resolve the hostage situation but found his efforts thwarted at every turn. In one instance, he contacted the United Nations to request that a commission be set up to investigate Iranian grievances, in return for the hostages being turned over to the Revolutionary Council as a first step toward their final release. On 23 February 1980, just one day before the UN commission was due to arrive, however, Ayatollah Khomeini vetoed this plan by proclaiming that only the *majlis* (parliament), which had yet to be elected, had the power to determine the fate of the hostages. In another instance, Bani-Sadr hoped to resolve the situation by arranging the extradition of the shah from Panama, where he had relocated after his medical treatment in the United States. However, these plans were soon foiled when the shah managed to flee to Egypt on 23 March 1980, thus avoiding extradition and dashing Bani-Sadr's hopes of ending the crisis.

Meanwhile, Washington was putting the pressure on Tehran as well. Financial restrictions were exerted on the country when President Jimmy Carter (b. 1924) froze all Iranian assets held in American banks (over $12 billion) on 14 November 1979, soon after the hostages were taken. Then, in April 1980, President Carter authorized a risky rescue attempt, which involved landing aircraft and troops in deserts near Tabas in eastern Iran. The ambitious covert operation failed when two of the helicopters developed mechanical difficulties, leading the commander to abort the mission. A helicopter and a transport aircraft collided, causing eight American service men to die. The political fallout of this disaster operation undoubtedly cost President Carter his reelection and intensified already strained ties with Tehran, which consequently delayed the release of hostages further.

Furthermore, this failed rescue mission resulted in a purge of the Iranian military, since some revolutionary leaders suspected that military officers might have helped the Americans escape radar detection as they entered Iranian air space. Bani-Sadr was, however, powerless to stop the military purging; his effectiveness was compromised at every turn. For instance, he was forced to accept the *majlis's* choice for prime minister, Mohammad Ali Rajai (1934–1981). Major political and personality differences prevented Bani-Sadr and Rajai from working as a team in resolving the crisis.

Through a diplomat in West Germany, the Rajai government let the United States know that it was now serious about negotiations to bring about the release of the hostages. One reason for this sudden shift in the hard-liners' attitude toward negotiations was the fact that Iran found itself in an imposed war with Iraq in September 1980.

### Settlement of the Hostage Crisis

Therefore, constructive negotiations began in earnest on 14 September 1980. However, the release of the hostages did not take place until 20 January 1981, which coincided with the inauguration of President Ronald Reagan (b. 1911) as president. Some believe the timing was no accident; Khomeini might not have wanted Carter to be credited with the release of the hostages. In return for the freedom of the hostages, the United States was to release the frozen Iranian funds held in American banks. Iran agreed to honor its loan commitments to the United States and to put $1 billion aside pending the resolution of claims made against Iran by U.S. companies, to be reviewed by the International Court of Justice.

American hostages in Tehran in December 1980. (BETTMANN/CORBIS)

Although the hostage crisis was settled peacefully, it served to strain Iranian relations with some other states. Some in Iran believed the settlement put Iran at a disadvantage financially and politically. In addition, it furthered antagonized the professional relations between Bani-Sadr and the Rajai government, since Bani-Sadr had been left out of the negotiations. Finally, this peaceful resolution did not, unfortunately, remove the tension and antagonism between the United States and Iran. These undercurrents have remained and are only recently ameliorating.

*Houman A. Sadri*

**Further Reading**

Bill, James A. (1988) *The Eagle and the Lion: The Tragedy of American-Iranian Relations*. New Haven, CT: Yale University Press.

Kreisberg, Paul H., ed. (1985) *American Hostages in Iran: The Conduct of a Crisis*. New Haven, CT: Yale University Press.

Milani, Mohsen M. (1994) *The Making of Iran's Islamic Revolution: From Monarchy to the Islamic Republic*. 2d ed. Boulder, CO: Westview Press.

Sick, Gary. (1985) *All Fall Down: America's Tragic Encounter with Iran*. New York: Random House.

## IRAN–UNITED STATES RELATIONS

The relations between Iran and the United States have experienced major transformations since the Iranian revolution of 1978–1979 and the overthrow of the pro-Western monarchy in Iran. In 1953, Shah Mohammad Reza Pahlavi (1919–1980) was restored to the throne (following his deposal by his popular prime minister, Muhammad Mosaddeq) by a military coup organized and funded by the United States and British intelligence agencies. The shah gradually developed close relations with the United States in political, economic, and military areas, and Iran became one of the most significant U.S. allies in the Third World.

The alliance between the two nations reached its zenith during the presidency (1969–1974) of Richard M. Nixon (1913–1994). The shah and President Nixon developed a close personal relationship. This helped cement the already close alliance between Iran and the United States, and Iran became the largest purchaser of advanced U.S. weaponry outside of the member nations of the North Atlantic Treaty Organization (NATO). Notwithstanding the shah's efforts to reap the benefits of his close ties with the United States, he was never able to establish legitimacy for his rule, largely due to the perception that he had become an agent of the West, promoting outside interests in the Middle East at the expense of his own nation. When the uprising in January 1979 succeeded in forcing the shah to flee Iran, the United States, as his closest benefactor, was dealt a heavy blow.

### The Hostage Crisis and Two Persian Gulf Wars

After a few months, diplomatic relations between the United States and Iran were strained beyond repair after a group of student militants stormed the U.S. Embassy in Tehran on 4 November 1979 and took its staff hostage. This action was ostensibly taken to protest the shah's admission to the United States for cancer treatment. The militants saw the shah's admission as yet another attempt by the United States to restore the shah to his throne after another popular uprising against his regime. The hostage crisis, which lasted 444 days, consumed President Jimmy Carter (b. 1924), who failed to gain the release of the hostages.

On 21 September 1980, in the midst of the hostage crisis, Iraqi President Saddam Hussein (b. 1937) took advantage of the widening chasm between Iran and the United States and invaded Iran, thus precipitating one of the longest and bloodiest wars of the twentieth century. The Iran-Iraq War (1980–1990) provided the United States with an opportunity to punish Iran by developing close ties with Saddam Hussein's regime. The most significant of Iraqi-U.S. ties were in the field of intelligence, where the United States provided crucial information to Iraq about Iranian troop deployments and movements and other types of satellite intelligence. The U.S. support of Saddam Hussein further strained Iran's relations with the United States.

The budding anti-Iran Arab coalition organized informally by the United States during the Iran-Iraq War was shattered after Saddam Hussein invaded Kuwait in August 1990. With the massive deployment of U.S. troops in the Persian Gulf and the ensuing war against Iraq, Iran emerged from its regional isolation. Even the United States began sending feelers toward Iran in the hope of gaining its support in the Persian Gulf War. Although Iran did not join the coalition of nations fighting against Iraq, it did not undertake any measures to undermine the U.S.-led war efforts. A window of opportunity to improve relations between Iran and the United States had opened.

### From Dual Containment to the Axis of Evil

Notwithstanding some hopeful developments in the immediate period of the Persian Gulf War, relations between the United States and Iran further deteriorated after the United States adopted its so-called dual containment policy during the first term of the presidency (1993–2001) of Bill Clinton (b. 1946). This

Iranians demonstrating outside the United States embassy in Tehran during the Islamic Revolution in 1979. (BETTMANN/CORBIS)

policy was designed to isolate both Iran and Iraq, preventing economic and trade ties as well as political relations between the United States and these two nations. It also called for punishment of non-U.S. third parties that invested in the petroleum industries of the targeted nations. The policy proved to be impractical and counterproductive. Most of America's major allies expressed varying degrees of opposition to this policy, especially when it affected their commercial interests and political sovereignty. Toward the end of Clinton's presidency, it was clear that dual containment had not achieved its goal with respect to Iran. As a consequence, the Clinton administration sought to find avenues to engage the moderate elements within the Iranian government who had come to power as a result of the landslide victory of Mohammad Khatami (b. 1943), the reformist cleric who became Iran's president in 1997. Years of mistrust and political animosity between the two governments again made improvements in relations impossible.

The U.S.-led war in Afghanistan and the campaign against terrorism again presented a unique opportunity for Iran and the United States to improve their relations. After an initial period of cooperation between the two nations, their relations deteriorated when President George W. Bush (b. 1946) included Iran as a node in his "Axis of Evil" State of the Union address in January 2002. Again, America's major allies took exception to this categorization and expressed their determined policy of engaging, not isolating, Iran.

Several areas of mutual interest should create close ties between the two nations. Iran is a significant oil producer, and its location makes it a major player in the Middle East and Central Asia/Caspian basin regions. Under the right circumstances, Iran can play a major role in stabilizing Afghanistan and can contribute to the Arab-Israeli peace process. However, its divided government and internal factional disputes have prevented it from advancing its foreign policy interests. In many ways, the current stalemate between the United States and Iran benefits neither nation.

*Nader Entessar*

### Further Reading

Alikhani, Hossein. (2000) *Sanctioning Iran: Anatomy of a Failed Policy.* London: I. B. Tauris.

Bill, James A. (1988) *The Eagle and the Lion: The Tragedy of American-Iranian Relations.* New Haven, CT: Yale University Press.

Cottam, Richard W. (1988) *Iran and the United States: A Cold War Case Study.* Pittsburgh, PA: University of Pittsburgh Press.

## IRAQ—PROFILE

**IRAQ—PROFILE** (2001 est. pop. 23.3 million). In 1916, Britain invaded the Ottoman provinces of Mosul, Baghdad, and Basra; in 1921 it united these provinces and renamed the country Iraq. As a modern state, Iraq is young, but the history of the land and its people dates back more than five thousand years. From 1921 to 1932, the country was known as the Kingdom of Iraq; after the overthrow of the monarchy in 1958, the official name was changed to the Republic of Iraq.

### History

Here, in ancient Mesopotamia, the Sumerian civilization appeared about six thousand years ago. The lush river valleys of the Tigris and the Euphrates had a plentiful water supply and allowed for the production of surplus food and the rise of city-states and kingdoms. The region of present-day Iraq was the cradle of civilization and the background against which many biblical events occurred. Some of the most notable

## IRAQ

**Country name:** Republic of Iraq
**Area:** 437,072 sq km
**Population:** 23,331,985 (July 2001 est.)
**Population growth rate:** 2.84% (2001 est.)
**Birth rate:** 34.64 births/1,000 population (2001 est.)
**Death rate:** 6.21 deaths/1,000 population (2001 est.)
**Net migration rate:** 0 migrant(s)/1,000 population (2001 est.)
**Sex ratio—total population:** 1.02 male(s)/female (2001 est.)
**Infant mortality rate:** 60.05 deaths/1,000 live births (2001 est.)
**Life expectancy at birth—total population:** 66.95 years, male: 65.92 years, female: 68.03 years (2001 est.)
**Major religions:** Shi'a Islam, Sunni Islam, Christianity
**Major languages:** Arabic, Kurdish, Assyrian, Armenian
**Literacy—total population:** 58%, male: 70.7%, female: 45% (1995 est.)
**Government type:** republic
**Capital:** Baghdad
**Administrative divisions:** 18 provinces
**Independence:** 3 October 1932 (from League of Nations mandate under British administration)
**National holiday:** Revolution Day, 17 July (1968)
**Suffrage:** 18 years of age; universal
**GDP—real growth rate:** 15% (2000 est.)
**GDP—per capita (purchasing power parity):** $2,500 (2000 est.)
**Population below poverty line:** not available
**Exports:** $21.8 billion (2000 est.)
**Imports:** $13.8 billion (2000 est.)
**Currency:** Iraqi dinar (IQD)

*Source:* Central Intelligence Agency. (2001) *The World Factbook* 2001. Retrieved 18 October 2001 from: http://www.cia.gov/cia/publications/factbook.

rulers in this area included the Babylonian Hammurabi (reigned 1792–1750 BCE), whose law code included the lex talionis ("an eye for an eye") better known in biblical law; the Assyrian king Tiglath-Pileser III (reigned 745–727 BCE), who carried the Israelites off into captivity; the Chaldean king Nebuchadnezzar (c. 630–562 BCE), who completed the conquest of the Jews; and the Achaemenid Persian rulers Cyrus the Great (c. 585–c. 529 BCE) and Darius the Great (550–486 BCE).

In 637 CE, the battle of Kadisiya (Arabic al-Qadisiyah, on the Euphrates River), between the Arab Muslims led by the caliph 'Umar (586–644) and the forces of the Zoroastrian Sasanid Persian empire, marked the introduction of Islam to present-day Iraq and opened up Iran and Central Asia as well to the Muslims.

Baghdad became the capital of the Islamic Abbasid dynasty (749/750–1258), which ruled the lands from North Africa to Iran. The dynasty ended with the Mongol invasions of 1258 and the subsequent sack of Baghdad. The area was then governed by various rulers until 1534, when it became part of the Ottoman empire (1453–1922). However, for nearly six hundred years, between the collapse of the Abbasids in the thirteenth century and the final years of the Ottomans, government authority was tenuous, and the area of modern-day Iraq was, in effect, autonomous.

Beginning with its League of Nations Mandate in 1920, the British government laid out the institutional framework for Iraqi government and politics. Britain imposed a monarchy and nominated King Faisal (1885–1933) of the Hashemite family from the Hejaz

area in modern-day Saudi Arabia as the first king of Iraq. The British drew the territorial limits of Iraq with little knowledge of the natural frontiers or traditional tribal and ethnic settlements. They also had a prominent role in the writing of a constitution and the structure of the Iraqi parliament. The Iraqi state became independent in 1932, but Iraq's disconnected ethnic, religious, and tribal social groups showed little allegiance to the central government. As a result, the Iraqi government has been challenged with forging a nation-state in a land plagued by ethnic, sectarian, and tribal divisions.

Iraq became a republic after a 1958 coup of army officers under the leadership of Abdul Karim Kassem (1914–1963) overthrew and executed King Faisal II (1935–1958). Between the overthrow of the monarchy in 1958 and the emergence of Saddam Hussein (b. 1937) in 1979, Iraqi history was characterized by coups, countercoups, and fierce uprisings on the part of its Kurdish minority.

Iraq invaded Iran in 1980, beginning the costly Iran-Iraq war (1980–1990). In 1990, Iraqi troops invaded Kuwait but were driven out in 1991 by an international

Oil is Iraq's major economic product. Here, a man works on the pipeline at the Dora refinery south of Baghdad in May 1999. (AFP/CORBIS)

force. The victors did not occupy Iraq, however; the regime of Saddam Hussein remained in control.

## Geography

Iraq is located in Southwest Asia, at the head of the Arabian/Persian Gulf. Iraq's longest border is with Iran (1,458 kilometers), followed by those with Saudi Arabia (814 kilometers), Syria (605 kilometers), Turkey (331 kilometers), Kuwait (242 kilometers), and Jordan (181 kilometers).

Iraq's two major rivers, the Euphrates and Tigris, whose headwaters are in Turkey, converge in the southern plains of Iraq and terminate in the Shatt al Arab waterway that flows into the Persian Gulf. The country is divided into four major geographic areas: the desert in the west and southwest, rolling uplands between the upper Euphrates and Tigris Rivers, highlands in the north and northeast, and alluvial reedy marshes along the Iranian border in the south, with large flooded areas in the central and southeast sections.

The climate varies from extreme cold in the north to subtropical weather in the south and southeast. Baghdad has cool winters and hot summers. The desert region experiences cool winters with dry, hot summers. The northern mountainous regions along the Iranian and Turkish borders are characterized by cold winters with occasionally heavy snows that melt in early spring, sometimes causing extensive flooding in central and southern Iraq.

Baghdad is the capital and largest city of Iraq, followed by Basra in the south and Mosul in the north. Iraq's oil industry is concentrated in the northern city of Kirkuk, and the towns of Karbala (with the shrine of the caliph Hasan, who was murdered there in 680) and An Najaf (with the shrine of ʿAli, Muhammad's son-in-law) are pilgrimage centers for all Shiʿa Muslims. There are eighteen governorates, or provinces, in Iraq, which are divided into districts and subdistricts. In the early 1970s, limited self-rule was granted to Kurds in three northern governorates officially known as autonomous regions.

## Politics

Political power in Iraq is concentrated in a one-party system dominated by the president. The provisional constitution of 1968 states that the Baʾath Party rules Iraq through the Revolutionary Command Council (RCC), which exercises both executive and legislative authority. The political system is designed to concentrate enormous powers in extremely few hands, with all power ultimately situated in the person of the president, who is also prime minister, chairman of the RCC, and secretary-general of the Regional Command of the Baʾath Party. The system is a dictatorial, totalitarian state, which allows no political dissent or freedom of expression or assembly.

## Economy

Oil was discovered north of Kirkuk on 15 October 1927, and the petroleum sector has dominated Iraq's economy since the 1950s. The oil boom in the 1970s funded large-scale development projects, increased public-sector employment, and significantly improved education and health care. Because financial awards, as well as positions of high social status in the workplace, were usually based on membership in the Ba'ath Party and not on merit, the oil economy also tied increasing numbers of Iraqis to the ruling party.

Civil war with the Kurds, damage incurred during the war with Iran and the Persian Gulf War, and U.N. sanctions, coupled with economic mismanagement, led to economic disaster in the 1990s. Oil remains Iraq's main resource, but a U.N. trade embargo in 1990 halted all of Iraq's oil exports. New U.N. resolutions in effect since August 1996 have allowed Iraq to export a limited amount of oil to meet humanitarian needs.

## People

Arabs form approximately 75 percent of Iraq's population, while Kurds form 20 percent; the remaining 5 percent are composed of Turkmen, Assyrians, and Armenians. Assyrians are Orthodox Christians who revolted against the Ottoman empire during World War I, after which they were later settled in Iraq with aid from the British. At least 95 percent of the Iraqi population adheres to some form of Islam. Shiʿa Muslims, mostly in the south, form 65 percent of Iraq's total population; 35 percent of Iraqis are Sunni Muslims. Most Iraqi Shiʿites are Arabs, and almost all Kurds are Sunnis. Fifteen percent of the population are Sunni Arabs, but they tend to hold the highest administrative positions. Christians form the remaining 3 percent and include the Assyrians, Chaldeans (Uniat Christians who adhere to papal authority), and Armenians. Yazidis, who are of Kurdish stock, follow a syncretistic Islamic faith, and a few Jews remain in Iraq.

Arabic is the official language. It is the mother tongue of about 75 percent of the population and is understood by most others. Kurdish is spoken in Al-Sulaimaniyya, Dahuk, and Irbil governorates. Minorities speak Turkic and Armenian languages.

## Culture

Iraq has for millennia attracted waves of ethnically diverse migrations due to its borders with non-Arab Turkey and Iran and because of the great agricultural potential of its river valleys. The influx of these peoples has enriched Iraqi culture but also has led to deep-seated ethnic and sectarian tensions.

Iraq's cultural zenith occurred when it was the center of the Abbasid dynasty, which created great scientific, literary, and architectural works. During the Abbasids, *The Thousand and One Nights* (or *Arabian Nights;* in Arabic, *Alf laylah wa laylah*) emerged, a collection of fables and folk stories. In the last century, Iraq has produced some of the Arab world's best-known poets, musicians, and artists, such as the Nazim al-Ghazali and Kazem al-Saher.

## Current Issues

Following the Persian Gulf War, the U.N. Security Council demanded that Iraq scrap all weapons of mass destruction and long-range missiles and allow U.N. verification inspections. U.N. trade sanctions remain in effect due to incomplete Iraqi compliance with these resolutions. Iraq has had disputes with Turkey over the Euphrates and Tigris Rivers; their headwaters are in Turkey, which has its own water development plans for the rivers. Since 1991, Iraq has had to deal with resistance from Shiʿite Muslims in the south and Kurds in the north. In many areas in the north, the Kurds have established de facto independent regions, under

A team of United Nations weapons inspectors at their Baghdad compound in November 1998. (AFP/CORBIS)

the protection of U.N.-created safe havens in this area. The future of Iraq remains uncertain. The debate over an Iraqi role in the attack on the World Trade Center in New York was raised after 11 September 2001. Nevertheless, the possibility of a U.S. military strike on Iraq seems possible as Iraq has refused U.N. weapons inspectors back into Iraq after their expulsion in 1998.

*Ibrahim Marashi*

### Further Reading

Cordesman, Anthony H. (1999) *Iraq and the War of Sanctions: Conventional Threats and Weapons of Mass Destruction.* Westport, CT: Praeger.

Helms, Christine Moss. (1984) *Iraq, Eastern Flank of the Arab World.* Washington, DC: Brookings Institution.

Longrigg, Stephen. (1953) *Iraq, 1900 to 1950.* London: Oxford University Press.

———. (1925) *Four Centuries of Modern Iraq.* London: Oxford University Press.

Marr, Phebe. *(1985) The Modern History of Iraq.* Boulder, CO: Westview Press.

Nonneman, Gerd. (1986) *Iraq, the Gulf States, and the War: A Changing Relationship, 1980–1986 and Beyond.* London: Ithaca Press.

Tripp, Charles. (2000) *A History of Iraq.* Cambridge, U.K.: Cambridge University Press.

## IRAQ—ECONOMIC SYSTEM

The government of Iraq regards data on national economic performance as a state secret, particularly since the Iran-Iraq War (1980–1990); therefore, information on the nation's current gross domestic product (GDP), GDP growth, and inflation and unemployment rates is unavailable from the government itself. (See Table 1 for estimates from the U.S. Energy Information Agency.)

**TABLE 1**

**Selected estimated data showing Iraq's national economic performance for 2000 through 2002**

(ID = Iraqi dinar)

| | |
|---|---|
| Official exchange rate | U.S.$1 = ID0.3 |
| Unofficial exchange rate, 2001 | U.S.$1 = ID1,900 |
| GDP, at market exchange rates, 2000 | $31.8 billion (around one-third of economic output for 1989) |
| Real GDP growth rate, 2001 | –10% |
| Real GDP growth rate, 2002 | 15% |
| Inflation rate, 2001 | 80% |
| Inflation rate, 2002 | 50% |
| Major export products, 2000 | Crude oil, oil products (regulated by U.N.) |
| Major import products, 2000 | Food, medicine, consumer goods (regulated by U.N.) |
| Merchandise exports, 2000 | $20.6 billion |
| Merchandise imports, 2000 | $11.2 billion |
| Merchandise trade balance, 2000 | $3.3 billion |
| Current account balance, 2000 | $1.3 billion |
| Oil export revenues, total export revenues, 2001 | 95% or more |
| Total external debt, 2000 | $60 billion |

SOURCE: Energy Information Agency, Washington, DC. Retrieved 13 March 2002, from: http://www.eia.doe.gov/cabs/iraq.html.

The economy of Iraq has been dominated by the oil sector since the 1950s. (Oil was discovered north of Kirkuk on 15 October 1927.) Until the imposition of United Nations sanctions beginning in 1990, most economic activities were derived from government expenditures, whose revenues came from the oil sector. Agriculture has had a minor role in Iraq's economy. Iraq's economy, infrastructure, and society, however, were devastated by its two recent wars.

During the Iran-Iraq War (1980–1990), massive expenditures caused financial problems, and Iranian attacks damaged oil-export facilities. The government resorted to austerity measures and incurred massive foreign-debt payments. Iraq's estimated economic losses from the war were $100 billion.

Iraq's invasion of Kuwait in August 1990 (the start of the 1990–1991 Persian Gulf War), and the subsequent economic sanctions imposed by the United Nations, combined with damage from military action, had dire effects on the Iraqi economy. The regime of Saddam Hussein (b. 1937) survived by funding Iraq's internal-security forces and awarding scarce resources to key internal government allies, thus exacerbating the current economic situation.

Iraq's GDP fell drastically after 1991, but increases in oil production led to an estimated Iraqi real GDP growth of 18 percent in 1999 and 4 percent in 2000. Iraq's inflation is estimated at around 80 percent (down from 100 percent in 2000). Under United Nations control, its merchandise trade surplus is over $3 billion. Iraq has a heavy debt burden, possibly as high as $140 billion. In addition to having erratic fiscal and monetary policies, the nation has no meaningful taxation system. The dinar was valued at 1,900 per dollar on the black market, as of August 2001, compared with around 900 dinars per dollar at the beginning of 2000.

In December 1996, the United Nations oil-for-food program was implemented, ameliorating living conditions for Iraqi citizens, many of whom had to balance two to three jobs to afford basic foodstuffs. Iraq was allowed to export limited amounts of oil in exchange for food, medicine, and necessary spare parts. In December 1999, the U.N. Security Council allowed Iraq to export oil to meet its humanitarian needs. Oil exports rose to more than three-quarters of their prewar level.

### Iraq's Prewar Economy

Industrial development halted after the 1958 revolution, during which the monarchy was overthrown. Socialist rhetoric, which called for nationalization of industry and redistribution of large landholdings, as well as allowed the Communist Party to operate openly in postmonarchy Iraq, scared away Iraqi private investors, and capital began leaving the nation.

After the 1968 coup of the Ba'ath Party, the government gave priority to industrial development. The Ba'ath Party, whose platform was based on Arab unity and socialism, began nationalizing many private industries. With increased oil-export revenues, the state pursued a policy of import-substitution industrialization to move the economy away from dependence on oil exports and to obtain foreign exchange. In the 1960s, investment in industry accounted for almost one-quarter of the development budget, about twice the amount spent under the monarchy in the 1950s. After 1968, the share allocated to industrial development grew to about 30 percent of development spending. With the outbreak of the Iran-Iraq War, this share decreased to about 18 percent.

After 1968, the government used central planning to manage the national economy. Budgeting and planning became obsolete in Iraq due to the extremely high revenues accrued from the oil boom in the 1970s. As a result, the government's role shifted from the allocation of scarce resources to the distribution of wealth. Economic planning focused on subsidies and social welfare rather than on economic efficiency.

### The Iran-Iraq War (1980–1990)

On the eve of the Iran-Iraq War, the petroleum sector dominated the Iraqi economy, accounting for two-thirds of GDP. The war diminished oil production, and by 1983 petroleum accounted for only one-third of GDP. The nonpetroleum sector of the economy also shrank, and real GDP dropped about 15 percent per year from 1981 to 1983.

Since economic-development planning depended on massive expenditures, the Iran-Iraq War brought central planning to a halt. The government resorted to ad hoc planning due to limited resources and deficit spending. In the late 1980s, the state relaxed its control of private-sector activities to increase domestic industrial and agricultural output. In 1987, Saddam Hussein shifted from a socialist economic ideology to a more open market, in response to the Iraq's increasing war debt.

At this time, approximately 95 percent of Iraq's exports were raw materials, primarily petroleum, while foodstuffs made up most additional exports. Half of Iraq's imports were capital goods. Prior to the 1991 Gulf War, the government traded with Japan, Germany, Turkey, Italy, France, the former Yugoslavia, Brazil, and Britain. Kuwait was Iraq's most important Arab trading partner.

### The Persian Gulf War (1990–1991) and Its Aftermath

The imposition of comprehensive U.N. sanctions in 1990 placed the Iraqi economy under siege. Rationing was introduced for foodstuffs, and large parts of the country's industrial sectors closed due to shortages of imported raw materials and spare parts. Agriculture received much greater attention than before, but although farmers were ordered to increase their acreage, they were hampered by the exodus of Egyptian farm workers and the lack of fertilizer. The overall effect of the war in Kuwait, combined with the economic sanctions, was to reduce the GDP by around 63 percent in 1991.

In theory, there have been no exports from Iraq since 1990, due to the U.N. sanctions. However, illegal exports range from $1 to 2 billion annually, with illegal trade conducted with Turkey, Iran, and Jordan. Iraq has also smuggled crude oil and petroleum products to Turkey, Jordan, Syria, Iran, and the United Arab Emirates, where it was used for domestic use. According to press reports, these illegal shipments have been estimated to provide Iraq with as much as $600 million to $2 billion per year in illegal revenues.

During late 1995 and early 1996, with oil reserves almost exhausted, the government began to privatize state institutions and to sell state property to ameliorate the most critical economic crises—maintaining the balance of payments and dealing with accumulated debts.

As a result of the food-for-oil program under U.N. Resolution 986, implemented in December 1996, Iraq earns $4 billion annually. Under this Resolution, Iraq can sell specified dollar amounts of crude oil over six-month periods in exchange for the purchase of humanitarian supplies. The distribution in Iraq of these supplies is under U.N. supervision. Proceeds are also used to pay compensation for Persian Gulf War victims, pipeline transit fees for Turkey, and funding for U.N. weapons-monitoring activities.

In November 2000, Saudi Arabia opened a border-crossing point with Iraq (the land border had been closed since 1990) to allow Saudi exports under the oil-for-food program. In January 2001, Iraq signed free-trade deals with Egypt and Syria, with the possibility of exporting oil via a pipeline to the Syrians.

A man works at the Kirkuk station on the Iraq-Turkey pipeline in May 1999. (AFP/CORBIS)

In February 2001, U.S. Secretary of State Colin Powell (b. 1937) proposed a system of smart sanctions, barring military-related items while allowing import of civilian goods. In early July 2001, the U.N. Security Council agreed to postpone indefinitely a vote on the U.S. plan, extending the oil-for-food program another five months.

### Oil

Iraq's oil reserves are estimated to be between 10 and 15 percent, or 112 billion barrels, of the world's proven oil reserves, the second largest in the world (after Saudi Arabia); there are also an additional approximately 215 billion barrels of probable and possible resources. Iraq's largest active fields are Rumaila and Kirkuk, but they are troubled by problems with technical matters, export terminals, and pipelines. Although the oil sector has dominated the economy, Iraq did attempt to create a more diversified industrial infrastructure before the war.

### Agriculture

One-fifth of Iraq's area consists of farmland. In the 1950s, Iraq was self-sufficient in agricultural production, but by the early 1980s, food imports made up approximately 25 percent of total imports. Iraq has the potential for agricultural growth, but restrictions on water flow, due to Syrian and Turkish dam building on the Tigris and Euphrates Rivers, have produced difficulties.

### Natural Gas

Iraq contains proven natural gas reserves. Since most of Iraq's gas is associated with oil, progress on increasing the nation's oil output directly affects the gas sector as well. Gas is both produced with oil and also used for reinjection for enhanced oil-recovery efforts.

### Banking and Finance

Commercial banks, primarily British, emerged during the British mandate (April 1920 to October 1932), although the traditional money dealers still offered limited banking services. In 1964, all banks were nationalized and consolidated; the banking system then consisted of the Central Bank, the Rafidayn Bank, and the Agricultural, Industrial, and Real Estate banks. The Rafidayn Bank had to balance the role of a commercial bank while acting as a government intermediary in securing loans from private foreign banks. In 2001, the United Nations urged Iraqi authorities to provide more food for the civilian population and to allocate a greater part of their oil revenues to improving the health infrastructure.

*Ibrahim al-Marashi*

### Further Reading

Al-Nasrawi, Abbas. (1967) *Financing Economic Development in Iraq: The Role of Oil in a Middle Eastern Economy*. New York: Praeger.

———. (1994) *The Economy of Iraq*. Westport, CT: Greenwood Press.

*Economist* Intelligence Unit. (2000) *Iraq: Country Report*. London: *The Economist*.

Marr, Phebe. (1985) *The Modern History of Iraq*. Boulder, CO: Westview.

## IRAQ—EDUCATION SYSTEM

Historically, Iraq's educational system was the product of a mostly urban-based community of religious scholars dedicated to instilling in its adherents the principles of the Qur'an, and the sunna (Way) of the Prophet Muhammad. Similarly, education in the shrine cities of the Shiʿa sect of Islam meant passing on the corpus of law and devotional practices of the Shiʿite imams to the students of the religious schools.

In Iraqi Kurdistan (northern Iraq, home of a large population of Kurds), Kurdish *tariqa*s (mystic brotherhoods) monopolized education in the countryside. There, instruction was less formal and consisted for the most part of the teachings of the Qur'an and sunna, heavily laced with the mystic nuances of a particular brotherhood, as well as the oral transmission of tribal genealogies and lore.

Up to the mid-nineteenth century, formal education in Iraq was centered on the *madrasah* (religious school). These ranged in type and sophistication from primary-level instruction, in which young boys (and infrequently, girls) were taught the Qur'an, to the more elaborate circles of learning, which drew mature students from far and wide in a scholarly network composed of individual sheikhs (professors of law and theology) and their followers, all drawing on chains of transmission of knowledge emanating from a rich Islamic past.

### Education in the Ottoman Period

Iraq's educational system was based on informal circles of learning consisting of teacher-student networks assembled in mosques or other religious centers, and constantly revitalized by the input of traveling scholars from all over the Islamic world. Education thrived on government sponsorship and, especially in the Ottoman period (1453–1922), remained tied to official patronage until the beginning of the twentieth century. Very few *ulama* (scholars of law, teachers of religion) were able to survive independently of the state, which, from the sixteenth century onward, became the main guarantor of Islamic networks of education, as well as its chief beneficiary. But changes were afoot. From the first part of the nineteenth century onward, both the structure and the systems of meaning of Iraq's education process were to suffer an eclipse, as other methods of education combined to change the worldview of Iraqis radically.

Education witnessed many changes in structure and organization throughout the nineteenth century, and much of what we now view as modern instruction had its beginnings in the later Ottoman era. A wave of military-influenced reforms occurred in the Ottoman empire; these were largely inspired by the desire to upgrade the armed forces to resist Western encroachment. Military preparatory schools were established throughout the empire, as were an Imperial Military College, School of Public Administration, School of Law, and other universities in Istanbul. Iraq came under the influence of reformist-minded *wali*s (provincial governors), who oversaw the creation of the *rushdiyya-I'dadiyya* (primary and secondary) system of schools (both military and nonmilitary).

Starting in 1870, Ottoman schools were established in Baghdad; they quickly spread to other provinces. Consisting of elementary and three- and four-year secondary schools, these institutions pursued the systematic teaching of mathematics, sciences, and foreign languages. After Ottoman Turkey was defeated in World War I, the British army entered Baghdad in March 1917, ushering in a new period of educational reforms.

## EDUCATION AND MODERNIZATION IN IRAQ

The following quote from Sati' al-Husary, first director general of the Ministry of Education, in 1923–1927, refers to the resistance mounted by the leadership of the religious schools or *madrasah*s to the institution of modern curricula in Iraqi schools.

> But I believe that anyone who has the true interests of the people at heart would not be sorry to see these [teaching] institutions decline, for they grouped the worst hygienic conditions with the stupidest teaching methods.
>
> *Source:* Hala Fattah. (2002) Personal Communication.

### The Religious Legacy and an Emergent Secular Ideology

The educational system of Iraq underwent a radical change under British administration, and this change was stepped up throughout the years of the Iraqi monarchy. Because education was viewed as the molder of a new Iraqi generation, it quickly became a contested field. Sati' al-Husary (1880–1968) was a preeminent Arab nationalist theoretician and first director-general of education. According to his memoirs, the struggle for public education in Iraq centered on the unremitting hostility of some of the more traditionalist groups to the promotion of a secularist agenda in Iraqi schools throughout the 1920s and 1930s. Al-Husary's opponents were for the most part from the Shi'a community of Iraq; they resented the highly centralized nature of the new system of education, which favored urban centers (chiefly Baghdad) over tribal areas (which were mostly Shi'ite), and they were even less receptive to the secularist, national ideology that formed its core. To be sure, religious education throughout Iraq, not only in the Shi'ite south, suffered a grievous decline under the monarchy, as modern curricula adopted by the centralizing state made important inroads in the older, *madrasah*-style educational system.

### Education during the Royalist Era

By 1950, the new educational system of Iraq had made deep strides among the population. A cornerstone of that system was free instruction at all levels,

## EDUCATIONAL IMPROVEMENTS

"Before the [Iraq-Iran] war, the government had made considerable gains in lessening the extreme concentration of primary and secondary educational facilities in the main cities, notably Baghdad. Vocational education, which had been notoriously inadequate in Iraq, received considerable attention in the 1980's. The number of students in technical fields has risen threefold since 1977, to over 120,090 in 1986. The BAATH regime also seemed to have made progress since the late 1960's in reducing regional disparities . . . Baghdad was the home of most educational facilities above the secondary level, since it was the site not only of Baghdad University, which in the academic year 1983–84 . . . had 34,555 students, but also of the Foundation of Technical Institutes with 34,277 students, Mustansiriyya University with 11,686 students and the University of Technology with 7,384 students. The universities in Basra, Mosul and Irbil, taken together, enrolled 26 percent of all students in higher education in th[at] academic year."

*Source:* Mokless Al-Hariri. *Iraq—A Country Study*. Library of Congress. Retrieved 11 February 2002 from: http://www.loc.gov.

with primary school compulsory for all Iraqi children. Teacher-training institutes also developed rapidly; of six thousand primary teachers in government schools, nearly a third were women. Vocational schools also flourished. Although no university had yet emerged, many bodies of higher education existed, such as the Law School, the Engineering College, the Royal College of Medicine, and the College of Agriculture. Finally, scholarships sent young Iraqis abroad to further their academic study; on their return, some of them joined the cadre of the emerging oil industry.

### Revolutionary Iraq and the Pursuit of Mass Education

The revolution of 1958, which overthrew the monarchy, accelerated changes already under way in the educational system, such as the universalization of learning for all Iraqis, no matter their background or gender. But it also added a different ideological interpretation to state curricula, by attempting to inculcate the principles of Arab nationalism in schools. Since most education was public, with few private institutions still in operation from monarchical times (such as the famed Baghdad College, an American-administered high school run by Jesuit priests), the experiment had some success.

After the coming to power of the Ba'ath regime in 1968, however, a pronounced shift toward an Iraqi identity became manifest. As a result of this emphasis, Iraq's rich archaeological and folkloric history, as well as its store of pre-Islamic history and traditions, was incorporated into a more comprehensive educational vision. Long a bastion of Arab nationalism, Iraq's education system introduced school curricula that began to promote the notion of a particularist identity.

In the late 1970s, flush with oil, the Iraqi state aggressively pushed to promote universal literacy, claiming, by the end of the 1980s, to have reached an astounding literacy rate of 95 percent. More significantly, the Iraqi commitment to raise the literacy rate had resulted in the expansion of the educational system in the 1970s, especially in the larger cities. By the end of the Iraq-Iran War in 1988, approximately 180,000 students had entered universities or colleges. Seven institutes of higher learning, including one university of technology, had been established (increasing to eleven in the 1990s), as well as eighteen technical institutes. Because there was a need for educated university graduates, the government, despite a steady shortage of manpower in the armed forces, exempted students from military service during the Iraq-Iran war. Between 1977 and 1988, the number of technical students increased almost 300 percent.

### Iraqi Education under Sanctions

During the Persian Gulf War (1990–1991), a system of United Nations–sponsored sanctions against Iraq, the most comprehensive in history, was put in place, inhibiting the state's normal economic activity and depriving its citizens of basic human needs. Because the U.N. initially banned Iraq from freely exporting its oil, state sponsorship of education was severely affected. Unable to fund schools and universities or to build new ones, Iraq was effectively hobbled, and its educational programs were arrested. Several international agencies and organizations attest to the alarming decline in the educational system of the country.

For instance, a 1996 UNESCO report speaks of a crumbling structure, with few teachers showing up to teach in primary schools (and those that did being paid derisory salaries in wildly inflated post-sanctions currency), a near-absence of reading materials, and an av-

A girl writing on the blackboard in her classroom in Iraq in 1996. (DAVID & PETER TURNLEY/CORBIS)

erage of one desk for four students. Some 40 percent of educational institutions had been destroyed or damaged, and many schools needed urgent repair. A UNICEF report in August 2000 noted that the situation had still not improved. Under the sanctions, the Iraqi government's education budget fell by 90 percent, from $230 million to $23 million, and as many as 83 percent of primary schools were in disrepair.

Iraqi medical education, formerly among the best in the region, continues to suffer from a physical breakdown of educational and health facilities, broken or obsolete equipment, and a dearth of the most basic medicines with which to treat patients. The facts are clear: The embargo on intellectual activity that has isolated Iraq from the outside world since 1990 is proving to be an unmitigated catastrophe for a state that devoted so much of its earlier history to making education a universal right for all Iraqis, and later boasted of having one of the best school systems in West Asia during the oil-boom days of the 1970s.

*Hala Fattah*

### Further Reading

Al-Hilali, Abdul-Razzaq. (1959) *Tarikh al-ta'lim fi al-iIraq fi al-ahd al-uthmani* (The History of Education in Iraq in the Ottoman Period). Baghdad, Iraq: Al-Tib'a wa al-Nashr Press.

Al-Husary, Sati'. (1960) *Al-bilad al-'arabiyya wa al-dawla al-uthmaniyya* (The Arab Lands and the Ottoman State). Beirut, Lebanon: Dar al-Ilm.

———. (1967). *Mudhakirrati fi al-iraq* (Memoirs in Iraq). Vol. 1. Beirut, Lebanon: Tali'a Press.

Baram, Amatzia. (1991) *Culture, History, and Ideology in the Formation of Baathist Iraq, 1968–89*. New York: St. Martin's Press.

Library of Congress. (1998) "Iraq: A Country Study." Retrieved 17 March 2002, from: http://lcweb2.loc.gov/frd/iqtoc.html.

Nakash, Yitzhak. (1994) *The Shi'is of Iraq*. Princeton, NJ: Princeton University Press.

Richards, Leila, and Stephen Wall, (2000) "Iraqi Medical Education under the Intellectual Embargo." *The Lancet* 355 (25 March): 1093–1094.

Roche, Josette Tagher. (2000) "Embargo Generation." *UNICEF Courier*. Retrieved 17 March 2002, from: www.unesco.org/courier/2000_07/uk.

## IRAQ—HISTORY

The modern nation of Iraq, established in 1932, is relatively young. But the land and its people have a history that dates back to the dawn of human civilization. Historians usually use the Greek term "Mesopotamia" to refer to the land between the Tigris and Euphrates Rivers in ancient times. It was not until the late sixth or early seventh century that the Arabs came to refer to this land as "Iraq."

### Ancient Mesopotamia (10,000 BCE–637 CE)

Most historians agree that agriculture, the domestication of animals, and sedentary life were first developed in the valleys of northern Mesopotamia and southern Anatolia around 10,000 BCE. This Neolithic revolution soon spread to southern Mesopotamia, where by 4000 BCE the world's first cities appeared, including Eridu, Nippur, Kish, and Uruk. The inhabitants at this time represented a variety of ethnic and linguistic groups, but those who had the most profound impact were the Sumerians and Semites. The Sumerians were responsible for the development of complex irrigation works, large temples (ziggurats), legal codes, state institutions, a sexadecimal system of calculation, and, most important of all, the world's first system of writing, known as cuneiform script. Politically, Mesopotamia was divided among a multitude of city-states whose growing competition for land and water gave rise to endemic warfare. It was not until 2350 BCE that the Semites of Akkad succeeded in unifying Mesopotamia into a single empire.

The Semites would continue to rule through a succession of expanding empires for more than fifteen hundred years. In addition to the Akkadians , these included the Amorites of Babylon, the Assyrians of Nineveh, and the Chaldeans, who reestablished the rule of Babylon. Under the Assyrians, the empire included the entire Fertile Crescent and Egypt as well as Mesopotamia, and under the Chaldeans, Babylon became one of the leading cities of the ancient world with such architectural accomplishments as the Gate of Ishtar, the Temple of Marduk, and the Hanging Gardens. In 539 BCE, Semitic overlordship of Mesopotamia was removed by the Achaemenid Persians. Under their rule, Mesopotamia became part of

## KEY EVENTS IN IRAQ HISTORY

**c. 10,000 BCE** Agriculture and sedentary life emerges in the region.
**c. 4000 BCE** The first cities in human history appear in the region.
**2350 BCE** The Semites of Akkad unify Mesopotamia as a single empire.
**539 BCE** The Persians displace the Semites as rulers.
**330–129 BCE** Alexander of Macedon defeats the Persians and the region comes under Seleucid rule.
**129 BCE–224 CE** During the Parthian period Greek influence continues.
**224/228–651 CE** The region comes under the rule of the Sasanid dynasty.
**637** The Arabs defeat the Sasanids at the Battle of al-Qadisiyah, opening the region to Muslim Arab rule.
**749/750–1258** The region is ruled by the Muslim Abbasid dynasty.
**762** Baghdad is founded.
**945** Baghdad comes under the control of the Buyid dynasty.
**1055** The region comes under Seljuk Turk rule for 50 years.
**1258** The Mongols destroy Baghdad and the region becomes an impoverished province.
**1508** Much of the region comes under Safavid rule.
**1534** The region comes under the rule of the Ottoman empire.
**1639** The Treaty of Qasr-I Shirin establishes the present-day boundary between Iraq and Iran.
**19th century** The Ottoman empire institutes reforms and British influence increases.
**1914–1918** During World War I, the British take Iraq.
**1920** Iraq is made a British mandate by the League of Nations.
**1921** The British agree to more Iraqi control and Faisal is made king.
**1932** Iraq becomes an independent nation.
**1936** The first of several military coups takes place.
**1950s** The Iraqi Communist Party becomes a leader of the nationalistic movement.
**1958** A military coup leads to a decade of political instability.
**1963** The Ba'ath Party comes to power but is quickly pushed aside.
**1968** The Ba'ath Party comes to power again.
**1972–1975** Iraq nationalizes the oil industry.
**1974** A Kurd rebellion is put down.
**1979** Saddam Hussein comes to power.
**1980–1990** Period of the Iran-Iraq War.
**1990** Iraq invades Kuwait.
**1991** In the Persian Gulf War, Iraq is driven out of Kuwait.
**1992** International sanctions are placed on Iraq.

a vast empire stretching from Egypt and Greece in the west to northern India and central Asia to the east. The Persians brought a relatively tolerant rule, excellent administration, and the dualistic Zoroastrian religion. In 330 BCE, Persian rule was temporarily interrupted by the conquest of Alexander of Macedon (356–323 BCE). It was under his Seleucid successors (321–129 BCE) that Greek influences spread widely. Although Greek government, religion, art, and culture existed side by side with their Mesopotamian counterparts, in time syncretism did take place. Greek influences continued well into the Parthian period (129 BCE–224 CE), which also witnessed the spread of universalist religions (Zoroastrianism, Judaism, Christianity). The Parthians were replaced by the Sasanid Persians, who inherited a destructive seesaw conflict with Rome and its successor, the Byzantine empire. The most important social changes during this period were the growth of Christianity (both Monophysites and Nestorians) and the continuous influx of Arabs from the southern deserts. In 580, the ruling family of the Arab kingdom of the Lakhmids (vassals to the Sasanids), converted to Christianity.

### Early and Middle Islamic Period (637–1534)

The unification of the Arabs in Arabia under the banner of Islam was the precursor to their conquest of the Middle East and beyond. With respect to Mesopotamia, the decisive Battle of al-Qadisiyah (Kadisiya) took place in 637. Taking advantage of Sasanid exhaustion due to their wars with the Byzantines, the Muslim Arabs scored a comprehensive victory, pillaging the capital Ctesiphon in its aftermath. During the rule of ʿAli ibn Abi Talib (c. 600–661), the son-in-law of the Prophet Muhammad (c. 570–632) and the fourth caliph, Syria and Iraq were used as bases for rival claimants to the caliphate. After ʿAli's murder, however, the Umayyad clan, under the leadership of Muʿawiyah (602?–680), gained control of the caliphate and moved the capital from Medina to Damascus. Despite being the wealthiest and most populous province, Iraq was subordinated to Syria, leading to discontent and numerous rebellions against Umayyad rule. Among the most important of these rebellions was that of Hasan (624–680), the son of ʿAli and grandson of Muhammad, whose death in the Battle of Karbala in 680 proved to be a defining moment in the development of Shiʿa Islam. Opposition to the Umayyads culminated in 749, when they were defeated by a broad coalition led by the Abbasid family. (The Abbasid dynasty ruled from 749/750 until 1258). The Abbasid takeover represents a real social and economic revolution that transformed the Islamic world, particularly Iraq. In 762, the caliph al-Mansur (reigned 754–775) founded the new capital of Baghdad, which, during the reign (786–809) of Harun ar-Rashid (c. 763–809), became a great cosmopolitan center of economic prosperity, artistic and literary creativity, and intellectual dynamism rarely matched anywhere in medieval times.

The fault lines in this golden age began to form as early as the mid-ninth century when interdynastic feuds; regional separatism; revolts by peasants, slaves and the urban poor; and the increasing dependence on Turkish mercenaries led to economic and political decline. In 945, Baghdad came under the control of the Buyid princes. These tribal people, who originated from the Caspian Sea area, were Shiʿites who nevertheless kept the Sunni Abbasid caliph as a figurehead. This attempt at compromise did not reduce the rising Shiʿite-Sunni tensions, which became a feature of Buyid rule. Another feature was the fragmentation of Iraq (and much of the Islamic world) into ever smaller political entities ruled by rival princes. An apparent turn of fortunes in 1055 instigated by the return of Sunni rule under the Seljuk Turks did not last long. Seljuk power waned after only fifty years, resulting in a return to fragmentation and decline. The most terrible disaster to strike Iraq, however, came in the form of the Mongol invasion. In 1258, under Hulegu Khan (c. 1217–1265), the Mongols took Baghdad, destroyed much of the city, looted its treasures, burned its priceless libraries, and engaged in widespread massacres. Iraq was reduced to an impoverished province well into the sixteenth century, during which political fragmentation was punctuated periodically by Turkic tribal invasions, notably by Timur (1336–1405) in 1393 and 1401.

### Ottoman Rule (1534–1918)

In 1508, most of Iraq came under Shiʿa Safavid rule when Shah Esmaʿil (1487–1524) entered Baghdad. The Safavid hold, however, remained tenuous, and in 1514, the Ottoman sultan Selim I (1467–1520) took Mosul and northern Iraq after defeating the Safavids at the Battle of Chaldiran. In 1534, the conquest of the nation was completed when Sultan Suleyman the Magnificent (1494/1495–1566) entered Baghdad. Iraq remained part of the Ottoman empire despite numerous attempts by the Safavids and their successors to capture Baghdad and the Shiʿa holy cities of Najaf and Karbala. The only exception to this was between 1623 and 1638, when Shah ʿAbbas (1571–1629) briefly reoccupied the nation. The land was divided into the three provinces of Mosul, Baghdad, and Basra. Overall conditions were improved through integration into the empire's vast trade networks, enhanced security, and a relatively stable administration and judicial system. During the seventeenth and eighteenth centuries, several local powers (like the Afrasiyabs in Basra, the Jalilis in Mosul, the Mutafiq tribes in the south, and the Kurdish tribes in the north) developed at the expense of central control. Still, Ottoman rule was never really threatened, particularly after the signing of the Treaty of Qasr-i Shirin with the Safavids in 1639. This treaty established the boundary between Iraq and Iran, which is virtually unchanged today.

During the eighteenth century, the Ottomans were increasingly pressed in Europe, the danger from Persia returned, and tribal raids grew bolder. This forced Istanbul to grant more autonomy to the governors of

Baghdad, who came to rely on Georgian slaves (Mamluks) as the backbone of their army. The Mamluks eventually seized control of the governorship of Baghdad, reaching the height of their autonomy by the end of the century. A temporary peace in Europe allowed the Ottomans to reestablish central control in 1831. During the mid-nineteenth century, the Ottomans embarked on a broad series of state reforms (known collectively as the Tanzimat), geared particularly toward greater centralization. In Iraq, the most significant reforms were put into effect by Baghdad's Governor Midhat Pasa (1869–1872), who rationalized the provincial administration and established freehold ownership of land, modern schools, a printing press, modern communications, and various urban and industrial construction projects. At this time Iraq also witnessed a qualitative rise in European (especially British) economic penetration. The growing commerce with Britain and British investments in river navigation, telegraph lines, and oil exploration aroused British imperial interests even prior to World War I.

## British Rule (1918–1932)

A British expeditionary force from India was already in place to invade Iraq when the Ottoman empire made its fateful decision to join World War I on the side of Germany in November 1914. The British easily took Basra and moved north along the Tigris and Euphrates Rivers. After encountering some stiff resistance (notably at Al Kut), they entered Baghdad in March 1917. Mosul was not seized until after the Armistice of Moudros in 1918. Despite the claims of General Mode that they had come as liberators, the British had, according to the Sykes-Picot Agreement of 1916, planned to divide the Arab provinces of the Ottoman empire with France. Immediately after the conquest, a British administration was set up over a bordered territory that had hitherto been socially, economically, and culturally part of the Arab Ottoman lands. In 1920, the new League of Nations awarded Britain a mandate over Iraq. Theoretically, this was to be a temporary period during which Iraq would be assisted until it could stand alone. Effectively, it was a cover for British rule over a territory deemed to be of vital interest due to its strategic location near India and its valuable oil resources.

Creating a nation in a land separated from its historic ties with Syria and Arabia and having an extremely diverse population was a challenge in its own right. But when the task was forced on a nation by an unpopular occupying power, it proved disastrous. The establishment of the mandate triggered a broad uprising in 1920, initiated by the tribes of the south. Despite a massive British show of force, it was not put down until the following year. At the Cairo Conference of March 1921, the British agreed to loosen their direct rule over Iraq through the establishment of a king and local administration. The choice of Faisal (1885–1933), son of Sharif Husayn of Mecca (whose attempt to create a united Arab kingdom after the war was foiled by French guns at Damascus), as king proved to be acceptable to a broad segment of Iraqi notables. Although Faisal was crowned in August 1921, the nation did not achieve formal independence until 1932.

## The Monarchy (1932–1958)

The independence of the new kingdom was threatened on several fronts. In addition to the ethnic, religious, regional, and tribal social divisions, which actively disrupted the formation of a cohesive nation, the integration into the international market gave rise to severe class divisions, especially in the countryside. Resentment focused on the British-Iraqi treaties that ensured a commanding role for Britain in vital areas like foreign policy, defense, and the exploitation of natural resources (especially oil). Faisal did well to balance the various conflicting interests and keep the developing anti-British movement in check. He insisted on a constitution, national referendums, and universal male suffrage. After his death in 1933, however, these tensions erupted in the form of sectarian violence, tribal uprisings, and a more militant nationalist movement. In 1936, the first military coup by General Bakr Sidqi took place, followed by others, often at the instigation of one political faction against another. Although the nation suffered from political instability, some important progress was made in areas like irrigation, oil export facilities, railroads, education, construction, and trade.

Arab nationalist officers led by Rashid Ali felt that World War II was an opportunity to disengage the nation from Britain and push for unity with Syria. In 1941, they seized power, forcing regent Abdul-Ilah and Prime Minister Nuri al-Sa'id to flee. Fearing German influence on this movement, the British occupied Baghdad and reinstated the previous government, causing further resentment. After the war, the marked increase in oil revenues did little to ease class divisions or resentment at the government's ties with Britain. During the 1950s, the Iraqi Communist Party came to play an important role in the nationalist movement, leading several mass uprisings in 1948, 1952, and 1956. The last was directed against Iraq's entry into a U.S.-British-led defense system known as the Baghdad Pact. Opposition to the monarchy was also stirred by Egypt's Gamal Abdel Nasser (1918–1970), who was emerging as a symbol of Arab independence from the West.

### The Republic (1958–1979)

In 1958, a group of army officers led by Brigadier Abdul Karim Kassem (1914–1963) overthrew the monarchy, declared a republic, and plunged Iraq into a decade of political instability. Initially, the takeover attracted enthusiastic popular support, particularly when the new government declared its withdrawal from the Baghdad Pact, the establishment of a more independent foreign policy by having diplomatic relations with the Soviet Union, and the initiation of a land-reform program to reduce the power of the big landowners and aid landless peasants. In less than a year, however, the revolutionary group began to fall apart. Among the issues that threatened the new regime were Kassem's refusal to join the United Arab Republic, his claims over Kuwait, growing hostility with the oil companies, a Kurdish rebellion in the north, and a rise in authoritarianism. The Baʿath Arab Socialist Party soon came to lead the opposition, and in 1963, Kassem was overthrown in a bloody coup that was accompanied by widespread executions and arrests, especially of Communists. The group seized power was led by ʿAbdul-Salam ʿArif, a pan-Arabist army officer and an admirer of Nasser. Within a couple of months, ʿArif kicked the Ba'athists, who were blamed for most of the repressive measures, out of his ruling coalition and began a series of nationalizations of banks and leading industries. The regime, however, never managed to gain any amount of popular legitimacy, and the fractious political atmosphere in Baghdad was accentuated by the continuing rebellion in Kurdistan and the 1967 Arab defeat at the hands of Israel. Taking advantage of the resulting unrest, the Ba'ath Party managed to rally enough support within the army to recapture power in a bloodless coup in 1968.

The new Ba'athist government was led by Colonel Ahmad Hasan al-Bakr (who assumed the presidency), Saddam Hussein (b. 1937), and a number of associates drawn mainly from their Takriti kinsmen. Although a civilian, Hussein had distinguished himself as an able party organizer and ruthless conspirator. During the next decade, he would build a powerful intelligence network and gradually assume more control at the expense of al-Bakr and the military. Mostly under his guidance, the Ba'ath Party came to dominate the military and most organizations and clubs, setting the stage for a totalitarian state. Initially, Ba'athist rule seemed focused on national unity, with an agreement on Kurdish self-rule reached in 1970 and the establishment of a National Progressive Front with the Communists and others in 1973. Between 1972 and 1975, in a highly popular move, Iraq nationalized the entire oil industry, placing huge revenues at the dis-

In a move that reduced sanctions, the U.N. Security Council voted on 31 March 2000 to allow Iraq to double expenditures on rebuilding its oil industry. (REUTERS NEWMEDIA INC./ CORBIS)

posal of the government. These revenues were used to extend and improve various social services and significantly raise the overall standard of living. They were also used, however, to strengthen the repressive apparatus of the government, especially the army and the intelligence services. In 1974, negotiations with the Kurdish Democratic Party over implementing Kurdish self-rule broke down, and war ensued. After defeating this latest Kurdish rebellion, the government turned to harassing other opposition groups, and by 1979 the Communist Party was outlawed and most of its members arrested or exiled.

### Dictatorship and War (1979–Present)

A few months after the tumultuous 1979 Islamic Revolution in Iran, al-Bakr relinquished power to Hussein. After executing his rivals in the Ba'athist leadership, Hussein turned to the perceived threat from revolutionary Iran. On 22 September, Iraqi forces invaded Iran, launching a destructive war. During the first year, Iraqi forces made important advances, especially in Khuzestan Province. The following year the tide had turned, and Iranian counteroffensives recaptured most territory. For the next six years, fierce fighting continued with little advantage to either side, although U.S. and French support for Iraq was beginning to have an effect. Fearing greater U.S. involvement and setbacks, Iranian leader Ayatollah Khomeini (1900–1989) reluctantly accepted a U.N.-brokered cease-fire. (Iraq did not officially agree to Iranian peace terms until after its invasion of Kuwait in 1990). The war did great damage to Iraq's economy, transforming it from a creditor to a nation with a debt of nearly $100 billion. The war also assisted in the establishment of dictatorial rule through a more thorough militarization of society and the development of Hussein's personality cult. Iraq, however, continued with an ambitious armament program (including chemical, biological, and nuclear weapons), and the peace did little to resolve internal and regional tensions. Fearing opposition from the army and angered by Kuwaiti oil policies (seen as depressing prices), Iraq invaded Kuwait on 2 August 1990 and then formally annexed it. After Iraq refused to withdraw, a 28-member coalition led by the United States (and including several Arab nations) launched an air and land war that liberated Kuwait in April 1991. The massive rebellion against Hussein's rule that followed was eventually crushed at great human cost. Iraqi infrastructure suffered massive damage during the air campaign, and the continuing U.N. economic sanctions (the most comprehensive in history) have crippled the nation. The northern Kurdish areas, with Allied protection, have since achieved autonomy from Baghdad. Nevertheless, Hussein's hold on power appears to have actually strengthened, and recently his son has been groomed to succeed him.

*Thabit Abdullah*

### Further Reading

Donner, Fred M. (1981) *The Early Islamic Conquests.* Princeton, NJ: Princeton University Press.

Farouk-Sluglett, Marion, and Peter Sluglett. (2001) *Iraq since 1958: From Revolution to Dictatorship.* Revised edition. London: I. B. Tauris.

Longrigg, Stephen H. (1925) *Four Centuries of Modern Iraq.* Oxford: Oxford University Press.

Marr, Phebe. (1985) *The Modern History of Iraq.* Boulder, CO: Westview Press.

Morony, Michael. (1984) *Iraq after the Muslim Conquest.* Princeton, NJ: Princeton University Press.

## IRAQ—HUMAN RIGHTS

**IRAQ—HUMAN RIGHTS** Iraq is a dictatorial, totalitarian state, with all political power concentrated in a repressive one-party apparatus dominated by the president, Saddam Hussein, and the Arab Socialist Baʿath Party. The state implements systematic human-rights abuses and internal repression through a network of internal-security organizations, secret intelligence services, Ba'ath party agencies, and police, military, and militia units. The state indiscriminately conducts these human-rights abuses against all sectors of the population. Officers and officials are regularly executed for their supposed involvement in subversive political activities. The government creates ethnically homogenous zones by expelling families from their homes and forcibly deporting them to other parts of the country. Freedoms of opinion, expression, association, and assembly are forbidden.

The vast Iraqi security apparatus maintains an order of repression through widespread terror, systematic use of torture, amputations, summary executions, forced "disappearances," and arbitrary arrests and detention. As socioeconomic conditions worsen under United Nations sanctions, the state punishes those accused of economic crimes and military desertion. Freedom of the press and expression is nonexistent, and Iraq's media outlets, such as television, radio, and newspapers, are government owned. Many foreign publications are banned, as is ownership of satellite dishes, computers, and typewriters.

### Background History

When the current regime took power in Iraq in a coup in July 1968, the first victims executed were the

Kurd refugees from Iraq living in tents in Turkey in 1991. (DAVID & PETER TURNLEY/CORBIS)

very military officers who had aided in the takeover. Non-Ba'athists were removed from state institutions. Even Ba'ath party members who were seen as potential rivals were executed. These practices continued throughout the 1970s, and increased when Saddam Hussein took over the presidency in 1979.

In 1971 the regime began a systematic campaign of deporting Iraqi Shiʿites and Kurdish citizens to Iran. They were accused of being Iranian, opposed to "pure Iraqi," and expelled, even though some of these families had been living in Iraq for 300 years. The campaign gathered additional momentum in the 1980s, due to the Iran-Iraq War (1980–1990). An estimated 250,000 to 300,000 people, including Arabs, Kurds, and Turkmen, were deported during this period. In 1975, after the Algiers Accord with Iran ended the shah's support of the Kurds, the regime systematically targeted Kurdish citizens, forcing thousands to flee to neighboring countries. In 1978 the Iraqi state executed thousands of members of the Iraqi Communist Party.

The state has also systematically eliminated opponents, who are accused of complicity in plots against the president. Many of them have included high-ranking civilian and military officials, tribal leaders, as well as members of Saddam Hussein's own family and al Majid clan. His two sons-in-law, Hussein Kamel and Saddam Kamel, defected to Jordan in August 1995, but returned because they believed the president's promise of a pardon. They were murdered in a gun battle on 23 February 1996, just three days after they came back. Not only were they killed, but forty relatives, including women and children, also died. Other members of Saddam's clan were also arrested, as well as mid-level military and civilian officials, for their association with the defectors.

**Religious Persecution**

Although Iraq's Shiʿite Muslims constitute about half of the country's population, Iraq's government has been traditionally dominated by the country's Sunni Muslim minority. The majority of the country's Shiʿite population lives in the areas south of Baghdad, with a large concentration in the southern marshland regions near the Iranian border.

Iraqi Kurds in the north and the Iraqi Shiʿites in the south launched an armed revolt against Saddam's regime at the end of the Gulf War. Iraqi troops crushed the uprising, razing Shiʿite mosques and other Shiʿite shrines and executing thousands. Thousands of rebels and Shiʿite civilians fled into the southern marshlands between the Tigris and Euphrates Rivers and continued the revolt. Ayatollah Abul-Qassem al-Khoie (1899–1992), Iraq's most respected Shiʿite leader, was put under house arrest after the failed uprising, and a few years later died under mysterious circumstances during his detention. In February 1999 security forces assassinated one of the leading Shiʿite clerics, Ayatollah Mohammad Sadiq Al-Sadr.

In 1992, in the aftermath of the Persian Gulf War (1990–1991), the allied forces opposed to Iraq imposed no-fly zones over both northern and southern Iraq, to deter Iraqi governmental aerial attacks on the marsh dwellers in southern Iraq and residents of northern Iraq. However, the Iraqi government conducted artillery attacks on villages in both areas, and a large-scale burning operation in the southern marshes. The government began a water-diversion project and other projects in the south, accelerating the process of large-scale environmental destruction. The army constructed canals to divert water from the wetlands, resulting in hundreds of square kilometers burned in military operations. Moreover, the diversion of supplies in the south limited the population's access to food, medicine, drinking water, and transportation.

The Assyrians, a Christian minority in Iraq, have also suffered from state-sponsored massacres from the 1930s. They have not only been targeted by the current state, but are also attacked by Kurdish groups who have traditionally been at odds with the Assyrians.

### Ethnic Persecution

The regime's ethnic hostility has been directed at three main targets: Kurds, Turkmen, and Kuwaitis. The Kurds have suffered the brunt of Iraq's dismal human-rights practices. For example, as Baghdad was making advances against Iranian forces during the final years of the Iran-Iraq War, the state turned its attention to the Kurds. In 1988, the Iraqi military attacked the Kurds in a campaign Baghdad called vAnfal," meaning "spoils of war," based on the eighth sura, or verse, in the Qur'an. The security apparatus demolished villages, executed thousands with firing squads, buried people in mass graves, and committed other atrocities. The Iraqi military attacked the Kurds with poison gas in the town of Halabja on 16 March 1988. Delivered over a three-day period, the gas left more than 5,000 dead and 30,000 injured. The campaigns against the Kurdish people by Iraq resulted in more than 4,000 villages destroyed and as many as 250,000 Kurds reported killed.

The Turkmen are a Turkic people, primarily living in the northern Iraqi city of Kirkuk and its surroundings. Not only have they been the victims of the Iraqi government's policies, but they also have come under attack from Kurdish parties who live in the same area.

Finally, six hundred Kuwaitis were taken prisoner during Iraq's occupation of Kuwait. The Kuwaiti government called for their immediate release and asked for the names of those who may have died in captivity to be revealed. Iraq disregarded the requests.

### The Future

The Iraqi government continues to employ torture, summary executions of suspected opponents, forced disappearances, arbitrary arrests, and denial of the basic right of due process. Current resistance to the central government is minimal as the Kurdish opposition continues with its infighting, and most of the Shi'ite opposition is limited to hit-and-run raids launched from Iran. Many attempted coup plans devised by Sunni opponents in the government have been foiled. A sustained series of U.S. attacks in the future may unite and encourage the opposition, just as these groups launched a coordinated, albeit unsuccessful, uprising after the Gulf War.

*Ibrahim Marashi*

### Further Reading

Committee against Repression and for Democratic Rights in Iraq (CARDRI). (1994) *Iraq Since the Gulf War: Prospects for Democracy*, edited by Fran Hazelton. London: Zed Press.

Hiltermann, Joost, ed. (1994) *Bureaucracy of Repression: The Iraqi Government in Its Own Words*. New York: Human Rights Watch.

Human Rights Watch. (1992) *Endless Torment: The 1991 Uprising in Iraq and Its Aftermath*. New York: Human Rights Watch.

Makiya, Kanan. (1993) *Cruelty and Silence*. New York: Pantheon Books.

———. (1998) *Republic of Fear: The Politics of Modern Iraq*. New York: Pantheon Books.

## IRAQ—POLITICAL SYSTEM

After the current government in Iraq came to power in a coup on 17 July 1968, removing 'Abdul Rahman 'Arif, another Ba'ath Party leader, Ahmad Hasan al-Bakr (1914–1982) became president and Saddam Hussein (b. 1937) vice-chairman. A provisional constitution, adopted on 16 July 1970, concentrated all executive and legislative powers in the Revolutionary Command Council (RCC), the chairman of which was also the president of the country. Iraq's political system is divided into three mutually checking branches, the executive, the legislative, and the judicial, but in reality the executive wields complete authority over the legislature and the judiciary.

The Arab Socialist Ba'ath (Resurrection) Party is in firm control of Iraq's political system. The government , dominated by the higher echelons of the Ba'ath Party, must sanction any formal political activity. Outlawed opposition political movements include Kurdish, Shi'a, and Communist parties.

### The Constitution

After the 1968 takeover, a constitution was drafted on 22 September 1968 and became effective on 16 July

A large mural featuring Iraqi leader Saddam Hussein is meant to build nationalism. (DAVID & PETER TURNLEY/CORBIS)

1970. Another constitution was drafted in 1990 but has not been adopted. The constitution states that Iraq is "a sovereign people's democratic republic" dedicated to Arab unity and socialism (Metz 1988: 177). Islam is the state religion, but freedom of religion and of religious practices is guaranteed. While both Arabic and Kurdish are official languages for administrative purposes, the constitution also states that the "national rights" of the Kurds and other minorities are to be exercised only within the framework of Iraqi unity. The 1970 constitution is officially designated as provisional, yet it has remained in force because a permanent constitution has never been promulgated.

### The President and Vice President

The president is the chief executive of the RCC and serves as the commander in chief of the armed forces and the head of state. The president has authority to appoint and dismiss members of the judiciary, civil service, and military. The constitution does not stipulate the president's term of office or provide for his successor.

Ahmad Hasan al-Bakr served as the first president, from 1968 to 16 July 1979, when he resigned (whether voluntarily or involuntarily is still debated). Saddam Hussein, the former vice chairman of the RCC, assumed the presidency. Saddam Hussein's power is based on a small group of supporters, especially relatives from the Talfah family from the town of Tikrit. He deals ruthlessly with suspected opposition to his rule, both external and from within the party. He is known for monopolizing power and promoting a cult of personality. The vice presidency is largely a ceremonial post, and the vice president is appointed or dismissed solely at the will of the president.

### The Council of Ministers

The Council of Ministers serves as the presidential executive arm. The council discusses presidential policies and subsequently creates specific programs based on these policies. The council's activities are closely monitored by the *diwan*, or secretariat of the presidency, from which executive orders are issued.

### The Cabinet

The president convenes all cabinet sessions. The cabinet usually consists of forty members, including the president and vice president. In addition to the president and the vice president, other senior members of the RCC serve on the cabinet, often, but not always, in the positions of minister of defense, minister of foreign affairs, minister of the interior, and minister of trade. Other ministerial positions include those for agriculture, communications, culture and arts, education, finance, health, higher education, industry, information, irrigation, justice, labor, oil, planning, housing, religious trusts, and transport.

**The Revolutionary Command Council**

The Revolutionary Command Council (RCC) was first formed after the July 1968 takeover. The constitution states that the RCC is the supreme body in the state and has the authority to promulgate laws, approve the government's budget, and deal with matters of national security, such as declarations of war. The RCC can override the constitution at any time and without judicial review. All who serve in the RCC must be members of the Ba'ath Party.

The president serves as chairman of the RCC. The RCC may dismiss any of its members by a two-thirds majority vote and can send to trial any members of the council, as well as any deputy to the president or any cabinet minister. The RCC has sweeping constitutional powers. It serves a legislative role in cooperation with or independently from the National Assembly. The powers of the National Assembly are defined by the RCC. The RCC also approves government decisions on national defense and internal security, such as declarations of war and ratifications of any international treaties or agreements. The chairman presides over the RCC's closed sessions and signs all laws and decrees issued by it. The RCC supervises the operations of cabinet ministers and the institutions of the state.

**State Security Apparatus**

The Iraqi state relies on a network of security and intelligence agencies, which protect it from internal enemies. These agencies are coordinated through the National Security Council, chaired by the president, and include the Iraqi army, the Special Security Service, the General Intelligence Directorate (Mukhabarat), Military Intelligence, the General Security Service, and the Office of the Presidential Palace. The responsibilities of different agencies overlap, so that no agency emerges as a threat to the power of the president. The Iraqi Department of General Intelligence is the most extensive arm of the state security system.

**Local Government**

There are eighteen governorates, each administered by a governor appointed by the president. Each governorate is divided into districts headed by district officers, with each district divided into subdistricts, which are administered by subdistrict officers. Mayors head cities and towns, while the president appoints the mayor of Baghdad and the mayors of other important cities.

**The National Assembly**

The Iraqi constitution provides for an elected, unicameral National Assembly, known in Arabic as al-Majlis al-Watani. The RCC first promulgated a draft law creating the Assembly in December 1979, and this took effect in March 1980. The first National Assembly was elected in June 1980, in the first parliamentary elections since Iraq became a republic in 1958.

The National Assembly consists of 250 members elected by secret ballot every four years. Two hundred twenty seats are elected by popular vote, and thirty seats are appointed by the president to represent the three northern provinces of Dahuk, Irbil, and Al-Sulaimaniyya, where Kurds who have demonstrated loyalty to the government are appointed as representatives. All Iraqi citizens over the age of eighteen years are eligible to vote for the candidates. There are 250 electoral districts, and one representative is elected to the Assembly from each of these constituencies.

Only members of the Ba'ath Party and pro-Ba'ath independent candidates are permitted to participate in the elections. Furthermore, a state-appointed election commission must approve the qualifications of all candidates for the Assembly. This system has maintained Ba'ath Party control over the National Assembly. To qualify as a candidate for National Assembly elections, individuals must be at least twenty-five years of age, must have Iraqi fathers and be Iraqi by birth, and must not be married to foreigners.

The National Assembly generally holds two sessions per year; the first session is held in April and May, and the second session in November and December. During these sessions, the Assembly carries out its legislative duties concurrently with the RCC. Its primary function is to ratify or reject draft laws proposed by the RCC. In addition, it has limited authority to enact laws proposed by a minimum of one-fourth of the Assembly, to ratify the budget and international treaties, and to debate domestic and international policy. However, its actual powers are restricted, and ultimate decision-making authority resides with the RCC.

**The Judiciary**

The RCC promulgated the laws that formed the judiciary, since the constitution guarantees an independent judiciary but has no provisions for the organization of courts. The judiciary is divided into civil, criminal, administrative, and religious affairs. The Ministry of Justice has jurisdiction over the courts, while the president appoints all judges.

**Political Parties**

Although the Ba'ath party is the only sanctioned political party, others have exerted an influence in the past. Some continue to have an effect despite their outlawed status.

***The Ba'ath Party*** Two Syrians, Michel Aflaq (1910–1989) and Salah ad Din al Bitar (1912–1980), founded the Ba'ath Party in Damascus in 1947. Several Iraqis who attended the meeting returned to Baghdad and formed the Iraqi branch of the Ba'ath.

During the 1950s, the Ba'ath was an outlawed party, and its members were subject to arrest if their identities were discovered. In the 1960s, the party was reorganized under the direction of General Bakr as secretary-general, with Saddam Hussein as his deputy. Both men were determined to bring the Ba'ath to power, and in July 1968, the Ba'ath finally staged a successful coup. After the takeover, when Bakr became president of the regime, he initiated programs aimed at the establishment of a nation based on the Ba'ath ideals of socialism and Arab unity.

The Ba'ath Party claims that about 10 percent of the population are supporters and sympathizers; of this total, full party members, or cadres, are at 0.2 percent of the population. Participation in the party is essential for social mobility.

The Ba'ath Regional Command is the party's top decision-making body, and its members are chosen by Saddam Hussein. Theoretically, the Ba'ath Regional Command makes decisions about Ba'ath Party policy based on consensus. In practice, all decisions are made by the party's secretary-general, Saddam Hussein.

***The Iraqi Communist Party*** The Iraqi Communist Party (ICP) was founded by Yusuf Salman Yusuf (1901–1949; known as Comrade Fahd, or the Leopard) in 1934. Although the ICP was legalized in 1973, the Ba'ath Party regularly suppressed it after 1963 and outlawed it altogether in 1985. The Ba'ath hierarchy had earlier perceived the ICP as a Soviet arm ready to interfere in internal affairs, but after the successful 1968 coup Ba'ath leaders joined ICP officials in calling for a reconciliation of their decade-long rivalry.

Despite several decades of arrests, imprisonments, repression, assassinations, and exile, in the late 1980s the ICP remained a credible force and a constant threat to the Ba'ath leadership. Because the ICP is a clandestine party fighting for the overthrow of the Ba'athist regime, its true membership strength may never be known.

***The Shi'a Parties*** The religious opposition to the Ba'ath originates from the devout Shi'a population, who form the majority of Iraq's population but are excluded from positions of power. The most important opposition party was Al-Da'wa al-Islamiyya. After the Ba'athist coup in 1968, Al-Da'wa opposed the regime's secular policies, which led to the party's state persecution. Al-Da'wa was banned in 1980, and membership in the organization was punishable by death.

All anti-Iraqi Islamic organizations, such as Al-Da'wa al-Islamiyya, moved their headquarters to Tehran. Iran set up an umbrella organization, the Supreme Assembly for the Islamic Revolution in Iraq (SAIRI), in November 1982. It is headed by the Iraqi cleric Hujjat al-Islam Muhammad Baqir al Hakim. SAIRI subsumed Al-Da'wa and other small Shi'a groups. It still launches military raids from Iran into southern and northern Iraq.

***The Kurdish Parties*** The Kurds have maintained a violent struggle against the central government in Baghdad almost since the founding of Iraq. The Kurdish Democratic Party (KDP) was formed in 1946 under the leadership of Mullah Mustalafa-al-Barzani (1904–1979), with assistance from the Soviet Union, in northern Iran. Here, a Kurdish territory, the Republic of Mahabad, was established. When the Republic was crushed by Iranian forces a few years later, the KDP moved its activities to northern Iraq. The Iraqi government then launched a military campaign against the KDP forces, which responded with guerrilla attacks on Iraqi government forces and installations with the support of Iran and the United States.

In 1975, the shah of Iran withdrew his support of the Kurds as part of the Algiers Accord (which also delineated the Shatt al Arab channel that forms the border between Iraq and Iraq) between Tehran and Baghdad, leading to divisions in the Kurdish movement. At this time, a breakaway faction emerged from the Kurdish Democratic Party (KDP), known as the Patriotic Union of Kurdistan (PUK), under Jalal Talabani (b. 1933). The PUK engaged in low-level guerrilla activity against the Iraqi government from 1975 to 1980. The war between Iraq and Iran in 1980 gave the PUK and the KDP the opportunity to intensify their military campaigns against the Iraqi government.

Most of the rural areas in northern Iraq were under the control of the guerrillas during the Iran-Iraq war years. Since the 1991 Gulf War, all central government functions in northern Iraq have been performed by local administrators, mainly Kurds, because the state withdrew its military forces and civilian administrative personnel from the area. A regional parliament and local government administrators were elected in 1992. This parliament last met in May 1995, when fighting between the PUK and the KDP disrupted normal parliamentary activity.

### Iraq Today

Iraq maintains tenuous control of northern Iraq, while a low-intensity revolt has been launched in the marshes of southern Iraq. As a response, Saddam Hussein built a series of canals to drain the marshes and contain this revolt. Saddam Hussein's popularity has diminished as Iraqis suffer from the hardships caused by the United Nations–imposed sanctions. His most loyal support comes from members of his al-Majid clan from Tikrit in northern Iraq and from the Special Republican Guard. Saddam Hussein will most likely be succeeded by one of his sons, Uday Hussein and Qusay Hussein.

*Ibrahim al-Marashi*

### Further Reading

Abu Jaber, Kemal. (1966) *The Arab Baath Socialist Party.* Syracuse, NY: Syracuse University Press.

Batatu, Hanna. (1978) *The Old Social Classes and the Revolutionary Movements of Iraq: A Study of Iraq's Old Landed and Commercial Classes and of Its Communists, Bathists, and Free Officers.* Princeton, NJ: Princeton University Press.

Devlin, John. *The Baath Party: A History from Its Origins to 1966.* Stanford, CA: Hoover Institution Press.

Ghareeb, Edmund. (1981) *The Kurdish Question in Iraq.* Syracuse, NY: Syracuse University Press.

Marr, Phebe. *The Modern History of Iraq.* Boulder, CO: Westview Press.

Metz, Helen. (1988) *Iraq, A Country Study.* Washington, DC: Federal Research Division, Library of Congress.

O'Ballance, Edgar. (1973) *The Kurdish Revolt, 1961–1970.* Hamden, CT: Archon Books.

Tripp, Charles. (2000) *A History of Iraq.* Cambridge, U.K.: Cambridge University Press.

## IRAQ-TURKEY RELATIONS

**IRAQ-TURKEY RELATIONS** Since the early twentieth century, when both Turkey and Iraq achieved independence in the aftermath of World War I, relations between the two states have been pragmatic. Given an overlapping history, complementary concerns, and sometimes conflicting values, Turkey-Iraq relations have been defined and informed by a relatively limited number of issues, each varying in significance. Some of the most important issues relate to Western interests.

### Pre–World War I Relations

Prior to World War I, neither Turkey nor Iraq existed as independent states. The Ottoman empire, ruled by the Anatolian Turks, included the Arabic province of Iraq, which had been incorporated into the empire by the Ottomans in 1534. For the following four hundred years, the Turkish sultan was both the political and spiritual ruler of the province of Iraq (the position of Islamic spiritual ruler, or caliph, having been wrested from the Mamluk regime of Syria and Egypt in 1517). Periodic attempts at rebellion in the Iraqi province failed, but over time, the slow demise of the Ottoman empire allowed Iraq greater freedom in its own affairs. World War I found the Ottomans on the side of the Germans, presenting the Western Allies with an opportunity to weaken the empire further and establish greater influence in the Middle East by supporting Arab nationalism through promises of independence. With British backing, the Arabs rebelled against the collapsing Ottoman empire, and the Middle East, Iraq included, achieved nominal independence.

### Relations from World War I to the Persian Gulf War

By 1923, Turkey had also consolidated its independence, expelling foreign powers from its vastly reduced territory, but maintaining positive relations with Western states for trade and developmental purposes. In Iraq, the League of Nations Mandate of 1920 gave control of the Iraqi province to the British, to the disappointment of Iraqi nationalists. From 1920 until Iraq achieved full independence in 1932, Iraqi relations with its former Turkish rulers were guided by the British and dealt primarily with British trade interests. Two main concerns existed for the British at this time, each economic in nature and giving substantial benefits to both Turkey and Iraq. The first was the construction of a transcontinental railroad bypassing the African trade route and linking British-held Kuwait to Europe. The second was the development of the Kirkuk oil fields, discovered in northern Iraq in 1927, and the shipment of its oil to Turkey's Iskenderun Gulf.

During the 1930s, Turkey-Iraq relations were at their most cordial, with both the Hashemite king Ghazi (1912–1939) of Iraq and Kemal Ataturk (1881–1938), the founder of the modern Turkish state and its leader since 1923, continuing to maintain close relations with the British. Although there was some conflict over border issues and resource questions, the relations of both states remained relatively stable, limited, and oriented toward the West.

From the late 1930s, after the deaths of both Ataturk and Ghazi, to the 1970s, Turkey and Iraq each suffered a series of military coups alternating with democratically elected governments with strong military elements. Relations between the two states focused on issues that remained significant for the rest of the twentieth century, transcending whatever regime happened to be in power, and institutionalizing the pragmatism of their ties. At times complementary, yet often at odds, the policy concerns of the two countries formed a basic pattern of behavior that was consistent on some fronts, although not necessarily friendly, and fluid on others. Islam, water issues, and the oil trade are examples of the former, whereas relations with the West and Kurdish minority questions are examples of the latter.

The 1940s saw differences emerging in Turkey-Iraq foreign relations, with Iraq shifting support away from Europe. Iraq took part in the first Arab-Israeli war (1948) and, in the early 1950s, examined the possibility of a union between itself and Syria. Turkey opted to look in the other direction, supporting the Western states and, after its ascension to the North Atlantic Treaty Organization (NATO) in 1952, placing itself firmly in the sphere of Western influence. Different foci in their extended foreign relations, however, did not preclude Iraq and Turkey from cooperating in common areas of interest. In 1955, both countries joined with Iran, Pakistan, and the United Kingdom to form the Baghdad Pact, a mutual-defense organization intended to contain the growth of Soviet influence in the region. This experiment ended when Iraq, after alienating many of its Arabic neighbors by joining the pact, found itself with a new military government and withdrew from the agreement.

The historically sensitive issue of water rights became a strong point of contention for the two countries beginning in the 1960s, when Turkey implemented a massive public-works project (the GAP project) aimed at harvesting the water from the Tigris and Euphrates Rivers through the construction of a series of dams, for irrigation and hydroelectric energy purposes. The intended level of control of common water resources by Turkey upon completion of the GAP project was unacceptable to Iraq, which remains dependent upon both rivers to supply a significant portion of its water needs.

First raised in the 1920s, the Kurdish question became a prominent concern of both Iraq and Turkey with the radicalization of a Kurdish independence movement and the formation of the Kurdistan Workers' Party (PKK) in the 1970s. Operating primarily out of Turkey, the PKK's revolutionary activity was aimed at the establishment of a Kurdish state in Turkey's southeast. For Iraq, the situation was less volatile, as divisions among the Kurds in northern Iraq prevented any real challenge to Baghdad's rule. However, as the Kurdish issue was a cross-border concern, it took center stage in Turkish-Iraq relations during the 1970s and the 1980s.

The establishment of military-backed regimes in Turkey and Iraq by 1980 helped strengthen relations on several core issues, as both governments supported secularist and antiradical policies, stable borders, and closer ties with the West—needed by Iraq for its conflict with Iran (1980–1990) and by Turkey in its desire to join the European Union (EU). The Iraqi invasion of Kuwait in 1990, under the orders of President Saddam Hussein (b. 1937), reversed this decades-long trend as Turkey again chose to support the West.

## Post–Persian Gulf War Relations

The pragmatism of Turkish-Iraqi relations is most evident in the post–Persian Gulf War era. While Turkey gained international praise for siding against Iraq and allowing United Nations forces to fly missions from its air bases, this favor did not compensate the country for the massive disruption of the Turkish economy resulting from the imposed U.N. sanctions. From 1991 until 2001, estimates of Turkey's economic losses ran between $30 billion and $40 billion. As Turkey's economy steadily declined in the 1990s, the government turned a blind eye toward increased trade between its southeastern provinces and Iraq. Oil and agricultural products were actively traded between the two states in explicit violation of the U.N. sanctions. By 2000, the Turkish government had even gone so far as to tax the illegal tanker trade in oil.

Iraq, for its part, often ignored Turkey's close ties with the United States, out of the desire to maintain relations with the country that, since the 1930s, had been one of Iraq's most significant trading partners and remained one of the few outlets for Iraqi goods, legal and illegal. Iraq also generally ignored the periodic incursions into its territory by Turkish forces pursuing PKK groups, a continuing threat to Turkey, but mostly harmless to Iraq, as Kurdish factions remained disunited.

While foreign relations diverged after the Persian Gulf War, Turkey-Iraq relations have remained closely defined by parameters established decades earlier, dependent upon both local circumstances and foreign influence.

*Sean M. Cox*

## Further Reading

Ahmad, Feroz. (1993) *The Making of Modern Turkey*. London and New York: Routledge.

Ciment, James. (1996) *The Kurds: State and Minority in Turkey, Iraq, and Iran*. New York: Facts On File.

Farouk-Sluglett, Marion, and Peter Sluglett. (2001) *Iraq since 1958: From Revolution to Dictatorship*. London: I. B. Tauris.

Stivers, William. (1982) *Supremacy and Oil: Iraq, Turkey, and the Anglo American World Order, 1918–1930.* Ithaca, NY: Cornell University Press.

**IRIAN JAYA** (2000 est. pop. 2.2 million). Irian Jaya, the easternmost province of the Republic of Indonesia, covers 421,981 square kilometers on the western half of the island of New Guinea, nearly 55 percent of the total area of Indonesia. Irian Jaya is encircled by other islands (Dolak, Misool, Salawati, Waigeo, Biak, Yapen, and Kelopom) and is bordered by the Seram and Banda Seas to the west, the Pacific Ocean to the north, the Arafura Sea to the south, and Papua New Guinea to the east. New Guinea is the second largest island in the world, after Greenland; from west to east it measures almost 2,500 kilometers, the distance from London to Istanbul.

The most populated and cultivated parts of the island are the Paniai Lakes district and the Baliam Valley to the east. The population comprises migrants from Java and indigenous people from diverse *suku* (tribes), such as the Dani of the Baliem Valley in the central highlands, the Asmat of the southern coastal region, and the Ekari of the Wissel Lakes region. The official language is Bahasa Indonesia, but at least 250 languages are spoken by the indigenous people, reflecting the isolation and small numbers of many of the tribes.

Irian Jaya is a tropical island with primeval rainforests, powerful rivers, beautiful beaches, lakes, and mountains. The highest mountain is Gunung Jayawijaya, with snowcaps covering its 5,000-meter-high peaks. The area is also rich in natural resources, including fish, timber, and precious metals. These, however, have become a source of conflict between the central government and local peoples.

## LORENTZ—WORLD HERITAGE SITE

The Lorentz National Park has been the largest protected region in Southeast Asia since its designation as a UNESCO World Heritage Site in 1999. Located at the intersection of two tectonic plates on New Guinea, the massive park is exceptionally biodiverse—including both snowcaps and a tropical marine environment.

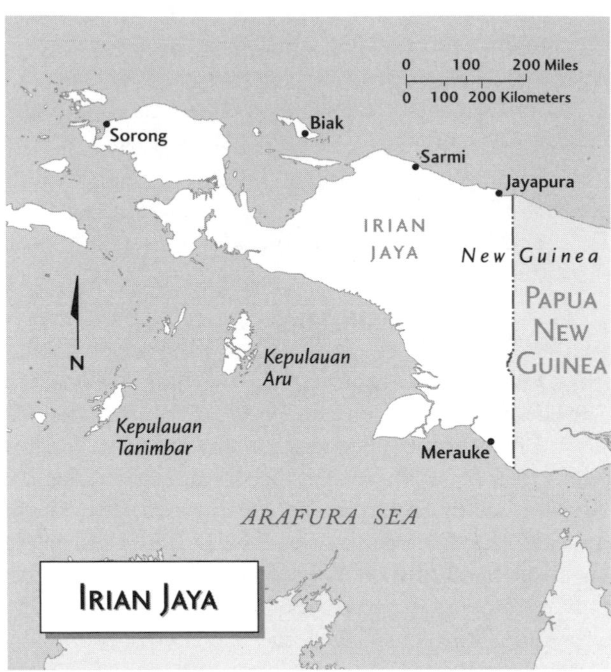


After a plebiscite in 1969, Irian Jaya became an Indonesian province, with its capital at Jayapura. However, frustrated by the exploitation of their natural resources, and poor social and economic conditions (e.g., high infant and maternal mortality rates), a growing number of Irian activists, who prefer to call themselves Papuans, consider the plebiscite illegitimate, and have demanded independence.

*Andi Achdian*

### Further Reading

*Ensiklopedi Nasional Indonesia.* (1994) Vol. V. Jakarta, Indonesia: PT Cipta Adi Pustaka.

Badan Pusat Statistik. (1996) "Statistics Indonesia." Retrieved November 2001, from http://www.bps.go.id.

**IRIAN JAYA CONQUEST** Irian Jaya, also known as Papua, has effectively been governed by Indonesia since May 1963, and its estimated 2 million inhabitants speak languages belonging to more than 200 distinct groups. The Netherlands ruled the western half of Papua island after transferring sovereignty of the rest of the archipelago to Indonesia in 1949. The Indonesian president Sukarno consistently argued that this territory was rightfully Indonesia's. The Netherlands, under U.S. pressure, finally acquiesced to Sukarno's demand, and an agreement was concluded on 15 August 1962, transferring power to the United

Nations on October 1962 and to Indonesia on 1 May 1963. The agreement stipulated that Indonesia hold an Act of Free Choice, but the 1969 plebiscite is widely regarded as fraudulent and unrepresentative (Indonesian military intelligence carefully selected 1,022 tribal leaders to endorse Indonesian rule). The U.N. "noted" the Act of Free Choice, but failed to give stronger endorsement of the heavily rigged process.

The Free Papua Movement (OPM or Organisasi Papua Merdeka) has resisted Indonesian rule since the mid-1960s (1,500 Indonesian paratroopers who entered Irian Jaya in early 1962 met stiff local resistance; 200 were either killed or went missing). Rejecting the 1969 Act of Free Choice, in 1971 the OPM announced the establishment of an independent government, and from the late 1970s to 1984 staged sustained guerrilla attacks. Indonesian armed forces broke the resistance by 1984 with advance knowledge of an attack on Jayapura. Retaliation by the Indonesian armed forces mirrored its tactics in Aceh and East Timor, and aerial bombardment affected thousands of civilians, causing them to flee into Papua New Guinea. OPM campaigns against mining operations reflect resentment over Indonesian exploitation of Irian Jaya's vast reserves of copper, gold, petroleum, and other resources. The OPM, however, suffers from serious divisions along tribal lines; as Robin Osborne argues, "For at least 20,000 years, for indigenous Melanesians of New Guinea, 'foreigners' were people of other language groups, even close neighbours" (Osborne 1986: 49).

Since the end of the Suharto era, the OPM and other independence supporters have adopted a peaceful strategy of using their new freedoms to push for recognition of Irian Jaya's distinct history. A government-sponsored conference in June 2000 backfired on Indonesia when delegates overwhelmingly resolved that West Papuan independence leaders had declared independence from the Dutch on 1 December 1961—before the transfer of power to Indonesia. (In 1961 Papuans elected to the new National Committee adopted emblems of state with Dutch approval.) The conference also concluded that this should prompt political review of Papua's status. The strategy of the independence movement is to correct "history" as the first step in reconsidering the province's future. Transmigration to Papua has been considerable, and more than 200,000 mainly Javanese settlers now live in the province, particularly in coastal areas.

*Anthony L. Smith*

### Further Reading

Emmerson, Donald K. (2000) "Will Indonesia Survive?" *Foreign Affairs* 79, 3(May/June): 95–106.

Malley, Michael. (1999) "Regions: Centralization and Resistance." In *Indonesia Beyond Suharto: Polity, Economy, Society, Transition*, edited by Donald K. Emmerson. New York: M. E. Sharpe, 71–105.

May, R. J., ed. (1986) *Between Two Nations: The Indonesia–Papua New Guinea Border and West Papua Nationalism.* Bathurst, Australia: Robert Brown and Associates.

Osborne, Robin. (1985) *Indonesia's Secret War: The Guerilla Struggle in Irian Jaya*. Sydney: Allen & Unwin.

## IRIOMOTEJIMA ISLAND

**IRIOMOTEJIMA ISLAND** (2000 est. pop. 2,000). Iriomotejima is located approximately 440 kilometers southwest of Okinawa. It is the largest island of the Yaeyama group, with an area of 289 square kilometers. Mountains average 400 meters and cover 70 percent of the island. The highest mountain is Komidake (470 meters). About 90 percent of the island is covered with tropical rain forests and mangroves flourish at the estuaries of the Urauchi and Nakama rivers. Because of repeated cases of malaria since 1637, people were forced to leave the island. The crested serpent eagle and the Iriomote wildcat are found in the island's forests. The latter, a species of mountain cat, was discovered in 1965 and was designated an endangered species by the Japanese government in 1994. The Iriomote National Park, which occupies several of the Yaeyama islands, is primarily located on Iriomotejima. The park has subtropical forests and vegetation, poisonous snakes, rare butterflies, and mangrove swamps. The island's economy depends mainly on farming and tourism, which began to flourish in the 1970s. The main agricultural products are wetland rice, sugarcane, and pineapples.

*Nathalie Cavasin*

### Further Reading

Okinawa Prefectural Government. (2000) *Nature in Okinawa.* Okinawa, Japan: Okinawa Prefectural Government.

Sugata Masaaki. (1995) *Nihon no shima jiten* (Dictionary of Japanese Islands). Tokyo: Mikosha.

Sutherland, Mary, and Dorothy Britton. (1984) *National Parks of Japan.* New York: Kodansha.

## IRON TRIANGLE

**IRON TRIANGLE** The Iron Triangle, about twenty miles northwest of Saigon in Vietnam, served as a base for attacks by the National Liberation Front (NLF) on the Saigon area and Tan Son Nhut Airport during the height of the American war in Vietnam (1965–1970). An area of 200 to 280 square kilometers of dense forests, its corners were the villages of Ben Suc, Ben Cat, and Cu Chi. The Triangle was also bordered by the Saigon and Thi Tinh Rivers. The area was so called because of its shape and because it was solidly under the control of the NLF and difficult to penetrate.

**Use by the Viet Minh**

The area had first been used by the Viet Minh during the Franco–Viet Minh War (1946–1954), and it comprised a vast and complex system of tunnels and underground facilities, including hospitals, living quarters, meeting halls, and command posts. From the tunnels, located near Cu Chi, the NLF was able to plan strategy and could avoid capture. The 240 kilometers of tunnels and underground facilities had allowed the Viet Minh and later the NLF to survive numerous military sweeps and massive bombings of the area. Some of the underground facilities were 6–9 meters deep and some of the passageways were as narrow as 60 centimeters by 60 centimeters.

**Operation Cedar Falls**

By 1966, the U.S. military in southern Vietnam considered the area a threat to its operations and to the safety of Saigon, and decided to destroy the Iron Triangle (referred to as War Zone D by the U.S. forces). Operation Cedar Falls was launched in January 1967. Approximately thirty thousand American and South Vietnamese (ARVN) troops took part in the search-and-destroy operation led by General William Westmoreland, among others. The primary aim of the mission was to eliminate the NLF presence and threat in the area. American military experts claimed this would require U.S. and ARVN troops to flush out and destroy the tunnels. In addition, all non-NLF inhabitants would have to be permanently relocated, and at least four villages would have to be razed.

One of the first missions of Operation Cedar Falls was the evacuation of the village of Ben Suc. On 8 January 1967, U.S. and ARVN troops surrounded the village. The estimated 3,500 residents of the village were rounded up and interrogated. Those considered noncombatants were evacuated to a refugee camp several miles from the village. Those suspected of being NLF troops were taken in as prisoners. Once the evacuation of Ben Suc was completed, U.S. demolition teams moved in to destroy the village itself. Tractors and bulldozers were brought in by helicopters in order to clear the surrounding jungle and to raze the village. Within a few days the forest had been cleared and the houses had been destroyed. This technique was used in other surrounding villages as well.

At Cu Chi, entrances to the tunnels were exposed and special U.S. military units, known as the Tunnel Rats, were sent in to destroy the tunnels and to capture any NLF troops in hiding. In addition the U.S. military used flooding and shelling to flush out any NLF troops in hiding. After the area had been defoliated and cleared, it was bombed and burned in order to destroy any remaining, undetected tunnels. Although considerable damage was done to the tunnels, NLF troops were quickly able to repair them and to continue to use them as protection.

Operation Cedar Falls lasted approximately eighteen days. It was followed by Operation Junction City and several others. Initially deemed a success by the U.S. military command, it failed to make the Iron Triangle safe, despite the amount of resources it received. The operation had created at least seven thousand Vietnamese refugees, resulting in stronger resentment of the U.S. presence in Vietnam.

**Evaluation**

Despite casualties of approximately 750 on the NLF side and 250 on the U.S. and ARVN side, there was very little fighting, as most NLF troops managed to escape and fled to sanctuaries in Cambodia. Within weeks, however, NLF activity resumed in the area. American intelligence units spotted NLF troops transporting supplies, on bicycle, toward Saigon. The NLF rebuilt camps and resumed operations. The Iron Triangle then served as the base from which the Tet Offensive was launched on Saigon (31 January 1968). The tunnels of Cu Chi were not successfully destroyed until they suffered repeated special B-52 bombings in 1970.

*Micheline R. Lessard*

**Further Reading**

Karnow, Stanley. (1983) *Vietnam. A History*. New York: Viking.

Schell, Jonathan. (1967) *The Village of Ben Suc*. New York: Knopf.

**IRRAWADDY DIVISION** (2002 est. pop. 7.2 million). The 35,138-square-kilometer territory that comprises the modern-day Irrawaddy (Ayeyarwady) Division is one of the most important political and economic regions in Myanmar (Burma). Flanked by the Arakan Yoma range in the west and the Irrawaddy River in the east, until the British annexation of Burma in the nineteenth century much of the territory consisted of wetlands and forests. Under British rule, however, large areas were cleared for paddy cultivation, leading to its preeminent position as the main rice producer in the country, a position it has retained into the twenty-first century.

The British encouraged immigration, changing the ethnic balance in an area that had previously been inhabited largely by Mons and Karens. In the 1990s, the population of the division was calculated by the government to be 5.84 million, including 1.19 million Karens, 60,000 Rakhines, and 160,000 inhabitants of other nationalities. The majority population of 4.43 million was classified as ethnic Burman. The Mon language disappeared more or less entirely in the division by the end of the twentieth century.

Many parts of the territory suffered severe disruption during World War II as well as during the insurgencies that broke out shortly after independence was granted in 1948. It was not until the 1970s that both the Karen and Communist insurgencies were suppressed throughout the division.

In the last two decades of the twentieth century, sectors of the local economy slowly revived. The capital of the division, Bassein (Pathein) in the western Delta region, is Myanmar's second busiest port. Other important centers are the road-rail junction towns of Henzada (Hinthada) and Myanaung, both of which lie farther north on the Irrawaddy River.

Agriculture and fisheries are the main industries. In addition to paddy and jute, crops such as pulses, groundnut, sesamum, coconut, bananas, chilli, and vegetables grow well in the alluvial soil. A variety of fish-based industries also developed. Fish-paste, dried fish, and prawns are all produced, and salt-making and fishing enterprises are located along the estuaries and Andaman seashore.

Manufacturing or heavy industries remained small-scale during the Burma Socialist Programme Party era (1962–1988), and included a jute mill at Myaungmya, a glass factory in Bassein, and the Myanaung Oil Field and Gas Turbine Power Generating Plant.

Under the State Law and Order Restoration Council government, which assumed power in 1988, major road and bridge building programs were introduced during the 1990s in an attempt to improve communications with Yangon and the rest of Myanmar. Particular emphasis was placed on expanding rice cultivation, which, it was intended, would produce an export surplus for the country, but economic progress in the division continued to be slow.

*Martin Smith*

### Further Reading

Adas, Michael. (1974) *The Burma Delta: Economic Development and Social Change on an Asian Rice Frontier, 1842–1941.* Madison, WI: University of Wisconsin Press.

Bunge, Frederica M., ed. (1983) *Burma: A Country Study.* Washington, DC: American University Foreign Area Studies, U.S. Government Printing Office.

Tinker, Hugh. (1967) *The Union of Burma: A Study of the First Years of Independence.* Oxford: Oxford University Press.

**IRRAWADDY RIVER AND DELTA** The Irrawaddy (Ayeyarwady) River is the major waterway of Myanmar (Burma). It originates at the confluence of two small rivers, the N'mai Kha and Mali Kha, in Kachin State and flows through the heart of the country before entering the Andaman Sea more than fourteen hundred kilometers to the south. Up to 1.6 kilometers wide in places, the river is navigable for much of its length.

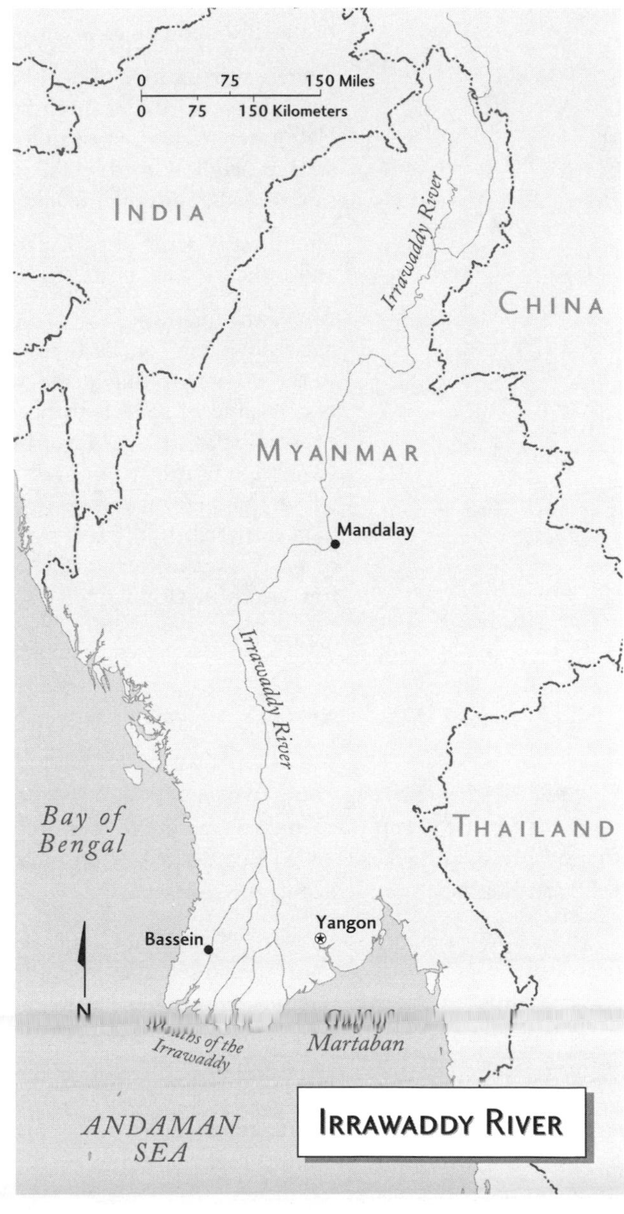

## NAVIGATING THE IRRAWADDY

The Irrawaddy is the major inland north-south transportation route in Myanmar. The following account describes one of two types of boats used to navigate the river in the 1800s.

> Of boats there are numerous kinds, from the small canoe to the large earth-oil or rice-boat; but all have a dug-out for the foundation whilst those in use on the Irrawaddy differ considerably from those found elsewhere. The Irrawaddy boats again are of two kinds. In one the keel-piece is a single tree hollowed out and stretched by the aid of a fire when green, a complete canoe in fact. From this ribs and planking are carried up. The bow is low with beautiful hollow lines. . . .
>
> The stern rises high above the water and below the run is drawn out fine to an edge. A high bench or platform for the steersman, elaborately carved, is an indispensable appendage. The rudder is a large paddle lashed to the larboard quarter, and having a short tiller passing athwart the steersman's bench. . . .
>
> The mast consists of two spars, it is in fact a pair of shears bolted and lashed to two posts rising out of a keel-piece. . . .
>
> Above the main yard the two pieces run into one forming the topmast. Wooden rounds run as ratlines from one spar of the mast to the other, forming a ladder for going aloft. The yard is a bamboo or line of spliced bamboos of enormous length and is suspended from the masthead by numerous guys or halyards, so as to curve upwards in an inverted bow. A rope runs along this from which the huge mainsail is suspended, running on rings, like a curtain, outwards both ways from the mast. There is a small topsail of similar arrangement: the sail cloth used is a common light cotton "stuff for clothing."
>
> *Source: Gazetteer of Burma.* (1893) New Delhi: Cultural Publishing House, 436–437.

Steamer service, carrying both passengers and goods, operates from the capital, Yangon (Rangoon), through Prome (Pyay) and Mandalay to Bhamo in Kachin State fourteen hundred kilometers to the north.

In its upper reaches, the river passes through mountain valleys and gorges, but beyond a major defile south of Bhamo the river begins to broaden. Here, as it crosses the Dry Zone of Myanmar, passage is seasonally interrupted by low water and shifting sandbanks. In these reaches are located the former royal capitals of Amarapura, Mandalay, Ava, Sagaing, and Pagan, testifying to the pivotal role the river has played in Myanmar's history and culture.

North of Pakokku, the Irrawaddy gains fresh impetus when it is joined by the Chindwin (Chindwinn) River through a network of channels. Flowing south, the river has created a long alluvial plain during thousands of years as it passes between the Arakan Yoma and Pegu Yoma ranges. On this stretch are located the historic oil fields between Chauk and Myanaung as well as the important road-rail-river junction at Prome.

Myanaung marks the upper gateway to the Irrawaddy Delta. In these lower reaches, the Irrawaddy flows through vast flatlands, dividing and subdividing on its way, before entering the Andaman Sea through eight major mouths. Yangon is further linked to the delta by the Twante Canal, constructed in 1883.

Amid a maze of creeks, mangrove forests, and agricultural land, road transportation is often difficult in the 33,670-square-kilometer delta region, which was largely a frontier area until British annexation in the nineteenth century. Silting and flooding remain annual problems, but the economy of this region, especially rice production, has become increasingly important to the nation over the past one hundred years. Local fishing industries are also located in several southernmost towns, such as Bassein (Pathein), Pyapon, Labutta, and Bogale.

For much of the twentieth century, the Irrawaddy was spanned only once—by the road-rail bridge at Sagaing. However, in a spate of building at the end of the 1990s, bridges were constructed at Maubin and Nyaungdon in the delta region, as well as at Prome, Chauk, and Myitkyina farther north.

*Martin Smith*

**Further Reading**

Adas, Michael. (1974) *The Burma Delta: Economic Development and Social Change on an Asian Rice Frontier, 1842–1941.* Madison, WI: University of Wisconsin Press.

McCrae, Alister, and Alan Prentice. (1978) *Irrawaddy Flotilla.* Paisley, U.K.: James Paton.

O'Connor, Vincent C. Scott. (1907) *Mandalay and Other Cities of the Past in Burma.* London: Hutchinson.

Tinker, Hugh. (1967) *The Union of Burma: A Study of the First Years of Independence.* Oxford: Oxford University Press.

**IRTYSH RIVER** The Irtysh River flows northwest for 4,248 kilometers (2,640 miles) through China, Kazakhstan, and Russia, and ends in western Siberia. It begins in the southwest slopes of the Chinese Altay mountain range (Xinjiang province) and it flows west into Kazak territory, where it is known as the Kara-Irtysh up to the point where it enters Lake Zaysan. Once it exits the lake, it is called Irtysh and continues its flow northwest within Kazakhstan, passing the cities of Ust'-Kamenogorsk, Semipalatinsk, and Pavlodar. A canal that was constructed in the 1960s from the Irtysh to Karaganda allows the use of the river's water for agricultural purposes in central Kazakhstan. Leaving Kazakhstan, the Irtysh river then crosses into Russia, passes the city of Omsk, and joins the Ob river.

The river is the principal source of water for almost four million Kazaks and a vital base for industry. China and Kazakhstan have been involved in discussions and negotiations regarding the future of the river. China's plans to build a canal on the upper part of the Irtysh (called Ertis He in China) in order to divert the water flow into the Xinjiang province of western China has caused concerns in Kazakhstan. At present, an agreement has been reached that allows China to divert only 10 percent of the river's flow—about one billion cubic meters—per year until 2020.

*Daphne Biliouri*

**ISE SHRINE** Located in Mie Prefecture, the Grand Shrine of Ise (Ise Daijingu) is the most important shrine in Japan. It comprises two main shrine complexes, Naiku (the Inner Shrine), which consecrates Amaterasu, the Sun Goddess, and Geku (the Outer Shrine), which enshrines Toyouke, an agricultural deity worshiped as parent to Amaterasu, together with more than 120 subordinate shrines. Naiku enshrines *Yata-no-kagami* (the Sacred Mirror), one of the three Imperial regalia. The two main shrines, built in the *shinmei* style, with plain wood and reed-thatched roofs, are ritually rebuilt every twenty years. Each building has an adjacent alternate site, where the new building is constructed with strict attention to detail. When completed, rites are held for the transfer of the deity to the new shrine. Following further rites, the shrine on the old site is disassembled and the materials distributed to affiliated shrines around the nation.

During the Tokugawa period (1600/1603–1868), branches of this shrine throughout Japan promoted pilgrimages to Ise, and large numbers of ordinary people, representing their local devotional groups, visited the shrine as part of a once-in-a-lifetime journey away from the farms and distant towns. In an average year, pilgrims numbered between 600,000 and 700,000; in the spontaneous mass pilgrimages of 1705 and 1830, however, they numbered between two and three million.

*James M. Vardaman, Jr.*

**Further Reading**

Bocking, Brian. (1995) *A Popular Dictionary of Shinto.* Surrey, U.K.: Curzon Press.

Holtom, D. C. (1965) *The National Faith of Japan: A Study in Modern Shinto.* Reprint ed. New York: Paragon.

Kanazaki Noritake. (2000) "Modern Tourism as it Developed in Japan since the Late Seventeenth Century." *Journal of Japanese Trade and Industry* 19, 5 (September/October): 27–31.

Picken, Stuart D. B. (1994) *Essentials of Shinto: An Analytical Guide to Principal Teachings.* Westport, CT: Greenwood Press.

**ISHIHARA SHINTARO** (b. 1932), Japanese novelist and politician. Born in Kobe, Ishihara Shintaro graduated from Hitotsubashi University with a law degree in 1956. In 1954, he published his first novel, *Hai iro no kyoshitsu* (The Gray Classroom), in *Hitotsubashi Bungaku*, a literary magazine. In 1955, he won two of Japan's most prestigious literary prizes, the Bungakukai Award for New Writers and the Akutagawa Award for his novel *Taiyo no kisetsu* (Season of Violence). Other novels include *Kiretsu* (The Crevice, 1958), *Sohei no Heya* (The Punishment Room, 1956), and *Kanzennaru Yugi* (Utter Decadence, 1957). In 1968, he entered politics and won a seat as a member of the Liberal Democratic Party (LDP) in the upper house of the Japanese legislature; in 1972, he was elected to the House of Representatives. Together with Sony Corporation Chairman Morita Akio (1921–1999), he coauthored an essay "'No' to ieru Nihon" (The Japan that Can Say 'No,' 1989). After an authorized translation raised concern among members of the U.S. Congress, Morita withdrew from the project. The book was published in English in 1991 under Ishihara's name. He coauthored with Malaysia's prime minister Mahathir Mohamad (b. 1925) another essay titled "An Asia That Can Say No" (1994). In 1995, he resigned from the LDP and in 1999 was elected governor of Tokyo.

*Nathalie Cavasin*

**Further Reading**

Ishihara Shintaro. (1991) *The Japan That Can Say No: Why Japan Will Be First Among Equals*. Trans. by Frank Baldwin. New York: Simon & Schuster.

Mohamad, Mahathir, and Shintaro Ishihara, eds. (1996) *The Voice of Asia: Two Leaders Discuss the Coming Century*. Trans. by Frank Baldwin. New York: Kodansha.

**ISHIKAWA** (2002 est. pop. 1.2 million). Ishikawa prefecture, in the central region of Japan's island of Honshu, combines rustic scenery with the high culture of old Japan. With an area of 4,197 square kilometers, the island has such picturesque geographical features as the Noto Peninsula and Hegurajima (Hegura Island), as well as several other small islands. Ishikawa is bordered by the Sea of Japan and Toyoma Bay and by Toyoma, Gifu, and Fukui prefectures. Ishikawa subsumed parts of the ancient provinces of Echizen, Noto, and Kaga and assumed its present name and borders in 1872.

The prefecture's capital is Kanazawa, situated on the southern plain of the Kaga region. Because it was not bombed during World War II, the city today exemplifies traditional Japanese architecture. Initially a fifteenth-century Buddhist temple town of the Ikko sect, after 1580 it became the castle town of the Maeda family, patrons of scholars and artists. The traditional crafts include Kutani-ware porcelain, decorated lacquer ware, and printed silk. Visitors are drawn to the garden Kenrokuen, the Nagamachi samurai quarter, the ruins of Kanazawa Castle, and numerous temples and museums. The other important cities of the prefecture are Komatsu, Kaga, and Nanao.

The fertile Kanazawa Plain is planted in rice, and the Noto Peninsula, also the site of rice paddies, is the center of a profitable fishing industry. Apart from some textile and heavy machinery plants, there is little other industry. Tourists are attracted to the Noto Peninsula, with its scenic rocky coast and unspoiled rural ways, as well as to the regional hotspring resorts, including Yamanaka, Yamashiro, and Awazu.

*E. L. S. Weber*

**Further Reading**

"Ishikawa Prefecture." (1993) *Japan: An Illustrated Encyclopedia*. Tokyo: Kodansha.

**ISHIM RIVER** The Ishim is a Siberian river that flows through northern Kazakhstan and the southern part of central Russia, between the two great rivers Tobol and Irtysh. It rises in the Niyaz Mountains, between Qaraghandy and Astana, the new Kazakh capital, and flows west for about 500 kilometers, before suddenly curving north to join the Irtysh in the Omsk region of southern Siberia. Its total length is about 2,140 kilometers, and it waters a rather small basin (compared with other Siberian rivers), which covers only 144,000 square kilometers. The main towns irrigated by the Ishim are Astana and Petropavlovsk in Kazakhstan and Ishin city in the Tyumen' region of Russia.

The Nura River, which flows near the Ishim upstream and shares much of its underground basin, suffers from mercury pollution from former Soviet industries situated in Qaraghandy. As the Nura is an endoreic river (a river with an inward-flowing basin), a channel was built in the mid-1990s to allow it to flow into the Ishim and thus increase the available water supply. When the mercury pollution was discovered, however, the government closed the channel, despite the water shortage in Astana.

*Patrick Dombrowsky*

**Further Reading**

Rey, Violette, and Roger Brunet. (1996) *Europes orientales, Russie, Asie centrale*. Paris: Belin; Montpellier, France: Reclus.

**ISKANDAR MUDA** (1590–1636), ruler of Aceh. Iskandar Muda (reigned 1607–1636), with the exalted title of *mahkota alam* (crown of the universe), is considered to have been the greatest ruler of the northern Sumatran principality Aceh. A ruthless and tyrannical ruler, reputed to have murdered his way to the throne, Iskandar Muda brought Aceh to the peak of its power and territorial expansion during the first half of the seventeenth century, dominating Sumatra and the Malay Peninsula except Portuguese Melaka.

In the three-way struggle for control over the Straits of Malacca and the Malay Archipelago between the Malays of Johor, the Acehnese, and the Portuguese at Melaka, Aceh appeared to have been the most successful because of Iskandar Muda and his powerful fleet.

In 1612, the kingdom of Aru, a vassal of Johor, was seized by the Acehnese. In 1613, Batu Sawar, the capital of Johor, was sacked by Iskandar Muda, and Sultan Alauddin (reigned 1597–1612) and his entire royal court suffered the humiliation of being brought as prisoners to Aceh. Alauddin's half-brother, Abdullah (Sultan Hammat Shah), was dispatched as a vassal ruler of Johor. Iskandar Muda then dominated the peninsular Malay kingdoms of Pahang (1617), Kedah (1619), and Perak (1620). In 1629, he attacked Portuguese Melaka with two hundred ships and a force of twenty thousand but failed to breach the fortress walls. Portuguese reinforcements from Goa repelled Iskandar Muda's Acehnese forces.

Iskandar Muda died in 1636. Nonetheless, Aceh remained a preeminent power during the reign of his successor, Iskandar Thani (1636–1641), a Pahang prince, but its territorial expansion was halted.

*Ooi Keat Gin*

*See also:* **Aceh Rebellion; Acehnese**

**Further Reading**

Andaya, Leonard Yuzon. (1975) *The Kingdom of Johor, 1641–1728*. Kuala Lumpur, Malaysia: Oxford University Press.

Lombard, Denys. (1967) *Le Sultanat d'Atjeh au Temps d'Iskandar Muda 1607–1636*. Paris: École Française d'Extreme-Orient.

Meilink-Roelofsz, Marie Antoinette Petronella. (1962) *Asian Trade and European Influence in the Indonesian Archipelago between 1500 and about 1630*. The Hague, Netherlands: Nijhoff.

**ISLAM—BRUNEI** As a Malay Islamic kingdom, independent Brunei Darussalam has undergone a profound Islamization of institutions and society. The temporal leader and head of religion in Brunei, the reigning sultan, Hassanal Bolkiah (b. 1946), wields absolute power. Just as the Sunnite orthodoxy is closely invigilated in Brunei Darussalam, so too the institutions of government share many of the features of Middle Eastern dynastic rule.

The date at which Islam entered Brunei is controversial, just as the date of conversion of a pre-Islamic ruler, likely a Hinduized maharaja, is unknown. By the early sixteenth century Brunei was a Muslim state. Nevertheless, Muslim merchants, including those from China, were active in Brunei by the thirteenth century. Conversion of the largely animist peoples outside of Brunei's royal center only gained ground in the last century, a process that continues to this day through marriage or active Islamic proselytization. However, more than is officially admitted, pre-Islamic beliefs frequently coexist with more doctrinal forms and practices.

Stemming from closer links with Mecca and the influence of pan-Islamic ideas promoted by the Ottoman sultan in the nineteenth century, a more scripturalized Islam took root in Brunei that superseded informal *tariqa*, or mystical, orders. Equally, the imposition of the British Residency system in Brunei between 1906 and 1959 introduced many innovations in the application and administration of Islamic law.

But with the rising tide of the Islamic resurgence in the 1980s, the religious authorities in Brunei have determinably harnessed the oil-rich state's resources to such pro-Islamic actions as the endowment of mosques and religious schools, sponsorship of the pilgrimage, and the mainstreaming of religious education in the nation's schools and universities. By the 1990s, Islam had been elevated as the leading prop of an arcane intellectual indoctrination in official history and religion termed Malay Islam Beraja (monarch), the mastery of which has become a loyalty test for all Brunei youths. In responding to the international Islamicist challenge, Islamic conservatism in Brunei has not only touched the style and demeanor of the sultan but has also stimulated the push for the total Islamization of Brunei society. For example, Arabized script, or Jawi, and even the Arabic language have seen new life in the Brunei education curriculum in a discourse where secular and liberal have become suspect categories. Still, civil law, which is based on British precedent and lifestyle, including gender relations, is more relaxed than in Brunei's Middle

The Omar Ali Saifuddin Mosque in Bandar Seri Begawan. (CHARLES & JOSETTE LENARS/CORBIS)

Eastern counterparts. Moreover, no apparent contradiction exists between ostentatious materialism, especially on the part of the Brunei royal family, and Islamic rectitude to which the *ummat*, or community of believers, are obliged to conform.

*Geoffrey C. Gunn*

### Further Reading

Iik Arifin Mansurnoor. (1992) "Islamic Reform in Brunei 1912–1915: Introductory Remarks." In *Essays on Modern Brunei History*, edited by Tan Pek Leng, Geoffrey C. Gunn, B. A. Hussainmiya, and Iik Arifin Mansurnoor. Gadong, Brunei Darussalam: Department of History, Universiti Brunei Darussalam.

Saunders, Graham. (1994) *A History of Brunei*. Kuala Lumpur, Malaysia: Oxford University Press.

**ISLAM—CENTRAL ASIA** Islam in Central Asia is a domestic religion, an experience of Muslim life in the household. The visitor's first impression is that there are few mosques and that few women wear veils. This does not mean that Islam is weak, only that under Communist pressure Muslim life made a strategic retreat into home and neighborhood. Islam is now reemerging into the public square: new mosques are going up everywhere, often with the help of gifts from Turkey, Pakistan, and Saudi Arabia. Islamic dress is seen again, notably among schoolgirls attending special classes for religious instruction. Where teachers are available, even public schools are offering Arabic as a subject. Each new republic has a Muslim directorate and an Islamic training center headed by a mufti (jurist) who is approved by the government. The Islamic revival has spawned "fundamentalist" reform movements against which the post-Soviet governments are on guard, although the extent of the threat they pose is disputed.

With the exception of Persian-speaking peoples in Tajikistan and Afghanistan, the native peoples of Central Asia are Turks of nomadic origin. Some of the Turkic peoples (those now called Uzbeks and Uighurs) settled centuries ago in bazaar towns and agricultural villages, building mosques and *madrasahs* (Islamic schools). Other Turks—Kazakhs, Kyrgyz, and Turkmen—remained pastoral nomads into the twentieth century. For them the Muslim life has always been lived primarily in the home and by extension at the "homes"— that is, the tombs or shrines (Arabic *mazar*)—of Sufi saints called *auliye* in Kazakh, the word deriving from the Arabic *wali*, "representative of God on earth." Dotting the arid landscape, these tombs and adjacent Muslim cemeteries far outnumber mosques; it has been said that in Central Asia the *mazar* is a holier place than the mosque. Groups and individuals make *ziyarat* (pilgrimages) to these shrines in search of the *baraka* (sacred power) of the Muslim saints, of the Prophet Muhammad and his family, and ultimately of God.

Central Asians are often accused of being weak and unobservant Muslims. They seldom deny the charge, exonerating themselves by pointing to historical circumstances: "We studied in Russian schools," "Our mullahs were fools," "Our father and mother were afraid to teach us the prayers for fear of the Communist Party," and so forth. The Kazakhs and Kyrgyz have additional excuses: "We were shepherds, roaming the steppe far from town," "We never had mosques," and so forth. Russian scholars concluded that religion in Central Asia is a survival of an archaic shamanism or animism overlaid with a thin veneer of Islam. In the West, most scholars adopted this Russian conclusion because the West is fascinated by primal religion and prefers shamans to Muslims. Such stereotypes have obscured an understanding of religion in Central Asia. Even where *shari'a* (Islamic law) is poorly understood, felt to be inconvenient, or perceived as a foreign Arab culture, the popular religion of the Turkic peoples is a genuine Muslim spirituality.

The minaret of the Khoja Mosque in Khiva, Uzbekistan. At 45 meters, the mosque is visible from anywhere in the city and is a major symbol of Islam in the region. (CHARELS & JOSETTE LENARS/CORBIS)

**Historical Background**

Religions crossed paths in Central Asia. Buddhists traveled from India to China by way of Central Asia, and the Manichaean religion made a strong impact. The Zoroastrians left archaeological evidence of their place in the history of Central Asian religion. As early as the fifth century CE, there were missions of Nestorian Christianity in Central Asia. Beginning in 652, Arab armies raided Transoxiana (the part of Central Asia to the north of the Amu Dar'ya River), and its major cities fell to the Arab general Qutayba ibn Muslim in the decade after 705. Bukhara became a center of Islamic civilization in the ninth century under the Samanids from Iran, as did Kashgar in the tenth century under the Karakhanids. To the north, the Turkic Oghuz people, later known as Turkmen and Seljuks, accepted Islam in 985 in return for the right to cross the Syr Dar'ya River into Muslim Transoxiana and Iran.

The Mongol invasion that began in 1219 put all of Central Asia under non-Muslim rulers. The Mongol empire tolerated all religions, and Muslims, Christians, and Jews lived side by side in Central Asian cities. In the fourteenth century, Emir Timur (Tamerlane) made Samarqand a pearl of Islamic architecture whose reputation was known in the West; he also wiped out the last vestiges of Nestorian Christianity in Central Asia.

The ancestors of today's Uzbeks and Kazakhs were the Kipchaks of the Golden Horde, who accepted Islam in the fourteenth century after a miraculous trial of fire between a band of traveling Sufis and the court shamans of Oz Beg Khan. In 1499–1500, the Uzbek ruler Muhammad Shaybani Khan conquered Transoxiana, which thus became the land of the Uzbeks, or Uzbekistan. Between the tenth and fifteenth centuries, the sedentary Turkic people in eastern Turkistan (today's Xinjiang province, northwest China) accepted Islam. Their descendants are the Uighurs. Today an underground Islamic movement struggles for the independence of Uighurstan from China.

The Islamization of Central Asia was complete in essentials by the fifteenth century. In the cities of Transoxiana and eastern Turkistan, Islam has been dominant ever since. Nomads, as always, were selective in their observance of the *shari'a*: among the Kazakhs, Islam was "*firmly*, albeit rather *superficially* established" (Akiner 1983: 301). In the eighteenth century, Russia's Catherine the Great deputized Tatar mullahs to "civilize" the Kazakhs, who, she imagined, would be more manageable subjects of the Russian empire if they were better Muslims, but this policy was short lived. In the late nineteenth century, the Russian Orthodox Church converted small bands of Kazakhs; the mission came to little, but Muslims in Central Asia still perceive the Russians as Christian invaders of the Muslim world.

**Religious Concepts**

The Turks readily adopted the conceptual structure of Islam, and the vocabulary of Central Asian religion comes largely from Arabic and Persian Islamic terms. The word for "God" is Allah in Arabic and Qudai in Persian. A few concepts from Turkic sources were used to translate Islamic ideas, such as Tengri (a Turkic deity who was equated with the heavens, as an alternate name for God). Very few non-Islamic terms have survived. The word for "spirit" in the Central Asian languages (Kazakh *aruaq*) comes from Arabic *(ruh)*, leaving no memory of archaic Turkic words for this fundamental concept. Thorough Islamization of religious vocabulary in Central Asia belies the stereotype that its people have a shamanistic worldview.

**Religious Roles**

Native *bakshi* (shamans) were healers and mediums who diagnosed and cured illnesses with the aid of their helping spirits while in a state of ecstasy or trance. When Islam came, the shaman tended to become a Muslim folk healer (Arabic *tabib*, Kazakh *tauip*). A male healer is also called a mullah when he learns to recite a few verses from the Qur'an, and the Uzbek *otin* is, in effect, a female mullah and healer. The shaman had always been a quixotic and socially marginal figure and therefore was open to easy ridicule by the Communist authorities; the few shamans who survived persecution failed to pass on their methods to their skeptical modern children. The Muslim *tabib*, however, was at the center of society, survived undercover in the Muslim home and neighborhood, and is enjoying a revival today. In every Central Asian neighborhood, there are one or more *tabib*s, often women, to whom the sick can resort when modern medicine fails them.

The mystical Sufis gave Islam in Central Asia its special quality, but Sufi spirituality tended to ossify over time into mundane social forms, losing its spiritual depth. The Sufis' ascetic discipline and inner search for the love of God can be seen in early Turkic poetry such as the *Diwan-i Hikmet*, attributed to Ahmet Yasawi, a twelfth-century Sufi master (Arabic *sheikh*, Persian *pir)*. Sufi movements inspired by such charismatic figures were organized later into *tariqa* (brotherhoods), the most important of which was the Naqshbandi order. There was profit to be made by the Sufi brotherhoods at the tombs of famous Sufi masters, both from Muslim pilgrims and from endowments of land, irrigation systems, and businesses that came to be attached to the shrines. Descendants of famous Sufis vied for control of the shrines of Ali in Balkh (Mazar-e Sharif) in northern Afghanistan, Zangi Baba in Shash (Tashkent), and Ahmet Yasawi in Yasi (Turkistan) in southern Kazakhstan.

The descendants of the Sufis are religious honor groups called *khoja*, a Persian word meaning "master" or "teacher" (Kazakh *qoja*, Turkish *hoca)*. In the Arab world, they are called *sayyid*, descendants of Ali, the fourth caliph and nephew of the Prophet Muhammad. Typically each *khoja* lineage preserves a *nasabnama* (genealogical manuscript) by which it proves its descent from Ali. The key links in these genealogies are the Sufi masters from whom a *khoja* group takes its name. Spiritual succession in Sufi communities tended to become hereditary over time; so that families claiming descent from a Sufi who had been called by the title *khoja* came to think of themselves as *khoja* bloodlines. They have a quasi-ethnic identity, calling themselves "Arabs" because of their descent from Muhammad, even though they speak no Arabic. Traditionally a Kazakh clan was the client of a *khoja* patron, who recited the Qur'an for them, taught their children, healed their diseases, prayed for rain, and so forth. Persecuted by the Communists, many *khoja*s have melted into modern society and no longer claim a religious role, but they are given the place of honor at banquets and referred to with respect because a harsh word from a *khoja* is believed to be a powerful curse. Whereas a *khoja* healer is believed to have special powers because of his or her descent from Muhammad, today's *khoja*s have only a shadowy awareness of their Sufi heritage. The social honor bestowed by descent from Muhammad has become more important to them than the spiritual values of the Sufi tradition from which they sprang.

When Russia conquered Central Asia after 1864, it brought European civilization with it, and a new elite of European-oriented Muslims emerged in Central Asian cities. This led to an Islamic renewal movement called Jadidism, which published progressive newspapers and opened "new method" schools where children were taught secular subjects as well as religious ones. The Jadidists were condemned by the *khoja*s and mullahs, who had a vested interest in the *madrasah*s, where Qur'anic recitation was the only instruction offered. The Jadidist renewal was cut short by the Communist Revolution, which had its own educational agenda and purged both the conservative mullahs and the forward-looking Jadidists. For the rest of the twentieth century, a domestic version of the Muslim life was taught to children in the home, when religious learning was passed on at all.

### Elements of Popular Religion Today

In Central Asia, memorial meals in honor of the dead are observed in the home according to the *shari'a*. An ancient pattern of ancestor veneration seems to have been at the root of funeral customs in both Arabian Islam and the Turko-Mongol tradition, so that the Turkic peoples readily adopted the Islamic funeral pattern as their own. After the death of a loved one, a feast is prepared for all the relatives and neighbors on the seventh and fortieth days after death, every Thursday between the death and the fortieth day, then on the anniversary of death. One or more mullahs recite the Qur'an (in Arabic) and add a blessing of dedication to the deceased, the family's ancestors, the prophets, and the local Sufi saints (in the vernacular language).

A related observance is that on every Thursday *qudayi nan* (sacred bread) is fried in oil, the aroma of which is thought to go up to the ancestor spirits. The family then dedicates the evening meal to its ancestors. Thursday is the day when the spirits are believed to leave their graves by the permission of God and return to their homes, waiting for the Qur'an to be recited and food to be dedicated in their memory. When someone in the house has a dream in which the ancestors appear, seven loaves of fried *qudayi nan* are distributed to neighbors, binding the Muslim neighborhood together in a common experience of the spiritual world. The woman of the household is the key person in this domestic cult of the ancestors. It is she who "emits the aroma" (Kazakh *iyis shigaradi*) of the sacred bread fried in oil, she who has her children distribute the seven loaves to the neighbors, and often she who has the dream that impels her to do so.

Pilgrimages or visits *(ziyarat)* to tombs and Sufi centers hark back to the medieval tradition of Muslim travels (Arabic *rihla*) in search of spiritual wisdom and power. The trip may be short, because almost every Central Asian town and village has a tomb or cemetery that is held in special reverence. More elaborate pilgrimages may be organized by families or by a healer with his patients. A common pattern is to prepare oneself by ritual ablutions, make a special request of God called an vintention" *(niyet)*, greet the saint upon arrival at the shrine, walk around the shrine up to seven times, pay one of the shrine mullahs to recite the Qur'an and say a blessing on one's behalf, leave a monetary contribution in a box designated for votive gifts and/or make an animal sacrifice, and promise specific acts of devotion if the saint answers one's prayer.

Important Sufi tombs may be referred to as "the second Mecca," thus relating the Islamic hajj (pilgrimage to Mecca) with *ziyarat* in local sacred space. It is widely believed in Central Asia that three visits to one of the major shrines is equivalent to the hajj. A visit to family graves at the local cemetery has a similar purpose, because the spirits of the Muslim dead are believed to be closer to God than are the living. In essentials, this pattern is similar to pilgrimage practices everywhere in the Muslim world, as is the funeral pattern mentioned earlier.

Personal observance of the five pillars of Islam (profession of faith, prayer five times a day, almsgiving, fasting during the holy month of Ramadan, and the hajj) is often neglected in Central Asia, but it is not absent or ignored altogether. In traditional extended families, the grandfather and grandmother are most likely to say the five daily prayers *(namaz);* the grandfather may do so at the neighborhood mosque. Although the Ramadan fast is becoming popular again, during the Soviet period it was only the elders who fasted; the Tashkent Muslim directorate, under pressure from the government, issued a *fatwa* (decree) that persons of working age need not fast.

In general this pattern persists today: elders perform the requirements of the *shari'a* vicariously, in effect, as surrogates for their family. If the grandchildren learn to say the *namaz* and recite verses of the Qur'an, it is the grandparents who teach them because the parents were the "lost generation," denied a religious upbringing in their Soviet schools. Or children may be sent to a neighborhood mullah or *otin* for Arabic lessons after school. Circumcision of boys at around the age of six years is now universal again and was widely practiced even during the Soviet period.

A standard practice of Muslim folk healers in Central Asia is the technique of diagnosing all manner of illnesses simply by taking the pulse and curing by reciting the Qur'an and breathing forcefully on the patient. The mullah or *tabib* does this to bring both the Qur'an and his or her ancestor spirits to bear on the patient's illness. Healers subscribe to the Islamic humoral theory of medicine, according to which an imbalance between hot and cold foods in the diet is the cause of disease, so that treatment often involves special diets or herbal remedies. For example, licorice root (native to the desert steppe) is chewed for stomach problems, and hummingbird nests soaked in horse fat are used to treat venereal disease. Wild rue or steppe sage *(adraspan)* is burned as incense or hung in the corner of the room to ward off evil spirits.

Representing the healer's spiritual power, the knife and whip are shamanic symbols that were long ago taken over by the Muslim healer, as was the ancient Turkic belief that each disease has a "master" (Kazakh *iye*, Uzbek *ege*) who must be overcome by the healer's spiritual energy (Kazakh *kiye*). Despite these shamanic elements, the Kazakh *tauip* today is more like the *tabib* elsewhere in the Muslim world than she is like the Siberian shaman.

Central Asian Muslims experience the spirit-world in dreams and dream-visions called *ayan*, the Arabic and Sufic word for "personal illumination." It is sought at the shrines of the Muslim saints, and someone who has neglected his or her Muslim duties will often be reminded to do so in a dream. The individual's conversion often begins with *ayan:* he or she will begin saying the five daily prayers after dreaming of the ancestor spirits. Healers say that *ayan* helps them diagnose and cure illness. Fortune-tellers called *balger* in all the Central Asian languages (Persian *pal*, divination) can see into the future when their ancestor spirits give them *ayan*. Modern folk healers influenced by Russian parapsychology and so-called New Age religion draw on the *ayan* tradition: some claim to be heirs of the shamans, and others go to Turkey and Pakistan to study Islam, claiming to be Sufis when they return.

### Religion and Ethnicity

That Muslim life in Central Asia survived the political turmoil of the twentieth century is due in no small part to religious memories sacralized by Islamic landscapes, the shrines of Sufi saints, and the cemeteries of Muslim ancestors. Except for elites influenced by Communism and now by Western secularism, the Central Asian peoples have a strong sense of their Muslimness. Their Turkic ancestors have been Muslims for centuries, so that they feel their ethnic identity as a Muslim identity, believing that their blood is Muslim. Soviet policy allowed Muslim ethnic groups to become nations in the modern sense even before the breakup of the Soviet Union. Ethnic and national consciousness understood in a Muslim way has given Central Asian Muslims a revived sense of their place in the Muslim world.

*Bruce G. Privratsky*

### Further Reading

Akiner, Shirin. (1983) *Islamic Peoples of the Soviet Union*. London: Kegan Paul.

Altoma, Reef. (1994) "The Influence of Islam in Post-Soviet Kazakhstan." In *Central Asia in Historical Perspective*, edited by Beatrice F. Manz. Boulder, CO: Westview Press.

Atkin, Muriel. (1989) "The Survival of Islam in Soviet Tajikistan." *Middle East Journal* 43: 605–618.

Azmun, Yusuf, ed. (1994) *Divan-1 Hikmet/Ahmed Yesevi*. Istanbul, Turkey: Tek-Esin.

Balzer, Marjorie, ed. (1990) *Shamanism: Soviet Studies of Traditional Religion in Siberia and Central Asia*. Armonk, NY: M. E. Sharpe.

Deweese, Devin. (1994) *Islamization and Native Religion in the Golden Horde*. University Park, PA: Pennsylvania State University Press.

Fathi, Habiba. (1997) "*Otines:* The Unknown Women Clerics of Central Asian Islam." *Central Asian Survey* 16: 27–43.

Gross, Jo-Ann, ed. (1992) *Muslims in Central Asia*. Durham, NC: Duke University Press.

McChesney, R. D. (1991) *Waqf in Central Asia: Four Hundred Years in the History of a Muslim Shrine, 1480–1889*. Princeton, NJ: Princeton University Press.

Muminov, Ashirbek. (1996) "Veneration of Holy Sites of the Mid-Sirdar'ya Valley." In *Muslim Culture in Russia and Central Asia from the 18th to the Early 19th Centuries*, edited by Michael Kemper, Anke von Kugelen, and Dmitriy Yermakov. Berlin: Klaus Schwarz Verlag.

Penkala, Danuta. (1980) "'Hot' and 'Cold' in the Traditional Medicine of Afghanistan." *Ethnomedizin* 6: 201–228.

Poliakov, Sergei. (1992) *Everyday Islam: Religion and Tradition in Rural Central Asia*. Armonk, NY: M. E. Sharpe.

Privratsky, Bruce. (2001) *Muslim Turkistan: Kazak Religion and Collective Memory*. London: Curzon Press.

Rakowska-Harmstone, Teresa. (1983) "Islam and Nationalism: Central Asia and Kazakhstan under Soviet Rule." *Central Asian Survey* 2: 7–87.

Tyson, David. (1997) "Shrine Pilgrimage in Turkmenistan as a Means to Understand Islam among the Turkmen." *Central Asia Monitor* 1: 15–32.

## ISLAM—INDONESIA

Islam has made important contributions to nation-building and socioeconomic development in Indonesia. Since the dawn of Islam in the Indonesian archipelago in the seventh century, the ulama (religious scholars) have played a significant role in the integration of its many ethnic communities. Successions of Western rulers caused various Muslim communities to band together to resist and repel the infidels *(kafir)* who, it was believed, only came to exploit the archipelago's economic resources and erode local cultural and religious values. Having been exposed to the Western way of life, twentieth-century Indonesian Muslims were acquainted with the concept of modernism, with "modern" social structures, schools, and print media. Islam became a bonding force against the imperial system, spurring communities to set aside cultural differences and work toward a common goal. Muslim organizations became keenly concerned with sociocultural, economic, and political life.

### Arrival and Propagation of Islam

Three successive processes led to the Islamization of the country: the arrival of Muslim traders who propagated Islam (seventh to twelfth centuries CE), the integration of foreign settlers into local communities (eleventh to twelfth centuries), and the creation of states ruled by Muslim sultans (thirteenth to seventeenth centuries). The religious landscape into which Islam came was one of indigenous beliefs: Hindu-Buddhist religions. But Islam that came through Hindu-Buddhist areas had already adapted to specific circumstances before coming to the archipelago, notably between Islamic Sufism and Hindu-Buddhist Sufism. Islam that was brought by traders whose approach was Sufistic was more tolerant; that made Islam easily welcomed. Furthermore, local traditions were soon Islamized, and Islamic teachings were localized. This made Islam in Indonesia different from Islam in other parts of the world.

**INDONESIA: THE LARGEST MUSLIM POPULATION OF ANY NATION**

The Top Ten in 2000

| Nation | Muslim Population | As a Percentage of the Population |
|---|---|---|
| Indonesia | 201 million | 88% |
| Pakistan | 140 million | 97% |
| India | 123.5 million | 12% |
| Bangladesh | 108 million | 83% |
| Turkey | 65.8 million | 99% |
| Egypt | 65.4 million | 94% |
| Nigeria | 63.3 million | 50% |
| Iran | 58.8 million | 89% |
| China | 31.8 million | 2.5% |
| Ethiopia | 30.9 million | 47% |

*Source:* CIA *World Factbook 2000.*

## Islam in Opposition to Colonialism

Since Islam was introduced by Muslim traders in the archipelago, it has been the basis for cultural integration. Several factors facilitated this integration, primary among them being internal and international trade, the preaching of religious teachers, and the use of Malay as the common language. Wandering teachers guided local sultans in the teachings of Islam. Their writings were disseminated across the country, creating an Islamic culture in the archipelago.

Dutch colonialists, who arrived in the seventeenth century, were perceived as a threat to the authority of local rulers and also affected the intellectual activities of the ulama. Islamic resistance to foreign rule became unavoidable, particularly as urbanization took place. Dutch rule began to be perceived as imperialistic exploitation and as an attempt to forcibly Westernize the country. As a result, Muslims were determined to overthrow the Dutch government. The ulama, along with students from their network of traditional religious schools *(pesantren)*, rose in support of this resistance. Peasant revolts broke out across the country. Local social associations were set up, including the Islamic Trade Association (Sarekat Dagang Islam, or SDI) in 1905, which became the Islamic Association (Sarekat Islam, or SI) in 1912, the first mass organization to participate in the indigenous economy and in the struggle for independence. In its anticolonialist activities, the SI was active at various levels. It campaigned against the suppression of Indonesians, and Islamic ideology became the foundation of its political struggle.

Muslims did not concentrate solely on politics, however. They were also concerned with social issues, primarily poverty and illiteracy. The "modernist" Muhammadiyah and "traditionalist" Nahdlatul Ulama (NU) were active in education and social development during their establishment in 1912 and 1926, respectively.

Furthermore, the unification of Indonesian communities as a result of the Dutch colonization provided new opportunities for solidarity among ethnic and Islamic groups that had different backgrounds and polities, and adhered to different approaches and strategies. At the time, during the last days of Japanese rule in 1945, Islamic political ideology could not provide a strong enough unifying focus, and secular nationalists eventually claimed the most powerful heroes and created the most powerful myths, pushing Muslim nationalists into the background.

As a result, Muslim nationalists experienced a crucial shift in their relationship with Japanese and Dutch rulers. From a position of subordination with the Dutch to one of favor with the Japanese, the secularist nationalists took over the leadership role. Both the secular and Muslim nationalists agreed to endorse the Pancasila ("Five Principles": belief in one God, humanitarianism, nationalism, democracy, and social justice) as the basis of the new state; the Muslims believed that Pancasila was based on Islamic law. Yet the Muslim nationalists soon realized that they were in fact marginalized, their factions fragmented, while secularists were in control of the government.

This became even clearer when the government used a divide-and-rule approach in dealing with Islamic

Muslims gather at the Indonesian parliament building in Jakarta on 10 April 2000 to offer their services in a jihad against Christians in Indonesia. (REUTERS NEWMEDIA INC./CORBIS)

factions. Sukarno (1901–1970), the first president of Indonesia, banned the Masyumi Party, the party of the Masyumi, a modern comprehensive confederation of Islamic organizations, in the belief that it supported Darul Islam, a movement for the establishment of an Islamic state, which continued in Aceh, West Java, and South Sulawesi. Instead, he created a new idea, Nasakom, which was meant to unite nationalists, Muslims, and Communists, an idea that was tolerated by the NU but not by Masyumi members. For the next two decades, the NU established its presence in the religious ministries and bureaucracy. After the 1965 alleged coup by Communists, the NU worked with Suharto (b. 1921) to expel not only Communists, but also other radical nationalists from the political arena. After Suharto replaced Sukarno as president in 1967, the NU was amalgamated with the Development Union Party (PPP), which Suharto controlled.

During the Suharto presidency, Islamic parties, as opposed to sociocultural Islamic organizations, remained marginalized. In particular, Suharto's economic modernization of the nation created discontent among Muslims, who were wary of the possible negative effects on the community. Suharto made Pancasila mandatory for all parties, thus preventing the revival of Islamic parties because no parties were allowed to be founded on religion, including Islam. Although the NU was the first to accept, it broke away from the PPP, renounced politics, and returned to its original mission as a socioreligious organization.

In 1990, Muslims established the All-Indonesian Association for Muslim Intellectuals (ICMI). Wanting to return to the center of power, intellectuals gathered in Malang, East Java, and appointed Bacharuddin Habibie (b. 1936), a figure close to Suharto, as president of the association. Cooperation with Suharto served the purposes of the Muslims, but Suharto's power had dwindled. After Suharto's dramatic fall from power, Habibie became president in 1998 and implemented democratic measures on behalf of the Muslim majority. He established a multiparty system, and several Islamic parties emerged, including the National Awakening Party (Partai Kebangkitan Bangsa, or PKB), which was founded by Abdurrahman Wahid (b.1940), leader of the NU. However, because of his closeness to Suharto and probably his non-Javanese origin, Habibie lost the 1999 presidential elections, which went to Wahid. Wahid remained in power until 23 July 2001, when the People's Consultative Assembly (MPR), the highest legislature of the nation, impeached him, and his vice president, Megawati Sukarnoputri (b. 1947), from a secularist group, was elected president by members of the MPR in its special session.

To what extent the government under Megawati will address the aspirations of the Muslim majority remains to be seen. The rivalry between the secularists and the Muslims is ongoing, and Islam continues to be a decisive factor in Indonesian politics. Having contributed to the evolution of modern Indonesia, Islam remains an important actor in the social and cultural identity of the nation.

*Andi Faisal Bakti*

### Further Reading

Bakti, Andi F. (1993) "Islam and Nation Formation in Indonesia." M.A. thesis. McGill University.

Forrester, Geoff, ed. (1999) *Post-Suharto Indonesia: Renewal or Chaos?* Singapore: Institute of Southeast Asian Studies.

Jones, Anthony H. (1987) "Indonesia: Islam and Cultural Pluralism." In *Islam in Asia: Religion, Politics, and Society*, edited by John L. Esposito. New York: Oxford University Press, 202–229.

Noer, Deliar. (1973) *The Modernist Muslim Movement in Indonesia 1900–1942.* Singapore: Oxford University Press.

Manning, Chris, and Peter van Diermen, eds. (2000) *Indonesia in Transition: Social Aspects of Reform and Crisis.* Singapore: Institute of Southeast Asian Studies.

## ISLAM—MAINLAND SOUTHEAST ASIA

Aside from Myanmar (Burma), three countries of mainland Southeast Asia have significant Muslim populations: Thailand, Cambodia, and Vietnam.

### Thailand

Thailand, a country with approximately 62 million citizens, of whom 95 percent profess Theravada Bud-

## THE INTERPLAY OF ISLAM AND BUDDHISM IN THAILAND

Islam is a minority religion in mainland Southeast Asia and in many communities Muslims must live alongside Buddhists, the majority religion in Thailand. The following extract pertaining to the village of Bang Chan in Central Thailand shows how the two groups differ in their spiritual approach to water.

> As a symbol of water for crops, Mother Water is taken seriously by both Muslims and Buddhists, though more so by Buddhists. As a symbol of physical and ritual purity, however, Mother Water is relevant only to the Buddhists. The reason, clearly, is that the Muslims have their own, more elaborate, system of purification through ritual bathing, and this system is well integrated into their daily ritual life. Village Islam thus has, as it were, no "need" for the purificational aspect of Mother Water. This is but one more illustration of the generalization that in all instances where Islam has taken a clear doctrinal or ritual stand on some issue, syncretism with other types of belief or ritual is likely to be at a minimum. The generalization does not hold nearly so strongly in the case of Buddhism, though perhaps a better formulation would be that Buddhism less often takes a "clear" stand on an issue. Another way of stating this difference at the general level is simply to say that Islam is more "compulsive" than Buddhism.

*Source:* Robert B. Textor. (1973) *Roster of the Gods: An Ethnography of the Supernatural in a Thai Village*. New Haven, CT: HRAFLex Books, 835.

dhism, has a population of about 4 million Muslims. The Muslims in Thailand make up two broad self-defined categories: Malay Muslims, who speak the Malay language and reside primarily in southern Thailand in a number of provinces bordering on Malaysia, and those who call themselves Thai Muslims and who reside in central and northern Thailand.

The majority of the Muslims in Thailand live in south Thailand. Prior to the nineteenth century, these southern Malay Islamic regions were informal tributary states tied to Thai monarchical authorities. After the nineteenth century, the Thai state began to take direct administrative control over these southern areas. The four southern provinces of Patani, Narathiwat, Satul, and Yala bordering Malaysia contain over 3 million Muslims. As in the other areas of the Malayan-Indonesia region, the form of Islam that took hold was based on the Sunni-Shafii tradition. However, since the time of its arrival, Islam has coexisted with earlier Hindu-Buddhist-animistic spiritual beliefs and practices. In addition, both Shi'a and Sufi elements influenced local forms of the belief system in this area.

Various Thai military governments from the 1930s through the 1970s adopted assimilationist policies toward these Malay Muslim regions through "development" or socioeconomic and education programs. However, these assimilationist policies were perceived by the Muslims as Buddhist-based attempts to subvert Islamic education and political, religious, and cultural ideals. Subsequently, a number of Islamic-based factions emerged during the 1960s and 1970s in southern Thailand and became engaged in separatist activities. These insurgency movements resulted in repressive military campaigns by the Thai government. Although there have been sporadic skirmishes in the recent past, since the 1990s the Malay Muslim communities of southern Thailand have largely turned away from extremist separatist movements, though they still want to preserve their "Malayness" and Islamic identity.

Because of historical and cultural conditions, the experience of Muslims in central and northern Thailand has been much different from that of the Malay Muslims to the south. Altogether there are approximately a half-million Muslims in central and northern Thailand. Historically, these Muslims of the central and northern corridors of Thailand have migrated, either voluntarily or by force, into these regions, bringing distinctive ethnic, social, and religious conventions. Thus, these Muslim communities are much more heterogeneous than the Muslims of the south. And unlike the Islamic population in the south, these Muslims are ethnic and religious minorities residing in the centers of a predominantly Thai Buddhist cultural environment.

By far the largest group of Muslims in central Thailand, especially in the capital city of Bangkok, are descendants of peoples from the southern provinces of Thailand and parts of Malaysia. As part of the assimilationist campaigns, the Thai government relocated Malay Muslims to central Thailand. Other communities of Muslims in central Thailand, including Chams, Indonesians, and Iranians, have a long-term history that extends back into the Ayutthayan period (1351–1767). Muslims from India, present-day Pakistan, and Bangladesh, and a small number of Arabs have also settled in the Bangkok area. In North Thailand, most of the Muslims came from the Islamicized portion of China, though there are also smaller numbers of Malay and South Asian Muslim migrants.

**Cambodia, Vietnam, and Laos**

The Muslim population and settlements in Cambodia and Vietnam are intimately related to the historical development of what was known as the Champa kingdom in mainland Southeast Asia. The kingdom of Champa lasted from the second to the seventeenth century CE and extended over the central and southern coastal regions of Vietnam. Persian and Arab Muslims traveled to Champa bringing both Shiʿa and Sunni traditions to the areas. Islam began to diffuse into the Champa region during the eighth or ninth century. Most of the Cham population converted to Islam and were ruled by Muslim religious and political officials. Following its defeat by Vietnam in 1471, Champa was gradually absorbed into the Vietnam state.

The Cham Muslims of Vietnam adopted many cultural features of the Vietnamese including housing style, clothing, lunar calendar, and the Sinitic twelve-animal cycle of years.

Traditionally, the Chams of Vietnam were involved in cultivating crops such as sugarcane, maize, bananas, coconut trees, beans, and various types of chili peppers. Unlike their patrilineal Vietnamese Buddhist neighbors, the Chams maintained matrilineal groups that were embedded within matriclans with totem-like symbols associated with the particular clan. The Cham Islamic tradition maintained in Vietnam was based on the Shiʿa tradition. Along with the Shiʿa tradition, other indigenous elements of animism and Hindu and Buddhist beliefs and practices were apparent among the Chams.

Continual Vietnamese state pressures for assimilation of these Muslims resulted in a considerable number of Cham refugees moving to Cambodia, establishing permanent communities in about seventy villages along or near the banks of the Mekong and Sap Rivers. By 1975, the population of Chams in Cambodia had grown to 250,000. Traditionally most of the Cambodian Cham practiced small-scale family fishing on the various rivers. They were well known for excellent construction of boats for use along the rivers, lakes, and canals in the region. The Cham refugees that settled in Cambodia maintained a very different form of the Islamic tradition from their Vietnamese counterparts. As these Cambodian Cham had had more contact with the main currents of Islam in Malaysia and Indonesian society, they gradually moved from a Shiʿa to a Sunni-Shafii form of Islam. They were also influenced by Sufism as well as by Sufistic, animistic, and Hindu-Buddhist religious elements. Sufistic traditions such as saint worship and praying at the tombs of Islamic saints were imported from Malaysian Islamic precepts and practices.

As a result of French colonialism and the war in Southeast Asia, the Chams of Cambodia and Vietnam began to develop their own ethnonationalist movements. Chams began to view their ethnic and religious cultural traditions as different not only from those of Europeans and Americans but from those of Vietnamese and Cambodians as well. These ethnonationalist movements resulted in tragic episodes for the Chams. Following the victories of the Khmer Rouge in Cambodia and Ho Chi Minh's regime in Vietnam, the Chams were relentlessly persecuted. Active genocidal policies were directed at the Cham Muslims by the Khmer Rouge, and some 90,000 Chams were executed by the Pol Pot regime. In Vietnam, the Cham Muslims have been subjected to intensive assimilation pressures directed by state authorities.

A small community of Muslims from India and other areas of South Asia has established a mosque in the center of Vientiane, Laos. This Muslim community has intermarried with the Laotian community.

Various reformist and mild forms of Islamic fundamentalism known as *da wah* (religious awakening) movements have influenced the Muslim populace of Thailand, Cambodia, and Vietnam. In Southeast Asia, these current Islamic trends correspond with the global impact of new forms of media, including increases in print journalism, television, and general improvements in literacy, especially within urban centers. Some Muslims from Thailand, Cambodia, and Vietnam have traveled to the Middle East for work or to participate in the hajj (the pilgrimage to Mecca that every Muslim is enjoined to undertake). They have become familiar with recent Islamic theology and political thought and have introduced these ideas into Southeast Asia. In the *da wah* movements in Southeast Asia, Muslims are called on to devote their lives to improving the social welfare of Muslims. They promote the revitalization of Islamic cultural and religious values and sponsor a variety of community-based social programs.

*Raymond Scupin*

*See also:* **Islam—Myanmar; Rohingya**

### Further Reading

Cabaton, Antoine, and George Meillon. (1971) "Indochina (Islam in)." *The Encyclopaedia of Islam,* edited by B. Lewis, H. A. R. Gibb, J. H. Kramer, E. Levi-Provencal, C. H. Pellat, and J. Schacht. Leiden, Netherlands: E. J. Brill, 1208–1212.

Che Man, W. K. (1990) *Muslim Separatism: The Moros of Southern Philippines and the Malays of Southern Thailand.* Oxford: Oxford University Press.

Keirnan, Ben. (1988) "Orphans of Genocide: The Cham Muslims of Kampuchea under Pol Pot." *Bulletin of Concerned Asian Scholars* 20: 2–33.

Pitsuwan, Surin. (1985) *Islam and Malay Nationalism: A Case Study of the Malay-Muslims of Southern Thailand.* Bangkok, Thailand: Thammasat University.

Scupin, Raymond. (1998) "Muslim Accommodation in Thai Society." *Journal of Islamic Studies* 9, 2: 229–258.

Taouti, Seddik. (1982) "The Forgotten Muslims of Kampuchea and Viet Nam." *Journal Institute of Muslim Minority Affairs* 4, 1: 3–13.

Thomas, Ladd. (1975) *Political Violence in the Muslim Provinces of Southern Thailand.* Singapore: ISEA.

## ISLAM—MALAYSIA

Islam is the official religion of Malaysia and the professed faith of half its population. Islam has played a significant role in the political and social development of Malaysia.

However, Malaysia has many ethnic cultures (Malays, Chinese, and Indians) and religious communities (Muslims, Buddhists, Confucianists, Hindus, and others). Ethnicity is often defined by religion; for example, Malays are generally considered to be Muslims. This distinction is reinforced by the constitution, which states that Malays who forsake Islam automatically forfeit their status as Malays. Conversely, non-Malays who embrace Islam can qualify for citizenship. The upholding of Islam as the official Malay identity defines the key role the religion has come to play in every sphere of Malaysian life, in its cultural definition, economy, and politics.

### Islam in Early Malay History

Islam has been a part of Malaysian history from the days of the Melaka sultanate (1400–1511). It was integrated into local culture in three major phases: the coming of Muslim traders (seventh–tenth centuries), the settlement and integration of these traders (eleventh–twelfth centuries), and the establishment of the Malay Islamic States (thirteenth–seventeenth centuries until the present).

Networks of Islamic organizations active in the peninsula began inspiring anticolonial feelings in the population. The area remained under British rule until the late nineteenth century, and the British rulers were perceived as infidels. The ulama (religious scholars) and their followers saw British representatives as agents sent to promote Christian evangelism. To prevent this domination of Malays, an Islamic identity was actively promoted. The creation of traditional religious schools (*pondoks* or *madrasahs*) was encouraged to teach the Islamic way of life. After World War II, the people of the Malayan Union strongly rejected the political entity that colonial rulers had established. The Islamic identity further brought a bonding of community leaders, which became crucial in mobilizing people against the British.

### Islam's Role in Malay Independence

With the return of fresh graduates from Islamic reformist schools in the Middle East, the pace of mobilization accelerated. The issues of political independence, economic prosperity, and education were championed and disseminated in schools and the media. The first popular journal was *Al-Imam* (the Leader), initially established in Singapore in 1906 and then in Penang. Published by a reformist group later known as the Young Group (Kaum Muda), it promoted *ijtihad* (religious reasoning) and rejected religious *takhyul* (myths), *taqlid* (blind imitations), *bid'ah* (unlawful religious innovations), and *khurafat* (superstition), practices accommodated by the Old Group (Kaum Tua). The Young Group accused non-Muslim communities in urban areas of monopolizing economic resources. These reformists promoted Malay Islamic nationalism but were eventually marginalized, especially during the Japanese occupation in the Second

## ISLAM IN THE MALAYSIA CONSTITUTION

The constitution of Malaysia establishes Islam as the official religion but also protects the religious freedom for all citizens.

The Constitution of Malaysia, Article number: 3

**(1)** Islam is the religion of the Federation; but other religions may be practised in peace and harmony in any part of the Federation.

**(2)** In every State other than States not having a Ruler the position of the Ruler as the Head of the religion of Islam in his State in the manner and to the extent acknowledged and declared by the Constitution, all rights, privileges, prerogatives and powers enjoyed by him as Head of that religion, are unaffected and unimpaired; but in any acts, observance or ceremonies with respect to which the Conference of Rulers has agreed that they should extend to the Federation as a whole each of the other Rulers shall in his capacity of Head of the religion of Islam authorize the Yang di-Pertuan Agong to represent him.

**(3)** The Constitution of the States of Malacca, Penang, Sabah and Sarawak shall each make provision for conferring on the Yang di-Pertuan Agong shall be Head of the religion of Islam in that State.

**(4)** Nothing in this Article derogates from any other provision of this Constitution.

**(5)** Notwithstanding anything in this Constitution the Yang di-Pertuan Agong shall be the Head of the religion of Islam in the Federal Territories of Kuala Lumpur and Labuan; and for this purpose Parliament may by law make provisions for regulating Islamic religious affairs and for constituting a Council to advise the Yang di-Pertuan Agong in matters relating to the religion of Islam.

*Source:* International Association of Constitutional Law. Retrieved 27 Feburary, 2002, from: www.eur.nl/frg/iacl.

World War, when both elitist and traditionalist groups suppressed them.

This discrimination was evident from the fact that when radical nationalists established the United Malays Nationalist Organization (UMNO) in 1946, and the Islamic nationalists established the Hizbul Muslimin party in 1948, the latter was banned while the former was not. The Pan-Malaysian Islamic Party (Partai Islam Se-Malaysia—PAS) was created within UMNO as a defection of the ulama faction in 1951 and was recognized as a political party four years later. The idea of an independent Islamic state resurfaced, but the British rejected the notion and instead set up the independent Federation of Malaya in 1957. Although Islam and Malay customs were guaranteed under the constitution, the new prime minister, Tunku Abdul Rahman (1903–1990), acceded to British preferences for a secular government. The PAS and other Islamic Malay groups protested against this government, and riots broke out on 13 May 1969. Five years later, the PAS forged a coalition with the government—Barisan Nasional (National Front). The government established an Islamic center within the prime minister's office as part of Islamic religious affairs.

### Islamization in Malaysia

Islam has a defining role in the political system of Malaysia, at both local and national levels. The adoption of the Islamic system of administration and government gave the religion an intrinsic role in all aspects of life. The government took measures toward Islamization, promoting Islamic principles in broadcasting and the print media and in public life in general. The use of Islamic references and names of former states suppressed during the colonial period was reinstated.

However, these measures were perceived as token formalities rather than a genuine attempt to practice Islamic values and teachings. Some attempts at Islamization were overzealous and merely stressed the symbolistic aspect of faith. As a result, so-called Islamic organizations mushroomed professing Sufi or otherwise spiritual traditions, and *dakwah/tabligh* (propagation) movements, youth associations, and political parties arose. The Muslim Youth Movement of Malaysia (Angkatan Belia Islam Malaysia—ABIM), for example, works to remove misconceptions about Islam. The Islamic Republic group, along with PAS, declares the goal of establishing an Islamic state willing to channel the aspirations of Muslims and non-Muslims. Darul Arqam (the House of Arqam, in reference to one of the prophet Muhammad's companions), a controversial movement later banned by the government, made significant efforts in community-based development, which the government perceived as a potential political threat. Jamaah Tabligh (an Islamic propagation group) is more concerned with Islamic missionary work among Muslim communities: members of the group encourage piety and abide by the traditions of the prophet Muhammad.

The Blue and White Mosque in Shah Aslam, Selangor State, Malaysia, in 1992. (BOB KRIST/CORBIS)

In 1977, the PAS was forced out of the National Front coalition because of its public demand for an Islamic state and implementation of the Islamic law *(shari'a)*. The PAS accused the government of insincerity in its Islamization initiatives. In 1982, Anwar Ibrahim (b. 1947), the former leader of ABIM, joined UMNO and attempted, with the support of the prime minister, Mahathir Mohamad (b. 1925), to implement Islamic principles within the administration. This heralded a new chapter in Malaysian history, with the Islamization of the administration, education system, legal system, and financial institutions. Through this policy of Islamization, Mahathir not only demonstrated his anti-Israel and pro-Palestinian feelings in his foreign policy, but was also critical of the West.

Anwar called for a stringent incorporation of Islamic ideas in the administration of the country and stressed the importance of responding to social demands. The Malaysian Reform Group (Jamaah Islam Malaysia), Darul Arqam, and ABIM also championed Islamic community development as well as people's economic welfare, particularly in the fields of basic needs and education. This approach was different from that of Mahathir, who was more concerned with large-scale development projects. Islamic leaders and scholars believed that such projects were detrimental to the Muslim community, fostering bureaucratic corruption, collusion, and nepotism and endangering the environment.

The concerns of various Muslim communities have also been stressed by the Jamaah Tabligh within the *dakwah* movement during the Islamic resurgence in Malaysia that began in the 1970s. Although this group does not operate as an organization per se and is not affiliated with any political party, it has followers in urban and rural areas, inside and outside Malaysia. All followers are required to travel from mosque to mosque, from home to home, in Malaysia and overseas and give informal talks encouraging worship and a return to the holy scriptures.

The approach of Malay (and Malaysian) society to community development in the last quarter of the twentieth century is rooted in both religious and secular ideas. While UMNO has been struggling for Malay Muslims, religious groups portray the former as narrow-minded, secular, even infidel. As a result, UMNO publicly addresses Islamic issues and portrays religious groups as fundamentalists, extremists, and fanatics. Both groups now attempt to approach Muslims and non-Muslims. The *dakwah* movement has been active in universities, where a significant proportion of faculty members belong to the movement, and it is attracting youngsters on and off campus.

During the 1990s and particularly during the 1997 economic crises in the region, the frustration over corruption, collusion, and nepotism intensified. The direct criticism of Mahathir's economic policy resulted in the sacking of Anwar from his position as deputy prime minister and minister of finance in September 1998. Although he denied all accusations, Anwar was charged, tried, and found guilty and imprisoned on charges of corruption, abuse of power, and immoral conduct.

The issue of Anwar Ibrahim has split the population along political lines—those who believe Anwar is a victim of a conspiracy, and those who support Mahathir. The former's supporters established a new coalition and a new party: the Justice Party (Partai Keadilan). This was founded by Dr. Wan Azizah Wan Ismail, Anwar's spouse, and is a coalition of reform and opposition parties, including the PAS. In 1999, Mahathir's party won the hastily arranged elections.

### Future Prospects

The struggle between the Islamic and secular groups clouds the future of the country and threatens the fabric of Malaysian society. However, the importance of implementing Islamic values in government is a key factor in reaching an agreement. The reinterpretation of *shari'a* and redefinition of the concept of an Islamic state could lead the way to a healthy relationship and peace in the country.

*Andi Faisal Bakti*

### Further Reading

Abdullah, Auni. (1991) *Islam dalam Sejarah Politik dan Pemerintahan Alam Melayu* (Islam and Political History of the Malay World). Kuala Lumpur, Malaysia: Nurin Enterprise.

Bakti, Andi F. (1993) "Islam and Nation State Formation in Indonesia." Master's thesis, McGill University.

Bastin, John Sturgis, and Robin W. Winks (1966) *Malaysia: Selected Historical Readings*. Kuala Lumpur, Malaysia: Oxford University Press.

Funsto, N. J. (1980) *Malay Politics in Malaysia: A Study of United Malays National Organisation and Party Islam*. Kuala Lumpur, Malaysia: Heinemann Educational Books.

Gill, Ranjit (1998) *Anwar Ibrahim, Mahathir's Dilemma: Blow-by Blow Account of the Sacking of Anwar Ibrahim as Deputy Prime Minister, His Dismissal from UMNO, and the Launch of His Reform Movement*. Singapore: Epic Management Services.

Hassan, Muhammad K. (1987) "The Response of Muslim Youth Organizations to Political Change: HMI in Indonesia and ABIM in Malaysia." In *Islam and the Political Economy of Meaning*, edited by William R. Roff. New York: Croom Helm, 180–196.

Lyon, M. L. (1979) "The Dakwah Movement in Malaysia." *Review of Indonesian and Malayan Affairs* 13, 2: 34–45.

Mauzy, D. K., and R. S. Milne. (1983–1984) "The Mahathir Administration in Malaysia: Discipline through Islam." *Pacific Affairs* 56, 4 (winter): 617–648.

Means, G. P. (1969) "The Role of Islam in the Political Development of Malaysia." *Comparative Politics* 1: 264–284.

Morais, J. V. (1983) *Anwar Ibrahim: Resolute in Leadership*. Kuala Lumpur, Malaysia: Arenabuku.

Mukmin, Mohd Jamil. (1994) *Melaka Pusat Penyebaran Islam di Nusantara* (Melaka as the Center of Islamization in the Archipelago). Kuala Lumpur, Malaysia: Nurin Enterprise.

Mutalib, Hussin. (1993) *Islam in Malaysia: From Revivalism to Islamic state*. Singapore: Singapore University Press.

Noer, Deliar. (1973) *The Modernist Muslim Movement in Indonesia, 1900–1942*. Singapore: Oxford University Press.

Osman, Muhammad Taib. (1997) *Islamic Civilization in the Malay World*. Kuala Lumpur, Malaysia: Dewan Bahasa dan Pustaka.

## ISLAM—MONGOLIA

Traces of Islamic culture are to be found throughout Mongolia, and Mongolians of Turkic and Muslim origin are also concentrated in Xinjiang (China) and Kazakhstan to the west and south of Mongolia. Although it is now a minority religion in Mongolia, Islam has been practiced there since at least the tenth century.

### Historical Context

Although the Mongols emerged historically as a distinct group only about 1080 CE, Islam appeared in Central Asia little more than a century after the Revelation to the Prophet Muhammad, 622 CE. The Battle of Talas (751 CE) established Arab, and hence Islamic, dominance of the area south of the Syr Dar'ya (known to the Greeks as the Jaxartes River). North and east of the river, in the central Siberian steppe (present-day north Kazakhstan, south Siberia, and parts of Mongolia), lived various nomadic groups speaking Altaic languages, related to modern Mongolian and Turkish, and professing Nestorian Christianity, Manichaeism, or shamanism. The largest of these groups, the Uighurs, adopted Manichaeism as a religion in 750 CE.

The Central Asian Samanid dynasty (864–999), based in Bukhara, established Sunni Islam as the region's dominant religion, although the area remained religiously mixed, with Muslims a minority in the population of Christians, Jews, Manichaeans, and Buddhists. The Samanids attempted to spread Islam, and with it their political power, among the Christian and shamanist Turks and Mongols in the steppe. Despite this, however, and despite the strong trade links that existed between the steppe and Central Asia, Islam made little headway east of the Altay and Tian Shan Mountains, which today separate Kazakhstan from Mongolia and China. In contrast, successive waves of Turko-Mongolian peoples spread west. In 1211, Kuchlug, head of the Mongol Naiman tribe, conquered the Samanid state in Central Asia and instituted attacks on Islam.

Mongolian power reached its height under the leadership of Genghis Khan (1167–1227), who took Bukhara in 1220. Genghis Khan's conquests in China resulted in the introduction of Buddhism into the steppe, adding to the religious mix. He also initiated the custom of inviting men of all faiths to his capital of Karakorum (now in the Inner Mongolian Autonomous Region of China) to debate religious affairs. The purpose of this appears to have been to establish a common religious "glue" by which the various peoples of the empire could be bound together.

Genghis Khan's empire was divided after his death between his sons. In the west, where Islam was long established as the religion of both governance and learning, the so-called Golden Horde was converted to Islam under Genghis Khan's grandson, Berke (1206–1267). Later Central Asian rulers such as Timur (Tamerlane, 1336–1405) were expected to be Muslim and to be descended from Genghis Khan. In the east, where Genghis Khan was succeeded first by his son Ogodei (1185–1241), then by a grandson, Guyuk (1206–1248), and from 1248 by a second grandson, Mongke (1209–1258), the religious situation was more fluid. We know from William of Rubruk, a Western traveler to the region, that in 1253 there were two mosques in Karakorum.

On 30 May 1254, Mongke initiated a debate between a Christian (William of Rubruk), a Muslim, and a Buddhist. The aim was to establish a state religion binding the Mongolian people together. This was followed by a debate in 1255 between Buddhists and Taoists. In 1256, Mongke adopted Mahayana (Tibetan) Buddhism as the religion of the Mongolian people, although Islam survived there for some time longer. As late as 1447, the ambassador of the Oirot Mongols to the Chinese Ming court was named Muhammad.

The successors of Khubilai Khan (1215–1294) gave the leader of Mahayana Buddhism the title Dalai Lama (most high priest). From this time on, Mongolian identity and culture were inextricably linked with Buddhism.

### Adoption by Kazakhs

Islam exists in Mongolia today because of the country's Kazakh minority, which is concentrated in the west of the country. People of this minority arrived as nomads in the west of Mongolia in the 1860s in response to Russia's advance into their traditional grazing areas. Whereas the Mongolian peoples came to identify with Buddhism, Turkic peoples such as the Kazakhs adopted Islam. The process was gradual, lasting one hundred years and ending with the complete conversion of the Kazakhs during the eighteenth century. The Kazakhs' nomadic pastoral way of life had much in common with the life of the Mongols. Some people have linked the name "Kazakh" to "Cossack" (Russian *kazakh),* meaning a people beyond the bounds of urban society.

It was Sufi missionary activity from the shrine town of Yasi (in Turkistan in present-day south Kazakhstan) that brought Islam to the Kazakhs in the eighteenth century. Although Islam came late to the Kazakhs, being Muslim is important to the Kazakhs, as it distinguishes them from Buddhist Mongols, or Buriyats, and from Christian Russians and aligns them with Muslim Tatars, Uighurs, and Uzbeks. The British missionary Henry Lansdell, writing in the 1880s, noted that Kazakhs were not overly religious unless it was suggested that they were other than Muslim, at which time they became very defensive of their Muslim identity.

The exact number of Muslim Kazakhs in Mongolia is impossible to state. This is in part due to the traditionally nomadic lifestyle of these people, who prior to the collapse of the Soviet Union (1991) crossed the borders separating the Soviet Union, China, and Mongolia in response to political changes in each country. A major emigration from the Soviet Union occurred during the 1920s, and other Kazakhs came from China after China recognized Mongolian independence in 1946 and during China's Cultural Revolution (1966–1976). There also were reverse trends as the political situation in China and the Soviet Union became more favorable. It is estimated that in 1989 there were 120,500 Kazakhs resident in Mongolia, accounting for 5.9 percent of the population. Another 1989 estimate gave a Mongolian Kazakh population of 130,000, of whom 10,000 lived in the capital, Ulaanbaatar. Since 1991 the government of Kazakhstan has encouraged a "return" of the Kazakh diaspora. Perhaps 60,000 Kazakhs had left Mongolia for Kazakhstan by 1994.

Kazakhs are concentrated in the western Bayan-Olgiy province bordering the Altay and Tuva Republics of Russia, where they form around 95 percent of the population, and in the Ili-Kazakh Autonomous Province in Xinjiang (China), where they form up to 75 percent of the population.

Muslims in Mongolia suffered from religious persecution during the 1930s, but there was relatively less to destroy than was the case for Buddhists. Kazakh Islam has always been of a less formal nature than has Islam in other areas. Although all mosques were destroyed in the persecution, no more than four (one in Ulaanbaatar) existed initially. Other Muslim institutions, such as *madrasahs* (law and theology colleges), were absent (traditionally in Kazakh society, Hadith, or customary law, took precedence over *shari'a*, or religious law). Owning a copy of the Qur'an was forbidden, but very few Kazakhs did own one. It has been estimated that at the beginning of the twentieth century, no more than one in two hundred Kazakhs could read, and traditionally the Qur'an had more the status of a talisman used for divination than of a sacred text.

### Post-Communist Resurgence

It has often been said that Mongolia under Communism became one of the most completely nonreligious societies on earth. Certainly, knowledge of the formal teachings of any religion was at a very low ebb. Kazakh Islam in Mongolia had however always existed at a level of folk practice rather than formal theology. Traditional Siberian practices such as divination by means of reading horses' bones, bride-price (or to avoid bride-price, *kalym*, ritual abduction), and the role of female divines in folk medicine, which were all associated with Islam, continued.

Since the end of one-party rule in Mongolia, formal Muslim life has experienced a resurgence. In 1990 the Mongolian Muslim Society was founded in Ulaanbaatar under the leadership of the Moscow-educated former Mongolian ambassador to China, Hajji Hadiryn Sayraan. A few Mongolian Kazakhs have made pilgrimages to Mecca, at least two mosques (in Ulaanbaatar and Olgiy) have opened, and Islamic literature has entered the country from India, Pakistan, and Turkey. There has been some political agitation for guaranteed Kazakh representation at the high government level, but this is not coupled with any Islamic ideology.

*Will Myer*

### Further Reading

Altay, H. (1991) "A Journey to Mongolia." *Journal of the Institute of Muslim Minority Affairs* (Jeddah, Saudi Arabia) 12, 1: 91–104.

Fox, R. (1925) *People of the Steppes.* London: Constable.

Bulag, H. (1998) *Nationalism and Hybridity in Mongolia.* Oxford: Clarendon Press.

Heissig, W. (1980) *The Religions of Mongolia.* Berkeley and Los Angeles: University of California Press.

Olcott, M. B. (1995) *The Kazakhs.* Stanford, CA: Hoover Institution Press.

## ISLAM—MYANMAR

When Myanmar (Burma) became part of British India, it had possessed a Muslim community since the beginning of the early modern period (from the fourteenth century), introduced by Muslim Chinese into northeastern Myanmar and by Muslim traders from Southwest Asia and India into Arakan and Lower Myanmar. Myanmar's Muslim population remained relatively small, however, until the establishment of British rule in the nineteenth century. Increased trade and the immigration of Muslim Indian laborers into Lower Myanmar and Muslim Bengali agriculturalists into Arakan to service the growing colonial economy encouraged a rapid growth in the Muslim population, indicated partly by large mosques that were built in Myanmar's major town-ports, including Sittwe (Akyab) and Yangon (Rangoon).

The Muslims of Myanmar are divided into three groups. The first group consists of the Rohingyas, the Bengali-speaking Muslim minority of Arakan state. This group has often been forced to flee to Bangladesh, the Middle East, and Malaysia because of communal violence between Muslim and Buddhist agriculturalists and hostile government policies (many Muslims of Arakan state have been defined as foreigners by the government and thus denied citizenship).

The second group consists of mainly Urdu-speaking Muslims who are descendants of Indian immigrants of the nineteenth and twentieth centuries. Indian Muslims tend to be strict in their observance of Orthodox Islam. Prior to 1962, this group was the most powerful of the three Muslim groups of Myanmar. They are concentrated in the Irrawaddy Valley and Yangon, the capital of both colonial and independent Myanmar, and are close to Myanmar's chief economic and political centers. After 1962, however, many Indian Muslims joined in the general Indian exodus from Myanmar that had begun in 1948.

The third group consists of Myanmar Muslims of various Burmese ethnic groups, heavily represented in Mandalay and Upper Myanmar. These Muslims share many cultural practices with Buddhists in Myanmar. Myanmar Muslim women expect equal treatment to men, reflecting the relative independence of women in Southeast Asian societies compared with many

A refugee camp in Cox's Bazaar, Bangladesh, which houses Muslims who have fled persecution across the border in Myanmar. (LIBA TAYLOR/CORBIS)

other Asian societies (and with Muslim societies in general). Purdah, the custom of keeping women's faces covered, is not generally practiced. Myanmar Muslim men are also monogamous, a custom that differs from other Muslim societies. Most significantly, Muslims in Myanmar adopted certain rituals involved in *nat* (spirit) propitiation. Some religious sites in Myanmar are held in reverence by both Muslims and Buddhists, for example, the famous Buddhermokan near Sittwe (Akyab) in Arakan.

*Michael Walter Charney*

*See also:* **Bangladesh—History; Bengali Language; Buddhism, Theravada—Southeast Asia; Hindi-Urdu; India-Myanmar Relations; Malaysia—History; Myanmar—Human Rights; Spirit Cult**

### Further Reading

Harvey, G. E. ([1925] 1967) *History of Burma: From the Earliest Times to 10 March 1824, the Beginning of the English Conquest*. Reprint ed. London: Frank Cass.

Yegar, Moshe. (1972) *The Muslims of Burma: A Study of a Minority Group*. Wiesbaden, Germany: O. Harrassowitz.

## ISLAM—PHILIPPINES

Muslim Filipinos (or as many prefer to be called, Philippine Muslims) represent about 4.5 percent of the Philippines population. They are concentrated in the islands of the Sulu archipelago, western and central Mindanao, and southern Palawan, and include some thirteen ethnolinguistic groups, though four of these—Maguindanao, Maranao-Ilanun, Tausug, and Samal—account for over 90 percent of the Muslim population. As in most of Southeast Asia, they are Sunni Muslims.

### Origins of Islam in the Philippines

Islam came to the Philippines in the thirteenth century, and by the middle of the fourteenth century there were settlements of Muslim Indian, Malay, and probably Arab traders and missionaries in Mindanao and Sulu and extensive commercial relations with the Islamic world to the west. The first to embrace Islam were the Tausug of the Sulu archipelago, and by the mid-fifteenth century a Sulu sultanate had been established at Buansa (Jolo) under Sultan Abu Bakr. At its peak, the Sulu sultanate extended from Basilan north to Palawan, east to the coast of Mindanao, and west to Borneo. Jolo was the center of a trading network that stretched west to Java and north to China.

In the sixteenth century, Sharif Muhammad Kabungsawan arrived from Johore and established himself in the Cotabato area of southern Mindanao, providing the foundation for the Maguindanao sultanate. From the Maguindanao-Ilanun area, Islam expanded along the coast from northern Mindanao to the Gulf of Davao and inland to Lake Lanao and

Three Muslim women of Basilan Island attend Friday prayer in June 2001. (AFP/CORBIS)

Bukidnon. Also in the sixteenth century, Islam spread from Brunei to the islands of Mindoro and southern Luzon. The Philippines thus became part of the *dar-al-Islam* (international community ["household"] of Islam) in Asia.

## Philippine Muslims and Colonial Forces

When the Spaniards arrived in the Philippines in 1565, they immediately came into conflict with the Moros ("Moors" or Muslims), beginning a bitter struggle for religious and commercial control in the Philippine islands that continued over some 350 years. Assisted by converted Christian *indios* (native Filipinos), the Spaniards reversed the expansion of Islam, vanquishing the Muslims from Luzon and the Visaya Islands, but they never gained effective sovereignty over Mindanao and Sulu.

When the United States took over control of the Philippines in 1898, the Moros continued to resist the foreign intrusion until a major military defeat in 1913. Subsequently, administration of Mindanao and Sulu passed from the U.S. Army to civilian authorities. Governance of Philippine Muslims initially came under the Bureau of Non-Christian Tribes. Under a "policy of attraction," the U.S. administration increased expenditures on infrastructure in Muslim areas and provided scholarships for Muslims to study in Manila and the United States. Many Muslims, however, saw this as an attempt to assimilate the Moros into mainstream, predominantly Christian, Filipino society, and there were intermittent outbreaks of armed resistance. In 1946, the Philippines became independent, but there was no independence constitution, and policies essentially followed those of the Philippine Commonwealth established under U.S. rule in 1935.

## Muslim Separatism

By the 1950s, increasing migration to Mindanao and consequent competition for land and political influence, combined with an Islamic resurgence reflected among other things in the proliferation of mosques and *madaris* (or *madrasahs*; Islamic schools), had brought new tensions in relations between Muslim and Christian communities. These tensions escalated during the 1960s, and in 1969 a Muslim independence movement was established. By the early 1970s, Muslim Mindanao and Sulu were in a state of armed insurgency, spearheaded by the Moro National Liberation Front (MNLF). This group, which demanded a separate Islamic state, or Bangsa Moro (Moro nation), received financial, logistical, and diplomatic support from the international Islamic community and was granted observer status with the Organization of Islamic Conference (OIC). The Marcos government made a number of concessions to Moro demands in the 1970s, including the codification of *shari'a* (Islamic law) for use in specific areas of jurisdiction in Muslim regions, the proclamation of Muslim holidays (proclaimed nationally but generally recognized only in Muslim areas), the revival of the historic barter trade between Malaysia and Muslim Mindanao, and the establishment of the Philippines Amanah Bank, which employed Islamic banking principles. With the signing of the Tripoli Agreement between the MNLF and the Philippine government in 1976, autonomous regions were created in western and central Mindanao and Sulu. Following the People Power Revolution of 1986, the Autonomous Region of Muslim Mindanao (ARMM) was established, though the MNLF refused to participate in the election that set it up. An Office of Muslim Affairs was also established within the Office of the President.

The Moro insurgency has continued, albeit on a reduced scale, since the 1970s; however, in 1996 a peace agreement signed between the MNLF and the Philippine government created a Special Zone of Peace and Development (SZOPAD) in the fourteen provinces claimed for the Bangsa Moro by the MNLF and provided for a Southern Philippines Council for Peace and Development (SPCPD) with limited powers of administration in the SZOPAD. The SPCPD was to be assisted by a *Darul Iftah* (religious advisory council). The OIC, which had helped bring about the 1996 agreement, was given a specific role in supporting its implementation and helping monitor the peace process. The 1996 agreement also provided for the drafting of legislation for an expanded ARMM, to be submitted to a referendum. In August 2001, the referendum was finally held, but of the fifteen provinces and fourteen cities covered by the agreement only one province and one city voted to join the four existing provinces in the ARMM. After this, the ARMM and MNLF chairman, Nur Misuari, lost office and briefly attempted to revive the armed struggle. He was arrested in Malaysia.

Two other Muslim groups—the Moro Islamic Liberation Front (MILF), which is a 1977 breakaway from the MNLF, and Abu Sayyaf, a group that has been heavily involved in kidnapping for ransom—have meanwhile continued the armed struggle for an Islamic Bangsa Moro. In 2002, peace negotiations with the MILF continued. The Ulama League of the Philippines has supported the peace process.

*Ronald J. May*

### Further Reading


Gowing, Peter G. (1979) *Muslim Filipinos: Heritage and Horizon*. Quezon City, Philippines: New Day Publishers.

Majul, Cesar A. (1973) *Muslims in the Philippines*. Quezon City, Philippines: University of the Philippines Press.

May, Ronald J. (2001) "Muslim Mindanao: Four Years after the Peace Agreement." In *Southeast Asian Affairs, 2001*. Singapore: Institute of Southeast Asian Studies, 263–275.

Mckenna, Thomas. (1998) *Muslim Rulers and Rebels*. Berkeley and Los Angeles: University of California Press.


## ISLAM—SOUTH ASIA

South Asia is home to more than 360 million Muslims, more than a third of the world's total. The majority of the populations of Pakistan and Bangladesh are Muslim (98 and 87 percent, respectively), as are 12 percent of Indians, almost all Maldivians, and tiny fractions of Sri Lankans and Nepalese.

The first Muslims to set foot in the subcontinent were Arab invaders who conquered parts of Sind and southern Punjab in 711. The Islamization process started with the establishment of the Delhi sultanate (1192–1526), a series of Turco-Afghan Muslim dynasties in Delhi. But the invaders-turned-rulers did not come to spread Islam, nor did they represent Islam's high culture. They came at the end of what was once the magnificent Abbasid caliphate (749/750–1258). The sultanate, theoretically subordinate to the Abbasids, proclaimed itself the protector and patron of Islam after the destruction of the Baghdad-based caliphate in 1258.

The Mughal dynasty (1526–1857), theoretically more secular and Indianized than the preceding sultanate, nevertheless named Muslim theologians to high government positions. Most of these rulers never identified themselves with India, despising its climate, religion, and people. But unlike Islam in Iran and the Ottoman empire (1453–1922), Indian Islam was saved from bureaucratization and state control by Indian pluralism. Most importantly, Islam came to India when the latter already possessed a developed civilization with well-structured peasant and village communities, urbanization, organized religions, and sociopolitical systems. Today, South Asia has all the principal varieties of Islam: scholasticism, Sufism (Islamic mysticism), scholastic-Sufi synthesis, Islamic modernism, and reformist or militant Islam. An appraisal of all the varieties is essential for an understanding of South Asian Islam.

### Sufis and Settlers

Although the bulk of Central Asian and Iranian warriors, Sufis, and fortune-seekers settled in northwestern India and elsewhere in the region, most South Asian Muslims are descendants of local converts. Persianized Turco-Afghans and Mughals constituted the bulk of the nobility and aristocracy *(ashraf)*, enjoying the lion's share of the state patronage during the Muslim rule. They not only alienated themselves from the popular culture and local traditions of the subcontinent; they also despised Hindus and the indigenous Muslims *(atraf)* as inferior. But the *ashraf* classes did not play the most decisive role in the Islamizing process. Had it been so, Delhi, Agra, and the adjoining districts in the core areas of Muslim rule would have Muslim majorities. It is interesting that peripheral eastern Bengal (Bangladesh) and western Punjab, Sind, North-Western Frontier, and Baluchistan (modern Pakistan), on the average, are more than 90 percent Muslim. During the thirteenth through sixteenth centuries, Sufis converted large sections of pre-agrar-

Muslims outside Dhaka's Baitul Mukarram National Mosque donate money to help flood victims in October 2000. (AFP/ CORBIS)

ian nomads and tribal people, as yet not integrated into the Hindu community, in the areas of present-day Bangladesh and Pakistan. The Islamization process accelerated in the sixteenth century, especially in eastern Bengal, due to the state patronage of Sufis who brought the Qur'an and the plow, creating a large number of peasant adherents of Islam. It is noteworthy that Muslim masses throughout the subcontinent still nourish the culture of saint-veneration, paying homage to Sufis and their tombs.

## The High Culture of Islam

Muslim rulers, elite, scholars, artisans, and artists brought elements of art and architecture, music and literature, food and attire, perfumes and jewelry, philosophy, and high culture from central Asia and Iran, including Sunni Islam and various mystic Sufi methods of meditation and prayer (*tariqas*). The Qutb Minar and Red Fort at Delhi, Agra Fort, Taj Mahal at Agra, and hundreds of beautiful buildings—mosques, palaces, tombs, and shrines—may be cited in this regard. The synthesis of Indian and Middle Eastern and Central Asian philosophy, literature, art, architecture, music, and painting gave a unique Indo-Islamic character to almost every branch of human endeavor and knowledge. Islamic philosophy and culture, monotheism, and the seclusion of women, for example, affected Indian religions and belief systems. The emergence of religious reformers such as Nanak (1469–1539), the founder of Sikhism; Kabir (1440–1518), an Indian mystic revered by Muslims, Hindus, and Sikhs; and Mahabir (fifteenth–sixteenth century), all of whom developed iconoclastic and monotheistic philosophies, may be attributed to the impact of Islam. Similarly, Muslim Sufis borrowed Hindu and Buddhist mystic ideas that were quite unknown in orthodox Islam. The development of the Urdu language and literature synthesizing Persian, Arabic, and Hindi literary traditions and styles, and especially the emergence of romantic Urdu love songs and poetry *(ghazal)* in northwestern India, with typical Islamic and Sufi imagery, would not have taken place without this Indo-Islamic fusion.

Major Sufi orders in India, such as the Chishti, Suhrawardi, Naqshbandi, and Qadiri, had their origins in Iran and central Asia. Many of them came along with the Muslim conquerors and some of them were themselves "warrior Sufis" who established Muslim rule by fighting local Hindu rulers, mostly in remote areas of eastern Bengal. Sufis in South Asia preached love and tolerance on the one hand, and syncretism (the fusion of multiple beliefs) and escapism on the other. While they were mainly responsible for the spread of Islam in the subcontinent, they arrived in the region after the decay of Islamic civilization had already begun in the heartland of Islam from the tenth century onward. So escapist, next-worldly, and syncretistic Islam—with Persian, Indian, Buddhist, and Hindu elements—came into being in the subcontinent. Sufis also absorbed Indian languages, music, yoga practices, and literary styles into Islamic practice. This explains why certain rituals and institutions among South Asian Muslims are unique to the region, unheard-of in the Islamic heartland.

## The Power of Orthodoxy

Islam in South Asia entered a crucial phase in the late sixteenth and early seventeenth centuries, during the reigns of the Mughal emperors Akbar (1542–1605; reigned 1556–1605) and Jahangir (1569–1627; reigned 1605–1627). Orthodox Muslim scholars and Sufis campaigned against the heterodoxy practiced by Akbar and Jahangir, and especially against Deen-i-Ilahi (the Religion of God), the syncretistic religion introduced by the former. Sufis belonging to the orthodox

Naqshbandi Tariqa under the leadership of Shaykh Ahmad Sirhindi (1564–1624) confronted the Mughal court. Sirhindi despised syncretism as heresy and considered any interaction with Hindus and other non-Muslims undesirable. Jahangir arrested him only to release him later, as the Shaykh had a large number of followers in the royal court. His overwhelming influence helped Muslim scholars reestablish orthodoxy in Indian Islam. He reaffirmed the views of al-Ghazali (1058–1111), a Sufi theologian who had rejected mathematics as "intoxicating" and "un-Islamic" and Greek philosophy as "dangerous."

It would be misleading, however, to suggest that Sirhindi and his followers alone were responsible for the isolationist and backward-looking nature of South Asian Islam. If the retrogression of South Asian Muslims is imputed to Sirhindi's influence, how does one explain the state of backwardness, next-worldliness, and the lack of scientific inquiry prevalent before his time? One cannot name a single university or institution for the study of science and technology in South Asia either during the Delhi sultanate or during Mughal rule, though leaders excelled in the building of beautiful mosques, forts, shrines and tombs. Unlike the Arab and Berber rulers of Egypt, North Africa, and Spain from the ninth to thirteenth centuries, who established universities and cultivated secular scientific knowledge, South Asian Muslim rulers, nomadic invaders from Central Asia, lacked the vision, education, and skill to contribute to science and high culture. They inherited only the retrogressive culture and institutions of the already decayed and degenerate Abbasid empire. The Mongol invasion of Baghdad in 1258 merely formalized the destruction of the empire and shattered the entire Muslim world, especially the vast region between the Nile and the Ganges.

## Sufism and the Sultanate

Meanwhile, Sufis had their heyday in the chaotic environment of plunder and pillage in Iraq, Iran, Central Asia, and India between the twelfth and sixteenth centuries. They preached mysticism, devotion, and escapism to large numbers of Sunni and Shiʿite devotees. Henceforth Sufism became the most important aspect of South Asian Islam. Many Sufis and most of their disciples preached syncretism, shunning the Qurʾanic exhortation to learn, study, and inquire. The Delhi sultanate remained unstable due to internal dissension and external invasions. The sultans were prejudiced against Hindus and some had no qualms about destroying Hindu temples or converting them into mosques. As for the Mughals, despite their generous patronage of secular art, architecture, music, painting, and literature—at least up to the late seventeenth century—Mughal rulers exclusively employed Islamic clergy as judges and jurists, and endowed Muslim shrines, seminaries, and mosques with land grants. Emperor Aurangzeb's reign (1658–1707) was a departure from the hitherto syncretistic and tolerant Mughal traditions. He antagonized liberal Muslims and many Hindus with his ultra-orthodoxy and the discriminatory poll tax on the majority Hindu community. Rebellions by Hindu rulers, especially in the Deccan and Maharashtra, ultimately led to the empire's decline and downfall.

## Shiʿite and Shiʿa Sufi Currents

Shiʿite Islam and Shiʿa Sufi orders came to the subcontinent mainly from Iran after the elevation of the sect as the state religion of Iran in the early sixteenth century. Shiʿite scholars and courtiers played important roles in the Mughal courts and elsewhere in northern and southern India and Bengal. There were several Shiʿite dynasties, in Kashmir and Golconda for example, during the precolonial period. Shiʿa sects represented include the Twelvers, Bohras, and Ismailis. The Ismailis, successors of the twelfth-century Assassins who in 1845 fled from Iran to India under the leadership of Aga Khan I (1800–1881), are also known as the "Aga Khani" community, renowned for their philanthropy and wealth. But South Asian history is replete with conflict between Shiʿite Muslims and Sunni Muslims. Their mutual hatred has been responsible for killings, pillage, and plunder, especially in north India and parts of Pakistan. There are followers of various Muslim sects and schools of thought, including the Ahmadiya (Qadiani), throughout the subcontinent. In the early 1970s, the Pakistani government, responding to popular demand, declared the Ahmadiya a non-Muslim minority community on the grounds that its belief system was heretical.

## The Growth of British Power

The onset of the British rule did not augur well for Indian Muslims. The consequential loss of political power, jobs, and state patronage as the most favored community turned the bulk of Muslims into disgruntled and confused masses or into the sworn enemies of the British. British expansion was slow, steady, ruthless, and calculating. British occupation of Bengal, Mumbai (Bombay), and Madras by the mid-eighteenth century and other regions by the early nineteenth frightened the feeble Mughals and hundreds of other Indian rulers. By then, raids by Hindu Maratha invaders from the west were frequent. The upshot was the growth of Muslim solidarity and militant reformist movements in British-occupied Bengal as well as in Indian-administered regions under the Mughals and some petty dynasties in northwestern India.

Shah Wali Allah (1702–1762), Sirhindi's great follower from Delhi, spearheaded the introduction of the orthodox, militant Islamic revivalist "Wahhabi" movement into the subcontinent. To secure the future of Islam in the subcontinent, this well-versed theologian invited Ahmad Shah Durrani (1722?–1773) of Afghanistan to fight the Marathas. Durrani routed the vast Maratha army and saved India from the Maratha menace at the battle of Panipat (1761). Meanwhile, Sikhs, Marathas, and Afghans had been vying for the control of the moribund Mughal empire. The exit of the Marathas allowed the Sikhs to occupy the Punjab, Kashmir, and parts of the Afghan territories in the northwest. Afterwards, the Sikh persecution of Muslims led to further mobilization of Muslim militants under the leadership of Wali Allah's son and successor, Shah Abdul Aziz (1746–1824).

**Rebellion and War**

In the early nineteenth century Abdul Aziz declared British India "Dar-ul-Harb" (an abode of war), making it obligatory for every pious Muslim to join the holy war against the British. One of his disciples, Sayyid Ahmad Brelwi (1786–1831), organized the jihad and moved to the northwest frontier to establish an Islamic state. Thousands of Muslims joined Brelwi's jihad to fight the Sikhs and then the British. Brelwi died fighting the Sikhs. His followers later supported the Indian Mutiny of 1857–1858. In 1867, a group of Brelwi's followers established the famous Deoband Madrasah (seminary) in north India. This ultraorthodox seminary produced thousands of traditionally educated graduates, some of whom joined Gandhi in the Freedom Movement or the Muslim separatist Pakistan movement. Thousands of Deoband-style *madrasahs* have been functioning throughout the subcontinent. (Afghanistan's Taliban, militant successors of the Indian Wahhabis, were graduates of such *madrasahs* in Pakistan.)

Several other reformers, such as Titu Meer (d. 1831) near Calcutta and Shariatullah (1781–1840) in eastern Bengal, started Puritan and militant anti-British movements. While the former died fighting at the hands of British troops, the latter organized the more successful and long-lasting Faraizi movement, to establish the *faraiz*, or obligatory rituals, discard syncretism, and fight the British.

**Branching Out**

Soon after Brelwi's death, his supporters split into several groups. One of his disciples, Karamat Ali Jaunpuri (1800–1873), shunned militancy after 1831, promoting loyalism and advising Indian Muslims to learn English and adopt orthodoxy by discarding syncretism. His main base was rural eastern Bengal (Bangladesh). He successfully neutralized the bulk of Faraizi supporters through peaceful reformism and by synthesizing the various Sufi *tariqas* into the Tayyuni movement. His brand of Sufism is still quite popular throughout Bangladesh and parts of Assam. Sir Syed Ahmad Khan (1817–1898), founder of the Aligarh Muslim University in north India, and Nawab Abdul Latif and Syed Ameer Ali of Bengal (d. 1928), contemporaries of Karamat Ali, were doing the same thing. Their movements ultimately promoted orthodoxy, "Islamic modernism," and separatism among Indian Muslims, who played the decisive role in the partition of the subcontinent in 1947 into Hindu India and Muslim Pakistan.

There have been scores of other Islamic movements and organizations throughout the region. The Jamaat-e Islami and the Tabligh Jamaat are the best known among them. The former has promoted a totalitarian Islamic state since 1941 and the latter Puritanism since the 1920s. The political use of Islam by civil and military dictators for the sake of legitimacy, and the mass frustration due to the failure of the welfare state in post-colonial Pakistan and Bangladesh are mainly responsible for the growth of political Islam and escapism or next-worldliness in these countries. The post–Cold War Islamic resurgence and Hindu revivalism, especially the demolition of the Babri Mosque by Hindu militants in 1992, are largely responsible for Muslim militancy in India. Last but not least, Islamic resurgence in neighboring Afghanistan under the Taliban, the terrorist attacks on America in September 2001, and the American retaliation against the Taliban regime, have had a tremendous impact on South Asian Muslims.

*Taj I. Hashmi*

**Further Reading**

Ahmad, Aziz. (1967) *Islamic Modernism in India and Pakistan, 1857–1964.* London: Oxford University Press.

———. (1964) *Studies in Islamic Culture in the Indian Environment.* Oxford: Clarendon.

Ahmad, Qeyamuddin. (1966) *The Wahabi Movement in India.* New Delhi: Manohar Publishers.

Ahmed, Rafiuddin. (1981) *The Bengai Muslims, 1871–1906: A Quest for Identity.* Delhi: Oxford University Press.

Eaton, Richard M. (1993) *The Rise of Islam and the Bengal Frontier.* Berkeley and Los Angeles: University of California Press.

Habibullah, A. B. M. (1961) *The Foundation of Muslim Rule in India.* Allahabad, India: Central Book Depot.

Hashmi, Taj I. (2000) *Women and Islam in Bangladesh.* New York: St. Martin's.

———. (1992) *Pakistan as a Peasant Utopia.* Boulder, CO: Westview.

Khan, Muin-ud-din Ahmad. (1965) *History of the Faraidi Movement in Bengal.* Karachi, Pakistan: Pakistan Historical Society.

Metcalf, Barbara D. (1982) *Islamic Revival in British India.* Princeton, NJ: Princeton University Press.

Mutalb, H., and Taj I. Hashmi, eds. (1994) *Islam, Muslims and the Modern State.* New York: St. Martin's.


**ISLAM—SOUTHWEST ASIA** The region now occupied by Afghanistan and Pakistan is unique in the Islamic world in the degree to which it looks both to the Middle East and to Central Asia. As a consequence of the latter connection, the region has remained orthodox, as has Muslim Central Asia itself. Although Iranicized in culture, the region is not Iranicized in religion. Shi'ites (the majority Muslim sect in Iran, though representing only 10 percent of the worldwide Islamic population) are only a small minority.

Afghanistan and Pakistan were both Buddhist prior to the appearance of Arab armies in the seventh century. They were at first comparatively untouched by the new religion of Islam. Arab armies swept through Afghanistan quickly, pressing on into Khorasan and points beyond, an expansion that culminated in the 751 Arabic victory on the Talas river against Tang China. That victory opened eastern Turkistan and even China itself to Islam. India was still only occasionally raided. Nowhere did the garrisons left behind by the Arabs, some quite large, and a scattered Islamic urban community, have much effect on the locals.

Real conversion began much later. It was long inhibited by the practice of taxing nonbelievers, turning them into a major fiscal resource of the state that would be lost if they converted. Nonbelievers, of course, had a financial interest in becoming Muslims, but their conversion was resisted by local governments. Social issues were important too. The form of Islam brought in by the Arabs was not attractive to former Buddhists. Only with the eleventh-century arrival of Sufism (mystical Islam), which offered a religious experience closer to what they were used to, and which was strongly influenced by Buddhism in any case, was real progress made.

## Early Islamic States

The first important Islamic state in Afghanistan was that of the Ghaznavids (977–1187). Its appearance marked the emergence of the Turks as a major force since its ruling family was descended from Turkic military slaves. Despite this, the Ghaznavids were associated with Iranian revival rather than Turkicization and played an important role in making Islam Iranian as well as Arabic. In promoting Iranian Islamic culture, the Ghaznavids, particularly Mahmud of Ghazna (971–1030), tried to avoid the doctrinal controversies of other parts of the Islamic world.

By his time serious penetration of India had begun, largely by Turkic warriors. Going on simultaneously with an overland advance were overseas contacts following Indian Ocean trade routes. Despite these advances, India, with traditions largely alien to those of the Middle East, proved resistant to Muslim penetration. For centuries, Islamic influence remained confined to the Punjab, an area first infiltrated by the Ghaznavids, and a few trading communities. Only gradually did Islam spread more widely in north India, in part due to the active efforts of the successors of the Ghaznavids, the Ghurids (1187–1215). Throughout India, the Buddhist or formerly Buddhist areas seem to have been the most receptive to the new religion.

A major turning point in the history of the region was the coming of the Mongols followed by the emergence of various Mongol successor states, including

The octagonal tomb of of Sufi leader Sheik Rukn-i-Alam in Multan, Pakistan. The tomb was built in 1320–1324 for the father of Sultan Muhammad Tughlaq. (ROGER WOOD/CORBIS)

the Timurid and Mughal empires. The Mongols controlled Afghanistan as well as Iran, but did not invade India. They were at first little interested in Islam and it was only after the breakdown of unified Mongol empire in 1259 that Islam began to make any real headway among them. The Iranian Il-Khans (1260–1335) officially converted to Islam under Ghazan (1271–1304), and under Oljeitu (1280–1316) began the process of official patronage of Shiʿa that resulted in the Shiʿite Iranian state of today. This change had little impact on Afghanistan since it was controlled by a competing khanate, that of Ca'adai (1260–1334), later a convert to Sunni Islam. Muslims in India could also remain orthodox since they were isolated from Mongol Iran under their own rulers. This included the various Delhi sultans, mostly of Turkic origin, although Iranicized, who gradually expanded their rule through much of India. Other Muslim regimes emerged there as well, including in Bengal, once a Buddhist stronghold. Throughout Muslim India, Sufism enjoyed great importance because of its ability to form a bridge between an Iranicized elite and Hindu converts.

**Islam under the Mughals and the British**

India's relative isolation changed radically due to the new wave of post-Mongol states. Timur (1336–1405), born a Muslim, led an invasion of India in 1398–1399, sacking Delhi and doing immense damage to local Islamic culture. The next wave was that of the Mughals, based in Afghanistan. Under Babur (1483–1530) and his successors, the Mughals became the first Islamic rulers to conquer all of India (except its extreme southern tip), although the majority of their subjects were non-Muslims.

The Mughals continued cultural patterns already established under the Delhi sultans. They promoted a court culture that was heavily Iranian but made one concession to their Turkic culture in encouraging use of the Turkic literary language of Central Asia, Chagatay, in which Babur himself wrote. More influential was their Iranian dialect, Urdu, the language of the *ordu*, or palace, now the second language of the Indian subcontinent and the official language of Pakistan. In religion they continued the toleration of almost all religious communities, even patronizing Shiʿite shrines when they could do so quietly. The Mughals were also accepting of the Hinduism of most of their subjects and of local cults combining Islam and Hindu beliefs, as long as it was done in acceptable ways. Personally, the Mughal emperors remained heavily influenced by the quiet introspection of Sufism.

The Mughal empire survived as the theoretically dominant power in India until 1858, although it no longer controlled Afghanistan by then and had been superseded by the British in much of north India. The British continued the system that the Mughals had created in ruling India and sought also to preserve the balance between the religions achieved under them. Although there were growing tensions between Muslims and non-Muslims in India, they remained in check during almost the entire period of British rule. Once the British were gone, the bloodshed began.

The intent of Mohandas Gandhi (1869–1948) and his followers was a united India, but this had become impossible, and British India was instead partitioned between a Muslim Pakistan and a Hindu India. As these two states were set up, and populations exchanged, there was considerable violence resulting in hundreds of thousands of deaths. The two states also went to war almost as soon as declared, and have engaged in several wars since. In 1956, Pakistan officially became an Islamic state and in recent years the power of Islam within it has grown. It has not, however, become fundamentalist, despite fundamentalism's growing influence.

**Islam in Modern Afghanistan and Pakistan**

While India was slowly moving toward religious conflict, Afghanistan was going its own way. Although Islam was certainly a factor in Afghanistan's ability to defend itself against British invasion in the nineteenth century, this was primarily a military success. Within Afghanistan, the divisions that existed were ethnic and not religious. This has changed as a consequence of decades of upheaval in the aftermath of the 1979 Soviet invasion and the failure to achieve stability following the Soviet withdrawal. Searching for a uniting ideology, many Afghans have turned to fundamentalism, resulting in the recent Taliban regime (1996–2001), which was entirely atypical of the past history of Islam in Afghanistan.

Nonetheless, how much of an aberration this episode will appear over the long term remains to be seen. The Islamic world is awash in a demographic wave of volatile young people, and until this generation grows up and quiets down there will be no peace. Playing a critical role in determining the future will be what happens in Pakistan. The government of Pervez Musharraf (b. 1943) is pro-Western, but as in most of the Islamic world, the real force is in the streets. A shift to Islamic radicalism in Pakistan would quickly find its echo in Afghanistan, which is now governed by a northern, largely Uzbek and Hazara minority, but still has a restive Pashtun majority. No one knows at this point exactly how the pieces will fall.

*Paul D. Buell*

**Further Reading**

Bulliet, Richward W. (1979) *Conversion to Islam in the Medieval Period, An Essay in Quantitative History*. Cambridge, MA: Harvard University Press.

Hodgson, Marshall G. (1974) *The Venture of Islam, Conscience and History in a World Civilization*. Chicago: University of Chicago Press.

Lapidus, Ira M. (1988) *A History of Islamic Societies*. Cambridge, U.K.: Cambridge University Press.

**ISLAM—WEST ASIA** Although people have practiced Islam in parts of West Asia (present-day Iraq, Iran, and Turkey) since its inception, different versions of the religion have been created by the region's differing cultures, language groups, and histories.

Islam was brought to modern Iraq during the reign of Abu Bakr (c. 573–634), the first successor to the Prophet Muhammad. Abu Bakr attacked and defeated the Persians near An Najaf in southern central Iraq in 634. In 642, under the caliph 'Umar (c. 585–644), the Muslim invaders again defeated the Persians, this time at the so-called victory of victories near modern Hamadan in northwestern Iran. This defeat resulted in the destruction of the old Sasanid empire (224/228–651 CE), whose religion had been Zoroastrian.

By contrast, Islam did not become a major force in the area of present-day Turkey until 1071, when the Muslim Seljuk Turks defeated the Christian Byzantines at the battle of Manzikert. Subsequently, as the Byzantine empire shrank, Turkish Muslim power grew.

Iraq was a battleground in the disputes surrounding who would govern the community of Muslim faithful, which split Muslims into Sunni and Shi'ite sects. (Today, Sunnis account for 90 percent of the

## SUPPORT FOR THE POOR

In many Islamic societies, the poor or otherwise disadvantaged are helped by taxes collected by the government and also charity given by individuals. This means that begging has a special meaning in Muslim societies.

> In 1949 I was traveling by bus from Tehran to Hamadan. At a certain ford the driver stopped. A blind woman, nursing a baby, arose from a brush shelter beside the road and approached the bus. The driver passed the hat, everyone put in a coin or a bill, and he handed the collection to the poor woman, who replied with an invocation to God to bless her benefactors. The blessing was returned by the occupants of the bus, and the driver drove on. (If, in visiting an oriental city, you find yourself pestered with beggars and remark, "There ought to be an institution to take care of these people," remember that there is an institution, and an old one, the zaka. Give, in moderation as the Muslims do, and take it off your income tax.)
>
> The zaka is not the only tax imposed in Muslim states. There is a special tax on Christians and Jews, which was abusively levied on Berber converts to Islam in the early days of the conquest of North Africa. There are also customs, gate taxes, market taxes, and other sources of revenue most of which appeared after Muhammad's death. But the zaka differs from those in that it was not originally designed to support the state, being rather a means of leveling out the income of the various elements in the community so that no one would go hungry, of financing the conversion of the heathen and of facilitating travel between the various parts of the Islamic world.
>
> *Source:* Carleton S. Coon (1951) *Caravan: The Story of the Middle East*. New York: Holt, 112.

world's Muslims.) Many of the most important sites in Shi'ite history are to be found on Iraqi soil, including the site of the battle of Karbala (10 October 680), when the Prophet's grandson Hussein was killed. Shi'ites annually mark this event at the Ashura festival (10 Muharram in the Islamic calendar).

Shi'ism has also always been strong in Iran, partly because its messianic tendencies grafted relatively easily onto the base of Zoroastrian culture and partly because this border region of the early empire attracted dissidents at a time when Shi'ism was a movement of social protest almost as much as a religious. A decisive moment in Iranian religious and cultural history occurred in the early sixteenth century, when the forces of Esma'il I (1487–1524) conquered the country. The new Safavid dynasty (1501–1722/1736) proclaimed Shi'ism the state religion. Shi'ism ceased to be a movement of social protest and was closely associated with the Safavid and later Qajar state (1784–1925).

A defining moment in Turkish Islam came with the capture of Constantinople by the Ottomans in 1453. The Ottoman empire (1453–1922), which at its height covered Southeast Europe, North Africa, and most of the Middle East, including modern Iraq, created a cultural synthesis of Turkish, Greek, Persian, and Arabic elements but was above all a Sunni state based on an ideology of universal empire. In the eighteenth century, Sultan Selim I (1467–1520) transferred the relics of the Prophet to Constantinople (modern Istanbul), and the title "caliph," implying leadership of the world Muslim community, came into use to describe the Ottoman rulers. Within the Ottoman and Persian states, the Muslim religion was the basis of all laws and of the education system. It was necessary to be Muslim to participate in government. However, during the nineteenth century, pressure from the West led to a decline in religious institutions. In 1826, the Tanzimat reforms, undertaken in the Ottoman empire to modernize society and limit the power of Muslim clerics, allowed Christians to participate in the administrative and legal systems and created state schools.

Iran also witnessed a gradual decoupling of religion and the state from the 1850s on. A gradual transfer of power from religious to secular authorities has been a recent feature of all three countries, although the 1979 Iranian revolution has challenged this trend.

### Turkey

Turkey emerged as a result of a nationalist struggle that began in 1919. Ironically, modern Turkey is much more Muslim than the Ottoman provinces it replaced. Roughly 2.5 million Christians left Turkey, to be replaced by Muslims from Europe. Turkey is now 98 percent Muslim. Estimates of the number of Shi'ites among these vary from 5 to 40 percent, a spread caused in part by widespread ignorance of the finer points of Muslim theology.

Theoretically, Turkey was to be ruled by the sultan-caliph, who based his legitimacy on his leadership of the Islamic community. However, real power lay in the hands of Turkish army officers, chief among them Mustafa Kemal (Kemal Ataturk; 1881–1938), who had seen that Islamic ideology had failed to bind the Arabs to the empire and who attributed the country's weakness to the Islamic institutions the sultan represented. A republic was proclaimed in 1923, and the following year the caliphate was abolished. Since then, Turkey has been constitutionally secular, with the army regarding itself as the guarantor of this secularity.

During the 1920s and 1930s, Ataturk drove through a program of modernization that involved assaults on Islamic institutions and traditions. Education and the courts were taken out of religious hands; pious endowments *(waqf)* were confiscated, Sufism outlawed, religious dress permitted only within the mosque, and Western dress enforced elsewhere. The government abolished the Muslim calendar, made Sunday the day of rest, and replaced Arabic with the Latin alphabet. Women were given legal equality with men. The number of mosques was reduced and the content of sermons supervised. In all, this amounted to the greatest attack on Islam anywhere outside the Soviet Union.

The Ortakoy Mosque with its towering minarets in Istanbul, Turkey. (MICHAEL NICHOLSON/CORBIS)

## PILGRIMAGE AND LOCAL TRADITIONS

All Muslims adhere to the basic beliefs and practices of Islam but in many places Muslims also worship personages of regional or local significance. The Kurds of West Asia are one people who follow this practice as described in the following extract.

> The typical indication of a shrine is either a low, quadrilateral, rubble wall about the grave or a cairn of stones. Those who visit the shrine with some purpose characteristically tie a piece of white rag on the end of a pole and lean the pole against the inner surface of the wall. Some shrines have bundles of these crude banners standing in them. The meaning of the rag is variable. In some cases the visitor will return and reclaim it, incorporating it in a charm, while in others it is simply the sign of a vow that the suppliant, if the shaykh buried there will bring about the desired favor, will sacrifice so many animals or give so much money to the poor. The most auspicious days, it might be noted, to visit a shrine are Wednesdays and Thursdays. The six most noted shrines near the town of Rowanduz are as follows:
>
> 1. Shaykh Piri Mawili near the village of Kani Kah. Shaykh Piri Mawili is said to have lived about two hundred years ago, "in the time of Kor Pasha."
>
> 2. Shaykh Sa'idi Galikarak near the village of Karak. The shrine is said to be very old, dating perhaps from the time of the Islamic conquest.
>
> 3. Shaykh Saran in the village of Saran itself. Shaykh Saran is said to have died about fifty years ago.
>
> 4. Shaykh Usu Shaykhan on the road to Kawlok. No one knows how old it is, but it is very ancient.
>
> 5. Shaykh Muhammad or Shaykh Balik, the second most famous shrine in the district, at Haiji Umran.
>
> 6. Shuwani Shaykh Muhammad or Shuwani Mala, The Shepherd of Shaykh Muhammad.
>
> *Source:* William M. Masters. (1953) "Rowanduz: A Kurdish Administrative and Mercantile Center." Ph.D. dissertation, University of Michigan, Ann Arbor, Michigan, 313.

In 1925, the Naqshbandi Sufis (an order of Sufis, or Islamic mystics) led a revolt among the Kurds, a non-Turkish ethnic group present in large numbers in eastern Turkey, but the revolt was ruthlessly suppressed.

Turkey's constitution banned religious parties, but from the 1960s there began to be calls for greater recognition of religion in public life. Religious parties have appeared by disguising their religious nature. Such parties, with messages of social justice and respect for traditional culture, have particularly appealed to recent migrants to urban areas, but they are led and often supported by the urban middle class. In part, the rise of these parties has been fed by resentment at the European Union's seeming preference for the membership claims of Christian countries over Turkey's

The leader of the Islamic Revolution in Iran, Ayatollah Khomeini, greets followers in Tehran in February 1979. (BETTMANN/CORBIS)

long-standing application. Recently the issue of whether female university students may wear Islamic head scarves has aroused political controversy. In addition, Sufi groups have reorganized in several cities.

### Iraq

As part of the Ottoman empire, Iraq experienced the modernizing trends of the Tanzimat reform. Arab nationalism, although not strong, was felt here, and neither the British nor the Turks who fought over the area in World War I could count on the support of the local population. At the time of Iraq's establishment by the British in 1921, the population was approximately 90 percent Muslim, with small Christian and Jewish communities. Roughly one-third of Iraqi Christians fled to Syria in 1933 following persecution.

Although the ratio of Shi'ites to Sunnis has been approximately 7 to 5 in Iraq, Sunnis have been politically dominant both under the British protectorate (until 1927) and subsequently. This has been particularly the case since a 1968 coup brought the Ba'ath Party to power.

For much of modern Iraqi history, the state has gradually taken over services traditionally provided by religious organizations (education, welfare, justice), although Islam has never faced the outright assault it did in Turkey.

The dominance of Sunni Arabs has left Shi'ites and Kurds relatively disadvantaged. Whereas among the Kurds political discontent is expressed through nationalism, in the Arab south this is expressed via the medium of Shi'ism. This situation is heightened by the presence of the Shi'i holy cities of An Najaf and Karbala on Iraqi territory. Ironically, Iraq has given shelter to Shi'ite leaders such as the Ayatollah Khomeini (1900–1989), who opposed the government of Iran, while suppressing outspoken leaders of its own Shi'ite community.

Antistate revolts articulated via Shi'ism have periodically broken out, notably in 1979 and after the expulsion of Iraqi troops from Kuwait in 1991. The regime's response has been both the suppression of Shi'ism and an increased Sunni religiosity on the part of political leaders.

### Iran

In 1920, Iran was 95 percent Shi'i, with small Baha'i, Christian, Jewish, and Zoroastrian communities. Traditionally, Shi'ism had kept politics at arm's length, but Iranian religious leaders began to become politically involved toward the end of the nineteenth century, their anger directed particularly against concessions granted by the Qajar shahs to Western economic interests (especially tobacco). Whereas in Turkey the constitutional movement was secular and nationalist, in Iran opposition to the power of the ruler came from the clergy, which was closely allied with the class of small shopkeepers most economically threatened.

A declining Islamic empire was taken over by a military strong man, Reza Pahlavi (1878–1944), in 1921. Fearful of a repetition of events in Turkey, the clergy opposed the creation of a republic, and Reza was proclaimed shah. However, he rapidly introduced secularizing policies similar to those of Ataturk. His son Mohammed Reza (1919–1980), who was placed on the throne by British and American interests after a short-lived socialist experiment, continued these policies in his so-called White Revolution of 1963.

One upshot of the fall of the leftist government in 1953 was that left-wing political parties were ruthlessly suppressed. Religion was now the only means of articulating political dissent, and during the 1960s two developments radically altered Shiʿi political thought. ʿAli Shariʿati (1933–1997), the philosopher whose thought most influenced Iran's Islamic revolution, created a synthesis of Marxist sociology and Shiʿi theology that for the first time provided religious justification for revolution, while the minor cleric Ruholla Khomeini, from his exile in An Najaf, Iraq, elaborated a theory of the ideal Shiʿite state.

As the shah's rule became increasingly oppressive, the urban middle class became attracted to Shariʿati's ideas. Migrants to the cities identified with Khomeini's formulation of a genuinely Shiʿite, just state untainted by foreign influences, although many senior clerics strongly disagreed with his formulation. The 1979 revolutionary slogan—Neither East nor West but Islam—expressed the anticolonial sentiment of the people, the desire for a genuinely Iranian political order, and frustration with the iniquities of the shah's regime. Popular dissatisfaction was expressed particularly toward the United States.

Since the establishment of the Islamic Republic of Iran in 1979, Iran has formally been a participatory constitutional democracy. However, Khomeini's insistence that legislation be vetted by a religious council has created tensions within the state, as power is split between the presidency and the Council of (Religious) Experts. The limits of Khomeini's conception have become increasingly clear.

### Present-Day Problems

In recent years, West Asian Muslims have faced similar pressures but have responded to them in a variety of ways. In Iran, Islam has become a substitute for nationalism and socialism. In Turkey, the government has, with limited success, presented nationalism as a substitute for Islam. In Iraq, where both Kurdish nationalism and Shiʿi Islam could threaten the governing class, a variant of Islamic socialism has held sway since 1968. All these countries feel the twin pressures of modernization and urbanization. Whereas a small group in each country is happy with the social changes, for most the experience has been deeply unsettling. They have therefore sought support from a form of their traditional culture and have sought to expand that culture into the alien secular environment, which in all cases was imposed from above by the state.

*Will Myer*

### Further Reading

Enayat, H. (1982) *Modern Islamic Political Thought*. London: Macmillan.

Esposito, J. (1991) *Islam and Politics*. Syracuse, NY: Syracuse University Press.

Momen, M. (1985) *An Introduction to Shiʿi Islam*. New Haven, CT: Yale University Press.

Owen, R. (1992) *State, Power, and Politics in the Making of the Modern Middle East*. London and New York: Routledge.

**ISLAM, KAZI NAZRUL** (1899–1976), Bengali poet and playwright. Kazi Nazrul Islam, known as the *bidrohi kobi* (rebel poet), was both a poet and a playwright who was deeply influenced by leftist ideology and who championed the working class. Many Bengalis consider Nazrul Islam a "nonconformist" who despite not having a formal education and not having traveled outside India acquired a worldly outlook. He took the Bengali literary world by storm with his poem *Bidrohi* (The Rebel). That poem, along with his many other patriotic poems and songs, inspired Bengalis during their struggle against the British and during the Bangladeshi war of liberation in 1971.

Nazrul Islam was born to an impoverished family in West Bengal, India. He lost his father at an early age and to support his family started working as a domestic servant and later as a baker's assistant. In 1917, at the age of eighteen, Nazrul quit high school and joined the Forty-Ninth Bengali Regiment. After the regiment was disbanded in 1919, Nazrul went to Calcutta to pursue his writing career.

Nazrul Islam is regarded as the greatest Bengali poetic force after the Nobel laureate poet Rabindranath Tagore. His chief works include *Agnibeena*, *Shonchita*, *Dolon Champa*, and *Chayanot*. Although Nazrul's life as a poet lasted a little over twenty years, he wrote three thousand songs, twenty-one books of verses, fourteen books of songs, six novels and collections of stories, four books of essays, three plays, four books of poems and plays for children, and three books of translations of Persian poetry and Qurʾanic verses. Many of his works remain uncollected in out-of-print journals and periodicals.

Tragically, Nazrul's literary career was cut short in July 1942 when he suffered a stroke and lost his speech. Within weeks his condition deteriorated further, and he lost contact with reality. He lived for another thirty-five years and died in Dhaka, Bangladesh.

*Mehrin Masud-Elias*

**ISLAMABAD** (1998 pop. 529,000). Soon after Pakistan achieved independence in 1947, the idea of the national capital of Islamabad was conceived by President Ayub Khan (1907–1974). Karachi had been contemplated as the capital because it was Pakistan's

The Parliament compound in Islamabad, which was closed off and guarded by soldiers during days of political instability in October 1999. (REUTERS NEWMEDIA INC./CORBIS)

commercial center, but it was not considered an appropriate administrative center. Therefore, the decision was to construct a new city at the eastern part of the Margalla Hills, which are located at the base of the Himalayas in northern Punjab region.

Islamabad, which officially became the capital of Pakistan in 1959, was designed to maximize its relationship with nature, thus adding to its natural beauty. Many streams flow through the landscape, over 6 million trees have been planted since Islamabad's inception, and, more recently, several lakes, such as Simly, Khanpur, and Rawal, have been added to the terrain.

*Houman A. Sadri*

### Further Reading

Adams, Francis, Satya Dev Gupta, and Kidane Mengisteab, eds. (1999) *Globalization and the Dilemmas of the State in the South.* New York: St. Martin's Press.

Cleveland, William L. (1994) *A History of the Modern Middle East.* Boulder, CO: Westview Press.

Cole, Juan R. I., ed. (1992) *Comparing Muslim Societies: Knowledge and the State in a World Civilization.* Ann Arbor, MI: University of Michigan Press.

Norton, Augustus Richard, ed. (1996) *Civil Society in the Middle East.* Leiden, Netherlands: Brill.

**ISLAMIC BANKING** Islamic banking refers to a modern banking system practiced in the Muslim world from about 1975, which pays no interest on deposits. Although the Qur'an condemns the taking of interest (*riba* in Arabic) on the grounds that it is exploitative and unjust, not all Muslim countries have instituted interest-free banking.

Today about 170 Islamic financial institutions worldwide, controlling over $150 billion in funds, follow this procedure, particularly in Saudi Arabia and the Gulf States; Iran and Sudan have recently implemented this system. Pakistan was scheduled to adopt it in 2001; in Turkey only a small minority of banks operate in this manner (3 percent of deposits nationally). In Kuwait, Morocco, and Malaysia, where Islamic banking is popular, depositors and borrowers can choose which sort of bank to patronize. Conventional banks such as Citibank also offer "Islamic services."

In countries with interest-paying and interest-free banks, Islamic banks can and do compete. Instead of paying interest on deposits and charging it on loans,

## HAWALA (TRANSFERRING DEBT)

Hawala is a form of Islamic debt exchange that is used to move money around the world cheaply without attracting government notice. The system gained worldwide attention in 2001, because Hawala was thought to be one of the ways in which the terrorist attacks of 11 September were financed.

A person wishing to transfer money gives it to a Hawala broker, and the two agree on a password. The Hawala broker then contacts a Hawala agent in the recipient's country, who gives the amount of money to whoever gives him the password. No real money is transferred between the Hawala agents, who receive a small fee paid at each end. Below is one of the Islamic rules that govern Hawala.

> If a debtor directs his creditor to collect his debt from the third person, and the creditor accepts the arrangement, the third person will, on completion of all the conditions to be explained later, become the debtor. Thereafter, the creditor cannot demand his debt from the first debtor.

*Source:* Middle East and Islamic Studies Collection, Cornell University. Retrieved 28 March 2002, from: http://www.library.cornell.edu/colldev/mideast/hawdrft.htm.

these banks seek profit- and loss-sharing arrangements with depositors and borrowers. One procedure is the *mudarabah* contract, which allows depositors to share the bank's profits rather than receive interest. Perhaps because of the frequent unfeasibility of this contractual procedure, Islamic banks make much more income from *murabaha*, a contract similar to an interest-bearing loan. A bank will, for example, buy a printing press from a client for $20,000, but leaves it on the client's premises. The client then buys it back later for $22,000, according to contract. The bank thus makes $2,000 on the transaction, and the client has his printing press.

*Paul Hockings*

**Further Reading**

Lewis, Mervyn, and Latifa M. Algaoud. (2001) *Islamic Banking*. Northampton, MA: Edward Elgar.

**ISLAMIC RENAISSANCE PARTY—TAJIKISTAN** Despite being proscribed by the government, the Islamic Renaissance Party (IRP) was formed in the Tajik Soviet Socialist Republic just before the dissolution of the Soviet Union. The IRP emerged as an important force for democracy in 1990 and was legalized soon after Tajikistan proclaimed its independence in September 1991.

The IRP soon came into conflict with Tajikistan's ruling Communist Party, and violence erupted. After the party was banned in 1993 for attempting to establish an Islamic state in Tajikistan, the leadership fled to Iran and Afghanistan and led the formation of the United Tajikistan Opposition (UTO). Until 1996 the UTO fought against the Tajik government in a war that cost tens of thousands of lives. A peace agreement was signed in March 1997, and the IRP and other parties of the UTO returned to Tajikistan. Despite an attempt to ban religious political parties, the IRP was registered as a political party in September 1999 and unsuccessfully ran a candidate in the country's presidential elections that November. The IRP went on to win two seats in the lower house of Tajikistan's parliament in March 2000. The IRP's platform is the revival of Islamic spiritual values in politics and society.

*Andrew Sharp*

**ISLAMIC REVOLUTION—IRAN** The Islamic Revolution in Iran began simmering during the Pahlavi dynasty (1925–1979) and boiled over in 1979. It represented the discontent of both the middle class and the lower class regarding the nation's rapid shift to secularism, its economic hardships, and the perception that foreign interests were controlling Iran.

Islam has strong roots in Iran, being introduced as a result of the Arab conquest in the seventh century. When the Islamic empire fell some two hundred years later, Islam was firmly entrenched within the communities of believers, which broke up into warring clans and dynasties. When the Safavid empire (1501–1722/1736) came to power in Persia (as Iran was known until 1935), it established Shiʿa Islam (one of the sects of Islam) as the state religion while the government operated under the auspices of a monarchy. The Safavid empire came to an end with several tribes vying for power. Ultimately, the Qajars won, beginning a dynasty that would last from 1794 to 1925.

In the beginning, the Qajar dynasty respected many of the wishes of the Islamic clerics, and the clerics were able to exercise influence in government affairs. At the same time, the Qajars worked to reaffirm the concept of the shah (king) being connected to God in order to legitimize their standing and position. However, during the reign of the third Qajar monarch, changes began that undermined the authority of the clerics. Many of these changes were at least partially due to the increased pressure and influence of Britain and Russia in Iranian affairs. In the late nineteenth century, the Qajars gradually started to adopt European methods of government in an effort to strengthen their system. Inadequate funds to run the government, however, resulted in the Qajars selling economic concessions to the British and Russians. The religious community strongly voiced its opposition to this by encouraging, in one instance, a boycott of tobacco when Britain was given a tobacco monopoly. In another instance, a cleric encouraged one of his disciples to assassinate the shah.

The economic troubles and foreign manipulations led the populace to question royal authority. This resulted in the Constitutional Revolution (1906), in which proponents demanded a constitution that would limit royal powers and institute the Majlis (Parliament). Although Muzaffar al-Din Shah, the fourth Qajar monarch, signed the constitution into law, he died soon after, and his successor fought its implementation.

Britain and Russia continued to meddle in Iranian affairs; they divided the nation into spheres of influence in 1907. With the advent of World War I, Iran found itself unable to prevent the war's being played out on Iranian soil as Russian, Turkish, and British troops fought one another on Iranian territory. Soon, Russia was dealing with pressures from its own revolution. Britain seized the opportunity to increase its

A young Iranian woman carries a photo of the late Ayatollah Khomeini at the 11 February 2000 celebration of the 1979 Islamic Revolution. (REUTERS NEWMEDIA INC./CORBIS)

influence and backed the ascension to power of Reza Khan (1878–1944). Reza Khan eventually had himself crowned shah (becoming Reza Shah Pahavi), founding the Pahlavi dynasty.

### Reza Shah Targets Clerics

Reza Shah's policies were designed to decrease the clerics' power. He organized a secular school system and borrowed Western ideas and technology to modernize Iran's cities and institutions. In addition, he established laws that excluded clerics from the justice system, and he monitored the administration of licenses to seminaries. Finally, he required the populace to wear European-style clothes and opened education and the workforce to women.

Initially, such reforms were welcomed because they were seen as improving the economic conditions of the nation. However, Reza Shah's repressive policies soon caused public approval to wane. He did not tolerate opposition; he jailed opponents and religious leaders or sent them into exile, censored the press, and executed bureaucrats and tribal leaders.

When World War II started, outside events again intruded on Iran. Iran's declaration of neutrality was unacceptable to the British and Russians, who invaded Iran. This resulted in the transfer of power from Reza Shah to his son, Mohammad Reza Shah Pahlavi (1918–1980). However, it took a while before the shah (as Mohammad Reza Shah Pahlavi was known) was in control of the nation, mainly because of the presence of foreign troops, who were also not appreciated by the masses. Premier Mohammad Mosaddeq (1880–1967) spearheaded a nationalist movement that compelled the shah to nationalize the oil companies. Eventually, popular opposition to the shah and support of Mosaddeq led to the former's exile and the latter being left in control of the country. The shah was able to return only with the support of the United States—a fact that was not forgotten by the Iranian masses.

The shah launched several ambitious five-year economic plans that were funded by oil revenues. He was equally ambitious in containing opposition. This led to several confrontations with Ayatollah Ruhollah Khomeini (1900–1989), a conservative cleric and harsh critic of the government.

In 1963, the shah arrested Khomeini after Khomeini criticized the shah and his policies. His arrest sparked riots, which the shah tried violently to suppress, resulting in many deaths. Soon, the shah was pressured by clerics to release the ayatollah, who continued to criticize the shah. Eventually, the shah exiled him; the ayatollah took refuge in Iraq and then France. In exile, the ayatollah mobilized opposition groups to organize and concentrate their criticism of the Shah. The ayatollah also further developed his concept of *veleyet-e-faqih* (rule of religious jurisprudence). This concept was significant because it would form the theoretical backbone of the new regime in Iran after the Islamic Revolution.

A booming economy and repressive social controls helped the shah maintain control. When the economy eventually declined as a result of the shah's overly ambitious programs, the country suffered runaway inflation. The result was increased opportunity for corruption and a growing gap between the rich and poor. The shah tried to correct the situation with new programs, but his efforts were seen as catering to the West and subverting Islamic values. The shah also was pressured to restrict his repressive tactics in order to placate international concern over human-rights violations.

### The Revolution Arrives

Iran was now ripe for revolution, as a middle-class protest movement seeking restoration of constitutional rule swept the nation. As the movement expanded its social base, it soon proclaimed Ayatollah Khomeini its leader and an Islamic state the ideal government. In November 1978, the shah tried to hold out the olive branch by arresting several of his officers involved in repression and by releasing several political prisoners. However, it was too little, too late, and the strikes started by the opposition continued. The shah opened a dialogue with the protest movement and agreed to appoint Shapour Bakhtiar (a National Front leader) as prime minister. Bakhtiar consented to the appointment only after the shah agreed to leave the country.

The new prime minister was unable to curb the revolutionary movement, as Khomeini had already declared that nothing less than a new political system was acceptable. Despite Bakhtiar's attempts to keep him out, Khomeini returned to Iran in early 1979. Immediately, he proclaimed the government illegal and set up a provisional government with Mehdi Bazargan as its prime minister. The main task of the provisional government was to produce a constitution. After the referendum result was announced, on 1 April 1979, Khomeini declared Iran to be the Islamic Republic of Iran. His concept of *veleyet-e-faqih* had become a political reality.

*Houman A. Sadri*

*See also:* **Khomeini, Ayatollah**

### Further Reading

Arjomand, Said. (1988) *The Turban for the Crown: The Islamic Revolution in Iran*. New York: Oxford University Press.
Kazemi, Farhad. (1980) *Poverty & Revolution in Iran*. New York: New York University Press.
Keddie, Nikki. (1981) *Roots of Revolution: An Interpretive History of Modern Iran*. New Haven, CT: Yale University Press.
Khomeini, Ruhollah. (1981) *Islam and Revolution*. Trans. by Hamid Algar. Berkeley, CA: Mizan Press.
Mottahedeh, Roy. (1985) *The Mantle of the Prophet: Religion and Politics in Iran*. New York: Pantheon Books.

## ISMAILI SECTS—CENTRAL ASIA

The Ismaili sect of Shiʿa Islam (Shiʿa Islam itself being the minority current of Islam, accounting for only some 10 percent of the world's Muslim population) separated from the mainstream of Shiʿa Islam in 765, when a minority of Shiʿites accepted Ismail, the son of the sixth Shiʿite imam, as the seventh and final imam. The Ismaili sect entered Central Asia around 1000 CE.

### Ismaili Areas in Central Asia

The Ismailis of Central Asia reside mainly in the ethnolinguistic area of the Pamir and eastern Hindu Kush Mountains, including the Pamirs in present-day Tajikistan, Afghanistan, and China, Dardistan Province in Pakistan, and Nuristan Province in Afghanistan. On the fringes of this area, the Ismailis are scattered in some places in Hazarajat in central Afghanistan and in isolated pockets in the Afghan provinces of Kunar and Lagman, as well as in some small communities in Herat and among the Turkmen of Balkh. Ismaili migrants also live in Kabul, Afghanistan, and Dushanbe, Tajikistan. The center of the Afghan Ismailis is the town of Pul-i Khumri (central Afghanistan), where they dominate local economic and political life.

It is difficult to provide exact up-to-date demographic data on the Ismailis of the Tajik Pamirs, but various records indicate that in the early 1990s the population of the region reached approximately 250,000. The number of Afghan Ismailis is estimated at anywhere between 100,000 and 500,000 people, and several thousand Ismailis live in the Chinese Pamirs.

The bulk of the Pamiri and Hazara Ismailis are village dwellers, dependent for their livelihood on irrigated and usually terraced fields in the valley bottoms. Those living in Afghan cities are often engaged in commerce or in the service sector. The Tajik Ismailis have the highest ratio of high school and university graduates in all of post-Soviet Central Asia.

### Ethnolinguistic Composition

The great majority of the several groups who live in the Pamirs speak different East Iranian languages. None of these is fixed in writing, and the language of culture and civilization is Tajiki (Persian). Before the late nineteenth century, the knowledge of Tajiki was confined almost exclusively to literate religious leaders.

The Ismailis of Badakhshan Province in Afghanistan refer to themselves as *panjtani* (followers of the five people of the *ahl al-bayt*, or the Prophet Muhammad's family). The Hazara Ismailis of Afghanistan are known as *qayani* after the father of the current head of the Afghan Ismaili community, al-Hajj Sayyid Mansur Nadiri, Nasir-Shah Qayani. The religious beliefs of the Hazara Ismailis shape their ethnic identity: They consider themselves a distinct ethnic group within the Hazara people, who are predominantly Twelver Shiʿites (Shiʿites who accept the twelve imams, rather than the seven of the Ismaili sect) of mixed Turkic-Mongolian and Iranian origin.

### Religious History

Nasir-i Khusrav (1003/1004–1072/1077) was the first Ismaili propagandist associated with the spread of Ismailism in the Pamirs; he was an important Persian writer sent on his mission to the eastern part of the Islamic world by the Fatimid (an Arab dynasty ruling in Egypt) caliph al-Mustansir (1029–1094). Khusrav is believed to have contributed significantly to the initial Islamization of the Pamirs. It is reported, however, that even three hundred years after his death the Ismaili propagandists from Khorasan in northeast Iran still encountered fire-worshipers in the Pamirs.

Due to its isolation, which lasted until the end of the nineteenth century, the Pamiri Ismaili community preserved a number of unique Ismaili manuscripts and developed religious practices specific to their cultural and geographical identity.

Pamiri Ismailis maintained more or less regular contacts with the Ismaili imam (the Aga Khan), whose seat is in India, only during the forty-year period from the mid-1890s to 1936. The mid-1890s marked the arrival of Russian troops in the Pamirs, which brought the end of Ismaili persecution at the hands of Afghans and Bukharans. In 1936, the Soviet-Afghan border was firmly sealed, which again isolated these Ismailis.

During the 1990s, a number of programs were developed by the Aga Khan Development Network, in collaboration with the government of Tajikistan and other international agencies, to promote social and economic development in the region. The current imam, Aga Khan IV (b. 1937), paid two visits to the area in 1995 and 1998, and there is now a growing awareness of and contact with the international Ismaili community and its institutions.

## Beliefs and Religious Practices

Apart from maintaining the general Ismaili tradition, the Pamiris developed their own practice of deeply venerating Nasir-i Khusrav. According to the 1944 proclamation issued by the Tajik Pamiri Ismaili authorities, the Ismailis based their understanding of religion on the *Vajh-i din*, one of Nasir-i Khusrav's treatises, which is sometimes ascribed by the Pamiri Ismailis to the teaching of al-Mustansir himself. This book is esteemed as a *maghz-i Qur'an* (kernel of the Qur'an), in which the esoteric aspects of the Holy Book are explained.

When Pamiri Ismailis describe their faith, certain points keep recurring, namely, the doctrine of the outer *(zahir)* and the inner *(batin)* meaning of life and, in particular, of religion, which is of utmost importance. Thus, one should strive for pure sincerity and reject what is done solely for outward appearance. Therefore, righteousness and abstinence from evil thoughts and acts are more important than the ostentatious manifestations of religiosity.

Ismailis strive to attain perfection whatever their tasks in life might be, for this path leads to the cognition of God and unity with him. Participation in religious ceremonies, as well as recitation of and listening to devotional religious poetry, is considered to be an educational activity helping a human being to reach his or her real origin—God. However, humans are not the only creatures traveling along this path. Although only humans possess reason *('aql)*, the faculty that puts them closer to God than all other beings, humans and nonhumans alike strive to get closer to their creator. However, if the lower soul *(nafs)* overwhelms a human being, he or she loses the privilege of possessing the faculty of *'aql*, or intellect, and his or her soul regresses to a lower, nonhuman state. The Pamiris have preserved pre-Islamic traditions, with a complicated system of cosmology linked to the Indo-European substratum, commonly occurring in other Iranian cultures as well.

## Community Organization

The Pamiri Ismailis believe that Ismailism is the most progressive and tolerant creed in the world because it is constantly adapting itself to the needs and requirements of the time through the mediation of the current imam, who guides his followers according to the prevailing circumstances.

In daily life, community religious authorities, or *pirs* (elders, masters), and their *khalifahs* (deputies) act as agents of the imam: they give believers guidance in matters of religion and accompany people in the events of life, especially during the rites of passage. They also give general moral guidance and counsel and are sometimes believed to have healing power. In their functions, they make use of the Qur'an and the *Vajh-i din*. Every Ismaili seeks to learn from a *pir*, or, if he is inaccessible, from his deputy. Usually this relationship is passed on to succeeding generations wherever they may live.

Since the mid-1950s, due to the pressure of the Soviet authorities in the Tajik Pamirs, *khalifahs* were elected by the people of a big village or a number of small neighboring villages. Before that, the position of *khalifah* tended to be hereditary. The *pirs* were always hereditary, but from the 1890s, the period that contacts between the community and the Aga Khan were reestablished, the *pirs'* succession had to be confirmed by the Aga Khan. The *pirs* left the Tajik Pamirs for Afghanistan in the 1930s for political reasons and due to the hostile climate of Soviet antireligious politics, and then the *khalifahs* became the main spiritual authorities in the area. In Afghanistan, the traditional hierarchy and system of *pirs* and *khalifahs* are still in place.

*Sergei Andreyev*

## Further Reading

Kreutzmann, Hermann. (1996) *Ethnizität im Entwicklungsprozeß: Die Wakhi in Hochasien.* Berlin: Dietrich Reimer Verlag.

Roy, Olivier. (1985) *Islam et modernité politique.* Paris: Éditions du Seuil.

Van den Berg, Gabrielle. (1997) "Minstrel Poetry from the Pamir Mountains: A Study of the Songs and Poems of the Ismailis of Tajik Badakhshan." Ph.D. diss. Leiden University.

**ISMAILI SECTS—SOUTH ASIA** An important Shiʿite Muslim community, the Ismailis arose in 765 from a disagreement over the successor to the sixth imam, Jaʿfar al. The Ismailis chose Ismaʿil and then traced the imamate through Ismaʿil's son Muhammad and the latter's progeny. The bulk of other Shiʿites, however, eventually recognized twelve imams, descendants of Ismaʿil's brother Musa al-Kazim. The two main Ismaili branches are the Musta'lis (Bohras) and the Nizaris (Khojas), both in India. The Nizaris, led by the Aga Khan, also have populations in Pakistan, Iran, Central Asia, East Africa, Europe, and North America.

By the middle of the ninth century the religiopolitical message of the Ismaili *daʿwa* (mission) aiming to win recognition for the Ismaili imam as the rightful interpreter of the Islamic revelation was disseminated in many regions by a network of *daʾi*s (missionaries). The earliest Ismaili missionaries arrived in Sind (in today's Pakistan) in 883, initiating Ismaili activities in South Asia.

By 909 the Ismailis had succeeded in installing their imam in the new Fatimid caliphate, in rivalry with the Abbasid caliphate (750–1258) established by Sunni Muslims. Around 958 an Ismaili principality was established in Sind, with its seat at Multan, where large numbers of Hindus converted to Ismailism. Ismaili rule ended in Sind in 1005, but Ismailism survived in Sind and received the protection of the ruling Sumra dynasty. The Sulayhids of Yemen, who acknowledged the suzerainty of the Ismaili Fatimid caliph-imams, played a crucial role in the renewed efforts of the Fatimids to spread the Ismaili cause in South Asia. In 1067 missionaries sent from Yemen founded a new Ismaili community in Gujarat in western India. The mission maintained close ties with Yemen, and this new Ismaili community evolved into the present Bohra community.

In 1094 the Ismaili community became divided over who would become the nineteenth imam; the two branches resulted from this division, each of which developed its own religious and literary traditions.

### Musta'li Ismailis (Bohras)

The Musta'li Ismailis founded their stronghold in Yemen, where in the absence of the imams the *daʾi*s acted as executive heads of the *daʿwa* organization and as community spiritual leaders. They were designated as *daʾi mutlaq* (*daʾi* with absolute authority).

The Musta'li *daʿwa* in South Asia remained under the strict supervision of the *daʾi* and the *daʿwa* headquarters in Yemen until the second half of the sixteenth century. In South Asia the Musta'li Ismaili *daʿwa* originally spread among the urban artisans and traders of Gujarat; the Hindu converts became known as Bohras.

Many were converted in Cambay, Patan, Sidhpur, and later in Ahmadabad, where the Indian headquarters of the Musta'li *daʿwa* were established. Early in the sixteenth century the headship of the Musta'li Ismailis passed to an Indian from Sidhpur, and later the headquarters of this Ismaili community were transferred permanently from Yemen to Ahmadabad, where the *daʾi*s could generally count on the religious tolerance of the Mughal emperors. By then the Ismaili Bohras of South Asia greatly outnumbered their coreligionists in Yemen.

In 1589 a succession dispute over the position of the *daʾi mutlaq* split the Musta'li Ismailis into the rival Daudi and Sulaymani branches, each of which followed a separate line of *daʾi*s. Subsequently the Daudi Bohras were further subdivided in India as a result of periodic challenges to the authority of their *daʾi mutlaq*. In 1624 a third Bohra splinter group appeared under the name of Aliyya, a small community of 8,000 still centered in Baroda. In 1785 the headquarters of the *daʿwa* organization of the Daudi Bohras were transferred to Surat, still a center of traditional Islamic and Ismaili learning for the Daudi Bohras.

The Bohras, like other Shiʿite Muslims, were periodically persecuted in South Asia, and many converted to Sunni Islam, the religion of the Muslim rulers of Gujarat and elsewhere. However, with the consolidation of British rule in India in the early nineteenth century, South Asian Ismailis were no longer subjected to official persecution. The total Daudi Bohra population of the world is currently estimated at around 700,000 persons, more than half of whom live in Gujarat. Since the 1920s Bombay has served as the permanent seat of the *daʾi mutlaq* of the Daudi Bohras and the central administration of his *daʿwa* organization.

The Sulaymani Ismailis, numbering around 60,000, are concentrated in northern Yemen, with only a few thousand Sulaymani Bohras living in South Asia, mainly in Mumbai (Bombay).

### Nizari Ismailis (Khojas)

In the late eleventh century, the Nizari Ismailis founded and organized a state with a network of mountain strongholds in Iran and Syria, which the Mongols destroyed in 1256. In the thirteenth century or a little earlier, the Nizari Ismaili *daʿwa* was introduced into the Indian subcontinent. The earliest Nizari *daʾi*s operating in South Asia apparently concentrated their efforts in Sind (modern-day Punjab in Pakistan), where Ismailism had persisted clandestinely since Fatimid times. Nizari *da'is* were referred to as *pirs* in South Asia. Pir Shams al-Din is the earliest figure associated with the commencement of Nizari Ismaili activities in Sind. The Nizari *da'wa* continued to be preached secretly in Sind by descendants of Shams. By the time of Pir Sadr al-Din, a great-grandson of Pir Shams, Nizari missionaries had established their own hereditary dynasty of *pirs* in South Asia with sporadic contacts with the Nizari imams who continued to reside in Iran.

Pir Sadr al-Din consolidated and organized Nizari activities in South Asia and strengthened the Nizari Ismaili, or Khoja, community in the Indian subcontinent. His shrine is located near Ucch, south of Multan. Sadr al-Din converted many Hindus from the Lohana trading caste and gave them the title of Khoja. The specific Nizari Ismaili tradition that developed in India is sometimes referred to by the vernacular translation of the Qur'anic term *sirat al-mustaqim*, rendered as Satpanth *(sat panth)* or the "true way."

Pir Sadr al-Din was succeeded by his son Hasan Kabir al-Din, who eventually settled in Ucch, which served as the seat of Nizari Ismailism in South Asia. Pir Hasan was reportedly affiliated with the Suhrawardi Sufi order, at the time prevalent in western and northern India. Multan and Ucch in Sind, where Ismailism had become established, were also the headquarters of the Suhrawardi and Qadiri Sufi orders. In the next two or three centuries Ismailism, in its Nizari form, reemerged in the subcontinent, in forms and ideas having much in common with Sufism. The nature of this relationship is not clear, but recent research suggests that the Ismailis along with the Sufis spearheaded the spread of Islam in rural areas of India. The Ismaili heritage and contribution to Islam in South Asia are best reflected in their literary traditions, preserved and developed over centuries and aptly called *ginan*, from the Sanskrit *jnan*, meaning reflective or contemplative knowledge.

After the death of Pir Hasan Kabir al-Din a section of the community seceded and established itself in Gujarat, becoming known as Imam Shahis. The majority continued to adhere to the authority of the Nizari imams.

***Ginans and Their Historical Context*** With scholars' growing realization that oral and so-called popular expressions of Muslim devotion and spirituality constitute a vital component of Islamic life and practice, there is increasing interest in the texts that preserve, in local languages, the devotional spirit of Muslim mysticism in the Indian subcontinent. In the South Asian context such texts represent part of the processes of conversion, negotiation, and transmission of established traditions of Muslim spirituality and ideas. The *ginans* emerged in a milieu where both oral and written traditions were well established. Because of their primary role in ritual and religious life, the performative and recitative elements of such devotional expressions were much more pronounced than was the case, for instance, for Sufi poetry.

Among the Nizari Ismailis *ginan* has come to refer to that part of their tradition whose authorship is attributed to the *pirs* who undertook conversion and preaching. It is important to distinguish the various strands making up the hagiography of the *pirs* and to isolate the elements that reflect traces of ancient tradition and form the nucleus of later narratives. These are rarely concerned with imparting objective records of the past; the true value of the *ginan* narratives lies in their dual perspective on the tradition: one level mirroring the impact and continuing influence of the earlier *pirs* on the community's collective memory, and the other revealing the community's beliefs and understanding at various stages in its history.

***Modern Period*** The forty-sixth Nizari Ismaili Imam Hasan Ali Shah (1817–1881), who received the honorific title of Aga Khan ("lord") from the monarch of Iran, Fath Ali Shah Qajar, emigrated from Iran to India in the 1840s and eventually settled in Bombay; he was the first Nizari Ismaili imam to live in India. Aga Khan I established elaborate headquarters and residences in Bombay, Poona, and Bangalore. As the spiritual head of a Muslim community, like other communities in British India, Aga Khan I was accorded recognition of his role in the legal framework of the empire. Aga Khan I tried to strengthen the religious identity of his followers. His successors to the Nizari Ismaili imamate adopted modernization policies and introduced new administrative and institutional frameworks for guiding the affairs of their Khoja and other Nizari followers. Sultan Muhammad Shah, Aga Khan III, the forty-eighth imam, led the Nizari Ismailis for seventy-two years (1885–1957), longer than any of his predecessors. He became well known as a Muslim reformer and statesman owing to his prominent role in Indo-Muslim and international affairs, as well as a wealthy sportsman and breeder of racehorses.

The Nizari Khojas, along with Bohras, were among the earliest Asian communities to settle in East Africa. Many from the Nizari Khoja communities of East Africa, India, and Pakistan have emigrated to Europe and North America since the 1970s. The Khojas today represent an integral part of the Nizari communities scattered in more than twenty-five countries.

They currently recognize Prince Karim Aga Khan IV as their forty-ninth imam. The present Nizari imam continued and substantially expanded the modernization policies of his grandfather and predecessor and developed new programs and institutions, including the prestigious Aga Khan award for architecture. Under the leadership of their recent imams, the South Asian and other Nizari Ismailis, numbering several millions, have entered the twenty-first century as a prosperous and progressive community with a distinct identity and a variety of regional traditions.

*A. Nanji and Farhad Daftary*

### Further Reading


Abdul Husain, Mian Bhai Mulla. (1920) *Gulzare Daudi, for the Bohras of India*. Ahmadabad, India: Amarsinhji Press.

Ali, Syed Mujtaba. (1936) *The Origin of the Khojahs and Their Religious Life Today*. Würzburg, Germany: R. Mayr.

Asani, Ali S. (1992) "The Ismaili *Ginans* as Devotional Literature." In *Devotional Literature in South Asia*, edited by R. S. McGregor. Cambridge, U.K.: Cambridge University Press, 101–112.

Daftary, Farhad. (1990) *The Isma'ils: Their History and Doctrines*. Cambridge, U.K.: Cambridge University Press.

Hamdani, Abbas H. (1956) *The Beginnings of the Isma'il Da'wa in Northern India*. Cairo, Egypt: Sirovic Bookshop.

Kassam, Tazim R. (1995) *Songs of Wisdom and Circles of Dance: Hymns of the Satpanth Isma'li Muslim Saint, Pir Shams*. Albany, NY: State University of New York Press.

Lokhandwall, Shamoon T. (1955) "The Bohras, a Muslim Community of Gujarat." *Studia Islamica* 3: 117–135.

Nanji, Azim. (1978) *The Nizari Isma'li Tradition in the Indo-Pakistan Subcontinent*. Delmar, NY: Caravan Books.

Schimmel, Annemarie. (1975) *Mystical Dimensions of Islam*. Chapel Hill, NC: University of North Carolina Press.

Shackle, Christopher, and Zawahir Moir. (1992) *Ismaili Hymns from South Asia: An Introduction to the Ginans*. London: School of Oriental and African Studies, University of London.


**ISTANBUL** (2002 pop. 10.3 million). Istanbul (called Byzantium until 330 CE and Constantinople until 1930), is an ancient city in northwest Turkey that straddles Europe and Asia. Istanbul lies on both sides of the Bosporus, a narrow, thirty-two-kilometer-long strait that separates the European and Asian parts of the city, so that the northern city is in Europe and the southern in Asia. The city was the capital of the Byzantine and Ottoman empires and also of the Turkish Republic until 1923, when the capital was moved to Ankara. Tourists, temporary workers, and transit passengers may increase the city's population to close to 12 million. Divided into twelve districts (*kazas*), Istanbul covers 240 square kilometers, three-quarters of it in Europe.

### History

Istanbul is largely a product of the millennia-long interaction between Eastern Europe and Asia and thus represents a unique mixture of Eastern European and Oriental cultures. Founded by Greeks around 660 BCE, the ancient city became a strategically important seaport due to its position on the Bosporus, which connects the Black Sea and the Sea of Marmara. Emperor Constantine the Great (d. 337) selected it as the capital of the Byzantine empire in 324 and renamed it Konstantinou polis (Constantine's city) in 330.

Constantinople became the largest and most prosperous city in Europe, benefiting from its strategic location and a vibrant trade. However, the city's wealth and situation made it an attractive prize, and through the centuries it was often attacked. For instance, in 1204, during the Fourth Crusade (1202–1204), the Crusaders captured and sacked the city, causing enormous damage. The Byzantines retook it in 1251, and for many centuries, Constantinople was the spiritual and political center of the Eastern Orthodox Church and the Byzantine empire. At first, the city was situated entirely on the European side and was encircled by a wall. This ancient part of the city was home to numerous Orthodox churches, palaces, and public buildings, with some Byzantine monuments, such as the magnificent church of Hagia Sophia (Saint Sophia or Holy Wisdom, today a museum) surviving today.

In 1453 the Turks under the Ottoman sultan Mehmed II (1432–1481) captured Constantinople, and soon afterward the city became the Ottoman capital. One symbol of the city, Hagia Sophia, built by the emperor Justinian (483–565) in 532–562, was converted into a mosque in the fifteenth century. The Turkish sultans nevertheless patronized ethnic and

**ISTANBUL—WORLD HERITAGE SITE**

Historical areas of Istanbul were designated as UNESCO World Heritage Sites in 1985 for their immense historical value, beauty, and the threat posed by increasing environmental and population pressures on the onion-domed Hagia Sophia, Hippodrome of Constantinople, and other masterpieces.

Galata Bridge and Galata Tower at the Golden Horn in northern Istanbul, in 1996. (STEPHEN G. DONALDSON PHOTOGRAPHY)

religious minorities and ordered the preservation of the city's major Byzantine churches and the retention of the Orthodox patriarchate. When in 1509 a devastating earthquake damaged many parts of the city, the Ottomans had the city rebuilt, adding numerous public buildings, including magnificent mosques, palaces, public baths, and gardens. As the capital of the Ottoman empire, Constantinople became the cultural center of the Middle East and for the next four centuries influenced the cultural, political, and economic development of the region.

Constantinople experienced a new wave of significant changes during the nineteenth and early twentieth centuries with the Tanzimat (Reorganization), the Ottomans' attempt to catch up with the West and to modernize the country. Textiles, weapons, shipbuilding, and other industries proliferated in the city, and Constantinople was significantly enlarged to take in new areas south of the Bosporus. In 1838 the first bridge was built across the Golden Horn, an inlet of the Bosporus, which forms Istanbul's harbor. In June 1883, a railroad, the renowned Orient Express, first connected Constantinople with Paris via Vienna.

During the Crimean War (1853–1856), in which Turkey was allied with France and Britain against Russia, French and British troops had been quartered in Constantinople. Yet close relations with the major great European powers did not last, and attempts to reform the country's political and economic systems met major resistance among conservative elements in Turkish society. In the early twentieth century, Turkey shifted its alliances and established close relations with Germany. The First World War left the Ottoman empire significantly weakened and unable to cope with separatist movements in its numerous provinces, combined with pressure from the European great powers, and Turkey collapsed.

At war's end in 1918, Britain, France, and Italy occupied the city until 1923, but then evacuated under pressure from the Turkish liberation movement led by Kemal Ataturk (1881–1938). In 1923, the Turkish republican government established Ankara as the capital of the secular Turkish Republic, but Constantinople (renamed Istanbul in 1930) has remained a major industrial, financial, and cultural city of the republic and by the end of the twentieth century was the largest city in Europe.

## Economy and People

Istanbul is one of the most important commercial centers in Turkey and southeast Europe. Its deepwater seaport and international airport enable it to serve as a transportation and communication hub for all the Black Sea countries, including the Russian Federation and Ukraine. The city's manufacturing sector involves petrochemicals, cement, machinery, food and tobacco processing, textiles, garments, and various other goods. Tourism is another important sector of Istanbul's economy, providing not only direct employment for more than 100,000 people, but also hard-currency earnings for the city and country. The number of tourists visiting Turkey rose steadily throughout the 1980s and 1990s, reaching 10 million in 2000 (official estimate), though the number of arrivals sharply declined in 2001. Most tourists to Turkey chose Istanbul as an entry point or destination of choice.

During the second half of the twentieth century, Istanbul became the fastest-growing city in Europe; its population almost doubled from approximately 2.3 million in the 1950s to 5.5 million in 1985 and in 2000 (official estimate) doubled to 10.1 million, approximately 15 percent of Turkey's total population. Only about half of the people who live in modern Istanbul were born in the city; the rest moved there from other parts of Turkey in search of jobs and better living standards. Due to the rapid population growth, many shantytowns called *gecekondu* ("set down by night") appeared on the city's outskirts. In the 1990s, Istanbul became an important transit hub for immigrants from the Middle East, South Asia, and Northern Africa on their way to Europe. The majority of the population are Turks, although there is a sizable minority that includes Greeks, Jews, Armenians, and Albanians.

*Rafis Abazov*

**Further Reading**

Behar, Cem, and Alan Duben. (1998) *Istanbul Households: Marriage, Family, and Fertility, 1880–1940.* Cambridge Studies in Population, Economy, and Society in Past Time, 15. Cambridge, U.K.: Cambridge University Press.

Celik, Zeynep. (1993) *The Remaking of Istanbul: Portrait of an Ottoman City in the Nineteenth Century.* Berkeley and Los Angeles: University of California Press.

Gerstel, Sharon, Julie Lauffenburger, and Garry Vikan, eds. (2001) *A Lost Art Rediscovered: The Architectural Ceramics of Byzantium.* University Park, PA: The Pennsylvania State University Press.

Lewis, Bernard. (1989) *Istanbul and the Civilization of the Ottoman Empire.* Centers of Civilization Series. Norman, OK: University of Oklahoma Press.

Mansel, Philip. (1995) *Constantinople: City of the World's Desire, 1453–1924.* London: John Murray.

Ousterhout, Robert, and Nezih Basgelen. (2000) *Monuments of Unaging Intellect: Historic Postcards of Byzantine Istanbul.* Champaign, IL: University of Illinois Press.

**ITO NOE** (1895–1923), Japanese writer and feminist. Ito Noe achieved notoriety as a freethinker whose autobiographical writing, political associations, and unconventional love relationships epitomized the "new woman" of modern Japan. Noe initially earned attention for her contributions to *Seito* (Bluestockings), a controversial feminist literary journal published from 1911 to 1916 by a small group of young Tokyo women also known as the Bluestockings. Noe joined the Bluestockings in 1912 when, as a teenager, she illegally fled from an arranged marriage in her Kyushu hometown to live with her former high school English teacher, Tsuji Jun, in Tokyo. The stories that Noe wrote about her arranged marriage and about the later failure of her love marriage to Tsuji Jun are some of her most significant contributions to *Seito.* Noe argued for women to have a choice about when to enter and when to leave a marriage. She also wrote essays championing the new woman, translated the works of Emma Goldman, and debated other Bluestockings over issues such as prostitution and charity work. She took the editorial helm of *Seito* in its last thirteen months of publication.

In 1916, Noe left Tsuji and their two children for the anarchist Osugi Sakae, winning him away from his wife and another lover. Noe bore five children with Osugi while working with him in labor organizing, writing, journal editing, and public speaking.

With Yamakawa Kikue, Noe participated in the socialist women's group Sekirankai (Red Wave Society). Both Noe and Osugi were murdered in the wave of police brutality following the great earthquake that devastated Tokyo in 1923. *The Collected Works of Ito Noe* was published in two volumes in Japanese in 1970, when the women's liberation movement renewed interest in Japanese feminist history.

*Jan Bardsley*

**Further Reading**

Bardsley, Jan. (2002) *The Bluestockings of Japan: Feminist Fiction and Essays from Seito, 1911–1916.* Ann Arbor, MI: Center for Japanese Studies.

**IWASHIMIZU HACHIMAN SHRINE** One of the oldest and most important Shinto shrines in Japan Iwashimizu Hachiman Shrine is located southwest of Kyoto on Mount Otokoyama. It is one of the main shrines dedicated to Hachiman, popularly viewed as the *kami* (deity) of war and learning. The shrine's main festival (and that of its numerous branch shrines throughout Japan) is on the fifteenth day of the ninth month.

The shrine was established about 859 CE by a Buddhist priest, Gyoko, and its buildings have been rebuilt several times. The current design is from 1634, when the shrine was patronized by the third shogun of the Tokugawa period (1600/1603–1868). One of the early patrons of the shrine was Minamoto no Yoshiie (Hachiman Taro), and the shrine was a favorite of Minamoto and Ashikaga shoguns because of its association with warrior values, as well as with their clan ancestors. The shrine was patronized by the imperial house, and homage is paid there annually, in the presence of an imperial envoy, for the defeat of Taira no Masakado and Fujiwara no Sumitomo, both accused, at different times, of plotting to usurp the throne. The shrine's original association with Buddhism was severed during the campaign to expel the buddhas in the early years of the Meiji Restoration (1868–1912).

*Michael Ashkenazi*

### Further Reading

Kanda, Christine Guth. (1985) *Shinzo: Hachiman Imagery and Its Development*. Cambridge, MA: Harvard University Press.

**IWATE** (2002 est. pop. 1.4 million). Iwate Prefecture is situated in the northern region of Japan's island of Honshu. Once on the untamed frontier, in the early 2000s it remains a bastion of early culture. With a population of 1,418,000 residents, Iwate occupies an area of 15,278 square kilometers. Its main geographical features are the Ou and Kitakami Mountains, which enclose the river Kitakamigawa plateau. Iwate is bordered by the Pacific Ocean and by Aomori, Akita, and Miyagi Prefectures. Once known as Mutsu Province, it assumed its present name and borders in 1876.

The prefecture's capital is Morioka. Although a bustling commercial city and home to Iwate University, it retains much of the flavor of its origins as the Edo period (1600/1603–1868) castle town of the Nambu family, famous for breeding fine horses. Its attractions include the old merchant quarter, the Hachiman shrine to the god of war, and the ruins of Morioka Castle. The prefecture's other important cities are Mikayo, Hanamaki, and Ichinoseki.

Iwate has a long history. In ancient times, it was home to the aboriginal Ezo people. In the Heian period (794–1185), the Fujiwara family assumed control of the province and established a capital at Hiraizumi, which became the military, political, and cultural center of all northern Japan. The Fujiwara became wealthy from the gold found in the area and they built splendid temples and palaces. In the late Muromachi period (1333–1573), control of the province passed to the Nambu family in the north and the Date family in the south. The Tokugawa shogunate (1600/1603–1868) oversaw the division of the area into some twenty domains.

Iwate's main agricultural activity is rice farming and livestock raising, along with lumber production and fishing. Mining makes the prefecture a leading source of iron and copper ore. A major tourist destination is Hiraizumi, today a small country town compared to its past days of splendor. Still standing are the temple known as Golden Hall (Konjikido), the first National Treasure to be so designated, and the Heian-style gardens and ruins of the Motsuji, once a complex of forty temples. Iwate's traditional crafts include the wooden folk toys known as Kokeshi dolls and Nambu cast iron made into bells, statues, and heavy kettles. The region's traditional dances include the deer dance *(shishi odori)* and sword dance *(kembai)*.

*E. L. S. Weber*

### Further Reading

"Iwate." (1993) *Japan: An Illustrated Encyclopedia*. Tokyo: Kodansha.

**IZMIR** (1997 pop. 2.0 million). Izmir (Smyrna), the third-largest city of Turkey and an important commercial center, is located on the Aegean coast of Anatolia, in the gulf of Izmir. Reputedly the birthplace of Homer, Izmir was an important city during the Classical Greek and Roman periods and was a provincial capital under the Byzantine empire. In 1081, it was conquered by the Seljuks, a Turkic empire that had invaded Anatolia a decade earlier. It was retaken by the Byzantines in 1097, but was lost to another principality, Aydinogullari, in 1344. The Ottomans took control of Izmir, along with the rest of Aydin territories, in 1390 under Sultan Beyazit I (reigned 1389–1402). After Beyazit's defeat by Timur (Tamerlane) at the Battle of Ankara in 1402, the Aydinogullari were able to briefly retake control, though they submitted sovereignty to the Ottomans once again in 1415.

Izmir maintained its importance throughout the Ottoman period, serving as a naval base, and has remained an important center for international trade. The city was noted for its cosmopolitanism. Its population was distinguished by ethnic and religious variety including Turkish-speaking Muslims, Ladino-speaking Jews, and Greek-speaking Orthodox Christians. In the nineteenth century Izmir was arguably the wealthiest city in the Ottoman empire. European capital promoted the development of advanced infrastructure, such as a modern port (1868), new industries, and gas streetlights (1864). Railways were built to connect

The city of Izmir, Turkey, on the Aegean Sea. (YANN ARTHUS-BERTRAND/CORBIS)

Izmir's port with its agricultural hinterland. In 1901 the German kaiser, Wilhelm II (reigned 1888–1918), donated a clock tower to the city, which today is its most famous landmark.

After the defeat of the Ottoman empire in World War I, Izmir became the center of an attempt by Greece to expand into western Anatolia. The Greek army landed in Izmir in May 1919, but this move precipitated a movement of Turkish nationalist resistance, which eventually forced the Greeks to withdraw from Izmir in 1922. As the Turkish army took control of Izmir, fires destroyed most of the city. Many non-Muslims fled with the Greek army, and the remaining Orthodox Christian population of the region was deported to Greece in the Greek-Turkish population exchanges agreed on in the treaty of Lausanne (1923).

Izmir has recovered from these traumas and is still an important trading and industrial city, with one of the highest standards of living in the country. It is home to several universities, an important archaeological museum, and NATO (North Atlantic Treaty Organization) installations.

*Howard Eissenstat*

### Further Reading

Eldem, Edhem, Daniel Goffman, and Bruce Masters. (1999) *The Ottoman City between East and West: Aleppo, Izmir, and Istanbul.* Cambridge, U.K.: Cambridge University Press.

Goffman, Daniel. (1990) *Izmir and the Levantine World, 1550–1650.* Seattle, WA: University of Washington Press.

**IZNIK** (2002 est. pop. 21,000). Iznik, a town in northwestern Turkey on the eastern shore of Iznik Lake, is surrounded by walls with four gates. Within the town are many historic baths, mausoleums, *madrasahs* or Muslim religious schools, mosques, minarets, and imarets or inns. Notable buildings include the fourteenth-century Green Mosque and the fourth-century Saint Sophia Cathedral.

The Macedonian Greek ruler Antigonus I (382–301 BCE), once a general of Alexander of Macedon (356–323 BCE), founded the town, which he named Antigoneia, in 316 BCE. Later renamed Nicaea, the town rose to prominence during the Byzantine empire, when influential Christian ecumenical councils met there. The First Nicene Council, held in 325, put forth the Nicene Creed as the description of the persons of the Trinity and condemned Arianism, a Christian heresy that disavowed Jesus' divinity. The Second Nicene Council, in 787, rescinded the ban on the veneration of images, which had been introduced during the iconoclastic controversies of 726 and 730.

In 1078 the Seljuk Turks conquered Nicaea. The Ottoman Turks captured the town in 1331 and gave it its present name of Iznik. From the late fifteenth to the early eighteenth centuries, Iznik was a famous production center for quartz-based tiles and clay pottery.

The colorful, abstract decoration of Iznik ware was painted in blue, turquoise and purple, and red, against a white ground. Iznik's ceramics industry was revived beginning in 1985. Some residents of Iznik grow olives, grapes, tomatoes, and peaches on nearby farmland, and fishers catch crayfish from Iznik Lake. The town has many hotels, restaurants, and cafes.

*Kevin Alan Brook*

### Further Reading

Atasoy, Nurhan, and Julian Raby. (1989) *Iznik: The Pottery of Ottoman Turkey*. London: Alexandria Press.

Carswell, John. (1998) *Iznik Pottery*. London: British Museum Press.

Eyice, Semavi. (1988) *Iznik: Tarihcesi ve Eski Eserleri (Nicaea: The History and the Monuments)*. Istanbul, Turkey: Sanat Tarihi Arastirmalari Dergisi Yayini.

**IZUMO SHRINE** Izumo Taisha (also known as Izumo no Oyashiro, the Grand Shrine of Izumo), one of the oldest and most influential shrines in Japan, is located in Kizuki, Shimane Prefecture, once the feudal Izumo domain. It enshrines the deity Okuninushi-no-mikoto, known popularly as Daikoku-sama.

Izumo Shrine is built in the archaic *taisha-zukuri* ("great-shrine building") style of shrine architecture. The present buildings date from 1744, although a major fire in 1953 necessitated some rebuilding. The main building, surmounted by a great thatched, slightly concave roof rising eighty feet above the foundation, is the largest shrine in Japan. During the month of October, by the lunar calendar, all the Shinto deities of the country are believed to depart their local shrines and gather at Izumo Taisha. Various rites are observed to welcome, honor, and later send off these deities on their return to their local shrines. This period, known throughout Japan as *kaminazuki* ("month when the gods are absent") is known at Izumo as *kamiarizuki* ("month when the gods are present").

The Great Shrine of Izumo in Shimane Prefecture, Japan. (SAKAMOTO PHOTO RESEARCH/CORBIS)

The shrine is popular among young couples for bestowing felicitous marital relations and is also thought to protect agriculture and offer good fortune.

*James M. Vardaman, Jr.*

### Further Reading

Boching, Brian. (1995) *A Popular Dictionary of Shinto*. Surrey, U.K.: Curzon Press.

Holtom, D. C. (1965) *The National Faith of Japan: A Study in Modern Shinto*. New York: Paragon Book Reprint.

Picken, Stuart D. B. (1994) *Essentials of Shinto: An Analytical Guide to Principal Teachings*. Westport, CT: Greenwood Press.

**JADE** Jade (Chinese *yu*), a dense, luminous stone of various colors including white, yellow, green, gray, mauve, and brown, has been an artistic medium from at least the fifth millennium BCE in China. The term "jade" is generally applied to two types of stones: nephrite, a crystalline calcium magnesium silicate from northeast China (Jiangsu Province) and Central Asia's Khotan and Yarkand regions, and jadeite, a green, glassy sodium aluminum silicate mineral of the pyroxene family from Myanmar (Burma). It is nephrite, however, that early Chinese artists utilized for ritual objects, personal items, and ornaments.

Prized for its innate beauty, jade came to be regarded as having moral virtues and magical properties and was believed to be the congealed semen of a celestial dragon. The Han dynasty scholar Xu Shen described jade as having five virtues: charity, epitomized by its bright warm luster; rectitude, as signified by its translucence; wisdom, as typified by its purity and penetrating sound when struck; courage, in that while it can be broken, it cannot be bent; and equity, represented by its sharp angles that injure none.

Special techniques for carving jade were devised because of jade's extreme hardness. Unlike other stones, which can be chiseled, jade must be fashioned through a laborious abrasion process utilizing drills and quartz sand. This labor-intensive process makes jade artifacts very costly. From earliest times, it seems that jade was the ultimate symbol of wealth and power. Thus, the finest workmanship and artistry were lavished on the precious stone.

The earliest artistic use of jade occurred in the Hongshan culture of the middle Huang (Yellow) River basin, Liaoning Province, dated to the fifth to fourth millennia BCE. Examples of jade carvings in this period include coiled dragons, owls, turtles, and cloudlike plaques. Jades are so predominant among Hongshan artifacts that some specialists have referred to the period as the Jade Age. In tombs, jade objects were positioned on, around, and under the body of the deceased. Thus, jade was regarded as having more than social status; it had ritual and protective properties as well.

Ritual use of jade in burials continued in China through the Western Han dynasty (206 BCE–24 CE). Most notable are the full jade body suits from Lingshan, Mancheng, Hebei Province, belonging to Prince Liu Sheng and his wife Princess Dou Wan. The two royal figures were covered from head to foot in outfits made entirely of jade plaques drilled at the four corners and fastened with gold wire. It is believed that these functioned as shrouds, protecting the body from decay and from attack by evil forces.

A jade carver holds a piece of carved jade in Changchun, China. (RIC ERGENBRIGHT/CORBIS)

Jade implements were important in statecraft during the Shang and Zhou dynasties (1766–256 BCE) in that various pieces came to signify specific courtly ranks. Because jade was associated with the imperial court and with great virtue, it became likened to the Confucian ideal of the perfect gentleman *(junzi)*.

From the Warring States period (475–221 BCE) on, jade was used more and more for secular items and personal adornment. By the Tang dynasty (618–907 CE), the secular use of jade was widespread. Jewelry, fine vessels, and utensils, as well as objets d'art having no particular religious connotation, were crafted from jade. Decorative and functional items such as bowls, cups, dishes, ewers, vases, containers, hair ornaments, beads, and bracelets received lavish, delicate ornamentation.

After centuries of Chinese jade working, the tradition spread westward through Central Asia into India and Turkey. There are fine Mughal pieces, known as Hindustan jades, many of which are embellished with intricate designs incorporating precious gems held in place with gold filigree.

*Katherine Anne Harper*

**Further Reading**

Born, Gerald M. (1982) *Chinese Jade: An Annotated Bibliography*. Chicago: Celadon Press.

Laufer, Berthold. (1946) *Jade: A Study in Chinese Archaeology and Religion*. South Pasadena, CA: P. D. Perkins with Westwood Press & W. M. Hawley.

Watt, James C. Y. (1989) *Chinese Jades from the Collection of the Seattle Art Museum*. Seattle, WA: Seattle Art Museum.

Yang, Xiaoneng, ed. (1999) *The Golden Age of Chinese Archaeology: Celebrated Discoveries from the People's Republic of China*. New Haven, CT: Yale University Press.

**JADIDISM** The term "Jadidism" denotes a range of modernist movements that flourished among the Muslims of the Russian empire between 1880 and 1920. Beginning as a movement of religious reform, Jadidism quickly acquired broad cultural, social, and ultimately political dimensions. The movement's name came from its advocacy of the *usul-i jadid* ("the new method"), new phonetic approach to teaching the Arabic alphabet, an indication of the centrality of educational reform to Jadidism. Historians refer to the proponents of Jadidism as Jadids, although the Jadids did not usually use this term themselves.

The late nineteenth century saw the rise of modernist movements throughout the Muslim world. While they existed in markedly different political contexts, these movements shared a concern over their societies' political and economic decline relative to Europe and a belief in the compatibility of Islam and modernity.

Jadidism originated in the intellectual ferment created in Tatar society by rapid economic change occurring in the mid-nineteenth century, including the emergence of a Tatar mercantile bourgeoisie with extensive trading networks in Russia, Siberia, and Central Asia. Religious scholars such as Abdunnasir al-Kursavi (1776–1812) and Shihabeddin al-Marjani (1818–1889) questioned the authority of traditional Islamic theology and argued for creative reinterpretation of Islam. But the efforts of the Crimean Tatar noble Ismail Bey Gaspirali (1851–1914) gave shape to Jadidism as a cultural movement. In 1883 Gaspirali received permission to publish the newspaper *Terjuman* (Interpreter) in his native Bakhchisaray. *Terjuman* became the standard bearer of Jadidism throughout the Russian empire and beyond, influencing cultural debates in the Ottoman empire as well. In 1884 Gaspirali opened the first "new method" elementary school, in which children were taught the Arabic alphabet using the new phonetic method of instruction. These schools quickly became the flagship of Jadid reform. The emphasis on enlightenment also gave rise to a boom in publishing among the Tatars, as Jadid authors wrote and translated (from Russian, French, Ottoman Turkish, and Arabic) thousands of books on various subjects.

At the turn of the twentieth century a Jadid movement emerged in Central Asia, where different social and political contexts imparted a distinct hue. The *ulama* (religious scholars) retained much greater influence in Central Asia, while the new mercantile class was much weaker. The market for publishing was also much smaller, and Central Asian Jadids were more strongly rooted in Islamic education. Nevertheless, they faced opposition from their own society as well as from a Russian state always suspicious of unofficial initiatives.

Jadidism's rhetoric of cultural reform was directed at Muslim society itself. The basic themes were enlightenment, progress, and "awakening" the nation to take its place in the modern, "civilized" world, which meant sovereign states possessing military and economic might. Given the lack of political sovereignty, however, it was up to society to lift itself up through education and disciplined effort. Jadid rhetoric was usually sharply critical of the present state of Muslim society, which the Jadids contrasted unfavorably to their own glorious past and the present of the "civilized" countries of Europe.

The single most important term in the Jadid lexicon was *taraqqi*, meaning progress. For the Jadids progress and civilization were accessible to all societies solely through disciplined effort and enlightenment. Nothing in Islam prevented Muslims from joining the modern world; indeed, Islam enjoined disciplined effort and enlightenment on Muslims. Only a modern person equipped with knowledge "according to the needs of the age" could be a good Muslim.

The new method of teaching the alphabet marked a shift in the understanding of the purposes of literacy and, ultimately, of knowledge. Literacy for the Jadids was a functional skill with no sacral connotations. The Jadids claimed that the true meaning of Islam could be acquired through a critical reading of the scriptures without recourse to the tradition of interpretation represented by the *ulama*. This claim had radical repercussions for the authority of the *ulama*, and for Islam itself.

Jadidism would have been impossible without the advent of print. Print allowed the new intellectuals to assert their claims to interpretation to a broad audience and thus to undermine the monopoly of the *ulama* over cultural debate. At the same time, newspapers and translations into Turkic or Arabic of European works made available to the Jadids new ways of thinking about the world and their place in it, so that when they looked at their own society they did so with new eyes.

The object of Jadid reform was the *millat*, the Muslim community, which quickly acquired national and ethnic overtones and led to the rise of nationalism and political radicalism. While Gaspirali was revered as the father of Jadidism, by the time of his death younger Jadids had grown wary of his political caution and were attracted to more radical political stances. The Russian revolution of 1917 radicalized Jadidism even further, and many Jadids came to espouse both nationalist and socialist agendas as the most efficient path to enlightenment and progress.

Jadidism provides a good argument for questioning the dichotomy between Islam and modernity, since it represented both. It was rooted in a long Islamic tradition of reform, but it also shared a post-Enlightenment understanding of the world and used such aspects of modernity as the press and schooling. New economic and social forces produced alternative understandings of the world and consequently new national and religious identities.

*Adeeb Khalid*

### Further Reading

Dudoignon, Stéphane A. (1996) "La Question scolaire à Boukhara et au Turkestan russe, du «premier renouveau» à la soviétisation (fin du XVIIIe siècle–1937) [The Education Question in Bukhara and Russian Turkestan, from the 'First Renewal' to Sovietization]. *Cahiers du Monde Russe* 37: 133–210.

Dudoignon, Stéphane A., Damir Is'haqov, and Rafyq Mohammatshin, eds. (1997) *L'Islam de Russie: Conscience communitaire et autonomie politique chez les Tatars de la Volga et de l'Oural depuis le XVIIIe siècle* (Communal Conscience and Political Autonomy among the Volga and Ural Tatars since the 18th Century). Paris: Maisonneuve.

Khalid, Adeeb. (1998) *The Politics of Muslim Cultural Reform: Jadidism in Central Asia.* Berkeley and Los Angeles: University of California Press.

## JAFFNA

**JAFFNA** (2002 est. population of the peninsula 480,000). Jaffna refers to the capital city, peninsula, adjacent islands, and hinterland of the northernmost region of Sri Lanka. It has been a major avenue of trade and migration between India and Sri Lanka since prehistoric times. After the collapse of the Anuradhapura kingdom and its conquest by the Chola dynasty, the area became a homogeneous Tamil-speaking Hindu region, and the city became the capital of a Tamil kingdom that periodically waged war with the Sinhalese kingdoms to the south. The area successively fell under Portuguese (1591), Dutch (1658), and British (1795) colonial rule. In the nineteenth century, it was integrated into the British Crown Colony of Ceylon. It remained part of the unified state when the colony gained its independence in 1948. Tamil claims of discrimination in favor of the majority Sinhalese Buddhists led to a separatist movement that erupted into a bloody civil war in 1983. The Liberation Tigers of Tamil Eelam (LTTE) emerged as the leaders of Tamil separatism through a violent contest with other separatists. The peninsula was occupied by the Indian army in 1987. When the Indian army withdrew in 1990, the LTTE established a harsh regime. The Sri Lankan army captured Jaffna in 1995. Despite government attempts to rehabilitate the region, fighting continued throughout 2001.

*Patrick Peebles*

### Further Reading

Abeyasinghe, Tikiri. (1986) *Jaffna under the Portuguese.* Colombo, Sri Lanka: Lake House Investments.

Rasanayagam, C. (1926) *Ancient Jaffna: Being a Research into the History of Jaffna from Very Early Times to the Portuguese Period.* New Delhi: Asian Educational Services.

## JAHANGIR

**JAHANGIR** (1569–1627), Mughal emperor. Sultan Salim, who ruled northern India under the name Nuruddin Muhammad and the title Jahangir, was born

## PLEASING THE EMPEROR (MUGHAL EMPEROR JAHANGIR)

"Mr Edwardes presented the Kinge [the Mughal Emperor Jahangir] a mastife, and speakinge of the dog's courage, the Kinge cawsed a younge leoparde to be brought to make tryall, which the dogge soe pinchtt, thatt fewer howres after the leoparde dyed. Synce, the Kinge of Persia, with a presentt, sent heather haulfe a dozen dogges—the Kinges cawsed boares to be brought to fight with them, puttinge two or three dogges to a boare, yet none of them seased; and rememberinge his owne dogge, sentt for him, who presently fastened on the boare, so disgraced the Persian doggs, wherewith the Kinge was exceedingly pleased."

*Source:* Letter from Kerridge, East India Company President at Surat (1612), as quoted in *The Sahibs* (1948), edited by Hilton Brown. London: William Hodge & Co., 158–159.

in Sikri in 1569. His mother was a Rajput princess, and his father was the great Mughal emperor Akbar (1542–1605). As a prince, Salim had sought to lead a rebellion against his father, but the two were later reconciled, and it was only with Akbar's death that Salim became emperor under the title of Jahangir (world seizer). Jahangir was fortunate in inheriting an extensive, prosperous, and politically stable empire from his father. Unfortunately, Jahangir's court was saturated with intrigue and corruption, and he faced a powerful rival in his eldest son, Prince Khusru, who was eventually subdued. His favorite wife, Noor Jahan, was the power behind the throne and placed her family members in important court positions. Her father received a title; the daughter of her brother married Prince Khurram, the eventual heir; and her daughter from her first marriage became the wife of Jahangir's youngest son, Prince Shahryar.

Western influence in India was growing, and Jahangir had contact with the Portuguese and the fledgling British East India Company. James I's ambassador, Sir Thomas Roe, was received warmly at court and managed to secure major concessions (1615–1618). Hunting and drinking were Jahangir's passions, and his rule did not leave any military or administrative landmarks. However, Jahangir was arguably the greatest of all Mughal connoisseurs of the arts and a lover of beauty—both natural and artistic. He took a keen interest in commissioning jewelry, calligraphy, and manuscript illustrations.

*Chandrika Kaul*

### Further Reading

Miles, Keith. (1988) *Jahangir and the Khan Dynasty.* London: Pelham.

Thackston, Wheeler M., ed. and trans. (1999) *The Jahangirnama: Memoirs of Jahangir, Emperor of India.* New York: Oxford University Press.

**JAINISM** Jainism, like Hinduism and Buddhism, is one of India's ancient, indigenous religions. The word "Jain" derives from the Sanskrit word *ji* meaning to conquer. The founder of Jainism was Vardhamana (c. 599–527 BCE), later known as Mahavira, who lived in Magadha (in present-day Bihar state). Mahavira, an

In Karhataka, India, a Jain priest stands before a figurine of Mahavira, the founder of Jainism. (CHARLES AND JOSETTE LENARS/CORBIS)

The Palitana Jain Temple in Gujarat, India, in 1987. (TIZIANA AND GIANNI BALDIZZONE/CORBIS)

unorthodox teacher, firmly opposed the prevailing religion of the day, the sacrificial Vedic religion, and the already dominant authority of the Brahman caste.

### Origins and Development

Mahavira was a contemporary of Siddhartha Gautama Buddha (c. 566–486 BCE), and like the Buddha he was the son of the king of a politically powerful clan, was educated as a prince, married, and fathered a child. Despite his royal upbringing, at the age of thirty he left his home to pursue a life of asceticism in search of spiritual salvation. First he joined the Nirgranthas ("Free from Bonds") ascetic sect founded by the teacher Parshavanatha, who lived during the ninth century BCE. The Nirgranthas were later absorbed into the order Mahavira founded. Parshavanatha is remembered as the twenty-third tirthankara ("ford maker"), or enlightened teacher, and Mahavira is the twenty-fourth in this long line of realized masters who attained enlightenment *(kevalajnana).* No doubt Jain beliefs and practices originated in remote antiquity, and the Jain connection to the Nirgranthas establishes the religion as far older than Buddhism. Jain mythology has it that the first tirthankara was Rshabhanatha, whose mother Marudevi attained *kevalajnana* upon seeing her son. According to Jain beliefs, she was the first human of this world to attain liberation.

During his long search for enlightenment Mahavira realized the necessity of renouncing all attachments and possessions, including even the one garment he wore. As a religious reformer he was critical of the Vedas and the Brahmans, seeing no relevance in the priestly class and their rites of sacrifice, particularly in the matter of freedom from the endless cycles of reincarnation and the attainment of transcendent knowledge. His teachings denied both a powerful god creator and a superhuman origin of the universe. He asserted that there was no creation per se; instead there was an unceasing evolution involving endless transmigration of souls. Upon achieving enlightenment, Mahavira spent his remaining life wandering unclothed and begging for food. According to tradition, he taught for thirty years with the patronization of kings and finally died of self-imposed starvation at the age of seventy-two.

In his teachings Mahavira stressed the need to fight passions and bodily senses to purify the soul and gain omniscience, the highest Jain goal. Many of his followers also became renouncers and abandoned worldly pleasures, renunciation being the way to conquer all passions. The body of believers was divided into two groups, the renouncers, composed of both monks and nuns, and the lay practitioners, whose position was subordinate to the renouncers. All Jains observed the three moral excellences or jewels *(triratna),* right knowledge, right intuition, and right conduct, including the practice of ahimsa (noninjury to any life-form). Lay followers were not expected to embrace the harsher requirements of the monks and nuns but were encouraged to develop twenty-one meritorious qualities, among them mercy, kindness, truthfulness, humility, modesty, and limiting possessions. Those who renounced, however, embraced five principles or greater vows *(vratas)*: (1) noninjury (ahimsa), (2) kindness and speaking the truth, (3) honorable conduct, (4) chastity in word and action, and (5) renunciation of worldly interests.

### Beliefs and Practices

Central to Jainism is the belief in reincarnation and karma (merit and demerit). The aim of the code of conduct is to avoid accruing new negative karma while destroying old negative karma. Jainism maintains that the self is polluted by karmic particles, bits of materials generated by a person's actions that attach to the soul and consequently bind the soul to material bodies through many births. When karmic particles are wiped from the self, enlightenment is attained and the soul no longer faces material rebirth. Mortification of the flesh protects against the acquisition of new negative karma and rids the body of old negative karma. Purification requires fasting, confession, penance, reverence for superiors, service to others, meditation, study, indifference to the needs of the body, and observation of vows.

The first principle, noninjury, or ahimsa, is viewed as especially necessary to free the soul of karma. The primary ethical virtue, ahimsa is the measure by which all actions are judged. A policy of ahimsa is assiduously followed, demanding great precautions to avoid harming or killing any life-form, including insects and microbes. In Jainism a person's negative karma is increased by interference with the spiritual progress of another. Thus many Jains cover their mouths, wearing a mask or cloth *(mul-patti)*, to prevent breathing in or swallowing insects. Many Jains do not eat or drink after dark to avoid inadvertent ingestion of insects. Eating meat, of course, is a violation of ahimsa, along with eating any foods that engender colonies of microbes. Not only are such foods considered unhealthful for the consumer, but also the microbes themselves are damaged by consumption. Similarly, wandering renouncers remain in one place during the monsoons, because while walking on muddy roads they might crush worms, snails, or waterborne creatures. Other renouncers refuse to travel by rail because of the possibility that the train's wheels might kill organisms on the tracks.

### Sects

Disputes among Mahavira's followers led to the formation of two sects. The division, which began around the second century BCE and was finalized in the first century CE, formed the Digambaras ("sky clad"), or naked ascetics, and the Svetambaras ("white clad"), who wear a simple white garment. The Digambaras believe nakedness is proof of the conquest of sin, asserting that sin cannot exist in the absence of shame. The Svetambaras protest that wearing a simple garment implies no shame or sin. The two sects are divided on the subject of women's enlightenment. Svetambaras assert that women can become enlightened, while Digambaras declare that only males can achieve enlightenment. Consequently women do not become naked ascetics, although according to Mahavira's teachings women are allowed to renounce the world and form orders of nuns. All renouncers are required to pluck out their hair rather than shave or cut it, hence Jains are often called hair pluckers. After twelve years of strict asceticism, a Jain renouncer may commit suicide through self-starvation.

### Influence and Role in Indian Society

Jainism has existed continuously in India for 2,500 years. Jain beliefs, particularly ahimsa, have had a significant influence on India's culture. Asoka (d. c. 238), a Buddhist emperor, stressed the practice of ahimsa in his reforms. In the twentieth century Mohandas (Mahatma) Gandhi (1869–1948) was influenced by the concept of ahimsa when he developed his policy of nonviolent resistance in India's struggle for independence. Historically ahimsa and vegetarianism have been important in Buddhism and Hinduism. Jains also have contributed to philosophy, logic, art, architecture, mathematics, astronomy, and literature.

Jains constitute the oldest religious minority still practicing in India. The 1981 Indian census counted some 3.2 million Jains, most of whom live in urban centers in the modern states of Maharashtra, Rajasthan, Gujarat, Madhya Pradesh, and Karnataka. Traditionally the Jains have avoided farming because cultivation of the soil may accidentally kill insects and violate the ahimsa restriction. Twenty-first-century Jains are mainly bankers, jewelers, merchants, moneylenders, and industrialists. As merchants and businesspeople they are known for their honesty. Even though the Jains are a wealthy community, they seek out and support humanitarian causes to relieve suffering. They are particularly renowned for operating centers dedicated to maintaining abused and sick animals and for endowing lavish temples.

*Katherine Anne Harper*

### Further Reading

Bhattacharyya, N. N. (1999) *Jain Philosophy: Historical Outline*. New Delhi: Munshiram Manoharlal Publishing.

Cort, John E., ed. (1998) *Open Boundaries: Jain Communities and Cultures in Indian History*. Albany, NY: State University of New York Press.

Dundas, Paul. (1992) *The Jains*. New York: Routledge.

Jain, Jagdishchandra. (1992) *Studies in Early Jainism*. New Delhi: Navrang.

Jaini, Padmanabh S. (1991) *Gender and Salvation: Jaina Debates on the Spiritual Liberation of Women*. Berkeley and Los Angeles: University of California Press.

**JAIPUR** (2001 est. pop. 2.3 million). The capital and largest city of Rajasthan state in northwestern India, Jaipur ("city of victory") is known as the pink city for its salmon-colored facades in the old-walled quarter. The fabled stronghold of a clan of rulers, it is today a vibrant, even tumultuous, city of wild contrasts. Jaipur was founded by the great warrior-astronomer Maharaja Jai Singh II (1693–1743). In 1728 with Mughal power receding, he decided to move from his hillside fort to a new site on the plains. Synthesizing Rajput and Mughal architectural styles, he laid out the city in rectangular blocks with surrounding walls and built a city palace and the world's largest stone observatory, all according to principles in the *Shilpa-Shastra*, a Hindu architectural treatise.

Among the city's architectural masterpieces are the Hawa Mahal ("hall of winds") palace, dedicated to the Lord Krishna, the Jamtar Mantar observatory, and the Ram Nivas gardens with the Central Museum, zoo, and art gallery. The Rambagh Palace, former home of the Maharaja of Jaipur, is one of India's most prestigious and romantic hotels. In commerce, cottage industries such as textiles, brass, lacquer, leather work, and jewelry prevail.

*C. Roger Davis*

### Further Reading

Gajwani, Gopi, and Kishore Singh. (2000) *Jaipur*. New Delhi: Crest Publishing House.

Parika, Nandakisor. (2000) *Jaipur That Was: Royal Court and the Seraglio*. Jaipur, India: Subodh Sahitya Sadan.

**JAKARTA** (2000 pop. 8.4 million). The Indonesian metropolis of Jakarta is situated on the northwest coast of Java and covers a territory of approximately 660 square kilometers. The present Indonesian capital has a history of nearly 500 years. It sprang up around a bustling pepper-trading port called Sunda Kelapa. In 1522 the Portuguese arrived, but before long they were driven out and the city was renamed Jayakarta, meaning "victorious city." For almost 350 years it was the center of Dutch colonial rule, known

The Hawa Mahal (Hall of Winds) in Jaipur. (WILDCOUNTRY/CORBIS)

as Batavia. In 1942 the Japanese invaded Java, and Batavia's name was changed back to Jayakarta. After World War II the Dutch returned, but in 1949, when Indonesian independence was eventually achieved, Indonesians made Jakarta the capital of the new republic, abbreviating its old name.

At that time Jakarta had a population of 900,000. Today the population is over 8 million, having increased almost tenfold. The population of greater Jakarta, the city plus the surrounding districts, is about 17 million.

As Jakarta has attracted people from many other parts of Indonesia and from abroad, it is a cosmopolitan city with a culture of its own. Over the last fifteen years Jakarta has undergone great changes, but it is still a place of extremes, where wide avenues intersect with unpaved streets and modern buildings stand a few blocks from overcrowded shacks. The city is sometimes under water for days because the canals, built by the Dutch to prevent flooding in below–sea level sections, cannot hold the pouring monsoon rains.

Jakarta is the main economic center of Indonesia. Engineering is the dominant sector of Jakarta's heavy industry, including shipbuilding, transport equipment, electrical and electronics products. Manufacturing includes rubber, chemicals, paper, and timber products. Textile and food industries are well developed. Jakarta has the principal Indonesian seaport of international trade, exporting rubber, tin, coffee, palm oil, and petroleum. Jakarta's Sukarno-Hatta International Airport is the center of international air traffic in Indonesia. The Presidential Palace, the army headquarters, the National Museum, and other governmental buildings are located in Jakarta.

*Dimitar L. Dimitrov*

### Further Reading

Jellinek, Lea. (1991) *The Wheel of Fortune: The History of a Poor Community in Jakarta*. Honolulu, HI: University of Hawaii Press.

Marcussen, Lars. (1990) *Third World Housing in Social and Spatial Development: The Case of Jakarta*. Brookfield, VT: Avebury.

## JAKARTA RIOTS OF MAY 1998

In Indonesia, the 1998 Asian economic crisis led to soaring inflation, plummeting currency, political violence, and the downfall of President Suharto (b. 1921). Unemployment rose to 20 million (11 percent).

The consequences were catastrophic. On 12 May, the turning point came. Security forces fatally shot six students of Trisakti University in Jakarta to bring the students under control. Crowds looted and burned the shops and residences of Chinese Indonesians, and Chinese-Indonesian women were targeted for systematic rape. There were reports of Chinese fleeing to Australia and Singapore. The mob violence resulted in over twelve hundred deaths. The Chinese were targeted by mobs because they were seen as the cause of all the problems. They dominated the corporate sector and retail trade. Indonesia had had a long history of anti-Chinese violence. The "anti-Chinese pogrom" of 1965 massacred 250,000 Chinese.

On 19 May, thousands of demonstrating students occupied the Assembly Building in Jakarta. About eighty thousand troops occupied Merdeka Square to prevent a large-scale demonstration. Meanwhile, Suharto was losing the support of Muslim leaders and his cabinet colleagues. On 21 May, he resigned.

The nation was aggrieved by the May events. The riots in Jakarta were the worst violence in Indonesia since 1965, when seven hundred thousand were killed over six months. The events of 1998 shattered the confidence of the Chinese-Indonesian community and sullied the image of Indonesia as a tolerant nation. The rule of Suharto, widely viewed as corrupt and authoritarian, was over.

*Patit Paban Mishra*

*See also:* **New Order; Suharto**

### Further Reading

Emmerson, Donald K., ed. (1998) *Indonesia beyond Suharto*. Armonk, NY: M. E. Sharpe.

Schwarz, Adam, and Jonathan Paris, eds. (1999) *The Politics of Post-Suharto*. New York: Council on Foreign Relations Press.

## JAMAʿAT-E-ISLAMI

The Jamaʿat-e-Islami ("Islamic party") is one of the oldest Islamist movements. It is a leading political force in Pakistan but has a more marginal presence in Bangladesh, India, and Sri Lanka. It treats Islam as a complete way of life that can be used as a guiding principle for all life's situations—whether on a personal level or on a national, political level—and as the only alternative to both Western liberalism and Marxism. Jamaʿat-e-Islami's highly structured organization has been a model for Islamist movements elsewhere in the world.

### History

Jamaʿat, as the party is often called, was created in 1941 by Abu'l-A'la Mawdudi (1903–1979), in the troubled context of preindependence India. It opposed both British colonial rule and the predominantly Hindu Indian National Congress. Opposed as well to the secular definition of Muslim nationalism put forward by the founder of Pakistan, Muhammad Ali Jinnah (1876–1948), Mawdudi defended the necessity of a truly Islamic state where *shariʿah* (Islamic law), interpreted in a very conservative way, would be the unique source of constitutional, penal, and family law and regulate the economic system. Jamaʿat also opposed religious esotericism.

Since 1947 Jamaʿat has been located in Lahore, Pakistan. Its leadership comes from educational and business sectors and contests the monopoly the *ulama* (religious scholars) hold over Qur'anic interpretation. It has a very small but very vocal membership (75 members in 1941; probably 15,000 in 1998); the party overall is hierarchical and disciplined. A single call from the emir, or president (Mawdudi from 1947 to 1972, Mian Tufail Muhammad from 1972 to 1987, and Qazi Husain Ahmad from 1987 to the present), mobilizes the whole party. Jamaʿat supervises a wide network of affiliated institutions, including relief organizations, schools, trade unions, publishing houses, and think tanks.

### Goals

The aim of Jamaʿat is to capture power. It has put forward candidates for nearly every election; it fought for civil liberties in the mid-1950s but also collaborated with Zia's military regime in 1978. Though electorally weak (never holding more than 4 percent of the seats in Pakistan's Assembly) due to its limited social base, it keeps a strong influence. The capacity of its student wing for street mobilization is feared by Pakistani government.

### Jamaʿat Outside of Pakistan

In Bangladesh, Jamaʿat was banned in 1971 for having opposed Bangladesh's drive for independence from Pakistan, but it has gained influence since 1991. In India, the Jamaʿat-e-Islami Hind concentrates on spreading Mawdudi's version of Islam, but in the disputed territory of Kashmir it has an important military force, Hezb-ul Mujahideen. In Great Britain, Jamaʿat-inspired organizations (such as the Islamic Foundation) act as a lobbying force and were prominent in the protests against the novelist Salman Rushdie when he was accused of blaspheming Islam by Iran's Ayatollah Khomeini in 1989.

*Amélie Blom*

### Further Reading

Ahmad, Mumtaz. (1991) "Islamic Fundamentalism in South Asia: the Jamaʿat-e-Islami and the Tablighi Jamaat." In *Fundamentalisms Observed*, edited by Martin Marty and Scott Appleby. Chicago: University of Chicago Press, 457–530.

Blom, Amélie. (1999) "Les partis islamistes à la recherche d'un second souffle." In *Le Pakistan, carrefour de tensions régionales*, edited by Christophe Jaffrelot. Brussels, Belgium: Complexe.

Nasr, Seyyed Vali Reza. (1994) *The Vanguard of the Islamic Revolution. The Jamaʿat-e-Islami of Pakistan*. London: I. B. Tauris.

**JAMI, ʿABDURRAHMAN** (1414–1492), Persian poet, scholar, mystic. Mowlana Nur od-Din ʿAbdurrahman ebn Ahmad Jami, a man of exceptional erudition, studied at the renowned Nizamiyya school in his native city of Herat in today's Afghanistan and later in Samarqand, where the sciences were patronized by the astronomer-prince Timurid Ulugh-Beg (ruled 1447–1449). In addition to poetry, Jami's writings included Qurʾanic commentaries and prophetic traditions (hadith), Arabic grammar, music, riddles, poetics, and prosody.

A profound affinity for mysticism made Jami an early adept of the Naqshbandi Sufi order and defined his literary work. Jami was held in the highest esteem by his contemporaries: the Ottoman sultan Bayazid II (ruled 1481–1512) tried to entice him to Istanbul, and the famous Timurid minister, scholar, and benefactor Mir 'Ali Shir Nava'i (1441–1501) was a close friend who wrote his biography.

Jami's poetry was renowned for its graceful style and vivid imagery. His fame rests on three lyrical collections (divans) composed in his youth, middle age, and old age; and on the *Haft aurang* (Seven Thrones, a name of the Great Bear constellation)—a compendium of seven long narrative poems in the tradition of Nizami's and Amir Khusraw Dihlavi's *Hamsa* (Five Poems). Three of these poems—*Silsilat al-dhahab* (Chain of Gold), *Tuhfat al-ahrar* (Gift to the Noble Ones), and *Subhat al-abrar* (The Rosary of the Devout)—are didactic works of a theological and ethical nature, illustrated with parables and instructive anecdotes. *Salaman and Absal* (translated into English by Edward Fitzgerald in 1856), *Layla and Majnun*, and *Yusuf and Zulikha* are allegorical romances permeated with mystical sentiments. The philosophical Alexander-romance *Khirad-nama-i Sikandari* (Book of the Wisdom of Alexander) completes the cycle.

Jami's prose writings are primarily scholarly in nature, but two have earned wide popularity: the biographical compendium of mystics *Nafahat al-uns* (Breath of Divine Intimacy) and the didactic collection of instructive anecdotes in rhymed prose *Baharistan* (*Abode of Spring*), which he modeled on Sa'di's (c. 1213–1292) *Gulistan* (Rose Garden). Jami's poetry and prose left a deep imprint on the literatures of Persia, Turkey, and Muslim India. He is considered the last great Persian author of the Classical period (tenth–fifteenth centuries).

*Marta Simidchieva*

**Further Reading**


Arberry, Arthur J. (1958) *Classical Persian Literature*. London: George Allen and Unwin.

———. (1956) *Fitzgerald's Salaman and Absal: A Study*. Cambridge, U.K.: Cambridge University Press.

Browne, Edward. (1964) *Literary History of Persia*. Vol. 3. Cambridge, U.K.: Cambridge University Press, 507–548.

Davis, Frederick. (1968) *The Persian Mystics: Jami*. Lahore, Pakistan: M. Ashraf.

Jami, 'Abdurrahman. (1887) *The Beharistan: Abode of Spring*. Benares, India: Kama Shastra Society.

Safa, Dhabih-Allah. (1990) *Tarikh-e adabiyat dar Iran* (History of Iranian Literature). Vol. 4. 6th ed. Tehran, Iran: Ferdows.


**JAMMU AND KASHMIR** In August 1947, the British territories on the Indian mainland and the princely states that were part of these territories were partitioned between India, which inherited the much larger portion, and the newly created state of Pakistan. The antagonisms that had made it impossible to hold the raj as a single entity survive to the present day in the enduring enmity between India and Pakistan. The problem, which originated in the controversial manner in which the fate of the princely state of Jammu and Kashmir was decided, stemmed from the actions of the wealthy ruler, the maharaja Hari Singh (1895–1961), of the Dogra Hindu dynasty.

In Jammu and Kashmir, where the maharaja ruled, the bulk of the population was Muslim and generally poor. The vast majority of the princely states were absorbed into either India or Pakistan. Some rulers of large states, as in the case of Hari Singh in Jammu and Kashmir, sought an independent status, but these requests were turned down by the British. On the basis of principles applied in the other princely states in 1947–1948, Kashmir should have been part of Pakistan. Generally, geographical compulsions, such as location, and the religious profile of the state would be the operative factors. Princely states with a Hindu majority would join India, while those with a Muslim majority would join Pakistan. Hari Singh's indecision provoked a rebellion in some parts of his territories, followed by an invasion by Pathan tribesmen supported by Pakistan. Hari Singh fled to India and

## AN UNFULFILLED PLAN FOR PEACE

The following statement was set forth at the fifty-seventh meeting of the Indian National Congress party in 1951. In 2002 conflict continues in Kashmir between Hindus and Muslims and Pakistani and Indian supporters of each.

> In regard of Kashmir, it has been the declared policy of the Government of India, with which the Congress is in entire agreement, that the people of Kashmir themselves should mould and decide their own future. The Congress welcomed an early plebiscite in Jammu and Kashmir under proper conditions which had been clearly stated by the Government of India. The Congress welcomes the constitution of a Constituent Assembly in the Kashmir State and hopes that through its labours the State will make even greater progress than it has done during the last two or three years.
>
> *Source:* Jagdish Saran Sharma. (1965) *India's Struggle for Freedom: Select Documents and Sources*. Vol. II. Delhi: S. Chand & Co., 176.

sought assistance to quell the rebellion and resist the invasion. More significantly, he agreed to let his state become part of India, a controversial decision that India claimed was valid but that Pakistan rejected as spurious and unacceptable. The Hindu maharaja's decision appeared to have been made under duress. From this dubious decision stems more than fifty years of hostility and three wars between India and Pakistan over the fate of Jammu and Kashmir.

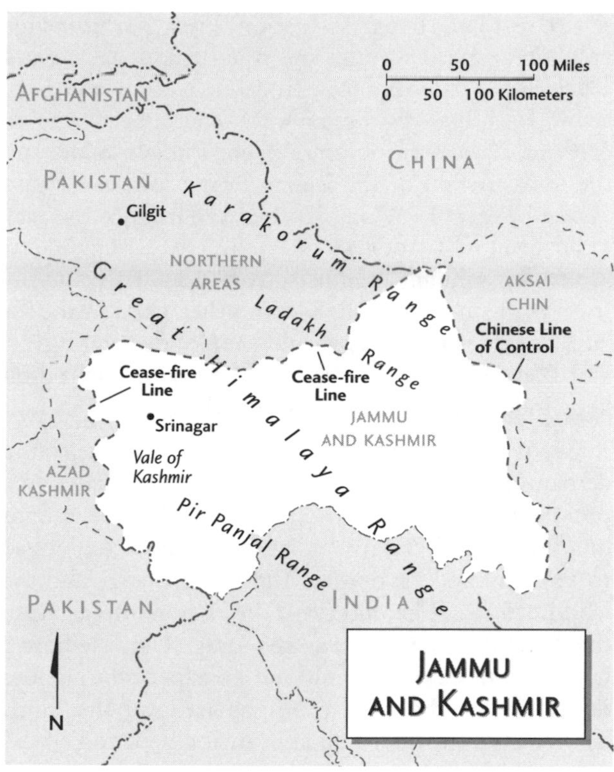


## The First Indo-Pakistan War over Jammu and Kashmir

The first Indo-Pakistan war over Jammu and Kashmir took place in 1947 in the wake of the independence of the two countries. A U.N.–mediated cease-fire took effect from January 1949 through the Karachi Agreement of 27 January 1949, signed by military representatives of the two countries defining the cease-fire lines in Jammu and Kashmir. In time this line came to mark the effective limits of the sovereignty of India and Pakistan. When the territories of Jammu and Kashmir were divided between India and Pakistan along the cease-fire line, India received the Kashmir valley; Jammu and Kashmir is thus the only Muslim-majority state in the Indian Union. Since the U.N. had in 1949 prescribed a plebiscite to determine the future of Jammu and Kashmir, the division was expected to be temporary. But that plebiscite was never held.

## Effects of the Division of Jammu and Kashmir

The cease-fire line in Jammu and Kashmir has become an extension of the international border between India and Pakistan. This leaves both India and Pakistan dissatisfied: India, as heir to the former state of the rulers of Jammu and Kashmir, insists on its rights to regions in Pakistan-controlled Azad Kashmir, to the north of Jammu and Kashmir. These territories are Swat, Gilgit, and the Northern Territories. Pakistan for its part insists on the plebiscite that was promised in 1949.

The situation became even more complicated in the early 1960s. After India's defeat at the hands of China in 1962, Pakistan signed the Sino-Pakistan agreement of 2 March 1963, setting the boundary between Pakistan-occupied Azad Kashmir and China's Xinjiang Province. Large extents of territory in Ladakh, to the east of Jammu and Kashmir, are now held by China but are claimed by India by virtue of being the heir to the rulers of Jammu and Kashmir.

## The Second and Third Indo-Pakistan Wars

Two years later came the second indecisive Indo-Pakistan war over Kashmir (1–23 September 1965), which ended after a cease-fire agreement. The Tashkent Declaration of 1 January 1966, signed by the Indian and Pakistani delegates with the then Soviet prime minister Kosygin as unofficial mediator, brought the second Indo-Pakistani war to an end. The two countries reaffirmed their commitment to solving their disputes by peaceful means and agreed to revert to their positions prior to 5 August 1965. The declaration proved to a mere temporary respite. In less than five years came the third Indo-Pakistan war in the Kashmir area, a war concurrent with the Indian intervention in East Pakistan and the successful separatist agitation that led to the creation of Bangladesh in 1971.

Talks between a triumphant Indian government and its defeated and humiliated Pakistani counterpart (28 June–2 July 1972) led to the Simla Agreement, through which both governments undertook to "respect" the line of control resulting from the cease-fire of December 1971.

## Continuing Problems in Jammu and Kashmir

Following the Simla Agreement of 1972, the Jammu and Kashmir problem lost some of its salience as a territorial dispute between Pakistan and India for a decade or so. But by the mid-1980s, the policy of benign (or not so very benign) neglect that India had pursued over this issue since the early 1970s faced a severe test in a changed situation. First, Kashmir's inhabitants experienced an upsurge of nationalism and a desire for independence from both India and Pakistan. Kashmiri dissidents were encouraged by the growing radicalization among the Punjabi Sikhs and the assassination of the Indian prime minister Indira Gandhi (1917–1984) in October 1984. Once the new radicalism took root in Kashmir, the struggle was joined by militant Islamists from outside, primarily from Afghanistan but also from other parts of the Islamic world, such as Libya and Iran, Sudan and Egypt, and Bangladesh. This process of internationalization kept Indo-Pakistan relations disturbed.

Second, the insurgents shifted their stance from a demand for Jammu and Kashmir's independence to a pro-Pakistan position. The Kashmiri Muslims, caught in a bitter conflict with Indian security forces, looked to Pakistan and beyond to Afghanistan, Iran, and the Middle East. The intervention of volunteers from these Islamic countries was encouraged and facilitated by Pakistan. Pakistan could not be expected to ignore events across the border on the basis of the Simla Agreement, an accord signed during a period of extreme weakness.

Equally important, the forces of democracy and nationalism that led to the collapse of the Soviet Union and the communist states of Central and Eastern Europe were at work in Kashmir itself. Although the Indian prime minister Rajiv Gandhi (1944–1991) adopted a more conciliatory policy in Jammu and Kashmir than had his mother, Indira Gandhi, the situation did not improve greatly. Indeed, the resort to terrorism by Kashmiri separatists led to the migration, forced or voluntary, of Hindus living in the Kashmir valley. The heavy-handed behavior of the Indian army in its response to the violence further antagonized the Kashmiris. Very soon, the Jammu and Kashmir issue returned to its pre-1972 form—an emotional factor in the domestic politics of both India and Pakistan, but especially in Pakistan. For both civilian and military leaders, Jammu and Kashmir was a useful rallying cry and a readily available issue with which to divert attention from failures in social and economic policies.

Whenever an opportunity to assert their rights presents itself, both India and Pakistan were quick to exploit it. Recently, improvements in mountain-climbing techniques have made it possible for both India and Pakistan to send troops into the remote, virtually uninhabited mountainous areas of Jammu and Kashmir, India, to the Siachen glacier, an undemarcated point on the line of control (in 1984 and thereafter), and Pakistan less successfully to the Kargil sector, across the line of control, in territory held by India (in 1999). The result has been confrontations on the border in one of the most inaccessible regions of Jammu and Kashmir, where the soldiers are more vulnerable to the bitter cold than to the weapons used by the opposing army.

India treats the fact that Kashmir is an integral part of India as beyond debate. Any attempts by Pakistan to raise the issue at a diplomatic level are dismissed as interference with India's internal affairs. Pakistan still insists on the plebiscite as originally envisaged by the U.N. Security Council resolution of 1949. For Islamabad, Kashmir is an unresolved international dispute. Thus, the public posture of the governments of India and Pakistan on the Jammu and Kashmir issue remains unchanged. It also remains the most dangerous issue in South Asia, and one that has the potential of a nuclear conflict.

In December 2001, an attack on the Indian parliament attributed to Kashmiri separatists brought India and Pakistan to the brink of another conflict. Indian troops were massed in Kashmir on the border with Pakistan. It took several weeks before the tensions eased.

*K. M. de Silva*

**Further Reading**

Amin, Tahir. (1995) *Mass Resistance in Kashmir: Origins, Evolution, and Options*. Islamabad, Pakistan: Institute of Policy Studies.

Behera, Navnita Chadha. (2000) *State, Identity and Violence: Jammu, Kashmir and Ladakh*. New Delhi: Manohar.

Gopal, Sarvapalli. (1979) *Jawaharlal Nehru, Vol. 2: 1947–56*. Delhi: Oxford University Press.

Gupta, Sisir. (1967) *Kashmir: A Study in India-Pakistan Relations*. Mumbai (Bombay), India: Asia Publishing House.

Jha, P. S. (1996) *Kashmir, 1947: Rival Versions of History*. Delhi: Oxford University Press.

Lamb, A. (1991) *Kashmir: A Disputed Legacy, 1946–1990*. Hertingfordbury, Hertfordshire, U.K.: Roxford.

———. (1994) *Birth of a Tragedy: Kashmir, 1947*. Hertingfordbury, Hertfordshire, U.K.: Roxford.

Wirsing, Robert G. (1994) *India, Pakistan and the Kashmir Dispute: On Regional Conflict and Its Resolution*. New York: St. Martin's.

**JAPAN—PROFILE** (2001 est. pop. 127 million). Japan, known as the Land of the Rising Sun, lies off the east coasts of Russia, Korea, and China. Its closest neighbor is Korea, from which it is separated by the Straits of Tsushima, a distance of about 200 kilometers. Made up of a number of islands, Japan is particularly small, being one and a half times the size of the United Kingdom.

## JAPAN

**Country name:** Japan
**Area:** 377,835 sq km
**Population:** 126,771,662 (July 2001 est.)
**Population growth rate:** 0.17% (2001 est.)
**Birth rate:** 10.04 births/1,000 population (2001 est.)
**Death rate:** 8.34 deaths/1,000 population (2001 est.)
**Net migration rate:** –0 migrant(s)/1,000 population (2001 est.)
**Sex ratio:** 0.96 male(s)/female (2001 est.)
**Infant mortality rate:** 3.88 deaths/1,000 live births (2001 est.)
**Life expectancy at birth—total population:** 80.8 years; male: 77.62 years; female: 84.15 years (2001 est.)
**Major religions:** Shinto and Buddhism
**Major language:** Japanese
**Literacy—total population:** 99% (1970 est.); male: not available; female: not available
**Government type:** Constitutional monarchy with a parliamentary government
**Capital:** Tokyo
**Administrative divisions:** 47 prefectures
**Independence:** 660 BCE (traditional founding by Emperor Jimmu)
**National holiday:** Birthday of Emperor Akihito, 23 December (1933)
**Suffrage:** 20 years of age; universal
**GDP—real growth rate:** 1.3% (2000 est.)
**GDP—per capita (purchasing power parity):** $24,900 (2000 est.)
**Population below poverty line:** Not available
**Exports:** $450 billion (f.o.b., 2000)
**Imports:** $355 billion (c.i.f., 2000)
**Currency:** Yen (JPY)

*Source:* Central Intelligence Agency. (2001) *The World Book Factbook 2001.* Retrieved 5 March 2002, from: http://www.cia.gov/cia/publications/factbook.

Although Japan was still an agriculture-based society in the middle of the nineteenth century, it changed, in about only sixty years, to a modern industrial nation. Today it has the world's second-largest economy, surpassed only by the United States, and enjoys one of the highest per capita incomes in the world. Its reliance on trade for wealth has led to a focus on manufacturing, and Japanese products are well known throughout the world.

### Geography

Japan is made up of four main islands—Hokkaido, Honshu, Shikoku, and Kyushu—along with some 7,000 smaller ones, so that altogether the island chain stretches about 3,000 kilometers from northeast to southwest. Because of its proximity to Siberia, Hokkaido has cold winters and heavy snowfalls, while the Ryukyu islands in the south, which stretch almost to Taiwan, are subtropical.

Japan's topography is very rugged, though some areas are favorable to agriculture. The largest such area is the Kanto Plain, on which Tokyo is situated. There are two other agricultural areas—the Nobi Plain (Nagoya area) and the Kansai Plain (Osaka, Kyoto, Nara area)—but these are some ten times smaller than the Kanto Plain. About 13 percent of Japan's land surface is devoted to agriculture today.

Approximately half the country is covered by mountains, with the Hida Range running through central Japan. Many of its peaks rise more than 2,000 meters and are volcanic in origin. The best known of

An exhibit at the Tokyo Motor Show, the largest auto exhibit in the world, in October 1999. (AFP/CORBIS)

these, with a summit of some 3,800 meters, is Mount Fuji (inactive since 1707), whose almost perfect cone shape is an enduring symbol of the country.

Japan is usually thought to be a highly urbanized nation, but this is only partly true. Cities cover less than 5 percent of Japan's land area. Its largest city is the capital, Tokyo, whose population numbers nearly 8 million, and the high concentration of population around Tokyo and other populous cities leads to considerable urban sprawl. In a fifty-kilometer radius of Tokyo there are more than 30 million people, around Osaka approximately 16 million, and around Nagoya 9 million. This high level of urbanization dates from the late nineteenth century but has become especially salient since 1950.

## Peoples

People first came to Japan from Korea, China, and the Pacific islands perhaps 200,000 years ago, or 600,000 years ago according to some archaeologists. The last glaciers receded about 15,000 years ago, and until that time land bridges in the north, west, and south intermittently connected Japan to the mainland. Archaeological evidence clearly shows that early waves of migrants reached the islands some 30,000 years ago and formed the Paleolithic (Old Stone Age) Japanese population. According to modern DNA analysis, the first wave of migrants came from Southeast Asia, with subsequent groups traveling from the Asian mainland. Hence, the modern Japanese are a mixture of both ethnic and racial groups, Southeast Asian and East Asian; remnants of the earlier groups, the Ainu people, today live in pockets in northern Japan. Thus the frequently heard Japanese claim that they are ethnically and racially homogeneous is not supported by the evidence.

## History and Culture

The first substantial Neolithic (New Stone Age) civilization of hunters and gatherers in Japan is the Jomon (roughly 10,000–300 BCE). Although the inhabitants remained primarily hunter-gatherers, the Jomon period saw the beginning of permanent settlements and early agriculture, particularly dry rice farming.

Around 300 BCE a new wave of migrants from the mainland arrived in Japan and eventually displaced (or absorbed) the Jomon, a process that took hundreds of years. The new group brought bronze and iron technology, and the period has been named Yayoi (after an excavation site in Tokyo). The technology and artifacts are typical of Northeast Asia and include mirrors, weapons, bells, and coins brought from the mainland. During the Yayoi period (c. 300 BCE–300 CE), the introduction of wet rice agriculture had a massive impact on Japanese society, in terms of increased food production, expanded areas of settlement, and establishment of a cooperative and hierarchical social order.

Shinto, the indigenous religion of Japan, existed from the earliest settlement of the islands. With its pantheon of gods *(kami)*, Shinto is animistic and is concerned with day-to-day matters such as keeping various spirits content. Although there is no substantial ethical code, the religion is grounded in a close relationship with the natural environment and communal life. As the titular head (chief priest) of this religion, the emperor still today performs ceremonies symbolic of planting and harvesting, and it is partly his place in Shintoism that has accorded him sacred status throughout Japan's history.

By the seventh century Japanese society began to be transformed through contacts with Korea and China. Among the important cultural practices borrowed from the mainland were Buddhism, Confucianism, and the concept of a strong centralized government. Borrowed, too, was the Chinese writing system, though it was modified to suit the spoken Japanese language.

Kyoto became the capital of Japan in 794, marking the beginning of a golden age in Japanese history. While Europe was just coming out of the Dark Ages, culture blossomed in Japan. Feudalism developed slowly in Japan as the centralized state under the emperor gradually lost its authority and regional groups of families, or clans, began to assert their power. This system prevailed for most of Japan's subsequent history. By 1185 the country was under the control of these warrior families, who in turn submitted to a military dictator with the title of shogun. Over the next

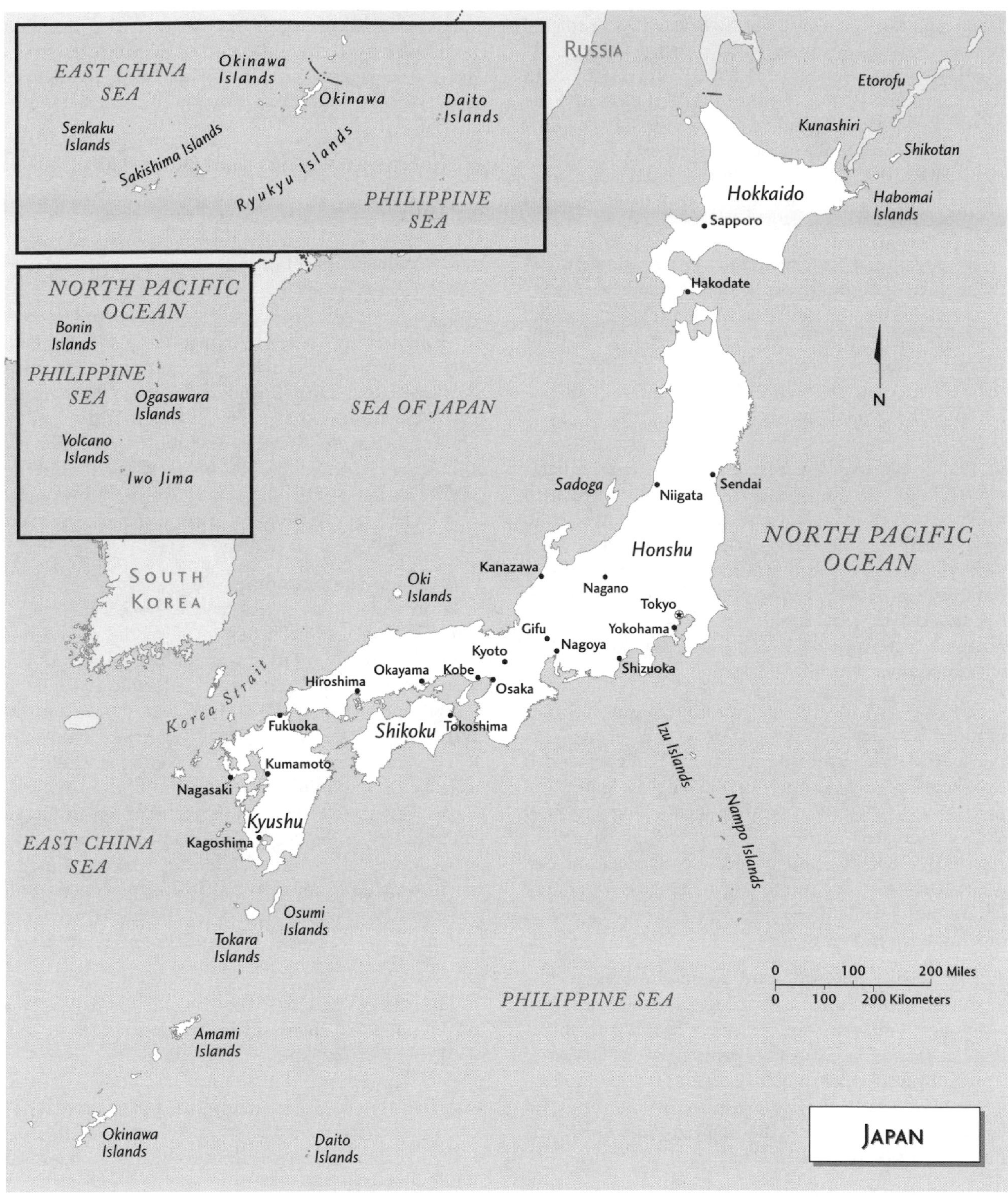


four hundred years, as the power of the shoguns waned, Japan broke into small feudal principalities; each was ruled by a daimyo, or feudal lord, and governed and policed by samurai warriors.

With mounting conflict among the daimyo and the various clans, Japan disintegrated into civil war by the mid-fifteenth century. In the mid-sixteenth century several powerful Japanese daimyo attempted to reunify

Japan, and the Tokugawa family eventually completed the unification by the early seventeenth century. At this time the leaders of this family, worried by both the continuing power of other regional clans and the growing Western influence (including the spread of Christianity and modern weapons) in Asia, decided to close Japan to foreigners. For more than 200 years thereafter Japan remained almost completely isolated from the rest of the world.

During the seventeenth and eighteenth centuries Japan developed many of its unique practices in government, literature, architecture, and religion, and the country remained relatively peaceful and stable. This peace was reinforced through a rigid totalitarian system of government, with the Tokugawa shoguns, based in the capital city of Edo (present-day Tokyo), as supreme leaders. As Europe and America became more insistent on trade during the mid-1850s, Japan's vulnerability to the West, because of its outdated military technology, became obvious to those who were aware of the threat, and the country was a potential target for colonization. Meanwhile, from a domestic standpoint the system of government that had worked well for some two centuries had, by the nineteenth century, become outdated and riddled with inequities.

The catalyst for change was the arrival of Commodore Matthew C. Perry (1794–1858) of the U.S. Navy, who sailed into Edo bay in 1853 and demanded that Japan open its ports to trade. The recognition of the country's vulnerability after such a long period of isolation created a tremendous drive for change in Japan. By 1868 the shogun and daimyo had handed power back to the emperor, who remained a symbol of continuity while the country went through a period of breakneck modernization.

This period, known as the Meiji Restoration, saw Japan move from a feudalistic, agricultural country to a modern, industrial one with a reasonably democratic constitution. Within sixty years Japan had electricity, railways, steamships, elections, and modern weapons. Its teachers were the major industrialized countries of the time—the United States, Britain, France, Germany, and Holland.

Japan was not content to remain a student, however, and by the late nineteenth century it exercised its growing power in a war with China (1894–1895), which it won. This victory eventually brought Japan into conflict with Russia, which it defeated in the Russo-Japanese War of 1904–1905. Underlying these conflicts was one of the fundamental truths about Japan—its home islands had few resources, and the country needed to import raw materials to maintain its industrial growth. Like the other major countries of the day, Japan sought to secure needed resources and markets through colonization and conquest.

Japan, however, was not accepted by the major Western countries as an equal, and its colonization of parts of China and Korea was strenuously resisted. By the 1930s Japan was on a collision course with the West. Faced with an embargo of raw materials, especially oil, from the United States and Britain, Japan gambled on war to secure these resources from East and Southeast Asia. The result was the surprise attack on Pearl Harbor in 1941 in an attempt to decimate American naval power while Japanese troops invaded Southeast Asia. Japan's leaders, however, underestimated the resolve of the United States and its allies. The result was the Pacific theater of World War II, ending with atomic bombs being dropped on the Japanese cities of Hiroshima and Nagasaki in August 1945 and Japan's subsequent unconditional surrender.

**Politics and the Economy**

Japan was in a shambles in late 1945. Much of its industrial base had been destroyed in the war, and it had lost the wealth of its empire. The country was occupied by the Allies under the leadership of General Douglas MacArthur (1880–1964), whose mission was to transform Japan into a peace-loving and stable ally of the West and to ensure that the country could not again become a military threat. One of the key decisions taken in this regard was to break up the large landholdings of the rich families and turn Japan into a nation of small farmers and entrepreneurs. Another was to provide Japan with a British-type constitution that included a unique provision (Article 9) whereby the Japanese renounced war and forswore the development of a military force.

The start of the Cold War and the outbreak of war in Korea in 1950 changed matters. Japan became part of America's front-line defense against the spread of world Communism. The country received economic aid to develop its manufacturing sector to supply motor vehicles, electronic goods, and clothing to the soldiers in Korea. Japan's economy began to boom in these areas.

Although there were labor problems in the 1950s and early 1960s, by the latter date Japan had become a peaceful, industrious nation focused on economic growth. The Liberal Democratic Party came into being in 1955 and, except for a brief period out of power in 1993–1994, has dominated ever since. Although the party is stable, there are multiple factions, each with its own leader, so that prime ministers regularly change while the same party remains in power.

The 1960s was a time of supergrowth in Japan's economy. Even faced with the "oil shocks" of the 1970s, the economy continued to grow, diversifying away from heavy industry into consumer electronics, computers, and robotics. Its trade surplus with other industrialized countries, principally the United States, led in 1985 to pressure on Japan to strengthen its currency. The result was a tremendous flow of Japanese money worldwide, as Japanese went on buying sprees. Japan seemed an unstoppable global economic power.

The massive loans made available to Japanese companies and individuals for both domestic and offshore investments led to the development of a "bubble" economy by the late 1980s. This resulted from easy credit made available by Japanese banks in the mid- to late 1980s, coupled with dramatic strengthening of the yen after 1985. Much of this money made its way into real estate speculation and the stock market, rather than productive industries. Many loans were secured by land, which led to an inflation in real estate values until Japanese land became the most expensive in the world. The stock market, too, became highly overvalued. The result, in the early 1990s, was a crash in both areas and an economic slump that continued into the twenty-first century. Japan's growth rate continues to hover around the 1 percent mark, far behind that of most other industrialized countries.

**Constitutional Reforms**

Constitutional reform has a long history in Japan. The principal area of debate is the nature of the country's military. Article 9 of the 1947 constitution renounces the maintenance of military forces or their use in international disputes. Today, however, Japan has the second-largest defense budget in the world after the United States as well as a well-equipped military, but avoids constitutional debate by calling the military a self-defense force. The charade has caused many in Japan to call for a change in the military's name and role.

Both the Gulf War and the terrorist attacks in New York and Washington, D.C., on 11 September 2001 have put increased pressure on Japan to use its military in international conflicts. In addition, Japanese leaders have been attempting to secure a permanent seat on the United Nations Security Council, which would probably require a greater commitment of military forces. Nevertheless, there is a strong pacifist group in Japan, dating from 1945, which inhibits reform in this area.

Other measures for reform are concerned with the way Japan is governed. Key areas here include reducing the power of the bureaucracy and making it subservient to politicians; making elections policy-based rather than focused on personalities and pork barreling; having elections contested between at least two major political parties rather than being dominated by the Liberal Democratic Party; and deregulating and decentralizing the governing system and giving ordinary people a stronger political voice. The reform movement has generally had little success, despite some optimism in the early 1990s, and today there are few areas of significant reform.

**Major Issues Today**

Japan is presently faced with myriad difficulties. While its companies continue to manufacture world-class products, cracks are developing throughout its economy and society. Japan is still coping with the bursting of the bubble economy. Many companies and banks were left with massive debt, much of it hidden, and the government has been attempting to take over these loans and restore business confidence. A major problem in this regard is the close connections between politicians, bureaucrats, and major corporations and interest groups. While this was viewed as a successful system during the period of high growth, today it is seen as a major obstacle to the government's making the hard economic decisions necessary to put the economy on the road to recovery.

The social system that supported Japan's rapid economic development is also being called into question. While workers are relatively well paid, they are expected to show tremendous dedication to the workplace. Men in particular must focus their lives on their companies. Because of the highly urbanized conditions in Japan, where land continues to be expensive, working people can anticipate extremely long commuting times, substantial overtime work, and little time for their families. Such dedication (or exploitation) is increasingly being called into question, particularly when companies no longer offer workers the generous benefits and certainty of lifelong employment typical of the boom years.

Japan's economic problems are also leading to questions about the way in which its fundamental social institutions are organized. The educational system, with its emphasis on competition and rote learning, is now being viewed by many as dysfunctional. The powerful bureaucracy in Japan, the pinnacle of achievement for young Japanese, whose roots go back to the samurai and a highly regimented feudalistic society, today often seems incapable of making effective decisions. Women, who until recently have been denied full participation in the economy, seem to be struggling to find new roles in modern Japan.

Perhaps the major issue confronting Japanese society today is its aging population. An extremely high birthrate in the late 1940s and early 1950s means that there will be massive retirements of Japanese in the first few decades of the twenty-first century, with concomitant problems of funding pensions, caring for elderly people, and possible substantial labor shortages. The aging of the population will have a massive impact on virtually every aspect of Japan's society and economy over the coming decades.

*Curtis Andressen*

### Further Reading

Andressen, Curtis. (2002) *Samurai to Sony: A Short History of Japan*. Sydney, Australia: Allen and Unwin.

Buckley, Roger. (1990) *Japan Today*. Cambridge, U.K.: Cambridge University Press.

Cortazzi, Hugh. (1990) *The Japanese Achievement*. London: Sidgwick and Jackson.

Dale, Peter. (1995) *The Myth of Japanese Uniqueness*. London: Routledge.

Frankel, Jeffrey, and Miles Kahler. (1993) *Regionalism and Rivalry: Japan and the United States in Pacific Asia*. Chicago: University of Chicago Press.

Hatch, Walter, and Kozo Yamamura. (1996) *Asia in Japan's Embrace*. Cambridge, U.K.: Cambridge University Press.

Henshall, Kenneth. (1999) *Dimensions of Japanese Society*. London: Macmillan.

Ishido, Kotaku, and David Myers, eds. (1995) *Japanese Society Today*. Rockhampton, Australia: Central Queensland University Press.

Reischauer, Edwin. (1993) *The Japanese Today: Change and Continuity*. Tokyo: Charles E. Tuttle.

Schirokauer, Conrad. (1989) *A Brief History of Chinese and Japanese Civilizations*. San Diego, CA: Harcourt Brace Jovanovich.

Simone, Vera, and Anne Feraru. (1995) *The Asian Pacific: Political and Economic Development in a Global Context*. London: Longman.

Wolferen, Karel van. (1993) *The Enigma of Japanese Power*. Tokyo: Charles E. Tuttle.

## JAPAN—ECONOMIC SYSTEM

Although endowed with few natural resources, Japan has achieved a world-class standard of living following its miraculous economic recovery from World War II. At current exchange rates, Japan's per-capita gross domestic product (GDP) in 1999 was $34,500, only slightly below that of the United States, a resource-rich country with 25 times as much land and twice the population. In 1999, Japan had only 2.1 percent of the world's population and 0.3 percent of the world's land, but its GDP was 13.4 percent of the world total.

The postwar economic miracle was characterized by phenomenal efficiency, but also by impressive economic equality. In 1960, 76 percent of respondents to a government survey considered themselves middle class, a figure that reached 90 percent by the early 1990s. As measured by salary gaps between various categories of employees (e.g., workers and managers; middle-school and college graduates), for example, Japan has had one of the lowest levels of income inequality in the world.

A high growth rate, relatively equal distribution of income, and low unemployment are hallmarks of the Japanese development experience. So too are a low crime rate and high rates of literacy and savings. Japan leads the world in life expectancy (77 years for men and 84 years for women, estimated for 2001). Other indicators of the quality of life, however, have been less favorable. Pollution was a serious problem in the 1960s. Long commutes to work, long working hours, and few vacation days meant Japanese workers had much less leisure time than their Western counterparts. Scarce land has resulted in high land prices, cramped living conditions, limited recreational space, and narrow roads. In 1996, residential land prices in Osaka were 18.5 times higher than in New York (commercial real estate was 2.8 times higher). For example, the cost of a detached house in Tokyo was 12.9 times annual income (9.5 times in Osaka) in 1994, but only 2.9 times annual income in New York. In 1995, the average size of a Japanese house was 93.3 square meters (the U.S. 1996 house size was 177.5 square meters). Most Japanese residential property is too small for a lawn or garden. Consumer prices in Japan have been consistently high compared to other developed countries. While Japan's resource constraints make such problems difficult to surmount, steady progress has occurred in most areas (due in no small part to the long economic stagnation). After falling steadily throughout the 1990s, residential land prices ended the decade at less than half their peak (1991) value. Japan's consumers also received a break in the form of lower prices and a greater selection of products and services.

### Historical Transitions

In Japan's transition from a closed, feudalistic society during the Tokugawa period (1600/1603–1868) to its modern status as a global, industrial giant, two turning points stand out: the Meiji Restoration (1868) and the Allied Occupation (1945–1952). Only

## EMPLOYMENT REALITIES IN JAPAN

The "lifetime-employment" guarantee enjoyed by many Japanese workers became far less practical in the harsher economic climate in Japan in the 1990s. The following excerpts from *White Paper on Labour, 1999*, a Japanese government report, outline some of the new realities facing employers and their young and middle-aged workers.

> Such factors as changes in younger people's attitudes about job changes and the growing diversity in employment patterns will have a significant impact on employment practices. Also, the continued decline in the number of children will make it difficult to fully compensate for structural changes through traditional adjustments at the labour market's entrance and exit. Instead, job changes will play a greater role than they have in the past. In addition, the lowering of the expected growth rate and the globalization of operations are likely to have the effect of weakening long-term employment practices.
>
> Nevertheless, support for long-term employment practices currently remains high among both companies and workers. Long-term employment practices will continue to be highly effective with respect to jobs in which teamwork is important, and in relation to vocational abilities that require a buildup over time. For Japanese companies and the Japanese economy and society as a whole, it will be important to focus in particular on stabilizing and maintaining employment, thereby improving employee morale and securing the flexibility needed for corporate growth. Hasty employment adjustments could cause companies to lose credibility and make it more difficult for them to obtain required workers. . . .
>
> In Japan, middle-aged workers have enjoyed a low unemployment rate and stable employment. Now, however, they are facing the most severe conditions ever. In order to eliminate unease about employment among middle-aged workers, it is of course important to steadily pursue improvements to employability, as well as job creation and the establishment of a labour market that facilitates reemployment. In addition to these efforts, however, there is a need for initiatives that utilize the vocational abilities that middle-aged workers have built up over time. It is also important that middle-aged workers be utilized in a way that maintains their connections to their traditional workplace or job (e.g., company or corporate group).

Ministry of Health, Labor and Welfare—Japan. *White Paper on Labour, 1999*. Retrieved 17 September 2002, from: http://www.mhlw.go.jp/english/wp/wp-l/2-3-3.html

four decades after the Meiji Restoration, Japan achieved modern economic growth and gained international respect as a leading military power. The Meiji period (1868–1912) resulted in significant economic reforms. These included the opening of the country to foreign trade and technology, privatization of land ownership, replacement of the rice tax with a monetary land tax, and the introduction of a modern money and banking system.

The Occupation brought radical reforms to many institutions. The three major economic reforms were the redistribution of agricultural land, the dissolution of the *zaibatsu* (large, family-owned industrial enter-

## JAPAN'S LARGEST COMPANIES

According to *Asia Week* the largest nineteen companies (on the basis of sales revenue) in Asia are Japanese firms. The top ten are as follows.

| Rank | Company | Sector | Sales ($ millions) |
|---|---|---|---|
| 1 | Mitsubishi | General Trading | 129,862.7 |
| 2 | Toyota | Cars, Trucks | 124,565.5 |
| 3 | Mitsui & Co. | General Trading | 121,974.7 |
| 4 | Itochu | General Trading | 112,603.3 |
| 5 | Nippon Telegraph & Telephone | Telecommunications | 105,113.6 |
| 6 | Sumitomo | General Trading | 93,533.1 |
| 7 | Marubeni | General Trading | 87,564.8 |
| 8 | Hitachi | Electronics, Machinery | 78,101.3 |
| 9 | Matsushita Electric | Appliances, Electronics | 71,277.4 |
| 10 | Sony | Electronics, Media | 67,874.4 |

*Source:* "The Asia Week 1000." (2001) *Asia Week* (9 November): 48–91.

prises), and the legalization of trade unions and collective bargaining. In the financial sphere, Joseph M. Dodge, an American banker and Occupation adviser, introduced a number of important policy changes known as the "Dodge line." These included the imposition of a balanced budget policy, an end to inflationary financing of public financial institutions, a return of foreign trade to private enterprise, lifting of price controls, termination of production subsidies, and the unification and pegging of the exchange rate (at ¥360 to the U.S. dollar). Professor Carl Shoup, another Occupation adviser, tried to implement a unified and nonpreferential tax system but was less successful.

Japan's recovery from wartime devastation and the recession induced by Dodge-line policies received a big boost from the "special procurements" demand of the Korean War (1950–1952), followed by a long period of high and sustained economic growth. From 1955 to 1965, GNP growth (in constant prices) averaged 9.5 percent. To put this in perspective, a growth rate of 8.6 percent would result in a doubling of real income in just nine years. Amazingly, super growth continued for almost a decade more. From 1965 to 1975, real GNP growth averaged 7.9 percent while the average per-capita GNP grew at an incredible 6.5 percent. This period includes the end of the Bretton Woods system of fixed exchange rates in 1971 (the "Nixon shock") and the first oil shock (1973–1974). These were traumatic events for Japan's export-led and import-dependent economy. The quadrupling of oil prices provoked the first year of negative growth in the postwar period and resulted in a massive restructuring of industry, drastic energy conservation measures, and an increasing reliance on nuclear power.

Japan's economy continued to grow at a very respectable pace in the decade and a half following the first oil shock. Real GNP growth averaged 4 percent between 1975 and 1990. The floating of the yen began a long period of appreciation, from ¥272 to the U.S. dollar in 1972 to a plateau of ¥210 in 1978. A period of yen depreciation followed the second oil shock in 1979, and recovery from the oil shock brought with it large current-account surpluses. As a result, trade frictions escalated. The Plaza Accord of September 1985 sought to reverse the yen's rise and shrink Japan's burgeoning trade surplus. While modest progress was made on the trade front, yen appreciation exceeded expectations, and it rocketed to a postwar peak of ¥94 to the dollar in 1995. The yen's rise was supported by a declining real price of oil, a positive U.S.-Japan inflation gap, and ongoing trade and capital liberalization.

It was the Bank of Japan's attempt to stem the yen's ascent that created the liquidity for financing the now infamous "bubble economy." During the bubble period (1985–1990), prices of such assets as stocks, bonds, land, and collectables doubled or tripled. Balance sheets ballooned. In fiscal 1991, the seven largest banks in the world (based on assets) were Japanese. Nomura Securities became the largest security company in the world. Starting in May 1989, monetary tightening by the Bank of Japan led to the collapse of the bubble and a liquidity crunch that led to a severe and protracted banking and economic crisis. The "lost decade" of the 1990s undermined faith in the continuing viability of the postwar economic system.

### Japanese Capitalism

Using the Anglo-American economic system as a point of reference, historians and social scientists have identified several distinctively Japanese institutions. With the collapse of the bubble economy, these institutions came under tremendous strain.

Three "golden treasures" characterize the traditional employment system: lifetime employment, seniority-based wages, and enterprise unionism. From the postwar period through the early 1990s, a lifetime employment guarantee was a standard feature of the implicit contract for employees of major corporations and government organizations. Smaller companies, although unable to offer the same employment security, often had a similar paternalistic attitude toward their employees. Wages in traditional organizations depended on initial entry conditions (education, gender, connections, industry, establishment size), position, and age. Typically, employees started out with salaries below market level, but received higher than market pay in later years. Some 95 percent of unions in Japan are enterprise unions (confined to the specific company for which union members work), and not organized on the basis of trade or industry as in other developed countries. Most unions belong to one of four major union federations and include both blue- and white-collar workers. In the 1990s, some economists began to see the golden treasures as golden chains, locking workers into a fixed and hierarchical system that seems increasingly ill suited for a fast-paced, flexible global economy.

Two other institutions of the traditional employment system deserve mention. One is the bonus system, whereby employees are given a lump sum payment two or three times a year. The size of the total annual bonus can be substantial, ranging from two to six times monthly base pay in normal years. A second institution is the annual "spring offensive" *(shunto)*, a coordinated and ritualized bargaining campaign by individual enterprise unions.

These institutions apply only to permanent employees, however. Japanese firms also take on large numbers of temporary employees, who receive lower pay and benefits, lack union protection, and may be laid off during business slowdowns. Women are another exception. In the traditional pattern, women work while young, but leave the work force in their twenties to marry and raise a family. A large proportion of the female work force are employed part-time, the result of the tax system, inflexible work conditions, a demanding educational system, seniority-based wages, and a host of discriminatory practices.

### Industry Groupings

Historically, Japanese corporations have had strong group affiliations of various types and purposes. *Zaibatsu* were powerful family-owned holding companies that dominated the Japanese economy prior to 1945. Under Occupation reforms, the holding-company structure was forbidden and individuals were prohibited from owning more than 1 percent of the shares of a single company. New group formations, however, soon emerged following dissolution of the *zaibatsu*. Horizontal (or financial) *keiretsu* are groups of independent firms with a trading company and a main bank at their core and an informal "presidents' club" as a coordination mechanism. Three financial *keiretsu* groups (Mitsubishi, Mitsui, and Sumitomo) are direct descendants of prewar *zaibatsu*. Rounding out the "Big Six" are three additional members (Fuyo, Sanwa, and Dai-Ichi Kangyo), postwar formations with substantial market shares but with a smaller number of affiliated firms and somewhat weaker ties. The vertical-production *keiretsu* is a manufacturer-supplier relationship in which a dominant manufacturing firm is supported by a network of subsidiaries, subcontractors, and affiliated companies. In the vertical-distribution *keiretsu*, a large manufacturing enterprise distributes its products through a network of affiliated retail stores. Still other variations on these basic group structures exist.

*Keiretsu* firms are held together by interlocking share ownership. Mutual shareholding prevents hostile takeovers and allows firms to honor their long-term commitments to workers. With few exceptions, board members of a Japanese corporation are senior executives of the company. There are, in fact, no corporations in Japan with a majority of outside directors. These features of the Japanese system leave individual stockholders with little influence on a company's management. The result is a form of capitalism different from that in the Anglo-Saxon world. In the Japanese firm, shareholders must take a back seat to other stakeholders. The Japanese corporation, it is often asserted, is run for the benefit of its permanent employees. In the 1980s, this system was widely praised. Japanese capitalism was said to promote long-term planning, since, unlike their Western counterparts, Japanese managers do not have shareholders constantly breathing down their necks.

### Banking and Finance

At the core of the *keiretsu* group is a main bank, which takes the lead in organizing funding for the affiliated firms. It is usually the largest holder of a firm's debt and holds up to 5 percent of its stock. This gives the bank a strong incentive to monitor the firm's activities and to provide useful information. It is in a good position to do this since it handles a disproportionate share of the firm's daily transactions. In times of financial distress, the main bank usually organizes the rescue operation. The main bank takes on many of the responsibilities that would be borne by large shareholders in the Anglo-American system.

The financial system of Japan's high-growth period (1955–1973) was characterized by highly segmented financial markets and indirect finance (i.e., borrowing through financial intermediaries). The private sector's slice of the financial pie was finely divided among a host of depository institutions, nondepository institutions, and securities-related financial institutions. Further categorization of private institutions depended on a host of characteristics (e.g., size and nature of its customers, types of products offered, maturity and structure of loans). Public financial institutions included postal savings, the trust fund bureau, two public banks, and eleven public finance corporations.

During the high-growth period, some 90 percent of investment funds were borrowed from financial institutions. Private banks dominated the system, accounting for 40 percent of total lending. Starting in the 1970s, financial liberalization began to whittle away at this "banker's kingdom." Barriers to intersector and international competition steadily eroded. Although capital markets have begun to play a more important role in industrial and public finance, depository institutions still hold a commanding position in the financial system. The main reason for this is the high proportion of private savings in deposit accounts, including the gargantuan postal savings system.

### Industrial Structure

Perhaps the most dramatic change in the Japanese economy in the last century has been the shrinking of the agricultural sector. At the start of the Meiji period, Japan was an agriculture economy. The agricultural sector provided 45 percent of Japan's GDP and employed 73 percent of its labor force. By 1955, those statistics had shrunk to 21 and 39 percent, respectively. In 1998, Japan's entire primary sector (agriculture, forestry, and fisheries) accounted for only 1.7 percent of GDP and 5.3 percent of employment (with most agricultural employees being part-time farmers). Although small in size, the agricultural sector wielded considerable political power in the postwar period as a mainstay of the ruling Liberal Democratic Party's support base. Its loyalty has been rewarded with generous price supports and subsidies, and large construction outlays. These and other barriers to trade have been sources of continuing international friction. Government policy has aimed at improving labor productivity by increasing the size of the average farm.

The share of the secondary sector (mining, manufacturing, and construction) in production and employment rose steadily before stabilizing in the mid-1970s. In 1998, the secondary sector accounted for 33.0 percent of GDP and 31.5 percent of employment. Manufacturing's share of GDP was 23.5 percent. In the manufacturing sector, large firms accounted for 52.2 percent of the total value of factory shipments (1998). The overwhelming number of firms in the industry (99.4 percent in 1998), however, were classified as small or medium-sized. Furthermore, small and medium-sized companies employed 74 percent of the industry's workers.

By the early 2000s, Japan had clearly entered the postindustrial stage of development. Japan's tertiary sector constituted 61.1 percent of GDP and 63.2 percent of employment (1998), and information technology had become the primary focus of its industrial policy.

Japan has often been described as having a dual economy. On one side of the divide are the large and efficient export-oriented firms—world-class corporations producing products such as automobiles, machinery, electronic goods, and semiconductors. On the other side are inefficient, domestic-oriented firms, which tend to be in such highly protected industries as agriculture, construction, and finance. Opinion is now widely shared that these inefficient sectors have been a profound drag on the economy. How to invigorate them without destroying the social compact is a great challenge.

### International Economic Relations

For a resource-poor country, Japan is surprisingly little dependent on foreign trade. In 1998, the export share of GDP was 10.2 percent; import dependency was 7.4 percent. Most European countries, in contrast, have dependency ratios over 20 percent. Japan's exports are dominated by manufactured goods; its imports are mostly primary products. Japan runs trade surpluses with most industrial countries and trade deficits with most of its primary product suppliers. The United States is Japan's biggest trade partner. In 1998, the U.S. absorbed 31 percent of Japan's exports and accounted for 24 percent of Japan's imports.

Since 1981, Japan has run continuous and generally rising trade surpluses, resulting in considerable friction, particularly with the United States. But Japan has also been active in promoting international and intraregional economic cooperation and has been the number one provider of overseas development assistance in the world. In 1998, 43.3 percent of Japanese aid went to Asia (down from a high of 98.3 percent in 1970), and the Japanese government has advocated closer and more open trading ties among Asian countries, seeking a more stable currency environment and a wider use of the yen as a settlement currency.

**Social Foundations and the Neoclassical Debate**

Some scholars argue that Japan's economic institutions are constructed on a fundamentally different social structure than those of Anglo-American design. The Japanese social system, in this interpretation, has feudal-period roots. It is claimed, for example, that Japanese business, government, and social institutions are patterned after the *ie* (household) or *mura* (village) concepts of social organization. In such organizations, individuals are bound together in lifelong, hierarchical relationships and, consequently, are compelled to accept group norms of behavior. In the Japanese system, social harmony and the pursuit of collective goals take precedence over individual interests. The dynamics of such organizations may well be different from those patterned on the more individual-centered Anglo-American model.

With its institutional rigidities and group dynamics, the Japanese economic system poses a challenge to neoclassical economic theory's paradigm of individual choice and its assumption that only unregulated markets deliver economically efficient outcomes. Many believe that Japan's success is an example of bureaucrat-led development—an example that has been successfully imitated by other Asian economies. The claim is that industrial and other policies, most notably those of the Ministry of International Trade and Industry (MITI), helped to propel the economy onto a faster and better growth path than would have been possible in a less regulated system. Neoclassical economists find such assertions hard to accept without convincing evidence that government action overcame recognized market imperfections (public goods, externalities, or Keynesian-style instabilities).

The importance of the bureaucracy in Japan's economic system cannot be lightly dismissed. The Japanese bureaucracy not only administers the nation's laws, but also drafts most of the legislation proposed in the Diet. The bureaucracy has consistently drawn top students from Japan's elite universities, and richly rewarded them. Scandals have cast light on the common business practice of showering key bureaucrats with gifts, speaker fees, and lavish entertainment. After retiring from government service, faithful bureaucrats can expect to "descend from heaven" *(amakudari)* into senior positions at private or public corporations. They may retire several times and receive generous, multiple pensions—practices one would not expect to find in a laissez-faire economy.

Nor is the power of the bureaucracy limited to enforcing formal laws and regulations. Japanese bureaucrats also rely on administrative guidance *(gyosei seido)*, an informal request for "voluntary" compliance with government policies. The more leverage the ministries exert over targeted firms, the more effective the administrative guidance.

An example of this approach is the Bank of Japan's policy of providing periodic loan targets for commercial banks. The "window guidance" policy, which was discontinued in 1991, rested on the rewards and punishments the central bank had at its disposal. Cooperative banks could borrow money at attractive rates, and, until 1995, were guaranteed a profit on Bank of Japan borrowing, since the spread between the interbank loan rate and the central bank discount rate was always positive. Recalcitrant banks probably found the discount window closed, had trouble getting Bank of Japan approval for new branches or products, and experienced more frequent and troublesome bank inspections.

**The Convoy System**

The literature on Japan's political economy concentrates on industrial and trade policies, but an arguably more important set of policies deals with the regulation of finance and macroeconomic activity. In this domain, the Ministry of Finance has traditionally reigned supreme. It prepares the budgets for the national government and the Fiscal Investment and Loan Program (FILP); designs the tax system and monitors tax collections; oversees customs, tariffs, and international finance; establishes financial system policies; and licenses and supervises, with some exceptions, all of the important financial institutions. An old exception is the postal savings system, which is regulated by the Ministry of Posts and Telecommunications.

As part of the "big bang" reforms following the banking crisis of the 1990s, the Ministry of Finance was forced to surrender some of its licensing and supervisory powers to a new Financial Agency under the prime minister's office. In addition, the new Bank of Japan Law, which took effect in April 1998, gave the central bank considerable independence in the design and conduct of monetary policy.

Bureaucrats refer to the Japanese system of financial regulation as the "convoy system." The image conveyed is a group of carefully selected ships, tightly linked under central command, moving at nearly identical speeds through dangerous waters. The Ministry of Finance, operating through the Bank of Japan, controlled the financial spigot. Four characteristics of the traditional financial system helped the ministry maintain convoy discipline. Capital controls protected domestic markets from external competition. Administered interest rates provided the incentive structure for domestic fund competition. Market segmentation allowed more precise channeling of the flow of funds. Finally, indirect finance gave the ministry direct control over the flow of funds and indirect control, through the *keiretsu* system, over the entire economy.

Is it a coincidence that the golden age of the convoy system (1955–1971) overlapped the period of high-speed growth? Maybe not. The convoy's low interest rate policy provided an inducement to "overinvestment." Other policies, such as tax incentives and consumer lending disincentives, may have stimulated the required "oversaving." This may have led to more capital deepening and per-capita income than would have been achieved by a more market-based system.

Whether or not the convoy system stimulated faster growth, the original convoy was ill suited for the choppy seas of the 1970s. Financial liberalization resulted in a soft form of convoy regulation. The big-bang reforms were designed to create a financial structure that was free, fair, and open. Could a convoy operate under such rules? The Ministry of Finance scarcely had time to contemplate the question when the ultimate shock occurred. In 1997 the collapse of several large commercial banks and the Asian currency crisis hit the convoy like a hurricane.

Macroeconomic stabilization was a key responsibility of convoy regulators. Demand management involved manipulation of several unique tools. Japan's underdeveloped bond market meant that open market operations could not be the primary instrument for monetary control, as in Western countries. Until the early 1990s, the Bank of Japan used discount loans and window guidance as its primary policy instruments. The primary tool for fiscal policy has been the highly flexible FILP budget. The Ministry of Finance has had enormous discretion in varying the amount of budget outlays within and between fiscal years.

## The Twenty-first Century

At the start of the new millennium, Japan found itself in a very difficult economic situation. The country had endured a decade of stagnation, going back to the collapse of asset values. Commercial banks and the government were burdened with enormous debts. Unemployment rates were at postwar highs, interest rates on savings near zero, and, with a rapidly aging population, pension funds under great stress. Whether the current economic system survives is a debatable point. What should be clear, however, is that the Japanese people will not give up. They are disciplined, hard working, frugal, and adaptable, and will surmount this crisis as they have others before it.

Some observers believe that the cumulative impact of the post-bubble changes in the Japanese economy may ultimately turn out to be as profound as that of the Meiji Restoration and the Occupation. They differ as to whether Japan's political-economic structure has been undergoing a "regime shift" or simply some costly modernization around a solid institutional core. But history suggests that the system that finally emerges will be a blend of both Western and Eastern values.

*James R. Rhodes*

*See also:* **Automobile Industry; Economic Stabilization Program; Electronics Industry—Japan; Farmer's Movement; Fishing Industry—Japan; Japanese Expansion; Japanese Firms Abroad; Japanese Foreign Investments; Ringi System; Whaling—Japan**

## Further Reading

Argy, Victor, and Leslie Stein. (1997) *The Japanese Economy*. New York: New York University Press.

Bank of Japan. (September 2000) *Guide to Japan's Money Stock Statistics*. Retrieved 22 May 2001, from: http://www.boj.or.jp/en/faq/data/exms.pdf.

Calder, Kent E. (1993) *Strategic Capitalism: Private Business and Public Purpose in Japanese Industrial Finance*. Princeton, NJ: Princeton University Press.

Flath, David. (2000) *The Japanese Economy*. New York: Oxford University Press.

Japanese Bankers Association. (2000) *Payment Systems in Japan*. Tokyo.

Johnson, Chalmers. (1982) *MITI and the Japanese Miracle.* Stanford, CA: Stanford University Press.

Katz, Richard. (1998) *Japan: The System That Soured (The Rise and Fall of the Japanese Economic Miracle).* Armonk, NY: M. E. Sharpe.

Pempel, T. J. (1998) *Regime Shift: Comparative Dynamics of the Japanese Political Economy.* Ithaca, NY: Cornell University Press.

Rhodes, James R., and Naoyuki Yoshino. (1999) "Window Guidance by the Bank of Japan: Was Lending Controlled?" *Contemporary Economic Policy* 17, 2, 166–176.

Suzuki, Yoshio, ed. (1987) *The Japanese Financial System.* Oxford: Clarendon Press.

Wade, Robert. (1990) *Governing the Market: Economic Theory and the Role of Government in East Asian Industrialization.* Princeton, NJ: Princeton University Press.

**JAPAN—EDUCATION SYSTEM** In the 1980s and 1990s, the Japanese education system received widespread international attention and praise for its accomplishments. Modern schooling was credited with contributing significantly to the country's modernization and economic development. Almost 90 percent of students graduated from high school, and the average level of student achievement was high by international standards.

While still impressive, Japan's education system is now undergoing significant changes. Underlying these changes is a shift in thinking about the purposes of education. Whereas the school system previously functioned to produce and differentiate human resources for the industrial and economic needs of postwar society, there is a growing consensus that the education system has many problems and shortcomings. The call for educational reform and the reports issued by advisory groups to the prime minister are not new to postwar Japan. There have been several series of reform debates and policy changes. The difference this time, however, is that reform debates are motivated by far-reaching social changes and a prolonged economic recession. Education for the twenty-first century must address issues such as globalization, aging and the low birth rate, technological innovations and the "information society," and the increasing diversification and internationalization of Japanese society.

### Historical Background

Before a modern education system was introduced into Japan in the second half of the nineteenth century, an extensive infrastructure of schools and private academies already existed during the feudal Tokugawa

## THE PRESSURE TO ACHIEVE IN JAPANESE

The following report from the Japanese newspaper *Yomiuri Shimbun* on 17 June 1951 indicates that pressure to achieve in school is not a recent development in Japan.

> Every time I meet one of my parents [complains an elementary-school teacher writing in the newspaper], I hear the same complaint—"Teacher, I wish you would pile on the homework a bit more. My boy simply won't sit down and study unless he's got to." Of course one understands the sincerity of the parents' desire to do the best they can for their child. But if the child, after giving all of his brain-power to his school work, comes home only to have to start work over again, the result will be a deep dislike for study of any sort. As long as this continues, the familiar problem of the child who seriously damages his health over entrance examinations will always be with us.

*Source:* R. P. Dore (1967). *City Life in Japan: A Study of a Tokyo Ward.* Berkeley and Los Angeles: University of California Press, 204.

period (1600/1603–1868). Children of aristocrats, the samurai warrior class, and urban merchants attended schools operated by and for their own respective classes. Regional government-operated fief schools prepared sons of samurai families for administrative work by training them in both military arts and Confucian studies. Commoners and farmers voluntarily attended so-called temple schools where they learned the three "Rs" and other basic skills under teachers who were not necessarily monks. Among these various schools, only the temple schools accepted females. By 1850, it was estimated that in Japan, as in leading European countries at this time, 25 percent of the population was literate.

In enacting the Education Law of 1872, the new Meiji government (1868–1912) began the task of creating a modern public-education system for all children, regardless of class. The aims of this new system were to help Japan catch up industrially with the West and to instill a sense of national, albeit emperor-centered, identity. After studying various Western school systems, the Meiji-era leaders adapted and combined aspects of several systems—the United States, France, Germany—for Japanese use and established a centralized Ministry of Education.

By 1890, the government had codified a nationalist educational philosophy in the Imperial Rescript on Education. This Rescript emphasized the Confucian values of hierarchical relationships and the pursuit of learning and morality. This philosophy persisted until Japan's defeat at the end of World War II, in 1945. During the time of the Rescript, a new Elementary School Law of 1900 established tuition-free compulsory education for four years, which was extended to six years in 1908.

Prior to and during World War II, the content of education became increasingly nationalistic and militaristic, and, therefore, reform of the education system was a priority for the U.S. Occupation authorities. The 1946 Report of the U.S. Education Mission to Japan, commissioned by the General Headquarters of the Occupation, recommended educational changes aimed at the production of citizens rather than subjects. Most of the Mission's recommendations were incorporated into the 1947 Fundamental Education Law (whose principles for education replaced those of the prewar Imperial Rescript) and into the 1947 School Education Law, which established a new school system. Respect for individual human rights, pacifism, and democracy replaced Confucian values as the guiding principles for education. The first article states: "Education shall aim at full development of personality, at rearing a people, sound in mind and body, who love truth and justice, esteem individual values, respect labor, have a deep sense of responsibility, and are imbued with an independent spirit as the builders of a peaceful state and society" (Ministry of Education, Science, Sports, and Culture 1999: 9). The new School Education Law subsequently formed a 6-3-3 school system (that is, six elementary, three lower secondary, and three upper secondary years), with coeducational nine-year compulsory schooling organized by the local boards of education under the supervision and control of the Ministry of Education.

## The Formal School System

Since the peak in the population of school-age children in the mid-1980s, there has been a steady decrease in enrollment rates due to a declining birth rate. This demographic phenomenon is having a lasting effect at all levels of the school system. For example, as average class size shrinks from forty-five students to thirty-eight to thirty, classroom management and teaching methods change. Another example is the effect on educational competition, discussed below in the section on postsecondary schools.

***Pre-Elementary Education*** Pre-elementary education is not compulsory, but a high percentage of Japanese children are enrolled. Sixty percent of all three-year-olds, 90 percent of four-year-olds, and 95 percent of five-year-olds attended either kindergarten *(yochien)* or nursery/day care centers *(hoikuen)* in 1996. Kindergartens operate under the supervision of the Ministry of Education and are usually open for about five hours a day. Day care centers are licensed by the Ministry of Welfare and are run for eight hours a day. Tuition at day care centers is adjusted to family income. Facilities, curriculum, teaching style, and activities at day care centers and kindergartens are similar. In both types of early education, the curriculum tends to be nonacademic, although pressure to become more academic is increasing among some groups. Recently, the declining population of children has forced many kindergartens to extend their hours and offer additional afternoon programs in an effort to compete with day care centers for enrollment.

***Compulsory Education: Elementary and Junior High School*** Compulsory education in Japan begins at the age of six years, when students enter elementary school, and ends upon completion of the third year of junior high school. Less than 1 percent of primary school children and a little over 5 percent of junior high school students attend private schools. Most students, in other words, receive their nine years of schooling in the mainstream public school system. Since the Ministry of Education determines curriculum standards, pace, and textbook content for all schools, both public and private, the degree of uniformity in educational experience is remarkable. In addition, students are not tracked by ability, and as long as they are attending classes, they are virtually assured of advancement to the next grade.

The school year begins with an opening ceremony in April and finishes with a closing ceremony in March. There is a forty-day summer vacation from mid-July to the end of August. Winter and spring vacations are fourteen days in December and March, respectively. Until recently, Japanese children attended sixty more days of school per year than American children. Half-day attendance on Saturdays is being slowly phased out by alternating six-day weeks and five-day weeks. By the year 2003, all public elementary and junior high schools will have completed the transition to a five-day school week.

The curriculum for elementary and junior high schools is also undergoing revision. By 2002, the required number of class hours for many subjects—Japanese language, social studies, mathematics, science, music, art, physical education, and special activities (assemblies, events, clubs)—was to be reduced. The thirty-five hours devoted to moral education will remain the same. Finally, integrated learning and information studies will be introduced.

With regard to cultural practices and implicit curriculum common to public schooling, coming-to-order procedures, small-group work structures, daily monitors who handle administrative tasks, and assignment of school clean-up duties are a few examples of classroom management and discipline strategies. These daily rituals are introduced to first graders and subsequently continued throughout a child's school career. Other examples are the custom of an annual visit to the home of every child by the homeroom teacher and, more generally, the cooperative relationship among home, school, and the community (including the police department). Activities such as after-school clubs or the sixth and ninth graders' three-day study trips by bus caravans to places of historical significance exemplify the emphasis on shared experiences that instill values of cooperation and awareness of group membership. What really distinguishes Japanese schooling from its Western counterparts is conventions such as these.

***Upper Secondary Schools*** Ninety-six percent of graduates of compulsory education continue on to upper secondary schools that require tuition and textbook fees. At this point, however, schools and curricula are no longer uniform. Through guided placement by junior high school advisers, students are directed to a school appropriate to their level, and they sit for that school's entrance examination. Since high schools tend to be ranked, the process of educational stratification begins at this stage. Entry into a particular high school is directly related to a person's future career path.

There are six types of high schools: elite academic, nonelite academic, vocational, evening, correspondence, and special education. Elite academic high schools, public and private, specialize in sending a high percentage of their graduates to the highest-ranking national and private universities. A majority of students attend nonelite academic high schools, and there is considerable diversity in terms of the percentage of graduates who proceed to universities, junior colleges, or special training schools.

There are several ways to obtain vocational or specialized training beginning at the high school level and, in some cases, continuing into postsecondary schooling. Vocational high schools, a part of the secondary school curriculum since 1893, are grouped by the Ministry of Education into the following categories: commercial, technology, domestic sciences, agriculture, medical, educational/social welfare, public health, arts and culture, and fisheries. Twenty-three percent of high school students attend specialized vocational high schools. In addition, about 31 percent of the nonelite academic high schools offer both vocational and general courses. In 1995, 4.3 percent of vocational graduates entered a four-year university, 6.6 percent joined a two-year college, and another 22.5 percent chose further education at a special training school. Approximately 60 percent obtained full-time employment.

Finally, evening and correspondence high schools, whose combined enrollment is about 4 percent of high school students, serve the needs of students who must work or, for reasons of health, cannot attend the day high schools.

***Postsecondary Schooling*** Postsecondary institutions include 604 universities with 438 graduate programs, 588 junior colleges, 62 technical colleges, and numerous other special training and miscellaneous schools. Junior-college programs are usually two to three years in length. Technical colleges, which include courses of study corresponding to upper secondary school, have five-year programs. Depending on the course of study, special-training and miscellaneous schools' programs range in length from a few months to five years. University undergraduate-degree programs are normally four years in length, two semesters per year. In addition, there are six-year programs in medicine, dentistry, and veterinary science. Postgraduate programs consist of two-year master's degree courses or five-year doctoral programs.

College admission rates have increased steadily throughout the postwar period, and in 1998, 55 percent of high school graduates matriculated to a university (41.6 percent) or junior college (13.4 percent). Seventy-five percent of these universities are private and educate about 73 percent of all university students. Among these, 34.9 percent of university students and 90.1 percent of junior-college students were female. Female students accounted for 24.8 percent of graduate program enrollment.

Universities are currently undergoing significant changes related to the economic recession and the declining birth rate. In the past, elite public and private universities maintained close connections to private companies, virtually ensuring the placement of their graduates. The name and reputation of the university mattered more than a student's actual skills and talents. Today, as many Japanese companies restructure and struggle to regain a competitive edge internationally, these firms have reconsidered their ties with universities. Increasingly, job candidates must demonstrate their abilities and assets to the prospective company.

By the year 2005, there is to be a place at a university for every student who wishes to attend. This means that, except for the most prestigious schools, it is the universities that are competing to recruit students rather than the students who are competing for admittance. This trend has stimulated many universities to redesign their programs to appeal to contemporary students. Faculty members, too, are under pressure to improve the educational environment through a better understanding of their students and the ways that students learn. The Central Council for Education, moreover, recently proposed a reform of the examination system that would give students choices about applying to public universities, based on the content of their future plans rather than on test scores. In addition, concerns about the financial survival of universities are inspiring many new opportunities for adult education, in the form of degree and nondegree programs.

***Educational Problems and Current Educational Reforms*** In addition to the changes occurring at the level of postsecondary schools, cultural values about the means and goals of education are shifting away from those of the previous fifty years. Schools are said to be too rigid, curricula too uniform, organizations too centralized, and children too stressed.

Criticisms such as these are buoyed by an intensification of problem behaviors and an increase in violent juvenile crime at younger ages. At the beginning of the 1980s, a fluctuation in school violence was followed by the identification of two new educational problems: bullying *(ijime)* and school-refusal syndrome *(tokokyohi*, a psychiatric category). While all three problems remain significant sources of research and public discussion, the more recent phenomena of collapse of order in classrooms *(gakkyu hokai)* and school nonattendance (a broad category that includes truancy) are also concerns. While statistics for school violence, bullying, and truancy have gradually risen over the last twenty years, the percentages are still low in comparison with schools in the United States.

To address these problems and other changes happening in education, such as the introduction of computers in schools, there is a growing consensus that local communities should control their own educational needs and decisions. It is also thought that more choices should be given to students, including early-graduation options. Current discussions emphasize helping all children to find and utilize their strengths in combination with teaching them how to serve the needs of their own communities and societies. Schools in the near future will have fewer children per classroom, and children will be partners in and responsible for their own learning.

***Special Education*** Compulsory special education for blind and deaf children began in 1948. In the late 1960s, various educators and parents set up special groups to study the problems and education of children with various disabilities. The range of schools was broadened to include other disabilities with the legal enactment in 1979 of compulsory education for developmentally disabled children. There are currently 71 schools for the blind, 107 schools for the deaf, and 810 schools for students with other significant disabilities, ranging in level from preschool to upper secondary education. In addition, 43 percent of public primary schools include special-education homeroom classes for children with intellectual or physical handicaps, speech problems, or emotional disturbances.

### The Teaching Profession

In the prewar period, teacher certification for primary education was controlled by normal schools that were established by the government and that had been given the mandate of training imperial servants. The postwar Fundamental Education Law, in contrast, included the notion that teachers were servants of the whole community. To ensure diversity among those in the teaching profession, various postsecondary schools were entitled to have a teacher-education course, making their graduates eligible to apply for certification. Consequently, although still authorized by the Ministry of Education, certificates for kindergarten, elementary, and junior high schools are obtainable at teacher-training universities and teaching-certificate courses in universities and junior colleges. Teachers for upper-secondary schools must receive training at universities or graduate schools or both. In addition to graduation from a two- or four-year institute and completion of professional training courses, a four-week and two-week minimum of student teaching for elementary and secondary levels, respectively, is required.

Upon graduation, a student automatically receives a teacher's certificate from the board of education in his or her university's prefecture. Although the certificate is valid throughout Japan, the holder must also pass an examination given by the board of education in the prefecture of his or her choice. Successful applicants are hired if there is a vacancy, and since the selection examination expires after one year, unemployed applicants must reapply and repeat the examination the following year.

According to the data supplied by the Ministry of Education in 1997, 80.7 percent of primary, 88.3 percent of junior high, and 89.3 percent of high school teachers have a four-year undergraduate degree. In addition, 1 percent of elementary, 2.5 percent of junior high, and 7.8 percent of senior high school teachers have completed a master's degree. Full-time female teachers made up 61.2 percent of elementary, 40 percent of junior high, and 23 percent of high school teachers in 1997.

### International Education

Internationalization and international education became serious issues in the 1980s, when economic success provoked demands for Japan to take a more active role in international affairs. One outcome was the creation in 1987 of a $400 million annual budget for the Japan Exchange and Teaching (JET) program. The JET program recruits college graduates from primarily Western countries and places them in Japanese public secondary schools and local government offices in a top-down bureaucratic effort to create mass internationalization.

There are currently a number of other programs that address international educational issues. The need for teaching the Japanese language to foreign children living in Japan and attending public schools increased by 50 percent between 1995 and 1998. Among these 17,000 children, 43.1 percent speak Portuguese as their native tongue, followed by 30.8 percent for Chinese and 10.1 percent for Spanish. The Portuguese- and Spanish-speaking children are mostly children of Japanese ancestry from Brazil and other South American countries. This influx of foreign children into the school system inspired NHK, Japan's public television station, to create a drama about the adjustment experiences of a Japanese-Brazilian girl and her classmates, and at least one public school is using this program in its moral-education classes to promote understanding of foreigners.

Aside from foreign children, Japanese children who have lived abroad with their families for a year or more experience varying degrees of difficulty when they return home. These children, known as *kikokushijo*, numbered 12,884 in 1998; 61 percent of *kikokushijo* were elementary school students. Most prefectures now have special programs to ease the reentry of these students into the Japanese cultural and educational environment.

Another aspect of international education is the variety of exchange and study-tour programs available to high school students. For example, in 1996 a total of 688 public and private high schools, with 130,669 students participating, took school trips abroad. The most popular destinations were Korea, China, the United States, and Australia. That same year, a total of 972 schools accepted a total of 1,280 foreign students for three months or more.

### Adult Education and Training

Systematic educational activities outside schools, also known as social education, have been practiced and promoted in Japan since the prewar period. The idea of lifelong learning became a major campaign of the Central Council for Education in the early 1980s. While social education had been defined by and organized under the Ministry of Education at national and local levels, universities and private educational establishments also began to expand their adult-education programs independently. Adult-education programs are offered in a variety of settings, including public halls and community centers, women's education centers, museums, libraries, and for-profit institutions of adult education. There are also institutions specializing in adult education, such as the Lifelong Learning Centers operated by local boards of education and the National Training Institute of Social Education. In addition, there are high school, university, and college extension courses, correspondence courses, and adult enrollment in higher education. Finally, the 1983 establishment of The University of the Air, which uses televised and radio-broadcast classes along with printed materials, offers anyone the opportunity to enroll in an institution of higher education.

The Japanese place a high value on education. They have referred to themselves as the society of educational credentialism. While educational achievement will remain a source of prestige in Japan, societal expectations for education are changing. Education should enhance personal fulfillment in a society that has more leisure time and an aging population. Schools should cultivate individual talents and creativity in each and every student, while also instilling in them a sense of responsibility to the larger society. It remains to be seen how Japanese educators will actually put these ideals into practice. It is clear, however, that all forms of education in Japan are undergoing diversification and localization, as well as increasing accountability and personal choice.

*Tetsuya Kobayashi and Diane Musselwhite*

### Further Reading

Cutts, Robert L. (1997) *An Empire of Schools: Japan's Universities and the Molding of a National Power Elite.* Armonk, NY: M. E. Sharpe.

Leestma, Robert, Robert L. August, Betty George, Lois Peak, and Cynthia Hearn Dorfman. (1987) *Japanese Education Today.* Washington, DC: U.S. Department of Education.

Lewis, Catherine C. (1995) *Educating Hearts and Minds: Reflections on Japanese Preschool and Elementary Education.* Cambridge, U.K.: Cambridge University Press.

Marshall, Byron K. (1994) *Learning to Be Modern: Japanese Political Discourse on Education.* San Francisco, CA: Westview Press.

McConnell, David L. (2000) *Importing Diversity: Inside Japan's JET Program.* Berkeley and Los Angeles: University of California Press.

Ministry of Education, Science, Sports, and Culture—Government of Japan (Monbusho). (1999) *Education in Japan: A Graphic Presentation.* Tokyo: Gyosei.

———. (1998) *Monbu tokei yoran (Heisei 10 nendo)* (Ministry of Education Statistical Handbook). Tokyo: Monbusho.

Okano, Kaori, and Tsuchiya Motonori. (1999) *Education in Contemporary Japan: Inequality and Diversity.* New York: Cambridge University Press.

Peak, Lois. (1991) *Learning to Go to School in Japan: The Transition from Home to Preschool Life.* Berkeley and Los Angeles: University of California Press.

Rohlen, Thomas P. (1983) *Japan's High Schools.* Berkeley and Los Angeles: University of California Press.

Shimahara, Nobuo K., and Sakai Akira. (1995) *Learning to Teach in Two Cultures, Japan and the United States.* New York: Garland.

Shimizu, Kazuhiko, ed. (2000) *Kyoiku Data Land.* Tokyo: Jijitsushinsha.

**JAPAN—HISTORY.** See **Heian Period; Heisei Period; Jomon Period; Kamakura Period; Muromachi Period; Nara Period; Showa Period; Taisho Period; Tokugawa Period; World War II.**

**JAPAN—HUMAN RIGHTS** At least until the 1990s, Japan was reluctant to promote human rights in either its domestic or foreign policies, arguably because the very concept of human rights—rights possessed simply by virtue of being human, or standards of human dignity beneath which people may not permit themselves to fall—derives from a Western liberal tradition that is alien to Japan, and indeed to Asia as a whole. But many of the features of modern industrial life—the factory system, post offices, the business suit—were imported from the West, and this did not prevent their rapid assimilation into everyday Asian life. At precisely the time that Western dress and manufacturing techniques were being introduced into Japan in the 1870s and thereafter, there were many across Japan who appreciated and promoted liberal rights ideas and, inspired by them, were critical of government policy. That they did not have more influence has more to do with a deliberate government policy to prevent the free circulation of dissident ideas than an inability to understand them.

### Establishment of an Independent Legal Profession

During the U.S. occupation of Japan following the end of World War II, the United States aimed to create democratic structures and eliminate the laws and practices that inhibited dissent. The postwar constitution was central to that task. Articles 10 through 40 define a set of human rights more extensive than any such document in the world did at that time. A network of locally appointed but centrally organized volunteers, the Civil Liberties Commissioners, was set up to promote the understanding of these human rights and to mediate in cases of rights infringement. Lawyers, who had previously been under the control of the Ministry of Justice, were converted into a self-governing profession within the Japan Federation of Bar Associations. Their primary duty, according to the Attorney Act of 1949, is "to protect fundamental human rights and to ensure social justice." Although the Civil Liberties

Commissioners have been unable to develop a critical role, the legal profession has been pivotal in the development of human-rights practice in Japan. Not only do lawyers publish extensively on human-rights issues, but they also are to be found actively involved in the whole range of rights-promoting activities.

### Japan and the United Nations' Human-Rights Instruments

Despite a promising start with the production of the Universal Declaration of Human Rights in 1948, the United Nations did not approve the twin international covenants on civil and political rights and economic, social, and cultural rights until 1966. Even then they did not become effective until ratified by thirty-five nation-states, which took another ten years. Japan was not among these initial ratifiers; neither was the United States. U.S. policy toward the international promotion of human rights was made clear in the early 1950s when John Foster Dulles, secretary of state from 1952 to 1959, declared the United States to be in favor of the promotion of human rights but through "persuasion, education, and example rather than formal understandings." Throughout the postwar period, Japan's foreign policy was devised within the framework set by the United States. Reflecting this, Japan ratified the two covenants in 1979 when there was evidence of wide international acceptability and President Jimmy Carter was promoting human-rights diplomacy.

Japan has been slow to ratify many of the most important international treaties by comparison with its Asian neighbor, South Korea, and a similarly advanced industrial country, Sweden. The official explanation for this stresses that Japan takes the treaty obligations seriously and makes sure that domestic law is fully consistent with the treaty text before ratification. Nongovernmental groups such as the legal profession contest this. They argue that Japan has repeatedly sought to avoid drawing attention to its poor human-rights record. A careful examination of domestic law does not, for example, explain the long delay in ratifying the Convention on the Elimination of all forms of Racial Discrimination (CERD), and Japan still has not ratified the first optional protocol of the International Covenant on Civil and Political Rights (ICCPR), which would permit appeals by individuals to the Human Rights Committee where domestic institutions failed to provide effective redress in cases of rights infringement by the state.

### Recent Developments

It is possible to detect a change in policy in the 1990s. Not only did the government ratify the Convention on the Rights of the Child (CRC), CERD, and the Convention Against Torture (CAT), but it also created a committee to produce a policy on human-rights education as part of the U.N. Decade for Human-Rights Education (1995–2004) and a committee to suggest reforms to enable more effective redress in cases of human-rights violations, both located in the prime minister's office. There have also been significant changes in Japan's policy toward *burakumin* (Japanese who face prejudice and discrimination because of supposed connections with the outcaste groups of the premodern era), Korean residents, women, and Ainu (the non-Japanese indigenous people of Hokkaido). Three factors drive this policy change. Since the early 1990s, Japan has sought a permanent seat on the U.N. Security Council, and the ministry of foreign affairs has been seeking to win domestic and international support for this. Second, during the 1990s the government submitted several reports to the United Nations that exposed it to international criticism and created an opportunity for domestic nongovernmental organizations (NGOs) to express their views on Japan's human-rights practices. The 1993 official report to the United Nations under the ICCPR stimulated twenty-three "counter reports" commenting on some or all of the official statement. Third, in the 1990s the indigenous NGOs sought to develop links with the international movement. Korean groups communicated with fellow Koreans in Seoul and California, Ainu groups came in touch with other "first peoples," and the Buraku Liberation League supported groups that aimed to create transnational human-rights awareness.

Could Japan take a lead in the promotion of human rights within Asia, the only region of the world with no regional framework? It has been constitutionally committed to rights for more than fifty years, and it has ratified the most important U.N. conventions and has an active human-rights NGO community. But the rest of Asia still remembers Japanese imperialism, and the periodic intemperate statements by right-wing politicians do nothing to assuage the fears of other Asian nations. Moreover, while there is increasing tolerance of groups such as the Ainu, Koreans, and immigrant workers, there is still no positive celebration of ethnic plurality. The Japanese government and society remain reluctant supporters of human rights.

*Ian Neary*

### Further Reading

Beer, L. W. (1984) *Freedom of Expression in Japan.* Tokyo: Kodansha International.

Goodman, R., and I. Neary, eds. (1996) *Case Studies on Human Rights in Japan.* Richmond, U.K.: Japan Library.
Neary, I. (2002) *Human Rights in Japan, South Korea, and Taiwan.* London: Routledge.

**JAPAN—MONEY** Money, in the classical definition, is any object that serves as a convenient means of payment or settlement. The financial assets that have been judged convenient by Japan's monetary authorities have varied over time with tastes, technology, institutions, and purpose; they have included bolts of cloth and bushels of rice. In the immediate postwar period, the most common definition of money was "cash currency in circulation" (bank notes and coins in circulation less vault cash in financial institutions). By 1955, the official definition was expanded to include "deposit money" (demand deposit minus checks and notes held at surveyed institutions). M1, or "narrow money," consists of cash currency plus deposit money. M1, which continues to be monitored by the Bank of Japan, is closely correlated with currency income and expenditure.

In 1967, recognition of the high degree of substitutability between demand and other deposits led to official recognition of "quasi money" (total deposits, less demand deposits, at surveyed institutions). Quasi money includes time deposits, deferred savings, installment savings, nonresident yen deposits, and foreign-currency deposits. M2, or "broad money," consists of M1 plus quasi money. The introduction of certificates deposit (CD) in 1979 provided another type of "near money." Since then, the most commonly used definition of money has been M2+CD.

In recent years, globalization and information technology have improved the liquidity of financial products. M3+CD has drawn increasing attention. M3 consists of M2 plus postal deposits (deposits made to savings account run by the Japanese post office), trust accounts, and deposits at various cooperative-type financial institutions. Since 1989, a variety of high liquid financial assets have been included in "broadly defined liquidity," the broadest category of official money.

Japanese money has several distinctive features. Consistent with a historical preference for cash payments, ordinary households do not use checkable deposits (deposits upon which a check can be written). Due to an efficient electronic payment system, payments by check constituted a mere 5 percent of noncash payments in 1997. Postal savings deposits in household portfolios, are an important part of broad-based money. In 1998, they made up 23 percent of M3+CD.

*James R. Rhodes*

**Further Reading**

Bank of Japan. (2000) *Guide to Japan's Money Stock Statistics.* Tokyo: Bank of Japan.
Japanese Bankers Association. (2000) *Payment Systems in Japan.* Tokyo: Japanese Bankers Association.
Suzuki, Yoshio. (1987) *The Japanese Financial System.* Oxford: Clarendon Press.

**JAPAN—POLITICAL SYSTEM** Modern Japan's political system can be formally divided into three periods centering around the emperor's Charter Oath of 1868, the Meiji Constitution of 1889, and the 1947 constitution. Each of these periods was, in turn, affected by less formal political movements, the meanings of which are still being hotly debated.

### The Charter Oath of 1868

In April 1868, the young Meiji emperor participated in a solemn Shinto ceremony in which he issued what is now known as the Charter Oath. This promised that deliberative councils would be established, public discussion encouraged, "evil practices of the past" ended, and knowledge sought "all over the world" so that "the foundations of imperial rule shall be strengthened." The document was intended both to reassure conservatives and to signal—particularly to the Western world—that the new leaders of the Meiji Restoration were prepared to modernize Japan. General enough to be reinterpreted as time went on, it was later cited by the Showa emperor (Hirohito, the Meiji emperor's grandson) in 1946 as a set of ideals Japan might use to recover from the war.

To help accomplish these aims, the Meiji government in its first five years ended the system of hereditary estates (or social classes), abolished feudal domains *(han)*, started a modern educational system, and organized a new army based on conscription rather than hereditary warrior privilege. On the negative side, a small (approximately 1,000 families) peerage was established, a strict press law was passed in 1869, legislation regulating public meetings was enacted in 1880, and the 1887 Peace Preservation Law gave the home ministry the power to censor "dangerous thoughts." Politically, the so-called Constitution *(Seitaisho)* of 1868 set up a Grand Council of State *(dajokan)*, a term that eventually stood for a government system allegedly modeled on that of the Nara and Heian periods (710–1185). A grand minister of state

## PREAMBLE TO THE CONSTITUTION OF JAPAN

Adopted on 3 Nov 1946

We, the Japanese people, acting through our elected representatives in the National Diet, determined that we should secure for ourselves and our posterity the fruits of peaceful cooperation with all nations and the blessings of liberty all over this land, and resolved that never again shall we be visited with the horrors of war through the action of government, do proclaim that sovereign power resides with the people and do firmly establish this Constitution. Government is a sacred trust of the people, the authority for which is derived from the people, the powers of which are exercised by the representatives of the people, and the benefits of which are enjoyed by the people. This is a universal principle of mankind upon which this Constitution is founded. We reject and revoke all constitutions, laws, ordinances, and rescripts in conflict herewith.

We, the Japanese people, desire peace for all time and are deeply conscious of the high ideals controlling human relationship, and we have determined to preserve our security and existence, trusting in the justice and faith of the peace-loving peoples of the world. We desire to occupy an honored place in an international society striving for the preservation of peace, and the banishment of tyranny and slavery, oppression, and intolerance for all time from the earth. We recognize that all peoples of the world have the right to live in peace, free from fear and want.

We believe that no nation is responsible to itself alone, but that laws of political morality are universal; and that obedience to such laws is incumbent upon all nations who would sustain their own sovereignty and justify their sovereign relationship with other nations.

We, the Japanese people, pledge our national honor to accomplish these high ideals and purposes with all our resources.

*Source:* International Court Network. Retrieved 8 March 2002, from: http://www.uni-wuerzburg.de/law/ja00000_.html.

*(dajo daijin)* presided over the minister of the right *(udaijin)* and the minister of the left *(sadaijin)*, and various vice ministers and councilors *(sangi)* headed the various administrative departments.

The *genro*, a group of leaders of the Meiji Restoration, was set up in 1875; a seven-member cabinet was established in 1885; and a Privy Council was formed in 1888. A civil service was also started, as were law codes heavily influenced by European advisers. Locally, the government attempted to extend its authority by appointing local officials and establishing assemblies whose membership was limited to the wealthy and whose authority to bring up sticky issues was limited. While considerable progress was made toward the establishment of a more civil society, most political decisions were still made by members of the former samurai class (particularly from the Satsuma and Choshu families) who had masterminded the Meiji Restoration itself.

Protestors outside the National Diet in Tokyo in August 2000 rallying against legislation concerning the official acceptance of signs of imperial rule. (AFP/CORBIS)

All this hardly went unchallenged. In 1877 the samurai followers of Saigo Takamori (1827–1877) rose up in a revolt that was only crushed after hard fighting; ironically, Saigo's doomed stance against the Meiji government made him into one of the great heroic figures of modern Japan. Peasants also protested, many violently, against the hardships caused by a new tax system that no longer gave breaks in years of poor harvests. Most significant for our purposes, the largely rural Jiyuto (Liberal Party) of Itagaki Taisuke (1837–1919) and the largely urban Kaishinto (Progressive Party) of Okuma Shigenobu (1838–1922) were both formed to demand more constitutional government. Pressure of this sort was one of the chief reasons that the Meiji government decided to promise as early as 1881 that there would soon be a new constitution. Framed particularly by Ito Hirobumi (1841–1909), who drew heavily from German sources, the promulgation of the Meiji Constitution on 11 February 1889 marked the end of this first era of the modern Japanese state.

### The Meiji Constitution of 1889

The new constitution clearly stated that Japan was to be "governed by a line of emperors unbroken for ages eternal." If his decrees were countersigned by a minister of state, the emperor had the official power to pick the prime minister, conduct foreign policy, command the military, dissolve the lower house of the Diet (the legislature), veto legislation, issue proclamations in place of laws, and consider constitutional amendments. The emperor continued to be advised by the *genro*; the last of these, Saionji Kimmochi, was active until his death in 1940. A Privy Council of various lifetime appointments and political figures became less important as time went on, but it also was an appointive body that had the right to advise the emperor on matters of state. A prestigious and powerful bureaucracy, chosen by civil-service examinations but largely composed of officials from former samurai families, proposed legislation, carried out policy decisions, and often provided prewar political leaders. The constitution authorized legal codes and an independent judicial system, but, as Article 29 put it, the Japanese were to enjoy freedoms of speech and association "within the limits of the law." Finally, military leaders also played an important part in creating Japan's prewar governments. During the 1900–1913 and 1936–1947 periods, only active-duty generals or admirals could legally head the Ministry of Military Affairs and hence be part of the cabinet.

The Meiji Constitution also established a legislature known as the Diet. This consisted of an appointed House of Peers and an elected House of Representatives. Both houses had to approve any proposed piece of legislation, but if a new budget was not approved, the government could use the previous year's budget. While voting in the first election of 1890 was limited to a very small number of property owners, universal suffrage for all males over twenty-five years of age was enacted by 1925. Political parties continued to be active, and in the so-called Taisho Political Crisis of 1913 these parties were even able to prevent the rather authoritarian Prime Minister Katsura Taro from using imperial edicts to build his cabinet. By 1926 Hara Takashi (Hara Kei), a commoner, had been appointed prime minister; by the 1920s, most prime ministers were appointed from one of the two major political parties.

Helped no doubt by a growing economy, foreign-policy successes, a weak Taisho emperor (the son of the Meiji emperor), and the growing popularity of liberal political ideals, commentators spoke hopefully about the changes in the formal political system apparently brought on by "Taisho Democracy." By the late 1930s, however, parliamentary democracy was in deep trouble. Politically, the Peace Preservation Law of 1887 was followed by a second, even stricter law that was passed in 1925 both to accompany the universal manhood suffrage bill and to counter what was considered to be the growing Communist threat. Economically, large numbers of Japanese (particularly tenant farmers) were doing so badly that they were naturally deeply resentful of the wealthy urban elite. Racially humiliating anti-immigration legislation passed by the United States in 1924, the collapse of the world economy that took place after the stock market crash of 1929, the high tariffs passed in the United States and elsewhere in the next few years, and the mounting opposition to Japan's military expansion all seemed to threaten Japan's existence. The police now began to arrest anyone deemed guilty of "dangerous thoughts."

Nationalist hotheads also assassinated unpopular leaders and, in February 1936, led an army rebellion that briefly occupied the center of Tokyo. With the Showa emperor too worried about the future of the throne to intervene and the various political parties apparently corrupt and fractious, many Japanese concluded that their only hope lay in allying with Germany and Italy. Even without formal changes in the political system, in other words, militarism became more popular. War followed.

### The New Constitution

After Japan's defeat, major political changes took place. Between 1945 and 1952, Japan was technically ruled by SCAP, a term that stood both for "Supreme Commander of the Allied Powers" (who for most of the period was General Douglas MacArthur) and his government. Working mostly through the formal Japanese government and bureaucracy, SCAP initiated a series of major political reforms that included the breakup of the military; a purge of top military, economic, and political leaders; a land-reform law that reduced the number of tenant farmers to perhaps 10 percent of the total farming population, legislation permitting unions to organize, an attempted breakup of some of the *zaibatsu*, or large industrial combines, and educational reforms designed to encourage liberal thinking. While not as severe as the reforms made in Germany, these various policies did try to create a more socially equal and politically aware civil society.

A new constitution lay at the center of these changes. Technically an amendment to the Meiji Constitution, this new one sprang from a draft written by SCAP officials unhappy with the more conservative proposals put forth by the Japanese government. It was promulgated in 1946 and went into effect in 1947. In this new document, the emperor was now "the symbol of the state and the sovereignty of the people . . . with whom resides sovereign power." All bodies such as the *genro* and the Privy Council were abolished, as was the peerage. At the insistence of the Japanese, the Diet—now the chief legislative body—kept the House of Councilors, half of whose members were elected every three years for a six-year term, and the House of Representatives, the members of which were to serve for no more than four years. Executive power lay in a prime minister who had to be a civilian and a member of the Diet. Like the Diet members, the prime minister and his cabinet could serve for up to four years unless (as in Great Britain) the Diet passed a no-confidence motion. An independent judiciary with the right of constitutional review and a far stronger set of human rights rounded out this new political system.

Four aspects of the new constitution were particularly striking. First, Article 14 of the new constitution explicitly outlawed discrimination not only on the basis of race, creed, social status, or family origin—this last aimed at discrimination against a racially Japanese outcaste group known as the Burakumin—but also on the basis of sex. Probably passed, ironically, in a rather sexist hope that women would be more likely to want peace than men, this amendment not only allowed women to vote for the first time, but also inspired other constitutional and legal provisions allowing them to own property, sue, hold public office, marry of their own free will, and divorce. Legislation of this sort naturally did not immediately change Japanese notions that separate, ascribed roles for women and men could be considered "equal." But there was at least substantial legal basis for women to argue that they should not be confined to the home or "office lady" jobs. By the beginning of the twenty-first century, women were seeking (and winning) legal redress for abuses such as employment discrimination and sexual harassment.

A second important innovation was Article 9. Claiming that they were "aspiring to an international peace based on justice and order," the article went on to say that "the Japanese people forever renounce war as the sovereign right of the nation" and that "land, sea and air forces, as well as other war potential, will never be maintained." Although the origins of this article remain obscure, Article 9 made it a good deal easier for SCAP to permit the Showa emperor to stay on the throne. The article also made a profound impression on the many millions of Japanese who were reacting against the general destruction of the war and the particular horror of two atom bombs. These Japanese reacted angrily when SCAP and the Japanese government decided that the Cold War (that is, the absence of the "international peace" cited earlier) made it constitutionally possible for Japan to have a highly sophisticated "Self-Defense Force." While this Self-Defense Force is gradually becoming less contentious, the government is careful to keep the military budget at a very low percentage of the gross national product and remains hesitant about sending troops overseas to United Nations peacekeeping forces.

A third key provision was one that let the Diet set up the electoral system. The House of Councilors has traditionally had some of its seats directly elected and some filled by proportional representation. Given also that this body has more limited powers than those of the House of Representatives, this system has not caused as many problems in the House of Councilors as it has in the House of Representatives. Here a failure to adjust electoral districts to population shifts have often meant that rural votes have had as much as four times as much impact as urban ones; this surely is one reason why the conservative Liberal Democratic Party was able to monopolize political power for much of the period. Another problem has been that the so-called multimember district (in which each voter has one vote but varied numbers of candidates can get elected) has allegedly contributed to the factionalism, "money politics," and corruption scandals often found in the Japanese political system. A 1994 reform tried to solve these problems by reducing the seats in the House of Representatives to five hundred, three hundred of which were elected in single-member districts and two hundred filled proportionally from eleven different districts. Voters now got two ballots so that they could vote both for a person and by party for the proportional seats. While it remains to be seen if these changes will radically alter Japanese politics over the long run, initially this system brought few changes to the political system.

Finally, Article 10 of the constitution left the requirements for citizenship largely up to the legislature. Given Japan's strong ethnic consciousness, this led to disputes over such things as immigration quotas, the ways in which the long-resident Korean minority in Japan has been treated, and the difficulties even foreigners who marry Japanese have had in becoming full citizens.

## Assessment of the System

Japan's political system has thus been controversial. Was the rise of militarism, for example, rooted in the less-than-perfect reforms of the Meiji period, or were hostile Western policies largely to blame? Was the Showa emperor constitutionally unable to prevent militarism from taking over, or—particularly if he can be given credit for intervening to make surrender possible in August 1945—should he also be blamed for the destruction of the country? There have been equally serious debates about postwar issues such as whether the 1947 constitution was imposed by SCAP; whether Japan was, as Chalmers Johnson puts it, a "capitalist development state" in which bureaucracy too tightly controlled the economy and foreign trade; and the whole question of whether Japan's notoriously slow judicial system (trials are before judges and can take years to settle) unfairly discourages ordinary citizens from filing civil suits. These questions have, in turn, been related to a politically charged debate over whether Japan's development can serve as a successful model for a modernizing country. While the answer to these questions depends in part on one's point of view, it is at least fair to say that even if open to criticism by ideal standards, Japan's postwar political system was surely a substantial improvement upon the past.

*Peter Frost*

*See also:* **Japanese Expansion; Meiji Period; Showa Period; Taisho Period**

## Further Reading

Johnson, Chalmers. (1982) *MITI and the Japanese Miracle: The Growth of Industrial Policy, 1925–1975.* Stanford, CA: Stanford University Press.

Kodansha. (1993) *Japan: An Illustrated Encyclopedia.* New York: Kodansha International Press.

Upham, Frank K. (1987) *Law and Social Change in Postwar Japan.* Cambridge, MA: Harvard University Press.

Urtis, Gerald L. (1999) *The Logic of Japanese Politics.* New York: Columbia University Press.

**JAPAN COMMUNIST PARTY** The Japan Communist Party (JCP) was founded 15 July 1922, with the encouragement and financial support of the Soviet Union. Throughout most of its history, the JCP has had a close ideological connection with, and taken its lead from, Moscow. Because the party has not identified with the goals and symbols of Japanese nationalism, it has been marginalized as a political force.

Historically, the JCP has been divided between advocates of peaceful coexistence and those favoring violent revolution. The latter ideology has gone out of fashion and now has few advocates. The party has vigorously opposed Japan's rearmament and its security alliance with the United States.

The JCP contests more seats in the general elections than it could possibly hope to win because it sees its mission as one of educating the public and raising political awareness. Communism has been popular among students and intellectuals, especially with respect to the peace movement.

The Japanese Communists were embarrassed first by the excesses of the Cultural Revolution (1966–1976) in China, then by the demise of the Soviet Union. Today, the JCP does not favor the model of the Communist state. Instead it limits its activities to speaking out on peace issues and against social inequities.

*Louis D. Hayes*

**Further Reading**

Hayes, Louis D. (2001) *Introduction to Japanese Politics.* 3d ed. Armonk, NY: M. E. Sharpe.

Hrebenar, Ronald J. (2000) *Japan's New Party System.* 3d ed. Boulder, CO: Westview Press.

**JAPAN SOCIALIST PARTY** Despite union support and ideological flexibility, the Japan Socialist Party (JSP) has never emerged as an effective political force. Founded on 28 January 1906, it was the first political party to be reestablished following World War II, but found itself ideologically divided. A leftist faction opposed the peace treaty ending the war on the grounds that it imposed on Japan an oppressive regime; also, it opposed the security alliance with the United States and Japanese rearmament. The rightist faction also opposed Japanese rearmament but favored the treaty and saw some virtue in the alliance with the U.S.

The Socialists did well in the election of 1947, but failed to win a majority. They formed a coalition government, but because Japan was experiencing serious economic conditions at the time, they were unable to rule effectively.

In the decades that followed, the JSP was Japan's largest opposition party, but was never in a position to capture control of the government. Among other reasons, it did not run enough candidates in parliamentary elections. Even if all JSP candidates had won, they would not have constituted a majority in parliament. In 1994 the Socialists formed a coalition government with the Liberal Democratic Party. But this government lasted only one year.

The JSP draws its support from organized labor, especially the Japan Teachers Union. However, the party's political leverage is limited by the fact that unions in Japan are organized at the individual company level rather than across an entire industry. Thus fragmented, unions are difficult to mobilize effectively during electoral campaigns. Public sector unions like the Teachers Union are more aggressive than industrial unions but they are not significantly more influential.

Members of the JSP have embraced ideologies ranging from advocacy of revolutionary socialism on the model of communist China to promotion of liberal democracy and human rights. Those embracing the latter philosophy split off to form the Democratic Socialist Party in 1960. The 1966–1976 Cultural Revolution in China was an embarrassment to the JSP, and the party tried to distance itself from both the Chinese and Soviet models of government.

In the mid-1980s, the JSP attempted to broaden its popular appeal by moving closer to the middle of the ideological spectrum. It largely abandoned its socialist agenda and in 1991 changed its name in English to the Social Democratic Party. But its efforts to redefine itself as a centrist party were ineffective. The party did poorly in the 1996 and 2000 elections, and for all practical purposes ceased to be an electoral force.

*Louis D. Hayes*

**Further Reading**

Hayes, Louis D. (2001) *Introduction to Japanese Politics.* 3rd ed. Armonk, NY: M. E. Sharpe.

Hrebenar, Ronald J. (2000) *Japan's New Party System.* 3rd ed. Boulder, CO: Westview Press.

**JAPAN-AFRICA RELATIONS** For most Japanese, the image of the African continent has been that of a remote and distant land. The majority of Japanese do not know that their economy has depended heavily on African natural resources. In fact, Japan's position as an economic superpower would not have been achieved without natural resources from the African countries. Before 1945, the Japanese had little interest in relations with Africa because Japan was concentrating on the West.

After 1945, however, Japan began to attend to the African continent. In order to recover from the disasters of war and to develop the national economy, the Japanese needed to develop a friendship with the Africans. Japan's African diplomacy is, however, problematic rather than easy. During the global antiapartheid movement, Japan, in contrast to other developed countries, accepted the racial policy instituted by the South African regime. As a result, many people in African countries have viewed Japanese diplomacy as supporting racism, a view that has been difficult to overcome.

## Pre–World War II

Japan-Africa relations prior to World War II were characterized by a lack of interest, if not disdain. Since the Meiji restoration in 1868, Japan had concentrated on its own modernization and industrial development by seeking to learn from the West. In 1897, Tomizu Hirondo (1861–1935), a professor at the University of Tokyo, advocated that Japan colonize African countries, because taking advantage of the natural resources available in Africa would create a golden era for Japan in the twentieth century. In his book *Afrika no zento* (The Future of Africa), he claimed that the African countries were as important to Japan as China was to the Asian region. No one in Japan, however, supported his view. The first official relations between Japan and Africa were initiated when Japan opened the Official African Residence in Cape Town, South Africa, in 1918. Before 1945, Japan also dispatched delegations to Ethiopia, Mozambique, and Madagascar.

## Post-1945

Japan's postwar African policy was determined by the search for economic resources. In the 1950s, most African countries were still under European colonial domination. While Japan sought to learn from the West, it pursued friendship with African nations. Japanese dual diplomacy with white and black Africa since the 1950s emphasized foreign relations with sub-Saharan Africa. (See Table 1.) In September 1951, Japan signed a peace treaty in San Francisco with the allied nations of the Western bloc, including Ethiopia, Liberia, Egypt, and South Africa.

It was not until African decolonization reached its peak in the 1960s that the opportunity for Japan to formalize its ties with Africa fully emerged. Japan's policy of dual diplomacy was very visible in the 1960s. In 1961, the white minority regime in South Africa agreed to reconfirm the Japanese as having "honorary white" status, meaning that the Japanese could do business with South Africa and live in white residential areas. At that point, Tokyo officially announced its intention to resume diplomatic relations with Pretoria, which had been disrupted by World War II.

**TABLE 1**

**Japanese Embassies in Sub-Saharan Africa**

| Country | Date established | Other countries served by the embassy |
|---|---|---|
| Ethiopia | April 1958 | |
| Ghana | 12 March 1959 | |
| Congo (Zaire) | 30 June 1960 | Congo (Brazzaville), Rwanda, Burundi |
| Nigeria | 26 December 1960 | |
| Senegal | 6 January 1962 | Mali, Mauritania, Gambia, Guinea-Bissau, Cape Verde |
| Ivory Coast | 22 February 1964 | Burkina Faso, Niger, Benin, Togo |
| Kenya | 1 June 1964 | Uganda, Seychelles, Somalia |
| Tanzania | 18 February 1968 | |
| Madagascar | February 1968 | Comoros, Mauritius |
| Zambia | 15 January 1970 | Botswana, Lesotho, Swaziland |
| Gabon | 21 November 1972 | Cameroon, Chad, Equatorial Guinea, Sao Tome & Principe |
| Liberia | January 1973 | Sierra Leone |
| Central African Rep. | 25 January 1974 | |
| Guinea | 20 January 1976 | |
| Zimbabwe | 2 May 1981 | Angola, Mozambique, Namibia |

SOURCE: Morikawa (1997: 65).

In the wake of Japan's recognition of South Africa in 1962, over sixty black African demonstrators were killed by white South African police in the Sharpeville massacre. There is no question that the white regime's decision to crack down on the demonstrators was bolstered by the vote of confidence represented by Japan's diplomatic decision to support South Africa at a time when South Africa was largely isolated from the industrialized world. The Japanese government, for its part, wanted to avoid criticism from black African countries rich in natural resources and so decided not to upgrade its consular office in Pretoria to the status of an embassy. For this reason, Japan reestablished a consular office rather than an embassy in Pretoria in 1961.

Despite the fact that the United Nations had moved to impose economic sanctions against South Africa in 1960, Japan continued to trade with South Africa, eager to gain access to South African uranium, man-

**TABLE 2**

**Bilateral Friendship Associations with Black African Countries**

| Country with which Japan established bilateral friendship associations | Date established |
|---|---|
| Nigeria | 1 February 1965 |
| Ethiopia (Ethiopian Association of Japan) | 27 April 1971 |
| Zaire | 3 June 1971 |
| Guinea | 29 May 1974 |
| Gabon | 19 March 1975 |
| Zambia | 20 December 1975 |
| Senegal | 25 February 1978 |
| Tanzania | 28 September 1978 |
| Malawi | 26 February 1983 |
| Somalia | 27 September 1983 |
| Liberia | 1 July 1984 |
| Mali | 31 July 1985 |
| Niger | 31 July 1985 |
| Mauritius | 5 December 1985 |
| Mozambique | 1 April 1986 |
| Ghana | 2 September 1987 |

SOURCE: Morikawa (1997: 65).

ganese, vanadium, and platinum. In the face of international objections, Japan opened a trade promotion office in Johannesburg. On 6 November 1962, the U.N. General Assembly passed a resolution to enforce economic sanctions against South Africa by a vote of sixty-seven in favor, sixteen opposed, and twenty-three abstentions. Japan was the only country in Asia to vote against the measure in 1962.

A significant date for Japan-Africa relations was 28 April 1964, when Japan was admitted as a full member to the Organization for Economic Cooperation and Development (OECD). In renewed efforts, Japan sought natural resources in Africa as a way to remain competitive in the postindustrial market. Membership in the OECD gave Japan greater access to international financial institutions such as the World Bank and the International Monetary Fund. On 31 August 1970, Keidanren, the most powerful business organization in Japan, formed the Committee on Cooperation with Africa. The priority for both government and business in Japan was to secure natural resources in black African countries. (See Table 2.)

After the end of apartheid, Japan has continued to have good relations with South Africa and has made little effort to improve relations with other African nations. Data indicate that Japan continues to discriminate against black African countries. According to the Ministry of Foreign Affairs, Japanese direct investment in South Africa in fiscal 1997 alone was around 16 billion yen, while Japanese loans to South Africa in 1996 alone totaled nearly 8 billion yen. On the other hand, Japanese direct investment in Kenya was only 5.7 million yen (total through 1998), and in Nigeria 48 million yen (cumulative total fiscal 1951–1998).

Japan's problematic diplomacy in Africa continues in the early 2000s. The Japanese government has tried to provide more official development assistance (ODA) to African countries to soften the criticism that it focuses only on Asian nations. During 7–15 January 2001, Prime Minister Yoshiro Mori made a symbolic visit to South Africa, Kenya, and Nigeria to promise to increase Japanese ODA.

*Unryu Suganuma*

### Further Reading

Ampiah, Kweku. (1997) *The Dynamics of Japan's Relations with Africa: South Africa, Tanzania, and Nigeria*. London: Routledge.

Hattori, Masaya. (2001) *Enjosuru kuni sareru kuni: Afurika ga seichosuru tameni* (Countries That Provide Aid and Countries That Receive Aid for Economic Growth in Africa). Tokyo: Chuo Koron Shinsha.

Morikawa, Jun. (1997) *Japan and Africa: Big Business and Diplomacy*. London: Hurst & Company.

Moss, Joanna, and John Ravenhill. (1985) *Emerging Japanese Economic Influence in Africa*. Berkeley and Los Angeles: University of California Press.

Owoeye, Jibe. (1992) *Japan's Policy in Africa*. New York: Edwin Mellen Press.

**JAPAN-FRANCE RELATIONS** Although the earliest contacts between Japan and France occurred in the late sixteenth century, prompted by the activities of Catholic missionaries, a formal bilateral relationship was not established until the signing of the treaty of friendship and trade in 1858. In the following year, the first French consul general arrived in Japan, while the first Japanese diplomatic mission reached France in 1862. In the last years of the Tokugawa regime, France sided with the shogunate and helped to lay the groundwork for Japan's modernization, notably in military matters. The Meiji Restoration of 1868, combined with the French defeat by Prussia in 1871, diminished the centrality of France as a model for Japan; nevertheless, French influence continued to be felt, for instance in legal reforms. The Tripartite Intervention that followed Japan's victory over China in 1895 soured Japanese popular sentiments toward France, but these events also indicated that Japan was becoming an imperial power on a par with France. Japan's next victory over Russia in 1905 led to the Franco-Japanese Agreement, and Japan joined the Triple Entente against Germany in World War I. From the 1920s, Indochina increasingly

Ai Sugiyama of Japan and Julie Halard-Decugis of France hold the women's doubles trophy which they won at the 2000 U.S. Open in New York City. (REUTERS NEWMEDIA INC./CORBIS)

became a bone of contention between the two countries as Japan sought to build up its naval forces lured by the rich natural resources of the region. Japanese troops finally entered and occupied Indochina in 1940, although the Vichyite French authority there was formally left intact until early 1945.

The San Francisco Peace Treaty revived the relations between Japan and France in 1952. In 1953, a bilateral Cultural Agreement followed. Shigeru Yoshida (1878–1967) became the first postwar Japanese prime minister to pay an official visit to France in 1954. In 1971, the Japanese emperor visited France, although the first official imperial visit did not take place until 1994. On the French side, Georges Pompidou was the first prime minister to visit Japan, in 1964, and Valéry Giscard d'Estaing was the first president to do so, in 1979. Although it was never seriously threatened, the bilateral relationship went through occasional difficulties, for example when France conducted nuclear tests in the Pacific in the 1970s, and again briefly in 1995. Lacking in focus, the postwar political relationship between the two countries verged on an indifferent friendship. The economic relations between the two countries continued to be marked by small bilateral trade volumes, and mutual cultural interest was the strongest underpinning of the postwar ties. French president Jacques Chirac furthered cultural exchanges in the early 2000s.

*Koichi Nakano*

### Further Reading

Le Centre d'études japonaises de l'Institut national des langues et civilisations orientales. (1974) *Le Japon et la France: images d'une découverte*. Paris: Publications orientalistes de France.

Comité des Sages. (1984) *Les relations franco-japonaises: bilan et perspectives du Comité des Sages*. Paris: Documentation française.

Medzini, Meron. (1971) *French Policy in Japan during the Closing Years of the Tokugawa Regime*. Cambridge, MA: Harvard University Press.

Sims, Richard. (1998) *French Policy towards the Bakufu and Meiji Japan, 1854–94: A Case of Misjudgment and Missed Opportunities*. Honolulu, HI: University of Hawaii Press.

## JAPAN-GERMANY RELATIONS

Relations between Japan and Germany go back to the early Edo period (1600/1603–1868), when Germans in Dutch service came to Japan to work for the Dutch East India Company. The first well-documented German visitors were the physicians Engelbert Kaempfer (1651–1716) and Philipp Franz von Siebold (1796–1866) in the 1690s and the 1820s, respectively. Siebold was allowed to travel throughout Japan, in spite of the restrictive seclusion policy the Tokugawa shogunate had implemented since the 1630s. Siebold became the author of *Nippon, Archiv zur Beschreibung von Japan* (Nippon, Archive for the Description of Japan), one of the most valuable sources of information on Japan well into the twentieth century.

Shortly after the end of Japan's seclusion in 1855, the first German traders arrived in Japan. In 1860 Count Friedrich Albrecht zu Eulenburg came to Japan as envoy from Prussia, the most powerful of the numerous regional states in Germany. After four months of negotiations, a treaty of amity and commerce was signed in January 1861 between Prussia and Japan—one of the infamous "unequal treaties" Japan was forced into by most of Europe's powers as well as the United States.

During the Meiji period (1868–1912), many Germans came to work in Japan as advisers to the new government and contributed to the modernization of Japan, especially in the fields of medicine (Leopold Mueller, 1824–1894; Julius Scriba, 1848–1905; Erwin von Baelz, 1849–1913), law (K. F. Hermann Roesler, 1834–1894; Albert Mosse, 1846–1925), and military affairs (K. W. Jacob Meckel, 1842–1906). The Constitution of the Empire of Japan, promulgated in 1889, was greatly influenced by the German legal scholars Rudolf von Gneist and Lorenz von Stein, whom the Meiji oligarch Ito Hirobumi (1841–1909) visited in Berlin and Vienna in 1882.

Japanese-German relations cooled down at the end of the nineteenth century due to Germany's imperialist aspirations in East Asia. The frictions culminated in 1895, when the Wilhelminian empire, together with Russia and France, prevented Japan from acquiring possessions on the Asian mainland (Triple Intervention). In World War I, Japan entered the conflict as an ally of Great Britain, France, and czarist Russia to seize the German colonial territories in Asia and the Pacific.

After World War I, cultural exchange between Japan and Germany was strengthened, but it was not until the rise of Nazism in Germany and militarism in Japan in the 1930s that political ties became closer again. Japan and Germany signed the Anti-Comintern Pact in 1936 and the Tripartite Pact, which also included Italy, in 1940. However, during the following years this seemingly close alliance never brought any real cooperation.

After their defeat in World War II, both Japan and Germany were occupied. Although Japan regained its sovereignty with the San Francisco Peace Treaty in 1952, Germany was split into two states. The Federal Republic of Germany (West Germany) restored diplomatic ties with Japan in 1955, and the German Democratic Republic restored ties as late as 1973. Postwar relations between Japan and both Germanys, as well as with unified Germany after 1990, have focused on economic questions. Germany, dedicated to free trade, continues to be Japan's largest European trading partner.

*Sven Saaler*

### Further Reading

Kreiner, Josef, ed. (1984) *Deutschland-Japan. Historische Kontakte* (Germany-Japan. Historical Contacts). Bonn, West Germany: Bouvier.

———. (1986) *Japan und die Mittelmächte im Ersten Weltkrieg und in den zwanziger Jahren* (Japan and the Central Powers in World War I and the 1920s). Bonn, West Germany: Bouvier.

Kreiner, Josef, and Regine Mathias, eds. (1990) *Deutschland-Japan in der Zwischenkriegszeit* (Germany-Japan in the Interwar Period). Bonn, West Germany: Bouvier.

Martin, Bernd, and Gerhard Krebs, eds. (1994) *Formierung und Fall der Achse Berlin-Tokyo* (Construction and Fall of the Berlin-Tokyo Axis). Munich, Germany: Iudicium.

Presseisen, Ernst L. (1958) *Germany and Japan: A Study in Totalitarian Diplomacy 1933–1941.* The Hague, Netherlands: Martinus Nijhoff.

## JAPAN-KOREA RELATIONS

Proximity and memory are the main factors that have shaped the relations between the Japanese archipelago and the Korean peninsula. Since the dawn of history, unceasing human and material exchanges have taken place between these two neighboring areas. Many elements of Japanese culture, like rice growing, seem to have originated in Korea, and Korean immigrants played an important role in the formation of the early Japanese state. On the other hand, the Japanese were involved in internal Korean rivalries, particularly in the fourth and fifth centuries. Under the unified Korean states of Shilla (668–935) and Koryo (935?–1392), bilateral trade developed, but formal Japanese-Korean relations were established only at the beginning of the fifteenth century, with the coming to power of the shogun Ashikaga Yoshimitsu (1358–1408) in Japan, and of the Yi (Choson) dynasty (1392–1910) in Korea.

### Early Relations

Those newly established formal relations put an end to the destruction Japanese pirates had wreaked on Korea during the second half of the fourteenth century. Furthermore, in 1443 the pirates lost one of their main strongholds when Korea concluded an agreement granting the So family, the lords of the island of Tsushima (part of Japan), in the Korean straits, a monopoly on the bilateral trade. This arrangement worked for 150 years, until the last decades of the sixteenth century. Then, between 1592 and 1598, the unifier of Japan, Toyotomi Hideyoshi (1537–1598), twice attempted to conquer Korea. The Koreans succeeded, with Chinese help, in stopping Hideyoshi, but the country was left devastated and exhausted.

Relations between the two countries were renewed in 1607. The So family regained its commercial privileges as main partner and only intermediary. A delegation from Tsushima, the Japan House (Japanese *wakan;* Korean *waegwan*), was opened in Pusan, and Korean embassies started coming to Japan. Between 1607 and 1811, twelve embassies consisting of several hundred people came to Japan, most of them crossing the archipelago from Tsushima to the shogunal capital of Edo. Korea was one of the few countries with which Japan had formal relations during the Edo period (1600/1603–1868). These exchanges make the period remembered as a rare time of friendship between the two lands.

### 1876–1910: From Opening to Annexation

During the Meiji period (1868–1912), Japan became a modern state and an imperialist power. Korea was one of the victims of this success. In the aftermath of the Meiji restoration (1868), the new Japanese government tried to redefine its relations with Korea, but Korea refused to change the old order. In 1876, Japan finally succeeded in opening her neighbor and in

## THE MODERNIZATION OF FISHING

The Japanese occupation of Korea affected many aspects of life, including the economy. The account below describes how the Japanese transformed fishing in the village of Sokp'o from a local activity to a major source of income for the villagers.

> Until the arrival of the Japanese in 1910 (their direct influence was not really felt in the village until four or five years later) Sokp'o had no sailboats, and fishing with hook and line and with nets was carried out near the coast at a relatively primitive technological level. All equipment was manufactured locally including hooks, although iron of course was obtained elsewhere.
>
> Large stone fish traps built where sandy beaches adjoin rock outcroppings take advantage of the great tidal range. They have been there as long as anyone can remember and have been handed down in a few families as an important source of food. In recent years the runs of mullet, shad, and corvenia along the coast that used to fill the traps periodically have dropped off sharply and some are no longer maintained. A good deal of work is required to put the stones back in place after a storm, and management and maintenance of the traps is now mainly done by the poor and the old who have no other work.
>
> Occasionally the traps still fill up with fish, and an excited crowd quickly gathers as the desperate fish begin to mill around more and more frantically. Many of the spectators help gather the fish as the tide goes out. Any fish that jumps over the stone wall or finds a gap in the rocks belongs to whoever catches it. The owner usually distributes a good portion to relatives and others to whom he may owe favors. If the catch is unusually large, he will use part of it to pay off obligations on the spot, keep a considerable portion for himself, and turn the rest over to the village.
>
> The inhabitants of Sokp'o bartered some of their fish during the late Yi dynasty period for food and a few manufactured goods that were brought to the coast by people from inland towns and villages. Under Japanese direction a revolution took place in fishing. A different kind of boat with sails was introduced and the villagers learned much more efficient "long line" techniques for catching ray, eel, corvenia, and croaker. They also learned various kinds of netting techniques from the Japanese, who supplied the fishermen with the necessary gear. The Japanese, in addition to building roads and a rail network, established coastal passenger and freight shipping service on a regular basis. Large city fish markets and canneries were built to handle the increased fish production. Sokp'o was too isolated to profit much from the expanded national market for fish, but trading with the immediate hinterland increased substantially.
>
> *Source:* Vincent S. R. Brandt. (1971) *A Korean Village between Farm and Sea*. Cambridge: Harvard University Press, 60–61.

## JAPAN TAKES CONTROL OF KOREA

In 1905 Japan made Korea a protectorate leading to its full annexation in 1910. The following declaration by the Japanese government of 22 November 1905 sets forth Japan's rationale for colonizing Korea.

> The relations of propinquity have made it necessary for Japan to take and exercise, for reasons closely connected with her own safety and repose, a paramount interest and influence in the political and military affairs of Korea. The measures hitherto taken have been purely advisory, but the experience of recent years has demonstrated the insufficiency of measures of guidance alone. The unwise and improvident action of Korea, more especially in the domain of her international concerns, has in the past been the most fruitful source of complications. To permit the present unsatisfactory condition of things to continue unrestrained and unregulated would be to invite fresh difficulties, and Japan believes that she owes it to herself and to her desire for the general pacification of the extreme East to take the steps necessary and to put an end once and for all to this dangerous situation. Accordingly, with that object in view and in order at the same time to safeguard their own position and to promote the well-being of the Government and people of Korea, the Imperial Government have resolved to assume a more intimate and direct influence and responsibility than heretofore in the external relations of the Peninsula. The Government of His Majesty the Emperor of Korea are in accord with the Imperial Government as to the absolute necessity of the measure, and the two Governments, in order to provide for the peaceful and amicable establishment of the new order of things, have concluded the accompanying compact. In bringing this agreement to the notice of the Powers having treaties with Korea, the Imperial Government declare that in assuming charge of the foreign relations of Korea and undertaking the duty of watching over the execution of the existing treaties of that country, they will see that those treaties are maintained and respected, and they also engage not to prejudice in any way the legitimate commercial and industrial interests of those Powers in Korea.

*Source:* John H. Maki. (1957) *Selected Documents, Far Eastern International Relations (1689–1951).* Seattle: University of Washington Press, 114.

imposing an unequal treaty, modeled on the treaties Japan itself had had to sign with the Western powers. The treaty of Kanghwa provided for the opening of three Korean ports to Japanese trade and residence and granted Japan commercial, financial, and judicial privileges. This was to be the beginning of a deepening Japanese involvement in the peninsula, which ultimately led to the annexation of Korea to Japan in 1910.

The annexation was not so much the result of a long-term policy as the outcome of the growing strategic importance of Korea for Japan. The peninsula was increasingly perceived as a vital element of Japan's security, as the archipelago's first line of defense against China and Russia. Accordingly, in the 1880s Japan tried to transform Korea into an independent and friendly state. For that purpose, Japan formed ties with Korean reformists, who saw in Japan's success a model

Japanese Prime Minister Keizo Obuchi and South Korea Prime Minister Kim Jong Il during a meeting on Cheju Island, South Korea, in October 1999. They are discussing the expansion of ties between the two nations. (REUTERS NEWMEDIA INC./CORBIS)

for their own country, and local reforms were encouraged and supported. But these were not enough to keep the Chinese away. In 1882, the Japanese delegation in Seoul was attacked by members of the military dissatisfied with the reforms (Imo mutiny). In 1884, the local reformists attempted to seize power by force, but failed (Kapsin political coup). These two incidents provided a pretext for Chinese military interventions, until in 1885 Japan and China agreed upon a mutual troop withdrawal (Tianjin convention).

This arrangement held for a decade, until the Sino-Japanese War (1894–1895). A Chinese military incursion to crush a peasant uprising (Tonghak rebellion) in the south of the Korean peninsula gave the Japanese an excuse to open hostilities. Along with the fighting, pro-Japanese reformist governments were set up, which adopted radical reforms (Kabo reforms). The Japanese victory may have eliminated Chinese influence from Korea, but it did not succeed in putting the peninsula inside the Japanese sphere of influence. Russia became Japan's new rival on the peninsula.

The decade before the Russo-Japanese war (1904–1905) was marked by dramatic events, such as the assassination of the Korean queen Min (1895) by a band led by the Japanese ambassador, and by compromises such as the Nishi-Rosen agreement (1898). These understandings allowed Japan to deepen its economic penetration of the peninsula. But the Russian advance in Manchuria also increased Japanese fears and reinforced Korea's strategic value. This perception was one of the main reasons for the war Japan launched against Russia in 1904.

After the victory over Russia, Japan was free to impose her will on Korea. The Korean-Japanese Convention of 1905 gave Japan full control over Korea's foreign affairs, making the peninsula a Japanese protectorate. Korean armed resistance was unable to stop the Japanese takeover. In October 1909, the Japanese resident-general, Ito Hirobumi (1841–1909), was assassinated in Harbin in northeast China by a Korean nationalist, An Chung-gun (1879–1910). On 22 August 1910, Japan forced a treaty of annexation on Korea. The Yi dynasty came to an end, and the country lost its independence.

### 1910–1945: The Colonial Period

The first decade of Japanese rule was a period of organization and consolidation. The government-general was essentially a military government that mercilessly repressed all signs of opposition. The land census and reorganization of land ownership caused great dissatisfaction among the peasants. Anger burst out on 1 March 1919 (Samil independence movement). Encouraged by the democratic spirit of the aftermath of World War I, large crowds demonstrated all over the country. The protests lasted for a few months and were answered by force. But once the movement was suppressed, Japan chose to soften its policy.

The 1920s were characterized by a relaxation of Japanese control. Limited political rights were granted to the population, and freedom of speech was expanded. These were also years of accelerated economic development. Rice production rose; roads, bridges, and railways were built; modern industries were created. Although the results were impressive, all this was done for Japanese colonial needs. For example, the quantity of Korean rice shipped to Japan grew regularly, leaving less and less rice for the local population.

After the outbreak of the second Sino-Japanese war in 1937, Korea and its population were mobilized for the Japanese war effort. Some 1.5 million Koreans were transported to Japan and forced to work there. At the same time, a policy of assimilation was enforced in Korea. Use of the Korean language was forbidden; all Koreans were forced to adopt Japanese names and to worship the Japanese emperor and gods. This was the outcome of the ideology that sustained the annexation of the peninsula and claimed that Korea was not a colony, but an inalienable part of the Japanese territory and nation. This was the reason that Koreans were also conscripted into the Japanese army. But Koreans were never granted equal-citizen rights and were subject to contempt and discrimination. Thousands of Koreans were massacred after the 1923 earthquake in Kanto, Japan, and tens of thousands of Korean women served as forced prostitutes of the imperial army.

### 1945–2002: Japan and the Two Koreas

On 15 August 1945, Japan surrendered, Korea regained its independence, and the country was soon divided into two separate states. The heritage of the colonial period weighed heavily on the relations between Japan and the two Koreas. The 700,000 Koreans living today in Japan are perhaps the most concrete manifestation of this heritage. On the diplomatic level, a treaty of normalization was concluded between Japan and the Republic of Korea (South Korea, ROK) in 1965. The two countries established diplomatic relations; Japan recognized the ROK government as the only lawful government on the peninsula and awarded South Korea important economic assistance, but no compensations or apologies for the colonial rule. The territorial controversy around the small island of Takeshima (Korean Tokto) in the Sea of Japan (Korean East Sea) was also left unresolved.

Although the 1965 treaty left open sensitive issues, it supplied the two countries with an agreed-on framework. Since then, economic, political, and human exchanges have deepened, and Japan-ROK relations have steadily improved. These links are reinforced by common strategic interests. Both countries are allies of the United States and harbor large American military bases, and both are diplomatically estranged from the Democratic People's Republic of Korea (North Korea, DPRK). Japan has no diplomatic relations with the DPRK, although normalization talks have been taking place intermittently since 1991.

The past still haunts relations between Japan and the Korean peninsula. North Korea wants Japan to apologize and provide compensation for the colonial period. South Korea would like to hear more explicit apologies than the "regrets" already expressed. In 2002, Japan and the ROK were to co-host the World Cup soccer tournament. Because of the sensitive nature of the relations between the two countries, the Soccer International Federation (FIFA) could not decide which one should hold the games; submitting to the historical record of colonialism, FIFA appointed both.

*Lionel Babicz*

#### Further Reading

Cumings, Bruce. (1997) *Korea's Place in the Sun: A Modern History*. New York and London: W. W. Norton.

Deuchler, Martina. (1977) *Confucian Gentlemen and Barbarian Envoys: The Opening of Korea, 1875–1885*. Seattle, WA: University of Washington Press.

Duus, Peter. (1995) *The Abacus and the Sword: The Japanese Penetration of Korea, 1895–1910*. Berkeley and Los Angeles: University of California Press.

Eckert, Carter J., Ki-baik Lee, Young Ick Lew, Michael Robinson, and Edward W. Wagner. (1990) *Korea—Old and New: A History*. Seoul: Ilchokak Publishers for the Korea Institute, Harvard University.

Elisonas, Jurgis. (1991) "The Inseparable Trinity: Japan's Relations with China and Korea." In *The Cambridge History of Japan*, John Hall Whitney, general editor; Vol. 4, John Hall Whitney editor, James L. McClain assistant editor. Cambridge, U.K.: Cambridge University Press, 235–300.

Lone, Stewart, and Gavan McCormack. (1993) *Korea since 1850*. New York: St. Martin's Press.

Ryang, Sonia, ed. (2000) *Koreans in Japan: Critical Voices from the Margin*. London and New York: Routledge.

Shin, Gi-Wook, and Michael Robinson, eds. (1999) *Colonial Modernity in Korea*. Cambridge, MA, and London: Harvard University Press.

## JAPAN–LATIN AMERICA RELATIONS

Latin America is geographically far from Japan, and the antipodes of Japan is found off the coast of southern Brazil. Despite the distance, Japan has maintained relations with Latin American countries in terms of labor migration and economic relations since the late nineteenth century.

Japan and Latin America have strong relations based on the history of Japanese migration. Among world regions, Latin America has the largest population of overseas Japanese and descendants of Japanese. Brazil is estimated to have 1.6 million Japanese and Japanese-Brazilians, while Peru (82,000), Argentina (30,000), Mexico (20,000), Bolivia (14,000), and Paraguay (7,000) also have Japanese communities (all estimates in 2000).

**Japanese Migration to Latin America**

The Japanese began to migrate to Latin America in the late nineteenth century at the end of national isolation and the lift of the ban on foreign travel. The first mass migration began in the 1890s, when 132 Japanese resettled from Hawaii's sugar plantations to Guatemala. In 1897, a group of thirty-five Japanese built the Enomoto Colony in Chiapas, southern Mexico, to grow coffee; however, the enterprise eventually failed. Some ten thousand Japanese were hired as plantation and mining laborers in Mexico during the first decade of the twentieth century. Diplomatically, Japan and Mexico entered into the Treaty of Amity, Commerce, and Navigation in 1888, which was the first equal treaty Japan was able to conclude with a non-Asian country. In 1899, 799 Japanese arrived at the port of Callao, Peru, as contract laborers in coastal plantations, marking the beginning of the era of migration to that country. Alberto Fujimori, who was the president of Peru from 1990 to 2000, is a son of Japanese immigrants.

Japanese migration to Brazil began in 1908 when a ship named *Kasatomaru* carried 791 Japanese to the port of Santos. They were hired as coffee plantation workers in the backcountry of Sao Paulo. After the initial contract expired, they either moved further inland to settle in Japanese enclaves or moved to Sao Paulo to engage in urban occupations as well as in farming on the urban fringe. The Brazilian government initially supported Japanese immigration to make up for a serious shortage of farm laborers, while the Japanese government assisted emigration to ease its domestic overpopulation. Japanese immigration continued until the early 1930s when it was prohibited by the Brazilian government. Under the new constitution of 1934, a quota system was introduced in accepting immigrants. This quota system appeared to resemble the Immigration Act of 1924 in the United States. Japanese immigration was prohibited partly because of an increasing number of Japanese immigrants while Brazil was suffering a labor surplus under a slow economy, and also because the Brazilian government began to encourage nationalism and disregard ethnic diversity.

Japanese migration to Latin America accelerated after Japan and the United States concluded the Gentlemen's Agreement (seven letters and memoranda between the U.S. Ambassador to Japan and the Japanese Foreign Minister in 1907 and 1908, under which Japan stopped issuing passports to those intending to go to the United States), and the United States enforced the 1924 Immigration Act cutting Japanese immigration. In the 1930s, however, the interest of the Japanese government shifted to Manchuria in northeastern China, where Japanese were sent as colonists. Total Japanese migration to Latin America prior to World War II totaled 244,000. Brazil received three quarters of the total Japanese immigrants to Latin America.

Although Japanese migration to Latin America stopped during World War II, mass migration resumed in the early 1950s. Many moved away to escape Japan's postwar devastation, and the Japanese government assisted emigration. Over 90 percent of the postwar emigrants chose Latin America. While Japanese migrants in the prewar period hoped to become rich and return home in glory, those who migrated to Latin America after the war intended to settle down. High economic growth in Japan in the 1960s increased Japan's demand for labor, and the emigration boom ended.

**Japanese Cultural Influence in Latin America**

Japanese migrants brought Japanese culture to Latin America, most clearly in Brazil. Japanese immigrants introduced intensive farming systems and Asian crops; they also introduced the concept of agricultural cooperatives. The Agricultural Cooperative of Cotia, established by Japanese farmers in 1927, developed into one of the largest agricultural cooperatives in Brazil. Systematic missionary work by Buddhist sects and Japanese new religions also began in the postwar period, especially in the 1960s. Missionary activity not only increased the numbers of Japanese adherents but also attracted non-Japanese believers; in the early 2000s there are over thirty Japanese religious sects in Brazil.

The flow of labor migration was reversed in the 1980s, especially during the so-called bubble economy of the late 1980s, in which booming labor demands and high wages in Japan attracted foreign workers. A stagnant economy and hyperinflation in Brazil and other Latin American countries contributed to the influx of Latin Americans of Japanese descent into Japan. Immigration law permitted people of Japanese descent to stay and work legally. The money remitted from

Japan, the amount of which is unknown, appears to have helped Latin American families and the economy.

In 1998, there were approximately 1.5 million officially registered foreigners in Japan, with Brazilians accounting for 14.7 percent and Peruvians 2.7 percent. A majority of those from Latin American countries entered Japan to engage in labor; they were the descendants of Japanese immigrants. The Latin American population in Japan continues to increase both in large cities and in less populated areas where there is a demand for factory workers. Latin American culture has made inroads in Japan.

### Japan's Trade Relations with Latin America

Japan and Latin America are trade partners, but the shares of Latin America in Japan's overall trade are low in comparison with Asia, North America, and Europe. Japan's exports to Latin America accounted for 4.7 percent of its total export value in 1999, while Japan's imports from Latin America accounted for 3.1 percent of its total import value. Panama, Mexico, Brazil, Chile, and Argentina are Japan's five leading trade partners from Latin America.

Japan was Brazil's third-largest export partner and was the destination for 6.7 percent of Brazil's exports. Japan was also the country of origin of 6.1 percent of Brazil's imports in 1995 and ranked fourth among Brazil's import trade partners. Japan exported machinery, automobiles, and auto parts and imported iron ore, aluminum, coffee beans, steel, paper pulp, and soybeans.

Japan was Mexico's third-largest export partner; exports to Japan accounted for 1.2 percent of Mexico's total exports. Imports from Japan accounted for 5 percent of Mexico's total imports, making Japan Mexico's second-largest import partner in 1995. Japan exported machinery, auto parts, and steel and imported machinery, oil, meat, and salt.

Japan was Peru's second-largest export partner and was the destination for 9.2 percent of Peru's exports; imports from Japan accounted for 7 percent of Peru's total imports, making Japan Peru's third-largest import partner in 1995. Japan imported copper ore and fish from Chile and exported automobiles and machinery to Chile. It is clear that Japan depends on the mineral and agricultural products of Latin America.

Japanese official development assistance (ODA) to Latin American countries amounted to $814 million in 1999, or 7.8 percent of the total. Latin American resources continue to attract Japanese investment, and direct investment, loans, and technical assistance from Japan have facilitated development projects.

A substantial amount of Japanese direct investment and government aid were directed to Brazil in the late twentieth century. Aluminum refineries were built at the mouth of the Amazon River. Eucalyptus plantations and paper pulp production were undertaken in Minas Gerais and Espirito Santo. The Serra dos Carajas Iron Mine project in eastern Amazonia has been partly financed by Japan. Japan has also helped with the reclamation of the inland savanna called *cerrado.* The Brazilian government launched a comprehensive development plan in the 1970s, which Japanese ODA helped finance. In addition to financial assistance, Japan has provided technical assistance, and a good portion of the products of the grain and coffee produced in newly developed large-scale farming regions that Japanese ODA has helped establish has been exported to Japan.

Those Japanese immigrants who departed from the port of Kobe for Brazil in 1908 spent nearly two months at sea. It is now possible to fly from Japan to Sao Paulo via Los Angeles in twenty-four hours. The distance between Japan and Latin America has been substantially reduced and there are many opportunities for cultural exchange. People in Japan enjoy Argentina's tango and Brazil's samba. There are Latin American soccer players and managers on Japanese teams. Japan-Latin America relations continue to improve in terms of the movement of people, goods, capital, information, and ideas in the early 2000s.

*Noritaka Yagasaki*

*See also:* **Japanese Foreign Investments**

### Further Reading

Collier, Simon, Thomas E. Skidmore, and Harold Blakemore, eds. (1992) *The Cambridge Encyclopedia of Latin America and the Caribbean.* Cambridge, U.K.: Cambridge University Press.

Noritaka, Yagasaki, ed. (2000) *Japan: Geographical Perspectives on an Island Nation.* Tokyo: Teikoku Shoin.

## JAPAN–PACIFIC ISLANDS RELATIONS

The archipelago of Japan is made of more than three thousand Pacific Islands. Most of them are tiny uninhabited spots of land, but they provide a sort of buffer zone between the four main Japanese islands and the non-Japanese Pacific islands. Historically, Hokkaido in the north and the Ryukyu Islands (included in Okinawa Prefecture, named for the largest of the

Ryukyus) in the south did not come under the control of the central government until the beginning of the twentieth century. This was the last step before the expansionist thrust of the early twentieth century toward the Asian mainland and the outer Pacific islands.

The great design of expanding Japanese territory and space step by step, rock by rock was inspired by the work of Japanese geographers at the beginning of the century. "South Seas fever" enflamed the national imagination and contributed to the myth that Japan could find in the South Seas islands the natural resources it lacked.

In 1917 a secret agreement between Japan and the United Kingdom, confirmed by the Treaty of Versailles (1919), provided the basis for the sharing of the German Far East possessions after World War I. In this way, Japan acquired sovereignty over the Marianna (except Guam), Marshall, and Carolina islands.

## The Pacific War

During the 1920s, Japan built naval bases on the Micronesian islands for its expanding fleet, which was progressively being freed from the constraints imposed by the Washington Naval Conference of 1922. (That conference had limited the number of military vessels Japan could have.)

On 7 December 1941, Japan attacked the U.S. forces in Pearl Harbor in Hawaii. Hong Kong, Guam, Wake Island, and the Gilbert Islands were seized within a month. The Japanese built a major base in Rabaul (New Britain, Papua New Guinea), from which they launched attacks on New Guinea and the Solomon Islands. The year 1942 was decisive, with the main sea battles in the Coral Sea (4–11 May), Midway (3–7 June), and Guadalcanal (August 1942–February 1943) being won by the U.S. forces. The Pacific islands were conquered by the U.S. forces, which leapfrogged toward Japan's main islands from Bougainville (November 1943) to Iwo Jima (February 1945). After the war, Japan surrendered sovereignty over Micronesia to the United States.

## Developments after World War II

After the war, Japan's energies were devoted to reconstruction and economic recovery. Japan was not part of any formal agreement between its former territories and the victorious Allied powers. The South Pacific became a U.S. lake under the ANZUS Treaty of 1952, which linked Australia, New Zealand, and the United States. Australia, New Zealand, the United Kingdom, France, and the United States set up the South Pacific Commission in 1947 for economic cooperation among their dependent territories. The Pacific islands gradually attained independence between 1962 and 1980. Australia and New Zealand became the leading regional powers and promoted the creation of the South Pacific Forum (SPF) in 1971 as a gathering of the independent island states of the region. The SPF promoted the creation of the South Pacific nuclear-free zone in 1986 (Treaty of Rarotonga). In 2001 the forum's membership included the following: Australia, the Cook Islands, the Federated States of Micronesia, Fiji, Kiribati, Nauru, New Zealand, Niue, Palau, Papua New Guinea, the Republic of the Marshall Islands, Samoa, the Solomon Islands, Tonga, Tuvalu, and Vanuatu.

During the Cold War, the main manifestations of Japan's relations with Pacific islands were commercial exchanges, Japanese fishing in these islands' economic exclusive zones (EEZ), and Japanese tourists.

## The Dawn of the Twenty-first Century

The end of the East-West confrontation in 1991, with the collapse of the Soviet Union, and the end of the French nuclear tests in Polynesia in 1995 dramatically changed the international role of the Pacific islands. They ceased to be pawns in a global competition and were left facing their own shortcomings and difficulties as poor, remote, and resourceless islands.

The former colonial powers have been all too happy to let Japan distribute a substantial amount of development aid to the island states. Since the 1990s, Japan has been contributing between $150 and $200 million annually in official development assistance (ODA) to the Pacific islands. It pursues an active bilateral diplomacy through grants (54.8 percent of ODA) and technical cooperation (33 percent) with most of them. It is also the third-largest contributor to Pacific Islands Forum activities (after Australia and New Zealand). At the end of the 1990s, Japan was the biggest bilateral aid donor to Samoa, the Solomon Islands, Tonga, and Vanuatu and the second biggest to Fiji, the Federal States of Micronesia, Kiribati, Nauru, Palau, Papua New Guinea, the Republic of the Marshall Islands, and Tuvalu. Japan is also the largest export market for the SPF countries, taking more than 30 percent of their exports (in minerals, forestry, fish).

In 1997 Japan initiated regular meetings between the leaders of Japan and the South Pacific states. The second meeting was held in April 2000. Three issues were discussed at this conference: sustainable development for the Pacific islands, promoting cooperation on regional and global problems, and strengthening

Japan's partnership with the South Pacific states. At the top of the cooperation agenda on global problems are climate change and global warming, which are matters of life and death for the island states, because rising sea levels are leading to land erosion and to the disappearance of some of the islands. The Pacific island states also expect Japan to pay attention to their own preoccupations when multilateral trade rules are being discussed in other forums.

Japan's aid policy is part of its global U.N. diplomacy: in 2000 Japan gave $3 million to the United Nations Development Programme (UNDP) to be spent on projects for the South Pacific, including projects aimed at advancing technologies and fighting infectious diseases. Paradoxically, Japan is also using aid to the South Pacific states as a means of gaining supporting votes in the United Nations on such controversial issues as whaling, Tonga and Fiji being considered as potential pro-whaling countries, or for its bid to become a permanent member of the U.N. Security Council.

The geographic location of the Pacific islands also explains why Japan is paying such attention to them. First, access to the region's rich resource of tuna has been an enduring reason for Japan's aid program. Japan is constantly trying to strike a balance between its own interests and those of the Pacific island states in this regard. Second, the island states are scattered on the sea links being used by Japanese ships coming from Europe carrying nuclear waste. These trips usually cause great discontent among the nuclear-sensitive populations of the Pacific, and Japan is keen to assuage these fears. Third, Japan is also interested in taking advantage of the location of the Pacific islands near the equator. Japan's NASDA (National Space Development Agency) built a monitoring facility on Kiritimati Island in Kiribati in 1977. In 2000 NASDA was granted authorization to renovate the runway and to build ports, road, and other facilities by March 2002 and to use the runway until 2020 as part of its space program to develop a reusable spacecraft. Last, Japanese tourists account for a huge majority of the visitors to the Micronesian islands and to the French overseas territories of New Caledonia and French Polynesia.

*Isabelle Cordonnier*

### Further Reading

Palm 2000. (2000) "Miyazaki Palm Declaration: Our Common Vision for The Future." Retrieved 7 February 2002, from: www.mofa.go.jp/region/asia-paci/spf/palm2000/palm-summit/seika/miya_dec.html.

Pelletier, Phillipe. (1996) "La géographie surinsulaire du Japon." *Hérodote* 4, 78–79: 20–95; 70.

## JAPAN-PHILIPPINES RELATIONS

Japan-Philippines relations are dominated mainly by issues that relate to trade and aid, and secondarily by security issues. For the Philippines, however, economic relations with Japan have implied collaboration with the enemy, especially in the immediate aftermath of World War II, and more recently in relation to problems about the large number of Filipino workers in Japan and about the environmental damage caused by Japan's dumping of hazardous waste in the Philippines.

### Relations before 1941

During the early 1900s, Japan's active expansionist policy in the Asia-Pacific region was hindered by the presence of American forces on Philippine soil and by the strong position of American business in the Philippines. Nevertheless, until 1941 the two countries developed active trade, as Japan sold its textile and industrial products in the Philippines market, while the Philippines provided abaca (Manila hemp), cotton, and other products to the Japanese. This trade was boosted by the sizable Japanese community in the Philippines, which grew in significance during the 1920s and 1930s. By the end of the 1930s, almost thirty thousand Japanese residents were living and working in the Philippines, mostly in Davao in the southern Philippines.

### Relations during World War II

By 1941 Japan had begun to express its ambitions in Southeast Asia and started to occupy the region bit by bit, including the Philippines, to establish the "Greater East Asia Co-Prosperity Sphere" and to assert its dominance over the area. Japan attacked the Philippines on 8 December 1941 and quickly advanced toward major strategic points. General Douglas MacArthur (1880–1964) evacuated his headquarters, Manila was declared an open city, and the Philippine president Manuel Luis Quezon y Molina (1878–1944) left for the United States to form a government in exile. In May 1942, Filipino and American forces led by General Jonathan Mayhew Wainwright (1883–1953), after a long and hard-fought defense of Bataan and Corregidor on Manila Bay, were forced to surrender. In an attempt to legitimize their occupation, the Japanese established an executive commission that included a number of influential Philippine politicians. In 1943 an independent Philippine Republic was declared, and Jose Laurel (1891–1959), a former senator and associate justice of the Commonwealth Supreme Court, became its president.

The Japanese occupation of the Philippines was one of the most depressing periods in the history of

## JAPAN, EAST ASIA, AND SOUTHEAST ASIA VERSUS THE WEST

On 5 November 1943 Japan and its "allies" in Asia (the Philippines, China, Thailand, Burma, Manchukuo) issued this declaration calling for Asian unity in the face of United States and British imperialism. Harsh Japan rule of these conquered nations during World War II forestalled any chance of such cooperation after the war.

> It is the basic principle for the establishment of world peace that the nations of the world have each its proper place and enjoy prosperity in common through mutual aid and assistance. The U.S.A. and the British Empire have in seeking their own prosperity oppressed other nations and peoples. Especially in East Asia they indulged in insatiable aggression and exploitation and sought to satisfy their inordinate ambition of enslaving the entire region, and finally they came to menace seriously the stability of East Asia. Herein lies the cause of the present war.
>
> The countries of East Asia, with a view to contributing to the cause of world peace, undertake to cooperate towards prosecuting the war of Greater East Asia to a successful conclusion, liberating their region from the yoke of British-American domination and assuring their self-existence and self-defence and in constructing a Greater East Asia in accordance with the following principles:—
>
> I. The countries of Greater East Asia, through mutual cooperation will ensure the stability of their region and construct an order of common prosperity and well-being based upon justice.
>
> II. The countries of Greater East Asia will ensure the fraternity of nations in their region, by respecting one another's sovereignty and independence and practising mutual assistance and amity.
>
> III. The countries of Greater East Asia, by respecting one another's traditions and developing the creative faculties of each race, will enhance the culture and civilization of Greater East Asia.
>
> IV. The countries of Greater East Asia will endeavor to accelerate their economic development through close cooperation upon a basis of reciprocity and to promote thereby the general reciprocity of their region.
>
> V. The countries of Greater East Asia will cultivate friendly relations with all the countries of the world and work for the abolition of racial discrimination, the promotion of cultural intercourse, and the opening of resources throughout the world and contribute thereby to the progress of mankind.
>
> *Source: Addresses before the Assembly of Greater East Asiatic Nations.* (1943) Tokyo: Ministry of Greater East Asiatic Nations, 63–65.

relations between the two countries, largely because of the atrocities Japanese troops committed against the local population, resistance groups, and prisoners of war; in addition, many Philippine women were forced to become so-called comfort women (prostitutes) for the Japanese forces. The Japanese occupation met strong opposition from major groups of Philippine society, and despite Japanese attempts to win the support of the local population and to suppress the resistance movement, Philippine guerrillas, often Communist led, never stopped their attacks against the Japanese.

### Relations Immediately after World War II

After General MacArthur's U.S. troops, together with Philippine guerrillas, recaptured the Philippines and defeated the Japanese in 1945, the civil government in exile, now led by President Sergio Osmeña (1878–1961), returned to Philippine soil. With American help, Osmeña's government gradually established control over the country.

In the aftermath of the war, the issue of collaboration with the enemy became a sensitive topic in the Philippines, and almost a decade elapsed before Japan and the Philippines could restore political and economic relations. In July 1956, ratification of two important documents, the Treaty of Peace with Japan and the Reparations Agreement between Japan and the Republic of the Philippines, opened a new chapter in the history of relations between these two countries.

### Relations to the Present

Significant growth in bilateral trade played a central role in the development of Japanese-Philippine relations in the postwar period, as rapid economic recovery in Japan in the 1950s and 1960s was based on the policy of export-oriented industrialization. The trade between the two countries quickly grew, and by the 1970s Japan had become one of the largest foreign investors in the Philippines. By the 1990s, Japan had also become one of the largest aid-donor countries to the Philippines. According to the Japanese Ministry of Foreign Affairs, cumulative Japanese loans to the Philippines reached $57.5 billion in 1999, and cumulative grants reached $17.9 billion in the same year.

By the end of the 1990s, Japan had become the Philippines' largest trading partner, with imports from Japan—mainly of manufactured electronics, machinery, and other products—totaling $6.13 billion in 1999 or 22.3 percent of all imports. At the same time, Japan had become the second-largest market, after the United States, for Philippine goods, with exports to Japan—mainly manufactured electronics, textiles, garments, and raw and processed agricultural products—totaling $4.66 billion or 14.6 percent of all exports.

Likewise, the number of Filipinos living and working in Japan has steadily increased. In 1998, the Philippine embassy in Tokyo reported that of the 245,518 Filipinos in Japan, 129,053 were Filipino entrants and residents, 36,777 were entertainers, 39,268 were spouses or children of Japanese nationals, and 40,420 were overstaying Filipinos. The Philippines has benefited from the significant number of workers in Japan who send remittances back to the Philippines; from 1990 to 1999, these amounted to $1.1 million. This amount applied only to bank-to-bank remittances and did not include remittances sent to the Philippines through other channels.

One important area of cooperation between the two countries has to do with the development of free trade in the Asia-Pacific region. The initiatives in this area include collaboration within the Asia Pacific Economic Cooperation framework and initiatives in the Japan–Association of South East Asian Nations (ASEAN) Comprehensive Partnership for regional prosperity and in the ASEAN + 3 (Japan, the People's Republic of China, and the Republic of Korea).

Several negative issues, however, have received public attention and have undermined the relations between the two countries. One is the trafficking of women to Japan. A significant number of Philippine migrants have been women looking for various opportunities in Japan; however, many women have been lured to Japan with promises of high salaries or prospective marriages, but were then treated harshly or forced into prostitution. Because the Philippine public has never forgotten the Japanese treatment of the comfort women, trafficking of women receives much public attention and mass-media coverage.

The other problem relates to environmental pollution in the Philippines, as a number of Japanese companies have illegally shipped hazardous waste there.

Since 2001, security issues have also become an important subject in Japan-Philippines relations, as the Philippines faces increasing violence and militancy from rebel and secessionist movements with links to several international terrorist organizations, and as Japan's role in international security and peacekeeping is becoming more prominent. After the terrorist attacks on the United States on 11 September 2001, Japan and the Philippines agreed to cooperate in actions against terrorism, and Japan agreed to provide financial assistance to Philippine security and defense forces.

*Rafis Abazov*

### Further Reading

Dela Cruz, Roland S. (1997) *Image and Reality: Philippine-Japan Relations towards the 21st Century.* Manila, Philippines: Institute of International Legal Studies, University of the Philippines Law Center.

Ikehata, Setsuho, and Ricardo Trota Jose, eds. (2000) *The Philippines under Japan: Occupation Policy and Reaction.* Manila, Philippines: Ateneo De Manila University Press.

Japanese Ministry of Foreign Affairs. (2002) *Japan Ministry of Foreign Affairs Official Website.* Retrieved 1 May 2002, from: http://www.mofa.go.jp/index.html

Philippines Department of Foreign Affairs. (2001) *Department of Foreign Affairs, Republic of the Philippines.* Retrieved 1 May 2002, from: http://www.dfa.gov.ph/.

Potter, David. (1996) *Japan's Foreign Aid to Thailand and the Philippines.* Houndmills, Basingstoke, Hampshire, U.K.: Palgrave.

Rodriguez, Ronald Bong. "Reality Check." Retrieved 1 May 2002, from: http://www.philippinestoday.net/September2001/reality901.htm.

Solidum, Estrella David. (1999) *ASEAN Engagements for Peace.* Manila, Philippines: Yuchengco Center for East Asia, De La Salle University.

Yu-Jose, Lydia. (1999) *Japan Views the Philippines, 1900–1944.* Honolulu, HI: University of Hawaii Press.


## JAPAN-RUSSIA RELATIONS

**JAPAN-RUSSIA RELATIONS** Japan and Russia, neighbors who rank as two of the great powers of Northeast Asia, have for more than a century vied with each other for influence in Korea and China. For the past half-century, Tokyo and Moscow have also faced each other on the global stage, at times seeking leverage from their bilateral relations but more often opposing each other as part of Cold War alliances. Even today they have not "normalized" relations. Mired in a dispute over four islands known in Russia as the Southern Kuriles and in Japan as the Northern Territories, they managed to reestablish diplomatic relations in 1956 but not to sign a peace treaty or to agree on boundaries. Although they have been negotiating about both territory and large-scale economic cooperation, nationalistic attitudes in both countries have long prevented a deal.

### Japanese-Russian Contacts before the 1850s

Japan and Russia first came into contact in the seventeenth century. After Russia's historic march through Siberia to the Pacific Ocean was diverted northward by China through the Treaty of Nerchinsk in 1689, Russian military colonizers sought provisions in Japan as a means to secure their presence in the East. Earlier in the century, however, Japan had decided to seclude itself from most foreign contacts, especially from the maritime West European powers jockeying for influence. Through the first half of the nineteenth century, Russia sought ways to pry open Japan, while Japanese through their window in Nagasaki (the one Japanese port open to certain foreign countries) heard rumors about the danger of a growing Russian presence in the North. Despite occasional contacts through shipwrecked Japanese fishermen and aggressive Russian naval vessels, a breakthrough came only after the U.S. navy opened Japan in 1853.

### Nineteenth- and Early-Twentieth-Century Relations

In the 1860s, both countries began far-reaching reforms after experiencing crushing military humiliations and awakening to national weakness. In the 1890s, they continued along parallel tracks, becoming leaders in rapid modernization. Both strengthened centralization and added nationalist assertiveness to their foreign-policy agendas. With Russia's construction of the Trans-Siberian railroad and Japan's defeat of China in the 1894–1895 Sino-Japanese War, the two countries confronted each other directly. The Russo-Japanese War of 1904–1905 fueled the two most powerful currents in Northeast Asia during the first half of the twentieth century: the rise of revolution in Russia after the country's defeat in World War I and the advance of colonialism in victorious Japan.

After the 1917 Bolshevik Revolution and the 1919 Japanese expeditionary force to the Russian Far East, a brief interlude of the friendly relations that had existed before World War I was impossible to revive. Eager to learn from European civilization, many Japanese were nevertheless drawn to Russia through its literary classics, while the two states found a common purpose in adjacent spheres of influence in Korea and northeast China. In Japan, a newly emerging intellectual stratum gravitated toward socialism, to the growing dismay of the Japanese government.

During Russia's civil war, Japan joined other countries in sending garrisons into Russia, which were later withdrawn once the Communists were firmly in charge. Indeed, until the Soviet Union blocked militarist Japan in two battles in 1938 and 1939, it appeared likely that Japan would turn northward from its invasion of China rather than shift toward Southeast Asia in its search for oil and a secure Asian hinterland from which to contend for global dominance.

### Post–World War II Relations

In 1945 as World War II came to an end, the Soviet Union scuttled the neutrality pact it had signed with Japan in 1941 and joined the United States in the last week of the war in the Pacific. Although at Yalta

## JAPAN CONSOLIDATES ITS CONTROL OVER MANCHURIA

As part of its colonial expansion in the early twentieth century, Japan used agreements, treaties, and conventions as well as military rule to control territory it gained militarily and to limit the power of rival nations. The following convention concerns Manchuria, which Japan had taken from Russia.

> The Imperial Government of Russia and the Imperial Government of Japan, sincerely attached to the principles established by the Convention concluded between them July 17/30, 1907, and desiring to develop the results of that convention with a view to the consolidation of peace in the Far East, have agreed to complete the said arrangements by the following agreements:
>
> Article I. For the purpose of facilitation of the communications and developing the commerce of the nations, the two High Contracting Parties engage mutually to lend each other their friendly cooperation with a view to the improvement of their respective lines of railroad in Manchuria, and to the perfecting of the connecting service of the said railways, and to refrain from all competition unfavorable to the attainment of this result.
>
> Article II. Each of the High Contracting Parties engages to maintain and to respect the status quo in Manchuria as it results from all the treaties, conventions or other arrangements hitherto concluded, either between Russia and Japan or between these two Powers and China. Copies of the aforesaid arrangements have been exchanged between Russia and Japan.
>
> Article III. In case any event of such a nature as to the menace to the above-mentioned status quo should be brought about, the two High Contracting Parties will in each instance enter into communication with each other, for the purpose of agreeing upon the measures that they may judge it necessary to take for the maintenance of the said status quo.
>
> *Source:* John V. A. MacMurray, ed. (1921) *Treaties and Agreements with and Concerning China, 1894–1919.* New York: Oxford University Press. Vol. I, 803–804.

the United States had approved the transfer of the Kurile Islands to the Soviets, along with Sakhalin Island, Moscow's occupation of the southernmost of the Kuriles, near Hokkaido, created a rallying cry for Japanese nationalists once they had regrouped under U.S. encouragement to hold the line against Communist expansionism. Japan argued that these islands were not part of the Kuriles and had never previously been under Moscow's control. Prolonged Soviet imprisonment and forced labor for hundreds of thousands of Japanese prisoners-of-war also started postwar relations on a negative note. Although widespread admiration for Russian literature and sympathy for socialism and the Russian-encouraged peace and neutrality movements offered opportunities for Moscow's foreign relations into the 1960s, Kremlin overoptimism about the prospects for revolution in Japan proved counterproductive.

This cartoon from 1904 or 1905 depicts Japanese troops crushing Koreans as they move toward Russia. (RYKOFF COLLECTION/CORBIS)

When in 1960 Moscow unilaterally abrogated the 1956 joint declaration that committed Moscow to return the two smallest islands nearest to Japan in the event of a peace treaty, the Liberal Democratic Party in Japan found a symbol for vigilance in international relations and for rebuilding Japan's self-defense forces. As the Japanese Left turned away from Moscow to Beijing, public opinion became intensely critical of the Soviet Union. The image of unfriendly bilateral relations and a negative national character lingered a decade after the demise of the Soviet Union in 1991.

Until Gorbachev's glasnost, Soviet media were filled with distorted stories about Japan—such as Japan's refusal to report the true nature of the "economic miracle," the growing influence of leftist political parties and labor unions that would soon turn Japan on a revolutionary course, and its lack of sovereignty vis-à-vis the United States. Yet from the 1970s, different images of Japan filtered through the propaganda. Its technological prowess became a reproof to the Soviet Union's failures in the new economy. Japan's success in combining rapid modernization with traditional culture appealed to intellectuals who bemoaned the loss of Russian cultural roots. In the late 1980s, those who objected to the militarization of Soviet foreign policy and the economy cited Japan's successful diplomacy and adaptation to global competition as proof that an alternative policy existed. Positive images of Japan played a role from 1988 to 1991 in fueling "new thinking" in diplomacy and domestic reform.

Despite generally cool relations in the 1960s–1980s, Moscow and Tokyo explored economic cooperation in ways that left enduring dreams. In the 1960s, Japanese companies began to invest in natural resources in eastern Siberia and the Russian Far East, assisting in the infrastructure to move coal, lumber, and other products to coastal vessels. In the mid-1970s, feasibility studies began for developing Sakhalin's offshore oil and gas deposits. After a decade of increasingly troubled relations as the Cold War intensified, Japanese local governments and business interests renewed their hopes for these projects at the end of the 1980s, embracing the concept of the Sea of Japan economic rim. Through a shift to a market economy and decentralization in Russia, many in Japan envisioned the start of regionalism in Northeast Asia, with powerful economic and even strategic consequences for their country's leadership aspirations. While Russian skeptics voiced vague hopes of joining the Asia-Pacific region through Japanese investment and trade, Japanese idealists saw the Russian Far East as one path for "reentering Asia," a popular slogan as Japan looked beyond its ties to the West after the Cold War.

Negotiations from 1986 to 2001 foundered on the territorial question, although the agenda was widening to incorporate common interests. In 1992 in secret and in 2001 through a public declaration, Moscow made it clear that it was prepared to return the two islands closest to Hokkaido with 7 percent of the land area of the four disputed islands. It favored a deal whereby Tokyo renounced its claim to the other islands. Already in 1989 Tokyo had agreed to discuss simultaneously economic ties as well as the territorial issue; in 1998 it suggested that it would settle for "residual sovereignty," or recognition that the land belonged to Japan even if its return took a long time; and in 2000 it appeared willing to postpone negotiations over the remaining two islands while signing a peace treaty and securing the return of the closest islands. Yet leaders on both sides were not prepared to relinquish any claims. In the Tokyo declaration of 1993, the Krasnoiarsk declaration of 1997, and the Irkutsk declaration of 2001, an upbeat tone was achieved, but neither side was ready for a compromise acceptable to the other. The symbol of territorial differences overshadowed other causes of abnormal relations.

**Recent Relations**

In the 1990s, economic ties suffered for reasons independent of territory. The Japanese generously provided humanitarian assistance in Russia's difficult transition from 1990 to 1993 but felt that Russia was not very grateful for the aid. In 1999 in the hope of a diplomatic payoff, Tokyo positioned itself to appear more supportive than the Western countries, who had been discouraged by Russia's default in 1998; Japanese investors, however, felt cheated in joint ventures with the Russians, and trade was declining. The sale of Japanese used cars in the Russian Far East had quickly become criminalized, as had the export of crabs and other marine products to Japan. Huge profits were made on the Russian side without providing much public revenue to counter the declining standards of living and the crisis conditions in the Russian Far East. Although a fishing agreement in 1998 was aimed at ending the practice of Russian patrol vessels firing on Japanese boats allegedly poaching, and a visa-free agreement allowed the original inhabitants of the disputed islands and their heirs to cross from Hokkaido, these steps did not reduce the distrust along the border.

Interfering with bilateral relations were the difficulties that leading officials had in recognizing the significance of the other country. The Soviet foreign minister, Andrei Gromyko, had long failed to recognize Japan's importance. Mikhail Gorbachev had moved more boldly in relations with other great powers; his trip to Japan was delayed until April 1991, when his standing at home did not permit compromise. Boris Yeltsin had rudely canceled a trip to Japan in September 1992, and by the time he visited in October 1993 nationalism had reawakened at home. The Russian military objected to a transfer of islands, fearing the loss of the Sea of Okhotsk as a haven for its missile-launching submarines. Japanese prime ministers came and went, with few secure enough to challenge the right wing of Japan's Liberal Democratic Party, which began to consider a compromise on the islands only after it became alarmed by the rise of China and the threat of instability from North Korea. When Ryutaro Hashimoto joined Boris Yeltsin at a "no-necktie summit" in November 1997, both sides appeared to be acting boldly, but at home they actually conveyed the message that the other side was about to abandon its position.

Only when, after 11 September 2001, Vladimir Putin shifted his position to support the United States in the war against terrorism did it become possible for the Japanese leader Junichiro Koizumi to see Russia as a partner. Before then, neither side took the other seriously as a balance among the great powers.

**Future Possibilities**

Japanese relations with Russia have been filled with dissatisfaction. The goal of "normalization" of relations remains illusive even as the benefits of good relations between the two countries become ever clearer: (1) expansion of trade would take advantage of enormous economic complementarities, such as Russian natural resources and Japanese manufactured goods and technical know-how; (2) joint development of the Northeast Asian region would use Japanese capital to exploit vast Russian resources; (3) stabilization of security on their mutual border and throughout the region would allow each country to diminish its military burden and to lessen its concerns over the Korean peninsula; (4) leverage in great-power relations would permit each country to balance relations with the United States and China; and (5) a rapprochement would support each country's model of development and national identity, as each seeks a return to what it regards as "normal" diplomacy by solving its problems with the other.

Lately Japanese-Russian relations have operated against the backdrop of the rise of China and U.S. unipolarity. Both Russia and Japan are looking for leverage in relations with those two countries, while hoping to develop closer relations with each other. After a century of seeing each other as threatening present or future military adversaries, they have begun military exchanges with the notion that this will be increasingly useful in the face of Chinese power. The United States has generally encouraged Japan to bolster Russia's democratization and market reforms, but as Washington has grown to doubt Moscow's commitment to those ideals, Tokyo's continued efforts at reconciliation raise some uncertainty. China stands to benefit from better Russo-Japanese relations through a quieter atmosphere in the North, so that it can concentrate on Taiwan, but it is distrustful. In 2000, the summit between North and South Korea made multilateral cooperation more essential, yet Japan's wariness about South Korea's making concessions without stopping the missile threat from North Korea differed from Russia's effort to rebuild ties with North Korea to gain leverage. Hopes for regionalism centered on development of Russian energy resources and resolution of the Korean impasse (both to be accomplished jointly with the United States and China) and on Russia's creating a sound economic and legal framework.

While at times over the past half-century leaders in the Kremlin have harbored hopes of splitting Japan from the United States, they would do well to expect only modest leverage through a more independent Japanese foreign policy in a context of economic globalization. Such leverage would give a boost to Russian aspirations for influence while not interfering with the need to combine the resources of multinational corporations for Russian development. It is up to Russia to foster an environment conducive to Japanese trust and investment.

Over more than three centuries of contact, Japanese and Russians can look back to few periods of sustained cooperation. In the second half of the nineteenth century, both nations turned to the West rather than to each other for models of change and for promising partners. In the first postwar decades, Moscow insisted that its socialist model was applicable to Japan as well as other countries. During the late 1980s and early 1990s, some in Japan proposed that Russia pay less attention to Western free-market ideals and borrow from Japan's state guidance and modified market economy. If comparisons may suggest that a shared preference for collective orientation over individualism could draw these nations together, most observers point instead to the contrasts in thinking: quality-oriented Japanese ways opposed to Russian reliance on quantity over quality; coercive top-down Russian exercise of power versus consensus building in Japanese organizations; and quiet Japanese confidence in continuities with the past unlike the frustrated Russian search for an elusive national identity. Even if the two nations need each other for stability and regional development, they are not likely to turn to each other as models.

Intense negotiations have begun to look beyond the territorial issue toward multilateral relations. Japan and Russia stand at opposite ends of Northeast Asia. Having squeezed China and Korea for many decades, they now face the challenge of economic integration through regionalism and globalization. The geographical reality is that Russia's Far East population is shrinking and now stands at barely 7 million, which Moscow cannot afford to support. Its dispersed natural resources from the northern reaches of eastern Siberia to the Sea of Okhotsk require Japanese investment for development. If Moscow and Tokyo could agree on a program for cooperation, the twenty-first century would proceed with the two sides bringing Northeast Asia together, in contrast to the past century when they split it apart.

*Gilbert Rozman*

## Further Reading

Hasegawa, Tsuyoshi. (1998) *The Northern Territories Dispute and Russo-Japanese Relations*, Vol. 1: *Between War and Peace, 1697–1985;* Vol. 2: *Neither War nor Peace, 1985–1998.* Berkeley, CA: International and Area Studies Research Series, no. 97.

Kimura, Hiroshi. (2000) *Japanese-Russian Relations under Brezhnev and Andropov: Distant Neighbors*, Vol. 1. Armonk, NY: M. E. Sharpe.

———. (2000) *Japanese-Russian Relations under Gorbachev and Yeltsin: Distant Neighbors*, Vol. 2. Armonk, NY: M. E. Sharpe.

Rozman, Gilbert. (1992) *Japan's Response to the Gorbachev Era.* Princeton, NJ: Princeton University Press.

Rozman, Gilbert, ed. (2000) *Japan and Russia: The Tortuous Path to Normalization, 1949–1999.* New York: St. Martin's Press.

Swearingen, Rodger. (1978) *The Soviet Union and Postwar Japan: Escalating Challenge and Response.* Cambridge, MA: Harvard University Press.

Verbitsky, Semyon, Tsuyoshi Hasegawa, and Gilbert Rozman. (2000) *Misperceptions between Japan and Russia.* Pittsburgh, PA: Carl Beck Papers, Center for Russian and East European Studies.

## JAPAN-TAIWAN RELATIONS

**JAPAN-TAIWAN RELATIONS** Relations between Japan and Taiwan have ranged from hostility in 1874, to colonial occupation in the late nineteenth and early twentieth centuries, to the current relationship of active commercial trade and diplomacy. Since 1972, official relations have been strained by the international acceptance of the People's Republic of China (PRC) as the legitimate government of China, but economic relations have continued and expanded in the face of this difficulty.

### Early Contacts

The first significant contact between Japan and Taiwan came when Japan sent a force to Taiwan in 1871 to punish the Taiwanese for the murder of a group of shipwrecked sailors from the Ryukyu Islands. China's foreign ministry accepted responsibility for the actions of the Taiwanese natives and paid an indemnity. In doing so, China asserted its sovereignty over Taiwan and effectively accepted Japan's control over the Ryukyus.

Some twenty years later, following the Sino-Japanese War of 1895, China was forced to cede Taiwan and neighboring islands to Japan, and Taiwan was formally colonized as part of Japan's Greater East Asia Co-prosperity Sphere in 1923. The indigenous Taiwanese population were thus brought into the Japanese empire as subjects (not citizens) and were indoctrinated much as the Korean population was, being forced to adopt Japanese names and wear Japanese clothing. This formal colonization ended with the Japanese defeat in 1945 at the end of World War II, but rather than becoming free Taiwanese the people came under the control of the Nationalist Chinese.

Because the Nationalist Chinese leader Chiang Kai-shek had participated in the Allied Cairo Conference with Franklin D. Roosevelt and Sir Winston Churchill, it fell to his forces to accept the surrender of Japanese forces on Taiwan. Thus the postwar relationship of Japan and Taiwan was between the former imperial power and the Chinese opposition, the former of which had been defeated by the United States, and the latter of which was losing its civil war against the Communists on the Asian mainland. Japan and Taiwan would be guided in the coming decades by the geopolitics between East and West and by the conflicts between Communism and capitalism, as much as by the actions and desires of their home governments.

### Role of Communist China

The role of the Chinese Communists shaped Japan-Taiwan relations for the next quarter-century. To counter what it perceived as a monolithic Communist threat, the United States sought to limit the opportunities upon which Moscow or Beijing could capitalize. The U.S. decision to support Chiang over China's Communist leader Mao Zedong was a political one; during World War II the Roosevelt administration had seen fit to ally itself with another Communist (Joseph Stalin), but in the case of China, the U.S. Congress favored Chiang. In any case, following the retreat of Chiang's forces to Taiwan in 1949, the United States pursued a policy of using its assets in the region to support the Nationalist government. One of those assets was Japan, which was still under U.S. administration at that time. Coincident with this was the need to keep Japan free from Communist influence; the fear of Communism was the dominant factor in Washington's East Asian policy.

The Truman administration (1945–1953) saw the establishment of close trade relationships between Taiwan and Japan as a means to preserve a stable, non-Communist Japan as well as to support the Japan that the United States was trying to develop. For Japan, Taiwan would be a better source of food and raw materials than other Southeast Asian nations such as Myanmar (Burma) or Malaysia. However, despite its desire to trade with Taiwan, Japan also favored ties with Communist China, which had more to offer despite the competing forms of government.

The key to Japan's willingness to trade with a Communist government lies in the Japanese business philosophy known as *seikeibunri*, a contraction for the Japanese words *seiji* (politics), *keizai* (economy), and *bunri* (separation). *Seikeibunri* provided a means of private Japanese business to continue economic ties with Taiwan when Japan and the United States wanted to do otherwise and was the basis for the continuation of these economic ties once diplomatic recognition of Taipei was abandoned. This stance, which came to be known as the Japan formula, explains a great deal of Japan's regional economic success.

The defeat of the Nationalist Chinese in 1949 seemed to the United States to be the harbinger of further Communist successes. Although the U.S. policy of "containing" Communism had called for steady pressure on the Soviet Union in the expectation that Communism would fail from its own flaws, President Harry Truman in mid-May 1950 approved an Asia policy that called for a "rollback" of Communism in China. The need for such a policy was punctuated five weeks later when the Korean War began, even as the Allied powers of World War II were negotiating a peace treaty with Japan.

Despite the Communist invasion of South Korea with its implications for other non-Communist nations in East Asia, not all of America's allies perceived the same degree of threat. In particular, Great Britain was at odds with U.S. policy regarding the two Chinas. London did not see the need for ties with the Nationalists and sought to have Taiwan ceded to the People's Republic of China; the British presence on Hong Kong may have been a motivating factor for this.

The U.S. desire for ties between Japan and Taiwan was fulfilled; by 1951 Japan and Taiwan accounted for about one-third of each other's trade. On the political side, the Japanese prime minister Yoshida Shigeru accepted the U.S. demand that Japan would not make peace with the PRC; for Yoshida, it was more valuable to end the U.S. occupation of Japan than to contest the bases of future Japanese foreign policy. Japan's acceptance of Taiwan over the PRC would contribute to the "two China" view preferred by the United States.

The Japanese position was supposedly laid out in a letter from Prime Minister Yoshida to the U.S. secretary of state John Foster Dulles. The "Yoshida Letter" (actually written by Dulles) accepted Nationalist rule in Taiwan and was the basis for a bilateral treaty between Tokyo and Taipei that took the place of Chiang's participation in the multilateral peace treaty with Japan. In retrospect, it shows the degree to which regional politics were at the convenience of Washington. This began to change once Japan signed the multilateral peace treaty and regained some degree of independence.

With the peace treaty signed, in 1952 Japan began unofficial trade agreements with the People's Republic of China. By 1956 Japanese trade with China exceeded that with Taiwan.

### U.S.-China Policy

The U.S. commitment to Taiwan was formalized in 1954 with the Mutual Defense Treaty. This treaty called for either party to support the other in the event of an attack by hostile forces, but it did allow either side to terminate the treaty after one year's notice. Coming after the Korean War, this treaty remained in effect through the conflict in Vietnam, during which military aid to Taiwan (and other nations in the region) more than doubled.

The Vietnam War led to a change in U.S. policy that was confusing to some and outrageous to others. Despite an ongoing armed conflict with a Communist nation (North Vietnam) supported by other Communist nations (the Soviet Union and the People's Republic of China), it became evident that U.S. policies seemed to be softening toward China. At the beginning of July 1971, the U.S. secretary of state Henry Kissinger met with Taiwan's ambassador, James Shen, to hear Taiwan's objection to the possibility of "dual representation" in the United Nations. The next day Kissinger left on a secret mission to Beijing to discuss a major change in U.S.-PRC relations. Dual representation was a political hot potato on many fronts; it would also face objection from South Korea and West Germany, due to their Cold War divided status.

A different view was held in Japan. In January 1971 Prime Minister Sato Eisaku announced to the Japanese parliament his desire for closer ties to Beijing. When it became known that the United States was involved in normalization of relations with the PRC, the Japanese response was enthusiastic. However, Japan's minister of foreign affairs did not believe that dual representation would be possible and so advised the U.S. embassy in Tokyo. The United States still sought a means for retaining the status quo with the Nationalist government while moving toward normalizing relations with Beijing, but support for Taiwan was eroding in the United Nations.

Only ten months later, the United Nations accepted the proposal to expel Taiwan; a vote on the U.S. plan for dual representation was not taken. A month later, in February 1972, the U.S. president Richard Nixon and the PRC premier Zhou Enlai issued the Shanghai Communiqué, which in addition to denouncing hegemony in the region declared that Taiwan was an integral part of China. This seemed to be at odds with Nixon's foreign policy report of the same month, which restated the United States's "friendship, our diplomatic ties, and our defense commitment" to Taiwan.

### Japan Formula

Japan formally offered diplomatic recognition to the PRC in September 1972. Japan had officially supported Taiwan as long as it was evident that the United States could prevent the PRC government from representing China in the United Nations. When it became evident that the PRC government had enough support to take over China's U.N. seat, Japan no longer supported Taiwan over the PRC. This did not mean that Japan sought to abandon Taiwan as a trading partner; it was just a formal recognition that Japan saw the People's Republic as having the advantage in any competition between the two Chinas.

That month the Japanese prime minister Tanaka Kakuei and Zhou Enlai agreed on essentially the same issues that Nixon and Zhou had. They announced work toward a peace treaty (since the People's Republic had not been a party to the multilateral treaty of 1951), and, most significant, China accepted the Japan formula, allowing continued Japanese trade with Taiwan. This Japan formula called for Japan and Taiwan to shift their relations from governmental to nongovernmental organizations. Rather than relying on the familiar governmental entities like the Japanese

Ministry of International Trade and Industry (MITI), trade between Tokyo and Taipei would be handled by such agencies as the Association of East Asian Relations in Taipei, the China External Trade Development Council, and the Japanese Interchange Association. Tokyo had too much at stake to give up its investment in Taiwan for better relations with the People's Republic. By 1972 Japan had $500 million invested in Taiwan, and trade was running at $800 million a year. The Japan formula provided a win-win-win situation for Japan and the two Chinas: Japan protected its investment, Taiwan got continued trade, and the People's Republic would receive Japanese credit, steel, and technology.

The importance of this Japan formula cannot be overstated, because in addition to allowing Japan to maintain economic relations with both Chinas it made the same thing possible for the United States. When the PRC paramount leader Deng Xiaoping traveled to Japan in October 1978 to sign the Sino-Japanese Peace Treaty, he hinted that the People's Republic would not object to a similar arrangement with the United States. This led to the eventual agreement that China would not object to continued U.S. economic, trade, and cultural relations with Taiwan, while the United States would recognize the PRC. This, of course, required that the United States withdraw from its Mutual Defense Treaty with Taiwan.

The U.S. decision to end the Mutual Defense Treaty with Taiwan led Congress to pass the Taiwan Relations Act in 1979. The ending of the U.S.-Taiwan relationship, foreseen for years, led to a new freedom in economic relations. The new order allowed the government in Taiwan to pursue the normal goals of diplomacy with other countries without official recognition or obligation. While lacking the diplomatic status of earlier years (and the forum of the United Nations), Taipei still had "informal offices" internationally through which it could participate in the international arena. Granted, it had to accept less-than-perfect agreements in many cases; nevertheless, it could still participate in the Olympics as "Chinese Taipei" alongside the People's Republic, and it earned membership in the Asian-Pacific Economic Cooperation forum (alongside the PRC) and the Asian Development Bank.

## Enhanced Japan-Taiwan Trade

The Japan formula did not hurt Taiwan's economic relations with Japan; trade continued, although much to Japan's favor. By 1980 Taiwan's trade deficit was $3.2 billion, with a cumulative $14.2 billion between 1972 and 1980. This imbalance led to Taiwan's embargoing Japanese goods, which resulted in a Japanese trade mission to resolve the imbalance. Japan reduced its exports to Taiwan briefly, which allowed a later increase in overall exports. This increased trade level continued until 1992.

In the early years of the Taiwan Relations Act, Taiwan and other "trading states" that had developed export-oriented economies along the Japanese model (such as South Korea, Taiwan, Singapore, and Malaysia) pulled away from other developing countries and established themselves in the global market. Between 1985 and 1989, Japan's trade with Taiwan increased threefold, and trends indicated that Japan would replace the United States as Taiwan's major trading partner.

By 1992 Japan's trade with Taiwan reached $30.7 billion (with Japan running a $12.9 billion trade surplus). Even as the economic relations between the two nations expanded, relations between Taipei and Beijing developed as well. In 1991 Taiwan and the People's Republic engaged in $7 billion in trade. Trade between the two Chinas grew during this decade in excess of 10 percent annually, and it stood at over $22 billion in 1998. The lack of diplomatic ties and restraints has enabled Taiwan and its trading partners to avoid the normal barriers of international trade and has simplified technology transfer between Taiwan and its trading partners.

In 1992 the government in Taiwan changed the name of its trade offices from the Association of East Asian Relations to the Taipei Economic and Cultural Representative Office; four of these quasi-consulates are located in the Japanese cities of Tokyo, Yokohama, Osaka, and Fukuoka. In 1994 MITI posted a minister to Taipei to further legitimize relations. As Taiwan's economy became one of the most prosperous in East Asia, investment became more expensive. This resulted in reduced Japanese imports from and exports to Taiwan, and subsequently Japan expanded investment in the less expensive developing nations in the region, such as Malaysia and Thailand.

As the government of Taiwan has begun to push for broader acceptance as a legitimate government, it has joined many international organizations of which Japan is also a member, including the Pacific Basin Economic Council and the Asia-Pacific Economic Cooperation forum. Japan and Taiwan continue to attempt to resolve the trade deficit issue through annual bilateral talks and to establish direct air travel facilities for tourist travel between the two nations. By the late 1990s, more than 1.5 million passengers and tourists made the trip annually.

Japan's economic involvement with Taiwan has contributed to the success of each and to the detriment of neither. Without the freedom to separate politics from economics, Japan would have been forced to choose sides in the competition between Taipei and Beijing, but *seikeibunri* removed that obstacle. Japan sought the greatest advantage for itself, whether that was to avoid ties with the People's Republic to accommodate the United States as Japan prepared for autonomy in 1951, to establish informal ties with the mainland while holding formal ties with Taiwan, or to reverse the arrangement and continue trade through nongovernmental agencies in Taipei.

*Thomas P. Dolan*

**Further Reading**

Fairbank, John K., Edwin O. Reischauer, and Albert M. Craig. (1989) *East Asia: Tradition and Transformation*. Rev. ed. Boston: Houghton Mifflin Company.

Gordon, Andrew, ed. (1993) *Postwar Japan as History*. Berkeley and Los Angeles: University of California Press.

Johnson, Chalmers. (1995) *Japan: Who Governs? The Rise of the Developmental State*. New York: W. W. Norton.

Kim, Young Hum. (1966) *East Asia's Turbulent Century*. New York: Meredith Publishing Company.

## JAPAN–UNITED KINGDOM RELATIONS

The history of relations between Japan and Great Britain can be divided into four stages: the beginning of full relations in the mid-nineteenth century, the alliance, interwar, and post–World War II.

Although the first contact between the two nations was in the early seventeenth century, full relations began in the last part of the Tokugawa period (1600/1603–1868). During the Meiji period (1868–1912), Britain played a major role in the modernization of Japan by helping in the establishment of the Japanese navy and the planning and construction of railroads and factories. Meiji leaders regarded Britain, the pioneer of the industrial revolution, as a model for modern economic and social institutions.

Meiji leaders sought treaty reform as another goal for Japan in its relations with the West. Revision of the Unequal Treaties sought to abolish foreigners' judicial and economic privileges. The Anglo-Japanese Commercial Treaty of 1894 prescribed termination of extraterritoriality, provided that Japan reformed its legal institutions along Western lines. Even though Japan did not get complete tariff autonomy until 1911, British treaties facilitated negotiations with other Western countries.

Japan and Great Britain were allies during the early twentieth century. The Anglo-Japanese Alliance (1902–1923), directed against Russian expansion in the Far East, assisted Japan in the Russo-Japanese War (1904–1905). It was renewed two times, which obligated Japan's participation in World War I as a British ally. After the war, the significance of the Alliance for Britain decreased, and the United States viewed Japan as a strong competitor in East Asia. At the Washington Conference (1921–1922), the United States forced Japan to end the Alliance, which was replaced by the Four Power Pact.

As Japan became an increasingly powerful nation, relations with Great Britain suffered, mainly because of political and economic disputes in Asia, especially trade disputes with China. After the Manchurian Incident of 1931, trade conflict became more intense, and at the conclusion of the Tripartite Pact of September 1940, Japan's ties with Germany and Italy strained relations further still. On 8 December 1941, Japan declared war against Great Britain and the United States, and attacked Britain's colonies in Southeast Asia.

Relations between Japan and Great Britain began to improve after World War II. Britain ratified the Multilateral Peace Treaty in 1952. In the 1960s, new trade treaties were concluded between the two countries. Exchange of royal visits in the 1970s symbolized more open communication between the two nations. Good relations continue in the early 2000s, with exchanges in every sphere.

*Hirohisa Yamazaki*

*See also:* **Heisei Period; Meiji Period; Showa Period; Taisho Period; World War II**

**Further Reading**

Brown, Kenneth Douglas. (1998) *Britain and Japan: A Comparative Economic and Social History Since 1900*. Manchester, U.K.: Manchester University Press.

Buckley, Roger. (1982) *Occupation Diplomacy: Britain, the United States, and Japan, 1945–1952*. Cambridge, U.K.: Cambridge University Press.

Lowe, Peter. (1969) *Great Britain and Japan, 1911–1915: A Study of British Far Eastern Policy*. London: Macmillan.

Nish, Ian Hill. (1985) *The Anglo-Japanese Alliance: The Diplomacy of Two Island Empires, 1894–1907*. London: Athlone Press.

Nish, Ian Hill, and Yoich Kibata, eds. (2000) *The History of Anglo-Japanese Relations*. New York: St. Martin's Press.

## JAPAN–UNITED STATES RELATIONS

The relationship between Japan and the United States, which dates from the mid-nineteenth century, is complex and multifaceted. Two of its most important aspects are security and economic relations.

### Relations until World War II

When Commodore Matthew Perry forced Japan to enter into trade and diplomatic relations with the West in 1853–1854, the event was a turning point in the transformation of the Japanese political system from the shogunate to the Meiji imperial system. The United States, however, paid little attention to the Asia-Pacific area until the end of World War I.

After 1918, Japan emerged as one of the five major world powers. The United States established the Washington Treaty System to restrict Japanese territorial expansion and the arms race in the Asia-Pacific area in the 1920s. This system was sustainable as long as Chinese nationalism did not become radical enough to challenge the status quo and Japan maintained its economic prosperity through cooperation with the United States. Though the U.S. immigration law of 1924 virtually prohibited Japanese immigration and damaged U.S.-Japanese relations, the spirit of cooperation and the benefit derived from the Washington Treaty System prevailed in the early 1920s.

But the Great Depression of 1929 demolished the Treaty System and precipitated Japanese military expansion into Manchuria and the Chinese mainland. In 1931 the Japanese army occupied Mukden, Manchuria (present-day Shenyang), and eventually extended its rule over all of Manchuria. The United States had no vital interest in Manchuria, and the Hoover Administration adopted a policy of nonrecognition. In the absence of strong U.S. opposition, Japan continued its expansion and established the puppet state of Manchukuo (in Chinese, Manchuguo) in 1934. In July 1937 the Japanese army advanced to the Marco Polo Bridge, beginning the full-scale Sino-Japanese war.

The United States did not intend to fight against Japan over China issues, but neither could Washington bear the prospect of the entire Asia-Pacific area under Japanese rule. In September 1940 Japan stationed its army in northern French Indochina, and in July 1941 moved into southern Indochina. The Japanese expansion in Asia, along with the expansion of Germany in Europe, would have led to a closed world, a world consisting of a series of exclusive economic blocs. In response to these developments, Washington forbade oil exports to Japan in August 1941. This prohibition significantly contributed to Japan's final decision to go to war against the United States and attack Pearl Harbor that December.

### THE UNITED STATES DECLARES WAR ON JAPAN AND ENTERS WORLD WAR II

"Whereas the Imperial Government of Japan has committed unprovoked acts of war against the Government and the people of the United States of America: Therefore be it

*Resolved by the Senate and House of Representatives of the United States of America in Congress Assembled,* That the state of war between the United States and the Imperial Government of Japan which has thus been thrust upon the United States is hereby formally declared; and the President is hereby authorized and directed to employ the entire naval and military forces of the United States and the resources of the Government to carry on war against the Imperial Government of Japan; and, to bring the conflict to a successful termination, all of the resources of the country are hereby pledged by the Congress of the United States.

*Source:* John M. Maki. (1957) *Selected Documents, Far Eastern International Relations (1869–1951).* Seattle, WA: University of Washington Press, 233.

***The Occupation Era, 1945–1952*** After Japan's defeat at the end of World War II, the United States played a dominant role in carrying out the Allied Occupation policies in Japan. It first employed punitive economic policies, but later tried to establish a self-sufficient economy in Japan. In February 1949, Joseph Dodge, an American financial adviser, implemented an austerity program to balance Japan's budget. This politically unpopular austerity program was called the Dodge Line.

The Dodge Line constituted a critical turning point in the Occupation, transforming the state-managed economy into a market-oriented, export-first economy. The fate of the Dodge Line depended on the revival of Japanese foreign trade, but with a world wide depression in 1949, Japan faced a severe economic downturn. Southeast Asian countries were Japan's natural market because of their great demand for

## OPENING JAPAN TO TRADE WITH THE UNITED STATES

This extract from Treaty No. 19, Treaty of Commerce and Navigation of 1860, sets the conditions for trade between Japan and the United States.

> The President of the United States of America, and His Majesty the Ty-coon of Japan, desiring to establish on firm and lasting foundations, the relations of peace and friendship now happily existing between the two Countries, and to secure the best interest of their respective Citizens and Subjects by encouraging, facilitating, and regulating their industry and trade, have resolved to conclude a Treaty of amity and commerce, for this purpose, and have therefore named, as their plenipotentiaries, that is to say:
>
> The President of the United States, His Excellency Townsend Harris, Consul General of the United States of America, for the Empire of Japan, and His Majesty the Ty-coon of Japan, Their Excellencies Ino-ooye Prince of Sinano and Iwasay Prince of Hego, who, after having communicated to each other their respective Full Powers, and found them to be in good and due form, have agreed upon and concluded the following Articles:
>
> Article First. There shall henceforth be perpetual peace and friendship between the United States of America, and His Majesty the Ty-coon of Japan, and His Successors.
>
> The President of the United States may appoint a Diplomatic Agent to reside at the City of Yedo, and Consuls or Consular Agents to reside at any or all of the Ports of Japan which are opened for American Commerce by the Treaty. The Diplomatic Agent and Consul General of the United States shall have the right to travel freely, in any part of the Empire of Japan from the time they enter on the discharge of their official duties.
>
> The Government of Japan may appoint a Diplomatic Agent to reside at Washington and Consuls or Consular Agents, for any or all of the ports of the United States. The Diplomatic Agent and Consul General of Japan, may travel freely in any part of the United States from the time they arrive in the country.
>
> Article Second. The President of the United States, at the request of the Japanese Government, will act as a friendly Mediator, in such matters of difference as may arise between the Government of Japan and any European Power.
>
> The ships of war of the United States shall render friendly aid and assistance, to such Japanese vessels, as they may meet on the high seas, so far as can be done without a breach of neutrality, and all American Consuls, residing at Ports, visited by Japanese vessels shall also give them such friendly aid as may be permitted by the Laws of their respective Countries, in which they reside.
>
> Article Third. In addition to the Ports of Simoda and Hakodate, the following Ports and Towns shall be opened on the dates respectively appended to them, that is to say:
>
> Kanagawa, on the (4th day of July 1859) . . .
>
> Nagasaki, on the (4th day of July 1859) . . .
>
> Nee-e-gata [Niigata] on the (1st of January 1860) . . .
>
> Hiogo [Hyogo] on the (1st of January 1863) . . .

CONTINUED ON NEXT PAGE

CONTINUED FROM PREVIOUS PAGE

> If Nee-e-gata is found to be unsuitable as a Harbour, another Port, on the West coast of Nipon, shall be selected by the two Governments in lieu thereof.
>
> Six months after the opening of Kanagawa, the port of Simoda shall be closed as a place of residence and trade, for American Citizens.
>
> In all the foregoing Ports and Towns, American Citizens may permanently reside, they shall have the right to lease ground, and purchase buildings thereon, and may erect dwellings and warehouses. But no fortification or place of military strength, shall be erected under the pretence of building dwellings or warehouses, and to see that this Article is observed, the Japanese authorities shall have the right to inspect from time to time any buildings, which are being erected, altered or repaired.
>
> The place which the Americans shall occupy for their buildings, and the Harbour Regulations, shall be arranged by the American Consul, and the Authorities of each place, and if they cannot agree, the matter shall be referred to, and settled by the American Diplomatic Agent and the Japanese Government.
>
> *Source: Compilation of Treaties in Force*. Washington, DC: Government Printing Office.

industrial goods and Japan's geographical proximity. Establishing a regional economic linkage, however, required political stability in Asia. By 1949, the United States had focused its attention on bringing political stability to Southeast Asia as a prerequisite for Japanese economic recovery.

The United States also emphasized demilitarization in the early stage of the Occupation. Because this left Japan defenseless, Washington realized that to ensure Japan's security it would have to maintain military bases and armed forces there, and in 1951 signed the U.S.-Japanese Security Treaty.

The United States successfully compelled Japan to accept American bases and to agree, reluctantly, to rearmament. But making military commitments is a double-edged sword, as it made the United States responsible for Japan's security. Moreover, for the Japanese retaining American bases was a sensitive issue, because they impinged on Japan's sovereignty. Consequently, the United States had to prevent the base issue from becoming the agenda of any heated debate in the Japanese Diet. Washington could not push Japan too hard concerning Japan's rearmament program since it might lead to the sensitive base issue. In short, Japan's reluctant acceptance of American bases guaranteed Japan's security while mitigating American pressure on Japan to rearm.

The Korean War, which broke out in June 1950, stimulated the Japanese economy. The Chinese Communists' intervention in the war and their military successes increased China's prestige in Asia. With China's increasing status, the United States believed that it would be difficult to retain Japan's pro-American orientation unless it took steps to preserve its own prestige. In response to these pressures, Washington articulated its commitment to maintaining Japan's security, sanctioning the use of force if necessary. Because Japan was an unreliable former enemy, Washington could not simply count on its good will, but had to stimulate Japan's own self-interest to encourage its alignment with the West.

Japan's primary task became to determine its minimum defense contribution without jeopardizing its ties with the United States. Japan was excellent at exploiting America's Achilles' heel: it manipulated U.S. security anxieties in Japan to induce more involvement in Japan's economic recovery and security. Japan also tried to induce aid from the United States in exchange for Japan's rearmament. As a weak ally in an unstable area surrounded by two giant Communist countries, Japan found its own perceived weakness to be the best asset with which to deal with the United States.

### Postoccupation Economic Relations

During the 1950s, both the American and Japanese governments tried to reduce Japan's trade deficit and integrate the Japanese economy into the Western bloc. Japan, however, could not enjoy full benefits of the General Agreement on Tariffs and Trade (GATT) because of restrictions imposed by other member states.

Workers preparing to hang U.S. and Japanese flags on the Old Executive Office Building in Washington, D.C., in honor of the visit of Japanese prime minister Zenko Suzuki in May 1981. (WALLY MCNAMEE/CORBIS)

Moreover, the United States severely curtailed Japanese trade with China.

Four factors helped the Japanese economic development in the early postoccupation period. First, the United States tolerated Japan's restrictions on imports and foreign investments. Few American businesses regarded the Japanese market as important. Second, Washington facilitated Japanese access to the American market. Third, American military spending in Japan and other parts of Asia helped revitalize the Japanese economy. Fourth, Japan was able to concentrate on economic growth because it was not hampered by excessive defense spending. During the 1950s, the United States and Japan had trade frictions only in specific sectors, including textiles, sundries, and silverware. The American textile industry was especially hard hit by heavy importation of cheap Japanese products. In January 1956, Japan began to adopt self-imposed export restraint.

As American economic supremacy gradually declined in the late 1960s, Washington could no longer keep its domestic market open to Japanese goods. The U.S.-Japanese textile negotiations between 1969 and 1971, which were designed to restrain imports of Japanese textiles, were symbolic incidents of this era. Americans were alarmed to realize Japan had recovered from World War II so quickly and, by the early 1970s, had become competitive with U.S. industries. During the 1970s, however, the United States was primarily concerned with competition from Western Europe.

Japanese economic growth gradually slowed beginning in the mid-1980s, and the United States started to focus serious attention on Japan as an economic competitor. Washington emphasized not only reducing Japanese imports to the United States but also expanding U.S. exports to Japan. In addition, Washington focused on unfair Japanese trade practices, considering it imperative to change the Japanese domestic system. By the late 1980s, Japan had an enormous trade surplus and the United States a towering deficit. Between September 1989 and June 1990, the two countries devised the Structural Impediments Initiative as a way to mitigate trade problems. Unlike earlier trade agreements, this one dealt with structural issues instead of focusing on particular items.

### Postoccupation Security Relations

The Security Treaty of 1951 had two major problems. First, it gave the United States the right to station its armies in Japan, but it did not oblige the U.S. to defend Japan or to consult with it over military operations. Second, the treaty allowed the American army to repress domestic rioting, a potential violation of Japan's sovereignty. In 1960, a new U.S.-Japan Security Treaty was concluded that abrogated the United States's right to intervene in domestic rioting and specified that the United States assumed official responsibility for Japan's defense. In turn, Japan was obligated to protect U.S. installations in Japan if they were attacked.

Japan did not become directly involved in the Vietnam War, but as a dependable ally of the United States it made significant contributions and reaped enormous economic benefits. Okinawa became a base for B-52s and a training base for U.S. Marines. America used its bases in mainland Japan for logistics, supplies, training, and rest and recreation. The U.S. withdrawal from Vietnam encouraged the United States to promote closer military cooperation with Japan. In November 1978, the United States and Japan began to review various aspects of military cooperation, such as the emergency defense legislation and logistic support.

### The 1990s and Afterward

The Cold War structure and America's preeminence in the world brought stability to post–World War II U.S.-Japanese relations. The Cold War made Japan depend on the United States strategically, and America's supreme power brought both military protection and economic well-being to Japan. However, the U.S. loss of dominance in the mid-1970s and the end of the Cold War in the early 1990s undermined the basis of stability in the countries' relations.

The 1990s were an unstable decade for U.S.-Japanese relations, a time during which these countries searched for a new principle to determine the orientation of their relationship.

During the 1990s, the U.S. economy revived, primarily due to the information technology (IT) revolution and the rapid development of IT-related industries, while Japan remained in deep political and economic turmoil. In July 1993, the Japanese Liberal Democratic Party, the long-term ruling party, lost its majority in the Diet, ending its thirty-eight-year rule over Japanese politics. A series of weak coalition governments followed, none bringing political stability, which contributed to Japan's economic recession. Economic crises in Southeast Asian countries in 1997 further undermined Japanese economic conditions. Currently, the world pays close attention to Japan's management of macroeconomic policy because of the negative effect of Japan's prolonged economic stagnation on the performance of the world economy, especially that of Asia.

The Japan-U.S. Framework for New Economic Partnership began in 1993 in order to redress trade imbalances. The negotiations stressed macroeconomic concerns, area-specific issues, structural problems, and a result-oriented approach. Washington demanded that Japan set the numerical target for its increase of imports, arguing that since the Japanese market was closed, the United States could not expand its exports to Japan. Japan strongly opposed this request on the grounds that it could lead to managed trade, and insisted that U.S. firms conduct more effective market research and produce goods suitable for Japanese consumers.

The gross national products (GNPs) of the United States and Japan combined constitute more than 40 percent of the world's total GNP, and their economic assistance makes up approximately 50 percent of the total amount of aid. Since U.S.-Japanese economic relations will continue to have a decisive impact on the health of the global economy, the U.S.-Japan Twenty-first Century Committee was established in July 1996 as a bilateral private-sector forum for dialogue and the consideration of policy proposals. Moreover, the two nations have worked together on such global threats as the deterioration of the earth's environment, communicable diseases, natural calamities, and terrorism.

The Persian Gulf War of 1991 reaffirmed the importance of the U.S. bases in Japan. The war forced the United States to restructure its strategic policy toward Asia as a whole. In February 1995 the United States published the Nye Initiative, a report on U.S. security strategy toward East Asia and the Pacific area compiled by defense expert Joseph Nye. It claimed there were 100,000 Americans associated with the military in Asia, of whom 60,000 were in Japan. The Nye Initiative defined U.S.-Japanese relations as the most important bilateral relationship in Asia, and Japanese security as the linchpin of U.S. security policy there.

Suspicions in 1994 that North Korea was developing nuclear weapons prompted Japan to reconsider its security policies. In September 1995, the abduction and rape of a twelve-year-old Japanese girl in Okinawa by American Marines sparked renewed criticism of the U.S.-Japanese Security Treaty. The threat of military conflicts among China, Taiwan, and the United States in 1995 and 1996 demonstrated military instability in Asia.

In April 1996, President Clinton held a summit with Prime Minister Hashimoto Ryutaro, with security as the principal agenda. They issued new guidelines for closer U.S.-Japan military cooperation. In May 1999 the Japanese Diet passed legislation supporting the guidelines. Japan formally approved conducting military-related action outside of Japan, including rear-area logistic support but not active combat operations, to enhance its own security interests.

Japan's neighbors, especially China, are closely watching the expanding role of the U.S.-Japanese alliance in the Asia-Pacific area and worry that Japan might again become a great military power. In the post–Cold War era, Washington redefined the security treaty with Japan to maintain a military presence in Japan partly because the continuous presence of the U.S. army would curb Japan's military behavior.

### The Near-Term Outlook

In 2001, Prime Minister Junichiro Koizumi visited Washington to meet with President George W. Bush, taking with him the sad statistics of the nation's economy. Japan faces the highest level of deflation since the Great Depression of the 1930s, and government debt has risen to 130 percent of the gross national product. Banks are the most important problem for Koizumi. Nonperforming loans total hundreds of billions of dollars. Koizumi openly expressed his pro-U.S. position in public, looking for outside support to implement his potentially unpopular reform agenda. President Bush, for his part, demonstrated support for Koizumi's economic reform policy. The terrorist attacks on the World Trade Center and the Pentagon in 2001 further promoted military cooperation between Japan and the United States. Japanese-U.S. relations continue to be one of the most important bilateral relationships in the twenty-first century, especially in the Asia-Pacific area. The peace and stability of the Asia-Pacific area depend on Japanese-U.S. cooperation and their efforts to contain destabilizing factors in this area.

*Yoneyuki Sugita*

### Further Reading


Borden, William S. (1984) *The Pacific Alliance: United States Foreign Economic Policy and Japanese Trade Recovery, 1947–1955.* Madison, WI: University of Wisconsin Press.

Buckley, Roger. (1992) *U.S.-Japan Alliance Diplomacy, 1945–1990.* New York: Cambridge University Press.

Cohen, Jerome B., ed. (1972) *Pacific Partnership: United States-Japan Trade: Prospects and Recommendations for the Seventies.* Lexington, MA.: Lexington Books.

Destler, I. M., et al. (1976) *Managing an Alliance: The Politics of U.S.-Japanese Relations.* Washington, DC: Brookings Institution.

———. (1979) *The Textile Wrangle: Conflict in Japanese-American Relations, 1969–1971.* Ithaca, NY: Cornell University Press.

Dower, John. (1999) *Embracing Defeat: Japan in the Wake of World War II.* New York: W. W. Norton.

Forsberg, Aaron. (2000) *America and the Japanese Miracle: The Cold War Context of Japan's Postwar Economic Revival, 1950–1960.* Chapel Hill, NC: University of North Carolina Press.

Green, Michael J. (1995) *Arming Japan: Defense Production, Alliance Politics, and the Postwar Search for Autonomy.* New York: Columbia University Press.

Hunsberger, Warren S. (1964) *Japan and the United States in World Trade.* New York: Harper & Row.

Iriye, Akira. (1972) *Pacific Estrangement: Japanese and American Expansion, 1897–1911.* Cambridge, MA: Harvard University Press.

———. (1981) *Power and Culture: The Japanese-American War, 1941–1945.* Cambridge, MA: Harvard University Press.

Koshiro, Yukiko. (1999) *Trans-Pacific Racisms and the U.S. Occupation of Japan.* New York: Columbia University Press.

LaFeber, Walter. (1997) *The Clash: A History of U.S.-Japan Relations.* New York: W. W. Norton.

Lincoln, Edward J. (1999) *Troubled Times: U.S.-Japan Trade Relations in the 1990s.* Washington, DC: Brookings Institution.

McKinnon, Ronald I., and Kenichi Ohno. (1997) *Dollar and Yen: Resolving Economic Conflict between the United States and Japan.* Cambridge, MA: MIT Press.

Neumann, William. (1963) *America Encounters Japan: From Perry to MacArthur.* Baltimore: Johns Hopkins Press.

Schaller, Michael. (1997) *Altered States: The United States and Japan since the Occupation.* New York: Oxford University Press.


## JAPANESE EXPANSION

Between 1895 and 1945, Japan built a colonial empire in East Asia and the South Pacific, exerted growing political and economic influence over areas of Asia beyond the borders of its formal colonial holdings, and eventually launched a war that extended the area of Japanese control to its greatest limits but ultimately resulted in the complete destruction of the empire.

While Japan's transition from a largely isolated country in 1853 into one of the world's major powers began with fears of being colonized, by 1905 a newly created Japanese state had successfully assumed a place alongside the Western imperialist powers. Japanese expansionism found its ultimate expression in a war to supplant Western colonial influence with a greatly enlarged Japanese colonial empire, defined as a "New Order in Asia."

### Colonial Empire

Following the establishment of the Meiji government in 1868, Japan's new leaders set out to establish formally Japan's boundaries under Western international law. The 1870s and 1880s thus witnessed the integration within Japanese borders of Hokkaido and the Kurile Islands in the north, the Ogasawara Islands off the Pacific coast, and the Ryukyu Islands in the south. Also driving the government's foreign policy was a desire to revise the unequal commercial and diplomatic treaties the old Tokugawa government (1600/1603–1868) had signed under duress during the 1850s. Establishing political and economic institutions patterned on Western practice was viewed as a necessary step toward convincing signatory nations to revise relations on a basis of equality; it was also seen as indispensable to building a Japan capable of guaranteeing its own independence.

Japan's leaders also became convinced that their nation's security would be threatened if any third power gained control of the Korean peninsula. Shortly after receiving British acquiescence to renegotiate the unequal treaties, rivalry with the Chinese Qing dynasty (1644–1912) over control of Korea erupted into the Sino-Japanese War of 1894–1895. A Japanese victory drove the Chinese out of Korea and brought Japan formal possession of Taiwan and participatory status in the unequal-treaty system that governed great-power relations with China.

The Russian presence just north of Korea in Manchuria, however, continued to concern Japanese leaders, and in 1902 Japan entered into an alliance with Great Britain directed at countering Russian influence in Northeast Asia. Japan's victory in the Russo-Japanese War of 1904–1905 brought control over what became known as the Guandong Leased Territory on China's Liaodong Peninsula and formal possession of southern Sakhalin. Japan's success also affirmed its status as a regional power and paved the way for the formal annexation of Korea in 1910. When Japan joined World War I as Britain's ally, it took control of Germany's colonial possessions in China and Micronesia. In 1915, the government also took an initiative known as the Twenty-One Demands to gain predominant political and economic influence over China, but this effort to exert influence beyond the formal boundaries of the new empire only provoked Chinese enmity and Western suspicions.

**The Search for a New Order**

After World War I, international conferences in Paris and Washington set out to revise the diplomatic practices of great-power relations and arms competition, which were viewed as central causes of the war. Open multilateral negotiations, free trade, self-determination, and arms limitation were to be the building blocks of a new order that would prevent a repeat of the Great War. Some Japanese viewed these reforms as an Anglo-American stratagem to perpetuate a status quo favoring their interests, but for the better part of the 1920s Japan was able to expand its interests on the Asian continent within the rules instituted in Paris and Washington.

Although the postwar settlement required that Japan relinquish control over former German concessions in China, the agreement also recognized the legitimacy of Japan's other colonial holdings and its control over the Guandong Leased Territory. Growing economic expansion on the continent during the 1920s further raised Japan's material stake in China's future. Some Japanese believed that the increasingly active Chinese nationalist movement and the prospects of a unified China threatened Japan's continental position. Others, particularly in the armed forces, feared that an invigorated Soviet Union would carry Communism into Northeast Asia. Finally, during the 1930s, the widely accepted belief in Japan's rightful role as the dominant power in East Asia increasingly intertwined with Pan-Asianist ideals postulating a national mission to liberate Asia from the yoke of Western imperialism.

Japan's response to these exigencies focused first on protecting its economic and security interests in Manchuria. By the beginning of the 1930s, many Japanese became convinced that Japan's interests could be better served through direct action than by continued adherence to the precepts of cooperative diplomacy. On 18 September 1931, against a backdrop of economic depression and domestic political uncertainty, Japanese army officers conspired to solve the "Manchurian question" by staging a swift military seizure of Manchuria and presenting their government and the world with their military occupation as a fait accompli. Extremely popular with the Japanese public, the Manchurian Incident strengthened the position of those favoring an independent foreign policy and reform of Japan's domestic political order. Following the army's lead, Japan's government in 1932 established the puppet state of Manchukuo and, in the face of international criticism, withdrew from the League of Nations in February 1933.

**Wartime Expansion**

Whereas Japan's expansion as a colonial power and pursuit of its interests in East Asia had occurred largely according to the prevailing practices of prewar imperialism and the postwar great-power style of cooperation elucidated in the Paris and Washington treaties, during the 1930s Japan became increasingly committed to establishing hegemony in East Asia. By the end of the decade, a confluence of domestic and international factors placed Japan increasingly at odds with those Western powers concurrently opposing German expansionism in Europe.

A skirmish between Chinese and Japanese troops north of Beijing on 7 July 1937 mushroomed into a general war that thereafter shaped Japanese policy making and eventually led to war with the Anglo-American powers. In 1938, Japanese leaders redefined the war in China as a noble crusade to construct a "New Order for East Asia," thereby placing Japan in direct conflict with the interests of the British and

Americans in China. In 1940, Japan joined in the Axis Pact with Nazi Germany and Fascist Italy and expanded its self-appointed mission to include incorporation of South and Southeast Asia into a Greater East Asian Coprosperity Sphere. Hostility with the Anglo-American powers grew as a result, and on 7 December 1941 Japan began the war in the Pacific with an air attack on Pearl Harbor and an assault on Western colonial holdings in East and Southeast Asia. Despite stunning initial successes, including the occupation of vast areas of the South Pacific, Japan's offensive soon stalled. The Allies' overwhelming counteroffensive culminated in 1945 with Japan's unconditional surrender and the complete collapse of both formal empire and regional hegemony.

### Explaining Japanese Expansion

Explanations of Japanese expansion tend to emphasize either the international context or Japan's domestic situation. Scholars who favor the former approach stress the reactive but rational nature of Japan's search for national security during a period of rampant colonization and great-power competition. While not necessarily disputing the importance of Western imperialism, other scholars view Japanese militarism and state economic imperatives as having driven the nation's imperialist expansion. While these two interpretative themes have analogs in broadly general theories of imperialism, Japan's experience as the only Asian country to colonize other Asians is unique. Given the fact that the wars launched by Japan on the continent and in the Pacific hastened the destruction of both Japanese and Western colonialism, Japan's imperial expansion clearly possesses specific and considerable significance for the history of the twentieth century.

*Roger H. Brown*

*See also:* **Russo-Japanese War; Sino-Japanese Conflict, Second; Sino-Japanese War**

### Further Reading

Beasley, William G. (1987) *Japanese Imperialism, 1894–1945.* Oxford, U.K.: Oxford University Press.

Duus, Peter. (1995) *The Abacus and the Sword: The Japanese Penetration of Korea, 1895–1910.* Berkeley and Los Angeles: University of California Press.

Duus, Peter, et al., eds. (1989) *The Japanese Informal Empire in China, 1895–1937.* Princeton, NJ: Princeton University Press.

———. (1996) *The Japanese Wartime Empire, 1931–1945.* Princeton, NJ: Princeton University Press.

Iriye, Akira. (1965) *After Imperialism: The Search for a New Order in the Far East, 1921–1931.* Boston: Harvard University Press.

Myers, Ramon H., and Mark R. Peattie, eds. (1984) *The Japanese Colonial Empire, 1895–1945.* Princeton, NJ: Princeton University Press.

Young, Louise. (1998) *Japan's Total Empire: Manchuria and the Culture of Wartime Imperialism.* Berkeley and Los Angeles: University of California Press.

## JAPANESE FIRMS ABROAD

The increasing international presence of Japanese firms beginning in the 1980s has generated a great deal of interest. At the end of the 1980s, Japanese companies made more investments abroad (in factories, banks, Hollywood picture studios, property, and hotels) than companies from any other country. While the 1990s saw a lessening of this overseas expansion, Japanese firms have become important players in the economies of North America, Europe, and mainland Asia. Indeed, their distinctive overseas behavior is due to the broader forces operating in the cultural, economic, and political environment at home.

One important factor that explains the differences between Japanese overseas operations and those of other countries is that, compared with the United States and Europe, for example, Japan is a latecomer to overseas investment. As a result of its defeat in World War II, Japan forfeited most of its foreign investments in 1946. After 1946, Japanese international economic strategy was based primarily on trade—on the development of exports and industrial self-sufficiency in raw materials for the domestic economy. Consequently, the giant Japanese trading companies *(sogo shosha)* were at the vanguard of overseas activities. Trading firms, such as Mitsui and Mitsubishi, acted as marketing agents for Japanese industry (textiles and steel products) in countries in Asia, North America, and Western Europe. At the same time, these firms were also responsible for acquiring strategic suppliers of materials such as coking coal and iron ore for the major steel firms. To conduct such global trade each *sogo shosha* maintained a large worldwide network of overseas offices connected to its headquarters by a sophisticated telex and telecommunications network.

### The Early Post–World War II Years

Until the late 1960s, the Japanese government's policy toward overseas operations by Japanese manufacturers was very restrictive in order to save scarce foreign exchange reserves. In addition, the relatively low domestic wage levels provided little stimulus for Japanese firms to look overseas for cheaper labor locations. As a result, Japanese manufacturing firms had a very low presence overseas throughout the 1960s. In the 1970s, however, trading houses became more involved in securing strategic energy resources following the oil shocks of that decade. Moreover, as Japanese exports and wages rose, Japanese manufacturers also began to move overseas. This was either to avoid trade barriers to the rush of Japanese exports in Southeast Asia and the United States, or to take advantage of cheaper wages in neighboring South Korea and Taiwan. As Japanese trade and offshore manufacturing grew, so did the overseas activities of banking, warehousing firms, and other service companies (construction and transportation companies).

## The Bubble Economy and Its Aftermath

In the 1980s, a number of developments in the Japanese economy combined to produce a dramatic takeoff in Japanese overseas production. The most important of these developments included the relaxation of Japanese government restrictions on overseas investments, the rapid increase in the value of the yen after 1985, the growing shortage (and increasing cost) of domestic labor, and a shortage of indigenous natural resources. The late 1980s also saw a spectacular rise of the Japanese stock market as well as the domestic property market, leading to sudden bloated values in corporate assets. This phenomenon was known as the bubble economy; it coincided with several years of strong balance-of-trade surpluses and very high rates of domestic savings. The net result was that Japan became the world's largest creditor and exporter of financial capital. Consequently, Japan's major banks, life insurance firms, and securities companies (stockbroking firms) also started rapidly expanding their overseas operations. Their intention was to expand their capacity to loan financial resources in the major financial markets of the world (New York and London) and invest in foreign bonds and property.

In the early 1990s, conditions dramatically altered as Japan's bubble economy burst, leading to stagnant growth at home. Since 1995, the number of overseas affiliate companies established by Japanese firms has declined. Manufacturing firms, however, have continued to search out lower-cost production locations and areas of market growth, such as Southeast Asia and China, in order to maintain their international competitiveness.

## Japanese Firms in North America

During the 1990s Japanese firms were established in all parts of the world and most had a globalization strategy that connected their organizations in the three major regions. In North America as well as in the world, the United States has been consistently the number-one country in terms of number of Japanese firms with a presence there. The growing presence of Japanese automobile firms in the United States has attracted widespread attention. The Honda Motor Company was the first Japanese automobile firm to begin producing automobiles in the United States (1982); it was followed by five other manufacturers. By the 1990s, these transplanted car assembly factories produced about 20 percent of the automobiles made in the United States. Japanese auto firms also operated in Canada (Toyota, Honda, and Suzuki), but Japan's major presence there has been in the timber and wood pulp sectors. Mexico has seen a number of electronics firms operate close to the U.S. border in special industrial zones (*maquiladoras*) aimed at exporting cheaper products and components into the lucrative U.S. market.

## Japanese Firms in Europe

In Western Europe, Japanese firms have been attracted by the size of the European Union market as a whole, especially as this region moves toward fuller unity. Most investment has occurred in the United Kingdom where Japanese firms are concentrated in automobiles (Nissan and Toyota) and electronics (Sony's color television factory in South Wales), as well as chemical products. These plants not only ensure access to the United Kingdom market but also to the continental European market. General machinery firms have chosen to go to Germany, while France is host to electronics, chemical products, and food processing companies. In Spain, Japanese firms are involved in automobile assembly and parts manufacturing, while in Italy it is clothing and textile products, as well as general machinery. Since the dissolution of the Soviet Union in 1991, some Japanese firms have expanded into Eastern Europe, for instance in automobile assembly.

## Japanese Firms in Southeast Asia

Starting in the late 1960s, Southeast Asian countries were targeted by electronics and machinery firms, and the relocation of complete production lines (video cameras, audio-visual products, and air conditioners) took place in large-scale factories aimed at worldwide as well as local markets. Around the mid-1980s, Southeast Asian countries began to be more relaxed about the operation of foreign companies in their countries; Malaysia and Thailand allowed Japanese automobile companies such as Toyota, Nissan, and Mitsubishi Motors to increase their production capacity. In the 1990s, China emerged as the most favorable investment location for Japanese firms. Although not large in value,

Japanese investment has also increased in Vietnam. Mention should also be made of the special role taken by Singapore and Hong Kong as centers for Japanese trade, banking, retailing, and service operations aimed at Southeast Asia and China, respectively.

### Friction with Host Nations

In all these regions there have been two major areas of controversy arising from the way Japanese firms have conducted their business. The first concerns labor practices and the impact of so-called Japanese-style management, as well as distinctive Japanese production techniques, including lean production, just-in-time delivery of parts, and flexible manufacturing assembly lines. Most accounts have shown that these practices have not been transferred abroad without some local adaptation that reflects the sociocultural background of the host country. A second area relates to localization and the relationship between assembly plants and their components suppliers. Japanese firms at home have been accustomed to very particular kinds of business ties with their domestic suppliers and have often found it difficult to quickly increase local procurement of parts or components when overseas. The strategy of importing from existing suppliers has been under severe pressure from governments in host countries. One response has been to persuade their traditional suppliers to move overseas. This offshore transfer is raising concerns about a hollowing out of the domestic manufacturing industry. Nevertheless, most companies have maintained research and development facilities in Japan, together with the very highest technology-intensive production.

### Future Directions

Despite an increasing convergence with Western corporations, Japanese firms as a group still differ in a number of significant ways from other multinationals in terms of their management style, strong links with the government, and sense of national mission. In the immediate future Asia is the preferred region for capital investment among Japanese companies. China looks particularly promising in the medium-term future, and Japanese firms expect positive changes in the business environment now that China has entered the World Trade Organization.

*David W. Edgington*

*See also:* **Quality Circles**

### Further Reading

Beechler, Schon L. and Allan Bird, eds. (1999) *Japanese Multinationals Abroad: Individual and Organizational Learning*. New York: Oxford University Press.

Edgington, David W., and R. Hayter. (2000) "Foreign Direct Investment and the Flying Geese Model: Japanese Electronics Firms in Asia-Pacific." *Environment and Planning A* 32: 281–304.

———. (2001) "Japanese Direct Foreign Investment and the Asian Financial Crisis." *Geoforum* 32: 103–120.

Encarnation, Dennis, ed. (1999) *Japanese Multinationals in Asia: Regional Operations in Comparative Perspective*. New York: Oxford University Press.

Hatch, Walter, and Kozo Yamamura. (1996) *Asia in Japan's Embrace: Building a Regional Production Alliance*. Cambridge, U.K.: Cambridge University Press.

Hollerman, Leon, and Ramon Hawley Myers, eds. (1996) *The Effect of Japanese Investment on the World Economy: A Six-Country Study, 1970–1991*. Stanford, CA: Hoover Institution Press.

Itagaki, Hiroshi. (1997) *The Japanese Production System: Hybrid Factories in East Asia*. Houndmills, U.K.: Macmillan.

Liker, Jeffrey K., W. Mark Fruin, and Paul S. Adler, eds. (1999) *Remade in America: Transplanting and Transforming Japanese Management Systems*. New York: Oxford University Press.

## JAPANESE FOREIGN INVESTMENT

A major feature of the world economy since the 1960s has been the rapid expansion of foreign direct investment (FDI). Strong world economic performance, substantial realignment of the exchange rates of major currencies, and technological developments in transportation and communication services have all contributed to unprecedented growth in FDI, particularly since the mid-1980s. The United States, Japan, Germany, the United Kingdom, and other developed nations have been the main investing countries. Among these nations, the increase of Japanese FDI has been particularly high since the mid-1980s, though it has declined since the economic recession of the 1990s. With the notable exception of Japan, most of the leading investing countries are also major recipients of FDI.

### The Development of Japan's FDI

The growth of Japan's role as a foreign investor has been extraordinary. With little involvement in the 1950s, Japan emerged with about 17 percent of the world's stock of foreign direct investment in the late 1980s. Total investment flows first began to gather momentum after 1965, rising from $227 million in 1966 to a peak of $3.49 billion by 1973. The investment boom slackened due to the oil crisis of 1973, but resumed again in 1978. After receding slightly in 1982, it rose steadily until 1985; between 1986 and 1989, it surged ahead at a rapid pace. By 1989, Japan was the single largest source of FDI, with outflows amounting to $67 billion. This was in comparison with $40 billion from the United States and $35 billion from the United Kingdom.

Factors that contributed to the high investment rates in the 1980s included Japan's increasing trade surplus; the 1980 deregulation of exchange controls that paved the way for banks, financial securities companies, and institutional investors such as life insurance firms to invest abroad; and the 46 percent appreciation of the yen between 1985 and 1987. Japan's foreign investment growth has been negative in the 1990s as a result of the bursting of the bubble economy at the end of 1989 and the resulting pessimistic economic forecast.

Most of the Japanese FDI is concentrated in Southeast Asia, China, Western Europe, and the United States. In the 1960s, in order to secure a stable supply of raw materials for manufacturing, Japan invested in petroleum drilling in Indonesia, iron-ore mining in Malaysia, and copper mining in the Philippines. Beginning in 1970, Japanese FDI began to concentrate in the newly industrialized economies (NIEs) of Taiwan, South Korea, Hong Kong, and China, in manufacturing activities such as textiles and consumer electronics. Both internal factors in Japan and external factors in the Asian countries played a role in promoting Japanese FDI. An increase in the price of Japanese products, particularly labor-intensive products, resulting from rising wages and appreciation of the yen led Japanese producers to shift their production to the countries where production could be carried out at a lower cost. The abundance of quality low-wage labor, FDI promotion policies such as export processing zones, and preferential taxes attracted Japanese FDI to Asia.

### FDI in Asia

In 1989, the share of Asia in overall Japanese FDI was 12.2 percent. Of that investment in Asia, the Asian NIEs, Southeast Asia, and China accounted for 98.6 percent of Japanese FDI in 1989. The largest recipients in Southeast Asia were Thailand, Malaysia, Indonesia, and Singapore in reported value of FDI. In 1989, Japan was the largest foreign investor in all the member countries of the Association of Southeast Asian Nations (ASEAN). Between 1990 and 1995 Malaysia, Indonesia, and Thailand continued to attract the most FDI in Southeast Asia, ranking third, fifth, and seventh respectively in the world based on cumulative FDI. Rising wages due to the shortage of labor and rising land prices in Japan provided additional incentive for overseas production. The distinguishing feature of Japanese firms in Asia in the early 2000s is that joint ventures between indigenous and Japanese partners are more common than in North America and Europe.

### FDI in the United States

The United States accounted for 48.2 percent of Japan's overall FDI in 1989, but in the 1990s, as a result of the fall in Japan's stock and land prices, FDIs were drastically reduced. The bulk of the Japanese investment in the United States is concentrated in manufacturing, particularly in electrical machinery and transport equipment. The Japanese automobile industry has made major investments in the United States and Canada; there are several major Japanese transplant assembly facilities, as well as some 270 automotive parts suppliers. Honda was the first automotive company to produce in the United States, arriving in 1982. By 1989, Nissan, Toyota, Mazda, and Mitsubishi had factories located in rural sites in the Midwest and South. The increasing threat of U.S. import barriers precipitated a massive onrush of Japanese manufacturing FDI in the period 1978 to 1984. Along with the desire to have a production presence in the United States to ensure market access, a number of Japanese firms, particularly in areas such as chemicals, optical goods, and electronics, acquired U.S. corporations to obtain a direct channel to coveted technology. The United States offers many attractions to foreign investors, including a large and growing market, few bureaucratic restrictions and regulations that impede corporate activity, an excellent social infrastructure, low energy costs, and an educated labor force. Most state and local governments have welcomed Japanese investment and have solicited Japanese firms.

### FDI in Europe

By the end of the 1980s, Europe accounted for 21 percent of the Japanese FDI. Japanese firms have invested in Europe because of trade restrictive measures.The United Kingdom was the favored FDI destination, followed by the Netherlands, Luxembourg, Germany, and France. Switzerland and Spain also received Japanese FDI. Relatively lower wages, favorable public investment incentives, and an absence of strong local rivals in automobiles and electronics explain the attraction of Britain. France offered a central location and a large internal market. Germany offered a good industrial relations record, high labor skills, and centrality. Spain, which has a large reservoir of cheap labor, had a relatively large Japanese production presence because of its high import barrier. In Britain, the Japanese have selected peripheral regions such as Wales, Scotland, and northeast England for locating firms. Machinery, electronics, and transport equipment dominate the FDI.

Historically, much of Japan's foreign investment has been induced by the need to avert potential market losses resulting from protectionist policies or by attempts to secure overseas raw materials. By setting up overseas plants, Japanese firms are able to retain much of their market share. Investments in low-wage countries in Asia and Latin America have helped Japan to retain the general export competitiveness of its products.

*P. P. Karan*

*See also:* **Asian Economic Crisis of 1997; Japanese Firms Abroad; Quality Circles**

**Further Reading**

Allen, G. C. (1981) *The Japanese Economy.* London: Weidenfeld and Nicolson.
Emmott, B. (1992) *Japan's Global Reach.* London: Century.
Flath, David. (2000) *The Japanese Economy.* Oxford: Oxford University Press.
Ito, T. (1992) *The Japanese Economy.* Cambridge, MA: MIT Press.
Karan, P. P. (2001) *Japan in the Bluegrass.* Lexington, KY: University Press of Kentucky.

**JAPAN INTERNATIONAL COOPERATION AGENCY (JICA)** The Japan International Cooperation Agency (Kokusai Kyoryoku Jigyodan) is one of two Japanese governmental organizations responsible for official development assistance (ODA). The other organization was formerly the Overseas Economic Development Fund (OEDF), which merged with the Japan Export-Import Bank in October 1999 to form the new Japan Bank for International Cooperation.

JICA's roles have been to administer grant aid, to provide technical aid, and to oversee the Japan Overseas Cooperation Volunteers (JOCV, or Seinen Kaigai Kyoryokudan), the Japanese equivalent of the U.S. Peace Corps. While Japanese ODA has traditionally been loan-based in order to ensure efficient use of funds by the recipient country, by fiscal year 1995, grant aid and technical assistance were nearly equal to lending. Japan gives grant aid to the world's poorest countries, as well as for general humanitarian projects. Thus, both JICA and the JOCV are influential in least developed countries (LDCs).

JICA's technical assistance takes a variety of forms. In many cases, consultants advise governments or public organizations in developing countries on engineering or other projects. JICA technical assistance also funds the feasibility studies that precede projects funded by either grant or loan aid.

Japan's ODA budget and policy priorities are set outside of JICA by the Ministry of Foreign Affairs, the Ministry of Finance, the Ministry of International Trade and Industry, and the Economic Planning Agency. The varying interests of these ministries have sometimes made for a disjointed approach that emphasizes foreign policy and commercial concerns to varying degrees.

In the late 1980s, the United States pressured Japan to untie its aid for fear that U.S. firms would be excluded from lucrative Japanese aid contracts in developing countries. The result was that most of JICA's grants were officially "untied," as were all Japanese ODA loans. In other words, non-Japanese as well as Japanese firms can bid to be contractors on most Japanese aid projects. In some cases, projects are LDC-untied, which means that LDC-based firms can compete with Japanese firms for contracts, but that developed country firms cannot. Most contracts are still won by Japanese firms, however, and there remains some dispute as to whether Japanese ODA is actually untied in practice.

*William W. Grimes*

**Further Reading**

Arase, David. (1995) *Buying Power: The Political Economy of Japan's Foreign Aid.* Boulder, CO: Lynne Rienner Publishers.
Orr, Robert. (1990) *The Emergence of Japan's Foreign Aid Power.* New York: Columbia University Press.

**JAPANESE LANGUAGE** The Japanese language ranks sixth in number of speakers worldwide after Chinese, English, Russian, Hindi, and Spanish. Most Japanese speakers are located within Japan, although there are also immigrant communities in the Americas and other parts of the world where a small number of Japanese speakers can be found. As Japan is said to be a linguistically homogeneous nation, most of its approximately 127 million residents do speak Japanese. It is important to remember, however, that Japan is also home to linguistic minorities such as the Ainu, Okinawans, and permanent foreign residents.

Scholars debate the origins of the Japanese language, and arguments have been made for links to Altaic languages (such as Mongolian), Korean, Dravidian languages (such as Tamil), Malayo-Polynesian languages, and Tibeto-Burmese. It seems probable that the Japanese language originated as a mix of languages from Central and Southeast Asia and had fully developed into a distinct language by the time of the Yayoi culture (300 BCE–300 CE).

While the Japanese use the Chinese system of writing, the Japanese language is not related to the Chinese language. The writing system was borrowed from Chinese during the fifth or sixth century, long after the development of spoken Japanese. The earliest known writings in Japanese date back to the eighth century.

### Pronunciation

Japanese has five vowels *(a, i, u, e, o)*, which are similar in pronunciation to the vowels of Spanish and Italian. Each vowel can also be elongated, doubling the duration of its pronunciation.

The sound system of Japanese is straightforward; there are few exceptions to established pronunciation rules, and each character in a word is pronounced. Unlike some languages, sounds are constant, and even long words can be sounded out easily. Sound units are composed of a consonant plus a vowel or a vowel alone. Only the consonant *n* can occur completely unattached to a vowel.

Japanese is a pitch-based language, unlike English, which is based on stress. Each syllable in a Japanese word is stressed equally, but the pitch of syllables rises and falls. Consequently, pronunciation of Japanese words is steady and even compared with English.

### The Written Language

The literacy rate in Japan is officially reported at 99 percent of the population, which shows the emphasis placed on the written language. Japanese utilizes four distinct systems of writing: kanji, hiragana, katakana, and *romaji* (romanization). These writing systems are used together, and occasionally all four are found in a single sentence. More commonly, two or three of the systems will be used in one sentence; it is extremely uncommon to find a sentence incorporating only one writing system.

Kanji is the Japanese name for the simplified pictographs borrowed from Chinese, which represent whole words and are not phonetic. Although elements of a kanji may at times offer clues to its pronunciation, there are no foolproof ways of knowing a particular kanji's pronunciation without memorizing its reading. Altogether there are approximately 50,000 kanji, but the Japanese government has limited to 1,945 the number necessary for daily use. Educated Japanese adults can usually recognize at least two to three thousand characters.

Kana, a term that covers both hiragana and katakana, originated from the simplification of kanji in the ninth and tenth centuries, and reflect phonological characteristics of Japanese. In other words, while kanji represent whole words, kana simply represent sounds that are combined to form words. There are forty-eight sound units that can be expressed in both hiragana and katakana. These units represent vowels, consonant-vowel combinations, and the single consonant *n*. Hiragana are a cursive style and are used mainly for verb and adjective endings and other grammatical markers. Katakana are much more angular. They are regularly used for onomatopoeias and loanwords from other languages, in a manner somewhat similar to italics in English.

The fourth writing system is the roman alphabet *(romaji)*, which is used primarily for company names and in advertising. For example, the company name Sony is always written in *romaji*. There are two systems of romanization, Hepburn and Kunrei, both of which are used in Japan and overseas.

Japanese can be written either vertically or horizontally. Traditionally, Japanese was written vertically from right to left; the first page of a Japanese book would be considered the last page of a Western book. This format continues in newspapers and some books, but many magazines and books are printed horizontally from left to right.

### Grammar

Japanese is a language with a flexible subject-object-verb word order. The only word order restriction is that the verb must come at the end of a sentence; otherwise, words can be randomly ordered because of the presence of conjugational suffixes and case particles that mark the function of words in a sentence.

Nouns in Japanese do not change for gender, case, or number. Verbs and adjectives in Japanese must be conjugated; verb conjugation is straightforward and there are few irregularities. There are no articles in Japanese.

An important aspect of the Japanese language is a complex system of honorific verbs. Because Japanese society is based on strict hierarchies, those hierarchies are expressed in the language. Humble verb forms are used when speakers refer to themselves, and exalted forms are used when addressing a person of higher rank or status. Positions can be based on social status, rank, gender, age, or any combination thereof. In addition, male and female speech is differentiated, with female speech usually taking more polite forms and male speech often coming across as more direct.

### The Future of Japanese

In addition to standard Japanese, based on the Tokyo dialect, there are a number of regional and local dialects of Japanese. Because mass media and compulsory education have familiarized people around the country with the standard dialect, most Japanese now speak both standard Japanese and their local dialect. The Kansai dialect, spoken in Kyoto and Osaka, is one of the most well-known dialects and is a source of pride for people from that region.

Another factor causing language change in Japan is the incorporation of a large number of loanwords. There are loanwords from a variety of languages, and since the end of World War II, the number of English loanwords has increased rapidly. Loanwords such as *apaato* (apartment), *hanbaagaa* (hamburger), and *basukettobooru* (basketball) are written in katakana. The increasing number of new loanwords being used in Japanese has caused confusion among older Japanese, who worry that Japanese is losing its traditional identity.

*Danielle Rocheleau*

### Further Reading

Hane, Mikiso. (1986) *Modern Japan: A Historical Survey.* Boulder, CO: Westview Press.

Loveday, Leo J. (1996) *Language Contact in Japan: A Socio-Linguistic History.* Oxford Studies in Language Contact. Oxford, U.K.: Clarendon Press.

Shibatani, Masayoshi. (1990) *The Languages of Japan.* Cambridge, U.K.: Cambridge University Press.

SWET [Society of Writers, Editors & Translators]. (1998) *Japan Style Sheet: The SWET Guide for Writers, Editors and Translators.* Berkeley, CA: Stone Bridge Press.

Tsujimura, Natsuko. (1996) *An Introduction to Japanese Linguistics.* Cambridge, MA: Blackwell Publishers.

## JAPANESE SPIRIT. See **Yamato Damashii.**

**JATIYA PARTY** The Jatiya Party (JP, but Jatiya Dal in its original form) was founded in 1983 as a vehicle for the Bangladesh leader Hussain Muhammad Ershad (b. 1930). It attracted some members of the Bangladesh Nationalist Party (BNP), who were willing to work with Ershad to maintain their political influence, as well as a few from the Awami League for the same reason. It is a centrist party, as is the BNP, and the economic and social programs of the two parties have little difference. The difference has been the BNP's dislike of the means Ershad used to gain power.

Ershad called a parliamentary election in 1986 in which the JP won a slight majority over the Awami League, thereby dispelling claims that the election was fixed. However, the Awami League withdrew from the parliament in 1988, forcing another election in which the JP won an overwhelming majority because no other significant party contested. Since the fall of Ershad in December 1990, the party has continued to contest, finishing third in the 1991 and June 1996 elections. Following the latter, Ershad led the party into a coalition with the Awami League, but the JP has now split. The faction led by Ershad has aligned with the BNP in the opposition; the other faction remains allied with the Awami League in the government.

*Craig Baxter*

**JATRA** *Jatra* ("journey") is a theatrical form of folk opera that relies heavily on dance and music, and is prevalent in the Bengal region of eastern India and present-day Bangladesh. This theater, which is devoted to the worship of Krishna, follows the tradition of classical ancient Indian theater, in which dialogue, dance, music, and gesture are all intermixed with the mythic content. But, whereas ancient drama had a larger secular content, *jatra* was narrowed down to the philosophy of personal and individual bhakti (devotion) to Krishna or Rama as god incarnate. Watching a *jatra* play is a way symbolically to perform a spiritual journey or a pilgrimage. The term also denotes the journeying *(jatri)* or wandering players.

The wave of bhakti was generated in Bengal and Orissa in the fifteenth century by, among others, the poet Chaitanya Mahaprabhu as a mass movement. In the earliest phase, the *jatra* plays were adaptations into local vernacular of such Sanskrit-tradition plays as *Vidagdha Madhavam*, written in northern India by authors including Roop Goswami. Goswami's play, adapted as *Radhakrishna Lila Kadamba*, continues to be a significant part of the *jatra* repertoire. Devotional verses of Bengali poets such as Lochan Das (1523–1589), Jagannath Vallabh, and Jadogunananda Das (around 1607) were adapted into *jatra*. Famous performance texts such as *Kaliya Daman*, *Nimai Sanyas*, and *Chaitanya Chandrodaya Kaumudi* (1712) were composed. Many *jatra* plays were about the lives of the great saints of the bhakti movement.

In the nineteenth century, *jatra* had more music than dance or gestures. The dance portions are mainly on the dalliance of Krishna with the *gopis* (village women tending cows), a standard motif. But the main emotional intensity in this theater was generated by the musical excellence of the verses used as dialogue. *Jatra*, like most medieval theater from other parts of India, made musical dialogue the most prominent feature of the performance.

The musical ensemble for *jatra* consists of the drum *(dhol)*, flute, and the harmonium—an Indian version of accordion—which was introduced during the nineteenth century. The singers were dressed in long white robes and the players in a conventional dress. The manager of the performers, the *adhikari*, generally is also the trainer and chief senior artist. In the twentieth century, however, the impact of the urban theater (an Indian version of Western naturalistic art) can be seen on *jatra*. There also was an attempt to use the *jatra* form to produce modern scripts with socialist and contemporary ideologies.

Like most traditional theatrical forms, *jatra* is becoming an endangered species in the twenty-first century, as audience tastes have changed and the social demand of the times is more for lighter entertainment than for deep devotion of the religious kind.

*Bharat Gupt*

### Further Reading

Gautam, M. R. (1980) *The Musical Heritage of India.* Delhi: Abhinav Publications.

Gupt, Bharat. (1994) *Dramatic Concepts: Greek and Indian. A Study of Poetics and the Natyasastra.* Delhi: D. K. Printworld.

Swami Prajnananda. (1965) *A Historical Study of Indian Music.* Calcutta, India: Anandadhara Publications.

**JAVA** (2000 pop. 120 million). The island of Java is the political and economic center of Indonesia. In conjunction with the island of Madura, usually included in its statistics, Java has a territory of 132,608 square kilometers. Java is divided into three provinces: West, Central, and East Java, and also includes two special territories: Jakarta and Yogyakarta. A volcanic mountain chain runs the length of the island. Java has over sixty volcanoes, of which more than a dozen are still active. The most important mineral resources are oil, iron ore, and salt. The climate is hot and wet, with a dry and a wet season. Natural forests have been reduced to about 3 percent of the land area. Valuable wood species are teak, coconuts, and spice trees. Endangered animal species include the gibbon, the one-horned rhinoceros, and the leopard. The main ecological problem is soil erosion.

With a density of approximately 905 people per square kilometer, Java is among the world's most densely populated areas. The ethnic composition of the population presents three main groups, each speaking their own language: Javanese, Sundanese, and

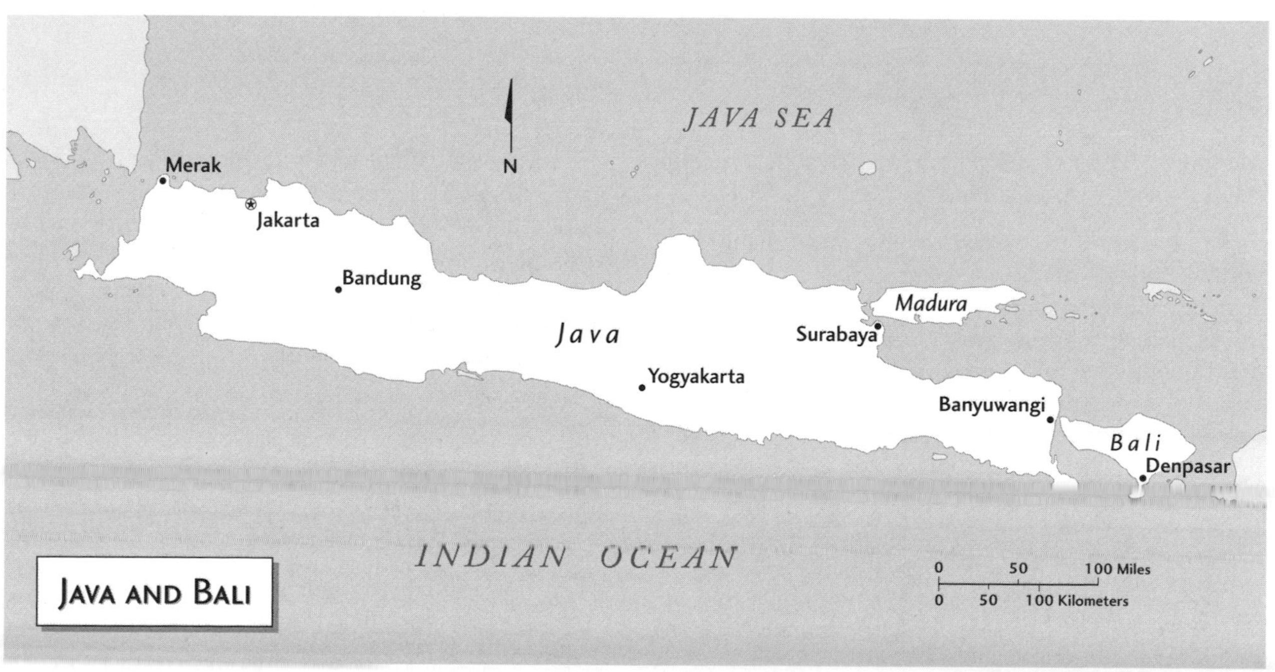


JAVA AND BALI

## FITTING IN—IN JAVA

*Tjotjog* is a key element of slametan, a system of Javanese rituals practiced by rural villagers. In the excerpt below, anthropologist Clifford Geertz explains the concept.

> At the base of this often quite involved system lies one of the most fundamental Javanese metaphysical concepts: *tjotjog*. To *tjotjog* means to fit, as a key does in a lock, as an efficacious medicine does a disease, as a solution does an arithmetic problem, as a man does the woman he married (if he doesn't, they get divorced). If your opinion agrees with mine, we *tjotjog;* if the meaning of my name fits my character (and if it brings me good luck), it is said to be *tjotjog*. Tasty food, comfortable surroundings, gratifying outcomes are all *tjotjog*. In the broadest and most abstract sense two separate items *tjotjog* when their coincidence forms an aesthetic pattern. It implies a contrapuntal view of the universe in which what is important is what natural relationship the separate elements—space, time, and human motivation—have to one another, how they must be arranged in order to strike a chord and avoid a dissonance.
>
> As in harmony, the ultimately correct relations are fixed, determinate, and knowable, and so religion, like harmony, is ultimately a science, no matter how much of an art its actual practice may be. The petungan system provides a way of stating these relationships and thus of tuning one's own actions to them, of avoiding the kind of disharmony with the general order of nature which can only bring misfortune.
>
> *Source:* Clifford J. Geertz. (1964) *The Religion of Java*. New York: The Free Press of Glencoe, 31.

Madurese. Most of the people are Muslim but some small pockets of Hinduism still survive in East Java.

Java is one of the oldest foci of human habitation, with specimens of *Homo erectus* dating from 800,000 years ago having been discovered there. The first major principality arose around the beginning of the eighth century. Hinduism, Buddhism, and Islam consecutively penetrated into Java between the first century CE and the sixteenth century. The Majapahit dynasty flourished there from the end of the thirteenth century to the sixteenth century; at its height its influence reached to Siam and Annam. By the end of the eighteenth century the entire island was under Dutch control. Today, Indonesia's three biggest cities are on Java: Jakarta (the nation's capital), Surabaya, and Bandung.

Java is one of the most fertile tropical places on earth. About 70 percent of the workforce engages in agriculture. Crops grown for domestic use include rice, maize, and cassava. A quarter of Java's land area is used for *sawah* agriculture (growing rice in flooded paddy fields). Cash commodities include rubber, coffee, tea, tobacco, and peanuts.

*Dimitar L. Dimitrov*

### Further Reading

Beatty, Andrew. (1999) *Varieties of Javanese Religion: An Anthropological Account.* New York: Cambridge University Press.

Knight, G. R. (2000) *Narratives of Colonialism: Sugar, Java, and the Dutch.* Huntington, NY: Nova Science Publishers.

Whitten, Tony, Roehayat Soeriaatmadja, and Suraya Afiff. (1996) *The Ecology of Java and Bali.* Hong Kong, China: Periplus Editions.

**JAVA SEA** The Java Sea is 162,662 square nautical miles and is bounded by Sumatra to the west, Borneo to the north, and Java to the south. Comprising the southern extension of the Sunda Shelf of continental Southeast Asia, it is 20–60 m deep and is sheltered from waves over 1.5 m. Influenced by monsoons, its surface currents reverse seasonally, and its tides range from under 1.5 m to 3 m. Mangroves dominate the Borneo shores while limited coral reefs lie off Java's north coast.

The Java Sea is Indonesia's second largest and most important marine region. On its southern shore is the heavily populated island of Java with Indonesia's largest ports at Tanjungpriok and Surabaya. Petroleum is produced in the western Java Sea, near the southeast coast of Sumatra. Fishing is economically important, and seafood processing facilities are located at Tanjungpriok, Cirebon, Pekalongan, Semarang, Surabaya, and Banyuwangi on the north coast of Java and at Banjarmasin in South Kalimantan. It is among Indonesia's most polluted seas, and erosion is a major problem on its southern shores.

*Wong Poh Poh*

**Further Reading**

Kent, George, and Mark J. Valencia, eds. (1985) *Marine Policy in Southeast Asia*. Berkeley and Los Angeles: University of California Press.

Morgan, Joseph R., and Mark J. Valencia, eds. (1983) *Atlas for Marine Policy in Southeast Asian Seas*. Berkeley and Los Angeles: University of California Press.

**JAVA WAR** The Java War lasted from 1825 to 1830, overlapping the Padri War (1821–1837) on neighboring Sumatra. The war cost 200,000 Javanese lives when Java's population was only around 3 million. As in the Padri movement, Islam helped unify opposition to Dutch rule in Java.

The Dutch policy of interfering in royal palace *(kraton)* affairs directly caused this uprising. Colonial authorities passed over Prince Diponegoro of Yogyakarta (1775–1835), eldest son of the previous sultan, recognizing instead the sultan's younger brother as his successor. Diponegoro sought to regain his rightful position, as revealed to him by the sea goddess Nyai Rara Kidul in a dream, and, more tangibly, as promised to him by Sir Thomas Raffles (1781–1826), lieutenant-governor of Java during the British interregnum. This Javanese mystical notion was combined with the prince's *pesantren* (Islamic school) education when he promoted Islam as the religion of Java by challenging the colonial unbelievers.

There was another provocation as well. The Dutch tried to restrict *kraton* wealth and power by declaring that it could not lease its land and that rentals must be repaid. A Dutch-built road from Malang to Yogyakarta was partly constructed over a sacred burial ground (the road also expedited Dutch troop movements). Diponegoro led resistance to the Dutch, assisted by the *priyayi* (aristocracy) of Yogyakarta, through a campaign of guerrilla warfare. Diponegoro was hailed as the *ratu adil* (just king) by many for whom the prince represented their anticolonial hopes. The Dutch countermeasure was to establish a series of linked forts from which effective raids were made. In 1829, Diponegoro's two most trusted advisers, Kiyayi Maja and Sentot, surrendered—a blow to the rebellion. In 1830, Diponegoro agreed to negotiations to end the conflict but refused to renounce his claim to the Yogyakarta throne. The Dutch tricked Diponegoro by falsely promising him safe conduct for the negotiations, but actually arrested him and exiled him to Makasar. While many hoped for Diponegoro's return, the Java War was the last of the *priyayi*-led rebellions; the *priyayi* were increasingly coopted by Dutch colonial authorities as agents of governance and were seen by the people as collaborators. The Dutch, in their campaign to destroy the power of the various *kratons* of Java and of traditional authorities elsewhere in the Indies, weakened the Yogyakarta sultanate by stripping away vast land holdings. However, Yogyakarta's royal family retained titular leadership of its traditional territory, and the current sultan of Yogyakarta, Hamenkubuwono X, remains the formal head of the province of Yogyakarta under a unique arrangement.

*Anthony Smith*

**Further Reading**

Frederick, William H., and Robert L. Worden, eds. (1992) *Indonesia: A Country Study*. Washington, DC: Library of Congress.

Spuyt, J., and J. B. Robertson. (1973) *History of Indonesia: The Timeless Islands*. Rev. ed. Melbourne, Australia: Macmillan.

Tarling, Nicholas, ed. (1992) *The Cambridge History of Southeast Asia: The Nineteenth and Twentieth Centuries*, 2. Cambridge, U.K.: Cambridge University Press.

**JAVANESE** Javanese is the language of the largest ethnic group of Indonesia with around 75 million speakers. It is mainly spoken in Central and East Java, as well as in northern coastal areas. Outside Java, many Javanese speakers are found in transmigration areas in Sumatra, Kalimantan, and Sulawesi. In Suriname (formerly Dutch Guiana, in South America) there is a Javanese immigrant community of some 60,000 descendants of indentured workers.

Javanese belongs to the Austronesian (Malayo-Polynesian) family. There is considerable dialectal variation, but the language of Central Java, more specifically the principalities of Surakarta and Yogyakarta, is commonly regarded as standard. A feature that Javanese shares with related languages such as Sundanese, Madurese, and Balinese is the possession of different speech levels or sets of vocabulary, the *ngoko-krama* phenomenon. The basic, informal level is *ngoko*, while *krama*—synonymous with politeness—is used when speaking to a social superior or a stranger. Three types of script are used for writing modern Javanese: Javanese, Perso-Arabic, and Roman script. Javanese script has evolved over more than 1,200 years and derives from an Indian script. Since World War II, however, Javanese script has rapidly given way to Roman script, which is currently the only script mastered by the majority of Javanese. Perso-Arabic script, with or without vowel diacritics, is associated with Islamic texts.

The charter of Sukabumi, dated 25 March 804 CE, marks the beginning of the Old Javanese language. The terms Old Javanese, Middle Javanese, and Modern Javanese do not reflect a neat historical succession. Old Javanese is used for all Javanese texts lacking Arabic loans or Muslim influence, whereas Middle Javanese denotes the language of Balinese *kidung* literature. In Bali, Old Javanese remains a living tradition to the present day. The earliest documents in Modern Javanese are two manuscripts of Islamic teachings current on the north coast of Java in the sixteenth century. In the early twentieth century Indonesian nationalists decided that Malay was more suitable than Javanese for a national language, and declared it so under the name of *Bahasa Indonesia* (Indonesian language) in 1928. A process of mutual interpenetration of the two languages is still in progress.

Javanese dancers in traditional costume in Bandung, West Java. (LINDSAY HEBBERD/CORBIS)

*Edwin Wieringa*

### Further Reading

Arps, Bernard. (1996) "Javanese Language, Literature and Theatre." In *Southeast Asian Languages and Literatures. A Bibliographical Guide to Burmese, Cambodian, Indonesian, Javanese, Malay, Minangkabau, Thai, and Vietnamese*, edited by E. Ulrich Kratz. London and New York: Tauris, 112–164.

Robson, Stuart. (1992) *Javanese Grammar for Students*. Clayton, Australia: Monash University.

Uhlenbeck, E. M. (1964) *A Critical Survey of Studies on the Languages of Java and Madura*. The Hague, Netherlands: Nijhoff.

**JAYAVARMAN II** (c. 770–834), founder of the unified Khmer state. Jayavarman II, a mysterious figure who left no inscriptions of his own, is credited with the foundation of a unified Khmer state in what is now Cambodia. Jayavarman II was often mentioned in the inscriptions of his successors, who regarded him as the founder of what became the powerful Angkorean kingdom. Scholars have established that when he was about twenty years old, Jayavarman came from Java and declared his independence from the Javanese kingdom. His early career combined military conquests and the formation of strategic alliances in which local powers transferred some of their influence to the newcomer.

The Sdok Kak Thom inscription, incised in the eleventh century, gives the details of what would later become Jayavarman's most enduring legacy. According to the inscription, in the year 802 CE, Jayavarman initiated a ritual whereby he became a "universal monarch." The ritual celebrated the cult of the *devaraja*, or "god king," which was associated with the Hindu divinity Siva. As Siva was a creator, keeper, and destroyer of worlds, the king assumed the role of an intermediary between the cosmic world and the world of human existence. Notions of a "universal monarch" and a "god king" endured to transcend the political culture of modern Cambodia.

*David M. Ayres*

**Further Reading**

Chandler, David. (1993) *A History of Cambodia*. 2d ed. Sydney: Allen and Unwin.

Mabbett, Ian, and David Chandler. (1995) *The Khmers*. Oxford: Blackwell.

Rooney, Dawn F. (1994) *Angkor: Temples of Cambodia's Kings*. Lincolnwood, IL: Passport Books.

**JAYAVARMAN VII** (1181–1220), king of Angkor. Jayavarman VII is recognized as the last great king of Angkor, the mighty kingdom that preceded modern Cambodia. A first cousin of Suryavarman II (d. 1150), who built the famed Angkor Wat, he assumed the throne at a time when the kingdom was in decline, having been invaded and overtaken in an attack by the Chams. It took four years of fighting for Jayavarman's army to drive the Chams out of Angkor. Unlike his Angkorean predecessors, who worshiped Hindu gods, Jayavarman VII was a Mahayana Buddhist. Jayavarman VII was the most prolific builder of Cambodia's Angkorean kings. He built roads that extended from the heart of his kingdom, and he built temples, hospitals, reservoirs, and rest houses. He built the walled city of Angkor Thom, with the Bayon at its center. He was also responsible for building Ta Prohm, Preah Khan, Ta Som, the Terrace of the Elephants, and Srah Srang. Much of the life, and death, of Jayavarman VII remains shrouded in mystery. It is possible that he is the leper king of Khmer oral tradition. Whatever the case, it is clear that regional power and influence of the Angkor kingdom declined after his reign.

*David M. Ayres*

**Further Reading**

Chandler, David. (1993) *A History of Cambodia*. 2d ed. Sydney: Allen and Unwin.

Mabbett, Ian, and David Chandler. (1995) *The Khmers*. Oxford: Blackwell.

**JESUITS IN INDIA** The Society of Jesus, founded in 1540 by Saint Ignatius of Loyola (1491–1556), is a Roman Catholic religious order known worldwide for its evangelical, charitable, and educational work as well as for its concern for social issues. Members (Jesuits) are bound by vows of poverty, chastity, and apostolic labors.

Saint Francis Xavier (1506–1552) was the first Jesuit to work in India; he represented the society in Goa on the west coast of India from 1540, where he worked among the *paravas*, a fisher caste, and made many converts. After his death his body was enshrined in the cathedral in Goa, where he is venerated by people of all faiths.

Jesuits published India's first printed book in 1556. Thomas Stephens (1549–1619), an English Jesuit stationed in Goa, wrote a Konkani grammar, a manual of Christian instruction in Konkani and Marathi, and *Kristapurana* (Christian Purana, 1615), a Marathi poem in the style of the Puranas. Roberto de Nobili (1577–1656), another linguist, wrote a Tamil catechism.

The Society of Jesus enjoyed many successes in India, but these were often tempered by momentary trials and setbacks. In 1744 Pope Benedict XIV (1675–1758) issued a papal bull suppressing the rites used by Indian converts. In 1759 the prime minister of Portugal, Marquês de Pombal (1699–1782), expelled all Jesuits from Portugal and Portuguese territories (including Goa), and in 1773 Pope Clement XIV (1705–1774) abolished the Jesuit order (it was reconstituted in 1814 by Pope Pius VII). Jesuit missionaries struggled with social issues, often involving caste. At first their evangelization targeted the lower-caste Hindus, who were known as "rice Christians" because their mass conversions were seen as tainted by desire for material comforts (such as food), but subsequent efforts, which focused on social change through education, attracted high-caste converts. By 1858 they had founded colleges in Goa, Mumbai (Bombay), Calcutta, and Cranganore. At the beginning of the twenty-first century, Jesuit missions in India are engaged in educational and social programs, having established over twenty colleges, more than one hundred high schools, and several technical, labor relations, and management institutes in India.

*Henry Scholberg*

*See also:* **Christianity—South Asia**

**Further Reading**

Bangert, William V. (1986) *A History of the Society of Jesus*. St. Louis, MO.: Institute of Jesuit Sources.

Correia-Afonso, John. (1997) *The Jesuits in India 1542–1773*. Anand, India: Gujarat Shahitya Prakash.

De Souza, Teotonioo, and Charles J. Borges, ed. (1992) *Jesuits in India: In Historical Perspective*. Macao, China: Instituto Cultural de Macau.

Neill, Stephen. (1985) *A History of Christianity in India, 1707–1858*. 2 vols. Cambridge and New York: Cambridge University Press.

**JEYARETNAM, JOSHUA BENJAMIN** (b. 1926), Singapore politician. Joshua Benjamin (J. B.) Jeyaretnam was born in Sri Lanka and was educated at University College London. He was called to the bar at Gray's Inn, London, and worked in the legal service in Singapore from 1952 to 1963, later engaging in legal practice there. He entered the political scene in Singapore when he revived the Workers' Party founded by David Marshall. In the 1972 election, Jeyaretnam advocated abolishing the Internal Security Act, which allows the government to detain anyone deemed to be a threat to internal security. In 1981, he became the first opposition member in the Singapore parliament since the withdrawal of Barisan Sosialis (Socialist Front) members in 1965. Lee Kuan Yew, then prime minister of Singapore, charged Jeyaretnam and his party with libel in a number of successful lawsuits. Consequently, both were burdened with a substantial debt. Jeyaretnam was returned to parliament by the constituents of Anson in the 1984 general election. In 1986 he was found guilty of making a false declaration concerning party accounts and fined S$2,500. This led to his expulsion from parliament; he was disqualified from membership in parliament until November 1991. He was also found guilty of abuse of privilege and contempt in January 1987 and fined S$13,000. Consequently, he was unable to participate in the August 1991 election.

Jeyaretnam contested in the 1997 general election and lost. He became one of the nominated members of parliament (NMP) because he polled one of the highest numbers of votes among the losing candidates. The prime minister and nine other ministers immediately sued him for statements he made at an election rally. The High Court's judgment on the suits by the prime minister, who was awarded S$100,000 in damages, was delivered in September 1997. In addition, Jeyaretnam had debts totaling S$547,508 in damages that he owed eight creditors who had sued him after they were defamed in an article in the Workers' Party publication. He lost his NMP nonconstituency seat in the parliament after a failed appeal of his bankruptcy in July 2001.

*Kog Yue Choong*

**Further Reading**

Mulliner, K., and Lian The-Mulliner. (1991) *Historical Dictionary of Singapore*. Metuchen, NJ: Scarecrow Press.

**JHARKHAND** (2001 pop. 26.9 million). Jharkhand is a new Indian state formed in 2000 from the southern half of the former state of Bihar. The name Jharkhand (or Jhaarkhand, Jhaakhand) has however existed since ancient times and has encompassed parts of West Bengal, Chhattisgarh, and Orissa, as well as Bihar. This area has also been called Khokhra, Nagdesh, Dasranya, and Ranchi, after the town of the same name, which is the capital of the new state. Jharkhand is administratively divided into eighteen districts. The state's area is 79,714 square kilometers. The region is mainly a hilly, forest-clad plateau lying between the basins of the Ganges, Sone, and Mahanadi Rivers. Much of the plateau is around 700 meters in elevation, though in the west it reaches 1,200 meters. The *sal* tree forests yield timber and medicinal plants, and the state is important for its coal and iron ore mines. Rice, maize, potato, pulse, and oil-seed are the main crops cultivated.

The British had little contact with this rather remote region at first, but with the decline of Maratha power early in the nineteenth century the East India Company acquired suzerainty, and in 1858 its authority was transferred to the Crown. During the British period Jharkhand was known as the Chota Nagpur (or Chutia Nagpur) division of the Bengal presidency.

This heavily forested area was populated primarily by warlike tribes who often fought against the British. The main tribal groups include Kol, Santal, Oraon, Munda, and Bhumij. Some tribes of the Jharkhand region first organized themselves collectively in 1915 for economic purposes, in a movement known since 1938 as Adivasi Mahasabha, under the leadership of Jaipal Singh. From 1947 to 2000 Jharkhand was part of the state of Bihar. The Adivasi Mahasabha, renamed the Jharkhand Party, won many seats in the Bihar Assembly in the first general election of 1952, but requests for the separation of Jharkhand from Bihar had been received as early as 1953. However, in the years that followed, the Jharkhand Party slowly lost its Assembly seats, eventually ceasing to exist as a distinct party.

Yet the quest for separate statehood was revived in 1973 with the formation of the Jhaarkhand Mukti Morcha Party (JMM), which by 1985 held thirteen seats in the Bihar Legislative Assembly. Since then JMM and other organizations have continued to gain popular support, culminating in the creation of the new state of Jharkhand in 2000.

*Paul Hockings*

**Further Reading**

Roy, Sarat Chandra. ([1912] 1970) *The Mundas and Their Country*. Mumbai, India: Asia Publishing House.

**JHELUM RIVER** The Jhelum (also Jhilam or Bihat) River is the most westerly of the five rivers that traverse Punjab and flow into the Indus River in Pakistan. Ancient Greeks called the river Hydaspes. It arises in the Himalayas some 80 kilometers south of Srinagar, flows northwest through Srinagar and the Vale of Kashmir, and then west and south until it joins with the Chenab. The length is 725 kilometers. The river is famed for its nine old bridges. In Pakistani Punjab the Jhelum is the basis of an extensive irrigation and canal system. In 1901 the Jhelum canal colony was established, with the intention of irrigating 457,000 hectares, and it quickly brought prosperity to the settler-farmers.

*Paul Hockings*

**Further Reading**

Ahmad, Khalid Bashir. (2001) *Jhelum, the River through my Backyard.* Srinagar, India: Bookman Publishers.

**JIANG JIESHI.** See **Chiang Kai-shek.**

**JIANG ZEMIN** (b. 1926), President of China. Born into an intellectual family in Yangzhou, Jiangsu Province, Jiang Zemin joined the Chinese Communist Party (CCP) in 1946 and occupied various economics-related Communist government positions, going to Moscow for a year's study in 1955. He continued working during the Cultural Revolution (1966–1976). As a supporter of reform, however, he did even better after 1978, becoming mayor of Shanghai in 1985 and, in 1987, Shanghai's CCP first secretary. During the nationwide demonstrations of 1989, he was able to defuse those of Shanghai peacefully. He was chosen by Deng Xiaoping (1904–1997) as CCP general secretary in June 1989 and became chairman of the Central Military Commission in November 1989. In March 1993 he became China's president, thus holding the three most senior positions in the Chinese party, military, and state.

After 1989, Jiang consolidated his power better than most observers anticipated he would. He followed reform policies, doing his best to strengthen the CCP's power and trying hard to stamp out widespread corruption within it. He played an active diplomatic role by traveling abroad many times and worked hard for China's accession to the World Trade Organization. He also aroused ire for such abuses as active suppression of the quasi-religious movement Falun Gong from mid-1999.

*Colin Mackerras*

Jiang Zemin arrives at Macau airport on 19 December 1999, the day Macau was transferred to Chinese rule after 400 years of Portuguese control. (AFP/CORBIS)

**Further Reading**

Gilley, Bruce. (1998) *Tiger on the Brink: Jiang Zemin and China's New Elite.* Berkeley and Los Angeles: University of California Press.

Tien, Hung-mao, and Yun-han Tien Chu, eds. (2000) *China under Jiang Zemin.* Boulder, CO: Lynne Rienner.

**JIANGSU** (2000 est. pop. 74.4 million). Accounting for only 1.1 percent of China's territory, Jiangsu is the fifth most populous and the fifth most densely populated province, with a population of some 74.4 million in 2000. Located on the eastern seaboard of China, it is the most low-lying province in that nation. It borders Shandong in the north, Anhui in the west, Zhejiang in the south, and Shanghai in the southeast. Jiangsu straddles the lower course of the Changjiang (Yangzi River) and has relatively mild temperatures and abundant precipitation. Both in terms of regional cultures and environments, Jiangsu is often considered a transitional zone between north and south China. Nanjing is Jiangsu's capital and largest city.

Rapid economic growth and persistent uneven development distinguish Jiangsu from other provinces. Since the Tang dynasty (618–907 CE), it has been one of the most prosperous provinces in China. Its early economic development was due in large part to an efficient water-transportation system consisting of numerous rivers and the Grand Canal as well as to sophisticated technologies in agriculture, industry, and trade. The post–Mao Zedong (1893–1976) economic reforms in China have further accelerated the growth of Jiangsu, whose gross domestic product (GDP) grew at an average rate of 15.1 percent from 1990 to 1999, compared with a national rate of 10.0 percent during the same period. In 1999 the GDP in Jiangsu was second only to Guangdong Province.

Jiangsu's recent economic growth is in no small part due to foreign investment and efforts in rural industrialization. "Open" cities and zones, such as Suzhou, Wuxi, and Kunshan, were designated to attract foreign investment. Equally important, rural industrial enterprises—often referred to as township-village enterprises (TVEs)—that benefited from the leadership or management by local government officials have fueled the economic growth of Jiangsu. The prominence of TVEs in Sunan (southern Jiangsu), which borders Shanghai and Zhejiang and is part of the agriculturally and industrially prosperous Changjiang (Yangzi River) Delta, has popularized a "Sunan model" of development emulated in other parts of China.

But perhaps the best-known story about Jiangsu is the persistent disparity between a prosperous and resource-rich Sunan and an impoverished Subei (northern Jiangsu). The gap between them is as large as that between the richest province and the poorest province in China and has widened further since the economic reforms. Though a transitional Suzhong (middle Jiangsu) seems to have emerged recently, Jiangsu remains a classic example of the simultaneous processes of economic growth and increasing spatial inequality during China's socialist transition.

*C. Cindy Fan*

**Further Reading**

Veeck, Gregory, ed. (1995) *Jiangsu in Transition: Issues and Challenges*. Armonk, NY: M. E. Sharpe. Special issue of *Chinese Environment and Development*.

Wei, Yehua Dennis, and C. Cindy Fan. (2000) "Regional Inequality in China: A Case Study of Jiangsu Province." *Professional Geographer* 52, 3: 455–469.

**JIANGXI** (2002 est. pop. 44.7 million). The southeastern China province of Jiangxi (Chiang-hsi, Kiangsi) covers an area of 166,600 square kilometers and borders on Hunan in the west, Hubei and Anhui in the north, Zhejiang and Fujian in the east, and Guangdong in the south. Hilly and mountainous areas account for three-fourths of the area, which is traversed by rivers that flow into Lake Poyang, China's largest freshwater lake, situated in a 20,000-square-kilometer lowland area in the north of the province. While the mountains in the province rise from 1,000 to 2,000 meters, the low area in the north rarely exceeds 50 meters above sea level. The climate is subtropical, with plenty of rain, averaging 1,500 millimeters annually. This makes the province perfect for agriculture. A total of 99 percent of the population are Han Chinese. The capital, Nanchang (1.5 million, 1995), is situated in the northern lowlands.

## LUSHAN—WORLD HERITAGE SITE

Mount Lushan in Jiangxi was designated a World Heritage Site in 1996 for its splendid landscape and important monuments to the Buddhist, Confucian, and Taoist faiths.

Jiangxi remained sparsely populated until the Tang dynasty (618–907 CE), when it was connected to the capital by the Grand Canal. During the Song dynasty (960–1279), Jiangxi became a center of political and cultural eminence and the resort of famous scholars, such as Zhu Xi (1130–1200). With the fall of the Song, the intellectual milieu declined, and in the following centuries the mountainous border regions became strongholds for antigovernment rebels. During the Qing dynasty (1644–1912), Jiangxi experienced peace and unprecedented wealth. This, however, was terminated with the Taiping Rebellion (1851–1864). In the early 1930s, Jiangxi became the battleground between the Communists and Nationalists, and from 1938 to 1945 the province was occupied by Japan.

Since 1949 economic development has grown steadily. Rice is by far the most important crop; most areas have two crops a year and some have three. Other major agricultural products are rapeseed, peanuts, and cotton, and, with a tea planting history going back to the eighth century, Jiangxi is one of the most important tea producers in China. Jiangxi also has a large production of pork, and timber and bamboo are exported to the rest of China. Industry is concentrated in the larger cities, and products include diesel engines, trucks, tractors, and aircraft. In the northeast the famous imperial kilns of the Ming dynasty (1368–1644), which produce Jingdezhen porcelain, are still operating.

*Bent Nielsen*

**Further Reading**

Alley, Rewi. (1962) *Land and Folk in Kiangsi: A Chinese Province in 1961*. Beijing: New World Press.

Litzinger, Ralph A. (2000) *Other Chinas, the Yao, and the Politics of National Belonging*. Durham, NC: Duke University Press.

Sweeten, Alan Richard. (2001) *Christianity in Rural China: Conflict and Accommodation in Jiangxi Province, 1860–1900*. Ann Arbor, MI: Center for Chinese Studies, University of Michigan.

Waller, Derek J. (1973) *The Kiangsi Soviet Republic: Mao and the National Congresses of 1931 and 1934*. Berkeley: Center for Chinese Studies, University of California.

Yang, Shangkui. (1981) *Chen Yi and the Jiangxi-Guangdong Base Area*. Beijing: Foreign Languages Press.

**JIKEY** *Jikey* is a form of Malaysian popular-music theater performed by Malay and Thai communities in the west coast border states of Kedah and Perlis. Its origins are unclear, but the genre may have developed from a form of Islamic chanting known as *dikir* or *zikir* and bears some resemblance to the Thai theatrical genre, *likay*. According to local folklore, *jikey* was introduced to the region by an Indian Muslim trader. This theory is supported by the presence of a turbaned Indian (Bengali) character, who appears at the beginning of each performance and dances, sings, and describes the plot to the audience.

*Jikey* is performed at night on a simple raised stage with minimal props and costume, by troupes ranging from twelve to sixteen performers, including musicians. The eclectic plots, which range from local legends and Thai folk tales to Middle Eastern tales derived from *bangsawan* theater, generally deal with the adventures of wandering royalty and frequently include ogres and clownish lower-class characters. Musical accompaniment is simple and might involve a small ensemble of *serunai* (double-reed oboe), a bossed gong, three *rebana* (frame drums), and a pair of *cerek* (wooden clappers). Other instruments may be used as available.

Like other theatrical genres of the region, *jikey* performances begin with consecration rituals *(buka panggung)*, introductory musical numbers *(lagu-lagu permulaan)*, and invocatory songs placating the local spirits *(hantu)*. The main play introduced by the Bengali character is always episodic. Each scene includes song, dance, and dialogue between the principal characters. The final scene, which begins with the performers lined up on stage to ask forgiveness of the audience for any infelicities in their performance, concludes with formal closing rituals *(tutup panggung)*.

*Margaret Sarkissian*

*See also:* **Dikir Barat**

**JILIN** (1998 est. pop. 26 million). In many ways, Jilin Province represents a very good example of "new" China in transition. Jilin is located in northeast China and has a short border with Russia and a long border with North Korea. It is the central province of the old Manchuria, whence came the Manchu people who conquered the Chinese empire in the mid-seventeenth century and who nominally ruled China until 1911. The province's capital, Changchun (meaning eternal spring), was the capital of the Japanese puppet state of Manchuguo between 1933 and 1945.

There is something of a frontier atmosphere in this province of 187,000 square kilometers. Its population is 90 percent Han Chinese, even though before 1907 Han Chinese were not permitted to live in this outpost of empire. Thus, the vast majority of the current Chinese in Jilin are descended from settlers who moved there during the twentieth century. Much of the remaining population is Man (the original Manchurians). There is also a large Korean minority population. The people of Jilin lack the reserve of those in southern China. They are known for their openness, their hospitality, and their ability to drink copious amounts of *bai jiu* (white liquor), the spirit of choice in most of China. The climate is similar to that of the northern part of North America; that is, the winters are long and severe, with temperatures dipping to –25° and –30°C. Jilin has four quite distinct seasons.

Jilin is an agricultural province. It supplies one-sixth of China's grain needs. Corn and wheat are the mainstays, while the ever-present rice is also a staple. Jilin also has ample forest resources, and wood products are a significant export. The province is a major oil producer. Since the Japanese occupation, Jilin has always been a highly industrialized province, being a center of automobile and chemical production. And while there is still a very large state-owned sector, in recent years the provincial government has welcomed foreign private investment, specifically in the automobile industry.

*Gerald Sperling*

### Further Reading

Howell, Jude. (1993) *China Opens Its Doors*. Boulder, CO: Lynne Rienner.

Kristoff, Nicolas D., and Sheryl Wudunn. (1994) *China Wakes*. New York: Times Books.

Spence, Jonathan. (1990) *The Search for Modern China*. New York: Norton.

**_JIN PING MEI_** *Jin ping mei* (Plum in a Golden Vase, The Golden Lotus) has been the most controversial Chinese novel ever since it was first published in the late Ming dynasty (1368–1644). Chronicling the rise and fall of a merchant, Ximen Qing, his wife, his five concubines, and assorted maids and prostitutes, the novel explores the corrosive effect of the "four vices" (drunkenness, lust, greed, and anger) on the social and moral fabric of society in vivid, intimate, and compelling detail. The intent and purpose of the novel's careful portrait of the pleasures, failings, and excesses of the denizens of a flourishing urban culture has elicited vastly different interpretations from changing generations of readers. The novel has been variously understood as a veiled attack on the abuses of historical elite and imperial figures, as a literary exposé of the corruption and decay of an entire age, as an exhortation toward the cultivation of Confucian sentiments such as filial piety, as a Buddhist-Taoist injunction toward renunciation of worldly desires, as a celebration of human instinct, as an alternately accurate or disparagingly misogynist representation of women, or as a literary masterpiece with few, if any, precedents in world literature.

Despite the sophistication of its narrative techniques and the punitive outcomes for excess, the novel's explicit representation of all manner of sexual practices elicited concern among paternalistic elite readers from its first appearance. At the end of the sixteenth century, a famous literary coterie, fearful that ordinary readers would be inclined to imitate rather than avoid the behavior represented in the novel, restricted circulation of the novel in manuscript form to their own circle. Upon subsequent publication under the pseudonym Lanling Xiaoxiao Sheng ("The Scoffing Gentleman of Lanling"), the novel was repeatedly proscribed in China and condemned as pornographic and, after being translated, in Europe as well. It nevertheless remained in print, albeit often in excised form.

In the wake of commercialization and the concomitant resurgence of interest in issues of gender and sexuality in the Chinese-speaking world in the 1980s, scholarly study of the novel intensified, as did interest among writers and filmmakers. Hong Kong filmmaker Claire Law's *The Reincarnation of Golden Lotus* and Chinese dramatist Wei Minglun's *Pan Jinlian* reassessed the most reviled character of the novel, the murderously manipulative Pan Jinlian, in light of feminist sexual politics.

*Patricia Sieber*

### Further Reading

Ding, Naifei. (2002) *Obscene Objects, Intimate Politics: On the Jin Ping Mei*. Durham, NC: Duke University Press.

Roy, David T., trans. (1993) *The Plum in the Golden Vase or Chin P'ing Mei*. Vol 1. Princeton, NJ: Princeton University Press.

**JINNAH, MOHAMMED ALI** (1876–1948), Indian Muslim leader and Pakistan's first governor-general. Mohammed Ali Jinnah, a Muslim Indian politician, played the leading role in the formation of the nation of Pakistan. Born in Karachi, Jinnah initially pursued a business career in London but soon switched to studying law at Lincoln's Inn and eventually became a barrister in Mumbai (then Bombay). His

A huge portrait of Mohammad Ali Jinnah being hung for Pakistan Day on 23 March 1993. (REUTERS NEWMEDIA INC./CORBIS)

career in politics began when he helped Parsi Dadabhai Naoroji win a seat in the Indian legislature. He joined the Indian National Congress in 1906 and in 1913 became a member of the Muslim League, working to increase cooperation between Hindus and Muslims. Jinnah contributed significantly to drafting the Congress-League Lucknow Pact of 1916.

After World War I, the political climate in India changed when Mohandas K. Gandhi (1869–1948) joined the Congress. Jinnah viewed Gandhi's ideas about noncooperation with the British as dangerous, but, unable to prevent the Congress from heeding Gandhi's message, Jinnah left the Congress in 1919. Nevertheless, he continued his political involvement and was elected to the viceroy's legislative council in Calcutta and New Delhi as an independent Muslim member from Bombay. While in London attending the first Round Table Conference on Indian constitutional reforms, Jinnah, along with Sir Shah Nawaz Bhutto, attained separate provincial status for Sind, which became the only province of British India with a majority Muslim population in 1935.

Jinnah returned to India to become the permanent president of the Muslim League. Empowered by its victories, the Congress blocked League members from positions in provincial cabinets in 1937. The situation led Jinnah to garner the support of Indian Muslims to achieve the status of Quaid-i-Azam (Great Leader). Three years later at the League's session in Lahore, Jinnah proposed a resolution creating a separate Muslim state, since he believed that Muslims could no longer achieve equality while remaining an ethnic minority.

From then on, Jinnah's efforts were focused on making the Lahore Resolution a reality. On 14 August 1947, Pakistan was founded following extensive and intensive negotiations with Britain, and Jinnah became its first governor-general. The next year, however, he succumbed to lung cancer and was unable to realize further his vision for Pakistan.

*Houman A. Sadri*

**Further Reading**

Cleveland, William L. (1994) *A History of the Modern Middle East.* Boulder, CO: Westview Press.

Haynes, Jeff, ed. (1999) *Religion, Globalization, and Political Culture in the Third World.* New York: St. Martin's Press.

**JIT, KRISHEN** (b. 1939). Malaysian theater director. The preeminent director in modern Malaysian theater, Krishen Jit has made seminal contributions to both Malay and English-language theater in a career that spans more than three decades. Educated in the University of Malaya and a Fulbright scholar at the University of California, Berkeley, Jit began his theater career with the Malaysian Theatre Arts Group in the 1960s and was the first Malaysian actor to take a lead role in Shakespeare's *Julius Caesar,* in what was then a British- and expatriate-dominated theater scene. Deeply affected by nationalist concerns following the country's 13 May 1969 race riots between Malays and ethnic Chinese, Jit broke with English-language theater. He directed exclusively for modern Malay theater until 1982. He cowrote an important nationalist manifesto for Malaysian theater for the National Cultural Congress in 1970, and was the leading theater critic until the mid-1990s.

In the 1970s, Jit eschewed naturalistic conventions and acting, and delved into experimental modes, physical theater, and contemporary reworkings of indigenous performance traditions. The performance of *Tok Perak,* a multimedia theater event, was a milestone in Malay theater in this period. Jit cofounded the Five Arts theater company, one of Malaysia's oldest professional theater and arts groups, and moved back into English-language theater. He has been involved with a more eclectic array of directorial styles within Kuala Lumpur's cosmopolitan and less nationalistic theater scene. His productions have been performed in theater festivals in Singapore, Tokyo, Cairo, and Berlin. He has also made pioneering contributions in theater education as the founding theater department chairman of the National Arts Academy as well as cofounder of the Flying Circus theater workshop in Singapore.

*Mohan Ambikaibaker*

**Further Reading**

Min, Chung Chee. (1999) "Krishen Jit—A Lifetime of Theatre." Retrieved 1 December 2001, from http://viweb.freehosting.net/vikrishenjit.htm.

**JIUZHAIGOU** The mountains, rivers, and waterfalls of Jiuzhaigou, a scenic nature reserve, make it one of the most beautiful areas in the world and a major sightseeing attraction in southwestern China. It is located in the northern part of Sichuan Province, about 400 kilometers north of Chengdu, the capital of Sichuan Province.

The word "Jiuzhaigou" has an interesting meaning. In Chinese, "*jiu,*" "*zhai,*" and "*gou*" mean "nine," "tribe," and "gutter," respectively. Because nine Tibetan tribes live there, people began to call the area Jiuzhaigou. Because Jiuzhaigou is located in the Min Shan Mountains, it lies 2,000 meters above sea level. More than one hundred rivers, waterfalls, and lakes, covering 650 square kilometers, are found in Jiuzhaigou. About 42 percent of Jiuzhaigou is forest land. In addition, a number of endangered animals, including the panda, live in Jiuzhaigou.

Because of its natural beauty, Jiuzhaigou has been called "the fairy-tale world" of China and has often been a film location for Chinese media. About 60,000 hectares of Jiuzhaigou were designated as a natural protective area in 1978 and were registered as a UNESCO Natural World Heritage Site in 1992. Because the number of people visiting Jiuzhaigou from all over the world has increased, in July 2001 the Chinese government began limiting visitors to twelve thousand a day.

*Unryu Suganuma*

### Further Reading

Amako, Satoshi, et al. (1999) *Iwanami Gendai Chugoku Jiten* (Iwanami Dictionary of Modern China). Tokyo: Iwanami Shoten.

"Jiuzhaigou Qiyueyiri Qidui Luke Shixing Xiangliang Jinru" (The Limitation of Visitors Entering Jiuzhaigou Starting on 1 July). (2001) *Renmin Ribao* (People's Daily), 27 June: 2.

**JODHPUR** (2001 est. pop. 846,400). Founded in 1459 by Rao Jodha, ruler of the Rathor clan of Rajputs, Jodhpur the city was the capital of the state of Marwar ("region of death") at the edge of the Thar Desert in northwestern India until 1949, when it became part of Rajasthan state. Jodhpur the state was founded about 1212; after 1561 it came under the Mughals, then the Marathas (a Hindu warrior caste) at the end of the eighteenth century, and in 1818 the British. Parts of the city are surrounded by an eighteenth-century wall. The massive hilltop fortress of Mehrangarh contains a palace and museum with a notable gem collection; it also offers a splendid view of Umaid Bhawan Palace, built of golden sandstone.

A road and rail junction, Jodhpur is an agricultural trade center and is famous for glass bangles, cutlery, dyed cloth, ivory goods, lacquers, leather goods, marble stonework, and carpet weaving. Called the blue city for the color wash of its old townhouses, it is the site of a university, the state high court, an air force college, and the University of Jodhpur medical college. Part of the 1994 film *Rudyard Kipling's Jungle Book* was shot here, and the riding britches called "jodhpurs" took their name from this city.

*C. Roger Davis*

The Umaid Bhawan Palace in Jodhpur. (BRIAN A. VIKANDER/CORBIS)

### Further Reading

Patankar, Aditya. (1996) *Jodhpur, Udaipur, Bikaner.* New Delhi: Rupa & Co.

**JOGJAKARTA.** See **Yogyakarta.**

**JOHOR** (2000 est. pop. of state 2.6 million; 2000 est. pop. of capital city 1 million). Johor (formerly known as Johore), a state in Malaysia, lies in the southern part of the Malay Peninsula, bordered by Indonesia on the southwest, Singapore on the south, and the Malaysian state of Melaka (formerly Malacca) on the west. Its coastline includes the Strait of Malacca and the South China Sea, and the narrow Johore Strait separates it from Singapore. With a land area of 18,986 square kilometers, Johor is the fifth-largest state of the Federation of Malaysia. Johor's capital city, Johor Baharu, is located in the southeast of the state.

The sultanate of Johore was founded by the sultan Mahmud Shah (d. 1528), once the sultan of Malacca, and his son Ala'ud'din (d. c. 1564), after the Malaccan sultanate fell to the Portuguese in 1511. The area remained largely undeveloped until the nineteenth century, due to the jungle and swamp that isolated it from the rest of the Malay Peninsula. In 1819, the British leased the territory of present-day Singapore from the sultan of Johore and thereby recognized the sultanate's independence. A later sultan, Abu Bakar (1843?–1895), succeeded in keeping Johore free of British rule.

In the early twentieth century, Johore received an important boost when large rubber, coconut-palm (for producing copra), and oil-palm plantations were established and tin and bauxite were discovered in the state. In 1914, it became a British protectorate, and in 1948 it joined the Federation of Malaya. Since 1970, Johor has been one of the fastest-growing states in Malaysia; it relies on agriculture, manufacturing, tourism, and mining, and it benefits from its proximity to Singapore.

*Rafis Abazov*

### Further Reading

Department of Statistics, Malaysia. (2001) "Official Website." Retrieved 3 April 2002, from: http://www.statistics.gov.my.

Lucas, Robert E. B., and Donald Verry. (1999) *Restructuring the Malaysian Economy: Development and Human Resources.* Houndmills, Basingstoke, Hampshire, U.K.: Palgrave.

Office of the Prime Minister of Malaysia. (2000) "Government of Malaysia." Retrieved 3 April 2002 from: http://www.smpke.jpm.my/.

**JOMON PERIOD** The Jomon is the period in Japanese prehistory between the Paleolithic and the Yayoi. Recent radiocarbon dates place the beginning of the Jomon period as early as 14,500 BCE; the period ends in the fourth century BCE except in Hokkaido, where the Epi-Jomon continued until the middle of the first millennium CE. "Jomon" in Japanese means "cord marked," and although not all Jomon pottery has this type of decoration, the beginning of the Jomon period is usually defined as coinciding with the appearance of ceramics in the islands of Japan. The economy of the Jomon period was primarily hunting, gathering, and fishing, and thus the presence of pottery but the absence of agriculture makes it difficult to fit the Jomon into the evolutionary schemes commonly used in Europe and North America. Similar foraging cultures with pottery are, however, known from mainland Northeast Asia, where they are sometimes termed Forest Neolithic.

### Jomon Subphases and Variations

The Jomon is usually divided into six subphases termed Incipient, Initial, Early, Middle, Late, and Final (with a seventh, the Epi-Jomon, being found only in Hokkaido). Considering the very long duration of the Jomon period and the ecological diversity of the Japanese archipelago, it is not surprising that there is

## JAPAN—HISTORICAL PERIODS

Jomon period (14,500–300 BCE)
Yayoi culture (300 BCE–300 CE)
Yamato State (300–552 CE)
Kofun period (300–710 CE)
Nara period (710–794 CE)
Heian period (794–1185)
Kamakura period (Kamakura Shogunate) (1185–1333)
Muromachi period (1333–1573)
Momoyama period (1573–1600)
Tokugawa or Edo period (Tokugawa Shogunate) (1600/1603–1868)
Meiji period (1868–1912)
Taisho period (1912–1926)
Showa period (1926–1989)
Allied Occupation (1945–1952)
Heisei period (1989–present)

An early Jomon period earthenware bowl. (SAKAMOTO PHOTO RESEARCH LABORATORY/CORBIS)

great cultural variation within the Jomon tradition. Rather than a single Jomon culture, it is more appropriate to speak of multiple Jomon cultures. These cultures were found as far north as Hokkaido but do not seem to have spread into Sakhalin until the Epi-Jomon phase. The Early Shellmound culture of the central Ryukyus probably originated in the Jomon tradition of Kyushu, but it is the most divergent of all Jomon cultures. The Sakishima islands of the southern Ryukyus were occupied by quite different cultures that appear to have their roots somewhere in Southeast Asia. The highest population densities in the Jomon period were found in central and eastern Honshu; western Japan was, in contrast, more sparsely populated. This difference is usually explained by the lower productivity of the broadleaf evergreen forests of western Japan.

Calibrated radiocarbon dates place the earliest pottery in Japan at about 14,500 BCE. Those dates make Jomon pottery the oldest in the world, but similar final Pleistocene dates have been reported from China and the Russian Far East, and it is not yet clear if Jomon ceramics developed in isolation or as part of a wider East Asian ceramic technology. Jomon pottery is not only very old but was produced in large quantities, especially in the latter half of the period. A deep cooking pot is the most common form; other vessels, such as shallow bowls and spouted "teapots," are much rarer.

**Life in the Jomon Period**

The diet of the Jomon peoples included a broad range of plant, animal, and marine foods. Remains of salmon bones from the Maeda Kochi site in Tokyo show that this fish was exploited from as early as the Incipient phase (14,500–8000 BCE). Shell middens are known from the Initial phase (8000–5000), and more than three thousand Jomon shell middens have been identified. These middens have produced a variety of shellfish as well as the remains of sea mammals and inshore and offshore fish. Deer and wild boar were the main terrestrial animal species exploited.

Hunting was conducted using bows and arrows as well as pit traps. The domesticated dog is present from the Initial phase and was probably also used in hunting. Nuts, roots, and berries are thought to have been the main plant foods exploited by the Jomon peoples. There is also increasing evidence that a number of plants were cultivated. These plants include hemp, *Perilla* (Japanese *shiso* and *egoma*), burdock, bottle gourd, barnyard millet *(Echinochloa utilis)*, azuki and mung beans *(Vigna angularis* and *V. radiatus)*, and the lacquer tree *(Rhus vernicifera)*. Rice, barley, broomcorn, and foxtail millet also appear to have been cultivated by the end of the Jomon period.

The semisubterranean pit house seems to have been the basic dwelling of the Jomon period, but ethnographic parallels suggest these buildings would have only been used in the winter months. A raised-floor structure is also commonly found at Jomon sites; these are usually interpreted as storehouses. Most Jomon sites are small clusters of a few pit buildings but many very large sites are also known, especially from the Early and Middle phases. Sannai Maruyama in Aomori Prefecture, the largest Jomon site discovered so far, has produced over six hundred pit buildings, but it is not clear how many of these were occupied simultaneously.

A great variety of ritual artifacts are known from the Jomon period. These artifacts include clay figurines and masks, phallic stone rods, and highly ornate lacquer and ceramic vessels. Stone and wooden circles are also known. The two stone circles at Oyu in Akita Prefecture have diameters of 45 and 40 meters. Jomon burials are mostly simple inhumations with few grave goods. The skeletons excavated from these burials are of a so-called "Paleo-Mongoloid" type that was broadly distributed across East Asia. The strong resemblance between Jomon and Ainu skeletal morphology suggests that the latter are descended from an earlier Jomon population in northern Japan. In cultural terms, however, Ainu society as known ethnohistorically appears to have been very different from its Jomon predecessor.

The Jomon period saw long-distance exchange in obsidian, jade, amber, asphalt, pottery, and probably also in shellfish meat. Most of these exchange networks were within the Japanese archipelago, but Jomon Japan was by no means isolated from the Asian mainland. The Siberian blade-arrowhead culture reached Hokkaido in the early part of the Jomon. Other influences arrived from the Korean Peninsula and across the Japan Sea; there was probably small-scale but steady gene-flow from the continent through the Jomon period. The discovery of over a hundred dugout canoes from Jomon sites suggests that these vessels were the main method of water transportation. That the Jomon people were not confined to rivers and coasts, however, is shown by several finds, including Early Jomon remains from Hachijo Island, some 200 kilometers from Honshu.

The Jomon is perhaps the most materially affluent hunter-gatherer culture known through archaeology. It is presently unclear, however, whether that material affluence was matched by the type of complex social organization known ethnographically from the northwest coast of North America and elsewhere.

*Mark Hudson*

**Further Reading**

Akazawa, Takeru, and C. Melvin Aikens, eds. (1986) *Prehistoric Hunter-Gatherers in Japan*. Tokyo: University of Tokyo Press.

Imamura, Keiji. (1996) *Prehistoric Japan: New Perspectives on Insular East Asia*. Honolulu, HI: University of Hawaii Press.

Kaner, Simon. (1990) "The Western-language Jomon: A Review." In *Hoabinhian, Jomon, Yayoi, Early Korean States: Bibliographic Reviews of Far Eastern Archaeology 1990*, edited by Gina Barnes. Oxford: Oxbow, 31–62.

Kenrick, Douglas M. (1995) *Jomon of Japan: The World's Oldest Pottery*. London: Kegan Paul International.

Naumann, Nelly. (2000) *Japanese Prehistory: The Material and Spiritual Culture of the Jomon Period*. Wiesbaden, Germany: Harrassowitz Verlag.

## JONES, WILLIAM

**JONES, WILLIAM** (1746–1794), British orientalist. William Jones was born in London but later settled in Calcutta, India. The son of a prominent mathematician, he was educated at Harrow College and Oxford. As a young man he became highly fluent in French and Persian, and he translated a biography of the Persian emperor Nadir Shah into French. His grammar of Persian (1771) was long the standard work in the field. He is said to have known thirteen languages thoroughly and twenty-eight others fairly well.

Jones came to India as a barrister, becoming a judge in the Supreme Court of Bengal in 1783. In 1784, following similar developments in Europe, he founded the Royal Asiatic Society of Bengal, the oldest scholarly society on the subcontinent. He collected rare Oriental manuscripts and befriended Indian scholars. He was one of the first to demonstrate the genetic connection between Latin, Greek, and Sanskrit, a language of which he was a devoted student. He was also the first to show the origin of the Brahmi script in some early Semitic alphabets and developed the first scientific Roman orthography for Indian languages. Several of his volumes of Asiatic researches were translated into French and German. He also completed nine large volumes of a digest of Hindu and Islamic law before his early death in Calcutta. Jones was knighted for his services to scholarship and the judicature.

*Paul Hockings*

**Further Reading**

Kejariwal, O. P. (1988) *The Asiatic Society of Bengal and the Discovery of India's Past*. New Delhi: Oxford University Press.

**JP.** See **Adalet Partisi.**

## JUCHE

**JUCHE** *Juche* (or *chuch'e*), the national Communist ideology of North Korea, is used to justify the personality cult of Kim Il Sung (1912–1994) and his son Kim Jong Il (b. 1942). It is the official state ideology of North Korea, as prescribed in the charter of the North Korean Workers' Party (NKWP). *Juche* (literally "subject") means thinking and acting to master the world. It is an anthropocentric ideology, based on the notion of the superiority of willpower and ideology over environmental conditions. While it is based on Marxism-Leninism, it is somewhat contradictory to Marxist analysis of the social conditioning of humankind. *Juche* and its twin notion of *chajusong* (self-determination) do not mean individualism, but a collective movement under the firm guidance of the NKWP and the leader *(suryong)*.

### History

Kim Il Sung first used the term *juche* in his speech "Eradicating Dogmatism and Formalism by Consolidating Juche," in December 1955. However, he later claimed to have originally developed *juche* in the 1930s, during his alleged struggle against the

A statue of North Korean leader Kim Il Sung in Pyongyang, North Korea, in 1975. Showing loyalty to Kim was one of the elements of the collectivist *juche* ideology. (MIROSLAV ZAJIC/ CORBIS)

Japanese occupation. As *juche* developed, it became an ideological and economic system underlying practically all of Kim Il Sung's and Kim Jong Il's thought. Much of this philosophy can be traced back to Stalinist and Maoist ideology, but during the ideological struggle between the Soviet Union and China in the 1960s *juche* became North Korea's "own style of socialism" *(urisik sahoejuui)*.

When Kim Il Sung and the NKWP took power in 1946, they introduced a system of Soviet-style Communism with the help of Russian advisers. This system included agrarian reform; nationalization of industry, banks, transportation, and communications; and modernization of North Korean society (for example, introduction of a law on equality of the sexes). After the Korean War (1950–1953), the collectivization of farming, commerce, and services completed the transition to a Soviet-style economy.

However, three problems led to the subsequent development of *juche* ideology. First, after the death of Josef Stalin (1879–1953), the personality cult in Communist countries was increasingly criticized, and a new basis for government was needed. Second, Kim Il Sung wanted to purge various opposing factions in the NKWP. Third, the rising differences between China and the Soviet Union, the two main supporters of North Korea, had to be addressed. In this situation, Kim Il Sung proposed *juche* as an ideological system in 1955. In 1956, he extended *juche* to the economic sphere, where it meant the development of a self-reliant economy. In 1962, *juche* was interpreted as the guiding thought for military defense, and in 1966 as the principle of political independence.

These extensions reflect the policy of equidistance between the Soviet Union and China. In 1970, in the fifth NKWP meeting, *juche* was introduced as the party's guiding principle, together with Marxism-Leninism, and in 1972 it was described as the leading guideline in the new Communist constitution. Throughout the 1970s and 1980s, *juche* experienced numerous variations; in the 1990s, it took the form of a careful ideological and economic opening process, in response to the economic problems experienced by North Korea in the wake of the collapse of the Soviet Union.

### Ideology

The ideology of *juche* is based on three axioms: economic autarky (self-sufficiency), military defense, and political independence. While reflecting the political position of North Korea between the Soviet Union and China, it also harkens back to nineteenth-century xenophobia and isolationism, the humiliation of Japanese occupation, and the threat posed by South Korea since the division. Contrary to an individualistic interpretation of the subject and the idea of self-reliance, *juche* stresses the monolithic development of the collective and the principle of the supreme leader *(suryongron)*.

The ideas of suffering and revolutionary spirit that evolved from the guerrilla war against Japan in Manchuria in the 1930s are prevailing in *juche*. Often, military metaphors are used—for example, in the three forms of economic-plan fulfillment through "speedy attack," "shock attack," and "exterminatory attack."

Mass movements along the lines of Mao's Great Leap Forward and Cultural Revolution are important means of ideological mobilization. For Kim Jong Il, the movement of the three revolutions—the economic, technical, and cultural changes necessary for the development of North Korea—became crucial in the power transition after his father's death in 1994. Kim Jong Il also developed the Red Flag Doctrine, based on a song allegedly sung by Kim Il Sung during the fight against the Japanese, to rally the masses to the defense of the supreme leader. After his death, Kim Il Sung was practically deified; the succession scheme is comparable to dynastic succession in pre-modern Korea.

*Juche* ideology is implanted in children from their early school days, but adults also have to participate in weekly sessions to learn *juche*. While *juche* is a national Communist ideology, from the beginning it was also promoted as the best Communist system the world over. Worldwide, *juche* is promoted by the Chotongpyung Liaison Committee, headquartered in Paris. Proselytizing among the Korean community in Japan is especially strong.

### Economics

As an economic system, *juche* is closely related to Soviet-style central planning. Economic decisions are formulated by a State Planning Commission under the political leadership of the NKWP's Central Committee; the market role is extremely limited. Plans are formulated in a reiterative process between plants and cooperatives, local planning commissions, ministries, and the State Planning Commission, implemented by the dual administrative and party structure, and controlled by the North Korean Central Bank. Spending is highly centralized, with 85 percent of the budget on the central level and 15 percent on the local level. Until the collapse of the Soviet Union, production focused on heavy industry and military and prestige goods (for example, the ubiquitous monuments for Kim Il Sung). Savings were raised mainly by socialist accumulation (forced domestic savings). Borrowing from Western countries and access to their technology in the early 1970s came to an abrupt halt with North Korea's default on its foreign debt in 1975.

Similar to Mao's strategy in China, mass movements should lead to leaps in economic development. In 1958, Kim Il Sung propagated the Flying Horse Movement *(chollima wundong)*, for the systematic mobilization of labor for the development of heavy industry. In 1960, he announced the *ch'ongsan-ri* method for ideologically motivated increases in productivity, named after "on-the-spot" guidance in a collective farm in South P'yongan province. In 1961, the *taean* work system, a form of economic management by the masses under the collective guidance of the party committee, was introduced.

### Results and Recent Developments

As an economic system, *juche* was disastrous. Forced industrialization, maintainable only through massive Soviet and Chinese aid, had by the late 1960s already resulted in declining growth rates. (Reliable statistical data have not been available since 1965.) After the collapse of the Soviet Union, famine and malnourishment became chronic despite international aid. Central planning declined due to the absence of resources, and illegal private markets flourished. After 1991, North Korea began a slow ideological change. While *juche* is still proclaimed as a superior ideology, an opening process for international and South Korean capital began. China's method of introducing economic reforms without relinquishing political power is being carefully studied. Today, North Korea resembles more and more a military dictatorship, and the role of *juche* as an effective ideological tool to mobilize the masses has practically disappeared.

*Bernhard Seliger*

### Further Reading

Hwang Eui-Gak. (1993) *The Korean Economies, A Comparison of North and South*. Oxford: Clarendon Press.

Kim Il Pyong. (1975) *Communist Politics in North Korea*. New York: Praeger.

Kim Il Sung. (1971–1994) *Selected Works*. P'yongyang, North Korea: Foreign Language Publishing House.

Kim Jong Il. (1992–1995) *Selected Works*. P'yongyang, North Korea: Foreign Language Publishing House.

———. (1997) *Guiding Light General Kim Jong Il*. P'yongyang, North Korea: Foreign Language Publishing House.

Scalapino, Robert A., and Chong-Sik Lee, eds. (1972) *Communism in Korea*. Berkeley and Los Angeles: University of California Press.

Yang, Sung Chul. (1999) *The North and South Korean Political Systems: A Comparative Analysis*. Seoul: Hollym.

**JUDAISM—CHINA** Chinese of the Jewish faith existed in China from the period of the first millennium. Jews of Kaifeng and Jewish sojourners in Shanghai and Harbin were practically invisible to the people of China. The former assimilated themselves into the Han population; the sojourners were isolated from most Chinese and departed after World War II. The memories of these communities are sharp among their descendants and among many scholars, however.

These scholars tend to agree that cloth traders and dyers using the Judeo-Persian written language migrated to Kaifeng at the end of the tenth century. They had arrived earlier in China overland along the Silk Road from Central and South Asia and by sea, possibly with Muslim traders. They converged on Kaifeng, the capital of the Song dynasty (960–1279), because it was the most important commercial and intellectual center in the country.

Although they built their first synagogue in 1163 and possessed sacred texts, including several Torah scrolls, their isolation from world Jewry, their efforts to conform to Chinese culture and religious practice, and the openness of the Chinese educational and bureaucratic systems to persons of talent led to their absorption. Information about their lives and practices comes from their descendants, but mainly from the writings of seventeenth-century Christian missionaries and Arab, Chinese, and Jewish travelers and inscriptions on stone steles. The Kaifeng Jews probably never accounted for more than two thousand people at any one time.

Beginning in the 1840s, an even smaller community of Arabic-speaking Baghdad Jews arrived in Shanghai and Hong Kong from India in the wake of the British control of Hong Kong and the grant of extraterritorial rights in the five major cities, including Shanghai. Never more than about 700 in number, these Jews enjoyed great influence through trade and real estate holdings. The Sassoon and Kadoorie families and their employees led the Jewish community by offering jobs to coreligionists and supporting the synagogue and educational institutions. With the exception of Silas Aaron Hardoon, an active participant in Chinese culture and politics, the Baghdadis considered themselves temporary visitors, and they departed after World War II.

The last and largest group of Jews, twenty thousand refugees, arrived in Shanghai, where no visas were required, between 1938 and 1942; they included Russians escaping from Japanese-occupied Harbin and Germans, Austrians, and others escaping Nazi terror. After World War II, most of these sojourners departed for Israel and the United States. Today, Jews still live in Hong Kong, and because of trade and diplomatic missions enough Jews reside in Shanghai, Beijing, and Hong Kong for the observance of major Jewish holidays.

*Brian Weinstein*

### Further Reading

Goldstein, Jonathan, ed. (1999) *The Jews of China: Vol. I—Historical and Comparative Perspective*. Armonk, NY: M. E. Sharpe.

———. (2000) *The Jews of China: Vol. II—A Sourcebook and Research Guide*. Armonk, NY: M. E. Sharpe.

Liu, Xinru. (1996) *Silk and Religion: An Exploration of Material Life and the Thought of People, AD 600–1200*. Delhi, India: Oxford University Press.

Pollak, Michael. (1998) *Mandarins, Jews, and Missionaries: The Jewish Experience in the Chinese Empire*. New York: Weatherhill.

## JUDAISM—SOUTH ASIA

Judaism, a monotheistic religion with a belief in a transcendent creator of the world, is essentially different from the predominantly polytheistic, iconocentric religions of South Asia. Nevertheless, Judaism and Hinduism share points of similarity. Both possess an orthodox system of codification, embodied in the rabbinical traditions of Judaism and in the Brahmanical traditions of Hinduism. Judaism is also rooted in nonorthodox traditions, as exemplified by Hasidic and cabalistic practices, while Buddhism and Hinduism have developed tantric and devotional traditions.

Judaism was never a significant religious force in South Asia, although throughout the centuries Jews had limited contact with members of local religions. Ancient South Asian Jewish communities have been found only in India, although it is possible that Jews lived in Sri Lanka at some stage. From the nineteenth century on Jewish communities have functioned in Burma (now Myanmar), Singapore, Malaya, Hong Kong and other parts of China, Thailand, and elsewhere. Established by Jews of Iraqi origin, these communities were frequented in the second half of the twentieth century by Jews who found a temporary haven there after the Holocaust as well as by occasional Jewish and Israeli businesspeople, some of whom were transient and some of whom eventually stayed.

### Historical Ties between Israel and South Asia

Linguistic evidence confirms the possibility of early commercial connections between Israel and South Asia in that the ships of King Solomon (c. tenth century BCE) transported cargo such as *kofim* (apes), *tukim* (peacocks), and *almag* (sandalwood or *valgum*), of Indian origin. Travelers' tales in the Talmud mention trade with India *(Hoddu)* and include specific Indian commodities, such as Indian ginger and iron, but they make no reference to Indian Jews. In the Book of Esther, the kingdom of King Ahasuerus (c. mid-fourth century BCE) stretched from *Hoddu*, generally accepted to be India, to *Kush*, generally accepted to be Nubia or Ethiopia.

From the ninth century CE Jewish merchants known as Radanites traded from the Middle East to South Asia and back. Documents discovered in the Cairo Genizah describe the trade in spices, pharmaceuticals, textiles, metals, gold, silver, and silks from the eleventh to the thirteenth centuries between

Arabic-speaking Jews and Hindu partners. However, the evidence does not indicate that Judaism was disseminated.

In the seventeenth century Jewish merchant centers were established in Madras, Calcutta, and other places. In addition an independent Jewish traveler, Hazrat Saeed Sarmad (d. 1659), carried on trade between Armenia, Persia, and India and practiced Judaism until he renounced a materialistic life to become an Indian saint. Sarmad was executed as a heretic by the Mughal emperor of India, Aurangzeb (1762–1839).

During the nineteenth century Jewish emissaries traveled to Asia from Palestine and other Jewish centers to make contact with the Jews in far-flung places, often in the belief that the scattered Jews were members of the legendary ten lost tribes. Several emissaries stayed in India for extensive periods and were influential in bringing the practices of Asian Jewish communities in line with those of other Jews. In the twentieth century some of the visitors to Asia were Zionist emissaries, who wanted to encourage Jews all over the world to emigrate to Israel.

## Jewish Communities in India

Three Indian Jewish groups, the Cochin Jews, the Bene Israel, and the Baghdadis, practice Judaism as a religion. All three groups adhere to the monotheistic nature of Judaism and observe the major festivals and commandments. The Judaism practiced in India developed several special Indian traits, however, such as eating Indian delicacies on particular festivals or the observance of specific wedding or burial customs, which reflect the influence of local customs. At times religious practices and beliefs were influenced by local Hindu, Muslim, or Christian behaviors.

***The Bene Israel*** According to the Bene Israel tradition, the ancestors of their community were members of the lost tribes of Israel who set sail from the Kingdom of Israel to escape persecution by enemy conquerors, possibly in the year 175 BCE. Their ship capsized off the coast of Konkan near Goa in India. The survivors lost all their possessions, including their holy books. Welcomed by the local Hindus, the Jews took up the occupation of pressing vegetable oil. They were called *Shanwar telis* ("Saturday oil people") because they refrained from work on Saturday in accordance with the dictates of the Jewish religion. They remembered the Jewish prayer "Hear! O Israel" declaring monotheism; they observed some of the Jewish holidays and fasts though not all; and they circumcised their sons as commanded by the Jewish religion. Unique customs adapted from South Asian practices characterized their Judaism, including the prewedding *mehendi* (henna body-painting) ceremony, the rites of the prophet Elijah (c. ninth century BCE), and the festival of Shila San (Festival of Stale Things) on the day after Yom Kippur (Day of Atonement), when the souls of the ancestors departed and alms were given to the poor.

From the eighteenth century on, the Bene Israel began a lengthy process of bringing their practices in line with other Jewish communities in the world. This process was aided by their contact with the British in India, a few of whom were Jewish, the resulting move to Mumbai and other cities, and access to the English language and higher education. The ultimate outcome of their identification with world Jewry was the gradual emigration of most members of the Bene Israel community to Israel during the last half of the twentieth century. During the 1960s their Judaism was questioned on halakic (Jewish legal) grounds, but the Bene Israel subsequently have been accepted as full Jews in every respect by the Israeli rabbinate. Some five thousand Bene Israel observe the Jewish religion in India, largely in the Maharashtra region, and nearly fifty thousand more live in Israel.

***The Cochin Jews*** The Jewish settlement on the Malabar Coast is ancient. One theory holds that they arrived with King Solomon's merchants; another account, repeated in South Indian legends, claims they arrived in the first century CE, when Saint Thomas (d. 53 CE) supposedly brought Christianity to India. Records noting that the ruler Bhaskara Ravi Varman (962–1020 CE) granted seventy-two privileges to the leader of the Jews, Joseph Rabban (c. late ninth century CE), document the Jewish settlement in Kerala. In 1344 the Jews moved from Cranganore to Cochin. After Vasco da Gama (c. 1460–1524) led an expedition to India in 1497–1498, some European and other Jews settled in Cochin to become part of the Paradesi ("foreigner" in Malayalam) Jewish community. The Paradesi synagogue was established in 1568. The subgroups of Jews in Cochin did not pray in each other's synagogues, and they did not intermarry. In 1954, the Cochin Jews emigrated as a community to the new state of Israel.

***The Baghdadi Jews*** From the eighteenth century on Jews from Baghdad and other cities in Iraq shifted their enterprises to India and other South Asian centers. Shalom Cohen (1762–1834), one of the first Jewish merchants to escape the deteriorating conditions in Iraq, settled in Calcutta in 1798. Other Iraqi Jews followed and established thriving businesses and magnificent Jewish community structures in the East. Among them was David Sassoon (1792–1864), who arrived in Mumbai in 1832. There he established two synagogues, Knesset Eliahu and Magen David. In Calcutta several Baghdadi synagogues operated with regular schedules. The Baghdadis kept up family and trade ties with other members of their community throughout South Asia. They identified with their British rulers, so when the British raj disintegrated in Asia, most Baghdadis emigrated to England, Australia, North America, or Israel. Fewer than three hundred Jews of Iraqi descent remain in South Asia.

### Jewish Manifestations

The Shinlung is the most prominent group of South Asians who, claiming descent from the lost tribes of Israel, have adopted forms of Judaism since the 1960s. Composed of Kuki and other tribes, the Shinlung group is found primarily in Mizoram and Manipur States in northeastern India, with an offshoot in Tiddim in Burma. This group, which calls itself "the Children of Menasseh," has established prayer halls and observes many Jewish practices. Over five hundred of its members have emigrated to Israel and converted to Judaism there. Groups claiming to descend from the ten lost tribes also have emerged in Andhra Pradesh and other regions of India.

Despite the relatively large numbers of Israeli and Jewish travelers visiting different locations in South Asia, no new Jewish communities have been established in South Asia. However, the Lubavitcher Hasidic movement holds an annual communal seder for Israeli and Jewish backpackers in Kathmandu, Nepal.

*Shalva Weil*

### Further Reading

Ezra, Esmond David. (1986) *Turning Back the Pages: A Chronicle of Calcutta Jewry*. London: Brookside Press.

Holdrege, Barbara A. (1996) *Veda and Torah: Transcending the Textuality of Scripture*. Albany, NY: State University of New York Press.

Narayanan, M. G. S. (1972) *Cultural Symbiosis in Kerala*. Trivandrum, Kerala, India: Kerala Historical Society.

Weil, Shalva. (1982) "Symmetry between Christians and Jewish in India: The Caananite Christians and the Cochin Jews of Kerala." *Contributions to Indian Sociology*, n.s., 16, no. 2: 174–196.

———. (1994) "Yom Kippur: The Festival of Closing the Doors." In *Between Jerusalem and Benares: Comparative Studies in Judaism and Hinduism*, edited by Hananya Goodman. Albany, NY: State University of New York Press, 85–100.

———. (1996) "Religious Leadership vs. Secular Authority: The Case of the Bene Israel." *Eastern Anthropologist* 49, 3–4: 301–316.

## JUDAISM—WEST ASIA

Until the mid-twentieth century, there were Jewish communities in all the countries of the Muslim Middle East. Jews belonged to all social classes, from very poor (the vast majority) to very rich, from sophisticated professionals to illiterates and beggars, and, along another spectrum, from deeply pious and learned to secular agnostic and leftist. Although Islam encouraged converts, it did not require, let alone force, conversion. Those who wished to retain their own religion could do so, as long as they paid the *jizya*, a capitation fee for non-Muslims, which was levied on various Christian and Jewish communities.

### Jews in West Asia before the Nineteenth Century

The situation of the Jews under medieval Islam compared favorably to that of the Jews in medieval Europe. Jews in the Islamic world were not outsiders; they had lived in the area long before the Muslim conquests and for the most part spoke the languages of those around them, initially Greek or Aramaic, and later Arabic, Persian, or (though to a lesser extent) Ottoman Turkish, both among themselves and with their non-Jewish neighbors. Hebrew was used only in the liturgy, and spoken or modern Hebrew is of recent origin, created by Zionist immigrants to Palestine at the end of the nineteenth century.

Although the picture has sometimes been painted in overly rosy terms, the Jews of the Middle East were rarely—certainly not until the nineteenth and twentieth centuries—subject to the persecutions and expulsions experienced by their contemporaries living in various countries of Europe. In no sense did Middle Eastern Jews live in constant fear of irrational or vicious sectarian rage. Thus when the Jews and the Muslims were expelled from Spain in 1492, both communities sought refuge and found new homes in Morocco and the Ottoman empire, adding to the Jewish population of the cities of North Africa, Egypt, and further east. It is also the case that the Jewish (and Christian) populations of the Middle East, although forming distinctive communities of their own, generally shared the norms of the majority Muslim population in such spheres as moral values, notions of right conduct, food, and domestic arrangements, including the seclusion of women, at least until the 1870s.

The communities also regularly interacted with one another. In Aleppo around 1900, for example, some 7 percent of the population of the old city was Jewish. Jews formed a majority in four of the city's traditional gated city quarters (the ones closest to the synagogue), but other Jews lived next door to Christians and Muslims in a further five city quarters. Jews sued Muslims for debt in the Islamic courts and won their cases if they could prove them; as further illustration of their faith in the Islamic legal system, they regularly brought cases against each other in the same courts. In Bab Tuma, a largely Christian suburb of Damascus, Christian, Jewish, and Muslim butchers' shops still stand next to one another; because the dietary laws are more or less identical and most Middle Eastern Christians do not eat pork, members of the various religions buy meat indiscriminately from one another's shops.

Family members of one of the thirteen Jews on trial for spying for Israel before the revolutionary court in Shiraz, Iran, wait outside the court. (REUTERS NEWMEDIA INC./CORBIS)

## Jews in West Asia from the Nineteenth Century Onward

In the nineteenth and twentieth centuries, the situation of the minority communities underwent some significant changes, partly because one result of the Ottoman reforms (called the Tanzimat) was an emphasis on the equality of all Ottoman subjects, and partly because of the greater intensity of European economic penetration throughout the region. A number of prominent Baghdad Jewish families, for example, became part of a great trading diaspora stretching from Manchester and London through Mesopotamia and the Persian Gulf, to India, Hong Kong, and Shanghai. The major trading families included the Sassoons, Kadouries, and Gabbays, who originated in Baghdad. When their business links with India, Hong Kong, Shanghai, London, and Manchester originated, in the late nineteenth century, the family members held British passports, deriving from their residence in England, India, Hong Kong, and other British countries. Wealthier Middle Eastern Christians also sent family members abroad, both for education and as representatives of their trading houses, with the result that when it came to appointing representatives for European firms or finding individuals to assist the European consulates in their relations with the local authorities and to act as vice-consuls and honorary consuls in the Middle East, the European powers often chose local Christians or Jews. France and Britain had *consuls de carrière* (full-time members of a country's foreign service) in Aleppo, but Austria-Hungary, for instance, was represented by several generations of the Picciotto family, Jews originally from Livorno who had settled in Aleppo in the late eighteenth century. Ironically, a leading businessman, Leopold Manasci, was appointed honorary consul of Germany in Aleppo in the mid-1930s, until an inquiry into his antecedents revealed that he was not suitable to serve as the Reich's representative in northern Syria.

In addition to this ready employment of members of the local minority communities (who were often also multilingual), a number of local Christians and Jews (although rather fewer than is often alleged) were either under the formal protection of a particular power or themselves possessed one or more European nationalities. Benefiting from a series of regulations on extraterritoriality known as the Capitulations (dating from the sixteenth century, originally guaranteeing non-Ottoman traders exemption from some local taxes, especially the *jizya,* and the right to be judged by their own consuls), such individuals had an edge over other local traders and businessmen, since they were not subject to the same tax regime. In the course of the nineteenth century, these arrangements occasionally aroused jealousies on the part of those who were not so well placed, and there were violent outbursts against the minority communities in Aleppo in 1850 and Damascus in 1860, often specifically targeting richer Christians and Jews.

Naturally the Jewish communities in the towns of the Middle East did not live in a vacuum. They were affected both by the various intellectual and philosophical debates among world Jewry in the nineteenth and twentieth centuries and by other political trends and tendencies that had more to do with their status as citizens of a particular nation than with their religious affiliation. Jews were pioneers in modern Arabic journalism, as writers of fiction (especially in Iraq and Egypt) and also as artists, musicians, and singers throughout the Arab world until the middle of the twentieth century. Many were also highly visible in the nationalist and independence movements and were prominent in the Communist movement in various Arab countries.

A vital catalyst in the provision of modern secular education (at little or no cost) was the Alliance Israélite Universelle, founded by French Jews in Paris in 1860, which by 1900 came to control a network of about one hundred schools from Morocco to Iran, with some 26,000 pupils and a teachers' training college in Paris. French was the principal language of instruction in the Alliance schools in French North Africa, Italian in Libya, and Arabic in Iraq and Syria. In addition, Hebrew newspapers of the *Haskala*, the Jewish enlightenment (a movement that began in the mid-nineteenth century and produced Reform Judaism), were becoming available in the Arab world and in Iran. Naturally, all this had a certain secularizing effect on the Middle Eastern communities. The *responsa* (traditional question-and-answer religious writings) literature of the early twentieth century reflects some of these concerns, although Oriental rabbis rarely took up the rejectionist positions, which did not admit the validity of reformed or "uncanonical" Jewish practices (in matters like conversion and services in vernacular languages) of many of their Orthodox European contemporaries.

Of all the currents competing for the attention of world Jewry in the first half of the twentieth century, Zionism seems to have held relatively little appeal for the Jews of the eastern Arab world, Iran, and Turkey, except for a rather large exodus of Yemenis to Palestine between 1881 and 1914. Along with their Christian contemporaries, Middle Eastern Jews migrated to Alexandria, Beirut, and Cairo and to Europe, the United States, and South America. By 1914, however, there were probably only ten to twenty thousand Jews of Middle Eastern origin in the area that became Palestine; Zionism, by and large, attracted the Jews of Central and Eastern Europe. Zionist associations in Egypt, Iraq, and Syria drew only small numbers. During the Palestine General Strike in 1936, the Iraqi broadsheet *Habazbuz* produced a cartoon showing the rabbi, the priest, and the mullah shaking hands and saying, "We are all Iraqis. Let us work hard together for the good of the country." In addition, the Alliance, still a major influence in the 1920s and 1930s, was suspicious of Zionism, since the Alliance's goals were to produce well-educated Jewish citizens imbued with French culture, rather than activists for the Zionist cause.

### Migrations to Israel

By the late 1960s the creation of Israel in 1948 and the Israeli wars of 1956 and 1967 had led to the departure of almost all the million or so Jews who had lived in the Arab world, Iran, and Turkey at mid-century. Most were obliged to go to Israel, but some, especially those from Algeria, Morocco, and Tunisia, went to France. Few of those who went to Israel would have done so of their own accord, and anecdotal and other evidence suggests that many were disappointed at the conditions they found there, particularly the disdain they endured at the hands of the European Jewish community. They generally had little choice, since they were stripped of their original nationality and their property in ways that, particularly in the cases of Iraq and Yemen, suggested an unusual degree of connivance between the Zionist authorities and the former host countries.

In the late 1940s there were about 1.1 million Jews in the Arab world, Iran, and Turkey. There are now about forty thousand: about six thousand in Morocco, twelve thousand in Iran, and nineteen thousand in Turkey, with a few hundred elderly people in Egypt, Iraq, Lebanon, and Syria. To an important extent, the communities have reconstituted themselves and continued their traditions in Israel, but, if only in terms of cultural diversity, pluralism, and tolerance, the loss to the regions where they lived for many thousands of years is irreparable.

*Peter Sluglett*

### Further Reading

Cohen, Mark R. (1994) *Under Crescent and Cross: The Jews in the Middle Ages*. Princeton, NJ: Princeton University Press.

Courbage, Youssef, and Philippe Fargues. (1997) *Christians and Jews under Islam.* Trans. by Judy Mabro. London: I. B. Tauris.

Deshen, Shlomo. (1994) "La Communauté juive de Bagdad à la fin de l'époque ottomane: Émergence de classes sociales et de la sécularisation." *Annales, Histoire, Sciences Sociales* 49: 681–703.

Deshen, Shlomo, and Walter P. Zenner, eds. (1996) *Jews among Muslims: Communities in the PreColonial Middle East.* New York: New York University Press.

Levy, Avigdor, ed. (1994) *The Jews of the Ottoman Empire.* Princeton, NJ: Darwin Press.

Stillman, Norman. (1991) *The Jews of Arab Lands in Modern Times.* Philadelphia and New York: Jewish Publication Society.

**JUDO** Judo is a nonaggressive Japanese martial art that developed in the late nineteenth century, split into rival approaches in the last half of the twentieth century and eventually became a global competitive sport. Judo was developed by Kano Jigoro (1860–1938) while a student at Tokyo University. He began to combine techniques from jujutsu with Western science and Asian philosophy. His goal was to produce a martial art that would serve as a vehicle for personal growth and the advancement of Japanese society. Judo uses techniques that turn an opponent's force against him and involve throwing, groundwork, and striking techniques.

Known as the "Father of Japanese Sports," Kano was an effective promoter of judo and sports in general. Before his death, he had set the stage for the emergence of judo as an international sport and as an Olympic event, with judo first appearing on the Olympic program in 1964. However, the popularity of judo as a sport also led many practitioners to abandon Kano's original vision and transform judo into a modern sport where the focus is on competition, scoring, and standardized methods and rules. The result has been a deep division among judo practitioners between the traditionalists who favor Kano's approach and methods and the modernists who favor training geared to competition rather than personal growth.

*Kevin Gray Carr*

### Further Reading

Kano, Jigoro. (1986) *Kodokan Judo*. New York: Kodansha.

Kiota, Minoru, and Kinoshita Hideaki. (1990) *Japanese Martial Arts and American Sports: Cross-Cultural Perspectives on Means to Personal Growth*. Tokyo: Bunsei Press.

Tegner, Bruce. (1967) *The Complete Book of Judo*. New York: Bantam Books.

**JUJUTSU** Jujutsu is a generic label for lightly armed and unarmed martial arts that emerged in Japan during the Edo period (1600/1603–1868). It is estimated that some seven hundred schools of jujutsu developed, with many based on earlier Japanese and samurai fighting techniques. Perhaps the greatest similarity shared by the schools was nevertheless a departure from the fighting techniques of the samurai—the emphasis placed on the use of motion and minimal force. Also important was the incorporation of ancient Japanese and Buddhist philosophy and the goals of mental and spiritual growth into the training and techniques of the different schools. To a significant extent, the emergence of jujutsu represented a decline and redefinition of the role of the samurai in Japanese society, with the government now controlling warfare and the merchant class increasing its influence.

In the twentieth century, the jujutsu schools declined in number and influence as the practice was suppressed by the Meiji government (1868–1912) and then resurrected as a source of nationalistic pride during World War II, which cost it favor after the war. Today, jujutsu remains a minor martial art, with many different schools. A basic conflict between schools that favor competition and those that favor personal growth remains, with no central organization to unify the art or promote it outside Japan.

*Kevin Gray Carr*

### Further Reading

Nelson, Randy F. (1989) *Martial Arts Reader*. New York: Overlook.

**JUMNA RIVER** The Jumna (or Yamuna) River rises in the Indian Himalayas in the north of Uttar Pradesh state, at the southwestern base of the Jamnotri Peaks, near the Jamnotri hot springs, at an elevation of 3,307 meters. It flows south to break through the Siwalik Hills by a gorge and out onto the Gangetic Plain at Faizabad, continuing on past Delhi, and then in a southeasterly direction past Agra to join with the Ganges River at the fort and city of Allahabad. This latter is a most sacred confluence, called *prayag*, or place of pilgrimage. Countless thousands come here to bathe and become sanctified each year.

The river's length is 1,384 kilometers, and it is the most important feeder of the Ganges. Its catchment area is estimated at 305,600 square kilometers. In its upper reaches, timber is floated down the stream, and in the lower reaches grain, cotton, and building materials are transported by barge. Near Faizabad it gives off the Eastern (constructed between 1823 and 1830) and the Western (constructed in 1350 and 1628) Jumna Canals. As a result of this loss of water, during the hot season the river itself is reduced to a mere stream above Agra. Here and elsewhere several railway bridges cross the Jumna.

*Paul Hockings*

**JUNK** The basic traditional Chinese ship style is the junk, a flexible design used in river and oceangoing vessels of various sizes. The design's predecessor seems to have been bamboo rafts, with flat ends and many internal compartments separated by bulkheads, a design that was easily adapted into a variety of easily maneuvered vessels; by the ninth century the junk was plying international waters in South and Southeast Asia. The use of multiple internal bulkheads created a series of watertight compartments that gave the junk further stability and seaworthiness. Older junks had no keels, relying on thick wales (planks) that ran

A river junk on the Chang (Yangtze) River in the Three Gorges area. (WOLFGANG KAEHLER/CORBIS)

along the sides of the vessel to provide rigidity. River junks usually had only one mast, though space was provided for oars in the forward section, with cabins and other types of superstructures always placed aft of the mast. These vessels could reach up to forty-six meters in length, though most were between eleven and thirty meters long, and were used for all kinds of transportation. In certain areas where rapids or narrow channels caused difficulties in navigation, articulated or twisted ships were built, though the basic junk design was retained.

Articulated ships could also be adapted for military use; incendiary devices placed in the forward portions of the vessel, which was brought up to an enemy position, were uncoupled and left to explode. Oceangoing junks had a design very similar to that of river junks but could reach fifty-two meters or more in length. The design of both types of junk provides for the greatest width of the ship to be at the rear, in a conscious imitation of aquatic birds. Many ships were built without the use of metal, the artisans preferring to use wooden pins. The flat-bottomed design also allowed comparatively large ships to dock in shallow waters or navigate up relatively small rivers or canals. Propulsion for Chinese vessels could be by sails or oars, or a combination of both. Evidence of the first true rudder, connected to the ship by a post and balanced on an axis, can be found on tomb models of Chinese ships from the first century CE. Junks are still commonly used today.

*Paul Forage*

**JURCHEN JIN DYNASTY** The Jurchen were a sedentary, Tungus-speaking people living in Manchuria and southeastern Siberia. In the eleventh century there were two groups of Jurchen. One was a little-assimilated group of "raw" tribesmen living more or less the traditional life. The other was the "cooked" Jurchen, who had interacted closely with the Kitan, the dominant political group at that time in north China and rulers of the Liao dynasty (906–1125), and with the many Chinese ruled by the Kitan.

The founder of the Jurchen state, the chieftain Aguda (1068–1123) of the Wanyan clan, was primarily a ruler of the "raw" Jurchen, but he had learned how to use cavalry effectively in warfare from the Kitan. (Horsemanship and war on horseback were then not part of Jurchen native tradition but soon became an important part of Jurchen culture and the real basis of their military power.) Aguda had also learned how to form a state in the Central Asian manner, by grafting heterogeneous elements, including Kitan tribesmen dissatisfied with their own government, around a Jurchen core.

After a series of raids conducted all along Liao's western frontiers, Aguda went over to a general attack and began taking the Liao subordinate capitals one by one, sometimes with the help of the native Chinese dynasty occupying the rest of China, the Northern Song (960–1126). Aguda died before completing his conquest of Liao, but his successor Wuqimai, or Taizong (1075–1135), not only completed his task, but even began a massive invasion of Song, his former ally. It had attempted to make gains in the north as Liao had collapsed at the expense of Jin.

The decades of war that followed nearly destroyed the Song, which had to be reorganized as a new dynasty, the Southern Song (1127–1279) under a collateral branch of the old imperial line, based in the city of Hangzhou in central China. Not just the old Liao domains, which had been confined to the northeast, but the entire north came under Jin control. China was divided between two equally powerful regimes, with a third regime, that of the Xi Xia state, occupying the northwest.

Even as the wars with Song continued, internecine struggle divided the Jin elite. In order to organize its new conquests, the Jin courts of Wuqimai and his successors had adopted Chinese forms of government. Many traditional elements of Jin society failed to understand why this was necessary; they felt that their vested interests were in danger and that they faced absorption by Chinese culture. This conflict was still unresolved at the time of the Mongol invasions, which was one of the reasons why the Mongols were able to conquer Jin with relative ease, in part with some of

## CHINA—HISTORICAL PERIODS

Xia dynasty (2100–1766 BCE)
Shang dynasty (1766–1045 BCE)
Zhou dynasty (1045–256 BCE)
  Western Zhou (1045–771 BCE)
  Eastern Zhou (771–256 BCE)
Spring and Autumn period (221–476 BCE)
Warring States period (476–221 BCE)
Qin dynasty (221–206 BCE)
Han dynasty (206 BCE–220 CE)
Three Kingdoms period (220–265 CE)
North and South Dynasties (265–589)
Sui dynasty (589–618)
Tang dynasty (618–907)
Five Dynasties period (907–960)
Song dynasty (960–1279)
  Northern Song (960–1126)
  Southern Song (1127–1279)
Jurchen Jin dynasty (1125–1234)
Yuan dynasty (1234–1368)
Ming dynasty (1368–1644)
Qing dynasty (1644–1912)
Republic of China (1912–1927)
People's Republic of China (1949–present)
Republic of China (1949–present)
Cultural Revolution (1966–1976)

the very same tribal allies that the Jurchen had used in their own rise.

The Jurchen emperor at the time of the dynasty's first Mongol crisis was Zhangzong (1168–1208), a Sinicizer. He had begun a new war with the Southern Song in 1207 in which Jurchen cavalry had proven far less effective than in the past, indicating a weakening of a native Jurchen tribal base that was having more and more difficulty maintaining its traditional life and the cavalry forces sanctioned by Aguda as part of this traditional life. The reign of Zhangzong also witnessed growing Jin problems with its other tribal groups, principally with the Kitan of the Sino-Mongolian frontier zone. In 1207, most of the peoples involved revolted, handing what is now Inner Mongolia over to the Mongols, who used it as a base for raiding and expansion.

The response of the Jin, who had once actively intervened in the steppe and had manipulated events there in its own interests, was to build fortifications. These proved no barrier whatever to the Mongols, who began a general assault on the Jin in 1211. During the next 23 years they conquered Jin territory piecemeal. They took the principal Jin capital of Zhongdu in 1215 and consolidated their rule in much of the north with a great deal of local help, including from Chinese warlords, the Kitan, and even Jurchen allies. The Jurchen court could only retreat to its domains along the Yellow (Huang) River, where it was able to hold out for another nineteen years thanks to Mongol preoccupation elsewhere, principally with a campaign in the west (1218–1223) and with the conquest of Xi Xia, and then an interregnum.

The end came when the Mongol khan Ogodei (1185–1241) gathered his resources and refocused Mongol attention on China. The Jin capital was then at Kaifeng. The Mongols assaulted it from several directions. The capital, swollen by refugees, was forced to extremities, and the Jin court fled south to Caizhou, where it attempted to organize further resistance. Kaifeng fell in 1233 and Caizhou in February 1234. The last Jin emperor killed himself.

Although their dynasty was at an end, the Jurchen, unlike the Tangus of Xi Xia, who were virtually exterminated resisting the Mongols, survived and prospered. The Jurchen had their own native scripts, based loosely on Chinese, and these survived into the sixteenth century. Later the same cultural groups that had given rise to the Jurchen produced the Manchu, who had their own "raw" and "cooked" components and who also tried to combine tribal vigor with a Chinese style of government. They had even less success than the Jurchen in maintaining their ethnic identity during their reign of China, and the once large Tungus population of Manchuria is all but extinct today.

*Paul D. Buell*

### Further Reading

Buell, Paul D. (1979) "The Role of the Sino-Mongolian Frontier Zone in the Rise of Cinggis-qan." In *Studies on Mongolia, Proceedings of the First North American Conference on Mongolian Studies*, edited by Henry G. Schwarz. Bellingham, WA: Center for East Asian Studies, 63–76.

Franke, H. H. (1994) "The Chin Dynasty." In *Alien Regimes and Border States, 907–1368*. Vol. 6 of *The Cambridge History of China*, edited by Herbert Franke and Denis Twitchett. Cambridge, U.K.: Cambridge University Press, 215–320.

Vorob'yev, M. V. (1975) *Chzhurchzheni i gosudarstvo Tszin' (X v.–1234g.): Istoricheskiy Ocherk*. (The Jurchen and the State of Jin [10th Century to 1243], a Historical Overview) Moscow: Nauka.

———. (1983) *Kultura Chzhurchenzhenei i gosudarstva Tszin (Xv–1234g)*. (Culture of the Jurchen and of the State of Jin [10th Century to 1234]) Moscow: Nauka.

**JUSTICE PARTY.** See **Adalet Partisi.**

**JUTE** Jute is a fiber that is extracted from the stems of plants in the genus *Corchorus* of the *Tiliaceae* order, which includes two jute species, white jute (*C. capsularis*) and upland jute (*C. olitorus*). Jute has been cultivated in India and Bangladesh since 800 BCE, but it was not grown as a major cash crop until 1838, when Dundee, Scotland, mills developed a jute-spinning machine. Jute plants are slender-stemmed annuals that are approximately 2.5 to 3.5 meters tall. The fiber is used to manufacture cordage and coarse fabrics that are used to make heavy-duty bags and carpet backing. Jute grows in alluvial soils and can survive in heavy flooding. It will only grow in areas with high temperatures, sand or loam soils, and annual rainfall over 1,000 millimeters. Large-scale jute cultivation is virtually confined to northern and eastern Bengal, mostly in the floodplains of the Ganges and Brahmaputra Rivers. More than 97 percent of the world's jute is produced in Asia, including 65 percent in India and 28 percent in Bangladesh. The world's largest jute mill is in Bangladesh. The jute industry has been threatened for more than four decades because synthetic fibers are cheaper to produce than jute.

A boat piled high with jute on the Hooghly River in Calcutta, India, in 1979. (SHELDAN COLLINS/CORBIS)

*Michael Emch, Aliya Naheed, and Mohammad Ali*

**Further Reading**

Wieldling, L. (1947) *Long Vegetable Fibers: Manila, Sisal, Jute, Flax, and Related Fibers of Commerce*. New York: Columbia University Press.

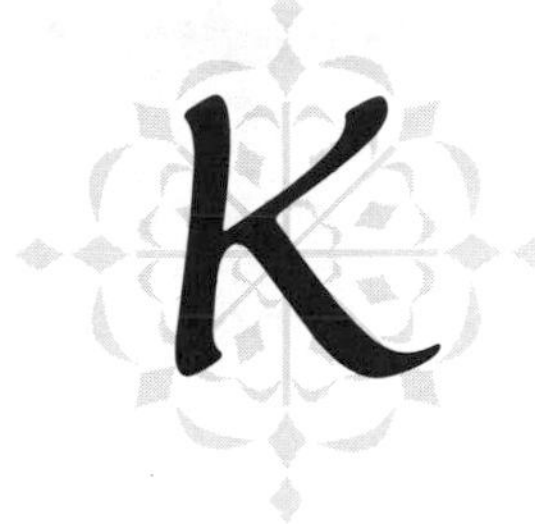

**K2, MOUNT** Mount K2 was so named in 1856 by its surveyor T. G. Montgomerie of the Survey of India, to designate it as one of the thirty-five peaks in the Karakorum range of the western Himalayas. One of its unofficial names is Mount Godwin Austen, after the British topographer who was only the second European to visit this remote and rugged area. Its other names include Qogir Feng in Chinese and Dapsong in Tibetan, and there are also several local names for the peak.

K2 is the second-highest mountain in the world, surpassed only by Mount Everest, which is also in the Himalayas. K2 rises to 8,611 meters, the highest peak in the Karakorum range. It lies athwart the borders between China and the state of Jammu and Kashmir, in an area heavily contested by India and Pakistan but now controlled by Pakistan. K2 is some 800 kilometers due north of Delhi. Although eight expeditions attempted to climb K2 between 1892 and 1954, the mountain was not ascended until 1954, when members of an Italian expedition managed to reach the peak.

*Paul Hockings*

### Further Reading

Ardito, Stefano, et al. (2001) *Peaks of Glory: Climbing the World's Highest Mountains.* Edison, NJ: Chartwell Books.

**KABADDI** *Kabaddi* is an Asian team sport of indeterminate origin, played extensively in the Indian subcontinent and Japan with some variation. Although it is believed to be more than four thousand years old, it has yet to establish itself as an international sport, being confined as it has been mostly to Asia.

The sport is played between two teams of twelve players each. Seven players begin the game for each team, and five players act as reserves. The *kabaddi* court measures 12.50 meters by 10 meters, divided by a line into two halves. Each team has to initiate moves of offense and defense alternately. The team who wins the toss sends into the opponents' area a "raider" who, while chanting "*kabaddi-kabaddi*" tries to touch any or all of the seven opponents. Those opponents who are touched by the raider are out of the game. The opponents try to capture the raider until the raider is out of breath and can no longer chant "*kabaddi-kabaddi.*" Points are awarded on the basis of opponents touched or raiders captured. The team scoring the most points within the scheduled time (a total of forty minutes of playing time with a five-minute break) wins. Because of its low cost and rugged skills, *kabaddi* is a popular sport among the rural masses in Asia.

*Ram Shankar Nanda*

**KABUKI** Kabuki is one of two major forms of commercial theater created by actors and playwrights for audiences of urban commoners during the Edo or Tokugawa period (1600/1603–1868) in Japan.

### History

In 1600, an attractive woman dancer, Okuni, captivated spectators in the capital city of Kyoto by singing sensuous love songs and acting in comic-erotic sketches. Her dance while dressed as a male samurai, called Kabuki (*kabuku*, "slanted"), was the rock or punk performance of the time. Later "ka-bu-ki" came to be written with the Japanese characters for "music-dance-acting," thus

Two Kabuki actors in the 1890s. One portrays a samurai and the other a woman. (MICHAEL MASLAN HISTORIC PHOTOGRAPHS/CORBIS)

identifying the three arts basic to Kabuki performance. Government edicts banning women and boys from the stage in 1629 and 1652, respectively, resulted in adult males taking female roles (*onnagata*, "woman's form"), a happenstance that contributed to creating Kabuki's unusual sensuous appeal.

During the Genroku era (c. 1688–1720), Sakata Tojuro (1644–1709) created the gentle style *(wagoto)* of acting romantic leads that suited the refined tastes of Kyoto audiences. His most famous role was in *Kuruwa bunsho* (Love Letter from the Licensed Quarter, 1678), written for him by Chikamatsu Monzaemon (1653–1724). The martial spirit of the city of Edo is reflected in the masculine style of bravura acting *(aragoto)* created by Ichikawa Danjuro I (1660–1704) and his son Danjuro II (1688–1738), in plays that featured heroes of superhuman strength. Danjuro I himself wrote *Narukami* (Narukami the Thunder God, 1684) and *Shibaraku* (Wait a Moment! 1692). Danjuro II melded the Kyoto and Edo acting styles when he created the dashing hero in *Sukeroku yukari no Edo zakura* (Sukeroku: Flower of Edo, 1713). In the nineteenth century, a new form of gritty "raw domestic dramas" *(kizewamono)* reflected the declining authority of the shogunate and the disintegration of feudal morality. In *Sakura hime azuma bunsho* (The Scarlet Princess of Edo, 1813), by Tsuruya Nanboku IV (1755–1829), and *Benten kozo* (Benten the Thief, 1862), by Kawatake Mokuami (1816–1893), the leading roles were thieves and murderers drawn from society's underclass.

### Characteristics

Kabuki developed over some three hundred years as a spectacular theater art for rich and poor alike. Dazzling productions in large, indoor theaters made use of mechanical stage lifts, revolving stages, and impressive stage tricks—flying in the air, real rain, and instant costume changes. Performances began at dawn and continued until dusk. Adjoining teahouses provided tea, sake, food, and tobacco, as spectators socialized and watched the dramas unfold on stage. Six programs a year matched Japan's calendar of religious festivals. The season began in November with the important "face showing" *(kao mise)* play that introduced the theater's acting company and ended the following September with an autumn "remembrance play" *(nagori kyogen)*, when spectators bid farewell to departing actors. The three plays in a program typically included a multiact history piece *(jidaimono)* that featured samurai or nobility, followed by a shorter domestic piece *(sewamono)* that dramatized the lives of commoners. A dance play accompanied by music in *nagauta*, *kiyomoto*, *tokiwazu*, or *takemoto* style followed either the first or the second play. This could be a solo dance *(shosagoto)*, such as *Musume Dojo-ji* (The Maid of Dojo Temple, 1756), to show off the skills of an *onnagata* actor, or a dance drama *(buyogeki)* like the highly dramatic *Kanjincho* (The Subscription List, 1841). Some dance plays were based on fifteenth- to sixteenth-century masked Noh plays, and about one-third of the repertory was adapted from plays written for the Bunraku puppet theater, Japan's other traditional commercial theater form.

Some important themes in Kabuki plays are the moral conflict between duty *(giri)* and human compassion *(ninjo)* and the plight of lovers driven by circumstance to take their lives *(shinju)*. Powerful acting techniques include a dynamic "frozen moment" pose *(mie)*, leaping exit *(roppo)* along the bridgeway *(hanamichi)* from the stage through the auditorium, beautifully choreographed fights *(tate* or *tachimawari)*, and musicalized speech in poetic passages written in phrases of seven and five syllables *(shichigo-cho)*. The black-robed stage assistant *(koken)* of Kabuki, who assists the actor with properties and costume on stage, is known throughout the world.

In the twenty-first century, Kabuki continues to be one of Japan's most honored theater forms. Monthlong programs can be seen at the Kabuki-za and the National Theater in Tokyo, the Shochiku-za in Osaka, and the Minami-za in Kyoto.

*James R. Brandon*

*See also:* **Bunraku**

### Further Reading

Brandon, James R. (1992) *Kabuki: Five Classic Plays*. Cambridge, MA: Harvard University Press.

Brandon, James R., ed. (1993) *Chushingura: Studies in Kabuki and the Puppet Theatre*. Honolulu, HI: University of Hawaii Press.

Ernst, Earle. (1956) *The Kabuki Theatre*. London: Secker & Warburg.

Gunji, Masakatsu. (1985) *Kabuki*. Trans. by John Bester. 2d ed. Tokyo and New York: Kodansha.

Kawatake, Toshio. (1990) *Japan on Stage: Japanese Concepts of Beauty as Shown in the Traditional Theatre*. Tokyo: 3A Corporation.

Kominz, Laurence R. (1997) *The Stars Who Created Kabuki: Their Lives, Loves, and Legacy*. New York: Kodansha.

Leiter, Samuel L. (1997) *New Kabuki Encyclopedia: A Revised Adaptation of Kabuki Jiten*. Westport, CT: Greenwood Press.

Malm, William P. (1963) *Nagauta: The Heart of Kabuki Music*. Rutland, VT: Charles E. Tuttle.

**KABUL** (2002 est. pop. 2.1 million). At the base of the Kabul River in Afghanistan and at the foot of the Khyber Pass in the Hindu Kush mountains lies the city of Kabul, the capital of Afghanistan. For thousands of years, the country of Afghanistan has been the crossroads of commerce, immigration, and invasion for India, Iran, Pakistan, and the area now comprising the Central Asian countries of Turkmenistan, Tajikistan, Uzbekistan, Kyrgyzstan, and Kazakhstan. Located on the eastern edge of modern-day Afghanistan, the populated areas of the Kabul River are thought to be over 4,000 years old.

The earliest reports of a city called Kabul come in ancient Indian songs dating back to 1000 BCE. In the ancient villages that are thought to make up modern-day Kabul, there was a particularly lush oasis that traders and merchants used as a stop for their camels. Its strategic location at the base of the Khyber Pass, which leads into Pakistan, and the availability of fresh water and arable land allowed a population to grow and prosper.

The number and variety of empires that used the city to control the numerous Afghan tribes mark the history of Kabul. Alexander the Great and his Greek army took over Kabul between 330 BCE and 326 BCE during his campaigns through Central and South Asia. The Arab conquests of the seventh century CE reached as far as Kabul. In the sixteenth century, Kabul was the capital of the Mughal empire from 1504 to 1526. From 1747 until 1979, Kabul was ruled by the Durrani kings;

## BEAUTIFUL KABUL

The description below from 1908 is far different than the images of Kabul 2002—which now show a city and region destroyed by over twenty years of war and political unrest.

> The Kabul river basin includes the most beautiful, if not the most fertile of the romantic valleys of Afghanistan. The great affluents of the north which find their way from the springs and glens of the Hindu Kush are as full of the interest of history as they are of the charm which ever surrounds mountain-bred streams, giving life to the homes of a wild and untamed people. The valleys of Ghorband and of the Panjshir are valleys of the Hindu Kush, scooped out between the long parallel flexures which are the structural basis of the system. With Kohistani villages below and battlemented strongholds above, breaking here and there into widened spaces where the ancient terraces of modern cultivation, and thick groves of apricot and walnut trees are grouped round the base of the foothills and the walls of the scattered villages, there is no more enchanting scenery to be found in the [Swiss] Alps than in these vales.

*Source: Imperial Gazetteer of India: Afghanistan and Nepal.* (1908) Calcutta: Superintendent of Government Printing, 2.

Afghans in the street in front of war-damaged buildings in Kabul in 1995. (BACI/CORBIS).

in 1979 it was occupied by the Soviet Union. The city remained under nominal Soviet control until the Soviet Union withdrew its troops in 1989, leaving the city in the hands of the Mujahideen rebel forces.

Mujahideen control was short-lived, as civil war soon broke out throughout the country of Afghanistan. Various tribal groups and political parties controlled Kabul until 1996, when the city came under control of the Taliban regime. The Taliban moved the capital of Afghanistan from Kabul to Kandahar and left Kabul in shambles. The Taliban lost control of Afghanistan in December 2001 to U.S. forces, sent by the U.S. government to remove the Taliban because of the Taliban's support of Osama bin Laden, the mastermind behind the 11 September attacks in New York City and Washington, DC.

Modern-day Kabul is undergoing massive reconstruction. The interim government of Hamid Karzai has received funding to rebuild the city and reestablish Kabul as the capital of Afghanistan.

*Jennifer Nichols*

**KABUL RIVER** The Kabul is a river approximately 700 kilometers (435 miles) long running mostly through eastern Afghanistan and a short distance in northwestern Pakistan. A tributary of the Indus River, it originates in the Sanglakh mountain range west of Kabul, the capital of Afghanistan. It then flows east, passing Kabul and the major cities of Jalalabad in Afghanistan and Peshawar in Pakistan. Soon thereafter it joins the Indus at Attock, not far from the Pakistani capital of Islamabad. It has several major tributaries, including the Lowgar and the Konar.

Agricultural civilizations have existed on its banks for several thousand years, and it was known as far as ancient Greece, where it was called Cophes. Alexander of Macedon had used its valley as the route for his aborted invasion of India in the fourth century BCE. In the nineteenth century major battles between the native guerrilla groups and British forces were fought along its banks, immortalized in Rudyard Kipling's poem "Ford o'Kabul River."

A hydroelectric plant was built on the river but came into disuse during the prolonged period of warfare started by the Soviet invasion in 1978. Because much of the river has been tapped for irrigation over the years, often inefficiently, due to poor infrastructure and continuing economic stagnation and warfare, much of the river west of the city of Kabul dries up in the summers. The Peshawar-Kabul highway—a major truck route between Afghanistan and Pakistan—passes through the Kabul River valley. The Kabul River is navigable by flat-bottomed light vessels downstream of Kabul city.

*Mikhail S. Zeldovich*

**Further Reading**

Afghanpedia. (2001) "Kabul River." Retrieved 27 December 2001, from: http://www.spinghar.com/afghanpedia.

Hopkirk, Peter. (1994) *The Great Game: The Struggle for Empire in Central Asia.* New York: Kodansha.

**KACHIN** "Kachin" is the collective name for a related family of highland peoples who live in northeastern Myanmar (Burma) as well as adjoining parts of China's Yunnan Province and northeast India. The Kachin language is classified as a branch of the Tibeto-Burmese linguistic group, and the Kachin people are culturally distinct from the Shan, Burman, and Chinese communities that inhabit many of the same areas.

Within Kachin state, six ethnic subgroups are regarded as the main branches of the Kachin peoples: the Jinghpaw, Maru, Lashi, Azi, Nung-Rawang, and Lisu. Elsewhere in Myanmar the Lisu are not included as Kachin. Moreover, there are significant variations in language and dialect among the different Kachin subgroups. In recent decades, this has led to the promotion of the dialect of the Jinghpaw majority as the standardized form of Kachin. The nationality term "Wunpawng" is also used by most Kachins to describe themselves.

The Kachins are thought to have been among the last migrants to arrive in present-day Myanmar, crossing the mountains from China within the past thou-

A Kachin couple in northern Myanmar in 1942. (BETTMANN/CORBIS)

sand years. Today Kachin-speakers are the majority ethnic group throughout much of the Kachin state and also parts of the northern Shan state where around 100,000 Kachins live. Population statistics are disputed, with Kachin leaders claiming a Kachin population in Myanmar of around 1 million, compared with government estimates of half that number.

Until the British annexation of present-day Myanmar in the nineteenth century, most Kachins were traditional spirit-worshipers, inhabiting the higher mountain regions where they practiced swidden (slash-and-burn) agriculture. Under British rule, however, many Kachins converted to Christianity and moved down to the plains. In modern Myanmar, most Kachins are Christians, predominantly Baptists.

Traditional customs nevertheless persist in many areas, including the *manau* celebration festivals, where costumed dancers progress in snaking columns around brightly decorated spirit posts. The Kachins have also retained a determined reputation for independence and for martial abilities in conflict. These were highlighted during World War II when many Kachins, nicknamed the "Amiable Assassins," fought on the Allied side against the Japanese occupation from 1941 to 1945.

A particular characteristic of the Kachin peoples is their unique clan system, which links all subgroups and individuals together. All Kachins have a familial tie through their clans, and there are customs prescribing which members of which clans can marry one another. The clan system was analyzed by the British anthropologist Edmund Leach, who published his famous study, *Political Systems of Highland Burma*, in 1954.

Despite the civil war that broke out in 1961, many traditional aspects of Kachin culture survived the following decades of conflict. Kachin communities, however, suffered enormous dislocation and loss of life before the 1994 cease-fire between the government and the insurgent Kachin Independence Organization.

*Martin Smith*

### Further Reading


Dell, Elizabeth, ed. (2000) *Burma: Frontier Photographs, 1918–35*. London: Merrell Publishers.

Fellowes-Gordon, Ian. (1971) *Amiable Assassins: The Story of the Kachin Guerrillas of North Burma*. London: Robert Hale.

Gilhodes, C. (1922) *The Kachins: Religion and Customs*. Calcutta, India: Catholic Orphan Press.

Leach, Edmund. (1954) *Political Systems of Highland Burma: A Study of Kachin Social Structures*. London: G. Bell & Son.

Lintner, Bertil. (1997) *The Kachin: Lords of Northern Burma*. Chiang Mai, Thailand: Teak House.

———. (1990) *Land of Jade: A Journey through Insurgent Burma*. Edinburgh, U.K.: Kiscadale.

Tegenfeldt, Herman. (1974) *A Century of Growth: The Kachin Baptist Church of Burma*. South Pasadena, CA: William Carey Library.


## KACHIN INDEPENDENCE ORGANIZATION

Founded in February 1961, the Kachin Independence Organization (KIO) is the leading armed opposition force among the Kachin people in northeastern Myanmar (Burma). An earlier Kachin uprising led by Burmese army mutineer Naw Seng in 1949 failed to find widespread support, but in the early 1960s a new generation of Kachin leaders quickly struck a popular chord.

Striking out from northern Shan State, by the mid-1960s KIO units had penetrated much of Kachin State. Fierce fighting with the Burmese army and rival Communist Party of Burma (CPB), as well as internal divisions, halted the KIO's advance. These events led to the deaths of KIO president Zau Seng and his two brothers in 1975. However, under the revived leadership of Brang Seng (1931–1994), a former high school headmaster, the KIO quickly reestablished itself as one of the most effective insurgent groups in the country, with an estimated 8,000 troops under arms.

Bolstered by control of the black market trade in jade, the KIO became a leading voice in the National Democratic Front, which it joined in 1983 following abortive peace talks with the Ne Win government. The KIO was also one of the main architects of the Democratic Alliance of Burma after the Burmese army's suppression of pro-democracy protests in 1988.

Following the CPB's collapse in 1989, however, the KIO came under increasing pressure. This was compounded by the cease-fires of local NDF allies as well as the defection of several hundred troops in Shan State who formed a rival Kachin Defense Army. Anxious to be part of political discussions within the country at large, KIO leaders agreed a cease-fire with the State Law and Order Restoration Council government in 1994 under a new strategy they termed "peace through development." In a major policy change, the KIO opened offices in the towns and began resettlement and development programs in several parts of northeastern Myanmar. Political problems, however, persisted for the KIO, partly due to the slow pace of reforms, and this saw a leadership struggle during 2001 in which the KIO president Zau Mai was replaced by another party veteran, Tu Jai.

*Martin Smith*

**Further Reading**

Lintner, Bertil. (1990) *Land of Jade: A Journey through Insurgent Burma*. Edinburgh: Kiscadale.

———. (1997) *The Kachin: Lords of Northern Burma*. Chiang Mai, Thailand: Teak House.

Smith, Martin. (1999) *Burma: Insurgency and the Politics of Ethnicity*. 2d ed. London: Zed Books.

Tucker, Shelby. (2000) *Among Insurgents: Walking through Burma*. London: Radcliffe Press.

**KACHIN STATE** (2002 pop. 1.3 million). Located in northeastern Myanmar (Burma), Kachin State is a land of deep mountains, forests, and rivers, as well as several areas of broad plains. Comprising eighteen townships and 699 wards or village-tracts, it is Myanmar's second largest ethnic minority state, with an area of 89,041 square kilometers. It is situated between the People's Republic of China to the east and north, Arunachal Pradesh in India to the northwest, the Sagaing Division to the west, and Shan State to the south. The capital is Myitkyina. Other important towns include Bhamo, Mohnyin, Mogaung, and Putao.

Kachin State was founded at the time of Myanmar's independence in 1948, but economic progress has been held back by ethnic and political conflict. Population statistics are disputed by the different parties, but in the 1990s the State Law and Order Restoration Council government estimated the population at 1.08 million people, of whom over 400,000 were Kachins (including Lisus), 310,000 Burmans, and 250,000 Shans. Historically, Kachins have tended to live more in upland areas, whereas Shans and Burmans have inhabited the plains and towns. However, there has been considerable civilian dislocation since the outbreak of insurgency in the 1960s and resettlement continued at the turn of the twenty-first century. There also are small local populations of Chinese and Indians, who play an important role in business.

Agriculture is the principal occupation of most inhabitants. Paddy, sugar cane, and groundnut are all commercially grown in the valleys and plains, and there is local cultivation of various fruits as well as orchids in the hills. Illicit opium production has also been a social problem in a number of areas.

The state also contains a variety of natural resources, including gold, silver, coal, lead, iron, copper, and jade. The world-famous jade mines are located at Hpakhant in the southwest of the state. Another important resource is timber, with teak and other valuable woods growing in the deciduous and evergreen forests that cover much of the territory.

Since the 1994 cease-fire by the Kachin Independence Organization (KIO), exploitation of all these resources has increased, and attempts have been made to upgrade the infrastructure of the state, which is handicapped by its distance from other markets. In the latter years of the twentieth century, the road between Myitkyina and Bhamo reopened; a bridge was constructed over the Irrawaddy River, near the capital; and various business enterprises were started, including the KIO-run sugar mill at Namti.

Economic development, however, continues to be slow. The spread of HIV/AIDS in the state became a matter of concern during the 1990s, accelerated by factors such as intravenous drug use and the rush of migrant workers to the jade mines at Hpakhant. Concerns were also expressed over a notable increase in logging as well as gold-dredging operations in the Irrawaddy River. Such extractive enterprises cause environmental degradation and put little investment into local communities.

Another field that has been targeted for economic expansion is tourism. The state is a region of unusual biodiversity, including the source of the Irrawaddy at the junctions of the Mali-Kha and N'Mai Kha rivers; the upper tributaries of the Chindwin River; Myanmar's largest lake, Indawgyi; and the country's highest mountain, Hkakabo Razi (5,881 meters). In these regions, species such as elephant, tiger, and musk deer, although under threat, were still relatively common at the beginning of the twenty-first century.

*Martin Smith*

### Further Reading

Lintner, Bertil. (1997) *The Kachin: Lords of Northern Burma.* Chiang Mai, Thailand: Teak House.

Smith, Martin. (1999) "Ethnic Conflict and the Challenge of Civil Society in Burma." In *Strengthening Civil Society in Burma: Possibilities and Dilemmas for International NGOs*, edited by Burma Center Netherlands. Chiang Mai, Thailand: Silkworm Books, 15–53.

Tinker, Hugh. (1967) *The Union of Burma: A Study of the First Years of Independence.* Oxford: Oxford University Press.

**KAEMA PLATEAU** The Kaema Plateau (Kaema Kowon), "the roof of Korea," stretches across north and south Hamgyong Province to the east and the provinces of North and South P'yongan to the west in North Korea. The height of the plateau ranges from 1,000 to 2,000 meters above sea level. It is the largest tableland on the Korean Peninsula, with an area comprising about 40,000 square kilometers. The plateau slants down on the side of the Amnok River (Yalu) in the northern sector and it builds a steep slope on the northern and eastern sides. The plateau stretches across several counties, including Kapsan, Changjin, and Musan, that are dissected by the tributaries of the Amnok and Tumen Rivers. Subsistence-level farming products such as foxtail millet, oats, soybeans, barnyard grass, and potatoes are produced using fire-field agriculture (slash-and-burn farming) on the west side of the plateau. Dams have been made to harness the power of the Hochon, the Changjin, and the Pujon Rivers, all of which flow northward into the Amnok River. The greatest benefit from the damming of these river basins has been the increase of hydroelectric power.

*Richard D. McBride II*

### Further Reading

McCune, Shannon Boyd-Bailey. (1980) *Views of the Geography of Korea, 1935–1960.* Seoul: Korea Research Center.

**KAESONG** (1993 pop. 335,000). Kaesong is located in southern North Korea (People's Democratic Republic of Korea), 160 kilometers (100 miles) southeast of the capital city of P'yongyang and 8 kilometers (5 miles) from Panmunjom near the Demilitarized Zone. The city has been under direct administration of the capital since 1955. Kaesong was the capital of the Koryo kingdom (918–1392) and an important commercial center during the Choson dynasty (1392–1910).

Chinese and North Korean officials at Kaesong in August 1951 where talks were held to end the Korean War. (HULTON-DEUTSCH COLLECTION/CORBIS)

The city prides itself on its rich cultural heritage. Major historic sites include the Southern Gate of the Kaesong fortress built between 1009 and 1029, the Sonjuk Bridge, the Kaesong Observatory, and several temples. The site of the Songgyun Institute, once the Koryo dynasty's premier educational institution, has been transformed into the Koryo Museum, which displays many artifacts unearthed in and around Kaesong. Of the Koryo royal palace of Manwoldae, built in 918 CE and destroyed in 1361 CE, only an elevated platform and foundation stones remain.

Several royal Koryo tombs are located on the outskirts of the city, such as the tomb of King Wang Kon (918–943), the founder of the Koryo dynasty, and the tomb of the thirty-first Koryo king, Kongmin (1352–1374), and his queen. Kaesong is known for the production of ginseng and products derived from it. Other industries include textiles, food processing, and machinery.

*Ariane Perrin*

### Further Reading

*Panorama of Korea.* (1999) P'yongyang, North Korea: Foreign Language Publishing House.

**KAFIRNIGAN RIVER** The Kafirnigan is a river in Tajikistan and a large tributary of the Amu Dar'ya, which it joins about 36 kilometers downstream of the confluence of the Pyandzh and Vakhsh Rivers. The Kafirnigan is 387 kilometers long with a basin area of 11,600 square kilometers. It rises in two branches from the southern slopes (partly from glaciers) of the Gissar Range and flows south through the Gissar Valley. The river is fed primarily by snow. The average annual discharge at the mouth is 156 cubic meters per second. In the lower reaches the banks are covered with reeds and *tugai* (riparian) forests.

The river's waters are used for irrigation. During the Soviet period, important irrigation development took place in the Kafirnigan River basin. Together with Uzbekistan, in 1940 Tajikistan built the large Gissar Canal, which carries water from the Dushanbe River into the basin of the Surkhandarya River (in Uzbekistan). The total irrigated area in the Kafirnigan basin is 49,000 hectares. Three of the nineteen dams (fourteen on the Amu Dar'ya) in Tajikistan are on the Kafirnigan.

*Bakhitor Islamov and Sharaf Arifkhanov*

**KAGAWA** (2002 est. pop. 1 million). Kagawa Prefecture is situated in the northeastern region of Japan's island of Shikoku, where it occupies an area of 1,883 square kilometers. Kagawa's primary geographical features are coastal lowlands in the north, the Sanuki Mountains in the south, and many small offshore islands. Kagawa is bordered by the Inland Sea and by Ehime and Tokushima Prefectures. Once known as Sanuki Province, it assumed its present name and borders in 1888.

The prefecture's capital is Takamatsu. In 1588, Ikoma Chikamasa (1526–1603) erected a castle to monitor Inland Sea maritime traffic and Takamatsu grew around this fortress. The Matsudaira family later took control of the castle town. With the initiation of a ferry route between Honshu and Shikoku, Takamatsu became the terminal, making it into the administrative and economic center of Shikoku. The completion of the bridge link to Honshu in 1988 rendered the ferry obsolete. The city manufactures machinery and processes foodstuffs, including *udon* noodles. Its more traditional crafts are lacquerware and tissue paper. Nearby is the Yashima Peninsula, a battlefield of the war between the Taira and Minamoto warrior clans in 1185. The prefecture's other important cities are Sakaide and Marugame.

Kagawa's main crop long has been rice, later supplemented by cotton, sugar, and salt, of which the prefecture once was the nation's largest source; the salt works were shut down in 1972. In the early 2000s, the economy also depends on fruit and livestock production, along with fishing. Shipbuilding is one of the few heavy industries; there is some processing of paper, textiles, and foodstuffs. Visitors are drawn to Inland Sea National Park, and historic Kotohira Shrine is a pilgrim destination.

*E. L. S. Weber*

**Further Reading**

"Kagawa Prefecture." (1993) *Japan: An Illustrated Encyclopedia*. Tokyo: Kodansha.

**KAGOSHIMA** (2002 est. pop. 1.8 million). Kagoshima Prefecture is situated in the southern part of Japan's island of Kyushu, where it occupies an area of 9,167 square kilometers. Situated in a subtropical region, it is often swept by typhoons. Among its geographical features are the major volcanoes Kirishimayama, Kaimondake, and Sakurajima, one of the world's more active. Offshore are various islands. Kagoshima is bordered by the Pacific Ocean and the East China Sea and by Kumamoto and Miyazaki Prefectures. In 1896 it subsumed the ancient provinces of Satsuma and Osumi and assumed its present name and borders.

The prefecture's capital is Kagoshima city, situated on Kagoshima Bay. In 1602, the Shimazu family erected a castle on the site, and the city flourished. It is the birthplace of Meiji Restoration leaders Okubo Toshimichi and Saigo Takamori. Saigo later led disempowered samurai in the 1877 Satsuma Rebellion, the last armed uprising against Meiji reforms. The city was severely bombed in World War II. It is the major departure port for Okinawa and other islands and is home to Kagoshima University. It produces *tsumugi* silk fabric, woodcrafts, and foodstuffs. The prefecture's other important cities are Sendai, Kanoya, and Naze.

The prefecture has a long history, as indicated by artifacts from the Jomon (14,500 BCE–300 BCE) and Yayoi (300 BCE–300 CE) cultures. Later it was inhabited by the Kumaso and Hayato tribes. From the Heian period (794–1185), Fujiwara regent families, Buddhist temples, and Shinto shrines owned landed estates in the region. Shimazu family rule lasted until the 1868 Meiji Restoration. Westerners, including the missionary Francis Xavier, first set foot in Japan in Kagoshima in the mid-sixteenth century.

Agriculture and forestry dominate the economy. Rice, sweet potatoes, and other vegetables are the leading crops, supplemented by the specialty crops of sugar cane, tea, tobacco, and citrus fruits and by the raising of livestock. Black Satsuma ceramics are a notable regional craft. Kirishima-Yaku National Park is popular with visitors.

*E. L. S. Weber*

### Further Reading

"Kagoshima Prefecture." (1993) *Japan: An Illustrated Encyclopedia*. Tokyo: Kodansha.

## KAIN BATIK

*Kain batik* ("cloth" in Bahasa Indonesia, *tik* from Bahasa Malaysia meaning "drops or dots") is cloth produced by a resist-dyeing technique. A resist medium, such as a combination of waxes or occasionally rice starch, is applied to cotton or silk cloth using a pen *(canting)* or a metal stamp *(cap)* to stop the penetration of dyes into the cloth in specific areas of the chosen design.

In preparation for the batik process the cloth is first carefully washed and may be soaked in vegetable oil to enhance the absorption of the dye. It is then starched so that the wax will not penetrate too deeply and pressed to give a smooth surface on which to apply the wax. A suitable resist medium, made from a combination of waxes, is then liquefied and applied to the cloth with a *canting*, a copper pen with one or several spouts, depending on the size and shape of the design. The untreated area of the cloth absorbs color in the dye bath; the waxed area remains undyed. The wax is then melted, scraped, or boiled away—an activity usually performed by men. For subsequent colors and additional design elements more wax is applied, up to four times. This style of batik is known as *kain batik tulis*. Each *kain panjang batik tulis* (a hip wrap worn by both men and women), generally 2½ by 1 meter, takes several months to create. *Kain batik tulis* was superseded in part in the mid-nineteenth century by the use of a *cap* with a waxed surface, facilitating increased production and using male labor. Special finishing treatments include gilding and glazing.

*Kain batik* is found in Java, southwest Sumatra, central Sulawesi, and Malaysia. Its origins are thought to be Indian; however, it may have been indigenous to Java. It is known to have been part of the court culture of central Java by the sixteenth century. Designs and colors were specific to different regions, and sumptuary laws governed the wearing of particular designs, especially in the royal courts of Yogyakarta until the early part of the twentieth century. Women still wear *kain panjung batik* throughout Southeast Asia, although silkscreen and machine prints of old and new designs are prevalent. *Kain batik* has become an icon of Javanese culture and is used by contemporary batik artists and in contemporary fashion and the decorative arts.

*Valerie Wilson Trower and Diana Collins*

### Further Reading

Heringa, Rens, and Harman C. Veldhuisen. (1996) "Diversification: Batik from Peranakan and Indo-European Entrepreneurs." In *Fabric of Enchantment: Batik from the North Coast of Java*, edited by A. L. Rich. Los Angeles: Los Angeles County Art Museum, 107–118.

Lee, Chor Lin. (1991) *Batik: Creating an Identity*. Singapore: National Museum.

Maxwell, Robyn. (2001) *Textiles of South East Asia: Tradition, Trade, and Transformation*. Oxford: Oxford University Press.

Van Roojen, Pepin. (1993) *Batik Design*. Amsterdam: Pepin Press.

Warming, Wanda, and Michael Gaworski. (1981) *The World of Indonesian Textiles*. New York: Kodansha International.

## KAIN SONGKET

The art of *kain songket* ("brocaded cloth"), the manufacture of silk and cotton fabric brocaded with gold or silver thread, has been known throughout western Indonesia since at least the seventh century, the time of the early Buddhist and Hindu kingdoms in Sumatra, Java, and Bali. Brocade weaving was most likely introduced to the archipelago by Indian craftsmen or merchants, along with many other crafts and art forms. The most luxurious silk brocades were worn by the nobility as part of their ceremonial attire; less valuable cotton brocades were used for classical dance costumes. Brocade weaving was the prerogative of noble women. With the introduction of cheaper raw materials, however, such as rayon and artificial silk in the 1930s, brocade manufacture gradually spread to the lower socioeconomic classes. In recent decades the Indonesian government has encouraged the manufacture of traditional local products. Home production has become an important economic activity, and brocade weaving has provided a decent, if not lucrative, income for many female household members, particularly in Bali and Lombok, where *kain songket* are still worn in numerous traditional rituals. The raw materials, mainly imported from abroad, are available even in small village markets.

*Martin Ramstedt*

### Further Reading

Hauser-Schäublin, Brigitta, Marie-Louise Nabholz-Kartaschoff, and Urs Ramseyer. (1991) *Textilien in Bali*. Singapore: Periplus Editions.

Nakatani, Ayami. (1999) "Eating Threads: Brocades as Cash Crop for Weaving Mothers and Daughters in Bali." In *Staying Local in the Global Village: Bali in the Twentieth Century*, edited by Raechelle Rubinstein and Linda H. Connor. Honolulu, HI: University of Hawaii Press, 203–229.

**KALIDASA** (flourished fifth century CE), Indian playwright and poet. Kalidasa was the greatest poet of India's classical age, which lasted from 500 BCE to 540 CE. Despite numerous legends about him, little is known of his life. He may have been a Brahman and a devotee of Siva. He excelled in all literary genres except the novel. Tradition associates him with the semilegendary king Vikramiditya, who is now thought to have been the great Gupta monarch Candragupta II. If correct, we have a ruling date for the king in Ujjain from 375 to 413 CE.

Kalidasa's best-known work, still sometimes performed, is the Sanskrit play *Abhijnana Shakuntala* (The Recognition of Shakuntala), which is the last of three dramas and a clever dramatization of part of the *Mahabharata*. Kalidasa's great skills in characterization, the construction of the plot and dramatic situations, and the clarity of his Sanskrit are the features that have brought praise to this love story. Kalidasa also wrote a comedy, *Malavikagnimitra*, about a king who falls in love with a maiden (despite already having a queen). Other plays included *Vikramorvasiya*, which is another love story based on a legend in the Vedas, and *Satapatha Brahmana*. Of his several poems, "Meghaduta" is one of the most fascinating in Sanskrit literature: just over a hundred verses telling of a minor folk deity who becomes separated from his master. In addition, another epic poem, *Raghuvamsa*, and several incomplete poems of Kalidasa's are extant.

*Paul Hockings*

**Further Reading**

Thapar, Romila. (1999) *Sakuntala: Texts, Readings, Histories*. New Delhi: Kali for Women.

**KALIMANTAN** (2000 pop. 10.4 million). Kalimantan occupies the southern three-quarters of the island of Borneo in Indonesia. It is divided into four provinces: West, Central, East, and South Kalimantan. The largest ethnic groups are the Malay-Indonesians, the Chinese, and the Dayaks.

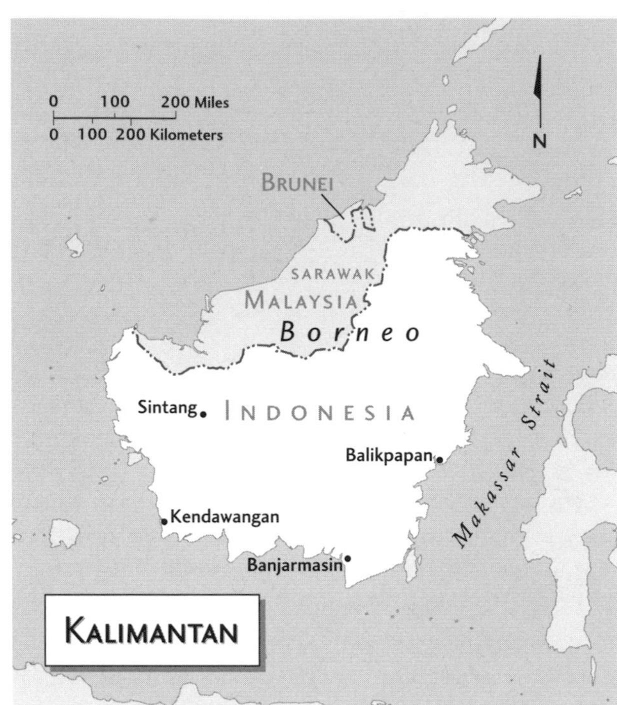


The history of Kalimantan is a patchwork of Chinese, Malayan, Hindu, Muslim, and Dutch influences. Hinduism reached Kalimantan around 400 CE, and the islands were ruled by Hindu kingdoms until, with the introduction of Islam, several sultanates emerged in the fourteenth century. The Dutch arrived on the island in the seventeenth century, and despite both Dutch and British interests in Kalimantan, the Dutch managed to strengthen their position as the main colonial power. The Japanese occupation of the island at the beginning of World War II ended Dutch rule. In 1945, Indonesia's independence ended the Japanese occupation and created Kalimantan as an official province of Indonesia.

Approximately 60 percent of the territory is forested. Kalimantan has one of the world's richest natural environments, including more plant species than in all of Africa. The fauna consists of species such as orangutans, crocodiles, giant butterflies, and freshwater dolphins. Kalimantan also contains great reserves of mineral resources: oil, natural gas, coal, gold, and uranium. Kalimantan is the second leading oil producer in Indonesia after Sumatra. Exports include oil, coal, and plywood. The oldest inscriptions in Indonesia have been discovered in Kalimantan. They are in Sanskrit and date from the beginning of the fifth century CE.

*Dimitar L. Dimitrov*

**Further Reading**

Cleary, M., and P. Eaton. (1992) *Borneo: Change and Development*. Singapore: Oxford University Press.

Guhardja, Edi, Mansur Fatawi, Maman Sutisna, Tokunori Mori, and Seiichi Ohta, eds. (2000) *Rainforest Ecosystems of East Kalimantan: El Niño, Drought, Fire, and Human Impacts.* New York: Springer.

**KALMAKANOV, BUKHARZHRAU** (1693–1789), Kazakh poet. The Kazakh poet Bukharzhrau Kalmakanov (or Bukhar-zhyrau Qalmaqanuly) was active at the court of Abylay (1711–1781), the khan of the Middle Horde. As his name-element *zhyrau* signifies, he was a poet and singer (*zhyr* means "song"), but he also acted as the khan's courtier and counselor. In his poems Bukharzhrau addresses political and topical themes, praising the khan for his deeds, advising him in his wars and negotiations with his neighbors, and urging the Kerey tribe to make peace with Abylay. The genre of poetry that he favored was the *tolghau*, a didactic and meditative poem, in which the poet expresses his views on the right form of living and utters words of wisdom generally taken from oral lore (proverbs, folk aphorisms). Bukharzhrau did not compose any epics, although the term *zhyrau* came to denote the singer of epics in the Kazakh language.

*Karl Reichl*

**Further Reading**

Gabdullin, M. G., et al., eds. (1968–1979) *Istoriia kazakhskoi literatury* (trans. *History of Kazak Literature*). 3 vols. Almaty, Kazakhstan: Nauka.

Maghauuin, Mukhtar, ed. (1971) *Aldaspan: XV–XVIII ghasyrlardaghy qazaq aqyn, zhyraularynyng shygharmalar zhyynaghy* (The Scimitar: A Collection of Poems by Kazak Aqyns and Zhyraus of the 15th–18th centuries). Almaty, Kazakhstan: Zhasuushy.

**KALYM** *Kalym* refers to the Central Asian tradition of the bride-price, a ransom paid by a man or his parents to the parents of the woman he chooses to marry. Payment is made after the parties negotiate an agreement in accordance with their social and financial status but before the wedding.

The custom of the *kalym* appeared in pre-Islamic times and was widely accepted and institutionalized in the Islamic period. The size of the *kalym* varies in different regions of Central Asia, and it should be distinguished from *mahr*, maintenance that the bridegroom provides for the bride, all of which remains the bride's personal and exclusive property. Kalym is distributed in three parts: one part to the fiancée, another part to her parents, and the third to be used by the fiancée's family for the wedding expenses.

A man from a poor family, or one who for another reason cannot pay the complete *kalym* in advance, may pay it in installments before and after the wedding. Traditionally *kalym* consisted of livestock, clothing and fabrics, and foodstuffs. In modern times the Central Asian *kalym* is usually given in the form of a cash equivalent, to hide the fact of negotiations for the *kalym* arrangement, which was legally forbidden. The practice of the *kalym* still occurs among rural Uzbeks, Turkmen, Tajiks, Karakalpaks, Kyrgyz, and other peoples of Central Asia.

*Kamoludin Abdullaev*

**KAMA SUTRA** *Kama Sutra* is a classic treatise on the science of sex. It was written by a famous Indian sage, Maharshi Vatsyayana, fifteen hundred years ago during the golden period of the Gupta dynasty. It is based on ancient Indian scriptures and treatises such as the Vedas—perhaps the world's oldest sacred text. The Vedas describe a fourfold purpose of human life—*dharma* (duty), *artha* (wealth), *kama* (pleasure), and *moksha* (liberation of the soul). Of them, *kama*, or sex, is considered indispensable for complete human self-fulfillment and happiness.

What makes Vatsyayana's *Kama Sutra* a unique work is its universal appeal and the value it places on the systematic treatment of sex both as a science and an art. It lays down scientific principles of various forms of lovemaking while fully taking the human anatomy and psychology into account. *Kama Sutra* lays out sixty-four lovemaking practices. Vatsyayana recommends maintaining absolute privacy while studying the art and practice of sex. His erotic arts are known as Panchali. A woman well versed in its sixty-four practices is known as a *ganika* (courtesan). A *ganika* is a woman much sought after by kings, the rich, and other men highly placed in society. She is compensated by generous offerings of money and precious gifts.

In *Kama Sutra*, male and female are each divided into three categories: man as rabbit, bull, and horse; woman as dove, mare, and she-elephant. The rabbit is handsome, tender, and soft-spoken. The bull is stout and well shaped, emitting semen with a salty odor; the horse is sturdy, long-faced, and sexually passionate. Similarly, the woman characterized by the dove is exceptionally beautiful, engaging, and soft-spoken; her discharges are as fragrant as the blossoming lotus. A mare woman is slim, tall, and easily seduced. She emits a fishy aroma. The she-elephant woman is fat, gluttonous, awkward in demeanor, and highly sexed. The size of the animal is related to the size of the genitalia. Thus, a happy and harmonious sexual relationship between a man and woman depends on having compatible qualities. Otherwise, *Kama Sutra* maintains, their sexual and married life will prove disastrous.

Vatsyayana describes eight steps to achieving sexual gratification. These include embracing, kissing, scratching with fingernails, biting, caressing, reversed coitus, and oral sex. He outlines three kinds of kissing by women: limited kiss, throbbing kiss, and probing kiss; five kinds of kissing by men: straight kiss, oblique kiss, evolving kiss, pressed kiss, and hard-pressed kiss. He also recommends the use of various Ayurvedic (India's traditional science of medicine) recipes for those men and women who cannot perform sexual intercourse successfully because of physical or psychological impediments. The text is remarkable, not only for providing detailed sexology, but also for being one of the very few ancient treatises referring to the geography of India. Vatsyayana imposes a kind of geographic determinism by maintaining that women have varying sexual proclivities relative to the climate of different regions of India they are native to.

*B. M. Jain*

**Further Reading**

Archer, W. G. (1963) *The Kama Sutra of Vatsyayana*. London: George Allen and Unwin.

Sinha, Indra. (1980) *The Love Teachings of Kama Sutra, with Extracts from Koka Shastra, Anamga Ronga* and *Other Famous Indian Works on Love*. New York: Crescent Books.

**KAMAKURA PERIOD** Japan's Kamakura period (1185–1333) was the first time a truly nonaristocratic regime held sway over the nation. Toward the end of the Heian period (794–1185), two warrior clans, the Taira (or Heike) and the Minamoto (or Genji), came to have increasing power, as various aristocratic and imperial factions came to depend on them for protection. The Taira wielded great influence from 1156 until 1185, when they were defeated by the Minamoto in the Battle of Dannoura, but the more powerful they became, the more they divorced themselves from their military roots, adopting the habits and lifestyle of the court nobles. The Minamoto did not make that mistake, and their rule marked a new cultural and political age.

In 1192 Yoritomo had himself appointed Sei-itaishogun (Barbarian-quelling Generalissimo), or shogun, by the emperor, and proceeded to establish a military government *(bakufu)* in Kamakura, some 400 kilometers away from the imperial capital in Kyoto. Minamoto control of the *bakufu* ended with Yoritomo, however: After his death, the Hojo family, natal family of Yoritomo's wife, established themselves as regents for the Minamoto shoguns, thereby usurping control.

Although the civil (imperial) government continued to exist during the Kamakura period, it was the military government that held real power in terms of land management, taxation, and policing. During the Heian period, more and more land had become exempt from taxation by the civil government; the Kamakura *bakufu* assigned a steward to all such estates and saw that the *bakufu* received a portion of the wealth from each. It also assigned constables to each estate to marshal the estate in times of conflict.

Culturally, the Kamakura period saw the flowering of popular, faith-oriented, sects of Buddhism. Pure Land Buddhism, which taught that the Western Paradise of the Buddha Amida could be attained through the recitation of the Buddha's name, became very popular as it promised relatively easy salvation for all. True Pure Land, introduced by the monk Shinran (1173–

## JAPAN—HISTORICAL PERIODS

Jomon period (14,500–300 BCE)
Yayoi culture (300 BCE–300 CE)
Yamato State (300–552 CE)
Kofun period (300–710 CE)
Nara period (710–794 CE)
Heian period (794–1185)
Kamakura period (Kamakura Shogunate) (1185–1333)
Muromachi period (1333–1573)
Momoyama period (1573–1600)
Tokugawa or Edo period (Tokugawa Shogunate) (1600/1603–1868)
Meiji period (1868–1912)
Taisho period (1912–1926)
Showa period (1926–1989)
Allied Occupation (1945–1952)
Heisei period (1989–present)

1262) in 1224 as an offshoot of Pure Land, simplified matters further by requiring only one such recitation, if made sincerely. The monk Nichiren (1222–1282) ascribed the same benefits to recitation of praise for the Lotus Sutra and denigrated other forms of Buddhism as false religion. Two schools of Zen Buddhism (in Chinese, Chan Buddhism), Soto and Rinzai, were also introduced during the Kamakura period and were adopted by the warrior class, who found their self-discipline and asceticism in keeping with warrior values. With Zen came the habit of drinking tea and the beginnings of the Japanese tea ceremony. In literature, war romances were popular, as were oral recitations of the *Heike monogatari* (Tale of the Heike), the story of the rise and fall of the Taira clan. The Buddhist theme of the evanescence of all things *(mujo)* permeates the tale.

*Francesca Forrest*

### Further Reading

Hall, John Whitney. (1970) *Japan: From Prehistory to Modern Times*. New York: Delacorte Press.

Hane, Mikiso. (1972) *Japan, A Historical Survey*. New York: Charles Scribner's Sons.

Maas, Jeffrey P. (1999) *Yoritomo and the Founding of the First Bakufu: The Origins of Dual Government in Japan*. Stanford, CA: Stanford University Press.

Sansom, George. (1958) *A History of Japan to 1334*. Stanford: CA: Stanford University Press.

Yamamura, Kozo, ed. (1990) *Medieval Japan*. Vol. 3 of *The Cambridge History of Japan*. New York: Cambridge University Press.

**KANAGAWA** (2002 est. pop. 8.6 million). Kanagawa Prefecture is situated in the central region of Japan's island of Honshu, where it occupies an area of 2,403 square kilometers. Its main geographical features are western mountains, southeastern plains, and the rivers Sagamigawa and Tamagawa. It is bordered by Tokyo and Sagami Bays and by Tokyo, Shizuoka, and Yamanashi Prefectures. Once known as Sagami Province, it assumed its present name in 1876 and present borders in 1893.

The prefecture's capital is Yokohama (2002 estimated population 3.5 million), beside the nation's major harbor. Yokohama was a small fishing village until 1858, when it was opened to Western ships and soon housed a residential compound of foreign diplomats and traders. In 1872, the nation's first railway linked its port to Tokyo. The 1923 earthquake leveled sixty thousand buildings and took twenty thousand lives. World War II bombing raids destroyed nearly half the city in 1945. Present day Yokohama is at the heart of the Keihin Industrial Zone, which extends to Tokyo. The prefecture's other important cities are Kawasaki, Yokosuka, Fujisawa, Sagamihara, and Hiratsuka.

During the Kamakura shogunate (1185–1333), Japan's military capital was in Kamakura, along the southeastern coast. During the Edo period (1600/1603–1868), the region linked Edo (Tokyo) to the western areas of Japan. Today as a major industrial center, Kanagawa produces automobiles, steel, electric appliances, and chemicals and processes petroleum and foodstuffs. Visitors are drawn to Kamakura's historical sites and to its mammoth Buddha statue. A vacation spot popular with Tokyo residents is the Hakone region of Fuji-Hakone-Izu National Park.

*E. L. S. Weber*

### Further Reading

"Kanagawa Prefecture." (1993) *Japan: An Illustrated Encyclopedia*. Tokyo: Kodansha.

**KANDAHAR** (2002 est. pop. of city 339,000). Kandahar, in southern Afghanistan, is the country's second largest city and capital of Kandahar province. Its strategic location—especially when linked with Kabul 483 kilometers to the northeast—has contributed to its political significance in the region since antiquity. It has also been a center for local trade and a nexus in extraregional trade networks since early times. It is the largest urban center of Afghanistan's Pashto-dominated south.

According to some sources, Kandahar was a city in the Achaemenid empire from the sixth through fifth centuries BCE. Other sources trace its origins to the Greek Alexandria Arachosiorum, founded by Alexander of Macedon in the fourth century BCE—the city's name apparently deriving from the eastern variation of Alexander (Iskander). Kandahar's independence from Safavid Persia in the eighteenth century was a critical event in the eventual rise of an Afghan state. The city was Afghanistan's capital for almost three decades in the eighteenth century and was later occupied by British forces twice during nineteenth-century Anglo-Russian struggles over Eurasia.

Kandahar had well-irrigated gardens and orchards and was famous for its grapes, melons, and pomegranates, but these were made inaccessible by land mines or destroyed outright in the conflict between the Soviets and the mujahideen, Islamic guerrilla fighters during the Soviet occupation. The city is of significant strategic importance in the region due to the

## KANDAHAR IN 1908

This 1908 description provides some understanding of the importance of Kandahar and of southern Afghanistan as a route for trade goods that flowed east and west across Asia.

> Kandahar is one of the principal trade centers in Afghanistan. There are no manufactures or industries of any importance peculiar to the city; but long lines of bazars display goods from Great Britain, India, Russia, Persia, and Turkistan, embracing a trade area as large probably as that of any city in Asia. The customs and town dues together amount to a sum equal to the land revenue of the entire province. The Hindus are the most numerous and wealthiest merchants in Kandahar, carrying on a profitable trade in with Bombay and Sind. They import British manufactures, e.g. silks, calicos, muslins, chintzes, broadcloth, and hardware; and Indian produce, such as indigo, spices, and sugar. They export asafoetida, madder, wool, dried fruits, tobacco, silk, rosaries, etc. In 1903-4 the exports to India from Kandahar were valued at nearly 35 lakhs, and the imports at 33 lakhs.
>
> *Source: Imperial Gazetteer of India: Afghanistan and Nepal.* (1908) Calcutta: Superintendent of Government Printing, 73.

major airport built in the early 1970s with development funding from the United States. It remains one of the most heavily land-mined urban centers in the world and was the center of Taliban rule in the late 1990s.

*Kyle Evered*

### Further Reading

Dupree, Louis. (1973) *Afghanistan.* Princeton: Princeton University Press.

Rashid, Ahmed. (2000) *Taliban: Militant Islam, Oil, and Fundamentalism in Central Asia.* New Haven, CT: Yale University Press.

**KANDY** (2001 pop. 105,000). Kandy is an ancient capital city situated in the central highlands of Sri Lanka, some 120 kilometers inland by rail from the capital of Colombo. Its hilly location is 560 meters above sea level. Kandy is chiefly famous among Buddhists for the Dalada Malagawa, the Temple of the Tooth, which enshrines as a relic a purported tooth of the Buddha. There are a dozen other Buddhist temples and several Hindu ones. In the center of the town is a beautifully placed artificial lake, constructed by the last king, Sri Vikrama Raja Singha (reigned 1798–1815), in 1806. Nearby, at Peredeniya, a fine botanical garden and the main campus of the University of Sri Lanka can be seen.

In 1472–1473, the city became the capital of a Sinhalese kingdom under Vimala Dharma (reigned 1592–

## KANDY—WORLD HERITAGE SITE

The picturesque hilltop city of Kandy was designated a UNESCO World Heritage Site in 1988. The sacred city, the last capital of the Sinhalese empire that ruled for 2,500 years, remains an important destination for Buddhist pilgrims.

A row of stores on a street in Kandy, Sri Lanka. (CHARLES & JOSETTE LENARS/CORBIS)

1604). In 1763, it was occupied by the Dutch. Forty years later, the British took possession of the territory, but the garrison was subsequently massacred, and it was only in 1814–1815 that Sri Vikrama Raja Singha was defeated and dethroned. From 1815 to 1948, the kingdom formed part of the British Crown Colony of Ceylon.

A particular style of ritual dancing, called Kandyan dance or "devil dancing," has developed in this area. It is typically marked by loud drumming and stamping with the feet splayed wide apart. It is best observed during the great annual religious procession through the city, called the Perahera.

*Paul Hockings*

**Further Reading**

Seneviratne, Henry L. (1978) *Rituals of the Kandyan State.* Cambridge, U.K.: Cambridge University Press.

**KANG YOUWEI** (1858–1927), Chinese reformer. Born in 1858 in Hainan, Guangdong Province, China, Kang Youwei was a precocious scholar who was impressed both by British-run port cities and later by the Meiji Restoration in Japan. Kang wrote directly to the Guang Xu emperor (1871–1908) in 1888 asking for a comprehensive reform to enhance China's power. Kang then became famous as a key figure in a long-running and complex debate over the relative merits of new or old texts of Confucian classics. He rallied more than one thousand scholars who were participating in official examinations in Beijing in 1895 and petitioned the emperor to refuse the Shimonoseki Treaty that China signed with Japan after the first Sino-Japanese War (1894–1895) and to carry out more radical reforms. He received his degree that year despite conservative opposition.

He then had a forum for his ideas, and he bitterly attacked the old ways in China and called for dramatic changes in the Qing dynasty's (1644–1912) system of government, all within the context of reinterpreting the Confucian classics. For a brief time, during the so-called Hundred Days Reform, the impetuous young emperor listened to Kang, but when the conservatives counterattacked, Kang had to flee China, and the pace of change thereafter overtook his once-radical ideas. Kang Youwei died in 1927.

*Charles Dobbs*

**Further Reading**

Hsiao, Kung-chuan. (1975) *A Modern China and a New World: Kang Youwei, Reformer and Utopian, 1858–1927.* Seattle, WA: University of Washington Press.

Lo, Jungpang, ed. (1967) *Kang Youwei: A Biography and a Symposium.* Tucson, AZ: University of Arizona Press.

The peak of Mount Kangchenjunga as seen from Darjeeling, India. (BRIAN A. VIKANDER/CORBIS)

**KANGCHENJUNGA, MOUNT** Mount Kangchenjunga (also Kinchenjunga), in the eastern Himalayan range, is the third-highest mountain in the world. The highest of its five peaks rises to 8,598 meters, only a few meters less than K2, also in the Himalayas. Its Tibetan name, Gangchhendzonga, means "Five treasures of the snows," in reference to its peaks, which the Sikkimese consider sacred.

The mountain rises on the Sikkim-Nepal border close to Tibet. The Zemu glacier lies on the eastern face of Kangchenjunga, or Kumbhkaran Lungur as it is called in Nepali. The mountain is best seen from the Indian hill-station of Darjeeling, making a grand spectacle on the northern horizon as it dominates all its surroundings.

Many attempts to scale Kangchenjunga from 1929 onward ended in failure and disaster. In 1955 a British expedition led by the Welsh mountaineer Charles Evans succeeded in ascending Kangchenjunga, but stopped a few meters short of the peak to honor the beliefs of the Lepcha inhabitants who consider the mountain a deity.

*Paul Hockings*

**KANGWON PROVINCE** (2002 est. combined pop. 3.2 million). Kangwon Province, one of two provinces divided between North and South Korea, is located on the central eastern coast of the Korean Peninsula. Its combined area is 28,050 square kilometers, with 16,898 square kilometers in the south and 11,152 square kilometers in the north. Until 1395 the province was known as Kangnung-do. It is among the least densely populated areas of Korea. The populations of Kangwon in North and South Korea are roughly 1.6 million, respectively. The capitals of Kangwon are Ch'un ch'on in the south and Wonsan in the north. Other important cities in the south include Kangnung and Wonju.

The province is widely known for its great natural beauty, especially along the coast and in the mountains. The Taebaek mountain range, the backbone of the peninsula, runs north-south along the east coast of the province, with its crest approximately 16 kilometers inland. This range is home to Mount Keumkang and Mount Sorak, two of the most scenic mountains in North and South Korea, respectively. Forest still covers 81 percent of the province.

During the World War II Japanese occupation and postwar period, the economy of southern Kangwon was based on mining, agriculture, and heavy industry. In recent years the mining industry has declined, and tourism has emerged as an important economic activity.

*Brandon Palmer*

**Further Reading**

Korea Overseas Information Services. (1994) *A Handbook of Korea.* Seoul: Korea Overseas Information Services.

**KANNO SUGA** (1881–1911), Japanese political activist. Kanno Suga was born in Osaka. Her mother died when she was ten, and her father remarried a woman who was the proverbial bad stepmother to Kanno. At fifteen, Kanno was raped. She became acquainted with socialism by reading an essay defending rape victims. At seventeen, she married into a merchant family in Tokyo to escape her stepmother. She did not return to Osaka until 1902 after her stepmother had left.

Kanno began working at a newspaper and became involved in a Christian women's movement fighting the legal brothel system. When the Russo-Japanese War broke out, she joined the Christian-socialist peace movement. In 1906, she took over a newspaper in Wakayama Prefecture and began a common-law relationship with socialist Arahata Kanson (1887–1981).

After moving to Tokyo, she attended a socialist-anarchist rally where prominent movement leaders were arrested in the Red Flag Incident of June 1908. When visiting her friends in prison she was arrested. After two months she was released and became acquainted with anarchist Kotoku Shusui (1871–1911). They started the publication of an anarchist journal, which was banned by authorities. Kanno was sent back to prison. While in prison, her involvement in a plot to assassinate the emperor was uncovered. With twenty-three others, Kanno was sentenced to death, and on 24 January 1911 she was hanged.

*Wim Lunsing*

**Further Reading**

Hane, Mikiso. (1988) *Reflections on the Way to the Gallows: Voices of Japanese Rebel Women*. New York: Pantheon.

**KANPUR** (2001 est. pop. 2.5 million). A major industrial city on the Ganges River in Uttar Pradesh State in northern India, Kanpur was called Cawnpore under British rule, from the ancient town Kanhpur ("city of the husband"), referring to the Hindu god Krishna. Acquired by the British in 1801, it grew rapidly from a village to 123,000 people by 1872 and almost two million by 1991. In the nineteenth century it hosted a large military base. Situated on major highways and railroads, it became a manufacturing center for textiles, leather goods, and ordnance, later supplemented by commerce and banking.

The city gained notoriety as the center of the Indian Mutiny or First War of Independence (1857–1858), a great uprising against British rule, in which native forces killed and dismembered British women and children as well as soldiers. The British press used the event to illustrate the barbarity of the Indian people. Equally brutal British reprisals followed.

Kanpur boasts several colleges and technological, sugar, and textile institutes, including the Indian Institute of Technology and the National Sugar Institute. Of historical and religious importance is the Valmiki Ashram (associated with the epic poem *Ramayana*), a Hindu glass temple; the Shri Radhakrishna Temple; and museums with antiquities dating from 600 to 1600 BCE.

*C. Roger Davis*

**Further Reading**

Mukherjee, Rudrangshu. (1998) *Spectre of Violence: The 1857 Kanpur Massacres*. New Delhi: Viking/Penguin Books India.

**KANSAI REGION** Kansai is a region in central Japan extending from the Sea of Japan to the Pacific Ocean. It includes the Kinki Region in Honshu (the prefectures of Kyoto, Osaka, Mie, Shiga, Hyogo, Nara, and Wakayama), and more broadly is extended to Fukui Prefecture and a part of Shikoku. The term "Kansai" usually connotes a cultural and historical viewpoint, whereas the Kinki Region is an administrative and geographical designation that has clearly defined boundaries. Kansai means "west of barriers" and was used in comparison to Kanto, "east of barriers." A barrier is a checkpoint or *seki* set up on the frontier between the emperor's residence and the outside world. During the Kamakura period (1185–1333), Kansai and Kanto were separated by three checkpoints, "Suzu station" (today Mie Prefecture), "Fuwa station" (Gifu Prefecture), and "Arachi station" (Fukui Prefecture).

Kansai has a rich cultural heritage and played an important role in politics, economics, and culture from ancient times. The capitals of Japan were located in Kansai, Heijo-kyo (Nara City) from 710 and Heian-kyo (Kyoto City) from 794 until the seventeenth century. Presently, Kyoto-Osaka-Kobe form the center of the Kansai Region—the second economic pole after Tokyo (in the Kanto Region).

*Nathalie Cavasin*

**Further Reading**

Tomohiko, Harada, and Sakudoo Yotaro. (1993) *The Culture and History of Kansai*. Trans. by Tsuneyoshi Matsuno. Osaka, Japan: TM International Academy.

**KANTO REGION** (2001 est. pop. 40.1 million). Located in the east central part of Honshu in Japan, Kanto contains the prefectures of Tokyo, Chiba, Saitama, Kanagawa, Gumma, Ibaraki, and Tochigi. It has an area of 32,421 square kilometers. It is referred to in contrast to the Kansai Region. Kanto is the most populated region and the political, economic, and cultural center of the nation. The region's core is the metropolitan area with Tokyo, Yokohama, Kawasaki, and Chiba. There are some criticisms about concentration of these different functions, and suggestions that it may be necessary to decentralize some of them to other locations in Japan for a more balanced regional development. The Japanese government has even considered transferring the capital.

The Keihin (Tokyo-Yokohama district) Industrial Area is Japan's leading commercial and industrial area. Agriculture is declining but still plays an important role in the region's economy. The Tone River has the largest basin of all Japanese rivers and is an important source of water for agriculture in the Kanto Plain as well as for urban and industrial use. Coastal fishing in the Pacific Ocean and Tokyo Bay has declined because of vastly increased catches by deep-sea fishing trawlers and also because of the pollution and land reclamation in Tokyo Bay.

*Nathalie Cavasin*

**Further Reading**

Yagasaki Noritaka, ed. (1997) *Japan: Geographical Perspectives on an Island Nation.* Tokyo: Teikoku-Shoin.

**KAO-HSIUNG** (2002 est. pop. 1.5 million). Kao-hsiung (in Pinyin, Gaoxiong) is Taiwan's second-largest city. It is situated on the southwest coast of the island. The city was founded during the Ming dynasty (1368–1644) and was under Dutch occupation from 1624 to 1660. In 1863, Kao-hsiung became a treaty port for trade with the European colonial powers. During the Japanese occupation (1895–1945) of Taiwan, Kao-hsiung was transformed into a major industrial center, and the port sustained heavy damage during World War II. The port was rebuilt, and in the 1970s and 1980s it became Taiwan's single-most important seaport, covering an area of 154 square kilometers. It has shipyards, steel mills, and other heavy industry, as well as Asia's biggest oil refinery with large petrochemical industries. Thus, it is not surprising that the city is among the most heavily polluted in Taiwan. The port also has a large fleet of fishing boats, and agricultural products are exported from Kao-hsiung by ship. Kao-hsiung is of strategic importance with its big naval base. The city enjoys equal status with Taipei and is administered directly by an executive committee *(yuan)* instead of the Taiwan provincial government. Kao-hsiung has a university and several higher education institutions and an international airport.

*Bent Nielsen*

**Further Reading**

Knapp, Ronald G. (1980) *China's Island Frontier: Studies in the Historical Geography of Taiwan.* Honolulu, HI: University Press of Hawaii.

Lu, Miaofang, ed. (1999) *Gaoxiong jianzhu san bainian* (The Architectural Beauty of Kao-hsiung 1683–2000). Gaoxiong: Gaoxiong shilu meishuguan.

**KAPITAN CINA** The Kapitan Cina (Chinese captains) were Chinese individuals appointed by local native chiefs and colonial authorities in Asia to mediate with the heterogeneous migrant Chinese populace in their provinces and colonies. The honorific title conferred upon an individual the highest status of leadership of the community.

In Melaka on the Malay Peninsula, the Kapitan system was first adopted in the sixteenth century, first by the Portuguese colonizers and then by the Dutch colonizers. This system continued during British rule and was extended to the Straits Settlements (consisting of Melaka, Penang, and Singapore) and then the Malay States. However, as British power consolidated throughout the peninsula, and as more Chinese immigrants poured into the urban centers, mines, and plantations, the political power of the Kapitan system was seen as a threat to the colonial administrators. It was thus phased out, first in the Straits Settlements and then in the Malay States by the beginning of the twentieth century. It was replaced by various administrative institutions such as Chinese Advisory Boards.

The responsibilities of the Kapitan Cina included looking after the general welfare of the Chinese populace, enforcing law and order, and collecting revenue for the authorities. As Kapitan Cina, they were supposed to transcend the clan and dialect differences among the Chinese populace. In reality, however, the Kapitan Cina were appointed from the dominant dialect groups, and their interests were subsequently better looked after. Minority groups, in turn, formed their own dialect organizations to pool their resources for collective self-help.

Before their appointment as Kapitan Cina, most of these individuals were already established leaders among their Chinese dialect groups. Many were also successful *towkays* (merchant-entrepreneurs) and "revenue farmers" who held monopoly rights to collect taxes on alcohol, opium, and so forth supplied to the workforce in the mines and plantations.

Neither funds nor manpower was usually extended to the Kapitan Cina by the colonial authorities in carrying out their official duties. For many Kapitan Cina, Chinese temples thus became their de facto administrative centers. Additionally, many forged close links with Chinese secret societies in order to enforce their authority and power. When secret societies were eventually banned (in 1890) by the colonial authorities, the Kapitan Cina redirected their attention to dialect organizations.

*Seng-Guan Yeoh*

### Further Reading

Lee, Kam-Heng, and Chee-Beng Tan, eds. (2000) *The Chinese in Malaysia.* Shah Alam, Malaysia: Oxford University Press.

Lynn, Pan, ed. (1998) *The Encyclopedia of the Chinese Overseas.* Singapore: Archipelago Press.

Wong, C. S. (1963) *A Gallery of Chinese Kapitans.* Singapore: Ministry of Culture.

Yen, Ching-hwang. (1986) *A Social History of the Chinese in Singapore and Malaya, 1800–1911.* Kuala Lumpur, Malaysia: Oxford University Press.

**KARABAG** Karabag (Karabagh, Karabakh) is a region in southeastern Azerbaijan, between the Caucasus and Karabakh mountain ranges. The chief towns are Xankandi and Shusha. Karabag contains many mineral springs as well as substantial deposits of limestone and marble. Farming, sheep herding, and light industries are the primary economic activities. The population is approximately 76 percent Armenian with a substantial Azeri minority and smaller Russian and Kurdish communities.

The region was part of the ancient kingdom of Caucasian Albania before being taken over by Armenia in the first century CE. It was ruled by the Armenian princes of Artsakh (as vassals to various Arab regimes from the seventh century) until conquest by the Seljuks under Alp Arslan (c. 1030–1072/73). It was first called Karabag (Turkish for "Black Garden") during the rule of the Ilkhanid Mongols in the 1300s. It was fought over by Turkey and Persia (Iran) before gaining independence under the Djevanshir family in the mid-1700s. The khanate of Karabag became a vassal to Russia in 1805 and was fully incorporated in 1822. Following the establishment of the Soviet Union it was attached to Azerbaijan as the Nagorno-Karabakh Autonomous Oblast (1923).

In the late 1980s, Armenia and Azerbaijan went to war over Karabag. By the end of 1993, Armenian forces had conquered much of the region, displacing over 1 million refugees. A cease-fire was reached with Russian aid in 1994. In 1996, the parliament of Nagorno-Karabakh declared independence, largely unrecognized by the international community. The ultimate disposition of the territory and refugees has yet to be resolved.

*Brian M. Gottesman*

### Further Reading

Croissant, Michael P. (1998) *The Armenia-Azerbaijan Conflict.* Westport, CT: Praeger.

"Kara Bagh." (1978) *The Encyclopedia of Islam.* Leiden, Germany: E. J. Brill.

**KARACHI** (1998 pop. 9 million). Before 1725 CE, Karachi, the capital of Pakistan's Sindh Province, was just a desolate geographic region, with the waters of the Arabian Sea lapping over it on three sides. It now boasts a population of over 9 million and is a commercial and industrial center for Pakistan.

Karachi is a city of contrasts where old and new elements blend together. Bazaars reflect the heritage of trade that is at the economic foundation of this city, while a nuclear power plant and higher learning institutions denote its place in the modern era. It also is home to the largest international airport in Pakistan as well as being the chief terminal point for Pakistan's railway transportation system.

Being located on the shores of the Arabian Sea makes Karachi the ideal shipping port. As a result, about 15 billion tons of cargo come through its harbor every year. The sea and Karachi's exceptional weather of constant sunshine throughout the year also

A broad view of Karachi, Pakistan. (NIK WHEELER/CORBIS)

make available recreational and sport activities, such as sailing, yachting, and scuba diving, to its inhabitants as well as foreign tourists to the area.

*Houman A. Sadri*

### Further Reading

Adams, Francis, Satya Dev Gupta, and Kidane Mengisteab, eds. (1999) *Globalization and the Dilemmas of the State in the South*. New York: St. Martin's Press.

Cleveland, William L. (1994) *A History of the Modern Middle East*. Boulder, CO: Westview Press.

**KARAKALPAKS** The Karakalpaks (or Qaraqalpaq) are an ethnic group living mainly in the Republic of Karakalpakstan, which occupies the northwestern part of Uzbekistan, bordering Kazakhstan in the north and Turkmenistan in the southwest. There are approximately 600,000 Karakalpaks (based on a 2001 estimate), and about 95 percent of them live in Karakalpakstan. The rest live in various regions of Afghanistan, Kazakhstan, Kyrgyzstan, and Russia. The Karakalpak language belongs to the Kipchak or Kipchak Nogay linguistic subgroup of the Central Turkic group of the Altaic language family (it is close to Kazak, with a strong Uzbek influence). Karakalpaks used the Cyrillic alphabet until 1992; however, under Uzbekistani government pressure, they changed to the Latin alphabet in the mid-1990s (the process is still incomplete due to financial restraints and other difficulties). The majority of Karakalpaks belong to the Hanafi school of Sunni Muslims, like the Kazakhs and Uzbeks. As a part of the independent republic of Uzbekistan, the Karakalpaks became independent from the Soviet Union on 1 September 1991.

### Early History

The Karakalpaks have a rich history, rooted in the ancient Turkic tribal confederations in Central Asia. There are several competing schools of thought that attempt to explain the origin of the Karakalpaks. One school, which includes many Karakalpak historians, believes that their ancestors derived from the early Turks, who arrived in Central Asia between the sixth and eighth centuries, and the Oghuz and Pechenegs, who controlled the territory that is now west Kazakhstan and south-central Russia between the eighth and tenth centuries. These historians claim that the name "Karakalpak," which means "Black Hat" in Turkic, may be seen in the twelfth-century Russian chronicles in the form *Chernyi Klobuki*, which means "Black Hats" in Russian.

The opposing school argues that this similarity in terminology has no significance and that the Karakalpaks probably began to distinguish themselves from other Central Asian Turkic tribal confederations in the sixteenth century. According to this theory, after the devastating Mongol invasion of 1219–1221, which resulted in the death or disappearance of a sizable proportion of the population as well as in the destruction of a significant portion of the irrigation system that had been developed by the settled population of the Khorezm khanate, the ancestors of the Karakalpak tribes came under the Nogay Horde, which occupied territory in the Northwestern Central Asian region, including present-day Turkmenistan, western Kazakhstan, and southern Russia. Probably around the fifteenth and sixteenth centuries, Islam established itself among these tribes (mainly through the activities of the Sufi orders), although early contacts with the Islamic world can be traced to the tenth and eleventh centuries.

By the sixteenth century, the Karakalpaks had begun clearly to differentiate themselves from the Kazakh, Turkmen, and Uzbek tribes and their neighbors and started calling themselves the Karakalpaks. The Karakalpaks controlled the territory of the lower delta of the Syr Dar'ya River, although they frequently moved north and south of this area due to pressure from neighbors and ecological changes, such as droughts and desertification. They gradually consolidated into an amorphous tribal confederation, building their economy on trade with neighboring states, agriculture, and animal husbandry. Throughout the seventeenth and eighteenth centuries, the Karakalpaks were subjects of the Bukhara khanate (1753–1920), the Kichi Dzhuz (one of the three Kazakh tribal confederations), and the Khiva khanate (1511–1920). In the eighteenth century, there was another important change as most of the Karakalpak tribes moved to the lower delta of the Amu Dar'ya River (this territory corresponds to the present Karakalpak state).

In the early nineteenth century, declining regional trade, technological backwardness, and the Khiva khanate's inability to secure political stability led to economic depression in the area populated by the Karakalpaks. These were the main factors that led the Karakalpaks to offer no or little resistance to Russia's advancement into their land. In 1873, the Karakalpaks' territory became a protectorate of the Russian empire as Russia advanced into Turkistan. Russian rule brought some positive changes, ending the numerous conflicts and political instability in this area, although emerging Russian capitalism aggravated the economic disparities in Karakalpak society.

### Soviet Rule

After the Russian empire collapsed in 1917, the Bolsheviks struggled to establish their dominance in Central Asia. They overcame the resistance of the Basmachi movement (a popular militant resistance often sponsored by the British government), and by 1920 they had established full control. In 1925, as the result of national delimitations in Central Asia, the Karakalpak Autonomous Province was established (as part of the Russian Federation), uniting most of the territory populated by the Karakalpaks into a single political entity. In March 1932, it was transformed into the Karakalpak Autonomous Soviet Socialist Republic (part of the Russian Federation). In December 1936, the Karakalpak Autonomous Soviet Socialist Republic was transferred to the Uzbek Soviet Socialist Republic.

Under Soviet rule, the Karakalpaks experienced major changes such as modernization, industrialization, urbanization, eradication of mass illiteracy, and establishment of a modern system of education. The Soviet authorities encouraged the creation of codified written languages, changing from the Arabic alphabet to the Roman alphabet (1928) and then to Cyrillic (1940), and promoted the development of literature, art, and science in the Karakalpak language. The literacy rate was lifted from 1.3 percent in 1926 to 98 percent in 1989; major diseases and the high child mortality rate were halted (at the beginning of the twentieth century, the Karakalpaks had been under threat of extinction due to the absence of medical services, high infant mortality, and epidemics); and a comprehensive social-welfare system was established. However, the Karakalpaks paid a heavy price for these changes, as the political opposition and pre–Soviet era intelligentsia disappeared in Stalin's brutal purges, and intensive agriculture, notably cotton growing, caused ecological disasters such as the Aral Sea's dramatic shrinkage, drinking-water pollution, and salinization of arable land.

### Independence

On 1 September 1991, Uzbekistan declared its independence from the Soviet Union. In December 1991, the founding member-states of the Soviet Union signed the historic document of dissolution of the U.S.S.R. This action peacefully ended almost seventy-two years of Soviet rule. The first post-Soviet constitution of Uzbekistan granted to the Karakalpaks the status of a "sovereign republic" with its own constitution and separate judiciary, but retained Tashkent's control over defense, foreign policy, and taxation, among other issues.

### Karakalpak Society

Most Karakalpaks live in predominantly rural areas and preserve many major features of their traditional life. Large families with more than four children are quite common; in 1999, the average size of a Karakalpak rural family was 6.7 people, down from 7.1 in 1989. Several generations often live in the same household or in close neighborhoods. Groups of extended families form a subclanic unit called the *koshe;* several *koshe*s make up the *uru*. People are still expected to trace their ancestors back as many as seven generations and to know their tribal affiliation. During major events and family gatherings, the *bakhsy* (folk singers) or the *zhyrau* (storytellers) are often invited to sing the songs of heroes, the *dastans* (epics), and to play traditional musical instruments, such as the *dutar* (a two-stringed, plucked instrument), the *kobuz* (bowed instruments), and various others. Many Karakalpak families still create such craft items as homemade rugs, carpet braids *(akkur)*, broad fringes *(zhanbau)*, and silver jewelry.

*Rafis Abazov*

### Further Reading

Allworth, Edward A. (1990) *The Modern Uzbeks, from the 14th Century to the Present: A Cultural History*. Stanford, CA: Hoover Institution Press, Stanford University.

Bartold, V. V. (1958) *Turkestan down to the Mongol Invasion*. 2d ed. London: Luzac.

Hanks, Reuel R. (2000) "A Separate Space? Karakalpak Nationalism and Devolution in Post-Soviet Uzbekistan." *Europe-Asia Studies* 52, 5: 939–953.

Kangas, Roger D. (2002) *Uzbekistan in the Twentieth Century: Political Development and the Evolution of Power*. Houndmills, Basingstoke, U.K.: Palgrave.

Reichl, Karl. (1992) *Turkic Oral Epic Poetry: Tradition, Forms, Poetic Structure*. New York: Garland.

**KARAKALPAKSTAN—PROFILE** (2002 est. pop. 1.6 million). Karakalpakstan, officially the Republic of Karakalpakstan (Qoraqalpokiston Respiblikasy in Karakalpak, Karakalpakia in Russian), is an autonomous republic within the Republic of Uzbekistan in central Asia. It is bordered by Kazakhstan in the north, Turkmenistan in the southwest, and Uzbekistan in the east. It also shares with Kazakhstan the southern portion of the Aral Sea. The nation has an area of 165,600 square kilometers, and it is the largest administrative entity in the Republic of Uzbekistan, occupying almost 37 percent of its territory. Karakalpakstan's capital city, Nukus, is located in the northeast of the nation, a few kilometers from the border with Uzbekistan.

According to its constitution, Karakalpakstan has a broad autonomy in cultural, economic, and social issues, although in reality it is under strict centralized control of Uzbekistan's government.

## Population

The population of Karakalpakstan is approximately 6 percent of the Uzbekistani population. It is a predominantly rural nation, with 48.4 percent of the population living in cities and towns. Nukus was home to about 254,000 people in 2002, up from 139,000 in 1985. The republic's population is young, with 37 percent below the age of fourteen and only 5 percent older than sixty-five. Karakalpakstan has a population growth rate of 1.6 percent or higher and a net migration rate of –2.18 migrants per 1,000 people. It is difficult to project the dynamics of population growth because of the remoteness of Karakalpakstan, scarce statistics, and a high infant mortality rate of more than 72 deaths per 1,000 live births in 1999. Karakalpakstan still has one of the lowest population densities in central Asia, standing at nine people per square kilometer. However, since the 1990s a number of young people have moved from rural areas to the areas around the capital in search of jobs and new opportunities.

Karakalpakstan is a multiethnic nation with a very diverse population. Karakalpaks make up approximately 32 percent of the population, Uzbeks around 30 percent, Kazakhs around 26 percent, and Turkmen around 4 percent; Russians, Tatars, Koreans, and other small groups make up the remaining 8 percent. Historically, the territory of Karakalpakstan was populated by ethnic groups of Turkic origin that migrated with their sheep and camels through the area. During Russian and Soviet rule, many Russians and people from different parts of the USSR were settled in the republic, many of them forcibly. Since 1991, the ethnic structure has changed slightly, as many urban Russians and other ethnic groups emigrated from Karakalpakstan, although the precise number is unknown.

In the late nineteenth and early twentieth centuries, the Karakalpaks were under the threat of extinction due to diseases, a high mortality rate, and the absence of medical services. After 1920, the Soviet government invested heavily in medical services and built a number of hospitals in the republic. The Soviet government also promoted the policy of population growth. For these and other reasons, the number of Karakalpaks almost doubled between 1926 and 1970 and again from 1970 to 1989, reaching 411,870 in 1989. According to the official estimates, there were around 600,000 Karakalpaks in 2001, most of them (around 95 percent) living in the republic.

## Society, Religion, and Culture

The Karakalpak language belongs to the Kipchak or Kipchak-Nogay linguistic subgroup of the Central Turkic group of the Altaic language family (it is close to Kazakh with strong Uzbek influence), and it is the official language of the nation, along with Uzbek. The majority of the population, including ethnic minorities, speaks Karakalpak and Uzbek, although during the Soviet era the Russian language was widely used in administration and education. After 1991, Turkey offered assistance to Uzbekistan, and consequently to Karakalpakstan, in shifting from the Cyrillic to Latin script (Soviet authorities initiated the shift from the Arabic alphabet to Latin in 1928 and then from Latin to Cyrillic in 1940).

The majority of Karakalpakstan's population (around 96 percent) is Muslim. The Karakalpaks embraced Islam mainly through the activities of the Sufi (Muslim mystic) orders in the thirteenth and fourteenth centuries, although some elements of shamanistic rituals from the pre-Islamic era may still be traced in the republic.

The people in Karakalpakstan strongly preserve major features of a traditional seminomadic society, and interethnic marriages and migration outside of the republic are still rare. Tribal affiliation still plays an important role in everyday life in Karakalpak society. Groups of extended families usually live together and form a subclanic unit called the *koshe;* several *koshe*s make up an *uru.* Soviet modernization contributed to the preservation of these traditional structures by encouraging the Karakalpaks to settle and to join the kolkhozy and sovkhozy (state-controlled collective farms) in the 1920s and 1930s. Whole families and *koshe*s settled collectively in the same place and joined the same kolkhozy. Karakalpaks, especially in rural areas, continue to keep ancient secrets of their traditional arts of homemade rugs, carpet braids *(akkur)*, broad fringes *(zhanbau)*, and silver jewelry for family use, for dowry, and increasingly for commercial sale in the market.

## Political System

The Karakalpaks are first mentioned in various sources in the sixteenth century. Their political organization resembled typical nomadic political entities, which were characterized by an absence of strong centralized political authority and rigid political organizations. The tribes and subtribal groups were governed by the *bii*s or *batyr*s (representatives of tribal nobility and armed leaders). Various historical sources mention that the Karakalpaks were subjects of the Bukhara khanate in the seventeenth century and then subjects of the Kazakh khans in the eighteenth century. In the late eighteenth and early nineteenth centuries, the Khiva khanate became increasingly active in the areas traditionally populated by the Karakalpak tribes, and by 1811 most of the Karakalpak tribes came under the rule of Khiva, in spite of their considerable resistance and uprisings. The Khiva khanate itself became a Russian protectorate in 1873. This development divided the Karakalpak tribes: those who lived on the right bank of the Amu Dar'ya River became subjects of the Russian empire, and those who lived on the left bank were still subjects of the Khiva ruler.

After the 1917 Bolshevik Revolution, the Karakalpak territory on the right bank of the Amu Dar'ya was incorporated into the Turkistan Autonomous Soviet Socialist Republic (TASSR), whereas a significant number of the Karakalpaks remained under the Khiva khanate, and later, after its abolishment, under the Khorezm People's Soviet Republic. In 1924, the TASSR government agreed to bring together the land populated by the Karakalpaks into one political entity, and in 1925 the Karakalpak Autonomous Province was established as a part of the Russian federation. This action united most of the territory populated by the Karakalpaks into a single political entity. In March 1932, the Karakalpak Autonomous Province was transformed into the Karakalpak Autonomous Soviet Socialist Republic (KASSR) within the Kazakh ASSR (still a part of the Russian federation). In December 1936, the KASSR was transferred to the Uzbek Soviet Socialist Republic. Under the Soviets, there was an attempt to replace the traditional political organization of the society with a system based on political parties, parliamentary legislation, and Communist ideology. Karakalpakstan preserved its one-party political system, dominated by the Communist Party, until 1991.

On 1 September 1991, Uzbekistan declared its independence from the Soviet Union, and in December 1991 the founding republics of the Soviet Union signed a historic document mandating the peaceful and voluntary dissolution of the USSR. On 8 December 1992, Uzbekistan adopted its first post-Soviet constitution. It granted the Karakalpak ASSR the status of a "sovereign republic," its own constitution, independence in administrative issues, and a separate judiciary. This constitution was influenced by the Soviet legal tradition, especially in arranging the center-province relations and defining the terms for cultural and political autonomy. Constitutionally, Karakalpakstan, as a part of the Republic of Uzbekistan, enjoys broad autonomy in internal administrative and cultural affairs, although the conduct of foreign policy and foreign trade is firmly in the hands of the central authorities in Tashkent, the capital of Uzbekistan. Karakalpakstan has its own government and, theoretically, the right to leave the Republic of Uzbekistan through national referendum, although the detailed procedure for the referendum was not established. Karakalpakstan, along with Uzbekistan, abandoned the one-party political system in 1991. At present, any political party is tolerated as long as it acts within the framework of the law, is loyal to the regime, and is officially registered by government authorities. According to official reports, at present there are several active parties in the republic. All of them are progovernment parties, approved by the Uzbekistani government, and often they act as the branches of larger Uzbekistani parties, such as the People's Democratic Party (formerly the Communist Party), Vatan Tarakiyoti (Fatherland Progress Party), Milly Tiklanish (Democratic National Rebirth Party), and others. However, tribal and ethnic political mobilization is still strong in Karakalpakstan and plays an important role in domestic politics.

## Economy

Karakalpakstan has a relatively small economy due to its small size (slightly larger than the state of New York), harsh climate, small population, and extremely limited natural resources. Agriculture and agricultural-product processing are the two main sectors of the national economy. Traditionally, most of the Karakalpaks were engaged in subsistence animal husbandry, raising sheep, goats, and cattle, and a few of them were engaged in crop cultivation (mainly around the Amu Dar'ya River). Most of Karakalpakstan is dry land unsuitable for crop cultivation without substantial irrigation, although vast areas in the west and northwest of the republic could be used as pasture for sheep and goats. The areas in the south traditionally have well-established irrigation systems, and these areas produce most of the cotton and silk. The areas in the north, mainly near the Aral Sea, were affected by salinization caused by the intensive use of water from the Amu Dar'ya River for the irrigation of cotton fields in other regions of Uzbekistan. In the 1980s and 1990s, almost the entire outflow of this river was taken for irrigation, causing shrinking of the Aral Sea from 68,000 square kilometers in 1960 to 33,800 square kilometers in 1992 (the sea's volume was reduced by around 75 percent). Despite this natural disaster the republic has significant economic potential because it has unexploited natural resources, including oil and possibly minerals.

After establishing the Soviet political system in the middle of the 1920s, the Soviet authorities introduced major economic changes throughout the Soviet Union. They nationalized most businesses, banned private ownership of land, and introduced central state planning and control over the economy. Most Karakalpaks were drawn to kolkhozy and were encouraged to abandon subsistence agriculture in favor of intensive agricultural production for the all-union market. Karakalpakstan significantly increased production of cotton, meat, wool, and other products for the Soviet market. Karakalpakstan established its industrial sector based mainly on agricultural-product processing. The government built new roads, electrical power stations, and new industrial enterprises. At the same time, private entrepreneurship was strongly discouraged, and cost inefficiencies and ecological downsides of large-scale production were ignored. Karakalpakstan relied heavily on subsidies from the central state budget due to price and other economic distortion and extensive centralized control.

After dissolution of the USSR, the government of Karakalpakstan, along with the government of Uzbekistan, adopted a policy of gradual change, slowly abandoning the centralized planning and easing state control over enterprises, dismantling collective farms, and privatizing most small and medium-sized enterprises. Subsidies to support local enterprises were significantly reduced, but unlike in Kazakhstan and Kyrgyzstan, they were not abandoned completely.

Karakalpakstan, along with Uzbekistan, experienced painful economic decline after independence as the Soviet market on which it had depended collapsed. It did not suffer in this regard as severely as neighboring Kazakhstan or Turkmenistan, however. Statistical data for Karakalpakstan are often unavailable, but its economic development is largely in line with Uzbekistan's as its economic policy is defined in Tashkent. According to the World Bank, Uzbekistan's agricultural sector accounts for 32.9 percent of gross domestic product (GDP), with industry accounting for 24.5 percent and services 37.8 percent. Between 1989 and 1999 average annual GDP growth in Uzbekistan was negative, declining at an annual average of around 1.0 percent, with industrial production declining at an annual average of 4.0 percent and agriculture 0.2 percent.

Agriculture is not only the most important sector of Karakalpakstan's economy, but also the source of income for almost half of the population. Animal herding provides everyday food and a mode of transportation; livestock are also an important export. The Karakalpaks migrate around vast prairies and deserts raising horses, sheep, goats, cattle, and camels. In 2000, livestock numbers in Karakalpakstan reached 383,800 cattle, 466,900 sheep, and 16,800 horses. Crop cultivation (cotton, rice, corn, vegetables) in Karakalpakstan is limited due to the extremely dry continental climate and a chronic water shortage. After privatization of the large state-controlled farms and the creation of a system of small private farming, crop production fell sharply. A combination of mismanagement and ecological disaster related to the declining level of the Aral Sea led to depression in the agricultural-product processing industries. Since 1991, many farmers have struggled to adapt to the new economic realities and have turned to a subsistence economy. In 2000, Karakalpakstan experienced its worst drought in decades, and its government requested food assistance of 80,000 metric tons of wheat and 3,000 metric tons of vegetable oil for distribution to 1.1 million people in rural regions.

The industrial sector is relatively small and includes light industry (leather goods and carpets), agricultural-product processing plants, food-processing plants, and mining. Oil, limestone, gypsum, asbestos, and marble are major natural resources of export significance. Karakalpakstan still relies largely on Russian technology in this sector of the economy, although Russian involvement began to diminish during the 1990s, and multinational corporations started to move into the mining sector.

Tourism is an underdeveloped sector of the economy, limited by lack of accommodation facilities and transport infrastructure. However, it has great potential, especially in adventure tourism, due to the fascinating history of the Silk Road and rare historical sites, including the ancient ruins of Toprak-Kala (dating to approximately the first or second century CE). The retail sector is also quite underdeveloped by Western standards and consists of numerous small shops and restaurants.

Electrical power is supplied by the Takhiatash and other electric power stations, covering the republic's needs and exporting the balance to other parts of Uzbekistan. However, due to inadequate maintenance and underinvestment, power cuts are frequent, and some remote areas still live without electricity, using instead diesel, wood, and dried cattle and camel dung as fuel. In the 1950s, a railway was built, connecting Uzbekistan with the Russian railway system via Karakalpakstan. Highways are unevenly distributed, and only 1,172 kilometers are paved, mainly in the southeastern part of the republic. In the north and northwest, horses and camels are still important modes of transportation.

Since the early 1990s, the government of Uzbekistan has been conducting a policy of economic liberalization and deregulation, encouraging the private sector and foreign investments. According to the Ministry of Macroeconomics and Statistics (MMS), the 9,069 small and medium-sized enterprises registered in Karakalpakstan in July 2000 accounted for 4.6 percent of all enterprises in Uzbekistan. Their total exports reached $33,105,000 in 1999. Karakalpakstan attracted 13.8 billion sums (the currency of Uzbekistan) of investments (official exchange rate in 2000: 141.4 sums per $1) or 9,100 sums per capita (fourth highest among regions in Uzbekistan). Karakalpakstan increasingly relies on the export of raw materials to the international market, and it is extremely vulnerable to fluctuations in world prices for its major export products—cotton and wool.

The economic changes of the 1990s, including the partial liberalization of the economy and abandonment of state guarantees of employment, hit the population of Karakalpakstan hard. According to the MMS, in Karakalpakstan the labor force stood at 484,000 in 2000, and the number of registered unemployed was around 8,700 or 2 percent. However, international assistance organizations and experts put the unemployment rate much higher, at 20–25 percent of the labor force. In 1999, the United Nations Development Programme (UNDP) Human Development Index put Uzbekistan in 106th place, behind Moldova and Cape Verde but ahead of Algeria, Vietnam, and Indonesia. According to the Uzbekistani national UNDP report, in Karakalpakstan the real GDP per capita was 42.4 percent lower than in Uzbekistan overall in 1999.

*Rafis Abazov*

### Further Reading


International Monetary Fund. (2000) *Republic of Uzbekistan: Recent Economic Developments Series.* IMF Staff Country Report, no. 00/36. Washington, DC: International Monetary Fund.

Ministry of Macroeconomics and Statistics of Uzbekistan and TACIS. (2000) *Uzbekistan: Economic Trends Quarterly.* Brussels, Belgium: European Commission, NIS/TACIS Service.

Nurmukhamedova, M. K., ed. (1986) *Istoriia Karakalpakskoi ASSR: sdrevneishikh vremen do nashikh dnei* (History of the Karakalpak SSR: From Ancient Times to the Present). Tashkent, Uzbekistan: Izdatelstvo "Fan."

Taube, Gunther, and Jeromin Zettelmeyer. (2000) *Output Decline and Recovery in Uzbekistan—Past Performance and Future Prospects.* Working Paper WP/98/132. Washington, DC: International Monetary Fund.

United Nations Development Programme (UNDP). (2001) *Uzbekistan 2000: Human Development Report.* Tashkent, Uzbekistan: UNDP.


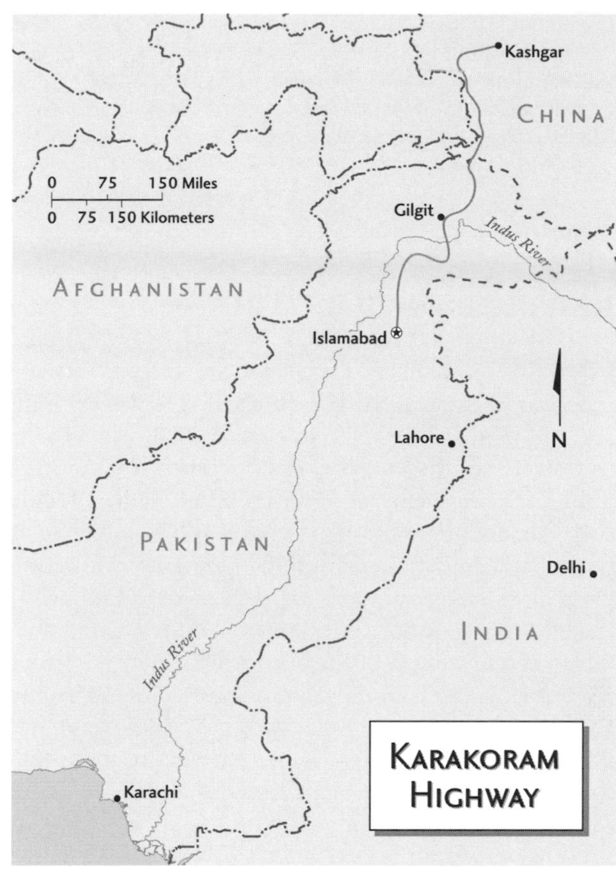


**KARAKORAM HIGHWAY** The Karakoram Highway, known to the Chinese as the Friendship Highway, is an engineering masterpiece. It is a stretch of highway that was built in the north of Pakistan, where some of the mountains extend to altitudes of seven to eight thousand meters. The Karakoram Highway runs along the Indus River and then dips into the Gilgit and Hunza valleys, culminating in a climb of 4,800 meters to the Khunjerab Pass, which serves as a dividing line between Pakistan and China. It took twenty years to complete the highway, which began in 1966 as the brainchild of both Chinese and Pakistani engineers to facilitate trade between China and Pakistan. Several hundred people lost their lives during its construction, which involved pushing, blasting, and leveling the terrain between Islamabad and Kashgar. The highway follows the path of what was once known as the Silk Road because of the caravans that followed it with loads of silk and other valuable trade goods.

The Karakoram Highway opened in Pakistan in 1982, finally opening to travelers to and from China in 1986. Today, heavy traffic flows between Pakistan and China's Xinjiang Province. Due to the many beautiful cities and sights along the way, which include Kohistan, Gilgit, Hunza, and Skardu, the Karakoram Highway is a popular way for visitors to travel in this area

*Houman A. Sadri*

### Further Reading


Ahmed, S. Z. (1998) *Travels in Shangri-La: Between Hindu Kush and Karakoram.* Trumbull, CT: A. E. R. Publications.

Cleveland, William L. (1994). *A History of the Modern Middle East*. Boulder, CO: Westview Press.

Haynes, Jeff, ed. (1999). *Religion, Globalization, and Political Culture in the Third World*. New York: St. Martin's Press.

Macfarlane, Allison, Rasoul B. Sorkhabi, and Jay Quade, eds. (1999) *Himalaya and Tibet: Mountain Roots to Mountain Tops*. Boulder, CO: Geological Society of America.

**KARAKORAM MOUNTAINS** The Karakoram Mountains extend 500 kilometers (310 miles) from India's Ladakh Himalaya, northwest through Pakistan to the Afghan Hindu Kush. The icy summits separate South Asia's Pakistan and part of India to the southwest from Central Asia's far western China and Tibet to the northeast. The colliding Indian Ocean and Eurasian tectonic plates have uplifted over forty peaks above 6,000 meters (20,000 feet) into numerous parallel ridges occupying 207,000 square kilometers (80,000 square miles). All four non-Himalayan 8,000-meter (26,250 feet) peaks are located here, of which K2 (8,611 meters; 28,251 feet) is second only to Mount Everest. The longest midlatitude glaciers (five exceed 48 kilometers; 30 miles) in length supply meltwater for 10 million downstream farmers along the Indus (South Asia) and Tarim (Central Asia) Rivers. The summer monsoon brings Indian Ocean moisture into the parched southern Karakoram, but high peaks create a rain shadow north of the crest where annual precipitation averages just 100 millimeters (4 inches).

Human settlement is concentrated on the moister southern slopes of the Pakistan Karakoram. The towns of Gilgit and Skardu number 40,000 people. The population in the Ladakh region of India is localized in Leh (9,000 people) and in over one hundred small villages throughout the mountains. Shi'ite Muslims predominate in Pakistan, while Tibetan Buddhists prevail in Ladakh. Minority Tajiks, Kyrgyz, and Uighurs are common in the more remote northern Karakoram. Subsistence farming and livestock raising dominate the economy. The primary crops are wheat, barley, buckwheat, corn, and potatoes. Apricots and walnuts are an important but declining food source.

Since 1975, Indian and Pakistani troops have fought on the Siacheen Glacier to adjudicate their international frontier. National pride, ethnic enclaves, and the headwaters of the mighty Indus River are at stake. In 1994, the governments of China and Pakistan opened the Karakoram Highway to the public. This renewed tourism, commerce, and immigration along this ancient Silk Road artery.

*Stephen F. Cunha*

**Further Reading**

Allan, Nigel J. R. (1988) "Highways to the Sky: The Impact of Tourism on South Asian Mountain Culture." *Tourism and Recreation Research* 13: 11–16.

Rowell, Galen. (1986) *In the Throne Room of the Mountain Gods*. San Francisco: Sierra Club Books.

The Karakoram Mountains as seen from the Dras Valley in Ladakh, northern India, in 1975. (CHARLES & JOSETTE LENARS/CORBIS)

**KARAKORUM** Karakorum (also known as Kharakhorin), located in Ovorhangai, Mongolia, on the Orhon River, was the thirteenth-century imperial capital of the successors of Genghis (or Chinggis) Khan. At its height, the city was a busy metropolis served by soldiers, merchants, and craftspeople, many of the latter imported from lands conquered by the Mongolian military. The ancient city, with an area of 400 meters by 400 meters, was protected from attackers by a fortified wall, and near each of the wall's four gates, four giant granite turtle sculptures were said to protect the city from a potentially more dangerous threat: periodic floods. Only one of these statues remains today. The town's most exotic monument was designed by the French sculptor Guillaume Bouchier, who lived in the twelfth century CE. The fountain he designed allegedly flowed with five different libations—honey, vodka, wine, cow's milk, and *airag* (fermented mare's milk).

Archaeological evidence from the eighth century demonstrates that Karakorum was not the first settlement on this site, neither was it the last. After being destroyed by Chinese invaders in the fourteenth century, the settlement and its building stones were recycled in 1586 to build the Erdene Zuu monastery, a Buddhist religious center. Although the ruined city was lost for several centuries, its precise location was redetermined by two Russian scholars in 1889.

*Daniel Hruschka*

**Further Reading**

Bawden, Charles R. (1968) *The Modern History of Mongolia.* London: Weidenfeld & Nicolson.

Morgan, David. (1990) *The Mongols.* Malden, MA: Blackwell Publishing.

**KARA-KUM CANAL** The V. I. Lenin Kara-Kum Canal, which diverts about 40 percent of the waters of the Amu Dar'ya across the Kara-Kum Desert to southern Turkmenistan, flows for almost 800 kilometers and in 1973 irrigated 440,000 hectares of land mostly used for cotton cultivation. The canal originates at Oba, Turkmenistan, 10 kilometers from the Afghan border and 10 kilometers from Kerki. The main areas of irrigation are the Mary, Tedzhen, and Ashkhabad (Ashgabat) oases.

The canal was approved in 1947, although engineering work was not begun in earnest until 1954. The initial 400 kilometers from the Amu Dar'ya to the Merv oasis was completed in 1959. By 1960 a further 140 kilometers to the Tedzhen oasis had been built. In 1962

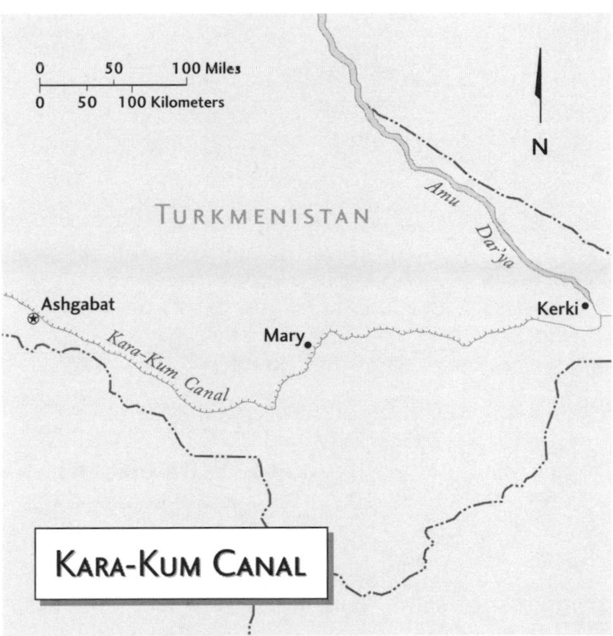


the canal reached Ashkhabad and in 1967 the 300-kilometer section from Tedzhen to Goek Tepe was completed. The canal ends at the Kopet Dagh Reservoir, which has a capacity of 190 million cubic meters. There are a further two reservoirs at Ashkhabad of 6 million cubic meters and 48 million cubic meters. The canal is navigable for 450 kilometers. Catfish, carp, and barbel are commercially fished from the canal's waters.

Although the canal has been described as one of the most impressive technical feats of Soviet engineering, it has been the cause of a number of environmental problems. Some estimates suggest that as much as 45 percent of the water entering the canal is lost to evaporation and seepage. These losses result in more diversion from the Amu Dar'ya and cause a major reduction in the Amu Dar'ya's flow, contributing to the disappearance of the Aral Sea. Seepage has also led to soil salinization due to a rise in the water table.

*Will Myer*

**Further Reading**

Allworth, Edward, ed. (1989) *Central Asia: 120 Years of Russian Rule.* Durham, NC: Duke University Press.

**KARA-KUM DESERT** The Kara Kum (Garagum) Desert (in Turkish *gara* means "black" and *gum* means "desert") is a large midlatitude desert occupying approximately 80 percent of the territory of the Republic of Turkmenistan and portions of southwestern Uzbekistan. Even though most of the desert is

composed of sand, sand dunes, and hard rocky surfaces (*takir* in Russian), portions have been used as pasture for camels and, during the Soviet period, as irrigated cotton acreage.

The Kara-Kum Canal, begun in 1954, runs along the southern part of the desert. It diverts water from the middle course of the Amu Dar'ya River westward, crosses the Murghab River delta in the southeastern portion of the desert, and runs along the northern foothills of the Kopet-Dag toward the Caspian Sea. It is approximately 1,400 kilometers long and provides most of the water for personal and agricultural uses in Turkmenistan.

Most of the canal is unlined, and waterlogging and soil salinization are major problems in areas of the desert around the canal because of seepage. The canal is also the greatest single contributor to the shrinking of the Aral Sea, as the canal diverts the largest amount of water among all the irrigation structures in the Aral Sea basin.

*David R. Smith*

### Further Reading

Pryde, Philip, ed. (1995) *Environmental Resources and Constraints in the Former Soviet Republics*. Boulder, CO: Westview Press.

**KARAOKE** The word *karaoke* (literally, "empty orchestra") refers to both amplified singing to prerecorded accompaniment and the equipment designed to enable that practice. Although various claims have been made to its exact origins, most scholars agree that karaoke's birth came in the early 1970s in Japan, when bars began to use professional recording machinery to accompany amateur singers. The tremendous popularity of karaoke throughout Japan, other areas of Asia, and many parts of the world made it a global phenomenon by the 1990s.

In Japan, karaoke's popularity stems from a longstanding tradition of amateur music-making at social gatherings. At these gatherings, singing is regarded as something both to participate in and to perform. The social etiquette surrounding karaoke in Japan emphasizes participation: all singers receive applause, but little critique. At the same time, an industry of singing lessons, amateur organizations, ranked competitions, and instructional publications and television programs emphasize song performance.

In 1978, karaoke extended from bars into homes through the development of a low-budget version called "home karaoke." This encouraged the development of karaoke as a hobby. In the meantime, karaoke equipment included an increasing number of vocal enhancers, including reverberation. The switch from audiotape to compact disc in 1983 resulted in greater ease and range of musical transposition, allowing people to sing a wider variety of songs. In the mid-1980s, videodisc and, later, laser disc use introduced video-projected images to karaoke. This shifted the experience from a strictly musical one to a visually enhanced, and some might say visually dominated, performance. In 1986, the development of karaoke "boxes" (business establishments that rent out private rooms equipped with karaoke machines) transformed commercial karaoke from a public performance into a private one. The spread of "boxes" and expansion of business into daytime hours extended karaoke beyond the late-night bar scene, into the everyday worlds of housewives, students, and even children.

In Asia, karaoke is regarded both as a local practice in the singing of local songs and as a Japanese import, especially as the manufacture of equipment, satellite broadcasting of songs, and online video networks all originate in Japan.

*Christine R. Yano*

### Further Reading

Kelly, Bill. (1998) "Japan's Empty Orchestras; Echoes of Japanese Culture in the Performance of Karaoke." In *The Worlds of Japanese Popular Culture*, edited by D. P. Martinez. Cambridge, U.K.: Cambridge University Press.

Man Kong Lum, Casey. (1996) *In Search of a Voice: Karaoke and the Construction of Identity in Chinese America*. Mahwah, NJ: Lawrence Erlbaum.

Mitsui, Toru, and Shuhei Hosokawa. (1998) *Karaoke around the World: Global Technology, Local Singing*. London: Routledge.

Yano, Christine R. (1996) "The Floating World of Karaoke in Japan." *Popular Music and Society* 2: 1–17.

**KARATE** Karate is a modern Japanese martial art that developed in the early twentieth century and is based on traditional Okinawan unarmed combat techniques. Karate involves the use of punching, striking, kicking, and blocking to ward off an opponent and to counterattack. Since the founding of the Nippon Karate Kyokai (Japan Karate Association) in 1957, karate has become a popular martial art and sport around the world, with an estimated 15 million practitioners. Important in the spread of karate to the West were the Bruce Lee and other kung-fu movies and television shows of the 1970s and 1980s. Other than Lee, those responsible for the development and spread of karate are the founder, the Okinawan Gichin Funakoshi (1868–1957), who brought karate to Japan, and Matsutatsu Oyama, who brought it to the United States in 1952.

Karate is now used as a form of physical training, as a form of self-defense, and as a competitive sport and is especially popular with women. Because of its rather late development, it is not so heavily imbued with the philosophical and spiritual elements of other Asian martial arts. Nonetheless, there are distinct schools of karate and a basic division between those who prefer the traditional noncontact style and those who prefer the contact sport style.

*Benny Josef Peiser*

**Further Reading**

Draeger, Donn F. (1974) *Modern Bujutsu and Budo.* New York: Weatherhill.

Funakoshi, Gichin. (1976) *Karate-Do Kyohan: The Master.* Trans. by T. Oshima. London: Ward Loch.

**KARBALA** (2002 est. pop. 550,000). Karbala is a city in central Iraq, eighty-eight kilometers southwest of Baghdad. It is one of the holiest cities of Shiʿa Islam (adherents of the Shiʿa branch of Islam today account for one-tenth of the world's Muslim population) and a center of pilgrimage. Prior to their mass expulsion during the Iran-Iraq War (1980–1990), people of Iranian descent constituted one-half of the city's population.

In 680 CE the plain upon which Karbala later rose was the site of a battle between the army of the Umayyad caliph (the spiritual and political leader of followers of Sunni Islam, the largest branch of Islam) and a small band led by Husayn ibn ʿAli (c. 626–680), the grandson of the Prophet Muhammad, the third imam of Twelver Shiʿia Islam (the dominant sect of Shiʿa Islam), and its foremost symbol of martyrdom. It is believed that after the defeat of his rebellion, Husayn's decapitated body was buried where it fell. A few years later his tomb had already become a center of pilgrimage, and by the mid-eighth century a shrine was built over it. The shrine was damaged and rebuilt several times, most notably in 1801 by desert nomads and in 1991 during Baghdad's suppression of the mass rebellion that followed the Persian Gulf War (1990–1991). Today the sanctuary surrounding the shrine, with its three minarets, gilded dome, mosque, and adjoining Shiʿa college, is one of the greatest in the Islamic world. Nearby is a smaller sanctuary and shrine built for al-ʿAbbas, Husayn's half-brother and standard bearer. Because popular Shiʿite belief guarantees paradise to all who are buried in Karbala, the outskirts of the city are dominated by large cemeteries. To the west of the city are the ruins of al-Ukhaydhir, an early Abbasid castle.

*Thaabit Abdullah*

**KAREN** Despite their large numbers, the Karen (Kayin) are one of the least documented peoples in the history of Myanmar (Burma). Even the modern Karen population figure is disputed. Karen nationalists claim a total of 7 million, whereas government statistics put the figure closer to 3 million. Part of the difference is due to the number of Buddhist Karens in the Irrawaddy Delta region who no longer speak Karen. A further factor is the diversity of Karen subgroups inhabiting different parts of the country. They share, however, many aspects of language, culture, and myth.

The Karen language displays many singular characteristics, usually being categorized on its own as a remote branch of Sino-Tibetan. Legend ascribes the migration of the Karen peoples into Burma from across the "River of Shifting Sands," identified by some Karens as the Gobi Desert. The first Karens are thought to have arrived in Upper Burma during the early centuries CE and then to have migrated southward through the Irrawaddy, Sittang, and Salween river valleys. In modern-day Myanmar, Karen-speaking peoples can be found from the Irrawaddy Delta in the west through the Pegu Yoma highlands in the center to the mountains of the Karen, Shan, and Kayah borderlands in the east. Here, in the hills above Toungoo, the greatest diversity of Karen subgroups live. An estimated 200,000 Karens also live in neighboring Thailand.

A twelve-year-old Karen boy poses with a rifle in a Karen rebel camp on 31 January 2000, the 51st anniversary of Karen Revolution Day. (REUTERS NEWMEDIA INC./CORBIS)

Around twenty subgroups have been identified among the Karens in Myanmar. By far the most numerous are the Pwo and Sgaw. Other large populations include the Pao (Taungthu), Kayah, and Kayan (Padaung). From these communities, four distinctive political identities emerged during the twentieth century: the mainstream Karen, the Pao, the Karenni of Kayah State, and the Kayan, who inhabit the Shan-Kayah borderlands.

Karen nationalism in its present-day forms first began during British rule. Following the inception of the Karen National Association by Christian Karens in 1881, the drive for self-determination accelerated. At the turn of the twenty-first century, perhaps only 20 percent of Karens were Christians; most Karens are Buddhists. During the colonial era, however, the British were initially perceived as protectors against historical aggression by their Burman neighbors, and many Karens joined the British army, fighting on the Allied side against the Japanese and Aung San's Burma Independence Army during World War II. Karens also achieved high office in government, notably Dr. San C. Po (1870–1946), who in the 1920s was the first to advocate the creation of an independent Karen homeland, to be known as Kawthoolei.

Po's dream, however, was never achieved, and it was not until 1952 that a much reduced Karen State was created in the Thai borderlands. Various Karen insurgencies have continued over subsequent decades, reflecting continuing demands for greater autonomy and political freedoms. Despite their long-standing sufferings in the conflict, many Karen communities, especially in the Thai borderlands, have continued to offer staunch resistance to central government control. This resulted in continuing Myanmar army offensives in border areas, the displacement of many Karen villages, reports of forced labor and other human-rights abuses, and the flight of more than 100,000 Karen refugees into Thailand.

*Martin Smith*

### Further Reading

Keyes, Charles, ed. (1979) *Ethnic Adaptation and Identity: The Karen on the Thai Frontier with Burma.* Philadelphia: Institute for the Study of Human Issues.

Marshall, Harry. (1922) *The Karen People of Burma: A Study in Anthropology and Ethnology.* Columbus, OH: Ohio State University Press.

Morrison, Ian. (1947) *Grandfather Longlegs: The Life and Gallant Death of Maj. H. P. Seagrim.* London: Faber and Faber.

San C. Po, Dr. (1928) *Burma and the Karens.* London: Elliot Stock.

Smeaton, Donald Mackenzie. (1887) *The Loyal Karens of Burma.* London: Kegan Paul, Trench and Co.

Smith, Martin. (1999) *Burma: Insurgency and the Politics of Ethnicity.* 2d ed. London: Zed Books.

Stern, Theodore. (1968) "*Ariya* and the Golden Book: A Millenarian Buddhist Sect among the Karen." *Journal of Asian Studies* 27, 2: 297–328.

**KAREN NATIONAL UNION** Since its establishment in February 1947, the Karen National Union (KNU) has been the leading opposition voice among the Karen people in Myanmar (Burma). Saw Ba U Gyi and the KNU's founders were largely pro-British intellectuals who advocated legal methods to achieve self-determination for a pan-Karen state. But after boycotting the 1947 general election, the KNU became increasingly marginalized from decisions affecting the country's future.

In January 1949, against a backdrop of rising intercommunal violence, the KNU resorted to armed struggle. Joined by defectors from the Karen Rifles in the Burmese army, KNU forces seized large areas of territory, including, at one stage, Mandalay and Toungoo. Saw Ba U Gyi was killed in a 1950 ambush and the KNU was forced back from the towns, but remained the largest insurgent force in lower Burma throughout the 1950s.

A damaging ideological split occurred in 1963–1964, and KNU president Saw Hunter Thamwe and several hundred followers made a unilateral peace deal with the military government of General Ne Win, who had seized power in 1962. For the next decade, leadership of the KNU in the Irrawaddy Delta and Pegu Yoma regions was taken over by a left-wing faction, the Karen National United Party (KNUP), headed by an ethnic Pwo Karen named Mahn Ba Zan. Meanwhile, the KNU's "Eastern Division" along the Thai border remained under the control of pro-Western nationalists, led by Bo Mya (b. 1926), a local Sgaw hill Karen. Mahn Ba Zan rejoined with Bo Mya in 1968.

After enduring repeated Burmese army offensives, the remaining KNUP/KNU forces in the Irrawaddy Delta and Pegu Yoma were destroyed by 1975, with only a few hundred soldiers escaping to KNU territory in the mountains in the east. Here, under Bo Mya's hard-line leadership, the reunited KNU flourished over a ten-year period, controlling much of the lucrative black market trade with Thailand. As a result, the KNU became the dominant force in the eleven-party National Democratic Front, which shared the KNU's headquarters at Mannerplaw. It was also into KNU territory that thousands of students and democracy activists fled after the military State Law and Order Restoration Council (SLORC) assumed power in 1988.

During the 1990s, however, the authority of the KNU was steadily undermined. Constant Myanmar army offensives as well as cease-fires by NDF allies and defections from KNU ranks (notably by the breakaway Democratic Karen Buddhist Army) saw many KNU base areas collapse, forcing around 100,000 Karen refugees to flee into Thailand. In 1995–1996, the KNU held unsuccessful peace talks with the SLORC government, and, in 2000, Bo Mya was replaced by Padoh Ba Thin as president. But five decades after its founding, the party is struggling for its very survival.

*Martin Smith*

**Further Reading**


Falla, Jonathon. (1991) *True Love and Bartholomew: Rebels on the Burmese Border*. Cambridge, U.K.: Cambridge University Press.

Smith, Dun. (1980) "Memoirs of the Four-Foot Colonel." Ithaca, NY: Cornell University Southeast Asia Program, Data Paper 113.

Smith, Martin. (1999) *Burma: Insurgency and the Politics of Ethnicity*. 2d ed. London: Zed Books.

Tinker, Hugh. (1967) *The Union of Burma: A Study of the First Years of Independence*. Oxford: Oxford University Press.


**KAREN STATE** (1997 est. pop. 1.3 million). The present-day Karen (Kayin) State was created in 1952 by parliamentary legislation to a background of political controversy. A mountainous and landlocked territory covering 30,383 square kilometers, Karen State consists largely of the former Salween Division under the British Frontier Areas Administration, with the addition of the adjoining Thandaung, Paan, Hlaingbwe, Kawkareik, and Kyain districts. With a capital at the then village of Paan (Hpa-an), it probably did not include even one-quarter of the Karen population in Myanmar (Burma) at that time.

As a result, Karen nationalist demands were not met and development in Karen State has been greatly hindered by the armed conflict that has continued ever since. The 1992 population was calculated by the government at 1.26 million, of whom over 700,000 were Karens (including 70,000 Paos), 220,000 Mons, and 170,000 Burmans, as well as small numbers of Shans, Indians, and other nationalities. Demographic statistics in Karen State are unreliable, however, because of the fighting of past decades. As many as one-third of the population is internally displaced from their homes, and over one hundred thousand refugees have fled into Thailand.

The state is dominated physically by the Dawna Range, which runs along the border with Thailand, before merging with steep mountains that continue northward above the town of Papun. These mountains are flanked by the Kayah and Shan states to the east and the Mandalay and Pegu (Bago) divisions to the north and northwest. The highest peak is Nattaung, which stands at 2,623 meters.

The most important river is the Salween (Thanlwin), which runs southward through the state into the broad plains area that adjoins Mon State in the southwest. Paddy, tobacco, betel nut, rubber, sesamum, groundnut, and sugar cane are the principal crops under cultivation. Natural resources include antinomy, copper, tin, and iron. Over half the land area is also covered with forests, but many of the most valuable teak and other timber reserves have been depleted by the logging trade with Thailand that accelerated during the 1990s and has been little controlled.

Under the State Law and Order Restoration Council government, which assumed power in 1988, there were attempts to upgrade the roads and local infrastructure. A principal objective was to speed up communication between the nearby estuary port of Moulmein (Mawlamyine) in Mon State and Thailand in the east through the border towns of Myawaddy and Three Pagodas Pass. This latter outpost was captured from insurgent Karen National Union (KNU) control in 1990.

Economic change, however, was slow, because of the continuing fighting as well as the lack of investment and long-term planning. In the mid-1990s, Paan was opened up to foreign tourists for the first time after a cease-fire by the New Mon State Party and a breakaway from the

KNU by the Democratic Karen Buddhist Army, which resettled several thousand villagers in surrounding areas. But despite its strategic position in the geopolitical region, at the beginning of the twenty-first century it seemed that progress in Karen State remained unlikely without peace and political reform.

*Martin Smith*

### Further Reading

Amnesty International. (1999) *Myanmar: The Kayin (Karen) State: Militarization and Human Rights*. London: Amnesty International.

Burma Ethnic Research Group and Friedrich Naumann Foundation, ed. (1998) *Forgotten Victims of a Hidden War: Internally Displaced Karen in Burma*. Chiang Mai, Thailand: Burma Ethnic Research Group and Friedrich Naumann Foundation.

Smith, Martin. (1999) *Burma: Insurgency and the Politics of Ethnicity*. 2d ed. London: Zed Books.

Tinker, Hugh. (1967) *The Union of Burma: A Study of the First Years of Independence*. Oxford: Oxford University Press.

**KARIMOV, ISLAM** (b. 1938), President of Uzbekistan. For over a decade, Islam Karimov has been the central figure in the politics of the Central Asian nation of Uzbekistan. Islam Karimov was born on 30 January 1938 in a town outside of Samarqand in present-day Uzbekistan. He graduated from the Polytechnic Institute in Tashkent in 1960 and worked as an engineer at the Tashkent Aviation plant from 1960 until 1966. At that point, having completed a degree program at the Institute of National Economics, Karimov took a job at the State Planning Agency (Gosplan), where he worked from 1966 to 1983. He was appointed minister of finance of the Uzbek Soviet Socialist Republic in April 1983 and rose to the rank of first secretary of the Communist Party of Uzbekistan in June of 1989. In March 1990, the Supreme Soviet elected him president, a position he carried over into the post-Soviet era.

President Karimov (right) at a press conference with U.S. Defense Secretary Donald Rumsfeld on 5 October 2001. Rumsfeld was in Uzbekistan to discuss the use of Uzbekistan territory to launch attacks against the Taliban in Afghanistan. (AFP/CORBIS)

Karimov was able to weather the breakup of the Soviet Union by declaring Uzbekistan independent in August 1991 and winning a December 1991 presidential election with 86 percent of the vote. He pushed through a referendum in March 1995 that extended his term and overwhelmingly won reelection in January 2000. In addition, by crafting a constitution that emphasized presidential authority, he has been able to maintain a tight grip on the political system of the nation. Furthermore, President Karimov has been able to thwart efforts on the part of a weak and divided opposition to seriously challenge his authority. The West has often criticized him for his nation's poor human rights record—to which he has responded that such actions are necessary to maintain stability.

*Roger D. Kangas*

### Further Reading

Karimov, Islam A. (1997) *Uzbekistan on the Threshold of the Twenty-First Century*. Tashkent, Uzbekistan: Uzbekistan Publishers.

Kangas, Roger D. (2001) "The Karimov Presidency: Amir Timur Revisited." In *Power and Change in Central Asia*, edited by Sally Cummings. London: Routledge.

**KARIZ IRRIGATION SYSTEM** *Kariz* (also known as *kareze* or *qanat*) is an ancient underground channel irrigation system invented in Persia (Iran). It is a sloping tunnel that brings water from an underground source in a range of hills down to a dry plain at the foot of these hills. Its advantage over an open-air aqueduct is that less water is lost by evaporation on its way from the hill to the plain.

In 714 BCE, when Sargon II invaded Armenia, he saw an irrigation system not yet known in Bet-Nahrain, called by its Arabic name *qanat* or the Farsi *kariz*. He brought the secret back to Assyria. *Qanat* irrigation was then spread over the Near East, as far as North Africa, and is still used.

In Tajikistan, as early as the fourth to fifth centuries BCE, a canal was constructed in the Vakhsh River Valley, near present-day Qurghonteppa (Kurgan-Tyube), which irrigated fifty square kilometers of land. Subterranean canals and reservoirs, with containers made of copper (known as *kariz*), were extensively constructed in the northern parts of Tajikistan in the ninth and tenth centuries CE. These *kariz* carried copious supplies of fresh water from the mountains to waterless plots of land, often many kilometers away. Sometimes as deep as forty meters, they were constructed underground to prevent evaporation of water as it crossed the sun-baked steppe. They were carefully engineered to bring the water to the surface at just the point it was required so that pumping was unnecessary.

In Turpan and Hami Prefectures of China's Xinjiang Uygur Autonomous Region, *kariz* comprising wells connected by underground channels were known as one of the three ancient projects in China, along with the Great Wall and the (Beijing-Hangzhou) Grand Canal. Although there is plenty of rainfall on the slopes of the Tengri-Tagh Mountains, the Turpan Basin is extremely dry and blazingly hot in the summer. Taking advantage of the natural incline of the land and the rich underground water source, the people of Turpan created a unique irrigation system. During the golden age of *kariz* development, 1,700 *kariz* covering a length of 4,400 kilometers were constructed in Turpan Prefecture. At present, *kariz* are facing dropping water levels and drying. Experts are worried about the future of *kariz*, the symbol of Chinese water culture.

In the high and dry plains of Afghanistan, agriculture is often impossible without irrigation. The Afghans have put in place a system for harnessing the water: the *kareze* tunnels.

*Bakhitor Islamov and Sharaf Arifkhanov*

## PATTADAKAL—WORLD HERITAGE SITE

A UNESCO World Heritage Site since 1987, Pattadakal, located in the state of Karnataka, typifies the seventh- and eighth-century blending of artistic and architectural forms in India. Nine ornate temples and one Jain sanctuary make up the Pattadakal site in Karnataka, with the Temple of Virupaksha being the most impressive in artistic and physical scope.

**KARNATAKA** (2001 est. pop. 52.7 million). Karnataka, a land of natural beauty and historical monuments, is the eighth largest state in India in terms of area (191,791 square kilometers) and population. It is situated on the western edge of the Deccan plateau surrounded on three sides by the neighboring states of Goa, Maharashtra, Andhra Pradesh, Tamil Nadu, and Kerala, with a coastline of approximately 300 kilometers on the western side along the Arabian sea. Karnataka got its name from a local word, *karanadu*, meaning lofty land, because it is located in a high plateau area.

Karnataka was formed in 1956 by combining territories from the erstwhile princely states of Mysore and Hyderabad and the British provinces of Bombay and Madras along with the small principality of Coorg. Originally named Mysore, it was given its present name on 1 November 1973. The state's formation marked the fulfillment of the aspirations of the Kannada-speaking people to merge in a cohesive sociopolitical unit.

The history of the area is associated with Bali and Sugreeva, characters from the popular Indian epic *Ramayana*. Subsequently, the region passed under the reigns of some of the most powerful Indian dynasties, including the later Muslim and British rules. Modern Karnataka bears traces of this long history in the form of well-preserved monuments and landmarks, of which the city of Mysore presents a good sample. Belur, Hampi, and Halebid contain remains of old buildings and rock carvings. The state is now divided into twenty-seven districts and it has a bicameral legislature. The Legislative Assembly has 224 members and the Legislative Council has 75 members.

The state's capital, Bangalore, is very attractive, with wide boulevards and modern shopping malls. Famous for key educational institutes and corporate offices, Bangalore is projected as the software capital of India. Apart from the fast-growing information technology industry, it has been a producer of telephones, aircraft, watches, and machine tools. The growth of Bangalore and similar industrial centers in the state has been facilitated by the steady generation of surplus hydroelectric power.

Karnataka's mineral resources include high-grade iron ore, copper, manganese, chromite china clay, limestone, and magnesite. The Kolar gold mines are a major Indian source for the precious metal. The state has a reputation for fine ivory and sandalwood handicrafts. The economy of Karnataka is predominantly rural and agrarian. Almost half of the state's income comes from the agricultural sector, with 71 percent of workers engaged in farming activities. The state accounts for a major share of coffee, millet, oil, and silk production in India. The people of Karnataka like to eat rice, fish, and a special pudding called *bittu*. Festivals celebrated in the state include Dasehra and, in particular, the Mysore Dasehra in the month of October, which draws huge crowds.

*Ram Shankar Nanda*

### Further Reading

Sivapriyananda, Swami. (1995) *Mysore Royal Dasara.* Delhi: Abhinav Publications.

Srinivasan, L. K. (1983) *Cultural Heritage of Karnataka.* Mysore, India: Government of Karnataka.

Ward, Philip. (1998) *Western India: Bombay, Maharastra, Karnataka.* Oleander Press.

**KARS** (2002 pop. 103,000). Kars, capital of the province of Kars (2002 pop. 323,000) in eastern Turkey, lies above the Kars River in a mountain range near the Russian border. Its position on a mountain top leaves the city open to high winds; one of the coldest regions in Turkey, it is covered by snow for at least five months of the year. Kars was inhabited by the Armenians in the ninth and tenth centuries, serving as the capital of the Bagratid dynasty. When the Armenian capital was transferred to nearby Ani, Kars lost some of its importance. Kars was conquered by the Seljuks in the mid-eleventh century, the Mongols in the thirteenth, and Timur (Tamerlane) in 1387. The Ottomans took Kars in 1534, and the city was of great military importance during the Ottoman-Safavid conflicts.

The Russians gained control over Kars in 1828 and 1855, but the city was transferred back to the Turks under subsequent peace treaties. In 1878, after eight months of war, the Treaty of Berlin transferred Kars to the Russians. It remained under Russian control until the Fifteenth Army Unit commanded by Kazim Karabekir Pasha recaptured the city on 30 October 1920. Kars was officially returned to Turkey in 1921. Today the city is an active military base.

*T. Isikozlu-E.F. Isikozlu*

### Further Reading

*Statistical Yearbook of Turkey, 1998.* (1998) Ankara, Turkey: Devlet Istatistik Enstitusu.

**KARSHI** (1998 est. pop. 190,000). Karshi, in the southern part of the republic of Uzbekistan in Central Asia, is an ancient city on the old trade route between Afghanistan and Samarqand. Situated in a fertile oasis of the Kashka Darya River, today Karshi is the administrative center of the Qashqadaryo Province on the Afghanistan border.

The Turks founded a fort here in the fourteenth century, at a site called Naksheb or Nesef, on a caravan route from Samarkand and Bukhara to Persia and India. Karshi was part of the Bukhara khanate (chiefdom) (1583–1740) and the Bukhara emirate (principality) (1747–1920). After the Uzbek Soviet Socialist Republic was formed (1924), Karshi received the name Bek-Budi in 1926 and in 1937 was renamed Karshi. Until 1991 the city was the administrative center of the Kashkadarya province of Uzbekistan and became the administrative center of Qashqadaryo Province in 1991, after the collapse of the Soviet Union.

Present-day Karshi is a large railway junction and gas-production center. It has cotton processing and carpet industries, major irrigation facilities, a state university, and a theater. The Kok-Gumbez Mosque was built in Karshi in the late sixteenth century.

*Natalya Yu. Khan*

### Further Reading

Allworth, Edward, ed. (1994) *Central Asia: 130 Years of Russian Dominance: A Historical Overview.* 3d ed. Durham, NC: Duke University Press.

Roy, Oliver. (2000) *The New Central Asia: The Creation of Nations.* New York: New York University Press.

**KARUN RIVER AND SHATT AL ARAB RIVER** The Karun River begins in the Zagros Mountains of western Iran and flows south to Iraq, where it empties into the Shatt al Arab. In Iran the Karun River extends for 720 kilometers, and by 1888 it had become a major route of foreign trade for Iran. Today it remains that country's primary inland navigation system. During World War II the construction of a rail line between the river port of Khorramshahr and the main Iranian railway system, however, caused the Karun trade route to lose its significance. Nowadays the Karun is used as a transportation corridor for oil exports and commodity imports, accessible only to shallow-draft vessels. The river also serves agricultural needs: Shushtar dam blocks the river to irrigate an area of 1,300 square kilometers. Due to its economic and strategic significance, control of the Shatt al Arab has long been contested. The earliest documented dispute was settled by a treaty signed in 1639, which was intended to establish a boundary between Iran (then Persia) and the Ottoman empire, including today's Iraq. Because of the vagueness of this and other treaties, the conflict over the Shatt al Arab has persisted. There has been continual treaty negotiation and annulment since World War I, and the increase in regional oil production in the 1960s and 1970s served to intensify the conflict. Control of the Shatt al Arab was one of the main reasons for the Iraqi invasion of Iran and the ensuing 1980–1988 war.

*Payam Foroughi and Raissa Muhutdinova-Foroughi*

**Further Reading**

Ionides, Michael G. (1937) *The Régime of the Rivers, Euphrates and Tigris: A General Hydraulic Survey of Their Basins, Including the River Karun*. London: E. & F. N. Spon.

**KAS** (2000 pop. 6,500). A lively Mediterranean coastal resort town in Turkey, Kas lies between Antalya and Fethiye. The economy depends entirely on seasonal tourism and civil service jobs. The easternmost of the Greek Dodacanese Islands, Kastellorizon (or Meis, as Turks call it), is just four kilometers offshore. Like many coastal towns that had Greek populations prior to 1922 (when Greece and Turkey repatriated their respective citizens), the local populace sustains ties with offshore Greeks that began a century ago out of economic necessity. The isolated location of both Kas and Kastellorizon fostered covert friendship and an economic interdependence that continues today. Many Greek-style buildings remain.

In ancient times (1200–600 BCE), Kas was known as Antiphellus, and it prospered because of trade in timber and sponges. A small amphitheater remains from this era. During the first and second centuries BCE, Antiphellus gained prominence as a safe harbor and an important city in the Lycian federation. More recently Kas was called Andifli, but until the advent of tourism in the 1960s it remained virtually landlocked by the Taurus Mountains. With the advent of tourism in the 1960s, a coastal road was built, making the town accessible for vehicles and ending centuries of dependence on sea trade.

The town has an abundance of pensions and hotels established by villagers who abandoned rural agriculture for tourism. But tourism has scarcely encroached on traditions like weddings, sacrifice holidays, or the custom of salting babies soon after birth, a practice believed to ward off evil.

*Suzanne Swan*

**Further Reading**

Bean, George E. (1978) *Lycian Turkey*. London: John Murray.

Clow, Kate. (2000) *The Lycian Way*. Istanbul: Garanti Bank.

**KATHMANDU** (2002 pop. 713,000). Built in 723 CE by King Gun Kamdev and the Newar peoples, Kathmandu, located in the southern Himalayas at an altitude of 1,220 meters (4,000 feet) near the Baghmanti and Vishumanti rivers, is the capital city of Nepal. Legend has it that the site was originally a lake that was made habitable when Manjusheree cut open the channel to south Chovar and let the water flow out of the lake. The original inhabitants, the Newars, are thought to be the descendants of several different ethnic groups.

During the seventeenth century, small city-states occupied the valley, and Nepal was an important trading

Durbar Square in Kathmandu in 1996. (STEPHEN G. DONALDSON PHOTOGRAPHY)

link between Tibet and the north Indian plains. The city's finest temples and palaces were built during the reign of the Malla kings in the seventeenth and eighteenth centuries. The city-states were unified in 1768 by Gorkha King Prithvi Narayan Shah when he captured Kathmandu and made it the capital. The shah closed the borders to the country in 1816, and the country remained isolated until the mid-twentieth century.

Places of interest in Kathmandu include the Freak Street area, which also is known as Jochne, but which received the name Freak Street from the hippie culture of the 1960s and 1970s, when travelers were in search of spiritual enlightenment. Durbar Square is located in the old Kathmandu area, with numerous temples and shrines. Located there is the Kasthamandap, the oldest building in the valley, supposedly built around the twelfth century. The Great Bell to ward off evil spirits, the Taleju Temple, the Jaganath Temple, and the Kala Bhairab are also located in Durbar Square. Another area of interest is the Hanuman Dhoka (Old Royal Palace).

*Stacey Fox*

### Further Reading


Gellner, David G., and Dedan Quigley, eds. (1999) *Contested Hierarchies: A Collaborative Ethnography of Caste among the Newars of the Kathmandu Valley, Nepal.* Oxford: Oxford University Press.

Vergati, Anne. (1995) *Gods, Men, and Territory: Society and Culture in Kathmandu Valley.* Columbia, MO: South Asia Books.


**KATHMANDU VALLEY** (2002 est. pop. 1.5 million). The Kathmandu valley, the site of modern-day Nepal's national capital, has long been among the most important administrative, economic, agricultural, and cultural centers in the Himalayan region. Lying at an elevation of approximately 1,350 meters, the valley is located in Nepal's middle hills, surrounded by peaks averaging 2,400 meters. Known for its deep alluvial soils deposited by a long-vanished lake, the Kathmandu valley has historically been one of the most productive agricultural regions of South Asia and one of the most densely populated areas in the Himalayas.

The Kathmandu valley rose to regional prominence mainly because of its role as an important entrepôt in the trans-Himalayan trade linking the Tibetan plateau and East Asia with the civilizations of the South Asian lowlands. In the Kathmandu valley, two of the most important trade routes from Tibet converged, and principal cities emerged at key points along these ancient transit corridors. Trade brought the valley great wealth, making it a center for architectural, religious, and artistic achievement.

## KATHMANDU VALLEY—WORLD HERITAGE SITE

Several religious monuments and classic royal buildings in the Kathmandu Valley were designated as World Heritage Sites in 1979 in recognition of their immense historical significance to the several cultures converging in Nepal.

### Early History

Details of the valley's prehistory remain obscure, but linguistic evidence suggests that the valley was settled by the ancestors of people who later became known as Newars. The historical record begins with Sanskrit inscriptions left by an Aryan Licchavi dynasty that occupied the valley in the fourth century CE and that ruled until the late ninth century. A range of Hindu and Buddhist sects flourished during Licchavi times, all of which benefited from royal patronage. Most of the Kathmandu valley's main religious structures are built on Licchavi foundations. Following the decline of Licchavi power, the Kathmandu valley went through several centuries of unstable political rule, punctuated by devastating raids by powers from neighboring Himalayan regions as well as from the northern Gangetic plain.

### The Malla Dynasty

The next major era began in the thirteenth century, with the establishment of several lines of Hindu kings adopting the honorific title "Malla." Once again, the Kathmandu valley was the seat of a prosperous, powerful state that rebuilt religious structures, strengthened administrative systems, and patronized the arts. After 1482, the unified Malla kingdom splintered into three antagonistic ministates, based in the valley's three primary cities of Patan, Bhaktapur, and Kathmandu. During the Malla era, Sanskrit gave way to Newari, still the vernacular of the Kathmandu valley, as the language of the court. Although all of the Malla kings were devotees of the valley's principal Hindu deity, Siva Pasupati, they also continued to patronize Buddhist shrines.

From the sixteenth century onward, each of the valley's city-states became not just a walled fortress but also a center for conspicuous patronage of temples, festivals, institutions, and artisans. Each Malla ruler sought to outdo his valley rivals in the grandeur of his palaces, religious ceremonies, temples, and public facilities such as water tanks. Almost all of the remaining traditional structures in each of the three cities' central Durbar Squares—along with the stunning examples of Newar craftsmanship in stone, metal, and wood—date from the Malla era. The art of metallurgy, already developed during Licchavi times, reached its pinnacle during the fourteenth and fifteenth centuries, with demand for Nepali cast bronze statuary and other ritual objects from as far away as China. But the competition that left a rich cultural legacy also served to make the Kathmandu valley desirable to outsiders and vulnerable to attack.

### The Shah Kings and the Rana Era

In 1744, Prithvi Narayan Shah (1722–1775), king of Gorkha—a small hill state west of the Kathmandu valley—captured a strategic hilltop fortress guarding the northern route into the valley, thereby setting in motion a decades-long war that ended with conquest of the Kathmandu valley. Gorkhali forces encircled the valley, played one Malla king off against another, and cut off trade and supply routes; in 1768, the Gorkhali forces finally stormed Kathmandu on the night of the annual Indrajatra festival when the walls were undefended. Prithvi Narayan Shah took control of the other cities in the valley, and he (and his successors) went on to conquer large parts of the central Himalayas, thereby establishing the modern state of Nepal, with Kathmandu as its capital.

The Shah kings gradually fell under the control of other powerful families in the Gorkhali court, eventually becoming mere figureheads. In 1846, Jung Bahadur Kunwar (1817–1877) seized control of the court at Kathmandu, declared himself and his offspring to be hereditary prime ministers, and claimed the honorific title of Rana. It was during the Rana era (1846–1951) that the Kathmandu valley most clearly began to realign itself with the shifting regional political economy. After the British conquest of India was complete, Nepal found itself on the periphery of a world imperial power.

Whereas earlier artistic and architectural practices had incorporated foreign influences into local traditions, during the Rana era, elites favored the wholesale importation of European styles and lifestyles. The Ranas eagerly acquired all the accoutrements of a Western-elite lifestyle—including the enormous European-style palaces that still dot the valley—even while prohibiting commoners from any contact with foreigners or foreign goods. During the Rana era, the gap between rulers and ruled became a chasm, severe travel restrictions were put in place, and the Kathmandu valley became virtually isolated from the rest of the world.

In 1951, Nepali nationalists overthrew the Rana regime, reinstated the Shah king, and initiated a series of experiments in democratic governance that continue to the present. Since 1951, the Kathmandu valley has become a regional center for international communications, foreign imports, and, since the 1970s, a popular tourist destination. In addition to government offices, the valley is also home to most of Nepal's institutions of higher education, international and local nongovernmental organizations, and media enterprises. Handmade carpets (developed originally in the Tibetan refugee community) and garments are the valley's main export industries. Today, the valley residents must contend with serious air- and water-pollution problems, suburban sprawl, and severely overburdened electrical, sewage, road, and water-supply systems.

*Mark Liechty*

### Further Reading

Slusser, Mary Shepherd. (1982) *Nepal Mandala: A Cultural Study of the Kathmandu Valley*. Princeton, NJ: Princeton University Press.

Stiller, Ludwig F. (1993) *Nepal: Growth of a Nation*. Kathmandu, Nepal: Human Resources Development Research Center.

**KATO TAKAAKI** (1860–1926), Japanese politician. Of samurai lineage from the Owari domain (present-day Aichi Prefecture), Kato Takaaki was one of imperial Japan's ablest diplomats and most powerful champions of parliamentary government. Graduating at the top of his class from Tokyo University, Kato joined Mitsubishi Enterprises in 1881 and at age twenty-three spent two years in London studying the shipping trade. In 1887, he entered the Foreign Ministry and became Japanese minister (1894–1899), then ambassador to London (1908–1912). As foreign minister (1900–1901, 1906, 1913, 1914–1915), he was Japan's most fervent supporter of the Anglo-Japanese alliance.

Kato orchestrated Japan's entrance into World War I and in 1915 presented China with a list of demands aimed at expanding Japanese continental privileges (the Twenty-One Demands). His greatest legacy, however, lies in his effort, as foreign minister, then prime minister (1924–1926), to shift the locus of policymaking from the extraconstitutional "elder statesmen" to the civilian cabinet. Under his leadership, the

Kenseikai Party (successor to the Doshikai, later renamed the Minseito) implemented universal male suffrage and army retrenchment (1925) and became the most powerful engine of social, political, and economic reform in interwar Japan.

*Frederick R. Dickinson*

**Further Reading**

Dickinson, Frederick R. (1999) *War and National Reinvention: Japan in the Great War, 1914–1919*. Cambridge, MA: Harvard University Press.

Duus, Peter. (1968) *Party Rivalry and Political Change in Taisho Japan*. Cambridge, MA: Harvard University Press.

**KAUTILYA** (flourished c. 300 BCE), Indian political author. Kautilya or Canakya is usually identified as the minister of the Emperor Candragupta Maurya (321–287 BCE). However, there have been reputable scholars who dated Kautilya's major work, the *Arthasastra* (if it is his), to around 300 CE, thus making it a work of the Gupta period (c. 320–c. 500 CE) rather than a Mauryan work. The book, a manual of practical politics, has often been compared to Machiavelli's *The Prince*. It covers numerous governmental and military topics: the education and discipline of princes, the qualifications of government ministers, the different kinds of spies, the regular duties of a king, the organization and superintendence of government departments, the administration and fortification of towns, regulation of prostitution, civil law, filling the king's treasury, salaries of government servants, seven elements of kingship, six lines of policy, vices of a king, calamities and disasters affecting the state, military campaigning, guilds and corporations, how to win wars, how to become popular in a conquered country, recipes for various mixtures (though not gunpowder) that might spread disease and aid in warfare, and a final description of Kautilya's plan of the work. It is written in Sanskrit and has many obscure technical terms, though in other respects its language is clear.

*Paul Hockings*

**Further Reading**

Kautilya. (1929) *Kautilya's Arthasastra*. Trans. by R. Shamasastry. Mysore, India: Wesleyan Mission Press.

**KAVERI RIVER** India's Kaveri or Cauvery River, 760 kilometers long, was originally called the Daksina Ganga, or "southern Ganges," and the whole of its course is holy to Hindus. It rises in Coorg District toward the southern end of the Western Ghats and flows across southern Karnataka and northern Tamil Nadu states in a southeasterly direction, to empty into the Bay of Bengal from a wide delta, which forms the richest agricultural land in Thanjavur District. Its chief mouth there, to the north, is called the Coleroon or Kolladam, and a second one to the south is Kaveri. The river is fed by a number of tributaries, including the Bavani, and is a major source of hydroelectric power.

Its drainage basin has been estimated at 71,740 square kilometers. In its tortuous course, the river creates three famous islands. One is Seringapatam, near Mysore City, the ruined capital of Tipu Sultan (1753–1799); a second is Sivasamudram, the site of an ancient city and the celebrated Falls of the Cauvery, a succession of rapids and broken cascades; and the third is Srirangam, 3 kilometers outside the city of Tirucciriappalli, the site of an important ancient temple dedicated to Vishnu. The only traditional form of navigation on the river was in basketwork coracles covered with buffalo hides. Ptolemy mentions the Kaveri River as Khaberos, and another ancient Sanskrit name was Ardhajahnavi.

*Paul Hockings*

**Further Reading**

Gough, Kathleen. (1981) *Rural Society in Southeast India*. Cambridge, MA: Cambridge University Press.

**KAWABATA YASUNARI** (1899–1972), Japanese novelist. Born the son of a doctor in Osaka, Japan, Kawabata Yasunari lost both parents, his grandmother with whom he lived, and a sister before he was nine, and then nursed his terminally ill grandfather. Determined early on to become a writer, Kawabata enrolled in the Japanese literature course at Tokyo Imperial University, where he came to the attention of well-known novelist Kikuchi Kan (1888–1948), who became his mentor. In the 1920s he helped to found the Shinkankaku-ha, or Neo-Sensationalist school, which went against the prevailing Realist trend in Japanese literature at that time and is characterized by unusual visual imagery and synesthesia.

Among Kawabata's most prominent works are "The Izu Dancer" ("Izu no odokiko," 1926), *Yukiguni* (*Snow Country*, 1948), *Senbazuru* (*Thousand Cranes*, 1951), *Meijin* (*The Master of Go*, 1954), and *Yama no oto* (*The Sound of the Mountain*, 1954). Kawabata constantly reworked even published pieces, later adding passages, and often leaving them incomplete. Characteristic of his works is a delicate balance between the human characters and the lyrically described natural background into which they seem constantly on the verge of disappearing. There is little in the way of plot or structure, but instead the works move from image to image, like the art of linked verse. Throughout his works is a preoccupation with death and loneliness and what he saw as the close relationship between beauty and sadness.

In 1968, he won the Nobel Prize for Literature. In 1972, Kawabata was found dead in a gas-filled apartment near his Kamakura home. It was generally assumed that he took his own life, although some close associates held it was an accident.

*James M. Vardaman, Jr.*

### Further Reading

Keene, Donald. (1984) *Dawn to the West: Japanese Literature of the Modern Era, Fiction.* New York: Holt, Rinehart and Winston.

Petersen, Gwen Boardman. (1979) *The Moon in the Water: Tanizaki, Kawabata and Mishima.* Honolulu, HI: University of Hawaii Press.

Ueda, Makoto. (1976) *Modern Japanese Writers and the Nature of Literature.* Stanford, CA: Stanford University Press.

**KAWASAKI** Kawasaki is a major Japanese manufacturer of ships, locomotives, railway cars, engines, aircraft, motorbikes, and missiles. In 1878, Kawasaki Shozo (1837–1912) founded the Kawasaki organization in Tsukiji in Tokyo as a shipyard. In 1881, the Kawasaki Hyogo shipyard was established in Hyogo, and in 1896 it was merged with the Tsukiji shipyard to form the Kawasaki Shipyard Corporation. The group adopted its present name in 1939 after expanding into the manufacture of locomotives, passenger coaches, freight cars, bridge girders, steel plates, and aircraft.

Kawasaki's production of freighters during World War II was augmented after the war by production of submarines and supertankers. After World War II, Allied Occupation authorities broke up Kawasaki. In 1950, the steel-making division was incorporated separately as the Kawasaki Steel Corporation. Kawasaki Dockyard merged in 1969 with two of its previous subsidiaries, Kawasaki Rolling Stock Manufacturing and Kawasaki Aircraft, to become Kawasaki Heavy Industries, a major corporation. Kawasaki remained until the 1970s one of Japan's leading shipbuilders. The company has constantly developed new technologies through the development and production of automated ships, the development of liquid natural gas (LNG) carriers, and future-oriented marine technologies.

*Nathalie Cavasin*

### Further Reading

Tsujimoto Yoshiaki. (2001) *Kobe wo kakeru: kawasaki shozo to matsukada kojiro* (Building Kobe: Shozo Kawasaki and Kojiro Matsukada). Kobe, Japan: Kobe Shimbun Publishing Center.

**KAYAH STATE** (2002 est. pop. 243,000). The Kayah (Karenni) State is the smallest ethnic minority state in Myanmar (Burma), but it has a unique history of independence. The inhabitants are predominantly ethnic Karen hill peoples. They take their collective name of Karenni from the largest subgroup, the Kayah, who were originally known as Karenni ("red" Karen) because of the color of their clothing. Other related subgroups include the Kayaw, Paku, Bre, Manu, and Kayan (Padaung), whose "long necked" women are famed for wearing brass coils around their necks. In valley areas, there are also many Shans, and modern-day immigration has brought in increasing numbers of Burmans and other nationalities.

The historic anomaly of the state began prior to British rule (1886–1948) when the local Karenni chieftains modeled their authority on the hereditary system of the neighboring Shan *Sawbwas* (princes). Subsequently, Karenni independence was recognized by both the British and Burman King Mindon in an 1875 treaty. As a result, the Karenni substates were never formally incorporated into British Burma.

At the British departure in 1948, the tradition of Karenni independence was recognized when the territory was granted the same political terms as Shan State with a similar right of secession after ten years. Armed conflict, however, began between the government and Karenni forces in August 1948, and this continued through the rest of the twentieth century and into the twenty-first. In 1951, the territory was renamed Kayah State by the government, and in 1959 the Karenni chiefs agreed to renounce their traditional powers as rulers.

Central government authority, however, has continued to be resisted. As a result of conflict, the present-day state is one of the poorest regions in Myanmar. Adjoining Thailand, Shan State, and Karen (Kayin) State, Kayah State is a mountainous territory with an area of 11,733 square kilometers, and it has few infrastructural links with its neighbors. The state is also dissected by two powerful rivers—the Salween and the Pun—making transportation difficult in many areas.

In the 1990s, the population was estimated by the government at 210,000 inhabitants, dwelling in six townships, but there has been considerable internal displacement during the fighting of past decades. Over ten thousand refugees have fled into Thailand.

The state's main produce is paddy. Other crops are grown in a variety of lowland and upland environments, including sesame, groundnut, fruits, and vegetables. Most economic investment by the government, however, has centered on Myanmar's largest hydroelectric power station at Lawpita, which is located west of the state capital, Loikaw. There are also marble mines near Loikaw, as well as wolfram, tin, and tungsten mines at Mawchi in the south of the state. Another important natural resource, the once abundant forest reserves—containing teak, pine, and a variety of other woods—were badly depleted by overlogging during the 1990s.

Armed opposition groups have impacted day-to-day affairs in the state. The largest force, the Karenni National Progressive Party (formed 1957), agreed upon a cease-fire with the government in 1995, but this broke down shortly afterward. In contrast, in the west of the state, the 1994 cease-fires by the rival Karenni State Nationalities Liberation Front (formed 1978) and allied Kayan New Land Party (formed 1964) both endured until the end of the twentieth century. Destruction and internal displacement, however, remained on a considerable scale within the state, which, in consequence, has some of the worst health, educational, and social indicators in any part of Myanmar.

*Martin Smith*

### Further Reading

Amnesty International. (1999) *Myanmar Aftermath: Three Years of Dislocation in the Kayah State*. London: Amnesty International.

Bamforth, Vicky, Steven Lanjouw, and Graham Mortimer. (2000) *Conflict and Displacement in Karenni: The Need for Considered Responses*. Chiang Mai, Thailand: Burma Ethnic Research Group.

Lehman, Frederick K. (1967) "Burma: Kayah Society as a Function of the Shan-Burman-Karen Context." In *Contemporary Change in Traditional Societies*, edited by J. Steward. Urbana: University of Illinois, 1–104.

Renard, Ronald. (1987) "The Delineation of the Kayah States Frontiers with Thailand: 1809–1894." *Journal of Southeast Asian Studies* 18, 1: 81–92.

Smith, Martin. (1999) *Burma: Insurgency and the Politics of Ethnicity*. 2d ed. London: Zed Books.

**KAYSONE PHOMVIHAN** (1920–1992), president of Laos. Kaysone was born in Savannakhet, the son of a Vietnamese civil servant father and Laotian mother. He studied law in Hanoi, where he became actively involved in the Viet Minh (Viet League, or fully, League for the Independence of Vietnam), an umbrella organization of Vietnamese Communists seeking independence from the French regime in Indochina (Laos had been a protectorate in the French Indochinese union since 1893). When the French returned to gain control of Laos following the Japanese occupation of the nation at the end of World War II, Kaysone fought to thwart their attempts but was unsuccessful.

Kaysone joined the Indochinese Communist Party in 1949 and became the defense minister of the Pathet Lao, or Lao Nation, a nationalist resistance movement. Kaysone assumed command of the Pathet Lao armed forces, precursor of the People's Liberation Army of Laos of which he later became commander, and waged guerrilla war to take control of Laos.

In 1953, Kaysone and Prince Souphanuvong (1909–1995) established northern Laos as the Pathet Lao stronghold and in 1955 formed the Lao People's Party, to which Kaysone was elected general secretary. In 1975 Kaysone became prime minister of Laos after the socialists gained control of the nation. As prime minister, he stressed the importance of leadership by the party and strict adherence to socialist doctrine. He strengthened Laotian ties with Vietnam and the Soviet Union while distancing the nation from the People's Republic of China. In the 1990s, after the breakup of the Soviet Union, Kaysone loosened restrictions on private ownership of land and the practice of Buddhism, promoted a market economy, and fostered cordial relations with China. Kaysone became president of the Lao People's Democratic Republic in 1991 and, following his death, remains revered by Lao citizens as a national hero.

*Linda S. McIntosh*

### Further Reading

*Kaysone Phomvihan: Revolution in Laos. Practice and Prospects.* (1981) Moscow: Progress Publishers.

Stuart-Fox, Martin. (1996) *Buddhist Kingdom, Marxist State: The Making of Modern Laos*. Bangkok, Thailand: White Lotus.

**KAZAK** The *Kazak* was a Kazakh-language newspaper published in Orenburg, Russia, between 1913 and 1918. After 1917 it became the principal organ of the Kazakh political party and the Kazakh autonomous government Alash Orda (The Horde of Alash). It first appeared on 2 February 1913 and continued as a weekly until 1915, when it was published twice a week. The initial print run was three thousand, but by 1916 it reached eight thousand, making it the most popular prerevolutionary Kazakh periodical. Subscribers included individuals from as far away as China and

Turkey. The editorial board included Akhmet Baitursynov (1873–1937), Mirzhaqyp Dulatov (1885–1935), Alikhan Bokeikhanov (1866–1937), and other well-known Kazakh writers, poets, and scholars.

*Kazak* focused its editorial attention on a variety of topics. Czarist colonization policies received significant attention, as did education and land, religious, and economic issues. In addition to the editors, the writer and social activist Zhusipbek Aimauytov (1889–1931), the scholar Mukhtar Auezov (1897–1961), and the writers Saken Seifullin (1894–1938), Maghzhan Zhumabaev (1893–1938), Sabit Donentaev (1894–1933), Sultanmakhmut Toraighyrov (1893–1920), Beiimbet Mailin (1894–1938), and Mustafa Shoqaev (1890–1940), leader of the Kokand autonomous government, wrote for the paper. *Kazak* also published articles advocating female emancipation and cessation of the bride-price, including articles by Nazipa Qulzhanova (1887–1934).

Following the February 1917 Russian Revolution *Kazak* became the official organ of Alash Orda, which opposed the Bolshevik seizure of power. It continued publication until its press was destroyed during the Russian civil war in September 1918.

*Steven Sabol*

### Further Reading

Bennigsen, Alexander, and Chantal Lemercier-Quelquejay. (1964) *La Presse et le Mouvement national chez les musulmans de Russie avant 1920.* Paris: Mouton.

Subkhanberdina, Ushkul-tai. (1993) *Qazaq, Alash, Saryarqa: Mazmundalghan bibliografiialyq korsetkish.* Almaty, Kazakhstan: Ghylym.

**KAZAKH UPLANDS** The region known as the Kazakh Uplands (Qazaqtyng Usaqshoqylyghy), or Kazakh Hillocky Country, is a plateau in eastern Kazakhstan between the Turanian Lowland to the west and the Altay Mountains to the east. The Ishim River, a major tributary of the Irtysh River, originates in the Kazakh Uplands and flows northwestward into the Irtysh and then north to join the Ob River in Siberia, eventually draining into the Arctic Ocean. The Nura River also flows through the Kazakh Uplands westward as it empties into Lake Tengiz in the central portion of the region.

The Kazakh Uplands represent the gradually eroded remains of a larger mountain chain in eastern Kazakhstan. Exposed rock layers have yielded a large amount of valuable raw materials for industrial use. It has developed as an important region for heavy industry based on large local coal and iron ore deposits. Several rare earth minerals, such as beryllium, molybdenum, antimony (used as alloys for strength and corrosion resistance), and uranium, are also found in the region. One of the largest copper deposits in the world is located near Dzhezkazgan in the western part of the Kazakh Uplands. Other large deposits of copper, lead, and zinc are found along the shoreline of Lake Balkhash in the southern part of the region.

*David R. Smith*

### Further Reading

Lydolph, Paul E. (1979) *Geography of the USSR: Topical Analysis.* Elkhart Lake, WI: Misty Valley Publishing.

**KAZAKHS** The Kazakhs are a central Asiatic Turkic people whose language belongs to the Kipchak group of the Altaic family. Most Kazakhs identify themselves as Sunni Muslims. According to a 1997 population estimate, approximately 9 million Kazakhs resided in the central Asiatic republic of Kazakhstan. In addition, there were about 1.1 million Kazakhs in China, 808,000 in Uzbekistan, 636,000 in Russia, 120,000 in Mongolia, 88,000 in Turkmenistan, 37,000 in Kyrgyzstan, 9,600 in Tajikistan, and 13,000 in other countries.

### Emergence of the Kazakhs

The Kazakhs emerged as a distinctive people in the fifteenth century. At the time, different parts of present-day Kazakhstan were controlled by Mongols, Uzbeks, and other Turco-Mongolian peoples. In the mid-fifteenth century, about 200,000 Uzbeks, dissatisfied with their leader, or khan, moved from an area of present-day Uzbekistan to an area between the Chu and Talas Rivers; before this time, the ancestors of this group had been converted to Islam by Sufi mystics who had spread Islam in central Asia. These separatist Uzbeks became known as Kazakh Uzbeks or "independent Uzbeks." They adopted a nomadic pastoral way of life, in contrast to the sedentary farming of their Uzbek forebears. In the late fifteenth and early sixteenth centuries, these people, now known simply as Kazakhs, formed a confederation called the Kazakh Horde, which controlled much of the steppe region.

The Kazakh pastoral nomads dwelled year round in portable, dome-shaped tents called yurts, with felt coverings over wooden frames that could be taken apart and reassembled after a move. They migrated seasonally to find pasturage for their livestock, which included horses, sheep, goats, cattle, and camels. They

Kazakh men riding horses in 1983 near Urumqi, Xinjiang Province, China. (CARL & ANN PURCELL/CORBIS)

lived primarily off their herds and especially savored fermented mare's milk *(koumiss)* and horse flesh.

The Kazakhs originally organized themselves into hordes *(ordas)* that were subdivided into tribes, clans, and lineages. Groups at various levels in the tribal hierarchy had chiefs or khans, but only rarely were all Kazakhs, or even one of their hordes, united under a single khan. Descent and membership in lineages and clans were traced patrilineally. Lineages and clans were subdivided into smaller camping groups that consisted of several extended families each. These families usually included parents, unmarried children, and married sons and their families.

**Russian and Soviet Periods**

The Russian advance onto the Kazakh steppe began in the early eighteenth century, and by 1848 Russia had taken control of the area. During the nineteenth century, as part of Russia's colonization program, about 400,000 Russians flooded into Kazakhstan to convert steppe pastures into farmland. In the early twentieth century, approximately a million Slavs, Germans, Jews, and others also immigrated to the region. These immigrants crowded Kazakhs off the best pastures and watered lands, rendering many tribes destitute.

On 26 August 1920, the Soviet government established the Kirgiz Autonomous Republic, which in 1925 changed its name to Kazakh Autonomous Soviet Socialist Republic. From 1927, the Soviet government pursued a vigorous policy of transforming the Kazakh pastoral nomads into a sedentary population. The Soviet regime's brutal imposition of collective farming on the traditionally pastoral nomadic Kazakhs resulted in a marked decrease in the Kazakh population. Between 1926 and 1939, more than 1.5 million Kazakhs died, mostly from starvation, disease, and violence. About 300,000 Kazakhs fled to Uzbekistan, 44,000 to Turkmenistan, and thousands to China. In addition, Stalin's purges destroyed much of the Kazakh intelligentsia. Another large influx of Slavs into Kazakhstan occurred from 1954 to 1956 as a result of the Soviet so-called Virgin and Idle Lands project, which opened up the vast grasslands of northern Kazakhstan to wheat farming. The Soviet Union also located its space-launch center and a substantial part of its nuclear-weaponry and nuclear-testing sites in Kazakhstan.

**Post-Soviet Period**

Kazakhstan declared its independence from the Soviet Union on 16 December 1991. In the early years of independence, significant numbers of ethnic Russians left Kazakhstan by emigrating to Russia, and many diaspora Kazakhs immigrated to Kazakhstan. Even by the mid-1990s, Kazakhs made up only 45 percent of their country's total population. By 1995, Kazakhs constituted about half the population of Almaty, the country's largest city and, until 1997, its capital.

Today, about three-fifths of Kazakh families live in rural areas. Most Kazakhs are settled farmers who still recognize membership in larger kin groupings based on patrilineal descent. In Xinjiang in northwest China, many Kazakhs still follow the nomadic way of life. Urbanization in Kazakhstan has resulted more from the immigration of foreigners than from the influx of Kazakhs into the cities from the countryside.

During much of their long nomadic period, the Kazakhs' adherence to Islam remained rather lax and informal. However, some young Kazakhs had studied Islamic theology in religious schools, known as *maktab*s or *madrasah*s, in the larger towns and cities. Consequently, there was an Islamic intelligentsia in the urban areas before the Soviet Communists took over in the early 1920s. Thereafter, Soviet authorities actively suppressed and discouraged religious teaching and practice in Kazakhstan. Since independence, Kazakhs have enjoyed freedom of religion, and there has been a religious revival.

Urban Kazakhs of both sexes dress in modern, Western clothing, while women and some men in rural villages continue to wear traditional costume. Some Kazakhs weave traditional carpets for home use and sale, and less-Russified Kazakhs often decorate their homes with *qoshma*s, bright-colored felt rugs.

Kazakhs, probably more than any other Central Asian people, show the impact of nearly two centuries of close contact with Russians. Unlike those Central Asians to the south of them, Kazakhs look more to Russia than to Islamic countries for inspiration in the post-Soviet period. Despite this, Kazakh scholars and intellectuals are actively working to reclaim Kazakh traditions and distinctive ways of life, including the literary and spoken language of a people whose experience has been greatly influenced by Russian culture, literature, language, and thought.

Oral epics formed the main literary genre among the largely illiterate Kazakhs until the nineteenth century. In the eighteenth century, the Russians established a series of outposts along the border of the Kazakh northern steppe. As a consequence of Russian contacts, some Kazakhs added written, poetic forms to their literature. Poetry remained the primary genre until prose stories, short novels, and drama were introduced in the early twentieth century, before the end of the czarist era in 1917. Today, urban Kazakhs can enjoy modern theaters that offer Uighur, Korean, and Russian musicals, opera, ballet, and puppet performances. They also enjoy cinemas and can participate in dance ensembles and music groups.

*Paul J. Magnarella*

**Further Reading**

Capisani, Giampaolo R. (2000) *The Handbook of Central Asia: A Comprehensive Survey of the New Republics*. London: I. B. Tauris.

Demko, George J. (1969) *The Russian Colonization of Kazakhstan, 1896–1916*. Bloomington, IN: Indiana University Press.

Olcott, Martha Brill. (1995) *The Kazakhs*. 2d ed. Stanford, CA: Hoover Institution Press.

Svanberg, Ingvar, ed. (1999) *Contemporary Kazaks: Cultural and Social Perspectives*. New York: St. Martin's Press.

**KAZAKHSTAN—PROFILE** (2001 est. pop. 16.7 million). Situated in central Asia, Kazakhstan, at 2,717,300 square kilometers, is the second largest of the Commonwealth of Independent States (CIS), the association of former Soviet states. It shares borders to the north and on the west with the Russian Federation, on the east with China, and on the south with Kyrgyzstan, Turkmenistan, and Uzbekistan. The Kazakhs are the largest of the country's 126 ethnic groups, accounting for 51 percent of the population, followed by Russians (32 percent), Ukrainians (4.5 percent), Germans, Uzbeks, Tatars, and others. The relative weight of the Kazakh ethnic group has increased since the country's independence, mainly due to the emigration of non-Kazakhs and the return of many ethnic Kazakhs to the country. Historically, Kazakhstan belongs to the Turkic-speaking world.

### Geography

The climate of Kazakhstan is sharply continental. Average temperature in January varies between –19° and –4°C, while the average July temperature fluctuates between 19° and 26°C.

The largest of the country's 8,500 rivers are the Ural and the Emba, which flow into the Caspian Sea; the Syr Dar'ya, which flows into the Aral Sea; and the Irtysh, Ishim, and Tobol, which all run across the republic to eventually reach the Arctic Ocean. The largest of its many lakes are the Aral Sea, Balkhash, Zaysan, Alakol, Tengiz, and Seletengiz. Kazakhstan shares the larger portion (2,340 kilometers) of the northern and half of the eastern Caspian seacoast.

Steppes comprise 26 percent of the territory of Kazakhstan. Deserts (44 percent) and semideserts (14 percent) cover 167 million hectares, and forests occupy 21 million hectares.

### Resources

The country is rich in minerals. The Tengiz oil field ranks as one of the largest in the world. Kazakhstan also has the world's second-largest deposit of

## KAZAKHSTAN

**Country name:** Republic of Kazakhstan
**Area:** 2,717,300 sq km
**Population:** 16,731,303 (July 2001 est.)
**Population growth rate:** 0.03% (2001 est.)
**Birth rate:** 17.3 births/1,000 population (2001 est.)
**Death rate:** 10.61 deaths/1,000 population (2001 est.)
**Net migration rate:** –6.43 migrant(s)/1,000 population (2001 est.)
**Sex ratio:** 0.93 male(s)/female (2001 est.)
**Infant mortality rate:** 59.17 deaths/1,000 live births (2001 est.)
**Life expectancy at birth—total population:** 63.29 years; male: 57.87 years; female: 68.97 years (2001 est.)
**Major religions:** Muslim, Russian Orthodox
**Major languages:** Kazakh (Qazaq, state language), Russian (official, used in everyday business)
**Literacy—total population:** 98%; male: 99%; female: 96% (1989 est.)
**Government type:** Republic
**Capital:** Astana; the government moved from Almaty to Astana in December 1998
**Administrative divisions:** 14 oblystar and 3 cities
**Independence:** 16 December 1991 (from the Soviet Union)
**National holiday:** Republic Day, 25 October (1990)
**Suffrage:** 18 years of age; universal
**GDP—real growth rate:** 10.5% (2000 est.)
**GDP—per capita (purchasing power parity):** $5,000 (2000 est.)
**Population below poverty line:** 35% (1999 est.)
**Exports:** $8.8 billion (f.o.b., 2000 est.)
**Imports:** $6.9 billion (f.o.b., 2000 est.)
**Currency:** Tenge (KZT)

*Source:* Central Intelligence Agency. (2001) *The World Book Factbook 2001.* Retrieved 5 March 2002, from: http://www.cia.gov/cia/publications/factbook.

phosphorite, and the phosphorite deposits of Zhanatas and Karatau are notable for their depth and quality. The republic is one of the greatest producers of aluminum in the world, and has an abundance of copper ore, salt, and construction materials.

### Political Structure

Nursultan Nazarbayev (b. 1940) was elected president in April 1990. On 1 December 1991, after the collapse of the Soviet Union, he was reconfirmed as president by nationwide ballot in newly independent Kazakhstan.

The constitution provides for a tripartite structure of government with power divided between the executive, legislative, and judicial branches. It establishes and sets out the powers and functions of the president, the parliament, the constitutional council, and local government and administration, and establishes an independent judicial system.

The political structure comprises the president (who is head of state); numerous presidential advisory bodies that focus on such areas as national policy, mass media, family and women, and human rights; and Parliament, consisting of the Senate and the Majlis. The republic has an array of political parties.

### History

Formed from different tribes, the Kazakhs were mainly pastoral nomads until the twentieth century. Russian influence in the region began in the sixteenth

century, when Cossacks settled along the Ural River in the west of the country. In the eighteenth century the Russian government sent large numbers of Russian peasants to the Kazakh territory. In 1866 the garrison town of Verny (now Almaty) was founded under Russian administration.

During the Soviet regime, Kazakhstan became the Kazakh Soviet Socialist Republic. The style of life changed dramatically during the period of collectivization and industrialization. Forced collectivization brought mass repression. Nearly 700,000 families died during that period.

During World War II, many people—including Russians, Ukrainians, Germans, and Tatars—were moved from the western USSR to Kazakhstan. This migration initiated the industrialization of Kazakhstan.

In the 1950s the Virgin Lands Project, designed to expand the use of Kazakhstan's vast territory, was implemented in northern Kazakhstan by the Soviet government. This brought thousands of people to Kazakhstan.

From 1959 to 1986 Dinmukhamed Kunaev (1912–1993) was first secretary of the Communist Party of Kazakhstan. His rule was controversial and mixed. His achievement was the direction of a high level of capital investment to the republic, which he was able to accomplish partly because he was a close friend of Leonid Brezhnev (1906–1982). He divided managerial positions between Russians (industry) and Kazakhs (agriculture). Under Kunaev's authority the republic achieved its most prosperous results.

In 1986 Kunaev was criticized for failing to meet economic goals by Mikhail Gorbachev (b. 1931), who at that time was general secretary of the Communist Party of the Soviet Union. Kunaev was replaced by Gennadiy Kolbin (1927–1998), who had previously held the post of first secretary of the Communist Party in Ul'yanovsk Oblast (in Russia). Many Kazakhs disagreed with Moscow's decision and demonstrated in Almaty. As a protégé of the central administration, Kolbin tried to keep reforms in the republic moving in the same direction as in the USSR as a whole.

In 1989 Nursultan Nazarbayev was appointed first secretary of the Communist Party of Kazakhstan. In March 1991 a referendum passed that favored preserving the USSR, but the coup in August destroyed any hope of saving the USSR as a country. The Republic of Kazakhstan formally became independent on 16 December 1991. It is a signatory to the agreement putting a formal end to the Soviet Union and creating the Commonwealth of Independent States.

**International Organizations and International Relations**

Kazakhstan has established diplomatic relations with over 120 countries. It is a full member of the United Nations, the International Monetary Fund, the International Bank for Reconstruction and Development, the United Nations Educational, Scientific and Cultural Organization (UNESCO), the International Atomic Energy Agency, the European Bank for Reconstruction and Development, the Asian Development Bank, the International Finance Organization, and the Islamic Development Bank. Kazakhstan has the status of an observer with the World Trade Organization.

*Yelena Kalyuzhnova*

**Further Reading**

Akiner, Shirin. (1997) *The Formation of Kazakh Identity: From Tribe to Nation-State*. London: The Royal Institute of International Affairs.

Kalyuzhnova, Yelena. (1998) *The Kazakstani Economy: Independence and Transition*. Basingstoke, U.K.: Macmillan.

Olcott, Martha Brill. (1995) *The Kazakhs*, 2d ed. Stanford, CA: Hoover Institution Press.

Pomfret, Richard. (1995) *The Economies of Central Asia*. Princeton, NJ: Princeton University Press.

## KAZAKHSTAN—ECONOMIC SYSTEM

Before 1991 Kazakhstan was part of the Soviet economic system, and its development was defined by the Union's needs, as was the case for the economies of all the republics constituting the Soviet Union. In accordance with the Union's labor specialization, only a few sectors (perhaps even just parts of sectors) of Kazakhstan's economy were relatively developed, namely, coal-production centers in the Karaganda and Yekibaztus areas, oil-production facilities at Emba, and copper mining at Balkhash and Karsakpau. For the Soviet economy Kazakhstan represented the single source of raw materials such as copper, zinc, chrome, and rare metal deposits. Kazakhstan was the second-largest oil producer in the Soviet Union, with the major oil fields of Tengiz (north Caspian Sea), Karachaganak (northwest Kazakhstan), Uzen (Manghystau region), Kumkol (central Kazakhstan), and Zhanazhol (near Aktyubinsk), as well as three major refineries.

The industrial sector was based on raw materials, but manufacturing production did not receive adequate development. Kazakhstan was heavily dependent on the other former republics of the Soviet Union, especially Russia.

From 1954 the Virgin Lands project (Northern Kazakhstan) was implemented; this project defined Kazakhstan's role as a main producer of grain (about one-fifth of the Soviet Union's grain). Kazakhstan was to specialize in grain and other crops, such as vegetables and potatoes.

Nevertheless, under Soviet rule, Kazakhstan gained significantly in human development and social conditions: whereas before the Soviet era few people received education through the secondary-school level, nearly all people did by the end of the Soviet era, for example. Kazakhstan's industrial sector and infrastructure benefited from Soviet investments.

**The New National Economy**

Since independence in 1991, Kazakhstan has begun a painful economic transformation. The gross domestic product (GDP) fell almost 50 percent from 1991 to 1995. For nearly two years Kazakhstan was unable to conduct its own monetary policy, remaining in a monetary union with Russia under the supervision of the powerful Central Bank in Moscow. Price liberalization (decontrol of prices and liberalization of domestic trade) paralyzed the Kazakstani economy, and hyperinflation created a cash shortage.

On 15 November 1993 the new national currency (the tenge) was introduced, but it was rapidly devalued after three weeks. The nonconvertibility of the tenge pushed Kazakstani enterprises to pay their former union partners in hard currency (such as U.S. dollars), which caused difficulties with the calculations of the value of deliveries between enterprises. As a result barter was expanded, interenterprise arrears were increased (as enterprises were unable to pay the businesses they owed money to because they themselves were waiting for payment), and output continued to decline. The economic crisis worsened in 1994, characterized by hyperinflation and a further collapse in output in the industrial and other sectors of the economy. In 1994, only 3 percent of a total industrial decline of 28.5 percent was connected to the narrowing sales market; the other 25.5 percent resulted from financial problems. In the same year, 26 percent of the rise in Kazakstani prices was caused by interenterprise arrears: Knowing that payments owed them were not forthcoming, enterprises required eventual payment in hard currency, which kept on rising in value in comparison to the tenge, thereby generating a price increase. By the first half of 1995, more than 54 percent of the rise in Kazakstani prices was caused by interenterprise arrears. Since the end of 1994 the National Bank of Kazakhstan has adopted a tight monetary policy.

After independence, following the unraveling of its existing trade links with other former Soviet republics,

Kazakhstan began to look for new international markets. Traditionally Kazakstani exports included raw materials, light industrial goods, machinery, and chemical products. From the former Soviet Union, Kazakhstan imported machinery and metal products, oil and gas, light industrial goods, and food. In the first years of independence Kazakhstan focused on the development of the oil and gas sector, which quickly became a major export item. In 1993 the Kazakstani trade deficit reached $615.6 million, four times higher than the previous year.

The economy needed a coherent strategy that would be able to prevent economic turmoil. The problem with all of the Kazakstani anticrisis programs of that time was the nation's unclear economic position and the absence of concrete aims for reform. The first years of the economic transition in Kazakhstan were also plagued by objective difficulties, such as the nation's dependence on members of the Commonwealth of Independent States (CIS; the confederation of former Soviet nations) and the fact that extraction of raw materials was the dominant industrial sector.

### Structural Reforms and Present Economic Performance

The Kazakstani government began privatization upon independence in 1991. The main challenge of this process was the interlocking of political and economic aspects. Privatization included three major steps: housing privatization (whereby government-owned housing was put up for sale), mass privatisation (whereby government-owned businesses were put up for sale), and privatization on the basis of individual projects. The most dominant method of privatizing state enterprises in industry, construction, transportation, and wholesale trade was the creation of joint-stock companies of both open and closed types. In some cases enterprises were purchased for speculative resale, using fluctuations in both the rate of exchange and the growing monthly rate of inflation. Corporate governance in many newly privatized enterprises remains weak. The privatization process is nearly complete; the government has now sold most of what it wanted to sell. Privatization revenue (revenue earned from the sale of state enterprises) was tenge 35.9 billion in 1999 (compared with tenge 50 billion in 1998).

The decline in output has been constant since 1991. Sectors such as chemicals, petrochemicals, food, and light industries began to disappear, and the industrial structure grew worse. From 1990 to 1997, production of various types of manufactured goods that are basic either as consumer goods or as industrial inputs were virtually eliminated. A decade of transition has eliminated much of the industrial base and left an economy dependent upon the exploitation of raw materials (especially oil), agriculture, and, to a lesser extent, food processing. Far from diversifying, the economy has become more dependent upon just a few sectors. Its risk exposure has thus increased, because its terms of trade are more vulnerable to price fluctuations in global oil and raw-materials markets. In short, a decade of transition has left Kazakhstan with many of the features of a resource-dependent economy. In the raw material sectors the situation is more positive, but the Asian and Russian financial crises (1997 and 1998, respectively) pushed Kazakhstan into recession and led to massive tax losses, as enterprises that were not working or were producing very little had little revenue from which to pay taxes.

When oil prices declined dramatically in 1998, the government decided to increase its emphasis on domestic processing of the country's mineral resources and particularly to stress the importance of finished-goods exports. A new industrial policy included light and chemical industries and mechanical engineering as major priorities.

The development of the banking sector in Kazakhstan has been impressive in comparison with other countries of the former Soviet Union. The Central Bank has managed to slow inflation through tight monetary policy and has tried to supervise the work of commercial banks as well as to create some measures for stimulation of small and medium businesses, including microcredits (microloans), credits for agriculture, and so on.

The security market is still rudimentary but it is the most advanced in the Central Asian region; Kazakhstan was the first country of the former Soviet Union to issue international bonds. In 1998 Kazakhstan embraced an ambitious pension reform dominated by a mandatory, privately managed pension scheme, the results of which remain to be seen.

In the late 1990s, Kazakhstan experienced a steady decline in the standard of living and a falling birth rate. However, from the end of 1999 Kazakhstan began to move out of economic crisis. The GDP grew because of the growth of world prices for oil and nonferrous metals, the devaluation of the tenge, and bumper crops of cereals. Agriculture, which has been badly affected by privatization, is important for the future of Kazakhstan due to the nation's sociodemographic structure (43 percent of the population is located in rural areas) and national traditions (many of the peoples of Kazakhstan were formerly nomadic). The rich harvest of 1999 played a crucial role in the fact that the GDP rose by

1.7 percent. However, the Kazakstani economy remains vulnerable to commodity-price fluctuation.

*Yelena Kalyuzhnova*

**Further Reading**

Kalyuzhnova, Yelena. (1998) *The Kazakhstani Economy: Independence and Transition.* Basingstoke, U.K.: Macmillan.

———. (1999) "An Assessment of Industrial Policy and Employment Prospects in Central Asia." In *Central Asia 2010: Prospects of Human Development.* New York: UNDP, 96–109.

Kalyuzhnova, Yelena, and Dov Lynch, eds. (2000) *The Euro-Asian World: A Period of Transition.* Basingstoke, U.K.: Macmillan.

Kaser, Michael. (1997) "The Central Asian Economies." In *Economic Survey of Europe, 1996–1997.* Geneva, Switzerland: ECE/UN, 179–209.

———. (1997) *The Economies of Kazakhstan and Uzbekistan.* London: Royal Institute of International Affairs.

Pomfret, Richard. (1995) *The Economies of Central Asia.* Princeton, NJ: Princeton University Press.

## KAZAKHSTAN—EDUCATION SYSTEM

The education system in Kazakhstan was strongly influenced by the Russian and Soviet education systems. In the late nineteenth and early twentieth centuries, the czarist government attempted to Westernize the Kazakh education system by sponsoring Russian-language schools and gymnasiums and encouraging the Kazakh elite to study at Russian universities. Yet a majority of ordinary people studied at local *maktabs* and *madrasahs*, where religious subjects were an important part of the curriculum. According to various estimates, at the beginning of the twentieth century the literacy rate stood at about 9 to 14 percent among the male ethnic Kazakhs and below 5 percent among the female ethnic Kazakhs. Since the early 1920s the Soviet government sponsored a free system of general and tertiary education that emphasized sciences,mathematics, and practical skills. Mass illiteracy in the republic was eradicated in the 1930s. In 1929, the alphabet of the written Kazakh language had been changed from Arabic to Latin; in 1940, it was changed from Latin to the Cyrillic script. In the 1970s and 1980s, Kazakhstan was able to maintain its literacy rate at about 98 percent, but could not catch up with the information technologies. In the 1980s, practically no schools in Kazakhstan had computers or access to computer technologies.

After the dissolution of the Soviet Union in 1991, there were three major changes in the education system of Kazakhstan. First, using the Kazakh language as the medium of instruction was increasingly emphasized. Second, there were significant cuts in the state funding of education. Third, the country made several attempts to reform the education system to meet economic changes and shifting labor market demands.

A young boy studies in a Kazakhstan classroom in 1996. (JON SPAULL/CORBIS)

The constitution of Kazakhstan (1995) stipulates that general education is mandatory and free, and that citizens have the right to receive a free tertiary education on a competitive basis. According to the constitution, the state sets uniform compulsory standards in education, as the Ministry of Education has to approve curriculum, textbooks, budgets, and so forth. This effectively put all public and privately funded education institutions under state control. Kazakh and Russian are the major languages of instruction, but the state provides support for education in other languages for ethnic minority groups (for example, Uzbeks, Germans). The constitution also stipulates separation of church and state, and no religious education is allowed in public schools.

At the age of three, children usually begin kindergarten, where they receive some basic reading and mathematics skills. At the age of seven, they begin an eleven-year compulsory education program, a primary four-year cycle, and a secondary seven-year cycle. The official figures for 1999 listed about 1,900 preschool establishments attended by 185,000 children. Approximately 8,280 elementary and secondary schools were attended by more than 3.1 million students. In addition, there were 244 specialized secondary schools (about 222,000 students), 131 gymnasiums and 85 lyceums (both are specialized elite schools), 62 evening schools, and 21 training centers. Approximately 85 percent of children of the relevant age group are enrolled in the secondary schools.

After completing secondary schooling, students may enter tertiary education institutions (universities and institutes), which usually offer five-year programs. Most of the education at the tertiary level is conducted in Kazakh or Russian, although throughout the 1990s there were some attempts to introduce English as a medium of instruction at some universities or at least at some faculties in major universities. According to the official statistics, in 1999 there were 132 tertiary education institutions, including 59 that were state-owned, attended by approximately 260,000 students, and 73 private institutions, attended by approximately 60,000 students. Private universities and some state-owned universities charge between $500 and $1,000 per academic year (2000–2001 academic year estimates).

After completing a five-year program, students may apply for a three-year *aspirantura* (postgraduate studies program), which combines course work and a dissertation. Upon completion of the *aspirantura*, students get the degree of *kandidat nauk* (equivalent to a master's degree). To receive a doctorate, students must have practical experience in the field (teaching or research) and complete an additional three- to five-year program.

During the 1990s, the education system in Kazakhstan experienced a serious crisis, as state funding dwindled, along with the quality and prestige of higher education. The Kazakh government has tried to reform the education system, emphasizing computerization, supporting private investment in educational institutions, and encouraging the introduction of new courses, which are in demand in Kazakhstan. Recently, the possible introduction of a U.S.-style credit system in some private universities has been under discussion.

*Rafis Abazov*

### Further Reading

Gurevich, L. (1999) *Sistemnye reformy vysshego obrazovaniia v Kazakhstane: Istoricheskie uroki v svete mirovogo opyta* (Systematic Reforms of Higher Education in Kazakhstan: Historical Lessons in the Context of International Experience). Almaty, Kazakhstan: Ekonomika.

Kusherbaev, K., ed. (1998) *Strategiia razvitiia vysshego obrazovaniia v Respublike Kazakhstan* (The Strategy of Development of Higher Education in the Republic of Kazakhstan). Almaty, Kazakhstan: Bilim.

Mamyrov, N. (1998) *Problemy razvitiia ekonomiki i obrazovaniia v Kazakhstane* (The Problems of Development in Economy and Education in Kazakhstan). Almaty, Kazakhstan: Daulr.

Sabdenov, O. (1994) *Nauka, obrazovanie, rynochnaia ekonomika* (Science, Education, Market Economy). Almaty, Kazakhstan: Bilim.

United Nations Development Programme. (1999) *Kazakhstan: Human Development Report, 1999*. Almaty, Kazakhstan: United Nations Development Programme.

UNESCO. (1999) *Monitoring Learning Achievements: Primary School Survey, May–June 1999*. Almaty, Kazakhstan: UNESCO.

## KAZAKHSTAN—HISTORY

**KAZAKHSTAN—HISTORY** The collapse of the Soviet Union in 1991 paved the way for the emergence of its largest Asian republic, Kazakhstan, as an independent state. Located in central Asia, early twenty-first century Kazakhstan borders Russia (north), China (east), Kyrgyzstan, Uzbekistan, and Turkmenistan (south), and the Caspian Sea and Russia (west). It is the world's ninth largest country, with an area of 2,719,500 square kilometers and a population of about 18 million. Because it is a neighbor of two nuclear powers (China and Russia) and has substantial oil and gas reserves, Kazakhstan is a potentially significant country in world politics.

As a state with a central political system and with its current geographical and ethnic characteristics, Kazakhstan is not a very old phenomenon. Its history is mainly the history of various nomadic groups and empires that ruled the region during the last two millennia.

### The Arrival of Turkic Peoples

Like the rest of central Asia, Kazakhstan today is populated mainly by Turkic speakers, but its indigenous inhabitants were Iranians. The seven-century-long migration of Turkic ethnic groups from regions of today's Mongolia and adjacent Chinese territory eventually "turkified" portions of central Asia by the thirteenth century. The nomadic Turkic peoples gradually replaced the Iranian people and populated those parts of central Asia that are now considered the nomadic regions (i.e., Kazakhstan, Kyrgyzstan, and parts of Turkmenistan). The other two current central Asian countries (Tajikistan and Uzbekistan) are considered sedentary regions as their populations are not primarily nomadic.

The seventh-century Arab invasion of central Asia introduced Islam to the region, but the nomadic population escaped the Arab occupation. The Arabs conquered only small parts of southern Kazakhstan in the eighth and ninth centuries and ruled there until the Mongols overran all of central Asia in the thirteenth century.

### The Turkic Era

The Turkic era (sixth–twelfth centuries) was a period of constant fighting among various Turkic ethnic groups who contested the control of today's central Asia; as a result, different groups ruled different regions,

## KEY EVENTS IN KAZAKHSTAN'S HISTORY

**6th–12th centuries** During the Turkic era, Turkic peoples from Mongolia migrate to Central Asia and compete for land and political dominance.

**8th–9th centuries** Islam is brought to Central Asia by Arabs.

**9th–11th centuries** Kazakhstan is ruled by the Oghuz Turks, Kimaks, and Kipchaks.

**1219–1221** The Mongols invade and conquer the ruling tribes and states.

**1511–1523** The Kazakh tribes are united as a single people and a distinct Kazakh ethnic identity emerges in the region with Islam the primary religion.

**16th century** The Kazakhs are divided into the Great Horde, Inner Horde, and Lesser Horde.

**18th century** Mongol rule ends in Central Asia and Russian incursions begin.

**1884** All of Kazakhstan is under Russian control.

**1918–1920** Kazakhstan forms an independent government, which is suppressed by the Soviets.

**1936** The Soviet Union establishes the five Central Asian republics.

**1986** Kazakh students riot in opposition to Soviet rule and are repressed.

**1991** Kazakhstan declares independence from the Soviet Union.

**1996** The capital is moved from Almaty to Astana.

whose territories frequently expanded and contracted. The three Turkic groups who had a major impact on the region were the Qaznavian (Qaznavy), who established the Qaznavian dynasty; the Seljuks, who established the Seljuk dynasty; and the Khawrazmshahians, who established the Kharazmshahian dynasty.

The first khanates (kingdoms) of central Asia, which ruled over parts of today's Kazakhstan, Uzbekistan, and Tajikistan, emerged under the control of various Turkic tribes in the second half of the sixth century and remained in power as loose federations of nomads until the eighth century, when the Qarluqs, another Turkic tribe, established a state in eastern Kazakhstan. This was overrun by a larger Turkic state, the Qarakhanid, whose territory included parts of eastern Kazakhstan and western China.

The Qarakhanids accepted the authority of the Arab Abbasid caliphs in Baghdad, but engaged in about a century of infighting as well as wars with the Seljuk Turks who dominated southern central Asia. The Qarakhanids' territory was gradually conquered in the 1130s by a Turkic federation of tribes from northern China, the Karakiti. From the ninth to the eleventh centuries, the Oghuz Turks governed western Kazakhstan, while the Kimak and Kipchak groups ruled over parts of its eastern region. The Karakiti state collapsed when the Mongols invaded central Asia in 1219–1221.

### The Mongol Era

The thirteenth-century Mongol occupation of central Asia ended the short-lived states of the rival Turkic ethnic groups in today's Kazakhstan. The Kazakh lands became part of the Golden Horde, the western branch of the Mongol empire. Rivalry among various Mongol khans led to the division of the empire into several khanates by the early fifteenth century. Mongol rule over Kazakhstan lasted until the eighteenth century.

Kazakhstan began to emerge only in the late fifteenth century, when the Kazakhs came to be recognized as a distinct ethnic group. The majority of the tribes forming the Mongol forces were Turkic. The demise of the Mongols as an empire in the fifteenth century led to the disintegration of their forces and the rise of rivalry over territories among the Turkic tribes formerly loyal to the Mongols. Late in the fifteenth century, some of them (including the Qebchaq, Naiman, Uzun, and Dulta tribes) stationed in current Kazakhstan emerged as Khazak tribes, which were united in the early sixteenth century by Khan Kasym (reigned 1511–1518). In the sixteenth century the Kazakhs formed three hordes, or clans, with their own local states: the Great Horde in southern Kazakhstan, the Inner (Middle) Horde in north central Kazakhstan, and the Small (Lesser) Horde in western Kazakhstan. Those states survived until their incorporation into the Russian empire in the first half of the nineteenth century.

### The Russian Era

Russia gradually conquered Kazakhstan through war and diplomacy. It began seizing western Kazakh territory in the seventeenth century when the Kazakhs were focused on the threat to their east posed by the Kalmyk, a Mongol group. The Small Horde sought Russian assistance in 1730; late in the eighteenth century, Russia subjugated the remnants of the Small and Inner Hordes in the Kazakh lands neighboring today's Siberia. The Russians captured the entire Inner Horde by 1798 and dismantled the Inner and Small Hordes in 1822 and 1824, respectively. Threatened by a southern Central Asian state, the khanate of Quqon, the Great Horde requested Russian protection in the 1820s, which led to its subjugation in 1847.

Having annexed that portion of Kazakhstan that had been under the control of the three Hordes, Russia was faced with the three Central Asian khanates of Quqon, Bukhara, and Khiva. By 1884, using both warfare and diplomacy, Russia conquered and annexed all of Central Asia, including the remaining parts of Kazakhstan. During the lengthy annexation process, the administrative structure of Central Asia changed several times. In the end, the areas between Siberia and the Aral Sea and Lake Balkhash, whose main inhabitants were the Kazakh groups, were annexed as one entity, and the rest of the region was annexed as another (Turkistan). The Russians faced various unsuccessful armed uprisings by Kazakhs seeking to regain their independence in the nineteenth century.

Russian rule changed the nomadic structure and ethnic makeup of Kazakhstan. The influx of Russian settlers turned many fertile Kazakh lands into farms, resulting in limited pasture for cattle breeding, the major economic activity of the Kazakhs, and forcing them to become sedentary. The Russians also created infrastructure (for example, roads and schools) and established some industries in Kazakhstan.

### The Soviet Era

The Bolshevik Revolution of 1917 and the establishment of the Soviet Union did not bring independence to Kazakhstan. The Soviet regime suppressed several antiwar, anti-Russian, anti-Soviet, and independence movements in Central Asia during the period 1917–1933, including the independent Kazakh government (1918–1920) created by a group of secular nationalists called the Alash Orda. The Soviets divided and redivided the region until 1936, when it finally settled on the establishment of the five so-called ethnically based republics. Henceforth Kazakhstan took its current geographical shape and borders.

The Soviet era had a major impact on the development of Kazakhstan and its ethnic makeup. Agriculture and industries were expanded significantly, but they were far less developed than in the European Soviet republics. Kazakhstan was therefore heavily dependent on those republics for agricultural and industrial products at the time of independence. The Soviet efforts to develop Kazakhstan's economy and the relocation of many industries from the European parts of the Soviet Union to Kazakhstan during World War II led to the massive migration of Russians and other Slavs to Kazakhstan. This migration made Kazakhstan the only Soviet republic where the "dominant" ethnic group (Kazakhs) was in the minority.

Kazakhstan was the Soviet republic least interested in freedom from the USSR, as reflected in its lack of a strong pro-independence movement before the fall of the Soviet Union. Soviet Secretary-General Mikhail Gorbachev's anticorruption campaign in Kazakhstan did however provoke limited anti-Soviet movements in the late 1980s. Hence the December 1986 replacement of the first secretary of Kazakhstan's Communist Party, Dinmukhamed Kunayev, an ethnic Kazakh, by Gennadiy Kolbin, an ethnic Russian from outside Kazakhstan, provoked riots (mainly by students), which Soviet forces brutally suppressed. In June 1989, Nursultan Nazarbaev, a reform-minded Kazakh, replaced Kolbin and became the president of the republic in October 1990. Nazarbaev remained a strong supporter of the Soviet Union, as he considered Soviet republics too interdependent to survive independence. He consolidated his power by winning an uncontested presidential election in December 1991, a few days before the dissolution of the Soviet Union.

### The Post-Soviet Era

Kazakhstan was the last Soviet republic to declare independence (15 December 1991). On 21 December, Kazakhstan and ten other former Soviet republics signed the Almaty Declaration, named after the country's capital, to create the Commonwealth of Independent States (CIS). In 1996, Astana became the new capital of Kazakhstan.

Like other former Soviet republics in transition from a socialist economy to free enterprise, Kazakhstan has experienced a decline in industrial and agricultural production and in living standards while suffering from growing unemployment and poverty. It has gradually shifted from its advocacy of democracy in the first years of independence to an authoritarian regime dominated by the Nazarbaev family and friends.

If developed fully, Kazakhstan's significant oil and gas reserves could help the Kazakhs address their current economic problems and build a more prosperous future. Russia's dissatisfaction with Kazakhstan's growing ties with the West, particularly the United States, and Russia's practical exclusion from the development of Kazakhstan's oil industry dominated by American oil companies could lead to serious conflicts between Kazakhstan and Russia. Accounting for about 40 percent of Kazakhstan's population, ethnic Russians have been losing to ethnic Kazakhs the preeminent social, economic, and political status they had enjoyed during the Soviet era. This situation creates the potential for Russia's manipulation of Kazakh Russian dissatisfaction to achieve its own objectives.

*Hooman Peimani*

**Further Reading**

Allworth, Edward, ed. (1989) *Central Asia: 120 Years of Russian Rule*. Durham, NC: Duke University Press.

Frye, Richard N. (1991) "Pre-Islamic and Early Islamic Culture in Central Asia." In *Turko-Persian in Historical Perspective*, edited by Robert L. Canfield. Cambridge, U.K.: Cambridge University Press, 35–52.

Olcott, Martha Brill. (1993) "Central Asia's Political Crisis." In *Russia's Muslim Frontier*, edited by Dale F. Eickelman. Bloomington, IN: Indiana University Press, 50–65.

Peimani, Hooman. (1998) *Regional Security and the Future of Central Asia: The Competition of Iran, Turkey, and Russia*. Westport, CT: Praeger.

Rywkin, Michael. (1990) *Moscow's Muslim Challenge: Soviet Central Asia*. Armonk, NY: M. E. Sharpe.

## KAZAKHSTAN—POLITICAL SYSTEM

Kazakhstan is a new nation, established as an independent, sovereign state only in 1991, when it emerged from the breakup of the Soviet Union. In its first decade of national independence, Kazakhstan's government demonstrated a strong commitment to establishing the foundation for an open, democratic form of government with a market-based economy. Kazakhstan won praise from the international community for this approach and for taking an unprecedented initiative in voluntarily relinquishing its status as a nuclear power. Kazakhstan's progress in the transition from a Communist-era system to a political system in accordance with international standards is significantly greater than that of its other Central Asian neighbors, which also became independent as a result of the breakup of the Soviet Union.

The political transition in Kazakhstan began as early as 1986, with the perestroika (restructuring) and glasnost (openness) reforms introduced under Mikhail Gorbachev (b. 1931), the last Communist Party leader of the USSR. True political reform in the Soviet Union began in 1988, when Gorbachev announced at the Nineteenth Conference of the Communist Party of the Soviet Union his intention to sponsor free elections. By December 1988, the Soviet government had adopted a new election law permitting national and republican multislate elections, the first free elections in the USSR since 1918.

In Kazakhstan's first free election in February 1990, Nursultan Nazarbaev (b. 1940)—then the first secretary of the Kazakhstan Communist Party—was elected chairman of the Kazakhstan Supreme Soviet, the Soviet-era parliament. A month later, parliamentary elections in Kazakhstan seated a new parliament. In one of its first official acts, the new parliament elected Nazarbaev president of the Soviet Republic of Kazakhstan in April 1990.

A short time later, the parliament passed the Kazakhstan Declaration of Sovereignty. Kazakhstan became a sovereign government, but remained within the USSR. As the Soviet Union began to unravel in autumn 1991, Nazarbaev scheduled a presidential election. Running without opposition, he won the election, easily becoming the country's first popularly elected president on 2 December 1991. Just two weeks later, Kazakhstan's parliament adopted the Kazakhstan Declaration of Independence. Kazakhstan became a sovereign and independent state with Nazarbaev as the head of state.

### Kazakhstan under Nazarbaev

Nazarbaev was a pragmatic and forward-thinking leader. Even during the Soviet period, he had sought to move Kazakhstan's government toward a market economy and a relatively open political system. During his early years in power, legislation was adopted to promote privatization in the economy and multiparty public participation in the political system. In 1992, a new constitution was adopted. It prescribed a representative government with a separation of powers among three coequal branches of government, based on popular sovereignty through free elections.

Despite the formal descriptions of checks and balances on power, however, the president exercised a decisive voice in agenda setting, policy, budgeting, and dispute resolution. This became clear in 1993, when disputes over economic policy emerged in Kazakhstan's legislature. The legislature was internally divided and yet, following its constitutional mandate, anxious to exercise greater control over economic issues, particularly privatization. The parliament eventually became deadlocked in a competition between those who supported Nazarbaev's market reforms and those who favored a partial restoration of the economic machinery of the Soviet period. In December 1993, a contingent of parliamentarians favoring reform voted to disband the deadlocked parliament. Nazarbaev recognized the vote immediately and, acting as head of state, dismissed the parliament and ordered that the legislative chambers be locked. With this act, Kazakhstan's Soviet-era parliament came to an end.

The election for a new parliament was held in March 1994. This new, more openly experimental deliberative body met in April 1994. The second Kazakhstani parliament quickly asserted its constitutional mandate to exercise control over legislation and the powers of the purse. A number of parliamentary committees began to exert direct influence over legislation related to privatization. Several parliamentary politicians assumed a watchdog function over the privatization process.

But the March 1994 parliamentary election had been a carefully structured process, with the most important decisions having been made during the nomination process rather than during the election itself. For these and other reasons, the election was criticized as fundamentally flawed by international election observers, particularly the Conference on Security and Cooperation in Europe (now known as the Organization for Security and Cooperation in Europe). Several unsuccessful candidates filed court challenges to the election. A challenge lodged by one unsuccessful candidate, Tatiana Kviatkovskaia, resulted in a constitutional-court ruling in March 1995. The court, ruling in favor of the plaintiff, rather surprisingly found the entire parliamentary election to be invalid. Nazarbaev vetoed this decision, but the court then overruled his veto. Yielding to the court, Nazarbaev dismissed the parliament.

Nazarbaev took advantage of the absence of a legislature to call a referendum to extend his own term of office. He easily won a five-year extension of his mandate in a referendum of 20 April 1995. A new constitution also won popular approval by nearly 90 percent of the voters in a referendum in August 1995. This new constitution granted expanded powers to the executive branch, established a bicameral parliament, and did away with the constitutional court in favor of a constitutional council. It gave the president an unambiguous mandate to issue decrees with the force of constitutional law. Parliamentary elections took place in December 1995.

**Kazakhstan's Governmental Structure**

Kazakhstan's bicameral parliament consists of the Senate and the *majlis*. The upper house, the Senate, has forty-seven seats, seven of which are appointed by the president. Other senators are popularly elected, two from each of the former oblasts and the former capital of Almaty. The senators serve six-year terms. Some senate seats come up for reelection every two years. The *majlis* has sixty-seven directly elected seats and ten party-list seats for a total of seventy-seven. *Majlis* deputies are elected to five-year terms. *Majlis* elections were held in fall 1999 and were next scheduled to be held in 2004.

For most of the period of the Soviet Union's existence (1917–1991), there was only one political party in Kazakhstan, the Communist Party. Although the Communist Party was not actually referenced in the Constitutions of the USSR, the Soviet Union maintained a one-party system with the Communist Party at the focus of activity. The Party served, in the words of a political slogan of the time, as the mind, honor, and conscience of society. It did not serve as a competitor in a competition of ideas. Competition of ideas existed, but the party's job was to direct and implement rather than to debate and deliberate. The period of perestroika and political reform in Kazakhstan inaugurated a period of experimentation with political movements. Eventually, political parties in Kazakhstan were legalized. During the 1999 presidential elections, there were nine political parties registered with Kazakhstan's Ministry of Justice. The Kazakh 1995 constitution specifically legalized political parties acting within the confines of the law. However, the registration of parties is complex and highly controlled.

**Kazakhstan's Political Parties**

Kazakhstan's most important political parties and political movements include (1) Otan, the "Fatherland" party, formed in March 1999 as a result of the combination of the Kazakhstan Liberal Movement, the Kazakhstan People's Unity Party, the Democratic Party, and the For Kazakhstan-2030 movement; (2) the Kazakhstan People's Congress, formed in October 1991 by the leaders of the Nevada-Semipalatinsk movement and Aral-Asia-Kazakhstan movement, the Union of Kazakhstan Women, the Birlesu independent trade union, the Kazakh Tili society, the Association of Young Builders, and national cultural centers; (3) the Kazakhstan Civil Party, formed in November 1998; (4) the Kazakhstan People's and Cooperative Party, formed in December 1994 on the initiative of Kazakhstan cooperatives; (5) the Kazakhstan Communist Party, re-formed in September 1991 as the successor to the Communist Party of the Soviet Union;

(6) the Kazakhstan Revival Party, formed in March 1995, and the Kazakhstan Social Party, formed in September 1991 following the reformation of the Kazakhstan Communist Party; (7) the Republican Political Labor Party, formed in 1996; (8) the Kazakhstan Republican People's Party, formed in December 1998 under the leadership of the former prime minister Akezhan Kazhegeldin; (9) the Kazakhstan Agrarian Party, formed in January 1999; (10) the Alash National Party, formed in May 1999; and (11) the Justice Party, formed in January 1998.

### Successes and Failures of the Political System

Kazakhstan's political system has functioned effectively in some areas. Kazakhstan established a legal foundation and regulatory system for a private economy. It introduced a national currency, the tenge, which became and has remained fully convertible. It established sound monetary and fiscal policies, particularly in taxation and spending. It actively encouraged international trade and foreign investment and established a regulatory structure for the private banking and financial sector. It turned major enterprises over to the private sector, including the majority of power-generation facilities and coal mines. It passed environmentally sound oil and gas legislation that meets international standards.

Kazakhstan's political reform has made less headway in other areas. Kazakhstan's agriculture remains without adequate investment in infrastructure such as roads, processing equipment, and farm inputs. Moreover, the banking system has virtually ignored agriculture, failing to provide much-needed credit for farm expansion. Kazakhstan adopted a private pension system, moving ahead of other former Communist countries, but the social safety net has worn thin in many areas. With a per-capita income of $1,300, most citizens have yet to see the benefits of macroeconomic reform and the resurgence of world prices for the country's significant oil, gas, and gold deposits. There have also been declines in the health status of the people of Kazakhstan, as well as declines in benefits for senior citizens and education opportunities. Dramatic increases in infectious diseases, such as drug-resistant tuberculosis, pose serious threats. Kazakhstan has drawn significant criticism from human-rights organizations for its inability to protect individual rights, provide for free and fair elections, combat nepotism and official corruption, and guarantee fundamental freedoms such as freedom of speech, the media, and political assembly.

*Gregory Gleason*

### Further Reading

Cummings, Sally N. (2000) *Kazakhstan: Centre-Periphery Relations.* London: Royal Institute of International Affairs.

Kazhegeldin, Akezhan. (2000) "Shattered Image: Misconceptions of Democracy and Capitalism in Kazakhstan." *Harvard International Review* 22 (Winter–Spring).

Nazarbaev, Nursultan. (2001) *Epicenter of Peace.* Hollis, NH: Hollis Publishing.

Olcott, Martha Brill. (1995) *The Kazakhs.* 2d ed. Stanford, CA: Hoover Institution Press.

**KEDAH** (2002 est. pop. 1.7 million). Kedah State is situated on the northwestern coast of peninsular Malaysia and borders Thailand. The state is commonly known as the "Rice Bowl of Malaysia." Recent government initiatives, however, have sought to diversify its mainstay economic activities, particularly in the areas of industry (e.g., Kulim Technological Park) and tourism (e.g., Isles of Langkawi).

In ancient times, Kedah was a well-known destination for trade. Lively commerce between India and Kedah existed some two thousand years ago, as indicated by contemporary Indian literature. Kedah was variously known in Tamil and Sanskrit as Kadaram, Kidaram, Kalagam, and Kataha. Its fame also reached civilizations in Greece and China.

Malaysia's most extensive archaeological site is also found in the Bujang Valley (in southern Kedah) where ruins of an ancient Hindu-Buddhist kingdom were uncovered. The oldest surviving written sources, in the form of stone inscriptions, bear witness to the region as an important landfall port (at Sungei Mas), and later, as an entrepôt (at Pengkalan Bujang) between India and China from as early as the fifth century CE. Additionally, artifacts in the form of bronzeware, ceramics, amber, glass, and beads originating from China, Indochina, Thailand, West Asia, and India indicate the vitality of these commercial links. Its importance, however, waned with the founding of the Melaka sultanate and the dawning of Islam from the fifteenth century CE onward.

*Seng-Guan Yeoh*

### Further Reading

Bonney, Rollins. (1971) *Kedah, 1771–1821: The Search for Security and Independence*. Kuala Lumpur, Malaysia: Oxford University Press.

Carstens, Sharon, ed. (1986). *Cultural Identity in Northern Peninsular Malaysia*. Athens, Ohio: Ohio University Center for International Studies.

**KELANTAN** (1995 est. pop. 1.3 million). Kelantan, located on the northeast coast of the Malay Peninsula, covers an area of 14,943 square kilometers. It is an agrarian state with lush paddy fields, fishing villages, and palm-fringed beaches. Its main cash crops are paddy, rubber, tobacco, and fruits. Fishing, livestock rearing, and timber production are also important economic activities, besides its handicraft cottage industry. The population is approximately 94 percent Malay, 4.5 percent Chinese, and 0.5 percent Indian. With its predominantly Malay population, Kelantan has kept its traditional character. Kota Baharu, its capital, is a center for the arts and crafts, particularly batik and silverwork, for which the state is famous. The womenfolk in Kelantan dominate life in the markets and hawker centers while their menfolk are mainly fishermen or farmers. The Kelantanese are Malaysia's most conservative Muslims and have voted a hard-line Islamic opposition into power.

Historically, Kelantan had always been a vassal. By the fourteenth century, Kelantan was under Siamese suzerainty. At that time, it was also under the influence of the Javanese Majapahit empire. During the fifteenth and sixteenth centuries, Kelantan was sending tribute to the Melaka sultanate and its successor, Johor. Problems of leadership and internal strife were part of Kelantan's history during most of the seventeenth and eighteenth centuries. In 1800, one local chief, Long Mohammad, proclaimed himself the first sultan of Kelantan. Upon the death of the heirless Sultan Mohammad, succession disputes again erupted. In 1909, through a treaty, Siam (Thailand) ceded its suzerainty of Kelantan, Kedah, Perlis, and Terengganu to the British. Together with Johor, these became the Unfederated Malay States. In 1948, the Unfederated Malay States became part of the Federation of Malaya. The federation gained independence from British colonial rule in 1957. Together with Sabah and Sarawak, the federation formed the country Malaysia in 1963.

*Yik Koon Teh*

**Further Reading**

Andaya, Barbara Watson, and Leonard Y. Andaya. (1982) *A History of Malaysia*. London: Macmillan.

Eliot, Joshua, and Jane Bickersteth, eds. (1995) *Indonesia, Malaysia and Singapore Handbook*. Bath, U.K.: Trade and Travel Publications Ltd.

Winstedt, Richard. (1966) *Malaya and Its History*. London: Hutchinson & Co. Ltd.

**KEMAL, YASAR** (b. 1922), Turkish novelist, journalist, short-story writer. One of Turkey's most prominent writers, Yasar Kemal draws his ideas from Turkish folklore, cultural traditions, and everyday life. Yasar Kemal's real name is Kemal Sadik Gogceli. He was born in the small village of Hemite (Gokceli) in the province of Adana. His father, while praying in a mosque, was shot dead in front of five-year-old Kemal, and the shock caused a speech impediment until the boy was twelve. He later lost his right eye in an accident. He finished elementary school in 1938, the first person in his village to do so. Kemal moved to Adana (the provincial capital) the same year to continue his education, but had to quit to support himself before he finished the eighth grade. Between 1941 and 1946 he held menial jobs until he became a schoolteacher. During the same period he studied folklore and wrote poems, which were published in several journals.

Kemal was arrested in 1950 for contributing to the organization of a communist party and spent a year in prison. The following year he earned fame as a journalist while working in Istanbul for the newspaper *Cumhuriyet*. In 1952 Kemal married his closest companion, Thilda, the English translator of his work. He received his first journalism award in 1955 from the Society of Journalists. In the same year Kemal's novel, a tale about a bandit and a folk hero, *Ince Memed* (Memed, My Hawk), was published and immediately became a national and international success. It earned him the Valik Literature Prize for best novel of the year in Turkey and has been translated into more than twenty-six languages. Kemal's other literary honors include the French Légion d'Honneur, the Prix du Meilleur Livre Étranger, and a spot on the shortlist for the Nobel Prize in literature. In 1962 Kemal became a member of the Workers' Party of Turkey but resigned in 1969. In 1971 he was imprisoned for twenty-six days, then released without being charged. Kemal took an active role in organizing the Writers' Syndicate of Turkey in 1973 and became its first chairperson in 1974. In 1995, following the publication of an essay in the German weekly *Der Spiegel* (The Mirror), which accused the Turkish government of oppressing the Kurds in Turkey, Kemal was accused of "separatist propaganda" undermining the "indivisible integrity of the state." Himself of Kurdish descent, Kemal, however, had not advocated a separate Kurdish state.

Kemal is considered Turkey's most influential living writer, who speaks for the persecuted and dispossessed. His novels and short stories, based on epic tales, folk songs, and popular literature, poetically describe the beauty of the Cukurova plain in southern Turkey and life in the countryside and coastal villages. His works include *Ince Memed II (They Burn the Thistles)*, the three-volume *Orta Direk* (The Wind from the

Plain), *Yer Demir Gok Bakir* (Iron Earth Copper Sky), *Olmez Otu* (The Undying Grass), and *Yilani Oldurseler* (To Crush the Serpent).

*T. Isikozlu-E.F. Isikozlu*

**Further Reading**

Kemal, Yasar. (1999) *Yasar Kemal on His Life and Art.* Trans. from the French by Eugene Lyons Hebert and Barry Tharaud. Syracuse, NY: Syracuse University Press.

**KENDO** Kendo ("way of the sword") is a Japanese martial art. It is the art and sport of sword fighting, although in its modern form the sword is actually a bamboo rod. Kendo developed more than a thousand years ago as a training technique for the samurai warrior class. After the samurai class was officially abolished in 1871, kendo began its transformation into a sport.

It was introduced into the secondary school curriculum in 1914 and became compulsory in 1931. From Japan, it spread to Korea (which Japan colonized from 1910 to 1945), where it remains popular, and to other nations in the Japanese diaspora. Kendo was employed as a hand-to-hand combat training exercise by the Japanese military before and during World War II and was banned by the occupying American officials after the war because it was believed to support Japanese militarism. It was revived in 1953, after the U.S. occupation ended, as a modern sport, and became popular with older people and women as well as young men.

Kendo contests take five minutes, with the first contestant to score two points being the winner. Points are scored by striking portions of the opponent's body with the bamboo sword. The areas on one's opponent that one must hit to score points are the head above the temple, either side of the trunk, the right forearm if the arm is at waist level, or either forearm if both hands are raised. The throat may be struck only by thrusting. The International Kendo Federation (IKF) is the sports governing body, with chapters in thirty nations.

*David Levinson*

**KERALA** (2001 pop. 31.8 million). The state of Kerala is located in southwestern India bordering the Arabian Sea. It was formed in 1956 by merging the British districts of Malabar and Calicut, the district of South Kanara, and the princely state of Travancore-Cochin. Though measuring only 38,863 square kilometers, Kerala is one of the most densely populated regions in the world. The mountains of the Western Ghats separate this narrow strip of tropical land, where access can be gained only through mountain passes, from the rest of the Indian peninsula to the east.

Kerala differs in many ways from the rest of India. Almost the entire population speaks Malayalam, a Dravidian language with significant Sanskrit influences, Kerala being the only Indian state to speak the language. Its population of Hindus (60 percent), Muslims (20 percent), and Christians (20 percent) enjoys interreligious harmony. Christianity supposedly came to Kerala in 52 CE, with the Apostle Saint Thomas, who founded one of the earliest Christian settlements in the world here. Islam also came not by conquest but through trade from Arabia. Hinduism as practiced here exhibits rather different customs from the rest of India, such as matrilineal inheritance. Other religions in Kerala include Buddhism, Jainism, and Judaism, although most Jews have now emigrated to Israel.

Kerala's traditional association with spice production attracted traders from the early Romans to the Chinese (first through fifteenth centuries CE) to Western Europeans (from 1498 onward). Kerala developed as an important entrepôt connecting Europe, Arabia, Persia, South Asia, Indonesia, and China. The major international ports were Cochin and Calicut. The European commercial and military intervention, beginning with the Portuguese, gradually eliminated trading rivals and finally culminated in British control. The British ruled Malabar in the north and indirectly controlled the princely states of Travancore and Cochin in the south.

Modern Kerala was the first major region in the world to have a democratically elected Communist government (1957). The present ruling coalition is headed by the Communist Party of India (Marxist). Today Kerala surpasses the rest of the country in literacy, health care, population control, equitable distribution of income, and popular participation in governance. Kerala's mortality and fertility indexes surpass China and are on a par with advanced Western countries. Though the state is the most advanced in India in its social indicators, it lags behind a number of other Indian states in terms of per-capita income.

*R. Gopinath*

**Further Reading**

Franke, Richard W., and Barbara H. Chasin. (1992) *Kerala: Development through Radical Reform.* San Francisco: Food First.

Menon, A. Sreedhara. (1979) *Social and Cultural History of Kerala.* New Delhi: Sterling.

The domed roof of the bazaar in Kerman in 1993. (K. M. WESTERMANN/CORBIS)

**KERMAN** (2002 est. province pop. 2.2 million; city pop. 419,000). In ancient times Kerman, a province in southeastern Iran, was known as Carmania (in Persian, "bravery and combat") and formed part of the province of Ariana in the Persian empire. The modern province has an area of about 186,000 square kilometers. The capital city, also Kerman, was founded as early as the third century CE by Ardeshir I, founder of the Sasanid dynasty.

Kerman's history was violent: Arabs, Buyids, Seljuks, Turkmens, Mongols, and Persians invaded and ruled it and left their mark on the region. The Safavid ruler Ganj Ali Khan (1005–1034 CE) especially contributed to Kerman's prosperity.

Kerman borders the modern provinces of Khorasan and Yazd to the north; to the south, Hormuzgan, the Persian Gulf, and the Gulf of Oman; east, Sistan and Baluchistan; and west, Fars. Western Kerman is mountainous, while northern and eastern Kerman is desert, with little water. Its most important permanently flowing river is the Halil. To alleviate the shortage of surface water, the province developed many subterranean water canals known as *qanat*, an ancient Iranian method of groundwater use and transport; some *qanat* systems have been in use for thousands of years. Due to its aridity, Kerman has a low population density, with ten major urban areas scattered throughout the province.

The language spoken in Kerman is Persian, with provincial and local differences and expressions. Turkish and Baluchi languages are also spoken by some regional nomadic tribes, who form a very small portion of the total population. Most people are Muslims, with some religious minorities such as Zoroastrians, who have been living in the area for thousands of years.

The economy of Kerman is based on agriculture and industry, as well as its rich copper mines. Agricultural products include grains, beets, henna, cumin, cotton, and citrus fruits; pistachios and dates are two of Kerman's major export items. Major nonagricultural exports are hand-woven carpets and rugs known as *gelim*. Kerman's carpets are known throughout the world for their delicacy, strength, and colors. The provincial capital, 1,060 kilometers from the Iranian capital of Tehran, is linked to it by road, rail, and air. Kerman also has good access to the Persian Gulf ports.

*Payam Foroughi and Raissa Muhutdinova-Foroughi*

### Further Reading

Iranhost. (2000) "Kerman." Retrieved 3 March 2002, from: http://iranhost.com/AboutIran/Kerman.htm.

SalamIran. (1998) "Province of Kerman." Retrieved 3 March 2002, from: http://salamiran.org/CT/Tourism/Map/kerman/index.html.

**KEUMKANG, MOUNT** Mount Keumkang (Keumkangsan, or "Diamond Mountain") is a range of spectacular peaks in Kangwon Province in eastern

North Korea. Keumkangsan includes some 12,000 individual peaks, as well as valleys and spectacular waterfalls. The highest peak within the range is Birobong, with a height of 1,698 meters. The range known as Manmulsan is unique in that its rugged terrain appears to change as light passes over and recedes from it. Keumkangsan is the northern extension of the Taebaek mountain range, which includes Soraksan (Mount Sorak) to the south. Like Soraksan, Keumkangsan has tremendous sentimental significance to Koreans because of its natural beauty and myths associated with it.

Keumkangsan's name is derived from a Buddhist poem that speaks of "the diamond mountain where the Bodhisattva lives." Legend holds that the region was originally controlled by nine dragons, which were defeated by the fifty-three Buddhas of the Yujeon Temple.

The region is largely undeveloped, although several archaeological and cultural sites exist there. The best-preserved of these dates from 670 CE during the Unified Shilla period (668–935 CE). In the late 1990s the region also became politically significant when the government of North Korea began to admit organized tours from South Korea. These tours were arranged by the Hyundai Corporation, which has begun economic development in North Korea.

*Thomas P. Dolan*

**KHAI HUNG** (1896–1947), Vietnamese writer. After graduating from senior high school, Tran Khanh Giu (Khai Hung) started teaching in a private institution called Thang Long School. The French authorities considered it an establishment in which liberal ideas and socialist doctrines were freely cultivated. It was there that Khai Hung made friends with patriots and writers who were to give a definite direction to the rest of his life. With a few young, politically and socially minded writers, he founded, in 1933, Tu Luc Van Doan, a literary, social, and political club. One year later, he published his first novel, *Nua chung xuan* (In Mid-Spring), followed by many more that made him into one of the most influential and popular authors of the time. In his novels, he attacked the traditional stratified society and showed the vacuity of Confucian virtues, which he felt were all there to make life miserable for everyone concerned. During this period, he was involved in many social endeavors. Finally, as the war portended drastic changes to the colony, Khai Hung launched himself into the political arena by joining the Dai Viet Party, which sought Vietnamese independence by collaborating with Japanese occupational forces. After the war, as the Communist Party was establishing its political control over Vietnam, he sided with the rival old Nationalist Party. Early in 1947, a few months into the Franco-Vietnamese war, Khai Hung was kidnapped and assassinated by parties unknown.

*Lam Truong Buu*

**Further Reading**

Thanh, Hoang Ngoc. (1991) *Vietnam's Social and Political Development as Seen through the Modern Novel*. New York: Peter Lang.

Woodside, Alexander B. (1976) *Community and Revolution in Modern Vietnam*. Boston: Houghton Mifflin.

**KHALKHA** Khalkha is the official language of Mongolia and is spoken by approximately 90 percent of its population, about 2.4 million in 2000. Khalkha is actually a dialect of Mongol. In addition to Khalkha, other important Mongol dialects include Dariganga, spoken in southern Mongolia, and Chakhar, Urat, Kharchin-Tumet, Khorchin, Ujumchin, and Ordos, all spoken in Inner Mongolia. Khalkha encompasses a number of dialect variants, but differences are as minor as the differences between Khalkha and the other Mongol dialects, all of which are mutually comprehensible. The real differences are historical rather than linguistic. When Khalkha's direct connection with China ended after 1911, Russian became a dominant influence; the other languages of the Mongol group, with the exception of Dariganga, continued to be influenced by Chinese. The Mongol languages of China also continued to use the Uighur script and a spelling that is somewhat archaic and less precise but has the advantage of deemphasizing phonological variations.

Prior to 1940, Khalkha was also written with the Uighur script, but since that time a slightly modified Cyrillic script has been used that better reflects the phonological patterns of everyday speech. Since 1991, the Uighur script has made a comeback. From the standpoint of Mongolian linguistic nationalism, a general return to the Uighur script would be extremely important. All speakers of Mongol would write the same way, although terminological differences would persist.

After more than sixty years of development as a distinct literary language, Khalkha has now become a sophisticated medium of exchange and a Mongolian national language in every sense. The evolution of Khalkha has accelerated since the end of Communist rule, with the introduction of new social and economic institutions and vocabularies to support them. Whole new sectors associated with concepts that simply did not exist in Mongolia prior to the 1990s, such as modern banking and computer science, have developed their own vocabulary. Most of the new terminology is based on Mongolian roots rather than borrowings. Nonetheless, in many highly technical areas the Mongols still have recourse to English, which has replaced Russian for them as the preferred language of international communication, at least until established Mongolian terminology has emerged.

*Paul D. Buell*

### Further Reading

Bawden, Charles. (1997) *Mongolian-English Dictionary*. London and New York: Kegan Paul.

Poppe, Nicholas. (1965) *Introduction to Altaic Linguistics*. Wiesbaden, Germany: Harrassowitz.

## KHAN, ABDUL GHAFFAR

(1890–1988), Pakistani politician. Abdul Ghaffar Khan played a major political role in the North-West Frontier Province (NWFP) of the Indian British empire (now part of Pakistan). He was born in 1890 at Charsadda (NWFP) into an important Pashtun family. He became very popular among the Pashtun population there for his movement devoted to the education of the illiterate. In the 1920s he joined the Indian National Congress, leading the provincial branch of the party in the Pashtun areas. As a member of the central executive committee of the Congress, he was jailed several times by the British.

In 1947 he opposed the partition of the Indian subcontinent into two different states (Pakistan and India). After the creation of Pakistan (1947), he became a member of the Pakistani National Assembly, but was later imprisoned and then expelled (1958) from Pakistan to Afghanistan because of his nationalistic radicalism. He struggled for the survival of the traditional way of life of the Pashtuns (who are the majority ethnic group in Afghanistan) and for their political reunification in a single state, called Pashtunistan. In 1970 he returned to Pakistan, having softened his political stance. He died at Peshawar, Pakistan, on 20 January 1988.

*Riccardo Redaelli*

### Further Reading

Bakshi, Shiri Ram. (1992) *Abdul Ghaffar Khan: The Frontier Gandhi*. New Delhi: Anmol.

Korejo, Muhammad Soaleh. (1994) *The Frontier Gandhi: His Place in History*. Karachi, Pakistan: Oxford Pakistan Paperbacks.

## KHAN, VILAYAT

(b. 1928), Indian musician. Vilayat Khan is a well-known exponent of Indian instrumental music. His many renditions on the sitar, a stringed instrument belonging to the lute family, have earned him international recognition. Born into a family of noted musicians in 1928 in East Bengal, Vilayat Khan spent his childhood in Calcutta. He later moved to Delhi after the death of his father, Ustad Inayat Khan, in 1938. Vilayat Khan was musically inclined at a very young age and showed great promise and determination. He cut his first album at the age of eight in 1936 and developed a distinctive style of his own in the course of his musical career. Vilayat Khan's music is marked by fluidity, sweetness, and a certain impatient energy of inventiveness. He is credited with forging the *gayaki ang* style of sitar playing, identifiable by its innovative deployment of vocal technique. By reducing the number of drone strings from seven to six, he created new tunings, making the sitar more supple and versatile. This unique style opened up new possibilities in Indian instrumental music. For his distinctive contribution Vilayat Khan has earned the title *aftaab-e-sitar*, "the radiant star of the sitar." He is known for his fierce and independent spirit, having declined state awards twice. A staunch defender of the purity and continuity of multiple local traditions, the sitar maestro has called for innovative experimentation within the existing repertoire of Indian classical music in view of its marked decline in recent times.

*Ram Shankar Nanda*

### Further Reading

Bose, Sunil. (1993) *Indian Classical Music*. New Delhi: Vikas.

Jairajbhoy, N. A. (1995) *The Raags of North Indian Music: Their Structure and Evolution*. Mumbai, India: Popular Prakashan.

Ramnarayan, Gowri. (1996) "Singing through the Sitar." *Hindu Folio Magazine* (December).

## KHARARKHI

Distilled alcoholic beverages, generically *khararkhi* ("black *arkhi*" in Mongolian), have a considerable antiquity among the Mongols and other Central Asians. In the thirteenth century they occurred in two forms: (1) various brandies and vodkas, mostly imported, judging from largely Turkic names (Mongolian *arkhi* is from Arabic via Turkic *arajhi*, meaning "properly distilled") and (2) various products of freeze distillation. In freeze distillation, a liquor is started in the normal way, and the product is then stored in an ice cellar as a semifrozen slush. Unfrozen portions are gradually ladled off and stored, yielding a concentrated drink of up to 60 proof. Most of the freeze distillates in the Mongol court dietary *Yinshan zhengyao* (Proper and Essential Things for the Emperor's Food and Drink) were intended for medicinal use and were to be cut with water. However, straight concoctions using fruit and other fermentables served concentrated for the simple pleasure of it were in use as well, with the Arabic *sharbat* tradition embracing a similar range of fruit drinks as one influence. Certainly, in the *Yinshan zhengyao*, Mongolian native drinks have been improved with more sophisticated Arabic traditions in mind.

The Mongols continued to drink distilled alcoholic beverages after their empire. There are no further references to freeze distillation, but the method must have continued in use since it is such an obvious one and well suited to Mongolian conditions. The range of ingredients was probably less exotic. Most of the true hard liquors continued to be imported from the sedentary world, better equipped to produce them, but easily portable distillation apparatus was generally available by the fourteenth century if not much earlier, judging from Mongol-era content in the popular encyclopedia *Zhujia biyong shilei* (Things That One Must Put to Use at Home), which clearly describes portable distillation apparatus of a type easily usable by Mongols.

In the twentieth century the Mongolian hard liquor of choice has become vodka, mostly imported from Russia, but the Mongols also make their own, too (for export), primarily from local wheat. Many varieties of moonshine exist, too. Almost any liquor that can be distilled is and with far better stills than the primitive ones in use among the Mongols prior to the twentieth century.

Under traditional conditions, alcoholism was uncommon among the Mongols. Hard liquors were available only sporadically and, in the case of those locally produced, only seasonally. This situation changed for the elite during the era of empire and has changed for Mongols generally in recent times. Alcoholism, as throughout the former Soviet bloc, is now a serious problem. Given the cheapness and ready availability of *khararkhi*, it is likely to remain so.

*Paul D. Buell*

### Further Reading

Buell, Paul D. (1990) "Pleasing the Palate of the Qan: Changing Foodways of the Imperial Mongols." *Mongolian Studies* 13: 57–81.

Buell, Paul D., and Eugene N. Anderson. (2000) *A Soup for the Qan: Chinese Dietary Medicine of the Mongol Era as Seen in Hu Szu-hui's Yin-shan Cheng-yao.* London: Kegan Paul International.

**KHASI** Khasi (Ki Khasi or Ri Lum) is the name of a tribe inhabiting the Khasi and Jaintia Hills of Meghalaya State in northeast India. Originally from Southeast Asia, Khasis migrated to the Khasi and Jaintia Hills, establishing small chiefdoms there by the mid-sixteenth century. British expansion into Assam in the early nineteenth century exposed the Khasis to missionary activities and Western cultural influence.

Khasis speak a Mon-Khmer language of the Austro-Asiatic family. Traditionally they practiced an animistic religion focusing on propitiation of spirits by a priest *(lyngdoh)* and a female priest (*Ka-soh-blei* or *Ka-lyngdoh*). Nowadays, however, the majority (67 percent) has adopted Christianity. The Khasis are divided into exogamous clans, each tracing their descent from an ancestress (*kiaw* or grandmother). The youngest daughter inherits the ancestral property. Although many have entered other occupations, agriculture, both intensive paddy cultivation and shifting agriculture *(jhum)*, is still the main economic activity.

There is much political and social turmoil among Khasis today, especially surrounding the vexatious question of political rights and limited economic opportunities in the region. Conflicts with nontribals resulted in formation of proactive groups such as the Khasi Students' Union (KSU) and the Federation of the Khasi, Jaintia, and Garo People (FKJGP). There is also increasing resentment of traditional Khasis against Christianity, giving rise to the Seng Khasi movement to preserve traditional religion.

*Sanjukta Das Gupta*

### Further Reading

Bareh, Hamlet. (1985) *The History and Culture of the Khasi People*. Guwahati, India: Spectrum Publications.

Dasgupta, P. K. (1984) *The Khasis: Life and Culture of a Matrilineal Tribe of Meghalaya*. New Delhi: Inter India Publications.

Nakane, Chie. (1967) *Garo and Khasi: A Comparative Study of Matrilineal Systems*. Paris: Mouton.

**KHIEU SAMPHAN** (b. 1933), Cambodian political figure. Khieu Samphan was an important member of the Communist Party of Kampuchea, which ruled Cambodia between April 1975 and January 1979—a period when more than 1.5 million Cambodians lost their lives. Born the eldest son of a Kompong Cham judge in 1933, Samphan attended the Collège Norodom Sihanouk and the Lycée Sisowath. He completed his studies at the University of Paris, where he wrote a thesis about Cambodia's economic development that many later mistakenly believed was a blueprint for the radical economic policies of the Khmer Rouge. It was during his time in Paris that Khieu Samphan became a dedicated Communist.

When he returned to Cambodia from France, Samphan taught at a private school and edited the left-wing newspaper *L'Observateur.* His writings about social justice and veiled criticisms of the injustices of the ruling regime made him a popular figure among Cambodia's students. In 1962 he was elected to Cambodia's National Assembly and was also appointed secretary of state for commerce. He was reelected in 1966, before disappearing into the maquis in 1967, fearing for his life after Sihanouk had begun to crack down heavily on Communists and suspected Communists.

Samphan occupied several important posts in the Democratic Kampuchea regime (1975–1979) and, after it was ousted by the Vietnamese, continued to represent the movement on the international stage. He played an important role in negotiating the 1991 Paris Peace Agreements, before withdrawing to the region of Cambodia's border with Thailand, where the Khmer Rouge continued its struggle against the ruling regime. Following the death of Pol Pot and the disintegration of the Khmer Rouge movement in the late 1990s, Samphan eventually surrendered to the Cambodian government. He was allowed to retire to the former Khmer Rouge stronghold of Pailin, to await a decision on whether he would be called to appear before an international genocide tribunal.

*David M. Ayres*

**Further Reading**

Chandler, David. (1991) *The Tragedy of Cambodian History: Politics, War and Revolution since 1945.* Bangkok, Thailand: Silkworm Press.

Heder, Steve. (1991) *Pol Pot and Khieu Samphan.* Clayton, Australia: Monash University Center of Southeast Asian Studies Working Paper 70.

**KHILAFAT MOVEMENT** The *khilafat* (caliphate) was the unique position occupied by the Muslim emperor of the Turkish (Ottoman) empire who was also the spiritual head (*khalifa* or caliph) of the Muslim community worldwide. The Khilafat Movement was a protest movement by Indian Muslims angry at the decision of the British and Allied governments after World War I to dismember the Ottoman empire and thus disperse the Islamic holy shrines and the rule of their spiritual leader, Abdul Hamid II. The Muslims had fought gallantly for the British during the war on the assurance that their religious interests would be protected, and Britain's treatment of the Turks after their loss in the war was seen as a betrayal of this trust.

Some Muslim leaders formed themselves into a *khilafat* conference; 27 October 1919 was designated as Khilafat Day; and a joint conference was called with Hindu leaders on 23 November over which Mohandas Gandhi presided. A *khilafat* deputation to the viceroy on 19 January 1920 proved unsuccessful, and in May 1920, by the Treaty of Sevres, peace terms were formally signed, sealing the fate of the Ottoman empire. The *khilafat* leaders formally joined ranks with the Indian National Congress and adopted Gandhi's noncooperation agenda, which saw nationwide mass peaceful protests by the Indians against British rule from 1920 to 1922. Thus the *khilafat* issue served to unite the Hindus and Muslims politically in the nationalist cause. The Jamiat-ul-Ulema issued a fatwa (religious decree) advising Muslims to boycott elections under the new constitution, boycott schools and colleges, give up titles, and refuse to serve in the army. Though *khilafat* leaders like the Ali brothers—Muhammad and Shaukat—contended that all Indian Muslims were equally enraged by these developments, it is also true to argue that to an extent an emotive issue was utilized by certain Muslim organizations to further political gains and that the issue itself and the distance from India meant that few Muslims could be directly inconvenienced by Allied actions. Meanwhile Turkey itself was undergoing a revolution with the Young Turk movement capturing power, ousting Hamid and abolishing the khalifat. By the early 1920s, therefore, the movement itself had run out of steam.

*Chandrika Kaul*

**Further Reading**

Brown, Judith M. (1972) *Gandhi's Rise to Power 1915–1922.* Cambridge, U.K.: Cambridge University Press.

Gopal, Ram. (1959) *Indian Muslims: A Political History.* London: Asia Publishing House.

Gordon, Richard. (1973) *Locality, Province, and Nation.* Cambridge, U.K.: Cambridge University Press.

Minault, Gail. (1999) *The Khilafat Movement.* New Delhi: Oxford University Press.

Moin, Shakir. (1970) *Khilafat to Partition.* New Delhi: Kalamkar Prakashan.

Niemeijer, A. C. (1972) *The Khilafat Movement in India.* The Hague, Netherlands: Nijhoff.

Robinson, Francis. (1974) *Separatism among Indian Muslims.* London: Cambridge University Press.

**KHIVA, KHANATE OF** The khanate of Khiva was a state centered in the basin of the Amu Dar'ya River in Central Asia from the early sixteenth century until 1920. Khiva was a successor state of the ancient and powerful state of Khorezm, founded by two descendants of Genghis Khan. The Uzbek chieftains Ilbars and Balbars conquered Khorezm, the land south of the Aral Sea and west of the Syr Dar'ya River, plus part of Khurasan, in 1511.

During much of Khiva's early history it was embroiled in wars between its own Uzbek and Turkmen populations and with its neighbors, Iran, Bukhara, and Turkmen nomads. At the same time the khanate government went through much change. Originally the khanate was a loose confederation of independent holdings all nominally owing allegiance to a great khan. By the early seventeenth century the confederation had been replaced by a system of powerful regional governors, or *inaq*s, who vied to control the khan. These *inaq*s were drawn from a powerful aristocratic class of Uzbek families, of whom the Qongrat and Manghits were the most powerful.

Khiva was handed a series of blows in the mid-eighteenth century as the khanate of Aral seceded in the northeast and Nadir Shah of Iran conquered the nation in 1740. In 1747 Iranian domination gave way to near anarchy as wars between the Qongrat and Manghit tribes, the khanate of Aral, and other Uzbek and Turkmen tribes tore the nation apart. The khanate hit a low point in 1767 when Yomut Turkmens captured the city of Khiva.

Muhammad Amin Inaq, a member of the Qongrat tribe, reconquered Khiva from the Yomut Turkmens and established his authority over the khan. During the reigns of Muhammad Amin's successors, Eltuzer and Muhammad Rahim, the Qongrat dynasty was established as Eltuzer deposed the khan and declared himself khan in 1804. Muhammad Rahim reunited Khiva by conquering the Aral khanate and breaking the power of the other Uzbek tribes.

Khiva was soon drawn into a fatal confrontation with Russia. The two clashed as early as 1839. In 1873 an overwhelming Russian force invaded Khiva. The resulting treaty made Khiva a protectorate of the Russian empire and stripped it of some territory but left Khiva's internal affairs intact. The Russian Revolution of 1917 sparked a short-lived seizure of power by Junaid Khan. Bolshevik and Khivan forces overthrew him in 1919 and abolished the khanate in 1920.

*Andrew Sharp*

### Further Reading

Becker, Seymour. (1968) *Russia's Protectorates in Central Asia: Bukhara and Khiva, 1865–1924*. Cambridge, MA: Harvard University Press.

**KHMER** The Khmer are the numerically and politically dominant ethnic group of Cambodia. They make up 90 percent of Cambodia's 12 million inhabitants, approximately 10.8 million people. Khmer also live in northeast Thailand, southern Laos, and southern Vietnam as minority groups. Khmer is also the name of the language this group speaks, a member of the Mon-Khmer group of the Austroasiatic ethnolinguistic family. The earliest-known inscription in the Khmer language is dated 612 CE. However, the Khmer did not begin to be unified as a people until the reign of the Angkorian king Jayavarman II (770–850, reigned 802–850).

Modern Khmer live much as their ancestors did. The majority of Khmer society is agrarian (85 percent), focusing on paddy rice cultivation. Prior to the twentieth century, each household practiced subsistence agriculture, using simple technology to farm. The Khmer traditionally established their villages near a water source, natural or man-made. Even today, the majority of the population inhabits one-third of Cambodia's arable land, primarily around the Tonle Sap (Great Lake), extending east and south to the Mekong River. The proximity to water also makes fish a staple of the Khmer diet.

The construction of a rural Khmer house has not changed over centuries. Khmer in rural areas continue to live in wood houses that are elevated off the ground for better air circulation and protection from wild animals and dangerous spirits.

### Social Organization

Khmer society is hierarchical, traditionally divided into royalty, nobility and officials, and the peasantry. These classes continue to dominate contemporary society. Royalty was viewed as having semidivine status; officials taxed and administered the majority of society; and peasants and landless laborers cultivated the land. Merchants were traditionally excluded from this system, since local traders were either women, whose social status was defined by gender, or of a different ethnicity, such as Chinese. Brahman priests and Buddhist monks were associated with royalty and occupied a prestigious category outside society's hierarchy. Slaves were used during Angkorian times (802–1431) to work on the king's and the nobility's estates, but slaves were usually not of Khmer descent.

Hierarchical relationships continue to define day-to-day relationships among individuals. Elders are authority figures, and their status depends not only on age but sex, wealth, political position, occupation, and religious piety. Social order is dependent on respecting elders and maintaining one's position in society; those positions are supported by Buddhist concepts of karma and merit. Disorder is viewed as dangerous and is exemplified by the wild jungles lurking on the edge of a village. Oral codes of conduct *(chbap)*, which are based on Buddhist teachings, help maintain the moral fiber of society.

In Khmer society, many roles are determined by gender. In rural areas men are responsible for plowing the fields, caring for large animals such as water buffalo, building houses, and other work with wood, while women plant the rice fields, care for smaller livestock, care for children, weave cloth, and cook meals. Men are seen as superior to women; a husband always assumes the position of elder in relation to his wife. Men are legally heads of households and responsible for providing money for the family, but women possess a great deal of authority in managing the household and are in control of monetary matters. Outside the home, women are traders at the market and participate in agricultural work, but men do the heavy tasks.

Kinship is traced through both the mother and father, and sons and daughters possess equal inheritance rights. The society is matrifocal (focused on the bride's family) in that the groom's family must pay a bride-price to the bride's family before the marriage occurs, newlyweds reside near the bride's parents, and the groom usually works for the father-in-law. Marriages are also arranged by parents and sometimes with the assistance of a matchmaker, demonstrating the importance of the elder in decision-making processes.

A Khmer refugee from Cambodia in a refugee camp in Thailand in 1988. (DAVID & PETER TURNLEY/CORBIS)

## Community Organization

The formal unit of social organization among the Khmer is the nuclear family, and there is little cohesion beyond the family unit. A weaker sense of kinship extends to grandparents, aunts, uncles, nephews, nieces, and first cousins. However, neighbors and relatives provide a network of cooperation if help for the construction of a house is required, for example. A patron/client relationship also exists in Khmer society to provide greater support. A patron provides monetary loans and physical protection, and in exchange the client will be politically loyal to the patron and give physical labor as requested by the patron.

Eighty-five percent of the population live in rural communities or villages. A village is defined by the presence of a Buddhist temple and a village headman, who is employed by the government. The *neak ta* cult of guardian spirits also loosely unites the village members, but solidarity among the community is weak.

## Religion

The Khmer are Theravada Buddhists but practice a popularized form of Buddhism infused with their animist beliefs. Buddhist concepts of karma and merit heavily influence daily life, and appeasement of the multitude of spirits in the Khmer belief system is considered very important. *Neak ta* are ancestral or guardian spirits that the Khmer pay homage to in their homes, villages, and the surrounding forests.

## Contemporary Khmer Society

Khmer daily life was primarily unaffected by external forces until the mid-nineteenth century, when Cambodia became a French colony. The French introduced cash crops such as rubber and changes to land ownership. Many rural Khmer lost land rights and were no longer self-sufficient, since they had to devote a portion of their land and energy to raising cash crops. World War II and the two Indochina wars disrupted Khmer life, and U.S. bombing of Cambodia in the early 1970s devastated the lives of many people. Cambodia began to experience food shortages.

The Khmer Rouge regime (1975–1979) caused the most severe changes. The regime intended to erase all Khmer traditional institutions, such as family, religion, and hierarchical relationships. The regime was responsible for the death of 2 million people (estimates vary widely), primarily through execution and starvation. It destroyed temples and animist shrines, separated families, and emptied urban areas. The years following the removal of the Khmer Rouge from power in 1979 have returned some stability to the Khmer, but military unrest persisted into the late 1990s, despite the fact that elections were held in 1993.

More than 800,000 people fled to Thailand and Vietnam in the 1970s and early 1980s. Some of the refugees then resettled in countries such as the United States, Australia, Canada, and France. The displaced Khmer have sustained their cultural traditions in their new countries. Khmer classical dance and musical performances are common, as the younger generations are learning these classical arts. Heritage language classes also teach the generations born outside of Cambodia the native language of their parents and grandparents. Khmer community networks exist globally, and the Internet assists in the maintenance of strong links among the Khmer diaspora.

*Linda S. McIntosh*

### Further Reading

Chandler, David P. (2000) *A History of Cambodia.* 3rd ed. Boulder, CO: Westview Press.

Ebihara, Mary M., Carol A. Mortland, and Judy Ledgerwood, eds. (1994) *Cambodian Culture since 1975: Homeland and Exile.* Ithaca, NY: Cornell University Press.

Ledgerwood, Judy. (1995) "Khmer Kinship: The Matriliny/Matriarchy Myth." *Journal of Anthropological Research* 51, 3: 247–261.

Mabbett, Ian, and David Chandler. (1995) *The Khmers.* Cambridge, U.K.: Blackwell.

Ovesen, Jan, Ing-Britt Trankel, and Joakim Ojendal. (1996) *When Every Household Is an Island: Social Organization and Power Structures in Rural Cambodia.* Uppsala Reports in Cultural Anthropology, no. 15. Uppsala, Sweden: Uppsala University.

**KHMER EMPIRE** With control over an area that once encompassed parts of modern Thailand, Cambodia, the Malay Peninsula, and the Lao People's Democratic Republic, the Khmer empire flourished in Southeast Asia between the sixth and mid-fifteenth centuries. Arising from lands originally ruled by the Kingdom of Chenla (550–800 CE), when Cambodia was called both Funan and Chenla, the Khmer empire reached its apex during the rules of Jayavarman II (802–850 CE), Yasovarman I (889–910 CE), Suryavarman I (1002–1049 CE), Suryavarman II (1112–1152 CE), and Jayavarman VII (1181–1201 CE).

Characterized by cultural expansion and conquest, the Khmer rulers were strongly influenced by Hindu traders from India. Jayavarman II originally established the Kingdom of Kambuja in honor of Kambu, the legendary first-century founder of the Kingdom of Funan, and the root of the current English term "Cambodia." After declaring his independence in 802 CE from the Javanese who controlled Cambodia, Jayavarman II climbed atop Phnom Kulen (Lychee Mountain) in northern Cambodia, where he proclaimed himself a *devaraja* (god-king). Identifying himself with the Hindu god Shiva, he then asserted power over rainfall and soil fertility, and began construction of a "temple mountain" to symbolize the holy mountain at the center of the universe. Both acts were to be repeated over the next four hundred years by Cambodian kings ascending the throne.

From their capital at Angkor, a city that encompassed nearly 120 square kilometers (75 square miles) of fertile plains north of the Tonle Sap (Great Lake), the Khmer leaders presided over a civilization that was one of the strongest and most advanced in the Greater Mekong subregion between the ninth and twelfth centuries. However, frequent infighting among rivals, as well as wars with Champa (a kingdom of southern Vietnam) and the Annamese of northern Vietnam left the Khmer weakened, and the empire eventually succumbed after repeated invasions by the Thais in the mid-1400s.

The longevity and success of the Khmer empire can be attributed, in part, to its location near the Tonle Sap and the major trade routes connecting the Bay of Bengal to southern China, as well as the ability of its leaders to regulate seasonal variations in the water supply through the use of huge canals and reservoirs, or *baray*. These made it possible to irrigate crops and to feed the population during the dry season. In addition, most of the Khmer kings appear to have ruled wisely, building schools, libraries, and roads that connected cities with rice-growing areas. Several rulers were also noted for their patronage of the arts.

The power of the Khmer empire is also a reflection of the artistic and religious significance of Angkor itself. Yasovarman I founded and relocated the Khmer capital from the banks of the Mekong to an island near the present-day provincial capital of Siem Reap, where it remained until 1431 CE. According to temple inscriptions, Yasovarman I thought so highly of his skills that it was as if he had created the arts and sciences.

Suryavarman I, known as the "King of the Just Laws," reunified and expanded the Khmer empire into Thailand and Laos. Consolidating his power by requiring all four thousand local officials to swear allegiance to him, he also continued construction of Angkor's irrigation system, building a huge *baray* near the current site of Angkor Wat. Nearly 8 kilometers long and 1.6 kilometers wide, the reservoir was capable of holding more than 567 million liters of water. Suryavarman I also made Buddhism the state religion, though people were permitted to continue worshiping Hindu gods if they wished.

Suryavarman II came to power in the twelfth century. Like Suryavarman I, he was an outsider who killed a rival in a battle for the throne. He also succeeded in uniting the kingdom through wars in Vietnam, Myanmar (Burma), and Champa. But Suryavarman II is best remembered as the king who commissioned Angkor Wat, a temple-mountain designed to represent Mount Meru, the mythical dwelling place of the Hindu kings. Characterized by extensive bas-relief statues of Khmer warriors, dancing girls, and mythological creatures from the *Ramayana*, the construction of Angkor Wat took thousands of laborers and artisans more than thirty years to build.

For much of the three decades following Suryavarman II's death, internal conflicts over succession and continuous warfare with Champa plagued the Khmer people. In 1177 CE, Angkor was captured by a Cham army and its inhabitants slaughtered. Demoralized by the loss of their capital, the Khmer empire nearly collapsed. However, Jayavarman VII, a relative of Suryavarman II and a devout Buddhist living in exile, rallied his people and not only drove the Chams out of Cambodia, but also conquered Champa and much of present-day Laos, Thailand, and Malaysia.

Jayavarman VII's reign marked the largest construction program in Cambodia's history; he built Angkor Thom as his new capital. Larger and more magnificent than the capital it replaced, Angkor Thom was surrounded by a stone wall with four-sided stone images facing in each direction. In the city's center, Jayavarman VII placed his own temple-mountain, the Bayon. One of the most photographed structures in Cambodia, the Bayon contains fifty towers of varying heights, each bearing stone faces and eyes that appear to stare straight at the viewer. Equally remarkable, the bas-relief walls depict ordinary Cambodian scenes from the twelfth century rather than the religious and royal icons depicted on every other Khmer building.

Following the capture of Angkor by a Thai army in 1431 CE, the Khmer rulers abandoned the site and relocated their capital to Phnom Penh, where it remains today. For the next four hundred years, Angkor remained buried in the jungle until it was "rediscovered" by the French explorer Henri Mouhot in the late nineteenth century. While much of the statuary and carvings have disappeared, the five towers of Angkor Wat are portrayed on the Cambodian flag, and the temple complex—the most visited tourist site in Cambodia—is considered a World Cultural Heritage site.

*Greg Ringer*

*See also:* **Angkor Wat; Cambodia—History; Jayavarman II; Jayavarman VII; Tonle Sap**

### Further Reading

Chandler, David P. (2000) *A History of Cambodia*. 3rd ed. Boulder, CO: Westview Press.

Dutt, Ashok, ed. (1985) *Southeast Asia: Realm of Contrasts*. Boulder, CO: Westview Press.

Greenblat, Miriam. (2000) *Enchantment of the World: Cambodia*. San Jose, CA: Khmer Pride.

Société d'Éditions Géographiques. (1939) *To Angkor*. Paris: Maritimes et Coloniales.

**KHMER ROUGE** The Khmer Rouge was a radical Maoist-oriented Communist party that ruled Cambodia from 17 April 1975 to 7 January 1979 and was responsible for the death of 2 million Cambodians (estimates vary widely). The Khmer Rouge had its roots in the Khmer People's Revolutionary Party, which was founded in 1951 by Vietnamese-influenced Cambodian radicals, and was renamed as the Workers' Party of Kampuchea (WPK) in 1960, as the Communist Party of Kampuchea (CPK) in 1971, and as the Party of Democratic Kampuchea in 1982. Prince Norodom Sihanouk called this movement *les Khmers rouges* ("the red Khmers") when they attempted to end his rule in the 1960s.

A number of future leaders of the movement, including Pol Pot, Ieng Sary, Thiuounn Mumm, Thiounn Prasith, Hou Yuon, Khieu Samphan, Khieu Thirith, and Khieu Ponnary, were radical young Cambodians who were studying in Paris in the 1950s. Many had joined both Ho Chi Minh's Indochinese Communist Party (ICP) and the French Communist Party. Returning to Cambodia, the students made contact with the Communist underground, at that time a group of approximately two thousand members of the Vietnamese-dominated ICP who were fighting the French in what is known as the first Indochinese War

(1946–1954). The movement suffered a series of setbacks during the 1953–1960 period, beginning with independence, which took away anticolonialism as their platform. Unlike their Lao and Vietnamese counterparts, Cambodian Communists did not participate in the 1954 Geneva Conference that ended the first Indochinese War. The Final Accords of the Geneva Conference called for the Viet Minh to withdraw their troops from Cambodia, and with them they took nearly one thousand Cambodian Communists, including the leader, Son Ngoc Minh, leaving a much reduced party infrastructure. Afterward Prince Sihanouk began arresting all known leftists. Pol Pot and other leftists went underground, working as teachers, bureaucrats, and journalists, while participating in clandestine party work and recruiting activities.

A Marxist-Leninist party organization was established in September 1960 to lead a Communist revolution, though Vietnamese-trained guerrilla fighters rather than the Paris-trained intellectuals dominated the leadership. The WPK had two platforms: ameliorating the country's landholding patterns, which kept the landless in a cycle of poverty and reinforced socioeconomic inequality, and continuing to wage a nonviolent struggle against the government, as the WPK had almost no armaments at the time.

In 1961 Sihanouk reversed his policies and endorsed three leading leftist intellectuals (all clandestine members of the WPK) for election into Parliament. Two, Hu Nim and Khieu Samphan, became government ministers responsible for economic affairs. But the WPK continued to be an illegal organization, and Communist-led strikes and student protests caused Sihanouk to launch another crackdown. After the party's second congress, in 1963, the new leaders fled Phnom Penh to the sparsely populated northeast of the country, where they began waging a violent struggle against the government.

The WPK received little external assistance, because both Beijing and Hanoi considered Sihanouk to be too important to their own goals (he allowed the North Vietnamese to use Cambodian territory for transport, logistics, and as a staging ground for the war in South Vietnam). In 1965 Pol Pot made a secret trip to Hanoi and Beijing to request material assistance; he was told that the Cambodian revolution would have to wait so as to not distract from the ongoing revolutions in Laos and South Vietnam. The North Vietnamese began to arm the WPK in the late 1960s, but never to the Khmer Rouge's satisfaction. The movement grew steadily from a few dozen men to a several thousand-strong fighting force due to peasant dissatisfaction, higher taxes, and the secret American bombing campaign that began in 1969.

In April 1970 U.S. President Richard Nixon authorized the invasion of Cambodia to stop Hanoi's supply lines and eliminate Viet Cong sanctuaries. The Vietnamese and Khmer Rouge retreated westward, where they routed the Cambodian army. Responding to Communist gains, in May 1970 General Lon Nol took over power while Sihanouk was in France. Wary of Lon Nol's ties to the United States, the Chinese brokered an agreement with the Khmer Rouge leadership that made Sihanouk their titular head, greatly improving the movement's public appeal. The WPK, renamed the Communist Party of Kampuchea, made huge gains following America's withdrawal from Indochina in 1973, and their peasant-based army captured Phnom Penh on 17 April 1975.

In power, the Khmer Rouge implemented a series of radical policies. Cities were evacuated, and all citizens were forced onto massive agricultural collectives. Many irrigation works were established to facilitate rapid agricultural growth. Private plots were collectivized, private property was made illegal, the commercial and banking sectors were shut down, and private markets were abolished, because all economic functions were controlled by a central plan.

Under the Khmer Rouge, there was a wholesale slaughter of intellectuals, artisans, doctors, lawyers, any members of the former Lon Nol regime, ethnic minorities, and any other political enemies. These executions, along with famine and disease, were behind Cambodia's staggering death toll during the Khmer Rouge regime.

Any economic gains from collectivization were not shared by the population, as nearly all surpluses were exported to China to pay for armaments. The xenophobic CPK, always concerned about Vietnamese domination, became more fearful upon Hanoi's calls for the establishment of an "Indochinese Union." The Khmer Rouge resisted and even provoked Hanoi by launching a series of border attacks. Hanoi made diplomatic protests but was rebuffed by both Phnom Penh and its patron, Beijing. In 1978 Hanoi launched a punitive strike into Cambodia and quickly withdrew.

The ease with which the battle tested Vietnamese were able to penetrate Cambodia led to a series of recriminations. Leaders from the eastern zone were summoned to Phnom Penh, where they were tortured and executed at the infamous Tuol Sleng Prison. In all, nearly one hundred thousand Khmer Rouge cadres and their families were executed at this time for treason.

The Khmer Rouge continued their attacks on Vietnam, and on 25 December 1978, after signing a mutual defense treaty with the Soviet Union, Vietnam intervened in Cambodia, driving the Khmer Rouge into enclaves along the border with Thailand. Hanoi occupied Cambodia with some one hundred thousand troops for ten years and installed a government comprising former Khmer Rouge leaders who had defected to Vietnam during the purges, as well as Cambodians who had trained in Vietnam since the 1950s.

Continuing to receive assistance from China, the Khmer Rouge regrouped near the Thai border and began an eleven-year guerrilla war. In 1982 the Coalition Government of Democratic Kampuchea (CGDK) was established with the backing of China, the United States, and members of the Association of Southeast Asian Nations. The coalition government, headed by Sihanouk, included the Khmer Rouge and two noncommunist guerrilla forces fighting the Vietnamese. Through the CGDK, the Khmer Rouge continued to hold Cambodia's seat in the United Nations. The well-armed Khmer Rouge fought the Vietnamese to a standstill, and in September 1989 the diplomatically isolated and financially burdened Vietnamese unilaterally withdrew. The Khmer Rouge was able to take advantage of the Cambodian government's weakness and controlled nearly one-third of the country by the time the U.N.-sponsored peace accords were signed in October 1991.

Though a signatory to the Paris Peace Accords and a member of the interim coalition government, the Khmer Rouge leadership refused to disarm or allow U.N. peacekeepers into their territory. The Khmer Rouge withdrew from the peace process and attacked U.N. Transitional Authority in Cambodia (UNTAC) personnel but in the end did not disrupt the May 1993 elections or stop the $2 billion UNTAC operation. After the elections, the coalition government of the incumbent Cambodian People's Party and the Khmer Rouge's former ally, the royalist FUNCINPEC (the French acronym for National United Front for an Independent, Neutral, Peaceful, and Cooperative Cambodia), renewed their offensive against the Khmer Rouge. The Khmer Rouge, having lost much of their aid from the Chinese after the Paris Accords, were able to continue to finance their war effort through the sale of gemstones and timber from the territory they controlled. But the movement faltered as royal amnesties and war weariness led to mass defections in the 1996–1998 period. Many top leaders, such as Ieng Sary, Khieu Samphan, and Nuon Chea, defected to the government side. As a result of these defections and fearful of others, Pol Pot ordered the murder of several top Khmer Rouge leaders, including Minister of Defense Son Sen. The remaining Khmer Rouge leadership then arrested Pol Pot and put him on trial, ostensibly as a bargaining chip to ensure the movement's survival. With Pol Pot's death on 15 April 1998, almost the exact anniversary of the Khmer Rouge capture of Phnom Penh, and the capture of the last remaining guerrilla leader, Ta Mok, the Khmer Rouge was no longer an effective fighting force. The government of Cambodia was under intense international pressure to turn over the former Khmer Rouge leaders to an international war crimes tribunal, but the Cambodian government refused on grounds of sovereign rights. The Cambodian government, most of whose leaders were former members of the Khmer Rouge, was concerned that they could be brought to trial as well, and hence wanted to control the scope of the trial. The United Nations was concerned that Cambodia did not have the legal capacity or expertise to try the Khmer Rouge leaders, and that the trials would be highly politicized, and entered into prolonged negotiations with the Cambodian government over establishing a tribunal in Cambodia that would include international jurists. In August 2001, the Cambodian Parliament passed a law establishing a war crimes tribunal for the remaining Khmer Rouge leadership, but it has fallen short of the law envisioned by the United Nations.

*Zachary Abuza*

**Further Reading**

Becker, Elizabeth. (1998) *When the War Was Over: Cambodia and the Khmer Rouge Revolution.* New York: Public Affairs.

Chanda, Nayan. (1986) *Brother Enemy: The War after the War.* New York: Harcourt Brace Jovanovich.

Chandler, David P. (1992) *Brother Number One: A Political Biography of Pol Pot.* Boulder, CO: Westview Press.

———. (1991) *The Tragedy of Cambodian History.* New Haven, CT: Yale University Press.

Jackson, Karl. (1989) *Cambodia, 1975–1978: Rendezvous with Death.* Princeton, NJ: Princeton University Press.

Kiernan, Ben. (1998) *The Pol Pot Regime: Race, Power, and Genocide in Cambodia under the Khmer Rouge 1975–79.* New Haven, CT: Yale University Press.

Shawcross, William. (1979) *Sideshow: Nixon, Kissinger, and the Destruction of Cambodia.* New York: Simon and Schuster.

**KHMU** Lao history indicates that the earliest inhabitants, predating the arrival of the Lao-Tais, were the Mon-Khmer, the Khmu being one subgroup of the Mon-Khmer peoples. Khmu belongs to the Khmuic branch of the larger Mon-Khmer line of the Austroasiatic language family. According to legend,

Khmu children in front of a thatched building in northern Laos in 1995. (BRIAN A. VIKANDER/CORBIS)

the Khmu are supposed to have come out of a certain round, red pumpkin *(ple' goek r-mwng)*. This pumpkin was born to a brother-sister couple (the only survivors of a big flood). When the people came out of the hole that was pierced with a glowing branding iron, the Khmu were the first to come through that hole, before everybody else emerged from the pumpkin. Therefore, the Khmu say that they are the "people from that burned hole *(hntu' srne')* in the pumpkin."

Today the Khmu number more than half a million people living throughout the north of Laos, particularly in the provinces of Luang Prabang, Oudomsay, and Phongsali, and in the bordering highland areas of Thailand, Vietnam, China, and Myanmar (Burma). The Khmu constitute the second-largest ethnic group in Laos after the Lao. The lowland Lao often call the Khmu the Lao Theung, which can be translated as "the Lao who live on the middle slopes of the mountains." Historical literature on Laos also knows the Khmu as Kha, a word carrying the connotation of "slave," which was used to designate other ethnic groups.

Most of the Khmu are still mountain dwellers who farm mountain fields where they plant rice, corn, cotton, vegetables, fruit, and tubers. The Khmu also depend on the upland forests for finding additional food, such as different leafy plants, mushrooms, bamboo shoots, fruits, and different types of animals and fish from mountain streams.

The Khmu, as well as other Austro-Asiatic peoples, have had a special relationship with the spirits *(hroey)* of the land. This relationship was institutionalized for many centuries as Khmu holy men performed elaborate rituals to pay respect to the spirits of the land in the Luang Prabang royal courts. The Khmu have a rich and varied nonmaterial cultural heritage that is expressed in their ritual traditions, legends, and stories, which are passed down from generation to generation.

With growing population pressure in Laos, new migrants from burgeoning farm families in the lowlands are expanding into the upland areas already occupied by Mon-Khmer groups, including the Khmu. The traditional way of life of the Khmu is threatened as conflicts over land tenure occur between the migrants and the upland populations.

*Olli Ruohomaki*

**Further Reading**

Chazee, Laurent. (1999) *The People of Laos: Rural and Ethnic Diversities.* Bangkok, Thailand: White Lotus.

Lebar, Frank M., Gerald Hickey, and John Musgrove. (1964) *Ethnic Groups in Mainland Southeast Asia.* New Haven, CT: Human Relations Area Files.

Lindell, Kristina, Jan-Ojvind Swahn, and Damrong Tayanin. (1998) *Folk Tales from Kammu.* Vol. 6, *A Teller's Last Tales.* London: NIAS-Curzon Press.

Simana, Suksavang, and Elisabeth Preisig. (1997) *Kmhmu' Livelihood: Farming the Forest.* Vientiane, Laos: Institute for Cultural Research.

Tayanin, Damrong. (1994) *Being Kammu: My Life, My Village*. Southeast Asia Program Series, no. 14. Ithaca, NY: Cornell University Press.

Tayanin, Damrong, and Kristina Lindell. (1991) *Hunting and Fishing in a Kammu Village*. London: Curzon Press.

**KHOMEINI, AYATOLLAH** (1902–1989), Islamic religious leader. Ayatollah Ruhollah Khomeini, an Islamic religious leader, was the architect of the Islamic Republic of Iran. Born to a cleric and property owner, Khomeini's name was originally Ruhollah Musawi, but he changed it to reflect his birthplace (Khomeini, a town south of Tehran). In 1920 Khomeini moved to Arak to study at a school run by Ayatollah Abd al-Karim Ha'eri. Two years later Ha'eri relocated to the Shiʿite holy city of Qom, and Khomeini followed him there. After completing his studies in ethics and spiritual philosophy, Khomeini taught Islamic philosophy and law. In 1929 he wed Khadijeh Saqafil, daughter of a well-known cleric, who bore him two sons and three daughters. Eventually his studies and publications resulted in his receiving the title of ayatollah ("likeness," or "sign," "of Allah"), one of the highest titles awarded clerics of the Shʿite sect of Islam.

Khomeini was imprisoned in 1963 for his speeches against Mohammad Reza Shah Pahlavi and his policies; his arrest caused major disturbances, which the shah contained with force. Under public pressure Khomeini was released to house arrest in Tehran and a year later was exiled to Turkey. Khomeini spent a year in Turkey before moving to Iraq, where there are several Shiʿite shrines. In exile he further developed the concept of *veleyet-e-faqih*, or rule of religious jurisprudence, which he had outlined in a previous work. His lectures on this subject culminated in the publication of *Hokumat-e Eslami* (Islamic Government).

In October 1978 Saddam Hussein ordered Khomeini to leave Iraq. He went to Paris to organize opposition groups against the shah and returned to Iran in January 1979, when the shah was forced to leave the country. He oversaw the establishment of the Islamic Republic of Iran on 11 February 1979. Ayatollah Khomeini appointed an Assembly of Experts to review and revise a draft constitution prepared by the provisional government, to reflect Khomeini's principle of *veleyet-e-faqih*.

He became Iran's first *faqih* (religious leader), a position he held until his death. His policies as *faqih* were anti-American and left little room for opposition to the regime he had established, although he tried to maintain a balance between conservative and moderate factions in Iran. Khomeini hoped to export revolutionary Islam to other countries, but with little success. Moreover, his tenure coincided with the Iran-Iraq War, which brought enormous hardships to Iran. Khomeini's reputation rests not only on the creation of the Islamic Republic of Iran but also on his challenge to the Western notion that religion and politics should be separate.

*Houman A. Sadri*

**Further Reading**

Dorraj, Manochehr. (1990) *From Zarathustra to Khomeini: Populism and Dissent in Iran*. Boulder, CO: Lynne Rienner Publishers.

Khomeini, Ruhollah. (1981). *Islam and Revolution: Writings and Declarations of Imam Khomeini*. Trans. by Hamid Algar. Berkeley, CA: Mizan Press.

Rajec, Farhang. (1983) *Islamic Values and World View: Khomeyni on Man, the State, and International Politics*. New York: University Press of America.

Roberts, Mark J. (1996) *Khomeini's Incorporation of the Iranian Military Microform*. Washington, DC: Institute for National Strategic Studies, National Defense University.

**KHON KAEN** (1999 est. province pop. 1.8 million). Khon Kaen is the name given to both a city and province in northeast Thailand. The province is located 450 kilometers from Bangkok and covers an area of approximately 10,886 square kilometers. The province has twenty districts and three subdistricts. It is the center for various regional development projects, but is also a transportation hub and education center, home of Khon Kaen University, founded in 1964.

The city of Khon Kaen was originally established near Phra That Kham Kaen. These early settlements never truly developed and were abandoned several times over the course of centuries. A ruler from Suwannaphum founded the present-day city in 1789 and gave it the name Kham Kaen, later changed to Khon Kaen.

Primary recent development in the area occurred in the 1960s, concurrent with Thailand's new national role in serving the needs of the United States Air Force during the U.S. war in Vietnam. An air base was located near the city. Transportation based in Khon Kaen serves the entire region. In addition to its highway system, the city has a major airport and is a stop on the northern railway line, which runs to Nong Khai, a gateway to Laos situated on the Mekong River.

*Linda Dailey Paulson*

**Further Reading**

Travel Thailand. (2001) "Khon Kaen." Retrieved 14 January 2001, from: http://www.travelthailand.com/isan/html/khonkaen/html/khonkaen.htm.

**KHOROG** (2000 est. pop. 22,000). The Tajikistan town of Khorog is located at an elevation of 2,200 meters in a narrow valley at the base of the Pamir Mountains, at the confluence of the Gunt and Pyandz Rivers. Khorog is the principal administrative, commercial, and population center of the semiautonomous region of Gorno-Badakhshan in southeastern Tajikistan. For much of each year the region suffers from geographical isolation from the outside world. Winter snows block the only road connections to Osh (Kyrgyzstan) and the Tajik capital of Dushanbe. Air connections to Dushanbe are intermittent due to weather and insufficient airport instrumentation. Political tensions have closed the route south into Afghanistan. Although the rain-shadow location yields only 150 millimeters of annual precipitation, abundant irrigation from melting snow and ice in the adjacent mountains supports wheat, sunflowers, barley, and many orchard crops. A small service industry, textile and food processing factories, a hydroelectric station, and government services employ a people of Mountain Tajiks (Pamiris) and Kyrgyz ancestry. The Pamir Botanical Gardens (founded in 1951) are nearby. Since Tajik independence in 1991, persistent food shortages have plagued this isolated corner of Central Asia.

*Stephen F. Cunha*

**Further Reading**

Cunha, Stephen F. (2002) "The Mountain Tajiks of Central Asia." In *Endangered Peoples of the World*, edited by Barbara Brower. Westport, CT: Greenwood Publishing Group.

Curtis, Glenn E., ed. (1997) *Kazakstan, Kyrgyzstan, Tajikistan, Turkmenistan, and Uzbekistan: Country Studies.* Washington, DC: Federal Research Division, Library of Congress.

Rakowska-Harmstone, Teresa. (1970) *Russia and Nationalism in Central Asia: The Case of Tadzhikistan.* Baltimore: Johns Hopkins University Press.

**KHUBILAI KHAN** (1215–1294), Mongolian ruler. Khubilai Khan (or Qubilai Qan), founder of the Yuan dynasty (1279–1368), as the Mongol khanate of China became known, was the last ruler of Mongol China to be born on the steppe. The second of four sons of Tolui (c. 1190–c. 1231), who was the youngest son of Genghis Khan, he began life as just another Mongol prince, until his elder brother, Mongke (d. 1259), came to the throne. Khubilai, then in his mid-thirties, became his brother's viceroy in China, a role he performed very successfully with the help of a variety of advisers savvy in local administrative tradition. Most but not all were Chinese and most went on to be among the founding ministers of Khubilai's new dynasty.

As Khan Mongke turned south to campaign against the Southern Song dynasty (1127–1279), Khubilai went along, in part because Mongke was becoming distrustful of his brother's independent power base. During a campaign lasting several years, much of it in difficult terrain at high altitude, Khubilai advanced as far as Yunnan where he helped establish a Mongol administration under Bukharan Sayyid Adjall (1211–1279).

**Khubilai Becomes Khan**

The sudden death of Mongke in 1259 found Khubilai heavily involved in his campaign. Anxious to assert his own candidacy for the now vacant Mongol imperial throne, Khubilai quickly hurried north and gathered his supporters. His principal rival was his younger brother Arigboke (d. 1266), who enjoyed more support in the Mongolian world as a whole. To forestall Arigboke, Khubilai convened a rump *quriltai* (assembly) and had himself elected khan. Arigboke quickly did the same and prepared for war.

The civil war lasted more than four years and ended with Khubilai's victory thanks to his superior resources. Khubilai now had unrestricted control in Mongol China and in most of Mongolia, including the old Mongol imperial capital of Karakorum, although his rule was never unchallenged in Inner Asia.

Once free of competitors, at least in the immediate vicinity of China, Khubilai set about building up his new successor khanate of China, initially confined to the north. Although Mongolian-style administration continued to function side by side with Chinese, khanate China increasingly had a Chinese structure, on paper at least. It was also given a Chinese capital, Daidu, founded (c. 1266) by Khubilai. Although Daidu (later modern Beijing) was considered the capital, strictly speaking, the khanate of China had no single capital since the court nomadized between summer pastures in Shangdu, Khubilai's old princely headquarters, and winter pastures near Daidu.

**Establishment of the Yuan Dynasty**

In 1271 Khubilai took a Chinese dynastic designation, Yuan, meaning "origin." The new Yuan dynasty quickly came to rule all China with the conquest of the Southern Song in 1279, reunifying China for the first time since the early twelfth century. But the conquest of Song did not mark the end of Mongol expansion. It continued toward Japan, into Vietnam, Burma, and across the sea to Java. For the first time in its history China became a base for a most aggressive sea power.

Although Khubilai had established a "Chinese" dynasty, his new regime was strongly aware of its Central Asian roots. Not only was the ruling family and much of the military if not civilian leadership Mongolian, but Khubilai continued to employ non-Chinese of every persuasion, not just Mongols, in his government to the extent that Persian and Turkic dialects were important as court languages. He also consciously pursued a cultural policy that sought to provide something for everyone. Nowhere is this clearer than in the official court cuisine, in which Mongol soups and roast wolf were served side by side with Iraqi-Persian, Turkic, Kashmiri, and other dishes. Khubilai also had a universal script created, the aPhags-pa alphabet, to write all the languages of his empire.

Another of the Inner Asian aspects of the Mongol Yuan dynasty was religion. Although Genghis Khan had flirted with Taoists and even a Zen monk, among other religious practitioners, and Christians from the West competed for imperial attention under Mongke, Khubilai and his house became converted to the Buddhist religion—and not to any of its Chinese varieties, but to Tibetan Buddhism, which was rich in shamanic traditions close to Mongol native beliefs. Tibetan Buddhism has remained the religion of the Mongols down to the present, pointing up the importance of this conversion.

Khubilai died in 1294, at a ripe old age. No subsequent ruler of Mongol China ever rose to his stature, and decline set in after his death. But despite this decline, Khubilai remains to this day the very symbol of the Oriental potentate and of China, thanks to Marco Polo. It was the China of Khubilai that the Portuguese and other Europeans went in pursuit of in the fifteenth and sixteenth centuries, inaugurating the age of Western ascendancy.

*Paul D. Buell*

**Further Reading**

Allsen, Thomas T. (1987) *Mongol Imperialism*. Berkeley and Los Angeles: University of California Press.

Buell, Paul D. (1993) "Saiyid Ajall." In *In the Service of the Khan, Eminent Personalities of the Early Mongol-Yuan Period (1200–1300)*, edited by Igor de Rachewiltz, Chan Hok-lam, Hsiao Ch'i-ch'ing and Peter W. Geier. Wiesbaden, Germany: Otto Harrassowitz, 466–479.

Buell, Paul D., and Eugene N. Anderson, appendix by Charles Perry. (2000) *A Soup for the Qan: Chinese Dietary Medicine of the Mongol Era as Seen in Hu Szu-hui's Yin-shan Cheng-yao*. London: Kegan Paul International.

Mote, F. W. (1999) *Imperial China, 900–1800*, Cambridge, MA, and London: Harvard University Press.

Rossabi, Morris. (1988) *Khubilai Khan: His Life and Times*. Berkeley and Los Angeles: University of California Press.

———. (1992) *Voyager from Xanadu, Rabban Sauma and the First Journey from China to the West*. New York: Kodansha International.

## KHUJAND

**KHUJAND** (2000 est. pop. 162,000). Khujand, on the left bank of the Syr Dar'ya River in the fertile Fergana Valley, is one of the oldest towns in Central Asia. It is the second-largest city in the republic of Tajikistan, a Central Asian state, and the administrative center of Viloyati Soghd (Soghd province) in northern Tajikistan.

Khujand was established around the fifth century BCE. In 329 BCE during his conquest of Central Asia, Alexander of Macedon founded a fortress named Alexandria Eskhat (the furthest) on the site of present-day Khujand. From the first century BCE Khujand was an important trading center on the great Silk Road, the major caravan route linking China and India with the Mediterranean, and later was part of the Bukhara (1583–1740) and Kokand (1710–1876) khanates or chiefdoms. Russia invaded the Kokand khanate in 1866, and Khujand became included in the Russian empire in 1868. From 1924 to 1929 the western part of the Fergana Valley including Khujand formed part of the Uzbek Soviet Socialist Republic, but in 1929 the region was turned over to the Tajik Soviet Socialist Republic. In 1936 the city was renamed Leninabad (city of Lenin), but it regained its original name—Khujand—in 1992, after the Soviet Union's collapse in 1991. Today the city is a major industrial center, famous for silk manufacturing and decorative and applied arts.

*Natalya Yu. Khan*

**Further Reading**

Roy, Oliver. (2000) *The New Central Asia: The Creation of Nations*. New York: New York University Press.

## KHUN CHANG, KHUN PHAEN

**KHUN CHANG, KHUN PHAEN** *Khun Chang, Khun Phaen* is one of the classics of Thai literature. It was written in verse during the reign of Rama II for *sepha* recitation (a method of solo recitation in which emotion is conveyed by changes in voice quality). Several different authors, each of whom was allocated various scenes, were involved in its composition, including the famous poet Sunthon Phu. The story is believed to have been based on fact. It tells of two men, the villain Khun Chang and the hero Khun Phaen, who had been childhood friends but later become bitter rivals for the love of Wan Thong. Wan Thong at different stages of the plot marries both her suitors, but when called upon to choose between them, is unable to do so and is therefore condemned to death.

Many of the convoluted twists in the plot are engineered by the protagonists' use of sorcery, while the work is also renowned for its use of images from nature in flimsily disguised passages of erotic description. A prose translation into English by H. H. Prince Prem Purachatra (Prem Chaya), *The Story of Khun Chang, Khun Phaen*, provides a good retelling of the story but conveys little of the aesthetic qualities for which Thais admire the work.

*David Smyth*

**KHUNJERAB PASS** A long, level, and open ridge at 4,700 meters that marks the frontier between China and Pakistan, the Khunjerab Pass is the continental watershed divide between the Indus River of South Asia and the internal drainage of Central Asia's Tarim Basin. The ridgeline unofficially separates the Afghan Hindu Kush from the Karakoram ranges. The pass is also the highest point on the 1,300-kilometer Karakoram Highway that connects Kashgar (Xinjiang, China) to Rawalpindi (northern Pakistan). In the local Tajik language, Khunjerab means River of Blood, after the rust-colored water that seeps from the pass. Local Pakistanis and Wakhi tribesmen simply call it "top."

The mostly paved Karakoram Highway that crosses this pass was built along an important artery of the ancient Silk Road. It has been operational since 1973 for construction workers and commerce. In May 1986, it opened to all travelers, starting a boom in tourism and Sino-Pakistani trade that continues today. The pass is normally open from 1 May until mid-November, although recurrent harsh weather, flooding, washouts, and landslides can delay travel. The broad summit area fringes the Khunjerab National Park (established in 1975), where Marco Polo sheep (*Ovis poli*) and snow leopards (*Uncia uncia*) abound. The border-post towns of Sost (in Pakistan, 96 kilometers south of the pass) and Pirali (in China, 49 kilometers north of the pass) are the customs, health, and immigration checkpoints.

*Stephen F. Cunha*

**Further Reading**

Allan, Nigel J. R. (1988) "Highways to the Sky: The Impact of Tourism on South Asian Mountain Culture." *Tourism and Recreation Research* 13:11–16.

Rowell, Galen. (1986) *In the Throne Room of the Mountain Gods*. San Francisco: Sierra Club Books.

**KHURASAN** (2002 est. pop. 6.1 million). Khurasan (translated as "sun rising") is the largest province of Iran, occupying one-fifth of the nation's territory. Located in northeast Iran, it covers an area of 324,000 square kilometers. To its north and east, Khurasan borders Turkmenistan and Afghanistan. To the west, it shares borders with Iran's internal provinces. Its capital is the city of Mashhad. Though most of its population speaks Persian, Turkmen, Kurdish, and some local dialects are also spoken. Besides Islam, the major religion of the province, a small number of its inhabitants profess the Baha'i, Christian, and Zoroastrian faiths.

After the conquest of Iran by the invading Muslim army, many Arabs settled in Khurasan. Khurasan was the first region of today's Iran to come under attack by invading Turkic nomads. Despite the successive hegemony of central Asian Turkic dynasties, however, Khurasan preserved its language and in fact emerged as a bastion of Persian literature. Not only did the inhabitants of Khurasan not succumb to the language of the nomadic invaders, but they imposed their own tongue on them. The region could even assimilate the Turkic Ghaznavids and Seljuks (eleventh and twelfth centuries), the Timurids (fourteenth–fifteenth centuries), and the Qajars (nineteenth–twentieth centuries).

The landscape of the region is mainly mountainous and arid. There have been periodic earthquakes in Khurasan; in 1997, an earthquake killed thousands of people and destroyed many villages. Agriculture is the major contributor to the economy, producing grains, beets, saffron, cotton, fruits, and refined sugar. The province is the site of light and heavy industries as well, including textiles, carpets, turquoise, and wool. Khurasan is rich in mineral resources, such as natural gas; the largest natural gas reserves in the world are said to be located there.

At the beginning of the eighth century, Abu Muslim (728–755) from Khurasan began his campaign against the Arab Umayyad dynasty (661–750). The province contributed to the power of the caliphs of the early Abbasid dynasty (749/50–1258). In the 1150s Khurasan was devastated by the Oghuz Turks and from 1220 to 1222 by the Mughals. In 1383 Tamerlane (1336–1404), emperor of the Mughal empire, invaded the province.

Khurasan was home to Al-Ghazali (1058–1111), the renowned Islamic theologian, philosopher, and mystic. Al-Ghazali was appointed professor at Baghdad in 1091, but after a spiritual crisis in 1095 he abandoned his career to become a Sufi mystic. He is credited with attempting to reconcile mysticism with Islam. His chief work, *The Revival of the Religious Sciences*, outlines a complete and orthodox system of the mystical attainment of unity with God.

*Payam Foroughi and Raissa Muhutdinova-Foroughi*

**Further Reading**

Daftary, Farhad. (n.d.) "Sectarian and National Movements in Iran, Khorasan, and Trasoxania during Umayyad and Early Abbasid Times." In *History of Civilizations of Central Asia.* Vol 4, pt. 1, edited by M. S. Asimov and C. E. Bosworth. UNESCO Publishing, Institute of Ismaili Studies. Retrieved 2 February 2002 from: http://www.iis.ac.uk/research/academic_papers/sectarian_national_movements/Daftary_Sectarian_National_Movements.pdf.

## KHUSHAL KHAN KHATAK

**KHUSHAL KHAN KHATAK** (1613–1689), Pashtun poet-warrior. Khushal Khan Khatak, a chief of the Khataks, one of the Pashtun tribes inhabiting the North-West Frontier Province in present-day Pakistan, is best known for his poetry in Pashtun, an Iranian language. Khushal Khan also wrote prose on subjects such as religion, society, politics, Pashtun-Afghan national unity, war, love, chivalry, philosophy, and even sports and falconry. Altogether, his works make up forty thousand verses. His *Tarikh-i-Murassa* (Jewel-Studded History), which his son, Afzal Khan (d. 1748?), compiled, sheds light on events of Mughal (1526–1857) rule in India during the mid-seventeenth century.

Khushal Khan was critical of Aurangzeb Alamgir (1618–1707), a Mughal ruler and son of Shah Jahan (1592–1666), who denied him chieftainship of the Khatak tribe and appointed other Pashtun warlords as local governors. Khushal Khan was contemptuous of Aurangzeb's religious fanaticism and greed for power: Aurangzeb jailed his father and killed his brothers to gain the throne of India. Khushal Khan spent most of his lifetime fighting against the Yousazais, a pro-Mughal fellow Pashtun tribe.

*Abdul Karim Khan*

**Further Reading**

Caroe, Olaf. (1965) *The Pathans, 550 BC–AD 1957*. London: Macmillan.

Kamil, Dost Muhammad Khan. (1968) *On a Foreign Approach to Khushal: A Critique of Caroe and Howell*. Peshawar, Pakistan: Maktabah-i-Shaheen.

MacKenzie, D. N. (1965) *Poems from the Divan of Khushal Khan Khattak*. London: Allen and Unwin.

## KHUSRAU, AMIR

**KHUSRAU, AMIR** (1253–1325), Indian poet. A renowned poet of medieval India, Amir Khusrau is a legendary figure in the history of Indian music, language, and poetry. Born in the village of Patiali in north India to Amir Saifuddin, a migrant from Transoxiana (a region northeast of the Khorasan), Khusrau settled in Delhi in 1260 after the death of his father. A close confidant of Sufi saint Nizamuddin Auliya (1236–1325), he also enjoyed the patronage of the Delhi sultan Ghiyasuddin Balban and his sons.

*Tuhfa-tus-Sighr* (Offering of a Minor), *Wastul-Hayat* (The Middle of Life), Khamsa-e-Khusro (Five Classical Romances), and *Nihayatul-Kamaal* (The Height of Wonders) are among his important works of poetry. His historical works such as *Khazain-ul-Futuh* (The Treasures of Victories), *Tughlaq Nama* (The Book of Tughluq), *Nuh Sipihr* (The Nine Heavens), and *Duval Rani-Khizr Khan* (Romance of Duval Rani and Khizr Khan) shed light on the social and political life of north India at that time.

Khusrau's *ghazals*, or lyrical poems, became very popular, and he is credited with fusing Indian and Persian elements, which influenced subsequent developments in Indian music. His dictionary of Hindi, Persian, and Arabic, *Khaliq-e-Bari*, helped to expand the vocabulary and the development of the Urdu language. Khusrau's accomplishments as musician, singer, and composer of Hindi and Persian verses earned him the sobriquet the Parrot of India.

*Patit Paban Mishra*

**Further Reading**

Government of India. (1976) *Amir Khusro, Memorial Volume.* New Delhi: Publication Division.

Mirza, Wahid. (1935) *Life and Works of Amir Khusrau*. Calcutta, India: Baptist Mission Press.

## KHUZESTAN

**KHUZESTAN** (2002 pop. 4.5 million). The discovery of oil at Masjed-e Soleyman in 1908 in the province of Khuzestan changed the fortunes of the region. Khuzestan lies in southwestern Iran bordering on Iraq and the Persian Gulf and occupies an extension of the Mesopotamian valley situated between the Zagros range and the sea. The province, with an area of 66,532 square kilometers, is a low alluvial plain formed by the deposits of the Karun and Karkheh rivers. Its climate is extremely hot, and rainfall is meager, but under irrigation the fertile northern and central lands produce sugarcane, dates, melons, and vegetables. Due to poor drainage, the low coastal areas in the south are covered with tidal salt marshes and mudflats.

The provincial capital Ahvaz is an important communications center: a river port on the Karun, an oil-pipelines nexus, and a link on the Trans-Iranian Railway

A water pipeline crosses over an oil pipeline and then under power lines in Khuzestan. (ROGER WOOD/CORBIS)

connecting the Persian Gulf with Tehran and the Caspian Sea. The discovery of oil in the province led to the establishment of the Abadan oil refinery south of Khorramshahr on an uninhabited island, which is now one of the world's largest oil-producing centers. The oil industry has almost recovered from the devastation of the 1980–1988 Iran-Iraq War. Khuzestan has the third largest oil reserves in the Middle East and the fourth largest in the world.

*Marta Simidchieva*

**Further Reading**

Fisher, W. D. (1968) *The Cambridge History of Iran.* Vol. 1, *The Land of Iran.* Cambridge, U.K.: Cambridge University Press, 33–38.

Held, Colbert C. (1989) *Middle East Patterns: Places, Peoples, and Politics.* Boulder, CO: Westview Press.

Savory, Roger M. (1986) "Khuzistan." In *Encyclopaedia of Islam.* Vol 5. Leiden, The Netherlands: E. J. Brill, 80–81.

**KHWAJA MUʿIN AL-DIN CHISHTI** (c. 1141–1236), Muslim leader of South Asia. One of the most significant Muslim personalities in premodern South Asia was Muʿin al-Din, the eponymous "founder" of the Chishti Sufi order (the most widespread and popular Islamic mystical order in India). As with other Islamic mystics, it is hard to reconstruct a factual account of his life; most anecdotal evidence comes from later hagiographic sources, which aimed to construct a behavioral paradigm that the Sufi community could emulate.

Muʿin al-Din did not write any books, but many statements are attributed to him in later writings. Some may reflect oral traditions linked to him. Muʿin al-Din's teachings are summarized in the following pearl about the qualities of a spiritual traveler: "generosity like the ocean, mildness like the sun, modesty like the Earth" (Lawrence 1992: 11). His disciples formed the so-called golden age of the Chishti order; his deputy, Qutb al-Din Bakhtiyar Kaki (d. 1236), established the order in Delhi and initiated Fardi al-Din Ganj-i Shakar (d. 1265), who became the master of Nizam al-Din Awliya (d. 1325).

Muʿin al-Din eventually settled in the Hindu state of Ajmer, where he died. His shrine complex established there became a major pilgrimage site, not just for Chishtis, but for Muslims from the entire subcontinent and even for Hindus. Mughal emperors often displayed their piety by undertaking pilgrimages to Muʿin al-Din's shrine. The emperor Akbar (reigned 1556–1605) is said to have walked on foot to Ajmer. In an even more fantastic account, Jahanara, Mughal princess and daughter of Shah Jahan (builder of the Taj Mahal), supposedly swept the saint's tomb with her eyelashes. The accuracy of these accounts may be questionable, but they convey the devotion to Muʿin al-Din attributed to the Mughal rulers of India.

The annual festival commemorating the death of Muʿin al-Din, called Urs (literally, "wedding night"), usually sees millions of devotees gathered in Ajmer.

*Omid Safi*

**Further Reading**

Lawrence, Bruce. (1992) *Nizam al-Din Awliya: Morals for the Heart.* New York: Paulist Press.

Nizami, K. A. (1954) "Cishti, Khwadja Muʿin al-Din Hasan." In *Encyclopedia of Islam, New Edition*, edited by Bernard Lewis, et al. Leiden, Netherlands: E. J. Brill.

Rizvi, S. A. A. (1991) "The Chishtiyyah." In *Islamic Spirituality: Manifestations*, edited by Seyyed Hossein Nasr. New York: Crossroad, 127–143.

Schimmel, Annemarie. (1974) *Mystical Dimension of Islam.* Chapel Hill, NC: University of North Carolina Press.

Trimingham, J. Spencer. (1971) *The Sufi Orders in Islam.* London: Oxford University Press.

**KHWARIZM** Since its earliest days Khwarizm was an agrarian outpost centered on an oasis and in contact with successive waves of nomadic peoples. Khwarizm is a region in central Asia extending south of the Aral Sea along the lower Amu Dar'ya river basin and bounded by the Kara-Kum and Kyzyl-Kum deserts and the trans-Caspian steppe. The region was ancient Chorasmia, which became a satrapy of the Persian empire in the fifth century BCE.

Khwarizm's remoteness meant that local rulers were often independent of regional powers. The Afrighids (305–995) held at bay the Sasanian emperors of Persia (third–seventh centuries) and then the Arabs, until internal strife allowed the Muslim conquerors to gain political control in 712. Within a century the Afrighids had converted to Islam and continued to rule from the city of Kath. The Ma'munids (995–1017) next claimed the crown and moved the capital to their stronghold Gurganj or Urganch, on the caravan route between Siberia and the Volga steppes.

During the early centuries of Islam, Khwarizm was an important center of learning. Among the world-famous scholars who found generous patronage at the Khwarizmian court were the philosopher and physician Ibn Sina (Avicenna; d. 980) and the polyhistor al-Biruni (d. 1051), a native of Khwarizm. The Ghaznavids (977–1186), however, annexed the province and left it in charge of Turkic slave governors, thus ending the rule of local dynasties. The Seljuks (1038–1194) continued the practice of slave governors, and their appointee Anushtigin Garchaʿi (c. 1077–1097) made the office hereditary. Anushtigin's descendants, the Khwarizm-shahs (c. 1077–1231), ruled a domain stretching from Afghanistan to Baghdad and south to the Persian Gulf, but they fell to the Mongols in the early 1220s.

Under the Golden Horde, Urganch became a thriving caravan trade center until Timur (Tamerlane, 1336–1405) destroyed it in 1388. A khanate established in the early sixteenth century by a new wave of Chinggizid nomads, the Uzbeks, was in constant rivalry with the Bukharan khanate and suffered many incursions by nomadic Turkmen raiders. In the nineteenth century a new dynasty of military chiefs of the Qungrat tribe held the nomads in check and vigorously resisted Russia's expansion into the area.

In 1873, however, the khanate became a Russian protectorate. The last khan was forced to abdicate in 1920, after the Bolshevik Revolution. The khanate was replaced by the short-lived Khoresmian People's Soviet Republic, which, four years later, was divided along ethnic lines between the Turkmen and Uzbek Soviet Socialist Republics. Presently the oasis is part of the Khorezm subdivision of Uzbekistan.

*Marta Simidchieva*

### Further Reading


Barthold, Wilhelm (Bartol'd, Vasilii Vladimirovich). (1977) *Turkestan down to the Mongol Invasion.* Trans. by T. Minorsky. 4th ed. London: E. J. W. Gibb Memorial Trust.

Becker, Seymour. (1968) *Russia's Protectorates in Central Asia: Bukhara and Khiva, 1865–1924.* Cambridge, MA: Harvard University Press.

Bosworth, Clifford Edmund. (1978) "Khwarazm." In *Encyclopaedia of Islam.* Vol 4. Leiden, Netherlands: E. J. Brill, 1060–1065.


## KHYBER PASS

**KHYBER PASS** The Khyber Pass is the northernmost strategically important mountain pass between Afghanistan and Pakistan, connecting Kabul with the historic Pakistani region of Peshawar. The pass is 56 kilometers long and some parts of it reach over 914 meters in elevation. Most of the pass can be more correctly described as a gorge formed by two rivers. Contained by sheer cliffs made mostly of limestone, the pass becomes a narrow defile as one approaches the Afghani border. A number of villages and old forts are perched on the rocks along the pass.

Traditionally, the Khyber Pass was both a crucial trading and invasion route. Persian and Macedonian armies probably followed the route in antiquity. Most recently, the pass was used and fought over by the British in the nineteenth century and the Soviet invasion forces in the 1980s.

The pass's value for trade is indicated by the presence of several market towns on the cliffs overlooking its winding road. The largest, Landi Kotal, is situated on the highest point in the pass (elevation 963 meters), where a powerful fort once stood. The pass had been used as a caravan route for thousands of years, helping tie Central Asian commercial centers of Bukhara, Samarqand, Merv (now Mary), and others with the prosperous marketplaces of the Indian subcontinent. In the fifth century BCE King Darius of Persia marched his huge army through the pass to the Indus River, probably enlarging it in the process. Future conquerors from Alexander the Great to Babur also passed through this road. In 1925 a railway was opened through the pass, featuring thirty-four tunnels and ninety-four bridges and culverts, increasing its commercial importance. There is also a fairly good hard-surface road in the pass. Today the Pakistani Khyber Agency has the authority over the pass, at least its Pakistani sector.

*Mikhail Zeldovich*

### Further Reading


"Khyber Pass." (2001) In Afghanpedia. Retrieved 27 December 2001, from: http://www.spinghar.com/afghanpedia.

Hopkirk, Peter. (1994) *The Great Game: The Struggle for Empire in Central Asia.* New York: Kodansha International.

**KILLING FIELDS** On 17 April 1975, the first day of Year Zero, the Khmer Rouge (Cambodian Communists) overthrew the military-led government of the Khmer Republic (Cambodia) and U.S.-backed General Lon Nol (1913–1985), after a five-year civil war that left 600,000 Khmer dead. Their leader, Pol Pot (1925–1999), otherwise known as "Brother Number One," then began a reign of terror that would eventually kill perhaps as many as 2 million Cambodians (estimates vary widely) of every socioeconomic class, religious belief, and ethnic group.

In only four years, nearly 25 percent of all the people in Cambodia lost their lives in the Khmer Rouge revolution and the state-sponsored violence it perpetuated as part of a social experiment gone amok. At its peak, more than thirteen hundred persons died each day—indiscriminately killed for reasons both personal and political. Men, women, and children succumbed to horrific conditions of abuse, overwork, and starvation. An additional 200,000 persons were tortured and executed without trial, judged as "class enemies" by the Khmer Rouge.

Many of the executions occurred at Security Prison 21 (Tuol Sleng, or S21), a former high school in the capital city of Phnom Penh. Anyone accused of working for the U.S., Russian, or Vietnamese governments was summarily executed, as were civil servants and soldiers associated with the former Cambodian government, teachers, doctors, lawyers, monks, dancers, and artists—even those who wore eyeglasses were arbitrarily slain, because they were assumed to be intellectuals. Victims were warned by signs at S21 not to cry while being subjected to electric shocks and beatings, and barbed wire outside the doomed prisoners' rooms prevented escape from punishment and execution. Outside the city, the bodies were dumped into the mass graves of Choeung Ek, the Khmer Rouge extermination camp located approximately 15 kilometers southwest of Phnom Penh that came to be known for this reason as the Killing Fields. Some fourteen thousand people were killed there. By May 2000, 520 such killing fields had been uncovered throughout Cambodia, containing more than ten thousand mass graves.

Between 1975 and 1979, the Khmer Rouge effectively dismantled the country's existing economic infrastructure and depopulated every urban area. Forcibly driving the 2 million residents of Phnom Penh and other towns into the rural countryside only two days after capturing the capital, Pol Pot effectively initiated one of the most brutal and radical transformations of a society ever attempted in recorded history. Cambodian survivors today relate stories of families forcibly separated and sent to agrarian collec-

The major product of the killing fields, a pile of skulls, in a deserted school in Siem Reap, Cambodia. (MICHAEL FREEMAN/CORBIS)

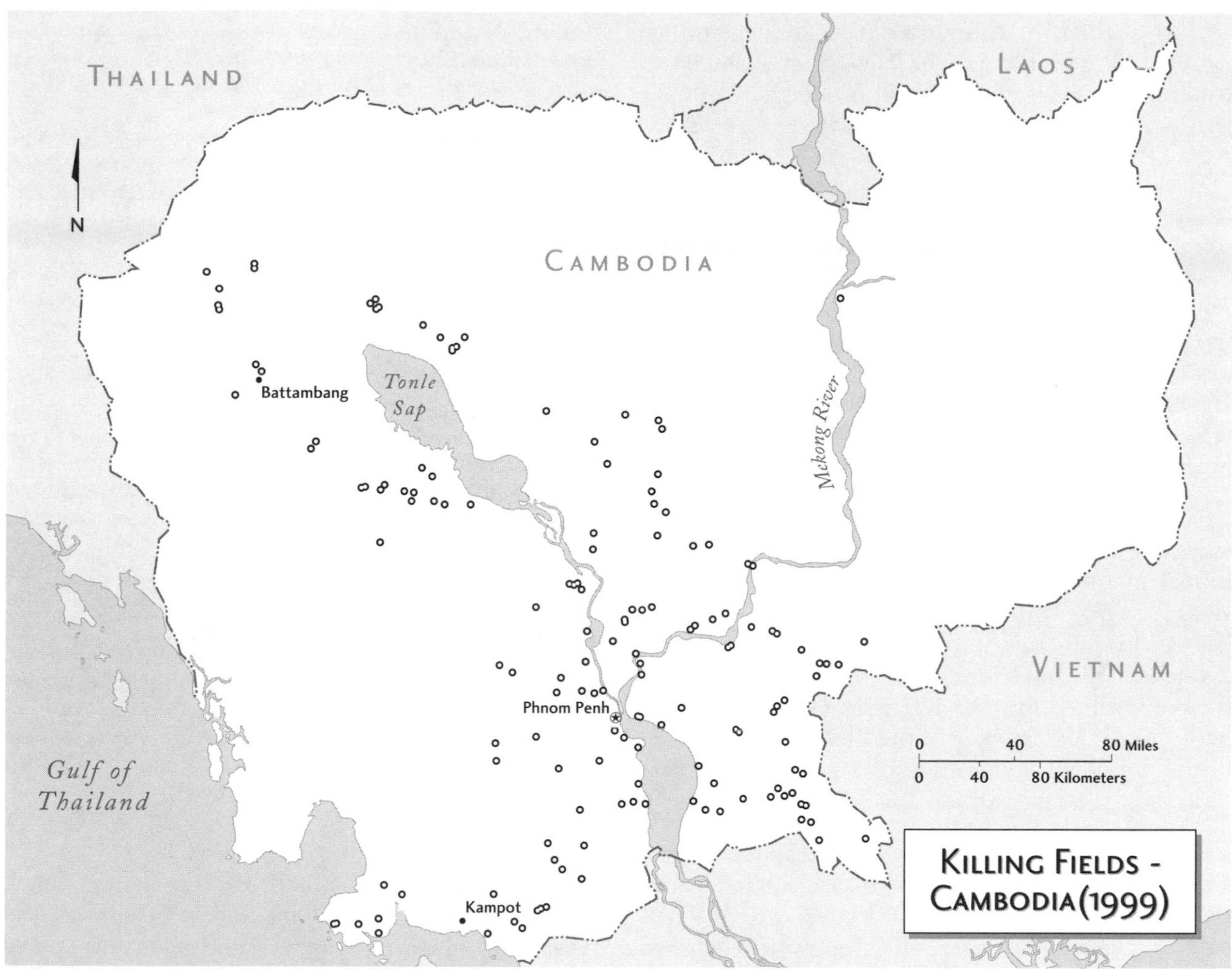


tives in different parts of the country, while monks not murdered outright were forced to disrobe and to marry. Children were co-opted into spying on—and often murdering—their parents and elders. Rural youths, often illiterate, were encouraged to punish those they found lacking in revolutionary spirit, while workers—forced to work twelve to fourteen hours a day—subsisted on meager bowls of watery soup with a few grains of rice for nutrition each day.

Symbols of Cambodian society were equally disrupted. Social institutions of every kind—stores, banks, schools, hospitals, churches, even the Khmer language and currency—were purged or torn down. Nothing was sacred outside the autarkic vision of Angka, the regime's mysterious organization that claimed to have "more eyes than a pineapple" and that maintained control through a constant atmosphere of fear and uncertainty.

Pol Pot's ideological intent was to create a purely agrarian society or cooperative. Practically isolated from the outside world, his "Democratic Kampuchea" was completely devoid of money, property, cities, all but the most primitive health care, traditional education, religion, and arts (including traditional dance and music). Pol Pot's harsh, utopian policies made the Cambodian revolution one of the most murderous in the twentieth century.

The revolution derived its energy, so the Khmer Rouge believed, from the empowerment of the rural poor, from their recent victory over the Phnom Penh military, and from what they thought was the intrinsic superiority of Cambodians to the hated Vietnamese. Pol Pot assumed that the Cambodian revolution would be swifter and more authentic than anything Vietnam could carry out, and his Chinese patrons said they agreed. By mobilizing mass resentments, as Mao Zedong had done in China, Pol Pot inspired tens of thousands of Cambodians—especially teenagers and those in their early twenties—to join in dismantling Cambodian society and liberating everyone from their past.

The methods he chose were naive, brutal, and inept. In 1976 a hastily written four-year plan sought to triple the country's agricultural production within a year—without fertilizer, modern tools, or material incentives. The plan paid no attention to Cambodia's physical geography nor did it use common sense. Already crippled by the preceding years of civil war, Cambodian farmers were expected to meet impossible quotas. Yet, Khmer Rouge workers, frightened of reprisals by their leaders if production failed to satisfy the goals, cut back the grain allotted for residents' consumption. As a consequence, tens of thousands of Cambodians starved to death, while many more collapsed from exhaustion and the absence of adequate medical equipment and care.

Sporadic violence flared between the once nominal allies, the Khmer Rouge and Vietnam, in 1977, as the former mounted occasional raids against Vietnamese villages along the border. Exasperated, Vietnam launched a full-scale war in 1978. Refused troops or assistance by the Chinese, Pol Pot's troops found themselves outgunned and outmaneuvered by the superior forces and training of the Vietnamese, who had in the preceding four decades defeated the militaries of France, the United States, and South Vietnam.

On Christmas Day, 1978, the Vietnamese entered Cambodia with more than 100,000 soldiers and ousted the Khmer Rouge regime. Pol Pot escaped to Thailand by helicopter when the Vietnamese entered Phnom Penh on 7 January 1979, leaving the city deserted. The Vietnamese quickly installed a new government, first under Heng Samrin (b. c. 1934) as president of the People's Revolutionary (Communist) Council of Kampuchea and then briefly under Prime Ministers Pen Sovann (b. 1936) and then Hun Sen (b. [officially] 1951), a former cadre in the Khmer Rouge who had fled the country in 1977 when he feared that he would be executed in S21.

After the Vietnamese liberated the Cambodian people, 600,000 Cambodians fled to Thai border camps to escape continued conflict and terror (though most have returned since the 1998 coup). Meanwhile, nearly 10 million land mines were sown throughout the countryside by opposing guerrilla groups during the late 1970s, more than one for every person in the country. As a result, though the years of genocide have effectively ended, the killing of Cambodians by Cambodians continues.

*Greg Ringer*

*See also:* **Cambodia—History; Khmer Rouge; Pol Pot**

**Further Reading**


Becker, Elizabeth. (1996) *When the War Was Over: The Voices of Cambodia's Revolution and Its People.* New York: Simon & Schuster.

Chandler, David. (1999) *Brother Number One: A Political Biography of Pol Pot.* 2d ed. Boulder, CO: Westview Press.

———. (1991) *The Tragedy of Cambodian History: Politics, War, and Revolution since 1945.* New Haven, CT: Yale University Press.

———. (2000) *Voices from S-21: Terror and History in Pol Pot's Secret Prison.* Berkeley and Los Angeles: University of California Press.

Deac, Wilfred. (1997) *Road to the Killing Fields: The Cambodian War of 1970–1975.* College Station, TX: Texas A&M University.

Hudson, Christopher. (1984) *The Killing Fields.* London: Pan Books.

Jackson, Karl D. (1992) *Cambodia 1975–1978: Rendezvous with Death.* 2d ed. Princeton, NJ: Princeton University Press.

Kiernan, Ben. (1998) *The Pol Pot Regime: Race, Power, and Genocide in Cambodia under the Khmer Rouge, 1975–79.* New Haven, CT: Yale University Press.

Morris, Stephen J. (1999) *Why Vietnam Invaded Cambodia: Political Culture & the Causes of War.* Palo Alto, CA: Stanford University Press.

Pran, Dith, and Ben Kiernan, eds. (1999) *Children of Cambodia's Killing Fields: Memoirs by Survivors.* 2d ed. New Haven, CT: Yale University Press.


**KIM DAE JUNG** (b. 1924), president of South Korea and winner of the 2000 Nobel Peace Prize. Kim Dae Jung, a long-time opposition leader, was elected president of South Korea in December 1997. He was born on 6 January 1924 in South Cholla Province, where he attended school, eventually graduating from high school in 1943. During the Korean War (1950–1953), Kim was captured by North Korean troops and sentenced to death as a traitor because he worked for the Japanese. Kim managed to escape his captors, finding his way back to Seoul.

Kim entered politics in 1960 as an opposition member in the national assembly. Eventually, in 1971 Kim ran as the New Democratic Party's presidential candidate against sitting president Park Chung Hee (1917–1979). Kim lost to Park by a narrow margin, thereby setting the stage for his becoming a vociferous critic of the Park regime. Park considered Kim such a danger that he had him kidnapped in Japan by the Korean Central Intelligence Agency and brought back to Seoul to stand trial by a secret military court for treason. Under heavy diplomatic pressure, Park rescinded Kim's death sentence, which was later commuted to three years' imprisonment, and Kim was released from jail.

Kim Dae Jung at the Asian Pacific Economic Cooperation Summit in Brunei in November 2000. (AFP/CORBIS)

Following the coup that brought Chun Doo Hwan (b. 1931) to power in 1979, Kim was again arrested, jailed, and sentenced to death. Kim's sentence was again commuted, and he was allowed to leave for the United States, where he was to receive medical treatment. Kim returned to South Korea in February 1985 and again became involved in Korean politics, first as an adviser to the Council for Promotion of Democracy and then as a member of the Reunification Democratic Party. Kim ran for the presidency in 1992, losing to Kim Young Sam. In 1997, he again stood as a candidate and, with support from Kim Jung Pil, leader of the opposition Democratic Republic Party, was elected president of South Korea.

Kim's election marked the first time that a peaceful transition of power took place in the South since the formation of the Republic of Korea. Kim's presidency was marked by a historic trip to P'yongyang, capital of North Korea, in June 2000 to open North-South dialogue on the possible reunification of Korea.

*Keith A. Leitich*

**Further Reading**

Kim Dae Jung. (1985) *Mass-Participating Economy: A Democratic Alternative for Korea*. Lanham, MD: University Press of America.

———. (1987) *Prison Writing*. Trans. by Choi Sung-il and David Malone. Berkeley and Los Angeles: University of California Press.

**KIM IL SUNG** (1912–1994), State leader of North Korea. The longest-serving head of state in the twentieth century, Kim Il Sung dominated North Korean politics for nearly fifty years, from his installation by Soviet occupying forces in fall 1945 until his death on 8 July 1994. Given his intense Stalinist personality cult and the extreme concentration of power under him, one could say that he *was* North Korean politics.

Born Kim Song Ju on 15 April 1912 near P'yongyang, he emigrated to Manchuria with his family in 1926. Imprisoned briefly for membership in the Communist Youth League in 1930, he joined (and some accounts claim later led) a guerrilla band fighting against the Japanese two years later. At this time, he took the nom de guerre Kim Il Sung, after an earlier Korean guerrilla leader. He went to the Soviet Union in 1941, or earlier, receiving military and political training in Moscow, the Soviet Far East, or both.

As chairman of the Soviet-supported People's Committee of North Korea in 1945, he quickly consolidated power and became the first premier of the Democratic People's Republic of Korea in September 1948. Eager to unify the two Koreas by force, he obtained conditional support for an invasion of South Korea from the Soviet leader Joseph Stalin and the Chinese leader Mao Zedong. After nearly conquering the South, his regime was almost destroyed by an American counterattack in fall 1950, and he was saved only by Chinese military intervention. Agreeing with the Chinese to an armistice in 1953, he never accepted a divided Korea, and until his death he worked to undermine what he viewed as an illegitimate U.S.-supported government in Seoul.

During the 1950s, Kim reconsolidated power and purged Communists he viewed as loyal to Beijing or Moscow. He sought to preserve a measure of independence by carefully balancing relations with the neighboring Communist giants through a policy often called equidistance. Up through the 1970s, his government pursued high growth by means of heavy industrialization and gradual collectivization of agriculture. Even so, the North was heavily dependent on aid from and barter trade with the Soviets and Chinese. Beginning in the 1950s, Kim propounded his opaque *juche* (self-reliance) philosophy, which purported to explain Korean uniqueness and in time

North Korean officers and officials seated in front of a portrait of Kim Il Sung on 14 April 2000, the eve of his birthday, celebrated as Sung Day in North Korea. (AFP/CORBIS)

eclipsed Marxism-Leninism as the state's core ideology. North Korean society became even more regimented than its Soviet or Chinese counterparts, and over all the godlike Kim personality cult (what historian Bruce Cumings calls an extreme form of corporatism) loomed large.

Economic growth halted in the 1980s, and Kim refused to consider a reform-and-opening policy like that employed in China. With the collapse of Soviet and Chinese support in 1990, the North Korean economy gradually fell apart. In 1972, Kim had begun to retire from some of his formal positions and to groom his son Kim Jong Il (b. 1941) as his successor. The elder Kim nonetheless retained ultimate authority and oversaw the ventures that were to mark North Korea as a "rogue state": arms sales to authoritarian regimes in the Middle East, international terrorism aimed at destabilizing South Korea, and the development of long-range missiles and nuclear weapons. The latter led to Kim's final crisis in 1994, and a second Korean War was averted when Kim agreed with the former U.S. president Jimmy Carter to halt the nuclear-weapons program in exchange for moderation of international economic sanctions and talks with the United States on nuclear and other issues. Kim died of a heart attack, and his funeral was an occasion for a mass outpouring of grief from a people who had known no other leader.

*Joel R. Campbell*

### Further Reading


Buzo, Adrian. (1999) *The Guerrilla Dynasty: Politics and Leadership in North Korea.* Boulder, CO: Westview.

Cumings, Bruce. (1993) "The Corporate State in North Korea." In *State and Society in Contemporary Korea,* edited by Hagen Koo. Ithaca, NY: Cornell University Press, 197–230.

———. (1998) *Korea's Place in the Sun: A Modern History.* New York: W. W. Norton.

Hunter, Helen-Louise, and Stephen J. Solarz. (1999) *Kim Il Sung's North Korea.* New York: Greenwood.

"Kim Il Sung." *Encarta Encyclopedia.* Retrieved 23 August 2001, from: http://encarta.msn.com/find?Concise.asp?ti+04C16000

"Kim Il Sung: A Brief Biography." (From official North Korea sources.) Retrieved 20 August 2001, from: www geocities.com/CapitolHill/Lobby/1461/kimilsungbio.htm

"Kim Il Sung: North Korean Leader." Retrieved 20 August 2001, from: http://clinton.com/SPECIALS/cold.war/kbank/profiles/kim/

Noland, Marcus. (2000) *Avoiding the Apocalypse: The Future of the Two Koreas.* Washington, DC: Institute for International Economics.

Suh, Dae-Sook. (1995) *Kim Il Sung: The North Korean Leader.* New York: Columbia University Press.


**KIM JONG IL** (b. 1941), leader of North Korea. Son of the founder of the People's Democratic Republic of Korea (North Korea), Kim Jong Il was born on 16 February 1941, probably in the Soviet Far East or Manchuria, although Pyongyang (the capital of North Korea) claims he was born on the sacred Mount Paektu. As a boy, he was sent to China during the Korean War (1950–1953) and later took pilot training in East Germany. Graduating from Kim Il Sung University in 1964, he went to work in the Korean Workers' Party secretariat, where he assisted with political purges in 1967. He married in 1966, divorced in 1971, and remarried in 1973. Groomed to succeed his father from 1973, when he became the unofficial Korean Workers' Party leader (referred to as the "party center"), Kim gradually became the second most powerful figure in North Korea.

Formally acknowledged as successor in 1980, he was thenceforth known as the "Dear Leader" and was absorbed into his father's personality cult. Information about him at this time is sketchy, but he reportedly was in charge of key party and personnel decisions and directed North Korea's foreign terrorism campaign. He was said to be highly interested in new production methods and was heavily involved in labor-mobilization campaigns. Foreign news reports described him as a hard-drinking playboy, much interested in movies and fast cars. He was invariably pictured with a bouffant hairdo, wearing a jumpsuit, square glasses, and elevator shoes.

Kim took power upon his father's death in July 1994 yet curiously remained out of public view for some time. Though already nominal military leader, he did not assume any of the elder Kim's military roles until he was named secretary general of the Korean Workers' Party in October 1997. North Korea's economy

South Korean President Kim Dae Jung (L) and North Korean leader Kim Jong Il raise hands on 14 June 2000 in Pyongyang. They had just concluded a meeting which produced a joint statement of cooperation. (REUTERS NEWMEDIA INC./CORBIS)

virtually collapsed under his rule, and, due to floods and drought, an extended famine greatly affected many rural areas. His government admitted that several hundred thousand people died, though foreign relief agencies felt that the numbers were much higher. Kim talked often about the need for economic changes and introduced modest liberalization, yet the Stalinist structure and *juche* (self-reliance) ideology inherited from his father remained essentially intact.

Kim also continued his father's nuclear and missile development programs, but in late 1994 he agreed to give up the former in exchange for a foreign-built nuclear reactor and assented to a moratorium for the latter in 1998. He became increasingly reliant on the Korean People's Army (KPA) for political support and maintenance of public order, and most of his appearances were at KPA events. Kim surprised many observers by his ebullient reception of South Korean leader Kim Dae Jung at a Pyongyang summit in June 2000. He agreed to a second summit to be held later in Seoul, South Korea.

*Joel Campbell*

**Further Reading**

Cumings, Bruce. (1997) *Korea's Place in the Sun: A Modern History*. New York: Norton, 414–417.

Eberstadt, Nicholas. (1994) "North Korea: Reform, Muddling Through, or Collapse?" In *One Korea?: Challenges and Prospects for Reunification*, edited by Thomas H. Henriksen and Kyung Soo Lho. Stanford, CA: Hoover Institution Press, 15–16.

Gill, B. K. (1996) *Korea versus Korea: A Case of Contested Legitimacy*. London: Routledge.

Hoare, James, and Susan Pares. (1999) *Conflict in Korea: An Encyclopedia*. Santa Barbara, CA: ABC-CLIO, 79.

Nahm, Andrew C. (1993) *Introduction to Korean History and Culture*. Elizabeth, NJ: Hollym, 137–139, 258, 261, 277–297.

Oberdorfer, Don. (1997) *The Two Koreas: A Contemporary History*. New York: Basic Books, 346–350.

**KIM MYONG-SUN** (1896–1951), Korean writer. Kim Myong-sun (pen name, Tansil) is considered to be Korea's first modern woman writer. Her first work, "Uisim ui sonyo" (Suspicious Girl), was published in the literary journal *Ch'ongch'un* (Youth) in 1917. The story mirrors Kim's own harsh and dismal life as the daughter of a rich man and his concubine, a former kisaeng (entertaining woman). Kim was born around 1896 in Pyongyang. After her mother died in 1907, she was raised by her stepmother. She graduated from high school in 1911 and went on to college but did not finish.

Throughout the 1920s Kim wrote many stories about love, a common literary theme of the period. Her protagonists were usually women conflicted by their love for the wrong men. Kim belonged to two important literary groups, Changjo (Creation) and Pyeho (Ruins), each centered in a literary journal of that name.

Kim wrote in every genre of literature from fiction to poetry and drama. She also acted in and starred in movies. Despite her talents, Kim lived most of her adult life in poverty. She published her last poem in 1939 and spent the remainder of her life in obscurity, disdained by Korean society for her sexually liberated lifestyle, which flouted traditional role expectations for women. She died in 1951 in a Japanese mental asylum.

*Jennifer Jung-Kim*

**Further Reading**

So, Carolyn P. (1994) "Seeing the Silent Pen: Kim Myong-sun, a Pioneering Woman Writer." *Korean Culture* 15, 2 (summer): 34–40.

**KIM PU-SHIK** (1075–1151), Korean historian and statesman. Kim Pu-shik was one of the most notable scholar-officials of Korea's Koryo dynasty (918–1392) and a figure of central importance in Korean historiography for his role as chief compiler of the *Samguk sagi* (A History of the Three Kingdoms). He came from a family of noteworthy scholar-officials of the mid-Koryo and traced his lineage back to the royal line of the Shilla kingdom (57 BCE–935 CE). Under several Koryo kings, Kim Pu-shik served key roles in the kingdom's administration, even leading a Koryo army to defeat a dynasty-threatening internal rebellion in 1136. His crowning achievement came with the compilation of the *Samguk sagi*, a history of the three kingdoms of ancient Korea (Shilla, Paekche, Koguryo), commissioned by Koryo's King Injong (1123–1146) and completed in 1145. Its importance today lies primarily in the fact that it is the oldest surviving native Korean history and the chief source for the history of the three kingdoms.

Kim Pu-shik was an unapologetically Confucian scholar, trained and nurtured in Chinese literary technique and tradition, and always espoused Korea's politically subservient role vis-à-vis China, a fact that has made him the prime target of much latter day Korean nationalist criticism. Yet Kim Pu-shik was also a practicing Buddhist, and his surviving magnum opus reveals a just pride in Korean achievements and recognition of Korea's unique cultural development.

*Daniel Kane*

**Further Reading**

Gardiner, K. H. J. (1970) "*Samguk sagi* and Its Sources." *Papers on Far Eastern History* 2 (September): 1–41.

Jamieson, John C. (1969) "The *Samguk sagi* and the Unification Wars." Ph.D. diss., University of California, Berkeley.

Kim, Kichung. (1996) "Notes on the *Samguk sagi* and *Samguk yusa*." In *An Introduction to Classical Korean Literature*. London: M. E. Sharpe.

**KIM SOWOL** (1902–1934), Korean poet. Sowol (his sobriquet) Kim Chong-shik was born in Korea and attended Osan Middle School near P'yongyang in today's North Korea, a famously activist, nationalist academy. He left when the academy was closed because of its involvements in the 1 March 1919 Independence Movement and went to Seoul, following his teacher and mentor Kim Ok. Sowol became a student at the Paejae Academy in Seoul and after graduation in 1923 left for Japan, to enter Tokyo Commercial College.

Sowol soon returned to Seoul, however, and tried for a time to make his way in the literary world. With Kim Ok's help, he published poems in a number of journals, including many in *Kaebyok* (Genesis). His single book of poems, *Chindallas kkot* (Azaleas), named for his most popular poem, came out in 1925, but he was unable to sustain himself as a writer, returned to his home area of Osan, and tried various small-scale business endeavors. He published few poems in the last years of his brief life. He died in December 1934, possibly a suicide.

Sowol's poems are noteworthy for their lyrical elegance, their folksong themes of loneliness and separation, and their stunning command of the expressive possibilities of the Korean language. While his best-known poems seem almost deliberately to overlook concerns about Korea's national identity during the Japanese colonial period, a subject that engaged many other writers, Sowol, in attending to particular place-names and to the routes or modes of transportation that connect them, seems to have addressed the subtle issue of how Korea was being remapped, reconfigured as a geographical space, by the colonial occupation and modernization.

*David McCann*

**Further Reading**

McCann, David R. (2001) "Korea the Colony and the Poet Sowôl." In *War, Occupation, and Creativity: Japan and East Asia, 1920–1960,* edited by Marlene J. Mayo and J. Thomas Rimer. Honolulu, HI: University of Hawaii Press.

**KIM YOUNG-SAM** (b. 1927), South Korean president. Kim Young-sam served as president of the Republic of Korea from 1993 until 1998, when he was defeated by longtime personal and political rival Kim Dae Jung. His presidency was noteworthy in two respects. Kim was the first civilian president in the postwar period, and he oversaw the first civilian transfer of power in South Korea's short history.

Kim was born in 1927 on Koje Island in South Kyongsang Province. After graduating from Seoul National University in 1952, he entered government service. His political debut came soon thereafter: he won a seat in the National Assembly in 1954 as a member of the ruling Liberal Party. Shortly after, however, Kim switched his political affiliation and defected to the opposition Democratic Party.

In 1972 Kim lost his bid to become the New Democratic Party's presidential nominee, as factionalism within the party divided support between Kim Dae Jung and himself. Although set back by his defeat, Kim became leader of the New Democratic Party in 1974, but he was expelled from the National Assembly in 1978 in the political crisis that enveloped the presidency of Park Chung Hee. Following the coup that

Kim Young-sam speaking to the media during the 1987 presidential election campaign. (DAVID & PETER TURNLEY/CORBIS)

brought Chun Doo Hwan to power, Kim was placed under house arrest until May 1983. Although banned from political activity, Kim became cochair of the Council for Promotion of Democracy in 1984 and became an adviser to the New Korea Democratic Party in 1986.

In the preceding year, Kim established a new political party, the Reunification Democratic Party, and ran as its presidential candidate against Roh Tae Woo and Kim Dae Jung. Defeated in the presidential election, Kim merged his Reunification Democratic Party with the New Democratic Republican Party to form the Democratic Liberal Party, of which he was chosen chairman.

Kim ran in and won the 1992 South Korean presidential election. Kim Young-sam's term in office can be best characterized by its cold relations with North Korea, the trials of former presidents Chun Doo Hwan and Roh Tae Woo, and the trial of his own son for corruption and tax evasion.

*Keith Leitich*

### Further Reading

Kim Young Sam. (1993) *Crusader for Democracy: The Life and Times of Kim Young Sam*. Seoul: Yonhap News Agency.

Oberdorfer, Don. (1997) *The Two Koreas: A Contemporary History*. Reading, MA: Addison Wesley Longham.

**KIM YU-SIN** (595–673), general and statesman of the Shilla kingdom. Kim Yu-sin was one of the primary architects of Shilla unification of the peninsula in 676 and is still revered as one of Korea's leading historical figures and national heroes.

Kim Yu-sin was born of a Shilla aristocratic family in 595, at a time of increasing rivalry between Korea's three dominant kingdoms (Paekche in the southwest, Koguryo in the north, and Shilla in the southeast), and was brought up in the tradition of strict military and Buddhist discipline common to the youths of Shilla nobility.

For almost two centuries the three Korean kingdoms had fought an ever-shifting struggle for territory on the Korean peninsula. By the early seventh century, with China unified under the Sui (518–618) and then the Tang (618–907) dynasties, their mutual struggle intensified to one for complete peninsular hegemony. After Shilla secured an alliance with the Tang dynasty, Kim Yu-sin in 661 led Shilla forces in a combined Shilla-Tang attack upon Paekche that culminated in that kingdom's defeat. The defeat of Koguryo, again through a Shilla-Tang alliance, soon followed in 668. The defeat of Koguryo, again through a Shilla-Tang alliance, followed in 668. Soon after these victories, however, Tang China moved to consolidate its power on the peninsula by creating Chinese protectorates of former Paekche and Koguryo territory, an event that soon led to war between Tang and Shilla. Though Kim Yu-sin would die before he could witness Korean unification with Shilla's defeat of Tang forces in 676, he is still viewed more than any other historical figure as the father of Korean unification. His tomb can still be seen in the historic city of Kyongju, the former capital of the Shilla kingdom.

*Daniel C. Kane*

### Further Reading

Adams, Edward B. (1991) *Korea's Golden Age: Cultural Spirit of Silla in Kyongju*. Rev. ed. Seoul: Seoul International Publishing House.

Chu, Yo-sop. (1947) *Kim Yusin: The Romances of a Korean Warrior of the 7th Century*. Seoul: Mutual Publishers.

Ilyon, Samguk yusa. (1972) *Legends and History of the Three Kingdoms of Ancient Korea*. Trans. by Tae-Hung Ha and Grafton K. Mintz. Seoul: Yonsei University Press.

McBride, Richard D., II. (1998) "Hidden Agendas in the Life Writings of Kim Yusin." *Acta Koreana* 1 (August): 101–142.

Yi, Ki-baek. (1984) *A New History of Korea*. Trans. by Edward W. Wagner with Edward J. Shultz. Seoul: Ilchokak Publishers.

**KINABALU, MOUNT** Mount Kinabalu, the highest mountain in Southeast Asia, is located in the Crocker Range of Sabah, a Malaysian state located on the island of Borneo. At 4,101 meters the mountain is a spectacular sight, described as a rectangular indented parapet rising above the rest of the range and Sabah. Botanists and zoologists have found Mount Kinabalu to be a reservoir of plants and animals. Half of the world's genera of flowering plants are to be found on Mount Kinabalu. Among these are the world's largest flowers, the *Rafflesia*, and well over one thousand species of orchids, including the slipper orchids for which Mount Kinabalu is renowned among orchid enthusiasts. Mount Kinabalu also has the largest variety of pitcher plants in the world.

Only the upper 300 meters of the mountain are bare; the rest is covered with vegetation, the type of which varies according to the elevation. Primary rainforest below 600 meters marks the boundary of the Kinabalu State Park, which was established in 1964 and covers about 76,700 hectares. The terrain above then ranges from rich lowland dipterocarp forest to montane oak/chestnut, shrub, and conifer forests be-

Mount Kinabalu rises behind the capital city of Kota Kinabalu, Sabah, Malaysia. (NIK WHEELER/CORBIS)

fore giving way to a mossy forest and finally the treeless alpine peak.

Mount Kinabalu is considered a young mountain and is actually younger than its surrounding rock. It is a great granite pluton (an intrusive body of igneous rock) that pushed its way through the Crocker Range between one and three million years ago. The rest of the range is approximately nine million years old.

The Dusun and Kadzan tribal people who live in the foothills of Mount Kinabalu hold the mountain sacred. They named it Aki Nabalu, which means "the revered place of the dead." Legend has it that the name of the mountain dates to the arrival of the Chinese in Sabah centuries ago. The word Kina is supposedly derived from the name Cina, or "China," and *balu* means "widow." A Chinese prince was believed to have climbed the mountain in search of a great pearl guarded at the summit by a dragon. According to the legend, he finds the pearl, kills the dragon, and marries a Kadzan girl but eventually leaves her and returns to China. His wife climbs to the "spirit mountain" to mourn the loss and is then turned to stone.

The first person documented to have climbed Mount Kinabalu, in 1857, was Sir Hugh Low, then a British colonial secretary stationed in Labuan. The highest peak on Kinabalu—Low's Peak—is named for him, although he never reached it. A zoologist, John Whitehead, was the first to reach the summit, in 1887.

*Ooi Giok Ling*

## MOUNT KINABALU—WORLD HERITAGE SITE

A nature reserve designated as a UNESCO World Heritage Site in 2000, Kinabalu National Park on the island of Borneo in Malaysia contains an astonishing variety of flora and fauna within its mountainous tropical rain forests.

### Further Reading

Hoebel, Robert. (1985) *Sabah on the Island of Borneo/Malaysia*. Hong Kong: Robert Rovera Ltd.

**KINKI REGION** (2001 est. pop. 22.2 million). The Kinki Region is located in the western part of Central Honshu in Japan and consists of Osaka, Hyogo, Kyoto, Shiga, Mie, Wakayama, and Nara Prefectures. It has an area of 33,075 square kilometers.

Most of the region has mountainous topography, but there are numerous coastal plains on the Inland Sea, Osaka Bay, and the Kii Channel. The Kii Peninsula in the southern part has a rainy climate and is warm in winter. The northern part facing the Sea of Japan is affected by northwest winds, and the winds off the Tsushima Strait bring heavy rainfall and snow. Rice, citrus fruits, vegetables, and floricultural products are cultivated. The Hanshin Industrial Zone, in and around Osaka-Kobe, is dominated by heavy industries such as metal, machinery, chemicals, and textiles. The area is characterized by many small and medium-scale factories specializing in the production of machine parts, blankets, and footwear. Efforts have been made to promote regional development. The city of Kobe is being rebuilt after the Great Hanshin-Awaji Earthquake of 1995. In the late 1990s, the new Kansai International Airport, built in Osaka Bay, was opened. Plans also focus on new technologies through industry, government, and academic linkages in the thirty-year Kansai Science City project that started in 1987.

*Nathalie Cavasin*

### Further Reading

Association of Japanese Geographers. (1980) *Geography of Japan*. Tokyo: Teikoku-Shoin.

Yagasaki Noritaka, ed. (1997) *Japan: Geographical Perspectives on an Island Nation*. Tokyo: Teikoku-Shoin.

Rudyard Kipling in the early 1900s. (UNDERWOOD & UNDERWOOD/CORBIS)

**KIPLING, JOSEPH RUDYARD** (1865–1936), British writer. Rudyard Kipling was born in Bombay, India. His parents, John Lockwood, the principal of an art school, and Alice Macdonald Kipling, sent him to England at the age of six (1871) for school where he was subjected to nightmarish treatment that left psychological scars (recalled in his novel *Stalky and Co.*, 1899). His experience at the United Services College in north Devon (1878–1882) was also unpleasant. In 1882, Kipling joined his parents in Lahore, India, where his father was curator of the museum. Seven years' experience in journalism as a reporter and editor of two Indian newspapers, the *Civil and Military Gazette* and the *Pioneer of Allahabad*, developed his superior writing skills. It also gave him a unique look at two very different societies—British colonialists and their Indian subjects, whose stories enriched his lifelong writing career. Kipling's first publication of poetry, *Departmental Ditties* (1886), met with success. His first volume of short stories, *Plain Tales from the Hills* (1887), which was followed by five more volumes (1888–1889), as well as the two *Jungle Books* (1894) and *Kim* (1901), brought him the indelible reputation of a great storyteller. Kipling won the Nobel Prize for Literature in 1907, the first British writer to be so honored. He lived the last years of his life in London.

*Abdul Karim Khan*

### Further Reading

Bauer, Helen Pike. (1994) *Rudyard Kipling: A Study in Short Fiction*. New York: Macmillan.

Ricketts, Harry. (2000) *Rudyard Kipling: A Life*. New York: Carroll & Graf.

**KIRKUK** (2002 est. pop. 729,000). Kirkuk, a city in northern Iraq, has been occupied for thousands of years, from at least the third millennium BCE. The city is bounded by the Little Zab River to the northwest, the Jabal Hamrin to the southwest, the Diyala River to the southeast, and the Zagros Mountains to the northeast. Kirkuk is strategically located as an entry to one of the few passes through the rugged Zagros Mountains and, hence, to the Iranian plateau. Medieval Arabs knew the city as Karkhina, the name that some inhabitants still used in the late twentieth century.

The area of Kirkuk was a region of contention between the Ottomans and Safavids from the sixteenth to nineteenth centuries. In 1555 the Treaty of Amasya assigned it to the Ottomans, and many Kurds in the region accepted Sunni Islam. Kirkuk became an important garrison town, commercial center, and source of petroleum products for the Ottoman army. In 1926 Kirkuk was incorporated into Iraq as part of the new province of the Mosul.

From ancient times Kirkuk was known for its sulfur, bitumen, and oil *(naft).* In 1927 a huge oil gusher discovered at Baba Gurgur near Kirkuk became the largest oil field in the world until the discovery of the Gawar field in Saudi Arabia in the 1950s. Between World War I and World War II, Britain allowed U.S. oil companies to participate in exploiting the Kirkuk fields to encourage American support of British imperialism. By 1935 oil production from the Kirkuk fields had made Iraq the eighth-largest producer in the world. In 1935, 1948, and 1949, pipelines were built from Kirkuk to the Mediterranean ports of Haifa, Tripoli, and Banias. In the 1980s two more pipelines traversing Turkey were extended to Dörtyol on the Mediterranean.

After the 1958 Iraqi Revolution the government aimed to nationalize oil production, which was achieved in 1972. Although the southern Iraqi oil fields, especially Rumaila, became more important in the 1970s, Kirkuk's oil was still significant at the end of the twentieth century. Throughout the 1960s, oil revenue, largely from the Kirkuk fields, provided around 27 to 40 percent of Iraq's total national income, 50 percent of all general revenue, and 90 percent of all foreign exchange.

Kirkuk remained a district of Mosul province until 1975, when it was reorganized as one of the eighteen *muhafaza* (governorates) of Iraq. From 1975 onward the Iraq government pursued a policy of Arabizing Kirkuk and removing the Kurdish and Turkmen people who formed the bulk of the population. Some 4,000 Kurdish villages and some 400,000 Kurds, a substantial number from Kirkuk, were deported to other regions of Iraq. After the conclusion of the Iran-Iraq war in 1988, in the ethnic cleansing campaign called *Anfal,* 180,000 Kurds were killed. After the Gulf War in 1991 the Iraqi government heightened its ethnic cleansing practices in the Kirkuk region to ensure that the region and the oil resources remained under Iraqi control in any future settlement with the Kurdish nationalist government. That part of the Kirkuk region not under Iraqi control was held by the the Patriotic Union of Kurdistan under the leadership of Jalal Talabani, one of two main Kurdish nationalist organizations. The partitioning of Kirkuk *muhafaza* and the allocation of its oil resources have remained unsettled disputes between the Kurds and the Iraq government since 1960.

In 1965, the population of the city of Kirkuk included 71,000 Kurds, 55,000 Turkmen, 41,000 Arabs, and several thousand Chaldeans and Nestorians. In 2000, due to massive migration, urbanization, and ethnic cleansing, it was difficult to estimate the population. Kirkuk *muhafaza* may have held 200,000 to 250,000 Turkmen, and Kirkuk city 65,000 to 75,000. The remainder of the population was Arab, due to the Arabizing policies of the Iraq government, which increased during the 1990s.

*Robert Olson*

**Further Reading**

Human Rights Watch Books. (1995) *Iraq's Crime of Genocide: The Anfal Campaign against the Kurds.* New Haven, CT: Yale University Press.

Longrigg, Stephen Hemsley. (1925) *Four Centuries of Modern Iraq.* Oxford: Clarendon Press.

Marr, Phebe. (1985) *The Modern History of Iraq.* Boulder, CO: Westview Press.

**KISHI NOBUSUKE** (1896–1987), prime minister of Japan. Born in Yamaguchi prefecture in November 1896 to the Sato family, Kishi was the second male in a family of ten children. During his teenage years, he was adopted into the family of his father's older brother in order to marry his cousin Yoshiko. Subsequently he took the family name Kishi.

Kishi attended Tokyo Imperial University and was offered a position on the law faculty upon graduating in 1920, but he entered the Ministry of Agriculture and Commerce instead. After assignments in the United States, Europe, and China, Kishi became the minister of commerce and industry in Tojo Hideki's cabinet. For this he was purged from politics after World War II. Regaining his political rights in 1948, Kishi entered the Liberal Party in 1953 and later helped form the Democratic Party in 1954. He worked behind the scenes in a conservative merger that led to the formation of the Liberal Democratic Party in 1955.

He was elected the prime minister of Japan in February 1957 and held that post until his resignation in July 1960, following demonstrations in Tokyo against the revision of the United States–Japan Security Treaty earlier that year. In addition to securing the revision of this treaty in an effort to strengthen bilateral relations, Kishi visited some thirty countries during his time as prime minister, including two successful visits to Southeast Asia and Oceania, the first visit of a Japanese prime minister to this region. In addition, Kishi proposed the creation of an Asian Development Bank with $700 million in funds for Southeast Asian development, using U.S. funds and Japanese know-how. The plan did not materialize due to a lack of interest on the part of the United States and Southeast Asian countries. Although Kishi resigned as prime minister in July 1960 and officially retired from politics in 1979, he exercised behind-the-scenes influence on Liberal Democratic Party politics until his death in 1987.

*Robert Eldridge*

### Further Reading

Hara Yoshihisa. (1995) *Kishi Nobusuke: Kensei no Seijika* (Kishi Nobusuke: The Ambitious Politician). Tokyo: Iwanami Shoten.

Kishi Nobusuke. (1993) *Kishi Nobusuke Kaikoroku: Hoshu Godo to Anpo Kaitei* (The Memoirs of Kishi Nobusuke: Conservative Merger and Security Treaty Revision). Tokyo: Kosaido Shuppan.

**KISHLAK** The word *kishlak*, from a Turkic word meaning "winter quarters," refers to settled agricultural villages in Uzbekistan, Tajikistan, and Kyrgyzstan. The *kishlak*, along with its nomadic counterpart, the *aul*, was an important social unit in Central Asia, traditionally inhabited by extended family groups.

*Kishlak*s are densely settled, crowding fifty or more houses into a relatively small area, a style that the Russians who came to the area called "nesting." Houses are built around courtyards that open directly onto the street, which is typically crooked. In mountainous areas *kishlak*s are often terraced. Before the Russian annexation of Central Asia, *kishlak*s were usually defended by walls, which like most of the *kishlak*s' buildings were made of mud brick. A *kishlak*'s fields lie outside and around the town, and a common irrigation system is maintained for the use of everyone in the community.

Until the Soviet period *kishlak*s were administered by village elders called *aksakal*s. Most *kishlak*s also housed a mullah, a Muslim cleric often called on to assist the *aksakal* in making decisions. During the Soviet period an attempt was made to replace *aksakal*s with soviets of workers' deputies.

*Andrew Sharp*

### Further Reading

Krader, Lawrence. (1966) *Peoples of Central Asia*. Bloomington, IN: Indiana University Press.

**KISTNA RIVER** Kistna or Krishna River, 1,370 kilometers long, rises in the Western Ghats of India near the town of Mahabaleshwar, only 65 kilometers from the Arabian Sea, at a source that is sacred to Hindus. The river flows eastward across southern Maharashtra, northern Karnataka, and Andhra Pradesh states to empty into the Bay of Bengal through two principal mouths, after crossing a broad delta valuable for its rice agriculture. In its lower course, an important irrigation work, the Bezwada Anicut, a dam with two canals, was begun in 1852 by Sir Arthur Cotton, just below a gorge where the Kistna bursts through the Eastern Ghats and the channel is over a kilometer wide. The river's two great tributaries are the Bhima and the Tungabhadra, and the Kistna is also joined by five other important rivers. The channel is too rocky, and the stream too rapid, to allow any navigation on the Kistna. During the dry season, the depth of water may be no more than two meters. The drainage area of the Kistna covers some 245,000 square kilometers in the central Dekkan plateau.

*Paul Hockings*

**KITES AND KITE FLYING** Kites are toys that fly in the air at the end of a line, and kite flying is a popular pastime in Asia. Many kinds of kites exist, but most have light bamboo frames covered with paper or cloth and are attached to a long string held in the hand. Brightly colored and decorated, Asian kites may take the shapes of birds, insects, butterflies, or geometric forms. One of the popular Chinese kite forms is the jointed dragon.

The oldest record of a kite is from the fifth century BCE in China. Plane-surface kites were diffused into Europe in the fifteenth century, and after the sixteenth century many other kinds of kites were introduced into Europe.

In East Asia kite flying is a traditional custom with religious meaning. In Japan and Korea people fly kites during the New Year celebrations. In China the ninth day of the ninth month is a holiday honoring kites. Koreans and Chinese sometimes write words representing evils on the surfaces of kites, then they burn the kites or let them fly away in the air after the New Year. The kites are thought to carry the evils away.

Kite flying is also popular in Thailand, where in March the air is filled with a variety of kites. Historically, the people of Thailand used kites at a ceremony to hasten the end of the rainy season, believing that the wind whistling through the bamboo frames of the kites blew away rain clouds. Kite fighting has survived as one of the major sports in Thailand, and the national championships are held in Bangkok every spring. Competitors attempt to bring their opponent's kites to the ground by severing the strings to which the kites are attached. There is also a kite championship in Malaysia. Participants demonstrate the height, sound, and beauty of their kites. Malays introduced kite flying to India, where, as in Japan, it remains popular.

*Hisashi Sanada*

Spectators watch a gigantic kite being flown at a festival in Ahmadabad, India, in January 1994. (HANS GEORG ROTH/CORBIS)

**Further Reading**

Kishino, Yuzo, Yoshio Kuroda, Yuichi Suzuki, and Takeo Fukagawa, eds. (1987) *Encyclopedia of Sports*. Tokyo: Taishukan.

Ohbayashi, Taryo, Yuzo Kishino, Tsuneo Sougawa, and Shinji Yamashita, eds. (1998) *Encyclopedia of Ethnic Play and Games*. Tokyo: Taishukan.

## KITES IN KOREA

This account of kite flying in Korea provides details of the activity in the late nineteenth century and also provides a glimpse into the rivalry that existed between the Koreans and Chinese.

> It is customary for all classes in Korea from His Majesty, the King, down to fly kites. Women sometimes fly kites from their yards, but it is said that anyone can tell a kite flown by a woman. The owner of a kite is often considered unable to fly it, and when he goes away, another who understands kite-flying will take the reel and play it.
>
> The Koreans say that the Chinese do not know how to fly kites, and that when a Chinaman grows tired after having sent up his kite with a heavy string, he will tie it to a tree and lie down and watch it.
>
> The time for kite-flying is the first half of the first month. After this time, if any one should fly a kite he would be laughed at, nor will any one touch a lost kite.
>
> On the fourteenth of the first month it is customary to write in Korean characters on kites a wish to the effect that the year's misfortunes may be carried away with them. Mothers write this for their child, with his name and date of birth. The letters are placed along bamboo frames so that they may not be seen by any one who might be tempted to pick the kite up. Boys tie a piece of sulfur paper on the string of such a kite, so that when the kite goes into the air the string will burn through and the kite fall.

*Source:* Stewart Culin (1895). *Korean Games with Notes on the Corresponding Games of China and Japan*. Philadelphia: University of Pennsylvania, Department of Anthropology and Paleontology, 12.

**KIZEL IRMAK RIVER** At 1,355 kilometers, the Kizel Irmak (Kizilirmak) River is the longest in Turkey. In ancient times it was called Halys, meaning "salty flowing water." It flows from the southern slopes of Kizildag east of Sivas to the southwest and then turns north through the industrial city of Kirikkale to the Kizil Irmak delta, where it empties into the Black Sea at Bafra in Samsun Province. It is fed by rain and snow. The river drains an area of 78,000 square kilometers and is dammed in four places. The river supplies farmers with rich sediment that also is used by potters in Avanos. At Kirikkale it picks up visible pollution from local industry. At the delta it forms several shallow lakes and waterways; people living in the delta region earn money by cutting the reeds that grow there. Agriculture and fishing are also important delta activities.

*David Levinson*

### Further Reading

Erdogan, Asli. (1996) *The Land of Kizilirmak*. Retrieved 16 April 2002 from: http://www.atlasturkey.com/990503/96 july/kizilirmak.

**KOBYZ** The *kobyz (qobyz)* is a Kazakh two-stringed, bowed instrument that is similar to a lute or fiddle. A comparable instrument is the *kiak*, familiar to the Kyrgyz; similar instruments are found among many other Central Asian peoples. The *kobyz*'s ancestry can be traced to ancient musical instruments dating back at least two thousand years. The modern *kobyz* dates from the eighth or ninth century CE. Typically, the *kobyz* is made from a single piece of wood, with a long neck and a pear-shaped body. A leather membrane covers the oblong part of the *kobyz* and is traditionally made from the skin of a camel, an animal revered throughout Central Asia. The strings and bow are made from horsehair. The instrument's body is angled, making a bridge unnecessary. It also lacks frets along the neck.

Most scholars believe that these instruments originally were plucked and that bows were used only later. Indeed, many scholars believe that bowing was developed in Central Asia. The music was played by using the fingers to shorten the strings rather than pressing them to the neck. A *kobyz* was often used by a shaman in ceremonies to fend off spirits; this practice has diminished along with shamanism among the Kazakhs. The *kobyz* is a solo instrument but is often played with accompanying vocalists.

Kazakh mythology traces the first *kobyz* to a certain Korkut, considered to be the father of Kazakh music. Korkut, a shaman in some versions, was unable to accept death and escaped from people, seeking truth and immortality in nature, only to discover that nature could not grant him eternal life. He fashioned the first *kobyz*, thus finding immortality in art and music.

*Steven Sabol*

### Further Reading

Beliaev, Viktor. (1975) *Central Asian Music: Essays in the History of the Music of the Peoples of the U.S.S.R.* Middletown, CT: Wesleyan University Press.

Lawergren, Bo. (1992) "The Ancient Harp of Pazyryk: A Bowed Instrument?" In *Foundations of Empire: Archaeology and Art of the Eurasian Steppes*, edited by Gary Seaman. Los Angeles: Ethnographic Press, University of Southern California.

Winner, Thomas. (1958) *The Oral Art and Literature of the Kazakhs of Russian Central Asia*. Durham, NC: Duke University Press.

**KOCHI** (2002 est. pop. 800,000). Kochi Prefecture is situated in the southern region of Japan's island of Shikoku, where it occupies an area of 7,107 square kilometers. Kochi's main geographical features are the Ishizuchi Mountains, intersected by river valleys. The prefecture is bordered by the Pacific Ocean and by Ehime and Tokushima Prefectures. Once known as Tosa province, it assumed its present name in 1871 and its present borders in 1880. The capital of the prefecture is Kochi city, situated on Urado Bay.

During the Sengogku (Warring States) period (1467–1568), the Yamanouchi and Chosokabe warrior families, among others, exerted power over the province. The town then grew around a castle erected there in 1603 by Yamanouchi Kazutoyo. During the late Edo period (1600/1603–1868), samurai from Tosa were active in the pro-imperial movement to overthrow the Tokugawa shogunate.

The city has relatively little industry aside from some production of cement, chemicals, steel, and ships, together with processing of lumber, paper, and foodstuffs. Kochi Castle, the scenic Katsurahama shore, and the Tosa Shrine are among local attractions. The prefecture's other important cities are Nankoku, Tosa, and Nakamura.

In the early 2000s, the prefecture's main economic activity remains agriculture, its subtropical climate sometimes allowing two plantings of rice per year. Fishing also is important, as are the processing of paper and lumber, harvested from the region's thick forests. Kochi is famous for breeding the fighting dogs known as Tosa-ken. Visitors are drawn to its scenic mountains and shore, part of Ashizuri-Uwakai National Park.

*E. L. S. Weber*

### Further Reading

"Kochi Prefecture." (1993) In *Japan: An Illustrated Encyclopedia*. Tokyo: Kodansha.

**KODAMA YOSHIO** (1911–1984), Japanese right-wing ideologist. Kodama was born in Nihonmatsu in Fukushima Prefecture and raised in Tokyo. In 1920, at the age of nineteen, Kodama went to Korea to live with relatives. There he worked industrial jobs. In

1928, he became very active in right-wing and nationalist societies. In 1932, he formed the *Dokuritsu Seinen Sha* (Independence Youth Society) in Japan, which was an ultra-right-wing youth group, and attempted to assassinate opposition cabinet ministers and Prime Minister Admiral Saito Makoto (1858–1936). Kodama was arrested and sentenced to spend three and a half years at the Fuchu Penitentiary. In 1937, he went to China and Manchuria on a fact-finding mission for the Japanese Foreign Ministry and also acted as guard and adviser to Wang Ching-wei (1883–1944), who was then chairman of the national government of China.

After resigning from his position over a disagreement with Tojo Hideki (1884–1948), Kodama returned to Shanghai as a naval air force procurement agent in order to build a network through his own agency, Kodama Kikan, for securing military materials for the Japanese war effort. During World War II, his agency bought and sold radium, cobalt, copper, and nickel, and he made a fortune. At the end of the war his industrial empire was worth $175 million. At the age of thirty-four, he became the second wealthiest man in Japan and was promoted to rear admiral by the Japanese government. At the end of World War II, he was appointed adviser to Prime Minister Higashikuni Naruhiko (1887–1990), but in early 1946 he was listed as a Class A war criminal, a designation given only to cabinet officers, ultranationalists, and high-ranking military persons, and was sentenced to jail. He spent two years in Tokyo's Sugamo Prison before he was released in 1948.

After his release from prison, Kodama became a behind-the-scenes force in politics and used his fortune to help finance conservative parties and politicians in Japan. When, in 1955, the Liberal Party merged with the Democratic Party to form the LDP (Liberal Democratic Party), Kodama emerged as its principal spokesman. In the late 1960s and early 1970s, Kodama became the most powerful figure in Japan. Then, in 1976, he was accused of involvement in the Lockheed scandal. According to his accusers, he had received about $2.1 million in payoffs from officials of the Lockheed Corporation who were looking for advantage in the Japanese market. Lockheed had solicited Kodama's help in selling Lockheed's TriStar L1011 in Japan, which faced tough competition from Boeing and McDonnell-Douglas. Kodama suffered a stroke and died in 1984, before the trial started.

*Nathalie Cavasin*

**Further Reading**

Boulton, David. (1978) *The Grease Machine*. New York: Harper and Row.

Dubro, Alec, and David E. Kaplan. (1986) *Yakuza*. London: Futura.

Ingells, Douglas J. (1973) *L-1011 TriStar and the Lockheed Story*. Fallbrook, CA: Aero Publishers.

Morris, Ivan. (1960) *Nationalism and the Right Wing in Japan: A Study of Post-War Trends*. London: Oxford University Press.

**KOHIMA** (2001 pop. 79,000). The capital of Nagaland State in northeastern India, Kohima was built by the British in the nineteenth century. It was the point of farthest Japanese advance into British India during World War II. Spread across a wide mountain ridge at an elevation of 1,495 meters, Kohima formed a pass through which the Japanese hoped to reach the plains of India. A war memorial, immaculate gardens, and a cemetery with twelve hundred bronze epitaphs dominate the town and commemorate the Allies who fell during the three-month Battle of Kohima, which ended in April 1944 after claiming over ten thousand lives.

Above Kohima, the old village Bara Basti—once an impregnable stronghold—boasts a wooden gate adorned with a scimitar of horns of buffalo to greet the visitor as a commemoration of the bravery of the Angami Nagas, one of the sixteen Naga tribes. A complex system of bamboo water pipes irrigates terraces growing twenty types of rice. The state museum is known for its log drum, woodcarvings, Naga jewelry, and figures displaying costumes and lifestyles of the Naga tribes, with their common love of music, dance, and pageantry.

*C. Roger Davis*

**Further Reading**

Hutton, J. H. (1921, 1969) *The Angami Nagas with Some Notes on Neighbouring Tribes*. Mumbai (Bombay), India: Oxford University Press.

**KOMEITO** The Komeito, or Clean Government Party, is the only party in postwar Japan with links to religion. Its sponsor, Soka Gakkai, is the laymen's affiliate of the Nichiren sect of Buddhism. Founded on 17 November 1964, it defined itself as the "party of ordinary people," oriented toward low-income groups and women.

With a basically conservative philosophy, the party stressed a commitment to fundamental values. It advocated a program of social welfare to elevate the status of those at the bottom of the social pyramid. In foreign policy, the party advocated greater Japanese involvement in the promotion of global peace. The Komeito's success at the polls was due in large measure to the effective local organizational strength of Soka Gakkai. The Komeito came under criticism for the energetic proselytizing of Soka Gakkai, efforts that bordered on pressure and intimidation.

In 1994, the Komeito joined with a group of defectors from the Liberal Democratic Party to form the New Frontier Party. This party in turn broke up in 1997. Former Komeito members began to explore ways to revive the party, and in November 1998 they joined with the New Peace Party to form the New Komeito.

*Louis D. Hayes*

**Further Reading**

Hayes, Louis D. (2001) *Introduction to Japanese Politics*. 3d ed. Armonk, NY: M. E. Sharpe.
Hrebenar, Ronald J. (2000) *Japan's New Party System*. 3d ed. Boulder, CO: Westview Press.

**KOMODO DRAGON** Descended from ancestors 100 million years old, the Komodo dragon *(Varanus komooensis)* is a member of the monitor lizard genus and inhabits the Indonesian archipelago, particularly Komodo Island National Park on the island of Komodo in south-central Indonesia.

An adult male Komodo dragon is the largest lizard in the world. Three meters long, weighing 135 kilograms, and having long talons, stout body, and a long tail, the Komodo dragon is a formidable predator. Carnivorous, these lizards can swallow their prey whole; their diet includes everything from small insects and lizards to pig, goat, buffalo, horse, and even an occasional human being. Although they can run fast enough to reach speeds of 20 kilometers per hour, Komodo dragons usually lie camouflaged waiting to attack. The olfactory and Jacobson's (in the roof of the mouth) sensory organs allow the animals to detect carcasses by perpetually flicking their forked yellow tongues, which taste and smell the surrounding air.

A Komodo dragon on Komodo Island, Indonesia. (WOLFGANG KAEHLER/CORBIS)

## KOMODO NATIONAL PARK—WORLD HERITAGE SITE

Komodo National Park was designated a UNESCO World Heritage Site in 1991 because the islands that form the park are the home of the Komodo dragon.

Once thought to be poisonous, the dragons can cause fatalities only through the saliva from their bite, which may produce septicemia (from the bacteria ingested when a dragon eats carrion). A Komodo dragon can live to the age of twenty years or even longer. Unfortunately they are presently on the endangered species list.

*Stacey Fox*

**Further Reading**

Auffenberg, Walter. (1981) *The Behavioral Ecology of the Komodo Monitor*. Gainesville, FL: University Press of Florida.
Lutz, Judy Marie, and Richard L. Lutz. (1996) *Komodo: The Living Dragon*. Salem, OR: Dimi Press.

**KOMPONG SOM BAY** Chhak Kampong Saom (Kompong Som Bay) is framed by the Chuor Phnom Kravanh (Cardamon Mountains) and Chuor Phnom Damrei (Elephant Mountains) on the northeast and the Gulf of Thailand to the south and west. Famed for its tropical beaches, and site of Cambodia's only deepwater port, Kampong Saom (Sihanoukville), the bay's natural advantages include deep water inshore and a string of islands stretching offshore across the mouth of the bay, which afford a degree of protection from storms. Proximity to Phnom Penh, as well as the major trading centers of Bangkok and Singapore, also makes the bay attractive for recreation and maritime traffic.

Constructed by King Norodom Sihanouk (b. 1922) in the late 1950s, Kampong Saom gained some notoriety when the SS *Mayaguez*, a merchant ship sailing between Hong Kong, Thailand, and Singapore in support of U.S. forces in Southeast Asia, was captured one week after Saigon fell to the North Vietnamese army in May 1975. Forced into the bay by Khmer Rouge

Men fishing from small boats in Kompong Som Bay in 1996. (KEVIN R. MORRIS/CORBIS)

gunboats, the *Mayaguez* was eventually released under pressure by the U.S. and Chinese governments.

At the beginning of the twenty-first century, with the assistance of the U.N. Development Program and the Asian Development Bank, efforts are underway to conserve the bay's biological diversity through the creation of ecotourism activities in Preah Sihanoukville (Ream National Park) near Sihanoukville. Such efforts are intended to mitigate the pollution and erosion associated with the port's operation and expansion.

*Greg Ringer*

**Further Reading**

Ringer, Greg. (2000) "Tourism in Cambodia, Laos, and Myanmar: From Terrorism to Tourism?" In *Tourism in South and Southeast Asia: Issues and Cases*, edited by C. Michael Hall and Stephen Page. Oxford, U.K.: Butterworth-Heinemann, 178–194.

**KONFRONTASI** In the early 1960s, Indonesian president Sukarno (1901–1970) grew openly critical of the West. He viewed the 16 September 1963 establishment of the Federation of Malaysia, including Malaya, Singapore, and former British Borneo (Sarawak and Sabah), as a continuation of colonial rule. In early 1963, Sukarno launched a military campaign to "crush" Malaysia in what was known as Konfrontasi—the Confrontation. Most of the guerrilla war happened in the rainforest of Borneo, with incursion into the Malayan peninsula in September 1964. Britain sent troops to help Malaysian forces seal the border on Borneo island, while Australia and New Zealand lent support. International condemnation forced Indonesia to abandon membership in the U.N. Sukarno's military campaign, largely intended to deflect attention from Indonesia's paralyzed economy, proved the death of Sukarno's regime. Unbeknownst to Sukarno, some leading army officers and foreign ministry bureaucrats contacted Malaysian officials in 1964 to scale down Konfrontasi. An alleged communist-led coup in September 1965, which saw the deaths of six leading generals, led to the successful countercoup by General Suharto (b. 1921). The ensuing military assumption of power removed Sukarno and effectively ended Konfrontasi, though this was not officially announced until 1966. At the height of Konfrontasi an estimated 15,000 to 30,000 Indonesian soldiers and irregulars tried to infiltrate the porous Malaysian border, while 50,000 British personnel were stationed in the Southeast Asian theater. British troops in Borneo, assisted by Malaysian forces, were spread thinly along the border to limit incursions.

*Anthony Smith*

**Further Reading**

Dewi, Fortuna Anwar. (1994) *Indonesia in ASEAN: Foreign Policy and Regionalism*. New York: St. Martin's Press; Singapore: the Institute of Southeast Asian Studies.

Gardner, Paul F. (1997) *Shared Hopes, Separate Fears: Fifty Years of U.S.-Indonesian Relations*. Boulder, CO: Westview Press.

Mackie, J. A. C. (1974) *Konfrontasi: The Indonesian-Malaysian Dispute, 1963–1966*. Kuala Lumpur, Malaysia: Oxford University Press.

Subritzky, John. (2000) *Confronting Sukarno: British, American, Australian, and New Zealand Diplomacy in the Malaysian-Indonesian Confrontation, 1961–5*. London: The Macmillan Press, Ltd.

**KONG XIANGXI** (1881–1967), Chinese politician. Better known to Westerners as H. H. Kong, Kong Xiangxi was born in 1881 in Taigu, Shanxi Province, China, and claimed to be a direct descendant (seventy-fifth generation) of Confucius (551–479 BCE). Educated at Oberlin College (Ohio), he also received a master's degree in economics from Yale. Kong was a loyal supporter of the Guomindang (Nationalist) government of Sun Yat-sen (1866–1925) and Chiang Kai-shek (1887–1975), who were his brothers-in-law. After 1928, he held various high positions in the Nationalist government, including prime minister (president of the Executive Yuan) from January 1938 to November 1939. In his long tenures as minister of finance (1933–1944) and president of the Central Bank of China, he made major reforms in China's monetary, financial, and fiscal systems. These reforms greatly benefited China's war against Japanese invasion, although they were also partially responsible for China's later hyperinflation. Criticized as the patron of widespread corruption among government officials and his family members (including his wife and children), he was removed from the Ministry of Finance in 1944 and the Central Bank of China in 1945. After the fall of the Nationalist government in 1949, Kong went to live in the United States, where he remained active in the China lobby until his death in 1967.

*Jody C. Baumgartner*

**Further Reading**

Coble, Parks M., Jr. (1986) *The Shanghai Capitalists and the Nationalist Government, 1927–1937*. Harvard East Asian Monographs, no. 94. 2d ed. Cambridge, MA: Harvard University Press.

Howard, Richard C., ed. (1971) *Biographical Dictionary of Republican China*. Cambridge, MA: Harvard University Press.

**KONOE FUMIMARO** (1891–1945), Japanese prince and politician. Konoe Fumimaro was a prominent politician between World War I and World War II and the prime minister of three cabinets between 1937 and 1941. Born in Tokyo of imperial ancestry, he held the title of prince. In his university years, Konoe came to view international relations as a class struggle between overbearing "have" nations and grasping "have-nots." The latter group, according to Konoe's world vision, included Japan, which he believed was held in its inferior status by the major powers and their handmaiden institution, the League of Nations.

Konoe's belief that a Japanese hegemonic role in Asia was essential to keep order in the region played into the hands of the military. In 1937, while prime minister, he ushered in a full-scale war to assert Japanese mastery over China. The China Incident, as this invasion was known among Japanese, began with a skirmish with Nationalist troops outside Beijing and eventuated in the capture of China's capital, Nanjing, and coastal provinces. Konoe also initiated wartime economic and military mobilization at home. Three years later his government signed the Tripartite Pact with Germany and Italy. He failed in his efforts to resolve the China Incident and to construct détente with Great Britain and the United States in the months before the Japanese invaded Pearl Harbor. When the German invasion of the Soviet Union and U.S. economic sanctions threatened his foreign agenda, Konoe resigned in October 1941 and was replaced by General Tojo Hideki (1884–1948).

In the final year of the war, Konoe engaged in maneuvering to terminate the conflict. Early in the Allied Occupation, General Douglas MacArthur (1880–1964) tapped him to draft a revision of the Meiji Constitution. However, Konoe's concepts of a reformed constitution fell far short of Occupation authorities' visions. For his prewar policies, the War Crimes Tribunal indicted Konoe as a Class A war criminal. On the day he was to report to prison, he committed suicide.

*Thomas W. Burkman*

**Further Reading**

Berger, Gordon M. (1977) *Parties Out of Power in Japan*. Princeton, NJ: Princeton University Press.

Fletcher, Miles. (1982) *The Search for a New Order: Intellectuals and Fascism in Prewar Japan*. Chapel Hill, NC: University of North Carolina Press.

Oka Yoshitake. (1992) *Konoe Fumimaro: A Political Biography*. Lanham, MD: Madison Books.

**KONYA** (2002 pop. 696,000). Konya is the capital of the province of Konya in south-central Turkey, the country's main agricultural region. The city is surrounded by fertile, well-irrigated plains, which have produced grains and cereals for millennia.

The earliest settlers were the Hittites, who called the city Kuwanna; they were followed by the Phrygians who used the name Kowania. In the third century Iconium (as it was known under the Greeks) became a Hellenistic city although the Phrygian population continued to maintain its cultural identity. After having been expelled from Antioch, St. Paul and St. Barnabas delivered sermons in Iconium in 47, 50, and 53 CE, but they were not favorably received and Christianity had little impact on the local population. In Byzantine times, Iconium served as a military base, subject to frequent attacks by the Arabs. After the Seljuks defeated the Byzantines at the Battle of Manzikert (1071), Iconium became a part of the Seljuk Empire. Seljuk Sultan Kilic Arslan I (1092–1107) later moved his capital to Konya after losing Nicaea to the Byzantines during the first crusade (1097). Konya was relatively free of the constraints posed by warfare, and under Seljuk rule the city flourished. This is especially true with regard to its architecture and tile work, which display a distinctly Seljuk style and remain a major tourist attraction today. In 1313, Konya was occupied by the Karamanid dynasty and officially became part of the Ottoman empire in 1475.

Konya is also the heart of the Mevlevi Sufi sect (known as the whirling dervishes) whose founder, the poet and philosopher Jalal-al-Din Rumi (1207–1273), is buried in Mevlana Museum; his shrine is a major pilgrimage site. An annual dervish festival takes place every December.

*T. Isikozlu-E. F. Isikozlu*

### Further Reading

Cahen, Claude, and Godfrey Goodwin. (1960) "Konya." In *The Encyclopedia of Islam*. 2d ed. Leiden, Netherlands: Brill.

*Statistical Yearbook of Turkey, 1998*. Ankara, Turkey: Devlet Istatistik Enstitusu.

**KOREA—HISTORY** Archaeologists generally posit 30,000 to 50,000 years before the present as the date for the Korean peninsula's earliest known inhabitants. These Paleolithic (Old Stone Age) peoples—who moved into the peninsula while the glacial climate of the ice ages made Korea contiguous with central China—inhabited caves, hunted and gathered for sustenance, used crude tools fashioned from stone or wood, and knew the use of fire. From about 8000 BCE, Neolithic (New Stone Age) populations appeared in Korea. Arriving in a series of migrations, they carried with them elements of the Siberian cultures from which they had emerged. These included shamanistic religious beliefs, communal or clan organization, and specialized pottery techniques represented by the so-called comb-pattern design. Neolithic habitations were mostly limited to coastal areas and along inland waterways.

Bronze culture arrived in Korea, probably via more advanced and Tungusic-speaking peoples who migrated into the peninsula from the northeast Asian steppe from around the eighth century BCE; around the fourth century BCE, the ancient states of Puyo and Choson appeared in the northern peninsula and in Manchuria. Rice production apparently began on the peninsula during this time. This period also saw the appearance of dolmens, imposing structures characterized by the piling of several large stones in a table-like formation, which probably served as both tombs and places of ritual.

Iron production was introduced via China around the fourth century BCE, as were elements of the advanced Chinese culture. The Chinese Han dynasty (206 BCE–220 CE) overcame the Korean tribal states to establish a network of colonies on the Korean peninsula and in present-day Manchuria from around 100 BCE, which went far in introducing Chinese technology, wealth, and concepts of rulership into a still rather primitive Korean peninsula.

By the first century BCE, the state of Koguryo appeared, perhaps as an offshoot of the Puyo state, which had occupied large portions of northeastern Manchuria along the Sungari River as early as the fourth century BCE. South of the Han River, the so-called Three Han States emerged, tribal confederations whose exact makeup remains debated. It was from the southern Han

**GOCHANG—WORLD HERITAGE SITE**

The cemeteries of Gochang, Hwasun, and Gangwha in South Korea, World Heritage Sites since 2000, contain hundreds of ancient dolmens—stone slab tombs structures—that date back to the first millennium BCE.

## KEY EVENTS IN KOREAN HISTORY

**c. 30,000–50,000 BCE** Humans first occupy the Korean peninsula.
**c. 8000 BCE** Neolithic peoples are living in Korea.
**8th century BCE** Bronze Age culture is present in Korea.
**4th century BCE** The states of Puyo and Chosen emerge in the north. Elements of Chinese culture enter Korea.
**c. 100 BCE** The Chinese Han dynasty establishes colonies in Korea.
**18 BCE–663 CE** Period of the Paekche kingdom in the southwest.
**37 BCE–668 CE** Period of the Koguryo kingdom in the north.
**57 BCE–935 CE** Period of the Shilla kingdom in the southeast.
**668 CE** The Shilla kingdom unifies the peninsula.
**c. 900 CE** The Shilla kingdom has weakened and provincial leaders have assumed control in parts of the peninsula.
**918–1392** The period of the Koryo kingdom with Korea reunified.
**1231** The Mongols invade Korea and Korea comes under Mongol control.
**c. 1368** Mongol rule ends with the rise of the Ming dynasty in China.
**1392–1910** Period of the Choson dynasty.
**1471** Confucianism is established as the ideology of the state.
**1592** Korea is invaded by Japan and again in 1598.
**1627** Korea is invaded by the Manchu and again in 1636 and comes under Manchu (Qing dynasty) control.
**1860s** Peasant revolts mark the emergence of the Tonghak movement.
**1894** Japanese and Chinese troops intervene to halt the Toghak-led revolt.
**1876** The Treaty of Kanghwa with Japan opens up trade with the west as treaties with the United States, Britain, and France follow.
**1905** Japan makes Korea a protectorate.
**1910–1945** Period of Japanese rule.
**1919** The March First Independence Movement fails to end Japanese rule.
**1945** Korea is liberated from Japanese rule and the peninsula is divided at the thirty-eighth parallel.
**1948** In a U.S.-backed election, Syngman Rhee is elected president of the First Republic of Korea while the People's Democratic Republic of Korea is established in the north.
**1948–1994** Period of rule of Kim Il Sung in North Korea.
**1950–1943** Period of the Korean War.
**1960** Syngman Rhee's presidency ends; he is replaced by Park Chung hee in a military coup.
**1960s** The South Korean economy begins several decades of rapid expansion.
**1966** *Juche* ideology emerges in North Korea.
**1970s** North Korea begins to experience economic difficulties.
**1981** Martial law is lifted in South Korea.
**1988** South Korea hosts the Summer Olympics.
**1992** Kim Young Sam becomes the first civilian president since 1960 in the south.
**1994** President Kim Il Sung of North Korea dies and is later replaced by his son, Kim Jong Il.
**1996** South Korea experiences a major economic crisis.
**1998** Kim Dae Jung is elected president of South Korea.
**2000** The first meeting between the leaders of the north and south takes place in P'yongyang, North Korea.

states, however, that more centralized kingdoms eventually developed.

From about the middle of the fourth century CE, three states began to emerge as primary contestants for power on the Korean peninsula: Koguryo in the north, Paekche in the southwest, and Shilla in the southeast. Paekche is traditionally dated to 18 BCE; Shilla emerged last as the strongest among various small tribal units in the south around the fourth century CE. It was the Shilla kingdom that unified the Korean peninsula when an alliance with Tang China gave it the commanding strength needed to prevail over its rivals in 668. The northernmost stretches of the kingdom of Koguryo, however, were not annexed by Shilla but instead broke off to become the kingdom of Parhae (Chinese Bohai). Founded by remnants of the Koguryo state, Parhae persisted as an independent kingdom until its defeat by the Khitans, a northern people, in 937.

### Unified Shilla (668–935)

Following Shilla's unification in 668, Korean culture entered a new stage. Buddhism, introduced into Korea during the Three Han States period, continued to be central to Shilla life, but institutional borrowing from Tang China, in the form of Confucian-inspired government administration, became more widespread. Shilla routinely sent delegates of scholars, artisans, and monks to China, bringing back Chinese learning and culture. Shilla's capital of Kyongju grew to upward of a million inhabitants, its rich cultural landscape still discernible today. This period also saw the introduction of Son (Chinese Chan, Japanese Zen) Buddhism, which gained great support among powerful provincial families.

The Shilla monarchy never succeeded in extending its control nationwide. By 750, provincial strongmen were emerging (sometimes called "castle lords"), armed with powerful private armies. By 900, the provinces, and their tax bases, had slipped from central control. The so-called successor states, Later Paekche and Later Koguryo, emerged in the provinces. It was the self-proclaimed king of Later Koguryo, Wang Kon (King T'aejo, 877–943), who was finally able to overcome his rivals and establish his new state, now shortened to Koryo, in 918. In 936, he crowned his victory, and ensured his legitimacy, by securing the abdication of Shilla's last king.

### Koryo (918–1392)

Koryo (from which the English word "Korea" is derived) extended the borders of the Korean state northward, farther than Shilla had been capable of doing, as far as the Yalu and Tumen Rivers, roughly to Korea's present-day borders.

The fourth king of Koryo, Kwangjong (925–975), took a momentous step when he adopted the Chinese civil service examination, which tested aspirants for government posts in the Confucian classics of Chinese tradition. In this way, Confucianism took its first sure steps toward becoming the orthodox doctrine of Korean social and government life.

Despite the increased reliance on Chinese-Confucian learning and institutions in the state bureaucracy, Buddhism retained a pivotal role in Koryo society and culture. Koryo-period Buddhist silk paintings are masterpieces of East Asian art. The entire Tripitaka (the Buddhist canon), carved into nearly 80,000 wooden tablets, was completed not once but twice; the second version survives at Haein Temple in South Korea. The Koryo period also saw the development of movable metal type, almost two centuries before its development in the West. Perhaps the crowning creative achievement of the Koryo period was the development of celadon ware, a porcelain typified by its unique blue-green hue and refined designs.

The Koryo dynasty faced a series of formidable aggressors during its 474 years in power. The first were the Khitans, the northern people who had defeated Parhae. They menaced Koryo as well, launching particularly brutal attacks in 1010 and 1018 before suffering a debilitating defeat. Only the Koryo agreement to pay tribute to another northern people, the Jurchen, prevented a similar large-scale invasion.

In 1170, aristocratic civilian rule in Korea was overthrown in a revolt by military leaders. This coup may be seen in part as a final act of open resistance against the growth of a Confucian-oriented and aristocratic officialdom, in which military figures were increasingly kept from leadership positions and high social status. The revolt may also be viewed as protest against the luxury and moral decline into which many in the military thought Koryo had sunk. In further bloodletting, another coup in 1196, led again by military elements, ensured the dictatorship of the Ch'oe house, which monopolized Koryo politics until the assassination of the last Ch'oe ruler in 1258 in the midst of the Mongol invasions.

The first in a series of Mongol invasions of Koryo came in 1231. Though the kingdom bravely resisted, it eventually surrendered to Mongol suzerainty. What ensued was a humiliating acquiescence to Mongol terms, including the intermarriage of the Koryo and Mongol ruling houses, large tribute payments, and even Koryo's assistance in two failed Mongol attempts to subdue Japan in 1274 and 1281. It was in the midst of this Mongol dominance that the Ch'oe house and power returned to the king and his civilian ministers. Meanwhile the Mongol (Yuan) dynasty in China continued to face a series of challenges posed by a more intensive native Chinese resistance. The establishment of the Chinese Ming dynasty in 1368 soon led to the end of Mongol suzerainty in Korea as well.

It was a Koryo general, Yi Song-gye (King T'aejo, 1335–1408), who finally toppled Koryo from within, first staging a court purge and then in 1392, with the compliance of literati (members of the educated class) officials, proclaiming himself the founder and first king of the new Choson dynasty.

### Choson (1392–1910)

The Choson dynasty, whose namesake was the ancient Bronze Age Korean state, was the longest lived of Korea's dynasties, ruling the country continuously until Japanese annexation in 1910. It witnessed the gradual but full implementation of Neo-Confucianism as the functioning ideology of public and private life. It also saw extreme social stratification emerge as a salient characteristic of Korean society, and factionalism become a prominent element of the nation's political landscape.

Yi Song-gye (or King T'aejo) situated the new Korean capital at Hanyang (present-day Seoul). Despite periodic turmoil in the form of succession struggles, during their first century Choson kings managed to diminish the privileged power of the aristocracy and establish Confucianism as the ruling ideology of the state, notably with the promulgation of a new national law code (the *Kyongguk taejon*) in 1471. They also succeeded in carrying out overarching land reforms that in effect nationalized land and helped set the foundation for a strong central government. The reign of King Sejong (1397–1450) stands out in particular for its cultural and institutional advancements, the most noteworthy being the development of the Korean alphabet (hangul), though it would not become widely used until the twentieth century due to the opposition of the learned aristocracy. Sejong also assembled the greatest Korean scholars of the day into the "Hall of Assembled Scholars" *(Chiphyonjon)*, a sort of think tank of the era. He instituted land surveys and directed the improvement of irrigation and farming techniques that greatly increased production.

Neo-Confucian principles, while increasingly serving to order social behavior, also served to weaken the power of the Korean monarchy by making it liable to checks and balances by literati officials. At numerous times during the Choson period, notably in the sixteenth century, this resulted in royal purges of literati officials in largely failed attempts to regain royal initiative.

In the social realm, Confucianism eventually stripped women of their power and identity outside the home, while segmenting society as a whole into a strict hierarchy of peasant, "middle people," and landed aristocrat (or *yangban*), with social mobility coming to a virtual halt. As the Choson period advanced, the rights and hereditary privileges of the *yangban* aristocracy were extended, including immunization from most taxation, all of which served to increase the burden on the peasantry and prepare the way for revolts in the nineteenth century. Buddhism during this period lost its official sanction and indeed became an all but proscribed sect.

In foreign affairs, Choson's first two centuries of peace contrasted sharply with the period of unprecedented national destruction brought on by the Japanese invasions of 1592 and 1598 and the Manchu invasions of 1627 and 1636. The Manchu attacks, preceding the ones that eventually toppled the Chinese Ming dynasty in 1644, resulted in Korean submission to the Manchu state (after 1644 the Qing dynasty).

The two centuries following the Japanese and Manchu invasions were also times of relative peace. One of the primary achievements of the period was the promulgation of a new tax system, the "Uniform Land Tax Law," which was finally instituted nationwide by 1708. By substituting a confusing array of taxes with a uniform tax based on land quality, government revenues increased and peasant tax burdens were greatly alleviated. This in turn stimulated commerce and the emergence of national markets.

Nevertheless, by mid-Choson, after centuries of aristocratic privilege, destructive factionalism, foreign invasion, and peasant misery, Korean social and political structures were under increasing strain. One response to this was the emergence of the Sirhak ("True Learning" or "Pragmatic") movement. As the name suggests, its proponents, including such scholars as Yi Ik (1681–1763) and Chong Yag-yong (1762–1836), through a wide-ranging examination of knowledge, rejection of dogma, and reliance on empirical fact, sought new approaches to Korea's ills. Though little successful in influencing policy, in their endeavors they added immeasurably to Korea's literary heritage.

A series of peasant revolts in the early nineteenth century were preludes to the rise of the Tonghak (or "Eastern Learning") movement. First appearing in the 1860s as a native religious movement combining ele-

## LADY HONG (1735–1815)

Memoirist Lady Hong, also known as Lady or Princess Hyegyong, was born into a prominent *yangban* (aristocratic) family caught in the quagmire of seventeenth-century political factionalism in Korea. Her husband was Crown Prince Changhon (1735–1762, also known posthumously as Sado, meaning "mournful thoughts"), heir to the throne of King Yongjo (reigned 1700–1776). The crown prince, however, was mentally ill and grew increasingly violent. Finally, in the summer of 1762, King Yongjo ordered his son to be imprisoned in a rice chest where the young prince perished from heat and starvation. King Yongjo was succeeded by his grandson (son of Sado and Lady Hong) who became King Chongjo (reigned 1776–1800).

Lady Hong wrote four separate memoirs in 1795, 1801, 1802, and 1805. The first memoir was written to her nephew, head of the Hong family. The other three memoirs were written to her grandson, King Sunjo (reigned 1800–1834). These four works vividly depict Lady Hong's childhood and palace life, political factionalism and Catholic persecutions of the late eighteenth century, and painful recollections of her husband's fight with the demons in his mind. Through her writings, it can be seen that Lady Hong was both powerless as the widow of the ill-fated Sado, yet influential as mother and grandmother to kings.

*Jennifer Jung-Kim*

*Source:* Ja Hyun Kim Haboush, trans. (1996) *The Memoirs of Lady Hyegyong: The Autobiographical Writings of a Crown Princess of Eighteenth-Century Korea.* Berkeley and Los Angeles: University of California Press.

ments of Confucianism, Buddhism, Taoism, and even Christianity, the movement soon took on antiestablishment notions, with calls for the punishment of corrupt officials, reform of tax laws, and rejection of Confucian notions of hierarchy. It was the specter of mass, Tonghak-led revolt in 1894 that initiated the intervention of Japanese and then Chinese troops, which in turn triggered the Sino-Japanese War of 1894–1895.

In Korea, as in other regions of the world, the coming of the Western powers marked a stark new chapter in national history. Choson Korea had for a long time maintained a policy of isolation from all but China and Japan (though it tolerated the presence of clandestine French Catholic missionaries until 1866). But as China and then Japan found themselves overwhelmed by Western pressures to open, Korea's opening too became inevitable. Despite victorious clashes with French and American forces (in 1866 and 1871), in 1876 Korea finally gave way before the pressure of Japan, which had greatly transformed itself since its opening by the West in 1858. The Treaty of Kanghwa (1876) between Japan and Korea was soon followed by treaties of amity and commerce with the various nations of the West, including the United States (1882), Great Britain (1884), and France (1886).

Unlike Japan, which was able to summon its national will and resources to bring about rapid Western-style modernization, Korea languished. Though various attempts at reform were attempted, they ended in failure and conservative backlash. Meanwhile, in the last quarter of the nineteenth century, Japan, China, and Russia emerged as primary rivals over Korea. While China continued to maintain jealously its traditional relationship with Korea, with the latter as a tributary state, Russia and Japan began to entertain territorial ambitions on the peninsula. This in turn heightened the anxieties of other Western powers. But Japan's victory over China in the Sino-Japanese War (1894–1895) and over Russia in the Russo-Japanese War (1904–1905) ensured Japanese hegemony in Northeast Asia. By the early twentieth century, as Russia and China both became mired in social and political upheaval, Western nations turned a blind eye as Japan encroached ever further on Korean sovereignty. Japan made Korea a protectorate in 1905 and annexed it in 1910.

### The Japanese Colonial Period (1910–1945)

Japan's colonial policy in Korea was ultimately one of assimilation—an attempt to eradicate all vestiges of Korean national identity. Though this policy waxed and waned in intensity, from shortly after annexation it was always central to Japanese planning. Ironically, this ideal of assimilation was pursued while denying Koreans the same rights and privileges as Japanese. Yet Japanese rule also constituted an era of tremendous industrial and institutional change that launched Korea decisively down the road toward modern development with a single-mindedness the Koreans themselves had been unable to achieve. Accomplishments included the construction of a national communication and transportation infrastructure, institutions of higher education, and development of important industries.

By 1910 Japanese troops had all but silenced Korean armed resistance to Japanese rule. National aspirations and frustrations continued to stew under the surface and finally erupted in the March First Independence Movement of 1919, during which a broad spectrum of Korean society rose up in massive anti-Japanese protests. Though this popular plea for independence ultimately failed, the movement did spark the emergence of Korean nationalist movements abroad, including the establishment of a Korean Provisional Government in Shanghai in April 1919 and a Korean Communist Party shortly thereafter. The 1919 independence movement also resulted in a more "enlightened" policy by the Japanese government in Korea, which for a period afterward tolerated the establishment of Korean nationalist organizations and expansion of the Korean vernacular press. This policy came to an end as Korea was increasingly industrialized and exploited to serve the Japanese war effort. From 1931 until the end of World War II, Korea was again ruled by a strict military regime with complete cultural assimilation the order of the day.

### Liberation, the Korean War, and National Division

The euphoria following Japan's defeat, and Korea's liberation, in 1945 was short lived as Soviet and American policy makers opted to divide Korea under a joint protectorship. The American decision to rely heavily on Japanese sympathizers to manage the country in the south was a source of immediate resentment.

In the north the Soviets began to groom a Communist leadership, headed by a young guerrilla leader named Kim Il Sung (Kim Il-song, 1912–1994). The cooling of U.S.-Soviet relations stalled negotiations for nationwide elections to bring an end to the protectorship, and when the Soviets refused to cooperate in a 1948 United Nations–brokered election, voting proceeded in the south alone, which thousands boycotted in protest. The winner was Syngman Rhee (Yi Sung-man, 1875–1965), a Princeton-educated conservative and lifelong friend of the United States, who was inaugurated president of the First Republic of Korea in 1948. That same year saw the formal establishment in the north of the People's Democratic Republic of Korea. By the following year most Soviet and United States troops had been withdrawn.

On 25 June 1950, North Korean forces crossed the border along the thirty-eighth parallel en masse, catching both South Korean and remnant U.S. forces by surprise. In a successful appeal to the United Nations, the United States oversaw the establishment of a U.N. force with a mandate to reunify the peninsula under a single Korean government. Initial U.N. success changed abruptly in the face of massive intervention by Chinese troops, and U.N. forces were driven back to the outskirts of Seoul. A strategic stalemate, and the unwillingness of the United Nations to risk a larger conflict with China and perhaps the Soviet Union, ultimately resulted in a 1953 armistice, with Korea divided along roughly prewar lines.

### Autocratic Rule and Ideological Conflict

"Autocracy" accurately describes the political situations in both North and South Korea from the Korean War until at least 1981, the year in which martial law was lifted in the south. Though this autocracy was more manifest in North Korea, following the Korean War, South Korea too was ruled by the autocratic regime of Syngman Rhee and then by a series of military governments, which took the Communist threat as primary justification for authoritarian rule.

North Korea was led by Kim Il Sung from 1948 until his death in 1994. Kim consolidated his initially tenuous hold on power through systematic purges of rival Communist factions, resulting in his rise to absolute power by 1960. From the 1960s, Kim Il Sung's rule was increasingly characterized by a cult of personality that credited him with fantastic exploits and even superhuman abilities. Closely tied to this was Kim Il Sung's appeal, notably after 1966, to *juche* ideology, characterized by an emphasis on self-reliance and ultranationalism, which has remained to this day a salient characteristic of North Korean life and thought.

Enjoying the lion's share of mineral resources, though lacking the agricultural base of the south, North Korea during the first two decades of its existence actually surpassed the south in economic development, and perhaps only massive U.S. aid to South Korea prevented the north from renewing a military drive for reunification. The situation in the north began to deteriorate in the 1970s, however, with the steady loss of foreign aid, heavy military expenditures, booming population, and low agricultural output. The collapse of the Soviet Union in 1990 and a series of natural disasters in the 1990s made things more critical. Massive food and medical aid, predominantly from Western nations, has helped stave off national catastrophe.

In South Korea, the Syngman Rhee presidency ended in violent student-led protests in 1960. Hopes for democratic civilian rule were soon dashed, however, when the South Korean general Park Chung Hee (Pak Chong-hui, 1917–1979) seized power in a military coup. Park's efforts to create a centrally engineered economy were largely successful, and from the mid-1960s the South Korean economy began a long and remarkable period of growth. During the 1980s, South Korea became known as one of Asia's "tiger economies," as it surged ahead in gross national product and industrial output, far surpassing North Korea, which now languished because of poor management and a lack of capital and material support. South Korea's hosting of the 1988 Olympic Games stands out as testament to that country's tremendous economic strides. Despite the south's miraculous economic advances, however, financial crises throughout Asia, combined with structural and managerial defects in Korea's centrally engineered economy, led to a severe economic crisis in South Korea in 1996.

Economic progress in the south naturally engendered calls for political plurality. Following Park Chung Hee's assassination in 1979, control passed to another military general, Chun Doo Hwan (Chon Tuhwan, b. 1931). In 1980, hundreds, perhaps thousands, of South Koreans died in the city of Kwangju protesting military rule. Free elections were finally held in 1987, though they still resulted in the election of a military man, Roh Tae Woo (No Tae wu, b. 1932). It was not until 1992 that Kim Young Sam (Kim Yongsam, b. 1927) became the first civilian president since Syngman Rhee. But in a greater test of democracy, in 1998 power transferred peacefully from Kim Youngsam to his elected successor, Kim Dae Jung (Kim Taejung, b. 1924).

In a move toward reunification, North and South Korean leaders Kim Jong Il and Kim Dae Jung read papers reporting on their 14 June 2000 summit meeting. (AFP/CORBIS)

North-south relations since 1953 have mostly been characterized by tense mistrust and ideological rancor. The death of Kim Il Sung and the eventual succession of his son Kim Jong Il (b. 1941) in the north, and the election of Kim Dae Jung as president in the south, marked a sea change in north-south relations, occasioned in part by Kim Dae Jung's "sunshine policy" toward North Korea, which stressed cordial relations and constructive dialogue. In June 2000, the first meeting between North and South Korean leaders occurred in the North Korean capital of P'yongyang, from where the leaders issued a joint communiqué calling for a peaceful resolution to national division.

*Daniel Kane*

*See also:* **Choson Kingdom; Confucianism—Korea; Korean War; Koryo Kingdom; Kwangju Uprising; March First Independence Movement; North Korea–South Korea Relations; Parhae Kingdom; Three Kingdoms Period; Tonghak; Unified Shilla Kingdom**

### Further Reading

Barnes, Gina L. (1999) *The Rise of Civilization in East Asia: The Archaeology of China, Korea, and Japan.* London: Thames and Hudson.

Cumings, Bruce. (1998) *Korea's Place in the Sun: A Modern History.* New York: W. W. Norton.

———. (1981) *The Origins of the Korean War.* 2 vols. Princeton, NJ: Princeton University Press.

Duncan, John B. (2000) *The Origins of the Choson Dynasty.* Seattle, WA: University of Washington Press.

Eckert, Carter J. (1997) *Offspring of Empire: The Koch'ang Kims and the Colonial Origins of Korean Capitalism, 1876–1945.* Seattle, WA: University of Washington Press.

Henthorn, W. E. (1963) *Korea: The Mongol Invasions.* Leiden, Netherlands: E. J. Brill.

Lee, Ki-baik. (1984) *A New History of Korea*. Trans. by Edward W. Wagner with Edward J. Shultz. Cambridge, MA: Harvard University Press.

Lee, Peter H., and William T. de Bary, eds. (1997) *Sources of Korean Tradition*. New York: Columbia University Press.

Lone, Stewart, and Gavan McCormack. (1993) *Korea since 1850*. New York: St. Martin's Press.

Nelson, Sarah Milledge. (1993) *The Archaeology of Korea*. Cambridge, U.K.: Cambridge University Press.

Pal, Hyung Il. (2000) *Constructing "Korean" Origins: A Critical Review of Archaeology, Historiography, and Racial Myth in Korean State-Formation Theories*. Cambridge, MA: Harvard University Press.

Robinson, Michael E. (1988) *Cultural Nationalism in Colonial Korea, 1920–1925*. Seattle, WA: University of Washington Press.

Shultz, Edward J. (2000) *Generals and Scholars: Military Rule in Medieval Korea*. Honolulu, HI: University of Hawaii Press.

Wagner, Edward W. (1974) *The Literati Purges: Political Conflict in Early Yi Korea*. Cambridge, MA: Harvard University Press.

**KOREA BAY** Korea Bay lies between the southwestern coast of North Korea's North and South P'yongan provinces and the Liaodong Peninsula of China, forming the northeast arm of the Yellow Sea. The water is shallow, and since the tidal land is wide along the shore of Korea Bay, with a big difference in the ebb and flow, there are salt fields in many places. During the wintertime, seasonal winds from the northwest have created large sand dunes on the seashore. The fishing industry in Korea Bay has not developed according to general expectations. Korean sources suggest that this is due to the unique conditions of the bay: shallow water and water temperature that is surprisingly lower than expected during cooler months. During the spring a warm current flows north past Cheju Island, causing several species of fish from Korea's Namhae (South Sea) to flourish. These include croakers, flatfish, cod, sciaenoid fish, small octopi, and crabs.

*Richard D. McBride II*

**Further Reading**

McCune, Shannon Boyd-Bailey. (1980) *Views of the Geography of Korea, 1935–1960*. Seoul, South Korea: Korea Research Center.

**KOREA INSTITUTE OF SCIENCE AND TECHNOLOGY** The Korea Institute of Science and Technology (KIST), known as Hanguk Kwahakweon in Korean, was one of the first modern research institutes in the developing world dedicated to industrial technology; it became a model for similar institutes in other developing countries, especially in Southeast Asia. The KIST was established in Seoul, South Korea, with a U.S. seed grant, at the behest of the South Korean president Park Chung Hee (1917–1979) and was organized to assist the nation's export drive. It has at least formal administrative independence and has conducted its work for both South Korean businesses and state-run laboratories on a contract basis.

Through the 1970s, the institute was Korea's most important research and development center and performed various industrial engineering projects under the direction of the ministry of science and technology. By the late 1980s, KIST was eclipsed by newer state-led laboratories such as the Electronics and Telecommunications Research Institute, and by corporate research and development, especially in electronics. Accordingly, KIST shifted to a supporting role in triad partnerships (corporate, academic, and government laboratories) or carried out specialized contract work for corporate clients. However, it was able to maintain a measure of political and research importance by playing a leadership role in the state's high-profile Group of 7 (G-7: Canada, France, Germany, Italy, Japan, United Kingdom, United States) industrial research projects, which were intended to elevate Korean technological advancement to the level of the most advanced industrial countries during the 1990s.

In 1981, KIST merged with the Korea Advanced Institute of Science (KAIS), a science and engineering graduate school established in 1971, to form the Korea Advanced Institute of Science and Technology (KAIST). Both institutes moved their major facilities from Seoul to the Daedok Science Town near Taejon. KIST was split off from KAIST in 1989 to resume its strictly research role.

*Joel R. Campbell*

**Further Reading**

Choi, Hyung Sup. (1986) *Technology Development in Developing Countries*. Tokyo: Asian Productivity Organization.

Hahm, Sung Deuk, and L. Christopher Plein. (1997) *After Development: The Transformation of the Korean Presidency and Bureaucracy*. Washington, DC: Georgetown University Press.

Hillebrand, Wolfgang. (1996) *Shaping Competitive Advantages: Conceptual Framework and the Korean Approach*. London: Frank Cass & Co.

Kim, Linsu. (1997) *Imitation to Innovation: The Dynamics of Korea's Technological Learning*. Boston: Harvard Business School Press.

Ungson, Gerardo, Richard M. Steers, and Seung-Ho Park. (1997) *Korean Enterprise: The Quest for Globalization*. Boston: Harvard Business School Press.

**KOREA STRAIT** The Korea Strait lies between the southeast coast of Korea and the north coast of Kyushu, Japan (the southernmost island), and the southeast coast of Honshu, Japan. It connects the East China Sea (Yellow Sea) to the East Sea (Sea of Japan). At the narrowest point, the strait is 195 kilometers wide; it is generally 90 meters deep. The strait bisects the Tsushima Islands, forming a western channel commonly called the Chosen Strait and an eastern channel called the Tsushima Strait. The western channel is slightly narrower and deeper. The warm Tsushima current passes through the Korea Strait in a northerly direction.

The Korea Strait was the site of the kamikaze winds that destroyed the Mongol armada in 1281, which had been preparing to attack and invade Japan. It was also the site of the Battle of Tsushima (27–28 May 1905), which ended with the annihilation of the Russian fleet by the Japanese during the Russo-Japanese War (1904–1905).

*Brandon Palmer*

**KOREA-JAPAN TREATY OF 1965** Japanese-South Korean normalization was a five-year process that took place between 1961 and 1965. Throughout the late 1940s and the 1950s, the Republic of Korea (ROK) was governed by Syngman Rhee (1875–1965) a man who had dedicated much of his life to publicizing the illegitimacy of Japanese rule in Korea. The Park Chung Hee regime (1961–1979) was different, as it included many Koreans who had been trained by the Japanese. This change in the administration breathed life into the possibility of Japan and the ROK signing a treaty of normalization.

The United States was a leading force between the two countries, commencing negotiations to reach this goal. Friendly relations between Japan and South Korea were necessary for the economic and political strength of both states; their healthy relations would help strengthen the U.S. containment policy against the Soviet Union. The treaty, ratified on 14 August 1965, provided the ROK with both grants ($300 million) and loans ($200 million); another $300 million arrived in the form of private investment.

The signing of the treaty boosted the Korean economy, but it ended the possibility of Koreans making further claims to the Japanese government for compensation. This latter concern has resurfaced in negotiations over the nature of compensation for former Korean comfort women, whom the Japanese military had forced into prostitution to serve its troops during World War II, as well as those with the North Koreans over normalization possibilities.

*Mark Caprio*

### Further Reading

Lee, Chong-Sik. (1985) *Japan and Korea: The Political Dimension*. Stanford, CA: The Hoover Institution, Stanford University.

**KOREAN LANGUAGE** The Korean language is spoken by approximately 72 million people around the world. In addition to the 42 million people in South Korea (Republic of Korea) and 20 million in North Korea (Democratic People's Republic of Korea; DPRK), Korean is spoken in Korean communities in China, Japan, United States, Canada, the former Soviet Union, and South America, among other places.

### Origins and Development

Korean is generally said to belong to the Altaic language group of central Asia, Siberia, and Mongolia. Some linguists maintain that Korean also belongs to the larger Ural-Altaic family, which includes Hungarian and Finnish. Archaeological and anthropological evidence, as shown in similarities in shamanism, language, and archaeological remains, supports the theory that Korean civilization is linked to that of its neighbors in central Asia and Siberia.

People on the Korean peninsula spoke different languages through the Three Kingdoms period (57 BCE–667 CE) until 668 when Shilla unified the lower two-thirds of the peninsula. When the Later Three Kingdoms arose and Shilla fell in 935 to Koryo (918–1392), the northern dialect of Kaesong (also called Kaegyong; the capital of Koryo) became dominant. The language of the Choson dynasty (1392–1910) was similar to the dominant language of Kaesong.

In the early 2000s, there are two official dialects of the capitals of Seoul, South Korea, and P'yongyang, North Korea. South Koreans call their official dialect *p'yojuno* (standard language), while North Koreans call theirs *munhwao* (cultured language). The two dialects are very similar and show only minor differences, as in the use of foreign loanwords. There are also numerous regional and provincial dialects, but they are also mutually understandable.

### Grammatical Features

Korean has fourteen consonants (five of which can be doubled) and ten vowels (with eleven additional vowel combinations or diphthongs). A morpheme is the smallest distinct unit of the Korean language, similar to an English syllable. A Korean morpheme must be formed of least one consonant and one vowel, but may have one or two additional consonants at the end.

Korean sentences are verb-final and are ordered subject-object-verb (I-flower-see), whereas English is subject-verb-object (I see a/the flower). The subject or object or both may be omitted in some cases, and in others, the subject and object order may be flipped to convey a specific meaning. The most important point is that the verb is always at the end, and every sentence must have a verb, although it need not have a subject or object.

Korean lacks articles such as *a* or *the*, but there are other means of distinguishing a specific noun. For example, *ku* (that) can be used similarly to the English word *the* when referring to something that has already been introduced into the conversation.

While there is a plural noun marker *(dul)*, it is often omitted. In the previous example, the listener must discern from context whether the speaker sees one flower or many flowers. Korean nouns are not masculine or feminine, as in French and Spanish. Korean also does not have specific masculine or feminine pronouns such as *he* or *she*.

The most commonly used pronouns are *I* or *we*. *You* is rarely used, as Koreans generally use the listener's name and/or title instead. Instead of *he/she/they*, a speaker might use the referent's name or title or both, or a generic phrase such as *this/that person*.

Korean is a highly agglutinative language with numerous suffixes that can be added to word stems and each other. These suffixes help clarify the meaning of a sentence. For example, markers can indicate the subject *(i/ga)*, topic *(un/nun)*, or object *(ul/rul)* of a sentence. The first marker in each example *(i, un, ul)* is used if the preceding morpheme ends in a consonant. If it ends in a vowel, the second marker *(ga, nun, rul)* is used. Modifiers precede the nouns they modify. For example, "the flower that is in bloom" would be expressed in Korean as "in-bloom flower."

Korean has different speech levels, specific to the relative social positions of the speaker, the subject of the sentence, and the listener. There are at least six levels of speech in contemporary Korean, but the four most commonly used levels are formal polite (deferential) style (verb stem + *[su]mnida*), informal polite style (verb stem + *ayo/oyo*), plain (essay) style (verb stem + *[nu]nda*), and casual style (verb stem + *a/o*.)

A verb stem is the root of any verb minus the *da* ending from its dictionary (infinitive) form. The use of *ayo/oyo* in the informal polite style and *a/o* in the casual style depends on the vowel harmony rule and the "bright" (*a* or the long *o*) or "dark" vowel (*u* and the short *o*) in the verb stem. Bright vowels combine with *a*, and dark vowels combine with *o*. This is called the vowel harmony rule because bright vowels complement other bright vowels.

A speaker will choose the speech level most appropriate to his or her relationship to the listener. The speaker also must consider the subject of a sentence in determining if subject honorifics are needed. For example, verbs and certain nouns must be changed to their honorific forms if the subject is older or in some other way superior to the speaker or listener.

Korean language is highly dependent on context. Because nouns and topics are often omitted, and pronouns are not commonly used, the listener must often infer the speaker's intent from nongrammatical clues such as nuance and conversation flow.

## Loanwords

Korean has numerous loanwords in its vocabulary, most of which are derived from Chinese. Chinese loanwords have corresponding Chinese characters, but in many cases there are also native Korean counterparts. In recent years, there have also been many loanwords from Japanese and English as well as some European languages. Japanese and English loanwords have become common because of the economic and cultural ties among Korea, Japan, and the United States. The loanword, however, may not retain the exact meaning it had in its original language.

North Koreans do not use as many foreign loanwords because of their relative isolation from other countries. This was further enforced by the North Korean *juche* ideology, which literally means "self-reliance" and refers to the official nationalist discourse of the DPRK.

## Writing Systems

Prior to the 1446 promulgation of the *hunmin chongum* (proper sounds to instruct the people), there was no native writing system. Official documents were translated into and written in classical or literary Chinese. Because of the difficulty of learning Chinese characters, literacy in Korea was generally limited to males of the upper class.

There were two native writing methods involving Chinese characters. *Idu* was a system utilized by clerks for administrative purposes and was widely used even into the nineteenth century. In *idu*, some Chinese characters were used for their meaning while others were used to stand for Korean syntax. *Hyangch'al* was another system that used Chinese characters, but only for their phonetic value. This system was used predominantly to record literature.

*Hunmin chongum* was used primarily by women and commoners. Official documents continued to be written in classical Chinese and *idu*. From the 1890s, *hunmin chongum* became revitalized as the official script and is known today as hangul.

The ease of learning this phonetic script is the reason why Korean literacy is nearly 100 percent. Nonnative speakers often can learn the basics of the modern Korean script in a matter of days. While Chinese characters *(hancha)* are used less and less in South Korea, and most newspapers are written in hangul, students learn 3,600 Chinese characters by the time they graduate from high school.

*Jennifer Jung-Kim*

### Further Reading

Korean Overseas Information Service. (1993) *A Handbook of Korea*. 9th ed. Seoul, South Korea: Korean Overseas Information Service.

## KOREAN WAR

**KOREAN WAR** The Korean War (1950–1953) was a civil struggle that originated in the division of Korea after World War II, and entered into a phase of conventional war on 25 June 1950, when North Korean forces crossed the dividing line and invaded the South. Soon the United States entered the fighting under the banner of the United Nations, along with small contingents of British, Canadian, Australian, and Turkish troops. In October 1950, Chinese forces in large numbers joined the war on the North's side. By the time a cease-fire agreement was signed on 27 July 1953, U.S. casualties were 33,629 dead and 103,284 wounded. South Korea had lost hundreds of thousands of soldiers and over a million civilian lives. Although no precise figures exist for Communist losses, North Korea suffered perhaps 3 million military and civilian casualties and the obliteration of nearly every modern building, and China lost almost 1 million soldiers. The 1953 armistice ended the fighting, but Korea remained divided for decades thereafter and subject to the possibility of a new war at any time.

The Korean War has been subject to frequent reinterpretation since it was fought in the early 1950s. For President Harry Truman (1884–1972), Korea was a "police action" that began, in the official American view, when North Korean forces backed by the Soviet Union launched a full-scale, unprovoked invasion across the thirty-eighth parallel. By the 1960s, Westerners had renamed it "the limited war," a conflict different from the world wars in being less than a total war and in being shaped by political decisions taken in Washington: mainly the Truman-MacArthur controversy, with President Truman seeking to limit the conflict to the Korean peninsula, and General Douglas MacArthur (1880–1964) seeking to extend the war to China. Under this interpretation Korea was a success for Truman's containment policy, but a failure for MacArthur's strategy—a stalemate yielding a substitute for victory.

### The Korean War after Vietnam

The U.S. war in Vietnam influenced another revision of meaning, as scholars in the 1970s increasingly came to see Korea as a civil war in which anticolonial nationalism confronted a status quo–oriented United States. Attention focused on the Korean experience of American and Soviet occupations after World War II, political and guerrilla conflicts (1945–1949) and small border wars (1949–1950), and Korea's colonial experience with Japan, during which time the military leaderships of North and South Korea were formed (northerners had been anti-Japanese guerrillas, whereas the high command of the South Korean Army had fought with Japan), with a corresponding deemphasis on the conventional "start" of the war in June 1950, and a significant spreading of responsibility for the initiation of this war.

### The Korean War Viewed from the 1980s

By the 1980s, however, Korea was "the forgotten war." Books and documentaries by that title proliferated, and the war entered an ambiguous realm: not World War II, not quite Vietnam either, more a question mark than a known quantity. Korean War veterans protested their exclusion from the American popular memory. This was also a decade of new light on the war, however, as scholars exploited reams of newly declassified documents. Most historians questioned the assumption that Joseph Stalin launched the war for his own purposes; the conventional assault in June 1950 was thought to be the idea of North Korea's Kim Il Sung (1912–1994), with perhaps more Chinese than Soviet support. The direct American role in suppressing left-wing politics in the South during its military occupation (1945–1948) was definitively proved, and captured Korean documents showed that the origins of the North Korean regime were much

U.S. marines on a road heading toward North Korea in November 1950. The mountainous terrain made movement difficult and also made soldiers in the open valleys easy targets for machine gunners in the hills. (BETTMANN/CORBIS)

more complex than had been thought, with significant indigenous and Chinese influence in addition to the Soviet role. Both Korean sides were deeply implicated in the border fighting that ensued from May through December 1949. New materials showed that the American decision to march into North Korea was taken by Harry Truman, not Douglas MacArthur, under a frankly stated "rollback" doctrine; Truman also thought long and hard about extending the war to China, and sacked MacArthur in April 1951 mainly because he wanted a reliable commander in place should that happen.

New Chinese materials also showed how difficult the decision to intervene in Korea was, with Mao Zedong (1893–1976) taking the lead but also deeply conflicted. Chinese materials also depicted a combined North Korean-Chinese strategy to lure United Nations forces deep into the interior of Korea after the famous amphibious landing at Inchon, hoping to stretch supply lines and gain time for a dramatic reversal on the battlefield. That reversal came as 1950 turned into 1951, when Sino-Korean forces threw U.N. troops back well below the thirty-eighth parallel and captured Seoul again; finally, General Matthew Ridgway (1895–1993) organized a successful defense that stabilized the front well south of the thirty-eighth parallel. U.N. forces then resumed the offensive, retaking Seoul and reestablishing a Korea divided roughly along the lines of the demilitarized zone that still exists today. Here the war could have ended, but it continued through two years of difficult peace negotiations.

### The Korean War after the Cold War

The 1990s have brought new interpretations, based mostly on newly declassified Russian documentation. These materials show more involvement by Stalin than most scholars had thought in the outbreak of conventional war in June 1950, although his involvement was ambiguous and wavering. Kim Il Sung held several secret meetings with Stalin and Mao in early 1950, hoping to gain their backing for a conventional assault on the South. Stalin was reluctant and worried, but ultimately supportive; the full record of Kim's discussions with Mao remains secret, but Beijing was also supportive, particularly because Kim had been a member of the Chinese Communist Party in the 1930s and had many Chinese allies from that period. Ultimately though, the dominant impetus—and responsibility—for taking the existing conflict to the level of conventional war was North Korea's.

All these are Western views. For Koreans in North and South, the likelihood of war came with the division of the ancient integrity of the Korean nation, through the unilateral action of the American officials in mid-August 1945, to which Stalin quickly acquiesced. For the South it was a just war to recover "lost territories" in the North and to resist Soviet and Chinese expansion. For the North it was a just war to resist American imperialism and reunify the homeland. For Koreans and thirty-seven thousand American soldiers, the war still continues today through a cold peace held only by the 1953 armistice, and with a hot war an ever-present possibility, given that more than a million soldiers still confront each other along the demilitarized zone. But in June 2000, the leaders of South and North Korea met for the first time since the country was divided, and the southern leader, longtime dissident Kim Dae Jung (b. 1925), has determined to try to bring a final end to the Korean War before he leaves office in 2003.

Eventually the Korean War will be understood as one of the most destructive and one of the most important wars of the twentieth century. In the aftermath of war two Korean states competed toe-to-toe in economic development, both turning into modern industrial nations. Finally, it was this war and not World War II that established a far-flung American base structure abroad and a national security state at home, as defense spending nearly quadrupled in the last six months of 1950, reaching a peak of $500 billion (in current dollars) that was never reached again during the Cold War. Today Koreans continue to seek reconciliation and eventual reunification of their torn nation, and Americans have a massive and expensive military-industrial complex that has lost its original raison d'etre with the collapse of the Soviet Union, but which continues apace as the primary American legacy of the Korean War.

*Bruce Cumings*

*See also:* **Kim Il Sung; North Korea–South Korea Relations**

### Further Reading


Chen, Jian. (1994) *China's Road to the Korean War*. New York: Columbia University Press.

Cumings, Bruce. (1981, 1990) *The Origins of the Korean War*. 2 vols. Princeton, NJ: Princeton University Press.

Stueck, William. (1995) *The Korean War: An International History*. Princeton, NJ: Princeton University Press.

Zhang, Shu Guang. (1995) *Mao's Military Romanticism: China and the Korean War, 1950–1953*. Lawrence, KS: University of Kansas Press.


## KOREANS

**KOREANS** Koreans are the people of the Korean peninsula in northeast Asia. The peninsula's northern boundary is formed by the Amnok (Yalu) and Tumen Rivers, which separate Korea from the Manchurian region of the People's Republic of China. There is also a short 16-kilometer border with Russia near the city of Vladivostok along the peninsula's northeast corner.

The Korean peninsula is currently divided into the Democratic People's Republic of Korea (North Korea) and the Republic of Korea (South Korea), which together have an area of 221,607 square kilometers, roughly the size of Great Britain. About 68 million Koreans lived in the two Koreas in 2000: 22 million in the north and 46 million in the south. Another 6 million live in other parts of the world, such as China, Japan, the United States, the former Soviet Union, and South America.

### Homogeneity

Koreans pride themselves on racial homogeneity based on an assumption of shared blood, common origins, culture, and language, as well as the perceived sharing of a common history and destiny. The Chinese people form the largest ethnic minority group in Korea today. Recently, many ethnic Koreans have returned

### THE CORE OF KOREAN NATIONAL CULTURE

"The great virtue which the Koreans possess is the innate respect and daily practice of the laws of human brotherhood. We have seen above how the various bodies, above all the family, form closely united corps to defend, support, second and help one another. But this sentiment of brotherhood extends well beyond the limits of kinship and association, and mutual assistance, generous hospitality toward all are distinctive traits of the national character, qualities which, it must be admitted, place the Koreans well above the peoples invaded by the egotism of our contemporary civilization."

*Source:* Christopher Dallet. (1954). *Traditional Korea*. New Haven: Human Relations Area Files, 149.

Korean officials light the torch to open the 1998 Olympic Games in Seoul, South Korea.

to Korea from such places as China's Yanbian region (in Korean, Yonbyon) in search of better lives.

Foreign invasions (Mongol invasions in the thirteenth century, Japanese invasions in 1592 and 1597, and Manchu invasions in 1627 and 1636) also contributed to this sense of racial unity. United efforts at defense helped forge a shared identity for Koreans.

**Origins**

The Korean Peninsula has been inhabited for half a million years, but these indigenous people are not thought to be the earliest ancestors of the Korean people. Instead, Koreans are believed to be descendants of Altaic immigrants from Central Asia who displaced the earlier residents in the Neolithic period (5500–800 BCE).

Evidence indicates that Koreans and Siberians share common roots. Based on archaeological findings of Scytho-Siberian bronze artifacts, the ancestors of the Koreans probably originated in Siberia and Central Asia, and the existence of iron implements from the same period indicates extensive exchanges with Sinitic (Chinese) iron culture. Furthermore, Korean shamanism is similar to Siberian shamanism. And while the Korean language is distinct, it is linguistically similar to other Altaic languages spoken in Mongolia, Manchuria, and Siberia.

According to the Korean foundation myth, Koreans trace their origins to the founding of Old Choson in 2333 BCE by Tangun. Tangun is said to have been the son of a deity and a female bear who became human after proving her patience and perseverance. The Tangun myth is significant because it points to non-Sinitic origins of Korean culture.

As with any culture, it is impossible to pinpoint the historical moment when a common ethnic or national consciousness was formed. People of prehistoric times did not think in terms of a shared nationhood. Over time, linguistically and culturally disparate groups merged to share a language, culture, and polity. By the time of the kingdoms of Koguryo (37 BCE–668 CE), Paekche (18 BCE–663 CE), and early Shilla (57 BCE– 668) CE), there was a clear sense of the peninsular peoples as being ethnically distinct from their Chinese neighbors. It was, however, not until the Unified Shilla kingdom (668–935) or the Koryo kingdom (918–1392) that the peninsula became unified. Unified Shilla controlled only the southern two-thirds of the peninsula, leading some to argue that the peninsula was not unified until Koryo extended the border northward. Unified Shilla, however, is to be credited with achieving linguistic, cultural, and political unity within its own borders.

**Cultural Characteristics**

The official adoption of Buddhism by Koguryo in 372, Paekche in 384, and Shilla in 534 helped each kingdom unite its people. Buddhism adopted some of the indigenous shamanic deities and bolstered royal authority by bestowing on kings religious and social legitimacy. There were many religious observances to ensure longevity for the king and kingdom. Religious architecture and artwork, especially sculptures and statues of the Buddha, flourished. Agricultural festivals had tremendous social, recreational, and religious importance. Today, Buddhism is still the most popular religion among South Koreans.

Confucianism is another important facet of Korean culture, past and present, in both Koreas. The Choson dynasty (1392–1910) became thoroughly Confucianized by the mid-seventeenth century (albeit a Koreanized form of Confucianism). Social order or hierarchy is a key aspect of Confucianism, characterized by patriarchy, respect for one's elders, and great value placed on education and position. These ideals are upheld in both Koreas today. For example, the symbol of the (North) Korean Worker's Party includes not only the hammer and sickle, but also the calligraphy brush, to signify the intellectual alongside the laborer and farmer. Patriarchy is embodied in North Korea's reverence for their two leaders, Kim Il Sung (1912–1994) and Kim Jong Il (b. 1941).

Nationalism is another key feature of the Korean people. In North Korea, nationalism is seen in the *juche* (self-reliance) ideology. In South Korea, there are different kinds of nationalism, such as conservative nationalism, *minjung* (people's) nationalism, and ultraconservative nationalism. Nationalism has been a democratizing force in South Korea, advocating national autonomy and reunification. The tendency to place nationalism above all else has upheld the interests of the elite and the state, marginalizing issues of class, gender, and region. Regionalism falls along provincial boundaries, which echo the earlier borders of Koguryo, Paekche, and Shilla. Regional discrimination was particularly prominent under the Choson dynasty and continues to be a problem today, especially in South Korea.

Koreans also share a sense of loss and longing called *han*. The loss of Korean sovereignty to Japanese colonial rule (1910–1945), the 1945 division of North and South under a Soviet-U.S joint trusteeship, the formation of separate states in 1948, and the Korean War (1950–1953) have engendered a strong sense of anxiety among Koreans. Despite recent attempts at reunification, the two Koreas remain deeply divided. For older Koreans, however, there is a strong imperative that they must see Korea reunified within their own lifetime.

*Jennifer Jung-Kim*

**Further Reading**

Clark, Donald N. (2000). *Culture and Customs of Korea*. Westport, CT: Greenwood Press.

Korean Overseas Information Service (1993). *A Handbook of Korea*. Seoul: Korean Overseas Information Service.

**KOREANS IN CENTRAL ASIA** The presence of a Korean minority in Central Asia resulted from the Stalinist ethnic purges of the 1930s, when the Soviet premier Joseph Stalin ordered the mass deportation of ethnic Koreans residing in the Vladivostok region and the Far East Maritime Province to the Central Asian republics of Kazakhstan, Kyrgyzstan, and Uzbekistan. Some 175,000 Soviet Koreans were forcibly removed from their homes, loaded onto railroad freight cars, and transported to Central Asia.

Following the annexation of Korea by Japan in 1910, Koreans had begun migrating to the Russian Far East and over time had integrated themselves into the local Soviet culture and economy. However, as tensions between the Japanese empire and the Soviet Union escalated over Manchuria and the Korean peninsula, Stalin became fearful that Koreans residing in the Russian Far East harbored pro-Japanese sympathies. Thus on 21 August 1937, he ordered the transfer of Koreans to Central Asia, and the forcible displacement occurred from September to November 1937.

During the long period of deportation, many children and elderly people died of malnutrition and disease. Scurvy, typhoid, diphtheria, dysentery, measles, and scarlet fever took the lives of those who were weak and infirm, as families were forced to live in unsanitary conditions aboard the freight trains, with little or no food for most of the trip. On their arrival in Central Asia, regional and local governments did what they could to feed and house the Korean refugees, but many families were forced to live in warehouses, barns, mosques, and converted prisons while they struggled to build homes for themselves.

Following World War II Koreans remained in the Central Asian republics and began integrating and assimilating into Soviet society, where they soon thrived as agricultural technicians, agronomists, and managerial professionals. To this day, there are still large Korean communities in Kazakstan and Uzbekistan.

*Keith Leitich*

**Further Reading**

Gelb, Michael. (1995) "An Early Soviet Ethnic Deportation: The Far Eastern Koreans." *Russian Review* 54, 3 (July): 389–412.

Huttenbach, Henry E. (1993) "The Soviet Koreans." *Central Asian Survey* 12, 1: 59–69.

Kho, Songmoo. (1987) *Koreans in Soviet Central Asia*. Helsinki: Finnish Oriental Society.

Ota, Natsuko. (2000). "Deportation of Koreans from the Russian Far East to Central Asia." In *Migration in Central Asia: Its History and Current Problems*, edited by Hisao Komatsu, Chika Obiya, and John Schoeberlein. JCAS Symposium Series 9. Osaka, Japan: Japan Center for Area Studies, National Museum of Ethnology, 127–145.

**KOREANS IN JAPAN** The Koreans constitute the largest minority group in Japan. Japan annexed Korea in 1910. The 1939 National Service Draft Ordinance on the eve of World War II resulted in

A young Korean boy studying a Korean book with his instructor in Chefoo, Hokkaido, Japan, in 1990. (BOHEMIAN NOMAD PICTUREMAKERS/CORBIS)

## KOREANS IN JAPAN

The integration of Koreans into Japanese society has always been a major social, economic, and political issue. The following description of Korean housing in Japan in the late nineteenth century indicates that house style was one cultural element that distinguished Koreans from Japanese.

> It will be seen by these brief extracts how dissimilar the Korean house is to that of the Japanese. And this dissimilarity is fully sustained by an examination of the photographs which Mr. Lowell made in Korea, and which show among other things low stone-walled houses with square openings for windows, closed by frames partly covered with paper, the frames hung from above and opening outside, and the roof tiled; also curious thatched roofs, in which the slopes are uneven and rounding, and their ridges curiously knotted[,] differ in every respect from the many forms of thatched roof in Japan.
>
> *Source:* Edward S. Morse ([1896] 1961) *Japanese Homes and Their Surroundings.* New York: Dover Publications, 345.

6 million Koreans arriving in Japan as conscripted laborers and military draftees to satisfy the manpower shortage. During the war, many Koreans also voluntarily migrated to Japan in search of better employment.

During the war, Koreans were given Japanese nationality. The introduction of the Alien Registration Order in 1952, whereby all non-Japanese were regarded as aliens, changed the status of Koreans. Since the legal process of becoming a naturalized citizen is complicated, many Koreans choose not to take up Japanese citizenship. As aliens, the Korean minority is denied many of the normal legal and social benefits enjoyed by the Japanese population.

Today approximately 687,000 Koreans live in Japan. They are slowly being Japanized, so much so that many don't speak Korean or even use their Korean name in public. Differences in status and racial prejudices have alienated the Koreans from the Japanese society at large. There are limited employment opportunities, and most Koreans hold low-paying jobs and suffer from exploitation from their Japanese employers. Some are involved in private businesses in the entertainment and service industries.

The Koreans are divided between supporters of North and South Korea. The Mindan (Association of Korean Residents in Japan) supports South Korea, and Chongryun (General Association of Korean Residents in Japan) supports North Korea. This division has created separate education systems. As a divided community with differing goals, it is difficult for the Koreans to fight for better social and economic conditions, and difficult for the Japanese government to implement any changes.

*Geetha Govindasamy*

### Further Reading

Mitchell, Richard. (1967) *The Korean Minority in Japan.* Berkeley and Los Angeles: University of California Press.

Ryang, Sonia. (1997) *North Koreans in Japan: Language, Ideology, and Identity.* Boulder, CO: Westview Press.

Wagner, Edward W. (1951) *The Korean Minority in Japan, 1904–1950.* New York: Institute of Pacific Relations.

Weiner, Michael. (1989) *The Origins of the Korean Community in Japan, 1910–1923.* Manchester, U.K.: Manchester University Press.

———. (1994) *Race and Migration in Imperial Japan.* London: Routledge.

**KOREANS, OVERSEAS** Some 5 million Koreans—more than 7 percent of the peninsula's population—live outside Korea. They are scattered among 140 nations, with about 93 percent living in China, the United States, Russia, and Japan. These overseas Koreans fall into two categories: first-generation emigrants, who were born in Korea and are culturally and linguistically Korean; and their descendants, who are ethnically Korean but who have adapted culturally and linguistically to their local environment and often can't speak Korean.

## The History of Korean Immigration

The first wave of overseas migration started in the second half of the nineteenth century and lasted until 1910. It was a large-scale movement, primarily to avoid famine and poverty. Koreans moved to Manchuria and the Russian Far East, where they pioneered wet rice farming. Another group, some seven thousand strong, went to North America as indentured laborers. Most worked on sugarcane farms in Hawaii, and some later migrated to the U.S. mainland and to Mexico and Cuba.

A second wave of several hundred Koreans left between 1910 and 1945, during Japan's colonial rule of Korea. Fleeing Japanese oppression, most moved to Manchuria and the Russian Far East. A number migrated to Japan in the hope of finding better employment, but during World War II the Japanese government conscripted laborers in Korea to work under quasi-military conditions in Japanese military industries to support the war effort.

By 1945, there were 2.4 million Koreans in Japan and more than 2 million in Manchuria. After Korea became independent, most Koreans in Japan went home, but 700,000 remain in Japan today.

The 1945–1970 period may have been the most difficult in Korea's history. The country split into North and South, and the Korean War raged from 1950 to 1953. The period from the 1950s to 1965 saw an attempt to rebuild the country, and there was little emigration. External migration was very difficult until 1965, when the U.S. immigration law was changed and many Koreans moved to America for better economic prospects. During this period Koreans had little contact with foreigners except Americans and did not consider emigration as an option.

During the 1970s and 1980s, Korea was industrializing fast, its economy was growing rapidly, and many Koreans were working overseas for Korean companies. Some decided to stay abroad to establish themselves in the developed world, particularly in the United States. A number of Korean students studying abroad also opted to stay, which caused a "brain drain" to the United States and other Western countries.

Since the early 1990s, immigration patterns have changed yet again. Korea's economy had peaked, and

A strip mall in Koreatown, Los Angeles, in 1997. (NIK WHEELER/CORBIS)

countries such as the United States, Canada, Australia, and New Zealand attempted to attract immigrants with money or useful skills. The resulting emigration of well-educated, prosperous Koreans contrasts sharply with that of forced laborers or citizens fleeing political persecution.

## Overseas Korean Communities

The largest number of overseas Koreans—2 million, or 39 percent—live in China. They are mainly concentrated near the Korean–Manchurian border, and most live in the Yenbien Korean Autonomous Prefecture of Jirin Province. Pioneer rice farmers and their descendants, they have formed communities with well-established education systems in which Korean is spoken and accepted as an official language.

The second-largest number of overseas Koreans—1.5 million, or 31 percent—live in the United States. Some are descended from of the early sugarcane laborers, but most are post-1965 immigrants and their families. Many were highly educated, with professional careers in Korea, but were unable to overcome linguistic and cultural barriers in America and wound up running small businesses such as grocery stores and laundries. California is home to most Koreans living in the United States—Los Angeles has a sizable Koreatown—followed by New York.

With 700,000, Japan has the third-largest number of overseas Koreans—about 14 percent. Most are descendants of the immigrants who were drafted as laborers for the war industry or who came to Japan seeking better jobs. They are concentrated in the industrial Osaka area and many no longer speak Korean, although they are ethnically and culturally Korean and identify themselves as such.

The fourth-largest number of overseas Koreans—460,000, or 9 percent—are in the former Soviet Union. They are mainly the descendants of immigrants who moved to Russia's maritime province before or during the Japanese takeover of Korea. Under Stalin, these Koreans were forcibly moved to Central Asia. In an area inhabited by Turkic nomads who raised livestock, the Korean immigrants introduced wet rice farming, as they had in Manchuria. The largest number of Koreans in the former Soviet Union, about 200,000, live in Uzbekistan. The Russian Republic and Kazakhstan have 100,000 each, and the other Central Asian republics have the remaining 60,000.

The remaining 340,000 overseas Koreans—about 7 percent—are scattered among Canada (70,000), Australia (40,000), Europe (60,000), Southeast Asia (25,000), and New Zealand (almost 10,000). Koreans are generally known as hardworking people and have established themselves quickly. Their communities have introduced aspects of Korean life such as kimchi (Korea's spicy vegetable pickle) and the martial art tae kwon do to their host countries and brought foreign culture back to Korea.

*Hong-key Yoon*

### Further Reading

Vasil, Raj, and Hong-key Yoon. (1996) *New Zealanders of Asian Origin*. Wellington, New Zealand: Institute of Policy Studies, Victoria University of Wellington.

National Council of Sport for All. (1994) *Segae hanminjok pyollam* (Koreans in the World). Seoul: National Council of Sport for All.

Yi, Kwang-kyu. (1997) *Kukjehwa Sidaeui Hanminjokui Chillo* (The Future of Korea in the Age of Internationalization). Seoul: Seoul National University Press.

**KOROGHLI** The epic of *Koroghli* is a cycle of oral epics found from the Balkans to Central Asia. The central hero of the cycle is called Koroghli (the son of the blind man) or Goroghli (the son of the grave), depending on whether it is told that the hero's father was blinded or that the hero was born in the grave after the death of his mother. In all versions the hero gathers a group of warriors around him with whom he performs various heroic exploits. In the versions collected from Turkish and Azerbaijani singers, the hero is a kind of minstrel outlaw who fights against the sultan or *padishah*. In the Central Asian versions (Turkmen, Uzbek, Karakalpak, Kazakh), Koroghli is depicted as a powerful ruler holding a splendid court with his group of brave retainers. This epic cycle is not only popular with the Turkic-speaking peoples but also with the Iranian-speaking Tajiks. In the various Turkic traditions, the epic is in a mixture of verse and prose, while in Tajik the epic is in verse. The epic cycle is thought to have originated in the sixteenth century, in connection with the Jalali movement in Turkey and Azerbaijan, directed against the Ottoman sultan and the Persian shah.

*Karl Reichl*

### Further Reading

Chadwick, N. K., and V. Zhirmunsky. (1969) *Oral Epics of Central Asia*. Cambridge, U.K.: Cambridge University Press.

Chodzko, Alexander, trans. (1842) *Specimens of the Popular Poetry of Persia, As Found in the Adventures and Improvisations of Kurroglou, the Bandit-Minstrel of Northern Persia*. London: Oriental Translation Fund.

Karryev, B. A. (1968) *Ѐpicheskie skazaniya o Ker-ogly u tyurko-yazychnykh narodov* (The Epic Tales about Koroghly among the Turkic-speaking Peoples). Moscow: Glavnaya redaktsiya vostochnoy literatury.

Karryev, B. A., and Y. A. Potseluevskiy, eds. (1983) *Gorogly: Turkmenskiy geroicheskiy ѐpos* (Gorogly: A Turkmen Heroic Epic). Moscow: Glavnaya redaktsiya vostochnoy literatury.

Nazarov, K., B. Shermukhammedov, and I. S. Braginskiy, eds. (1987) *Gurugli: Tadzhikskiy narodny ѐpos* (Gurugli: A Tajik Folk Epic). Moscow: Glavnaya redaktsiya vostochnoy literatury.

Reichl, Karl. (1992) *Turkic Oral Epic Poetry: Traditions, Forms, Poetic Structure*. Albert Bates Lord Studies in Oral Tradition, no. 7. New York: Garland.

**KORYO KINGDOM** A series of uprisings near the end of the ninth century led to the fragmentation of the declining Unified Shilla kingdom (668–935 CE). In the northern part of the Korean Peninsula, rebel leaders established the later Koguryo kingdom (901–918) with the aim of regaining the glory and vast territory of the former Koguryo kingdom (37 BCE–668 CE). With Wang Kon (877–943) as Koguryo's leader, the Shilla king abdicated in 935, the later Paekche kingdom (892–936 CE) bowed to Koguryo's superior military force the following year. The peninsula was thus reunified. Wang Kon (King T'aejo, 877–943) married Shilla royalty, changed the kingdom's name to Koryo, derived from "Koguryo" and from which "Korea" derived, and became the first king of the Koryo dynasty (918–1392).

Koryo's northern border extended to the Yalu River. Across the border, the Liao kingdom of the Khitans conquered Parhae in 926 and then became a threat to Koryo. Liao attacked repeatedly until peace was achieved in 1022 without loss of territory. Domestically, Koryo began to prosper more rapidly to reach its height in the 1100s. From the outset, the government adopted Buddhism as the state religion, like Shilla before it. Temple construction flourished, as did Buddhist sculpture, painting, and wood-block printing, including the six thousand chapters of the *Tripitaka* (Three Collections). Inspired by vigorous Buddhist faith, the arts and scholarship flowered under the centralized Chinese-style government. The ceramics industry, which produced exquisite Koryo celadons, was particularly distinctive.

By the end of the twelfth century, however, Koryo's power began to wane. Powerful aristocratic clans and the military vied with the royal family for political power. In 1170, a revolt of the military leaders resulted in the complete overthrow of aristocratic rule, assumption of power by military leaders, and a puppet role for the throne. The powerful Mongols overran Liao to the north and became a threat to Koryo. Consecutive invasions forced the royal family to flee to Kanghwa Island, west of present-day Seoul. Hoping for divine intervention, the king ordered a new set of Buddhist canon woodblocks produced to replace the *Tripitaka* destroyed by the Mongols. This extant replacement, the *Tripitaka Koreana*, consists of 81,137 wooden blocks of exquisite workmanship. By 1259, however, the Mongol conquest was complete. Under Mongol suzerainty, which lasted for a century, Koryo was stripped of its political freedom. Kings had to marry Mongol princesses, and Mongol officials supervised the activities of the Koryo government.

The library at Haein-sa Temple in Taegu, South Korea, which houses the *Tripitaka*. (LEONARD DE SELVA/CORBIS)

## KOREAN KINGDOMS AND DYNASTIES

Koguryo kingdom (37 BCE–668 CE)
Paekche kingdom (18 BCE–663 CE)
Shilla kingdom (57 BCE–935 CE)
Unified Shilla (668–935 CE)
Koryo kingdom (dynasty) (918–1392)
Choson dynasty or Yi dynasty (1392–1910)

In the fourteenth century, rebellions broke out throughout China, and the Mongols were finally driven from power, which freed Koryo from Mongol domination. Koryo made efforts to reform its government but was stymied by opposing pro-Mongol and pro-Ming China factions. This was not the only problem to hinder Koryo recuperation. Most of the land was now in the hands of military officers and government officials favored by the Mongols. There was rising animosity between the Buddhist clergy and Confucian scholars, and highly organized Japanese marauders raided the country.

This was the situation in 1388 when the king dispatched an outstanding military general, a member of the rising new class of nobles of the pro-Ming faction, as part of an expedition of forty thousand men to attack the Ming. When this general, Yi Song-gye (1335–1408), reached the northern border, he turned his men around, marched into the undefended capital, and took control of the government. Four years later, General Yi (King T'aejo, reigned 1392–1398) ascended to the throne, ushering in the Chosun dynasty (1392–1910).

*David E. Shaffer*

*See also:* **Buddhism—Korea; Wang Kon; Yi Song-gye**

### Further Reading

Eckert, Carter J., et al. (1990) *Korea: Old and New.* Seoul: Ilchokak Publishers.

Han, Woo-keun. (1970) *The History of Korea*. Trans. by Lee Kyung-shik. Seoul: Eul-yoo Publishing.
Henthorn, William E. (1971) *A History of Korea*. New York: Free Press.
Joe, Wanne J., and Hongkyu A. Choe. (1997) *Traditional Korea: A Cultural History*. Elizabeth, NJ: Hollym.
Koo, John H., and Andrew C. Nahm, eds. (1997) *An Introduction to Korean Culture*. Elizabeth, NJ: Hollym.
Lee, Ki-baik. (1984) *A New History of Korea*. Trans. by Edward W. Wagner. Seoul: Ilchokak Publishers.
Nahm, Andrew C. (1983) *A Panorama of 5000 Years: Korean History*. Elizabeth, NJ: Hollym.
———. (1988) *Korea: Tradition & Transformation*. Elizabeth, NJ: Hollym.

**KOTA KINABALU** (2000 est. pop. 354,000). Kota Kinabalu ("fort of Kinabalu," formerly Jesselton) is a city on the northwest coast of Borneo Island; it lies between rain forest, mountains, and offshore coral reefs that are a national park. The city takes its name from the nearby Mount Kinabalu, at 4,101 meters the highest peak in the Malay Archipelago; Kinabalu means "sacred place of the dead," and the inhabitants of the region regard the heavily forested mountain as a holy site.

An important commercial, educational, and cultural center in eastern Malaysia, Kota Kinabalu is the capital of the state of Sabah, the second-largest state of the Federation of Malaysia. It is situated 1,600 kilometers east of Malaysia's capital, Kuala Lumpur, on the coast of the South China Sea.

In the nineteenth century, Kota Kinabalu was a small, sleepy town until it was destroyed by anti-British rebels led by Mat Salleh in 1897. In 1899, the British North Borneo Company established a colonial settlement and a deepwater seaport, naming it Jesselton, after Sir Charles Jessel, then a director of the British North Borneo Company. During World War II, the city was occupied by Japanese troops, but by the end of the war it was in ruins due to extensive Allied bombing.

In 1946, Jesselton replaced Sandakan as the capital of what then was British North Borneo, and in 1968 it was renamed Kota Kinabalu. Between the 1960s and 1990s, Kota Kinabalu grew significantly and became an important commercial center in Sabah state, with well-developed agriculture, furniture manufacturing, wood processing, and lately tourism. Kota Kinabalu has an international airport, which was recently modernized, and is connected with the rest of Borneo Island through a well-maintained network of highways and railroads.

*Rafis Abazov*

### Further Reading

Department of Statistics, Malaysia. (2001) "Official Website." Retrieved 3 April 2002 from: http://www.statistics.gov.my.
Kaur, Amarjit. (1998) *Economic Change in East Malaysia: Sabah and Sarawak since 1850*. New York: St. Martin's Press.
Leong, Cecilia. (1982) *Sabah, the First 100 Years*. Kuala Lumpur, Malaysia: Pecetakan Nan Yang Muda.
Lucas Robert E. B., and Donald Verry. (1999) *Restructuring the Malaysian Economy: Development and Human Resources*. Houndmills, Basingstoke, Hampshire, U.K.: Palgrave.
Office of the Prime Minister of Malaysia. (2000) "Government of Malaysia." Retrieved 3 April 2002 from: http://www.smpke.jpm.my/.
Roff, Margaret Clark. (1974) *The Politics of Belonging: Political Change in Sabah and Sarawak*. Kuala Lumpur, Malaysia, and New York: Oxford University Press.

**KOTO** Originally used for court music *(Gagaku)* and called *gakuso*, the koto is a heterochord zither related to the Chinese *Zheng*, the Korean *Kayagum*, and the Vietnamese *Dan tranh*. Practiced as an independent genre known as *Tsukushi-goto* on Kyushu Island through the sixteenth century, the koto was popularized by Yatsuhashi Kengyo (1614–1685) in seventeenth-century Kyoto. Today, the instrument is central to the *sokyoku* (koto instrumental) and *sankyoku* (chamber) repertoire maintained by two major schools, Yamada Ryu and Ikuta Ryu.

With a vaulted *kiri* (paulownia) wood sound box 180 to 190 centimeters long and 48 centimeters wide, the koto has thirteen strings of equal gauge, originally of silk but now more frequently of nylon. Movable bridges, most commonly of ivory or plastic, support the strings and determine pitch. The tunings are pentatonic (five-tone scale), covering two-and-a-half octaves. Three ivory picks *(tsume)* with leather rings are attached to the underside of the player's thumb and first two fingers of the right hand. The shape, rounded or square, indicates the school. The left hand manipulates pitch and sound quality. Innovations include a seventeen-string bass koto, *jushichi-gen*, introduced around 1920 by Michio Miyagi (1894–1956), who is therefore considered the father of modern koto.

*Kevin Olafsson*

### Further Reading

Adriaansz, Willem. (1971) "Koto," subentry 4–2 of "Japan." In *New Grove Dictionary of Music and Musicians*, edited by Stanley Sadie. London: Macmillan, 526–532.
———. (1980) "The Yatsuhashi Ryu: A Seventeenth-Century School of Koto Music." *Acta Musicologica* 43, 1–2: 55–93.
Harich-Schneider, Eta. (1973) *A History of Japanese Music*. London: Oxford University Press.

Johnson, Henry M. (1993) "Koto Manufacture: The Instrument, Construction Process, and Aesthetic Considerations." *Galpin Society Journal* 49 (March): 38–64.

Kishibe, Shigeo. (1969) *The Traditional Music of Japan*. Tokyo: Japan Cultural Society.

Thrasher, Alan. (1995) "The Melodic Model as a Structural Device: Chinese Zheng and Japanese Koto Repertories Compared." *Asian Music* 26, 1: 97–117.

**KOUTA** *Kouta* (short song) is a type of Japanese vocal music, the most widely known form of which is a song accompanied by a *shamisen* (three-stringed lute) and performed by female musicians, usually geisha, at traditional, small-scale, Japanese social events. The term, however, has not always been so applied but has been used to denote a variety of other song forms throughout the history of Japanese music.

From the tenth to the twelfth centuries, *kouta* was generally used to indicate all manner of short or colloquial songs, in contrast to the longer, more formal pieces that were a common part of court rituals. By the sixteenth century, however, the term had become exclusively associated with a type of short song that used verses of four lines based around groups of five and seven syllables (7+5+7+5 / 7+7+7+7 / 7+7+7+5 / or 7+5+7+7); this is noted in several important *kouta* compilations of the period, including *Kangin shu* (1518) and *Soan Kouta shu* (late sixteenth century). By the Edo period (1603–1868), the term had evolved to include both certain types of unaccompanied folk songs and some of the *shamisen* songs common in the Kabuki theater of the time. In the Meiji period (1868–1912), the term became associated with the short *shamisen*-accompanied song that is common today. This type of *kouta*, generally one to three minutes in duration, is sung by a female vocalist in a small chamber known as an *ozashiki;* usually the singer accompanies herself on the *shamisen*. The instrument is plucked with the nails—unusual, in that most *shamisen* music calls for a special plectrum—and maintains the rhythm, above which the vocal melody provides subtle musical ornamentation to augment the seven-and-five-syllable verses. Although this type of *kouta* was primarily the cultural property of the geisha, it filtered into the public domain in the 1950s and 1960s. Today, although *kouta* does not attract the level of interest it once did, it represents a musical tradition that embodies a broad spectrum of Japanese emotions and images.

*Terauchi Naoko*

**Further Reading**

Crihfield, Liza. (1979) *Kouta: "Little Songs" of the Geisha World*. Rutland, VT: Charles E. Tuttle.

Fujie, Linda. (1996) "Kouta." In *Worlds of Music: An Introduction to the Music of the World's People*, edited by Jeff T. Titon. New York: Schirmer Books, 384–391.

Hirano, Kenji. (1989) "Kouta." In *Nihon Ongaku Daijiten* (Encyclopedia of Japanese Music), edited by Kenji Hirano et al. Tokyo: Heibonsha, 89, 453–455.

Kurata, Yoshihiro. (1989) "Kouta." In *Nihon Ongaku Daijiten* (Encyclopedia of Japanese Music), edited by Kenji Hirano et al. Tokyo: Heibonsha, 553–555.

**KOZHIKODE.** See **Calicut.**

**KUALA LUMPUR** (2002 pop. 1.5 million). Kuala Lumpur (or "KL," as it is commonly known) is the federal capital city of Malaysia. In comparative historical terms, Kuala Lumpur is a young city. Its genesis is traced to the middle of the nineteenth century, when a settlement of Chinese tin miners grew up on the muddy confluence of two rivers (Gombak and Klang); hence its place name: "Kuala Lumpur" means "muddy confluence." Although Malay and Sumatran

The Kuala Lumpur stock exchange in 2001. (MACDUFF EVERTON/CORBIS)

village settlements had existed in the vicinity, Kuala Lumpur's meteoric rise as a major trading center and, later, as the colonial and postcolonial capital, is attributed to a number of fortuitous factors. Among others, they include a boom in tin prices and the pioneering entrepreneurship of various individuals. In particular, Yap Ah Loy, a Hakka Chinese immigrant who had come to seek his fortune in the Malay States, is customarily credited with playing an influential role in Kuala Lumpur's formative stages. From 1868 to 1885, he ruled the town as the third Chinese *kapitan*.

In 1880, recognizing the growing commercial importance of Kuala Lumpur, the British relocated their state administrative capital 35 kilometers from Klang. In 1896, Kuala Lumpur was chosen to become the capital of the Federated Malay States (FMS) when this political unit (comprising Perak, Selangor, Negri Sembilan, and Pahang) was formed to standardize governmental policy and practice. This initiated the modernization of the town as the British put into place municipal planning practices and erected ornate administrative buildings. Following the Japanese occupation of British Malaya between 1939 and 1945, Kuala Lumpur became the capital of the Federation of Malaya created in 1948. When the country achieved political independence from Great Britain in 1957, Kuala Lumpur was the natural choice as the capital for the new nation.

It achieved city status in February 1972 and was ceded to the federal government by the Selangor state government in 1974. In the 1990s, its landscape and skyline were transformed dramatically. The enforced demolition of squatter colonies, the completion of the light rail transit system and the ring roads, and a construction boom in the property market are some of the driving forces of this transformation into a bustling metropolis. Emblematic of these changes is the Petronas Twin Towers, at 452 meters the tallest building in the world when it was completed in the late 1990s. Moreover, in keeping with city hall's efforts to project Kuala Lumpur as a recognizable world-class city, the motif of "The Garden City of Lights" pervades its official discourse and transformative activities.

*Yeoh Seng-Guan*

### Further Reading

Gullick, John Michael. (2000) *A History of Kuala Lumpur, 1857–1939*. Kuala Lumpur, Malaysia: Malaysian Branch of the Royal Asiatic Society.

———. (1994) *Old Kuala Lumpur*. Kuala Lumpur, Malaysia: Oxford University Press.

Khoo, Kay-Kim. ed. (1996) *Kuala Lumpur: The Formative Years*. Kuala Lumpur, Malaysia: Berita Publishing.

Lim, Heng-Kow. (1978) *The Evolution of the Urban System in Malaya*. Kuala Lumpur, Malaysia: Penerbit Universiti Malaya.

**KUBLAI KHAN.** See **Khubilai Khan.**

**KUCHING** (2000 pop. 496,000). Kuching is today the capital city of Sarawak, Malaysia's largest state, situated on the island of Borneo. Pangiran Mahkota, a nobleman of Brunei and governor of Sarawak in the 1830s, founded the city. Pangiran Mahkota was in Kuching during the arrival of James Brooke (1803–1863), the first White Rajah of Sarawak. Kuching was formerly known as Sarawak, as it was located in the valley of the Sarawak River. The river, town, and country shared the appellation Sarawak until 1872. It is a common practice among the natives of Sarawak to name places and people after the river that flows there. Its name was changed to Kuching, after the name of a rivulet that flowed at the east end of the town before joining the Sarawak River, by Charles Brooke in 1872. The name, which means "cat" in the Malay language, is said to derive from a lychee-like fruit tree, called *mata kuching* (*Nephelium nalarense*) that grew on the hill opposite the stream that ran there. Some sources say that the name originated from the Chinese word *gu chin* which means "harbor."

Kuching has a long history as a trading center, primarily for antimony (which in the Malay language is known as *serawak*) and jungle produce. Currently timber and petroleum are its main resources. Since 1963, when Sarawak became part of the Federation of Malaysia, Kuching has changed and developed into a modern city.

*Shanthi Thambiah*

### Further Reading

Alice Yen Ho. (1998) *Images of Asia: Old Kuching*. Kuala Lumpur, Malaysia: Oxford University Press.

Pollard, Elizabeth. (1972) *Kuching Past and Present*. Kuching, Malaysia: Borneo Literature Bureau.

**KUKAI** (774–835), Japanese Buddhist monk. Kukai, also known as Kobo Daishi, was born in Shikoku; at age seventeen, he went to Kyoto to attend the university, where he studied Chinese classics. Renouncing the life of the scholar-noble, he became a mountain ascetic and eventually encountered the Great Sun Sutra, one of the central texts of Shingon esoteric Buddhism. This stimulated a desire to travel to China to study the deeper meaning of the sutra.

Sailing to China in 804, Kukai reached Chang'an, where he studied Sanskrit before approaching Huiguo, the master he had been seeking. Within three short months, Kukai received the formal transmission of the major esoteric teachings, becoming the dharma heir of Tantric Buddhism. When Kukai returned to Japan in 806, he brought translations of texts of esoteric Buddhism and the ritual implements necessary for transmission of the dharma lineage. Saicho, eventual founder of the Tendai school of Japanese Buddhism, initiated a correspondence with Kukai by asking to borrow certain texts which Kukai had copied in China.

Gaining patronage at the imperial court in Kyoto, Kukai spread the teachings of Shingon esoteric Buddhism, founded a monastic center on Mount Koya in 816, and was granted the prestigious Toji temple as headquarters for Shingon training. Credited with creating the kana syllabary, constructing various waterworks, and originating the eighty-eight-temple pilgrimage on Shikoku, as a scholar Kukai is remembered for his ten-volume *Ten Stages of the Development of the Mind.* It came to be believed that Kukai remains in eternal samadhi in the Okunoin, the inner shrine on Mount Koya.

*James M. Vardaman, Jr.*

**Further Reading**

Kashiwahara, Yusen, and Koyu Sonoda, eds.(1994) *Shapers of Japanese Buddhism.* Trans. by Gaynor Sekimori. Tokyo: Kosei Publishing.

Tsunoda, Ryusaku, et al. (1958) *Sources of Japanese Tradition.* Vol. 1. New York: Columbia University Press.

## KULI, MAKTUM

**KULI, MAKTUM** (1733?–1782?), Classical Turkmen poet. Maktum Kuli (Makhtumkuli, Maxtumquli, Magtymguly) is probably the most important Turkmen classical poet. He was born sometime in the fourth decade of the eighteenth century and died sometime in the ninth decade. His father was the famous poet Azadi. Maktum Kuli studied for three years in the *madrasah* of Khiva and during his life traveled widely in central Asia. The poet, who also used the pseudonym Firaqi (the separated one), left a rich body of work of over ten thousand verse lines. Many of his poems are of mystic inspiration, and a great part of his poetry is devoted to religious and moral themes (for example, the Last Judgment, mortality, the corruption of the rich and powerful, falseness, and deceit found among all walks of life). There are poems dealing with the poet's personal experiences with death (the death of his father and his sons, who died in childhood), love, loneliness, and aging. Maktum Kuli also composed poetry on political and social issues in which he urges the Turkmen tribes to unite against the threat of subjugation emanating from the Persian shah, the khan of Khiva, and the emir of Bukhara.

*Karl Reichl*

**Further Reading**

Kor-Ogly, Kh. (1972) *Turkmenskaja literatura* (Turkmen Literature). Moscow: Izd. Vysshaya shkola.

Magtymguly (Maktum Kuli). (1993) *Saylanan aserler* (Selected Works). Ashkhabad, Turkmenistan: Magaryf.

Makhtoumkouli Firaqui (Maktum Kuli). (1975) *Poèmes de Turkménie.* Trans. by Louis Bazin and Pertev Boratav. Paris: Publications Orientalistes de France.

## KULOB

**KULOB** (2002 est. pop. 81,000). Kulob (Kulyab), the third-largest city in southwestern Tajikistan, lies in the mountains north of the Amu Dar'ya River. The city is situated in the Yaksu River valley, in the piedmont zone of the Khazaratish range, 200 kilometers southeast of Tajikistan's capital Dushanbe. In the thirteenth–fourteenth centuries Kulob was founded as a trading post on the caravan route linking the Hisor (Gissar) valley in southern Tajikistan with Persia. Kulob was part of the Bukhara khanate (1583–1740) and the successive Bukhara emirate (principality) (1747–1920).

In 1934, the city became the administrative center of the Kulyab province of the Tajik Soviet Socialist Republic (established in 1929). After the 1991 dissolution of the Soviet Union, the newly independent Tajikistan's southern provinces of Kulob and Qurghonteppa (Kurgan-Tyube before 1991) merged in 1992 into Khalton province, with the capital city in Qurghonteppa. Though deprived of its capital status, Kulob has remained the largest city of the province. The Kulob region was the hardest hit during the civil war in Tajikistan (1992–1997). Kulob is Tajikistan's key cotton-producing and industrial center.

*Natalya Yu. Khan*

**Further Reading**

Allworth, Edward, ed. (1994) *Central Asia. 130 Years of Russian Dominance: A Historical Overview*. 3d ed. Durham, NC: Duke University Press.

Lubin, Nancy, and Barnett Rubin. (1999) *Calming the Ferghana Valley: Development and Dialogue in the Heart of Central Asia*. New York: The Century Foundation Press.

Roy, Oliver. (2000) *The New Central Asia: The Creation of Nations*. New York: New York University Press.

**KUM RIVER** At 401 kilometers, the Kum River is the third longest river in South Korea and the sixth longest on the Korean peninsula. It originates from a valley in Mount Shinmu east of the city of Chonju in north Cholla province in southwest Korea and weaves its way north into northern Chungchong province. It then arches west into south Chungchong just north of the city of Taejon and flows southwest back into north Cholla to its mouth at the city of Kunsan on the East China Sea. Its main tributaries are the Muju, Miho, Namdae, and Chongja Rivers. In 538, the Paekche kingdom (18 BCE–663 CE) established its last capital, Sabi (now Puyo), on the southern bank of the Kum River. Sabi served as the cultural center of Paekche until it fell to the Shilla kingdom. The Kum River basin is only 6,107 square kilometers but is currently home to roughly 4 million people. The river is navigable for 130 kilometers from its mouth, making it an important highway for transporting rice grown on the Honam plain. In 1980 and 1990, dams were built to control the seasonal floods.

*Brandon Palmer*

**KUMAMOTO** (2002 est. pop. 1.9 million). Kumamoto Prefecture is situated in the western region of Japan's island of Kyushu, where it occupies an area of 7,408 square kilometers. Its main geographical features are the active volcano Asosan, a generally mountainous south and northeast encircling a broad central plain, and part of the Amakusas, a group of about one hundred offshore islands. Kumamoto is bordered by the Amakusa Sea and by Fukuoka, Oita, Miyazaki, and Kagoshima Prefectures. Once known as Higo Province, it assumed its present name and borders in 1876.

The prefecture's capital is Kumamoto city, the Higo Province seat of power since the seventh century. In 1588, Kato Kiyomasa (1562–1611) was assigned to restore order after a long samurai uprising. In 1607, he completed Kumamoto Castle, one of Japan's most massive fortresses. The city later came under the control of the Hosokawa family and then was a Meiji era (1868–1912) military post. Today the city is home to Kumamoto University. The prefecture's other important cities are Yatsushiro, Arao, and Hitoyoshi.

Excavations of the prefecture's numerous ornamented tombs, similar to the wall-mural tombs of the Asian continent, indicate cultural exchanges during ancient times. During the Kofun period (300–710 CE), this was Kumaso tribe territory. Various warlords ruled from the late eighth century until the late sixteenth century. In 1637, Kyushu's Shimbara uprising of discontented peasants and masterless samurai spread to the Amakusa Islands, a hiding place for persecuted Japanese Christians.

In present-day Kumamoto Prefecture, the primary economic activity is agriculture, with rice, vegetables, and fruit, particularly mandarin oranges, the chief crops. Also important are dairy and livestock herding, as well as forestry. The regional industrial base is relatively small. Visitors are drawn by the volcano Asosan and the coastal scenery of the Amakusa Islands.

*E. L. S. Weber*

**Further Reading**

"Kumamoto Prefecture." (1993) *Japan: An Illustrated Encyclopedia*. Tokyo: Kodansha.

**KUMAR, DILIP** (b. 1922), Indian cinema actor. Yusuf Khan (screen name Dilip Kumar) was born in Peshawar. He came to Pune after a quarrel with his father and worked as an assistant in the army canteen. Devika Rani, the actress, introduced him into the world of Indian cinema. His acting career began with the movie *Jwar Bhatta* in 1944. The "tragedy king of the Hindi cinema" has left an indelible impression on the public mind for his roles in *Aan*, *Andaz*, *Dag*, *Devdas*, *Ganga Jamuna*, *Karma*, *Kohinor*, *Madhumati*, *Mughal-e-Azam*, *Naya Daur*, *Paigam*, *Ram aur Shyam*, *Saudagar*, and *Shakti*. His penetrating eyes, cultured voice, and histrionic talent have created a special niche in the annals of Indian cinema. In 1967, he married the actress Saira Banu.

He was awarded the coveted Dadasaheb Phalke award. The Pakistani government awarded him the *Nishan-e-Imitiaz*, the national award of excellence. This generated a lot of controversy because of the political animosity between India and Pakistan; Indian political parties like Shiva Sena told Kumar to return the award, but he refused. Kumar preferred to act in India and declined an offer to work in David Lean's *Lawrence of Arabia*. He has a great passion for soccer. Although Hindu communal organizations have accused him of supporting Pakistan, soft-spoken Dilip Kumar by sheer charisma and contribution to Hindi cinema has been one of India's most popular actors.

*Patit Paban Mishra*

**Further Reading**

Kumar, K. Naresh. (1995) *Indian Cinema: Ebbs and Tides*. New Delhi: Har-Anand Publications.

Rajadhyaksha, A., and Paul Willmen, eds. (1998) *Encyclopedia of Indian Cinema.* Bloomington, IN: Indiana University Press.

Vasudevan, Ravi S., ed. (2000) *Making Meaning in Indian Cinema.* Oxford: Oxford University Press.

**KUNAEV, DINMUKHAMED** (1911–1993), Kazakh Communist leader. Born in the rural region around Alma-Ata (now Almaty), Dinmukhamed Akhmedovich Kunaev worked his way through the ranks of the Communist Party of Kazakhstan (CPKaz). After World War II, he assumed a leadership role in the Council of Ministers of the Kazakh Socialist Soviet Republic. In the late 1950s, Nikita Khrushchev (1894–1971), the general secretary of the Communist Party of the Soviet Union (CPSU), initiated an agricultural reform program for northern Kazakhstan. The Virgin Lands campaign, as it was called, met with some initial failures, resulting in the sacking of several top Kazakh officials. In December 1959, Kunaev was appointed first secretary of the CPKaz and placed in charge of the agricultural reform program. However, by March 1962, Kunaev was blamed for continued shortcomings and was eventually removed from office in December 1962. Khrushchev's own ouster in October 1964 gave new life to Kunaev's career, and the Kazakh was reappointed by the new general secretary, Leonid Brezhnev (1906–1982), to be the CPKaz first secretary. In the early 1970s, Kunaev was elevated to full membership in the CPSU Politburo, the primary decisionmaking organization of the Soviet Union, thus becoming one of the most powerful Central Asian figures in the Soviet Union.

With the death of Brezhnev in 1982, and the eventual accession of Mikhail Gorbachev (b. 1931) in March 1985, Kunaev's fortunes waned. Gorbachev considered Kunaev to be representative of the corrupt, ossified CPSU old guard and removed him from office in December 1986. Gorbachev replaced Kunaev with an ethnic Russian, Gennadiy Kolbin (b. 1927), prompting ethnic riots in Alma-Ata. Kolbin's eventual successor, Nursultan Nazarbaev (b. 1940), partially rehabilitated Kunaev in the early 1990s, although the elder statesman never returned to active politics again. Dinmukhamed Kunaev died in 1993, after Kazakhstan's independence.

*Roger D. Kangas*

**Further Reading**

Colton, Timothy J., and Robert C. Tucker, eds. (1995) *Patterns in Post-Soviet Leadership.* Boulder, CO: Westview.

Olcott, Martha Brill. (2002) *Kazakhstan: Unfulfilled Promises.* Washington, DC: Carnegie Endowment.

**KUNANBAEV, ABAI** (1845–1904), Kazakh writer, poet, lyricist, social philosopher. Born in Kazakhstan in Semey province, Abai Kunanbaev (Ibragim Qunanbaiuly ) was educated at home and then sent to a *medressa* (Muslim religious school) where he learned Arabic and Persian and became acquainted with Eastern literature and poetry. His father ordered him home to train as his successor as clan chieftain, but appalled by what he regarded as his father's autocratic and brutal leadership, Kunanbaev broke with his family and at the age of twenty-eight returned to his studies in Semey city. While there, he actively participated in the city's intellectual life, studied Russian and Western classics by Pushkin, Goethe, and Byron, among others, and translated many of them for the first time into Kazakh. He also began writing poetry and prose and reinterpreted Krylov's Russian fables to suit Kazakh cultural sensibilities.

Kunanbaev's works were influenced by his belief in human reason. He was attracted to Western Enlightenment thinking and wove criticism of Kazakh culture into his works, most notably in his collection of poems called *Qarasozder* (often translated as the Book of Words). He criticized Russian colonial policies and encouraged his fellow Kazakhs to embrace education and literacy to escape from colonial oppression.

Most scholars consider Kunanbaev the first Kazakh to use poetry and prose to broaden the Kazakh literary milieu and to express social and political ideas designed to arouse the Kazakh nation. His writings, first published five years after his death and many times afterward, deeply influenced early-twentieth-century Kazakh activists. His life has been retold in films, operas, and novels, the best known being Auezov's *Abai zholy* (The Path of Abai).

*Steven Sabol*

**Further Reading**

Auezov, Mukhtar. (n.d.) *Abai.* Moscow: Foreign Languages Publishing House.

Nurgaliev, R. (1995) *Abai: Entsiklopediia* (Abai: Encyclopedia). Almaty, Kazakhstan: Atamura.

Winner, Thomas. (1958) *The Oral Art and Literature of the Kazakhs of Central Asia.* Durham, NC: Duke University Press.

**KUNASHIRO ISLAND** (2000 est. pop. 4,100). Kunashiro Island (or Kunashir, as the Russians know it) is a long, narrow volcanic island located approximately twenty kilometers from the eastern coast of the Japanese prefecture of Hokkaido. It is separated from this larger island by the Nemuro Kaikyo. It is 122 kilometers in length and ranges from 6.3 to 32 kilometers in width, with a total area of 1,500 square kilometers. The highest volcano is the Mont Chacha (Tiatia), which is 1,822 meters high.

The mineral deposits found on the island are tin, zinc, lead, copper, nickel, sulfur, and metallic sulfides. It has a maritime climate with an annual average temperature of 7°C. It is also characterized by abundant precipitation throughout almost the entire year, which encourages the island's rich flora. The annual average precipitation is 110 centimeters. Forestry, mainly of conifers, and mining were an important part of the island's economy until World War II. Located on the southwestern side of the island are the main fishing ports of Tomari (Golovnino) and Furukamappu (Yuzhno-Kuril'sk). The fishing products characterizing Kunashiro are green and brown kelp, salmon, trout, king crab, and scallop. Livestock farming prospered before World War II, but nowadays people do it as their second activity. The harsh weather and poor infrastructure make farming very difficult. The common practice is to cultivate small gardens for family consumption.

The Ainu people inhabited the island from the beginning of 1600s. The island was occupied by the Soviet Union in August 1945. At that time, approximately 7,000 Japanese people resided there. As of 2001, Kunashiro Island was still disputed territory, under the administration of the Russian Federation but claimed by Japan.

*Nathalie Cavasin*

### Further Reading

Hasegawa Tsuyoshi. (1998) *The Northern Territories Dispute and Russo-Japanese Relations.* Vol. 1: *Between War and Peace, 1697–1985.* Berkeley and Los Angeles: University of California Press.

———. (1998) *The Northern Territories Dispute and Russo-Japanese Relations,* Vol. 2: *Neither War, nor Peace.* Berkeley and Los Angeles: University of California Press.

Ministry of Foreign Affairs. (1996) *Japan's Northern Territories.* Tokyo: Ministry of Foreign Affairs.

Stephan, John J. (1974) *The Kurils Islands, Russo-Japanese Frontier in the Pacific.* Oxford: Clarendon Press.

**KUNLUN MOUNTAINS** The Kunlun Mountains are a range that is about 2,300 kilometers long and that follows an east-west direction on the northwestern border of the Tibetan Plateau. The mountain range stretches from the Pamir Highlands in Central Asia to central China, where it forks out into three ranges, the Altun Shan range, the Arkatag mountains, and the Hoh Xil mountains. The Kunlun range constitutes the border between Tibet and the Xinjiang Uighur Autonomous Region and extends into Qinghai Province. The width of the range differs in various locations but seldom exceeds 200 kilometers. The height of the mountains varies between 4,000 and 7,000 meters, and in the higher western part, where the range is composed of three parallel ridges, peaks like Kongur and Muztag reach over 7,700 meters. The southern slopes fade into the 1,500-meter lower Tibetan Plateau, while the northern slopes are extremely steep. On the Tibet-Xinjiang border, the Kunlun range has a glaciated area of about 4,000 square kilometers, and the glacial streams of the northern slopes are important for the oases in the Taklimakan desert. The area is mainly populated by pastoral nomads whose economy is based on yak, sheep, goats, and, to a lesser extent, cattle. There is only a little farming in the region.

*Bent Nielsen*

### Further Reading

Gasse, F., and E. Derbyshire, eds. (1992) *Environmental Changes in the Tibetan Plateau and Surrounding Areas: A Selection of Papers from the International Symposium on the Karakorum and Kunlun Mountains, Kashi, China, June 5–9, 1992.* Amsterdam: Elsevier.

Zhu, Zhenda, and Dieter Jäkel. (1991) *Reports on the 1986 Sino-German Kunlun Shan Taklimakan Expedition.* Berlin: Gesellschaft für Erdkunde zu Berlin.

**KUOMINTANG.** See **Guomindang.**

**KURDS** The Kurds are known in the West as the victims of both Saddam Hussein's oppression and the ethnic cleansing practices of the Turkish Armed Forces (TAF), which warred against the Partyia Kakaran Kurdistan (Kurdistan Workers' Party, or PKK). The Kurds have long lived in contiguous regions that they refer to as Kurdistan, that is, "The Land of the Kurds," now largely within the confines of four Middle Eastern countries: Turkey, Iraq, Iran, and Syria. A half million Kurds also live in former countries of the Soviet Union, especially in Armenia and Azerbaijan.

The Kurds in Turkey number approximately 15 million and make up 21 percent of the population. Half of the Kurdish population lives in fourteen predominantly Kurdish provinces of the southeast; the other half lives in the large cities of Istanbul, Ankara, and Izmir and in the western provinces. From 1980 to 2000, some 3 million Kurds fled from the southeast and east to the western provinces in the wake of Turkish persecution. Iran has the second-largest Kurdish population; Kurds number around six and a half million, or 10 percent of the population, and live predominantly in the provinces of West Azerbaijan, Ardalan, and Bakhtaran (formerly Kermanshah). Hundreds of thousands of Kurds also live elsewhere in Iran, especially in the cities of Tabriz, Tehran, Isfahan, and Shiraz.

In 2000, Iraq's Kurdish population was estimated at approximately 4 million, or 22 percent of the population. From 1920 to 1975, Kurds lived predominantly in the provinces of Mosul, Kirkuk, Arbil, Sulaymaniya, and Diyala. In 1975, eighteen governorates replaced the provinces, and three of them—Sulaymaniya, Dohuk, and Arbil—formed the Autonomous Kurdish Region. In 1992, the Kurdish Regional Government (KRG) was created. In 2000, more than a million Kurds lived in regions of Iraq outside the control of the KRG, especially in Baghdad, which had a population of a half million. In Syria more than a million Kurds live predominantly in the region along the border with Turkey. The cities of Damascus, Aleppo, Hims, and Hama all have Kurdish populations.

### Language

The Kurdish language belongs to the Iranic language group and hence is part of the Indo-European family. In Turkey, Kurds speak the northwestern dialect called Kurmanji. There are also some 4 million Zazaki (Dimili) speakers; most Zazaki speakers speak Kurmanji as well. Many Kurds in Turkey speak only Turkish. In Iran, Kurds speak four Sorani subdialects. In Iraq, Kurds speak Kurmanji and subdialects of Sorani.

### History

Wherever they reside in the Middle East, educated Kurds consider themselves an ancient people associated with the Urartian (thirteenth through seventh centuries BCE), Medes (625–550 BCE), and Neo-Babylonian (612–539 BCE) cultures. Many Kurds think they were ancestors of the Medes, although scholarly evidence does not support this claim. Xenophon (writing c. 401–400 BCE) first used the word *Karduchoi* to describe a people living in Bohtan, the region between Lake Van and the present-day border between Turkey and Iraq. Many scholars think the Karduchoi were ancestors of the Kurds.

Starting in the 640s, historians of the Arab conquests gave ample coverage to the Kurds and their

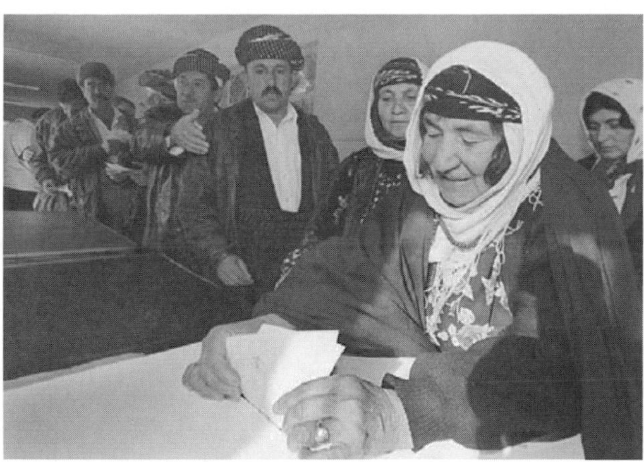

A Kurd woman votes in the 3 February 2000 election in the city of Suleimaniyeh in northern Iraq. (AFP/CORBIS)

dynasties, the most important of which included the Shaddids (951–1075), Hansanwayhids (959–1095), Marwanids (984–1083), Annazids (991–1117), Barrids (1101–1312), Zangids (1127–1250), Kurkborids (1144–1232), and Ardalans (1168–1861). Salah ad-Din, the Saladin of the West, who established the Ayyubid dynasty (1169–1260), was a Kurd. Many Kurdish principalities were destroyed by the Seljuk invasions (1055–1258). During the Seljuk period the term Kurdistan first appeared in Arabic texts.

***The Ottoman (1300–1923), Safavid (1501–1724), and Qajar (1795–1925) Periods*** From the sixteenth to the twentieth centuries, the Ottoman, Safavid, and Qajar empires dominated the Kurds. After the battle of Chaldiran in 1514, the Kurds and Kurdistan acted as bulwarks for the Ottomans against the Safavid Shi'is for the next four centuries.The semiautonomous Kurdish emirates in Turkey and Iraq were crushed during the Ottoman reform period (1839–1876), and the hereditary rulers (emirs, *pirs*) were replaced by religious leaders called *shaykh*s. This change resulted in a new governance in Kurdistan in which religious persons, primarily leaders of the Naqsbandi *tarikqat* (Muslim Brotherhood), exercised political authority.

Some historians consider a Naqsbandi *shaykh*, 'Ubaydallah of Nehri (d. 1883), to be the leader of the first rebellion in which Kurds demanded political autonomy. Further Kurdish attempts to gain greater political autonomy occurred in the early 1890s. Kurds participated in the ethnic cleansing of Armenians from the 1890s through the genocide of 1915, and many grew wealthy and powerful as a result of acquiring abandoned Armenian lands. After the creation of the Republic of Turkey in 1923, the new Turkish government left powerful Kurdish leaders *(aghas)* in control of much of Kurdistan in return for their loyalty to the state. Nevertheless, Kurds launched the large rebellions of Shaykh Said (1925), Ararat (1930), and Dersim (1937–1938), which were met with brutal suppression. Not until the 1980s under the banner of the PKK did the Kurds of Turkey again commence armed conflict with the state. War raged from 1984 to 2000; over forty thousand people, mostly Kurds, were killed; thirty-six hundred villages and hamlets were destroyed, and some two million Kurds were forced to flee to the large towns of Kurdistan in Turkey's eastern provinces. The capture of the PKK leader, Abdullah Ocalan, in February 1999, and his sentencing to death on 29 June, seemed to indicate that the armed conflict, at least on the PKK's part, was ending. As of 2000, however, the death sentence had not been carried out. The challenge of Kurdish nationalism remained the most significant problem confronting the Turkish state.

### The Kurds in Iran

In Iran, the Kurds became increasingly separate from Kurds in the Ottoman empire after the treaty of Zuhab in 1639. During the seventeenth and eighteenth centuries, Kurds moved throughout Iran as they followed their leaders, who were dispersed by order of the ruling powers. The division and control of Kurdistan remained a central focus of the Ottomans and Iranians in the nineteenth and twentieth centuries. As in Turkey, Iran's main objective after 1921 was to crush ethnic groups, principally the Kurds.

The Kurds of Iran, under the leadership of Komala-e Zhian-e Kurdistan (Committee for the Resurrection of Kurdistan), with the aid of the Soviet Union, succeeded in establishing the Kurdish Republic of Mahabad, which lasted from 23 December 1945 to 17 January 1946. After the Soviet Union withdrew its support, the Iranian government crushed the Republic. Nevertheless, the Kurdish Republic of Mahabad has been a symbol of hope for all Kurds who still work and fight for an independent Kurdistan.

After the assumption of power by the Islamic Republic of Iran in 1979, warfare continued between the Islamic Republic and the Kurds until the end of the century. From the inception of the Islamic Republic to 2000, Kurdish leaders negotiated with Tehran for political autonomy. Their efforts received a setback when the leader of the Kurdistan Democratic Party of Iran (KDPI), Abulrahman Qassemlou, was assassinated by Islamic Republic agents in 1989 in Vienna, where he had gone to negotiate with Islamic Republic officials. Relationships between Tehran and the Kurds soured again when Islamic Republic officials assassinated Sadegh Sharafkhani, the leader and Secretary-General of the KDPI, and six companions in Berlin in 1992. The election of Mohammad Khatami in August 1997 resulted in promises of economic aid, but there was little movement on the Kurds' demands for political autonomy.

### The Kurds in Iraq

In Iraq, the Kurds played a crucial role in the establishment of the modern state. After World War I, Kurds were a majority of the population in the province allocated to Iraq under British mandate by the 5 June 1926 treaty between Turkey, Iraq, and Britain. The British wanted to use the Kurds to control the Saudi Arabian–originated Hashemite dynasty that the British installed in Iraq in 1921 to head the Sunni Arab government in Baghdad. From 1926 to 1958, the Iraq government chafed against this arrangement. After the Iraqi revolution in 1958 through the remainder of the twentieth century, there was intermittent war between Baghdad and the Kurds.

After Shaykh Mahmud, leader of the first Kurdish rebellion, Molla Mustafa Barzani was the most important leader of the Kurdish nationalist movement in southern Kurdistan. He was leader of the Kurdistan Democratic Party (KDP) from its inception in the 1930s to his death on 1 March 1979. Leadership then went to Molla Mustafa's two sons, Maʿsud and Idris. After the death of Idris in 1987, Maʿsud took the reins of power and still held them in 2000.

During the 1991 Gulf War, Allied forces led by the United States created a safe haven in part of northern Iraq and extended air cover for the entire region above the thirty-sixth parallel. As a result, from 1992 onward, much of Kurdistan Iraq in the governorates of Dohuk, Arbil, and Sulaymaniya was controlled by the Kurdish Regional Government (KRG). After 1992, both the leaders of the KDP and the Patriotic Union of Kurdistan (PUK) took pains to stress that the Kurds in northern Iraq did not demand independence, but rather political autonomy in the state of Iraq. Whether the KRG in southern Kurdistan could maintain its de facto independence well into the twenty-first century remained unclear in 2000, but Kurds throughout Kurdistan and in the diaspora hoped that the Kurdish entity in southern Kurdistan and northern Iraq would mature into an independent state.

### The Kurds in Syria

The international border delimited between Turkey and Syria in 1921 left several hundred thousand Kurds in Syria. From 1930 to the 1980s, Kurds, like many other ethnic groups in Syria, were beset with many problems, which made it difficult for them to organize against the government. In the 1980s, Kurds in Syria once again began to play a major role in the Kurdish national movements. Late in 1979, just before the 1980 military coup in Turkey, Abdullah Ocalan escaped to Syria where for the next twenty years he received the support of the Syrian government and of the Kurds of Syria in his war against the Turkish government. During this period, up to 20 percent of the PKK guerrillas fighting in Turkey were Kurds from Syria. Turkey threatened to invade Syria in October 1998 if it did not evict Ocalan and 400 PKK fighters from Syria. Ocalan, as mentioned earlier, was captured in 1999. The eviction of Ocalan and the PKK from Syria reduced Syria's ability to use the PKK "card" against Turkey to compel Ankara to increase the downflow of Euphrates river water from Turkey to Syria, as did Turkey's military and intelligence alliance with Israel (officially announced in early 1996). This alliance, in turn, compelled Syria to enter into negotiations with Israel in early 2000, which demonstrated the paramount role of the Kurdish question in the pursuit of peace in the Middle East.

*Robert Olson*

**Further Reading**


Chamoy, F. B. (1868–1875) *Chéref-nâmeh ou Fastes de la nation Kourde*. 2 vols. French translation of Sharaf Khan Bidlisly's *Sharafname*. St. Petersburg, Russia: Commisionaires de l'Académie impériale des sciences.

Entessar, Nader. (1992) *Kurdish Ethnonationalism*. Boulder, CO: Lynne Rienner.

Gunter, Michael M. (1999) *The Kurdish Predicament in Iraq: A Political Analysis*. New York: St. Martin's Press.

Hassanpour, Amir. (1992) *Nationalism and Language in Kurdistan, 1918–1985*. San Francisco: Mellen Research Press.

Izady, Mehrdad. (1992) *A Concise Handbook: The Kurds*. Washington, DC: Crane Russak.

McDowall, David. (1996) *A Modern History of the Kurds*. London: I. B. Tauris.

Olson, Robert. (1989) *The Emergence of Kurdish Nationalism and the Sheikh Said Rebellion: 1880–1925*. Austin, TX: University of Texas Press.

———. (1996) *Imperial Meanderings and Republican By-Ways: Essays on Eighteenth Century Ottoman and Twentieth Century History of Turkey*. Istanbul, Turkey: Isis Press.

———. (1998) *The Kurdish Question and Turkish-Iranian Relations: From World War I to 1998*. Costa Mesa, CA.: Mazda Press.

McDowall, David, ed. (1996) *The Kurdish Nationalist Movement in the 1990s: Its Impact on Turkey and the Middle East*. Lexington, KY: University Press of Kentucky.


**KURMANJAN DATKA** (1811–1907), leader of the Alay mountain Kyrgyz. Kurmanjan Datka exercised skilled governance and diplomacy during the turbulent period when control over the southern Kyrgyz passed from the collapsing khanate of Quqon to expanding czarist Russia. Born into an ordinary family of the Kyrgyz Mungush tribe east of Osh, Kurmanjan was strong-willed and independent. She divorced her first husband in 1832 and married Alimbek, a Quqon governor, assisting him in his work until his murder in 1861. In recognition of her influence over the Alay Kyrgyz, in 1863 the emir of Bukhara, and later Khan Khudayar of Khiva, awarded Kurmanjan the high title *dadkhwah* (Kyrgyz: *datka*).

In 1876, with the Quqon khanate fallen to Russian forces and most of the Kyrgyz withdrawn to secure mountain pastures, Kurmanjan Datka negotiated with General Skobelev for the safety of her people and persuaded the Kyrgyz to submit peacefully to Russia. Called "Queen of the Alay," she governed her people as a loyal Russian subject for another three decades and received the rank of colonel. She was a fine orator and a wise judge who was much sought after for settling disputes. Kurmanjan Datka continued to live as a nomad in the Alay mountains, riding on horseback and living in felt tents, until her death at age ninety-six. She is buried in Osh, Kyrgyzstan.

*D. Prior*

**Further Reading**


Iuvachev, I. (1907) "Kurban-Dzhan-datkha, kara-kirgizskaia tsaritsa Alaia" (Kurmanjan Datka, Kyrgyz Queen of the Alay). *Istoricheskii Vestnik* (Historical Bulletin) 110, 12 (December): 954–980.

Usenbaev, Kushbek. (1960) *Prisoedinenie iuzhnoi Kirgizii k Rossii* (The Annexation of Southern Kirgizia to Russia). Frunze, Kyrgyzstan: Kirgizskoe gosudarstvennoe izdatel'stvo.


**KUROKAWA KISHO** (b. 1934), Japanese architect. Kisho "Noriaki" Kurokawa's stature was established early. By 1959, he had published a study of industrial housing in the Soviet Union. (Over three dozen books in Japanese and a dozen in English followed.) Kurokawa became known globally the following year as one of the founders of Metabolism, a postwar movement concerned with exploiting technological advances in a new, adaptable architecture. His 1970 Nakagin Capsule Building in Tokyo confirmed him among Japan's leading architects. In the building, rooms made from shipping containers ("capsules") were attached to a fixed core and were theoretically easily removed or reconfigured.

Kurokawa's Toshiba IHI Pavilion for Expo '70, the first modern international architecture exposition held in Asia, was one of the earliest buildings designed using computers, reflecting his ongoing fascination with technology. Throughout his career, however, he countered the rational with a love of poetry and philosophy. In the 1980s, Kurokawa brought these approaches together in his theory of Symbiosis—a postmodern challenge to all architects to look beyond Western precedents. Kurokawa has embraced regional culture over sentimental traditionalism, in projects ranging from studies of the physical character of streets to nuanced interpretations of *sukiya*, the "artless simplicity" of teahouse architecture.

Kurokawa's learned approach brought him commissions from the art world, including highly regarded museums in Hiroshima, Nagoya, Wakayama, Belgium, and Holland. The diversity of his practice is demonstrated by his proposal for revitalizing Tokyo and by his designs for ecological cities in Japan and China. The 1998 Kuala Lumpur Airport summarizes Kurokawa's strengths: finely detailed, high tech, and framing lush natural spaces.

*Dana Buntrock*

**Further Reading**

Kurokawa, Kisho. (1977) *Metabolism in Architecture*. London: Studio Vista; Boulder, CO: Westview Press.

———. (1991) *Intercultural Architecture: The Philosophy of Symbiosis*. London: Academy Editions; New York: American Institute of Architects Press.

———. (1994) *The Philosophy of Symbiosis*. London: Academy Editions.

Sharp, Dennis, ed. (1998) *Kisho Kurokawa: From the Age of the Machine to the Age of Life*. London: BookART.

**KUTAHYA** (2002 province pop. 714,000; 2002 city pop. 181,000). Kutahya, the capital of the province of Kutahya, on the Porsuk River in northwestern Turkey, was once the largest city of ancient Phrygia, when it was known as Cotyaeum, city of Cotys or Cybele. After the Battle of Manzikert (1071) it fell under Seljuk rule. Kutahya was later captured by the Greeks, recaptured by the Seljuk ruler Kilic Arslan II (1155–1192) in 1183, lost to the Byzantines, and retaken by the Seljuks in 1233–1234. In the fourteenth century, Kutahya was transferred to the Ottomans when Ottoman Sultan Yildirim Bayezid (1389–1402) married Dewlet Khatun, daughter of Suleyman Shah Celebi (c. 1363–1398) of the kingdom of Germiyan-oghullari. After the Mongols defeated the Ottomans in 1402, Timur (Tamerlane) made his son governor. Kutahya fell to the Karamanids in 1411 but was recaptured by the Yakub Germiyani, ruler of the Germiyan-ogullari kingdom, with help from the Ottomans. When Yakub died in 1429, he left Kutahya to Ottoman sultan Murad II (1421–1451).

Kutahya flourished under the Ottomans. Sultan Selim I (1512–1520) brought Persian and Armenian potters from Tabriz to Kutahya after capturing Persia in 1514, and Kutahya acquired a reputation for ceramic tiles rivaling those of Iznik. Today Kutahya continues to produce ceramic tiles, which are considered its greatest tourist attraction.

*T. Isikozlu-E.F. Isikozlu*

**Further Reading**

Bosworth, C. E. (1960– ) "Kutahiya." In *The Encyclopaedia of Islam*. 2d ed. Leiden: E. J. Brill, 539

*Statistical Yearbook of Turkey*. (1998) Ankara, Turkey: Devlet Istatistik Enstitusu.

**KWANGJU** (1999 pop. 1.3 million). Kwangju is the capital of South Cholla Province (Cholla namdo) in southwestern Republic of Korea (South Korea). It has a total area of 744.22 square kilometers. The administratively autonomous Kwangju Metropolitan City, however, occupies only 478.37 square kilometers, with the rest of the area divided among Changsong, Tamyang, and Hwasun counties and the city of Naju.

Kwangju is located in the fertile basin of the Kungnak River (a tributary of the Yongsan River). Kwangju is also surrounded by six mountains. Populated since prehistoric times, Kwangju was a part of the Paekche (18 BCE–663 CE) and Later Paekche (892–936) kingdoms during the Three Kingdoms period. In between, it was a part of the Later Shilla Kingdom (668–892). Prior to 940, the region was also known as Mujin or Muju.

Some of the key industries based in Kwangju are telecommunications and information technology; material, electrical, biotechnology, and environmental engineering; energy; manufacturing; export; and service sectors.

Kwangju has been the site of two historic uprisings. In 1929, students rose up against the Japanese colonization of Korea (1910–1945). In 1980, civilians protested Chun Doo Hwan's 1979 coup and ensuing events, such as the imprisonment of dissident Kim Dae Jung.

*Jennifer Jung-Kim*

**Further Reading**

Nilsen, Robert. (1997) *South Korea Handbook*. Chico, CA: Moon Publications.

Storey, Robert, and Alex English. (2001) *Korea*. 5th ed. Berkeley, CA: Lonely Planet Publications.

**KWANGJU UPRISING** One of the darkest moments in the history of South Korea, the Kwangju Uprising has had a long-lasting impact on domestic Korean politics. What began as a mass protest by students and residents of the city of Kwangju in South Cholla Province against indiscriminate attacks by South Korean Special Armed Forces on students and bystanders led to full-scale battle between students and the Special Armed Forces units from 18 to 27 May 1980.

In the months following the assassination of President Park Chun Hee in October 1979, opposition politicians and students increasingly demanded the lifting of martial law and the setting of a date for presidential elections. As the number of student-led protests grew nationwide, Major General Chun Doo Hwan ordered the arrest of the student leaders as well as leading opposition political figures, including the "three Kims" (Kim Dae Jung, Kim Young Sam, and Kim Jong Il), instituted full martial law, and closed the National Assembly at bayonet point. The army then moved in and occupied college campuses, closing all universities.

Following the announcement of martial law, government soldiers arrested Kim Dae Jung and his closest political advisers. The news of the arrest of Kim Dae Jung ignited student-led demonstrations in Kim's hometown of Kwangju, and as a result, clashes between students and riot police broke out. Special Armed Forces arrived to help subdue the demonstrators; however, following three days of indiscriminate attacks on protesters and residents that left hundreds either injured or dead, residents of Kwangju seized military vehicles and weapons from munitions depots and fought a pitched battle with the Special Armed Forces in the city center that left hundreds, perhaps thousands, wounded or dead. Unable to control the demonstrators, the Special Armed Forces units withdrew to the outskirts of Kwangju. The following day thirty thousand residents gathered in front of the provincial administration building to support the demands of the students that the government release those in detention, that troops withdraw from Kwangju, and that compensation be paid to the families of the dead and wounded. After a four-day standoff, the army with support of Special Armed Forces units moved back into Kwangju with tanks and percussion bombs to reimpose martial law. In the ensuing action, the remaining student demonstrators were either captured or killed.

In succeeding years citizens of Cholla Province voiced their opposition to Presidents Chun Doo Hwan and Roh

As the uprising is put down by South Korean soldiers, students are tied together and led away on 27 May 1980 in Kwangju. (BETTMANN/CORBIS)

Tae Woo for their role in authorizing the attack on Kwangju and its citizens. The Korean student movement maintained a fervent anti-American bias, believing that the United States either supported or acquiesced to the massacre of students and residents of Kwangju.

*Keith Leitich*

*See also:* **Chun Doo Hwan; Kim Dae Jung; Kwangju; Roh Tae Woo**

### Further Reading

Clark, Donald N. (1988) *The Kwangju Uprising: Shadows over the Regime in South Korea*. Boulder, CO: Westview Press.

Warnberg, Tim. (1987) "The Kwangju Uprising." *Korean Studies* 11: 33–54.

———. (2000) *The Kwangju Uprising: Eyewitness Press Accounts of Korea's Tiananmen*, edited by Henry Scott-Stokes and Lee Jai Eui. Armonk, NY: M. E. Sharpe.

**KYE** There has long been a history of communal cooperation for mutual benefit among the villages and townships of Korea. This was once most apparent in reciprocal labor arrangements *(pumassi)* at key points in the planting, harvesting, and kimchi-making seasons. It was also demonstrated in the organized groups of friends, family, and acquaintances who gathered together on a regular basis to share a subject of interest, invest money, or prepare for some future event such as a wedding, funeral, or parent's birthday party or funeral. These meeting groups were loosely known as *kye*. Usually such a group would designate a leader, a set number of members, and a fee payable at each meeting to cover costs and expenses. *Kye* mainly provided an essential venue for socializing and also for a limited form of social welfare, but some were set up with the aim of investing or mobilizing a large amount of capital. The most common way in which this was achieved was through the creation of a rotating credit association. Every month all the members would be expected to contribute a set amount of money or rice to the *kye*, the sum of which was given to one of the members. The *kye* would then continue until all the members had received a monthly total to spend as they chose.

In the cities and urban landscapes of modern Korea, many of the more traditional forms of social and community organization have become outdated. In

## A DEATH KYE DOCUMENT

This is a translation of a death kye document of 1651 kept in Puan County in North Cholla province. It outlined the rules of a local funeral kye started in 1651.

> If a member's parents die, then the other members will collect 10 hama of rice between them and give to the member.
>
> If a member doesn't attend the regular kye meeting, he has to pay 5 dwae (4.5 kg) of rice.
>
> The kye shall have a leader and the leadership shall rotate through the members with a new leader every year.
>
> There will be a manager who takes care of the rice. If he is careless in his duty he will be receive 50 strokes on his buttocks with a wooden stick.
>
> If a member creates a bad relationship with the other members he will receive 5 mal (45 kg) of rice and ejected from the kye.
>
> If one of the member's family members die, the member will receive 1 pil of cloth.
>
> If a member needs to discuss anything, they can discuss it with the leader and reach a decision with him about funeral arrangements, etc.

contrast, perhaps because of its flexibility and the social, economic, and networking opportunities it offers, the *kye* has both adapted and flourished during the painful upheavals of urbanization and modernization. In particular, socially premised *kye* are often portrayed as being essential for the maintenance of geographically dispersed networks of kin, friends, classmates, and business associates. The *kye* remains a fundamental and deeply embedded institution within Korean society.

*David Prendergast*

### Further Reading

Janelli, Roger. (1988) "Interest Rates and Rationality: Rotating Credit Associations Among Seoul Women." *Journal of Korean Studies* 6: 159–185.

Kennedy, Gerard F. (1977) "The Korean *Kye*: Maintaining Human Scale in a Modernizing Society." *Korean Studies* 1: 197–222.

Moon, Okpyo. (1990) "Urban Middle Class Wives in Contemporary Korea: Their Roles, Responsibilities, and Dilemma." *Korea Journal* (November–December): 30–43.

## KYOIKU MAMA

*Kyoiku* mama (education mama) is a stereotypical term referring to Japanese mothers who go to extraordinary lengths to develop their children's aptitude (particularly boys) and place them on the best educational track directed toward entry into a top-ranked university and subsequent employment with a prestigious company. Depicted as having sacrificed both career and personal aspirations, these mothers devote themselves to their children's education, staying at home full time to make lunches, clean and mend school uniforms, and help their children prepare for the following day's lessons at school. They also arrange for supplemental lessons at cram schools or private tutoring, continually urging their children to study hard and improve their academic performance. During important examination periods, other activity in the home is kept to a minimum in order to create a quiet place to study. As children study late into the evenings, mothers prepare and deliver snacks to them to symbolically show support and mutual involvement. Ultimately, if their children do well at school, the devotion and efforts of these mothers are deemed successful. Extreme versions of this stereotype portray zealous and intensely competitive mothers preparing infant children for entrance examinations to prestigious preschools or kindergartens that offer students an inside track to an affiliated high-ranking university.

*Dawn Grimes-MacLellan*

*See also:* **Japan, Education System**

### Further Reading

Dickensheets, Tony. (1998) "The Role of the Education Mama." In *Education and Schooling in Japan since 1945*, edited by Edward R. Beauchamp. New York: Garland, 277–282.

## KYONGGI PROVINCE

(1999 pop. 9 million). Kyonggi Province (Kyonggido), in the northwest region of South Korea (Republic of Korea), has an area of 10,188 square kilometers. The province borders part of the demilitarized zone (DMZ) to the north and the Yellow Sea to the west. Seoul (the nation's capital) and Inchon (a port city) are both located within Kyonggi Province, but the two cities are independent administrative units and thus are autonomous from Kyonggi.

Kyonggi Province is composed of twenty-three cities and eight counties *(kun)*. The region is heavily populated and industrialized because of its proximity to Seoul. The satellite cities of Songnam, Anyang, Suwon, and Puchon are also busy urban centers.

Seoul (formerly Hanyang) was the capital of the Choson dynasty (1392–1910); as a result, Kyonggi is home to many historical points of interest, such as Kanghwa Island, where the royal court fled during the Mongol invasions. Kanghwa's fortress later protected Korea's west coast from foreign incursions during the nineteenth century. Another historic site is Panmunjom, in the DMZ; since the Korean War (1950–1953), Panmunjom has been the site of ongoing negotiations and peace talks between North and South Korea.

There are also numerous ski resorts, golf courses, and fishing lakes for sports enthusiasts. The province is home to three major theme parks, including the Korean Folk Village (Minsokch'on), where visitors can observe traditional Korean folk customs.

Manufacturing, automotive parts, aircraft, electronics, medical equipment, and satellite communications are among the diverse industries in Kyonggi Province. The province is also important agriculturally, most notably for rice, fruits, beef, and poultry. Kyonggi's coastline hosts fisheries and salt production. Kyonggi is also home to many artisans who carry on centuries-old traditional methods of producing pottery; the province has abundant clay sources.

*Jennifer Jung-Kim*

### Further Reading

Austin, Audrey. (1991) "Kanghwa Island." *Korean Culture* 12, 3: 42–47.

Nilsen, Robert. (1997) *South Korea Handbook*. Emeryville, CA: Moon.

**KYOTO** (2002 est. pop. 1.5 million). Located in southern Kyoto Prefecture in central Honshu, 50 kilometers northeast of the industrial port of Osaka, Kyoto was the residence of the Japanese emperor and imperial court from 794 to 1868. Originally named Heian-kyo ("capital of tranquillity and peace"), the city was constructed in the 790s after a fire destroyed much of the former capital city at Nara. During later centuries the city was also called Saikyo ("western capital") to distinguish it from the shogun's capitals at Kamakura and Edo (Tokyo). In 1997 Kyoto's population was 1.5 million, making it the seventh-largest urban center in Japan, after Tokyo, Yokohama, Osaka, Nagoya, Sapporo, and Kobe.

## KYOTO—WORLD HERITAGE SITE

Parts of Kyoto, the capital of imperial Japan between 794 and 1868 CE, were designated a UNESCO World Heritage Site in 1994. The development of wooden architecture and traditional gardens over one thousand years of Japanese history is vividly presented in Kyoto.

The original plan for the city of Kyoto was, like the earlier capital at Nara, modeled after Changan—the capital of the Tang dynasty (618–907) in China. The city was laid out on a grid pattern 23.4 square kilometers in area. During the Kamakura period (1185–1333), the city lost some of its importance as political and military power shifted to the Minamoto shogun's headquarters at Kamakura. During the Muromachi period (1333–1573), Kyoto regained some of its status, as both the shogun and the emperor took up residence in the city. It was during this period that many of the city's great temples were constructed, including the Nanzenji, Kinkakuji (Temple of the Golden Pavilion), and Ginkakuji (Temple of the Silver Pavilion). With the victory of Tokugawa Ieyasu (1543–1616) at the battle of Sekigahara in 1600, the seat of political power was again moved, as the new shogun established his capital at Edo in eastern Honshu. During the Tokugawa period (1600/1603–1868), Kyoto retained some of its stature because of the presence of Nijo Castle—a temporary residence for the shogun during his visits to the imperial court and inspection tours of central Japan. The city also continued to grow as an artistic and religious center during this time.

After the Meiji Restoration of 1868 and the transfer of the nation's symbolic and administrative governance to Tokyo, Kyoto was forced to remake itself, emerging as one of the most modern cities of the Meiji period (1868–1912); it claimed the first streetcars in Japan, as well as a thriving industrial quarter. Spared

The entrance to the Fushimi-Inari Shinto Shrine, one of many shrines and temples in the city of Kyoto. (DAVID SAMUEL ROBBINS/CORBIS)

by U.S. bombers during World War II, Kyoto survived the conflict to become an important center of higher education and culture, and a major transportation hub. While tourism, finance, and education are the leading industries in Kyoto, the city is also home to light industry and numerous producers of traditional Japanese products, including porcelain, textiles, and works of art. The city also boasts numerous museums, Buddhist and Shinto temples, and historic sites, making it an important center in the preservation of traditional Japanese culture.

*Robert John Perrins*

### Further Reading

Kaneko, Anne, and C. Andrew Gerstle, eds. (1994) *Kyoto: A Celebration of 1,200 Years of History*. London: Japan Research Center, School of Oriental and African Studies.

Lowe, John. (2000) *Old Kyoto: A Short Social History*. New York: Oxford University Press.

Plutschow, Herbert. (1983) *Historical Kyoto: With Illustrations and Guide Maps*. Tokyo: Japan Times.

Röpke, Ian Martin. (1999) *Historical Dictionary of Osaka and Kyoto*. Lanham, MD: Scarecrow Press.

Waley, Paul, and Nicholas Fiévé, eds. (2000) *Japanese Capitals in Historical Perspective: Place, Power, and Memory in Kyoto, Edo, and Tokyo*. Surrey, U.K.: Curzon.

## KYRGYZ

**KYRGYZ** The Kyrgyz are a largely Muslim people of Turko-Mongol origins whose language, Kyrgyz, is a member of the central, or Kipchak, branch of the Turkic linguistic group. The Kyrgyz language is divided into northern and southern dialects, and there are also historical and cultural differences between northern and southern Kyrgyz people. In 2001, about 2.5 million Kyrgyz lived in the central Asian nation of Kyrgyzstan, although Kyrgyz also inhabit Uzbekistan, Kazakhstan, Tajikistan, northwestern China, and other nations. Traditionally pastoral nomads, some Kyrgyz live in the steppe and others live at the edges of mountains. Many other contemporary Kyrgyz are city dwellers.

### History

Kyrgyz have been divided into clans for many centuries. The word "Kyrgyz" derives from the Turkic words *kyrk* (forty) and *yz* (clans). Clan membership is determined by paternal ancestry. Kyrgyz tribes settled in the area of Kyrgyzstan between the thirteenth and sixteenth centuries. Some of the early Kyrgyz were traders along the Silk Road, and others were farmers and herders. Many were forced into Tajikistan by the Oirat Mongols in 1685.

The Uzbeks' khanate of Quqon ruled the Kyrgyz during much of the nineteenth century. During the 1860s, many Kyrgyz allied with the Russian empire against the khanate of Quqon. By 1876, most of the territory of present-day Kyrgyzstan had been taken by the Russian czar. Many Russians and Ukrainians came to settle in Kyrgyzstan. The new Slavic immigrants were given prime farmland at the expense of the Kyrgyz, who were driven from the lowlands into higher terrain where the land is less suitable for herding and farming. Mining and manufacturing industries also came to Kyrgyzstan during the czarist period. Some Kyrgyz migrated to Afghanistan and Tajikistan.

In 1916, the Kyrgyz revolted against Russian rule, but the Russians retaliated with great force, and many Kyrgyz fled to China to escape repression. Czarist rule came to an end in 1917, but Russian domination did not. On 14 October 1924, the Soviets created the Kara-Kyrgyz Autonomous Region, which was soon renamed the Kyrgyz Autonomous Republic. The Kyrgyz Soviet Socialist Republic was established on 5 December 1936.

Soviet dictator Joseph Stalin (1879–1953) ordered the destruction of many animal herds and forced the Kyrgyz to collectivize their farms, which changed the Kyrgyz lifestyle from nomadic to more settled and caused widespread famine. Another consequence of Soviet rule over the Kyrgyz was the dramatic growth in literacy. Prior to 1917, most Kyrgyz schools were *madrasahs* (Islamic religious schools), and almost all Kyrgyz were illiterate. But after the founding of the Soviet Union, all religious schools were forcibly closed, and children were required to attend public schools. This led to almost universal literacy and exposed the Kyrgyz people to new ideas as the Kyrgyz became familiar with the Russian language, Cyrillic alphabet, and Russian culture.

Kyrgyzstan declared its independence on 31 August 1991, following the collapse of the Soviet Union. Many Kyrgyz revived their old traditions and customs, but fluency in Russian is still prevalent. The Kyrgyz forged new ties with the outside world, including Turkey, Israel, and the United States.

Poverty increased sharply among the Kyrgyz of Kyrgyzstan during the 1990s, affecting approximately 55 percent by 2000.

### Traditional Culture

Nomadic Kyrgyz traditionally lived in *yurtas*, or yurts (felt tents), and although most Kyrgyz today live in more permanent structures, *yurtas* are still used to entertain guests during special events. Kyrgyz women make felt carpets called *shyrdaks* that often decorate the *yurtas*. Some of today's Kyrgyz still live a seminomadic

The "group" nature of Kyrgyz culture is demonstrated by the large number of guests at this wedding celebration in the Alaisky region of Kyrgyzstan in 1995. (JANET WISHNETSKY/CORBIS)

lifestyle, residing in *yurta*s during the summer months and returning to their permanent houses in the autumn.

Kyrgyz are known for their hospitality, offering traveling guests samples of the rich Kyrgyz cuisine. *Kymys* (in English, koumiss), a popular Kyrgyz beverage, is fermented mare's milk. Kyrgyz also drink tea, vodka, and *bozo* (a fermented millet drink). Other components of Kyrgyz cuisine include meats (especially lamb), potatoes, bread, rice, pasta, and yogurt.

For centuries, Kyrgyz have practiced the arts of storytelling and singing, and a rich heritage of oral literature accompanied by music has developed. The primary Kyrgyz folk instrument is the *komuz*, a three-stringed lute. In the years following Kyrgyzstan's independence, the three-part epic poem *Manas* emerged as a key element of Kyrgyz literature. *Manas* was preserved over the centuries by wandering bards called *manaschi*. Several versions of *Manas* have assumed written form, and *Manas* has become a major component of modern Kyrgyz identity and government ideology. Popular pastimes among Kyrgyz men include hunting with the aid of *berkut* (steppe eagles) and playing games of skill on horseback.

The extended family remains vital to rural Kyrgyz, but for many urbanized Kyrgyz the basic family unit is the nuclear family. Kyrgyz women used to be restricted to household chores (cooking, cleaning, hosting, and raising children) and crafting but now have more career opportunities.

The practice of bride stealing, in which a woman is taken (often involuntarily) by a man to be married, was common until Soviet times and has revived in recent years among rural Kyrgyz, despite the fact that it is prohibited by Kyrgyzstani law.

## Religious Beliefs

The principal religions among Kyrgyz are Islam and ancient folk beliefs, including shamanism, animism, and totemism. Islam was well established among Kyrgyz by the eighteenth century. The vast majority of modern Kyrgyz are at least nominally Sunni Muslims. Islam is practiced in a relatively pure form among the southern Kyrgyz, whereas elements of shamanism and animism still persist among the northern Kyrgyz. However, some southern Kyrgyz are practitioners of Sufism, a mystical school of Islamic thought.

Under Soviet rule, Islam was officially discouraged, and atheism was encouraged. But in the mid-1980s, Islam began to grow in popularity again, and by 2001 there were over two thousand mosques in Kyrgyzstan.

*Kevin Alan Brook*

## Further Reading

Akiner, Shirin. (1986) *Islamic Peoples of the Soviet Union.* 2d ed. London: KPI.

Mayhew, Bradley, Richard Plunkett, and Simon Richmond. (2000) *Central Asia.* 2d ed. Hawthorn, Australia: Lonely Planet.

Soucek, Svatopluk. (2000) *A History of Inner Asia.* Cambridge, U.K.: Cambridge University Press.
Stewart, Rowan, and Susie Weldon. (2002) *Kyrgyzstan.* Hong Kong: Odyssey Publications.

**KYRGYZSTAN—PROFILE** (2001 est. pop. 4.8 million). Kyrgyzstan is a mountainous, landlocked central Asian country; more than half of its land area is above 2,500 meters in elevation. Kyrgyzstan borders Kazakhstan on the north, Tajikistan on the south and west, and the Xinjiang Uygur Autonomous Region of the People's Republic of China on the east. Its total area is 198,500 square kilometers. High mountains whose peaks range from 4,880 to 7,200 meters, glaciers and snow, valleys, and river basins dominate the landscape, with few lowland areas. There are several mountain rivers in Kyrgyzstan and one large lake, the Issyk-Kul. The country has a continental climate with little rainfall and hot, dry summers and low winter temperatures. Kyrgyzstan became independent of the former Soviet Union on 31 August 1991. The country's official name is the Kyrgyz Republic and its capital is Bishkek (formerly Frunze).

### History

Most scholars believe the Kyrgyz people to be of mixed Mongolian, Eastern Turkic, and Kipchak descent. The formation of the Kyrgyz as a distinct ethnic group was completed in the sixteenth century, when they started migrating to modern-day Kyrgyzstan. In the seventeenth century, the Kyrgyz territory came under the control of the Mongols until the Manchus overthrew them in 1758. In the nineteenth century, the Kyrgyz lands became part of the Quqon

## KYRGYZSTAN

**Country name:** Kyrgyz Republic
**Area:** 198,500 sq km
**Population:** 4,753,003 (July 2001 est.)
**Population growth rate:** 1.44% (2001 est.)
**Birth rate:** 26.18 births/1,000 population (2001 est.)
**Death rate:** 9.13 deaths/1,000 population (2001 est.)
**Net migration rate:** –2.66 migrant(s)/1,000 population (2001 est.)
**Sex ratio:** 0.95 male(s)/female (2001 est.)
**Infant mortality rate:** 76.5 deaths/1,000 live births (2001 est.)
**Life expectancy at birth—total population:** 63.46 years, male: 59.2 years, female: 67.94 years (2001 est.)
**Major religions:** Muslim 75%, Russian Orthodox 20%, other 5%
**Major languages:** Kirghiz (Kyrgyz)—official language; Russian—official language
**Literacy—total population:** 97%, male: 99%, female: 96% (1989 est.)
**Government type:** republic
**Capital:** Bishkek
**Administrative divisions:** 7 oblastlar (singular—oblast) and 1 city
**Independence:** 31 August 1991 (from Soviet Union)
**National holiday:** Independence Day, 31 August (1991)
**Suffrage:** 18 years of age; universal
**GDP—real growth rate:** 5.7% (2000 est.)
**GDP—per capita:** (purchasing power parity): $2,700 (2000 est.)
**Population below poverty line:** 51% (1997 est.)
**Exports:** $482 million (f.o.b., 2000 est.)
**Imports:** $579 million (f.o.b., 2000 est.)
**Currency:** Kyrgyzstani som (KGS)

*Source:* Central Intelligence Agency. (2001) *The World Book Factbook 2001.* Retrieved 5 March 2002, from http://www.cia.gov/cia/publications/factbook.

khanate, Turkic rulers of a powerful kingdom in present-day eastern Uzbekistan. When the Quqon khanate started to lose power, mostly due to expanding Russian influence, the Kyrgyz people came into contact with the Russians. The Kyrgyz territory was incorporated into the Russian empire in 1876 as part of the Quqon khanate, and the region remained under the rule of czarist Russia until the Bolshevik Revolution in 1917. In 1918, the territory of the Kyrgyz was included in the Turkistan Autonomous Soviet Socialist Republic within the Russian Federation. On 14 October 1924, the Kara-Kirghiz Autonomous Oblast (political subdivision) was created within the Russian Federation; in 1925 the oblast was renamed the Kirghiz Autonomous Oblast with its capital at Bishkek. Bishkek was renamed Frunze in 1925. On 1 February 1926, the Kirghiz Autonomous Oblast was raised to the status of the Kirghiz Autonomous Soviet Socialist Republic. On 5 December 1936, the Kirghiz Soviet Socialist Republic was established, and Kirghizia became one of the fifteen union republics of the Soviet Union. On 15 December 1990, Kyrgyzstan declared its sovereignty.

## Politics and Administration

Kyrgyzstan has six oblasts, each having its own provincial capital. In the north, there are four oblasts: Talas (capital: Talas), Chu (capital: Bishkek), Issyk-Kul (capital: Przheval'sk), and Naryn (capital: Naryn). These four administrative regions have dominated the political life of the country during the Soviet era and after independence. In the south there are two oblasts: Osh (capital: Osh) and Jalal-Abad (capital: Jalal-Abad). These two administrative regions, dominated by the fertile lands of the Fergana Valley, were politically under represented during the Soviet era.

The president of the republic, Askar Akaev (b. 1944), was elected on 28 October 1990 and started his third term of office in October 2000. The president shapes the political life of Kyrgyzstan. Kyrgyzstan has a bicameral legislative assembly, the Zhogorku Kenesh (Supreme Council). The upper chamber is the Assembly of People's Representatives, and the lower chamber is the Legislative Assembly.

Kyrgyzstan was one of the countries of central Asia most determined to realize a successful post-Soviet transition toward a democratic political order and a market economy. During the first half of the 1990s, the republic was seen as an island of democracy, because there were several different political parties and movements, such as Ashar (Mutual Help), Asaba (Banner), Erkin Kyrgyzstan (Free Kyrgyzstan), the Kyrgyz Democratic Wing, Osh Aymagy (Osh Oblast), and

Adolat (Justice). President Akaev also adhered to economic reform guidelines established by international economic organizations such as the World Bank and the International Monetary Fund. Akaev, who was a physicist, had never been part of the Soviet party hierarchy, and as such he was distinguished from other central Asian republican leaders. However, in the latter part of the 1990s, Akaev gradually drifted to more authoritarian policies by increasing his presidential powers and putting pressure on the opposition.

## Economy

The Kyrgyz economy is primarily agricultural. The agricultural sector accounts for around 30 percent of the gross domestic product (GDP) and employs 40 percent of the active population. The main crops are grain (wheat, barley, maize), cotton, vegetables, fruits, tobacco, sugar, and silk. Kyrgyzstan also has the world's largest natural-growth walnut forest. In addition to crops, animal husbandry is common in Kyrgyzstan. Cattle raising and sheep and horse breeding remain key agricultural activities in all areas of the republic.

Kyrgyzstan has important reserves of various minerals such as coal, mercury, uranium, zinc, lead, gold, and antimony. It has some limited oil and natural gas as well.

Kyrgyz industry accounts for about 30 percent of GDP and employs about 30 percent of the active population. With its fast-flowing rivers, Kyrgyzstan has abundant hydroelectric power. In addition to the production of electricity, mining, engineering, metalworking, light manufacturing, food and thread, and construction are other key industries.

## People

The Kyrgyz people are basically rural, with their traditional occupations of agriculture and stock breeding. About 90 percent of all Kyrgyz live in Kyrgyzstan, even though Tajikistan, Uzbekistan, China, and Afghanistan have small Kyrgyz communities. The Kyrgyz make up about 56 percent of the population of the Kyrgyz Republic, followed by Russians (18 percent), Uzbeks (13 percent), Ukrainians (2 percent), Germans (1 percent), and other smaller groups (10 percent).

Kyrgyz speak a Turkic dialect called Kipchak, which belongs to the Altaic family of languages. The Kyrgyz are Sunni Muslims of the Hanafi school. However, Islam came to the Kyrgyz at a relatively late date; their widespread conversion dates only from the second half of the seventeenth century. In Kyrgyz society, Islam is mixed with some of the pre-Islamic practices and beliefs of shamanism. Furthermore, loyalties at the level of tribe and clan are still important in the private and public lives of the Kyrgyz people. There are three clan groupings, or wings, in Kyrgyzstan: the *sol* (left wing) is in the north and west; the *ong* (right wing) and *ichkilik* (insider) are in the north. A Kyrgyz belongs to one of these groups and then to a particular tribe.

The north-south division in the republic further distinguishes the Kyrgyz people from one another. In northern Kyrgyzstan, people are historically nomadic, more sophisticated, economically better off, less traditional, and less religious, whereas in southern Kyrgyzstan, people are sedentary and agricultural, economically poorer, more religious, and more conservative.

However, despite these differences, the Kyrgyz nevertheless consider themselves one people. This is the basic theme of the Kyrgyz oral epic *Manas*. Manas was a famous Kyrgyz warrior, and the epic tells of various Kyrgyz tribes and their survival despite numerous hardships. The Manas legend has been a binding force among the diverse Kyrgyz for centuries. One of the meanings of the word Kyrgyz is "forty clans," and today the forty spreading beans of the Kyrgyz flag represent these Kyrgyz clans.

## Current Issues

After more than a decade of independence, Kyrgyzstan faces several economic, political, and social problems. Shortly after independence, President Akaev started implementing an economic reform program to enable transition to a market economy. He was the first Central Asian leader to break out of the ruble zone by introducing a Kyrgyz national currency, the som. Akaev started a privatization program in industry as well as in agriculture by legalizing the sale of land. However, the immediate results of these reforms were not promising. There were drastic falls in GDP and industrial and agricultural output. Inflation and unemployment increased dramatically. Corruption and crime rates rose. The sudden end to the transfers and subsidies from the budget of the Soviet Union and the collapse of inter-republican trade resulted in a sharp fall in government revenues. As a result, social services came close to breakdown. In the early 2000s, most Kyrgyz people faced the threat of real poverty.

As economic problems increased, President Akaev has become more concerned with political stability. He has increased his presidential powers and grown less tolerant of opposition groups and the media. He is also concerned about potential inter-ethnic unrest in Kyrgyzstan and about Russian emigration from the republic. The departure of Russians results in a shortage of much-needed professional and technical skills, further complicating the economic problems. In order to prevent Russian emigration, the Kyrgyz leadership declared Russian the second state language. This official bilingualism is to remain in effect until 1 January 2005.

*Pinar Akcali*

### Further Reading

Bohr, Annette. (1996) "Kyrgyzstan and the Kyrgyz." In *The Nationalities Question in the Post-Soviet States*, edited by Graham Smith. 2d ed. New York: Addison Wesley Longman, 385–409.

Caspiani, Giampaolo. (2000) *The Handbook of Central Asia: A Comprehensive Survey of the New Republics*. London: I. B. Tauris.

Olcott, Martha Brill. (1997) "Kyrgyzstan." In *Kazakhstan, Kyrgyzstan, Tajikistan, Turkmenistan, Uzbekistan: Country Studies*, edited by Glenn E. Curtis. Washington, DC: United States Government Printing Office.

Soucek, Svat. (2001) *A History of Inner Asia*. Cambridge, U.K.: Cambridge University Press.

## KYRGYZSTAN—ECONOMIC SYSTEM

Despite nearly seventy years of Soviet industrialization Kyrgyzstan's economy remains primarily agricultural. According to World Bank statistics, agriculture contributed an estimated 44.2 percent to gross domestic product (GDP) in 1997. Grain production generally accounts for more than 50 percent of agricultural production. Other products such as hay, forage, potatoes, and vegetables are also grown, primarily in the southern regions of Osh and Jalalabad. Livestock production, which once contributed significantly to the overall agricultural output, has declined since independence, partly because of the reduction in state subsidies and partly because of unregulated sale or consumption by the rural population. Agriculture employed more than 48 percent of the labor force in 1998, although, given the mountainous topography, only 7 percent of the land is arable. Private family farms cultivated an estimated 35 percent of the arable land in 1998, while the remainder was farmed collectively in the old Soviet style. The percentage of agriculture's contribution to GDP declined 4.6 percent during the 1990–1996 period, but the agricultural sector rebounded beginning in 1997 and registered growth rates of 15 percent and 12 percent in 1996 and 1997, respectively.

### Industry, Services, and Foreign Trade

Industry accounts for approximately 16 percent of GDP. Manufacturing, including food processing, textiles, machinery, and nonferrous mineral products, has remained largely stagnant since the breakup of the Soviet Union. The sector employed an estimated 10 percent of the working population in 1997. Kyrgyzstan has considerable mineral resources, including gold, coal, tin, mercury, zinc, tungsten, and uranium. The gold deposit at Kumtor, the eighth-largest in the world, has made a sizable contribution to GDP since 1998. The construction industry also benefited from the development of the Kumtor site, but construction growth declined after the completion of projects related to the mining industry in 1997. The energy sector is dominated by the hydroelectric production for which Kyrgyzstan has an ideal topography. Oil and gas deposits are small, and the country depends on imports from Kazakhstan.

In 1997 the services sector accounted for an estimated 33 percent of GDP. The sector is the economy's second-largest employer. Foreign trade accounted for approximately 10 percent of GDP in that year.

### Economic Policy

Designed to satisfy the requirements of industrial centers outside its territory, Kyrgyzstan's economy has suffered a significant decline since the breakup of the Soviet Union. The process of restructuring the economy has been slow and uneven, despite substantial financial support from Western countries and major global donor agencies such as the World Bank, the International Monetary Fund (IMF), and the European Bank for Reconstruction and Development (EBRD). In 1993 President Akayev introduced an ambitious economic reform program, calling for macroeconomic stabilization, privatization, trade and price liberalization, and a new currency, the som, introduced in May. The conservative parliament opposed the program, which touched off a power struggle that led to the president's decision to disband the parliament and introduce constitutional amendments in 1994 and 1995. His victory resulted in the resumption of the economic reform program largely supported and financed by the IMF and the World Bank. Since 1995 the government has embarked on reforms of the banking sector and the tax structure and has privatized large enterprises. The reform program suffered a setback in the aftermath of the collapse of the Russian economy in 1998 and the decline in the price of gold, a major foreign-exchange earner for Kyrgyzstan.

### Privatization

The privatization of the economy entered its third phase in 1998, with the aim of selling shares in large enterprises such as the Kyrgyztelecom and the energy company, Kyrgyzenergo. Although the government retains controlling stakes in these and other large enterprises, the entire process has yet to be completed. The first stage of privatization included small enterprises in service and retail sectors and was largely completed by 1995. The second stage, designed to sell shares of medium-sized enterprises, came to an abrupt halt in 1997, as allegations of corruption and nepotism resulted in an audit of previously privatized enterprises. The public received privatization coupons to be used toward the purchase of company shares. Unfortunately, the privatized industries have remained either stagnant or completely insolvent because the Soviet-era inter- and intra-enterprise order system has collapsed.

### Fiscal Reform

Decline in output and insufficient tax revenue collection have combined to create a chronic budget deficit since independence. According to the IMF, the budget deficit was 9.9 percent of GDP in 1998 and was estimated at around 10 percent of GDP in 1999. A new three-year Poverty Reduction and Growth Facility program was signed with the IMF in February 2000. It replaced the Enhanced Structural Adjustment Facility program in effect since 1992 and accurately predicted a budget deficit of 7.4 percent of GDP in 2000, to be reduced to 4.6 percent by 2002. Inflation has been pegged at 20 percent, 9.9 percent, and 5.0 percent for 2000, 2001, and 2002, respectively. Thus far, the targets have not been met. Between 1994 and 1998 inflation amounted to 51.6 percent. An estimated 60 percent of government spending is devoted to social-welfare programs. The government has been planning to introduce private land ownership, but the issue has generated considerable controversy, which has delayed the process.

Real GDP declined by nearly 50 percent between 1991 and 1995. Growth returned to the economy in 1996 as a result of foreign investment projects in the mining sector and as positive agricultural growth. GDP continued to grow in 1997 but suffered a decline in 1998, achieving only 2 percent real growth. Private consumption has constituted an estimated 65 percent of GDP in recent years, but the continued economic uncertainties will adversely affect the level of consumption for some time to come. A 1997 World Bank survey revealed that an estimated 60 percent of the Kyrgyz population lives in poverty, the majority residing in the impoverished south of the republic.

### External Sector

Much like the other central Asian republics, Kyrgyzstan's trade with the Commonwealth of Independent States (CIS) has declined since independence. The figure for 1998 indicated an export contraction of nearly 30 percent in CIS trade. In dollar terms the trade with CIS members accounted for 44 percent of exports and 52 percent of imports. In 1997 many of Kyrgyzstan's exports were nonferrous metals, notably gold (36 percent), followed by electricity (14 percent), food processing (13 percent), machine construction (10 percent), and agriculture (8 percent). Oil and gas topped the import list at 25 percent, followed by machine construction (22 percent), chemical and petrochemical production (14 percent), and food processing (12 percent). The major non-CIS trading partners included China, the United States, Germany, Switzerland, and Turkey.

Kyrgyzstan has accumulated a sizable foreign debt since 1993: nearly $1 billion in 1998, or 54 percent of GDP. In 1999 the government reallocated $60 million to prevent a possible default on servicing its loan. More than $600 million is owed to multilateral institutions. The government restructured its loans to Turkey and Russia in 1996 and 1998, and the EBRD allowed it to delay payments on the $75 million partially due in 1999. To prevent further defaults, the IMF extended an additional loan of $29 million in 1999. A total of $99.1 million was earmarked for the three-year period from January 2000 through December 2002. Between 1992 and 1999 the World Bank disbursed an estimated $500 million to help the republic's transition to a market economy. Foreign direct investment, which is also critical in preventing further decline of the economy, amounted to nearly $400 million between 1993 and 1999.

The Kyrgyz national currency, the som, was the first currency to be allowed to float freely in central Asia. Since its introduction in 1993 the som experienced a steady nominal depreciation from $1 to 4 som to $1 to 42 som in 1999. In real terms the som lost more than 50 percent of its value by 1998. Kyrgyz foreign reserve currency has fluctuated since 1998, as the government has attempted to address its foreign debt and current account obligations. The reserves in early 1999 could cover only three months of imports. Foreign reserves amounted to $163 million, 70 percent of which was held in dollars.

*Mehrdad Haghayeghi*

### Further Reading

European Bank for Reconstruction and Development. (1996, 1997, 1998, 1999) *Transition Report.* London: European Bank for Reconstruction and Development.

International Monetary Fund. (2000) *The Kyrgyz Republic—Recent Economic Trends.* Washington, D.C.: International Monetary Fund.

Pomfret, Richard. (1995) *The Economies of Central Asia.* Princeton: Princeton University Press.

World Bank. (1993, 1996) *Krygzstan: Country Profile.* New York: The World Bank.

## KYRGYZSTAN—EDUCATION SYSTEM

The education system in Kyrgyzstan today is a synthesis of Soviet-type public education, Western-type private high schools and colleges, and newly emerging Muslim religious schools. The collapse of Communism and the emergence of democratization encouraged multiple forms of education, although the government plays a key role in regulating public education. The Ministry of Education is responsible for developing curriculum, setting national standards and educational policy, developing certification examinations, and awarding degrees. The ministry is divided into departments for general education, higher education, and material support. Below the ministry level, the education hierarchy includes the six provinces and the separate city of Bishkek, representatives from each of which provide input to the ministry on local conditions. The level of basic local administration is the district *(raion);* the district education officer hires faculty and appoints school inspectors and methodology specialists.

### Instruction

General education has traditionally been accessible to nearly all children in Kyrgyzstan. In primary and secondary grades about 51 percent of students are female; that number increases to 55 percent in higher education, with a converse majority of males in vocational programs. There is little difference in school attendance between urban and rural areas or among the provinces. Higher education, however, became more accessible to urban and wealthy segments of the population as a consequence of independence in 1991.

In line with the reform of 1992, children start school at the age of six and are required to complete grade nine. The general education program has three stages: grades one through four, grades five through nine, and grades ten and eleven. Students completing grade nine may continue into advanced or specialized (college preparatory) secondary curricula or into a technical and vocational program. The school year is thirty-four weeks long, extending from the beginning of September until the end of May. The instruction week is twenty-five hours long for grades one through four and thirty-two hours for grades five through eleven.

In 1992 about 960,000 students were enrolled in general education courses, 42,000 in specialized secondary programs, 49,000 in vocational programs, and 58,000 in institutions of higher education. About 1,800 schools were in operation in 1992. That year Kyrgyzstan's state system had about 65,000 teachers, but an estimated 8,000 teachers resigned in 1992 alone because of poor salaries and a heavy workload that included double shifts for many. Emigration has also depleted the teaching staff. In 1993 the national pupil-teacher ratio for grades one through eleven was 14.4 to 1, slightly higher in rural areas, and considerably higher in the primary grades. The city of Bishkek, however, had a ratio of almost 19 to 1.

Despite restructuring there is a shortage of schools, and 37 percent of general education students attend schools operating in two or three shifts. Construction of new facilities has lagged behind enrollment growth, the rate of which has been nearly 3 percent per year.

General education is financed by district budgets, and college preparatory and higher education programs are financed by the national budget. For the former category of expenditures school principals negotiate their requirements with district officials, but the central government sets norms based on previous expenditures and on the relative resources of the provinces.

### Curriculum

The language of instruction remains Russian, but the Kyrgyz language is becoming increasingly important as nonindigenous citizens leave the country and textbooks in Kyrgyz slowly become available. In 1992 the first major curriculum reform provided for mandatory foreign language study (English, French, or German) beginning in grade one; computer science courses in grades eight through eleven (a program hampered by lack of funds); and replacement of Soviet ideology with concepts of market economy and ethnic studies. The reformed curriculum requirements also leave room for elective courses, and instructional innovation is encouraged.

### Higher Education

In 1997 Kyrgyzstan had forty-three institutions of higher learning, almost all of them located in Bishkek. Seven of the institutions were private and the remainder state funded. Approximately 4,700 faculty were employed there, of which only 150 had doctoral degrees and 1,715 were candidates, the step below the doctorate in the Soviet system, which is still used in Kyrgyzstan. The language of instruction remained predominantly Russian in the mid-1990s, although the use of Kyrgyz has increased yearly. Long-term plans call for a more Western style of university study, so that universities can begin to offer a baccalaureate degree. In 1992 President Akayev created a Slavic University in Bishkek to help Kyrgyzstan retain its population of educated Russians, for whom the increased "Kyrgyzification" of education was a reason to emigrate. Because Russian students from outside the Russian Federation had lost their Soviet-era right to free education in Russian universities, Akayev hoped to provide a Russian-language institution for Russian-speaking students from all the Central Asian states.

The multicultural character of educational policy was underlined in the establishment of Bishkek Humanities University in 1994. The Humanities University has three major departments: the Department of Kyrgyz Philology with a major in Kyrgyz language and literature; the Department of Russian Philology with a major in Russian language and literature; the Department of Oriental Studies and International Relations with majors in Turkish, Korean, Japanese, Arabic, Persian, and Chinese languages; and the Department of German Philology with majors in German and English.

In 1996 the Kyrgyz Turkish Manas University was established as a sign of advancing cultural ties between predominantly Muslim Kyrgyzstan and the Muslim world. The official teaching languages of the university are Kyrgyz and Turkish. The university admitted one hundred students in the 1997–1998 academic year and five hundred students in the 2000–2001 academic year. The university is sponsored by the government of Kyrgyzstan and the Turkish National Lottery Administration. All education is free of charge, and some financial aid is provided to all students.

As soon as market reform began in Kyrgyzstan in 1992, the need for new managers with knowledge of market institutions became urgent. The government encouraged the establishment of the Bishkek International School of Management and Business, which was reorganized under the Academy of Management headed by the president of the Kyrgyz Republic on 19 March 1997. The Academy of Management is a government-sponsored university with a strong similarity to U.S. business schools that offer business training and masters of business administration degrees. At the same time it functions as the government academy, providing continuing education for government managers, as well as courses for managers and owners of private businesses.

During the transition from state socialism, the Kyrgyz education system experienced a drastic change. Ideologically there was a shift from justifying Communism and castigating capitalism to promoting market-economy ideology. Structurally there was an emergence of new forms of educational institutions. Despite the difficulties of the first years of transition the government managed to continue educational reforms. Achievements include an increase in public expenditures for education from 4 percent of gross domestic product in 1993 to 5 percent in 1997; an increase in the enrollment ratio for all levels of education from 61 percent in 1993 to 71 percent in 1997; and an increase in the number of universities from eighteen in 1993 to forty-three in 1997. Among discouraging trends, on the other hand, was a decline in the tertiary enrollment ratio for women from 62 percent in 1993 to 51 percent in 1997.

*Pavel Krotov*

### Further Reading

*Human Development Report for Central and Eastern Europe and the CIS.* (1999) New York: Published for the United Nations Development Programme.

*Kyrgyzstan—Social Protection in a Reforming Economy.* (1993) Washington, DC: World Bank Papers.

Oruzbaeva, B. O., chief ed. (1982) *Kirgizskaia Sovetskaia Sotsialisticheskaia Respublika: Entsiklopediia* (Kirgiz Soviet Socialist Republic Encyclopedia). Frunze, Kyrgyzstan: Glavnaya redakziya Kirgizskoi Sovetskoi Enciklopedii.

## KYRGYZSTAN—HISTORY

The ancestors of today's Kyrgyz people were nomadic pastoralists living in the upper reaches of the Yenisey River in Siberia before migrating south to the Tian Shan region around the tenth century CE. They were ruled by various Turkic peoples until 1685, when they were conquered by the Mongols, who ruled the region until 1785, when they were displaced by the Manchus. In the early nineteenth century, the territory inhabited by the Kyrgyz was under the control of the khanate of Quqon. The Russians moved into the area in the mid-nineteenth century, and by 1876, the Kyrgyz were incorporated into the Russian empire as part of Russian Turkistan. The Russian empire exercised dominance over the khanate from 1876 until the Bolshevik Revolution of 1917, after which the entire Central Asian region commonly known as Turkistan was incorporated into the Soviet Union. The Kyrgyz staged major uprisings against Russian rule, but all failed, and many Kyrgyz migrated to the Pamirs and Afghanistan. In 1916, Russia's suppression of a massive Kyrgyz revolt led to many Kyrgyz deaths and a large immigration to China. In 1918, Kyrgyzstan was included in the newly created Turkistan Autonomous Soviet Socialist Republic.

### The Soviet Period

In 1924, the Kara-Kyrgyz Autonomous Region was established, renamed the Kyrgyz Autonomous Republic in 1926. The nomadic Kyrgyz tribes were forced to settle beginning in the 1920s, when the Soviets began to establish urban centers and impose agricultural collectivization. Kyrgyzstan was granted union republic status in 1936. Although some local self-rule was allowed in the 1920s, in the early 1930s, Joseph Stalin (1879–1953) launched massive purges of local cadres and cruelly collectivized the largely nomadic society.

In the Osh region, on the eastern edge of the fertile and densely populated Fergana Valley, a major ethnic conflict broke out between Kyrgyz and Uzbek residents in June 1990, leading to scores of deaths. That region, although a part of Kyrgyzstan, is populated mostly by ethnic Uzbeks. The conflict led many in Kyrgyzstan to demand the ouster of Kyrgyz Communist Party leader Absamat Masaliyev for mishandling the Osh events. When the Kyrgyz Supreme Soviet convened in October 1990, a democratic bloc of deputies narrowly defeated Masaliyev's bid for the post of president, a new office created by the progressive Soviet Communist Party General Secretary Mikhail Gorbachev (b. 1931), and elected Askar Akaev, ending Masaliyev's career.

### The Post-Soviet Period

A forty-six-year-old ethnic Kyrgyz, Akaev was a well-respected computer engineer and mathematician who was president of the Kyrgyz Academy of Sciences. Because of this respect he was elected in 1989 to the newly created Soviet Congress of People's Deputies and served in its smaller Supreme Soviet legislative body. Similarly, he was elected a full member of the Soviet Communist Party Central Committee in 1990, a high-ranking party post. He opposed an August 1991 coup attempt against Gorbachev by Communist reactionaries and moved after the coup's collapse to suspend Kyrgyz Communist Party activities. Afterward, the Kyrgyz Supreme Soviet declared Kyrgyzstan an independent democratic state and scheduled a direct presidential election for October 1991. Akaev was overwhelmingly reaffirmed as president in this election. After the dissolution of the Soviet Union in early December 1991, Kyrgyzstan and other Central Asian states joined Russia and other former Soviet republics on 21 December 1991 in founding a cooperative group called the Commonwealth of Independent States (CIS). Akaev was reelected as president in December 1995, winning 72 percent of the vote in a three-way race. Legislative elections held that same year, although marred by some irregularities, were judged by international observers to be largely free and fair. Socialist-oriented parties won the largest proportion of party-contested seats, reflecting popular discontent with economic decline and with scandals associated with several democrats, although the Kyrgyz Communist Party also showed poorly. Ethnic Kyrgyz won most seats. Akaev criticized the electoral process, stating that he would have preferred a mixed system of voting that included party lists, a social organization list, and quotas for women and ethnic minorities, so that the legislature would be representative in its composition.

About 95 percent of voters approved a 1996 referendum on constitutional changes that gave Akaev greater powers to veto legislation, as well as the power to dissolve the legislature and appoint all ministers (except the prime minister) without legislative confirmation while making impeachment more difficult. Despite those new restrictions on its powers, in 1997–1998 the legislature showed increasing signs of independence from executive power. Moving to further weaken it, Akaev spearheaded another referendum on 17 October 1998 that further curtailed its power. The referendum also provided for private land ownership, opposed by most in the legislature, and upheld freedom of the press.

In July 1998, the Kyrgyz Constitutional Court decided that Akaev could run for a third presidential term, even though the constitution permitted only two terms, on the technicality that Akaev's October 1991 election had occurred before the enactment of the current constitution. The Central Electoral Commission reported that Akaev won 74.5 percent of 1.46 million votes cast, but many international observers reported major irregularities, including bribing of voters, governmental intimidation of voters, media bias and intimidation, ballot box stuffing, and manipulation of vote tabulations. Monitors from the Organization for Security and Cooperation in Europe concluded that the election represented a further setback to democratization, although it hailed the democratic sentiments of many election officials and voters as promising for the future. Feliks Kulov, a major opposition leader who had been disqualified from running because he refused to take a Kyrgyz language competency test that was required for running, was convicted of corruption by a military tribunal in January 2001 and sentenced to a seven-year prison sentence. According to many observers, the irregularities of the election and the efforts to quash the opposition mark the growing authoritarianism of Akaev's rule.

### Economic and Foreign Policy

Foreign assistance has been a significant factor in Kyrgyzstan's budget. The International Monetary Fund and the World Bank have been major lenders to support economic reforms and stabilization; in fact, debt servicing has become an increasing burden to the Kyrgyz state budget. The United States and other developed nations also have provided major humanitarian and economic aid. After independence, the Kyrgyz economy declined by over 50 percent of GDP until beginning to recover in the late 1990s. The Russian financial crisis and declining world gold prices harmed the Kyrgyz economy in late 1998, contributing to reduced Kyrgyz exports to Russia, increased budget deficits, and increased inflation. The economy improved somewhat in 2000. Crime and corruption are threats to economic recovery. A major fraud shook the state natural-gas company and contributed to the failure of several banks in 1999. Illegal drug production in Kyrgyzstan, and drug trafficking, particularly along routes leading from Afghanistan through Tajikistan's Gorno Badakhshan region to Kyrgyzstan's city of Osh, increasingly threaten Kyrgyzstan's legitimate economy and the rule of law. In his inauguration address on 9 December 2000, Akaev pledged to carry out a ten-year economic development program that would create a new "Silk Road" transport network linking Kyrgyzstan to the outside world, combat corruption, and raise standards of living.

Akaev's March 1999 foreign-policy concept called for close relations with ancient Silk Road route nations, including China, former Soviet republics, and Turkey, Iran, India, and Pakistan. Akaev has stressed that landlocked Kyrgyzstan must rely on its neighbors for access to world markets. Akaev has stressed close relations with Russia, hoping for economic and trade benefits and security ties to alleviate concerns about Chinese and Uzbek intentions. Akaev and Boris Yeltsin (b. 1931) signed a Friendship and Cooperation Treaty in 1992, and Akaev gave early support to the 1992 CIS Collective Security Treaty, which called for mutual military assistance in case one of the signatories is attacked. Akaev has urged that the CIS cooperate on economic and security matters. Seeking amicable ties with China, Akaev joined leaders from Russia, Kazakhstan, and Tajikistan in 1996 and 1997 in signing agreements with China on demarcating and demilitarizing the former Soviet-Chinese border.

## Outside Threats and Kyrgyzstan's Military

Although Akaev preferred that Kyrgyzstan not be faced with the expense of maintaining its own armed forces, he established a defense ministry and armed forces in 1992. Kyrgyzstan's armed forces numbered about ninety-two hundred ground, air force, and air defense troops in 2000. Most of the troops are ethnic Kyrgyz conscripts, although some officers are Russians. Kyrgyzstan has about three thousand border troops. In joining NATO's Partnership for Peace (PFP) in June 1994, Akaev hoped that the PFP would provide aid in working out Kyrgyzstan's defense doctrine, converting defense industries, abating environmental problems, and overcoming natural disasters. Kyrgyz officers and troops frequently participate in PFP exercises.

Kyrgyzstan faced a major threat to its territorial integrity when several hundred Islamic extremist guerrillas and others invaded Kyrgyzstan in July–August 1999. The guerrillas seized hostages, including four Japanese geologists, and several Kyrgyz villages, stating that they would cease hostilities if Kyrgyzstan provided a safe haven for refugees and would release hostages if Uzbekistan released jailed extremists. The guerrillas were rumored to be seeking to create an Islamic state in south Kyrgyzstan as a springboard for a jihad in Uzbekistan. Some observers argued that the guerrillas were trying to seize major drug-trafficking routes in southern Kyrgyzstan. Kyrgyzstan called out reservists and admitted that its military was unprepared for combat. With air support from Uzbekistan and Kazakhstan, Kyrgyzstan succeeded in forcing virtually all the guerrillas into Tajikistan. According to some observers, the guerrilla incursion indicated both links among terrorist cells in Kyrgyzstan, Uzbekistan, and Russia (Chechnya) and the weakness of Kyrgyzstan's security forces. After the incursion, Kyrgyzstan worked to upgrade its defense capabilities and stepped up its defense cooperation with Russia, the CIS, and NATO's PFP.

A reported five hundred insurgents launched another attack in early August 2000, taking foreigners hostage and causing thousands of Kyrgyz to flee the area. Uzbekistan provided air and some other support, but Kyrgyz forces were largely responsible for defeating the insurgency by late October 2000. Hailing the performance of professional (rather than conscript) troops in halting the incursion, Kyrgyzstan in early 2001 considered both downsizing the military and converting it completely to contract-based forces.

*Jim Nichol*

### Further Reading

Anderson, John. (2000) "Creating a Framework for Civil Society in Kyrgyzstan." *Europe-Asia Studies* 52, 1; 77–93

Bohr, Annette, and Simon Crisp. (1996) "Kyrgyzstan and the Kyrgyz." In *The Nationality Question in the Post-Soviet States*, edited by Graham Smith. London: Longman, 385–409.

Elebayeva, Ainura, Nurbek Omuraliev, and Rafis Abazov. (2000) "Shifting Identities and Loyalties in Kyrgyzstan: The Evidence from the Field." *Nationalities Papers* 28 (June): 343–349.

Hunter, Shireen T. (1996) *Central Asia since Independence*, Washington Papers, no. 168. Westport, CT: Praeger, published with the Center for Strategic and International Studies.

Khamidov, Alisher. (2001) "Kulov Verdict Indicates Akayev Moving in Authoritarian Direction." *Eurasia Insight* (29 January).

Luong, Pauline Jones. (2000) "After the Break-Up: Institutional Design in Transitional States." *Comparative Political Studies* 33 (June): 563–592.

Olcott, Martha Brill. (1996) "Kyrgyzstan." In *Kazakstan, Kyrgyzstan, Tajikistan, Turkmenistan, and Uzbekistan: Country Studies*, edited by Glenn E. Curtis. Washington, DC: U.S. Government Printing Office, 99–193.

———. (1996) "Kyrgyzstan: Surviving on Foreign Support." In *Central Asia's New States: Independence, Foreign Policy, and Regional Security*. Washington, DC: United States Institute of Peace, 87–112.

Organization for Security and Cooperation in Europe (OSCE), Office for Democratic Institutions and Human Rights. (2000) *Kyrgyz Republic: Parliamentary Elections, February 20 and March 12, 2000*. Warsaw, Poland: OSCE.

———. (2001) *Kyrgyz Republic: Presidential Elections, October 29, 2000*. Warsaw, Poland: OSCE.

Soltobaev, Aziz. (2001) "Kulov Jailed—Political Opposition Turned into Criminals." *Central Asia/Caucasus Analyst, Biweekly Briefing* (14 March).

## KYRGYZSTAN—POLITICAL SYSTEM

Bordering Kazakstan to the north, China to the east, Uzbekistan to the west, and Tajikistan to the south, Kyrgyzstan is a presidential republic that declared independence in 1991, shortly before the collapse of the Soviet Union. Its first elected president, Askar Akayev (b. 1944), was elected by the parliament in October 1990 and then elected in nationwide elections in October 1991. He was reelected to a second term in December 1995 and to a third term in October 2000.

### Background

The Kyrgyz lived a pastoral-nomadic life along the upper reaches of the Yenisey river before migrating south to the Tian Shan region around the tenth century. Ruled by various Turkic peoples until 1685, the Kyrgyz tribes came under Mongol rule until 1785, when the Manchus conquered the region from the east. In the early nineteenth century the territory inhabited by the Kyrgyz came under the control of the khanate of Kokand. The Russian empire exercised dominance over the khanate from 1876 until the October Revolution of 1917, after which the entire Central Asian region commonly known as Turkistan was eventually incorporated into the Soviet Union. In 1918 the newly created Turkistan Autonomous Soviet Socialist Republic included Kyrgyzstan. In 1924 the Kyrgyz Autonomous Oblast (region) was established, and two years later, it was renamed the Kyrgyz Soviet Socialist Republic.

The Kyrgyz tribes were forced to settle beginning in the 1920s, when Soviet administrative rule began to establish urban centers and impose agricultural collectivization. Subsequently, ethnic Russians dominated the government structures until the late 1950s. Not until Leonid Brezhnev headed the Soviet Union (1962–1982) did Soviet central authority finally allow an ethnic Kyrgyz elite to assume the republic's top posts. Brezhnev encouraged a patrimonial system and demanded loyalty to Moscow in exchange for partial transfer of power to local cadres. This arrangement fostered systemic corruption that still persists.

The Soviet Union's election of Mikhail Gorbachev in 1985 and the subsequent introduction of perestroika and glasnost allowed the emergence of informal political and social movements and organizations with various agendas. Although the Communist Party opposed these movements, it could not control the growing demand for greater political freedom or contain ethnic hostility. In 1989 one such organization, Osh Aymagi, called for the distribution of vacant land among the ethnic Kyrgyz to alleviate acute housing shortages in the southern region of Osh. Uzbek and Kyrgyz inhabitants clashed violently in disputes over land and housing, with casualties estimated at one thousand. In October 1990, two months after the Osh disturbances, the Kyrgyz Supreme Soviet called for the selection of a new president to restore normalcy. Askar Akayev, a physicist by profession, replaced Abasamat Masaliyev and abolished the post of First Secretary of the Communist Party.

Akayev called for liberalization of the polity and encouraged political pluralism. Later he introduced sweeping economic reforms that accelerated the republic's transition to a market economy. In 1991 Akayev replaced the Council of Ministers with a Western-style cabinet and appointed reformist politicians. A combination of parliamentary hostility and allegations of high-level corruption led to an open confrontation between the reform-minded president and the largely Communist-oriented parliament. In 1994 a referendum led to the dissolution of the old unicameral parliament in favor of a bicameral legislature. Since 1995 Akayev has curbed the earlier press and political freedoms, forcing the opposition to limit its criticism of the government and its policies.

### Constitution and Institutions

The first post-Communist constitution of Kyrgyzstan, adopted on 5 May 1993, called for the separation of powers and a limited government. Subsequently, however, several amendments increased presidential powers to parliament's detriment. These amendments included a provision for creating a small 105-seat bicameral assembly, the Jogorku Kenesh, to replace the 313-seat Supreme Soviet. The new parliament had a permanent thirty-five-member lower house and a seventy-member People's Assembly (upper house). In October 1998 yet another referendum was held to amend the constitution to allow Akayev to stand for a third term. The voters also approved a constitutional provision calling for an increase in the representation in the lower house to sixty-seven and a reduction in the membership of the upper house to thirty-eight. These changes took effect in 1999.

Parliament members are elected for a five-year term. The president is elected directly for a five-year term with tenure in office limited to two terms. He is head of state and commander-in-chief and holds extensive executive powers. The prime minister is appointed by the president, subject to confirmation by the parliament. Although the constitution calls for an independent judicial branch, Akayev is largely in control. The president nominates appointments to the highest judicial bodies, the Constitutional Court, the Supreme Court, and the Higher Court of Arbitration. In 1996 President Akayev established the Security Council, which functions as an inner cabinet. Unlike the cabinet of ministers, this thirteen-member council is not accountable to the parliament and has become the main instrument of policy making in the republic.

The Kyrgyz political structure also allows for the establishment of a multiparty system. Since 1991 a number of political parties ranging from nationalist to social democratic and Communist have been registered by the justice ministry. However, the relative power of these parties has been significantly diminished as a result of constitutional amendments increasing the power of the executive branch. The Party of the Communists of Kyrgyzstan has been one of the largest opposition parties. The Ar-Namys (Dignity) Party, established by a presidential opponent, Felix Kulov, in 1999, has been kept under strict scrutiny and its leader jailed. Nationalist parties such as Asaba and Erkin have also been marginalized.

## Regional and International Relations

Kyrgyzstan became a member of the Central Asian Union, joining Kazakhstan, Uzbekistan, and Tajikistan, in January 1994. Designed to create a single economic space, the union has accomplished very little in this respect. Several perennial disputes continue to hamper efforts to bring about meaningful regional economic reforms that would benefit each republic. Border disputes, outstanding water, gas, and electricity bills, and competition for regional leadership have driven a political wedge between the member countries. In addition to these issues, the growth of militant Muslim activities has become a source of friction between Uzbekistan and Kyrgyzstan. In the summer of 1999 a group of Uzbek Muslim activists crossed into Kyrgyzstan from Tajikistan and held several Japanese hostages for more than three months.

Kyrgyzstan's structural dependence on Russia has forced the republic to be extremely flexible in its dealing with Moscow. Akayev has signed bilateral and multilateral security treaties with Russia. In 1996 Kyrgyzstan joined a customs union treaty with Kazakstan, Russia, and Belarus, which has yet to produce positive economic results. But Kyrgyzstan's admission to the World Trade Organization in 1999—which requires strict adherence to its membership provisions—has drawn criticism from Russia, whose trade regulations do not conform to international conventions.

Kyrgyzstan has also established ties with China and is a signatory to the Shanghai Five treaty, which unites China, Kazakstan, Kyrgyzstan, Russia, and Tajikistan. These parties signed the treaty in April 1997 as a security guarantee to reduce tensions along the old Chinese-Soviet border. To appease China, Kyrgyzstan has curbed the activities of Muslim Uighur separatists on its territory, a policy that has led to many arrests and extraditions. Xinjiang Uygur, an autonomous region in northwestern China, is home to a relatively large Uighur population, and an estimated 40,000 Uighur Chinese live in Kyrgyzstan.

At the same time, Akayev has established close ties with the European countries whose assistance has been critical in facilitating economic transition. The United States, together with major international donor agencies, has provided economic and technical assistance since 1993. Akayev has embraced the Partnership for Peace program, and Kyrgyz troops have been participating in a Central Asian peacekeeping battalion, which has held joint exercises on an annual basis since 1996.

*Mehrdad Haghayeghi*

## Further Reading

Alworth, Edward. (1986) *Central Asia: 120 Years of Russian Rule.* Durham, NC: Duke University Press.

Dawisha, Karen, and Bruce Parrot, eds. (1987) *Conflict, Cleavage, and Change in Central Asia and the Caucasus.* Cambridge, U.K.: Cambridge University Press.

Fierman, William, ed. (1991) *Central Asia: The Failed Transformation.* Boulder, CO: Westview Press.

Haghayeghi, Mehrdad. (1996) *Islam and Politics in Central Asia*. New York: St. Martin's Press.

Mandelbaum, Michael. (1994) *Central Asia and the World.* New York: Council on Foreign Relations Press.

**KYUSHU** (2001 pop. 13.4 million). Kyushu is located at the westernmost part of the Japanese archipelago and consists of numerous islands stretching toward Taiwan to the southwest. It is made up of the prefectures of Fukuoka, Nagasaki, Saga, Kumamoto, Oita, Miyazaki, and Kagoshima. When the Kyushu region is referred to as a larger administrative unit, it includes Okinawa Prefecture and has a total area of 44,420 square kilometers. Historically, Kyushu has been the contact point between Japan and foreign culture.

The northern part of Kyushu is characterized by a coastal climate with warm temperatures and rainfall, the Inland Sea coast has a typical Inland Sea climate, and the southern part has a Pacific Ocean coastal climate. Typhoons often hit Kyushu in August and September. The geography of Kyushu is very diverse and is characterized by volcanoes, coastal plains, and hot springs. The active volcano Mount Aso (1,592 meters) in Aso Kuju National Park has the world's largest caldera, or crater. Others active volcanoes are Unzendake and Sakurajima. The latter is a stratovolcano composed of the peaks Kitadake (1,117 meters), Nakadake (1,060 meters), and Minamidake (1,040 meters). Most of the plateaus in southern Kyushu are covered with volcanic ash and pumice *(shirasu).* Heavy rains very often cause landslides. Agriculture on the *shirasu* is difficult because of frequent drought, so to cope with this, irrigation projects have been developed. Agriculture has become more commercialized and diversified since World War II, and the products include rice, vegetables, sweet potatoes, tobacco, mandarin oranges, tea, and strawberries, which are grown in greenhouses. Southern Kyushu is a leading producer of beef in Japan, and fishing is important particularly on the west coast. Tourism is also an important economic activity.

Kyushu leads the nation in industrial production in many fields, accounting for almost one-third of the nation's shipbuilding, motorcycle manufacturing, and production of integrated circuits. The Kita-Kyushu Industrial Area is a major industrial area of Japan. Its development began in 1901 with the mining industry (Yawata Iron Mill); however, the iron and steel industries have since declined because of competition from China and South Korea. New industries, including electronics, precision instruments, and information and communication technologies, now account for an increasing share of this area's economic activity. When a part of Yamaguchi Prefecture is added, this region is called "Kyushu-Yamaguchi Economic Sphere." Traditional industries such as furniture making, ceramics, and distilled liquor *(shochu)* are also still important. Most of the high urban functions (information technologies, leisure activities, and international exchange) are centered in and around Fukuoka city, which had a 2001 population of 1.28 million. Secondary cities are Kitakyushu (2001 pop. 1 million), Kumamoto (2001 pop. 650,000), Kagoshima City (2001 pop. 543,000), Oita (2001 pop. 436,000), and Nagasaki (2001 pop. 421,000).

*Nathalie Cavasin*

### Further Reading

The Association of Japanese Geographers, eds. (1980) *Geography of Japan*. Tokyo: Teikoku Shoin.

Kyushu Economic Research Center, eds. (1999) *Outline of Kyushu Economy 1999–2000.* Fukuoka, Japan: Kyukeicho.

Yagasaki Noritaka, ed. (1997) *Japan: Geographical Perspectives on an Island Nation.* Tokyo: Teikoku Shoin.

**LABU SAYONG** The *labu Sayong* (water calabash) is a Malay earthenware container. It takes its shape from the gourd or starfruit and is used as a water container. The clay used for Malay pottery is a terra-cotta clay found by streams, riverbanks, and paddy fields. A potter's wheel is not used in Malay pottery making. The *labu* is coated with river silt with a high iron content, and the surface of the pottery is burnished to a smooth polish with a pebble, a technique carried out by potters at the town of Sayong on the Perak River in West Malaysia. At Sayong, a pot is placed inverted on a rack made from tree branches, with a fire pit below, and after four to five hours the pot is placed into the glowing embers. The color can range from yellowish brown to rust-red, depending on the iron content. A pot is usually decorated with foliage motifs. It was traditionally part of the paraphernalia used in rituals performed during a healing ceremony whereby the water kept in the *labu* was blessed with incantations. Traditional Malay pottery sites are found on or near ancient routes that connect the tributaries of the Perak and Pahang Rivers. One such site is Sayong.

*Shanthi Thambiah*

A woman making a *labu Sayong* in the village of Kepala Bendang, about 300 kilometers north of Kuala Lumpur. The vessels are the main source of income for the 500 people in the village and in 2000 sold for from $1.30 to $21 each. (REUTERS NEWMEDIA INC./CORBIS)

### Further Reading


Winstedt, R. (1925) *Malay Industries: Arts and Crafts*. Kuala Lumpur, Malaysia: Government Press.

Wray, Leonard. (1903) "The Malayan Pottery of Perak." *Journal of the Anthropological Institute of Great Britain and Ireland* 33.


**LAC LONG QUAN** (b. 2879 BCE), mythological founder of the kingdoms of Vietnam and southern

China. Lac Long Quan is the mythological descendant of Than Nong (Shen Nong in Chinese) and the founder of the first Vietnamese kingdom, which received the name Van Lang. His name means the dragon (*long*) king or chief (*quan*) of the Lac family or clan. According to legend, Shen Nong sent his great-great grandson, King De Minh (De Ming in Chinese), on an inspection tour of south China. Arriving at the Wu Ling Mountains in Hunan, De Minh married an immortal woman and sired several sons. Loc Tuc, one of his younger sons, ruled over the south of China under the title of King Duong Vuong. His land was called Xich Quy.

In 2879 BCE, Loc Tuc's son, Lac Long Quan, was born. He too married an immortal woman, Au Co, who gave birth to a pouch containing one hundred eggs, producing one hundred children. Legend has it that after he succeeded his father to the throne of Xich Quy, he told his wife that their marriage could not last because he was of the dragon race and therefore belonged to the water, whereas she, an immortal, belonged to the mountains. He suggested that she take fifty of their children and establish them in the mountains, while he would live on the coastal plains with the other fifty. He then sent one of his children to rule over a southern part of his kingdom, in a country called Van Lang (Vietnam). That son's descendants were known as the Hung kings. There were eighteen in all, and they ruled from approximately 2879 BCE to 258 BCE.

*Truong Buu Lam*

**Further Reading**

Taylor, Keith W. (1983) *The Birth of Vietnam.* Berkeley and Los Angeles: University of California Press.

**LACQUERWARE** Wares made of wood, porcelain, or metal to which lacquer has been applied are known as lacquerware. Lacquer is the sap or resin of the lacquer *(rhus verniciflua)* or varnish tree. The tree is native to central and southern China and possibly to Japan. When applied to wood, porcelain, or metal, the lacquer gives the wares a hard, smooth, transparent, and shiny surface. True or Far Eastern Asian lacquerware has been used since ancient times in China and Japan. The natural sap of the lacquer tree has been used as a protective and decorative varnish for art objects as well as those used in everyday living. The lacquer is applied in thin layers on the wooden objects or inlaid on metal wares. When solidified, lacquer also has been used as a medium for sculpture. Like porcelain, lacquerware has been much appreciated not only in Asia but also Europe, where it has been collected since the sixteenth and seventeenth centuries. Lacquerware includes beautifully decorated items, and many that were household utensils provided waterproof and durable service in Asian households. They would have been popular in Asia where wood was once plentiful. Wood fashioned into lacquerware provided great versatility, as evident from the wide range of objects included among the wares.

East Asian lacquer is not at all similar to the type of lacquer that is the basis of some of the varnishes used in the "japanning" of European furniture from the sixteenth century onward. There are differences in chemical composition and also sources, since the English resin lac or shellac comes from a substance deposited on trees by certain species of insects.

Two broad classes of lacquer objects are distinguished. In one category, the lacquer has been applied largely for the purposes of protection and decoration. Therefore, the lacquer application does not change the form of the objects, such as wooden chairs, so decorated. In the second category, the objects are made mostly of leather, supported by a nonlacquer core or substrate. These objects include lacquer boxes and containers. The core can be hemp cloth, wood, or metal, but it is encased in a lacquer coating thick enough to modify the form of the object. The lacquer coating gives the objects a plump, fleshy shape that can be decorated by carving or by using techniques of inlay and painting.

Lacquer objects, including all those in the second category and also those in the first category in which lacquer forms a significant part of the decoration, are works of art. Other objects, such as lacquered chopsticks, would be essentially lacquered. Lacquer as an art form developed in China. There was pictorial or surface decoration and also carving of the lacquer. After the tenth century, the techniques of *qiangjin* (engraved gold), *diaotian* (filled in), and *diaoqi* (carved lacquer) gradually evolved. Lacquer art dates from about 1600 BCE, during the Shang dynasty in China (1766–1045 BCE). Carved lacquer is a uniquely Chinese achievement. It is considered lacquer art in its pure form.

In Japan, lacquer art surface decoration is paramount. During the Nara period (710–794 CE), lacquerware with gold and silver foil inlay was produced. This was considered to have been transmitted from Tang (618–907 CE) China. *Makie* (gold or silver) lacquer is a unique and supreme achievement of Japanese decorative art. Japanese Negoro ware is also well known. These are objects with a thin layer of lacquer

## LACQUERWARE

Lacquerware is an important export from some nations in Southeast Asia. The following excerpt describes in much detail how lacquerware was made for personal use in Myanmar (Burma) in the late 1800s.

> Drinking cups and boxes for carrying the necessary ingredients for betel-chewing are made of lacquered-ware and are manufactured principally in Upper Burma, but they are also made to some extent in the Prome district. A box of the required size and shape is prepared of exceedingly fine bamboo wicker-work; the finer this is the more valuable is the box. On this is evenly applied a coat of dark pure vegetable oil, known as thit-tsee and obtained from the *Melanorrhoea usitatissima*, which is allowed to dry thoroughly. When it is dry a paste composed of pure sawdust, thit-tsee and rice-water is thickly and evenly laid on and when this is dry, the box is fastened to a rude lathe and carefully smoothed with a piece of silicious bamboo, which is used instead of sand-paper. The next coat consists of a paste of finely-powdered bone-ashes and thit-see which is allowed to dry and smoothed in the same way and the grounding is now complete. In colouring the boxes three colours only are used but of different shades. For *yellow*, yellow orpiment is carefully pounded and washed several times, being allowed to dry between washing, until a pure and impalpable powder remains, reduced three parts in bulk from the raw powder; with this is intimately mixed a small portion of a kind of tragadcanth and the whole dried in the sun. This is worked with a vegetable oil called shan-tsee to the proper consistency and a little thit-tsee is added but not enough to injure the colour. For *green* finely-ground indigo is added to the orpiment in a sufficient proportion to give the required shade and the rest of the process is the same. *Red* is prepared from finely-ground vermillion mixed with a little thit-tsee and worked up with shan-tsee. A coat of the colour and shade intended for the foundation is thickly and evenly applied and when it is thoroughly dry the pattern which is to appear in the next shade or colour is engraved with a style and the colouring matter applied all over the box. When it is dry the box is placed on the lathe and the second colour removed by means of a bit of silicious bamboo so that it remains only in the lines of the engraved pattern. A similar process is followed for the different colours till the design is complete. Lastly one or two coats of a varnish of eight parts thit-tsee (wood-oil) and one part shan-tsee are applied.
>
> *Source:* (1983) *Gazetteer of Burma*. (1893) New Delhi: Cultural Publishing House, 419.

that has usually worn away, leaving a surface that has the appearance of an abstract painting. In Korea, lacquer surfaces were decorated with metal foil inlay during the Unified Shila period (668–935 CE), which was more or less contemporary with the Tang period in China. Subsequently, Korea developed its own style of lacquerware, the finest of which appeared during the Koryo (918–1392) and early Choson (1392–1910) periods, with fine mother-of-pearl inlay often in combination with tortoiseshell. Another area in East Asia that is well known for its tradition of fine lacquer manufacture is the Ryukyu Islands. Now part of Japan, the islands were once a kingdom, and the growth and decline of the lacquer industry actually paralleled that of the kingdom, which began in the fourteenth century and ended in 1872. Chinese lacquer techniques were a major influence on Ryukyuan lacquer objects.

Lacquerware comprised large and small objects from chopsticks, bowls, cups, and vases to coffers, bamboo baskets, and containers, as well as screens and even suits of leather armor. The lacquer vases produced in Soochow, China, resembled fine porcelain with their intricate carvings on wood stained in coral and then lacquered. These were made for the emperor during the Ch'ien Lung period (1736–1796) of the Qing dynasty (1644–1912). They were among the treasures used in the summer palace. Other types of lacquerware include the Japanese ware in black and gold lacquer inlaid with gold, silver, and mother-of-pearl. Chinese and Japanese screens of lacquered, painted, and gilt wood are familiar not only in Asian homes and institutions today but also in fine arts museums. These screens are often painted by hand, sometimes by well-known artists or copyists. Korean suits of armor of the seventeenth and eighteenth centuries, made of gold-lacquered small plates, gilt-copper brown lacquer plates, and scarlet, are prized collectors' items.

Modern lacquerware from Japan and Korea is highly finished in appearance when compared to that still produced in China and other parts of Southeast Asia. The Straits Chinese or Peranakan society in Southeast Asia reproduced lacquered basketry, originally produced in China, for carrying special gifts offered to deities in temples or during occasions such as weddings and festivals. Lacquerware items remain important in most East and Southeast Asian households, although they tend to be more expensive than either ceramics or plastic.

*Ooi Giok-Ling*

**Further Reading**

Clifford, Derek. (1992) *Chinese Carved Lacquer.* London: Bamboo Publishing Ltd.

Cocks, A. S. (1980) *The Victoria and Albert Museum.* Leicester, U.K: Windward.

Garner, Harry M. (1972) *Ryukyu Lacquer.* London: School of Oriental and African Studies, University of London.

Watt, James, C., and Barbara Brennan Ford. (1991) *East Asian Lacquer.* New York: The Metropolitan Museum of Art.

**LADAKH** (2001 est. pop. 118,000). Ladakh, formerly called Middle Tibet, is a mountainous district of Jammu and Kashmir that forms the northernmost area of the Indian Republic. It covers 82,665 square kilometers of very high and rugged country, and is the biggest administrative district anywhere in India. Elevations range from 3,000 to 5,000 meters. Aside from its mountains, the most important physical feature of Ladakh is the great valley of the Indus River, which crosses the entire district as it flows northwestward from its source in Tibet, thus separating the Karakoram Range from the Zanskar Range. Near Leh, the district headquarters, the Indus is 3,350 meters above sea level. The observatory at Leh is said to be the most elevated one in Asia. It records a mean annual temperature of 4.4°C, dropping in the coldest months (January and February) to about –8°C.

The culture is basically a Tibetan one, with numerous lamaistic monasteries. But while the bulk of the population are Lamaistic Buddhists, the Baltis in the west are Shiʿite Muslims. There is very little arable land, but this remote region abounds in valuable minerals: lead, gold, copper, sulfur, coal, iron, borax, gypsum, and precious stones. Ladakh has long been an area involved in trans-Himalayan trade, difficult as this is.

*Paul Hockings*

**Further Reading**

Rizvi, Janet. (1996) *Ladakh: Crossroads of High Asia.* 2d ed. New Delhi: Oxford University Press.

———. (1999) *Trans-Himalayan Caravans: Merchant Princes and Peasant Traders in Ladakh.* New Delhi: Oxford University Press.

**LAHORE** (1999 est. pop. 7 million). Lahore is the capital of the Punjab province of Pakistan and is the country's cultural and industrial center and its second-largest city. There are contrary views as to the origin of its name. According to folklore, Lahore was established by Loh, the son of Rama, the renowned hero of the Hindu epic the *Ramayana*. However, others believe it derives from the word *loh-awar*, which means a fort as strong as iron and which refers to the fort built to protect the city.

Historically, Lahore has played a significant role in the region. It has been the capital of Punjab province for almost a thousand years. The city first achieved this status during the Ghaznavid dynasty (977–1187). It continued as such under the rule of Muhammad of Ghor as well as under several sultans of Delhi. Qutb-ud-din Aibak became the first Muslim sultan in the area after being crowned in Lahore in 1206. From 1524 to 1752, the Mughal dynasty (1526–1857) raised the level of prominence of Lahore by adding considerably to its architecture and size. Akbar (reigned 1556–1605) was responsible for overseeing the construction of the Lahore Fort, which was built over an old fort. In addition, he had a red-brick wall with twelve impressive gates constructed around the city. Shah Jahan (1592–1666) and Janhangir (reigned 1605–1627) contributed palaces, tombs, and gardens to the city landscape and enlarged the fort. The last great Mughal, Aurangzeb, had the famous monument the Badshahi Mosque built along with the Alamgiri gateway to the fort.

The eighteenth century witnessed constant invasions throughout the region, which laid Lahore open to capture by Ranjit Singh (reigned 1801–1839) in 1799. His control over Lahore afforded him the legitimacy that he needed to become emperor. Unfortunately, the Sikh era was not kind to Lahore; the existing structures were not well maintained, and few new ones were built. When the British arrived in Lahore in 1849, they initially constructed practical facilities for the administration of the capital. Later, however, they worked to preserve some of the ancient structures and eventually added their own Victorian style of architecture, named Mughal-Gothic, to the city.

### FORT AND SHALAMAR GARDENS IN LAHORE—WORLD HERITAGE SITE

Shah Jahan's Mughal gardens and fort were designated UNESCO World Heritage Sites in 1981 and added to the list of World Heritage Sites in Danger in 1999 when the garden's water tanks were destroyed. It is hoped that growing international awareness will help preserve the beautiful terraced gardens and gilded marble fort.

The Budshahi Mosque in Lahore. (CORBIS)

In 1940, Lahore was the site of a significant Muslim League session during which the Lahore Resolution was proposed. This resolution called for a separate state for the Muslim population of India, leading to the creation of Pakistan on 14 August 1947. Lahore is now a major industrial and cultural center and home to several leading institutions of higher education. Its mix of numerous styles of architecture, from ancient to modern, is a significant tourist attraction.

*Houman A. Sadri*

### Further Reading

Alter, Stephen. (2000) *Amritsar to Lahore: Crossing the Border between India and Pakstan*. Columbia, MO: South Asia Books.

Mizra, Jasmin. (2002) *Between Chaddor and Market: Female Office Workers in Lahore*. Oxford: Oxford University Press.

Tahir, M. Athor. (1999) *Lahore Colours*. Oxford: Oxford University Press.

**LAKSAMANA** *Laksamana* is a Malay honorific title given to the supreme military commander, the counterpart of the highest Malay state official, the *bendahara*. This is expressed in the saying "The *bendahara* rules the land, the *laksamana* rules the sea." Since the Malay states were generally maritime empires, the position of *laksamana* became equated with "admiral." He was the "ruler of the sea" and the "warden of the coast." It is unknown when the term first came to be used, but it probably derives from Laksmana, the name of Rama's half-brother in the *Ramayana*. The oldest written Malay version of the Indian *Ramayana* dates from between the thirteenth and seventeenth centuries. In this epic it is told that Laksamana drew a magic figure (*baris Laksamana*, i.e., "Laksamana's line") to protect Sita against the assaults of Ravana.

At the court of Perak (and perhaps also at other Malay courts) the *laksamana*, when ashore, was also in charge of the sultan's harem. During processions the *laksamana*'s post was by the sultan's palanquin. When the sultan rode in state upon an elephant the *laksamana* followed, bearing the ruler's sword. Considering the *laksamana*'s position and functions, it is worth noting that in the *Ramayana*, Laksamana behaves toward Rama more like a servant than a prince. In the Malay version of the *Ramayana*, Laksamana is furthermore presented as a great ascetic, which might explain why he could be entrusted with the task of looking after the sultan's harem.

According to the *Sejarah Melayu* (Malay Annals), which depicts the world of Melaka in the fifteenth and early sixteenth centuries, the association of the name with the office was fortuitous. Hang Tuah, the legendary fifteenth-century Malay hero, was always comparing himself to the epic Laksamana. In time he was nicknamed Laksamana and finally given the name as a title. This title later went to his successors with his office of warden of the coast. In the *Sejarah Melayu*, which were probably commissioned by a Melaka *bendahara*, the activities of the *bendahara* steal the spotlight from all other senior officials. The importance of the *laksamana*'s office, however, cannot be ignored, because of his military prominence, commanding the *orang laut* fleets. The Orang Laut—the sea and river peoples in the western half of the Malay-Indonesian archipelago—were crucial to Melaka's security and prosperity, for they represented a strong naval power and transported sea products to Melaka's busy market. After the Portuguese conquered Melaka in 1511, the *laksamana*'s position in the sultanate of Johor, Melaka's successor state, became more important than that of the *bendahara*'s.

*Edwin Wieringa*

*See also:* **Bendahara**

### Further Reading

Andaya, Barbara Watson, and Leonard Y. Andaya. (1982) *A History of Malaysia*. London: Macmillan Education.

Gonda, J. (1973) *Sanskrit in Indonesia*. New Delhi: International Academy of Indian Culture.

Wilkinson, R. J. (1959) *A Malay-English Dictionary (Romanised)*. New York: St. Martin's Press.

Zieseniss, A. (1937) "Funktion und Stellung des Laksamâna am Hofe der malaiischen Sultane." *Acta Orientalia* 15: 72–75.

**LAKSHADWEEP** (2001 est. pop. 61,000). Lakshadweep is an Indian union territory (capital, Kavaratti) that includes the Laccadive, Minicoy, and Amindivi islands, which are scattered in the Arabian Sea some 300 kilometers off the Malabar Coast of South India. An isolated and picturesque archipelago of twelve tropical atolls and three reefs and submerged sand banks, Lakshadweep's thirty-six small islands cover a total area of only thirty-two square kilometers located between between 8° and 12°N latitude, 71° and 74°E longitude. The coral archipelago is built on the submarine Chagos Ridge, like the Maldives archipelago farther south. The Amindivi Islands occupy the northern part of Lakshadweep, the Laccadive Islands the central part, and Minicoy is the southernmost island.

Due to their exposed location, the islands were ruled by the Portuguese, Indian rajas, Tipoo sultans, and British rulers until the islands were absorbed into independent India. Ten of the islands are inhabited; island-to-island traffic is either by boat or helicopter. Though originally Hindu, the population has followed the Muslim faith since the fourteenth century. They are classified as Scheduled Tribes (ethic subgroups who have faced discrimination and economic privations). They speak Malayalam, except on Minicoy, where they speak a Sinhalese dialect. The isolation of Lakshadweep's population has meant that they suffer from health and education deficits when compared with mainland Peninsular India. Lakshadweep is seriously overpopulated, with nearly two thousand persons per square kilometer, and this overpopulation is causing tremendous economic problems as the economy is mainly based on coconut products, fisheries, and tropical fruit and vegetable gardening, though dairies and poultry farms were established in the 1980s. Tourism was introduced in 1988 with the opening of the resort on Bingaram Island, intended to diversify the narrow and backward economy. This formerly uninhabited island is ringed by a fringed coral reef. The favorable dry and sunny tourist season is from October to April. At other times of the year, the channels between the islands are often affected by harmful currents. Heavy monsoon storms also visit the Lakshadweep islands and seas.

*Manfred Domroes*

### Further Reading

Mukundan, T. K. (1979) *Laksha Dweep: A Hundred Thousand Islands*. Gurgaon, India: Academic Press.

**LAND MINES** First identified as a humanitarian concern in Afghanistan and Cambodia in the late 1980s, land mines have become an international issue. Afghanistan, Cambodia, and Angola are the world's most seriously affected countries; other Asian countries adversely affected by land mines include Myanmar (Burma), Iran, Iraq, Jordan, Laos, Lebanon, Sri Lanka, Tajikistan, Turkey, and Vietnam.

Land mines continue to endanger civilians long after wars end. The Convention on the Prohibition of the Use, Stockpiling, Production, and Transfer of Anti-Personnel Mines and on Their Destruction was signed in Ottawa in 1997; by March 2001, 139 states had signed and 111 had ratified. Important Asian states that have not signed include Pakistan, India, and China. The treaty, negotiated outside regular disarmament forums, was an outstanding achievement, and the 1997 Nobel Peace Prize was awarded to the International Campaign to Ban Landmines (ICBL) and its coordinator, American activist Jody Williams (b. 1950).

Although not a subject of the convention, antivehicle land mines and unexploded ordnance (UXO) are nevertheless significant threats. In Laos, and more recently in Afghanistan, for instance, so-called bomblets—small submunitions from U.S. cluster bombs—often fail to explode after hitting the ground, posing great risk for civilians.

In addition to causing injury and death, land mines can force nomads to change their traditional migration patterns (as in Afghanistan), prevent agricultural cultivation (as in Cambodia), or block important infrastructure. In Afghanistan and Cambodia, land mines became a significant concern when repatriated refugees returned to areas with massive mine problems.

Since the late 1980s, new humanitarian projects have been designed to increase awareness of the risks associated with land mines. Unfortunately, these efforts have been less successful among populations who have lived with mines for years. In many cases, civilians will enter a minefield by compulsion, searching for basic means of survival. Although the cost is often high and progress slow, Humanitarian mine clearance operations have made a significant impact. A 1999 U.N. report states that the Afghanistan program had cleared 166 square kilometers of an identified 311-square-kilometer high-priority area. By mid-2000,

## UNICEF ON LAND MINES

"Land mines pose particular dangers for children. Naturally curious, children are likely to pick up strange objects, such as the infamous toy-like 'butterfly' mines that Soviet forces spread by the millions in Afghanistan. In northern Iraq, Kurdish children have used round mines as wheels for toy trucks, while in Cambodia, children use B40 anti-personnel mines to play 'boules', notes the report."

"Land mines also have more catastrophic effects on children, whose small bodies succumb more readily to the horrific injuries mines inflict. In Cambodia, an average of 20 per cent of children injured by mines and unexploded ordnance die from their injuries. Children who manage to survive explosions are likely to be more seriously injured than adults, and often permanently disabled. Because a child's bones grow faster than the surrounding tissue, a wound may require repeated amputation and a new artificial limb as often as every six months—although the prosthesis is not likely to be available. Moreover, competing demands for scarce medical services also mean that children injured by mines seldom receive the care they deserve. Only 10–20 per cent of children disabled by mines in El Salvador receive any rehabilitative therapy."

*Source:* UNICEF article on the United Nations report *Impact of Armed Conflict on Children*, by Graça Machel. Retrieved 11 October 200l, from: http://www.unicef.org/graca/mines.htm.

however, some countries with substantial landmine or UXO problems, including Vietnam and Tajikistan, still lacked clearance capacity.

*Kristian Berg Harpviken*

**Further Reading**

Harpviken, Kristian Berg, and Mona Chr. Fixdal. (1997) "Anti-personnel Land Mines: A Just Means of War?" *Security Dialogue* 3, 28 (September): 151–165.

International Campaign to Ban Landmines. (1999) *Landmine Monitor Report 1999: Toward a Mine-Free World.* New York: Human Rights Watch.

## LANGUAGE PURIFICATION

Purification is a conscious, deliberate attempt to remove from a language the elements that are borrowed from a "foreign" language or even from a dialect of the language. Borrowing and purification are products of language contact and conflict and occur on all levels of language use and structure.

Asia is an area of intensive language contact and conflict. The continent has the largest number of languages, 2,165, which constitutes 32 percent of the total 6,703 languages of the world (1996 data). In Asia, some of the world's most important classical languages—Arabic, Chinese, Persian, and Sanskrit—have strongly influenced other tongues. Although the phenomenon has occurred in premodern societies as well, purifying language from "foreignisms" has turned into "purist movements" in modern times. Thus purism is closely tied to Asia's nationalist movements from Korea in the east to Kurdistan in the west and is often a nationalist response to domination, assimilation, and "linguistic imperialism."

Purification varies in scope, forms, and intensity. For instance, while classical Tibetan and Chinese are known for their conservatism, Japanese has been more receptive to loans from diverse languages. In each language, too, purist attitudes and behaviors constitute a spectrum, ranging from "linguistic chauvinism" or "linguistic xenophobia" to moderate purges of "foreign" elements. Purist movements are, at the same time, important trends in the formation of standard national languages such as Baluchi, Korean, Mongolian, Nepali, and Tamil.

Loanwords are the main, but not only, targets of purification. Vietnamese and Korean, for example, finally discarded the Chinese writing system in the latter part of the twentieth century, while Japanese continues to use it in mixed and modified forms. In West Asia, Turkey, under the rule of nationalists, replaced the Arabic script with the Roman in 1928 but was less successful in its sweeping purge of Arabic and Persian loanwords. Extremist purists in Kurdish have tried to purge phonemes and letters of the alphabet that they consider to be imposed by Arabic.

Languages in all parts of Asia are experiencing increasing contact and conflict in the unceasing process of globalization, the formation of a "world linguistic order," characterized by unequal relations among languages, proliferation of new communication technologies, and ongoing ethnic, nationalist, and religious conflicts. Under these conditions, which also perpetrate "language death" and "linguicide" (the deliberate killing of a language), speakers of endangered tongues resist by various means, especially purification.

*Amir Hassanpour*

**Further Reading**

Grimes, Barbara F., ed. (1996) *Ethnologue: Languages of the World.* Dallas, TX: Summer Institute of Linguistics.

Jernudd, Björn H., and Michael J. Shapiro, eds. (1989) *The Politics of Language Purism.* Berlin: Mouton de Gruyter.

## LAO PEOPLE'S REVOLUTIONARY PARTY

The Lao People's Revolutionary Party (LPRP) has been the sole party governing Laos since 1975. The Laotian prince Souphanuvong (1901–1995) and Kaysone Phomvihan (1920–1992), both influenced by the Indochinese Communist Party, emerged as Laos's communist leaders and cofounded the party in 1955 as the Lao People's Party. In 1956, the party was renamed the Lao People's Revolutionary Party (LPRP) and operated in secrecy. The party emerged to govern Laos when the communists took power in 1975. The LPRP is Marxist-Leninist and, like other Lao institutions, is influenced by the North Vietnamese model. The party planned to transform Lao society into a socialist one by completely eliminating traces of French colonialism and American imperialism through the leadership of the party in all aspects of society. Power was held by the small politburo of the party's central committee and a secretariat that was abolished in 1991.

The relaxation of socialist ideology began in the 1980s due to the failure of communist initiatives with *chintanakan mai* (New Economic Mechanism). *Chintanakan mai* lifted restrictions and introduced new policies such as private land ownership and a free market economy to Laos. At the fifth party congress in 1991, many party veterans such as Souphanuvong retired from the central committee, but the party remained in complete power. After the death of Kaysone in 1992, leadership passed to the third most powerful man in the party, General Khamthay Siphandon, the current president. The LPRP continues to govern Laos with a membership of approximately 1.1 percent of the population.

*Linda McIntosh*

### Further Reading

Stuart-Fox, Martin, ed. (1982) *Contemporary Laos: Studies in the Politics and Society of the Lao People's Democratic Republic.* New York: St. Martin's Press.

———. (1996) *Buddhist Kingdom, Marxist State: The Making of Modern Laos.* Bangkok, Thailand: White Lotus.

**LAO SHE** (1899–1966), Chinese author and playwright. Lao She, pen name for Shu Qingchun, was one of modern China's most celebrated humorists; his satirical novels, short stories, and plays are highly appreciated. He is also renowned for his sympathy with the underprivileged. After graduating from Beijing Teacher's College, in 1924 he went to England, where he taught Mandarin Chinese, studied at the School of Oriental and African Studies, and was inspired by reading the novels of Charles Dickens. When he returned to China in 1930, Lao had already written three novels and had achieved a reputation as a humorous writer, and he continued to write while teaching. By his death in 1966 in the early stages of the Cultural Revolution (1966–1976), Lao had written more than twenty plays in praise of the Communist Chinese regime. Among his most famous works are the 1938 novel *Luotuo Xiangzi* (Xiangzi the Camel, also known as *Rickshaw Boy*) and the 1957 play *Chaguan* (Teahouse).

*Bent Nielsen*

### Further Reading

Kao, George, ed. (1980) *Two Writers and the Cultural Revolution: Lao She and Chen Jo-hsi.* Hong Kong: Chinese University Press.

Wang, David Der-wei. (1992) *Fictional Realism in Twentieth-Century China: Mao Dun, Lao She, Shen Congwen.* New York: Columbia University Press.

**LAOS—PROFILE** (2001 pop. 5.6 million). The landlocked and multiethnic Lao People's Democratic Republic has passed through many vicissitudes of history. It has maintained its unity and national identity in spite of foreign invasions and interference, poverty, and ideological conflict.

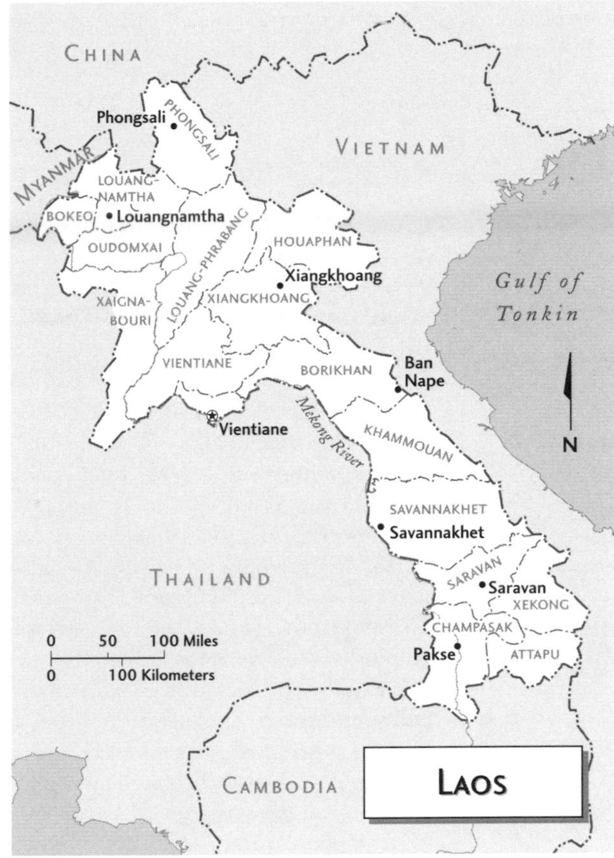


### Geography

Situated in the northern part of the Indochinese peninsula in mainland Southeast Asia, Laos is bordered by China in the north, Myanmar (Burma) in the northwest, Thailand to the south and west, Vietnam to the east, and Cambodia to the south. It is 236,800 square kilometers in area. Some 1,835 kilometers of the Mekong river flows through it from north to south. Rugged lands, dense forests and mountainous terrain dominate most of the country. Two-thirds of the country is thick subtropical forest. Laos has a tropical monsoon climate, with a rainy season from May to October and a dry season from November to April.

### People

With an average of nineteen people per square kilometer, Laos is one of the least densely populated countries in Asia. There are four broad population groupings in Laos: the Lao Lum (valley Lao, 68 percent), the Lao Theung (mountainside Lao, 22 percent), Lao Sung (mountaintop Lao, including Hmong and Yao, 9 percent), and ethnic Chinese and Vietnamese (1 percent). Diverse ethnic groups have settled in Laos in different periods of its history. The Lao Lum, originally a Tai people from southern China,

## LAOS

**Country name:** Lao People's Democratic Republic
**Area:** 236,800 sq km
**Population:** 5,635,967 (July 2001 est.)
**Population growth rate:** 2.48% (2001 est.)
**Birth rate:** 37.84 births/1,000 population (2001 est.)
**Death rate:** 13.02 deaths/1,000 population (2001 est.)
**Sex ratio:** 0.98 male(s)/female (2001 est.)
**Infant mortality rate:** 92.89 deaths/1,000 live births (2001 est.)
**Life expectancy at birth:** total population: 53.48 years, male: 51.58 years, female: 55.44 years (2001 est.)
**Major religion:** Buddhist
**Major languages:** Lao (official), French, English, and various ethnic languages
**Literacy:** total population: 57%, male: 70%, female: 44% (1999 est.)
**Government type:** Communist state
**Capital:** Vientiane
**Administrative divisions:** 16 provinces, 1 municipality
**Independence:** 19 July 1949 (from France)
**National holiday:** Republic Day, 2 December (1975)
**Suffrage:** 18 years of age; universal
**GDP—real growth rate:** 4% (2000 est.)
**GDP—per capita:** (purchasing power parity): $1,700 (2000 est.)
**Population below poverty line:** 46.1% (1993 est.)
**Exports:** $323 million (f.o.b., 2000 est.)
**Imports:** $540 million (f.o.b., 2000 est.)
**Currency:** kip (LAK)

*Source:* Central Intelligence Agency. (2001) *The World Book Factbook 2001.* Retrieved 5 March 2002, from http://www.cia.gov/cia/publications/factbook

migrated to Laos from the seventh century onwards. Belonging to the Mon-Khmer stock, the Lao Theung are the oldest inhabitants; they arrived in prehistoric times. Emigration from Laos became frequent after Laos became Communist in the latter part of 1975. At the start of the twenty-first century, 10 percent of the world's Lao population lived in Thailand, the United States, France, Canada, and Australia. About 80 percent of the population in Laos itself lived in rural areas. Lao is the nation's official language. The Marxist government sanctions Buddhism as the state religion.

### History

A number of kingdoms, centered on urban settlements, arose in the beginning of the first century BCE. Parts of Laos came under the control of the Mon kingdoms of Dvaravati and Funan before the seventh century CE, but Prince Fa Ngoum (1353–1373), a Lao, founded the first unified state, Lan Xang (land of a million elephants) in 1353. The powerful Lan Xang kingdom ruled Laos and areas of the Cambodian plateau, northeastern Thailand, and parts of Yunnan. In 1559 Laos lost control over the Vientiane region to Bayinnaung (1550–1581), the ruler of the Burmese Toungoo dynasty; the area remained under Burmese control until 1637, when the Lan Xang kingdom reasserted itself. Internal dissension and powerful neighbors brought its decline in 1713, and it splintered into the three kingdoms of Luang Prabang, Vientiane, and Bassac. Laos became a French protectorate in 1893. During World War II, the Japanese took control of Laos and declared it independent; after the war, the Franco-Laotian Convention of July 1949 granted Laos internal autonomy only, leaving France in control of Laos's foreign and defense affairs. The Pathet Lao, a Communist nationalist movement, opposed the reestablishment of French control, and Laos was soon engulfed in the First Indochina War. Civil war continued through the 1960s, with the only hopes for peace pinned on the outcome of the conflict in Vietnam. On 2 December 1975, the Pathet Lao succeeded in establishing the Lao People's Democratic Republic. Suffering from the effects of three decades of war, Laos became dependent on Vietnam, with whom it signed a twenty-five-year treaty of friendship in 1977.

Toward the end of 1980s, Laos's leadership moved away from ideological rigidity and began a program of liberalizing the economy. A new liberal constitution was promulgated in August 1991, and relations with China, Thailand, the United States, and other Western countries improved. Laos became a member of the Association of Southeast Asian Nations (ASEAN) in July 1997. In spite of these advances, charges of human-rights violations are still made, with the allegation that the government has been responsible for the disappearance of some 300,000 people from 1975 to 2001. In March 2001, the Lao National Assembly decided to retain party chairman Khamtay Siphandone as president but made Boungnang Vorachit the premier.

### Economy

The people of Laos have one of the lowest per capita incomes in the world (300 dollars), with about 46 percent of the population living below the poverty line. However, using the purchasing-power parity measure, gross domestic product per capita is estimated to be a much higher $1,700, reflective of the relatively low cost of living in the country. About 70 percent of the people are farmers; common crops include rice, sweet potatoes, and coffee. Laos is rich in natural resources, including tin, copper, gold, lead, and timber. Its main items of export are electricity, timber and wood products, tin, textiles, and coffee, and its leading trade partners are Thailand, Vietnam, and Japan. Laos imports petroleum products, machinery and equipment, vehicles, cement, and steel. Although Asia's regional economic crisis of the mid-1990s hurt Laos, by the middle of 2000 its economy had stabilized. As a member of Mekong River Commission Council (MRCC), which Laos joined in 2001, Laos expects to boost rice production. At the start of the twenty-first century, its currency, the kip, hovered at between 7,500 and 8,000 to one U.S. dollar.

### Culture

Interaction with the Khmer, Thai, and Indians has enriched the indigenous culture of Laos. Classical Lao literature, inscriptions, and language show Sanskrit and Pali influence. Themes from Indian literature are in abundance in folk songs, dramas, and theater. The Lao version of the *Ramayana*, the *Phra Lak Pha Lam*, reflects the environment and culture of Laos. It is a dance-drama performed to the accompaniment of Lao classical music.

Laos is a largely rural nation. Here, men stand with their cattle in the village of Pan Phanom in Luang Prabang Province. (BOHEMIAN NOMAD PICTUREMAKERS/CORBIS)

***Religion*** According to tradition, Buddhism came to Laos during the reign of the Indian emperor Asoka (reigned c. 265–238 BCE). Sculptures of Buddha in a standing position are distinctively indigenous. Lao religious life also is marked by belief in wandering spirits and souls of departed ones *(phi)*.

***Festivals*** Popular festivals include Boun Pimai, which celebrates the Lao New Year over the course of several days in April. In Luang Prabang, Boun Pimai celebrations include ablutions for Buddhist icons. Boun Bang Fai celebrates the start of the rainy season in May. At this festival, giant homemade bamboo rockets are launched skyward to summon the rains. The festival of Haw Khao Padap Din, which occurs in August, is a time to pay respects to the dead. November is the occasion of a huge festival at the temple of That Luang (the national symbol of Laos) in Vientiane. It takes place on the week of the full moon.

***Music*** Although Laos has a long history of classical music, decades of warfare and instability have led to its decline. Folk music remains popular; the most common form of musical instrument is the *khean*, or Lao panpipe, seven pairs of pipes made of bamboo. It provides the music for the most popular folk dance, the *Lamvong*, or Circle Dance, a folk dance in which couples move in circles.

### Laos in the Twenty-first Century

In the early twenty-first century, Laos continues to move prudently from ideological orthodoxy to economic pragmatism. There are signs of relative openness in society, although the regime still does not tolerate dissent. It is evident that the predictions of some pundits that Laos would cease to exist as a nation-state were wrong. Tentatively, Laos is moving toward a better future.

*Patit Paban Mishra*

*See also:* **Music, Folk—Laos; That Luang Festival.**

### Further Reading

Davies, Ben. (2001) *Laos: A Journey Beyond the Mekong.* Bangkok, Thailand: Luna Publications.

Mishra, Patit Paban. (1999) *A Contemporary History of Laos.* New Delhi, India: National Book Organization.

Murphy, Dervla. (1999). *One Foot in Laos.* London: John Murray.

Stuart-Fox, Martin. (1996) *Buddhist Kingdom, Marxist State: The Making of Modern Laos.* Bangkok, Thailand: White Lotus Co.

———. (1997) *A History of Laos.* Cambridge, U.K.: Cambridge University Press.

ETC Asia Co. (2000) "Laos Culture and Travel Information: Festivals." Retrieved 13 September 2001, from: http://visit-mekong.com/laos/background/festivals.htm.

## LAOS—ECONOMIC SYSTEM

**LAOS—ECONOMIC SYSTEM** Laos is one of the poorest countries in Asia. This is a result of such factors as a small population, the burden of a colonial past, and the adverse effects of geography. The socialist Pathet Lao (Lao Country party) government has opened the country to a limited form of market forces and is sustaining free-market conditions for its people, but that system has brought with it problems. For example, with a market-determined exchange rate, there was a dramatic and quite severe fall of the kip, Laos's currency, in 1998–1989.

### Economic Geography of Laos

Laos is a landlocked country bordered by Vietnam to the east, China to the north, Cambodia to the south, Myanmar (Burma) to the northwest, and Thailand to the west and south. Borders are generally not firmly established and often follow geographical features; hence, cross-border movement is difficult to regulate and cross-border economic transactions may be beyond the reach of governments.

Much of the country is mountainous and heavily forested. The people are spread thinly across its extent, with only Vientiane (population of the city proper approximately 190,000) and the much smaller centers of Savannakhet, Pakse, and the ancient capital of Luang Phrabang representing major urban centers. Transportation links are very few, although recently these have been improved. The paucity of the infrastructure makes it very difficult for central authorities to control patterns of development within regions.

There are both east-west and north-south divisions within the country. The southern regions possess the advantages of greater forest cover and of more fertile lands. They enjoy greater access to more flourishing markets based upon the exploitation of forest goods and of an agricultural surplus not available in northern provinces. Most of the population, meanwhile, is concentrated on the western border with Thailand, which is a region offering much greater opportunities for trade and communication than the eastern border with Vietnam which, while important for political reasons, remains an undeveloped zone economically. A small number of links across borders represent important nodes for development and communication. The link between the Thai town of Nong Khai and the Lao capital Vientiane, represented by the Australian-financed Friendship Bridge across the Mekong river, has become a vital conduit of commerce, and many Vientiane households routinely tune in to Thai television and radio broadcasts.

The country itself is ethnically diverse, and the principal ethnic groups are themselves composed of a variety of elements. The main ethnic groups are usually divided into three main categories, each of which has differential access to political power and economic opportunities. The most populous group are the Lao Loum (lowland Lao), who represent some 60 percent of the population; next are the Lao Thoeng (midland Lao), with 30 percent of the population; finally there are the Lao Soung (Lao of the highlands), with 10 percent of the population. Lao Soung and even Thoeng are sometimes referred to as *kha* (slaves), which is an offensive term and reflects popular public perception of them; they remain underrepresented at all governmental levels. Lao Thoeng are the oldest inhabitants of the country; they coexisted and borrowed from their Mon and Khmer neighbors. Toward the end of the first millennium CE, the Tai-speaking peoples migrated to the region and eventually enforced political superiority, forcing the Lao Thoeng upland, away from prime agricultural positions. Upland Lao have mostly migrated to Laos over the last century or so, largely from southern China and as a result of persecution of some kind or another; they wish to continue the swidden (slash-and-burn) agriculture that is their tradition. Some of these peoples have been active in growing and trafficking in opium to raise income and to sustain an armed struggle for independence. Groups such as the Hmong were involved in the Vietnam War

(1954–1975) on behalf of the United States and against the interests of the eventually victorious Pathet Lao government. Subsequently, many thousands have emigrated to the United States and elsewhere. The dispersal of an already small population has been a significant factor in the reduction of the level of human capital in the country.

Various attempts have been made by successive central administrations to bring the upland Laos and other ethnic groups into the mainstream of Lao political life—although this does not mean that upland Lao or women or other groups are appropriately represented within political life. However, as in neighboring Thailand, these attempts have been contested on the grounds that they are intended to change or damage the peoples' traditional lifestyle or otherwise infringe on their customs. That local officials are often obliged to act at a distance from central authority, with all the dangers of the potential for corruption or malfeasance that this represents, has exacerbated the situation. As in the case of the majority of mainland southeast Asia, certain remote regions are effectively under the control of unofficial local leaders who can operate beyond the reach of the law with respect to such activities as illegal logging, gambling, and cultivation of narcotics.

The Mekong river, which is a principal part of the western border of the country, represents a significant source of potential hydroelectric power and hence a stimulus to economic development. Already, a large station has been built at Nam Ngum, although the effects of the Asian financial crisis have significantly reduced demand for power regionally and so total capacity remains superfluous. Various mineral deposits have been surveyed, but these remain mostly unexploited owing to difficulties with infrastructure or else are worked only in a primitive fashion. Manufacturing is at a very low level and agriculture is primarily at the subsistence level; hence, exports are much lower than necessary imports. Foreign aid assistance represents a considerable source of income and skills within the economy.

### Historical Patterns of Economic Development

Lao of the lowlands are a Tai people who began to migrate to mainland Southeast Asia, probably from southern China and northwestern Vietnam, from perhaps as early as the eighth century CE. However, evidence of settled Lao communities is sparse, and it is not until the end of the first millennium CE that evidence of settlements is unambiguous.

The Tai practiced a form of political and economic organization that emphasized the two-way connections between a prince or other official and his followers in a complex web of personal interaction and loyalties upon which geography had little bearing. In other words, the physical location of people and their leaders was of less importance than the personal, familial, or social ties which bound them together. There was little incentive therefore to attempt to delineate formal borders or to institute taxation schemes. Instead, institutions such as corvée labor were formalized to provide a tangible outcome to the accumulation of a surplus. Surplus labor could be used for public works, such as building temples. This system proved durable and did not change in essence until the arrival of the Europeans, when it was perverted by the French colonists who required that corvée labor be used to their direct benefit. The French also taxed the population. The requirement to provide both labor and taxes to rulers who seemed to provide nothing in return was met with outrage; indeed, Lao historians still have nothing good at all to say about colonization.

The period of colonization spawned and was succeeded by the spread of Communism throughout the region, and the armed struggle against the colonialists led to the intervention of other Western powers, notably the United States in its war against Vietnam and its unofficial offensives against Laos and Cambodia. Subsequently, Laos received per capita the heaviest aerial bombardment ever recorded. Ultimately, victory was achieved by the Pathet Lao, considerably supported by the Vietnamese. The Pathet Lao immediately instituted a series of revolutionary social and economic policies, including collectivization of agriculture and the abolition of many traditional practices and the much-revered lifestyle of monks. (Soon after coming to power, however, the Pathet Lao realized the necessity of embracing Buddhism, which it did.)

Contrary to the tenets of Marx, the party sought the institution of a socialist state without what had been considered to be the necessary intermediary step of capitalist development. The resources available to the Pathet Lao administration, therefore, were inadequate to rapid modernization. Given the numerous constraints and the war-weariness of the country, it is not surprising that the measures instituted were extremely difficult to enact and in some cases deeply resented. Political opposition was a part but not the whole of this. The agricultural system of rice farming, for example, is not amenable to the type of collectivized agriculture developed with a view to the very different conditions of the steppes of the Ukraine, while the demands for administrative and managerial competence necessarily enforced upon the population were far more than they could generally accommodate. Aid from the Soviet bloc, meanwhile, was much lower than had been arriving from the Western world. Regulations on economic freedom and personal mobility persuaded many within the Chinese and Vietnamese communities within Vientiane and elsewhere to return to their homelands, taking as much capital with them as possible.

The period until 1986, when the New Economic Mechanism was announced and introduced, was therefore characterized by the inability of the government to enforce its developmental aims and subsequent disillusionment of the population. Difficulties were exacerbated by the Chinese-Vietnamese war of 1979, which forced Laos to take sides against one of its key allies and led to isolation from China.

Vietnam's *doi moi* (Renovation) economic plan (1986) and China's increasing economic liberalization under Deng Xiaoping helped to inspire a similar movement in Laos. This was formalized in the New Economic Mechanism of 1986, which aimed to provide a unique Lao solution to the problems of market development by combining a measure of economic freedom with a closed political system. This has led to improved ties with the outside world, most notably with Thailand, from which most external stimulus to growth has derived and is likely to continue to derive. Subsequently, such economic gains as have been achieved have outstripped even more the ability of the administration to deliver them equitably, and so income disparities and gender inequalities have been rising.

## Economic Systems of Laos

The diversity and division within Laos have led to the development of a variety of more or less closed economic systems within and across its borders. These range from rice agriculture and some cash cropping in lowland regions, swidden (slash-and-burn) agriculture in the highlands, and some manufacturing and service activities for the small urban class. One important system that links Laos with its neighbors is border trading, which consists of numerous informal and occasionally illicit trading arrangements organized by small-scale traders particularly on the borders with southeastern China and eastern Thailand.

For those activities over which the government is able to exercise some authority, activities are regulated in accordance with specific policy goals. The further away from the center that activities take place, the less likely they are to receive government support or for the activities to support government policy. An important developmental goal for the Lao government will be to integrate the activities of the periphery into a national economic system or systems that can provide a more equitable distribution of income and opportunities than presently exists or that is customarily provided by a market-driven system.

## Constraints to Development

It is clear that the various economic systems pursued in Laos today are both inadequate to fulfill political national objectives and to compete internationally in a globalizing world. While there is plenty of advice from international bodies on how to liberalize trade, invite inward investment, and change (or "reform") government practices, there are difficulties attempting these initiatives. Difficulties include:

1. The small size and density of the population, together with the low levels of wealth, which means that there is little prospect for developing an indigenous manufacturing industry or for creating a domestic market with sufficient demand to attract foreign investment.
2. The paucity of the country's infrastructure—measured both in terms of lack of transportation links, social-welfare provision, and the ability of government to enact and enforce its policies, together with the underdeveloped nature of the human capital (that is, the low levels of education and training)—makes both the extraction of natural resources and the distribution and marketing of goods more demanding and expensive.
3. The lack of a modern business environment, including a firmly established legal framework and the presence of essential supply-chain components (for example, office supplies, market research, and advertising services, as well as skilled labor and manufacturing supplies) adds risk and delay to all business processes.

The most likely method of overcoming the problems is some form of integration with Laos's neighbors. This means setting up systems that will allow Laos to take advantage of the complementary advantages available in the region (for example, entrepreneurial competence and capital from Thailand and organized labor pools from Vietnam and China) in return to access to the resources within Laos.

## Future Prospects

Future economic prospects depend to a considerable extent upon whether the states can deal with external forces and create mutually beneficial partnerships and alliances. In a market-led economy featuring openness to the world economic system, the Lao government's relationship with significant trading partners such as Thailand and China will be of considerably more importance than the relationship with the politically important partner, Vietnam. Indeed, there is likely to be friction with Vietnam as competitiveness succeeds cooperation in relations between the two states. Laos will also need to manage its relationships with global players such as the International Monetary Fund and the World Bank. Over-precipitous opening of the economy will not benefit the Lao people, since very few will be able to secure the fruits of economic opportunities in a competitive environment. The government must continue to try to draw the country together and seek to develop its human capital while identifying and strengthening industries that might provide sustainable comparative advantage. The Seventh Congress of the Lao People's Revolutionary Party, which took place in March 2001, reiterated commitments to creating a market economy in Laos while giving few if any concessions to political liberalization. However, the acknowledgment of difficulties with the economic planning process and of critical lack of resources gives some support to the belief that a greater cooperative effort will be possible in the future. Identifying which officials seem set to occupy leading positions within the party remains of considerable importance since there remains little in the way of transparency or openness in political circles. While personalities continue to rank in importance with policies, prospects for the future remain needlessly clouded.

*John Walsh*

### Further Reading


Asian Development Bank. (1998) *Country Assistance Plan (CAP): Lao PDR, 1999–2001.*

Jemdal, Randi, and Jonathan Rigg. (1999) "From Buffer State to Crossroads State: Spaces of Human Activity and Integration in the Lao PDR." In *Laos: Culture and Society*, edited by Grant Evans. Chiang Mai, Thailand: Silkworm Books, 35–60.

"Lao Chief Lists Country's Failures." (2001) *The Nation* (13 March).

Stuart-Fox, Martin. (1998) *The Kingdom of Lan Xang: Rise and Decline.* Bangkok, Thailand: White Lotus.

Thalemann, Andrea. (1997) "Laos: between Battlefield and Marketplace." *Journal of Contemporary Asia.* 27, 1: 85–105.

Walker, David. (1999) "Women, Space and History: Long Distance Trading in Northwestern Laos." In *Laos: Culture and Society*, edited by Grant Evans. Chiang Mai, Thailand: Silkworm Press, 79–99.


## LAOS—EDUCATION SYSTEM

**LAOS—EDUCATION SYSTEM** The Lao educational system has a long history, extending from early, traditional temple education to contemporary education in the transitional economy of the Lao People's Democratic Republic. The current regime faces complex challenges in improving education in the context of the country's increased global connections and amid economic problems exacerbated by the Asian economic crisis of 1997.

### Historical and Political Background

A major motif of Lao history is the country's remarkable survival as a distinct political and cultural entity despite small population and being landlocked and surrounded by large, powerful neighbors such as China, Vietnam, Thailand, and Myanmar. The original Lao kingdom that flourished between the fourteenth and eighteenth centuries was known as Lan Xang (land of a million elephants). Seriously weakened in the early eighteenth century when it broke into three smaller kingdoms, Lan Xang fell into the Siamese orbit and then under French colonialism.

### Traditional Temple Education

As in neighboring countries such as Thailand and Cambodia, Buddhist priests traditionally provided basic education, moral training, and the fundamentals of a literary culture to children in village temples. But given the limited roles of women in the Buddhist priesthood, this system did discriminate against women. Because education at temple schools provided preparation for becoming a monk, it was limited to males because females could not become monks. Women's education was informal in the family context for rural women or in royal compounds for elite women.

### French Colonial Influence on Lao Education (1893–1975)

After Laos became a French colony in 1893, the traditional Buddhist educational system became less important as the French introduced elitist, secular French-language education oriented to the "civilizing" mission of the colonial power. In 1946, only a miniscule 2 percent of Lao school-age children were enrolled in school. The reason for the low enrollment was French unwillingness to support education in the countryside. Even after Laos gained nominal independence in 1949, the elitist, French-language educational system continued to dominate until genuine independence was finally achieved in 1975. U.S. influence during the 1954–1975 period led to considerable expansion of Lao education with the establishment of high schools, vocational schools, and teacher training institutions. Enrollments in 1971–1972 were seventeen times higher than in 1946.

## EDUCATION AND NATIONALISM IN LAOS

Phoumi Vongvichit, a leading Laotian intellectual, reflects on education and nationalism in Laos.

> The leading idea in my research and writing of this book *Lao Grammar* is for the grammar of Lao to belong to the nation, and to the people, and for it to be progressive, modern, and scientific. . . . Every principle, and every term used herein is intended to be simple, so that the general populace, of high or low education, may easily understand and utilize the principles and various terms in the easiest possible way.
>
> Every country in the world has its own principles of speech and writing, its own linguistic principles which may demonstrate the style and honor of the nation, and demonstrate the cultural independence of the nation, along with independence in political, economic, and other arenas.

*Source:* Phoumi Vongvichit quoted in "Lao as a National Language" by N. J. Enfield. (1999) In *Laos: Culture and Society*, edited by Grant Evans. Chiang Mai, Thailand: Silkworm Books, 269–270.

**Educational Reforms of the Lao PDR (1975 to Present)**

The Lao People's Democratic Republic (Lao PDR), established 2 December 1975, initiated three major reforms. The first was to consolidate independence and replace French schooling with a Lao-language, mass-education system. Reflecting this commitment, 1996–1997 primary school enrollments were over three times higher than in 1971–1972. Expansion was hampered, however, by a lack of qualified teachers and poor infrastructure.

The second major reform occurred in 1986 when the Lao PDR adopted a new economic policy (the New Economic Mechanism, or NEM) calling for increased use of market mechanisms in the economy and decreased state and central planning. This meant that education had to be rationalized to serve the needs of an increasingly privatized economy. This reform also permitted privatization within the education system in order to expand opportunity and reduce the financial burden on the government.

The third major reform began in 1991 and continued throughout the 1990s. In the initial stages of socialism, responsibility for education had become highly decentralized, resulting in growing regional disparities. In 1991 education began to be recentralized, with greater authority resting with the Ministry of Education.

With the opening of the Lao economy following the collapse of the Soviet Union in 1991, the Lao government actively sought international educational assistance from agencies such as the World Bank, the Asian Development Bank (ADB), and bilateral donors such as the Nordic countries and Switzerland. The country has used such external funds for enhancing physical infrastructure, developing textbooks, and providing training of educational administrators, teacher educators, and teachers for Lao nationals. Partly thanks to external assistance, Lao expenditures on education in 1996–1997 represented 2.9 percent of GDP, a figure higher than that of China, the Philippines, and Indonesia. In 1996–1997, 15.8 percent of the national budget went to education, putting Laos ahead of countries such as Malaysia, India, and Indonesia, and nearly equal to Korea.

Lao primary education currently lasts five years, followed by three years of lower secondary, three years of upper secondary, and then three to seven years of tertiary education, depending on the field. In 1995, the National University of Laos (NUOL) was established by consolidating four existing tertiary institutions.

### Major Contemporary Problems Facing Lao Education

Despite the major reforms initiated during the twenty-five years of socialism, major educational problems persist. Relatively few Lao young people complete the various levels of education. For the 1996–1997 school year, 20 percent received no education at all, while only 13.9 percent completed primary education, 8.6 percent lower secondary, 4.8 percent upper secondary, and 4 percent tertiary education.

Given the country's sparsely populated remote areas and many ethnic minorities, access to education is problematic, and significant regional disparities exist. The 1995 national census indicates that 47.5 percent of the population were of diverse ethnic minorities. As a result, roughly half of those entering grade one are taught in a language that is not their native tongue.

There are also serious gender issues in Lao education, exacerbated by high fertility levels in Laos and heavy household burdens for women and female children. The government's establishment of a special Gender and Ethnic Minorities Education Unit within the Ministry of Education reflects its concern about such access issues.

Girls practice dancing at a school in Vientiane, Laos. (NIK WHEELER/CORBIS)

Though the Lao PDR devotes considerable funds deriving from international assistance to education, recurrent funding of education is low compared to other countries in the region. It is thus often difficult to sustain educational projects initiated with external assistance.

Since 1998 the Lao government has faced a severe economic crisis. Major inflation and a significant devaluation of the Lao kip (the nation's currency) have adversely affected the economy and the government's ability to finance improvements in education. Despite these serious problems mainly related to formal schooling, the Lao PDR excels in areas such as fostering strong moral education, quality parenting, social cohesion, and a sense of national identity. As well, the adverse effects of media are carefully controlled and restricted.

*Gerald Fry*

### Further Reading


Asian Development Bank. (1993) *Lao People's Democratic Republic*. Education in Asia and Pacific Series, no. 1. Manila, Philippines: Asian Development Bank.

———. (2000) *Lao People's Democratic Republic: Education Sector Development Plan Report*. Manila, Philippines: Asian Development Bank.

Bounyavong, Outhine. (1999) *Mother's Beloved: Stories from Laos*. Seattle, WA: University of Washington Press.

Chazée, Laurent. (1999) *The Peoples of Laos: Rural and Ethnic Diversities*. Bangkok, Thailand: White Lotus.

Enfield, N. J. (1999) "Lao as a National Language." In *Laos: Culture and Society*, edited by Grant Evans. Chiang Mai, Thailand: Silkworm Books, 258–290.

Ngosyvathn, Mayoury. (1995) *Lao Women: Yesterday and Today*. Vientiane, Laos: Ministry of Culture.

Stuart-Fox, Martin. (1997) *A History of Laos*. Cambridge, U.K.: Cambridge University Press.

World Bank. (1995) *Lao PDR: Social Development Assessment and Strategy*. Washington, DC: World Bank.


**LAOS—HISTORY** The modern boundaries of Laos date only from 1907, and include only a fraction of the people who have historically called themselves Lao. Throughout its history, the classical Lao kingdom of Lan Xang (fourteenth–eighteenth centuries) and its successor kingdoms covered territory that now falls within northeastern Thailand. Any history of Laos cannot avoid, therefore, including territory and people that no longer fall under the jurisdiction of modern Laos.

## KEY EVENTS IN LAOS HISTORY

**500 BCE** The culture of the Plain of Jars flourishes.
**c. 500 CE** Small Indian-influenced kingdoms emerge.
**14th–18th centuries** Period of the Lan Xang Kingdom.
**18th century** Lan Xang splits into three antagonistic kingdoms, which fall under Siamese domination.
**1893** France forces Siam to cede all Lao territories east of the Mekong.
**1907** A treaty between France and Siam establishes the present frontiers of Laos.
**1945** The Japanese displace the French, and Laos declares its independence.
**1946–1954** Period of the First Indochinese War.
**1946** France regains power, the Laos government is forced into exile, and the Kingdom of Laos is established.
**1949** Laos is granted limited independence.
**1950** Nationalists declare the government of the Pathet Lao.
**1953** Laos becomes an independent nation.
**1957–1958** Laos moves toward reunification with reintegration of the two Communist provinces.
**1959–1960** A series of coups destroys the coalition government and civil war begins.
**1963–1973** During the Vietnam War, Laos remains a divided nation and the government is under U.S. control.
**1975** The Lao People's Democratic Republic is formed.
**1977** Laos signs a 25-year Treaty of Friendship and Cooperation with Vietnam.
**1980s** Political and economic reforms encourage capitalism and open elections.
**1994** The first bridge across the Mekong River is opened near Vientiane.
**1997** Laos joins ASEAN.
**1997–1998** The economy is damaged by the Asian economic crisis.

In modern Laos, lowland or ethnic Lao comprise not much more than half the population. The remainder is made up of people speaking other Tai dialects, Austroasiatic languages, Hmong-Mien, and Tibeto-Burman languages. The history of Laos, therefore, is also a history of these ethnic groups, the last two of which only began entering Laos from southern China early in the nineteenth century.

Human occupation of Laos goes back to the Stone Age. Bronze and Iron Age cultures developed both in northeast Thailand and on the Plain of Jars. The culture of the Plain of Jars flourished around 500 BCE and was characterized by massive carved stone mortuary urns, the "jars" after which the plateau is named. We know little about these people, but it is likely that they were ancestors of the Khamu, the largest Austroasiatic-speaking group in northern Laos.

### The Lao Kingdom of Lan Xang Hom Khao

By the middle of the first millennium CE, small Indianized kingdoms were being established in the middle Mekong basin. Over the next few centuries, Tai-speaking peoples began spreading into northern Laos, forcefully founding their own principalities *(meuang)*. In the early thirteenth century the kingdoms of the middle Mekong were absorbed into the expanding Khmer empire. Within a century, however, as Khmer power declined, larger Tai kingdoms were established. Among these was the Lao kingdom of Lan Xang Hom Khao (A Million Elephants and the White Parasol), a title signifying both military might and royal kingship.

For two centuries, Luang Prabang was the capital of the Lao kingdom. During this time, Theravada Buddhism became established as the dominant religion; it legitimized kingly rule in return for royal patronage. As Lao settlers continued migrating south, the center of population shifted. In the face of Burmese invasions in the mid-sixteenth century, King Xettathirat (1533–1571) moved the Lao capital to Viang Chan (Vientiane).

The seventeenth century marked the apogee of Lao power. The first European merchants and missionaries to reach the Lao capital left glowing reports of the wealth and pomp of the court of King Surinyavongsa (1615–1694). Already, however, the balance of power was shifting in mainland Southeast Asia to the maritime kingdoms that could benefit from increasing trade with China and the West. In the early eighteenth century, Lan Xang split into three antagonistic kingdoms, each of which soon fell under Siamese domination.

### French Occupation and World War II

In 1827, King Anuvong (1767–1828), the last ruler of Vientiane, made a desperate attempt to free his kingdom from Siamese suzerainty. Bangkok's response was swift. The Lao were defeated and their capital was sacked. French explorers who reached the Lao territories in the 1860s found a beautiful but impoverished land. It was the situation of these territories astride the Mekong that attracted the French, for they hoped the river would provide navigable access to China. That hope proved ill-founded, but the French were determined to expand their Indochina empire.

In 1893 France forced Siam to cede all Lao territories east of the Mekong. A subsequent treaty in 1907 established the present frontiers of the Lao state. As their new possession provided little economic benefit, the French allowed Laos to remain a sleepy backwater. Some ethnic minorities fought the imposition of French rule, but among the lowland Lao, nationalist feelings were slow to develop.

Laos was woken from its slumber by World War II. Siam, renamed Thailand in 1939, took advantage of French weakness to seize Lao territories west of the Mekong. In response to the pan-Thaiism emanating from Bangkok, the French deliberately encouraged Lao nationalism. When in April 1945 the Japanese overthrew the French administration, the king of Luang Prabang (1885–1959) was forced to declare the independence of Laos.

Six months later Japan surrendered. The king promptly abrogated his declaration of independence, but nationalists of the Lao Issara (Free Lao) quickly took advantage of the power vacuum to establish an independent government under the leadership of Prince Phetxarat (1890–1959). This lasted only six months before the French forcibly reoccupied Laos, forcing the Lao Issara to seek exile in Thailand. From there they waged a diplomatic and guerrilla campaign against continued French control of their homeland.

## Impact of the Indochinese Wars

With the outbreak of war in Vietnam in 1946, the French recognized that some concessions to Lao aspirations were inevitable. The country was unified as the Kingdom of Laos, with the king of Luang Prabang as head of state. A constitution was drawn up, with Laos designated a member state within the French Union. Greater though still limited independence granted in 1949 was enough to convince the moderate wing of the Lao Issara led by Prince Souvanna Phouma (1901–1984) to accept an amnesty and return home to take part in the political process.

The radical wing refused an amnesty and instead joined forces with the Viet Minh, the Communist-dominated revolutionary movement fighting the French in Vietnam. In August 1950, close to the Lao-Vietnamese frontier, the radical nationalists, under the leadership of Souvanna Phouma's half brother, Prince Souphanouvong (1909–1995), proclaimed their own government of Pathet Lao (Land of the Lao), the name by which the Lao revolutionary movement was known thereafter.

For the next four years, Laos was caught up in the First Indochinese War. At first it was relatively sheltered, as the Pathet Lao were militarily weak. In April 1953, however, Viet Minh forces struck deep into Laos, threatening the royal capital of Luang Prabang. The king refused to leave the city, and the Viet Minh eventually withdrew. As they left, they handed over large areas of northeastern Laos to the Pathet Lao. It was to prevent a second such invasion that the French established a base at Dien Bien Phu, in Vietnam. And it was the fall of Dien Bien Phu in May 1954 that ended the First Indochinese War.

In the meantime, however, France had granted full Lao independence in October 1953. Two years later, in December 1955, the Kingdom of Laos was granted full membership of the United Nations. Under the terms of the Geneva Agreements that formally concluded the First Indochinese War, the Pathet Lao were assigned two provinces in northeastern Laos as regroupment areas for their forces. These were to be reintegrated into the Kingdom through fair and free elections to be held within two years.

The process of reintegration did not, however, proceed easily. Negotiations continued throughout 1955, without success. In December, elections were held in all but the two provinces under Pathet Lao control, and Souvanna Phouma formed a new government. Immediately he entered into new negotiations with Souphanouvong with a view to accepting the Lao Patriotic Front as a legitimate political party that could take part in a coalition government of national unity. In doing so, however, he encountered concerted opposition from the United States.

By early 1956 the United States had replaced France as the dominant Western power in Cambodia, Laos, and South Vietnam, countries that it was determined to save from Communism. In the context of the Cold War, any government including Communists was anathema to Washington, and over the next two years the U.S. embassy in Vientiane did all in its power to torpedo Souvanna Phouma's negotiations with Souphanouvong. Souvanna pushed resolutely on, however, and on 19 November 1957, the Lao National Assembly unanimously endorsed formation of a government of national union in which the Pathet Lao were given two ministries in a cabinet of fourteen. Supplementary elections the following May gave them representation in parliament, much to American alarm.

The immediate American response was to throw its weight behind both the political right and the Royal Lao Army (RLA). In July 1958, American aid was withheld from the coalition government. Souvanna was forced to resign, to be replaced by a more conservative leader. Negotiations to integrate two Pathet Lao battalions into the RLA meanwhile collapsed, allowing Pathet Lao troops to return to the Lao-Vietnam border area, where they could again be supplied by the North Vietnamese.

In December 1959 military strongman General Phoumi Nosavan (1920–1985) mounted a coup d'état. A military-dominated government took power and Pathet Lao members of the National Assembly were imprisoned. New elections were held, blatantly rigged to ensure that no leftist candidates were elected, even from areas under Pathet Lao control. All pretense of coalition between conservatives and Communists was at an end, and fighting recommenced.

The descent into civil war horrified many Lao. On 9 August 1960, Captain Kong Lae (b. 1934), commander of an elite paratroop battalion, staged a coup in the name of national reconciliation and neutrality. Souvanna Phouma was again named prime minister. The United States, however, threw its weight behind General Phoumi, who assembled his forces and, in the Battle of Vientiane, seized the capital. The neutralists withdrew to the Plain of Jars, where they joined forces with the Pathet Lao. The country was again divided, with two governments: one in Vientiane recognized by the West, and one on the Plain of Jars recognized by the Communist bloc.

This was the situation faced by the new administration of U.S. President John F. Kennedy in 1961. Laos, rather than Vietnam, had become the Cold War flash point in Asia. Kennedy decided to seek a political resolution of the crisis. A new international conference was convened in Geneva, which in July 1962 agreed on the neutrality of Laos and formation of a second coalition government, again with Souvanna Phouma as prime minister. But already it was too late. Political polarization had gone too far, and Laos could not avoid being dragged into the war the United States was fighting in Vietnam. Within a year the coalition had collapsed, and Lao neutrality was but a mask behind which North Vietnam and the United States fought a clandestine war in Laos.

This war was fought in two theaters. In northern Laos, particularly in the region of the Plain of Jars, Pathet Lao forces, massively reinforced by Vietnamese "volunteers," were opposed by a secret army, trained and equipped by the U.S. Central Intelligence Agency. This secret army was recruited mainly from among the Hmong and other ethnic minorities and was commanded by the Hmong general Vang Pao. The second theater was the Ho Chi Minh Trail, the network of jungle tracks through southeastern Laos along which North Vietnamese troops infiltrated south to join the fighting in South Vietnam. In both areas the United States conducted a secret bombing campaign, which, by the time the war ended with the cease-fire of February 1973, left Laos the most heavily bombed country, per capita, in the history of warfare.

During the decade from 1963 to 1973, the United States ensured that Souvanna Phouma remained prime minister, while Souvanna turned a blind eye to violations of Lao neutrality. During this period, the U.S. Agency for International Development constituted what amounted to a parallel administration in Laos, while massive amounts of military and economic aid kept the country afloat. While it spared the towns along the Mekong River, the war had a devastating impact. Tens of thousands died, with casualties among the Hmong particularly high.

### The Lao People's Democratic Republic

Yearlong negotiations led in 1974 to formation of a third coalition government, this time with half the ministries held by the Pathet Lao, to reflect their greater military and political strength. Like earlier coalitions, however, it lasted barely a year. Communist seizures of power in Cambodia and South Vietnam in April 1975 opened the way for the Pathet Lao to dispense with the pretense of coalition government in Laos. On 2 December 1975, the six-century-old Lao monarchy was swept aside to make way for the Lao People's Democratic Republic, but only after thousands of Royal Lao civil servants and military officers had been incarcerated in reeducation camps. Souphanuvong was named president of the new republic, but real power lay in the hands of Kaysone Phomvihan (1920–1992), secretary-general of the Lao People's Revolutionary Party (LPRP), which had secretly been the guiding force behind the Pathet Lao throughout what they called their "thirty-year struggle" for power since 1945. Kaysone was half Vietnamese and enjoyed close relations with the Vietnamese Communist leadership. In 1977 Laos signed a twenty-five-year Treaty of Friendship and Cooperation with Vietnam. Relations were also close with the Soviet Union.

At first the new government instituted a hard-line policy along strict Communist lines. Economic controls were placed on the production and distribution of goods, and the government nationalized what little industry there was. Personal freedoms were curtailed and limitations placed on the practice of religion. The previous constitution and legal framework were abolished and replaced by the arbitrary rule of the LPRP and people's courts. As the bubble economy that had been maintained by American aid collapsed, and more and more people were sent off for reeducation, thousands of Lao fled across the Mekong into Thailand. Eventually some 300,000 people (10 percent of the population) fled, including many Hmong and most of the country's educated class.

Centralization of power in the upper echelon of the Lao People's Revolutionary Party and a desperate lack of qualified personnel made it difficult to administer the country efficiently. Drought and the decision to cooperatize agriculture only exacerbated the situation. Then in January 1979 Vietnamese forces occupied Cambodia, overthrowing the Khmer Rouge regime of Pol Pot, China reacted by attacking Vietnam, and Laos found itself once again embroiled in the animosities of its neighbors. Laos sided with Vietnam, making a new enemy of China and bringing an end to China's much-needed economic assistance.

In the face a deteriorating security situation (anti-Communist Lao insurgents were operating out of Thailand and China), the Party was forced to rethink its economic policies. The agricultural cooperatization program was terminated, and the government admitted that, given the stage of Lao economic development, there was after all a place for private enterprise and initiative. Social controls were loosened, and even Party members began attending Buddhist festivals. As the economy improved and the international situation became less threatening, the Party felt secure enough to hold its Third Congress, its first since coming to power.

Reforms in both the structure of the Party and the government, including a crackdown on corruption, were followed by the decision further to reform the economy—but only after furious debate within the Party. Under what became known as the New Economic Mechanism *(chintanakan mai)*, capitalist foreign investment was welcomed. Meanwhile relations were mended with Thailand and China. As the economy began moving inexorably toward a free market system, the first elections were held for the Supreme People's Assembly in March 1989. Two years later a constitution was finally promulgated and elections held for the new National Assembly in December 1992.

By this time Communism had collapsed in Eastern Europe and the Soviet Union, and Laos could only look to Vietnam and China for political support. For desperately needed foreign aid to meet chronic deficits in both the budget and balance of payments, however, Vientiane turned to international lending institutions and Western aid donors. In the 1990s the country enthusiastically embraced regional integration. In April 1994 a first bridge across the Mekong was opened near Vientiane, road construction was stepped up, and Laos embarked on an ambitious program of hydroelectric dam construction.

All this was cut short by the Asian economic crisis of 1997–1998. Investment dried up and the Lao currency collapsed. This did not stop Laos from joining the Association of Southeast Asian Nations in July 1997, but it did lead to a slowdown of economic reform, as the more conservative military took control of the Party (following the death of Kaysone, and his replacement by General Khamtai Siphandone as Party and state president). Laos thus entered the new millennium with some trepidation, in desperate need of both economic and political reform, neither of which seemed likely.

*Martin Stuart-Fox*

*See also:* **Laos—Political System; Pathet Lao; Souphanuvong; Souvanna Phouma**

### Further Reading

Brown, MacAlister, and Joseph J. Zasloff. (1986) *Apprentice Revolutionaries: The Communist Movement in Laos, 1930–1985*. Stanford, CA: Hoover Institution.

Evans, Grant. (1998) *The Politics of Ritual and Remembrance: Laos since 1975*. Chiang Mai, Thailand: Silkworm Press.

Evans, Grant, ed. (1999) *Laos: Culture and Society*. Chiang Mai, Thailand: Silkworm Press.

Ngaosyvathn, Mayoury, and Pheuiphanh Ngaosyvathn. (1998) *Paths to Conflagration: Fifty Years of Diplomacy and Warfare in Laos, Thailand, and Vietnam, 1778–1828*. Ithaca, NY: Southeast Asia Program Publications, Cornell University.

Stuart-Fox, Martin. (1996) *Buddhist Kingdom, Marxist State: The Making of Modern Laos*. Bangkok, Thailand: White Lotus Press.

———. (1997) *A History of Laos*. Cambridge, U.K.: Cambridge University Press.

———. (1998) *The Lao Kingdom of Lan Xang: Rise and Decline*. Bangkok, Thailand: White Lotus Press.

———. (2000) *Historical Dictionary of Laos*. 2d ed. Lanham, MD: Scarecrow Press.

**LAOS—POLITICAL SYSTEM** The major motif of Laos's political history has been the struggle

## THE FOUNDING OF THE LAO PEOPLE'S DEMOCRATIC REPUBLIC

Below is the statement from the Declaration of the National Congress of People's Representatives of 2 December 1975, the day of founding of the Lao People's Democratic Republic:

> This victory signifies a fundamental change in the destiny of our nation and society, opening a new era of rapid and vigorous progress of our motherhood on the road of independence, unity and prosperity, and ensuring the well-being, freedom and happiness of all the ethnic groups for all time.

*Source:* Kaysone Phomvihane. (1981) *Revolution in Laos.* Moscow: Progress Publishers, 9.

for unity and political independence. Laos as a political identity dates back to 1353, when King Tiao Fa Ngum, a national hero, unified the country and formed the kingdom of Lan Xang (the land of a million elephants). This kingdom was a conservative, traditional monarchy for centuries, until 2 December 1975, when, after a successful revolutionary struggle, the country was transformed into the Lao People's Democratic Republic.

### Pre-Colonial Laos

The major challenges facing ancient Laos were threats from its neighbors, particularly the Siamese and the Burmese. Lan Xang achieved its greatest glory under the reign of King Surinyavongsa (reigned 1683–1695). At this time, Laos controlled more territory than at any other time in its history, including what is now northern and northeastern Thailand. Following Surinyavongsa's rule, succession disputes resulted in Lan Xang's breaking up into three separate kingdoms (1707–1713). The subsequent weakness caused Laos to fall into the Siamese orbit within a century (1779).

***The French Colonial Period, 1893–1949*** Through actual armed confrontation between the French and the Siamese in 1893, the French gained complete control of Siamese Laos. Thus, "French Laos" became a reality in 1893 and, importantly, led to the reunification of the country.

Auguste Pavie served as France's first commissioner-general for Laos, and he was determined to "make of Laos a French country" (Stuart-Fox 1997: 23). Examples of the attempt to do this included the education of elite Lao in the French language and the mandating of French as the language of instruction in schools. French treatment of Laos could be termed adverse neglect. Both a head tax and corvée labor caused resentment among the Lao. Not surprisingly, numerous rebellions against the French ensued, resulting in the eventual formation of the Lao Issara (Lao independence) movement.

### "Independence," the Neocolonial Period, and Revolutionary Struggle, 1949–1975

At the end of World War II, the French returned to the region to resume their control of Laos. On 19 July 1949, Laos became "independent" under the French Union, with French influence continuing until 1975. As the result of the Geneva Agreements, Laos in reality became a torn country, with the Pathet Lao (a Communist revolutionary movement) taking control of so-called liberated areas in the northeast of the country. Thus, Laos was drawn into the vortex of the Cold War, and civil war continued until 1975.

### The Current Political System of the Lao People's Democratic Republic

The major pillars of the ideology of the victorious socialist regime were peace, independence, democracy, welfare, and unity. These are not simply slogans but fundamentally reflect the political culture of modern Laos under the leadership of the Lao People's Revolutionary Party (LPRP). After assuming power, the Party even introduced a policy to reform the Lao language, to make it both easier to learn and more egalitarian, eliminating many feudalistic aspects of the language. For example, many honorific titles and status identifiers were removed.

In 1986, the Lao also moved to implement economic reforms to allow for free-market mechanisms *(chintanagan mai).* After the collapse of the Soviet Union in 1991 and the loss of aid from the Eastern-bloc countries, the LPDR began to foster relations with the West, leading to considerable multilateral and bilateral assistance in the 1990s.

***Nature of the Lao Power Structure and System of Governance*** Interestingly, it was not until 1991 that a new constitution was introduced. The national symbol was at the same time changed from the hammer and sickle to the That Luang Buddhist temple, reflecting the regime's early realization that it would be pragmatic to embrace Buddhism, given the popularity of the religion among the masses.

Laos remains a one-party state but does have an elected National Assembly (formerly known as the Supreme People's Assembly). Basically, national policy is determined at Party Congresses (held every four to five years), and the National Assembly debates and discusses the laws necessary to implement those policies. The government ministries are then responsible for administering the laws. There is usually a balance in the power structure within each ministry between strategically placed Party people and technocrats, which provides a rather unusual system of checks and balances.

The Party Congress elects the Central Committee and the Politburo. The most powerful political body is the Politburo, still dominated by an older generation with revolutionary experience, but who generally have limited formal education. It has eight members, who are drawn from the Party's Central Committee, which is currently composed of forty-nine members. The members of the Politburo hold key positions in the power structure of the country. Six members of the current Politburo are generals. Their average age is approximately sixty-six.

To be elected to the National Assembly, it is not necessary to be a member of the Party. Numerous non-Party candidates are commonly elected. Elections for the National Assembly take place every five years, with the last one having been held in 1997. The National Assembly appoints the president, who in turn appoints the prime minister and cabinet.

Media (controlled by the state) discussions of politics are always dominated by the phrase *pak lae lat* (party and state). Interestingly, the word "Communist" is never used. Free expression in terms of opposition to the current one-party political system is simply not tolerated.

***Lao Political Leaders*** General Khamtai Siphandon (b. 1924), who has been LPRP chairman since 1992, has been president of the LPDR since 1998. General Sisavat Keobounphan, prime minister since 2001, cofounded the Lao People's Army with Khamtai. Laos's most revered political figure is the late Kaysone Phomvihane (1920–1992), a revolutionary hero who was the nation's major political leader (serving first as prime minister and then as president) until his death.

***Local Politics and Governance*** Local authorities have considerable independence in decision making, and the 1991 constitution "has left governors, mayors, and district and village chiefs free to 'administer their regions and localities without any assistance from popularly elected bodies'" (Brown and Zasloff 1995: 224). Both women and minorities have served as governors.

## Major Challenges Facing the Lao Polity and Party

Currently the LPRP faces some of its most serious challenges since coming to power. A major question currently being discussed internationally is how effective the Lao political system will be in dealing with the economic challenge stemming from the aftermath of the 1997 Asian economic crisis, which led the Lao currency to fall in value approximately ninefold by June 1999.

With its amalgam of socialist politics, capitalist market mechanisms, and Buddhism, Laos has a unique political system. The LPDR, with a highly favorable ratio of people to natural resources, also has the potential to become a Switzerland of Southeast Asia. To achieve such a goal, it must have inspiring political leadership. The future of the current political system depends fundamentally on the extent to which it remains faithful to its revolutionary ideals and demonstrates genuine commitment to and success in improving the welfare of the Lao people.

*Gerald Fry*

## Further Reading


Brown, MacAlister, and Joseph J. Zasloff. (1995) "Government and Politics." In *Laos: A Country Study*, edited by Andrea Matles Savada. 3d ed. Washington, DC: Federal Research Division, Library of Congress, 203–258.

Butler-Diaz, Jacqueline, ed. (1998) *New Laos, New Challenges*. Tempe, AZ: Program for Southeast Asian Studies Monograph Series, Arizona State University.

Cordell, Helen, comp. (1991) "Politics and Administration." In *Laos*. World Bibliographical Series, no. 133. Oxford, U.K.: Clio Press, 98–106.

Dommen, Arthur J. (1991) "Laos." In *Yearbook on International Communist Affairs*. Stanford, CA: Hoover Institution, 191–199.

Evans, Grant. (1990) *Lao Peasants under Socialism*. New Haven, CT: Yale University Press.

———. (1998). *The Politics of Ritual and Remembrance: Laos since 1975*. Honolulu, HI: University of Hawaii Press.

Kaysone Phomvihane. (1981) *Revolution in Laos: Practice and Prospects*. Moscow: Progress Publishers.

Maha Sila Viravong. (1964) *History of Laos*. New York: Paragon.

Ngaosyvathn, Mayoury, and Pheuiphanh Ngaosyvathn. (1994) *Kith and Kin Politics: The Relationship between Laos and Thailand.* Wollongong, Australia: Journal of Contemporary Asia Publishers.

Savada, Andrea Matles, ed. (1995) *Laos: A Country Study.* 3d ed. Washington, DC: Federal Research Division, Library of Congress.

Stuart-Fox, Martin. (1996) *Buddhist Kingdom, Marxist State.* Bangkok, Thailand: White Lotus.

———. (1997) *A History of Laos.* Cambridge, U.K.: Cambridge University Press.

Stuart-Fox, Martin, and Mary Kooyman. (1992) *Historical Dictionary of Laos.* Metuchen, NJ: Scarecrow Press.

Zasloff, Joseph J., and Leonard Unger, eds. (1991) *Laos: Beyond the Revolution.* New York: St. Martin's Press.

**LAOS-THAILAND RELATIONS** The lowland peoples of Laos and Thailand are both ethnically Thai and share important cultural traits such as cooperative, wet-rice cultivation and a belief in Theravada Buddhism. The Lao and Thai languages, while different in important ways, are mutually intelligible. Since Laos became communist in 1975, however, the languages have diverged significantly. Over time the Lao Isaan language of northeast Thailand has become Thai-ized, while Lao has become more egalitarian and simplified to facilitate enhanced literacy. Approximately one-third of Thailand's current population is ethnically Lao.

At the apogee of its power in the 1600s, the Lao Kingdom of Lan Xang (land of a million elephants) controlled much of present-day northeast and northern Thailand. In the early 1700s, succession conflicts caused Lan Xang to split into three independent kingdoms. Subsequent weakness led to Laos falling under the Siamese orbit in 1779. In both 1778 and 1828, Siamese armies sacked the Lao capital, Vientiane, and during the 1778 attack they captured the precious Emerald Buddha. Also many Lao were relocated to Siam to serve as corvée labor. In 1893, Siam began to lose its Lao territories to the French and Laos eventually became part of colonial French Indochina.

Laos achieved independence in 1951 but was subsequently drawn into the Cold War and conflict in Vietnam. Thailand and the United States actively supported the rightist faction in Laos, while the Soviet Union, North Vietnam, and China supported the revolutionary Pathet Lao. U.S. bombers, using Thai air bases, continually bombed Laos for eight years (1965–1973), making it the most bombed country in history. The United States also paid Thai mercenaries to fight against the leftist Pathet Lao. After prolonged civil war, the Lao People's Democratic Republic (Lao PDR) was founded on 2 December 1975.

Relations between the Lao PDR and Thailand were tense for the next fifteen years, reflecting their Cold

The Thai-Lao Friendship Bridge crosses the Mekong River near Nong Khai, Laos. (NIK WHEELER/CORBIS)

War alignments. In early 1988, there was a three-month border war between the two countries. With the Soviet collapse and the end of major Soviet economic support, Laos liberalized its policies toward Thailand and other noncommunist countries. In the 1990s Laos-Thailand relations improved greatly, and Thailand became Laos's major economic partner, source of external investment, and also supplier of tourists. As Thai influence in Laos increased, there was considerable concern about excessive Thai cultural and linguistic influence. In this regard the Lao-Thai relationship mirrors the Canada–United States relationship.

After the Asian economic crisis, ignited by the devaluation of the Thai baht on 2 July 1997, Thai investments in Laos dropped dramatically to only 4.8 percent of total international investment (1999), and Laos increasingly turned to its socialist neighbors, China and Vietnam, for economic and political support. Both Thailand and Laos have demonstrated skill in "bamboo diplomacy"—remarkable flexibility in adjusting to complex, changing, and threatening situations—a means of preserving their cultural identities and sovereignty.

*Gerald W. Fry*

### Further Reading

Ngaosyvathn, Mayouri, and Pheuiphanh Ngaosyvathn. (1994) *Kith and Kin Politics: The Relationship between Laos and Thailand.* Manila, Philippines, and Wollongong, Australia: Journal of Contemporary Asia Publishers.

———. (1998) *Paths to Conflagration: Fifty Years of Diplomacy and Warfare in Laos, Thailand, and Vietnam, 1778–1828.* Ithaca, NY: Southeast Asia Program Publications, Southeast Asia Program, Cornell University.

This Vietnam War liberation poster which hangs in a war museum in Laos symbolizes the strong relations between the two nations. (TIM PAGE/CORBIS)

## LAOS–VIETNAM RELATIONS

In 1479 a Vietnamese army invaded the Lao kingdom of Lan Xang and sacked its capital, Luang Prabang. Although Vietnam at times exercised political control over the Plain of Jars in the north, not until 1953 was Luang Prabang again threatened by a Vietnamese army. At that time the city was spared, and the Vietnamese had Lao allies in the form of the Pathet Lao, the Lao revolutionary movement.

Throughout the First (1946–1954) and Second (1954–1975) Indochina Wars, both the political and military wings of the Pathet Lao enjoyed close relations with their Vietnamese counterparts. Vietnamese Communists advised the fledgling secret Lao People's Party (later the Lao People's Revolutionary Party). Vietnamese "volunteers" trained, equipped, and fought alongside Lao People's Liberation Army forces. At the same time, right-wing elements within the royal Lao government and military developed friendly relations with the Republic of (South) Vietnam.

With the formation of the Lao People's Democratic Republic in December 1975, relations with the unified Socialist Republic of Vietnam became even closer. In July 1977 the two countries signed a twenty-five-year Treaty of Friendship and Cooperation, under the terms of which not only did Vietnam supply Laos with economic advice and assistance but also Vietnamese troops were stationed in Laos. In fact up to fifty thousand Vietnamese troops remained in Laos until 1989, when they were withdrawn at the same time that Vietnamese forces were withdrawn from Cambodia, as a precondition for improved relations between Hanoi and Beijing.

The strength of Lao-Vietnamese relations was demonstrated in 1979 when Laos sided with Vietnam against China in the aftermath of the Vietnamese invasion of Cambodia. This led to difficult relations with China, which did not improve for several years. Meanwhile relations with Vietnam continued to be multifaceted, covering everything from training of party cadres and advice on economic planning to media, communications, and provision of educational materials. As between communist states, relations operated on three levels: government to government, party to party, and military to military, and in the early 1980s Laos was little more than a client state of Vietnam. What led to the loosening of the Vietnamese embrace was the need to diversify sources of foreign aid and investment, and that meant improving relations with Thailand and the West.

Close relations between Laos and Vietnam continued into the 1990s, however, based on the twin foundations of common revolutionary experience as comrades-in-arms and commitment to a common ideology. This was particularly so after the collapse of the Soviet Union and the return of Cambodia to a multiparty political system. Though Laos opened up its economy to foreign, especially Thai, investment, political and military relations with Vietnam remained paramount. For Laos the relationship reinforced regime security; for Vietnam it kept alive old ambitions to dominate Indochina.

Following the Asian economic crisis of 1997–1998, Laos again turned for assistance and advice to Vietnam. Given the dominance of the military in the upper echelons of the Lao People's Revolutionary Party, relations are likely to remain close well into the new millennium.

*Martin Stuart-Fox*

### Further Reading

Brown, MacAlister, and Joseph J. Zasloff. (1986) *Apprentice Revolutionaries: The Communist Movement in Laos, 1930–1985*. Stanford, CA: Stanford University Press.

Ngaosyvathn, Mayoury, and Pheuiphanh Ngaosvyathn. (1998) *Paths of Conflagration: Fifty Years of Diplomacy and Warfare in Laos, Thailand, and Vietnam, 1778–1828*. Ithaca, NY: Cornell University Press.

Stuart-Fox, Martin. (1996) *Buddhist Kingdom, Marxist State: The Making of Modern Laos*. Bangkok, Thailand: White Lotus.

———. (2000) *Historical Dictionary of Laos*. 2d ed. Lanham, MD: Scarecrow Press.

———. (1997) *A History of Laos*. Cambridge, U.K.: Cambridge University Press.

**LAO-TAI LANGUAGE** Lao is the official language of the Lao People's Democratic Republic. Lao is spoken by the political majority, the Lao Loum or Lowland Lao, and by other ethnic groups as a second language. The Lao Loum are composed of the Tai Lao, primarily occupying river valleys, and upland Tai groups, together making up 68 percent of the 5.4 million inhabitants of Laos (1999). Other Tai groups in Laos include the Tai Lue, Tai Daeng, Tai Dam, Phu Thai, and Saek.

Lao is a monosyllabic, tonal language, and its structure is based on the initial consonant, vowel nucleus, optional final consonant, and tone. Lao has six tones: low, mid, rising, high, low falling, and high falling. Polysyllabic words found in Lao have been borrowed from Pali, Sanskrit, and French. Lao has also borrowed from Vietnamese, especially since 1975.

There are many regional dialects of Lao, such as Luang Prabang dialect, Xieng Khouang dialect, and Vientiane dialect. These regional dialects vary in phonology, tones, and vocabulary. Vientiane dialect, the language spoken in the capital, may be considered the national standard, but its use is not enforced. Lao has its own written script originating from the Khmer script, consisting of thirty-three consonants and twenty-eight vowels.

The socialist regime has attempted to standardize the written language. Phoumi Vongvichit, a Pathet Lao revolutionary and a strong supporter of Lao identity and culture, wrote the book *Lao Grammar* in 1967 prior to the revolution and influenced the standardization of Lao grammar and spelling. His work also simplified the language to facilitate literacy efforts and eliminated feudalistic aspects of the language associated with Lao royalty to affirm the revolution's egalitarianism.

Lao is a member of the Southwestern Tai language group in the Tai-Kadai ethnolinguistic family. Tai languages range west from Assam province in India, with the written Ahom language, east to Hainan Island in China, inhabited by the Li. Tai speakers are found in northern Myanmar (Burma), Thailand, Laos, northern Vietnam, and southern China. Tai-speaking peoples began to inhabit Laos and other parts of Southeast Asia a thousand years ago after migrating from the area around southern China and northern Vietnam and established autonomous political entities two hundred years later.

The Lao government claims that the country's literacy rate (reading and writing at a fourth-grade level) is 85 percent. However, other agencies, including the World Bank and UNESCO, set the adult (age fifteen and over) illiteracy rate at about 44 percent, with the male adult (age fifteen and over) illiteracy rate 30 percent and the female adult illiteracy rate 50 percent. Ethnic minorities of the Lao Thoeng and Lao Soung ethnic categories experience lower literacy rates due to the lack of formal educational institutions in their villages and because they speak a different native language.

*Linda McIntosh*

### Further Reading


Enfield, N. J. (1999) "Lao as a National Language." In *Laos: Culture and Society*, edited by Grant Evans. Chiang Mai, Thailand: Silkworm Books, 259–313.

Hudak, Thomas John. (1997) *William Gedney's Tai Dialect Studies: Glossaries, Texts, and Translation.* Michigan Paper on South and Southeast Asia, no. 45. Ann Arbor, MI: Center for South and Southeast Asian Studies, University of Michigan.

Kerr, Allen D. (1972) *Lao-English Dictionary.* Bangkok, Thailand: White Lotus.

UNESCO. (1998) "UNESCO World Education Report, 1998: Teachers and Teaching in a Changing World." Retrieved 7 February 2002, from: http://www.litserver.literacy.upenn.edu/explorer/stats-basic.html.

World Bank. (2001) "World Bank Group." Retrieved 7 February 2002, from: http://www.worldbank.org/html/extdr/regions.html.


**LAO-TZU.** See **Laozi.**

**LAOZI** "Laozi" (c. sixth century BCE) is both the name of a philosopher and of the work attributed to him, which is also entitled *Daodejing* (in Wade-Giles, *Tao Te Ching*, meaning "The Way and Its Power"). Taoists (or Daoists) often celebrate anonymity. It may be the case that the author or authors of the *Daodejing* were able to preserve their anonymity. However, every text needs its author and every philosophical approach needs its founder, and so the name Laozi denotes the founding author of Taoism.

There is a good deal of controversy concerning whether there actually was a historical person named Laozi. When Laozi's biography was written in the *Records of the Historian (Shiji)*, the historical data concerning Laozi was already very obscure. The biography implies that Laozi may have been one of three people: Li Er, also called Li Dan; Lao Laizi; and Dan the Historian. Some ancient texts attribute sayings to a fellow known as Lao Dan that are passages found in the *Daodejing* or that reflect Taoist attitudes. Literally, "Laozi" means the "old master," and it could simply

## *DAODEJING*

Below is the opening chapter of Laozi's *Daodejing* ("The Way and the Power").

1. The Tao that can be trodden is not the enduring and unchanging Tao. The name that can be named is not the enduring and unchanging name.

2. (Conceived of as) having no name, it is the Originator of heaven and earth; (conceived of as) having a name, it is the Mother of all things.

3. Always without desire we must be found,
If its deep mystery we would sound;
But if desire within us be,
Its outer fringe is all that we shall see.

4. Under these two aspects, it is really the same, but as development takes place, it receives the different names. Together we call them the Mystery. Where the Mystery is the deepest is the gate of all that is subtle and wonderful.

*Source:* Lao Tze. (1891) *Tao Te Ching.* Translation and commentary by James Legge. Oxford: Oxford University Press, 1.

A classic drawing of Laozi riding a sacred cow. (BETTMANN/CORBIS)

be a general term for any and all old masters who taught the way of nature (*dao* in English is often seen as Tao). Because the character for "master" also means "boy," when the *Daodejing* was chanted as a sacred text in the Han dynasty (206 BCE–220 CE), a legend developed that Laozi was born at the mature age of sixty, gray haired and able to speak. For the follower of temple Taoism, Laozi, or Lord Lao, is considered to be the human incarnation of the cosmic Way.

There is an old legend that Confucius went to see Laozi, but he left baffled, not being able to comprehend him. This legend has been used both to argue that Laozi must have been a historical person and that there was no such person. After reading the *Daodejing*, one might realize that the academic debates concerning the historicity of Laozi are moot. The important things to be grasped are the profound ideas expressed in the text and their affect on the development of Chinese culture, politics, art, and poetry.

The *Laozi* has been translated more often than the Bible. The phrases "A thousand mile journey begins with the first step" and "he who knows does not speak" come from the *Laozi*. The *Laozi* is clearly giving guidance to a ruler and his high ministers. The text advocates a type of limited anarchy. The ruler is unknown to the masses; he does not personally undertake projects; he does not micromanage affairs. He does nothing, yet everything is completed. The *Laozi* describes the way of nature and suggests that people, especially the ruler, follow the model of nature, especially water. Water exhibits the power *(de)* of nature in that it returns *(fan)* to the source; it nourishes all things without discrimination or possessing them; it is soft, frictionless, and feminine, yet it wears down mountains. One of the most paradoxical concepts in the *Laozi* is "acting by not acting" *(wei wu wei)*. If the root images of the *Laozi* are grasped, then this expression is not as paradoxical as it first seems. "Not acting" is not literally doing nothing at all, but acting naturally. It is not acting artificially in a contrived manner, but acting without resistance in a spontaneous manner.

*James D. Sellmann*

**Further Reading**

Kaltenmark, Max. (1965) *Lao Tzu and Taoism*. Stanford, CA: Stanford University Press.

Lau, D. C. (1971) *Lao Tzu: Tao Te Ching*. Middlesex, U.K.: Penguin Books.

Mair, Victor H. (1990) *Tao Te Ching: The Classic Book of Integrity and the Way (Lao Tzu)*. New York: Bantam Doubleday Dell Publishing Group, Inc.

**LAXMIBAI** (d. 1858), Indian nationalist. Laxmibai—or the Rani (queen) of Jhansi, as she is also known—came to prominence in India after the British East India Company sought to consolidate its power in the mid-nineteenth century. Under the leadership of Lord Dalhousie, the company adopted a policy called the "doctrine of lapse," which allowed the British to annex an Indian state if the ruler did not have a male heir. This policy, in effect from 1848 to 1856, led to the British annexation of many Indian states. Resistance to the policy, and events surrounding the Great Mutiny of 1857, brought the Rani of Jhansi, the widow of the last ruler of the state of Jhansi, into the political spotlight. Jhansi "lapsed" to the British in 1853. In the period following this debacle, Jhansi was faced with political challenges from rival claimants to its throne, specifically the rulers of Orchha and Datia. This saga was unfolding as war continued to rage in northern and central India in late 1858. After being politically cornered, Laxmibai, together with Nana Sahib (the adopted son of Baji Rao II, the last Maratha ruler) and his artillery expert Tatia Tope, fought the British army until she was killed while fighting on horseback. Remembered as the "Joan of India," the Rani of Jhansi remains a major figure in the pantheon of Indian nationalist icons.

*Vivek Bhandari*

**Further Reading**

Bayly, Chris A. (1988) *Indian Society and the Making of the British Empire.* New York: Cambridge University Press.

Keay, John. (2000) *India: A History.* New York: Atlantic Monthly Press.

**LE DUAN** (1908–1986), Vietnamese politician and nationalist. Le Duan was born in Quang Tri province in Central Vietnam. In 1928 he joined the Revolutionary Youth League (Thanh Nien), and in 1930 he helped found the Indochinese Communist Party (ICP). Following the 1931 uprisings in northern Vietnam, he was arrested and convicted of sedition. He received a twenty-year prison sentence but was pardoned and released in 1936 after the Popular Front's victory in France.

Le Duan rose in the ranks of the ICP, but he was arrested again in 1940 and sent to Poulo Condore prison (Con Dao Island) until 1945. Following his release, he briefly worked with the Ho Chi Minh government in Hanoi. In 1946 he was sent to southern Vietnam, where he became secretary of the Central Office for South Vietnam (COSVN). While in southern Vietnam, Le Duan led the Viet Minh military in its efforts against the French.

Le Duan, on the right, with Pham Van Dong, prime minister of North Vietnam, in 1969. (BETTMANN/CORBIS)

In 1957 he returned to Hanoi as a prominent member of the Politburo. He became secretary-general of the Lao Dong (Workers') Party in 1959. Following Ho Chi Minh's death in 1969, Le Duan became one of the most influential members of the Lao Dong Party. He became secretary-general of Vietnam's Communist Party in 1976 and served in that position until his death in 1986.

*Micheline R. Lessard*

**Further Reading**

Duiker, William. (1981) *The Communist Road to Power in Vietnam.* Boulder, CO: Westview Press.

Karnow, Stanley. (1983) *Vietnam: A History.* New York: Viking.

Le Duan. (1994) *Selected Writings.* Hanoi, Vietnam: The Gioi Publishers.

**LE DUC ANH** (b. 1920), president of the Democratic Republic of Vietnam. Le Duc Anh was born in Truong Ha, near the city of Hue in central Vietnam. He was president of the Democratic Republic of Vietnam (North Vietnam) from 1992 to 1997. Le Duc Anh joined the Vietnamese revolutionary movement in 1937 and became a member of the Indochinese Communist Party in 1938. He joined the Vietnamese army in 1945 and was promoted to the position of general in 1984. He was deputy commander during military campaigns against South Vietnam in 1975. In 1978, he was field commander of the Vietnamese forces responsible for the attack on Phnom Penh in Cambodia. In 1979, he became the highest-ranking commander of Vietnamese troops in Cambodia. His political career paralleled his military career and soon after he became deputy minister of defense.

Due to his accomplishments and to the patronage of Le Duc Tho (1911–1990), Le Duc Anh was admitted to Vietnam's Politburo in 1981. He became minister of defense in 1987 and served that position until 1991. In 1992, he was elected president of Vietnam by the Vietnamese National Assembly. In 1997, months after having suffered a stroke, Le Duc Anh announced he would not be a candidate for the presidency at the Tenth National Assembly.

*Micheline R. Lessard*

**Further Reading**

Duiker, William J. (1995) *Vietnam: Revolution in Transition.* Boulder, CO: Westview Press.

Kolko, Gabriel. (1997) *Vietnam: Anatomy of a Peace.* London: Routledge.

**LE DUC THO** (1910–1990), Vietnamese revolutionary and founder of the Indochinese Communist Party. Le Duc Tho was born in Nam Ha Province in northern Vietnam. He was the son of "a French functionary" in the colonial government in Vietnam, so he probably was born into upper-middle-class status at least. He was educated in French schools before he joined the revolution against France. He became an influential member of the Lao Dong (Communist) Party Political Bureau and Secretariat, often guiding party directives, and served as the chief negotiator for the Democratic Republic of Vietnam (DRV) at the Paris peace talks between the DRV and the United States from May 1968 until January 1973. Tho spent time in the French island prison of Poulo Condore in the 1930s and served as the party chief commissar for the Indochinese Communist Party (ICP) southern region of Vietnam during most of the First Indochinese War (the war between Vietnam and France, 1946–1954). During the Second Indochinese War (the war between the United States and Vietnam, 1955–1975), Tho played a major role in directing the war in South Vietnam for the DRV. For his efforts in negotiating the Paris Peace Accords, Tho received, with the U.S. chief negotiator, Henry Kissinger, the 1973 Nobel Peace Prize. He refused to accept the award because the war in Vietnam continued. He returned to Vietnam to guide the final DRV push to take Saigon in 1975. After the war Tho remained an active member of the Vietnamese Communist Party Central Committee and also directed the Party Organization Department for the country. Tho retired from public life in 1986.

Le Duc Tho in Ho'Ville, Vietnam, in 1985. (TIM PAGE/CORBIS)

*Richard B. Verrone*

**Further Reading**


Buttinger, Joseph. (1968) *The Smaller Dragon: A Political History of Vietnam*. New York: Praeger.

Karnow, Stanley. (1991) *Vietnam: A History*. New York: Viking Press.

Tucker, Spencer C., ed. (1999) *Vietnam*. Lexington, KY: University Press of Kentucky.


**LEE KUAN YEW** (b. 1923), Singaporean statesman. During his tenure as prime minister of Singapore from 1959 to 1990, Lee Kuan Yew led the country's transformation into a modern, clean, green entrepot city-state with highly successful manufacturing, financial and banking, and communications sectors. Under colonial rule prior to the 1960s, Singapore was known for its considerable squalor, poverty, disease, and ignorance and had a reputation as a hotbed of communist radicalism.

Lee studied in the United Kingdom at the London School of Economics and Cambridge University, earning double first honors. Returning to Singapore, in 1954 he founded the People's Action Party to fight for Singaporean independence. In 1959, at the age of thirty-five, he became prime minister, only eleven years after taking his first degree at Cambridge.

Lee emphasized the development of Singapore as a multicultural, multiracial nation with a distinctive identity. He personally practiced this ideal, speaking six different Asian languages as well as English. He favored social engineering, social conservatism, and Asian values. A pragmatist, Lee wanted to create an effective socialism in Singapore. Noted for his corruption-free leadership, Lee was nevertheless seen by many in the West as practicing an authoritarian democracy with harassment of opposition groups and little tolerance of dissent.

Lee Kuan Yew in September 1965. (BETMANN/CORBIS)

Lee was one of the few world leaders to give up power voluntarily (in 1990), providing for a smooth succession in political leadership. He will be remembered as a transformative leader of the twentieth century who helped Singapore become one of the world's most competitive economies.

*Gerald W. Fry*

### Further Reading

Josey, Alex. (1968) *Lee Kuan Yew*. Singapore: Donald Moore Press.

Razak, Mohamed Najib Tun. (1998) "Lee Kuan Yew." *Asiaweek* (12 June).

Sheridan, Greg. (1997) "Lee Kuan Yew and Goh Chok Tong: Old Tiger, Young Tiger." In *Tigers: Leaders of the New Asia-Pacific*. St. Leonards, Australia: Allen & Unwin, 59–83.

**LEE TENG-HUI** (b. 1923), President of Taiwan. Lee Teng-hui was the first Taiwanese native to lead the government and Nationalist Party of Taiwan. Under his presidency, democracy was fully established on Taiwan. Born in 1923 when Taiwan was a Japanese colony, Lee Teng-hui received a Japanese education until the end of World War II when Taiwan returned to Chinese control. In the 1950s, Lee was among the first generation of Taiwanese students to undertake graduate studies in the United States. He alternated between studying in the United States and working for the Joint Commission for Rural Reconstruction, a combined Chinese Nationalist–American effort at land reform on Taiwan. Taiwan's land reform stressed legal procedures along with agricultural improvement projects and contrasted sharply with the Communist Party's populist, confiscatory, and often violent land reform on the Chinese mainland.

In 1968, Lee earned a Ph.D. in agricultural economics from Cornell University. Back in Taiwan he emerged as a rising Taiwanese figure in the Nationalist Party. His appointments included mayor of Taipei and governor of Taiwan and then, in 1984, vice president. Lee's elevation marked acceptance by the mainlander Nationalist Party that its future was tied to Taiwan and needed support from the Taiwanese majority. When President Chiang Ching-kuo, who did much to further Lee Teng-hui's career, died unexpectedly in January 1988, Lee succeeded him. He served as president until 2000 and earned the deep enmity of the leaders of the People's Republic of China on the mainland for his strong advocacy of Taiwan's continuing political separation from China.

Constitutionally barred from a third term as president, Lee was forced into retirement in 2000 but has remained a significant force in Taiwan's politics. His open support for Chen Shui-bian, the leader of the Democratic Progressive Party (DPP) who succeeded him as president, exacerbated his differences with the Nationalist Party's leadership. In the run-up to the 2001 parliamentary elections, the party expelled Lee from membership, and he responded by organizing a political party called the Taiwan Solidarity Union, which captured thirteen seats. So, Lee has become identified with a minority party in parliament that is sympathetic toward the DPP and its policies.

*David D. Buck*

### Further Reading

Clough, Ralph N. (1978) *Island China*. Cambridge, MA: Harvard University Press.

Garver, John W. (1997) *Face Off: China, the U.S., and Taiwan's Democratization*. Seattle, WA: University of Washington Press. Hung-mao Tien. (1989) *The Great Transition: Political and Social Change in the Republic of China*. Stanford, CA: Hoover Institute Press.

Lee Teng-hui. (1999) *The Road to Democracy: Taiwan's Pursuit of Identity*. Tokyo: PHP Institute.

Rigger, Shelly. (1999) *Politics in Taiwan: Voting for Democracy*. London: Routledge.

**LEH** (1999 est. pop. 15,000). The most northerly town in India, Leh is the capital of Ladakh district in eastern Jammu and Kashmir State. Located in the mountainous region often called "the roof of the world," Leh was built as a terminus for caravans from Central Asia. At 3,523 meters, it is one of the highest permanently inhabited towns on earth. In the sixteenth century, King Sengge Namgyal shifted his court here to be closer to the head of the Khardung La-Karakorum corridor into China. Within a generation, the town had become one of the busiest markets on the Silk Road. In the 1920s and 1930s, the bazaar received over twelve camel trains daily. The prosperity ended with the closing of the Chinese border in the 1950s but resumed when the border was opened up to foreign tourists in 1974. In the winter, the economy is supported by military families from nearby bases, a reminder of the sensitive borders nearby. Leh is dominated by the nine-story medieval Tibetan-style palace of the Ladakhi royal family. Its Dukhar temple houses a thousand-armed image of the goddess Tara. Other notable structures include a Mughal mosque and several ancient, still-functioning Buddhist monasteries. The annual Ladakh Festival features a spectacular march of monks, troupes, and refugees, with dancing, archery, polo, concerts, ceremonies, and exhibitions.

*C. Roger Davis*

**Further Reading**

Michell, George, and Philip Davies. (1989) "Leh." In *The Penguin Guide to the Monuments of India.* Vol. 1. New York: Viking, 120–121.

Rivzi, Janet. (1999) *Trans-Himalayan Caravans: Merchant Princes and Peasant Traders in Ladakh.* New Delhi: Oxford University Press.

**LENINSHIL ZHAS** The principal newspaper of the Kazakh SSR Communist Youth Union, or Komsomol, the *Leninshil zhas* was published five times a week. The roots of the *Leninshil zhas* are found in the prerevolutionary Kazakh youth organization *Birlik* (Unity) and its newspaper, *Sary arka* (often translated as "The Wide Steppe"). *Birlik* followed the editorial line of the Kazakh political party Alash Orda (The Horde of Alash [mythical founder of the Kazakh people]), which advocated greater political and cultural autonomy for Kazakhs.

*Leninshil zhas* was first published on 22 March 1921 as *Zhas Alash* ("Young Alash"), with the goal of educating Kazakh young people in the virtues and attitudes sanctioned by the Communist Party and the government. On 8 February 1924 the name was changed from *Zhas Alash* to *Leninshil zhas* to honor Vladimir Lenin and to weaken the nationalist tendencies among Kazakh intellectuals.

Numerous Kazakh writers, poets, and scholars published articles in its pages, including Akhmet Baitursynov, Saken Seifullin, Turar Ryskulov, and Mukhtar Auezov. During the 1950s many articles were devoted to the Virgin and Idle Lands program and to agricultural and industrial development in Kazakhstan. In March 1991 the newspaper's name was changed back to *Zhas Alash*, and presently it generally supports current Kazakh government policies.

*Steven Sabol*

**LEOPARD, CLOUDED** The clouded leopard (*Neofelis nebulosa*), the largest of the arboreal (tree-living) cats, inhabits the tropical forests of Southeast Asia, from Nepal to Sumatra and Borneo. Its name refers to the dark cloud-shaped markings on its golden-brown coat. Its tail is ringed with black stripes.

The head and body measure about one meter in length, and the long tail acts as an effective balancing aid. A stocky body, powerful limbs, and sharp claws make the clouded leopard an expert climber. Its primary prey is primates, which it stalks through the trees, but it also eats birds, small mammals, and fish. Its extremely long, sharp canine teeth enable the hunting of still larger game such as deer and wild pigs.

Clouded leopards are largely nocturnal. They live an average of fifteen years, and females produce litters of two to four cubs. They are considered sacred by a number of Southeast Asian peoples. Clouded leopards are an endangered species protected under the Convention on International Trade in Endangered Species, but illegal hunting for their coats, teeth, and bones continues and deforestation is eroding their habitat. Secretive and hard to study in the wild, they have also proved difficult to breed in captivity.

*Lucy D. Moss*

**Further Reading**

Alderton, David, and Bruce Tanner. (1998) *Wild Cats of the World.* London: Sterling Publications.

**LEOPARD, SNOW** The snow leopard or ounce inhabits the harsh, high mountain environments of Central Asia from Russia and Mongolia south to China, Tibet, and the Indian subcontinent. This includes part or all of the upper reaches of the Himalaya, Karakoram, Hindu Kush, Pamirs, Kunlun Shan, Tian Shan, Altay Shan, and Sayan Mountains. Experts place the snow leopard in the genus *Panthera* or, citing its unique skull and vocal apparatus, classify it as the lone member of the genus *Uncia* (*Uncia uncia*).

A mature snow leopard is 2.1 meters (7 feet) long, including its 0.9-meter (3-foot) tail, which is used for balance on rocky and snowy terrains. The leopard attains a 0.6-meter (2-foot) shoulder height, weighs 20 to 40 kilograms (40 to 90 pounds), and lives for 15 to 18 years. The cubs are born two to three to a litter in early spring following an average gestation of ninety-three days, and they remain with their mothers for eighteen months. The animal's small head has tiny ears and a heavy brow. Large paws support powerful limbs that are short in relation to the body size. The rosettes and spot markings common to all leopards are more muted on the snow leopard, and its soft, wooly textured fur is 5 centimeters (2 inches) on the top and sides and up to 10 centimeters (4 inches) on the underparts of the animal. Weakly developed fibroelastic tissue in the throat prevents this cat from emitting a load roar.

Snow leopards hunt argali, bharal, markhor, and ibex in rock outcrops, canyons, plateaus, and mountain ridge tops at heights of between 2,000 and 5,500 meters (6,500 and 18,000 feet). They also pursue numerous birds and hare along with marmots, yak, musk deer, and domestic stock. During winter they descend, with their prey, into the more protected upper margins of lowland forests.

By most estimates only five thousand snow leopards remain, although inaccessible terrain and this mammal's highly furtive character make it difficult to take an accurate census. Despite legal protection in 90 percent of its range, it remains an endangered species on *The 2000 World Conservation Union Red List of Threatened Animals*. Unless poaching for its fur and for its bones, purported to have healing powers, is halted, the snow leopard may become extinct in the wild.

*Stephen Cunha*

### Further Reading

Jackson, Ronald, and Ashiq Ahmad, eds. *Proceedings of the Eighth International Snow Leopard Symposium*. Seattle, WA: International Snow Leopard Trust and World Wide Fund for Nature–Pakistan.

**LHASA** (2000 est. pop. 400,000). Presently capital of the Tibet Autonomous Region of the People's Republic of China and historically the capital of the Tibetan state, Lhasa is situated in the central Tibetan province of U on the Kyushu River at a height of 3,650 meters, with a population of about 200,000 for the central city and 400,000 for the whole municipality.

The name Lha-sa (pronounced Ha-sa) in Tibetan means divine ground, and Lhasa has always combined a religious and a political role. There are two main

Barkhor Jokhang Temple I Lhasa in July 1996. (STEPHEN G. DONALDSON PHOTOGRAPHY)

## LHASA IN THE 1840s

The following description of Lhasa written by two French missionaries in the mid-nineteenth century provides a good example of Western attitudes about Asia and about Buddhism.

> The morning after our arrival at Lha-Ssa, we engaged a Thibetan guide, and visited the various quarters of the city, in search of a lodging. The houses at Lha-Ssa are for the most part several stories high, terminating in a terrace slightly sloped in order to carry off water; they were whitewashed all over, except the bordering around the doors and windows, which are painted red or yellow. The reformed Buddhists are so fond of these two colours, which are, so to speak, sacred in their eyes, that they especially name them Lamanesque colours. The people of Lha-Ssa are in a habit of painting their houses once a year, so that they are always perfectly clean, and seem, in fact, just built; but the interior is by no means in harmony with the fine outside. The rooms are dirty, stinking, and encumbered with all sorts of utensils and furniture, thrown about in a most disgusting confusion. In a word, the Thibetan habitations are literally whited sepulchers; a perfect picture of Buddhism and all other false religions, which carefully cover, with certain general truths and certain moral principles, the corruption and falsehood within.
>
> *Source:* Huc Evariste-Regis and Joseph Gabet. ([1851] 1987) *Travels in Tartary, Thibet, and China, 1844–1846.* New York: Dover Publications, 168–169.

phases in its existence. Lhasa was established as the capital by the first Buddhist king, Songtsen Gampo (609?–649), in the seventh century CE to house the sacred image of Buddha, or Jowo. Using geomancy, it was determined that the heart of Tibet, where the image should be kept, was in an island on a lake on the site of today's Lhasa. After subduing the local demon of the lake, a temple was built for the statue and called the Jokhang (House of the Lord Buddha). The Jokhang is to this day Lhasa's holiest shrine. The next phase was in the seventeenth century, when Lhasa was reestablished as the capital of the Dalai Lamas. The Potala Palace was built on the Marpo-Ri, or Red Hill, as the center for the joint religious and secular government of Tibet.

Around the Jokhang is the Barkhor, or circumambulation path, along which pilgrims walk or prostrate themselves. The Norbulingka, summer palace of the Dalai Lamas, lies to the west. Other sites include the ancient Ramoche temple. The historic monasteries of Ganden, Drepung, and Sera, headquarters of the dominant Yellow Hat sect of the Dalai Lamas, are close to Lhasa and have wielded enormous influence over the town.

Since Chinese rule, modern Lhasa has expanded, dwarfing the Tibetan area, large parts of which have been knocked down. Lhasa suffered during the Tibetan uprising in 1959 and was extensively damaged during the Cultural Revolution in the 1960s. In the 1980s, the Chinese started restoration work, and a Chinese city expanded in the area to house the administration and business. Today, the Tibet Heritage Fund has helped to preserve some areas of historic Lhasa around the Barkhor.

Modern Lhasa has been described variously as drab, featureless, or like a bustling frontier town. Under the Chinese plan of modernizing Tibet and developing its economy, small-scale manufacturing, beer brewing, and now the Internet have come to the city. Lhasa's importance as a pilgrim center for Tibetans and as a tourist spot has allowed it to preserve some of its main features, while the Chinese plan for Tibet has created a completely new city. China has ambitious plans for Lhasa as part of its policy of developing the western regions of the People's Republic, including building the world's highest railroad linking Lhasa to the nearest railhead in Qinghai Province.

*Michael Kowalewski*

**Further Reading**


Batchelor, Stephen. (1987) *The Tibet Guide.* London: Wisdom.

Chandra Das, Sarat. ([1902] 1970) *Journey to Lhasa and Central Tibet.* Reprint ed. New Delhi, India: Manjusri.

Dowman, Keith. (1999) *Power Places of Central Tibet.* London: Routledge & Kegan Paul.

Larsen, Knud, and Amund Sinding-Larsen. (2001) *The Lhasa Atlas.* London: Serindia.

Richardson, Hugh. (1994) *Ceremonies of the Lhasa Year.* London: Serindia.


**LI BAI** (701–762), Chinese poet. Li Bai, or Li Bo, also known as Taibai and style named Qinglian, is often mentioned along with Du Fu as one of the two greatest Tang dynasty (618–907) poets. Although Li's hometown is recorded as a site in present-day Jiangyou District, Sichuan Province, his ancestors were said to be merchants from Central Asia, where it appears that he was actually born.

Li Bai is known in Chinese poetic history as the "Transcendent of Poetry." This epithet captures some of Li's personal and poetic style; his preoccupation with transcendence and with supramundane realms is directly related to his close association with Taoist beliefs, practices, and practitioners. The fantasy of knight errantry forms another aspect of Li Bai's temperament and style. Upon encountering painful experiences, he turned to drinking, and his poetry is characterized by a cyclical alternation between high spirits and despondency. Enamored of hyperbole, Li wrote with an impetuous exuberance, mostly "ancient style" poems and quatrains in simple language. Li also made significant contributions to landscape poetry.

*Timothy Wai Keung Chan*

**Further Reading**


Kroll, Paul W. (1986) "Li Po's Transcendent Diction." *Journal of the American Oriental Society* 106, 1: 99–117.

Owen, Stephen. (1981) "Li Po: A New Concept of Genius." In *The Great Age of Chinese Poetry: The High T'ang.* New Haven, CT: Yale University Press, 109–146.

Waley, Arthur. (1984) *The Poetry and Career of Li Po, 701–762 A.D.* London: G. Allen and Unwin.


**LI HONGZHANG** (1823–1901), Chinese official. Li Hongzhang was a leading Chinese official of the latter half of the nineteenth century. A Confucian scholar, Li served under Zeng Guofan (1811–1872) and helped suppress the Taiping Rebellion (1851–1864) and Nian Rebellion (c. 1852–1868). He was appointed governor of Zhili Province and remained in that position for a quarter of a century, serving in many respects as an unofficial prime minister of China.

Li was one of the prime movers behind the flawed Self-Strengthening Movement, which was an effort by the Qing dynasty (1644–1912) to restore power to resist Western encroachments, especially after the Second Opium War. Although he recognized the need to modernize and to borrow appropriately from the West, he was not capable of accepting or instituting changes necessary to meet the challenge of late-nineteenth-century imperialism. Still, Li helped establish the Jiangnan Arsenal, the Nanjing Arsenal, the Tianjin Machine Factory, the China Merchants Steam Navigation Company, the Imperial Telegraph Bureau, and the Beiyang Fleet. Li was unable to stop Japan in the 1894–1895 conflict, although he did negotiate the peace and was responsible for the protocols that ended the western occupation of Beijing after the Boxer Rebellion (1900). He also helped accelerate the trend of power away from the capital and hence the coming warlord period of the 1920s and 1930s.

*Charles Dobbs*

**Further Reading**


Chu, Samuel C., and Kwang-ching Liu, eds. (1993) *Li Hongzhang and China's Early Modernization.* New York: M. E. Sharpe.

Spector, Stanley. (1964) *Li Hongzhang and the Huai Army: A Study in Nineteenth-Century Chinese Regionalism.* Seattle, WA: University of Washington Press.


**LI PENG** (b. 1928), Chinese premier. Born in Chengdu, Sichuan Province, in October 1928, Li Peng is the orphaned son of a Chinese Communist Party (CCP) worker and was adopted by Chinese premier Zhou Enlai (1898–1976). Li was trained as a power engineer in Moscow from 1948 to 1955. After his return to China, he was the director and chief engineer

Li Peng, on a four-day visit to Kenya in November 1999, is greeted by Kenyan President Daniel arap Moi. (AFP/CORBIS)

at several power plants from 1956 to 1966 and later in various bureaucratic or party positions relating to power generation. In 1979, partly due to the backing of his stepmother, CCP Central Committee member Deng Yingchao (1904–1997), Li began a swift ascent up the hierarchy, first as deputy minister of power production (1981), then as a member of the Central Committee (1982) and vice-premier in charge of energy and communications (1983). In 1985, he became a member of the Standing Committee of the CCP Politburo and in 1988 became premier, a post he held until 1998.

Li achieved his greatest notoriety during the Tiananmen Square incident of 1989. Strongly opposed to the student takeover of the square, he was seen as patronizing during meetings with student leaders and was hectored at a televised meeting with hospitalized hunger strikers. He sided with other hard-liners against Zhao Ziyang (b. 1919), who was removed as party leader. Later, news media and students frequently referred to him as the "butcher of Beijing" for being the first official to publicly support the People's Liberation Army's bloody crackdown during the night of 3–4 June.

After 1989, Li cooperated with CCP leader Jiang Zemin and economics czar Zhu Rongji to rein in China's high inflation and begin sweeping reforms of state-owned enterprises. Elected chair of the National People's Congress despite an unprecedented two hundred negative votes in 1998, Li remains an influential voice in policy making.

*Joel Campbell*

**Further Reading**

Lam, Willy Wo-Lap. (1999) *The Era of Jiang Zemin*. New York: Prentice-Hall.

Salisbury, Harrison E. (1992) *The New Emperors: China in the Era of Mao and Deng*. Boston: Little, Brown & Co.

**LI SHIZHEN** (1518–1593), Chinese physician and pharmacologist. Li Shizhen is best remembered for his *Bencao Gangmu* (Compendium of Materia Medica), one of the most frequently mentioned books in the Chinese herbal medical tradition. He was born in 1518 at the height of the Ming dynasty (1368–1644); his grandfather was an itinerant doctor and his father a traditional physician. As a result of these influences and a bout with tuberculosis when he was twenty, Li decided to become a doctor at the age of twenty-four. At the age of twenty-nine he took a position in government practicing medicine, but, having found many problems with existing herbal literature, he left this position within the year and began work on the *Bencao Gangmu.* He traveled throughout China, experimenting with various herbs, collecting local folk remedies, and consulting virtually every medical book available (over eight hundred). His fifty-two-volume book took twenty-seven years to produce and was completed in 1578. The book describes 1,892 medicines (374 of which were new) and 11,096 prescriptions. Finally published in 1596 (three years after his death), the book has been translated either whole or in part into Japanese, Latin, French, English, Russian, and German and was a standard text on Chinese herbal medicine until 1959.

*Jody C. Baumgartner*

**Further Reading**

Lu Gwei-djen. (1976) "China's Greatest Naturalist: A Brief Biography of Li Shizhen." *American Journal of Chinese Medicine* 4, 3: 209–218.

Wang Zhenguo, Chen Ping, and Xie Peiping. (1999) *History and Development of Traditional Chinese Medicine.* Beijing: Science Press.

**LIANG QICHAO** (1873–1929), Chinese scholar and essayist. Liang Qichao was a reform-minded Chinese scholar and essayist who rose to prominence following the humiliating defeat of China in the Sino-Japanese War (1894–1895). In 1898, he was among the leading participants of the ill-fated "Hundred Days of Reform" sponsored by the progressive Guangxu emperor. Following the reactionary restoration of Empress Dowager Cixi, Liang fled to Japan, where, for the next fourteen years, he edited a series of influential journals and wrote an impressive range of persuasive and inspiring essays and monographs. His writings at this time advocated political reform or revolution and introduced his contemporaries to Western liberalism, nationalism, and science.

In the aftermath of the Republican revolution of 1911, Liang returned to China and formed the moderate Progressive Party (Jinbudang) that contended with the ruling Guomindang in the nascent National Assembly. He twice served as a cabinet-level minister. With the onset of warlordism in 1917, Liang withdrew to a life of teaching and scholarship during which he wrote prolifically on Chinese culture, literature, and history. These later writings reflected his predominant aspiration for a new cultural synthesis in China that would combine the most worthy and enduring elements of Chinese Confucianism with the social and political principles of Western liberalism.

*Michael C. Lazich*

**Further Reading**

Huang, Philip C. (1972) *Liang Ch'i-ch'ao and Modern Chinese Liberalism.* Seattle, WA: University of Washington Press.

Tang Xiaobing. (1996) *Global Space and the Nationalist Discourse of Modernity: The Historical Thought of Liang Qichao.* Stanford, CA: Stanford University Press.

**LIAONING** (2002 est. pop. 44.6 million). Liaoning Province is in the southern part of Northeast China. Bounded by the Yellow and Bo Hai Seas in the south, with a coastline 2,187 kilometers long, it has a total area of 145,900 square kilometers. Jilin Province, Inner Mongolia, and Hebei Province surround it. The Liao River, the principal waterway of the province, flows through the middle part of Liaoning from north to south. The Yalu River on the eastern fringe forms the boundary between China and North Korea. The Liaodong Peninsula juts out between the Yellow and Bo Hai Seas from the landmass. Liaoning has a zigzag coast and many rocky islands and fine natural harbors. It has a population of 40.57 million (1996). Ethnic groups living there include Man, Mongolians, Koreans, and Xibo.

Liaoning has a temperate continental monsoonal climate, with hot, rainy summers, long, cold winters with little snow; and short, windy springs. It has an average annual temperature of 6–11°C, a frost-free period of 130–180 days, and a mean annual precipitation of 400–1,000 millimeters, which decreases notably from southeast to northwest.

Liaoning grows sorghum, maize, rice, and soybeans and the cash crops of cotton, tobacco, and peanuts. It is also the major tussah-silk grower of China. The apples of southern Liaoning and the pears of western Liaoning are known throughout China. The province also produces ginseng and antlers, valuable ingredients for traditional Chinese medicine. The fishery industry is developed along the coast.

Liaoning has rich mineral resources, especially iron ore and coal mines. Fushun and Fuxin, popularly called the "coal capital" and the "coal sea," produce top-quality coal as the largest open-cast mining centers in China. With a well-grounded heavy industry, Liaoning is one of China's major industrial bases. It leads the country in the production of iron and steel, aluminum, sulfuric acid, soda ash, heavy machinery, magnesia, and talcum. With its railway mileage exceeding 4,000 kilometers of tracks, Liaoning has the densest network of rail lines in the country.

Shenyang, the provincial capital, is the largest city of Northeast China, with a population of more than 6.5 million, and is one of its economic, communications, and cultural centers. Shenyang is known throughout China for its machine-building industry.

Dalian, the most famous city in Liaoning, lies at the southern tip of the Liaodong peninsula. One of the most beautiful cities in China, it is a tourist paradise, with European-style architecture framing its skyline and miles of beaches along the oceanfront.

*Di Bai*

**Further Reading**

China Handbook Editorial Committee, comp., (1992) *Geography, China Handbook Series.* Trans. by Liang Liangxing. Beijing: Foreign Languages Press.

Hsieh Chiao-min, and Max Lu, eds. (2001) *Changing China: A Geographical Appraisal.* Boulder, CO: Westview Press.

**LIBERAL DEMOCRATIC PARTY—JAPAN** The Liberal Democratic Party (LDP) has dominated Japan's postwar politics. It was formed in 1955 when the Liberal and Democratic Parties combined. Despite its name, the LDP is a conservative party with strong ties to business. Except for a short period following World War II when the Japan Socialist Party organized a coalition government, the LDP held power until 1993, when it lost control of the lower house of the Diet, the national legislature, to a coalition of seven parties. But this setback was only temporary; the LDP regained control in 1996.

The LDP's philosophy has two key elements: a commitment to economic growth and the maintenance of good relations with the United States, including supporting the security alliance between the two countries. Under LDP leadership, Japan followed U.S. policy guidance during the Cold War. Aligning itself with the United States allowed Japan to prosper economically, but Cold-War antagonisms restricted commercial opportunities with the Soviet Union and especially with China.

The LDP has traditionally been divided into factions, usually five in number. These factions are made up of members of the Diet who are committed to following the leadership of a senior party leader. In return for their support, faction members can expect to receive substantial amounts of money from their leaders. Individual LDP Diet members use this money to maintain a local electoral organization and to do favors for constituents.

Factions govern the process whereby party leadership and important government posts are filled. Competition among factions has been intense. In fact, competition among LDP factions has been a more significant aspect of Japanese postwar politics than competition among parties has been. The leader of the most powerful faction plays an important role in the selection of the prime minister. Ministerial positions in the cabinet are allocated through a bargaining process on the basis of faction strength.

The LDP lost control of parliament in 1993, following a series of highly publicized scandals involving bribery and corruption charges against top officials in the party. The substantial weakening of the Japanese economy in the 1990s also contributed to the LDP's decline in popular support. But opposition parties had problems of their own and failed to form a cohesive alternative. The LDP regained control of the government following the 1996 election, but lacking a majority in parliament, it had to form a coalition. After the 2000 election, the LDP continued to rule through a coalition.

*Louis D. Hayes*

**Further Reading**

Hayes, Louis D. (2001) *Introduction to Japanese Politics.* 3d ed. Armonk, NY: M. E. Sharpe.

Hrebenar, Ronald J. (2000) *Japan's New Party System.* 3d ed. Boulder, CO: Westview Press.

**LIGHT, FRANCIS** (c. 1740–1794), British officer and founder of Penang. Francis Light started his career as a naval officer. At the age of twenty-three he became the ship's captain for the firm Jouruain, Sullivan and De Souza in Madras. It was through this voyage that Light reached the Malay Peninsula. Light traveled extensively in the Malay Peninsula and Sumatra, learning the Malay and Siamese languages in order to conduct trade negotiations.

At the time Light was in Kedah (in the northwestern Malay Peninsula), Siam was constantly threatening it. At this time too the British East India Company (formed in 1600 for conducting spice trade with the East Indies) was interested in securing a trading port at the Eastern of Bay of Bengal. It was also the British government's interest to control the spice trade and compete with the Dutch monopoly. Light found that Penang, at that time a part of Kedah, was a sustainable port and that it would serve the British interest well.

The sultan of Kedah, who was aware that the British were in his land, asked Light if the British army would help him handle the attacks from Siam. Light used this opportunity well and signed a pact with the sultan stating that the sultan would give Penang to the British and that in return the British would protect Kedah from their vantage point in Penang, if Kedah were attacked.

On 11 August 1786, Light inaugurated Penang and named it Prince of Wales Island (however, this name was not popular), and named the new port Georgetown. At the time Light arrived, the population in Penang was one thousand; by 1804 it had risen to twelve thousand. The inhabitants of Penang were conducting trade with Great Britain and India, trading mainly cloth, metalware, and opium. After expending much effort in developing the state, Francis Light died in 1794.

*Mala Selvaraju*

**Further Reading**

Ryan, N. J. (1974) *The Making of Modern Malaysia and Singapore.* Kuala Lumpur, Malaysia: Oxford University Press.

**LIJIANG, OLD TOWN OF** The old town of Lijiang, one of the largest traditional towns left in China, is located in the southwest of the country in the part of Yunnan Province that borders on Tibet and Sichuan. The town, at the center of Lijiang Prefecture, sits on a high plateau, just south of the 5,000-meter-high Jade Dragon Mountain. Lijiang has a long history, taking its present form in 1253, when members of Khubilai Khan's (1216–1294) Mongol army set-

## LIJIANG—WORLD HERITAGE SITE

The Old Town of Lijiang, a masterwork of Chinese feudal architecture, was designated a UNESCO World Heritage Site in 1997. So intact that its intricate ancient waterworks are still in use today, the site demonstrates several centuries of different cultural influences and adaptation to the difficult mountain topography.

tled in the area. They, along with the Naxi, one of several ethnic groups that populate the region, developed the town around a market square that still exists to this day. From the 1300s until 1723, the town was gradually incorporated into the Chinese empire. As other groups, including the Tibetan and Han, came to settle in Lijiang, a distinct architectural style developed, characterized by two-story sun-baked brick and clay-tile houses with carved wooden windows. Also unique is the town's centuries-old water system, which is still in use. Lijiang's inhabitants divert streams from the mountain's glaciers into a network of swift canals that run through the town streets. In 1997, UNESCO added the old town of Lijiang to its World Heritage Site list.

*Elizabeth VanderVen*

### Further Reading

Agland, Phil. (1994) *China: Beyond the Clouds*. Washington DC: National Geographic Society.

Goullart, Peter. (1955) *Forgotten Kingdom*. London: John Murray Publishers, Ltd.

Rock, Joseph. (1947) *The Ancient Na-khi Kingdom of Southwest China*. 2 Vols. Cambridge, MA: Harvard University Press.

**LIM CHIN SIONG** (1933–1996), Singapore politician. Lim Chin Siong was a great orator in Chinese. He was one of the conveners of the People's Action Party at its founding when he was twenty-one years old. As a trade unionist, he was a charismatic leader who cared deeply for the welfare of workers.

Lim Chin Siong was involved in organizing strikes and boycotts among workers and Chinese middle-school students in the early 1950s, when Singapore was trying to break free of British colonialism. He contested the 1955 general election and was one of three PAP members, one of whom was Lee Kuan Yew, elected into the Legislative Assembly. In 1959, when PAP came into power, he was appointed political secretary to the finance minister, Goh Keng Swee. He was sacked from his post two years later when he joined twelve PAP assemblymen to oppose the party leadership. He then became the secretary-general of the newly formed Barisan Sosialis. The PAP government accused him of being a communist "open-front" leader with links to the Malayan Communist Party and arrested him in 1963. He was placed in detention until 1969, when he decided to quit politics and resigned from the Barisan Sosialis. He went to London and stayed there for ten years before returning to Singapore, where he lived until his death.

*Kog Yue Choong*

### Further Reading

Drysdale, John. (1984) *Singapore: Struggle for Success*. Singapore and Kuala Lumpur, Malaysia: Times Books International.

"SDP Pays Tribute to Lim Chin Siong." (1996) *The Straits Times* (8 February).

"SM: Chin Siong Taught Me the Meaning of Dedication to a Cause." (1996) *The Straits Times* (9 February).

Wang Hui Ling. (1996) "Lim Chin Siong Cremated." *The Straits Times* (10 February).

**LIM CHONG EU** (b. 1919), Malaysian physician and politician. Born in Penang, Malaysia, Lim Chong Eu began his career as a medical officer in the armed forces in China from 1944 to 1945. In 1946, he served as the personal physician of General Chen Cheng, chief of staff of the Chinese armed forces. Between 1946 and 1947, he lectured in English literature at the Fudan University in Shanghai.

In 1957, he returned to Malaysia to practice medicine at his father's dispensary in Penang, remaining there until 1950, and then serving from 1950 to 1951 as a medical officer in the Malayan Air Force. By 1951, he was involved in local politics and had joined the Penang Straits Settlements Council as a councillor. In the same year, he founded and served as vice-chairman of the Penang Radical Party. In 1953, he became the party's chairman but refused to defend the post in June 1954.

Instead, he joined the Malaysian Chinese Association (MCA), another Chinese political party. In January 1955, he was elected councillor of the Penang Straits Settlements Council for the area of Kelawai. In March 1955, he was appointed a member of the

Alliance National Council, a coalition of three political parties, each representing a racial group in Malaysia. (MCA was the party representing the Chinese.) In the same year, he became the Alliance chief whip in the federal Legislative Assembly.

Lim Chong Eu became the president of the MCA in 1958, when he defeated the incumbent, Datuk Tan Cheng Lock. Lim, however, resigned from the presidency of the MCA in 1961, when the party failed to secure from the Malay political party, the United Malay National Organisation (UMNO), certain rights for the Chinese.

He then founded and became vice president of the United Democratic Party (UDP), thus assuming the position of a leader of the Chinese political opposition in Malaysia. In 1963, he became the UDP's secretary-general. He was elected as the member of Parliament for the constituency of Tanjung in the 1964 general elections and in the same year was elected assemblyman for the Penang State Legislative Assembly for the Kota seat.

In 1968, he founded and became vice president of the Gerakan Party. He was reelected to both his parliamentary and state assembly seats during the 1969 elections. The Gerakan Party subsequently joined the Barisan Nasionalis, a newly named coalition of political parties, each representing a racial group.

Datuk Lim Chong Eu was chief minister of the state of Penang, Malaysia, from 11 May 1969 until October 1990 and served as the president of the Gerakan Party in 1971. In the 1974 general elections in Malaysia, he was elected to a third term to both his parliamentary and state assembly seats. He held his seat, the constituency of Kota in the state of Penang, for three terms, during the general elections in 1978, 1982, and 1986. In the 1990 general elections, he lost the state assembly seat to the leader of an opposition party, Lim Kit Siang, of the Democratic Action Party, by 706 votes.

**Further Reading**

*New Malaysian Who's Who.* 2d ed. (1995) Kuala Lumpur, Malaysia: Kasuya.

Pan, Lynn, ed. (1999) *The Encyclopaedia of the Chinese Overseas.* Cambridge, MA: Harvard University Press.

**LIM, SHIRLEY** (b. 1944), Chinese-Malaysian writer. Shirley Lim is an award-winning Chinese-Malaysian writer who immigrated to the United States and became a prominent academic and literary figure, especially in Asian-American literary circles. Her work examines relocation, belonging, and hybrid identity, both in the Asian and American contexts, and analyzes cross-cultural and minority gender experiences. Born in a small village in Malaysia, she overcame poverty, going on to higher education at the University of Malaya and Brandeis University. She rose to fame when her debut collection of poetry, *Crossing the Peninsula,* became Malaysia's first winner of the Commonwealth Poetry Prize in 1980. Widely anthologized for her poetry and short stories, Lim has also written a memoir, *Among the White Moonfaces,* and a novel, *Joss and Gold. Among the White Moonfaces* won the American Book Award in 1996, as did a feminist anthology she edited, *The Forbidden Stitch: An Asian American Women's Anthology,* in 1990. Her work has recently been included in the English Language Syllabus of the National Secondary School Curriculum in Malaysia. Lim has had a distinguished academic career in the United States and in 2002 was professor of English and Women's Studies at the University of California, Santa Barbara.

*Mohan Ambikaibaker*

**Further Reading**

Lim, Shirley. (1998) *What the Fortune Teller Didn't Say.* Albuquerque, NM: West End Press.

———. (1996) *Among the White Moonfaces: Memoirs of a Nyonya Feminist.* Singapore: Times.

———. (1985) *No Man's Grove.* Singapore: National University of Singapore.

———. (1984) *Another Country and Other Stories.* Singapore: Times.

**LIN BIAO** (1908–1971), Chinese soldier and politician. Lin Biao was among the youngest and perhaps best of the Communist generals during China's long civil war with the Nationalists (Guomindang) and the anti-Japanese resistance. Lin played a critical role in helping the forces of Mao Zedong (1893–1976) defeat the Nationalists in Manchuria and largely settle the civil war. He showed a genius for partisan warfare.

However, Lin's accomplishments were limited by periodic and severe illnesses, and he was often forced to take leave from his official duties. Still, he was, for a time, a great favorite of Mao, and after Lin became minister of defense in 1962, Mao relied on Lin to keep the army loyal and under control of the Communist Party in the period leading up to and during the Cultural Revolution (1966–1976). Indeed, Mao named Lin as a successor, but that may have been a ploy to isolate Lin and make him more dependent on Mao's favor. Perhaps at the peak of his ascendancy, Lin either attempted a coup d'etat or merely tried to flee to save his life, and it was reported that he, his wife, and some fellow travelers died in 1971 in a plane crash while seeking sanctuary in the Soviet Union.

*Charles Dobbs*

**Further Reading**


Teiwes, Frederick C. (1966) *The Tragedy of Lin Biao: Riding the Tiger during the Cultural Revolution, 1966–1971*. London: Hurst.

Yao, Ming-le. (1983) *The Conspiracy and Death of Lin Biao*. Trans. by Stanley Karnow. New York: Alfred Knopf.


**LINGAYAT** The Lingayats are a Hindu sect concentrated in the state of Karnataka (a southern provincial state of India), which covers 191,773 square kilometers. The Lingayats constitute around 20 percent of the total population in that state and are also common in Bijapur, Belgaum, and Dharwar.

The Lingayats do not call themselves Hindus. They are known as Virasaivas because of their single-minded and deeply passionate devotion to Siva (a deity who is venerated both by upper- and lower-caste Hindus, as well as other marginal groups in Hindu society), manifested in a lingam, or male phallus form. Followers carry the lingam either around their necks or across their chests; children may have the image tied to one arm. The *Lingadharanachandrika*, the religious treatise of the Lingayats, makes it compulsory for all devotees to wear a lingam on their body, even in death.

The Lingayat religious movement challenged the deep-rooted Brahmanic system on which high Hinduism or Vedic Hinduism rested. Beginning in the twelfth century as a miniscule socioreligious movement in north Karnataka and founded by a government minister named Basavanna, the religion gained momentum over a period of time throughout Karnataka.

Basavanna assimilated the tenets of dominant Saivite (Siva-worshiping) religious traditions prevalent during his time in Kashmir, Gujrat, and Tamil Nadu and transformed them so that they retained their functionality within the broad framework of Lingayat religion. The Lingayat religious doctrine emphasizes the mutual dependence between Siva and individual human beings. Siva is believed to have constituted the Parama Sakti (ultimate cosmic force), that is, Siva and the cosmic force are considered to be identical. Lingayat religious doctrine holds that prior to the creation of the cosmos, Siva was absolute self in terms of purity, beyond space and location, beyond pattern, nameless, shapeless, and deedless.

Through this philosophy, Basavanna and other Lingayat preachers tried to combat the polytheistic forces of Brahmanic Hinduism. Basava's monotheism not only dethroned the Vedic deities (venerated by the followers of Vedic Hinduism), but also exposed the falsities of the Brahmanic interpretations of the Hindu scriptures. Consequently, Lingayat religion favored a social order that was devoid of the caste system and social servitude. As a result, it initially countenanced the conversion of men and women from all Hindu castes, including the lowest.

The movement's egalitarianism struck at the core of the Brahmanic tradition: It disavowed caste segregation and hierarchy, the system of fourfold division of society, the multitude of gods and goddesses, ritualism, and the notions of pollution and rebirth. The Lingayat movement, however, went beyond a merely negative critique of the Brahmanic order. It developed its own opposing and parallel structures, involving reinterpretations of monotheism, the guru (spiritual teacher), the lingam, the *jangama* (itinerant priest), and *kayaka* (calling).

The Lingayat religious culture, which stresses the principles of individuality, equality, and fellowship, created a political awareness among its followers. Though the Lingayat culture was an apolitical culture in the early decades of the twentieth century, it envisaged a populist style of politics that assigned the community the role of political critic. The communitarian social outlook of the Lingayats found expression in the creation of the state of Karnataka in 1956. Because of their numbers, the Lingayats in the early 2000s decide the political fortunes of the major political parties in Karnataka.

*Rajshekhar Basu*

**Further Reading**


Hunashal, S. M. (1947) *The Lingayat Movement: A Social Revolution in Karnatak*. Dharwar, India: Karnatak Sahitya Mandira.

Ishwaran, Karigondar. (1983) *Religion and Society among the Lingayats of South India*. Delhi: Vikas.

Parvathamma, C. (1971) *Politics and Religion. A Study of Historical Interaction between Socio-Political Relationships in a Mysore Village*. Delhi: Sterling Publishers.


**LINH NHAT** (1905–1963), Vietnamese novelist. Linh Nhat is the pen name of Nguyen Tuong Tam, who was one of Vietnam's most prominent novelists in the first half of the twentieth century. Born in central Vietnam in 1905, he was an ardent nationalist and in 1933 with Khai Hung (1896–1947) cofounded the Self-Strengthening Literary Group to promote Vietnamese vernacular literature. Linh wrote primarily about the plight of the urban bourgeoisie constrained by both traditional Vietnamese culture and French colonialism. His writings, critical of arranged marriages, were applauded by women's organizations. A prolific author, Linh's most famous works include *Autumn's Sunlight* (1934), *Breaking Away* (1934), *A Lonely Life* (1936), *Two Golden Afternoons* (1937), *Two Friends* (1938), *White Butterfly* (1939), *Cau Moi Hamlet* (1958), and *Thanh Thuy River* (1961). These novels were some of the first major works in vernacular Vietnamese and set the standard for the genre. During World War II, Linh had some contact with Japan; he hoped that Japan would grant Vietnam independence. Linh fled arrest by the French authorities to southern China, where he lived for more than a year. He returned to Vietnam in September 1945 with other nationalists. Although Linh was critical of the Republic of Vietnam (South Vietnam) regime, his works were banned after 1975 because of his staunch anticommunist stance. It was not until December 1987, when the Vietnam Communist Party issued Resolution Five, that writers and artists were given more intellectual freedom and bans were lifted on many literary works, including those by anticommunist writers such as Nhat Linh. Linh's works remained popular in South Vietnam.

*Zachary Abuza*

### Further Reading

Marr, David. (1984) *Vietnamese Tradition on Trial.* Berkeley and Los Angeles, CA: University of California Press.

## LION, ASIATIC

Once a symbol of royalty in West Asia, the lion was hunted and killed only by kings in ancient Mesopotamia (modern Iraq). Today the Asiatic, or Indian, lion *(Panthera leo)* is virtually extinct in Iran and Iraq but survives in the Gir Forest National Park in India. The Asiatic lion is the same species as the African lion, which includes the Cape Lion, the Masai lion, the Senegal lion, the Barbary lion, the Somali lion, and the Persian lion, *Panthera leo persica*, once native to southwestern Asia. During Pleistocene times, a million or more years ago, lions lived over much of the earth, but they disappeared from North America about ten thousand years ago, from the Balkans about two thousand years ago, and from Palestine during the Crusades. Scarcely any still exist in western Asia where they once flourished, as they did too in central and northern India; but the Gir Forest, in Gujarat, western India, is a sanctuary created in 1913 for the protection of Indian lions. Their tourist appeal may ensure their survival here, but local herders are now their chief enemy.

Lions average 275 centimeters in length, whether in Africa or India (the largest-known Indian specimen was 292 centimeters long, the largest-known African one 323 centimeters). The male weighs up to 200 kilograms. Lions have not been domesticated except in isolated instances for circuses and film work; but the two hundred or more inhabiting Gir Forest today seem remarkably tame and tolerant of tourists. They eat large animals including cattle but are not normally manhunters unless sick.

As is the case with the African lion, the Indian female begins breeding at about three years of age; there is no particular breeding season, and she produces two or three cubs every one-and-a-half or two years, after a gestation of about 116 days. The color of the Asiatic lion's coat is the same sandy brown as that of African lions, but the male's mane tends to be a little thinner, and the coat otherwise somewhat thicker, than in the African varieties.

*Paul Hockings*

## LITERATURE—CAMBODIA, KHMER

The earliest dated stone inscription in the Khmer language, which could be regarded as the beginning of Khmer, or Cambodian, literature, is from 611 CE and was found in Takeo province. Over a thousand inscriptions in Old Khmer and Sanskrit that were produced throughout Cambodia and the former Khmer regions of northeast Thailand, southern Laos, and southern Vietnam between the seventh and fourteenth centuries survive. The Cambodian inscriptions are of great significance for general history as well as for the history of art and linguistics.

### Classical Literature

The period of inscriptional literature ended after the decline of the Angkor empire in the fourteenth century. The four centuries from the abandonment of Angkor in 1432 to the establishment of the French protectorate in 1836 were considered to be the dark ages in the history of Cambodia, but it was in this period that the literary works regarded as classics appeared. Written on palm leaves, classical Khmer literature was exclusively composed in verse. Prose was not regarded as an artistic medium and was reserved for practical documents such as legal texts and chronicles. There are more than fifteen forms of verse composition, each with its own strict rules on syllable length and internal and external rhyme schemes. As with other kinds of Khmer art, the beauty of Khmer poetry lies in the delicacy and richness of harmonious ornamentation. Several techniques, such as the use of high-style vocabulary, paired synonyms, alliteration, and assonance, must be skillfully manipulated to produce the most euphoric effect. Therefore, literary production was only in the hands of the intelligentsia, who had sound knowledge of the Khmer, Sanskrit, and Pali languages. Indian literary influence was undoubtedly very strong, but always the Khmer authors modified what they adopted to suit their own traditions and tastes.

Classical Khmer literature, which was composed by kings, court poets, and Buddhist monks, can be divided into ten categories. The most important genres include verse novels and didactic poems. The best-known and earliest verse novel is the *Reamker*, the Khmer version of the Indian epic *Ramayana*, written between the sixteenth and eighteenth centuries. The story of Rama, which was adapted to match the culture and beliefs of the Cambodians, has pervaded all art forms: the bas-reliefs at Angkor, the frescoes on temple walls, the shadow theater, the masked dance, and the chief repertoire of the Royal Ballet. Apart from the classical *Reamker*, popular versions of *Reamker* also exist that were recited by storytellers in public performance. The *Cbap*, or the Code of Conduct (didactic poetry written to encourage good social behavior consistent with the observance of Buddhist morality), was also highly influential. The *Cbap* has enjoyed remarkable popularity; it was constantly written, copied, and memorized from the early seventeenth century right up to the present. Two of the most famous examples are *Cbap Proh* (Code of Conduct for Men) and *Cbap Srey* (Code of Conduct for Women).

During the early eighteenth century, the *Satra Lbaeng*, verse novels recounting the Buddha's birth stories, developed. The oldest example, *Khyang Sang* (The Conch Shell), dates from 1729. Portraying the Buddhist concept of karma, many of the *Satra Lbaeng* were used by monks as texts to teach Khmer boys to read and write. Later, they came to be dramatized both in the court and the popular dance drama. A number of Khmer verse novels also draw their story lines from old local folktales and legends. A favorite with Cambodians is *Tum Teav*, the story of the ill-fated romance between Tum and Teav, based on a true love story said to have occurred in the fifteenth century. Unlike other verse novels, which are Hindu-Buddhist in their inspiration, *Tum Teav* is almost free from supernatural and mystical elements, and ordinary Khmer life is described with striking realism.

### Early-Twentieth-Century Literature

During the early part of the twentieth century, the Khmer novel emerged as a result of Western influence. The appearance of the first two novels, *Sophat* (The Story of Sophat) and *Tik Tonle Sap* (The Water of the Tonle Sap), during the last years of the 1930s marked a new era in the history of Khmer literature. These innovative and realistic literary works, reflecting the life of the emerging middle class, aroused considerable interest among the public. From 1940 to the end of the colonial era in 1953, more than fifty novels were published, with the main trend being toward romanticism. Many of them were created with serious social and political motives, and nationalism was the main inspiration for writers, although patriotic sentiment had to be shown in an indirect way. Among the best early novels are *Kulap Pailin* (The Rose of Pailin), *Phka Srapon* (The Faded Flower), and *Mealea Duongjit* (The Garland of the Heart).

### Postindependence Literature

After independence in 1954, the novel underwent tremendous growth and became the most popular literary genre in Cambodia. Between 1953 and 1975, almost one thousand titles were published. Love stories constituted a major portion of the postindependence novels, with the favorite theme being the arranged marriage. Another outstanding type was the historical novel; these were written mainly to cultivate a spirit of nationalism and loyalty toward the monarchy. The adventure novel, packed with exciting battles, was also very popular among the Khmer readers. The authors of these novels were heavily influenced by Western adventure novels as well as by Chinese epics and films. In the late 1950s, the social novel appeared after the government and the Association of Khmer Writers introduced literary competitions. The award-winning novels mostly dealt with such contemporary social problems as the struggle of Khmer women in modern society and the life of the urban working class. An outstanding example is *Preah Athit Thmey Reah Loe Phaendey Chas* (The New Sun Rises on the Old Land), which reflects the struggle of the working class against oppression and exploitation by urban capitalists.

### Khmer Rouge and Later Periods

Khmer literature degenerated during the Khmer Rouge regime between April 1975 and January 1978.

As a result of revolutionary policies, at least 1.5 million Cambodians were killed, including a great many writers and literary scholars, as well as members of the reading public. Schools were closed, libraries were demolished, books were deliberately destroyed, and writers were not able to express their ideas and feelings. Literature, in the form of poetry and proverbs, was written to support Khmer Rouge ideology and values. After 1979, cultural and literary activity was reorganized by the government of the People's Republic of Kampuchea. Khmer poems and novels of the 1980s were written to support the socialist policy of the government and to encourage the Cambodians to participate in the work of national security and reconstruction. Their recurring themes are the tragic life during the Pol Pot years, the heroic acts of soldiers in the revolutionary army fighting against the Khmer Rouge and the noncommunist resistance factions, and Cambodian-Vietnamese friendship and solidarity. In Europe and America, Khmer refugee writers also produced novels, stories, and collections of poems with the principal theme of the dramatic events between 1975 and 1979 and their suffering and nostalgia for the homeland. From 1980 on, the horrors of the Khmer Rouge reached a much wider audience through the autobiographical accounts of survivors written in English and French. Among the first was Pin Yathay's *L'Utopie Meurtière*, published in Paris in 1980. This book is considered by general readers as well as scholars of Cambodian studies as one of the best of the surviviors' accounts. Later, it came out in English under the title *Stay Alive, My Son.*

In the 1990s the Association of Khmer Writers was reestablished, and two literary competitions have been organized since 1995. Khmer fiction in this decade developed in two directions: one returning toward the novelistic tradition of the postindependence period, and the other continuing the socialist influence from the former decade.

*Klairung Amratisha*

*See also:* **Angkor Wat; Buddhism, Theravada—Southeast Asia; Cambodia—History; Ramayana**

### Further Reading

Amratisha, Klairung. (1998) "The Cambodian Novel: A Study of Its Emergence and Development." Ph.D. thesis. University of London.

Jacob, Judith M. (1995) "Cambodia (Kampuchea)." In *Southeast Asia: Traveler's Literary Companion*, edited by Alastair Dingwall. Lincolnwood, IL: Passport Books.

———. (1996) *The Traditional Literature of Cambodia.* Oxford: Oxford University Press.

Jarvis, Helen, comp. (1997) *Cambodia.* Oxford: Clio Press.

Khing Hoc Dy. (1990) *Contribution à l'Histoire de la Littérature Khmère.* Vol. 1, *L'Epoque Classique XVe–XIXe Siècle.* Paris: L'Harmattan.

———. (1993) *Ecrivain et Expression Littéraires du Cambodge au XXème Siècle.* Paris: L'Harmattan.

———. (1994) "Khmer Literature since 1975." In *Cambodian Culture since 1975: Homeland and Exile*, edited by May M. Ebihara, Carol A. Mortland, and Judy Ledgerwood. Ithaca, NY: Cornell University Press.

## LITERATURE—CENTRAL ASIA

It is difficult to imagine Central Asia without literature. Of the epic literature and poetry produced by numerous Central Asian ethnic groups, scholars are most familiar with Turkish and Persian literature and, to a certain extent, writings and oral compositions in Arabic and Urdu. Some of the oldest forms are odes to Tengri, the predominant monotheistic belief system of the eleventh through thirteenth centuries. Next came the *chorchok* (also known as *sav, jir, dastan*), oral histories, as well as didactic stories drawn from that genre.

Poetry writing was one of the earliest pastimes in Central Asia. Folk poets still perform poetry at teahouses, as they accompany themselves with a stringed musical instrument generally known as the *kobuz.* Other performers often join in, contesting for top honors and monetary and other awards. This musicopoetic competition has always been an eagerly awaited entertainment feature at special occasions such as weddings and funerary feasts. Or a traveling minstrel may recite and act out an entire epic, such as the *Manas* (c. 995, the national epic of the Kyrgyz people, centering on a heroic figure called Manas), *Iskandarnameh* (The Book of Alexander the Great, by the Persian poet Nezami, c. 1141–1203), or *Shahnameh* (The Book of Kings, compiled by the Persian poet Firdawsi, c. 935–c. 1020).

### Poetry Written by Rulers

From the Samanid rulers of the ninth century through the sixteenth-century rulers of the Uzbeks and Timurids, a new ruler usually issued a collection of his poems in a specially prepared volume in order to win the respect and allegiance of his subjects. This collection was duplicated by scribes and read aloud at teahouses. The ruler's prestige was increased when people enjoyed such poetry on aesthetic grounds, an especially desirable achievement if the new ruler was establishing a dynasty to replace a previous one. *Hikmet*, by Shibani Khan (d. 1510) of the Uzbeks, is an example of such poetry written in the early sixteenth century.

### Mirrors for Princes

Manuals prepared to instruct future rulers and to improve the abilities of reigning kings, termed "Mirrors for Princes," include such works as the *Kutadgu Bilig* (published in English as *Wisdom of Royal Glory*), the *Kabusnameh* (*A Mirror for Princes*, eleventh–twelfth centuries), and *Siyasatnameh* (The Book of Government). The *Kutadgu Bilig* was written by Yusuf of Balasagun and dedicated to Tavgach Bugra Khan of the Karakhanid dynasty (999–1212), in 1170. The *Kabusnameh* was produced shortly afterward as a series of admonitions from the ruler to his son and heir, detailing how to extract the most from the earthly pleasures in his realm. The *Siyasatnameh* was presented by Nizam al-Mulk (1018/19–1092), the prime minister of Alp Arslan (c. 1030–1072), the Seljuk ruler, as his testament and as a defense of his own political actions.

### *Dastan*s and Other Oral Compositions

The form of epic poem known as the *dastan* is the principal repository of the ethnic identity, history, customs, and value systems of its composers and their peoples. The events commemorated in a *dastan* may date from a very early period. For the Central Asians, the oral record, particularly as preserved in *dastan*s, is an integral part of identity, historical memory, and the historical record itself. The oral tradition in Central Asia precedes the common era and has been preserved across multitudes of generations. It stands, as it always has, as the final line of defense against any attempts to dominate the Central Asians culturally or politically.

Stylistically Central Asian *dastan*s differ from Islamic epic poetry, the bulk of which appeared and spread after approximately the twefth century, and especially since the fifteenth century. In Central Asia, the tradition of expression and celebration of ancestral exploits and identity predates the use of the word *dastan*, which appears as a later borrowing into Turkic dialects.

Certainly the idea of marking important events with versified narrations or songs is not new. In fact, each significant event in the lives of Central Asians had its own type of "marker" song. The *suyunju* celebrated good news, including the birth of the *alp* (leader), especially after a tribe or individual had experienced difficulties. The *yar-yar* was sung at weddings. More than merely celebrating the union of the bride and groom, however, it also signaled the beginning of other courtships at the wedding feast. The *koshtau* was sung on the departure of the *alp* for a campaign and the *estirtu* when an *alp*'s death was announced. The *yogtau* was sung at *yog ashi*, the memorial feast (after burial) to lament the death of the *alp*.

The term *jir*, as in *batirlik jiri*, is equivalent to *dastan* and includes all these components. In most cases, the celebration of the *alp*'s tribulations and ensuing victory is referenced by the name of the *alp* only. Oghuz Khan, Manas, Koroglu, Kirk Kiz are some examples of *alp*s whose exploits are recorded in epics of the same name. At other times, the term *batir* or *alp* is appended to the name of the individual thus honored: Kambar Batir, Chora Batir, Alp Er Tunga. However, despite the prevalent use of the terms *jir* and *kokcho* (still used in various portions of Central Asia), the term *dastan* is employed throughout this work when referring to this type of epic composition, in keeping with the usage of the secondary literature.

When celebrating the *alp*, the exemplary individual's attributes were always compared to natural phenomena, since he or she possessed rare qualities. Thus the *alp* can run as swift as lightning; his hair glows as bright as the sun; his body, in his prime, is as sturdy as the strongest tree; his punch is mightier than a thunderbolt. Such nature imagery draws upon the values of shamanism, the dominant belief system of Central Asian Turks prior to the arrival of Islam in the eighth century. Moreover, the use of the term *bahsi* (also *ozan*) to designate the reciter of the epic also has shamanistic connotations.

Traditionally, a *dastan* is composed by an *ozan* in order to celebrate a memorable event in the life of his people. The *ozan* will usually set the events in verse and recite them while accompanying himself on a stringed instrument. The *dastan* typically depicts the *alp* fighting against the collective enemies of his people and tribe. Under his leadership the longed-for victory is achieved. The trials and tribulations endured by this preeminent leader, though aggravated by one or more traitors, are in due course alleviated by a full supporting cast. Nor is the theme of love a stranger to the plot. Often the loved one is abducted by the enemy, only to be rescued after much searching, fighting, and sacrifice. There are attempts by the foes and the traitors to extort favors of various sorts from the lovers, but this does not deter the resolve or the eventual triumph of the principal personages. The traitors, frequently from the same tribe as the *alp*, collaborate with the enemy or abuse the trust of their people and their leaders. However, none of this prevents the inescapable success of the *alp* in the end. The traitors receive their due, being now and then executed for their sins but customarily forgiven and allowed to roam the earth in search of reconciliation between themselves and God.

Reference to similar past experiences is standard and reinforces the very important link to earlier *dastans*.

Motifs or whole episodes from earlier *dastans* may be repeated, sometimes with variations, in new *dastans*. Religious motifs emerge in descriptions of practices and beliefs. Among the Islamic practices earlier modes of worship are apparent. The narration of the *dastan*, in verse or prose, may also allude to supernatural powers.

The *dastan* travels with the Central Asians and, like its owners, it is not limited by geographic frontiers. Indeed, the idea of boundaries in the Western sense was alien to the nomadic societies of Central Asia and imposed on them late in their history. The necessity to undertake biannual migrations in search of fresh pastures for the livestock complicated the definition of a rigidly defined homeland. In the event that the heirs of a *dastan* face new threats to their freedom, the importance of the *dastan* is reinforced. Should the enemy somehow prevail, the *dastan*, by providing an unbreakable link to the past, affords the inspiration to seek independence once again.

### Conversion Literature

Before the arrival of Islam in the tenth through thirteenth centuries, several dominant belief systems coexisted in Central Asia, including Tengri, Zoroastrianism, and Buddhism. Special literature was created or translated for the purpose of disseminating each newcomer religion, when it arrived. These missionary works were rendered into the Central Asian languages dominant at the time that the religion reached the region and, in some cases, were translated out of them for dissemination in other regions. For example, Buddhism made its way from India into China by way of the Uighurs, who translated sacred Buddhist texts from Sanskrit into Uighur and then into Chinese. Christianity established a small foothold in western Central Asia with the *Codex Cumanicus* (c. 1300), a Latin guide to the language of the Cumans, a people of Central Asia, which included passages from the Bible in translation.

In eastern Central Asia, the Ghaznavids (977–1187) and Karakhanids held sway as the Islamization of the region got underway. In the central area of Central Asia, the Seljuk or Oghuz Turks (1038–1157) and the Timurids (fifteenth–sixteenth centuries) were the dominant powers. The Mongol Golden Horde khanates (fourteenth–sixteenth centuries) held the northwestern region. Farther west were the Ottoman Turks (1453–1922), who were sometimes involved in Central Asian affairs. These polities and dynasties all directly or indirectly participated in the proliferation of Central Asian literary traditions.

Under these rulers, Islam popularized two new literary genres in Central Asian polities. The first dealt with the myths associated with the conversion of Central Asian populations to Islam, and the second was concerned with the struggle of Islam against the extant belief systems in Central Asia, in the form of tales of battles during the conversion process. The Persian poet Mawlana Jalal ad-Din ar-Rumi (1207–1273) was one such figure making use of the genre. Rumi relied on his voluminous poetry to spread the word of his Sufi (Islamic mystic) sect.

### Philosophy, Astronomy and Other Sciences, and Mathematics

The rulers of polities provided the patronage and favorable environment for the production of masterpieces, by which the rulers would be remembered for eternity. Therefore, regardless of the nature and objectives of the writing, Central Asians adhered to certain rules in their works. This is evident even in books not entirely devoted to belles lettres. Among them are the writings of the Turkish philosopher Abu Nasr al-Farabi (c. 878–c. 950) and the Arab historian Muhammad ibn Jarir at-Tabari (c. 839–923), who wrote in Arabic and Turkish. Their works were translated into Western languages and published from the sixteenth century on. Ulugh Beg (1394–1449), the grandson of the Turkic conqueror Timur (1336–1405), ruled Samarqand and the environs and was the author of astronomical and mathematical works that influenced European studies, when, beginning in the seventeenth century, they were translated into Latin and printed in Oxford, England.

Reportedly of Uighur descent, Mir Ali Shir Nava'i (1441–1501) was one of the premier literati and statesmen of his time. He wrote voluminously and with apparent ease in Chagatay, a Turkic dialect, and in Persian and long served as prime minister of the Timurid ruler Huseyin Baykara (reigned 1469–1506) of Herat and Khorasan. Much of his tasteful poetry remains untranslated, but among his prose works, *Muhakemat al-lughateyn* (Consideration of Two Languages) has been translated into English. Babur (1483–1530), another direct descendant of Timur, established the Mughal empire in India. He was also an accomplished author in Chagatay; his memoirs are still highly praised and regarded. Jami (1414–1492), a Persian poet and mystic, was Nava'i's friend and fellow man of letters of the period in Herat.

### The Czarist Period

As Russian armies proceeded to invade Central Asia, the literature began to reflect the struggle between the invaders and the defenders. The Russian invasion attempts were not always successful. In 1506, Shibani Khan of the Uzbeks sent a quatrain to Muhammed Amin, the khan of Kazan, congratulating the latter for turning back the Russian attack on Kazan. Shortly afterward, *dastans* were pressed into service as well. The 1552 variant of the Chora Batir *dastan* described the fighting over Kazan. In 1905, Ismail Gaspirali, (1851–1914), an influential Tatar journalist, wrote a poem to admonish his detractors: "If my arrow would hit the target / If my horse should win the race / Chorabatir is valiant / If my arrow could not reach its target / And my horse cannot win the race / Tell me, what could Chorabatir do?" (Paksoy 1986: 265).

## The Basmachi and the Semi-Independence Period

During the nineteenth century, when the greatest portion of Central Asia fell under Russian armies, the response of the Central Asian leadership was to have medieval Central Asian literature collected and published. In 1916, the Basmachi (Turkistan National Liberation Movement) began fighting, at first spontaneously, later in a planned and coordinated manner, to construct a Turkistan polity. For a time, the movement was successful. According to Zeki Velidi Togan (1890–1970), a prime mover of the initiative, the *dastan Koroglu* not only kept morale high but also served as a role model because the historical Koroglu (sixteenth century) had fought for freedom against all odds.

When Central Asian peoples could not openly circumvent Russian censorship, they resorted to writing highly coded satire. The journal *Molla Nasreddin* is a prime example. Named after a "people's philosopher" who lived prior to the thirteenth century, it was founded by Jelil Memmedkuluzade (1866–1937) and published in Tbilisi, Tabriz, and Baku from 1906 to 1920. Exercising an enormous influence on its readership, it spawned dozens of emulators across continents. When Mikhail Gorbachev instituted perestroika, the Soviet policy of economic and governmental reform, in the mid-1980s, the journal was reprinted in Baku, as a reminder of what had gone before. Those who reprinted *Molla Nasreddin* had the same objective as its founder, Memmedkuluzade: autonomy and freedom.

## The Soviet Period

When the 1917 Bolshevik revolution began, Central Asian people were endeavoring to commit their vast and ancient literature to print. After 1924, when Central Asia was divided among various Soviet Socialistic Republics, the Oriental Institutes, now Sovietized, worked to regain control of the process. One method they used was to collect and record on paper the oral literature as if the materials were intended for publication, but then to bury the collected manuscripts in a myriad of inaccessible archives. Some manuscripts were supposedly lost, their reciters who had carried on the oral tradition murdered. When other methods failed, the Soviet bureaucracies charged with the "management" of Central Asian literature began mounting court trials of books during 1950–1952. The court trials were designed to purge national cultures of those elements deemed incompatible with a Marxist-Leninist world view. Typically, attacks would begin with derogatory comments in a local newspaper or national newspaper. This would be picked up by the local Communist Party and then by various local, political, social, academic, or literary organizations, and finally by an organization of national standing. The culmination of the attack would be the universal condemnation of local intellectuals, who would be charged with idealizing the bourgeois-nationalist aspects of their national literature. At this time, traditional literatures of the countries of the USSR were banned. After the accession of Nikita Khruschev (1894–1971) to Communist Party leadership, the publication process resumed—but with new methods. Rather than allowing the originals to be disseminated, the Oriental Institutes insisted on issuing approved sanitized versions. Also, purported *dastans* on such themes as Ode to the Tractor and Ode to the Collective Farm were issued to replace the traditional ones.

One solution used in the 1930s to circumvent censorship was fiction literature. During the 1980s, the genre continued to survive in works like *Olmez Kayalar* (Immortal Cliffs) by Mamadali Mahmudov, *Kuyas ham Alav* (Sun Is Also Fire) by Alishir Ibadinov, *Singan Kilich* (Broken Sword) by Tolongon Kasimbekov, *Baku 1501* by Azize Caferzade, and *Altin Orda* (Golden Horde) by Ilyas Esenberlin. Despite being fiction, all these novels contain, to various degrees, footnotes with historically accurate information and provide details of how Central Asia was invaded by Russian armies. The Soviet apparatus, spearheaded by the Oriental Institutes, tried to pressure these and other authors to rewrite portions of their novels to cast the Soviet Russians in a better light. Failing that, the Soviet bureaucrats endeavored to have the authors recant their written assertions. Despite the efforts of the Soviet bureaucracies, defiant works kept appearing.

A number of authors took advantage of the Soviet state's atheism policy to disseminate views not otherwise printable. Aliser Ibadinov, in his *Kuyas ham Alav*, insisted on the necessity of remaining true to ancestral beliefs, which predated not only Soviet ideology but also Islam. This Ibadinov accomplished by portraying how Central Asians resisted the spread of Islam.

## The Post-Soviet Period

Some Central Asian authors were sent to Soviet jails simply for writing. In some cases, world attention focusing on the plight of these writers managed to get them freed. One such case involves Mamadali Mahmudov, who was imprisoned by the Uzbeks for including criticisms of the Soviet government in his writings. One of the reasons that the government was willing to free him was, perhaps, that Mahmudov was simply quoting passages from older works, such as the *Dastan Dede Korkut* (committed to paper in the sixteenth century although dating from a much earlier period). After the Uzbek Republic declared independence in the post-1991 era, Mahmudov was rewarded for his earlier work by being given the newly instituted Cholpan Prize. Named after a Central Asian author who perished in Stalin's Soviet jails, the Cholpan Prize was meant to honor Mahmudov's skill in transmitting historical documentation and narration under the guise of fiction. In 1999, Mahmudov was abducted and jailed once again. To what extent his new incarceration is due to his past sins of the Soviet period is yet to be understood. His case has been taken up by various groups and governments, including Amnesty International, Helsinki Watch, Human Rights Watch, and Digital Freedom Network.

Perhaps the ancient literature of Central Asia is continuing to serve the original intent of its creators. The following poem was printed in *Muhbir* (Tashkent, November 1982), the official organ of the Uzbek Communist Party Authors' Union. The message is still valid:

> Give me a chance, my rebellious dreams
> My father has erected his statue in my memory
> May years and winds be rendered powerless
> May his legacy not be erased from my conscience
>
> Give me a chance, my rebellious dreams
> Grant my father a holy Dastan
> May years and winds be rendered powerless
> May his remembrance never be allowed to fade

*H. B. Paksoy*

### Further Reading


Baykara, Huseyin. "Risale-I Huseyin Baykara." (1991) *AACAR Bulletin* 4, 2 (Fall).

Bosworth, C. E. (1973) *The Ghaznavids: Their Empire in Afghanistan and Eastern Iran, 994–1040*. Beirut, Lebanon: Librairie du Liban.

Dankoff, Robert, ed. and trans., in collaboration with James Kelly. (1982, 1984, 1985) "Compendium of the Turkic Dialects (Diwan Lugat at-Turk)." In *Sources of Oriental Languages and Literatures*, edited by Sinasi Tekin. Cambridge, MA: Harvard University Press, Part I (1982) xi, 416; Part II (1984) iii, 381; Part III (1985), 337 + microfiche.

DeWeese, Dewin. (1994) *Islamization and Native Religion in the Golden Horde*. University Park, PA: Pennsylvania State University Press.

Mano Eiji, ed. (1995) *Babur-nama (vaqayi)* (Memoirs of Babur). Kyoto, Japan: Syokado Nakanishi.

Hacib, Yusuf Has. (1983) *Wisdom of Royal Glory (Kutadgu Bilig): A Turko-Islamic Mirror for Princes*. Trans. by Robert Dankoff. Chicago: University of Chicago Press.

Hanaway, W. L. (1988) "Epic Poetry." In *Persian Literature*, edited by Ehsan Yarshater. Ithaca, NY: Bibliotheca Persica.

Levend, Agah S. (n.d.) *Ali Shir Nevai*. 4 Vols. Ankara, Turkey: Türk Tarih Kurumu Basimevi.

Nava'i, Ali Shir. (1966) *Mukhamet al-lughateyn* (Consideration of Languages). Trans. by Robert Devereux. Leiden, Netherlands: Brill.

Nizam al-Mulk (1960) *Siyasatnama: The Book of Government, or Rules for Kings*. London: Routledge & Kegan Paul.

Noldeke, Theodor. (1930) *Shahnama*. Mumbai, India: Executive Committee of the K. R. Cama Oriental Institute.

Paksoy, H. B. (1986) "Chora Batir: A Tatar Admonition to Future Generations." *Studies in Comparative Communism* 19, 3–4 (autumn–winter): 253–265.

———. (1989) *Alpamysh: Central Asian Identity under Russian Rule*. Hartford, CT: AACAR.

———. (1999) *Essays on Central Asia*. Lawrence, KS: Carrie.

———, ed. (1992) *Central Asian Monuments*. Istanbul, Turkey: ISIS Press.

———, ed. (1994) *Central Asia Reader: The Rediscovery of History*. Armonk, NY: M. E. Sharpe.

Schamiloglu, Uli. (1986) "Tribal Politics and Social Organization." Ph.D diss. Columbia University.

Subtelny, Maria Eva. (1979) "The Poetic Circle at the Court of the Timurid Sultan Husain Baiqara, and Its Political Significance." Ph.D. diss. Harvard University.


**LITERATURE—CHINA** From earliest times, literature in China was considered to include philosophical and historical writing along with prose and poetry; literature was writing that met social needs or expressed one's deepest feelings, or both. Oral literary forms were often respected, and most written forms through time regularly drew material from the folk tradition; conversely, the dominant written forms helped shape the ethics and aesthetics of popular oral traditions as well.

## NOBEL PRIZE FOR GAO XINGJIAN

In 2000, the Nobel Prize for Literature was awarded to Chinese writer Gao Xingjian for his novel, *Soul Mountain*. The novel, which was translated into English by Mabel Lee and published by HarperCollins, is an account in various literary forms of Gao's travels (physical, mental, and spiritual) through modern China and a less than favorable comparison with the China of the past. Gao was born in 1940 and became known in China for his writings on the Cultural Revolution, which he burned for fear of being imprisoned. After that his work was both tolerated and repressed by the government, and in 1987 he immigrated to France. His book is based in part on his travels for a year and a half through southern China.

*David Levinson*

### Earliest Forms and Functions

China's earliest extant texts presumably reflect the spoken language of the time, but writing was increasingly reserved for the social and political elite; consequently, the language of classical literature (*wenyan*, or "cultured language") was not allowed to reflect changes as spoken language developed through time. Thus the language of formal literature became archaic and demanded extensive study for thorough comprehension. Its difficulty was enhanced by the welter of allusions to a broad range of earlier literature, which adorned the work of learned writers. Although classical Chinese literature required years to master, the preservation of a standard written language and its rich literary tradition served to link successive generations of writers and readers of diverse backgrounds throughout China and elsewhere throughout East Asia to produce what is arguably the world's richest literary tradition. Those who succeeded came to be called *wenren* (people of culture), or literati, in contrast to the bulk of the Chinese people, who could merely read practical texts or who were illiterate. The high status associated with high levels of education, like many of China's literary forms and genres, had remarkable tenacity, lasting hundreds of years until the twentieth century, when Western influences swept through Chinese culture as well as through its political system.

### Dominant Literary Forms—Poetry

Unquestionably, the dominant Chinese literary form was always poetry. Among the oldest preserved writings are hymns and dances from the courts of the Shang (1766–1045 BCE) and Zhou (1045–256 BCE) dynasties, twelfth and eleventh centuries BCE. These and folk songs make up the earliest collection assembled around 600 BCE, the *Shijing* (Classic of Poetry/ Book of Songs), which was memorized by generations of budding writers for the imagery of its poems and for the moral teachings each poem was thought to embody. Most were read as oblique references to contemporary political events and social situations.

For two thousand years, this collection has been identified with the Confucian school of moralistic teaching; this poetic tradition grew up in the states of the north China plain, the Confucian homeland. By around 400 BCE, a second tradition was developing farther south, around the Chang (Yangtze) River. These poems more closely reflect religious, even ecstatic, practices and beliefs. This tradition, preserved in the collection *Chuci* (Songs of Chu), contributed a more diverse prosody as well as fantastic images and motifs to the maturing poetic tradition. Marked by a caesura in each line, this form may have influenced the development of the prosy *fu*, or rhapsody, during the Han dynasty (206 BCE–220 CE); it died out when the political power of the north became dominant.

A new form, *shi*, or lyric poetry, was to develop toward the end of four centuries of unified Han rule. Written in equal numbers of lines of five syllables (or words, in largely monosyllabic early Chinese), *shi* were often composed in couplets; later, seven-syllable lines also became common. Poems in this form served as the vehicle for the most profound philosophical speculation as well as deep emotion and even literary play.

## THE CHINESE VIEW OF WESTERN APPRECIATION OF LITERATURE

The extract of text written by the Protestant missionary Mary Isabella Bryson in 1890 provides an interesting insight into the Chinese opinion of Western civilization.

> But what is the business of the man who is approaching us, carrying two large deep bamboo baskets, each with a tiny flag attached to one of them bearing the legend, "Respect Printed Paper"? As he proceeds, a door here and there opens, and a manservant comes out with a waste basket, emptying its contents into the large basket carried by the collector of scraps. This man is employed by some Chinese benevolent society to go round and collect even the smallest scraps of printed paper so that they may be carried to some temple courtyard, and destroyed by fire in a furnace set apart for the purpose, for the kitchen stove would be considered too secular of a place for performing such a sacred duty. This is one of the works of merit which the Chinese believe accumulate for them a sort of balance, to be set against the sins for which they have committed when they are judged by the king of the infernal regions at the end of life.
>
> Probably few things have contributed so much to the idea that foreigners are uncivilized barbarians as our light regard for our own printed or written paper. They see us using it in all sorts of ignominious ways. We wrap parcels in it, and frequently carelessly tread it underfoot, consequently the Chinese not unnaturally conclude that we can have nothing of the name of a language or literature, or we should not treat the printed page in so disrespectful of a manner.

*Source:* Mary Isabella Bryson. (1890) *Child Life in China.* London: William Clowes and Sons, Limited, 58–59.

They served as the cornerstone of virtually all writers' collected works—and reputations. The "classical" form of such poetry, *gushi,* reached maturity in the third century and was used as a vehicle for poets' most intensely felt emotions until the twentieth century. During the Tang dynasty (618–907), a highly formalized version became popular, the *lushi* (regulated poetry), written in eight lines of either five or seven syllables. Over fifty thousand *shi* are preserved from the Tang period, a high point in poetic expression; from the subsequent Song dynasty (960–1279), hundreds of thousands still exist.

China's most famous poets include three who were contemporary, Wang Wei (d. 761), Li Bai (often romanized Li Bo or Li Po, 701–762), and Du Fu (712–770), all members of the educated elite of the Tang period. Although their differences are sometimes exaggerated for the sake of contrast, each is identified with a major philosophical school of the times: Wang Wei with Buddhism, Li Bai with Taoism, and Du Fu with Confucianism. This is because many of Wang Wei's poems reflect the stillness of meditation, Li Bai's works express the mental freedom associated with philosophical Taoism, and Du Fu frequently addressed the calamities of the day, particularly the sufferings caused by the An Lushan rebellion that began in 755. In this, Du Fu was performing the duties of the faithful Confucian minister of state, although his stern advice brought him dismissal from office.

Also during the Tang, another new form of poetic expression developed in the entertainment districts of the Tang capital, the *ci,* or song lyric. Such poems had lines of irregular lengths to match melodies then popular and most frequently extolled romantic love. After the music was forgotten, poets continued to write new words, often having far more philosophical import, to these old song patterns, and they do so today. Even Mao Zedong (1893–1976) wrote his revolutionary verse to *ci* song patterns hundreds of years old.

**Dominant Literary Forms—Historical Writing**

Most early Chinese prose constitutes what later would be considered historical writing. Rarely is it in the form of connected accounts; instead it records facts, primarily the words and deeds of both important individuals and important groups in early Chinese society. The most famous, *Shiji* (The Historical Records), compiled by Sima Qian (145–87? BCE), is also considered a model for prose style. Its strength lies in its presentation of biographical material with an eye to demonstrating how individuals fulfilled (or failed in) social roles. This approach led, in later histories, to a tendency to type individuals at the expense of the psychological detail that might distinguish them.

**Dominant Literary Forms—Philosophical Writing**

Philosophical writing, especially the early canonical works of major schools, were also considered part of the literary canon. The period during which Confucius (Kong Qiu, termed Kong Fuzi or Master Kong, 551–479 BCE) lived was considered the time of the "Hundred Schools," because of the lively philosophical debates of the time, during which few schools seemed to be mutually exclusive in their ideas and texts were quoted relatively freely among them. Most philosophical writings from that time were collectively produced; identifying authorship is thus a futile effort. The most important school of thought to emerge was Confucianism. Its moral teachings and political values were adapted to fit the needs of the Han state, and its ideology, though frequently modified, remained nominally dominant until the fall of China's final dynasty, the Qing (1644–1912). The Confucian school claimed many of the writings of highest antiquity, such as ritual texts and the *Yijing* (Classic of Changes), to take the position of guardians of China's cultural traditions.

The second most important school is Taoism. An early gnomic text known as the *Laozi*, or more commonly in recent decades, the *Daodejing* (or *Tao-te ching*, The Classic of the Way and of Virtue), apparently began as an allusive treatise on proper governing, but it has often served as a source of inspiration for poets when read as a mystical text. References to such early philosophical works recur throughout Chinese writing until the present day.

## "IMMORTAL BY THE RIVER"

Written by Su Shi (1037–1101)

I was drinking that night on Eastern Slope,  
I sobered up and got drunk again,  
and when I went back it seemed about midnight.  
My servant boy was snoring  
it sounded like the thunder,  
When I knocked at the gate, no one answered,  
then I leaned on my staff  
and listened to the river.

I've always resented how this body  
has never been my own,  
will the time ever come when I can forget  
being always busy?  
The night ended, the winds calmed,  
the wrinkled waves grew flat,  
I'll set off from here in my small boat,  
on river and lakes lodge the rest of my days.

*Source:* Stephen Owen (1997) *Anthology of Chinese Literature, the Beginnings to 1911.* New York: W. W. Norton, 578.

**Dominant Literary Forms—Fiction**

Chinese fiction began as an informal mode of philosophy, through parables and brief moralistic tales. Called *xiaoshuo* (lesser discourses), fictional narratives in the classical language served as an elegant amusement for some. But especially after vernacular-language writings developed around 1300, highly educated authors increasingly used fiction as a vehicle for social and political commentary. This is despite the conventional evaluation of fiction as less artistic than poetry, hence less worthy of serious consideration as an art form. The earliest fictional genre has been termed *zhiguai*, or "records of anomalies." These terse accounts, which began to appear around 250 CE, are generally anonymous and have been collected into a number of popular anthologies without regard to period of composition or authorship. Such anecdotes record the appearance of ghosts, uncanny events involving animals or plants, or magical objects. A subset, termed *zhiren* (records of persons), includes observations about the habits of eccentric individuals, their witty remarks, and critical evaluations of their literary and artistic skills. Later examples of the form tend to be longer, with more fully developed plots and characterization. Nearly five hundred of the best known and finest are assembled in *Liaozhai zhiyi* (Liaozhai's Notes on Strange Matters) by Pu Songling (1640–1715). Many have to do with intrusions of the ghostly and the supernatural into the lives of lonely scholars, seemingly projecting the aspirations and fears of this group into the realm of the supernatural.

A somewhat longer fictional form, also written in the formal language, was the *chuanqi xiaoshuo*, or classical tale (literally, "transmissions of the strange"), which became popular during the Tang and subsequent Song periods. Romantic in subject matter, the best known involve romantic liaisons between young scholars and beautiful women, heroic acts of larger-than-life men and women knights-errant, and satirical attacks on contemporary figures and points of view. Justly famous is *Yingying zhuan* (The Story of Yingying) by the poet Yuan Zhen (779–831), a sad tale of unwise passion between young lovers, presumably based on personal experience.

Although material from oral traditions can be discerned in these classical-language narratives, folk literature is usually assumed to have played a larger role in the development of vernacular fiction. Professional entertainers had been active from the earliest times; through the Tang period, most were known for singing and dancing. But by the Song period, the capital was home to narrators of a variety of coherent tales, ranging in subject matter from historical and religious figures to romantic adventures of knights-errant, criminals, and illicit lovers. Literati summaries of these narrations may have circulated in written versions as book printing became increasingly common after around 1000 CE, but the earliest extant vernacular short stories date from around 1550. From that time onward, these stories, subsequently termed *huaben xiaoshuo* (oral tales fiction), became an artistic form for literati writers, whose works constitute examples of the most complicated fiction in the language.

Some of these stories take up the lives of common people during traumatic historical events such as invasions by foreign peoples; others explore the complex motivations of adulterous couples or the events leading up to heinous crimes. Feng Menglong (1574–1646), the editor of the most outstanding collection of 120 stories, described their content as most effectively limited to one individual or a single event.

The Chinese vernacular novel developed around the same time, presumably on the basis of unrefined lengthy historical narratives termed *pinghua* (plain[ly told] tales), written between around 1280 and 1450. The first novel was *Sanguo zhi yanyi* (Romance of the Three Kingdoms), attributed to Luo Guanzhong (c. 1330–1400), although its earliest edition appeared only in 1522. It traces a terrible period during the third century when China was wracked by civil war and ultimately, but temporarily, divided into three warring states. The novel focuses on human motivations and shortcomings as one leader after another struggles to unite the country.

Within a few decades, by the middle of the sixteenth century, many other novels had appeared. Most narrated historical periods, with endless scenes of battlefield carnage and palace intrigues, focusing on the human motivations behind historical events. Others included tales of individual bandit heroes (*Shuihu zhuan*, or Outlaws of the Marsh) or adventures of a magical monkey during his quest for Buddhist scriptures (*Xiyou ji*, or Journey to the West). They were popular among the educated elite, but a genuine breakthrough in narrative writing came with the circulation, in manuscript form, of *Jin Ping Mei* (The Plum in the Golden Vase) in the late 1580s. This novel is set in the household of a wealthy merchant and explores the tortuous relationships between its male protagonist and his many wives and lovers. The work of a literatus of prodigious knowledge, it is jammed with quotations from and allusions to all forms of popular culture, songs, proverbs, jokes, and slang expressions. It is infamous for its descriptions of sexual behavior, but all are couched in flowery euphemisms.

By around 1600, a number of novel genres had appeared: romantic but artistically refined encounters between men and maids, pious tales of religious figures, fantastic journeys, and, of course, the ever-popular novelistic versions of the lives of historical figures and ruling houses. But the high point of Chinese fiction came with the development of the literati novel during the eighteenth century, the most outstanding being *Shi'tou ji* (Story of the Stone, also known as *Honglou meng*, or Dream of Red Mansions/the Red Chamber) by Cao Xueqin (1715–1764). Like other literati novelists, Cao worked on his masterpiece for several decades; indeed, he died before it was completed. Story of the Stone presents a lovingly detailed description of life in a declining but still extravagantly wealthy household, presumably based on the author's childhood experiences. It is also an engaging but ultimately tragic love story involving three cousins, a boy and two dissimilar teenage girls. But the novel's dominant theme is the disparity between appearance and reality, a theme that abounds with religious significance as various characters struggle with the competing appeals of Buddhist detachment and the realm of emotional commitments. Other literati novels explore the frustrations of young men who aspire to the high status of the literati but who fail in the increasingly sharp competition for limited places among the political elite.

### Dominant Literary Forms—Drama

Drama evolved from the religious fairs and puppet entertainments of antiquity into fully developed combinations of plot, instrumental and vocal music, acting, and physical display around 1250. The first major form was the *zaju* (variety show), of the Mongol Yuan period (1279–1368). Each play had only one singing role, and the story was presented from the perspective of this one character. Early playwrights, including Guan Hanqing, Ma Zhiyuan, and Bai Pu, rapidly developed characterization and plotting in this form, with the result that their plays later were widely read among the literati. The highlight of the form was the sequence of five plays collectively known as *Xixiang ji* (The Story of the Western Wing) by Wang Shifu (flourished 1250–1300), based on the Tang-period story *Yingying zhuan.*

Literati developed their own dramatic form during the sixteenth century, in the Ming period (1368–1644). Termed *chuanqi*, or romances, these lengthy plays interwove contrasting plots and subplots with all the major characters singing; consequently the form became known for the rich poetry of its many arias. Although many deal with romantic attachments and were based on earlier *chuanqi* classical-language tales, major plays such as *Taohua shan* (Peach Blossom Fan) by Kong Shangren (1648–1718) and *Changsheng dian* (Palace of Long Life) by Hong Sheng (1645–1704) examine the nature of love and commitment as the lovers' world collapses around them. Perhaps the most famous is *Mudan ting* (The Peony Pavilion) by Tang Xianzu (1550–1617); it questions the arbitrariness of dreams and wakefulness, even of life and death, in the face of powerful human emotions.

### Modern Developments

Although traditional literature continues to be admired and to influence contemporary writers, influences from Western cultures have made a dramatic impact over the last 150 years. Twentieth-century Chinese literature is marked by experimentation in both form and content, movements that began during the waning years of the Qing period as nineteenth-century novelists turned ever more to contemporary events and social problems as subject matter. Generally considered the preeminent pioneer of China's new literature, Lu Xun (1881–1936) brought European-style psychological realism into his explorations of contemporary social problems, beginning with his story *Kuangren riji* (Madman's Diary) in 1918. This trend for "critical realism" was followed by several decades during which China's writers were exhorted by their political leaders to become ever more instrumental in bringing about revolutionary change. One of the more successful of these writers was Ding Ling (1904–1985). Because many of her writings use a first-person narrator superficially like herself, unsophisticated male readers misconstrued her work as inappropriately subjective for wartime literature.

The death of Mao in 1976 and the increasing internationalization of Chinese culture heralded striking developments in modernist and postmodernist fiction in both the mainland and Taiwan. Among the most noteworthy writers in this category are Mo Yan (b. 1956) from northeast China, whose *Hong gaoliang jiazu* (Red Sorghum, 1988) was made into a widely heralded film, and Wang Wen-hsing (b. 1939), who grew up in Taiwan. The idiosyncratic style and vulgar expressions of his irreverent novel *Jiabian* (Family Catastrophe, 1972) outraged moralistic critics at the time, but the novel has since been heralded as a masterpiece. In marked contrast to old Chinese practice, many outstanding contemporary writers are women, including Wang Anyi (b. 1954) from Shanghai and Zhu Tianwen (b. 1956) from Taipei.

*Robert E. Hegel*

*See also:* **Chuci; Ding Ling; Drama—China; Du Fu; Four Books; Li Bai; Lu Xun; Poetry—China; Shi**

### Further Reading


Cao Xueqin. (1973–1986) *The Story of the Stone.* 5 vols. Trans. by David Hawkes and John Minford. Harmondsworth, U.K.: Penguin.

Chang, Kang-i Sun, and Haun Saussy, eds. (1999) *Women Writers of Traditional China: An Anthology of Poetry and Criticism.* Stanford, CA: Stanford University Press.

Ding Ling. (1989) *I Myself Am a Woman: Selected Writings of Ding Ling.* Edited by Tani E. Barlow with Gary J. Bjorge. Boston: Beacon Press.

Idema, Wilt, and Lloyd Haft. (1997) *A Guide to Chinese Literature.* Ann Arbor, MI: University of Michigan Center for Chinese Studies.

Lao She. (1999) *Blades of Grass: The Stories of Lao She.* Trans. by William A. Lyell and Sarah Wei-ming Chen. Honolulu, HI: University of Hawaii Press.

Lau, Joseph S. M., and Howard Goldblatt, eds. (1995) *The Columbia Anthology of Modern Chinese Literature.* New York: Columbia University Press.

Lu Xun. (1990) *Diary of a Madman and Other Stories.* Trans. by William A. Lyell. Honolulu, HI: University of Hawaii Press.

McDougall, Bonnie S., and Kam Louie. (1997) *The Literature of China in the Twentieth Century.* New York: Columbia University Press.

Mo Yan. (1993) *Red Sorghum.* Trans. by Howard Goldblatt. New York: Viking.

Owen, Stephen, ed. and trans. (1996) *An Anthology of Chinese Literature.* New York: Norton.

Tang Xianzu. (1980) *The Peony Pavilion.* Trans. by Cyril Birch. Bloomington, IN: Indiana University Press.

Wang Shifu. (1991) *The Moon and the Zither: The Story of the Western Wing.* Edited and translated by Stephen H. West and Wilt L. Idema. Berkeley and Los Angeles: University of California Press.

Wang Wen-hsing. (1995) *Family Catastrophe.* Honolulu, HI: University of Hawaii Press.

**LITERATURE—INDIA** Some of the earliest literature in the world originated in India, beginning with writings in Vedic Sanskrit (an Aryan language), which may well be the oldest literature in any Indo-European language (Hittite being its only competitor for this position). Because of India's warm, damp climate and insect life, however, few existing manuscripts are as old as a thousand years; ancient literature was passed down by word of mouth and by the incredible rote learning of the Brahmans. If there was any literature in the Indus Valley earlier than that produced by the Aryan speakers, it is not known to have survived; only unreadable inscriptions (dating roughly from 2700–1500 BCE), so short that they never exceed two dozen characters, have been preserved from this time. These are presumed to be brief business documents.

### The Vedas

The Rig Veda is the oldest of the four Vedas, long religious texts composed in an early form of Sanskrit around 1500–1000 BCE. It was followed by three other Vedas; taken together, these books, called the Samhitas, are something like a bible, being collections of liturgical texts of diverse origin, style, date, and authorship. The Rig Veda, the most important Veda, contains 1,028 hymns, ranging in length from just one to fifty-eight stanzas. The hymns are addressed mostly to the gods, among them the sovereign Varuna, the fire god Agni, and the warrior god Indra.

The Yajur Veda has two sections: the Black Yajur Veda with magical formulas and commentaries and the White Yajur Veda with formulas that were once part of a larger text. The Sama Veda (Book of Melodies), is the oldest text on Indian music. The last of the Vedas, the Atharva Veda, is a collection of corrective magic. By about 500 BCE the form of these Vedic texts was essentially fixed.

### The *Brahmanas*

The *Brahmanas* (c. 1000–800 BCE) are exegetical commentaries on the four Vedas, two for the Rig Veda, ten for the Sama, one for the Atharva, and two for the Yajur Veda. The *Brahmanas* were the first texts to justify the superior status of the priesthood in Vedic society, by placing Brahman priests above rulers and warriors. The *Brahmanas* include some texts called *Aranyakas*, ("forest texts," that is, fit for recitation in isolation), as well as the better-known Upanishads (speculations). The fourteen principal Upanishads were perhaps written during the ninth through sixth centuries BCE, the earlier ones in prose, the later ones versified, to explain the esoteric meaning of sacrifice. Additional Upanishads were written later, as condensations of religious teachings. Their total number is hence indeterminate, though it approaches two hundred.

### The Tripitaka

During the fifth through third centuries BCE the Tripitaka (Three Baskets), the Buddhist canon in the Pali language (closely related to Sanskrit), was fixed for all time. It was soon to become the most influential body of literature in the eastern half of Asia and has remained so until the present day, especially in its Chinese and Japanese translations.

### Secular Sanskrit Writing

The first significant secular document in Sanskrit was a linguistically sophisticated grammar by Panini, which fixed the structure of Sanskrit, in the fourth century BCE. Probably during the reign of the emperor Candragupta Maurya (d. c. 297 BCE), the text of the great epic *Mahabharata*, the world's longest poem, was established (c. 300 BCE). The *Mahabharata* contains about 100,000 distychs (two-line stanzas); it deals with a great war that possibly occurred around 900 BCE and was fought on the plain of Kurukshetra, in the Punjab. One section of the poem is particularly well known as the *Bhagavad Gita*, a debate of high moral caliber between the deities Arjuna and Krishna, which was probably inserted into the poem at a later date. Another later inclusion in the *Mahabharata* was an abridged version of the *Ramayana*.

The *Mahabharata* is made up of a number of distinct sections, incorporating tales, fables, and parables, as well as disquisitions on morals, politics, and law; in fact it is a sort of encyclopedia. Yet the poem cannot be considered a historical document. It took hundreds of years to complete, is of unknown authorship, and in its final form probably dates to the second century CE. There are numerous later adaptations and translations of the story, in several languages, including those of Bali and Java.

The second great and lengthy Sanskrit epic, the *Ramayana*, is dated around 200 BCE and probably assumed its final form some two centuries later. Both epics must have incorporated material from extant folklore. Tradition has Valmiki as the author of the *Ramayana*, and it indeed appears more like the work of one person than does the *Mahabharata*. The *Ramayana* includes seven books, the first and last of which were later additions.

The *Ramayana* has only a handful of leading characters: Rama, who is a prince, his wife Sita, Rama's faithful half-brother Lakshmana, the Lankan demon Ravana, and Hanuman, the king of the monkeys. The characters and their moral dilemmas are richly drawn against a background of courtly life. A historical substratum of the story in the *Ramayana* may refer to the "Aryanization" (the northern cultural influence) of Central India. The poem had a wide influence on later literature, and there are versions in languages other than the original Sanskrit.

In this early era the image of the social structure of India was in a sense fixed by two books. During the late fourth century BCE, Kautilya wrote the *Arthasastra* (Treatise on the Good), which was rediscovered only in 1909 and is reminiscent of Machiavelli's *Il principe* (*The Prince*, 1513). In the second century CE came the *Manusmrti*, a compilation of the laws of Manu, India's legendary first man. This treatise on religious law and social obligation described in detail a society, quite possibly utopian, in which there were four caste blocks or *varna*s, each of which had its own occupations, status, and religious duties. This work exercised an immeasurable influence on Indian society for the next two thousand years, and the *varna* model is still a popular image, or simplification, of Hindu caste society.

The outpouring of Sanskrit devotional literature continued with the major Puranas, eighteen in number (c. fourth century CE). Only two are of great importance, the Bhagavata Purana (some 12,000 verses in length) and the Vishnu Purana. Each Purana is a compendium of myths and legends, heroic polemics, and philosophizing, a mine of information about early Hinduism. Roughly contemporary with the main Puranas was the famous and internationally influential anthology of anonymous fables and folktales the *Pancatantra*, which had been translated into most western European languages by the eighteenth century.

## Indian Literature in Other Languages

In the middle of the third century BCE, the first inscriptions in Tamil (a Dravidian language) in the Brahmi script appeared, and then, around 150 CE, there was established in South India the Tamil Sangam, a series of three academies of poets and philosophers, which lasted for decades. While its historicity is shrouded, the Sangam set the stage for an outpouring of medieval poetry in Tamil. Some of this was devotional, but much was secular in its appeal, including the first known works of Indian women authors.

A popular work of poetry was the *Purananuru*, an anthology of four hundred poems praising various Tamil rulers. Equally important was the *Kural*, an influential collection of moral maxims, compiled by Tiruvalluvar around the third to fourth century.

## Sanskrit Plays and Novels

At about the same time as the third Tamil Sangam, Sanskrit drama flowered in northern India. In the fourth or fifth century lived the greatest of all Sanskrit poets, Kalidasa. The best-known plays that have survived from this era are *Shakuntala* and *Mrichchakatika* (The Little Clay Cart), the former written by Kalidasa and the latter a comedy possibly written by him.

In the sixth or seventh century, Dandin's early Sanskrit novel, the *Dasakumaracharita* (Story of Ten Princes) appeared. It was a forerunner of the picaresque novel. Even earlier was a distinguished Tamil novel of epic dimensions, the *Silappadigaram* (The Stolen Anklet), by the prince Ilangovadigal (between the second and fifth centuries CE).

## Medieval Indian Literature

During the Indian Middle Ages Sanskrit writings on science and philosophy flourished. There were works from the many schools of philosophy, from great mathematicians, surgeons, and astronomers. Perhaps the best known, if least scientific, work of this period was the *Kama Sutra*, a treatise on love, by Vatsyayana, who wrote it in a legal style of Sanskrit in about the third century CE, as a guide to the attainment of sexual pleasure.

The Middle Ages witnessed an outpouring of religious and philosophical literature, not just in Sanskrit, which was still the prime liturgical and scholarly language, but also in a number of regional languages.

Logic, metaphysics, devotional poetry, and commentary steadily developed.

In the period 850–1330 a new philosophical literature appeared in today's Karnataka, the *Kavirajamarga.* This was Jain literature, written in the medieval Kannada language. At the end of the twelfth century the first novel in Kannada, *Lilavati,* was written by Nemichandra. It was followed by other allegorical novels, as well as by Kesiraja's grammar of the medieval Kannada language in the thirteenth century.

## Early Indian Poetry

Around 1020 CE Dravidian literature in the Telugu language appeared with the grammarian Nannaya Bhatta and the poet Nannichoda. At about the same time the Malayalam language became differentiated from Tamil. A century later the oldest known manuscript written in Bengali proclaimed the birth of that literature. Mukundaraj, who lived around the turn of the thirteenth century, was the first man to write poetry in Marathi. In the early fifteenth century two Bengali poets brought that literature into prominence: Chandidas and Vidyapati, the latter writing in Sanskrit as well as Bengali. Contemporary with them were two Telugu poets, Srinatha and Potana, as well as the best loved of the Hindi poets, Kabir (1440–1518). His was a medieval regional language closely related to Sanskrit. Although Kabir was a low-caste Hindu, he drew much of his inspiration from Sufism and criticized caste, ritualism, and idolatry.

Kabir was followed in 1540 by the first important Muslim poet of India, Mohamed of Jais (a town near today's Allahabad), who created the allegorical poem *Padmavat* in Hindi. Contemporary with Kabir was one of the greatest Indian female poets, the Rajput Mirabai, who wrote in both Hindi and Gujarati. A century before, Lalla, another female poet, had been writing in Kashmiri, while Manichand, also a woman, had written a historical novel in Gujarati. In 1574 the Hindi version of the *Ramayana*, by the poet Tulsidas (c. 1532–1623), appeared, a forerunner of numerous versions of the *Ramayana* in regional languages.

By this time there was a strong Persian cultural influence in some parts of India. A ruler of the Muslim province of Golconda (later Hyderabad), Mohammed Quli Qutub Shah, was a poet who wrote in both Persian and Urdu, which was a new dialectal form of Hindi containing much Persian vocabulary and written in an Arabic script. In later centuries Urdu poetry flourished in northern India.

In 1604 the Adi Granth, the canonical text of the Sikh religion, was established in Punjabi. Thirty years later, also in northwestern India, appeared a work of Urdu prose, the *Sab Ras* of Vajhi. In southern parts of the subcontinent, the middle of the seventeenth century saw the writing of the Kannada poem *Rajasekhara* (1657), by Sadakshara Deva; the works of the Gujarati storyteller Premanand (1636–1734); and the influential Marathi-language poems of Tukaram (1607–1649). Another Telugu poet and bard was Tyagaraju (1767–1847), who influenced both Tamil and Malayalam verse.

## Printed Indian Literature

With the arrival of the printing press in south India, Tamil literature underwent something of a renaissance. Arunachala Kavirayar (1712–1779) wrote *Rama Nataka Keerthanaigal* (The Tragedy of Rama) in 1728 (at the age of sixteen); the Italian Jesuit C. G. E. Beschi (1680–1746) wrote the Tamil poem *Tembavani* (an epic about the life of St. Joseph) in 1724 under the pen name Viramamunivar (published only in 1853). Another interesting author was the eighteenth-century "Indian Pepys," Anandaranga Pillai, a Tamil living in the French colony of Pondicherry. His fascinating and lengthy diary has been published in Tamil, French, and English.

During the eighteenth century Urdu poetry flowered at the hands of Vali, Hatim, Sauda, Inch'a, and Nazir (1740–1830). By the time of Nazir, British hegemony in India was well established, along with the spread of regional printing presses, the first modern universities, and the ever-widening influence of European literary forms, especially those in English.

## Modern Novels

English influence is evident even in those writers who chose to publish works in their native languages. Bengal in particular saw a literary and intellectual renaissance in both English and Bengali, for example, in the novels of Bankim Chandra Chatterjee (1838–1894) and in the works of India's first Nobel Prize winner, the poet and dramatist Rabindranath Tagore (1861–1941).

A parallel literary renaissance occurred in Hindi at the beginning of the twentieth century, with the novels of Premchand (1880–1937). Tamil novels were also written under English influence. The sources of this influence were the novels of Dickens, Thackeray, Scott, Hardy, and many others, which were widely read in India.

India was also the setting for works of British writers who visited or lived and worked in this bulwark of the empire, such as Rudyard Kipling (1865–1936) and E. M. Forster (1879–1970), author of *A Passage to India.* In the mid-twentieth century John Masters (1914–1983) wrote a number of popular novels about the British in India; his own family had served there for five generations. By the late twentieth century British memoirs and novels set in India had become a flourishing cottage industry in the United Kingdom.

But the novel also became a domesticated form in Hindi, Urdu, Bengali, Marathi, Malayalam, and Tamil. Indian literary forms continued to be modernized throughout the twentieth century, aided by the ease of publication and the ever-increasing size of the reading public. An unexpected development was the emergence of numerous world-class, prize-winning Indian novelists writing in English, beginning with Tagore, but these authors often no longer resided in India. Kamala Markandaya and R. K. Narayan are but two of a host who write for a worldwide English readership. Preeminent today are the New York–based Salman Rushdie, originally from Bombay (author of *Midnight's Children*, 1980, and the controversial *Satanic Verses*, 1988), and the Delhi-based writer Arundhati Roy, originally from Kerala (author of *The God of Small Things*, 1997). Some of their recent novels have been translated into dozens of languages.

### Oral Literatures of India

As mentioned earlier, the bulk of classical Indian literature was memorized by the Brahmans rather than recorded in written form. But India is also home to dozens of other literatures that are oral in nature and passed on from one generation to the next solely by rote learning in a local language—just as the early Sanskrit texts were. Only during the past two centuries have folklorists and other scholars, most of them Westerners, taken the trouble to record some of this literature, and coverage has hence been spotty.

This oral literature exists in a large number of languages. Collections published as texts in English translations include *Folktales of India* (1987), edited by Brenda E. F. Beck et al.; *Myths of Middle India* (1949); *Folk-Tales of Mahakoshal* (1944); *Folk-Songs of Chhattisgarh* (1944); *Folk-Songs of the Maikal Hills* (1944); *Tribal Myths of Orissa* (1954); and *Folklore of the Santal Parganas* (1909). Several long ballads, of epic proportion, have been recorded in Tamil dialects, among them the so-called bow songs of the far southern tip of India.

*Paul Hockings*

### Further Reading


Basham, A. L., ed. (1975) *Cultural History of India.* Oxford: Clarendon Press.

Beck, Brenda E. F., Peter J. Claus, Praphulladatta Goswami, and Jawaharlal Handoo, eds. (1987) *Folktales of India.* Chicago and London: University of Chicago Press.

Blackburn, Stuart H. (1988) *Singing of Birth and Death: Texts in Performance.* Philadelphia: University of Pennsylvania Press.

Bompas, Cecil H. (1909) *Folklore of the Santal Parganas.* London: David Nutt.

Bonnefoy, Yves, and Wendy Doniger, eds. (1991) Part 7: "South Asia, Iran, and Buddhism." In *Mythologies* 2, edited by Yves Bonnefoy and Wendy Doniger. Chicago: University of Chicago Press, 797–910.

Clark, T. C., ed. (1970) *The Novel in India: Its Birth and Development.* Berkeley and Los Angeles: University of California Press.

Embree, Ainslie T., and Stephen Hay, eds. (1988) *Sources of Indian Tradition.* 2d ed. New York: Columbia University Press.

Emeneau, Murray B. (1984) *Toda Grammar and Texts.* Memoirs of the American Philosophical Society 155. Philadelphia: American Philosophical Society.

Hockings, Paul. (1997) "Badaga Epic Poetry." In *Blue Mountains Revisited: Cultural Studies on the Nilgiri Hills*, edited by Paul Hockings. New Delhi and New York: Oxford University Press.

Queneau, Raymond, ed. (1956) *Histoire des Littératures I: Littératures anciennes, orientales, et orales.* Paris: Gallimard.

Roy, Arundhati. (1997) *The God of Small Things.* New York: Random House.

Rushdie, Salman. (1980) *Midnight's Children.* New York: Vintage Books.

Shanmukham Pillai, M., and Jakka Parthasarathi. (1992) *The Divine Pilgrimage: The Story of Perumal Cuvami (A Folk-Ballad from Palm-Leaf Manuscripts).* Madras, India: Institute of Asian Studies.

Stutley, Margaret, and James Stutley. (1977) *Harper's Dictionary of Hinduism: Its Mythology, Folklore, Philosophy, Literature, and History.* New York: Harper & Row.


## LITERATURE—INDIA, TAMIL

Of the four Dravidian literary languages, Tamil has the oldest recorded history. Its earliest records, inscriptions in an Asokan Brahmi script, date to around 254 BCE. Tamil literature, preserved in copper-plate inscriptions and on palm-leaf manuscripts, covers more that 2000 years. It is the only Indian language with an uninterrupted continuity between its classical and modern forms. Its vigorous literary development begins with short bardic poems about love and war. The grammar, *Tolkappiyam*, is characterized by richness and rigor in phonetics and phonology, morphology, semantics, prosody, and conventions of literary composition.

### Predevotional Literature

The bardic corpus (200? BCE–250? CE) is represented by two large collections of poems in two main genres: *agam* (love poetry) and *puram* (war poetry).

The collections *Ettuttogai* (Eight Anthologies) and *Pattuppattu* (Ten Songs) are both of very high quality. The postclassical period (250–600 CE) is exemplified by the *Tirukkural* (c. fifth century), a collection of 1,330 couplets on ethical order, social activities, and pleasure, and by the *Silappadigaram* (The Stolen Anklet, fifth–sixth century), a narrative-dramatic poem ascribed to Ilangovadigal. *Silappadigaram* is a tragic story about Kannagi, a woman who proves the innocence of her husband, who has been accused of the theft of a golden anklet belonging to the queen, but only after her husband is executed. In anger, Kannagi destroys the city with fire before being taken up to heaven as a goddess.

### Devotional Literature

Tamil is famous for the devotional literature of Saiva and Vaishnava poets (poets devoted to Siva and Vishnu, respectively). The two greatest Saivia poets were Appar (seventh century), also known as "The Lord of the Divine Speech," and Manikkavasagar (ninth century), whose mystical poems stress the love of the soul for God and his response with grace, as well as his immanence in all things. The lives of the sixty-three Saiva saints were told in *Periyapuranam* (The Great Purana) by Sekkilar (twelfth century) in 1,286 stanzas. Among the Vaishnava poets, the best known is the female poet Andal (eighth century), who sang about her love for and intense devotion to Krishna, an incarnation of Vishnu.

Kamban's (c. 1180–1250) magnificent poem *The Descent of Rama (Iramavataram)* in 40,000 lines is based on the Sanskrit *Ramayana*. According to many scholars, Kamban was the greatest of all Tamil poets.

### Modern Literature

Modern Tamil literature may be said to begin with the first genuine novel *Kamalambal* (*Fatal Rumour*, 1895) by B. R. Rajam Iyer (1872–1898), and the patriotic and lyrical poetry of S. Subrahmanya Bharati (1882–1921), the national poet of the Indian state of Tamil Nadu. Contemporary Tamil writing begins in the 1930s, with 1933 representing a watershed in the development of Tamil poetry and prose. In that year, *Manikkodi* (The Jewel Banner), a literary journal that has become a legend, was founded in Madras and soon attracted the best creative writers and critics of the period.

Tamil poetry went though decisive changes after 1959, when C. S. Chellappa (b. 1912) began publishing his review *Eluttu* (Writing), which opened its pages to things new and experimental. By 1965, avant-garde poetry, dissociated from stock phrases, traditional conventions, classical meters, and repetitive themes, was firmly established in Tamil writing, represented by poets like S. Mani (b. 1936), T. S. Venugopalan (b. 1929), S. Vaitheeswaran (b. 1935), and Shanmugan Subbiah (b. 1924).

The novels of T. Janakiraman (1921–1982) are rich, colorful, and realistic portrayals of rural life. *Amma vantal* (*The Sins of Appu's Mother*, 1972) has become a classic. In honesty, courage, social involvement, realism, and skill, Rajam Krishnan (b. 1925) is a superb novelist. She is noted for her scrupulous documentation, psychological insight, realistic approach, and great thematic variety. She has published many novels, including *Kurincitten* (*Honey of the Kurinci Flower*, 1953) on the life of a tribal community in the Nilgiri Hills of South India.

D. Jayakanthan (b. 1934) is in many respects the most complex and the most widely read author among Tamil prose writers. Strongly influenced by Freud and Marx, as well as by Mohandas (Mahatma) Gandhi, in his later writings he has become a great humanist, uncommitted to any particular ideology. The heroine of *Some People at Some Time* (*Cila nerankalil cila manitarkal*, 1970) is sexually exploited by her old sadistic uncle and ostracized by society. Almost the entire work is set within her interior monologue. In her figure, Jayakanthan has created an unforgettable character—a courageous and tragic woman.

L. S. Ramamirtham (1916) is a master craftsman and unsurpassed stylist who explores character and emotion with striking and multifaceted imagery. In 140 stories and 6 novels, his major concerns are language, emotions, and Hindu religious philosophy. Similes and metaphors of startling beauty abound in his works. Among his novels, *Apita* (*The One Who Cannot Be Touched*, 1970) is the Indian illustration of Goethe's "The eternal feminine raises us to spiritual heights," while *Putra* (*The Son*, 1965) expresses the author's belief in the indestructible chain of all life. Among Tamil writers, Jakanthan and Ramamirtham, though different in language, theme, and style, deserve highest praise.

*K. V. Zvelebil*

### Further Reading

Zvelebil, Kamil V. (1973) *The Smile of Murugan. On Tamil Literature of South India*. New York: E. J. Brill.

———. (1974) *Tamil Literature*. Wiesbaden, Germany: Otto Harrassowitz.

———. (1995) *Lexicon of Tamil Literature*. New York: E. J. Brill.

**LITERATURE—JAPAN** Japanese literature has flourished from the early eighth century to the present in a myriad of genres and styles reflecting the nation's cultural periods. The *Kojiki* (Records of Ancient Matters), the earliest Japanese text, was completed in 712. A history based on oral traditions, this work provides a justification for the supremacy of the imperial family and its right to rule and includes myths of creation documenting the foundations of the Yamato state, those clans along the Inland Sea that formed the nucleus of the early Japanese nation.

In the creation myths in *Kojiki*, the god and goddess Izanagi and Izanami describe creation in terms of the union of male and female and emphasize the importance of rituals and purity. They see humanity as part of nature and stress harmony over conflict. A second cycle of myths concerning Amaterasu, the sun goddess, and Susanoo, the storm god, describes solstice rituals and depicts an agrarian society. These myths are also political narratives reflecting a conflict between the Izumo culture on the Sea of Japan coast and the Yamato culture across the mountains from it. A parallel history, the *Nihon shoki* (Chronicles of Japan from the Earliest Times to 697 CE), compiled in 720, contains much of the same material as the *Kojiki* but is presented more formally in imitation of Chinese dynastic histories.

### The *Manyoshu* and Its Poets

Within a generation of the appearance of the *Nihon shoki*, the first collection of poetry in Chinese, the *Kaifuso* (Fond Recollections of Poetry), was published in 751, and shortly thereafter, the first collection of poetry in Japanese, the *Manyoshu* (Collection of Ten Thousand Leaves), appeared around 756. The *Manyoshu* contains 4,516 poems arranged in twenty books. Drawing on ancient oral traditions of poetry, this collection is noted for the scope and variety of its verse, including poetry in the *tanka* (short song) and *choka* (long song) forms.

The first great poet of the *Manyoshu* is Nukata Okimi (c. 630–after 690). Her poem on the seasons, celebrating the primacy of autumn over spring, and her poems of love provided a model for later poets. Kakinomoto Hitomaro (flourished 685–705) wrote both public and private poetry. His public poems, such as one commemorating an imperial excursion to Yoshino, celebrated the great events of court, while his poem on separating from his wife is a masterpiece of private poetry expressing personal feelings of grief. "Dialogue on Poverty," a poem by Yamanoue Okura (660–c. 733), condemns social injustice, criticizing the state for allowing people to live in destitution. The *Manyoshu* also contained poems written by people of the lower classes from Azuma, the eastern lands encompassing the area around present-day Tokyo. After the *Manyoshu*, poets no longer created such a wide range of poetry.

### Literature in Japanese Courtly Society

The Heian period (795–1185) marks one of the richest flowerings of Japanese literature. While men generally wrote in Chinese, which was admired as the language of scholarship, women writing in Japanese created a series of masterworks. *Taketori monogatari* (The Bamboo Cutter's Tale, 909 CE) is often regarded as the grandparent of Japanese prose fiction. Other developments included poem tales *(uta monogatari)*, such as *Ise monogatari* (*Tales of Ise*, probably written in several stages, the earliest versions late ninth century), which were characterized by a mixture of prose and poetry. Diary literature also became popular, beginning with *Tosa nikki* (Tosa Diary, c. 936) and including *Kagero nikki* (translated as *The Gossamer Years*) and *Izumi Shikibu nikki* (The Diary of Izumi Shikibu), both probably early eleventh century.

These developments culminated in Murasaki Shikibu's *Genji monogatari* (*Tale of Genji*, completed c. 1010), the world's first novel, often considered the finest work of Japanese literature. Composed of fifty-four chapters, this romance details the lives of three generations at court and centers on the activities of Hikaru Genji, the epitome of the Japanese courtier. The *Genji* presents a portrait of life in the Japanese court during the eleventh century, revealing the social, ethical, and aesthetic values of Japanese court society. *Eiga monogatari* (Tales of Courtly Splendor, early eleventh century) represents a genre of historical fiction.

The first decade of the tenth century saw the imperially commissioned compilation of the *Kokin waka shu* (Collection of Ancient and Modern Songs), which defined the standard for court poetry and served as a model for later imperial anthologies. Ki no Tsurayuki (d. c. 945), one of the editors, wrote a preface in Japanese, which was the earliest statement of Japanese poetics. Tsurayuki called for formality and elegance as the sine qua non of Japanese court poetry. The collection, in twenty books, has the poems arranged by topic, the greatest number being seasonal poems and love poems.

During this period a significant body of Chinese prose and poetry continued to be written. Sugawara no Michizane (845–903) brought the composition of

Chinese poetry to its peak. The collection *Wakan roei shu* (*Japanese and Chinese Poems to Sing*, 1013) and others featured a mixing of Japanese and Chinese poetic forms. In prose fiction, *Nihon ryoiki* (miraculous stories from the Japanese Buddhist tradition, which were compiled c. 822), a collection of morality tales written in Chinese, promoted Buddhism.

### Literature in Japanese Warrior Society

Toward the end of the twelfth century, a bloody civil war broke out between two warrior clans, the Taira and Minamoto, bringing courtly society to an end and ushering in the warrior society of medieval Japan. The great war epic *Heike monogatari (Tales of the Heike)* described that war and laid the foundation for a new genre of *gunki mono* (war literature). The accounts presented in *Tales of the Heike* were originally recited by blind troubadour-priests known as *biwa hoshi*. From its opening homily, which reminds the reader of the transience and futility of human endeavor, to the concluding chapters, where Lady Kenreimon'in, the lone survivor, is left to ponder thoughts she cannot forget or bear to remember, the narrative is strongly liturgical in its rhythms.

In contrast to narratives of the great deeds of warriors are the accounts of recluses, men who chose to withdraw from worldly affairs. Faced with the brutality and violence of war, these hermits sought an alternative way of life. The most celebrated of such accounts is the essay *Hojoki* (*An Account of My Hut*, 1212), by Kamo no Chomei (1155?–1216), which describes the struggle, frustration, and pain of living in the world and contrasts that experience with the serenity of life as a hermit. More than a century later, another hermit priest, Yoshida Kenko (1283–1350), wrote *Tsurezuregusa* (translated as *Essays in Idleness*, c. 1330), describing his life of solitude and nostalgia for the lost glory of courtly society.

In poetry, the *Shin kokin waka shu* (New Collection of Ancient and Modern Songs, 1205) was compiled by Fujiwara Teika (1162–1241). This eighth imperial anthology of poetry was dedicated to the idea that old vocabulary should be used to create a new poetry, in this case characterized by elaborate poetic techniques. Reflecting an age of turbulence, poetry took on a darker tone. New aesthetic values included *sabi* (the quality of being old and tarnished) and *yugen* (the quality of mystery and depth). The *Shin kokin waka shu* collection may represent the high water mark of *tanka*, and from it emerged *renga* (linked verse).

The late fourteenth and early fifteenth centuries saw the emergence of the Noh theater under the guidance of Kan'ami (1333–1384) and his son Zeami (1363–1443), with the patronage of the shogun (military ruler) Ashikaga Yoshimitsu (1358–1408). Originating in festival entertainments, Noh was elevated by Kan'ami and Zeami to the epitome of aesthetic and aristocratic performance. The strong influence of Zen Buddhism can be seen in the austere quality of performance. Although the costumes are elaborate, there are few props; the tempo of the plays is slow and dignified, while the texts themselves are spare. The aesthetics of Noh harmonize the values of elegant courtly society with the values of vigorous warrior society.

Both prose and poetry continued to be written in Chinese throughout the medieval period, mostly by priests from the five great Zen temples, and their work is known collectively as *gozan bungaku* (literature of the five mountains).

### Literature of Unified Japan

After centuries of warfare, Japan was unified by Tokugawa Ieyasu (1543–1616) at the beginning of the seventeenth century, and peace and national isolation ensued for two-and-a-half centuries. The work of three writers, Matsuo Basho (1644–1694), Ihara Saikaku (1642–1693), and Chikamatsu Monzaemon (1653–1724), dominated the seventeenth century.

Basho followed the poetic conventions of his day, but in his middle years he established a style of his own, elevating the seventeen-syllable form (which we know today as haiku) to the level of serious poetry. Basho's best verse is characterized by simplicity of language and engagement with nature and is significantly influenced by Zen. Basho freed poetry from unremitting elegance to celebrate rustic beauty. His many travel diaries combine prose and poetry.

Saikaku came from the merchant culture of Osaka and represented that class, which was becoming a patron of the arts. A series of fictions written during the last decade of his life established his reputation. Beginning with works depicting the lives of amorous heroes and heroines, parodying the romances of the courtly period, he moved on to more serious explorations of the concerns of the newly wealthy townspeople. His twin themes were love and money. He explored all aspects of love—romantic, commercial, homosexual, illicit, and tragic. In the area of money, he showed how the merchant makes his fortune and how he can lose it, usually by being blinded by love. In these fictions, Saikaku created a sensitive picture of urban society.

Chikamatsu was a seminal playwright for both the Kabuki (a theatrical form using male actors and combining music, dance, décor, and stage effects to produce a spectacle) and Bunraku (a theatrical form where characters are represented by dolls manipulated simultaneously by as many as three men) theaters, which became the most popular forms of drama. He wrote historical plays *(jidai mono)* celebrating the exploits of the heroes of the past, as well as domestic plays *(sewamono)*, based on contemporary events such as love suicides. His love-suicide plays became so popular, and so many couples were inspired by them to commit suicide, that the government banned the use of the term "love suicide" in the titles of plays. Because Tokugawa society was rigid and repressive, Chikamatsu developed the theme of the conflict between duty *(giri)* and the urge to follow one's personal feelings *(ninjo)*.

**Literature during the Meiji Restoration**

Following the Meiji Restoration of 1868, which ended shogunal rule of Japan as well as Japan's isolation from most of the rest of the world, Japanese literature began to modernize in several stages. First, translations of Western fiction were introduced as models, works such as *Robinson Crusoe* and *Around the World in 80 Days* being among the most popular.

Tsubouchi Shoyo (1859–1935) provided the second step toward modernization by writing *Shosetsu shinzui* (The Essence of the Novel, 1885–1886), an essay analyzing Western fiction and providing a blueprint for writing works in imitation of Western fiction. In the 1880s, writers like Futabatei Shimei (1864–1909) began to employ techniques such as interior monologue and psychological realism. By the first decade of the twentieth century, romanticism was being practiced by Kunikida Doppo (1871–1908), and naturalism was advocated by Tayama Katai (1872–1930) and Shimazaki Toson (1872–1943).

The best writers, however, remained aloof from literary movements. Natsume Soseki (1867–1916) explored the concept of the self in relation to society, in works such as *Kokoro*. Mori Ogai (1862–1922) wrote historical fictions, including *Sansho Daiyu* (Sansho the Bailiff), and Nagai Kafu (1879–1959) wrote eloquent elegies on the dying culture of old Edo.

Every writer of the new age had to find a balance between the new literature and the long, proud traditions of the old. Perhaps more than anyone else, Akutagawa Ryunosuke (1892–1927) maintained this balance by mining ancient Japanese fiction and retelling its stories in a Chekhovian mode by adding a modern psychosocial aspect.

**Literature in Contemporary Japan**

The two great writers of the mid-twentieth century, whose careers spanned the Second World War, were Tanizaki Junichiro (1886–1965) and Kawabata Yasunari (1899–1972). In the years before the war, Tanizaki wrote a series of erotic and grotesque stories, often historical fictions, exploring perverse aspects of human psychology. Following the war came his greatest work, *Sasame yuki* (translated as *The Makioka Sisters*), an elegy on the indolent lifestyle of upper-class society in the Osaka region in the years immediately before World War II. Following the war, Tanizaki produced several studies of aging and sexuality, including *Kagi (The Key)* and *Futen rojin nikki (Diary of a Mad Old Man)*. Kawabata Yasunari dabbled in modernist techniques of writing, but created a highly traditional aesthetic in works such as *Yukiguni (Snow Country)*. Largely in recognition of his ability to convey traditional Japanese aesthetics, he was awarded the Nobel Prize in 1968.

The years following the Second World War saw a great resurgence of writing. Dazai Osamu (1909–1948) captured the despairing mood of the immediate postwar years in works such as *Shayo* (*The Setting Sun*, 1947) and *Ningen shikaku* (*No Longer Human*, 1948). Mishima Yukio (1925–1970), who came of age during the war, wrote brilliant, often troubled works such as *Kikakuji (Temple of the Golden Pavilion)*, exploring human psychology and motivation. Although in many ways innovative as a writer, Mishima held conservative and nationalistic political views that led to his celebrated suicide in 1970. Ibuse Masuji (1898–1993), generally known as a humorist, also produced *Kuroi ame* (*Black Rain*, 1965–1966), which raised the experience of the nuclear bombing of his native Hiroshima to mythic proportions. Abe Kobo (1924–1993) claimed to reject tradition and wrote about what it meant to be modern and live in a technological world, most notably in *Suna no onna* (*Woman in the Dunes*, 1962).

Women writers have come to play an increasingly major role in the literary world. Oba Minako (b. 1930) balances both traditional and modern views, including a global perspective, by writing about her experience of living for twelve years in Sitka, Alaska. She calls into question the very definition of national literatures by creating characters and settings that are not Japanese. Feminist and gender issues also form major themes in her work. Oe Kenzaburo (b. 1935) exemplifies the liberal, socially committed writer. Whether dealing with the loss of childhood innocence in a short story, "Shiiku" ("Prize Stock," 1959), the personal tragedy of the birth of his brain-damaged son in *Kojinteki na taiken* (*A Personal Matter*, 1964), or his nonfiction works such as *Hiroshima Noto (Hiroshima Notes*, 1964) and *Okinawa Noto* (Okinawa Notes, 1969), he is a writer with a social conscience and a global perspective. For this he received the Nobel Prize for Literature in 1994. In recent years a new generation of writers, including Murakami Haruki (b. 1949), Yoshimoto Banana (b. 1964), and Yamada Emi (b. 1959), have challenged and enlarged the boundaries of the literary world.

Poetry began the process of modernization in 1882 with the publication of *Shintaishi sho* (Selections of Poetry in the New Form), a collection of nineteen poems, fourteen translated from English and five composed in Japanese in the new form—free verse. This became a model of a new form of poetry, which would be experimented with and developed through translations and original works.

The new form of poetry came into its own with the emergence of Hagiwara Sakutaro (1886–1942). His collection *Tsuki ni hoeru* (*Howling at the Moon*, 1917) established his reputation, and although he often wrote in the traditional styles, Hagiwara is best known for his colloquial poetry in free verse. His poems experiment with musical rhythms and onomatopoeia. Takamura Kotaro (1883–1956) spent his youthful years in the United States, England, and France and is best known for a series of poems celebrating his love for his wife. In *Chieko sho* (translated as *Chieko's Sky*, 1941), he describes her insanity and death. Nishiwaki Junsaburo (1894–1982) is widely regarded as being responsible for both the resurgence of modern poetry and for the internationalization of the poetic perspective in the postwar years.

Traditional Japanese poetry has survived in the modern world. Surely the most popular *tanka* poet in modern times has been Ishikawa Takuboku (1886–1912), who wrote in both the traditional and free-verse styles. His reputation is based on two collections of traditional poems, *Ichiaku no suna (A Handful of Sand*, 1910) and *Kanashiki gangu (Sad Toys*, 1912). These poems, expressing immediate experiences with great emotional intensity, frequently depart from the conventions of traditional *tanka* in mood, subject, and vocabulary.

Yosano Akiko (1878–1942) represents the emergence of women in modern poetry. Her collection, *Midaregami* (Tangled Hair, 1901), is remarkable for its defiant sensuality, unusual syntax, irregular meter, and vocabulary that was new to *tanka* poetry. Masaoka Shiki (1867–1902) wrote both *tanka* and haiku but is known chiefly for leading a revival of Basho's poetry and for modernizing haiku. Following Shiki, modern haiku developed in several directions, the main line represented by the conservative ideas of Takahama Kyoshi (1874–1959) and the journal *Hototogisu*. Traditional poetry continues to thrive in Japan.

Like poetry, drama has developed in modern Japan in a broad spectrum, including traditional forms of Noh, Bunraku, and Kabuki, and also including modern Western forms of theater. The traditional forms survived the Meiji Restoration and World War II; they continue to be popular, and leading actors and playwrights in all forms have created adaptations and incorporated new material keeping these forms vital in the contemporary world. In the early years of the twentieth century, the Shingeki (new drama) movement began to create a modern theater. This movement has always struggled to maintain a balance between introducing works by Western playwrights and works by Japanese dramatists. In the early years the focus was on works by Tolstoy, Shakespeare, Ibsen, and Chekhov. In 1924, Osanai Kaoru (1881–1928) founded the Tsukiji Shogekijo, Japan's first modern theater, and concentrated on producing plays. Kishida Kunio (1890–1954) founded the Bungakuza theater, which focused on theatrical literary works. While never widely popular, Kishida's work was seminal in the creation of modern theater in Japan.

During the postwar years, Kinoshita Junji (b. 1914) wrote many plays based on traditional Japanese folktales, using language that reflected a wide range of Japanese dialects. *Yuzuru* (Twilight Crane, 1949) is his best-known play. Mishima Yukio, although better known as a novelist, produced works for the theater in every form from traditional Noh and Kabuki to the most contemporary forms. His work reflects a strong sense of what it means to be Japanese. In contrast, Abe Kobo has written a series of theatrical experiments focusing on movement, light, and sound while nearly eliminating dialogue. These plays depict contemporary urban society with no clue that they might be Japanese.

Japanese literature today is a remarkably rich and bewildering array of work in which all forms and genres are vigorous and which maintains traditional forms and styles while also being on the leading edge of literary development in a global sense.

*Stephen W. Kohl*

*See also:* **Haiku; Poetry—Japan**

## Further Reading

Brower, Robert, and Earl Miner. (1961) *Japanese Court Poetry*. Stanford, CA: Stanford University Press.

Kato, Shuichi. (1979–1983) *A History of Japanese Literature*. 3 vols. Tokyo and New York: Kodansha International.

Keene, Donald. (1984) *Dawn to the West*. 2 vols. New York: Holt, Rinehart and Winston.

———. (1993) *Seeds in the Heart*. New York: Henry Holt.

———. (1976) *World within Walls*. New York: Holt, Rinehart and Winston.

Konishi, Jin'ichi. (1984) *A History of Japanese Literature*. Princeton, NJ: Princeton University Press.

**LITERATURE—KOREA** Korean literature consists of oral literature, literature written in classical Chinese or in any of several hybrid systems employing classical Chinese, and literature written in the Korean script (hangul). Classical Chinese was the literary language of the scholar-bureaucrats who constituted the Korean elite from early times to the end of the Choson kingdom. Hangul, though promulgated in 1446, did not gain universal acceptance in Korea as a literary script until the twentieth century. Korean literature is generally divided into the following periods: Three Kingdoms (57 BCE–667 CE); Unified Shilla (667–918 CE); Koryo (918–1392); early Choson (1392–1592); later Choson (1592–1910); and modern (1910–present).

### Three Kingdoms

Recorded Korean history begins with the three kingdoms of Shilla (57 BCE–935 CE), Koguryo (37 BCE–668 CE), and Paekche (18 BCE–663 CE), which together occupied the Korean peninsula and part of Manchuria. The earliest surviving examples of Korean literature in a Korean text (a handful of ancient songs attributed to Koreans appear in Chinese histories) date from the sixth century and are recorded in the *Samguk yusa* (Memorabilia of the Three Kingdoms, 1285). These are the *hyangga* (native songs). This diverse group of songs includes works with oral origins as well as those composed and written down by individuals, primarily Buddhist monks and the Shilla warrior youth known as *hwarang*.

### Unified Shilla

In 668 the Shilla state, for the first time in Korean history, unified the Korean peninsula under one ruling house. Over the next three centuries the *hyangga* form continued to develop. One of the best-known examples, "Ch'oyong ka" (Song of Ch'oyong, 879 CE), is a shaman chant, reflecting the influence of shamanism in Korean oral tradition and suggesting that *hyangga* represent a development of shaman chants into Buddhist invocations. Buddhism, officially recognized by Shilla in the sixth century, became the dominant system of thought in Unified Shilla; it exercised great influence over literature and Shilla art in general.

*Hanshi*, poetry composed in classical Chinese and following Chinese principles of poetry, but written by Koreans, became widespread among the literati of Unified Shilla. In contrast with *hanshi*, there also existed by this time a rich oral tradition consisting of lyric folk songs, shaman chants, myths, legends, and folktales. The diverse genre of folk song comprises work songs, ceremonial songs, and, most numerous, songs both happy and sad that deal with problems encountered in daily life. Among this third group is "Arirang," probably Korea's best-known folk song.

### Koryo

In 935 CE Wang Kon, king of the new Koryo state, extended his control over the entire peninsula, founding the Koryo Kingdom, which would survive until 1392. Koryo literature is distinguished by lyric folk songs, increased sophistication and diversity of poetry in Chinese, the prose miscellany called *shihwa*, and the appearance of *shijo*, a terse, intensely personal song that would be recorded and composed in hangul following the promulgation of that script early in the Choson kingdom.

Koryo lyric folk songs, often called *changga* (long songs) or *pyolgok* (special songs), are a diverse body of anonymous works such as Buddhist songs and shaman chants as well as songs composed by individuals. Many survived as court music but originated in orally transmitted folk songs, and thus combine folk song onomatopoeia and rhythms with refinements in diction and music.

*Hanshi* reached an early zenith in the works of Yi Kyu-bo (1168–1241), which achieve a consummate balance of the universal and the particular. The brevity, revelation, and self-reference of his poems characterize many other *hanshi* as well.

While poetry was the most widespread and popular form of literature, prose writing achieved popularity with the emergence of *shihwa* (talks on poetry), collections of random thoughts on life and poetry. Meant to entertain, these miscellanies combine the factuality of public records with the more poetic language of essays. A good example is *P'ahan chip* (Collection for Dispelling Idleness, 1260), a posthumous compilation of works by Yi Il-lo (1152–1220). This and other collections prefigure the early Choson miscellany known as the *chapki*, which is weighted more heavily toward folktales and anecdotes.

## Early Choson

Early Choson is the designation for the period extending from the founding of the Choson kingdom in 1392 to the Japanese invasions of 1592–1598. The two most important historical developments affecting early Choson literature were the promulgation of hangul by King Sejong in 1446 and the adoption of neo-Confucianism as the state ideology. Neo-Confucianism, with its emphasis on exemplary Chinese texts, meant that Korean literati would continue to study and use classical Chinese as a literary language. In fact, because mastery of Chinese ensured their monopoly on learning, the literati continued for the most part to write in Chinese for centuries after the creation of hangul. For its part, hangul in theory gave all Koreans a literary language of their own; in actuality, until the 1900s it was used primarily by women and commoners, most of whom were not literate in Chinese. One of the first works written in the new native script was *Yongbi och'on ka* (Songs of Dragons Flying to Heaven, 1445–1447), an *akchang* (set of lyrics and chants accompanying court music) celebrating the supposed virtues and moral authority of the Choson founders.

For recognition and advancement, Choson literati wrote in Chinese; for their own pleasure and amusement, and to express their innermost thoughts, they often wrote in Korean. Of the works they composed in hangul, *shijo* are the most numerous. *Shijo* were originally sung, and still are today. Three of the greatest *shijo* practitioners were Chong Ch'ol (1536–1593), Yun Son-do (1587–1671), and Kim Su-jang (1690–?).

The other major vernacular poetic tradition in Korea is the *kasa*. Appearing in the mid-1400s, *kasa* are generally longer than *shijo* and are variously narrative as well as lyrical. Chong Ch'ol, in addition to his accomplishments with *shijo*, is considered by many to have perfected the *kasa* form, as seen in his "Kwandong pyolgok" (Song of Kangwon Scenes, 1580).

Women have until recently occupied a low profile in Korean literary history. They almost certainly composed some of the traditional folk songs that have survived, and they should be credited with much of the oral tradition that is inspired by native shaman beliefs and rites (in Korea most shamans are women). But not until early Choson do we have examples of literature by identifiable women writers. In Choson times and earlier, women were discouraged from educating themselves in Chinese. And even after the creation of hangul gave Korean women an accessible literary language, the Confucian emphasis on women's place in the home made women reluctant to attach their name to their writings or to circulate them outside the home. Still, a few aristocratic women such as Ho Nansorhon (1563–1589), as well as *kisaeng* (professional entertaining women) such as Hwang Chin-i (c. 1506–1544), managed to lift the veil of anonymity that for so long had shrouded premodern women's literature. These women have left us a small but eloquent body of *shijo*, *kasa*, and *hanshi*.

It is also in early Choson that we see what is often considered the first example of Korean fiction: *Kumo shinhwa* (New Stories from Golden Turtle Mountain) by Kim Shi-sup (1435–1493), consisting of five short romances written in Chinese. The aforementioned *chapki*, or literary miscellany—a collection of random writings such as character sketches, poetry criticism, anecdotes, and folktales—developed around the same time. A good example is the *P'aegwan chapki* (Storyteller's Miscellany) of O Suk-kwon (flourished 1525–1544).

Surviving examples of folk drama suggest that a rich variety of dramatic works existed by mid-Choson. The most important genre was the mask dance, a combination of song, speech, and dance that originated in local village festivals. Like much folk and oral literature elsewhere, mask dances expose the foibles of the powerful and elite, in Korea's case the aristocratic gentry known as *yangban*. Also serving as comic relief for the common people were puppet plays, which, like the mask dances, were performed in the open so as to be accessible to all.

## Later Choson

From later Choson we have more writing by commoners and women and a corresponding increase in works surviving in hangul. It was against the background of the Japanese invasions of 1592 and 1597 and the feeble response by the Choson state that Ho Kyun (1569–1618) wrote *Hong Kil-dong chon* (Tale of Hong Kil-dong, c. 1610), usually cited as the first Korean fictional narrative written in hangul. A variety of fictional works in hangul followed, many originating in the oral tradition and most of them anonymous. By the eighteenth and nineteenth centuries these works had gained widespread popularity among commoners. Some 600 fictional works in hangul survive. A new fictional form that appeared late in the 1700s was the *kajok sa sosol*, or family saga. These works are forerunners of the multivolume novels widely read in modern Korea.

In contrast with the variety of vernacular fiction that is solidly grounded in Korean soil are romances such as *Kuun mong* (A Nine-Cloud Dream, c. 1689) by Kim Man-jung (1637–1692), which is situated in ninth-century Tang China. *Kuun mong* is often honored as the first Korean novel written in hangul, but evidence increasingly suggests it was written in classical Chinese and that only hangul translations have survived.

Among the comparatively small amount of later Choson fiction written in Chinese, the works of Pak Chi-won (1737–1805), a *shirhak* (practical learning) scholar, stand out. *Ho Saeng chon* (Tale of Ho Saeng) and *Yangban chon* (Tale of a *Yangban*) are penetrating satires of the *yangban* class.

Writing by women was virtually unknown outside the home, but in the mid-1900s scholars began to discover a large amount of writing in hangul by later Choson women: diaries, travelogues, memoirs, biographies, and especially long instructive *kasa* passed down from mother to daughter and kept for generations within the family. *Shijo* by *kisaeng* and other women survive as well. Also dating from this period is *Hanjungnok* (A Record of Sorrowful Days), by Princess Hyegyong (1735–1815), a series of memoirs about her long life at court.

Poetry in Chinese would be written until the fall of the kingdom in 1910, but Korean-language verse continued to be favored for its greater expressive potential. Yun Son-do and Kim Su-jang, mentioned earlier, are the great *shijo* poets of later Choson. Kim himself was not a scholar-bureaucrat of the aristocracy but a functionary, reflecting the increasing production of literature by commoners during this period. It is perhaps these commoners who authored the majority of the great number of anonymous *shijo*, almost half of all surviving *shijo*.

As with *shijo*, more *kasa* were composed by women and commoners in later Choson than in early Choson. *Kasa* composed by commoners often describe the harshness of peasant life, criticize immoral individuals (and, by implication, an unjust society), or describe relations between the sexes.

Especially popular in the oral tradition was *p'ansori*, a long narrative partly sung and partly spoken by an itinerant performer *(kwangdae)* accompanied by a lone drummer. The *p'ansori* performances, developing in the southwestern part of the peninsula in the late seventeenth century, appealed especially to commoners, who were familiar, for example, with the Hungbu and Ch'unhyang stories, which became part of the *p'ansori* repertoire. Most of the *p'ansori* works conformed outwardly to Confucian values but implicity criticized the application of those values in real life.

### The Modern Period

The development of a modern literature in Korea was conditioned by two watershed events: (1) the modernization movement that swept East Asia at the turn of the twentieth century, and (2) the annexation of Korea by Japan in 1910. The modernization movement exposed young Koreans to enlightenment ideals such as literacy, education, equality, and women's rights and spurred many of them to study in Japan, where they encountered (in Japanese translation) new literary models. Annexation inspired a wave of nationalism that finally legitimized hangul as the literary language of all Koreans, and it forced Korean writers to come to grips with the necessity of preserving their own language and literature in an increasingly repressive colonial environment.

Modern Korean literature is dated by most to 1917, the date of publication of Yi Kwang-su's *Mujong* (Heartlessness). This novel is considered distinctly modern in its use of language and its psychological description. The first generation of writers of modern Korean literature were for the most part young men born around the turn of the century who had received their higher education in Japan and had there been introduced, in Japanese translation, to literature from the West. There resulted an influx of Western literary models into Korea, primarily realism in fiction and symbolism, imagism, and romanticism in poetry. The new generation of writers tended to gravitate toward literary journals (most of them short-lived) in which they published poetry, short fiction, and essays (both critical and personal, the latter form termed *sup'il*). Novels maintained the mass readership they had enjoyed since late Choson times; while novels continued to be serialized in newspapers, they were considered lowbrow entertainment by the literary elite. Important among the first generation of fiction writers were Yi Kwang-su (1892–1950?) for his enlightenment and nationalist agenda, Yom Sang-sop (1897–1963) for his psychological realism, Kim Tong-in (1900–1951) for his modernization of the Korean language and his art-for-art's-sake views, and Hyon Chin-gon (1900–1943) for his fictional slices of life of colonial Korea.

Early modern poetry is best represented by Kim Sowol (1902–1934), Chong Chi-yong (1903–?), and Han Yong-un (1879–1944). Kim (known better by his pen name, Sowol, than his given name, Chong-shik) utilized traditional Korean folk song rhythms to produce lyrics of exceptional melody. Chong Chi-yong was a master technician, drawing on both native and foreign sources for a rich bank of images in poems that are redolent of solitude, nostalgia, and nature. Han was a man of action, actively opposing the Japanese occupation, working to reform Buddhism, and attempting to instill in his readers a sense of their cultural identity.

Proletarian literature was tolerated by the Japanese colonial authorities from the mid-1920s to 1935. This literature is cited today more for its historical interest than its literary value. Subsequently, many Korean fiction writers looked to the past or the countryside for their inspiration. A variety of new voices appeared: Hwang Sun-won (1915–2000), Korea's most accomplished short fiction writer; Kim Tong-ni (1913–1995), considered by Koreans the possessor of a uniquely Korean zeitgeist; Ch'ae Man-shik (1902–1950), a writer of wit and irony who employed a direct, conversational style; Yi T'ae-jun (1904–?), a polished stylist; Kim Yu-jong (1908–1937), who utilized an earthy, colloquial style rooted in the oral tradition; and Yi Sang (1910–1937), an avant-garde poet as well as a modernist fiction writer. Their combined efforts led in the mid- to late 1930s to an early high point in modern Korean fiction.

Korean literature after 1945 has to a large extent been conditioned by the realities of modern Korean history. Korean literati from premodern times to the present day have often felt a need to bear witness to the times, and authors from 1945 on have been no exception. The literature of the 1950s and 1960s is a good example. Reacting to the devastation inflicted on the peninsula by the Korean War (1950–1953), writers produced poems and stories portraying not just a shattered landscape but traumatized psyches and corrupted values. The stories of Son Ch'ang-sop (b. 1922) and the poems of Kim Su-yong (1921–1967) are excellent illustrations. The late 1960s and early 1970s gave voice to a new generation of writers, educated in their own language (their parents' generation had been educated in Japanese, and the literary language of their grandparents' generation was more often than not Chinese). With little or no experience of the period of Japanese occupation and exhibiting a sardonic attitude toward the authoritarian rule that marked South Korean politics from 1948 to 1987, they produced fiction and poetry that display a more free-wheeling use of language and a powerful imagination. Fiction writers Kim Sung-ok (b. 1943) and Ch'oe In-ho (b. 1945) are representative. Their contemporaries Ch'oe In-hun (b. 1936) and Yi Ch'ong-jun (b. 1939) are known for the intellectual rigor of their fiction.

The 1970s brought to the fore a collection of powerful voices that exposed the social ills attending South Korea's industrialization under President Park Chung Hee. There is no better fictional treatment of this subject than Cho Se-hui's (b. 1942) *Nanjangi ka ssoaollin chagun kong* (A Little Ball Launched by a Dwarf, 1978), perhaps the most important one-volume novel of the post-1945 period. Yun Hung-gil (b. 1942) wrote of the scars of the civil war and of citizens coerced into supervising "subversive" neighbors. Hwang Sog-yong (b. 1943) wrote of itinerant construction workers, urban squatters, and refugees from North Korea. Cho Chong-nae (b. 1943), in his ten-volume novel *T'aebaek sanmaek* (The T'aebaek Mountains, 1989), took a revisionist approach to modern Korean history. The 1970s also marked the debut of Yi Mun-yol (b. 1948), perhaps the most important Korean novelist at the century's end. Yi is concerned with retrieving Korean tradition amid the territorial division of the peninsula, the legacy of colonialism, and the challenges posed by modernization and urbanization.

Among the most important works of modern Korean fiction are the multivolume novels called *taeha sosol* (great-river fiction). These works have precedents in the family saga of premodern times and usually feature a historical background and several generations of family life. In addition to Cho Chong-nae's *T'aebaek sanmaek*, the most important examples are *Im Kkok-jong* (1939) by Hong Myong-hui (1888–?), about a bandit leader of that name; *T'oji* (Land, 1994) by Pak Kyong-ni (b. 1927); *Chang Kil-san* (1984) by Hwang Sog-yong, also about a bandit leader thus named; and *Honpul* (Spirit Fire, 1996) by Ch'oe Myong-hui (1947–1999).

So Chong-ju, Shin Kyong-nim, Kim Chi-ha, and Ko Un stand out among poets of the post-1945 era. So (1915–2000) is Korea's most important modern poet, a master of the Korean language who mined Korean history and culture and the Buddhist worldview to produce short, revelatory lyrics and longer prose-poems, all of them inspired by native Korean tradition and, earlier in his career, French symbolism. Ko, Kim, and Shin have all exhibited a populist streak, and have incorporated the spirit of political activism in their poetry.

Modern Korean drama, like fiction and poetry, was subject to considerable Western influence early in the 1900s. Among the earliest examples of modern drama is *San twaeji* (Boar, 1926) by Kim U-jin (1897–1926). *T'omak* (Piece, 1932) by Yu Ch'i-jin (1904–1973) marked the advent of a new realist drama. Perhaps the most important contemporary playwright, O T'ae-sok (b. 1940), blends an innovative, Western-influenced style with texts drawn from Korean history and folklore recent and past. A good example is *Ch'unp'ung ui ch'o* (Ch'un-p'ung's Wife, 1975).

The most noteworthy trend in Korean literature at the end of the twentieth century is the prominence achieved by women fiction writers. Long marginalized by the overwhelmingly male literary establishment, Korean women writers, building on the pioneering efforts of writers such as Ch'oe Chong-hui (1912–1990), have since the 1970s gained both critical and commercial success through the technical and thematic innovations of Pak Wan-so (b. 1931), O Chong-hui (b. 1947), Ch'oe Yun (b. 1953), and others.

Little is known of literature produced in the Democratic People's Republic of Korea (North Korea). Around one hundred established writers migrated from southern Korea to what is now North Korea following Korea's liberation from Japanese colonial rule in 1945, but their works were unavailable in the Republic of Korea (South Korea) until the democratization movement of the late 1980s in South Korea. A full account of literature in North Korea must await reunification of the Korean peninsula. In the meantime, fiction writers in South Korea have begun to chronicle the experiences of Northern defectors to the South.

*Bruce Fulton*

*See also:* **Drama—Korea; Poetry—Korea**

### Further Reading


Fulton, Bruce. "Korea." In *The Columbia Companion to Modern East Asian Literature*, edited by Joshua Mostow. New York: Columbia University Press. Forthcoming.

Fulton, Bruce, and Ju-Chan Fulton, trans. (1997) *Wayfarer: New Fiction by Korean Women*. Seattle: Women in Translation.

Kim, Chong-un, and Bruce Fulton, trans. (1998) *A Ready-Made Life: Early Masters of Modern Korean Fiction*. Honolulu, HI: University of Hawaii Press.

Kim, Hunggyu. (1997) *Understanding Korean Literature*. Trans. by Robert J. Fouser. Armonk, NY: M. E. Sharpe.

Kim, Kichung. (1996) *An Introduction to Classical Korean Literature*. Armonk, NY: M. E. Sharpe.

Lee, Peter H., ed. (1981) *Anthology of Korean Literature: From Earliest Times to the Nineteenth Century*. Honolulu, HI: University of Hawaii Press.

Lee, Sung-Il, trans. (1998) *The Moonlit Pond: Korean Classical Poems in Chinese*. Port Townsend, WA: Copper Canyon Press.

Myers, Brian. (1994) *Han Sorya and North Korean Literature: The Failure of Socialist Realism in the DPRK*. Ithaca, NY: Cornell East Asian Series.

O'Rourke, Kevin, trans. (1999) *Looking for the Cow: Modern Korean Poems*. Dublin, Ireland: Dedalus.

———. (1993) *Tilting the Jar, Spilling the Moon: Poems from Koryo, Choson, and Contemporary Korea*. Dublin, Ireland: Dedalus.


## LITERATURE—LAOS

The emergence of traditional Lao literature began after the founding of the first Lao kingdom, known as Lan Xang (1353–1694), during which many classic works, both secular and religious, were composed. The neighboring Hindu and Buddhist cultures influenced traditional Lao literature, which was composed in a number of poetic forms.

### Early Lao Literature

The early manuscripts consisted of accordion-style folded paper or palm leaves, onto which Buddhist monks engraved the text with a metal stylus. The manuscripts were stored in Buddhist temple libraries or in private homes of the elite. Today they are preserved in temples as well as in the National Library in Vientiane, Laos, the National Library in Bangkok, Thailand, and in libraries in Europe.

The temple was the center for Lao literature since both secular and religious festivals were held on temple grounds. Monks and village elders might spend several days reciting both secular and religious stories to the public at these festivals. All levels of society enjoyed traditional Lao literature in this public forum.

***Secular Literature*** Secular literature was written in Lao script, and the content was mainly folk tales, legends, and historical annals. Secular literature began as an oral tradition, but over the years the stories and legends were recorded on paper, although the identities of the writers and the dates they wrote are unknown. For example, the legend of Khun Bhorom traces the life of Khun Bhorom, the founding father of the Lao people. Some folk stories were risqué and humorous, such as the tale of Xieng Mieng, a cunning, lazy man who loved to outwit the king; it continues to be a popular story of the Lao people. Historical records traced the founding of a kingdom, acts of a king, and major events affecting the kingdom. One example is the *Muang Phuan*, a historical record of the kingdom of the Phuan people.

***Religious Literature*** Religious literature was based on Hindu and Buddhist works, which were transformed into Lao. Lao characters replaced the Indian characters in the stories, and the settings were changed to Laos, often near the Mekong River. Popular religious stories included the five hundred *Jataka* tales, or stories of the Buddha's previous lives. Another fifty tales of the Buddha's past lives that influenced religious Lao literature came from the literature of the Lanna kingdom (1259–1931) and indirectly from the Mon kingdom Haripunchai (660–1281), both located in present-day northern Thailand. The Vinaya and the

Abhidhamma Buddhist texts also influenced Lao religious literature.

Popular religious stories were morality tales that focused on pious deeds. This type of literature aimed to teach people how to behave and how to accept their station in Lao society and in the greater Buddhist realm. The Indian Hindu epic *Ramayana* became *Pha Lak Pha Lam* in Lao literature; it was a favorite at the Lao court (as well as the Siamese and Khmer courts) and was portrayed in classical dance performances.

After the breakup of the Laos kingdom into three small kingdoms in the seventeenth century, classic Lao literature continued to be produced until well into the nineteenth century.

**Emergence of Modern Lao Literature (1893–1954)**

The Siamese and then the French, who came to dominate Laos, did little to improve education or the field of literature during the nineteenth century. The French began to introduce secular education with a Western-based curriculum in Laos during the 1930s, and the first lycée (French-model high school) opened in 1947. The French system moved away from the religious nature of traditional schools and literature and focused on teaching students that they were French subjects. Lao royalty and elite usually received a Western education in France and other European nations.

Fiction was introduced during this period. The first Lao novel, published in 1944, was a detective story, *Pha Phoutthahoop Saksit* (The Sacred Buddha Image), by Somchine Nginn. The first Lao newspapers—*Lao Nhay* and *Pathet Lao*—appeared during the 1940s, and the first Lao news agency was called Agence Lao Presse.

**Modern Lao Literature (1954–1975)**

After World War II, Lao literature split into two camps, reflecting the political ideologies of the royalists and the Communists. Royal Lao writers included Pakian Viravong (who wrote under the pen name of Pa Nai), Dara Viravong (Duang Champa), and Duangdueane (Dok Ket) Viravong. These writers were children of Maha Sila Viravong, the famous Lao historian. Duangdueane Viravong married Outhine Bounavong (1942–2000), another royalist writer. Writers in this camp continued to be influenced by French writers and then in the 1960s by Thai writers. In the 1970s, Maha Sila Viravong founded a magazine devoted entirely to Lao literature, *Phai Nam*.

Literature of the Communists, or the Lao Patriotic Front *(Neo Lao Hak Sat)*, such as *Rains in the Jungle*, was written in traditional Lao poetic forms in an attempt to reach the common people. The Lao Patriotic Front also began to publish a report with stories written by soldiers and party members. Seri Milamay (Seriphap) was a revolutionary writer who received the Southeast Asian Writers Award for his work.

**Postrevolutionary Literature (1975–Present)**

Since the Communist takeover in December 1975, the government has strictly controlled Lao writers. Literary criticism is nonexistent in Laos, and anything of a critical nature is usually published anonymously in Thailand. Royalist writers spent time in reeducation camps before being allowed to continue to write for the new regime. Outhine was the first Lao writer to have his short stories published in English, and works by other writers have been translated into Thai, Russian, and Vietnamese.

Revolutionary writers still active after the revolution include Chanti Dueansavan and Sonvanthone Bouphanovong, while Saisuwan Phengphong and Bounthanong Somsaiphon are writers who became popular after the revolution. Their works have been translated into Thai.

With the introduction of the New Economic Mechanism *(Jintanakan Mai)*, censorship has relaxed, but Lao literature faces many obstacles. One is the lack of funding for producing books. Printing presses are located in the nation's capital, Vientiane, and the costs of publication are high. The country's lack of infrastructure and its rugged terrain hinder efforts to send materials to all parts of the country. The inadequate number of schools affects the illiteracy rate, which in turn affects the dissemination of literature. These hindrances have, however, enabled traditional forms of Lao literature to persist. Palm-leaf manuscripts were used until the mid-twentieth century, and temples continue to be education centers for traditional Lao literature and settings for festivals where literature is still recited.

*Linda S. McIntosh*

**Further Reading**

Anonymous. (1967) *Rains in the Jungle*. Vientiane, Laos: Neo Lao Hak Sat (Lao Patriotic Front).

Koret, Peter. (1999) "Contemporary Lao Literature." In *Texts and Contexts: Interaction between Literature and Culture in Southeast Asia*, edited by Luisa Mallari-Hall. Quezon City, Philippines: University of Philippines Press, 77–103.

———. (1994) "Lao." In *Traveler's Literary Companion to Southeast Asia*, edited by Alastair Dingwall. Brighton, U.K.: In Print, 120–153.

———. (1995) "Whispered So Softly It Resounds through the Forest, Spoken So Loudly It Can Hardly Be Heard: The Art of Parallelism in Lao Literature." In *Thai Literary Traditions*, edited by Manas Chitakasem. Bangkok, Thailand: Chulalongkorn Press, 265–298.

La-Font, P. B. (1989) "Laos." In *Southeast Asian Languages and Literatures: A Select Guide*, edited by Patricia Herbert and Anthony Milner. Honolulu, HI: University of Honolulu Press, 67–76.

Peltier, Anatole-Roger, trans. (1999) *The White Night Jar: A Lao Tale*. Vientiane, Laos: Institute of Research in Culture, Ministry of Culture.

Outhine Bounyavong. (1999) *Mother's Beloved*. Chiang Mai, Thailand: Silkworm Books.

Xay Kaignavongsa, and Hugh Fincher. (1993) *Legends of the Lao*. Vientiane, Laos: Geodata Systems.

## LITERATURE—MYANMAR

Burmese literature falls into three periods: monarchic (until 1885), colonial (1886–1948), and postindependence (1948 to the present). Although Burma was a parliamentary democracy right after independence, most of its subsequent history has been of military rule, one-party rule, or both.

The earliest example of writing using Burmese script is probably the Prince Raja Kumar's stone inscription, written around 1112 in four languages: Pyu, spoken by a group related to the Burmese; Mon, spoken by settlers of Lower Burma; Pali, the Indian language of Theravada Buddhism; and Burmese. The Burmese alphabet in this inscription is ultimately derived from the ancient Indian Brahmi script.

Appearing later solely in the Burmese language, these inscriptions are mostly records of donations. They mention the kinds of donations, the identity of donors, the occasions, and the locations. The inscriptions end with prayers or curses, written to scare people and prevent them from destroying the donor's act of merit. At this time, there were also texts written on terra-cotta plaques and in ink on stucco. Both of these forms usually appear beneath depictions of scenes from the *Jataka* tales (Burmese *Zat*, didactic stories of the Buddha's past lives).

Although the early stone inscriptions are written in prose, verse began to replace the prose after the thirteenth century, especially in palm-leaf manuscripts and in *parabaik* (folding tablets made of paper, cloth, or metal). This resulted in the appearance of longer forms of verse, including *pyui'* (epics), *mo'kvan*‘" (poems on historic occasions), *yadu* (lyrical odes on the seasons, love, and so forth), and *e" khyan*‘" (poems for the young princes and princesses).

At first, the writers were usually monks writing religious tales, such as the life story of the Buddha and the *Jataka* tales in *pyui'* form. Later writers wrote nonreligious tales in *pyui'* form. *Mo'kvan*‘", on the other hand, is a verse form that courtiers used to record and eulogize the exceptional achievements of the king. *E" khyan*‘" is a verse form used in composing success stories of a child's parents and grandparents; these were sung as lullabies for princes and princesses to give them confidence and encouragement. *Yadu* is the shortest verse form, the style adopted by kings, monks, and those in the palace, including laypeople. Writers used the *yadu* form to write about personal affairs, the beauty of nature, and weather. Still other verse forms include "*khyui*" (four-stanza verse), *te"thap*‘ (lyric of eighteen lines), *bo" lay*‘ (plaintive song), and *lvam" khyan*‘" (poem or song of longing), which are closely related to songs.

Verses on country life and verses composed by people in the countryside begin to appear in the seventeenth century. Padāsa Rājā (1684–1744), a minister of the king, wrote verses about the countryside in the form of *'khyan*‘" (classical song). Some country people themselves also wrote about village youths in the style of *auin*‘ *khyan*‘" (folk song) addressed to their close friends.

After 1300, prose was written on many subjects. Buddhist monk Rhan'Maha Silavamsa (1453–1518) wrote *Pārāyana vatthu* (Stories Leading to Nirvana) based on Buddhist sermons and Buddhist texts, and many narratives based on Buddhism followed. The entertaining Buddhist narrative sermons of U" Punna (1807–1867), a literary figure known for his humorous writings, allowed people to enjoy both literary style and stimulating thoughts on Buddhism. While *Pārāyana vatthu* became the basis for Buddhist narratives, Rhan'Maha Silavamsa's *Rajavan'ky U* (Famous History) became the forerunner of later Burmese historical texts.

To satisfy the Burmese readers' thirst for knowledge, expositional texts also began to appear. Among those, the *Rājadhamma san*‘*gaha* (Precepts Incumbent on a King), written by Yo" Atvan‘"van U" (1729–1823), was a suggestion for modern administration. Also, travelogues such as *Putake Capīn´ Itālyam sva" mhat´tam"* (Journal of a Trip to Portugal, Spain, and Italy) by U" Khrim´' (1828–1883) and *Lan'dan*‘ *sva" ne zin*‘ *hmat*‘ *tam*‘" (Journal of a Trip to London) by Kan‘" van‘ Man‘" kri" U" Kon‘" (1821–1908) appeared in the nineteenth century.

Rhvēton´ Sīhasū (1708–1748), a palace attendant, on the other hand, wrote *Ratana' kre" mum vatthu* (Treasured Mirror Stories) purely to entertain readers. Scholars consider this original composition the first Burmese legend, since the characters in the narrative are human beings, *nats* (supernatural animist beings), and dragons.

In the later part of the monarchy, plays and dramas to be performed in the palace were written both in prose and verse. U" Kran´ U (1773–1828) and U" Punna wrote plays that lasted all night—the former based on the author's own ideas and the latter on Buddhist literature.

In the mid-nineteenth century, printing technology came to Burma, and printed materials replaced palm-leaf and *parabaik* literature. Newspapers and books were published both in Lower and Upper Burma. By the time the British conquered Burma (1885), printing was already well underway.

## Literature during British Colonial Rule

Under the British, the Burmese began to translate Western literature. Readers came to understand more about Western popular literature when, in 1902, U" Phui" JU translated Daniel Defoe's *Robinson Crusoe* into Burmese. In 1904, James Hla Kyō (1863–1913) added his own story to sections of Alexandre Dumas's *The Count of Monte Cristo* and turned it into *Mōn' Ran' Mōn' Ma May' Ma Vatthu* (The Story of Maung Yin Maung and Ma Me Ma), which scholars consider the first modern Burmese novel.

Many other Burmese novels appeared at this time. Most were romantic with moral lessons until 1920. However, *Cabay' ban' vatthtu* (Jasminc Plant Story) and *Rhve Pran n' Cui" vatthu* (The Story of Shewei Pyi So) by U" Lat' (1866–1921) were unusual in that the characters were true to life. After the anticolonialist movements in 1920, people started to write with a political or social agenda in mind.

Around 1930, university students created *khet' cam'"* ("test the age") literature, whose style and topics differ from those of earlier times. Sippam Mon' Va (1899–1942) became a successful *khet' cam'* writer. Books on Western political thought published by the the Naga"nī Association, founded by young people in 1937, opened the political eyes of the Burmese.

While prose was developing, verse also bloomed. Sa khan' Kuito'mhuin'" (1875–1964) was the most famous poet of the colonial period; he wrote about Burmese culture and the fight for independence, and he encouraged anticolonialist movements. His *Le" khyui" kri"* (Longer Four-Stanza Verse) poems followed ancient forms, but the language was closer to that of the countryside. Students from Rangoon University writing *khet' cam'"* literature focused on writing in a simple style so that literature would be accessible to most people.

## Burmese Literature after Independence

After independence, various literary styles appeared in response to the unstable political situation. A struggle developed between those who believed in literature for literature's sake and those who leaned toward leftist themes.

In 1962, the Revolutionary Council took power, and freedom of the press declined under the Burma Program Socialist Party. A Censorship Board was established so that literature that attacked party policy could be banned. Literary awards were presented only to authors whose topics supported party policy.

At present, the Censorship Board still controls publishing policy, but Burmese literature is alive despite the tight censorship. Authors must now write about political and social conditions indirectly to make their works acceptable to the Censorship Board, and the quality of the literature has even improved. Currently, literary criticism is playing a new role in Myanmar. Literature is now being viewed from the perspective of literary skills and values instead of from political perspectives, as before. In line with developments in world literature, the terms "modern" and "postmodern" have appeared in the Burmese literary world.

*Saw Tun*

## Further Reading

Allot, Anna. (1988) "Burmese Literature." In *Far Eastern Literature in the Twentieth Century, a Guide Based on the Encyclopedia of World Literature in the Twentieth Century*, edited by Leonard S. Klein. Harpenden, U.K.: Old Castle, 1–8.

Badgley, John H. (1981) "Intellectuals and the National Vision: The Burmese Case." In *Essays on Literature and Society in Southeast Asia; Political and Sociological Perspectives*, edited by Tham Seong Chee. Singapore: Singapore University Press, 36–55.

Bode, Mabel Haynes. (1966) *The Pali Literature of Burma*. Prize Publications Fund, no. 2. London: Royal Asiatic Society.

Esche, Annemarie. (1979) *Marchen der Volker Burmas*. Leipzig, Germany: Im Insel-Verlag.

Herbert, Patricia M., ed. (1991) *Burma*. Oxford, U.K.: Clio Press, 206–213.

Pe Maung Tin, U. (1977) *Mran' m, c, pA s, muin'"* (History of Burmese Literature). Yangon, Myanmar: Khittaya Press.

**LITERATURE—PHILIPPINES** Philippine literature, written in Filipino, English, Spanish, and Philippine languages (e.g., Cebuan, Ilocano, Tagalog, Hiligaynon, Pampangan, Hanunuo-Mangyan, and Bontok), has been influenced by colonization, economic and social systems, religion, and political movements. An oral tradition continues to exist through epics, riddles, poems, and legends of the country's around sixty ethnolinguistic groups, reflecting a culture linked with the Malay of Southeast Asia and the influence of Indian, Arabic, and Chinese cultures. With the colonization of the islands by Spain and the United States, Western forms such as the novel, short story, essay, and full-length play were introduced. However, resistance to colonization also produced a tradition of radical literature. Philippine literary texts have been records of everyday life, historical documents, receptacles of values, and either participants in the colonial discourses of the colonizers, or testaments to freedom and sovereignty.

### Precolonial Literature (1564)

Among the literary forms during the precolonial period were riddles and proverbs, at the heart of which were the *talinghaga* (metaphor); the Hanunoo-Mangyan *ambahan* (a poetic form chanted without a predetermined musical pitch); the Tagalog poetic form *tanaga;* myths, fables, and legends; mimetic dances and rituals that at times involved a plot (for example, the *Ch'along* of the Ifugao); and epics, such as *Lam-ang* and *Labaw Donggon*. Created in communal societies, the subject matter and metaphors came from common village experiences. Literature was essential in daily life, rites of passage, and survival. Songs provided rhythm at work, rituals healed the sick, and epics validated community beliefs. Each member of the community was a poet or storyteller, and the conventions of oral literature—formulaic repetition, character stereotypes, and rhythmic devices—facilitated transmission.

### The Spanish Colonial Period (1565–1897)

Literature during Spanish colonial rule consisted of both religious and secular literature, prevalent during the first two centuries, and a nineteenth century reformist and revolutionary literature that reflected the clamor for change and independence. Spanish colonial rule resulted in the establishment of a feudal system and the imposition of the Catholic religion. Religious orders monopolized printing presses; the first book, *Doctrina Cristiana* (Christian Doctrine, 1593), was published by the Dominicans. The first printed literary work in Tagalog, the poem "May bagyo ma't may rilim" (Though There Be Storm and Darkness) was published in *Memorial de la vida Cristiana*, (1605), by friar lexicographer Francisco Blancas de San Jose. In 1704, Gaspar Aquino de Belen published "Ang mahal na passion ni Jesu Christong panginoon natin" (The Passion of Jesus Christ Our Lord), a narrative poem of the life of Christ.

Literature reaffirming religious values was dominant, including forms such as the *sinakulo*, a play on the passion of Christ, the *ejemplo*, which spoke of saints, and the *komedya*, which featured battles between Christians and Moors. Nationalist literary historians believe that these feudal and colonial discourses contributed to the country's colonization because they promoted beliefs and values such as acceptance of one's destiny, deferring to authority, superiority of the colonizer, and the supremacy of the Catholic religion over Muslim beliefs.

Spanish ballads, which inspired the *komedya*, also influenced narrative poetry, including the *awit*, with its four mono-rhyming dodecasyllabic lines, and the *korido*, with its four mono-rhyming octosyllabic lines. The most significant *awit* was "Pinagdaanang buhay ni Florante at Laura sa cahariang Albania" (The Life of Florante and Laura in Albania, 1838), by Francisco Baltazar (1788–1862). It is considered the first nationalist literary text and is known for its indictment of colonial rule, its popularity, and its skillful manipulation of language.

The growth of a nationalist consciousness resulted in literature that called for reform. Written by *ilustrados* (Filipino students in Spain), many of these works either parodied religious literature or introduced new literary forms to better articulate issues. Marcelo H. del Pilar (1850–1896) criticized religious orders using the *pasyon* and prayers, using monetary currency to describe the friar in the poem "Friar Ginoong Barya" (Hail Father Coins) a parody of "Aba Ginoong Maria" (Hail Mary, a popular prayer). National hero Jose Rizal (1861–1896) wrote the novels *Noli me tangere* (Touch Me Not, 1887), and *El filibusterismo* (The Subversive, 1891), works that portrayed Philippine society with a critical view, introduced realism, and are considered to be among the most important works in Philippine literature.

The revolutionary organization Katipunan published in its newspaper *Kalayaan* essays and poems emphasizing that the Philippines was a free land before the coming of the Spaniards, thus justifying the need for a revolution. "Ang Dapat Mabatid ng mga Tagalog" (What the Filipinos Should Know), by Andres Bonifacio (1863–1896), rallied Filipinos in the struggle against Spain. The essay "Kalayaan" (Freedom), by Emilio Jacinto (1875–1899), asserts that freedom is a basic right of all human beings. Along with the revolutionary love songs of the period *(kundiman)*, these anticolonial and nationalist discourses contributed to the Filipinos' struggle for independence.

### The American Colonial Period (1898–1946)

Philippine independence, declared by the revolutionary government on 12 June 1898, proved to be short-lived, ending with the invasion of U.S. forces. Resistance was evident in allegorical plays known as the *drama simboliko* (symbolic drama). In *Tanikalang Guinto* (Golden Chains, 1902), by Juan Abad (1872–1932), and *Kahapon, Ngayon at Bukas* (Yesterday, Today, and Tomorrow, 1903), by Aurelio Tolentino (1868–1915), characters represent the Motherland (Inangbayan, Pinagsakitan) and revolutionary Filipinos (Taga-ilog, K'Ulayaw, Tanggulan). In many of these allegorical plays, the lead male character, who pretends to be dead but is actually alive, represents the revolutionary forces still fighting in the mountains. The anticolonial and nationalist discourses found in drama can similarly be found in poetry, whether written in Spanish, such as the poetry of Fernando Ma Guerrero (1873–1929) or in Tagalog, such as that of Jose Corazon de Jesus (1836–1932). While there were novels that dwelled on romantic love and adventure, and were reminiscent of the *komedya*, such as *Nena at Neneng* (1903), by Valeriano Hernandez Pena (1858–1922), many novelists gave a critical portrayal of society. *Pinaglahuan* (1907), by Faustino Aguilar (1882–1995), and *Banaag at Sikat* (1903), by Lope Santos (1879–1963), focused on the exploitation of the working class and introduced socialist ideas. These novels participated in the anti-imperialist discourses of such organizations as the Union Obrero Democratico (Democratic Workers' Union)

The imposition of English as the medium of instruction resulted in the dominance of literature in English. Although Filipino writers mastered the craft of poetry and fiction using Western aesthetics, several chose to portray the countryside, thus emphasizing local color. Collections such as *How My Brother Leon Brought Home a Wife* (1941), by Manuel Arguilla (1910–1944), may have painted idyllic portraits, but the emphasis on rural life was also read by critics as a protest against the industrialization brought about by U.S. colonial rule. A pioneering novel in migrant literature was *America Is in the Heart* (1946), by Carlos Bulosan (1913–1956); it focused on racial discrimination and the exploitation of workers in the United States.

During this period magazines such as *Liwayway* (1922, Tagalog), *Bisaya* (1930, Cebuano), *Hiligaynon* (1934, Ilongo) and *Bannawag* (1934, Iloko) became the primary outlet for short stories written in indigenous languages. Literary production was influenced by market and editorial policies, resulting in many works that used formulaic plots and deus ex machina endings. However, skillfully written stories such as "Greta Garbo" (1930), by Deogracias Rosario (1894–1936), "Kung Ako'y Inanod" (If I Am Swept Away, 1907), by Marcel Navarra, and "Si Anabella," (Anabella, c. 1936–1938), by Magdalena Jalandoni, indicted the colonial way of thinking, explored psychological realism, and created complex characters.

The tension between colonial and anticolonial forces in Philippine society was echoed in literature, with the "art for art's sake" philosophy of the poet Jose Garcia Villa (1906–1997) on the one hand and the social consciousness of Salvador P. Lopez (1911–1993), as emphasized in his essay "Literature and Society," on the other. Much work during this period was both a result of and a response to U.S. colonial rule and capitalist values.

The cultural policy of the Japanese occupation (1942–1945), which encouraged Tagalog writing, resulted in a harvest of works. These were compiled in the collection *Ang 25 Pinakamabubuting Katha ng 1942* (Twenty-Five Best Stories of 1942). By following the guidelines of the policy however, many of the works focused on everyday life that seemed untouched by war. Exceptions were several stories where males were conspicuously absent or characters seemed to be waiting for loved ones, making it possible for critics to read in these stories references to the Filipino guerrillas fighting the Japanese forces. Literature, through satirical skits performed by stage actors, and poems, songs, and plays performed by the guerrillas played an important part in the anti-Japanese movement.

### Contemporary Literature

Contemporary literature has been influenced by various critical theories, among them New Criticism, which emphasizes the literary work as a verbal construct, and Marxism, which produces works political in intent and content. Experimental and eccentric form and language can found in poetry collections such as Jose Garcia Villa's *Have Come, Am Here* (1942) and *Piniling mga tula ni AGA* (Selected Works of AGA, 1965), by Alejandro G. Abadilla (1904–1969). Among the works that focused on economic and social issues were the novel *Ilaw sa hilaga* (Light from the North, 1948), by Lazaro Francisco (1898–1980), the poetry collection *Isang dipang langit* (A Stretch of Sky, 1961), by Amado V. Hernandez (1903–1973), and the novel *Dagiti mariing iti parbangon* (Those Who Are Awakened at Dawn, 1957), by Constante Casabar (b. 1929). The production of works that were anti-imperialist and revolutionary in content, such as Hernandez's prison poems, alongside works emphasizing a revolution in form, such as the comma poems of Villa, reflected a society that, although independent since 1946, had remained feudal, economically dependent on foreign capital, and heavily influenced by U.S. culture.

The search for national identity, an upsurge of nationalism, and debates on the national language have shaped Philippine literature. This is evident in the novels of Nick Joaquin (b. 1917), Francisco Sionil Jose (b. 1924), N. V. M. Gonzalez (1917–2000), and Edgardo M. Reyes (b. 1938), and in the poetry of Rio Alma (b. 1945) and Rolando Tinio (1937–1997). While Joaquin's search for identity led him to works that glorified a past era, Reyes's work centers on the poverty that led people to migrate to the city from the countryside, and the continuing exploitation they faced in urban centers. Two landmark collections, *Mga agos sa disyerto* (Streams in the Desert, 1964) and *Sigwa* (Storm, 1972), contain works that participate in discourses on class, gender, and imperialism.

Literature from the 1980s and 1990s saw renewed interest in regional language, the publication of anthologies of feminist and gay literature (for example, *Filipina I*, 1984), and programs geared toward developing writers among peasants and workers in the hope of creating a truly national literature.

*Maria Josephine Barrios, with notes from Bienvenido Lumbera*

## Further Reading

Lumbera, Bienvenido, and Cynthia Lumbera. (1997) *Philippine Literature: A History and Anthology*. Pasig, Philippines: Anvil Publishing.

Riggs, Stanley. (1901) *The Filipino Drama*. Manila, Philippines: Intramuros Administration.

# LITERATURE—SOUTH ASIA, BENGALI

The Bengali language is as old as English, emerging from eastern dialects of Middle Indo-Aryan (standard colloquial Sanskrit, or Prakrit), sometime before 1000 CE. The earliest surviving literary texts in Old Bengali are mystic *caryapad*, "play-part" songs, dating between 1000 and 1200 CE and preserved in a single manuscript of Sanskrit commentary in the Nepal Darbar Library. These songs, composed in syllabic rhyming couplets with caesuras in mid-line, treat esoteric practices of yoga and tantrism in paradoxical, sometimes vulgar, code language. Their imagery, derived from everyday village life, is meant to reveal and conceal the inner meaning of the spiritual masters' *(acaryas)* yearnings for spiritual union and experiences in the process of attaining self-realization. These songs conclude with a signature couplet *(bhaita)* in which the poet identifies himself and comments obliquely on his theme. The *carya*-style song never disappeared entirely from Bengali folk culture.

Contemporary *baul* songs have forms and thematic concerns similar to those of *carya*-style songs. *Baul*s are members of a heterogeneous (Hindu and Muslim) syncretic sect of West Bengal and Bangladesh, originating in the sixteenth century CE, whose nondualistic beliefs and practices derive from Hindu Vaishnava, Buddhist Tantric, and Muslim Sufi teachings. The *bauls* traditionally led a wandering life, singing their distinctive devotional songs and playing folk instruments, especially at fairs and festivals, as their main source of livelihood. The *baul*s form a tolerated but marginalized subcaste in Bengali society; in the late 1900s, however, a number of the more talented and ambitious performers among them, such as Purna Chandra Das Baul, have become recording artists with international reputations. *Baul* songs have greatly influenced Bengali literary culture; Rabindranath Tagore (1861–1941), Bengal's Nobel Prize winner in literature, was much affected by the songs of Lalon Fakir (d. 1890), the most celebrated *baul* of all time.

## The Old and Middle Bengali Periods

Although mystic, devotional song was not always thought to possess high literary value, religious themes predominated in Bengali poetry through the Old and Middle Bengali periods (c. 950–1350 and 1350–1800 CE, respectively). Poetry predominated as there was no prose to speak of until nearly 1800. Under Hindu rulers of the Pala and Sena dynasties (eighth to twelfth centuries), Bengal developed its own schools of Vedic Sanskrit studies and Buddhist Tantrism in monasteries, temples, and other learning centers. After Turkish invaders overran the Bengali kingdom of Nadia in 1201, the Muslim *darbar* (court) established in Gaur continued to provide patronage for over 200 years to court poets of the Middle Bengali period, who composed narrative poems of the exploits of gods such as the Vedic deity, Dharma, and the competing cults of the pre-Vedic goddesses Chandi, consort of Siva, and Manasa, a daughter of Siva and queen of serpents. The most popular narrative poetic themes, however, were from the *Ramayaa*, the legends of the god Rama, rendered into Bengali by poets such as the fifteenth-century Krittivas Pandit; the epic *Mahabharata*, chanted in Bengali by professional court poets; and tales of Lord Krishna, the most remarkable version of which, the secularized Srikrishnakirttana by Chandidas, dates from about the sixteenth century. In this rendition, a dramatic series of Bengali dialogue-songs interspersed with Sanskrit verses, Krishna and his lover Radha are not divine or mythical beings but youthful villagers carrying on their illicit affair with a full range of human emotions.

**Role of Chaitanya**

Bengali popular imagination was galvanized by the charismatic Vaishnava revivalist Chaitanya (1486–1533) who, though he composed only one poem, the Sanskrit Siksastaka (Lesson in Eight Verses), continues to exert influence over Bengali literature to this day. Born into a learned Brahman family in Navadvip, Nadia, the boy trained as a Vedic scholar. At age twenty he took initiation from a Vaishnava teacher and was transformed into a *bhakta*, a devotional mystic, who sought union with God by identifying with Radha and singing the names of her beloved Lord Krishna. The Vaishnava revival started by Chaitanya swept through Bengal, dissolving religious and caste barriers among his followers; for three centuries poets composed *Caitanyamagal*, narrative poems recounting Chaitanya's life and teachings, as well as *kirttan*, folk-influenced lyrics celebrating the love of Radha and Krishna. The *bauls* arose in Nadia during this period as a folk outgrowth of Chaitanya's movement, and both Sufi and Vaishnava poets composed or transcribed folk versions of tales of local Muslim saints, creating legends of syncretic deities with both Hindu and Muslim names and jointly celebrated festivals.

**Transition to the Modern Bengali Period**

Three centuries of Muslim governance, from Delhi or through semi-independent local rulers, had already enriched Bengali literature and language through the influence of Persian and Arabic, the languages of law, administration, and Islamic cultural life. With the advent of European trade and missionary activity in the early eighteenth century, followed by printing presses and the first Bengali type fonts (designed by an officer of the British East India Company), poetry as a literary genre, widely available in inexpensive printed form, began to diverge from traditional forms of song and narrative recitation. Prose developed first through vernacular translations of catechisms and Bibles, physicians' handbooks, grammars and readers for Bengali language instruction to Europeans, and legal documents translated from English for purposes of provincial governance. Bengali culture, especially in the port of Calcutta and smaller market towns, was energized by European contact; colleges and universities modeled on the British system proliferated. Intellectuals, with English or traditional Sanskrit and Persian educations, soon distinguished themselves as prose stylists and founded the first Bengali periodicals to disseminate their work and foster greater intellectual exchange and social reform. The Modern Bengali period (1800 to the present) was underway.

**Notable Prose Stylists**

Rammohan Roy (1772–1833), polemicist, religious reformer, translator, grammarian, and forerunner of the nineteenth-century "Bengal Renaissance," wrote essays and treatises with equal facility in Bengali and Persian. Essayist, literary scholar, and social reformer Iswarchandra Vidyasagar (1820–1891), renowned for the clarity and concision of his prose, wrote treatises that shaped laws against polygamy and in favor of widow remarriage. Devendranath Tagore (1817–1905), hailed as Maharishi (Great Sage) by the educated public, refined an epistolary style and contributed to the new periodicals impelling Bengal's literary renaissance. Innovative plays on social themes, influenced by Shakespeare as well as Sanskrit drama, were staged in private and later in public theaters in Calcutta. English literary works studied in the new colleges were translated into Bengali, and some poets, most notably Michael Madhusudhan Dutta (1824–1873), ventured to write English verse. Despite his multilingual gifts and ambition to *become* as well as write in English, Dutta's greatest poem, the *Meghanadbadh Kavya (Meghnad's Fall)*, is in Bengali, in traditional Sanskrit epic cantos; however, its rebellious hero Meghnad, brother of Ravana, the demon defeated in the *Ramayana*, is modeled on tragic Western characters such as Homer's Achilles and Milton's Satan. Dutta's true literary revolution, though, came in his final book, with the first Bengali sonnets, a form well-suited to the language's inherent concision and ease of rhyming, and in his use of a massive, multilingual vocabulary and allusions from many literatures.

The nineteenth century also saw the first recognized literary contributions by women. East Bengali village matron Rassundari Devi (1810–?), her days spent in exhausting rounds of housework and childrearing, clandestinely taught herself to read from her sons' primers and by scratching letters on the smoke-blackened kitchen walls; her two-part autobiography, *Amir Jaban* (1876 and 1909), was an astonishing achievement of clear, succinct narration. The first Bengali novel, *Phulmani O Karuar Bibaran (The Story of Phulmani and Karuna)*, published in 1852, was also by a woman, Calcutta-born Hannah Catherine Mullens (1826–1861), a Christian who may have been of English descent. Bengal's first prominent prose fiction writer was Bankimchandra Chatterjee (1838–1894), who brought a lively imagination to realistic character development and an informal and often colloquial style. His best-selling novels focused on upper-middle-class Victorian-era Bengali domestic life, as well as the first stirrings of anti-British nationalism; they endure as popular classics today. The Tagore family dominated literature from the mid-1880s until the mid-twentieth century. Dwijendranath, the eccentric eldest of Devendranath Tagore's fourteen children, wrote plays and an allegorical verse fantasy, *Swapnamayi* (The Dreamer), which owed much to *The Faerie Queene* and *Pilgrim's Progress*. Swarnakumari Devi (1856–1932), an elder sister of Rabindranath, was one of Bengal's first renowned literary women, writing novels, dramas, and poetry, and editing *Bharati* (India), the monthly magazine started in 1877 by her elder brothers.

## Rabindranath Tagore

But it is the protean genius Rabindranath Tagore (1861–1941) who towers over all other literary artists of the language. Musician, actor, painter, social reformer, and educator as well as writer, he produced a vast output that included some sixty collections of poetry and other works, including novels, short stories, essays, plays, dance-dramas, and songs so distinctive that the style *Rabindra-sangit* (Tagore songs) is named after him. In 1913 he received the Nobel Prize, which led to worldwide recognition for Bengali literature. Two works available in English translation are the novel *Ghare Baire* (Home and the World), featuring multiple first-person limited points of view, a narrative strategy new to Bengali; and the self-translated *Gitanjali* (Song Offering), the poetry collection that won Tagore the Nobel Prize. This volume is a free rendering, disappointingly stripped of all specific Bengali literary, historical, and mythological allusions and echoes, based on Tagore's notion of what Western readers could relate to, so that the poems read more like Emersonian transcendentalist texts than Bengali songs. But Tagore was influential in abandoning formal literary language and adopting the standard colloquial speech of real people in his writings. Most of Tagore's work has not yet been rendered into English translations that capture the originals' subtleties, but Bengalis revere him; he is the only poet who has composed the national anthems of two countries, India and Bangladesh.

## Other Major Writers

After Tagore, notable writers include the immensely popular novelist Saratchandra Chattopadhyay (1876–1938); Begum Rokeya Sakhawat Hossain (1880–1932), polemicist, educator, and pioneering Muslim feminist, whose utopian short story, "Sultana's Dream" (1905), and opinion pieces collected in *Avarodbhasini* (Secluded Women), battled verbally against the cruelties of purdah, the oppressive seclusion of women; novelist Bibhutibhushan Bandyopadhyay (1889–1950), author of *The Apu Trilogy* (as it is called in English), which was filmed by Satyajit Ray (1920–1992), writer and cinematographer whose own father, Sukumar Raychaudhuri (1887–1923), penned *Abol-Tabol* (which roughly translates to "helter skelter"), a beloved volume of children's nonsense verse in Bengali; and the popular Calcutta novelist and short story writer Ashapurna Devi (b. 1909), author of an epic trilogy beginning with *Pratham Pratisruti* (First Promise). Notable poets include the East Bengali modernist Jibanananda Das (1899–1954); Kazi Nazrul Islam (1899–1976), a Muslim orphan nurtured on Persian verse who went on to become poet laureate of Bangladesh; East Bengali folk poet Jasim Uddin (1903–1976); and Begum Sufia Kamal (1911–1999), poet, social reformer, and educator, whose poetry collection, *Mor Jaduder Samadhi Pare* (Where My Darlings Lie Buried), became the defining voice of Bangladesh's 1971 freedom struggle. Mahasweta Devi (b. 1926) has written voluminously on the struggles of eastern India's oppressed and neglected tribal peoples; her stories and novellas, translated by the postcolonial scholar Gayatri Chakravorty Spivack, have received the University of Oklahoma's prestigious Neustadt Prize. Another chronicler of the Bangladesh Liberation War was Jahanara Iman (1929–1994), whose 1971 diary-memoir, *Ekattarer Dinguli* (literally, Days of '71, but translated as *Of Blood and Fire*), was a best-seller in both the Bengali original and in English translation.

Since the 1947 independence and partition of India and the creation of the nation of Bangladesh in 1971, Bengali literature has more closely allied itself to Western forms, both in prose (fiction and memoir) and poetry, while West Bengali and Bangladeshi writers maintain vital contacts among themselves. Magazine and book production by the more prosperous publishers in the two major literary centers, Calcutta and Dhaka, has been computerized; there are also flourishing literary publishing ventures in Bengali expatriate communities, particularly in London and New York City.

*Carolyne Wright*

*See also:* **Bangladesh; Poetry—India**

**Further Reading**

Rahman, Shamsur, and Sunil Gangopadhyay, eds. (1988) *Dui Banglar Bhalobasar Kabita* (Love Poetry from Both Bengals). Calcutta, India: Model Publishing House.

Rashid, M. Harunur, ed. (1986) *A Choice of Contemporary Verse from Bangladesh*. Dhaka, Bangladesh: Bangla Academy.

Sen, Sukumar. (1979) *History of Bengali Literature*. Calcutta, India: Sahitya Akademi.

Tagore, Rabindranath. (1987) *Selected Poems*. Trans. by William Radice. London: Penguin Books.

Tharu, Susie, and K. Lalita, eds. (1991 and 1993) *Women Writing in India*. 2 vols. New York: The Feminist Press.

## LITERATURE—SOUTH ASIA, SANSKRIT

Although almost entirely unknown to the average Western reader, the corpus of literary texts composed in Sanskrit constitutes one of the oldest continuing and most copious literary traditions in the world. The complete body of Sanskrit texts is of a size unparalleled, until modern times, by literature in any language except Chinese. It includes, in the broadest possible definition of "literature," all of the religious, philosophical, legal, historical, medical, inscriptional, technical, and scientific texts associated with the intellectual, theological, and political elites of South and Southeast Asia, from its beginnings in the middle of the second millennium BCE, through its period of greatest efflorescence in the sixth to thirteenth centuries, to the present. This corpus contains such relatively well-known works as the *Bhagavad Gita*, the *Kama Sutra*, the great Sanskrit epic poems the *Mahabharata* and the *Ramayana*, the laws of Manu, the Buddhist Lotus Sutra, and many individual works of immense size, such as the Puranas.

This entry concerns the compositions in poetry and prose that the Sanskritic tradition generally refers to generically as *kavya* or *sahitya*, writings in which the formal elements and the aesthetic response of the audience are as important as their content. This corpus is ancient, large, and still alive to some extent. It includes various genres in prose and verse, ranging from collections of short, pithy verses, or *subhashitas*, on a wide range of subjects, to lengthy narrative poems on epic, romantic, and religious themes, and a large body of plays ranging from short, one-act comic pieces to lengthy emotionally wrought dramas on various themes.

### History

From a Western viewpoint the history of Sanskrit literature can be traced back to the earliest-known compositions in the language, the hymns of the Rig Veda, which date from perhaps the middle of the second century BCE. Some of these hymns, particularly those invoking deities associated with phenomena of nature such as the dawn, the sun, or fire, are among the finest examples of religious poetry in any language. Some of the dialogue hymns and those that narrate stories have been associated by scholars with the origins of drama and the copious story collections for which Sanskrit literature is justly famous.

In the traditional Indian view, however, the Vedas, although regarded with an unparalleled reverence, are not primarily literary texts. For the majority of traditional Indian literary scholars and audiences the origin of poetry is traced to the divine inspiration of the legendary poet-seer Valmiki, who, in the wake of an intense emotional experience, composed his famous epic narrative poem the *Ramayana* in perhaps the fifth century BCE. The *Ramayana* is thus often regarded as the first true poem.

The corpus of Sanskrit literary texts begins to build in the first centuries BCE. Among the earliest are the two surviving narrative poems of the Buddhist poet Asvaghosa (flourished first–second century CE), the *Buddhacarita*, a poetic biography of the historical Buddha, and the *Saundarananda*, an account of the conversion of a prince to Buddhism, and a collection of dramas on themes drawn from Sanskrit epics and other sources attributed to the playwright Bhasa. Highly styled poetic composition is also found in Sanskrit royal inscriptions from the first centuries CE.

### The Flowering of Sanskrit Literature

One of the earliest (although of uncertain date) poets of the efflorescence of Sanskrit literature, and by more or less general consensus the single greatest literary master of the Sanskrit language, is the poet and playwright Kalidasa, who is often associated with the imperial court of the Guptas, perhaps around the fifth century CE. This artist, sometimes known in modern times as "the Shakespeare of India," left four major poetic works and three dramas. Of the former, two, the *Raghuvamsa* and the *Kumarasambhava*, are considered masterpieces of the genre known as *mahakavya* or "great poems," long, multicanto narrative poems based on themes drawn from the epics and the Puranas. The first of these is a poetic rendering of the history of the great dynasts of the Raghu dynasty, including a retelling of the career of its most illustrious son, Rama. The second is an account of the courtship and marriage of the great divinity Siva and his wife, the goddess Uma or Parvati. A third piece, the *Meghaduta* or "Cloud Messenger," is an example of a shorter genre *(khandakavya)* composed in a single poetic meter; it consists of the romantic message of a lovelorn demigod to his distant wife, which he imparts to a passing cloud. This piece is among the most imitated works of Sanskrit poetry and has inspired a whole subgenre of messenger poetry.

The dramas of Kalidasa are equally highly esteemed; one of them, *Shakuntala*, is often considered by Indian and Western critics alike to be perhaps the finest single work of the Sanskrit literary canon. This romantic play, based on an episode in the *Mahabharata*, captured the imagination of poets and scholars in late-eighteenth-century Europe and was showered with praise in a famous verse by Goethe in 1792.

Perhaps because of the genius, prolific production, and exalted reputation of Kalidasa, the genres he favored acquired considerable prestige in succeeding centuries. Thus the *mahakavya* form finds numerous exponents, some of whom established it as a major genre between the sixth and eighth centuries.

Drama, too, particularly the longer subgenres of multiact plays based on epics and invented themes, was further developed by early masters such as Bhatta Narayana (the *Venisamhara*), Shriharsha (the *Ratnavali*), and above all Bhavabhuti (the *Mahaviracarita*, the *Uttararamacarita*, and the *Malatimadhava*) during roughly the same period. Noteworthy also among the older dramas is a charming romance, the *Mrichchakatika* or "Little Clay Cart," attributed to a king Shudraka, whose date is a matter of continuing scholarly debate.

Along with the development of these verse forms (the dramas are largely verse interspersed with prose dialogue), early authors set high standards for the development of prose *kavya* in the form of lengthy narrative romances. Noteworthy here are the *Dashakumaracarita* (Adventures of the Ten Princes), by the writer and literary critic Dandin; the *Vasavadatta* of Subandhu; the historical prose poem the *Harshacarita;* and the romance the *Kadambari* of Banabhatta.

### Narratives and Fables

The genres, periods, and authors of Sanskrit literature are far too numerous to summarize completely here. One important genre was the narrative tale and fable literature, which was highly developed in India and which traveled widely throughout Europe and Asia from this point of origin. Noteworthy works include the *Pancatantra*, a collection of moral beast fables; the riddling stories of the *Vetalapancavimshati;* and the great *Kathasaritsagara* (Ocean of Stories), by the eleventh-century Kashmiri poet Somadeva.

Although Sanskrit literature reached what was perhaps its pinnacle by the twelfth century CE, it by no means ended then. Poets and storytellers in many genres continued to compose abundantly in Sanskrit for many centuries afterward and continue to produce poems, stories, and plays in this ancient language down to the present day.

*Robert P. Goldman*

*See also:* **Kalidasa; Literature—India**

### Further Reading

De, Sushil Kumar, and S. N. Dasgupta. (1947) *History of Sanskrit Literature*. Calcutta, India: University of Calcutta Press.

Dimock, Edward C., Jr., Edwin Gerow, C. M. Naim, A. K. Ramanujan, Gordon Roadarmel, and J. A. B. van Buitenen. (1974) *The Literatures of India: An Introduction*. Chicago: University of Chicago Press.

Keith, Arthur Berridale. (1920) *A History of Sanskrit Literature*. Oxford: Oxford University Press.

Winternitz, Moriz. (1963) *History of Indian Literature*. Trans. by S. Ketkar and H. Kohn. Calcutta, India: University of Calcutta Press.

## LITERATURE—SRI LANKA, SINHALESE

Sinhalese literature, or literature written in Sinhala, the language of the Sinhalese people of Sri Lanka, is distinguished from literature in other modern South Asian languages by its antiquity, its historical association with Buddhism, and the pervasive influences of long colonial domination in Sri Lanka. Buddhist monasteries became the center of intellectual activity after the conversion of the Sinhalese king to Buddhism in the third century BCE and remained so until modern times. The language and its literature declined under colonial governments (1505–1948) but have revived in recent times.

### Classical Sinhala

Buddhist texts in the Pali language were at first preserved orally by monks; the monks also composed commentaries on these texts, including historical records, in Sinhala. The early literature is lost, but there are references to it in Pali texts and later writing in Sinhala. The *Mahavamsa*, the great chronicle of Sinhalese kings composed in Pali in the fifth century CE, apparently drew on Sinhala commentaries. The ancient sources praised the kings' literary ability. The Pali chronicle *Culavamsa* (41: 55) describes King Moggallana II (531–551 CE) as "having poetic gifts without equal." The oldest extant prose work in Sinhala dates to the tenth century and is attributed to King Kassapa V (913–923 CE).

The restoration of Sinhalese rule by Vijayabahu I in 1070 after Sri Lanka's conquest by invaders from South India was followed by a cultural revival. Vijayabahu himself was considered a poet and patron of literature (*Culavamsa* 60: 80). King Parakramabahu II (1236–1271), another ruler who restored order after a foreign invasion, was the author of the *Kavsilumina*, one of the great poems of the classical period. Works in the thirteenth and fourteenth centuries were written in an ornate style with many words and literary conventions adapted from Sanskrit in what is considered the high point of literature in Sinhala. On the other hand, Gurulugomi in the thirteenth century wrote prose literature in a "pure" form of Sinhala known as Elu and limited the use of Sanskrit and Pali loan words. Sinhala diverged from other South Asian languages in this development of prose. Buddhist monks wrote commentaries and paraphrases of doctrinal texts, historical chronicles, works on grammar and rhetoric, stories of the life of the Buddha, and many translations of Sanskrit works. In the fifteenth century Sinhalese poets wrote in a style closer to the ordinary language than earlier poets did and wrote on more secular subjects. At the end of the sixteenth century, literature flourished under the patronage of the state and Buddhist monastic orders.

**Colonial Domination**

All this changed after the Portuguese conquered the southwest coastal region of the island, where the Sinhalese government had its capital. The Portuguese persecuted Buddhists, destroyed monasteries and libraries, and rewarded Christian converts. Buddhist monks and laymen moved from the coastal regions to the interior. For over two hundred years a Sinhalese kingdom survived at Kandy in the hilly interior, constantly threatened by Portuguese, Dutch, and finally British conquerors. Pali and Sanskrit scholarship declined, and popular literature developed, much of it influenced by Tamil sources. At the end of the eighteenth century Buddhism and classical literary forms revived under royal patronage in the Kandyan kingdom.

In 1815, the British annexed the Kandyan kingdom, and the island was united under Christian, English speaking rulers. The British supported Sinhalese (and Tamil) schools but only for elementary education and primarily for the purpose of encouraging conversion to Christianity. Many educated Sinhalese preferred English literature and disregarded literature in Sinhala.

Nevertheless, Sinhalese printing presses began to reprint classical works in Sinhala, woks that had been preserved in village temples on palm-leaf manuscripts, and a literary revival began. Printing also made literature available to a nonscholarly audience, and journals, pamphlets, and newspapers discussed politics and literature in Sinhala. By the late nineteenth century there were frequent controversies over literary styles. Monks and others continued to write in classical styles, whereas Pali texts and foreign literature were translated into a more popular idiom of Sinhala.

Modern fiction in Sinhala has its origins in propagandistic Christian stories in the 1870s. The first novels, often romantic fantasies or morality tales, appeared in the 1890s and became popular in the early twentieth century. Detective fiction also became popular. The most popular author was Piyadasa Sirisena (1875–1946), whose writings emphasized the destructive effects of English influence on Sinhalese culture. His counterpart in theater was the playwright John de Silva (1857–1922). Poets in the early twentieth century continued to use traditional forms until a new generation of poets called the Colombo school rejected classical poetics and themes. They introduced modern themes in poems of romantic love and social criticism, and they were in turn succeeded by writers directly influenced by contemporary Western poets.

**Independent Sri Lanka**

W. A. Silva (1892–1957) and other novelists attracted popular followings in the 1940s and 1950s with escapist narratives and simple plots. The greatest of Sinhalese novelists, Martin Wickramasinghe (1891–1976), initially was not popular. His *Gamperaliya* (1944) tells the story of the disintegration of village life under the impact of modern conditions. It is considered the first serious novel in Sinhala, and it contributed to raising the standards of fiction in Sinhala. Wickramasinghe was the most influential literary critic of his period.

Another writer and critic, Ediriweera Sarachchandra (1914–1996), devoted himself to raising the reputation of literature in Sinhala among the English-educated elite, as well as to encouraging serious fiction in Sinhala. Studies by faculty at the University of Ceylon (established 1942) increased scholarly interest in literature in Sinhala.

Throughout much of the twentieth century, literature written in Sinhala was somewhat overshadowed by works written in English. Two outstanding and, indeed, internationally influential writers were Leonard Woolf (1880–1969), the husband of Virginia Woolf and author of a novel, *The Village in the Jungle* (1914), drawing on his experiences in the Ceylon civil service, and Michael Ondaatje (b. 1943), a distinguished contemporary writer born in Sri Lanka who now lives in Canada.

Radical changes occurred in 1956, when Sinhala became the medium of education for most schools and universities in the nation and the Department of Cultural Affairs (which became the Ministry of Cultural Affairs in 1970) moved literature in Sinhala away from both Western influences and the classical past. Wickramasinghe emphasized traditional Sinhalese-Buddhist values in his later works; he and other writers accused Sarachchandra and others based at the universities of being too influenced by Western literature.

At the beginning of the twenty-first century literature in Sinhala has come under increased political pressure. Sarachchandra was physically assaulted by government supporters after he wrote a satire following the 1977 election that blamed the government's social and economic policies for the deterioration of cultural values. The civil war that began in 1983 has led to increased use of Sinhala in public life, but also to censorship, a surge in Sinhalese chauvinism, and violence against writers. It may be that, as in the past, literature in Sinhala flourishes in times of crisis.

*Patrick Peebles*

### Further Reading

Godakumbura, Charles Edmund. (1955) *Sinhalese Literature.* Colombo, Sri Lanka: Colombo Apothecaries' Co.

Sarachchandra, Ediriweera. (1950) *The Sinhalese Novel.* Colombo, Sri Lanka: M. D. Gunasena.

Wickramasinghe, Martin. (1948) *Sinhalese Literature.* Trans. by E. R. Sarathchandra. Colombo, Sri Lanka: M. D. Gunasena.

## LITERATURE—THAILAND

The earliest examples of Thai (Siamese) writing are stone inscriptions dating from the thirteenth century. The most famous of these is a four-faced pillar inscribed by King Ramkhamhaeng (flourished c. 1279–c. 1317) of Sukhothai in 1292. Although the content deals with the history and social organization of the kingdom of Sukhothai, it is generally regarded as a part of Thai literary history. Another important work believed to date from this period is the *Trai Phum Phra Ruang* (The Three Worlds of Phra Ruang), a Buddhist cosmology that describes, in prose, the worlds of desire, form, and formlessness.

### Classical Literature

Classical literature is written in verse and can be traced back to the Ayutthaya period (1350–1767). One early example, believed to date from the late fifteenth century, is the historical poem *Lilit Yuan Phai* (The Defeat of the Yuans), which recounts the victory of the Ayutthaya kingdom over the northern kingdom of Lanna. More difficult to date is the epic *Lilit Phra Lor* (The Story of Prince Lor), one of the most admired works of classical literature. It tells the story of Phra Lor's love for the two daughters of a hostile neighboring ruler; their illicit meeting is discovered, and all three lovers are subsequently killed in battle. The reign of King Narai (d. 1688) was a golden period, when poetry flourished at the court, and new verse forms, involving complex rhyme schemes, emerged. His reign saw the composition of two famous works drawn from Buddhist tales, *Samutthakhot Kham Chan* (The Story of Prince Samutthakhot) and *Su'a Kho Kham Chan* (The Tiger and the Cow). Some of the masterpieces of the *nirat* genre (travel poetry), such as *Nirat Hariphunchai* and the poet Siprat's *Khlong Kamsuan*, describing his journey into exile in Nakhon Sri Thammarat, also date from this period.

After the death of King Narai, the Ayutthaya kingdom became embroiled in war with the Burmese. In 1767, the capital was overrun and razed, resulting in the loss of most of its recorded literary material. King Taksin (1734–1782) established a new Thai kingdom based at Thonburi and began the task of literary restoration, but it was only after he was overthrown and a new dynasty established at Bangkok, under King Rama I (1737–1809), that real progress was made. The only complete version of the *Ramakien* was composed during his reign, by, as was customary at the time, groups of anonymous poets working on different sections. Literary revival continued during the reign of his son, Rama II (1768–1824), with the appearance of the epic poem *Khun Chang, Khun Phaen* and various works composed for dramatic performance, such as *Sang Thong*, *Kraithong*, and *Inao*, all of which take their title from the names of the main protagonists. The literary career of Sunthorn Phu (1786–1856), Thailand's most famous poet and author of several famous *nirat* poems and the lengthy poem *Phra Aphaimani*, is also associated with the reign of Rama II.

### Modern Literature

King Rama III (d. 1851) showed little interest in literature, but under his successor, Rama IV (King Mongkut, 1804–1868), printing technology was introduced into the nation by Western missionaries. This, together with the emergence of a potential reading public due to the growth of the education system, had, by the latter part of the nineteenth century, created the conditions for the emergence of prose fiction.

The first novels and short stories appeared in journals such as *Lak Witthaya*, which were edited by Western-educated Thai princes or aristocrats; the contents were often serialized translations of popular Western writers of the day, such as Marie Corelli, Charles Garvice, Sax Rohmer, Arthur Conan Doyle, and H. Rider Haggard. The first Thai novel, *Khwammaiphayabat* (Non-Vendetta), by Luang Wilatpariwat, which appeared in 1915, was a deliberate response to the translation of Marie Corelli's novel, *Vendetta*, which had appeared in *Lak Wittaya* in 1901. By the mid-1920s, there was a growing demand for original Thai stories; most popular were adventure stories, often with masked villains, and romantic stories, typically involving a poor boy–rich girl theme, in which the plot was brought to a happy conclusion by a series of improbable coincidences. Novels, both then and now, were typically serialized in a magazine first and then reprinted later as a complete volume. By the 1930s, a number of writers were beginning to look beyond providing readers with escapist entertainment and attempting to address serious social issues; two classics of the period are Siburapha's *Songkhram Chiwit* (The War of Life), written in 1932, which dealt with poverty, inequality, and the lack of freedom of speech, and K. Surangkhanang's *Ying Khon Chua* (The Prostitute), published in 1937, which, sensationally for the time, presented the prostitute-heroine as a sympathetic and virtuous character.

In the late 1940s, a number of writers, including Siburapha, were influenced by socialist realism; for a brief period, works highlighting social injustice and criticizing an exploiting ruling class appeared. But freedom to write such works was short-lived, and many writers were either imprisoned or stopped writing during the literary "dark age" of the 1950s and 1960s. One serious writer who did manage to escape interference from the authorities was Khamsing Srinawk (Lao Khamhom); yet some of the elegantly crafted stories in his collection *Fa Bor Kan*, published in English as *The Politician and Other Stories*, are rather more subversive than they appeared at first reading.

By the late 1960s, a new generation of writers was rediscovering the political fiction of twenty years earlier; the works of Siburapha and some of his contemporaries became a model for many aspiring writers, whose work became known as "literature for life," that is, literature that was intended to create, or lead toward, a better life for the masses. Such literature flourished in student and academic circles after the overthrow of the military government in 1973, but, with its often simplistic treatment of issues, it had little broad appeal and soon disappeared. With rapid economic and social change sweeping through Thai society in the 1980s, new and more complex themes presented themselves; in the award-winning *Kham Phiphaksa* (The Judgment, 1982), for example, Chart Korbjitti chronicles the gossip and social hypocrisy that turn a lowly villager into an outcast within his own community. As one of the nation's most successful and accomplished writers, Chart is one of the few who can make a living entirely from writing; nevertheless, with a number of literary prizes to be won each year and considerable media attention, the literary scene remains vibrant.

*David Smyth*

*See also:* **Bidyalankarana; Khun Chang, Khun Phaen; Nirat; Ramakien**

### Further Reading

Anderson, Benedict R. O'G. and Ruchira Mendiones. (1985) *In the Mirror: Literature and Politics in the American Era.* Bangkok, Thailand: Editions Duang Kamol.

Barang, Marcel. (1994) *The 20 Best Novels of Thailand: An Anthology.* Bangkok, Thailand: Thai Modern Classics.

Hudak, Thomas. (1994) "Thailand." In *Traveller's Literary Companion to South-East Asia*, edited by Alastair Dingwall. Brighton, U.K.: In Print Publishing, 55–119.

## LITERATURE—TURKEY

**LITERATURE—TURKEY** Turkish literature is traditionally said to begin with the Kokturk inscriptions of the eighth century. Found in the region of the Orhon River in northern Mongolia, these inscriptions are the major written source for the history of all Turkic languages. Yet their influence on various national literatures in these languages can be dated only from the end of the nineteenth century, when the inscriptions were discovered.

Although today modern Turkish literature in the Republic of Turkey is considered to have developed from Ottoman Turkish literature, conceptualizing Ottoman Turkish literature as the traditional predecessor to modern Turkish literature is problematic. The influence of Ottoman Turkish literature on modern Turkish literature is overshadowed by the influence of Western literatures.

### Development of Ottoman Literature

In Anatolia during the thirteenth and fourteenth centuries, under the patronage of several Turkish frontier states, a written language based on the Oghuz branch of Turkic languages was developed. The first written compositions in this language were Islamic treatises translated from Arabic and Persian. Under the influence of Islamic literary genres and themes, this literary production reached its culmination in the fifteenth and sixteenth centuries, with the centralization of the Ottoman state. The Ottoman sultans and bureaucratic elite supported a class of learned men, most of whom were involved in writing poetry. Poets as well as prose writers were either associated with the court or were supported by other patrons who rewarded their literary accomplishments. This so-called court literature served to legitimize the claims of patrons to bravery, justice, and religious integrity. Authors of this state-sponsored literature were educated in Arabic and Persian literatures and languages and in Qur'anic and literary sciences.

During the Ottoman empire, the words for literature were *si'ir* (poetry) and *insa* (prose). Poetic genres were defined according to rhyme scheme and length. *Aruz*, a version of an Arabic metric system containing long and short syllables, was so influential in written literature that it completely displaced the older syllabic metric system typical of Turkish oral poetry. Lyric and panegyrical (eulogistic) poems (*gazel* and *kaside*, respectively) were compiled in poetry collections called *divan*. Several authors chose to display their poetic prowess by composing romances in verse *(mesnevi)* on various Islamic themes, such as Joseph and Potiphar's wife. Manuscript copies of story compilations such as *Sindbadname*, *Camasbname*, and *Forty Viziers* are also preserved in library collections.

Ottoman poetry was defined by a set of formal and thematic elements that poetically expressed a mystical understanding of life. Although on the surface the poetry may appear repetitive and lacking in originality, a closer examination of Ottoman Turkish literary production reveals a self-referential literature driven by an urge toward perfection of formal qualities. Authors composed works in competitive response to their predecessors as well as their contemporaries.

Ottoman literature existed mainly in the form of manuscripts. Ibrahim Muteferrika (1670–1745) established the first printing house (1729), but by the end of the eighteenth century it had published only seventeen books (none a work of literature). Printing developed only by the second half of the nineteenth century.

### European Influence on Ottoman Literature

By the end of the eighteenth century, European influence became evident. After the observations of the great traveler Evliya Chelebi (1611–1681), the first major literary account of Europe appeared between the lines of the lyric romances, *Huban-name* and *Zenan-name* (Book of Boys and Book of Women by Fazil-i Enderuni [d. 1810]). In the nineteenth century educational reforms in the Ottoman empire allowed several Ottoman students to study in a rapidly changing Europe. The ideals of modernization appealed to the Ottoman ruling elite, who saw them as the roots of European technical superiority. Restructuring educational institutions after European models generated a need for translations of European textbooks from European languages, primarily French and German. Along with this development, the literature of the empire gradually came under the influence of Western literary forms at the expense of Eastern forms. Throughout the nineteenth century new literary forms imported from the West and imbued with ideals such as democracy and freedom lived side by side with the classical Ottoman Turkish literary tradition, often engaging in debate with it.

In 1859 the first literary translations from French appeared: an edition of French poems and their translations, *Terceme-i Manzume* (Translations of Verse by Sinasi, 1826–1871); conversational pieces from Voltaire, Fontenelle, and Fenelon, *Muhaverat-i Hikemiyye* (Philosophical Dialogues) by Munif Pasa (1830–1910); and a version of Fenelon's *Les Aventures de Telemaque* (1699), *Terceme-i Telemak*, by Yusuf Kamil Pasa (1808–1876). These three books, which are really adaptations rather than literal translations, initiated a flurry of translations. Sinasi later published the first Turkish work for the theater, a comedy titled *Sair Evlenmesi (Wedding of a Poet)*. The first Turkish short story, by Ahmet Mithat Efendi (1844–1912), appeared in 1870; the writer later published a series of such stories in *Letaif-i Rivayat* (The Best of the Stories, 1895). Semseddin Sami (1850–1904) wrote the first Turkish novel, *Taassuk-i Talat u Fitnat* (Love of Talat and Fitnat, 1872).

With the establishment of theater companies such as the Gedikpasa Ottoman Theater (1870), founded by an Ottoman Armenian artist, Agop Efendi (1840–1902), several dramas, mostly adaptations of Molière's plays, were staged with great success. Ahmed Vefik Pasa (1823–1891) translated sixteen plays of Molière, replacing several of his characters with Greek, Armenian, and Turkish characters.

Ahmet Mithat employed traditional minstrel storytelling techniques in his didactic fictional works emulating French novels. Other early novelists, such as Recaizade Ekrem (1847–1914), had a more ornate style. After writing and staging the most popular political play of the period, *Vatan yahut Silistre* (The Motherland, or Silistre, 1873), Namik Kemal (1840–1888) wrote the novel *Intibah* (Awakening, 1876).

*Intibah* is the best example of early Turkish novels that portray social and political problems in the envelope of impossible love stories. The novelists of the period criticized the Westernization fad among elite circles and advocated a combination of Eastern and Western lifestyles in which the West represented the technical aspects of progress and development while the East represented the moral.

Later, under the influence of realist and naturalist literary movements in France, a group of authors established a movement called Edebiyat-i Cedide (New Literature, 1869–1901). The most prominent member of this movement, Halit Ziya Usakhligil (1866–1945), wrote realist novels, perfecting the form with *Ask-i Memnu* (Forbidden Love, 1900). Even though his works followed the dictum of art for art's sake, a consciousness of decline as well as a philosophy of populism informed the thematic inclinations of poets of this movement such as Tevfik Fikret (1867–1915), who also revolutionized classical prosody through his innovations in *aruz* meter.

Gaining momentum under new parliamentary governance, nationalism as an ideology overtook the debates about Islamism and Ottomanism, further problematizing the trend toward Westernization and defining the character of modern Turkish literature. After the second parliament in 1908, a nationalist literature developed in reaction to ongoing nationalist movements among non-Muslim communities of the Ottoman empire. A group of authors based in Thessalonica published the journal *Genc Kalemler* (Young Pens, 1911). A linguistic nationalism, constructed around an idea of a Turkish Islam and an original homeland in Central Asia, was launched in this journal by authors such as Omer Seyfettin (1884–1920) and Ziya Gokalp (1875–1924). This movement was preceded by the publication of a book of poetry by Mehmet Emin Yurdakul (1864–1944), which was tellingly entitled *Turkce Siirler* (Turkish Poems, 1899) and proposed establishing a pure Turkish language. While Ziya Gokalp was the ideological leader of the nationalist Turkish literature movement, Omer Seyfettin crafted a new Turkish discourse closer to spoken language through his short stories on nationalistic themes.

**Literature under the Turkish Republic**

After the establishment of the Turkish Republic (1923), Yakup Kadri Karaosmanoglu (1889–1974), Halide Edip Adivar (1884–1964), and Resat Nuri Guntekin (1889–1956) continued employing similar themes in fiction. Karaosmanoglu's *Yaban* (The Outsider, 1932), Adivar's *Sinekli Bakkal* (*The Clown and His Daughter*, 1936), and Guntekin's *Yesil Gece* (Green Night, 1928) not only display a revolutionary break in the careers of these authors, but their texts are also symptomatic of a period of reorientation in Turkish literature. With their ideological orientation, these novels establish the major themes of modern Turkish literature until the 1950s. By then the Ottoman cultural legacy had already been defined as the "Other." During the 1940s, Sait Faik (Abasiyanik) (1907–1954) developed a straightforward language in his short stories, which focus on personalities from different subcultures in Istanbul, downplaying the national ideal as a core theme. In his short stories and novels, Sabahattin Ali (1906–1949) reflected a socialist realist depiction of Turkish society, developing a counterargument to the established nationalist discourse in his work.

Writers of nationalist literature disrupted attempts to reformulate classical poetic meter, and a set of poets hailed the syllabic meter as the national poetic meter of the Turkish Republic. Following a sentimentalist path, these poets drew on the tradition of oral folk poetry to describe the beauties of the Turkish landscape and Turkish villagers. Social themes were also handled in syllabic meter by poets such as Necip Fazil Kisakurek (1905–1983), Ahmet Hamdi Tanpinar (1901–1956), and Cahit Sitki Taranci (1910–1956). Under the impact of Futurism (an Italian movement advocating the expression of dynamism and movement), Nazim Hikmet (Ran) (1902–1963) experimented with free verse. His socialist realist perspective on Turkish realities, as well as his experimentation with different genres that combine poetry and prose, proved to be a fountainhead for modern Turkish poetry.

Nazım Hikmet spent many years in prison as a result of his Communist philosophy, finally escaping from Turkey in 1951. Prison experiences were the fate of many thinkers, authors, and poets, mostly leftist, including the novelist Kemal Tahir (1910–1973) and the satirist Aziz Nesin (1915–1993). Such attempts by the state to suppress freedom of speech further radicalized literature.

The publication of *Garip* (The Loner, 1941), a collection of poems in free verse, defined another vein of Turkish poetry characterized by free verse, playfulness, and a populist spirit. The leader of this movement was Orhan Veli Kanik (1914–1950). Oktay Rifat (1914–1988) and Melih Cevdet Anday (b. 1915), who were also outstanding poets of this movement, subsequently focused on more esoteric themes in line with the Second New Movement. Poets of this movement, such as Ece Ayhan (b. 1931) and Edip Cansever (1928–1986), employed symbolism to express psychological states and initiated a distant relationship with Ottoman lyric poetry by drawing on its rich imagery. The stylistic and thematic characteristics of socialist realism and the Second New Movement dominated Turkish poetry.

*Bizim Koy* (Our Village, 1950) by Mahmut Makal (b. 1930) spurred interest in village life, portrayed in the form of a socialist realist critique of the prevalent modernist-nationalist discourse. Under the impact of the village-realism movement, several authors who had come into close contact with provincial people while in prison shifted their interest from city life—the lair of nationalist modernization—to Anatolia. In his serial novel *Ince Me* (Memed, My Hawk, 1960), the prolific author Yasar Kemal (b. 1922) created a groundbreaking Turkish narrative style that originated from oral legends.

Politically engaged authors dominated the literary scene more and more after the military coups following 1960. They searched for new techniques in realism to elucidate sociopolitical themes in their novels and poems. Attila Ilhan (b. 1925) advanced a unique vocabulary of imagery in his poetry and novels, and in his serial novel *Aynanin Icindekiler* (Inside the Mirror, 1973) he wrote a history of Turkey from the second half of the nineteenth century on. Adalet Agaoglu (b. 1929) depicted the impact of social and political events of the 1960s and 1970s on individuals. Sevgi Soysal (1936–1976), like Agaoglu a woman novelist, depicted representative characters to present class conflict in cities.

This realism was countered by the monumental work of Oguz Atay (1934–1977): *Tutunamayanlar* (The Misfits, 1971) was a critique of Turkish nationalism in the form of a Joycian narrative. But the real challenge to realism appeared much later, after the 12 September 1980 military coup. As strict censorship under the military regime was abolished, new thematic trends and narrative techniques appeared. Latife Tekin (b. 1959) recounted the experience of the Turkish radical left in her novels, the first of which appeared in 1983, *Sevgili Arsiz Olum (Dear Naughty Death)*. The influence of magical realism in her novels blurs didactic tendencies.

During the 1990s, while these critical perspectives continued, historical novels experienced an unprecedented revival. This trend was initiated by the publication of *Beyaz Kale* (*The White Castle*, 1985) and *Kara Kitap* (The Black Book, 1990), both by Orhan Pamuk (b. 1952). The new millennium has witnessed an increase in historical novels dealing mostly with the Ottoman empire, such as the latest popular novels of Ahmet Altan (b. 1950), for example, *Isyan Gunlerinde Ask (Love in the Days of Revolt, 2001)*.

Diverging from the dominant tendencies of various forms of realism, Yusuf Atilgan (1921–1989) reflected the influence of existentialism in his *Aylak Adam* (Free Man, 1959), with its alternative perspective on Turkish realities. Later Bilge Karasu (1930–1995) developed his own narrative style, using a stream-of-consciousness technique. His fractured narrations reveal a concealed gay identity, while his focus on the use of language is shared, in a different form, by another author, Murathan Mungan (b. 1950). Mungan's poetry, short stories, and plays draw on legends and fairy tales of eastern Anatolia. Metin Kacan (b. 1961) also displays a sensitivity to the use of language in his *Agir Roman* (Heavy Novel 1990), specifically through the slang of communities that live on the slopes surrounding Istanbul.

Criticism in Turkish literature has developed both in academic institutions and the popular press. While academic criticism tended to neglect post-1950s literature, popular criticism focused on radical leftist literature until the 1980s. In the realm of popular criticism, the subjective approach of Nurullah Atac (1898–1957) and the 1940s humanist criticism of Sabahattin Eyuboglu (1908–1973) come together in the highly popular works of Fethi Naci (b. 1927). Recently the English literature specialists Berna Moran (1921–1993) and Jale Parla (b. 1945) have introduced critical theoretical approaches for the evaluation of Turkish literature, and Marxist criticism continues to generate valuable analyses.

Both Ottoman and nationalist Turkish literature embraces a wide array of generic, stylistic, and thematic trends. Moreover, modern Turkish literature's dialogue with Western literary forms is enriched today by a new interest in a variety of Third World literary traditions. Turkish literature is entering a new phase. Debates on Turkish literary history, the republication of several early Republican literary works with commentaries, the compilation of various anthologies, the publication of several literary journals, an interest in pre-Republican Turkish literatures, and a considerable break with traditional Western literary influence all point to yet another period of reevaluation of a rich literary tradition.

*Selim Kuru*

**Further Reading**

Adivar, Halide Edip. (1935) *The Clown and His Daughter.* London: Allen & Unwin.

Andrews, Walter G. (1976) *An Introduction to Ottoman Poetry.* Minneapolis, MN: Bibliotheca Islamica.

———. (1985) *Poetry's Voice, Society's Song: Ottoman Lyric Poetry.* Seattle, WA: University of Washington Press.

Evin, Ahmet V. (1983) *Origins and Development of the Turkish Novel.* Minneapolis, MN: Bibliotheca Islamica.

Finn, Robert. (1984) *The Early Turkish Novel, 1872–1900.* Istanbul, Turkey: Isis Press.

Gibb, E. J. W. (1963–1984) *A History of Ottoman Poetry.* Cambridge, U.K.: Trustees of the E. J. W. Gibb Memorial.

Halman, Talat Sait. (1982) *Contemporary Turkish Literature: Fiction and Poetry.* Rutherford, NJ: Fairleigh Dickinson University Press.

———. (1976) *Modern Turkish Drama: An Anthology of Plays in Translation.* Minneapolis, MN: Bibliotheca Islamica.

Hébert, E. L., and B. Tharaud, trans. (1999) *Yasar Kemal on His Life and Art.* New York: Syracuse University Press.

Karasu, Bilge. (1994) *Night.* Trans. by Guneli Gun with the author. Baton Rouge, LA: Louisiana State University Press.

Kemal, Yasar. (1961) *Memed, My Hawk.* Trans. by Edouard Roditi. New York: Pantheon.

Nazim Hikmet (Ran). (1982) *Human Landscapes.* Trans. by Randy Blasing and Mutlu Konuk. New York: Persea Books.

Pamuk, Orhan. (1991) *The White Castle.* Trans. by Victoria Holbrook. New York: Braziller.

Silay, Kemal, ed. (1996) *An Anthology of Turkish Literature.* Bloomington, IN: Indiana University Press.

Stone, Frank A. (1973) *The Rub of Cultures in Modern Turkey; Literary Views of Education.* Bloomington, IN: Indiana University Press.

## LITERATURE—VIETNAM

Vietnamese literature refers to a body of writing that has evolved over many centuries and is linked with the history, culture, and language of the Vietnamese people. Vietnamese history is marked by long periods of domination by foreign powers; Chinese rule stretched for nearly a millennium from the second century BCE to the tenth century CE. The efforts by Vietnamese kings and lords to regain territorial integrity was partly realized in the tenth century, making the unity of Vietnam an ideal for which to fight. In the modern period, Vietnam was colonized by the French, who withdrew only in the mid-twentieth century. More recently, the Vietnam War renewed the historical experience of protracted agony for the people of Vietnam. Understandably, Vietnamese poets, scholars, and writers have sought to record the impact of this troubled legacy on the national consciousness. Vietnamese literature owes its creative impulse and continued vitality to this sense of a shared destiny in the face of interruptions and invasions. Writings originating in the Vietnamese culture are realistic, communicating the human need to participate in life despite its harshness. A similar spirit is also evident in the folk literature of Vietnam, which is a rich storehouse of tales, proverbs, songs, and legends, providing ample evidence of the imaginative resources of the Vietnamese people.

### Traditional Literature

Traditional Vietnamese literature is said to have its beginnings in the ancient period (tenth–fifteenth centuries) and to last until the eighteenth and nineteenth centuries. The beginning of this literature was tied to the Chinese occupation of Vietnam, when poetry was the favored literary genre. Monks, kings, scholars, and civil servants were the first poets in Vietnam, and they wrote in a literary language called *Han*. While the script and style were distinctly Chinese, in subject matter and perspective the poems were Vietnamese. At the outset, the themes were religious and philosophical, written under the influence of Chan (Zen) Buddhism and Confucianism. Gradually, however, poetry came to reflect the secular and aesthetic aspects of human experience as well. Many of these early poems have been lost because of foreign invasions and (in some instances, such as after the Ming occupation of 1407–1427) a deliberate policy of destruction by the new rulers. The extant poems, however, express the transience of life and delineate themes of birth, aging, sickness, and death. There was also a strand in early poetry that depicted aspects of court life, as well as the simple joys of nature. With the assertion of a Vietnamese identity by rulers of the Ly (1010–1225), Tran (1225–1400), and Le (1427–1791) dynasties, the community life of Vietnam became the principal theme for poetic exploration, as illustrated in the life and achievement of Nguyen Trai (1380–1442). The form of the early poems mostly followed strict metrical patterns set by Chinese models and was restricted by notions of decorum deemed necessary for the practice of literary art. An interesting later development was writing in *nom* characters, a demotic version of Chinese *Han* ideograms used to transcribe Vietnamese words. This type of writing became popular as a new mode of expression and paved the way for a vibrant vernacular literature that broke away from the elitist, imitative literature written in Chinese. In time, classical works were translated into a growing corpus of *nom* literature that was diffused among different strata of Vietnamese society. Prose forms for easy communication were devised. Verse narratives, a typical Vietnamese form, became popular, culminating in *The Tale of Kieu* by Nguyen Du (1765–1820), a poem of 3,254 lines considered to be Vietnam's national epic poem. *The Tale of Kieu* occupies a unique place in Vietnamese literature. It is the tale of a young woman of noble character who sacrifices everything out of loyalty to her family and for love. Her sufferings and resilience find an echo in every Vietnamese heart. In addition to long narratives in verse, short poems with eclectic forms were composed by poets from diverse backgrounds. A good example is the work of the woman poet Ho Xuan Huong (1768–1839), who in lines of power and beauty protested against traditional institutions.

### Modern Literature

Modern Vietnamese literature was written in the wake of Vietnam's contact with the West. This contact increased after the French began their formal occupation of Vietnam toward the end of the nineteenth century. For administrative reasons, the French favored the use of *quoc ngu* (the romanized Vietnamese script), which was instrumental in spreading literacy and culture. The rise of newspapers and magazines gave a new direction to Vietnamese cultural life, and the practice of literature was no longer restricted to the learned. With the growth of an educated Vietnamese public, circulation of innovative forms such as serialized novels increased rapidly. The nationalist resistance to the colonial regime used the *quoc ngu* script and writings to further its goal of forging a distinctive Vietnamese identity. Prose became a versatile medium of political and aesthetic expression, and ideas from other cultures stimulated the native intellectual climate. Literature in *quoc ngu* signaled a break with tradition and gave rise to novelty and experimentation. New journals like *Dong Duong Tap Chi* (The Indochina Review) in 1913 and *Nam Phong* (South Wind) in 1917, which were instigated by the colonial administration, prefigured publications by nationalist and progressive intellectuals. Traditional poetry was challenged by the individualistic efforts of poets like Nguyen Khac Hieu (1888–1939), who popularized a movement for the reform of poetry that culminated in the New Poetry Movement of the 1930s. The novel and short story utilized the emergent prose medium. Ho Bieu Chanh (1884–1958) in the south and Hoang Ngoc Phach (1896–1973) in the north introduced readers to new prose fictional forms. Phach's only novel *To Tam* (Pure Heart; 1925) is regarded as the first Vietnamese novel.

Since 1975, an attempt to redefine literary practice has raised methodological questions concerning the terms "social" and "socialist" as they were used to describe the outlook of writers in their efforts to portray the traumatic experiences of the Vietnamese people. Influential writers of the period were Duong Thu Huong (b. 1947), Bao Ninh (b. 1952), Nguyen Huy Thiep (b. 1950), and Pham Thi Hoai (b. 1960). Beginning with the innovative efforts of the Tu Luc Van Doan (Independent Literary Group) writers between 1930 and 1935 until the creative mediation of the diasporic writers of modern times, Vietnamese literature has come a long way in shaping its distinctive identity.

*Ram Shankar Nanda*

*See also:* **Chu Nom; Ho Xuan Huong; Khai Hung; Poetry—Vietnam; Tu Luc Van Doan**

### Further Reading

Durand, Maurice, and Nguyen Tran Huan. (1985) *An Introduction to Vietnamese Literature.* Trans. by D. M. Hawke. New York: Columbia University Press.

Jamieson, Neil. (1993) *Understanding Vietnam.* Berkeley and Los Angeles: University of California Press.

Marr, David. (1981) *Vietnamese Tradition on Trial, 1920–1945.* Berkeley and Los Angeles: University of California Press.

Thong Huyn Sanh, ed. (1996) *An Anthology of Vietnamese Poems: From the Eleventh through the Twentieth Centuries.* New Haven, CT: Yale University Press.

Vien, Nguyen Khac. (1977) *Glimpses of Vietnamese Literature.* Trans. by Primerose Gigliesi and Robert Friend. Hanoi, Vietnam: Foreign Languages Publishing House.

## LITERATURE—WEST ASIA, PERSIAN

Islamic literatures have been expressed in two languages more than others: Arabic and Persian. Persian literature flourished not just in Persia (Iran), but also in Central Asia, Turkey, Afghanistan, and South Asia. A great deal of debate surrounds the rise and nature of Persian literature in the aftermath of the Arab conquest of Persia in the seventh century. Some scholars have argued that post-Islamic Persian literature is part and parcel of the attempt of Iranians (and, subsequently, other Persian speakers) to express their own identity as non-Arabs. At least some of these early expressions are no doubt connected to protonationalist *shu'ubi* movements in the early eras of Islam. Other scholars have identified Persian literature as quintessentially mystical, epitomized in the poetry of great masters such as Rumi (c. 1207–1273) and Hafiz (d. 1389). The truth, as usual, would seem to lie in neither extreme, nor in a convenient middle point. It is true that much of classical Persian literature is characterized by a high degree of Sufi (that is, Islamic mystic) imagery. However, the origin of much Sufi imagery can be traced to regal court poetry, which was subsequently applied to lover-beloved or spiritual master-disciple relationships.

There is also some ambiguity about the origin of this new Persian literature. The thirteenth-century literary historian Muhammad ʿAufi relates that Bahram Gur, a pre-Islamic Sassanian Iranian king who flourished in the fifth century, was the first to compose Persian poetry. Earlier figures from the eleventh century (Thaʿalibi and Ibn Khurdadhbih) had also claimed.that Bahram Gur was the first. The accuracy of such claims may be questioned; one is on much firmer ground in tracing the blossoming of Persian literature to the Samanid dynasty (864–999 CE).

An important figure in this early stage was the poet Rudaki (d. 940). He was affiliated with the Samanid ruler Amir Nasr ibn Ahmad. The *Chahar-maqala* of Nizami Arudi (d. 1174, an important author from Samarqand) states that once when the Samanid king had taken a longer than usual excursion from the much-loved Transoxiana city of Bukhara, the courtiers pleaded with Rudaki to write a line that would move the king to return home. The result was this much-loved and oft-recited line:

The Ju-yi Muliyan we call to mind

We long for those dear friends long left behind

*(Arberry 1958: 33)*

**Firdawsi's Book of Kings**

The next grand figure of Persian literature was Firdawsi (d. 1020 or 1026), whose monumental *Shahnameh* (Book of Kings) is the quintessential recollection of pre-Islamic Persian glory. Although not a historical text per se, this text has radically shaped the way that many later Iranians have come to imagine their historical heritage. Ironically, Firdawsi did not receive the compensation he was hoping for from the Ghaznavid Sultan Mahmud. Mahmud, a Turk who had positioned himself as the defender of Sunni Islam, was not impressed by the extensive glorification of pre-Islamic (largely Zoroastrian) Persian kings. A devastated Firdawsi responded with a scathing critique of the miserly sultan. Still, history seems to have verified Firdawsi's boast that through his thirty years of toiling over the composition of the *Shahnameh*, he resurrected Persian language and literature.

After Firdawsi, Persian literatures gradually became infused with the imagery of Sufism, the mystical expression of Islam. Almost from the start, the mystics sought to express the ineffability of their spiritual experiences through the terse and often-ambiguous medium of poetry. As early texts such as the *Asrar al-tawhid*—written by Ibn Munawwar in the twelfth century about the great early Sufi Abu Saʿid ibn Abi 'l-Khayr (d. 1049)—clearly demonstrate, poetry was often recited in Sufi gatherings. There were many significant Sufi-influenced Persian writings in this period. As with Firdawsi, medieval masters find a receptive audience even in contemporary Iran. One of the identifying features of Persian literature has been its continuity, to the point that even elementary school education in Iran today includes reading poetry from a thousand years ago.

Among other great figures such as Anvari, Nizam al-Mulk, Nasir Khusrau, Sana'i, al-Ghazali, Ibn Sina, ʿAttar, Nizami of Ganja, and Amir Khusrau, the next monumental figure is Saʿdi (c. 1213–1292). If Firdawsi has become the identifying mark of a nationalist Iranian consciousness, Saʿdi more than any other figure has contributed to the articulation of a distinctly Persian, Islamic, spiritually influenced humanistic ethic that can perhaps best be represented by the term *adab* (cultured etiquette). Saʿdi's *Gulistan* (Rose Garden) and *Bustan* (Orchard) are two classics of Persian literature. The *Gulistan* in many ways has become the model of prose works that are interspersed with lines of poetry here and there. The chapters of this important text deal with kingship, Sufi teachings, virtues of silence, old age and youth, and passionate love.

**Rumi the Master**

Living roughly a generation after Saʿdi was the most luminous of all Persian Sufi poets, Mawlana (Our Master) Jalal al-Din Muhammad Balkhi, simply called Rumi in most English sources. Had he not composed a single line of poetry, he would still be recognized as one of the most important figures of Persian culture due to his elevated rank as a much-loved Sufi exemplar whose legacy has forever shaped the spiritual lives of Muslims in Iran, Turkey, Afghanistan, and South Asia. What is more relevant here is that he also composed masterful works of poetry: the *Masnavi* is perhaps the most widely read of all Persian didactic Sufi poems. His *Divan of Shams of Tabriz* contains 33,135 lines of passionate love poetry. The *Fihi ma fihi* is a prose collection of Rumi's table talks, gathered by his students. Rumi's literary output is now being transmitted to the West: in the past twenty years various translations and "versions" of Rumi's poetry have made Rumi the top-selling poet in America, according to the *Christian Science Monitor*.

Although Rumi is undoubtedly the master of explicitly Sufi poetry, the absolute pinnacle of lyric love poetry *(ghazal)* was to be achieved by Shams al-Din Hafiz, often called *Tarjuman al-asrar* (interpreter of mystical secrets) and *Lisan al-ghayb* (tongue of the unseen realm). Hafiz's *Divan* contains almost five hundred short love poems, often held to be the absolute finest example of Persian poetry. His poems are characterized often by a delicious ambiguity: one is never sure if the subject of the poem is a wine minstrel, a spiritual teacher, an earthly beloved, or God. Chances are that all of them are intended at the same time. Both Hafiz and his legion of admirers seem to revel in this deliberate ambiguity, which has characterized so many of the best examples of Persian literature.

No doubt some will object to such a selective reading of Persian literature that essentially stops in the fourteenth century. Much has been left out in the preceding, most of all prose works of ethics and philosophy, history, and other subjects. Also, a reading of Persian literature that ends at the fourteenth century tends to perpetuate historiographic models of a "golden age" inevitably followed by "decline," which have been so problematic in depicting many facets of Islamic society. These shortcomings are freely acknowledged. But it is no exaggeration to state that this literature, the grandest aesthetic achievement of Persian speakers, is also the single greatest contribution of Persian societies to humanity.

*Omid Safi*

**Further Reading**

Arberry, A. J. (1958) *Classical Persian Literature*. London: Allen & Unwin.

Browne, Edward G. ([1902] 1997) *A Literary History of Persia*. 4 vols. Reprint ed. Oxford: Oxford University Press.

Jalal Al-Din Rumi, Maulana. (1925–1940) *The Mathnawí of Jalalu'ddin Rum*. Trans. by Reynold A. Nicholson. London: E. J. W. Gibb Memorial Series.

Sa'di, Shaykh Muslih Al-Din. (1965) *The Gulistan*. Trans. by Edward Rehatsek. New York: G. P. Putnam's.

Yarshater, Ehsan, ed. (1988) *Persian Literature*. Albany, NY: Bibliotheca Persica.

**LIU SHAOQI** (1898–1969), People's Republic of China president. Liu Shaoqi was a tragic political figure, symbolizing the political struggle occurring in China over the first fifty years of the People's Republic of China (PRC). Liu joined the Chinese Communist Party (CCP) in 1921 when he was studying in Moscow. After he returned to China, he became one of the CCP leaders working underground among workers. Along with Li Lisan (1899–1967), Liu organized a strike by 400,000 workers in 1922. In 1934, Liu participated in the Long March and played an important support role for Mao Zedong (1893–1976) during the Yan'an period.

After the PRC was founded in 1949, Liu was named chairman of the National People's Congress (NPC) in 1954. In 1956, he made a bold proposal to reform the Chinese economy, a move that eventually cost him his life. Along with Deng Xiaoping (1904–1997), Liu insisted that China's socialism should concentrate on increasing the productivity and development of the national economy. In 1959, Liu was promoted to the posts of president of China and chairman of the Defense Committee. He was also in charge of the daily work of the PRC and CCP before the Cultural Revolution. However, Liu began to struggle with Mao in 1960 regarding the national economic policy.

At the beginning of the Cultural Revolution in 1967, Liu was labeled as "taking the capitalist road" and arrested. Liu was physically abused by the Red Guards (students who adulated Mao during the Cultural Revolution), kicked out of the CCP, and died in Henan Province in 1968. In February 1980, the CCP rehabilitated his name, but only after fourteen years of humiliation.

*Unryu Suganuma*

**Further Reading**

Baum, Richard. (1994) *Burying Mao: Chinese Politics in the Age of Deng Xiaoping*. Princeton, NJ: Princeton University Press.

Fairbank, John King. (1987) *The Great Chinese Revolution: 1800–1985*. New York: Harper and Row.

Fairbank, John King, and Merle Goldman. (1998) *China: A New History*. Enlarged ed. Cambridge, MA: Belknap Press of Harvard University Press.

**LOCKHEED SCANDAL** One of postwar Japan's worst political scandals broke in 1976 when it was discovered that Lockheed Aircraft had made illegal payments to airlines in Japan and other countries as a way to boost airplane sales and avoid bankruptcy. In Japan's case the scandal led to the prosecution of seventeen people for illegal activities. The money was funneled through three channels, the Marubeni Corporation (Japan's third-largest general trading company), All-Nippon Airways (ANA—Japan's major domestic airline), and Kodama. Those indicted in 1976 included Kakuei Tanaka (1918–1993), a former Liberal Democratic Party (LDP) prime minister (in office 1972–1974) and a central figure in this affair; a former secretary of Tanaka's; a former chairman of Marubeni and two of its executives.

Tanaka had influenced the Ministry of Transportation and ANA to buy Lockheed L-1001 Tri-Stars instead of McDonnell-Douglas DC-10s, on which ANA had already taken an option. Around 1974, Tanaka was arrested for having accepted 500 million yen in bribes in violation of the Foreign Exchange Control Law. Following earlier corruption charges that involved real estate and construction companies, he resigned as prime minister in November 1974. In 1976, investigations in the Lockheed scandal revealed that through a right-wing fixer, Yoshio Kodama (1911–1984), business people and LDP leaders had received bribes.

Tanaka was convicted on 12 August 1983 by the Tokyo District Court. He was sentenced to four years in jail and fined 500 million yen, the amount of the bribe he had received. When the Tokyo High Court dismissed his appeals, he appealed to the Supreme Court, which eventually dropped his case when he died in 1993.

Miki Takeo (1907–1988) became prime minister from 1974 to 1976 and pursued the investigation into Lockheed corporate bribery, but political turmoil caused his government to fall.

The Lockheed case, the most serious scandal until the Recruit affair in 1988, revealed a side of Japanese politics and its lack of transparency that underlined the need for political reform. Japanese critics have referred to this close connection of elites formed of politicians, businessmen, and bureaucrats as "structural corruption."

*Nathalie Cavasin*

**Further Reading**

Curtis, Gerald. (1999) *The Logic of Japanese Politics: Leaders, Institutions, and the Limits of Change.* New York: Columbia University Press.

Hunziker, Steven, and Ikuro Kaminura. (1996) *Kakuei Tanaka: A Political Biography of Modern Japan.* Singapore: Times Editions.

Markkovits, Andrei S., and Mark Sliverstein. (1988) *The Politics of Scandal: Power and Process in Liberal Democracies.* New York: Holmes & Meier.

Mitchell, Richard H. (1996) *Political Bribery in Japan.* Honolulu, HI: University of Hawaii Press.

**LON NOL** (1913–1985), leader of the Khmer Republic. Lon Nol is remembered as the leader of the Khmer Republic (1970–1975), which preceded the rule of the Khmer Rouge in Cambodia. He was born on 13 November 1913 in the village of Prey Chraing in Prey Veng Province, close to the Vietnamese border. Lon Nol was the son of a minor government official, Lon Hin. After completing primary school in Cambodia, he was sent to Saigon, where he attended the Lycée Chasseloup-Laubat. He left school in 1934 and joined the Judicial Service, eventually becoming a magistrate in Siem Reap Province in northwestern Cambodia. He later transferred to the Administrative Service, taking up a post in Kompong Cham Province. Lon Nol's efficiency quickly came to the attention of his superiors, and he rapidly rose through the ranks of what was a French colonial administration.

Lon Nol at Cham Car Mon palace in Phnom Penh in 1975. (FRANCOISE DE MULDER/CORBIS)

In September 1947, Lon Nol, then the governor of Kratie Province, helped to found the Khmer Renewal Party. The party failed to win any seats in the elections of 1947, with Lon Nol placed last in polling for the seat he contested in Kompong Cham. The setback did not halt his rise through Cambodian government circles. He became police chief, transferred to the Royal Cambodian armed forces, and eventually became chief of the General Staff. He became minister of defense in October 1955.

Lon Nol's political rise accelerated sharply after the 1966 elections. A largely conservative national assembly appointed him as Cambodia's prime minister. He was remembered for his calm and quiet attitude and for the comprehensive dossiers he held on all of his friends, foes, rivals, and potential rivals. He was also remembered as a fervent Buddhist and as a devoted ally of Cambodia's national leader, Prince Norodom Sihanouk.

Along with Sihanouk's cousin, Prince Sisowath Sirikmatak, Lon Nol surprisingly led a coup against Sihanouk in March 1970, which would eventually lead to the rise of the Khmer Rouge. Lon Nol eventually became the leader of the Khmer Republic that succeeded Sihanouk's initial reign. His regime, supported by the United States, was embroiled in a bloody civil war against the local Communists, who had aligned themselves with the deposed Sihanouk and who were supported by North Vietnam and China. Lon Nol's regime was riddled with corruption. Lon Nol preferred to ignore the problem, ensconcing himself in a world of clairvoyants and mystics. In 1975, with his regime on the verge of collapse, he fled Cambodia. On 17 April 1975, as Communist soldiers marched victoriously into Cambodia's capital, Phnom Penh, Lon Nol was making a new home for himself in Hawaii. He would remain there until his death in 1985.

*David M. Ayres*

**Further Reading**

Chandler, David. (1991) *The Tragedy of Cambodian History: Politics, War, and Revolution since 1945*. Bangkok, Thailand: Silkworm Press.

Corfield, Justin. (1994) *Khmer Stand Up! A History of the Cambodian Government, 1970–1975*. Clayton, Victoria, Australia: Monash University Centre of Southeast Asian Studies.

Deac, Wilfred. (1997) *Road to the Killing Fields: The Cambodian War of 1970–1975*. College Station, TX: Texas A&M University Press.

**LONG MARCH** The Chinese Communists' six-thousand-mile journey of retreat (1934–1935) across such provinces as Hunan, Guangxi, Guizhou, Yunnan, Sichuan, and Shaanxi has been glorified by the leaders of the Communist Party of China (CCP) as the "Long March." As a result of the retreat, the Communist revolutionary base was relocated from southeast to northwest China, an area beyond the control of the Nationalist troops under Chiang Kai-shek (1887–1975), leader of the Guomindang (Nationalist Party). Historians have considered the march a milestone in the history of modern China—the point at which the Chinese Communist movement started to forge its own path, independent of Comintern control, and the time that Mao Zedong (1893–1976) became the undisputed leader of the CCP. (Comintern, an association of national Communist parties founded

A speaker addresses a crowd of Chinese Communists in March 1938 after they had completed the Long March. (HULTON-DEUTSCH COLLECTION/CORBIS)

in 1919 for the stated purpose of promoting world revolution, actually worked like an agent of the Soviet Union to control the international Communist movement, including the CCP.)

### The Formation of the Soviet in Jiangxi Province

The CCP was founded in the early 1920s. In 1924, the Guomindang agreed to form a "united front" (alliance) with the CCP in return for Soviet aid. But in 1927, after the Guomindang experienced some success in its expedition against warlords in the north, a bloody purge was carried out against all Communists in areas under the Guomindang's control. Communist movements in China were forced to go underground. In the early 1930s, there were up to fifteen Communist rural bases in south central China, but their links with the central committee of the CCP in Shanghai were shattered because of the purge. The CCP, whose leadership was dominated by a group of Moscow-trained Chinese students known as the Twenty-Eight Bolsheviks, came to rely all the more on Russia's support. In 1931, the central committee relocated from Shanghai to the Jiangxi Province (northern China) and the Chinese Communists declared the local government a soviet. Mao's influence in the Jiangxi Soviet was overshadowed by that of the Moscow-trained Chinese leaders, many of whom were adherents of the Soviet orthodoxy of revolution by urban workers. (Mao, by contrast, held that the revolution could be achieved by relying on the peasants who made up the bulk of China's population.) By redistributing and expropriating land in these soviet regions, Communist leaders enlisted support from the Chinese lower class and increased the popularity of the CCP in these regions.

Between 1930 and 1934, the Nationalists had launched a series of military encirclement campaigns against the Communists in an attempt to annihilate their bases. Using the tactics of guerrilla warfare developed by Mao Zedong, the Communists managed to fight off four campaigns, but in early 1934 the Communist central committee removed Mao from CCP leadership.

In October 1933, the Nationalists launched a fifth campaign against the Communists. With advice from German experts, Chiang Kai-shek mobilized about 700,000 men to build a series of cement blockhouses around the Communist troops. Slowly encircling the soviet areas in Jiangxi, the Nationalists enforced an economic stranglehold. About a million people died as a result of the economic blockade and the subsequent military conflicts. The Communists, using positional warfare tactics (the strategy of simple defense from one's military bases, abandoning the former tactics of guerrilla warfare) against the better-armed Nationalist forces, suffered severe losses and were nearly crushed. By mid-1934, the Red Army was defeated. It had to move or be crushed.

### The Communist Retreat, or Long March

On 15 October 1934, 86,000 Communist military personnel, as well as 30,000 Communist Party officials and civilian party members, broke through the blockade and fled westward. Along the route of retreat, core concerns were where the troops should go and who should lead the march, as the direction and leadership of the march were unclear. In the first three months of this journey of retreat, mainly under the leadership of Zhu De (1886–1976) and Zhou Enlai (1898–1976), the Communists were subjected to frequent bombardments and attacks by the Nationalist forces and suffered great losses. But on the way northwest, Mao's tactics of guerrilla warfare were gradually adopted. The demoralized Communists reached Zunyi, Guizhou Province, in early 1935, where Mao managed to gather enough support to establish his dominance in the CCP leadership. In a session lacking a quorum of the CCP Politburo (Political Bureau), Mao defeated the Soviet-trained faction and became the actual leader of the Communist Party. The era of Comintern direction of party leadership was ended.

Under Mao's leadership, the Communists proceeded toward Shaanxi. This Jiangxi contingent was later joined by the Second Front Army headed by He Long from its base in Hunan. In June 1935, the Fourth Front Army under Zhang Guodao (1897–1979), from the base in the Sichuan-Shaanxi border, also joined Mao's troop. After a bitter power struggle between Mao and Zhang, Zhang's group decided to move toward southwestern China, while Mao's troops headed toward northern Shaanxi, northwest China, where Gao Gang (1902–1955) had established another Communist base. Most of the route was mountainous, with few motor roads and little access to resources. To maintain marching speed, the Communists had to discard their heavy equipment, including medical and food supplies, along the route.

The march lasted for about a year. The Chinese Communists crossed eighteen mountain ranges and twenty-four rivers, averaging about seventeen miles a day. After a journey of about six thousand miles over mountains and dales, rivers and forests, the troops arrived at Shaanxi in October 1935, with only about eight thousand survivors. Although the Long March had set out from Jiangxi with about 100,000 followers and had gathered many new recruits along the retreat, by the time it had reached Zunyi in January 1935, half had been lost. When these survivors finally reached Shaanxi in October 1935, only the leaders and a very small number of the troops remained, a small proportion of those who had set out from Jiangxi. Along the route of retreat, some had left to mobilize the peasantry, some had died on the way, and others had simply abandoned the endeavor.

In the middle of 1936, the remnants of several Red armies gathered in northern Shaanxi, with Yenan as their headquarters. By December 1936, the Red Army numbered about thirty thousand men. The mountains and difficult terrain made the new base secure and enabled the Red Army to reorganize its strategy against the Nationalists.

### The Significance of the Long March

During the Long March, Mao Zedong secured his leadership role in the CCP. Before that, the core of the leadership had been the Twenty-Eight Bolsheviks, Soviet-trained leaders who believed that revolutions in China should be urban based and who had strong connections with the Comintern. These men regarded Mao's belief in guerrilla warfare and rural-based revolution as unorthodox. Under the military threat of the Nationalists, the Chinese Communists ignored the Soviet advisers and forged their own tactics. It was during this period that Mao started to develop his own version of Communist theory in writings and established himself as a theorist.

The rise of Mao as the CCP's new leader during the Long March brought dramatic changes in party-mobilization policy. Mao's views overrode the Soviet orthodoxy of a narrowly defined proletarian revolution and became the party's new key to establishing itself in the countryside. The Communists had gained local peasant support along the route of the March. From then on, the CCP made it a doctrine that imported Marxism was less important in China than China's own unique historical circumstances and economic situation. Mao believed that China's revolution should be guided and supported by the huge rural-based population, not the small number of working-class people in the cities.

The Long March allowed a new batch of CCP leaders to emerge on China's national political scene. Most of the later prominent leaders of the CCP, including Deng Xiaoping (1904–1997), Zhou Enlai, Liu Shaoqi (1898–1969), Zhu De, and Lin Piao (1906–1971), participated in the march. After 1949, these Long March veterans became top-ranking political leaders of the People's Republic of China.

The establishment of the CCP's new territorial base in northern Shaanxi had significant implications for the second Sino-Japanese War (1937–1945), as well as for Nationalist-CCP relations. After arriving in Shaanxi province in late 1935, Mao and the CCP leaders found that they were surrounded by desert on the west and the Huang (Yellow) River on the east. Although the geographical environment and the absence of motor roads in northwest China made Shaanxi a defensible area, the lack of food and other resources also meant that the new base was vulnerable to Nationalists' attacks. But when the second Sino-Japanese War broke out, the northwest became an important base from which a war of resistance was organized. The Long March inspired increased Chinese nationalism that bolstered morale in the face of advancing Japanese troops, and it helped to transform and consolidate the CCP's position inside and outside China.

*Stephanie Po-yin Chung*

### Further Reading


Harrison, James P. (1972) *The Long March to Power: A History of the Chinese Communist Party, 1921–1972.* New York: Praeger.

Liu Po-cheng et al. (1978) *Recalling the Long March.* Peking: Foreign Language Press.

Salisbury, Harrison. (1985) *The Long March: The Untold Story.* New York: Harper & Row.

Short, Philip. (2000) *Mao: A Life.* New York: Henry Holt.

Snow, Edgar. (1968) *Red Star over China.* New York: Grove Press.

Wilson, Dick. (1982) *The Long March, 1935: The Epic of Chinese Communism's Survival.* New York: Penguin Books.


## LONGBOAT RACING

Longboat racing is a national sport in both Thailand and Laos. Longboat races normally are held in late September through November when rivers are high. They serve as a traditional rite to mark the end of Buddhist Lent (which occurs during the rainy season). Popular Thai longboat races are held in October in Chiang Khan, Nong Khai, and Sakon Nakhon, areas along the Mekong River or its tributaries. Key longboat races also are held in Luang Prabang and Vientiane in Laos. The history of this popular sport goes back six hundred years to the Ayutthaya kingdom. Participation was considered excellent training for warriors. It was also a sign of masculinity.

The boats are made from dugout tree trunks and are quite long, accommodating up to sixty rowers seated two across. The boats are often elegantly carved, with prominent, elevated heads that are often in the form of a *naga* (serpent). The *naga* is considered king of the river and a source of fertility. The races are thought to please the river gods and goddesses.

The races are held in any area with rivers, drawing many spectators. Prizes and trophies are given for the top-finishing boats, for the most beautiful boats, and on special occasions for beauty queens associated with the boats.

*Gerald W. Fry*

### Further Reading

*Thailand: Land of Cultural Treasures.* (2000) Bangkok, Thailand: Tourist Authority of Thailand.

Thanapol Chadchaidee. (1994) *Essays on Thailand.* 4th ed. Bangkok, Thailand: Thai Charoen Press.

**LONGMEN GROTTOES** Carved into limestone cliffs near Luoyang, Henan Province, China, the Longmen (Dragon Gate) Grottoes are one of China's three most important Buddhist statuary sites. More than 1,350 caves, together with more than 2,100 grottoes and niches, numerous pagodas, and thousands of inscriptions, make Longmen an important repository of Buddhist imagery and texts dating from the fifth to the twelfth century.

A colossal seventeen-meter-high image of the Buddha Vairocana (Cosmic Buddha, source of all the phenomenal universe) was carved into the cliffside in the seventh century (Tang dynasty, 618–907 CE), largely funded by the imperial family, notably Empress Wu Zetian (625–705). Two disciples, Ananda and Kasyapa, along with guardian kings on adjoining walls, flank the seated Buddha. The open niche measures over thirty meters by thirty-six meters. Other important sites within Longmen include the Cave of Ten Thousand Buddhas (carved 680), which actually contains more than fifteen thousand small Buddha figures; the Lotus Flower Cave (527), housing the smallest Buddha images; the Medicine Prescription Cave (575), with more than 120 prescriptions for ills ranging from headaches to madness; and the Bingyang Cave (500–523), which the Emperor Xuan Wu (reigned 499–515) dedicated to his parents, recording that it took 802,336 men to complete the work. In the year 2000, UNESCO designated Longmen a World Heritage Site.

*Noelle O'Connor*

### Further Reading

Siren, Osvald. (1998) *Chinese Sculpture from the Fifth to the Fourteenth Centuries.* Vol. 2. Rev. ed. Bangkok, Thailand: SDI.

Whitfield, Roderick, and Ann Farrar. (1990) *Caves of the 1,000 Buddhas.* New York: Braziller.

## LONGMEN GROTTOES—WORLD HERITAGE SITE

Designated a UNESCO World Heritage Site in 2000, the Longmen Grottoes in the Henan province of China illustrate the heights that stone-carved art reached in the Northern Wei and Tang dynasties. The Buddhist art is carved into the walls of these incredible caves.

**LOUANGNAMTHA** (2000 est. pop. 145,000). Located in the northwest corner of Laos, Louangnamtha is one of the country's sixteen provinces. Covering an area of 3,500 square miles (9,300 square kilometers), Louangnamtha is relatively small and sparsely populated. The only city in the province, Nam Tha, has just 20,000 residents but serves as the region's political and commercial center. Nearly 200 miles (320 kilometers) north of the Laotian capital, Vientiane, Louangnamtha is remote—much closer to the borders of China and Myanmar (Burma) than to the major cities of Laos. As is the case with the rest of Laos, the region's economy is primarily dependent on agriculture. However, with increasing international investment and aid coming into the country, economic diversification in Louangnamtha will likely occur.

Mountainous and forested, Louangnamtha is mostly pristine, although plans for a new "economic highway" through the region will likely change that soon. Timber operations, most owned by international companies, also pose a potential conflict between economic development and attempts to sustain natural resources.

Recently, Laos's communist government has relaxed many controls and opened up the country to tourism. Louangnamtha's rugged terrain is perfect for trekking. The region also has one of the country's few protected wildernesses, the massive Nam Ha Conservation Area. Louangnamtha offers great cultural diversity too. The so-called hill tribes, such as the Hmong, Lahu, and Akha, make up a large proportion of the region's population.

*Arne Kislenko*

*See also:* **Hmong**

**Further Reading**

Nguyen, Thi Dieu. (1991) *The Mekong River and the Struggle for Indochina*. Westport, CT: Praeger.

Stuart-Fox, Martin. (1986) *Laos: Politics, Economics and Society*. Boulder, CO: Lynne Rienner.

Zasloff, Joseph J. and Leonard Unger, eds. (1999) *Laos: Beyond the Revolution*. New York: St. Martin's.

## LU, MOUNT

Mount Lu (Cottage Mountain), is situated in China's northern Jiangxi Province and covers an area of over 300 square kilometers. Its highest peak, Hanyangfeng, is 449 meters above sea level. To its north is the Chang (Yangtze) River and to the southeast is Lake Poyang. Over three thousand species of plants can be found on its slopes, and the mountain encompasses approximately ninety peaks.

Famed scenic areas include the Peak of the Five Old Men; the Three Step Falls, which cascades over 150 meters; Great Tianchi Lake; the Flower Path; and the Cave of the Immortals, where the mythic Lu Dongbing achieved immortality. Mount Lu also houses the White Deer Cave Academy, one of China's oldest academies, and the East Forest Monastery (fourth and fifth century) where Pure Land Buddhism is said to have originated. The Incense Burner Peak inspired the Tang dynasty (618–907 CE) poet Li Bai (701–762). Guling town houses villas dating from the early twentieth century, when Mount Lu became a popular retreat for wealthy Chinese and Europeans. For hundreds of years, Mount Lu's beauty has inspired poets and painters. In 1996, it was declared a UNESCO World Heritage Site.

*Noelle O'Connor*

*See also:* **Buddhism; Chang River; Jiangxi; Li Bai; Tang Dynasty**

**Further Reading**

Bush, Susan. (1983) "Tsung Ping's Essay on Painting Landscape and the 'Landscape Buddhism' of Mt. Lu." In *Theories of the Arts in China*, edited by Susan Bush and Christian Murck. Princeton, NJ: Princeton University Press, 132–164.

Grant, Beata. (1994) *Mt. Lu Revisited: Buddhism in the Life and Writings of Su Shi (1037–1107)*. Honolulu, HI: University of Hawaii Press.

## LU XUN

(1881–1936), Chinese writer. Lu Xun was the pen name of Zhou Shuren, a Chinese fiction writer, essayist, poet, translator, scholar, and patron of the arts who is widely considered to be the most influential man of letters in twentieth-century China. Born in Shaoxing, Zhejiang Province, Lu Xun went to Japan in 1902 to study medicine. As his autobiographical essays claim, he left medical school in 1905 to devote himself to a spiritual healing of the nation through literature. Returning to China in 1909, Lu Xun took up work at the Ministry of Education and also taught at schools in Shaoxing, Hangzhou, and Beijing. In 1918, he published *Kuangren riji* (Diary of a Madman), celebrated as the first piece in modern Chinese vernacular.

Lu Xun's collections of fiction, *Nahan* (Outcry, also known as Call to Arms, 1923) and *Panghuang* (Wondering, 1926), include short stories such as *A Q zhengzhuan* (The True Story of Ah Q) and *Zhufu* (New Year's Sacrifice), which portray with humor and sarcasm the delusions of villagers during the upheavals of the early twentieth century. As the stories offer a poignant criticism of contemporary social mores, they have come to represent of the ideals of the May Fourth Movement, an influential trend during the 1910s and 1920s that saw a new social order. In parallel, Lu Xun experimented with other forms of writing, starting with the prose-poems in *Yecao* (Wild Grass, 1927). After 1927, he wrote mostly essays, contributing to the burgeoning of the genre in twentieth-century Chinese literature. Altogether he published sixteen volumes of essays on subjects varying from sketches of everyday life to pointed political commentary. Lu Xun also influenced the literary scene through his journal editing and prolific translations, mostly of Russian and Japanese writers.

After moving to Shanghai in 1927, he used his status to support writers and other artists. Believing in the power of visual art to carry social messages, he advanced the woodblock print movement and collaborated with his brother Zhou Zuoren in publishing art prints. Despite his concern with social issues, he remained politically unaffiliated, engaging in debates with the poet Guo Moruo to the left and the essayist Lin Yutang to the right. In 1931, however, he joined the League of Leftist Writers, a fact used a decade later by Mao Zedong (1893–1976) to posthumously declare Lu Xun as the paragon of Communist writers.

*Yomi Braester*

**Further Reading**

Lee, Leo Ou-fan. (1987) *Voices from the Iron House: A Study of Lu Xun*. Bloomington, IN: Indiana University Press.

Pusey, James Reeve. (1998) *Lu Xun and Evolution*. Albany, NY: State University of New York Press.

**LUANG PRABANG** (2001 pop. 15,000). Surrounded by mountains on and around a peninsula between the Mekong and Nam Khan rivers, Luang Prabang is one of the most beautiful, historic, and least explored ancient capitals of Asia. Today the third or fourth biggest city in Laos, Luang Prabang was originally the center of Lane Xang ("land of a million elephants"), an empire that stretched across much of present-day Laos, northeastern Thailand, and southern China approximately 700 years ago. The name itself is taken from the Phra Bang, a golden image of the Buddha, which remains a revered object of the Lao people. Although the whereabouts of the authentic Phra Bang are a mystery, and little remains of the original city, Luang Prabang continues as a center of Lao history and culture. Renowned for its magnificent temples and the former Royal Palace, the city also boasts a unique mix of Lao and French architecture, a legacy from the country's colonial past. So rich is Luang Prabang's history that the city was designated a UNESCO World Heritage site in 1995, with 33 temples and 111 buildings protected or scheduled for restoration. Luang Prabang retains a magical, unspoiled quality. Quiet and small, with only about 15,000 residents, the city is widely regarded as the best-preserved historic town in Southeast Asia. Luang Prabang also stands as evidence of a glorious era in Laos's troubled history.

*Arne Kislenko*

**Further Reading**


Berger, Hans G. (2000) *Het Bun Dai Bun: Luang Prabang—Rituale einer glucklichen Stadt.* Munich: Knesebeck.

Sepul, Rene, and Cici Olsson. (1998) *Luang Prabang.* Trans. by Ed Lamot. Vientiane, Laos: Raintrees.

Stuart-Fox, Martin. (1997) *A History of Laos.* Cambridge, U.K.: Cambridge University Press.

## LUANG PRABANG—WORLD HERITAGE SITE

The town of Luang Prabang is noted for the attention given to the preservation of its many temples and other historic buildings. It was designated a UNESCO World Heritage Site in 1995.

**LUCKNOW** (2001 pop. 2.2 million). The capital of Uttar Pradesh, India's most populous state, Lucknow is a major commercial and cultural center 270 miles southeast of Delhi. In 1590 the Mughal emperor Akbar named it the seat of the governor of Awadh. Muslims constituted its ruling families. Modern Lucknow, known as the city of nabobs, was largely created by Oudh princes, descendants of the Persian adventurer Saadat Khan, who governed the province as a gift of the Mughal court beginning in 1732. The Mughal emperor Asaf-ud-Dawlah moved the court from Faizabad to Lucknow in 1775 and turned it into a center of Urdu poetry, courtly diction, music, and dance. The early nineteenth century saw the continued building of palaces and mosques and the cult of the sophisticated courtesan. The British annexed the area in 1856.

Today music festivals and dance made famous by the Oudh court continue in Lucknow. The city produces silver and *bidri* (ornamental metal) work and

## HOUSING THE COLONEL IN LUCKNOW (OR LAKNAU)

"Colonel Martin's other residence . . . is a palace on a very extensive scale, but in which the singularity of the Colonel's taste is chiefly discernible. . . . Under the principal apartment are subterraneous rooms, intended for the hot season. This plan of living underground during the hot months being quite experimental, it would perhaps have been more reasonable to make the trial on a less expensive scale. The heat and smoke and smell, arising from the number of lamps necessary to light the dark chambers and passages, seemed alone sufficient to render the success of the scheme more than doubtful. In the middle of the largest of these dark rooms the Colonel had already raised his tomb, and the number of lights to be burned there, night and day, *for ever*, and the sum to be allotted for this purpose, were already mentioned."

*Source:* Thomas Twining, *Travels in India, a Hundred Years Ago, with a Visit to the United States* (1792), as quoted in *The Sahibs* (1948), edited by Hilton Brown. London: William Hodge & Co., 238.

trades in copper, brass, and cotton. It is an important rail junction with an impressive station reflecting Mughal and European influences. Also noteworthy is the Great Imambara, the tomb of the nabob Asaf-ud-Dawlah. Most residents are Hindus, but Lucknow is the principal Shi'ite Muslim center in India and still home to many Sunni Muslims.

*C. Roger Davis*

### Further Reading

Hay, Sidney. (1994) *Historic Lucknow.* New Delhi: Asian Educational Services.

## LUDRUK

*Ludruk* is a secular East Javanese folk-theater genre, performed by amateur and professional troupes for mass audiences. Its contemporary form began emerging in the 1930s, although evidence suggests that its roots go back several hundred years. *Ludruk* has become increasingly popular since World War II, heavily influencing many television productions.

Starting with a comic prologue, *Ludruk* consists mainly of spoken dialogue; songs and dances are performed at the opening of the performance and between the acts. *Ludruk* is usually accompanied by a gamelan—a traditional Indonesian percussion orchestra. The melodramatic stories often highlight social problems and social injustice, seen from the perspective of the masses. Clowns figure prominently; they mock the airs of social superiors and criticize their wrong behavior. Often the plot revolves around love and typically can involve the marriage of a lower-class beauty to the son of a rich man or the desperation of a youth of humble background who wins the heart of an upper-class beauty forbidden to marry him. Except for these female roles, all other women are characteristically played by men.

*Martin Ramstedt*

### Further Reading

Hefner, Carl J. (1994) *Ludruk Folk Theatre of East Java: Toward a Theory of Symbolic Action.* Ann Arbor, MI: University of Michigan Press

Peacock, James L. (1968) *Rites of Modernization: Symbolic and Social Aspects of Indonesian Proletarian Drama.* Chicago: University of Chicago Press.

## LUNA Y NOVICIO, JUAN

(1857–1899), Filipino painter and revolutionary. Juan Luna y Novicio was the older brother of Antonio Luna (1866–1899), a general of the Filipino forces during the Philippine-American War. Juan learned the rudiments of painting under Don Agustin Saez. He became a sailor, and his sea travels inspired him to continue pursuing painting. He enrolled at the Academy of Fine Arts in Manila under the tutelage of Don Lorenzo Guerrero and further trained in Spain under Don Alejo Vera.

In 1884, his masterpiece, *Spolarium,* won first prize at the National Exposition of Fine Arts in Madrid. His friend Dr. Jose Rizal, national hero of the Phillipines after his execution in 1896, praised his success as a triumph of Filipino talent in the face of Spanish prejudice toward Filipinos. Juan created other notable paintings in the academic style such as *Daphne and Cleo, Death of Cleopatra, Las Damas Romanas* (The Roman Women), *Españas y Filipinas* (Spain and the Philippines), *Peuple et Roi* (Purple and Red), *Vanidad* (Vanity), *Inocencia* (Innocence), and *El Pacto de Sangre* (The Blood Compact).

In 1885, he moved to Paris and in the following year married a woman belonging to the prominent Pardo de Tavera family. In 1892, he was arrested for murdering his wife because of her infidelity but was eventually released on the grounds of insanity, as the judge in the case felt that because Luna was such a talented artist, it was a shame to send him to prison. In 1894, he returned to the Philippines, and two years later, he and his brother Antonio were arrested for allegedly conspiring to overthrow the colonial government. They were pardoned in 1897, and days after their release, they left for Europe.

During the Philippine-American War (1899–1901), Juan served as a diplomatic agent for Emilio Aguinaldo, the president of the fledging Philippine Republic. While stopping at Hong Kong on his way home, he died from a heart attack and was buried there. Afterward his remains were brought to the Philippines and interred at San Agustin Church.

*Aaron G. Ronquillo*

### Further Reading

Cruz, E. Aguilar. (1975) *Luna.* Manila, Philippines: Department of Public Information.

Da Silva, Carlos. (1997) *Juan Luna y Novicio, First Internationally Known Filipino Painter.* Manila, Philippines: National Historical Institute.

Ocampo, Ambeth. (1990) *Rizal without the Overcoat.* Pasig City, Philippines: Anvil.

Pilar, Santiago. (1980) *Juan Luna: The Filipino As Painter.* Manila, Philippines: Eugenio Lopez Foundation.

Quirino, Carlos. (1992) *Juan Luna.* Manila, Philippines: Tahanan Books for Young Readers.

———. (1995) "Luna, Juan." In *Who's Who in Philippine History.* Manila, Philippines: Tahanan Books, 133.

**LUZON GROUP** (2002 pop. of Central Luzon 85.2 million). The largest island group in the Philippine archipelago, the Luzon group includes the main island of Luzon and the island provinces of Palawan, Marinduque, Oriental and Occidental Mindoro, Batanes, Canandu-anes, Masbate, and Rombkon. Together, these cover more than 109,000 square kilometers.

The Luzon group is divided into five regions based on geographic location and ethnolinguistic groupings of the population. Region 1, Ilocos Region, consists of Ilocos Norte, Ilocos Sur, La Union, and Pangasinan.

Region 2, Cagayan Valley, consists of Cagayan, Isabela, Nueva Vizcaya, Quirino, and Batanes. In 1981, several provinces formerly in Regions 1 and 2 (Abra, Apayao, Benguest, Ifugao, Kalinga, and Mountain province) were reconstituted into the Cordillera Autonomous Region, home to indigenous ethnic groups and cultural minorities with common historical and cultural heritages.

Region 3, Central Luzon, includes Nueva Ecija, Tarlac, Pampanga, Zambales, Bataan, and Bulacan. Angeles City and Olongapo City, in the provinces of Pampanga and Zambales, respectively, are independent of, although located in, those provinces.

Region 4, Southern Tagalog, consists of Rizal, Laguna, Cavite, Batangas, Palawan, Oriental Mindoro, Occidental Mindoro, Marinduque, Aurora, Quezon, and Romblon.

Region 5, Bicol Region, includes Camarines Norte, Camarines Sur, Albay, Sorsogon, Catanduanes, and Masbate. The national capital, Manila, is located in this region, in an enclave called the National Capital Region, which itself has twelve cities and five municipalities.

Luzon has a myriad of topographical features ranging from mountain ranges to volcanoes. At 2,928 meters, Mount Pulog is the highest mountain in Luzon. Several lakes and rivers, such as Laguna Lake, the largest lake in the Philippines, as well as a few active volcanoes, notably Mount Mayon in Albay and Mount Pinatubo in Zambales, are also in Luzon. Pinatubo's eruptions in 1991 and 1992 were so powerful that volcanic material rising into the upper atmosphere was carried around the world. Aside from the vast mineral and natural resources of the Luzon group, central Luzon is also the rice bowl of the Philippines, where most of the country's rice is produced.

Luzon is populated by people of different cultural and linguistic backgrounds. Tagalog, a member of the Austronesian family, is the most widely spoken language, though each region has its own local language.

Despite the diverse population, Catholicism is the predominant religion, with a few Protestant denominations and other local religions. The Luzon group is home to one of the simplest-living ethnic groups in the Philippines, the Negritoes, occupying the hinterlands, while the most modern metropolis in the country, Metro Manila, is also in Luzon.

The capital city of the Philippines, Manila was a bustling community engaged in trade prior to the arrival of the Spanish. After the Spanish established themselves in Manila in 1572, the city became a launching point for further expeditions into the rest of Luzon to spread Catholicism and Western civilization. It was also in Luzon that the revolution for Philippine independence started and where Philippine independence was proclaimed in 1898.

*Aaron Ronquillo*

### Further Reading

Action Asia. (1999) *Adventure and Travel Guide to the Philippines.* Hong Kong: Action Asia.

Department of Tourism, Philippines. (1994) *The Philippines: Spirit of Place.* Manila, Philippines: Department of Tourism.

Höbel, Robert. (1981) *The Philippines.* Hong Kong: Robert Rovena Ltd.

Lancion, Conrado, Jr. (1995) *Fast Facts about Philippine Provinces.* Manila, Philippines: Tahanan Books.

Mayuga, Sylvia, et. al. (1988) *Philippines.* Hong Kong: APA Publication.

**MACAO** (2002 est. pop. 465,000). A Portuguese colonial outpost in southern China for more than four centuries (1557–1999), the territory of Macao (Macau), or as it is known in Chinese, Aomen, consists of a narrow peninsula in southern Guangdong Province and the islands of Tiapa and Coloane. In 1996 the population of Macao was 415,850. Coupled with the territory's minute size (23.5 square kilometers, or 9 square miles), this makes it one of the most densely populated places in the world.

The Portuguese name "Macao" was possibly derived from either the Ma Kwok (Cantonese) temple that has stood in the city since the fourteenth century or the Cantonese term "Ama-ngao" ("Bay of the Goddess A Ma," the patron of sailors and fishermen). The Portuguese first settled Macao in 1557 and named the site Provacão do Nome de Deos na China, or "Settlement in the name of God in China." It is not known why the Chinese authorities allowed the Portuguese to establish a settlement. Possible explanations are that the territory was both small and not of any value and that the presence of the foreigners would facilitate trade, or that the Portuguese were being rewarded for their perceived assistance in driving off local pirates. Regardless of the reason, the territory became an important base of operations for Portuguese merchants in East Asia from the sixteenth to nineteenth centuries. Reporting to authorities in Goa, India, the Portuguese governor in Macao oversaw a vibrant trade with the Ming and later Qing empires, and his city was an important headquarters for the Jesuit missionary movement in East Asia.

Other European powers, particularly the Dutch, were envious of Portugal's position in Macao, and on several occasions the colony had to defend itself from attacks launched by the Dutch East India Company. The Macao colony did provide shelter for the families of Dutch and English merchants who were involved in the China trade at Guangzhou (Canton), 100 kilometers to the north; regulations there forbade merchants from permanently residing in the city and family members from accompanying them on trading missions. With the expulsion of all foreigners (except for a small number of Dutch traders) from Japan in 1635, Macao became the center of Sino-European trade until the end of the eighteenth century.

After the Opium War of 1840 and the opening of four new ports to foreign trade, Macao's importance as a point of commerce on the China coast declined. The Portuguese, however, remained in Macao, although much of the trade with the Qing empire shifted to Hong Kong and Shanghai. In 1845 the governor of Macao, João Ferreira do Amaral, ended the established practice of paying the Chinese an annual rent of 500 silver taels and evicted Chinese customs officials from the colony. In 1887 Portugal and China signed a treaty that formally recognized Portuguese sovereignty over Macao. Although now a foreign-controlled possession on the China coast, Macao's economy and importance continued to decline with Hong Kong's growing importance. During the Pacific War, Macao enjoyed a brief revival as a safe haven due to Portuguese neutrality in the worldwide conflict.

In 1987 the governments of Portugal and the People's Republic of China concluded negotiations for the return of Macao to Chinese rule. The reversion of Macao to the "motherland" on 20 December 1999 was an important event for the Chinese leadership in

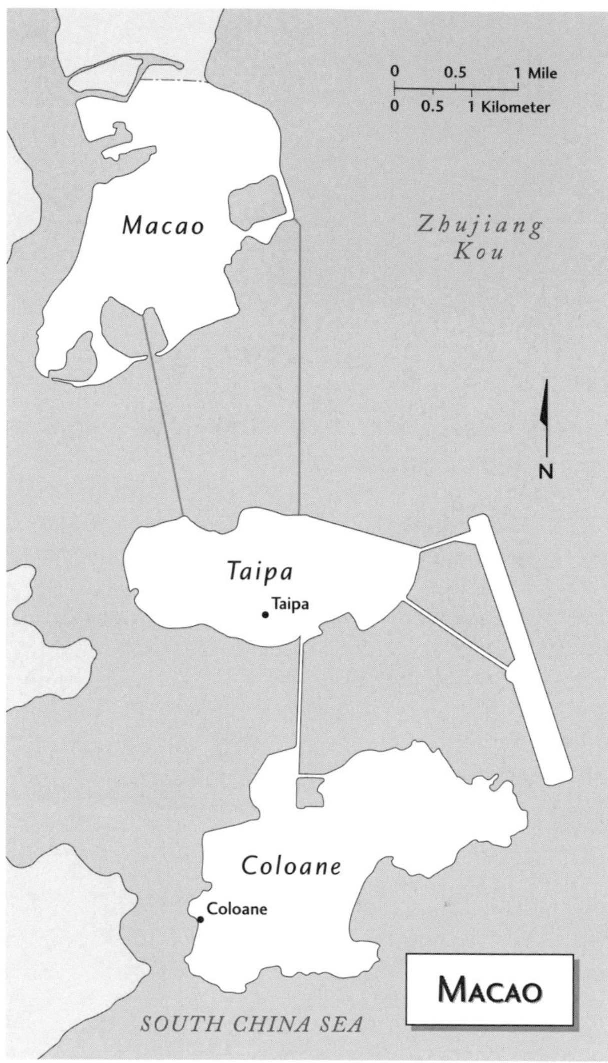


Beijing and for many Chinese. The return of the last of the foreign-controlled territories to Chinese authority—like the earlier handover of Hong Kong in 1997—ended almost two centuries of unequal treaties that were a source of humiliation for many Chinese and signified that a new and strong China had at last come of age as an equal player on the world stage. The Beijing government hopes that successes in the Hong Kong and Macao Special Administrative Regions under the "one country, two systems" banner will eventually pave the way for the reunification of Taiwan and the People's Republic of China.

Apart from trade, some light manufacturing, and the local fishing industry, the economy of the Macao Special Administration Region is dominated by tourism and gambling. In the mid-1990s the colony was plagued by violence as Chinese criminal gangs, or triads, from Hong Kong moved into Macao prior to the handover of Hong Kong. These gangs fought for control of the colony's gambling establishments, prostitution, and drug trade. The Macao Special Administration Region continues to serve as a popular holiday destination for the residents of Hong Kong, and the former colony's economy is being more closely integrated into that of the neighboring Zhuhai Special Economic Zone.

*Robert John Perrins*

**Further Reading**

Boxer, Charles R. (1968) *Fidalgos in the Far East, 1550–1750*. 2d ed. Hong Kong: Oxford University Press.

Cheng, Christina Miu Bing. (1999) *Macau: A Cultural Janus*. Hong Kong: Hong Kong University Press.

Guillen-Nuñez, Cesar. (1984) *Macau*. Hong Kong: Oxford University Press.

Gunn, Geoffrey C. (1995) *Macau, 1575–1999: An Economic and Political History*. Nagasaki, Japan: Nagasaki tonan Ajia kenkyujo.

Porter, Jonathan. (1996) *Macau the Imaginary City: Culture and Society, 1557 to the Present*. Boulder, CO: Westview Press.

Roberts, Elfed V., Sum Ngai Ling, and Peter Bradshaw. (1992) *Historical Dictionary of Hong Kong and Macau*. Metuchen, NJ: Scarecrow Press.

Yee, Herbert S. (2001) *Macau in Transition: From Colony to Autonomous Region*. New York: Palgrave.

## MACAPAGAL, DIOSDADO (1910–1997),

President of the Republic of the Philippines. Born to a poor family on 28 September 1910, Diosdado Macapagal worked his way through law school and joined the largest U.S. law firm in Manila while the Philippines was still a U.S. colony. After independence he joined the Department of Foreign Affairs, rising to the position of second secretary of the Philippine embassy in Washington, D.C. While in Washington, Macapagal conducted graduate work in economics, earning a Ph.D. in 1957. He was twice elected to the Philippine Congress, serving from 1949–1956, and was vice president from 1957–1961. According to Marcos biographer James Hamilton-Paterson, in 1961 Macapagal successfully challenged incumbent president Carlos Garcia after making a tacit agreement with Ferdinand Marcos that if elected he would only serve one term, after which he would support a Marcos candidacy. In 1965, when it became clear that Macapagal was going to renege and run for reelection, Marcos ran as the opposition candidate, easily defeating the incumbent president, who ran a poor campaign. As president, Macapagal supported land redistribution but lacked the political support to implement sweeping reform. In 1963 he proposed legislation giving the government greater power to expropriate landed estates, but members of the elite resisted the reforms, and Congress watered down the proposal, which was inadequately funded and poorly implemented. Although considered personally honest, Macapagal's administration was tainted by corruption, and he was threatened with impeachment when he protected political allies from prosecution. Out of office, Macapagal ran as a delegate and was elected president of the 1971 Constitutional Convention. Before the body was able to draft a new constitution, however, President Marcos declared martial law, rendering the convention powerless. Macapagal died in 1997, but his political legacy continues. His daughter, Gloria Macapagal Arroyo, became president in February 2001 following the impeachment trial of President Joseph Estrada.

*Zachary Abuza*

**Further Reading**

Hamilton-Paterson, James. (1999) *America's Boy: A Century of Colonialism in the Philippines*. New York: Henry Holt.

## MACARTHUR, DOUGLAS (1880–1964), U.S. military leader.

Asia was central to the career of Douglas MacArthur, one of the most celebrated, yet controversial, U.S. military leaders. He had four tours of duty in the Philippines between 1903 and 1942. A visit to military installations in eleven Asian countries in 1905–1906 as an aide to his father, Lt. Gen. Arthur MacArthur, Jr., convinced him of the importance of Asia to America's future.

Asia was the site of MacArthur's worst defeats and greatest victories. Commanding U.S. and Filipino forces, MacArthur was unable to defend the Philippines against the Japanese invasion in 1941. Ordered to Australia by President Franklin Roosevelt in 1942, he declared, "I shall return." Implementing a brilliant island-hopping strategy that avoided Japan's main forces, MacArthur made good on his promise, landing on Leyte island in October 1944.

As supreme commander of the Allied Powers in Japan, MacArthur oversaw the rebuilding of Japan and the establishment of democracy, laying the foundation for Japan to become a major industrial nation. With the outbreak of the Korean War in 1950, MacArthur was appointed commanding general of U.N. forces. His amphibious landing at Inchon turned the war against North Korea. MacArthur's push to the Yalu River, however, brought China into the war and led to a policy dispute with President Harry Truman. Relieved of command in April 1951, MacArthur returned to the United States to a hero's welcome.

*Robert L. Youngblood*

**Further Reading**

James, Clayton D. (1970–1980) *The Years of MacArthur*. 3 vols. Boston: Houghton Mifflin.
Manchester, William. (1978) *American Caesar: Douglas MacArthur 1880–1964*. Boston: Little, Brown.
Petillo, Carol M. (1981) *Douglas MacArthur: The Philippine Years*. Bloomington, IN: Indiana University Press.
Spanier, John W. (1965) *The Truman-MacArthur Controversy and the Korean War*. New York: W. W. Norton.
Weintraub, Stanley. (2000) *MacArthur's War: Korea and the Undoing of an American Hero*. New York: The Free Press.

## MACAULAY, THOMAS B. (1800–1859), English politician, writer, member of the Supreme Council of India.

Thomas Babington Macaulay was a precocious scholar, with an extremely retentive memory. After studying at Trinity College, Cambridge, he began training in the law, but soon abandoned his studies to concentrate on writing for periodicals, chiefly the *Edinburgh Review*. In 1830, he entered Parliament as a Whig. In 1843, he accepted a lucrative post on the Supreme Council of India to help bolster the family finances when his father's business failed. He arrived in Madras, India, in June of that year with his sister.

His period in India was notable for two things. First, he took the lead in the creation of a criminal code, which established English common law as the basis of the Indian legal system. Second, he intervened in the debate about whether public funds should be used to promote the study of English language and learning or of traditional Eastern subjects and languages. Macaulay dismissed the achievements of Indian learning and argued in his famous "Minute on Education" (1835) that universities should teach the English language, science, and Western literature in the English language. His argument prevailed and played an important part in establishing English as the official language of India.

Macaulay returned to England in 1838, never to revisit India. Although he reentered Parliament, his final years were devoted to his *History of England*, which he left unfinished at his death in 1859. He was one of the greatest essayists of nineteenth-century English literature.

*Chandrika Kaul*

**Further Reading**

Trevelyan, George Otto. (1876) *The Life and Letters of Lord Macaulay*. 2 vols. London: Longmans, Green.

## MACHINERY AND EQUIPMENT INDUSTRY—CHINA

China's machinery industry started in the 1860s with three government-sponsored military factories. By the start of the twenty-first century, it contributed over 5 percent of world total production and ranked fifth in the world.

### History of Development

By 1933 China possessed 226 machine-building plants, 63 plants for manufacturing electrical equipment, and 34 shipbuilding and locomotive repair plants, which provided 2 percent of China's total industrial gross output. In Manchuria and North China, which came under Japanese occupation between 1931 and 1940, the Japanese expanded the machinery industry substantially to support their war effort. Manchuria had a total of 968 plants in 1940. In the interior areas that remained under the control of the Nationalist government during the war with Japan, the state and private industrialists built many machine-building factories, but only 77 remained in operation by 1944.

In 1945 the Soviet army occupied Manchuria and dismantled half the machinery factories. Industrial production was further disrupted by the 1946–1949 civil war between the Chinese Nationalists and Communists. At the founding of the People's Republic of China (PRC) in 1949, the machinery industry accounted for only 2.7 percent of total gross industrial output, not much of an increase since 1933.

The industry was given high priority in the Communist government's development plans, given its importance for national defense and for the technological transformation of the national economy. With the stimulus of the Korean War (1950–1953) and the inflow of Soviet technical assistance, the industry regained 1947 levels in 1952. It was assigned 26 percent of total investment in industrial capital construction in the first five-year plan (1953–1957), or 6.9 million yuan renminbi (RMB). Imports of machinery and transport equipment were given high priority. Foreign experts were invited to China, and many Chinese technicians were sent abroad for training. A number of comprehensive institutes were established, as were several new machinery industries, including heavy machines, mining equipment, machine tools, tractors, bearings, and electric equipment.

The launching of the Great Leap Forward of 1958–1960 led to a sharp rise in quantity of machinery produced, but much of it proved unusable because quality was sacrificed in the frenzy to increase production exponentially. Imports of machinery and transportation equipment, 94 percent from Communist countries, reached a peak of $840 million in 1960. The economic disaster of the Great Leap Forward, coupled with the withdrawal of Soviet assistance after the open rift between China and the Soviet Union, led to years of readjustment and recovery between 1961 and 1965. While imports plunged to a low of $100 million in 1963, the machinery industry successfully absorbed and adapted previously imported technology, and the value of its output attained 9.7 billion yuan RMB in 1965, far surpassing the level of 3.5 billion in 1957. In 1966 the industry contributed 12 percent of total gross industrial output.

The outbreak of the Cultural Revolution in 1966 disrupted scientific research, because government agencies were paralyzed and many scientists and technicians suffered persecution. But with the PRC government's seating in the United Nations in 1972 and the establishment of diplomatic relations with Japan and a number of Western countries thereafter, technical imports under licensing agreements from the technologically advanced capitalist economies assumed importance. In 1973 imports of machinery and transportation equipment from non-Communist countries ($501 million, or 63 percent) first surpassed those from Communist countries ($296 million).

The end of the Cultural Revolution in 1976 and the beginning of economic reform after 1978 accelerated China's technical imports. Whereas earlier the bulk of the industry's production was geared toward the industrial and defense sectors, now much more attention was paid to its development for agricultural production and consumer goods. Emphasis shifted from import of complete sets of plants and equipment to import of single techniques, and from building new enterprises to the technical transformation of existing enterprises. In addition to licensing agreements, joint ventures, wholly foreign-owned enterprises (legal since 1980), and cooperative enterprises served to import advanced techniques. By 1996, there were nearly 5,300 officially

New red tractors at the factory in Luoyang, Henan, China. (LOWELL GEORGIA/CORBIS)

approved foreign-funded ventures, with a total direct investment of approximately $5.5 billion.

The industry grew at an average annual rate of 16 percent from 1984 to 1989, and 24 percent from 1990 to 1995. Growth has slowed since: 10 percent in 1997 and again in 1999; 4.34 percent in 1998. With rising internal demand, an expansionary monetary policy, and the deepening reform of the state-owned enterprises, the industry is expected to expand at an annual rate of 11 percent or higher from 2000. Machinery production in 2000 rose by 14.7 percent over production in 1999.

### Current Configuration

Currently, there are twelve major sectors in China's machinery industry: automotive, electrical equipment, heavy and mining machinery, petrochemical and general machinery, agricultural machinery, construction machinery, internal combustion engines, machine tools, instruments and meters, basic machinery parts, food processing and packaging machinery, and environmental protection machinery. As of 1997 there were 120,000 enterprises and 122 scientific research institutes, colleges, and universities, employing 20 million people. The Machinery Industry Bureau (formerly the Ministry of Machinery Industry) is responsible for overall planning of the modernization of the industry and for determining key areas for its improvement.

At the end of 2000, China's machinery industry contributed over 5 percent of world total production and ranked fifth in the world. Considerable technological advancement has been accomplished through imports and indigenization. Advanced manufacturing methods have been widely adopted in areas such as casting, forging, welding, heat treatment, and surface protection, while microelectronic technology has been spreading along with the Computerized Integrated Manufacturing System (CIMS).

Before 1973 machinery and equipment amounted to only 2 to 5 percent of China's total exports. China remained a net importer of machinery and equipment during the period of economic reform since 1978. A trade deficit in machinery and equipment peaked close to $30 billion in 1993 and 1994. Imports accelerated from the mid-1980s up and exports from the early 1990s. In the late 1990s, as the industry became more sophisticated and competitive, the trade deficit dropped significantly. Exports of machinery and electronics increased by an annual rate of 32.7 percent between 1985 and 1998, from $1.68 billion to $66.54 billion, and assumed first place among China's leading export commodities. In 2000 total trade in machinery and electronic products, dominated by information technology products, electronics, home appliances, and complete equipment for power generation and engineering, equaled $208.2 billion, or 43.9 percent of total foreign trade volume.

### Technical Capabilities Shortfall

Technical levels in many sectors of the Chinese machinery and equipment industry remain below those of the advanced economies. The tenth five-year plan (2001–2005) aims to transform China's machinery industry from a large producer (quantitatively large but technologically not the most advanced or sophisticated) to a strong producer (state-of-the-art technology), from a large importer to a large exporter, and from an equipment department of the national economy to a sector serving the needs of both the nation and the consumers.

*Robert Y. Eng*

### Further Reading

Cheng, Chu-yuan. (1971) *The Machine-Building Industry in Communist China.* New York: Aldine-Atherton.

Jain, Ashok, V. P. Kharbanda, Qiu Cheng-ben, and Huang Ai-lan. (1995) *Industrialization in India and China: A Comparative Study of Machine Building and Electronic Industries.* New Delhi: Har-Anand Publications.

## MADHYA PRADESH

**MADHYA PRADESH** (2001 est. pop. 60.4 million). Madhya Pradesh is a central Indian state (named from a Hindi translation of the old British unit called Central Provinces). It is entirely landlocked, being bounded on the south by Maharashtra, on the east by Chhattisgarh, on the north by Uttar Pradesh and on the west by Gujarat. It is virtually bisected from east to west by the Narmada River. The state was formed in 1956, and its reduced area was 273,994 square kilometers in 2000, when the eastern third of the state was sliced off to create Chhattisgarh state. The landscape consists of forested hills with extensive plateaus and steep slopes. The Vindhya and the Satpura Ranges cover much of the northern and southern parts of the state, respectively. The capital is Bhopal (2001 est. pop. 1.4 million), though the largest city is Indore (2001 est. pop. 1.6 million). Although there are numerous towns, three-quarters of the inhabitants are rural. The greatest disaster in modern times in this state was the deadly gas leak on 3 December 1984, at the Union Carbide plant in Bhopal. This killed some 2,500 residents and injured another 2,000. Most survivors have received virtually no compensation.

Madhya Pradesh was a part of the Mauryan Empire in the fourth to third centuries BCE. Later it was a part of Harsha's Empire (seventh century, and then of the Delhi Sultanate (eleventh century). In 1527 the Mughal empire extended into this area when Babur conquered Chanderi; and in the later seventeenth century, a Bhopal State was formed when the Afghan chief Dost Mohammad conquered the area. In 1817 this was annexed by the East India Company, and was administered by the British until 1947.

Cultivated crops include cotton, rice, wheat, pulses, linseed and other oilseeds, castor, soybean, millet, mustard and tobacco. The diverse industries are located mostly in the western half of the state, and include electronics, aluminum, rayon, fertilizer, petrochemicals, paper, tires and tubes, industrial gases, and cables. But the state is primarily agrarian, with low productivity.

Land use in 1991 was 43.2 percent agriculture, 30.7 percent forest, and 26.1 percent other purposes. Some 93 percent of the population are Hindus, and 86 percent speak Hindi as their first language. Tourist sites of outstanding historical importance include Sanchi, Ujjain, Gwalior, Indore, and Bhopal. The state has 448 colleges but no university of major stature.

*Paul Hockings*

**Further Reading**

Russell, R.V., and Hira Lal ([1916] 1969). *The Tribes and Castes of the Central Provinces of India.* 4 vols. Oosterhout: Anthropological Publications.

**MADRAS** (2002 est. pop. 4.3 million). Now officially Chennai, Madras is a large city on the southeast coast of India. Its name came from the Arabic *madrasa,* "a religious school," but recently the ancient Tamil name of the town *(Cennai)* has been asserted by local politicians. In the early days of its European settlement, it was known as Fort St. George, in reference to the main fortification, which still stands. In 1639 territory was given to Francis Day of the East India Company by a deputy of the Raja of Chandragiri, who was the last local representative of the foundering royal house of Vijayanagar. This grant was later confirmed afresh, in 1762, by the Nawab of Arcot (Arkattu).

From a small fort built there in 1644, the town slowly expanded as it became the most important trading center in that part of India. Among the town's more notable governors were Elihu Yale (1687–1691), who gave a small grant to found the noted American university that bears his name; Thomas Pitt (1730–1735); and Sir Thomas Munro (1820–1827). This was the first settlement of any size belonging to the East India Company, and St. Mary's Church, built in 1678–1680, was the first English church in Asia. Even older, however, is the Roman Catholic Cathedral of San Thome, built by the Portuguese in 1547 and resting place of the mortal remains of St. Thomas. But the antiquity of the town goes back even further, for St. Thomas's Mount is mentioned by Marco Polo in the thirteenth century. According to legend, the apostle was martyred on this spot while kneeling on a stone, which now forms the altar in the cathedral. The seventeenth century Parthasarathi and Kapaleshvara Temples are the two main Hindu temples within the city.

Madras is located where the Cooum and Adyar rivers empty into the Bay of Bengal. It was the capital of Madras Presidency (at first called Carnatic, then just Madras) from early in the nineteenth century. At Independence the presidency disappeared as a political unit, to be replaced by Madras Province and several other states. Today Madras is the capital of Tamil Nadu State, and its approximately 6 million people make it the fourth-largest city in India. It has many industries, several universities, and a multiplicity of government offices. It is a hub for railroad and bus transportation and has an important airport. It is also a major seaport, but this too is a twentieth-century development.

*Paul Hockings*

**Further Reading**

Michell, George, and Philip Davies. (1989) "Madras." In *The Penguin Guide to the Monuments of India.* New York: Viking Press, 1: 446–448; 2: 542–554.

**MADRASAHS** A *madrasah* is an institution of higher education where advanced Islamic sciences are taught. Distinguished from *maktab,* which is an elementary school for the study of Islamic subjects, *madrasah* is the traditional equivalent of a college. The origin of *madrasah* may be traced back to early mosques in the Muslim Middle East, where clerics performed both religious and educational duties. By the early eighth century, prominent mosques evolved into complexes that provided lodging and other services for out-of-town students interested in receiving religious instruction, in addition to providing a place of worship for the believers. *Madrasah*s were financed primarily through religious endowment land, *waqf,* which provided a steady income to subsidize clerics, students, and pay for the upkeep of the mosques and other buildings within the complex. Early *madrasah*s focused entirely on the study of the Qur'an and Hadith (Sayings of the Prophet Muhammad). This gradually led to the development of the discipline of Islamic jurisprudence and four prominent legal schools of interpretation within the Sunni tradition: Maleki, Shafi'i, Hanbali, and Hanafi. With the expansion of Islamic civilization beyond the Arabian Peninsula, various *madrasahs* provided religious education following one of these traditions. In addition to classical Islamic subjects *(fiqh)*, *madrasahs* also offered a number of subjects in science and philosophy.

Western colonial expansion brought about a sizable decline in the status of *madrasahs* within the Muslim world, as modern education began to replace the traditional religious schools. However, the success of the Iranian Revolution in 1979 and the growth of Islamic fundamentalism have brought about a partial renewal of traditional Islamic education in some parts of the Middle East, North Africa, and South Asia.

*Mehrdad Haghayeghi*

**Further Reading**

Eickelman, Dale. (1985) *Knowledge and Power in Morocco: Education of a 20th Century Notable*. Princeton, NJ: Princeton University Press.

Mottaheheh, Roy. (1985) *The Mantle of the Prophet: Religion and Politics in Iran*. New York: St. Martin's Press.

Talas, Asad. (1939) *La Madrasa Nizamiyya et son histoire*. Paris: Paris University Press.

**MADURAI** (2001 est. pop. 1 million). Madurai is one of the oldest cities in India—it has a demonstrable history of some twenty-five hundred years. In ancient times, it was known as Mathura, as cited in the *Mahabharata*. One of the early descriptions, in the fifth-century *Silappadigaram*, is that of its fiery destruction. The city lies in south central Tamil Nadu state on the Vaigai River.

For many centuries, the city was the capital of the Pandya kingdom. The chief attraction in the city has long been the great temple of Sri Minakshi, the "fish-eyed goddess," who is associated with fertility. The temple compound also contains the even larger shrine of her consort, Sundareshvar. Much of the temple was constructed by the ruler Tirumala Nayak (1623–1660), but parts of the interior are much older and so are some of the bronze icons they contain. Although the inside of the shrines is rather dark, the outside presents a splendid view from a number of vantage points. The outer walls form a parallelogram of 258 by 222 meters, surrounded by nine massive pyramidal gateways *(gopuram)*, of which the tallest is 46.3 meters high. All are elaborately decorated with hundreds of three-dimensional human figures. Perhaps the most remarkable sight within the temple is the Hall of a Thousand Pillars (actually 997 pillars), nearly all of which differ from each other.

Today, the city does a considerable trade in tea, coffee, and cardamom, all grown on the hills to the west. Local crafts include making silk cloth, woodwork items, brassware, and muslin weaving.

*Paul Hockings*

The Sri Minakshi Temple, c. 2000. (CHRIS LISLE/CORBIS)

**Further Reading**

Michell, George, and Philip Davies. (1989) "Madurai." In *The Penguin Guide to the Monuments of India*, Vols. 1 and 2. New York: Viking Press, 448–452; 554–556.

**MADURESE** The Madurese originate from the 5,304 square kilometer island of Madura, which is part of Indonesia's East Java province. There are about 10 million Madurese, making them the third-largest ethnic group in Indonesia after the Javanese and the Sundanese. However, more than half of the Madurese have moved to other parts of Indonesia, particularly to mainland East Java, where they have integrated with the Javanese. The harsh, arid, and unfertile land of the island of Madura, which can only be used during the rainy season, causes the migration of the Madurese to other areas. Reports show that by 1994, only about 3 million people were left in Madura. Many have also transmigrated to areas such as Kalimantan, Sumatra, and Sulawesi.

Madurese migrants in Indonesian cities are easily identified because they stay exclusively in their own areas, maintaining their language and customs. The Madurese are Muslims and are notable in their adherence to their religious leaders or *kiyai* (Islamic clerics), who also become their informal political and social leaders. The *kiyai* have an elevated status for Madurese. The fanatical supporters from East Java province of Indonesia's former cleric president, Abdurrahman Wahid, counted Madurese in their numbers.

Madurese men are protective of their women, and should their wife or girlfriend suffer an offense from another man, then the Madurese man must settle it by *carok* (a life and death duel) using a *clurit* (a 30- to 40-centimeter half-circle knife). Madurese men must master *carok* as a martial art. Those who fully master this martial art are called *orang jago* and given *blater* (brave man) status. Traditional music and dances *(remo)* are regularly held in Madurese society to formally honor members of the *blater* group.

Migrant Madurese are usually small traders. In west and central Kalimantan, their presence has created difficult relations with the local people such as the Dayak, Malay, and Chinese. There have been a number of pogroms against the Madurese, including the brutal killings in 2001 in which thousands were beheaded in Central Kalimantan province after local Dayak people accused the Madurese of taking their land and of denigrating local customs and cultures.

*Abubakar Eby Hara*

**Further Reading**

Wiyata, A. Latief. (2001) "Carok: Institusionalisasi Kekerasan Dalam Masyarakat Madura" (Carok: Institutionalization of Violence in Madurese Society). Ph.D. diss. Gadjah Mada University, Yogyakarta, Indonesia.

**MAGNETISM** Among the greatest Chinese contributions to physics were the discovery of magnetism and the development of the compass. Though references to magnetism in Chinese sources do not date before the third century BCE, knowledge of the phenomenon was clearly widespread by this time, and experiments were being undertaken and documented by the first century CE. There were many early lodestone devices, such as the "south-pointing spoon" of the first century CE (which may have been invented a century earlier), and there are several intriguing references to the use of magnets to make "automatic" chess boards.

But magnetism seems to have been used predominantly in geomancy until the tenth century. Geomancy, or feng shui, was concerned with regulating human dwellings in relation to those currents of the spirit of the earth that affect people. The fact that knowledge of the compass was reserved for imperial magicians greatly restricted its spread, and it seems that for many centuries the compass served only as a tool for divination. Even when the compass passed into more general use, the primacy of canal and river traffic slowed the spread of the device to ocean-going vessels. Nevertheless, there were many adaptations and improvements in the form of compasses, which culminated in their use in navigation by the eleventh century.

Two of the most critical components in the development of the compass were the use of a needle rather than a lodestone or piece of metal and the discovery of magnetic declination (the deviation between true or geographic north and the direction that a compass needle points). The magnetization of needles was an important step in the development of the compass, because needles could float or be suspended by a thread and turn with a great degree of freedom. Also, steel holds magnetization longer than iron, and it was relatively easy at an early date to make small needles of steel; such compasses with steel needles could be used on long voyages. Steel came to China from India in the fifth century, but the Chinese quickly began to produce their own supplies. There is evidence to suggest that magnetized needles were used as early as the fourth century CE, and their superiority in the construction of compasses was quickly recognized.

The discovery of declination was also relatively early, sometime between the seventh and tenth centuries. While the influence of nonscientific divinatory practices was clearly prominent in the development of the compass, much research and experimentation went into magnetism from the fifth century on.

*Paul Forage*

### Further Reading

Needham, Joseph. (1986) *The Shorter Science and Civilisation in China.* Vol. 3. Edited by Colin A. Ronan. Cambridge, U.K.: Cambridge University Press.

**MAGSAYSAY, RAMON** (1907–1957), Filipino statesman. Ramon Magsaysay was born 31 August 1907, in Iba, Zambales Province, in the Philippines. He was educated at the University of the Philippines (1927) and later transferred to the Institute of Commerce at Jose Rizal College (1928–1932), where he was awarded a degree in commerce. When World War II erupted, Magsaysay—having taken an interest in auto mechanics—joined the motor pool of the Thirty-First Infantry Division of the Philippine Army. When the Japanese overran the nation, he helped to organize the Western Luzon Guerrilla Forces. In January 1945, Magsaysay was involved in clearing the Zambales coast of the Japanese prior to the landing of American forces.

After the war, he was appointed by the U.S. Army as military governor of Zambales, and in 1946, Major

## RAMON MAGSAYSAY ON PHILIPPINES FOREIGN POLICY

In the following extract from an article written in 1956 Philippine president Ramon Magsaysay set forth the basics of Philippines foreign policy that linked Philippine interests to those of the United States.

> In shaping its foreign policy the Philippines is primarily moved by three considerations: . . . first, the strengthening of our national security by suppressing subversion from within and building strength against attacks from without through participation in collective security arrangements with other free nations; second, the utilization of the machinery of our foreign relations for the promotion of our foreign trade and economic cooperation in order to strengthen our domestic economy and to contribute our share to the economic development of a free world; and third, the development of our political and cultural relations with countries of the free world with particular emphasis on our relations with our Asian neighbors through our membership in the United Nations and by participation in regional conferences, such as the Manila Conference of 1954 (SEATO) and the Asian-African Conference in Bandung (1955).
>
> In the pursuit of our objectives and in the choice of our methods our government finds itself closely associated with the United States of America. It is an association immediately dictated by our community of objectives, the most urgent of which is the defense of our freedom against Communist aggression. But our policy of close relations with the United States is not a mere artificial creation of government policy makers, and it is not dictated exclusively by the accident of common purposes. It is the product of experience in serving the national interest.

*Source:* Ramon Magsaysay. (1956) "Roots of Philippine Policy." *Foreign Affairs* 35 (October): 29–30.

President Ramon Magsaysay in November 1953. (BETTMANN/CORBIS)

Magsaysay was discharged from the army and was elected representative of Zambales, serving until 1950. In 1950, Magsaysay condemned his own Liberal Party for being corrupt and insisted on acceding to the demands for social and political reform that had been responsible for sparking the rebellion by the Hukbalahap (Huk), a group of peasant-rebels fighting for democratic rights throughout the nation. Magsaysay was appointed secretary of national defense in 1950, and for the next three years, with American aid, he not only cleaned up military corruption, but also launched an extensive sweep to eliminate the insurgents of the Huk rebellion. Unfortunately, many labor leaders, educators, and diplomats, along with an array of innocent people, were arrested and deprived of their rights under Magsaysay's policy.

In November 1951, Magsaysay was responsible for keeping national elections clean by deploying soldiers to oversee the election process. During the Korean War, he also sent Philippine forces to fight under the U.N. command.

Ramon Magsaysay enjoyed a reputation of being energetic and honest; as a result, he was immensely popular with the people. On 10 November 1953, having quit the Liberal Party to join the Nacionalista Party and having U.S. support, he was elected the third president of the Philippines.

Aside from quelling the Huk rebellion, Magsaysay's presidency is remembered for the signing of the Laurel-Langley Agreement, which maintained the economic submissiveness of the Philippines to U.S. monopolies, as well as for the negotiation of the Agricultural Commodities Agreement with the United States in 1957, an accord that helped keep the nation's economy locked into a colonial pattern. Magsaysay was also responsible for establishing the Anti-Subversion Law, which limited citizens' democratic rights. Finally, he was a primary player in establishing the Southeast Asia Treaty Organization (SEATO). Ramon Magsaysay was killed in a plane crash on 17 March 1957.

*Craig Loomis*

*See also:* **Huk Rebellion**

### Further Reading

Gray, Marvin M. (1965) *Island Hero: The Story of Ramon Magsaysay.* New York: Hawthorn Books.

Romulo, Carlos P., and Marvin M Gray. (1956) *The Magsaysay Story: A Political Biography.* Manila, Philippines: Solidarida Publishing House.

**MAGUEY** Maguey is a crop that produces fiber for use in clothing textiles, rope, and heavy matting. The Spanish introduced the New World maguey (*Agave salminae*, also known as agave) and the pineapple to the Philippines. Although there were small plantings throughout the country, the maguey has never flourished in the Philippines. Traditionally, a number of fiber sources have been used in the home and for the handicraft industry. Maguey produces a fiber similar to that of the abaca, the latter perhaps the most significant fiber crop grown in the Philippines.

Maguey plantings are distributed throughout most Philippine provinces, especially in those regions with pronounced dry seasons, although the plant has never developed into a major export crop. The cultivation of maguey peaked in the early twentieth century, when over 50,000 acres were planted. Farms growing maguey were usually small; most of these were on Cebu, an island in the central Philippines. Since then acreage has dropped drastically; fewer than 10,000 acres were planted in the 1960s, and by 2000 production was so insignificant that maguey was no longer reported in any official economic statistics. What little fiber the crop does yield serves the domestic market; little goes to the export trade.

*Kog Yue Choong*

### Further Reading

Wernstedt, Frederick L., and Joseph Earle Spencer. (1967) *The Philippine Island World.* Berkeley and Los Angeles: University of California Press.

## MAGWE DIVISION

(2002 est. pop. 4.7 million). Magwe (Magway) Division, located in the central dry zone of Myanmar (Burma), has an area of 44,820 square kilometers. The town of Magwe, 530 kilometers from the national capital of Yangon (Rangoon), is its capital. The division is bordered by Mandalay Division to the east, Sagaing Division to the north, Chin State and Rakhine State to the west, and Pegu (Bago) Division to the south. Magwe's 1993 population was comprised of 3.75 million Burmans, 90,000 Chins, and 40,000 of other ethnicities.

Magwe Division is a center for the production of edible oils from the sesamum and groundnuts grown in the region; other crops are rice, maize, cotton, pulses, and tobacco. Oil was discovered in this region, and for centuries crude earth oil was extracted from shallow wells, many held by hereditary ownership and others by royalty. The Burmah Oil Company, formed in 1886, developed mechanized drilling to exploit Magwe Division's main oil fields of Yenangyaung, Chauk, and Mann (near Minbu). Until the mid-1930s, Yenangyaung was Myanmar's foremost oil field. The division's other industrial plants include cement, fertilizer and cigarette factories, and cotton textile mills. The division's main north-south transport artery is the Irrawaddy River, together with road, rail, and air links.

*Patricia M. Herbert*

### Further Reading

Greenwood, Nicholas. (1995) *Guide to Burma.* 2d ed. Old Saybrook, CT: Globe Pequot Press.

Longmuir, Marilyn. (2001) *Oil in Burma.* Bangkok, Thailand: White Lotus.

## MAHABHARATA

The monumental Sanskrit poem the *Mahabharata*, attributed to the legendary poet-seer Krsna Dvaipayana Vyasa (fifth century? BCE), although perhaps not the oldest epic poem to have survived from antiquity, is certainly the longest and undoubtedly among the most influential in the world. Its complex characters and its grim and involuted plot have left a profound and indelible impression on the peoples and cultures of South and Southeast Asia for at least two millennia, influencing the arts, literature, and religious, political, and social lives of many hundreds of millions of people throughout this vast region. One section of the immense text, the *Bhagavad Gita*, has come to be regarded as a seminal text of classical Hindu ethics.

The *Mahabharata*, as it has come down to us in a large number of manuscripts from virtually all the regions and in virtually all the indigenous scripts of South Asia, is a lengthy epic narrative ranging (depending on the textual version) from some 100,000 to perhaps 120,000 Sanskrit couplets, although a few passages are in prose.

### The Central Narrative

At its narrative heart, the poem is a political and military history recounting the origins of the ruling family (known variously as the Bharatas, the Pauravas, and the Kurus or Kauravas) of an early Indian kingdom that appears to have flourished in central northern India in the vicinity of the modern city of Delhi, probably around the beginning of the first millennium BCE.

The story involves a bitter succession struggle between rival claimants for the ancestral throne of this kingdom and culminates in a brutal and bloody civil war that leaves most of the aristocratic characters in the epic drama dead and the world of the Bharatas in ruins. The struggle originates in a complex set of displacements and disqualifications that muddy the clear stream of dynastic succession so that the sons, respectively, of a pair of royal brothers, each of whom is forced to give up his claim to the throne, are pitted against one another in increasingly implacable rivalry and enmity.

The poem casts the struggle not only in political terms but also as a conflict over dharma, righteousness itself. The protagonists of the poem, and the parties more clearly associated with dharma, are the sons of King Pandu, known as the Pandavas. Their rivals (sometimes called the Kauravas for the sake of convenience) are their first cousins, the sons of Pandu's older brother Dhritarashtra, who had to forgo sovereignty because of congenital blindness. As a consequence of a curse, Pandu cannot father children. His five heroic sons are, however, sired by a series of powerful Vedic divinities and are therefore regarded as earthly incarnations of these gods. The eldest and heir apparent to the throne, Yudhishthira, is the incarnation of the god of righteousness, Dharma. His brothers Arjuna and Bhima are the children of, respectively, the Vedic warrior and wind gods Indra and Vayu, and the two youngest Pandavas, Nakula and Sahadeva, are the twin sons of the twin divinities, the Asvins. Their antagonists, the sons of Dhritarashtra, are led by the eldest brother, the angry and vengeful Duryodhana, who is regarded as an incarnation of a demonic being.

The two parties are rivals from childhood, and the Pandavas must endure threats, abuse, and assassination attempts by Duryodhana and his allies. At length a seeming resolution is reached when the kingdom is divided, with Duryodhana ruling in the ancestral capital of Hastinapura, and Yudhishthira, the eldest Pandava, building a fabulous new capital city at nearby Indraprastha. This device does not, however, long appease the envy and enmity of Duryodhana. He invites Yudhishthira to a rigged gambling match where he divests him of all his property, his brothers, and their common wife, the princess Draupadi. This ultimate catastrophe is averted at the last moment through the wit of Draupadi, but as a consequence of a second round of dicing, the Pandavas are forced to withdraw in exile to the forest for a period of twelve years and spend a thirteenth year incognito. They fulfill these conditions, but Duryodhana is obdurate in his refusal to share power with them. The two sides set about securing allies and preparing for battle. Complex bonds of loyalty obligate many of the epic's most powerful and venerable figures to ally themselves reluctantly with Duryodhana; the Pandavas, through the intervention of Arjuna, the foremost hero among the five brothers, manage to secure the latter's close friend and virtual alter ego, their cousin Krishna, as a noncombatant adviser and charioteer.

The long-brewing war at last breaks out, attended by massive slaughter on both sides, but at length the Pandavas, although outmatched by Duryodhana's forces, manage to achieve a Pyrrhic victory largely by adhering to the sagacious though often ethically questionable advice of Krishna. Yudhishthira reigns disconsolately over his hard-won but devastated kingdom for some years, until he and his brothers, along with their long-suffering wife Draupadi, abandon the world and trek off into the Himalayas in an attempt to enter heaven. The four younger Pandavas and Draupadi fall dead on the path, with only the supremely righteous Yudhishthira managing to enter the heavenly realm in his earthly body. Ultimately, however, all the heroes are reunited in paradise.

### Cultural Significance of the Epic

This spare narrative, central though it is to the work, does scant justice to the dense layering of meaning and richness of substance that characterize the text of the epic that has come down to us. The core narrative was used as a frame around which was attached a huge corpus of secondary texts incorporating a considerable amount of the systematized knowledge of ancient India. This takes the form of discourses and stories placed in the mouths of various characters, detailing mythological, cosmological, historical, theological, philosophical, political, social, and scientific knowledge preserved by the culture. Thus the *Mahabharata* is not merely an exciting story of treachery, intrigue, and war but a virtual encyclopedia of ancient India.

With its concentration on and magnification of the role of Krishna, who emerges in the poem as an earthly incarnation of the supreme Lord Vishnu, the poem has become one of the major early textual sources for Vaishnavism (worship of Vishnu), one of the sectarian forms of Hinduism. The triumph and salvation of the Pandavas are represented as artifacts of their (especially Arjuna's) devotion to and faith in Krishna. The *Bhagavad Gita*, a section of the epic's sixth book in which Krishna exhorts Arjuna to fight his righteous war and reveals himself as the all-loving god, became one of the central texts of Hindu devotionalism.

Although traditional Indian culture has always been cautious about the message of the *Mahabharata*, with its focus on intrafamilial conflict, the text lies close to the heart of the tradition and powerfully influenced the social, religious, political, and artistic sensibility of South and Southeast Asian peoples for two millennia or more.

*Robert P. Goldman*

*See also:* **Ramayana**

### Further Reading

Brockington, John L. (1998) *The Sanskrit Epics*. Leiden, Netherlands: Brill.

Hiltebeitel, Alf. (1999) *Rethinking India's Oral and Classical Epics: Draupade among Rajputs, Muslims, and Dalits*. Chicago: University of Chicago Press.

Hopkins, E. Washburn. (1902) *The Great Epic of India*. New York: Charles Scribner's Sons.

Van Nooten, Barend A. (1971) *The Mahabharata, Attributed to Krsna Dvaipayana Vyasa*. New York: Twayne.

**MAHALLA** The term *mahalla* is used by Uzbeks. It originated in Arabic and translates as encampment, neighborhood, or community. The term *guzar* is often used in place of *mahalla* among the Tajiks living in Uzbekistan; the term *avlod* is used by Tajiks living in Tajikistan. There are many other variants in existence throughout the Muslim world. Familiar institutions are not uncommon internationally, but they tend to flourish more in societies that deemphasize contractual social relations. As such they are more common in Eastern societies.

The *mahalla* is a social institution, providing goods and services to its constituent members, such as tables, utensils, and other practical items. A *mahalla* can also be considered a small economy of sorts because of the interactive nature of its activities. Events such as weddings, funerals, birthdays, and so on are times where gifts are exchanged among participants. Whether the gift is in the form of goods, such as food, or services, such as entertainment or religious functions, there is a constant flow of material between members. This exchange of goods and services helps reinforce the members' loyalty to their community by adding a dimension of economic necessity to the familiar basis.

Today the entire population of Uzbekistan belongs to one of the more than ten thousand *mahalla*. No other institution in Uzbekistan has as much influence as the *mahalla*, and as such it is the definitive social, economic, and political institution of Uzbekistan. Presently the government of Uzbekistan employs the *mahalla* as part of its means of maintaining power. The *mahalla* is the primary site and source of state welfare assistance, with the local leader *(hokim)* having total control over who receives what and how much. In short, *mahalla* are the center of Uzbek daily and economic life. They are largely based upon kinship, but that is not as strict a designation as it once was. They represent the basic administrative division of the country and the primary vehicle for the exercise of its power. The *mahalla* serve as a means of surveillance and as vehicles for the construction of national identity. *Mahalla* and their members are required to participate in all national festivals and cultural celebrations. The rural *mahalla* have a greater degree of control over their economic fate than their urban counterparts due to their greater distance from the central power structure.

*Anthony Bichel*

### Further Reading

Carlisle, Donald S. (1991) "Uzbekistan and the Uzbeks." *Problems of Communism* 40, 5: 23–44.

Poliakov, Sergei P. (1992) *Everyday Islam: Religion and Tradition in Rural Central Asia*. London: M. E. Sharpe.

**MAHANADI RIVER** The Mahanadi River, 89 kilometers long, is known as one of the "great rivers" of India, crossing the state of Orissa and cutting through the Eastern Ghats by way of a gorge some 50 kilomenters long. The Mahanadi's catchment area is estimated at 113,440 square kilometers, and in the rainy season it carries an immense amount of water, up to 51,000 cubic meters per second at the Naraj gorge. The river rises in Raipur District of Chhattisgarh, just south of Raipur city. After flowing eastward and passing the city of Cuttack (where in the rainy season it is 3 kilometers wide), the river enters the Bay of Bengal through a number of deltaic channels and two main estuaries. In the delta region is an extensive system of irrigation canals for the cultivation of rice. From July to February the river is navigable by boats for 740 kilometers from the sea.

*Paul Hockings*

### Further Reading

Mahalik, N. K. (2000) *Mahandi Delta: Geology, Resources, and Biodiversity*. New Delhi: AIT Alumni Association, Indian Chapter.

**MAHARASHTRA** (2002 est. pop. 98.6 million). Maharashtra, the third largest state of the Indian Union in terms of area and population, lies on the west coast of India facing the Arabian Sea. The state shares its boundary with Gujarat, Madhya Pradesh, Andhra Pradesh, Karnataka, and Goa. A 720-kilometer by 80-kilometer coastal expanse called Konkan forms a continuous band along the coast. Parallel to this runs the Western Ghats mountain range, which is flanked, on its eastern side, by the fertile plateau that forms the dominant physical environment of the state. Three major rivers—Godavari, Bhima, and Krishna (Kistna)—flow through this region.

The soil of the plateau is rich and supports the extensive cultivation of cotton, sugarcane, peanut, and tobacco along with different varieties of mangoes, grapes, oranges, and bananas. The coastal region produces rice and coconuts in abundance. The state receives its rainfall mainly from the southwest monsoon which is very active in the coastal belt, but loses its vigor once it approaches the central parts.

Maharashtra's early history stretches from the time of the Mauryan empire in the third century BCE to the reign of the Yadavas in the thirteenth century. The high point of this history comes with the rise of Sivaji in the seventeenth century, who succeeded in establishing an independent Maratha kingdom despite repeated Muslim attacks. Sivaji's successors ruled the territory with occasional reverses till the British took control of the region in early nineteenth century. At the time of independence the state was part of the

Bombay presidency under the British. It got its present identity on 1 May 1960 when all the Marathi-speaking areas from neighboring states were united to form Maharashtra. The state has thirty-three administrative districts and has a bicameral legislature. It has a representation of nineteen members in the Upper House (Rajya Sabha) and forty-eight members in the Lower House (Lok Sabha) of the Indian Parliament.

More than 60 percent of the people in Maharashtra depend on agriculture for a living. In addition to a thriving agricultural sector, Maharashtra has a well-developed industrial base. Because of its convenient location as the link between northern and southern India, it functions as a bridgehead of financial and commercial activities. Mumbai (Bombay), the capital of Maharashtra, is the business capital of India and the largest stock exchange in the country. It has a big textiles market and a busy port. Many small and medium industries have grown around the city and it showcases products from all over India. Food products, breweries, tobacco and related products, textiles, plasticware, petroleum and coal products, paper, rubber, basic chemicals and chemical products, and crude oil are some of the items manufactured and marketed from Maharashtra. Major corporate houses in India are Mumbai-based. The city is also well known for its film industry, which is the chief source of the popular Hindi cinema.

*Ram Shankar Nanda*

**Further Reading**


Kulkarni, A. R. (1999) *Maharastra: Society and Culture*. Columbia, MO: South Asia Books.

Sirsikar, M. (1995) *Politics of Modern Maharastra*. Sangam Books.

Prime Minister Mahathir Bin Mohamad in Kuala Lumpur in October 2001. (AFP/CORBIS)

**MAHATHIR MOHAMAD** (b. 1925), prime minister of Malaysia. Mahathir Bin Mohamad has significantly shaped his country's political landscape while also serving as an unofficial spokesman for the so-called Third World. Throughout his career, Mahathir has been an outspoken critic of the industrialized nations' foreign policies directed at developing nations, while espousing the virtue of Asian morals.

Mahathir was born in Alor Setar, capital of the state of Kedah in northern Malaysia. The youngest of nine children, he grew up in a stable, financially secure family, and his father held a prestigious position as schoolmaster of an English language school. He studied medicine, but his passion was politics. He joined the dominant United Malays National Organization (UMNO) party and aligned himself with the majority Malay population's needs. His book *The Malay Dilemma*, published in Singapore in 1970, which criticized the then-current Malay government, promoted a strident Malay nationalism and articulated his ideological beliefs. In the *Malay Dilemma*, Mahathir asserted that Malays were the indigenous people of Malaysia and demanded a policy of affirmative action to elevate their economic status to a level equal with the Chinese-Malaysians. At the same time, Mahathir also criticized certain Malay cultural traits and presented a theory steeped in Social Darwinism to explain the Malays' economic backwardness. Mahathir's open letter to Prime Minister Tunku Abdul Rahman in 1969 led to his expulsion from UMNO, but by 1972 he was reinstated.

After 1972, Mahathir's political star rose rapidly. Tun Abdul Razak, the second prime minister, appointed him to a cabinet position in 1974, and he became deputy prime minister in 1976 under the third prime minister, Hussein Onn. By 1981, Mahathir had himself become prime minister. During the 1980s, Mahathir consolidated his power and became more authoritarian by successfully staving off political opponents through arrests and detention. He also eliminated the supreme court as a source of opposition, first by altering the constitution to weaken the court's power of review and then by forcing the resignation of several high-ranking members. In the 1990s, Mahathir promoted his economic plan, *The Way Forward* or *Vision 2020*, which proclaims that Malaysia will rank as a fully developed nation by the year 2020. Mahathir's *Vision* proposed a difficult economic growth rate that Malaysia has not been able to maintain. Nevertheless, Malaysia has prospered under Mahathir and the country's economic prospects remain solid.

*Allen Reichert*

### Further Reading

Khoo Boo Teik. (1995) *Paradoxes of Mahathirism: An Intellectual Biography of Mahathir Mohamad*. Kuala Lumpur, Malaysia: Oxford University Press.

Milne, R. S., and Diane K. Mauzy. (1999) *Malaysian Politics under Mahathir*. London: Routledge.

Mohamad, Mahathir. (1998) *The Way Forward*. London: Weidenfeld & Nicolson.

**MAHMUD OF GHAZNA** (971?–1030), Afghan conqueror and emperor. Mahmud of Ghazna was an emperor during the Ghaznavid dynasty (977–1187) in Afghanistan. It was during his reign that the Ghaznavid dynasty amassed its greatest wealth and territory. The son of a Turkish slave who fled to Ghazni after a failed revolt against his masters, Mahmud rose to power by defeating his elder brother for control of Afghanistan and the Khorasan region of Iran. Using his military expertise, Mahmud extended his territory to the west and north of Afghanistan, as well as to the Punjab region. Mahmud led several raids into India, ransacking temples and converting the natives to Islam. With the wealth gained from his pillaging, he transformed his capital, Ghazni, into a cultural center, establishing universities and supporting scholars and poets; the well-known historians Al Biruni and Al Utbi, as well as the great poet Firdawsi (c. 935–c. 1020) were in residence at Ghazni. A devout Muslim, Muhmad also built a grand mosque. Mahmud died in 1130, after which the empire began a downward spiral until its dissolution in 1186.

*Houman A. Sadri*

### Further Reading

Adamec, Ludwig W. (1997) *Historical Dictionary of Afghanistan*. 2d ed. Lanham, MD: Scarecrow Press.

Edwards, David B. (1996) *Heroes of the Age: Moral Fault Lines on the Afghan Frontier*. Berkeley and Los Angeles: University of California Press.

**MAHMUD SHAH** (d. 1528), sultan of Melaka. The sudden death of Sultan Alauddin Riayat Shah (reigned 1477–1488) led to the installation of Mahmud Shah, his younger son and a nephew of the influential *bendahara* (prime minister) Tun Perak, who sought to perpetuate his dominance in the royal court by promoting the more pliant of the late sultan's sons.

Mahmud (reigned 1488–1511) was neither an able nor a forceful ruler. Philandering, obstinate, and impulsive, he left the affairs of state to Tun Perak and other ministers. Mahmud's ineptness notwithstanding, Melaka remained at the peak of its power, wealth, and prestige at the beginning of the sixteenth century, which attracted the covetous attention of the Portuguese.

In facing the Portuguese challenge, Melaka lacked strong leadership and mass support. Malay-Tamil rivalry resurfaced in court with the appointment of Tun Mutahir as *bendahara* in 1500, and intrigues and conspiracies led to his execution. The foreign mercantile community that dominated Melaka's trade and commerce—and hence its wealth—followed only its self-serving economic interests. The Melakan aristocracy shared in this wealth but little trickled down to the common people.

Despite a gallant defense by Mahmud and his son Ahmad, Melaka fell to the Portuguese in August 1511. Mahmud fled, initially to Muar, then to Pahang, and finally to Bintan in 1513. Between 1515 and 1524 he launched five campaigns to recapture Melaka but failed. He died in Kampar in 1528. His surviving sons, Muzaffar and Alauddin, established the Perak sultanate and the Johor-Riau empire, respectively.

*Ooi Keat Gin*

### Further Reading

Cortesao, Armando, ed. (1944) *The "Suma Oriental" of Tome Pires*. 2 vols. London: Hakluyt Society.

Meilink-Roelofsz, Marie Antoinette Petronella. (1962) *Asian Trade and European Influence in the Indonesian Archipelago between 1500 and about 1630*. The Hague, Netherlands: Nijhoff.

Muhammad Yusuf Hashim. (1992) *The Malay Sultanate of Malacca: A Study of Various Aspects of Malacca in the 15th and 16th Centuries in Malaysian History*. Trans. by D. J. Muzaffar Tate. Kuala Lumpur, Malaysia: Dewan Bahasa dan Pustaka.

*Sejarah Melayu or Malay Annals*. (1983) Trans. by C. C. Brown. Kuala Lumpur, Malaysia: Oxford University Press.

Wheatley, Paul. (1966) *The Golden Khersonese: Studies in the Historical Geography of the Malay Peninsula before* A.D. *1500.* Kuala Lumpur, Malaysia: University of Malaya Press.

**MAILIN, BEIIMBET** (1894–1938), Kazakh writer. Beiimbet Mailin was not only a writer but also a poet, a dramatist, and an educator in Soviet Kazakhstan. Born in the Kustanay region (now Qostanay) of Kazakhstan to a family of poor nomads, Beiimbet Mailin began his education in local religious schools when he was seven years old. In 1913 he started teaching at the local *madrasah* (seminary) in his native village. The same year he published his first poem, *Musylmandyq belgisi* (Notes of a Muslim) and continued to teach in various *madrasahs* and in the Russian-Kazak school in Kustanay. Following the 1917 Russian Revolution he was active in the Kazakh political party *Alash Orda*. After the Bolshevik victory in the Russian Civil War, he published his first full collection of poetry in 1923, and in 1926 he became the editor of *Qazaq Adebieti* (Kazakh Literature). During the 1920s and 1930s, he published some of his best-known works, including *Kommunistka Raushan* (The Communist Raushan) and the screenplay *Amangel'dy* (For the Noted Kazak Warrior). Between 1933 and 1936 his collected works were published in four volumes.

In 1938 he was arrested during the Stalinist purges and executed. His work was rediscovered in 1957, and a new six-volume edition of his collected works appeared between 1960 and 1964.

*Steven Sabol*

**Further Reading**

Sarabalaev, Baqyt. (1988) *Beiimbet Mailin.* Almaty, Kazakhstan: Mektep.

**MAJAPAHIT** Majapahit was the last medieval Hindu-Javanese empire to wield much influence in Southeast Asia. When emissaries from Mongol China appeared at Singhasari in 1289, the great warrior-king Kertanagara promptly arrested and expelled them. This provoked a punitive Chinese expedition to eastern Java in 1292; it arrived to find that Kertanagara had been killed in an uprising engineered by a prince of the displaced house of Kadiri. Kertanagara's son Vijaya was forced to flee to a village on the Brantas River named Majapahit (bitter fruit). Vijaya enlisted the support of the newly arrived Chinese forces to drive the Kadiri usurper out of Singhasari and recover the throne. He then compelled his Chinese supporters to withdraw and depart homeward.

The village of Majapahit became Vijaya's new capital. Gajah Mada was appointed prime minister in 1331, and under his direction Majapahit filled the political vacuum left by the fall of the Srivijaya empire and the dissolution of its temporary successor, Singhasari. As early as 1365, Majapahit could claim domination over most of Sumatra and the Malay Peninsula. Its hold on the latter extended as far north as Kedah, Langkasuka, and Pantai. Majapahit's influence extended to much of what now comprises Indonesia, extending to territories on the south and west coasts of Borneo, and to southern Celebes and the Moluccas. Some even claim that Majapahit power was felt as far away as the Indo-Chinese peninsula, in Siam, Cambodia, and Annam, though this is doubtful. The infiltration of Islam from the Straits of Malacca into the Southeast Asian archipelago gradually undermined the influence of Majapahit. In 1478 the Muslim coastal state of Demak invaded Majapahit itself, and by the late fifteenth century Majapahit was reduced to little more than an eastern Javanese state with a glorious past.

*Kog Yue Choong*

**Further Reading**

Harrison, Brian. (1954) *South East Asia—A Short History.* London: MacMillan & Co. Ltd.

Prapanca, Mpu, Rakawi of Majapahit. (1995) *Desawarna (Nagarakrtagama).* Trans. by Stuart Robson. Leiden, Netherlands: KITLV (Royal Institute of Linguistics and Anthropology) Press.

**MAK YONG** If "feminism" had been a term in the Malay court four hundred years ago, Mak Yong would have been seen as a feminist dance drama. This is because, except for the comedians, all parts were played (and still are today) by young women. The dance drama was meant for entertaining female royalty (queens and princesses) in the absence of their men when the latter were away at war. The "female space" was necessary to protect these women from falling into disgrace because their concerned husbands and fathers feared that they might commit immoral activities with male performers in their absence. The presence of women only was necessary to safeguard aristocratic honor. The women were free to do and say what they wanted without being conscious of male presence.

The dance originated in Patani (south Thailand) and spread southward into Kelantan in Malaysia. Mak Yong, originally performed as soul worshipping of ancestors, combines elements of romantic drama, dance, and operatic singing. There are no written texts, and hence no two performances are ever the same. The music that accompanies the dance is played on a *rebab* (bowed lute), *tawak-tawak* (two hanging gongs), and *gendang* (two double-headed drums). There is a marked Middle Eastern flavor in the combination of a solo voice, a chorus, and musical instruments in Mak Yong.

A *pawang* (shaman) initiates the rituals of stage opening prior to a performance. The stories performed are from the old Malay tales, all of which are original and date back to the golden age of the Malay kingdoms of great culture and power. In the past, Mak Yong was a court entertainment, and the Malay Palace was the patron. Mak Yong would be performed four or five times a week at the royal residence. Today, Mak Yong has become a traditional drama for the common people.

*Nor Faridah Abdul Manaf*

**Further Reading**

Harris, Mark. (1990) *National Museum Kuala Lumpur: History and Culture of Malaysia.* Kuala Lumpur, Malaysia: Syarikat S. Abdul Majeed.

Ismail, Yahaya. (1989) *The Cultural Heritage of Malaysia.* Kuala Lumpur, Malaysia: Dinamika Kreatif Sdn. Bhd.

Yousof, Ghulam-Sarwar. (1994) *Dictionary of Traditional South-East Asia Theatre*. Kuala Lumpur, Malaysia: Oxford University Press.

**MAKHAMBET UTEMISOV** (1804–1846), Kazakh poet. Makhambet Utemisov (Maxambet Otemisuly) was a distinguished Kazakh poet and political activist. He is remembered for his leading part in the insurrection of the Kazakhs against the oppressive rule of the khan of the Inner Horde, Zhangir, as well as against Russian colonialism, in 1836–1837. The rebellion was crushed, and Makhambet had to flee with a price on his head. He was murdered in 1846.

Although Makhambet was sent to a Russian school in Orenburg, where he learned to read and write, his poetry stands in the tradition of oral Kazakh poetry. More than fifty poems attributed to him have been transmitted, some in writing, some orally. The first publication of one of his poems dates from 1908. Most of Makhambet's poems have a political and moral message, often protesting the unjustness of the khan's rule. In one directed against Khan Zhangir, Makhambet calls the khan a wolf, a snake, and a scorpion. A number of poems are of a warlike and heroic nature, some addressed to his companion-in-arms Isatay Taymanov. Makhambet also composed meditative poems (termed *tolghau* in Kazakh), on themes such as the decay of morals or the transience of human life.

*Karl Reichl*

**Further Reading**

Gabdullin, M. G., et al., eds. (1968–1979) *Istoriia kazakhskoi literaturi* (History of Kazakh Literature). Vol. 2. Almaty, Kazakhstan: Nauka.

Makhambet. (1989) *Ereuwil atqa er salmay: Olengder* (Put No Saddle on an Enduring Horse: Poems), edited by Qabibolla Sydyzov. Almaty, Kazakhstan: Zhazuushy.

**MAKLI HILL** One of the largest necropolises in the world, with a diameter of approximately 8 kilometers, Makli Hill is supposed to be the burial place of some 125,000 Sufi saints. It is located on the outskirts of Thatta, the capital of lower Sind until the seventeenth century, in what is the southeastern province of present-day Pakistan. Legends abound about its inception, but it is generally believed that the cemetery grew around the shrine of the fourteenth-century Sufi Hamad Jamali. The tombs and gravestones spread over the cemetery are material documents marking the social and political history of Sind.

Imperial mausoleums are divided into two major groups, those from the Samma (1352–1520) and Tarkhan (1556–1592) periods. The tomb of the Samma king, Jam Nizam al-Din (reigned 1461–1509), is an impressive square structure built of sandstone and decorated with floral and geometric medallions. Similar to this is the mausoleum of Isa Khan Tarkhan II (d. 1651), a two-story stone building with majestic cupolas and balconies. In contrast to the syncretic architecture of these two monuments, which integrate Hindu and Islamic motifs, are mausoleums that clearly show the Central Asian roots of the later dynasty. An example is the tomb of Jan Beg Tarkhan (d. 1600), a typical octagonal brick structure whose dome is covered in blue and turquoise glazed tiles. Today, Makli Hill is a United Nations World Heritage Site that is visited by both pilgrims and tourists.

*Kishwar Rizvi*

**Further Reading**

Cousens, Henri. (1929) *The Antiquities of Sind, with Historical Outline*. Calcutta, India: Government of India.

Lari, Yasmeen, and Suhail Zaheer Lari. (1997) *The Jewel of Sindh: Samma Monuments on Makli Hill*. Karachi, Pakistan: Heritage Foundation and Oxford University Press.

Mir Ali Sher Qani Thattavi. (1967 [1872]) *Maklinama*. Reprint ed. Hyderabad, India: Sindhi Adabi Board. Schimmel, Annemarie. (1983) *Makli Hill: A Center of Islamic Culture in Sindh*. Karachi, Pakistan: University of Karachi.

**MALAY STATES, UNFEDERATED** Located on the Malay Peninsula in Southeast Asia, the Unfederated Malay States (UMS), were Johor, Kedah, Perlis,

Kelantan, and Terengganu. The main difference between the five UMS and the four Federated Malay States (FMS) was that British control was somewhat looser in the unfederated states. While British influence extended to all of the nine Malay states, which were ruled by sultans, internal government remained largely under the control of the traditional rulers. In each state, a British adviser was responsible to the British high commissioner. The four northern states of the UMS (except for Johor) were originally under the sphere of influence of Siam (now Thailand) and were among the poorest on the peninsula. In 1909, the king of Siam signed a treaty transferring the states to British control, but the sultans refused to join the FSM for fear of losing their de facto executive power; hence they maintained a modicum of independence. Johor also remained outside the FMS because its sultan, Abu Bakar, insisted on remaining independent.

The Union of Malaya, composed of the nine states of the USM and the FSM, was set up in 1946 and became the Federation of Malaya in 1948. In 1957, it achieved independence from Britain and joined the commonwealth. The next year, the name was changed to the Federation of Malaysia.

*Ho Khai Leong*

**Further Reading**

Ryan, N. J. (1969) *The Making of Modern Malaysia and Singapore.* Kuala Lumpur, Malaysia: Oxford University Press.

**MALAY SULTANATE.** See **Melaka Sultanate.**

**MALAYAN EMERGENCY** The Malayan Emergency was a reaction, through legal regulations, to counter the guerrilla war initiated by the Malayan Communist Party (MCP), led by Chin Peng, the party's secretary general, against the British Commonwealth administration and Malay forces. The war lasted from 1948 to 1960. The decision to undertake a guerrilla war was made by the MCP in response to British proposals for the Malayan Union Constitution and the 1948 Federation of Malaya agreement, which the MCP feared would put in place a strong anticommunist central government.

Political events elsewhere, such as Mao Zedong's guerrilla tactics against Chiang Kai-shek's forces in China, Indonesia's war with the Dutch government to gain independence, and the beginning of the Cold War between the Soviet Union and the United States, prompted the MCP to openly revolt against the British in order to achieve independence and establish a communist Malaya. The MCP began attacking and terrorizing plantation workers and isolated estates, derailing trains, and burning workers' houses and buses. The Communists were jungle based and supported by the Chinese population, who lived mainly in cities and at the fringes of jungles. An underground organization called Min Yuen acted as a spy network and provided supplies, food, and information to the Communists.

A state of emergency was declared in parts of the states of Perak and Johore on 18 June 1948 by High Commissioner Sir Edward Gent after three British planters were found murdered in Sungai Siput, Perak. By 23 June, the whole country was in a state of emergency. The MCP, which had been legalized by the British at the end of World War II, was banned. The British also tried to thwart the Communists by establishing a national registration system. Those people without an identification card were considered illegal and were seen as Communist sympathizers. Furthermore, under the Briggs Plan (named for Sir Harold Briggs, a retired general appointed to coordinate and direct military and civilian operations during the emergency) to cut off interaction between the Min Yuen and the Chinese population of Malaya, the British resettled nearly 500,000 Chinese squatters from outlying areas to newly created and protected villages. This deprived the Communists of their supplies and information from the Chinese population. More important, the British used psychological warfare to win the "hearts and minds" of the population by seeking to unite the racially divided Malayan people to fight the Communist insurrection.

Other drastic measures taken by the British eventually cut off supplies and support to the Communists, who were trapped in the jungle and constantly hunted by British special forces. The Communists failed largely because of lack of support from the majority Malay community, who opposed the MCP due to its predominantly Chinese-based support. Eventually, the MCP tried to negotiate for peace at the Baling Talks of 1955, but the talks broke down because Chin Peng refused to dissolve the MCP. The MCP finally lost its struggle when Malaya was granted independence in 1957. The newly formed Malayan government declared the end of the emergency on 31 July 1960. The MCP surrendered on 2 December 1989 to the Malaysian government and agreed to terminate all activities.

*Geetha Govindasamy*

*See also:* **Malayan Union**

**Further Reading**

Cloake, John Templer. (1985) *Templer, Tiger of Malaya: The Life of Field Marshall Sir Gerald Templer*. London: Harrap.

Clutterbuck, Richard. (1984) *Conflict and Violence in Singapore and Malaysia, 1945–1983*. Rev. ed. Singapore: Graham Brash.

Coates, John. (1992) *Suppressing Insurgency: An Analysis of the Malayan Emergency, 1948–1954*. Boulder, CO: Westview Press.

Jackson, Robert. (1991) *The Malayan Emergency: The Commonwealth Wars 1948–1966*. London: Routledge.

Short, Anthony. (2000) *In Pursuit of Mountain Rats: The Communist Insurrection in Malaya*. Singapore: Cultured Lotus.

Stubbs, Richard. (1989) *Hearts and Minds in Guerrilla Warfare: The Malayan Emergency 1948–1960*. Singapore: Oxford University Press.

## MALAYAN PEOPLE'S ANTI-JAPANESE ARMY

**MALAYAN PEOPLE'S ANTI-JAPANESE ARMY** The Malayan People's Anti-Japanese Army (MPAJA) was a guerrilla army that was part of the Malayan Communist Party (MCP). When Japan attacked Malaya in 1941, the MPAJA was the foremost local force carrying out guerrilla attacks against the Japanese. Because the Chinese population was harshly treated during the Japanese occupation of Malaya, the MPAJA membership consisted mostly of Chinese who were anti-Japanese. From 1942 onward, following their defeat in Singapore by the Japanese, the British forces in Malaya collaborated with the MCP by providing supplies and personnel with two objectives in mind: to train and equip the MPAJA to fight the Japanese and to prepare for an eventual Allied invasion of Malaya.

Even though the MPAJA was unsuccessful in driving the Japanese out of Malaya, it gained invaluable experience in guerrilla warfare and established a basis for future resistance against the British during the Malayan Emergency (1948–1960), a successful British counter, through civil, police, and military programs, to Communist insurrections. As part of the support network for independence, the fighters developed links with the rural communities on the fringes of the jungle. The MPAJA also constructed bases and hideouts in the jungle and accumulated a large quantity of weapons. When the war ended in 1945, the Japanese surrendered, and an Allied invasion of Malaya became unnecessary. In the same year, the MPAJA guerrilla fighters emerged from the jungle, and the British who returned to Malaya legalized the MCP. Unfortunately, MPAJA links with the rural community, as well as the training and weapons provided by the British, proved valuable to the MCP in fighting the British during the Malayan Emergency.

*Geetha Govindasamy*

**Further Reading**

Andaya, Barbara Watson. (2001) *A History of Malaysia*. 2d ed. Hampshire, U.K.: Palgrave.

Clutterbuck, Richard. (1984) *Conflict and Violence in Singapore and Malaysia*. Rev. ed. Singapore: Graham Brash.

Kratoska, Paul, ed. (1995) *Malaya and Singapore during the Japanese Occupation*. Journal of Southeast Asian Studies, Special Publication Series, no. 3. Singapore: National University of Singapore.

Zakaria, Haji Ahmad. (1977) *Political Violence in Malaysia: The Malayan Emergency and Its Impact*. Kuala Lumpur, Malaysia.

## MALAYAN UNION

**MALAYAN UNION** Prior to World War II, Malaya (now Malaysia) comprised three different administrative governments: the Federated Malay States (Perak, Selangor, Pahang, and Negeri Sembilan), the Unfederated Malay States (Kedah, Kelantan, Perlis, Terengganu, and Johor), and the Straits Settlements (Melaka, Penang, and Singapore). During the Japanese occupation of Malaya, British authorities prepared a plan proposing a centralized government comprising these peninsular possessions, to be known as the Malayan Union.

The official arrangement of the Malayan Union was announced in a 1946 White Paper. Under this new system the Federated and Unfederated Malay States, and Melaka and Penang, were to be centralized under a British governor. Singapore, however, because of its strategic location, rapid economic development, and large Chinese population, was to remain a separate British colony. The centralized government was to consist of a governor, a legislature, and an executive board. The position of the Malay sultans would remain, although their sovereignty would be ceded by the British. Citizenship under the scheme offered equality of rights to all irrespective of race or creed, and also allowed dual citizenship.

The plan received widespread criticism and opposition from the Malays, the sultans, and also British officers who had served in Malaya, including Frank Swettenham and Sir George Maxwell. The Malays were reluctant to share their rights and political power with other peoples, namely the Chinese and the Indians. The sultans were dissatisfied with the way Sir Harold MacMichael, the British officer in charge, handled the negotiations: the sultans were coerced, threatened, and blackmailed.

As a result of this opposition about two hundred Malays representing forty-one associations gathered in Kuala Lumpur and formed the United Malays National Organization to protest the proposed Malayan Union. As a result of their efforts and criticism at home the British government decided to scrap the proposal, replacing it with a milder plan to form the Federation of Malaya. The new proposal was seen as more palatable because citizenship is given to immigrants who have stayed more than ten years in Malaya. Apart from that, the sultans remain as leaders of Islam and Malay society.

*Mala Selvarju*

**Further Reading**

Emerson, R. (1964) *Malaysia*. Kuala Lumpur, Malaysia: University of Malaya Press.

Ryan, N. J. (1974) *The Making of Modern Malaysia and Singapore*. Kuala Lumpur, Malaysia: Oxford University Press.

## MALAY-INDONESIAN LANGUAGE

The national languages of Malaysia and Indonesia—Bahasa Malaysia and Bahasa Indonesia, respectively—are the Malay language as spoken in those countries; Malay is also spoken in Singapore and parts of the Philippines. In both Malaysia and Indonesia, knowledge of the language is necessary for gaining citizenship.

According to historical records, the rulers of the Srivijaya empire in Malaya used and popularized the Malay language in the seventh century, and it has remained the most important language of the archipelago ever since. Bahasa Malaysia and Bahasa Indonesia share common words, idioms, and roots, and both belong to the Western Malayo-Polynesian branch of Austronesian or Malayo-Polynesian, one of the world's largest language families. The Malay language is phonetic in character, with few prefixes and suffixes for verbs and nouns. It does not have gender, person, number, or tense, and verbs are not conditioned on the basis of conjugation, declension, or tense. Bahasa Malaysia and Bahasa Indonesia have been written with a common reformed spelling system since 1972.

### Bahasa Malaysia

Malay as spoken in Malaysia—Bahasa Malaysia—is the national language and an important element in promoting nationalism and intracommunal harmony. Knowledge of the Malay language is essential for becoming a Malaysian citizen, and it is now the sole official language of the country. According to a census taken in 2000, in the total population of 22.3 million, Malays made up 66.1 percent, Chinese 25.3 percent, and Indians 7.4 percent. The Malaysian territories are more homogeneous than Indonesia, and Malay is used throughout the country. Although a significant number of Chinese and Indians speak other languages such as Hakka, Mandarin Chinese, and Tamil, they have increasingly learned Bahasa Malaysia. The government of Malaysia has promoted English as a second language, and it is widely used in business and academic circles.

Britain, which ruled over the country as a colonial power, was more benevolent toward the Malays than were the Dutch toward Indonesians. The first Malay printing press was established in Malaya in 1848, and it published several works in Malay: autobiographies, studies of folk traditions, poetry, court chronicles, epics, the Qu'ran, other Islamic texts, and legal digests.

There was a resurgence of Malay nationalism during the Japanese occupation (1941–1945), when various publications in the Malay language awakened Malayans to their subjugation and repression. Although some Malay authors of the era at first supported the Japanese occupation, they changed their emphasis after the end of the war and in 1948 founded an association, The Generation of 50, to promote the Malay language. The publication of essays, short stories, and novels analyzing issues of social concern were given prime importance at this time.

When the Federated Malay States became independent in 1957 and subsequently when the Federation of Malaysia emerged in 1963, the government declared Bahasa Malaysia the sole official language. This language is understood and spoken in all parts of the country, and no party or political group of significance questions its status in the national polity.

### Bahasa Indonesia

In addition to Malay, more than 250 other languages or dialects are spoken in Indonesia; these include Acehnese, Batak, Sundanese, Javanese, Sasak, Tetum of Timor, Dayak, Minahasa, Toraja, Buginese, Halmahera, Ambonese, and Ceramese, all of which were influenced by Malay. Their vocabularies and idioms, like those of Bahasa Indonesia, have indigenized a number of words from Sanskrit, Arabic, Persian, Portuguese, Dutch, and English. The speakers of all these languages use Bahasa Indonesia as their lingua franca.

Bahasa Indonesia was systematized and organized in the twentieth century. At a youth congress held in Jakarta, Indonesia, in 1928, delegates pledged to promote Malay and to nurture it as their national language. Several political parties supported this resolution, and thereafter this language became the common medium for spreading revolutionary struggle.

The Japanese occupation actually fostered the acceptance of the Indonesian language. The conquerors banned the use of the Dutch language and ordered the arrest of anyone speaking Dutch. The textbooks for primary and secondary education, which had previously been written exclusively in Dutch, were translated into Bahasa Indonesia. The Japanese thought that the use of the Indonesian language in schools and official proceedings would promote anti-Dutch sentiments and would aid in the eventual acceptance of the Japanese language. But the policy of replacing the Dutch language with Japanese was never carried out.

With Japanese support, scholars of the era established the Komisi Bahasa Indonesia (Commission for Indonesian Languages), which systematized the Indonesian language and published a literary magazine highlighting linguistic, cultural, and political issues. The commission simplified the spelling of words borrowed from Sanskrit, Arabic, Dutch, and English, which were pronounced and spelled differently in different parts of Indonesia.

Article 36 of the 1945 constitution of Indonesia declared Bahasa Indonesia the language of the state, although in 1959 President Sukarno (1901–1970) explained that areas of Indonesia possessing languages of their own were entitled to use them as well. Both Presidents Sukarno and Suharto (b. 1921) nurtured the development of Bahasa Indonesia at the literary, academic, and official levels, not only as the language of Indonesians but as a bond to forge solidarity and kinship with the Malay world.

According to a 1990 census by the Central Bureau of Statistics, the use of Bahasa Indonesia falls into three categories: 15 percent use it for daily communication, 68 percent can speak it but do not use it every day, and 17 percent cannot understand it. The Indonesian government has set 2010 as the year in which all Indonesians will understand Bahasa Indonesia.

*Ganganath Jha*

### Further Reading

Alisjahbana, S. Takdir. (1976) *Language Planning for Modernization: The Case of Indonesian and Malaysian.* The Hague, Netherlands: Mouton de Gruyter.

Kaidir, Anwar. (1980) *Indonesian: The Development and Use of a National Language.* Yogyakarta, Indonesia: Gadjah Mada University Press.

Wong Hoy Kee, Francis. (1971) "The Development of a National Language in Indonesia and Malaysia." *Comparative Education* 7, 2: 73–80.

Belarus
Ukraine
Moldova
Romania
Bulgaria
Greece
Turkey
Black Sea
Istanbul
Ankara
Adana
Nicosia
Cyprus
Lebanon
Israel
Syria
Jordan
Egypt
Georgia
Caucasus Mts.
T'bilisi
Armenia
Yerevan
Azerbaijan
Baku
Caspian Sea
Kazakhstan
Astana
Aral Sea
Syr Dar'ya
Amu Dar'ya
Kara-Kum
Lake Balkash
Almaty
Bishkek
Kyrgyzstan
Tashkent
Fergana Valley
Uzbekistan
Turkmenistan
Ashgabat
Dushanbe
Tajikistan
Pamirs
Tian S
Taklima
Deser
R
Tehran
Iran
Iraq
Baghdad
Euphrates
Tigris
Zagros Mountains
Kuwait
Persian Gulf
Qatar
Saudi Arabia
United Arab Emirates
Oman
Yemen
Red Sea
Eritrea
Djibouti
Somalia
Ethiopia
Sudan
Kabul
Afghanistan
Peshawar
Islamabad
Jammu and Kashmir
Himalay
Lahore
Indus River
Pakistan
Karachi
New Delhi
Nep
Kath
Ganges River
India
Mumbai
Arabian Sea
Madra
Lakshadweep
Sr
La
Colombo
Maldives
Male
N
0
500
1000 Miles
0
500
1000 Kilometers
Uganda
Kenya
Democratic Republic of the Congo
Rwanda
Burundi
Tanzania
Zambia
Zimbabwe
Mozambique
Madagascar
Mauritius
Port Louis
Réunion
60°E
INDIAN